Microsoft® Office 365

IN PRACTICE

2019

Randy Nordell
AMERICAN RIVER COLLEGE

Kathleen Stewart
MORAINE VALLEY COMMUNITY
COLLEGE

Annette Easton
SAN DIEGO STATE UNIVERSITY

Pat Graves
EASTERN ILLINOIS UNIVERSITY

D1274793

Mc
Graw
Hill
Education

©Chris Ryan/Getty Images

MICROSOFT OFFICE 365: IN PRACTICE, 2019

Published by McGraw-Hill Education, 2 Penn Plaza, New York, NY 10121. Copyright © 2020 by McGraw-Hill Education. All rights reserved. Printed in the United States of America. No part of this publication may be reproduced or distributed in any form or by any means, or stored in a database or retrieval system, without the prior written consent of McGraw-Hill Education, including, but not limited to, in any network or other electronic storage or transmission, or broadcast for distance learning.

Some ancillaries, including electronic and print components, may not be available to customers outside the United States.

This book is printed on acid-free paper.

2 3 4 5 6 7 8 9 LMN 21 20

ISBN 978-1-260-07990-6 (bound edition)
MHID 1-260-07990-2 (bound edition)
ISBN 978-1-260-81853-6 (loose-leaf edition)
MHID 1-260-81853-5 (loose-leaf edition)

Managing Director: *Terry Schiesl*
Director: *Wyatt Morris*
Senior Product Developer: *Alan Palmer*
Executive Marketing Managers: *Tiffany Russell & Corban Quigg*
Content Project Manager: *Harvey Yep*
Buyer: *Susan K. Culbertson*
Designer: *Matt Backhaus & Egzon Shaqiri*
Cover Image: *©Chris Ryan/Getty Images*
Compositor: *SPi Global*
Printer: *LSC Communications*

Library of Congress Control Number: 2019933451

mheducation.com/highered

dedication

Bob and Lanita, thank you for generously allowing me to use the cabin where I completed much of the work on this project. Don and Jennie, thank you for teaching me the value of hard work and encouraging me throughout the years. Kelsey and Taylor, thank you for keeping me young at heart. Kelly, thank you for your daily love, support, and encouragement. I could not have done this without you. I'm looking forward to spending more time together on our tandem!

—Randy

Thank you to the members of my writing team for your collegiality and encouragement on this work. I also want to thank the development, editing, production, and marketing staff at McGraw-Hill for your efforts and support on this series. And I am indebted to reviewers, instructors, and students who have made comments, critiques, and suggestions.

—Kathleen Stewart

George, thank you for your support and patience as I worked on this book. Your love sustains me, and your encouragement and support inspires me. Timothy and Megan, and Amanda and Tu, George and I are so happy for all of you. Best wishes as you start your life adventures together!

—Annette Easton

Brent, thank you for your steadfast love and support that mean so much to me. Thank you to my friends who shared their expertise, project ideas, and encouragement while I worked on this book.

—Pat Graves

brief contents

contents

CHAPTER 2: WORKING WITH FORMULAS AND FUNCTIONS

ACCESS

CHAPTER 1: CREATING A DATABASE AND TABLES

POWERPOINT

about the authors

RANDY NORDELL, Ed.D.

AMERICAN RIVER COLLEGE

Dr. Randy Nordell is a Professor of Business Technology at American River College in Sacramento, California. He has been an educator for over 25 years and has taught at the high school, community college, and university levels. He holds a bachelor's degree in Business Administration from California State University, Stanislaus, a single subject teaching credential from Fresno State University, a master's degree in Education from Fresno Pacific University, and a doctorate in Education from Argosy University. Randy is the lead author of the *Microsoft Office 365: In Practice, Microsoft Office 2016: In Practice,* and *Microsoft Office 2013: In Practice* series of texts. He is also the author of *101 Tips for Online Course Success* and *Microsoft Outlook 2010.* Randy speaks regularly at conferences on the integration of technology into the curriculum. When not teaching and writing, he enjoys spending time with his family, cycling, skiing, swimming, backpacking, and enjoying the California weather and terrain.

KATHLEEN STEWART, M.S. Ed., M.B.A.

Kathleen Stewart is retired from her role as professor and department chairperson for the Information Management Systems Department at Moraine Valley Community College in Palos Hills, Illinois. She has a master's degree in occupational education from Southern Illinois University in Carbondale and an M.B.A. from Loyola University in Chicago. She has authored Microsoft Office texts for many years for McGraw-Hill and has been involved in corporate training in the Chicago area. When not occupied by a writing project, she enjoys traveling, working on her golf game, literacy tutoring, and exploring cultural activities in the city.

ANNETTE EASTON, Ph.D.

Annette Easton is retired from her role as department chair and associate professor of management information systems at San Diego State University. She taught for over 28 years at the university level and served as a School Board Trustee for eight years. She holds a bachelor's degree in business administration from Fresno State University, and a doctorate in management information systems from the University of Arizona. Annette has published articles on information technology education, electronic meeting systems, and integrating new technologies into the information systems curriculum. She co-authored Cases for Modern Systems Development, and has been an author of Access textbooks for McGraw-Hill Education since 2013. When not writing, she enjoys traveling and improving her golf game with her husband, spending time with her family, and cooking.

PAT GRAVES, Ed.D.

Pat Graves is a professor emeritus at Eastern Illinois University in Charleston, Illinois. She taught at the high school level before receiving her doctorate in education from the University of Memphis. At Eastern Illinois University, she taught in the School of Business for 20 years. Pat has been an author for McGraw-Hill Education since 2002. She is the PowerPoint author for the *Microsoft Office: In Practice* series published in 2013, 2016, and 2019. When not writing, she travels, spends time with family and friends, enjoys the music city of Nashville, and appreciates the peacefulness of the Tennessee mountains.

What We're About

We wrote *Microsoft Office 365: In Practice, 2019 Edition* to meet the diverse needs of both students and instructors. Our approach focuses on presenting Office topics in a logical and structured manner, teaching concepts in a way that reinforces learning with practice projects that are transferrable, relevant, and engaging. Our pedagogy and content are based on the following beliefs.

Students Need to Learn and Practice Transferable Skills

Students must be able to transfer the concepts and skills learned in the text to a variety of projects, not simply follow steps in a textbook. Our material goes beyond the instruction of many texts. In our content, students practice the concepts in a variety of current and relevant projects *and* are able to transfer skills and concepts learned to different projects in the real world. To further increase the transferability of skills learned, this text is integrated with SIMnet so students also practice skills and complete projects in an online environment.

Your Curriculum Drives the Content

The curriculum in the classroom should drive the content of the text, not the other way around. This book is designed to allow instructors and students to cover all the material they need to in order to meet the curriculum requirements of their courses no matter how the courses are structured. *Microsoft Office 365: In Practice, 2019 Edition* teaches the marketable skills that are key to student success. McGraw-Hill's Custom Publishing site, **Create,** can further tailor the content material to meet the unique educational needs of any school.

Integrated with Technology

Our text provides a fresh and new approach to an Office applications course. Topics integrate seamlessly with SIMnet with 1:1 content to help students practice and master concepts and skills using SIMnet's interactive learning philosophy. Projects in SIMnet allow students to practice their skills and receive immediate feedback. This integration with SIMnet meets the diverse needs of students and accommodates individual learning styles. Additional textbook resources found in SIMnet (Resources and Library sections) integrate with the learning management systems that are widely used in many online and onsite courses.

Reference Text

In addition to providing students with an abundance of real-life examples and practice projects, we designed this text to be used as a Microsoft Office 365 reference source. The core material, uncluttered with exercises, focuses on real-world use and application. Our text provides clear step-by-step instructions on how readers can apply the various features available in Microsoft Office in a variety of contexts. At the same time, users have access to a variety of both online (SIMnet) and textbook practice projects to reinforce skills and concepts. Both SIMnet and this text are updated with the most current Office 365 features. For the most current updates, please refer first to SIMnet.

instructor walkthrough

Textbook Learning Approach

Microsoft Office 365: In Practice, 2019 Edition uses the *T.I.P. approach:*

- **T**opic
- **I**nstruction
- **P**ractice

Topic

- Each Office application section begins with foundational skills and builds to more complex topics as the text progresses.
- Topics are logically sequenced and grouped by topics.
- Student Learning Outcomes (SLOs) are thoroughly integrated with and mapped to chapter content, projects, end-of-chapter review, and test banks.
- Reports are available within SIMnet for displaying how students have met these Student Learning Outcomes.

Instruction (How To)

- *How To* guided instructions about chapter topics provide transferable and adaptable instructions.
- Because *How To* instructions are not locked into single projects, this textbook functions as a reference text, not just a point-and-click textbook.
- Chapter content is aligned 1:1 with SIMnet.

Practice (Pause & Practice and End-of-Chapter Projects)

- Within each chapter, integrated Pause & Practice projects (three to five per chapter) reinforce learning and provide hands-on guided practice.
- In addition to Pause & Practice projects, each chapter has 10 comprehensive and practical practice projects: Guided Projects (three per chapter), Independent Projects (three per chapter), Improve It Project (one per chapter), and Challenge Projects (three per chapter). Additional projects can also be found in the Library or Resources section of SIMnet.
- Pause & Practice and end-of-chapter projects are complete content-rich projects, not small examples lacking context.
- Select auto-graded projects are available in SIMnet.

Chapter Features

All chapters follow a consistent theme and instructional methodology. Below is an example of chapter structure.

Main headings are organized according to the *Student Learning Outcomes (SLOs).*

SLO 1.1

Creating, Saving, and Opening Docume

In Microsoft Word, you can create a variety of document types of Word enables you to create, edit, and customize high-quality ments. You can create Word documents from a new blank doc plates, or from existing documents. Word enables you to save do

ate letters, memos, reports, flyers, brochures, and mailings without a va knowledge. This chapter covers the basics of creating and editing a Wo

STUDENT LEARNING OUTCOMES (SLOs)

After completing this chapter, you will be able to:

SLO 1.1 Create, save, and open a Word document (p. 3).

SLO 1.2 Customize a document by entering and selecting text, usin and using *AutoComplete*, *AutoCorrect*, and *AutoFormat* fe

SLO 1.3 Enhance a document using paragraph breaks, line breaks, non-breaking spaces (p. 10).

SLO 1.4 Edit a document using cut, copy, paste, the *Clipboard*, and and repeat features (p. 15).

SLO 1.5 Customize a document using different fonts, font sizes, and

SLO 1.6 Enhance a document using text alignment and line and pa (p. 28).

SLO 1.7 Finalize a document using Word's research, proofing, and tools (p. 32).

SLO 1.8 Apply custom document properties to a document (p. 38).

A list of Student Learning Outcomes begins each chapter. All chapter content, examples, and practice projects are organized according to the chapter SLOs.

WORD

CASE STUDY

Throughout this book, you have the opportunity to practice the application features presented in each chapter. Each chapter begins with a case study that introduces you to the Pause & Practice projects in the chapter. Pause & Practice projects provide a chance to apply and practice key skills in a realistic and practical context. Each chapter contains three to five Pause & Practice projects.

Placer Hills Real Estate (PHRE) is a real estate company with regional offices throughout central California. PHRE encourages agents to use standard formats for their business documents. This ensures consistency in document appearance while also allowing agents to personalize their correspondence to customers and colleagues. In the Pause & Practice projects for this chapter, you create a business document related to the real estate business.

The *Case Study* for each chapter is a scenario that establishes the theme for the entire chapter. Chapter content, examples, figures, Pause & Practice projects, SIMnet skills, and projects throughout the chapter closely related to this case study content. The three to five Pause & Practice projects in each chapter build upon each other and address key case study themes.

How To instructions enhance transferability of skills with concise steps and screen shots.

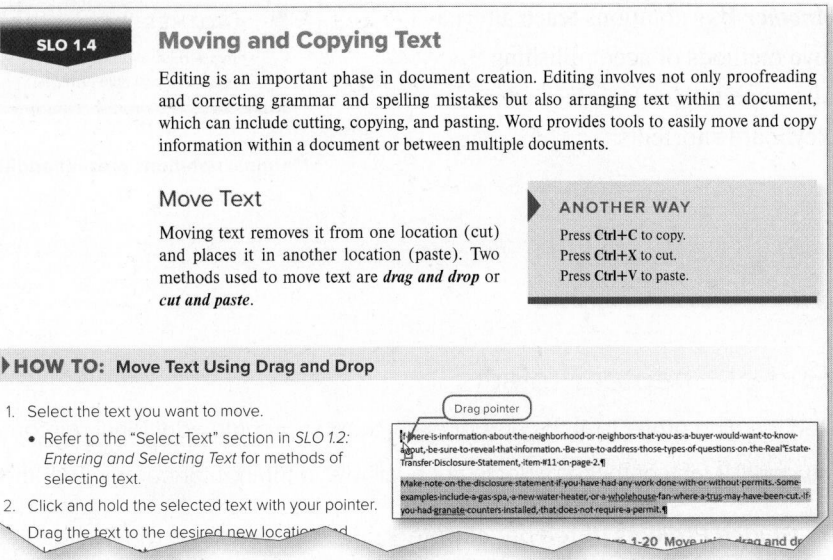

How To instructions are easy-to-follow concise steps. Screen shots and other figures fully illustrate How To topics.

Students can complete hands-on exercises in either the Office application or in SIMnet.

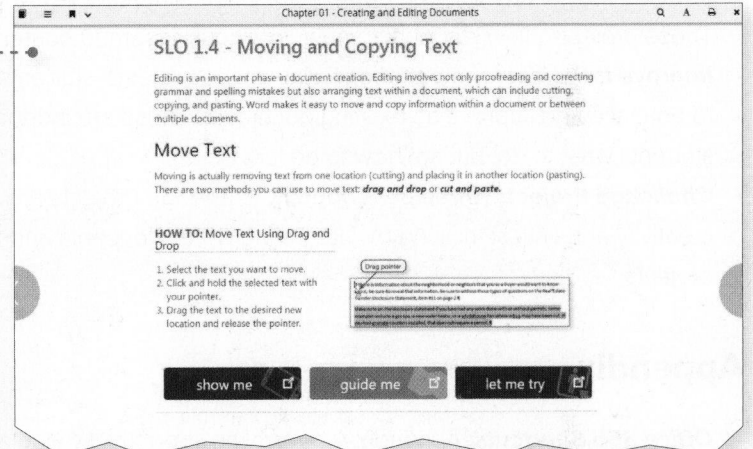

Pause & Practice 1-1: Create a business letter in block format with mixed punctuation.

Pause & Practice 1-2: Edit the business letter using copy, paste, and *Format Painter*. Modify the font, font size, color, style, and effects of selected text.

Pause & Practice 1-3: Finalize the business letter by modifying line spacing and paragraph spacing, changing paragraph alignment, translating text, using research and proofing tools, and adding document properties.

Pause & Practice projects, which each cover two to three of the student learning outcomes in the chapter, provide students with the opportunity to review and practice skills and concepts. Every chapter contains three to five Pause & Practice projects.

> **MORE INFO**
>
> The *launcher* (also referred to as the *dialog box launcher*) is referred to throughout this text. Click the launcher in the bottom-right corner of a group to open a dialog box or pane for additional options.

More Info provides readers with additional information about chapter content.

Another Way notations teach alterna-
tive methods of accomplishing
the same task or feature, such as
keyboard shortcuts.

Marginal notations present additional information and alternative methods.

End-of-Chapter Projects

Ten learning projects at the end of each chapter provide additional reinforcement and practice for students. Many of these projects are available in SIMnet for completion and automatic grading.

- *Guided Projects (three per chapter):* Guided Projects provide guided step-by-step instructions to apply Office features, skills, and concepts from the chapter. Screen shots guide students through the more challenging tasks. End-of-project screen shots provide a visual of the completed project.
- *Independent Projects (three per chapter):* Independent Projects provide students further opportunities to practice and apply skills, instructing students what to do, but not how to do it. These projects allow students to apply previously learned content in a different context.
- *Improve It Project (one per chapter):* In these projects, students apply their knowledge and skills to enhance and improve an existing document. These are independent-type projects that instruct students what to do, but not how to do it.
- *Challenge Projects (three per chapter):* Challenge Projects are open-ended projects that encourage creativity and critical thinking by integrating Office concepts and features into relevant and engaging projects.

Appendix

- *Office 365 Shortcuts:* Appendix A covers the shortcuts available in Microsoft Office and within each of the specific Office applications. Information is in table format for easy access and reference.

Additional Resources
in SIMnet

Students and instructors can find the following resources in the Library or Resources sections in SIMnet.

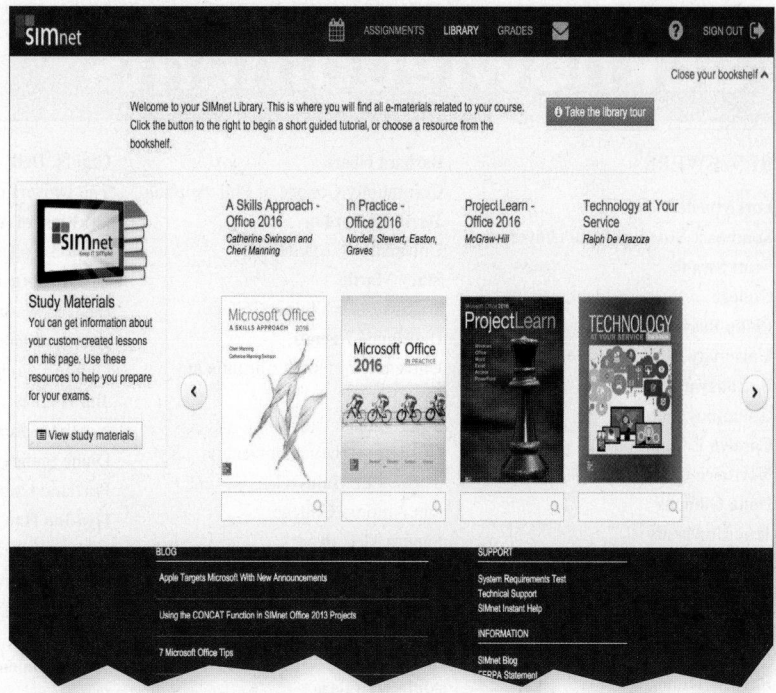

Student Resources

- **Data Files:** Files contain start files for all Pause & Practice, Capstone, and end-of-chapter projects.
- **SIMnet Resources:** Resources provide getting started and informational handouts for instructors and students.
- **Check for Understanding:** A combination of multiple choice, fill-in, matching, and short answer questions are available at the end of each SIMbook chapter in SIMnet to assist students in their review of the skills and concepts covered in the chapter.

Capstone Projects

- **Integrating Applications:** Projects provide students with the opportunity to learn, practice, and transfer skills using multiple Office applications.
- **Integrating Skills:** Projects provide students with a comprehensive and integrated review of all of the topics covered in each application (Word, Excel, Access, and PowerPoint). Available in individual application texts.

Appendices

- **Business Document Formats:** Appendix B is a guide to regularly used business document formatting and includes numerous examples and detailed instructions.

Instructor Resources

- **Instructor's Manual:** An Instructor's Manual provides teaching tips and lecture notes aligned with the PowerPoint presentations for each chapter. The manual also includes the solutions for online **Check for Understanding** questions.
- **Test Bank:** The extensive test bank integrates with learning management systems (LMSs) such as Blackboard, WebCT, Desire2Learn, and Moodle.
- **PowerPoint Presentations:** PowerPoint presentations for each chapter can be used in onsite course formats for lectures or can be uploaded to LMSs.
- **SIMnet Resources:** These resources provide getting started and informational handouts for instructors.
- **Solution Files:** Files contain solutions for all Pause & Practice, Capstone, Check for Understanding, and end-of-chapter projects.

acknowledgments

REVIEWERS

Lori Mueller
Southeast Missouri State University

Scott Straub
College of Western Idaho

Philip Reaves
University of Western Georgia

B. Bhagyavati
Columbus State

Carolyn E. Johnson
Northern Oklahoma College

Dona Gibbons
Troy University

Denise Sullivan
Westchester Community College

Suzanne Marks
Bellevue College

Phyllis Fleming
Middlesex County College

Salli DiBartolo
Eastern Florida State College

Teresa Roberson
Northwest-Shoals Community
College

Amy Chataginer
Mississippi Gulf Coast Community
College

Dr. Lucinda Stanley
Wor-Wic Community College

Bill Dorin
Indiana University Northwest

Anita Laird
Schoolcraft College

Sue Bajt
Harper College

Ralph Argiento
Guilford Technical Community
College

Annette D. Rakowski
Bergen Community College

Beth Deinert
Southeast Community College

Jo Stephens
University of Arkansas Community
College Batesville

Terry Beachy
Garrett College

Vincent Kayes
Mount Saint Mary College,
Newburgh

Kimberly Madsen
Kellogg Community College

Nicolas Rouse
Phoenix College

Barbara Hearn
Community College of Philadelphia

Terribeth Gordon
University of Toledo

Stacy Martin
Southwestern Illinois College

Dr. Hamid Nemati
University of North Carolina at
Greensboro

Beverly Amer
Northern Arizona University

Michael L. Matuszek
San Antonio College

Sandra Metcalf
Grayson College

David Cook
Stephen F. Austin State University

Donnie W. Collins
Andrew College

Frank Whittle
Dutchess Community College

Robert LaRocca
Keiser University

Adnan Turkey
DeVry University

Sheryl S. Bulloch
Columbia Southern University

Richard Flores
Citrus College

Dmitriy Chulkov
Indiana University Kokomo

Mary Locke
Greenville Technical College

Sherrie Drye
North Carolina A&T State
University

Andrew Smith
Marian University Indianapolis

Crystal Theaker
Chandler-Gilbert Community
College

Pam Cummings
Minnesota State Community and
Technical Colleg

Tina LePage
Chandler-Gilbert Community
College

Darenda Kersey
Black River Technical College

Amy Rutledge
Oakland University

Brian Fox
Santa Fe College

Trey Cherry
Edgecombe Community College

Gigi N. Delk
The University of Texas at Tyler

Dr. Richard A. Warren
Vernon College

Debra Morgan
Eastern Washington University.

Pamela Bilodeau
Olympic College

Jim Hughes
Northern Kentucky University

Diane Shingledecker
Portland Community College

Hyo-Joo Han
Georgia Southern University

Becky McAfee
Hillsborough Community College
Home

Karen Donham
University of Arkansas at
Monticello

Craig Bradley
Shawnee Community College

Elodie Billionniere
Miami Dade College

Joan Rogers
Hillsborough Community College

Genalin F. Umstetter
Delta College

Michael Kato
University of Hawaii

Ann Konarski
St. Clair County Community
College

Dr. Mark W. Huber
University of Georgia

Kathleen Morris
The University of Alabama

Rebecca Leveille
American River College

Dory Eddy
Colorado Christian University

Masoud Naghedolfeizi
Fort Valley State University

Joe Vargas
Santa Barbara Business College

Donna Kamen
Truckee Meadows Community
College

David Sanford
Northwood University Home

Ken Werner
Alaska Vocational Technical Center

Gigi Simonsen
Northeast Community College

Paula Gregory
Yavapai College

Mordechai Adelman
Touro College

Ron Oler
Ivy Tech Community College of
Indiana

Sandra LaFevers
Joliet Junior College

Sherilyn Reynolds
San Jacinto College

Melissa Nemeth
Indiana University

Barbara Garrell
Delaware County Community
College

Astrid Todd
Guilford Technical Community
College

Deedee Flax
Dodge City Community College

Elizabeth P. Sigman
Georgetown University

Preston Clark
Cornell University

Sara Rutledge
Mount Aloysius College

Robyn Barrett
St. Louis Community College

William Neiheisel
Gwinnett College

Sheila Gionfriddo
Luzerne County Community
College

Teodoro Llallire
Fairleigh Dickinson University

Tracy Driscoll
Bishop State Community College

Sam McCall
St. Philip's College

Joyce King
Bay College

John Schrage
Southern Illinois University
Edwardsville

John Maloney
Miami Dade College

Lisa Friesen
Southwestern Oklahoma State
University

Shelley Ota
University of Hawaii

Heidi Eaton
Elgin Community College

LaVaughn Hart
Las Positas College
Sandy Keeter
Seminole State College
Kathy J. Schaefer
Southwest Minnesota State University
Edward Hall
Seward County Community College
Saiid Ganjalizadeh
The Catholic University of America
Melinda Norris
Coker College
Phillip Dickson
Black River Technical College
Kathy Powell-Case
Colorado Northwestern Community College
Marianne Daugharthy
College of Western Idaho
Ann Taff
Tulsa Community College
Lydia Slater
Rock Valley College
Seyed Roosta
Albany State University
Pamela Silvers
Asheville-Buncombe Technical Community College
Phillip Davis
Del Mar College
Logan Phillips
Tulsa Community College
Dianne Hill
Jackson College
Jeff Harper
Indiana State University
Carla K. Draffen
West Kentucky Community & Technical College
Colin Onita
San Jose State University
N. T. Izuchi
Quinsigamond Community College
Camille Rogers
Georgia Southern University
Luy Parker
California State University, Northridge
Homer Sharafi
Prince George's Community College
Bill Courter
Jackson College
Robert Wardzala
University of Findlay
Lindsey Huber
Northern State University
David Rosenthal
Seton Hall University

Sandro Marchegiani
University of Pittsburgh
Linda Johnsonius
Murray State University
Barbara Bracken
Wilkes University
Marie Hassinger
Susquehanna University
Rich Cacace
Pensacola State College
Arcola Sullivan
Copiah-Lincoln Community College
Angela Mott
Northeast Mississippi Community College
Tony Hunnicutt
College of the Ouachitas
Stephen D. Ross
Mississippi Delta Community College
Alex Morgan
De Anza College
Aaron Ferguson
University of Maryland University College
Patricia White
University of Maryland University College
Anne Acker
Jacksonville University
Pam Shields
Mt. Hood Community College
Nancy Lilly
Central Alabama Community College
Mandy Reininger
Chemeketa Community College
Alison Rampersad
Lynn University
Jeanine Preuss
South Puget Sound Community College
Timothy J. Lloyd
University of Maryland University College
Betsy Boardwine
Virginia Western Community College
Meg Murray
Kennesaw State University
Lynne Lyon
Durham College
Peter Meggison
Massasoit Community College
Sujing Wang
Lamar University
Alla Zakharova
University of South Alabama
Rachel E. Hinton
SUNY Broome Community College

Rhoda A. M. James
Citrus College
Gena Casas
Florida State College at Jacksonville
James D. Powell
College of the Desert
Sue Joiner
Tarleton State University
Dawn Nelson
University of Dubuque
Carlos Jimenez
El Paso Community College
Diane Smith
Henry Ford College
Steven Brennan
Jackson College
Mehran Basiratmand
Florida Atlantic University
Sharolyn Sayers
Milwaukee Area Technical College
Charles Wunker
Webber International University
Doreen Palucci
Wilmington University
Kristy McAuliffe
San Jacinto College
Rob Lemelin
Eastern Washington University
Nancy Severe
Northern Virginia Community College
Julie Becker
Three Rivers Community College
David Childress
Kentucky Community & Technical College System
Carolyn Kuehne
Utah Valley University
Carolyn Carvalho
Kent State University
Irene Joos
La Roche College
Dr. Shayan Mirabi
American InterContinental University
Zhizhang Shen
Plymouth State University
Kirk Atkinson
Western Kentucky University: WKU
Nisheeth Agrawal
Calhoun Community College
Dr. Bernard Ku
Austin Community College
Jennifer Michaels
Lenoir-Rhyne University
William Barrett
Iowa Western Community College
Naomi Johnson
Dickinson State University

Gilliean Lee
Lander University
Clem Lundie
San Jose City College
Cynthia C. Nitsch
MiraCosta College
Beth Cantrell
Central Baptist College
Bernice Eng
Brookdale Community College
Paul Weaver
Bossier Parish Community College
William Penfold
Jamestown Community College
Kathrynn Hollis-Buchanan
University of Alaska
Carmen Morrison
North Central State College
Marie Campbell
Idaho State University
Jpann G. Becento
Navajo Technical University
Annette Yauney
Herkimer College
Judy Jernigan
Tyler Junior College
Elise Marshall
University of North Florida
Karen Waddell
Butler Community College
Allison Bryant
Howard University
William Spangler
Duquesne University
Henry Bradford
Massasoit Community College
Julie Haar
Alexandria Technical & Community College
Martha Balachandran
Middle Tennessee State University
Cheryl Jordan
San Juan College
Mary Kennedy
College of DuPage
Pengtao Li
California State University Stanislaus
Odemaris Valdivia
Santa Monica College
Joyce Quade
Saddleback College
Pam Houston
Oglala Lakota College
Marc Isaacson
Augsburg University
Penny Cypert
Tarrant County College

Manuel T. Uy
Peralta Colleges
Bonnie Smith
Fresno City College
Brenda Killingsworth
East Carolina University
Ember Mitchell
Dixie State University
Emily Holliday
Campbell University

Holly Bales
International Business College in
Indianapolis
Elizabeth Sykes
Golden West College

TECHNICAL EDITORS

Karen May
Blinn College

Andrea Nevill
College of Western Idaho
Richard Finn
Moraine Valley Community
College
Chris Anderson
North Central Michigan
College
Gena Casas
Florida State College

Leon Blue
Pensacola State College
Amie Mayhall
Olney Central College
Patrick Doran
University of Wisconsin Milwaukeex

Thank you to the wonderful team at McGraw-Hill for your confidence in us and support throughout this project. Alan, Wyatt, Tiffany, Corban, Debbie, Harvey, and Julianna, we thoroughly enjoy working with you all! A special thanks to Debbie Hinkle for her thorough and insightful review of the series. Thank you to all of the reviewers and technical editors for your expertise and invaluable insight, which helped shape this book.

—Randy, Kathleen, Annette, and Pat

Windows 10, Office 365/2019, and File Management

CHAPTER OVERVIEW

Microsoft Office 2019 and Windows 10 introduce many new and enhanced features. Office 2019 includes the Office features added to Office 365 since the release of Office 2016. The integration of Office 2019 and Windows 10 improves file portability and accessibility when you use *OneDrive*, Microsoft's free online cloud storage. Office 2019, Office 365, Office Online, Office mobile apps, and Windows 10 enable you to work on tablet computers and smartphones in a consistent working environment that resembles your desktop or laptop computer.

STUDENT LEARNING OUTCOMES (SLOs)

After completing this chapter, you will be able to:

SLO Intro. 1 Explore select features of Windows 10 (p. Intro-2).

SLO Intro. 2 Use basic features of Microsoft Office and navigate the Office working environment (p. Intro-12).

SLO Intro. 3 Create, save, close, and open Office files (p. Intro-19).

SLO Intro. 4 Customize the view and display size in Office applications and work with multiple Office files (p. Intro-28).

SLO Intro. 5 Print, share, and customize Office files (p. Intro-32).

SLO Intro. 6 Use the *Ribbon,* tabs, groups, dialog boxes, task panes, galleries, and the *Quick Access* toolbar (p. Intro-37).

SLO Intro. 7 Use context menus, mini toolbar, keyboard shortcuts, and function keys in Office applications (p. Intro-41).

SLO Intro. 8 Organize and customize Windows folders and Office files (p. Intro-46).

CASE STUDY

Throughout this book, you have the opportunity to practice the application features presented in the text. Each chapter begins with a case study that introduces you to the Pause & Practice projects in the chapter. These Pause & Practice projects give you a chance to apply and practice key skills in a realistic and practical context. Each chapter contains three to five Pause & Practice projects.

American River Cycling Club (ARCC) is a community cycling club that promotes fitness. ARCC members include recreational cyclists who enjoy the exercise and camaraderie as well as competitive cyclists who compete in road, mountain, and cyclocross races throughout the cycling season. In the Pause & Practice projects, you incorporate many of the topics covered in the chapter to create, save, customize, manage, and share Office files.

Pause & Practice Intro-1: Customize the Windows *Start* menu and *Taskbar*, create and save a PowerPoint presentation, create a folder, open and rename an Excel workbook, and use Windows 10 features.

Pause & Practice Intro-2: Modify an existing document, add document properties,

customize the *Quick Access* toolbar, export the document as a PDF file, and share the document.

Pause & Practice Intro-3: Copy and rename files, create a folder, move files, create a zipped folder, and rename a zipped folder.

SLO INTRO. 1

Using Windows 10

Windows 10 is an *operating system* that controls computer functions and the working environment. Windows 10 uses the familiar *Windows desktop*, *Taskbar*, and *Start menu*. The Windows operating system enables you to customize the working environment and to install applications (apps), such as Microsoft Office. Visit the *Microsoft Store* to download additional apps similar to how you would add an app to your smartphone. Your *Microsoft account* stores your Microsoft settings, enabling you to download apps from the Microsoft Store, and to connect to Microsoft Office, *OneDrive*, and *Office Online*.

Windows 10

The Windows 10 operating system controls interaction with computer hardware and software applications (apps; also referred to as programs). *Windows 10* utilizes a *Start menu* where you select and open an app. Alternatively, you can open apps using the *Taskbar*, the horizontal bar that displays at the bottom of the Windows desktop. When you log in to Windows 10 using your Microsoft account, your Microsoft account synchronizes your Windows, Office, and *OneDrive* cloud storage among computers.

Microsoft Account

In Windows 10 and Office 365/2019, your files and account settings are portable. In other words, your Office settings and files travel with you and are accessible from different computers. You are not restricted to using a single computer. When you sign in to Windows 10 using your Microsoft account (user name and password), Microsoft uses this information to transfer your Windows and Office 2019 settings to the computer you are using. Different types of Microsoft accounts exist: Personal, Education, and Business.

Figure Intro-1 Create a Microsoft account

Your Microsoft account not only signs in to Windows and Office but also to other free Microsoft online services, such as *OneDrive* and *Office Online*. As a student, you can get a free education Microsoft account at https://products.office.com/en-us/student/office-in-education. Also, you can create a free personal Microsoft account at https://signup.live.com (Figure Intro-1).

Windows Desktop and Taskbar

The Windows desktop is the working area of Windows. When you log in to Windows, the desktop displays (Figure Intro-2). The *Taskbar* displays horizontally at the bottom of the desktop. Click an icon on the *Taskbar* to open apps and folders (see Figure Intro-2). Pinning is used to add shortcuts to the *Taskbar* or the *Start* menu. You can pin the *Settings, File Explorer,* and other frequently used apps to the *Taskbar* (see "Customize the Taskbar" later in this section).

Figure Intro-2 Window desktop and *Taskbar*

Start Menu

Windows 10 utilizes a redesigned *Start* menu (Figure Intro-3) that you open by clicking the **Start button** located in the bottom left of the *Taskbar*. From the *Start* menu, you open apps, files, folders, or other Windows resources. The *Start* menu is divided into two main sections. The left side of the *Start* menu displays the *Account, Documents, Pictures, Settings,* and *Power* buttons. This section also displays *Recently added* and *Most used* items, as well as an alphabetical listing of all apps installed on your computer. The right side of the *Start* menu displays tiles (large and small buttons) you click to open an application or window.

Figure Intro-3 Windows *Start* menu

You can customize which apps and items appear on either side of the *Start* menu, arrange and group apps on the *Start* menu, resize the *Start* menu, and display the *Start* menu as a **Start page** when you log in to Windows. See "Customize the Start Menu" later in this section for information about customizing the *Start* menu.

Add Apps

Windows 10 uses the term **apps** generically to refer to applications and programs. Apps include the Windows 10 Weather app, Microsoft Excel program, Control Panel, Google Chrome, or *File Explorer*. Many apps are preinstalled on a Windows 10 computer, and additional apps can be installed on your computer. Install an app, such as Office 2019 or Quicken, by downloading it from a web site. These apps are referred to as **desktop apps** or **traditional apps**.

The **Microsoft Store** app is preinstalled on Windows 10 computers. Install apps such as Netflix, Yelp, and Spotify from the Microsoft Store. These apps are referred to as **modern apps** and look and function similar to apps you install on your smartphone. Many apps in the Microsoft Store are free, and others are available for purchase.

▶ HOW TO: Add an App from the Microsoft Store

1. Click the **Start** button to open the *Start* menu.
2. Click the **Microsoft Store** button (tile) to open the Microsoft Store app (Figure Intro-4) and click the **Apps** tab.
 - If the *Microsoft Store* tile is not available on the *Start* menu, locate the *Microsoft Store* button in the alphabetic listing of all apps.
3. Search for and select an app in the Microsoft Store (Figure Intro-5).
 - The Microsoft Store includes different categories of apps.
 - You can search for apps by typing keywords in the *Search* box in the upper-right corner.
 - When you select an app, information about the app displays.
4. Click the **Get**, **Buy**, or **Free trial** button to install the app.
 - You must have a payment method stored in your Microsoft account to purchase apps from the Microsoft Store.
5. Click **Launch** to open the installed app.
 - When you install an app, the app displays in the *Recently added* area on the *Start* menu and *All apps* list of applications.

Figure Intro-4 *Microsoft Store* app on the *Start* menu

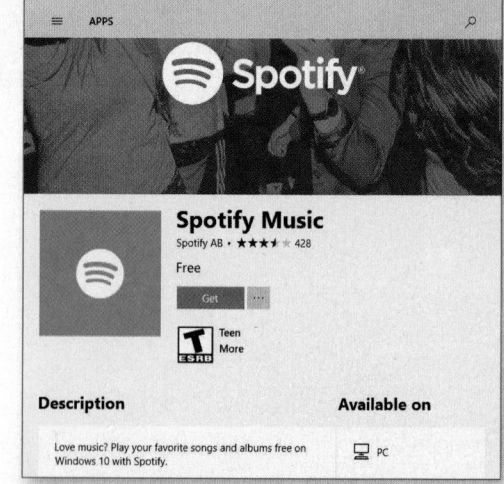

Figure Intro-5 Install an app from the Microsoft Store

Customize the Start Menu

When you start using Windows 10 or after you have installed apps, you can customize what appears on your the *Start* menu. When you **pin** an app to the *Start* menu, the corresponding app tile remains on the right side of the *Start* menu. Pin the apps you most regularly use, unpin the apps you don't want displayed on the *Start* menu, and rearrange and resize app tiles to your preference.

▶ HOW TO: Customize the Start Menu

1. Click the **Start** button to open the *Start* menu.
2. Move an app tile on the *Start* menu by clicking and dragging the app tile to a new location. The other app tiles shuffle to accommodate the placement of the moved app tile.
3. Remove an app tile from the *Start* menu by right-clicking the app tile and selecting **Unpin from Start** from the context menu (Figure Intro-6).
 - The app tile is removed from the right side of the *Start* menu, but the program or task is not removed from your computer.

Right-click app to display context menu

Figure Intro-6 Unpin an app from the *Start* menu

4. Pin an app tile to the *Start* menu by right-clicking the app in the alphabetic listing of apps in the *Start* menu and selecting **Pin to Start** (Figure Intro-7).
 - Drag the newly added app tile to the desired location on the *Start* menu.

Figure Intro-7 Pin an app to the *Start* menu

5. Resize an app tile by right-clicking the app tile, selecting **Resize**, and selecting **Small**, **Medium**, **Wide**, or **Large**.
 - Some apps only have *Small, Medium,* and *Wide* size options.
6. Turn on or off the live tile option by right-clicking the app tile, selecting ***More,*** and selecting **Turn Live Tile on** or **Turn Live Tile off**.
 - Live tile displays rotating graphics and options on the app tile. When this option is turned off, the name of the app displays on the tile.

Settings button
Start button
Figure Intro-8 *Settings* button on the *Start* menu

7. Uninstall an app by right-clicking the app you want to uninstall and selecting **Uninstall**.
 - Unlike the unpin option, this option uninstalls the program from your computer, not just your *Start* menu.
 - The *Uninstall* option is not available for some pre-installed Microsoft Windows apps.
8. Resize the *Start* menu by clicking and dragging the top or right edge of the *Start* menu.
9. Customize *Start* menu settings by clicking the **Start** button, selecting **Settings** button (Figure Intro-8) to open the *Settings* window, clicking the **Personalization** button, and clicking the **Start** option at the left (Figure Intro-9).
 - Click the **X** in the upper-right corner to close the *Settings* window.

Figure Intro-9 Use full screen *Start* menu

Customize the Taskbar

The *Taskbar* is the horizontal bar located at the bottom of the Windows desktop, and you can quickly open an app by clicking an icon on the *Taskbar* rather than opening it from the *Start* menu. You can customize the *Taskbar* by pinning, unpinning, and rearranging apps. The right side of the *Taskbar* is the *System Tray,* which displays smaller icons of system applications that automatically run in the background of the Windows operating system.

▶ HOW TO: Customize the Taskbar

1. Pin an app to the *Taskbar* by clicking the **Start** button, right-clicking an app, clicking **More**, and selecting **Pin to taskbar** (Figure Intro-10).

 - You can also pin an app to the *Taskbar* by right-clicking an app from the alphabetic listing of apps in the *Start* menu.

2. Unpin an app from the *Taskbar* by right-clicking an app icon on the *Taskbar* and selecting **Unpin from taskbar** (Figure Intro-11).

 - You can also unpin apps from the *Taskbar* by right-clicking an app in the *Start* menu, clicking **More**, and selecting **Unpin from taskbar**.

3. Rearrange apps on the *Taskbar* by clicking and dragging the app to the desired location on the *Taskbar* and releasing.

Figure Intro-10 Pin an app to the *Taskbar*

Figure Intro-11 Unpin an app from the *Taskbar*

> ▶ **MORE INFO**
>
> If using a touch screen, press and hold an app on the *Start* menu or *Taskbar* to display the app options.

File Explorer

The *File Explorer* in Windows 10 is a window that opens on your desktop where you browse files stored on your computer (Figure Intro-12). You can open a file or folder, move or copy items, create folders, and delete files or folders. Click the **Start** button and select **File Explorer** to open a *File Explorer* window. Alternatively, right-click the **Start** button and select **File Explorer**.

Figure Intro-12 *File Explorer* window

> ▶ **MORE INFO**
>
> You can pin the *File Explorer* to the *Taskbar* for easy access to this window.

The *File Explorer* has different areas:

- **Navigation pane**: The *Navigation* pane displays folders on the left. The **Quick access** area at the top of the *Navigation* pane displays shortcuts to favorite folders. You can pin or unpin folders in the *Quick access* area of the *Navigation* pane.
- **Navigation buttons**: The navigation buttons (*Back, Forward, Recent location,* and *Up*) are located directly above the *Navigation* pane and below the *Ribbon.* Use these buttons to navigate a File Explorer window.
- **Folder pane**: When you select a folder in the *Navigation* pane, the contents of the folder display in the *Folder* pane to the right of the *Navigation* pane. Double-click a folder or file in the *Folder* pane to open it.
- **Ribbon**: The *Ribbon* is located near the top of *File Explorer* and includes the *File, Home, Share,* and *View* tabs. When you click a tab on the *Ribbon,* the *Ribbon* displays the options for the selected tab. Other contextual tabs display when you select certain types of files. For example, the *Picture Tool Manage* tab opens when you select a picture file in the *Folder* pane.
- **Quick Access toolbar**: The *Quick Access* toolbar is above the *Ribbon.* From the *Quick Access* toolbar, click the **New Folder** button to create a new folder or click **Properties** to display the properties of a selected file or folder. You can add buttons, such as *Undo, Redo,* and *Rename,* to the *Quick Access* toolbar.
- **Search**: The *Search* text box is located on the right of the *File Explorer* window below the *Ribbon.* Type key words in the *Search* text box to find files or folders.

OneDrive

OneDrive is a cloud storage area where you store files in a private and secure online location that you access from any computer. With Windows 10, the **OneDrive folder** is one of your storage location folder options, similar to your *Documents* or *Pictures* folders (Figure Intro-13). You can save, open, and edit your *OneDrive* files from a *File Explorer* folder. Your *OneDrive* folder looks and functions similar to other Windows folders. *OneDrive* synchronizes your files so when you change a file stored in *OneDrive* it is automatically updated on the *OneDrive* cloud.

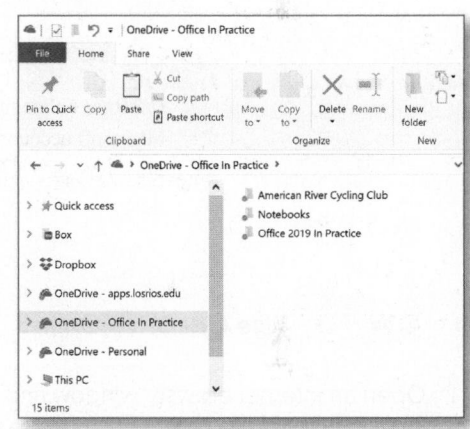

Figure Intro-13 *OneDrive* folder in a *File Explorer* window

When you store your files in *OneDrive,* you have the option of storing the files on *OneDrive* only (in the cloud) or syncing the files to your computer so they are saved on both your computer and on the cloud. You can customize which *OneDrive* folders and files are cloud only (not stored on your computer) and which folders and files are synced to your computer.

▶**HOW TO:** Customize OneDrive Settings

1. Open a *File Explorer* window using one of the following methods:
 - Click the **Start** button and select the **File Explorer** button.
 - Click the **File Explorer** button on the *Taskbar* (if available).
 - Right-click the **Start** button and select **File Explorer**.

2. Right-click the **OneDrive** folder in the *Navigation* pane of the *File Explorer* window and select **Settings** to open the *Microsoft OneDrive* dialog box.

 - Alternatively, right-click the **OneDrive** icon (if available) in the *System Tray* (right side of the *Taskbar*) and select **Settings**.

3. Click the **Account** tab and click the **Choose folders** button to open the *Sync your OneDrive files to this PC* dialog box (Figure Intro-14).

 - Check the **Sync all files and folders in OneDrive** box to sync all files and folders to your computer.
 - You can also select only those folders to sync in the *Or sync only these folders* area by selecting or deselecting the check boxes. Use this option to save storage space on your computer.

4. Click **OK** to close the *Sync your OneDrive files to this PC* dialog box and click **OK** to close the *Microsoft OneDrive* dialog box.

Figure Intro-14 Customize *OneDrive* folders to sync to your computer

OneDrive Online

In addition to the *OneDrive* folder on your computer, you can also access your *OneDrive* files online using an internet browser such as Microsoft Edge, Google Chrome, or Mozilla Firefox. When you access *OneDrive* online using a web browser, you can upload files, create folders, move and copy files and folders, and create Office files using *Office Online* (*Office Online* is discussed in *SLO Intro.2: Using Microsoft Office 2019*).

> **MORE INFO**
>
> *OneDrive* online may display differently and include different features depending on the type of Microsoft account you have: personal, education, or business.

▶HOW TO: Use OneDrive Online

1. Open an internet browser window and navigate to the *OneDrive* web site (www.onedrive.live.com), which takes you to the *OneDrive* sign-in page.

 - Use any internet browser to access *OneDrive* (Microsoft Edge, Google Chrome, Mozilla Firefox).

2. Click the **Sign in** button in the upper-right corner of the browser window.

3. Type your Microsoft account email address and click **Next** (Figure Intro-15).

4. Type your Microsoft account password and click **Sign in**. The *OneDrive* page displays.

 - If you are on your own computer, check the **Keep me signed in** box to stay signed in to *OneDrive* when you return to the page.
 - The different areas of *OneDrive* are listed under the *OneDrive* heading on the left (Figure Intro-16).
 - Click **Files** to display your folders and files in the folder area.
 - At the top of the page, buttons and drop-down menus list the different actions you can perform on selected files and folders.

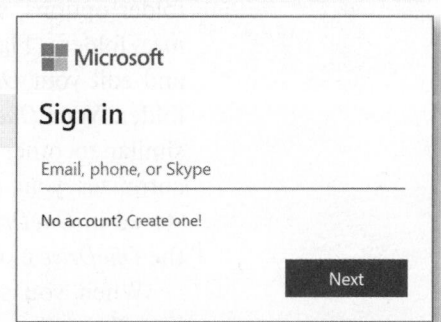

Figure Intro-15 Log in to *OneDrive* online

Figure Intro-16 *OneDrive* online environment

Cortana

In addition to using the search tools in *File Explorer,* you can also use **Cortana**, which is the Windows search feature. While the search feature in *File Explorer* searches only for content on your computer, *Cortana* searches for content on your computer, on the internet, and in the Microsoft Store. You can either type keywords for a search or use voice commands to search for content.

When you open *Cortana,* other content, such as weather, upcoming appointments, and popular news stories, displays in the *Cortana* pane.

▶HOW TO: Search Using Cortana

1. Click the **Cortana** search area on the *Taskbar* to open the *Cortana* pane (Figure Intro-17).
 - If the *Cortana* search area is not on the *Taskbar,* click the **Start** button, right-click **Cortana** in the list of apps, and select **Pin to taskbar**.
2. Type keywords for your search in the **Type here to search** area at the bottom of the *Cortana* pane.
 - You can also click the microphone icon and speak to enter keywords as the search.
 - Content from your computer, the internet, and the Microsoft Store displays in the *Cortana* pane (Figure Intro-18).
 - The search results are grouped into categories such as *Best match, Photos, Search suggestions, Store,* and *Places.* These categories vary depending on the search results.
3. Click a result in the *Cortana* pane to view a file, search the internet, or view apps in the Microsoft Store.
 - The buttons at the top of the *Cortana* pane filter your search by *Apps, Documents, Email,* and *web.*
 - The *More* button displays a drop-down list of additional filter options.
4. Click the **Menu** button at the top left to display other content options in the *Cortana* pane (see Figure Intro-18).
 - The other content options are *Home, Notebook,* and *Devices.*

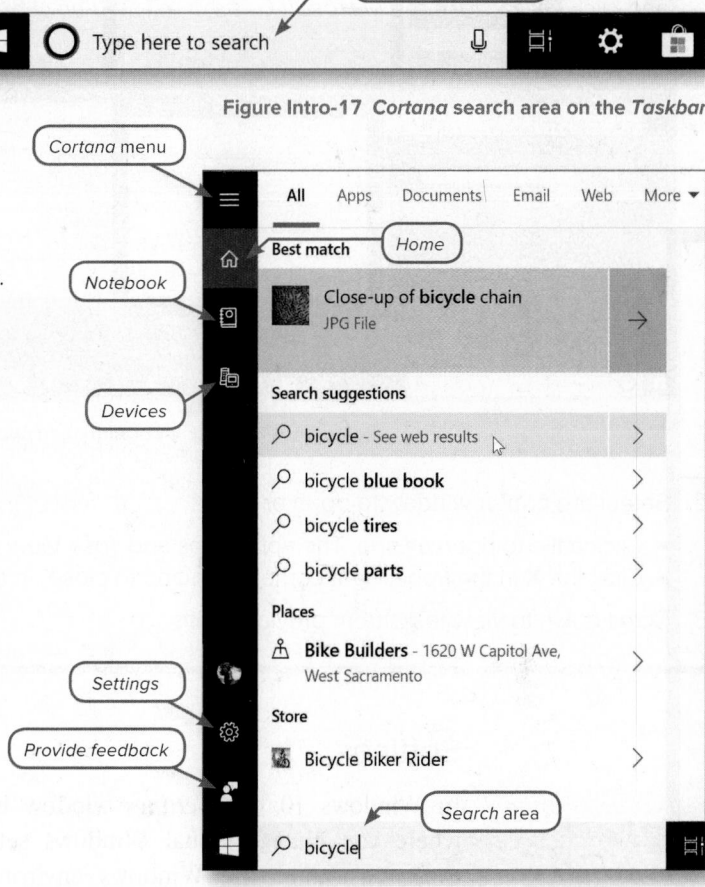

Figure Intro-17 *Cortana* search area on the *Taskbar*

Figure Intro-18 Use *Cortana* to search your computer, the internet, and the Microsoft Store

Task View

Task View displays all open apps and windows as tiles on your desktop, and you can choose which item to display or close. This feature is very helpful when you have multiple items open and need to select or close one. Additionally, *Task View* displays a timeline of tasks you've worked on in Windows. Scroll down in *Task View* to display previous days.

▶HOW TO: Use Task View

1. Click the **Task View** button on the *Taskbar* (Figure Intro-19).
 - All open apps and windows display on the desktop (Figure Intro-20).

Figure Intro-19 *Task View* button on the *Taskbar*

Figure Intro-20 *Task View* with open apps and windows displayed on the desktop

2. Select the app or window to open or close.
 - Click a tile to open an app. The app opens and *Task View* closes.
 - Click the **X** in the upper-right corner of an app to close an app. *Task View* remains open when you close an app.
3. Scroll down to view tasks from previous days.

Settings

In Windows 10, the **Settings** window is where you change global Windows settings, customize the Windows environment, add devices, and manage your Microsoft account. Click the **Settings** button (Figure Intro-21) on the *Taskbar* or *Start* menu to open the *Settings* window (Figure Intro-22). The following categories are typically available in the *Settings* window. *Settings* categories and options may vary depending on the version of Windows you are using and updates to Windows.

- *System*: Display, notifications, and power
- *Devices*: Bluetooth, printers, and mouse

Figure Intro-21 *Settings* button on the Start menu

- **Phone**: Link your Android and iPhone
- **Network & internet**: Wi-Fi, airplane mode, and VPN
- **Personalization**: Background, lock screen, and colors
- **Apps**: Uninstall, defaults, and optional features
- **Accounts**: Your account, email, sync, work, and family
- **Time & Language**: Speech, region, and date
- **Gaming**: Game bar, DVR, broadcasting, and Game Mode
- **Ease of Access**: Narrator, magnifier, and high contrast
- **Cortana**: Cortana languages, permissions, and notifications
- **Privacy**: Location and camera
- **Update & Security**: Windows Update, recovery, and backup

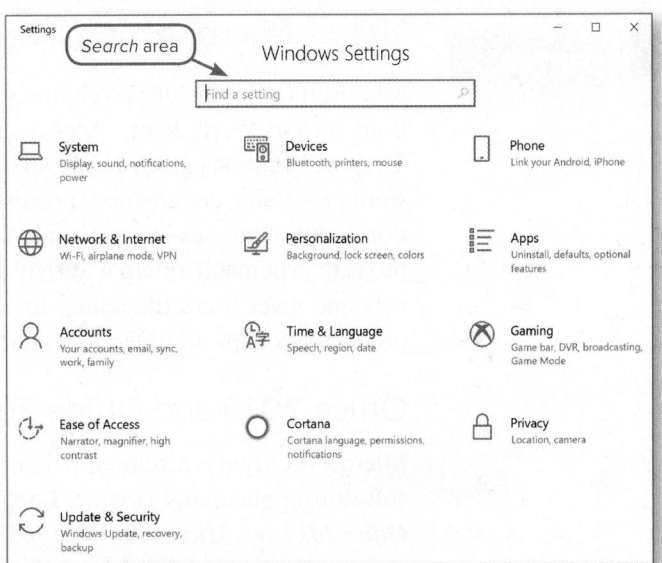

Figure Intro-22 *Settings* window

MORE INFO

If you can't find an item in *Settings,* use the *Search* dialog box (*Find a setting*) to type keywords. If *Settings* is not available on the *Taskbar,* you can find it in the list of apps on the *Start* menu.

Action Center

The **Action Center** in Windows 10 provides a quick glance of notifications and buttons to open other commonly used settings and features in Windows. The *Action Center* displays notifications such as emails and Windows notifications. Click an action button to turn on or off features or open other windows or apps such as the *Settings* menu (*All Settings* button) or OneNote (*Note* button). Click the **Action Center** button on the right side of the *Taskbar* (last button in the *System Tray*) to open the *Action Center* pane, which displays on the right side of your screen (Figure Intro-23).

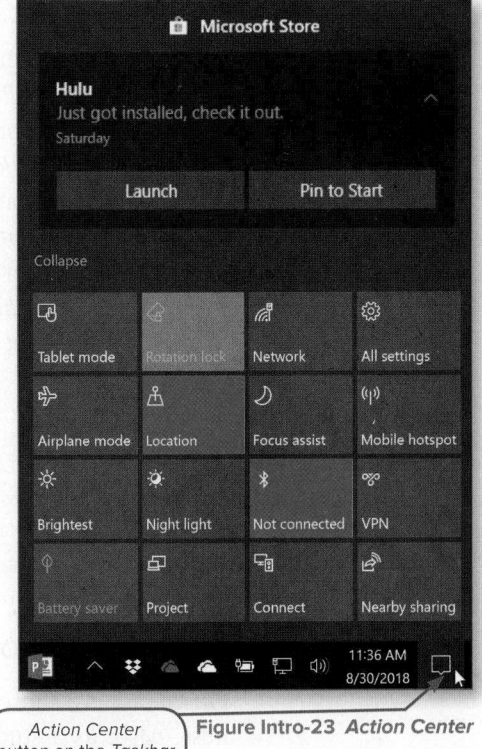

Action Center button on the *Taskbar*

Figure Intro-23 *Action Center*

ANOTHER WAY

Windows+A opens the *Action Center.* The *Windows* key is typically located near the bottom-left corner of the keyboard.

Using Microsoft Office

Microsoft Office includes common software applications such as Word, Excel, Access, and PowerPoint. These applications give you the ability to work with word processing documents, spreadsheets, presentations, and databases in your personal and business projects. Microsoft offers a variety of Office products and gives users the ability to work with these productivity apps on different technology devices.

Figure Intro-24 Microsoft Office application tiles on the *Start* menu

Office 2019 and Office 365

Microsoft Office is a suite of personal and business software applications (Figure Intro-24). *Microsoft Office 2019* and *Microsoft Office 365* are similar software products; the difference is how you purchase the software. Office 2019 is the traditional model of purchasing the software, and you own that software for as long as you want to use it. Office 365 is a subscription that you pay monthly or yearly, similar to how you purchase Netflix or Spotify. If you subscribe to Office 365, you automatically receive updated versions of the applications when they are released.

The common applications typically included in Microsoft Office 2019 and 365 are described in the following list:

- *Microsoft Word*: Word processing software used to create, format, and edit documents such as reports, letters, brochures, and resumes
- *Microsoft Excel*: Spreadsheet software used to perform calculations on numerical data such as financial statements, budgets, and expense reports
- *Microsoft Access*: Database software used to store, organize, compile, and report information such as product information, sales data, client information, and employee records
- *Microsoft PowerPoint*: Presentation software used to graphically present information in slides such as a presentation on a new product or sales trends
- *Microsoft Outlook*: Email and personal management software used to create and send email and to create and store calendar items, contacts, and tasks
- *Microsoft OneNote*: Note-taking software used to take and organize notes, which can be shared with other Office applications
- *Microsoft Publisher*: Desktop publishing software used to create professional-looking documents containing text, pictures, and graphics such as catalogs, brochures, and flyers

> MORE INFO
>
> Office 365 includes regular updates that include new and enhanced features, while Office 2019 does not include these regular updates. So, differences in features may exist between the Office 2019 and Office 365.

Office 365 Products, Versions, and Update Channels

Office 365 is a subscription to the Office applications and can be purchased for home or business. Also, as a student, you can get Office 365 for education free (https://products.office.com/en-us/student/office-in-education). The Office applications that come with an Office 365

Intro-12

subscription can vary depending on the Office 365 product subscription you have. With an Office 365 subscription, you can install the Office applications (both PC and Mac) on multiple computers and mobile devices.

Another advantage of an Office 365 subscription is regular updates that enhance the functionality of the apps. The version and build of your Office 365 is determined by the update channel, which is the frequency of updates. This is typically set by your school or business. If you have Office 365 Home or Personal, you determine the update channel. If you have an Office 365 for education or business, the college or business determines the update channel. The following are common update channels:

- *Semi-annual Channel*: Receives updates two times a year in January and July
- *Semi-annual Channel (Targeted)*: Receives new feature updates earlier than the Semi-annual Channel. These semi-annual updates are rolled out in March and September.
- *Monthly Channel*: Receives new feature updates as soon as they are available, which is typically every month

▶HOW TO: View Your Office 365 Product Information

1. Open an Office application and open a blank or existing file if necessary.
2. Click the **File** tab to open the *Backstage* view.
3. Click **Account** at the left to display *User Information* and *Product Information*.
 - The *Product Information* area displays the Office 365 product installed on your computer (Figure Intro-25).
 - The *About [Application]* area displays the version, build, and update channel.
 - The *Version* number indicates the year and month of the most recent update. For example, "Version 1808" means 2018 and the eighth month (August).
4. Click the **Update Options** button to select an update option: *Update Now, Disable Updates, View Updates,* or *About Updates.*
 - Click the **Update Now** button to manually check for Office 365 updates.
5. Click the **What's New** button to view the new features included in the most recent Office 365 updates for your update channel.
6. Close the **Back** arrow to close the *Backstage* view and return to the file.

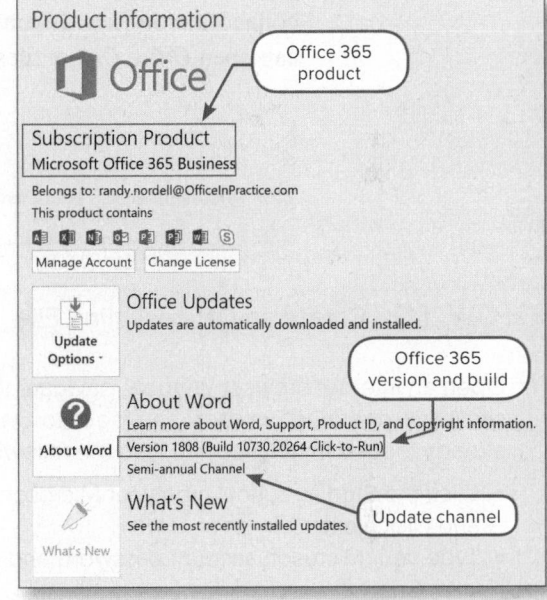

Figure Intro-25 *Product Information* displayed in the *Account* area on the *Backstage* view

Office Desktop Apps, Office Mobile Apps, and Office Online

Office desktop apps are the full-function Office 2019 or 365 programs installed on your computer (PC or Mac). Both Office 2019 and Office 365 are considered Office desktop apps. Because of the increased popularity and capabilities of tablets and mobile devices, Office software is also available for both tablets and smartphones. *Office mobile apps* are the Office 365 programs that can be installed on tablets or other mobile devices. Office mobile apps do not have the full range of advanced features available in Office desktop applications, but Office mobile apps provide users the ability to create, edit, save, and share Office files using many of the most common features in the Office suite of programs.

The *Office Online* apps are free online apps from Microsoft that work in conjunction with your Microsoft account and *OneDrive* (Figure Intro-26). With *Office Online*, you can work with Office files online through a web browser, even on computers that do not have Office 2019 or 365 installed. Click the **App** launcher in the upper-left corner of *OneDrive* to display the *Office Online* applications. This list of *Office Online* apps may display differently depending on the type of Microsoft account you are using.

You can access *Office Online* from your *OneDrive* web page to create and edit Word documents, Excel workbooks, PowerPoint presentations, and OneNote notebooks. *Office Online* is a scaled-down version of Office and not as robust in terms of features, but you can use it to create, edit, print, share, and collaborate on files. If you need more advanced features, you can open *Office Online* files in the desktop version of Office.

Figure Intro-26 *Office Online*

▶HOW TO: Create an Office Online File

1. Open an internet browser Window, navigate to the *OneDrive* web site (www.onedrive.live.com), and log in to *OneDrive*. If you are not already logged in to *OneDrive,* use the following steps.
 - Click the **Sign in** button, type your Microsoft account email address, and click **Next**.
 - Type your Microsoft account password and click **Sign in** to open your *OneDrive* page.
2. Click the **New** button and select the type of *Office Online* file to create (Figure Intro-27).
 - A new file opens in the *Office Online* program.
 - The new file is saved in your *OneDrive* folder (both online and on your computer).

Figure Intro-27 Create an *Office Online* file from your online *OneDrive* page

3. Rename the file by clicking the file name at the top of the file, typing a new file name, and pressing **Enter** (Figure Intro-28).
 - You can also click the **File** tab to open the *Backstage* view, select **Save As**, and choose **Save As** or **Rename**.
 - Click the **Open in *[Office application]*** button (for example, **Open in Excel**) to open the file in the Office desktop application (see Figure Intro-28).
4. Close the browser tab or window to close the file.
 - *Office Online* automatically saves the file as you make changes.

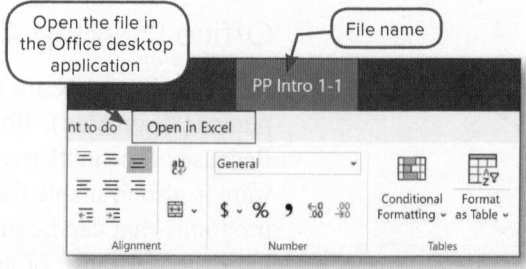

Figure Intro-28 Rename an *Office Online* file

Open an Office Desktop Application

When using Windows 10, you open an Office desktop application by clicking the application tile on the *Start* menu or the application icon on the *Taskbar*. If your *Start* menu and *Taskbar* do not display the Office applications, click the **Start** button and select **Word**, **Excel**, **Access**, or **PowerPoint** from the alphabetic list of apps to launch the application (Figure Intro-29).

You can also use *Cortana* to quickly locate an Office desktop app (Figure Intro-30).

Figure Intro-29 Open an Office desktop app from the *All apps* area on the *Start* menu

Figure Intro-30 Use *Cortana* to find and open an app

> **MORE INFO**
>
> Add commonly used apps to your Windows *Start* menu and/or *Taskbar* to save time. See the "Customize the *Start* Menu" and "Customize the *Taskbar*" sections in *SLO Intro.1: Using Windows 10*.

Office Start Page

Most of the Office applications (except Outlook and OneNote) display a ***Start page*** when you launch the application (Figure Intro-31). From this *Start* page, you can create a new blank file (for example, a Word document, an Excel workbook, an Access database, or a PowerPoint presentation), create a file from an online template, search for an online template, open a recently used file, or open another file. These options vary depending on the Office application.

Figure Intro-31 Excel *Start* page

▶HOW TO: Use the Office Start Page

1. Open an Office application from the *Start* page or *Taskbar*.

2. Open a file listed in the *Recent* area on the left side of the *Start* menu by clicking the file name. The file opens in the working area of the Office application.

 - The *Recent* area on the left side of the *Start* page displays recently used and pinned files.

3. Open a new blank file by clicking the **Blank *[file type]*** tile (*Blank workbook, Blank document,* etc.) to the right of the *Recent* area (see Figure Intro-31).

 - You can also press the **Esc** key to exit the *Start* page and open a new blank file.

4. Open an existing file that is not listed in the *Recent* area by clicking the **Open Other *[file type]*** link (Figure Intro-32). The *Open* area on the *Backstage* view displays.

 - Click the **Browse** button to open the *Open* dialog box where you can locate and open a file.
 - Select a different location (*OneDrive* or *This PC*) and select a file to open.

5. Open a template by clicking a template file on the right or searching for a template.

 - Search for a template by typing keywords in the *Search* area on the *Start* page.
 - Click a link to one of the categories below the *Search* area to display templates in that category.

6. Pin a frequently used file to the *Start* page by clicking the **pin** icon (see Figure Intro-31).

 - The pin icon is on the right side of items listed in the *Recent* area and at the bottom right of templates displayed in the *Templates* area (to the right of the *Recent* area).
 - Pinned files display at the top of the *Recent* area.

Figure Intro-32 *Open Other Workbooks* link on the *Start* page

> ▶ **MORE INFO**
>
> In Access, you have to open an existing database or create a new one to enter the program.

Backstage View

Office incorporates the ***Backstage view*** into all Office applications (including *Office Online* apps). Click the **File** tab on the *Ribbon* to open the *Backstage* view (Figure Intro-33). *Backstage* options vary depending on the Office application. The following list describes common tasks you can perform from the *Backstage* view:

- ***Info***: Displays document properties and other protection, inspection, and version options.

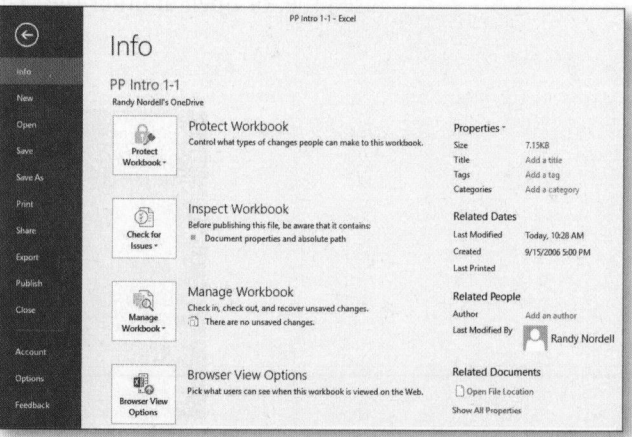

Figure Intro-33 *Backstage* view in Excel

- *New*: Creates a new blank file or a new file from a template or theme.
- *Open*: Opens an existing file from a designated location or a recently opened file.
- *Save*: Saves a file. If the file has not been named, the *Save As* dialog box opens when you select this option.
- *Save As*: Opens the *Save As* dialog box.
- *Print*: Prints a file, displays a preview of the file, or displays print options.
- *Share*: Invites people to share a file or email a file.
- *Export*: Creates a PDF file from a file or saves it as a different file type.
- *Close*: Closes an open file.
- *Account*: Displays your Microsoft account information.
- *Options*: Opens the *[Application] Options* dialog box (for example, *Excel Options*).

> **MORE INFO**
>
> Options on the *Backstage* view vary depending on the Office application you are using.

Office Help—Tell Me

In all the Office 2019/365 applications, **Tell Me** is the help feature (Figure Intro-34). This feature displays the commands in the Office application related to your search. The *Help* fea-

ture in older versions of Office displayed articles describing the feature and how to use it. The *Tell Me* feature provides command options that take you directly to a command or dialog box. For example, if you type *PivotTable* in the *Tell Me* search box in Excel, the results include the option to open the *Create PivotTable* dialog box, as well as other options such as *Recommended PivotTables* and *Summarize with PivotTable*.

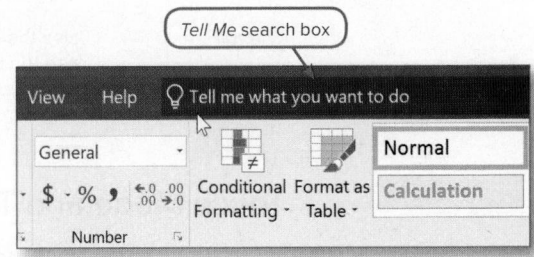

Figure Intro-34 *Tell Me* search box

▶**HOW TO: Use Tell Me**

1. Place the insertion point in the **Tell me what you want to do** search box at the top of the *Ribbon* (see Figure Intro-34).

2. Type keywords for the command or feature for which you are searching.

3. Select an option from the search results list (Figure Intro-35).
 - When you select a search result, it may apply a command, open a dialog box, or display a gallery of command choices.

Figure Intro-35 *Tell Me* search results

> **ANOTHER WAY**
>
> **Alt+Q** places the insertion point in the *Tell Me* dialog box.
> The previous *Help* feature is still available in Office. Press **F1** to open the *Help* pane on the right.

Mouse and Pointers

If you are using Office on a desktop or laptop computer, use your mouse (or touchpad) to navigate around files, click tabs and buttons, select text and objects, move text and objects, and resize objects. Table Intro-1 lists mouse and pointer terminology used in Office.

Table Intro-1: Mouse and Pointer Terminology

Term	Description
Pointer	Move your mouse to move the pointer on your screen. A variety of pointers are used in different contexts in Office applications. The following pointers are available in most of the Office applications (the appearance of these pointers varies depending on the application and the context used): • *Selection pointer:* Select text or an object. • *Move pointer:* Move text or an object. • *Copy pointer:* Copy text or an object. • *Resize pointer:* Resize objects or table columns or rows. • *Crosshair:* Draw a shape.
Insertion point	The vertical flashing line indicating where you type text in a file or text box. Click the left mouse button to position the insertion point.
Click	Click the left mouse button. Used to select an object or button or to place the insertion point in the selected location.
Double-click	Click the left mouse button twice. Used to select text.
Right-click	Click the right mouse button. Used to display the context menu and the mini toolbar.
Scroll	Use the scroll wheel on the mouse to scroll up and down through your file. You can also use the horizontal or vertical scroll bars at the bottom and right of an Office file window to move around in a file.

Touch Mode and Touch-Screen Gestures

The user interface in Windows 10 and Office 2019 has improved touch features to facilitate the use of Windows and the Office applications on a tablet computer or smartphone. On tablets and smartphones, you can use a touch screen rather than using a mouse, so the process of selecting text and objects and navigating around a file is different from a computer without a touch screen.

In Office 2019/365, *Touch mode* optimizes the Office working environment when using a computer with a touch screen to provide more space between buttons and commands. Click the **Touch/Mouse Mode** button on the *Quick Access* toolbar (upper left of the Office app window) and select **Touch** from the drop-down list to enable *Touch* mode (Figure Intro-36). To turn off *Touch* mode, select **Mouse** from the *Touch/Mouse Mode* drop-down list.

Figure Intro-36 Turn on *Touch* mode

 MORE INFO

The *Touch/Mouse Mode* button displays on the *Quick Access* toolbar when using a touch-screen computer.

Table Intro-2 lists common gestures used when working on a tablet or smartphone (these gestures vary depending on the application used and the context).

Table Intro-2: Touch-Screen Gestures

Gesture	Used To	How To
Tap	Select text or an object or position the insertion point. Double tap to edit text in an object or cell.	
Pinch	Zoom in or resize an object.	
Stretch	Zoom out or resize an object.	
Slide	Move an object or selected text.	
Swipe	Select text or multiple objects.	

> **MORE INFO**
>
> Window 10 has a ***Tablet mode*** that optimizes all of Windows and apps for touch screens. When you turn on the *Tablet mode* feature in Windows, the *Touch mode* in Office apps turns on automatically. Click the **Action Center** button on the Windows *Taskbar* and click the **Tablet mode** button to turn on this feature in Windows.

SLO INTRO. 3

Creating, Saving, Closing, and Opening Office Files

Creating, saving, opening, and closing files is primarily done from the *Start* page or *Backstage* view of the active Office application. Both the *Start* page and the *Backstage* view provide many options and a central location to perform these tasks. You can also use shortcut commands to create, save, and open files.

Create a New File

When you create a new file in an Office application, you can create a new blank file or a new file based on a template (in PowerPoint, you can also create a presentation based on a theme). On the *Start* page, click **Blank *[file type]*** to create a new blank file in the application you are using (in Word, you begin with a blank document; in Excel, a blank workbook; in Access, a blank desktop database; and in PowerPoint, a blank presentation).

▶ HOW TO: Create a New File from the Start Page

1. Open an Office application. The *Start* page displays when the application opens (Figure Intro-37).

2. Click **Blank** *[file type]* to open a new file.

 - The new file displays a generic file name (for example, *Document1*, *Book1*, or *Presentation1*). You can rename and save this file later.
 - When creating a new Access database, you are prompted to name the new file when you create it.
 - A variety of templates (and themes in PowerPoint only) display on the *Start* page, and you can search for additional online templates and themes using the *Search* text box at the top of the *Start* page.

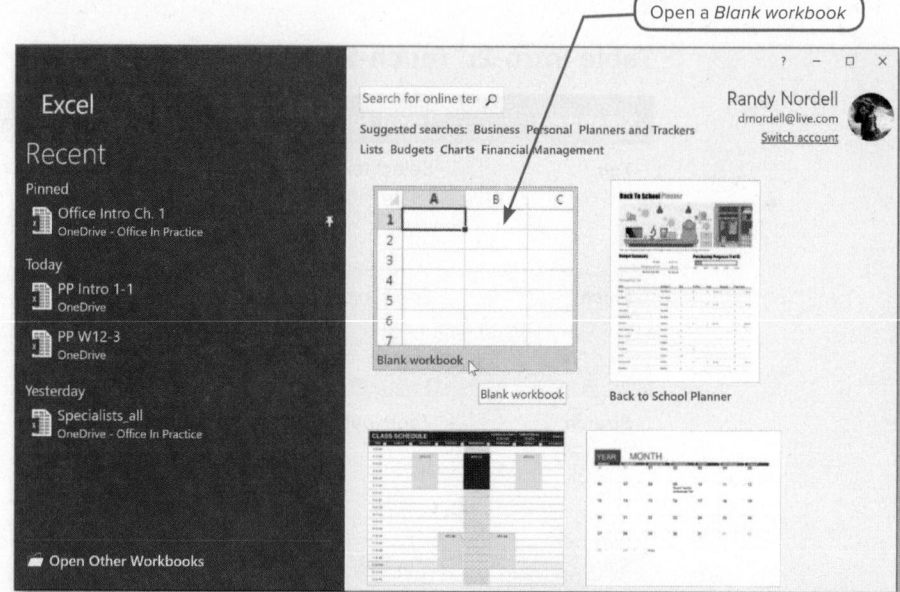

Figure Intro-37 *Start* **page in Excel**

▶ **MORE INFO**

Esc closes the *Start* page opens a blank file in the Office application (except in Access).

If you have been using an application already and want to create a new file, you create it from the *Backstage* view. From the *Backstage* view, the new file options are available in the *New* area.

▶ HOW TO: Create a New File from the Backstage View

1. Click the **File** tab to display the *Backstage* view.

2. Select **New** on the left to display the *New* area (Figure Intro-38).

3. Click **Blank** *[file type]* to open a new blank file or select a template or theme to use.

 - The new file displays a generic file name (*Document1*, *Book1*, or *Presentation1*). You can name and save this file later.
 - When you are creating a new Access database, you are prompted to name the new file when you create it.

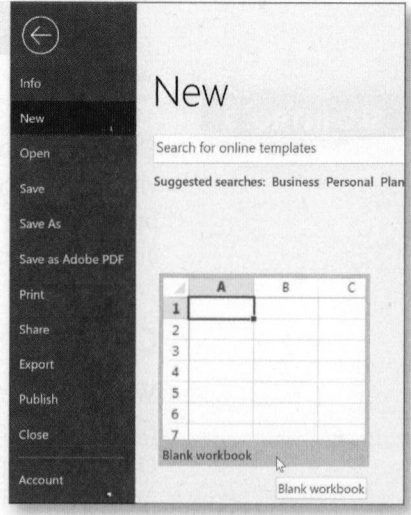

Figure Intro-38 *New* **area on the** *Backstage* **view in Excel**

Save a File

In Access, you name a file as you create it, but in Word, Excel, and PowerPoint, you name a file after you have created it. When you save a file, you type a name for the file and select the location to save the file. You can save a file on your computer, an online storage location such as *OneDrive,* or portable device, such as a USB drive.

▶ HOW TO: Save a File

1. Click the **File** tab to display the *Backstage* view.

2. Select **Save** or **Save As** on the left to display the *Save As* area (Figure Intro-39).

 - If the file has not already been saved, clicking *Save* or *Save As* takes you to the *Save As* area on the *Backstage* view.

3. Click the **Browse** button to open the *Save As* dialog box (Figure Intro-40).

 - Alternatively, type the file name in the *Enter file name here* text box and click **Save**. To change the save location, click the **More options** link to open the *Save As* dialog box or select a save location at the left (*OneDrive* or *This PC*) and select a folder from the list of folders (see Figure Intro-39).

4. Select a location to save the file in the *Folder* list on the left.

5. Type a name for the file in the *File name* area.

 - By default, Office selects the file type, but you can change the file type from the *Save as type* drop-down list.

6. Click **Save** to close the dialog box and save the file.

Figure Intro-39 *Save As* area on the *Backstage* view in Excel

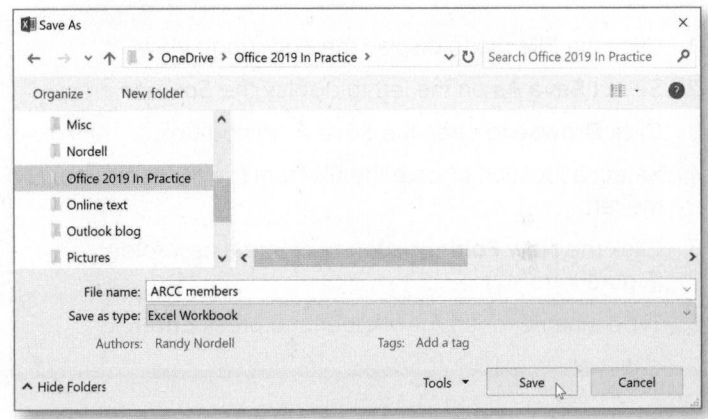

Figure Intro-40 *Save As* dialog box

AutoSave

AutoSave is a new feature that automatically saves a file that is stored on *OneDrive,* Microsoft's cloud storage area. The *AutoSave* feature turns on by default when you save a file to *OneDrive,* and changes made to the file are automatically saved as you work on a file.

Office 2019 Note: The *AutoSave* feature is not available in Office 2019.

This feature displays in the upper-left corner of the file (Figure Intro-41). Click the **AutoSave** button to turn it on or off. When *AutoSave* is on, the save options on the *Backstage* view change from *Save* and *Save As* to **Save a Copy.**

Figure Intro-41 *AutoSave* feature

Create a New Folder When Saving a File

When saving files, it is a good practice to create folders to organize your files. Organizing your files in folders makes it easier to find files and saves time when you are searching for a specific file (see *SLO Intro.8: Organizing and Customizing Folders and Files* for more information on this topic). When you save an Office file, you can also create a folder in which to store that file.

> ▶ **HOW TO:** Create a New Folder When Saving a File
>
> 1. Click the **File** tab to display the *Backstage* view.
> 2. Select **Save As** on the left to display the *Save As* area.
> 3. Click **Browse** to open the *Save As* dialog box.
> 4. Select a location to save the file from the *Folder* list on the left.
> 5. Click the **New Folder** button to create a new folder (Figure Intro-42).
> 6. Type a name for the new folder and press **Enter**.

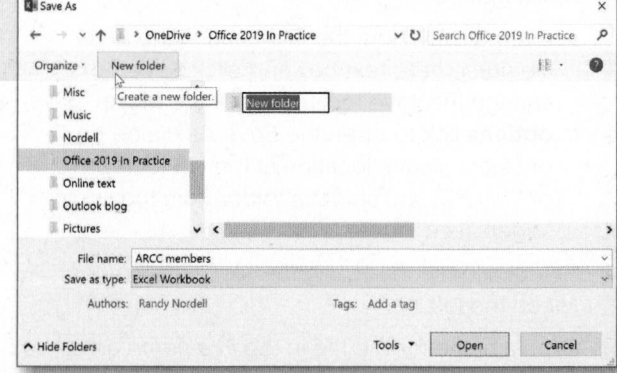

Figure Intro-42 Create a new folder

> ▶ **ANOTHER WAY**
>
> **F12** opens the *Save As* dialog box (except in Access). On a laptop, you might have to press **Fn+F12**. See more about the *Fn* (Function) key in *SLO Intro. 7: Using Context Menus, the Mini Toolbar, and Keyboard Shortcuts.*

Save As a Different File Name

After you have saved a file, you can save it again with a different file name. If you do this, you preserve the original file, and you can continue to revise the second file for a different purpose.

▶HOW TO: Save As a Different File Name

1. Click the **File** tab to display the *Backstage* view.
2. Select **Save As** on the left to display the *Save As* area.
3. Click the **Browse** button to open the *Save As* dialog box (see Figure Intro-42).
4. Select a location to save the file from the *Folder* list on the left.
5. Type a new name for the file in the *File name* area.
6. Click **Save** to close the dialog box and save the file.

> **MORE INFO**
>
> If *AutoSave* is turned on, **Save a Copy** is the save option on the *Backstage* view rather than *Save* and *Save As*.

Office File Types

By default, Office saves a file in the most current file format for that application. You also have the option of saving files in older versions of the Office application. For example, you can save a Word document as an older version to share with or send to someone who uses an older version of Word. Each file has an extension at the end of the file name that determines the file type. The *file name extension* is automatically added to a file when you save it. Table Intro-3 table lists common file types used in the different Office applications.

Table Intro-3: Office File Types

File Type	Extension	File Type	Extension
Word Document	.docx	Access Database	.accdb
Word Template	.dotx	Access Template	.accdt
Word 97-2003 Document	.doc	Access Database (2000-2003 format)	.mdb
Rich Text Format	.rtf	PowerPoint Presentation	.pptx
Excel Workbook	.xlsx	PowerPoint Template	.potx
Excel Template	.xltx	PowerPoint 97-2003 Presentation	.ppt
Excel 97-2003 Workbook	.xls	Portable Document Format (PDF)	.pdf
Comma Separated Values (CSV)	.csv		

Close a File

You can close a file using the following different methods:

- Click the **File** tab and select **Close** on the left.
- Press **Ctrl+W**.
- Click the **X** in the upper-right corner of the file window. This method closes the file and the program if only one file is open in the application.

When you close a file, you are prompted to save the file if it has not been named or if changes were made after the file was last saved (Figure Intro-43). Click **Save** to save and close the file or click **Don't Save** to close the file without saving. Click **Cancel** to return to the file.

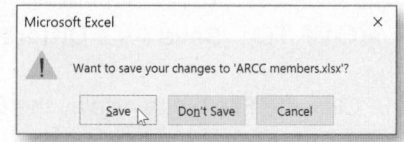

Figure Intro-43 Prompt to save a document before closing

Open an Existing File

You can open an existing file from the *Start* page when you open an Office application or while you are working on another Office file.

▶ **HOW TO:** Open a File from the Start Page

1. Open an Office application to display the *Start* page.
2. Select a file to open in the *Recent* area on the left (Figure Intro-44).
 - If you select a file in the *Recent* area that has been renamed, moved, or is on a storage device not connected to the computer, you receive an error message.
3. Alternatively, click **Open Other *[file type]*** (for example, *Open Other Presentations*) to display the *Open* area of the *Backstage* view (see Figure Intro-44).
 - Click the **Browse** button to open the *Open* dialog box (Figure Intro-45).
 - Select a location from the *Folder* list on the left.
 - Select the file to open and click the **Open** button.
 - If the file opens in *Protected View,* click the **Enable Editing** button to enable you to edit the file.

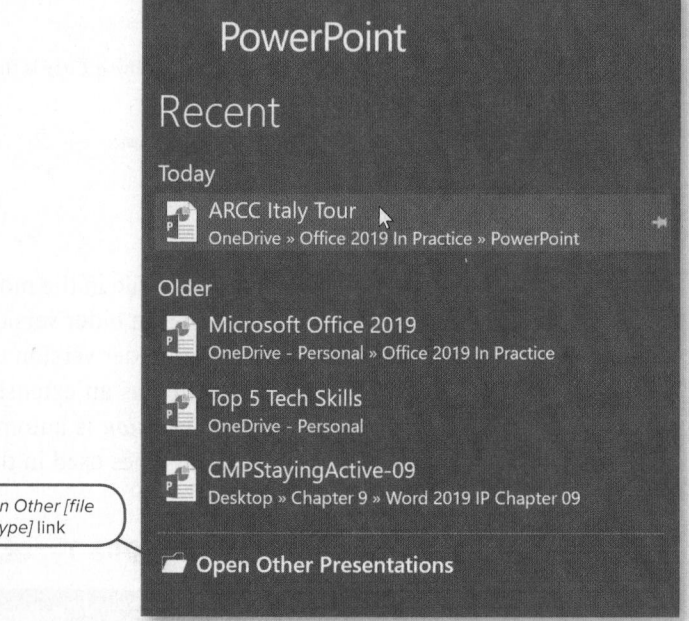

Open Other *[file type]* link

Figure Intro-44 Open a *Recent* file from the *Start* page

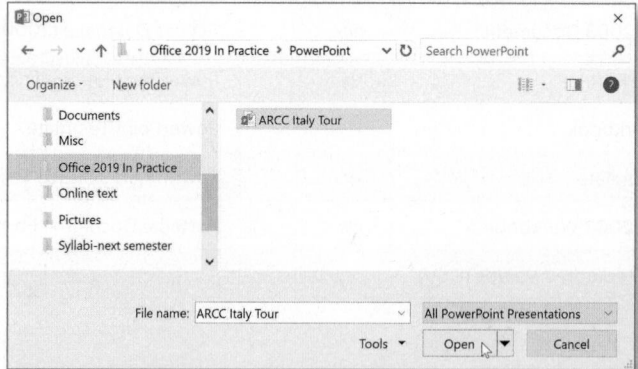

Figure Intro-45 *Open* dialog box

When working on a file in an Office application, you might want to open another file. You can open an existing file from within an Office application using the *Open* area on the *Backstage* view.

▶**HOW TO:** Open a File from the Backstage View

1. Click the **File** tab from within an open Office application to display the *Backstage* view.
2. Click **Open** on the left to display the *Open* area on the *Backstage* view (Figure Intro-46).
3. Click the **Browse** button to open the *Open* dialog box.
 - Alternatively, select a file to open from the list of *Recent* files on the right of the *Open* area on the *Backstage* view.
4. Select a location from the *Folder* list on the left.
5. Select the file to open and click the **Open** button.
 - If the file opens in *Protected View,* click the **Enable Editing** button to enable you to edit the file.

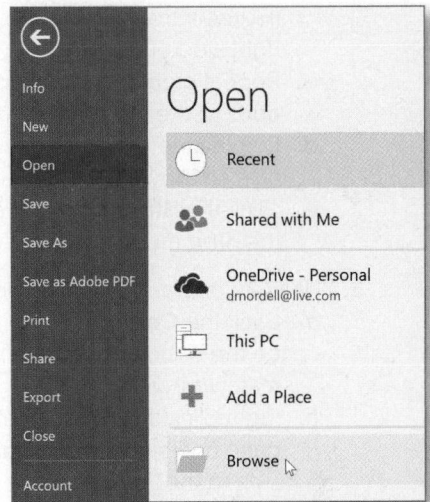

Figure Intro-46 *Open* area on the *Backstage* view

You can also open a file from a *File Explorer* folder. When you double-click a file in a *File Explorer* folder, the file opens in the appropriate Office application. Windows recognizes the file name extension and launches the correct Office application.

PAUSE & PRACTICE: INTRO-1

For this project, you log in to Windows using your Microsoft account, customize the Windows *Start* menu and *Taskbar,* create and save a PowerPoint presentation, create a folder, open and rename an Excel workbook, and use Windows 10 features.

File Needed: **ARCC2020Budget-Intro.xlsx** *(Student data files are available in the* Library *of your SIMnet account.)*
Completed Project File Names: *[your initials] PP Intro-1a.pptx* and *[your initials] PP Intro-1b.xlsx*

1. Log in to Windows using your Microsoft account if you are not already logged in.
 a. If you don't have a Microsoft account, you can create a free account at https://signup.live.com.
 b. If you are using a computer on your college campus, you may be required to log in to the computer using your college user name and password.

2. Pin the Office apps to the *Start* menu. If these apps tiles are already on the *Start* menu, skip steps 2a–e. You can pin other apps of your choice to the *Start* menu.
 a. Click the **Start** button at the bottom left of your screen to open the *Start* menu.
 b. Locate *Access* in the alphabetic list of apps, right-click the **Access** app, and select **Pin to Start** (Figure Intro-47). The app displays as a tile on the right side of the *Start* menu.

 c. Repeat step 2b to pin **Excel**, **PowerPoint**, and **Word** apps to the *Start* menu.
 d. Display the *Start* menu and drag these Office app tiles so they are close to each other.
 e. Click the **Start** button (or press the **Esc** key) to close the *Start* menu.

 Figure Intro-47 Pin *Access* to the *Start* menu

3. Use *Cortana* and the *Start* menu to pin Office apps to the *Taskbar*.
 a. Click the **Cortana** button (to the right of the *Start* button) on the *Taskbar* and type Access. *Cortana* displays content matching your search.
 b. Right-click the **Access** option near the top of the *Cortana* pane and select **Pin to taskbar** (Figure Intro-48). The app pins to the *Taskbar*.

 c. Click the **Start** button to open the *Start* menu.
 d. Right-click the **Excel** tile on the right side of the *Start* menu, click **More**, and select **Pin to taskbar**. The app pins to the *Taskbar*.
 e. Use either of the methods described above to pin the **PowerPoint** and **Word** apps to the *Taskbar*.
 f. Drag the Office apps on the *Taskbar* to rearrange them to your preference.

 Figure Intro-48 Use *Cortana* to find an Office app and pin it to the *Taskbar*

4. Create a PowerPoint presentation and save the presentation in a new folder.
 a. Click the **PowerPoint** app tile on your *Start* menu to open the application.
 b. Click **Blank Presentation** on the PowerPoint *Start* page to create a new blank presentation.
 c. Click the **Click to add title** placeholder and type American River Cycling Club to replace the placeholder text.
 d. Click the **File** tab to open the *Backstage* view and click **Save As** on the left to display the *Save As* area.
 e. Click **Browse** to open the *Save As* dialog box (Figure Intro-49).

 f. Select a location to save the file from the *Folder* list on the left. If the *OneDrive* folder is an option, select **OneDrive**. If it is not, select the **Documents** folder in the *This PC* folder. You can also save to a portable storage device if you have one.
 g. Click the **New Folder** button to create a new folder.

 Figure Intro-49 *Save As* area on the *Backstage* view in PowerPoint

h. Type American River Cycling Club as the name of the new folder and press **Enter** (Figure Intro-50).

i. Double-click the **American River Cycling Club** folder to open it.

j. Type [your initials] PP Intro-1a in the *File name* area.

k. Click **Save** to close the dialog box and save the presentation. Leave the file and PowerPoint open. If you saved your file to OneDrive, you may receive a notification about automatic saving.

Figure Intro-50 Create a new folder from the *Save As* dialog box

5. Open an Excel file and save as a different file name.

a. Click the **Excel 2019** app button on the *Taskbar* to open the *Start* page in Excel.

b. Click the **Open Other Workbooks** link on the bottom left of the Excel *Start* page to display the *Open* area of the *Backstage* view.

c. Click **Browse** to open the *Open* dialog box (Figure Intro-51).

d. Browse to your student data files and select the **ARCC2020Budget-Intro** file.

e. Click **Open** to open the workbook. If the file opens in *Protected View,* click the **Enable Editing** button.

f. Click the **File** tab to open the *Backstage* view.

g. Click **Save As** on the left to display the *Save As* area and click **Browse** to open the *Save As* dialog box. If this file is stored on OneDrive, click **Save a Copy** rather than *Save As*.

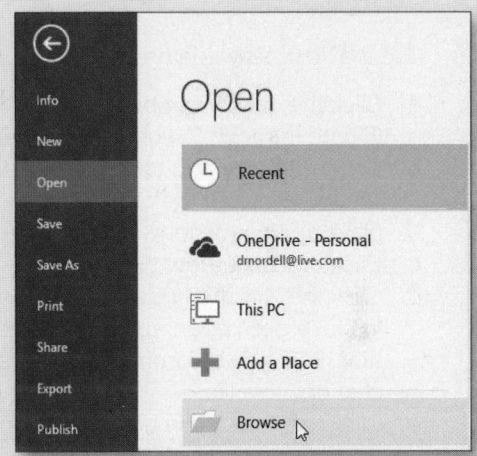

Figure Intro-51 *Open* area on the *Backstage* view

h. Locate the **American River Cycling Club** folder (created in step 4h) in the *Folder* list on the left and double-click the folder to open it.

i. Type [your initials] PP Intro-1b in the *File name* area.

j. Click **Save** to close the dialog box and save the workbook. Leave the file and Excel open.

6. Use the *Tell Me* feature in Excel to find a command.

a. Click the **Tell Me** search box on the *Ribbon* of the Excel window and type PivotTable (Figure Intro-52).

b. Click **PivotTable** to open the *Create PivotTable* dialog box.

c. Click the **X** in the upper-right corner of the *Create PivotTable* dialog box to close it.

7. Open the *Microsoft Store* app, the *Action Center*, and the *Settings* window.

a. Click the **Cortana** search area and type Microsoft Store.

b. Click **Microsoft Store** at the top of the *Cortana* pane to open the *Microsoft Store* app.

c. Click the **Apps** tab in the top left and browse the available apps in the Microsoft Store.

Figure Intro-52 Use the *Tell Me* feature to find a command

d. Click the **Minimize** button in the upper-right corner of the *Store* window to minimize this app (Figure Intro-53). The app is still open, but it is minimized on the *Taskbar*.

Acton Center button

Minimize button

e. Click the **Action Center** button on the right side of the *Taskbar* to display the *Action Center* pane on the right (Figure Intro-54).

f. Click **All settings** to open the *Settings* window.

Figure Intro-53 *Minimize* button on an app window

g. Click the **Find a setting** search box, type Printer, and view the search results.

Figure Intro-54 Windows 10 *Action Center*

h. Click the **Minimize** button to minimize the *Settings* windows to the *Taskbar*.

8. Use the *Task View* feature to open and close apps and windows.

a. Click the **Task View** button on the left side of the *Taskbar* (Figure Intro-55). All open apps and windows display tiled on the Windows desktop.

b. Click the **Store** app to open it. *Task View* closes and the *Store* app displays on your Windows desktop.

Task View button

c. Click the **Task View** button again.

d. Click the **X** in the upper-right corner to close each open app and window. You may be prompted to save changes to a file.

Figure Intro-55 *Task View* button on the *Taskbar*

e. Click the **Task View** button again or press **Esc** to return to the desktop.

Working with Files

SLO INTRO. 4

When you work with Office files, a variety of display views are available. You can change how a file displays, adjust the display size, work with multiple files, and arrange windows to view multiple files. Because most people work with multiple files at the same time, Office makes it easy and intuitive to move from one file to another or to display multiple document windows at the same time.

File Views

Each of the different Office applications provides you with a variety of ways to view your document. In Word, Excel, and PowerPoint, the different views are available on the *View tab* (Figure Intro-56). You can also change views using the buttons on the right side of the *Status bar* at the bottom of the file window (Figure Intro-57). In Access, the different views for each object are available in the *Views* group on the *Home* tab.

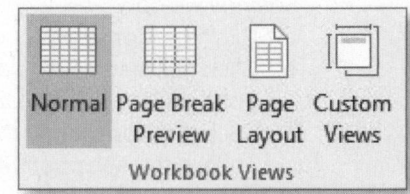

Figure Intro-56 *Workbook Views* group on the *View* tab in Excel

Figure Intro-57 PowerPoint views on the *Status* bar

Table Intro-4 lists the views that are available in each of the different Office applications.

Table Intro-4: File Views

Office Application	Views	Office Application	Views
Word	*Read Mode* *Print Layout* *web Layout* *Outline* *Draft*	**Access** *(Access views vary* *depending on active* *object)*	*Layout View* *Design View* *Datasheet View* *Form View* *SQL View* *Report View* *Print Preview*
Excel	*Normal* *Page Break Preview* *Page Layout* *Custom Views*	**PowerPoint**	*Normal* *Outline View* *Slide Sorter* *Notes Page* *Reading View* *Presenter View*

Change Display Size

Use the ***Zoom*** feature to increase or decrease the display size of your file. Using *Zoom* to change the display size does not change the actual size of text or objects in your file; it only changes the size of your display. For example, if you change the *Zoom* level to 120%, you increase the display of your file to 120% of its normal size (100%), but changing the display size does not affect the actual size of text and objects in your file. Decrease the *Zoom* level to 80% to display more of your file on the screen.

You can increase or decrease the *Zoom* level several different ways. Your *Zoom* options vary depending on the Office application.

- ***Zoom level*** *on the Status* bar (Figure Intro-58): Click the **+** or **−** button to increase or decrease *Zoom* level in 10% increments.
- ***Zoom group*** *on the View tab* (Figure Intro-59): The *Zoom* group includes a variety of *Zoom* options. The options vary depending on the Office application.
- ***Zoom dialog box*** (Figure Intro-60): Click the **Zoom** button in the *Zoom* group on the *View* tab or click the **Zoom level** on the *Status* bar to open the *Zoom* dialog box.

Figure Intro-58 *Zoom* area on the *Status* bar in PowerPoint

Figure Intro-59 *Zoom* group in Excel

Figure Intro-60 *Zoom* dialog box in Word

Manage Multiple Open Files and Windows

When you are working on multiple files in an Office application, each file is opened in a new window. *Minimize* an open window to place the file on the Windows *Taskbar* (the bar at the bottom of the Windows desktop), *restore down* an open window so it does not fill the entire computer screen, or *maximize* a window so it fills the entire computer screen. The *Minimize, Restore Down/Maximize,* and *Close* buttons are in the upper-right corner of a file window (Figure Intro-61).

Figure Intro-61 Window options buttons

- *Minimize*: Click the **Minimize** button (see Figure Intro-61) to hide the active window. When a document is minimized, it is not closed. It is reduced to a button on the *Taskbar* and the window does not display. Place your pointer on the application icon on the Windows *Taskbar* to display thumbnails of open files. Click an open file thumbnail to display the file (Figure Intro-62).

- *Restore Down/Maximize*: Click the **Restore Down/Maximize** button (see Figure Intro-61) to decrease the size of an open window or to maximize the window to fill the entire screen. This button toggles between *Restore Down* and *Maximize*. When a window is restored down, change the size of a window by clicking and dragging a border of the window. You

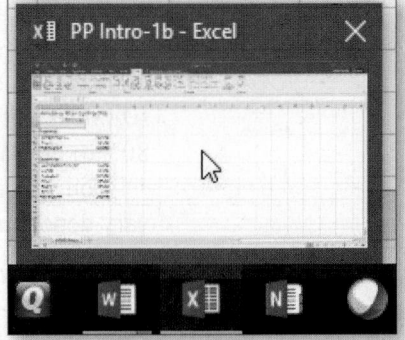

Figure Intro-62 Display minimized file on the *Taskbar*

can also move the window by clicking and dragging the title bar at the top of the window.

- *Close*: Click the **Close** button (see Figure Intro-61) to close the window. If there is only one open file, the Office application also closes when you click the *Close* button on the file.

You can switch between open files or arrange open files to display more than one window at the same time. The following are several methods to do this:

- *Switch Windows button*: Click the **Switch Windows** button [*View* tab, *Window* group] (not available in Access) to display a drop-down list of open files. Click a file from the drop-down list to display the file.

- **Windows Taskbar.** Place your pointer on an Office application icon on the Windows *Taskbar* to display the open files in that application. Click a file thumbnail to display it (see Figure Intro-62).
- **Arrange All button**: Click the **Arrange All** button [*View* tab, *Window* group] to display all windows in an application. You can resize or move the open file windows.

Snap Assist

The **Snap Assist** feature in Windows provides the ability to position an open window to the left or right side of your computer screen and fill half the screen. When you snap an open window to the left or right side of the screen, the other open windows tile on the opposite side where you can select another window to fill the opposite side of the computer screen (Figure Intro-63).

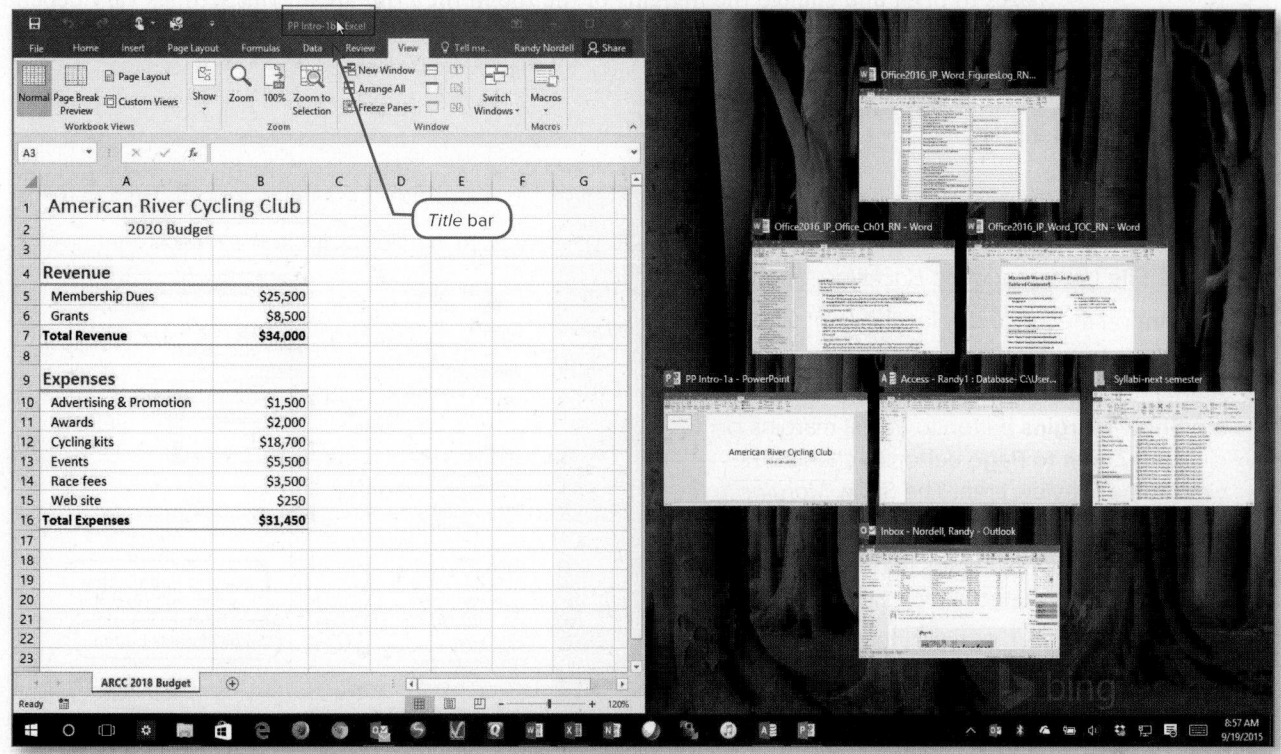

Figure Intro-63 Windows *Snap Assist* feature

▶HOW TO: Use Snap Assist

1. Click the **title bar** of an open window.
2. Drag it to the left or right edge of the computer screen and release the pointer.
 - The window snaps to the side of the screen and fills half of the computer screen (see Figure Intro-63).
 - The other open windows and apps display as tiles on the opposite side.
 - If you use a touch-screen computer, press and hold the title bar of an open window and drag to either side of the computer screen.
3. Select a tile of an open window or app to fill the other half of the screen.

> ### MORE INFO
>
> *Snap Assist* also enables you to snap a window to a quadrant (quarter rather than half) of your screen. Drag the **title bar** of an open window to one of the four corners of your computer screen.

Printing, Sharing, and Customizing Files

Use *Backstage* view in any of the Office applications, to print a file and to customize how a file is printed. You can also export an Office file as a PDF file in most of the Office applications. In addition, you can add and customize document properties for an Office file and share a file in a variety of formats.

Print a File

Print an Office file if you need a hard copy. The *Print* area on the *Backstage* view displays a preview of the open file and many print options. For example, you can choose which page or pages to print and change the margins of the file in the *Print* area. Print settings vary depending on the Office application you are using and what you are printing.

▶ HOW TO: Print a File

1. Open the file you want to print from a Windows folder or within an Office program.
2. Click the **File** tab to open the *Backstage* view.
3. Click **Print** on the left to display the *Print* area (Figure Intro-64).
 - A preview of the file displays on the right. Click the **Show Margins** button to adjust margins or click the **Zoom to Page** button to change the view in the *Preview* area. The *Show Margins* button is only available in Excel.
4. Change the number of copies to print in the *Copies* area.
5. Click the **Printer** drop-down list to choose from available printers.
6. Customize what is printed and how it is printed in the *Settings* area.
 - The *Settings* options vary depending on the Office application and what you print.
 - In the *Pages* area (*Slides* area in PowerPoint), select a page or range of pages (slides) to print.
 - By default, all pages (slides) are printed when you print a file.
7. Click the **Print** button to print your file.

Figure Intro-64 *Print* area on the *Backstage* view

> ▶ **ANOTHER WAY**
>
> Press **Ctrl+P** to open the *Print* area on the *Backstage* view.

Export as a PDF File

Portable document format, or **PDF**, is a specific file format that is often used to share files that are not to be changed, or to post files on a web site. When you create a PDF file from an Office application file, you are actually exporting a static image of the original file, similar to taking a picture of the file.

The advantage of working with a PDF file is that the format of the file is retained no matter who opens the file. PDF files open in the Windows Reader app or Adobe Reader, which is free software that is installed on most computers. Because a PDF file is a static image of a file, it is not easy for other people to edit your files. When you want people to be able to view a file but not change it, PDF files are a good choice.

HOW TO: Export a File as a PDF File

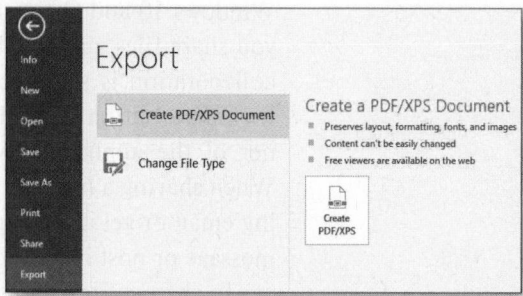

1. Open the file you want to export as a PDF file.
2. Click the **File** tab and click **Export** to display the *Export* area on the Backstage view (Figure Intro-65).
3. Select **Create PDF/XPS Document** and click the **Create PDF/XPS** button. The *Publish as PDF or XPS* dialog box opens.
 - XPS (XML Paper Specification) format is an alternative to a PDF file. XPS is a Microsoft format and is not widely used.
4. Select a location to save the file.
5. Type a name for the file in the *File name* area.
6. Click **Publish** to close the dialog box and save the PDF file.

Figure Intro-65 *Export* a file as a PDF file

MORE INFO

Microsoft Word can open PDF files, and you can edit and save the file as a Word document.

If Adobe Acrobat is installed on your computer, *Save as Adobe PDF* displays as an option on the *Backstage* view.

Document Properties

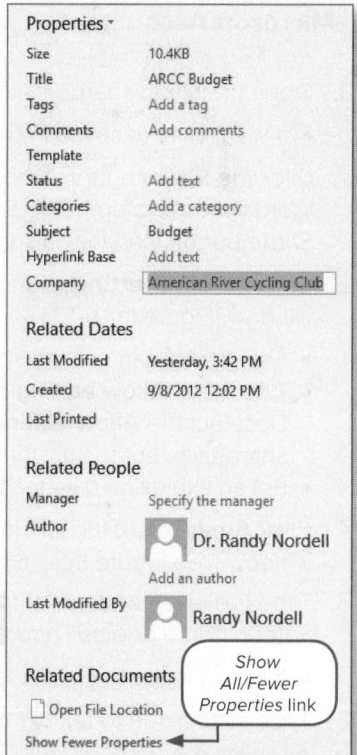

Document properties are hidden codes in a file that store identifying information about that file. Each piece of document property information is called a *field*. You can view and modify document properties in the *Info* area of the *Backstage* view.

Some document properties fields are automatically generated when you work on a file, such as *Size*, *Total Editing Time*, *Created*, and *Last Modified*. Other document properties fields, such as *Title*, *Comments*, *Subject*, *Company*, and *Author*, can be modified. You can use document property fields in different ways such as inserting the *Company* field in a document footer.

HOW TO: View and Modify Document Properties

1. Click the **File** tab and click **Info** (if not already selected). The document properties display on the right (Figure Intro-66).
2. Click the text box area of a field that can be edited and type your custom document property information.

Figure Intro-66 Document properties

3. Click the **Show All Properties** link at the bottom to display additional document properties.
 - Click **Show Fewer Properties** to collapse the list and display fewer properties.
 - This link toggles between *Show All Properties* and *Show Fewer Properties*.
4. Click the **Back** arrow to return to the file.

Share a File

Windows 10 and Office have been enhanced to help you share files and collaborate with others. Because collaboration is so important and commonly used, the *Share* button is available in the upper-right corner of the application window, except on Access. When sharing a file with others, you can send a sharing email or get a sharing link to paste into an email message or post in an online location.

To share a file, it must first be saved in *OneDrive*. If you try to share a file that is not saved in *OneDrive*, Word prompts you to save your document to *OneDrive* before sharing it. Depending on the type of Microsoft account you're using, the sharing options display in a *Send Link* window (education and business Microsoft accounts) (Figure Intro-67) or the *Share* pane (personal Microsoft account). The *Send Link* window or *Share* pane displays a variety of sharing options.

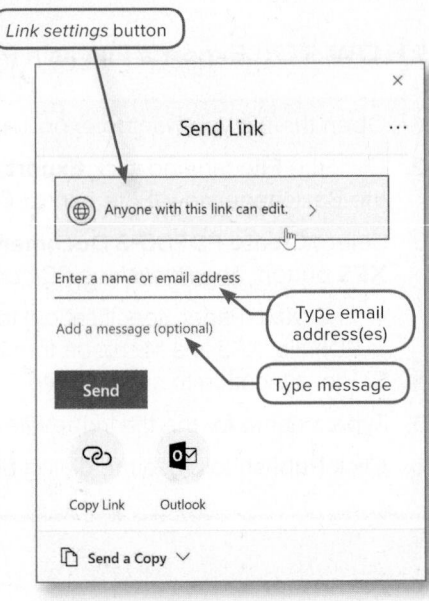

Figure Intro-67 *Send Link* window

▶ HOW TO: Share an Online File (Education and Business Microsoft Accounts)

Figure Intro-68 *Share* button

1. Open the file to share.
 - If the file is not saved in *OneDrive*, save the file to *OneDrive*.
2. Click the **Share** button (Figure Intro-68) in the upper-right corner of the Word window to open the *Send Link* window (see Figure Intro-67). The *Share* button icon may display differently in Office 2019.
3. Click the **Link settings** button (see Figure Intro-67) to open the *Link settings* window (Figure Intro-69).
 - Select who can use the sharing link.
 - Check the **Allow editing** box to enable recipients to edit the shared file. Deselect the **Allow editing** box to enable recipients to open and view the shared file, but restrict them from editing it.
 - Set an expiration date for the sharing link if desired (optional).
4. Click **Apply** to set the sharing link options and to return to the *Send Link* window (see Figure Intro-67).
5. Type the email address of the person with whom you are sharing the file in the *Enter a name or email address* area.
 - If typing multiple email addresses, separate each with a semicolon.
6. Type a message to recipient(s) in the *Add a message* area. This is optional.
7. Click the **Send** button. An email is sent to people you invited.
8. Click the **X** to close the confirmation window.

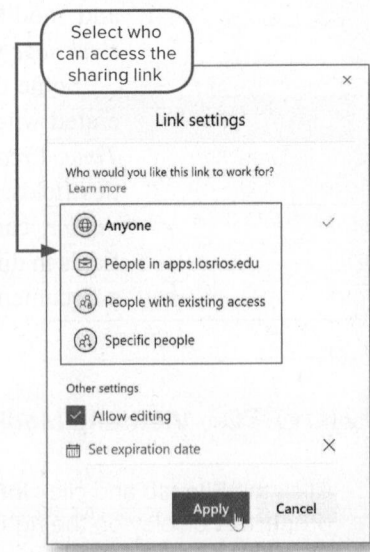

Figure Intro-69 *Link settings* window

If you're using a personal Microsoft account, the *Share* pane opens at the right after you click the *Share* button.

Share button

▶ HOW TO: Share an Online File (Personal Microsoft Account)

1. Open the file to share.
 - If the file is not saved in *OneDrive,* save the file to *OneDrive*.
2. Click the **Share** button in the upper-right corner of the Word window to open the *Share* pane to the right of the Word window (Figure Intro-70). The *Share* button icon may display differently in Office 2019.
3. Type or select the email address of the person with whom you are sharing the file in the *Invite people* area.
4. Select **Can edit** or **Can view** from the *Permission* drop-down list.
 - *Can edit* enables users to edit a shared document.
 - *Can view* enables users to open and view a shared document but restricts users from editing the document.
5. Type a message to recipient(s) in the *Message* area.
6. Click the **Share** button. An email is sent to people you invited.
7. Click the **X** to close the *Share* pane.

Figure Intro-70 Share a *OneDrive* file

Creating a sharing link (hyperlink) is another way to share a file with others rather than sending an email through Word. You can create and copy a sharing link and email the sharing link to others. You have the option of creating an *Edit link* or a *View-only link*.

▶ HOW TO: Create a Sharing Link (Education and Business Microsoft Accounts)

1. Open the file to share.
 - If the file is not saved in *OneDrive*, you are prompted to save the file to *OneDrive*.
2. Click the **Share** button in the upper right of the Word window to open the *Send Link* window.
3. Click the **Link settings** button to open the *Link settings* window (see Figure Intro-69).
 - Select who can use the sharing link.
 - Check the **Allow editing** box to enable recipients to edit the shared file. Deselect the **Allow editing** box to enable recipients to open and view the shared file, but restrict them from editing it.
 - Set an expiration date for the sharing link if desired (optional).
4. Click **Apply** to set the sharing link options and to return to the *Send Link* window.
5. Click the **Copy Link** button to open the window that displays the sharing link (Figure Intro-71).
6. Click the **Copy** button to copy the sharing link.
7. Click the **X** to close the confirmation window.
8. Paste the copied sharing link in an email, Word document, or other online location.

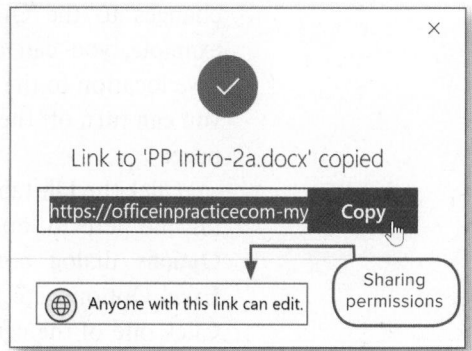
Figure Intro-71 Copy sharing link

If you're using a personal Microsoft account, the *Share* pane opens at the right after you after you click the *Share* button.

▶ **HOW TO: Create a Sharing Link (Personal Microsoft Account)**

1. Open the file to share.
 - If the file is not saved in *OneDrive*, you are prompted to save the file to *OneDrive*.
2. Click the **Share** button in the upper right of the Word window to open the *Share* pane to the right of the Word window.
3. Click **Get a sharing link** at the bottom of the *Share* pane (see Figure Intro-70).
4. Click the **Create an edit link** or **Create a view-only link** button (Figure Intro-72) to create a sharing link.
 - *Can edit* enables users to open, view, and edit a shared document.
 - *Can view* enables users to open and view a shared document but restricts users from editing the document.
5. Click the **Copy** button to copy the sharing link (Figure Intro-73).
6. Click the **Back** arrow to the left of *Get a sharing link* at the top of the *Share* pane to return to the main *Share* pane, or click the **X** to close the *Share* pane.
7. Paste the copied sharing link in an email, Word document, or other online location.

Figure Intro-72 Create a sharing link

Figure Intro-73 Copy a sharing link

▶ **ANOTHER WAY**

You can also share a file through email by clicking the **Send as attachment** link at the bottom of the *Share* pane. The email share options require the use of Microsoft Outlook (email and personal management Office application) to share the selected file through email.

Program Options

Use program options to apply global changes to the Office program. For example, you can change the default save location to the *OneDrive* folder or you can turn off the opening of a *Start* page.

Click the **File** tab and select **Options** on the left to open the *[Program]* **Options** dialog box (Word Options, Excel Options, etc.) (Figure Intro-74). Click one of the categories on the left to display the category options on the right. The categories and options vary depending on the Office application.

Figure Intro-74 *Excel Options* dialog box

Using the Ribbon, Tabs, and Quick Access Toolbar

Use the *Ribbon*, tabs, groups, buttons, drop-down lists, dialog boxes, task panes, galleries, and the *Quick Access* toolbar to modify your Office files. This section describes different tools used to customize your files.

The Ribbon, Tabs, and Groups

The **Ribbon**, which appears at the top of an Office file window, displays the many features available. The *Ribbon* is a collection of **tabs**. Each tab includes **groups** of commands. The tabs and groups available vary for each Office application. Click a tab to display the groups and commands available on that tab.

Some tabs always display on the *Ribbon* (for example, the *File* tab and *Home* tabs). Other tabs are contextual, which means that they only appear on the *Ribbon* when you select a specific object. Figure Intro-75 displays the contextual *Table Tools Fields* tab that displays in Access when you open a table.

Figure Intro-75 Contextual *Table Tools Fields* tab displayed

> **MORE INFO**
>
> The *Ribbon* may appear slightly different depending on the version of Office you are using.

Ribbon Display Options

The *Ribbon* displays by default in Office applications, and you can customize the appearance of the *Ribbon*. The **Ribbon Display Options** button is in the upper-right corner of an Office application window (Figure Intro-76). Click the **Ribbon Display Options** button to select one of the three options:

- *Auto-Hide Ribbon*: Hides the *Ribbon*. Click at the top of the application to display the *Ribbon*.
- *Show Tabs*: Displays *Ribbon* tabs only. Click a tab to open the *Ribbon* and display the tab.
- *Show Tabs and Commands*: Displays the *Ribbon* and tabs, which is the default setting in Office applications.

Figure Intro-76 *Ribbon Display Options*

> **MORE INFO**
>
> **Ctrl+F1** collapses or expands the *Ribbon*. Also, double-click a tab name on the *Ribbon* to collapse or expand it.

Buttons, Drop-Down Lists, and Galleries

Groups on each of the tabs contain a variety of *buttons*, *drop-down lists*, and *galleries*. The following list describes each of these features and how they are used:

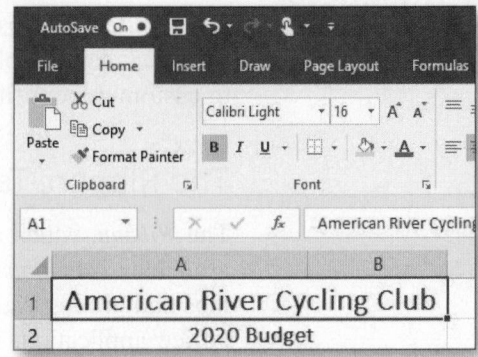

- **Button**: Applies a feature to selected text or an object. Click a button to apply the feature (Figure Intro-77).
- **Drop-down list**: Displays the various options available for a command. Some buttons are drop-down lists only, so when you click these buttons a drop-down list of options appears (Figure Intro-78). Other buttons are *split buttons*, which have both a button you click to apply a feature and an arrow you click to display a drop-down list of options (Figure Intro-79).

Figure Intro-77 *Bold button in the Font group on the Home tab*

- **Gallery**: Displays a collection of option buttons. Click an option in a gallery to apply the feature. Figure Intro-80 is the *Styles* gallery. Click the **More** button to display the entire gallery of options or click the **Up** or **Down** arrow to display a different row of options.

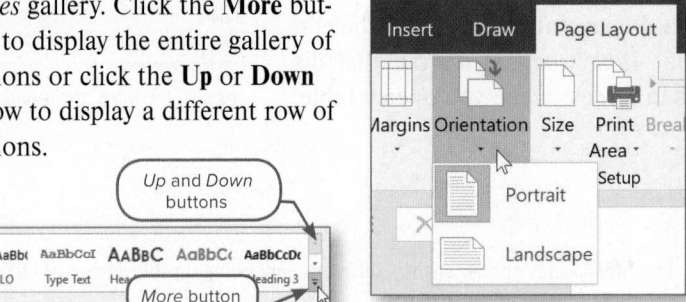

Figure Intro-80 *Styles gallery in Word*

Figure Intro-78 *Orientation drop-down list*

Figure Intro-79 *Merge & Center split button— button and drop-down list*

Dialog Boxes, Task Panes, and Launchers

Office application features are also available in a *dialog box* or *task pane*. A *launcher*, which is a small square that displays in the bottom right of some groups, opens a dialog box or displays a task pane when clicked (see Figure Intro-82).

- **Dialog box**: A new window that opens to display additional features. Move a dialog box by clicking and dragging the title bar. The title bar appears at the top of the dialog box and displays the title. Figure Intro-81 shows the *Format Cells* dialog box that opens after you click the *Alignment* launcher in Excel.

Figure Intro-81 *Format Cells dialog box*

- **Task pane**: Opens on the left or right of an Office application window. Figure Intro-82 shows the *Clipboard* pane, which is available in all Office applications. Task panes are named

according to their purpose (for example, *Clipboard* pane or *Navigation* pane). You can resize a task pane by clicking and dragging its left or right border. Click the **X** in the upper-right corner to close a task pane.

Figure Intro-83 *Align Left ScreenTip*

ScreenTips

ScreenTips display descriptive information about a button, drop-down list, launcher, or gallery selection. When you place your pointer on an item on the *Ribbon*, a *ScreenTip* displays information about the selection (Figure Intro-83). The *ScreenTip* appears temporarily and displays the command name, keyboard shortcut (if available), and a description of the command.

Figure Intro-82 *Clipboard* pane

Radio Buttons, Check Boxes, and Text Boxes

Dialog boxes and task panes contain a variety of options you can apply using *radio buttons*, *check boxes*, *text boxes*, *drop-down lists*, and other buttons (Figure Intro-84).

- **Radio button**: A round button you click to select one option from a group of options. A selected radio button displays a solid dot inside the round button. Radio buttons are mutually exclusive.

Figure Intro-84 *Page Setup* dialog box in Excel

- **Check box**: A square button you click to select one or more options. A check appears in a selected check box.
- **Text box**: An area where you type text.

A task pane or dialog box may also include drop-down lists or other buttons that open additional dialog boxes. Figure Intro-84 shows the *Page Setup* dialog box in Excel, which includes a variety of radio buttons, check boxes, text boxes, drop-down lists, and command buttons that open additional dialog boxes (for example, the *Print* and *Options* buttons).

Quick Access Toolbar

The *Quick Access toolbar* is located above the *Ribbon* on the upper left of each Office application window. It contains buttons to apply commonly used commands such as *Save*, *Undo*, *Redo*, and *Open*. The *Undo* button is a split button (Figure Intro-85). You can

Figure Intro-85 *Quick Access* toolbar

click the button to undo the last action performed, or you can click the drop-down arrow to display and undo multiple previous actions.

Customize the Quick Access Toolbar

You can customize the *Quick Access* toolbar to include commands you regularly use, such as *Quick Print*, *New*, and *Spelling & Grammar*. The following steps show how to customize the *Quick Access* toolbar in Word. The customization process is similar for the *Quick Access* toolbar in the other Office applications.

▶ HOW TO: Customize the Quick Access Toolbar

1. Click the **Customize Quick Access Toolbar** drop-down list on the right edge of the *Quick Access* toolbar (Figure Intro-86).

2. Select a command to add to the *Quick Access* toolbar. The command displays on the *Quick Access* toolbar.
 - Items on the *Customize Quick Access Toolbar* drop-down list with a check display on the *Quick Access* toolbar.
 - Select a checked item to remove it from the *Quick Access* toolbar.

3. Add a command that is not listed on the *Customize Quick Access Toolbar* by clicking the **Customize Quick Access Toolbar** drop-down list and selecting **More Commands**. The *Word Options* dialog box opens with the *Customize the Quick Access Toolbar* area displayed (Figure Intro-87).

4. Click the **Customize Quick Access Toolbar** drop-down list on the right and select **For all documents** or the current document.
 - If you select *For all documents*, the change is made to the *Quick Access* toolbar for all documents you open in Word.
 - If you select the current document, the change is made to the *Quick Access* toolbar in that document only.

5. Select the command to add from the alphabetic list of commands on the left and click the **Add** button.
 - If you can't find a command, click the **Choose commands from** drop-down list and select **All Commands**.
 - The list on the right contains the commands that display on the *Quick Access* toolbar.

6. Rearrange commands on the *Quick Access* toolbar by selecting a command in the list on the right and clicking the **Move Up** or **Move Down** button.

7. Click **OK** to close the *Word Options* dialog box.

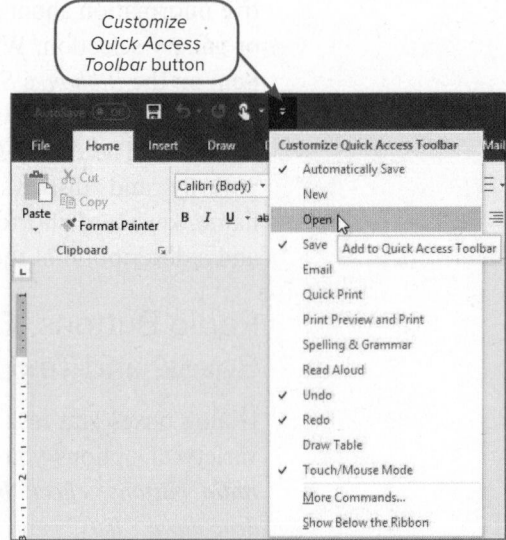

Figure Intro-86 Add a command to the *Quick Access* toolbar

Figure Intro-87 Customize the *Quick Access* toolbar in the *Word Options* dialog box

SLO INTRO. 7

Using Context Menus, the Mini Toolbar, and Keyboard Shortcuts

Most of the commands used for formatting and editing your files display in groups on the tabs. But many of these features are also available using context menus, the mini toolbar, and keyboard shortcuts. Use these tools to quickly apply formatting or other options to text or objects.

Context Menu

A *context menu* displays when you right-click text, a cell, or an object such as a picture, drawing object, chart, or *SmartArt* (Figure Intro-88). The context menu is a vertical list of options, and the options are contextual, which means they vary depending on what you right-click. Context menus include options that perform an action (*Cut* or *Copy*), open a dialog box or task pane (*Format Cells* or *Insert*), or display a drop-down list of selections (*Filter* or *Sort*).

Mini Toolbar

The *mini toolbar* is another context menu that displays when you right-click or select text, a cell, or an object in your file (see Figure Intro-88). The mini toolbar is a horizontal rectangular menu that lists a variety of formatting options. These options vary

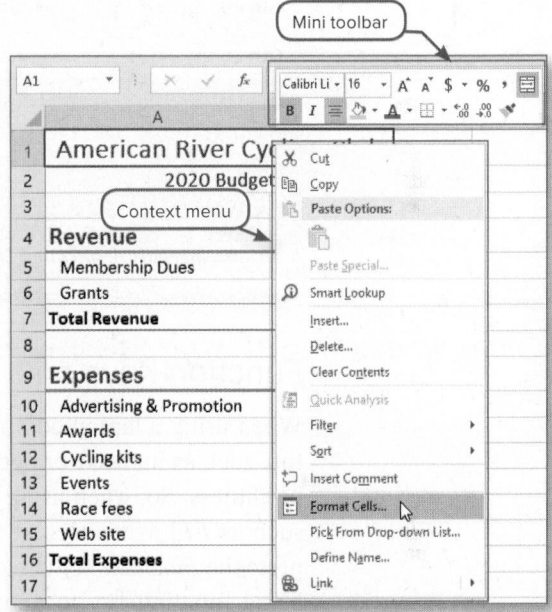

Figure Intro-88 Context menu and mini toolbar

depending on what you select or right-click. The mini toolbar contains a variety of buttons and drop-down lists. The mini toolbar typically displays above the context menu, and it automatically displays when you select text or an object, such as when you select a row of a table in Word or PowerPoint.

Keyboard Shortcuts

You can also use a *keyboard shortcut* to quickly apply formatting or perform commands. A keyboard shortcut is a combination of keyboard keys that you press at the same time. These can include the **Ctrl**, **Shift**, **Alt**, letter, number, and function keys (for example, **F1** or **F7**). Table Intro-5 lists common Office keyboard shortcuts.

Table Intro-5: Common Office Keyboard Shortcuts

Keyboard Shortcut	Action or Displays	Keyboard Shortcut	Action or Displays
Ctrl+S	Save	Ctrl+Z	Undo
F12	*Save As* dialog box	Ctrl+Y	Redo or Repeat
Ctrl+O	*Open* area on the *Backstage* view	Ctrl+1	Single space
Shift+F12	*Open* dialog box	Ctrl+2	Double space
Ctrl+N	New blank file	Ctrl+L	Align left
Ctrl+P	*Print* area on the *Backstage* view	Ctrl+E	Align center
Ctrl+C	Copy	Ctrl+R	Align right
Ctrl+X	Cut	F1	*Help* pane
Ctrl+V	Paste	F7	*Spelling* pane
Ctrl+B	Bold	Ctrl+A	Select All
Ctrl+I	Italic	Ctrl+Home	Move to the beginning
Ctrl+U	Underline	Ctrl+End	Move to the end

> **MORE INFO**
>
> See *Appendix A: Microsoft Office Shortcuts* (online resource) for additional Office keyboard shortcuts.

Function Keys on a Laptop

When using a laptop computer, function keys perform specific Windows actions on your laptop, such as increase or decrease speaker volume, open Windows *Settings*, or adjust the screen brightness. So, when using a numbered function key in an Office application, such as *F12* as a shortcut to open the *Save As* dialog box, you may need to press the **Function key** (**Fn** or **fn**) on your keyboard in conjunction with a numbered function key to activate the Office command (Figure Intro-89). The *Function key* is typically located near the bottom left of your laptop keyboard next to the *Ctrl* key.

Figure Intro-89
Function key

PAUSE & PRACTICE: INTRO-2

For this project, you work with a document for the American River Cycling Club. You modify the existing document, add document properties, customize the *Quick Access* toolbar, export the document as a PDF file, and share the document.

File Needed: **ARCCTraining-Intro.docx** *(Student data files are available in the* Library *of your SIMnet account.)*
Completed Project File Names: **[your initials] PP Intro-2a.docx** and **[your initials] PP Intro-2b.pdf**

1. Open Word and open the **ARCCTraining-Intro** file from your student data files. If the file opens in *Protected View*, click the **Enable Editing** button.

2. Save this document as [your initials] PP Intro-2a in the *American River Cycling Club* folder in your *OneDrive* folder.
 a. In *Pause & Practice Intro-1*, you created the *American River Cycling Club* folder in *OneDrive* or other storage area. Save this file in the same location.
 b. If you don't save this file in *OneDrive*, you will not be able to complete steps 7 and 9 in this project.

3. Use a button, drop-down list, and dialog box to modify the document.
 a. Select the first heading, "**What is Maximum Heart Rate?**"
 b. Click the **Bold** button [*Home* tab, *Font* group].
 c. Click the **Underline** drop-down arrow and select **Double underline** (Figure Intro-90).
 d. Click the **launcher** in the *Font* group [*Home* tab] to open the *Font* dialog box (Figure Intro-91).
 e. Select **12** from the *Size* area list or type 12 in the text box.
 f. Click the **Small caps** check box in the *Effects* area to select it.
 g. Click **OK** to close the dialog box and apply the formatting changes.
 h. Select the next heading, "**What is Target Heart Rate?**"
 i. Repeat steps 3b–g to apply formatting to selected text.

Figure Intro-90 Apply *Double underline* to selected text

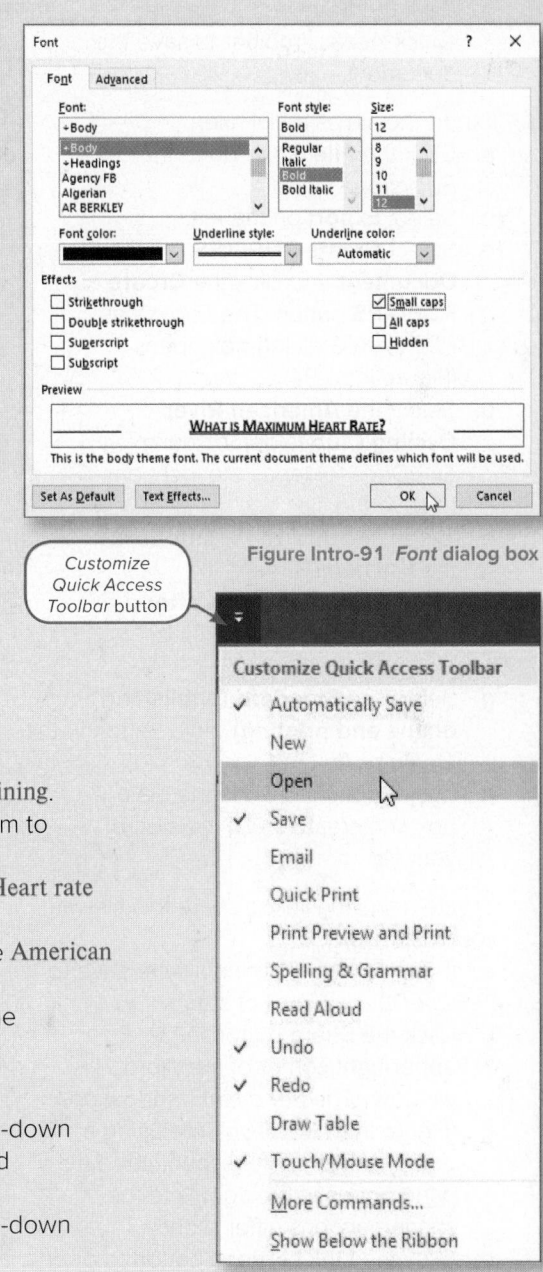

Figure Intro-91 *Font* dialog box

4. Add document properties.
 a. Click the **File** tab to display the *Backstage* view.
 b. Select **Info** on the left (if not already selected). The document properties display on the right.
 c. Click the **Add a title** text box and type ARCC Training.
 d. Click the **Show All Properties** link near the bottom to display additional document properties.
 e. Click the **Specify the subject** text box and type Heart rate training.
 f. Click the **Specify the company** text box and type American River Cycling Club.
 g. Click the **Back** arrow on the upper left to close the *Backstage* view and return to the document.

5. Customize the *Quick Access* toolbar.
 a. Click the **Customize Quick Access Toolbar** drop-down arrow and select **Open** if it is not already selected (Figure Intro-92).
 b. Click the **Customize Quick Access Toolbar** drop-down arrow again and select **Spelling & Grammar**.

Figure Intro-92 *Customize Quick Access Toolbar* drop-down list

c. Click the **Customize Quick Access Toolbar** drop-down arrow again and select **More Commands**. The *Word Options* dialog box opens (Figure Intro-93).

d. Select **Insert Comment** in the list of commands on the left.

e. Click the **Add** button to add it to your *Quick Access* toolbar list on the right.

f. Click **OK** to close the *Word Options* dialog box.

g. Click the **Save** button on the *Quick Access* toolbar to save the document.

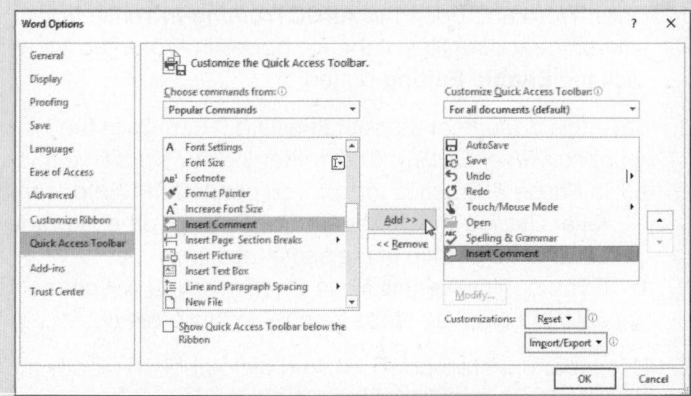

Figure Intro-93 Customize the *Quick Access* toolbar in the *Word Options* dialog box

6. Export the file as a PDF file.
a. Click the **File** tab to go to the *Backstage* view.
b. Select **Export** on the left.
c. Select **Create PDF/XPS Document** and click the **Create PDF/XPS** button. The *Publish as PDF or XPS* dialog box opens (Figure Intro-94).
d. Select the **American River Cycling Club** folder in your *OneDrive* folder as the location to save the file.
e. Type [your initials] PP Intro-2b in the *File name* area.
f. Deselect the **Open file after publishing** check box if it is checked.
g. Select the **Standard (publishing online and printing)** radio button in the *Optimize for* area.
h. Click **Publish** to close the dialog box and create a PDF version of your file.

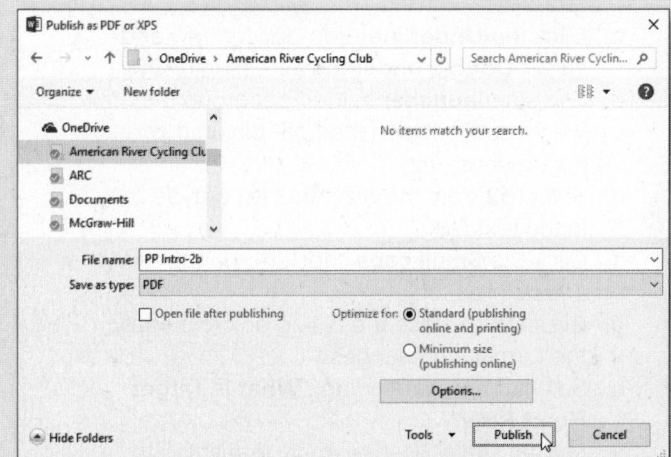

Figure Intro-94 *Publish as PDF or XPS* dialog box

7. Create a sharing link to share this file with your instructor.
a. If you don't have the ability to save to *OneDrive*, skip all of step 7.
b. Click the **Share** button in the upper-right corner of the Word window. The *Send Link* window opens (Figure Intro-95). If you are using a personal Microsoft account, the *Share* pane opens at the right, and the sharing options differ slightly.
c. Click the **Link settings** button to open the *Link settings* window.

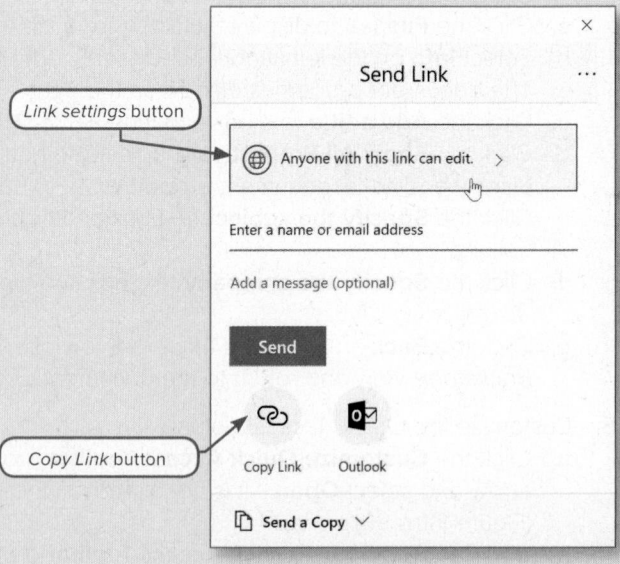

Figure Intro-95 *Send Link* window

d. Click the **Anyone** button and check the **Allow editing** box (if necessary) (Figure Intro-96).

e. Click **Apply** to return to the *Send Link* window.

f. Click the **Copy Link** button to create a sharing link.

g. Click **Copy** to copy the sharing link and click the **X** in the upper-right corner to close the sharing link window (Figure Intro-97).

h. Use your email account to create a new email to your instructor. Include an appropriate subject line and a brief message in the body.

i. Press **Ctrl+V** to paste the sharing link to your document in the body of the email and send the email message.

8. Save and close the document (Figure Intro-98).

Link to 'PP Intro-2a.docx' copied

https://officeinpracticecom-my Copy

Anyone with this link can edit.

Figure Intro-97 Copy a sharing link

Link settings

Who would you like this link to work for?
Learn more

- Anyone ✓
- People in apps.losrios.edu
- People with existing access
- Specific people

Other settings

- ✓ Allow editing
- 📅 Set expiration date ✕

Apply Cancel

Figure Intro-96 *Link settings* window

Figure Intro-98 PP Intro-2a completed

Organizing and Customizing Folders and Files

The more you use your computer to create and edit files, the more important it is to create an organized system to locate and manage files. Use *folders* to store related files to make it easier to find, edit, and share your files. For example, you can create a folder for the college you attend. Inside the college folder, create a folder for each of your courses. Inside each of the course folders, create a folder for student data files, solution files, and group projects. Folders can store any type of files; you are not limited to Office files.

Create a Folder

In *SLO Intro. 3: Creating, Saving, Closing, and Opening Office Files*, you learned how to create a new folder when saving an Office file in the *Save As* dialog box. You can also create a Windows folder using *File Explorer*. You can create folders inside other folders.

▶ **HOW TO:** Create a Windows Folder

1. Click the **File Explorer** on the *Taskbar* or click the **Start** button and select **File Explorer** to open a *File Explorer* window.
 - Your folders and computer locations display on the left in the *Navigation* pane.
2. Select the location in the *Navigation* pane where you want to create a new folder.
3. Click the **Home** tab and click the **New folder** button [*New* group]. A new folder is created (Figure Intro-99).
 - The *New Folder* button is also on the *Quick Access* toolbar in the *File Explorer* window.
4. Type the name of the new folder and press **Enter**.

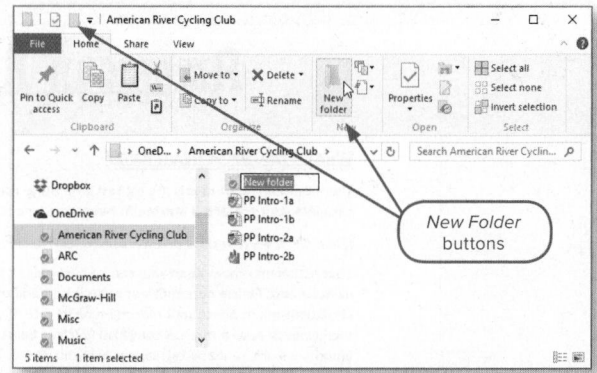

Figure Intro-99 Create a new Windows folder

ANOTHER WAY

Ctrl+Shift+N creates a new folder in a Windows folder.

Move and Copy Files and Folders

Moving a file or folder is cutting it from one location and pasting it in another location. Copying a file or folder creates a copy, and you can paste in another location so the file or folder is in two or more locations. If you move or copy a folder, the files in the folder are moved or copied with the folder. Move or copy files and folders using the *Move to* or *Copy to* buttons on the *Home* tab of *File Explorer*, keyboard shortcuts (**Ctrl+X, Ctrl+C, Ctrl+V**), or the drag-and-drop method.

To move or copy multiple folders or files at the same time, press the **Ctrl** key and select multiple items to move or copy. Use the **Ctrl** key to select or deselect multiple non-adjacent files or folders. Use the **Shift** key to select a range of files or folders. Click the first file or folder in a range, press the **Shift** key, and select the last file or folder in the range to select all of the items in the range.

▶HOW TO: Move or Copy a File or Folder

1. Click the **File Explorer** on the *Taskbar* or click the **Start** button and select **File Explorer** to open a *File Explorer* window.
2. Select a file or folder to move or copy.
 - Press the **Ctrl** key or the **Shift** key to select multiple files or folders.
3. Click the **Home** tab in the *File Explorer* window.
4. Click the **Move to** or **Copy to** button [*Organize* group] and select the location where you want to move or copy the file or folder (Figure Intro-100).

Figure Intro-100 Move or copy a selected file or folder

 - If the folder is not available, select **Choose location** to open the *Move Items* or *Copy Items* dialog box.
 - To use keyboard shortcuts, press **Ctrl+X** to cut the file or folder or **Ctrl+C** to copy the file or folder from its original location, go to the desired new location, and press **Ctrl+V** to paste it.
 - To use the drag-and-drop method to move a file or folder, select the file or folder and drag and drop to the new location.
 - To use the drag-and-drop method to copy a file or folder, press the **Ctrl** key, select the file or folder, and drag and drop to the new location.

> **ANOTHER WAY**
>
> Right-click a file or folder to display the context menu and select **Cut, Copy**, or **Paste**.

Rename Files and Folders

You can rename a file or folder in a *File Explorer* window. When you rename a file or folder, only the file or folder name changes. The contents of the file or folder do not change.

▶HOW TO: Rename a File or Folder

1. Click the **File Explorer** on the *Taskbar* or click the **Start** button and select **File Explorer** to open a *File Explorer* window.
2. Select the file or folder you want to rename.
3. Click the **Rename** button [*Home* tab, *Organize* group] (see Figure Intro-100).
4. Type the new name of the file or folder and press **Enter**.

> **ANOTHER WAY**
>
> Select a file or folder to rename, press **F2**, type the new name, and press **Enter**. You can also right-click a file or folder and select **Rename** from the context menu.

Delete Files and Folders

You can easily delete files and folders. When you delete a file or folder, it is moved from its current location to the **Recycle Bin** on your computer. The *Recycle Bin* stores deleted items. If a file or folder is in the *Recycle Bin*, you can restore it to its original location or move it to a different location. You also have the option to permanently delete a file or folder. If an item is permanently deleted, you do not have the restore option.

▶ HOW TO: Delete Files and Folders

1. Open a *File Explorer* window and select the file or folder you want to delete.
 - You can select multiple files and folders to delete at the same time.

2. Click the **Delete** drop-down arrow [*Home* tab, *Organize* group] to display the list of delete options (Figure Intro-101).
 - The default action when you click the *Delete* button (not the drop-down arrow) is *Recycle*.

3. Delete a file by selecting **Recycle**, which moves it to the *Recycle Bin*.
 - *Recycle* deletes the item(s) and moves it (them) to the *Recycle Bin*.
 - When you *Recycle* an item, you are not prompted to confirm the deletion. To change the default setting, select **Show recycle confirmation** from the *Delete* drop-down list. A confirmation dialog box displays each time you delete or recycle an item.

4. Delete a file permanently by clicking the **Delete** drop-down arrow and selecting **Permanently delete**. A confirmation dialog box opens. Click **Yes** to confirm the deletion.
 - *Permanently delete* deletes the item(s) from your computer.

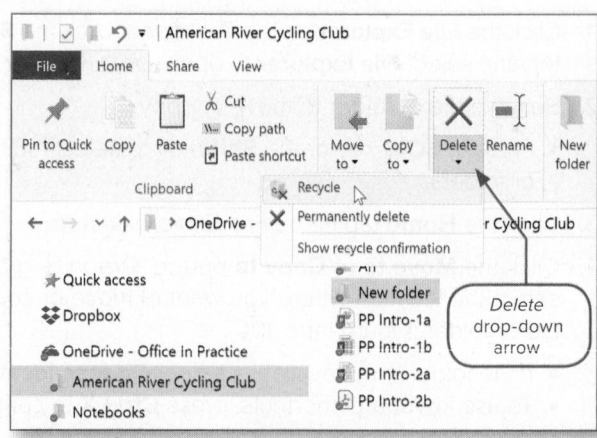

Figure Intro-101 Delete selected folder

> ▶ **ANOTHER WAY**
>
> Press **Ctrl+D** or the **Delete** key on your keyboard to recycle selected item(s).
> Press **Shift+Delete** to permanently delete selected item(s).

Create a Zipped (Compressed) Folder

If you want to share multiple files or a folder of files with classmates, coworkers, friends, or family, you can *zip* the files into a *zipped folder* (also called a *compressed folder*). For example, you can't attach an entire folder to an email message, but you can attach a zipped folder to an email message. Compressing files and folders decreases their size. You can zip a group of selected files, a folder, or a combination of files and folders, and then share the zipped folder with others through email or in a cloud storage location such as *OneDrive*.

▶ HOW TO: Create a Zipped (Compressed) Folder

1. Open a *File Explorer* window.

2. Select the file(s) and/or folder(s) you want to zip (compress).

3. Click the **Zip** button [*Share* tab, *Send* group] (Figure Intro-102). A zipped folder is created.
 - The default name of the zipped folder is the name of the first item you selected to zip.

4. Type a name for the zipped folder and press **Enter**. Alternatively, press **Enter** to accept the default name.
 - The icon for a zipped folder looks similar to the icon for a folder except it has a vertical zipper down the middle of the folder.

Figure Intro-102 Create a zipped folder

Extract a Zipped (Compressed) Folder

If you receive a zipped folder via email or download a zipped folder, save the zipped folder to your computer and then *extract* its contents. Extracting a zipped folder creates a regular Windows folder from the zipped folder.

▶ **HOW TO:** Extract a Zipped (Compressed) Folder

1. Select the zipped folder to extract.
2. Click the **Compressed Folder Tools** tab.
3. Click the **Extract all** button (Figure Intro-103). The *Extract Compressed (Zipped) Folders* dialog box opens (Figure Intro-104).
4. Click **Extract** to extract the folder.
 - Both the extracted folder and the zipped folder display.
 - If you check the **Show extracted files when complete** check box, the extracted folder will open after extracting.

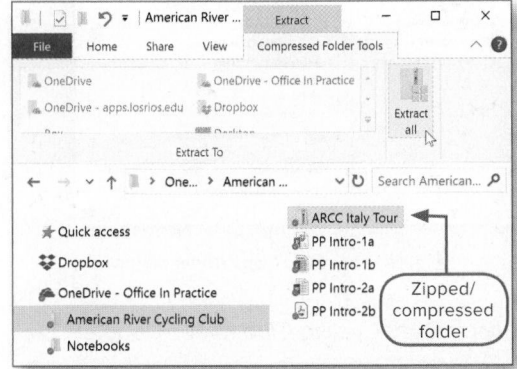

Figure Intro-103 Extract files from a zipped folder

Figure Intro-104 *Extract Compressed (Zipped) Folders* dialog box

For this project, you copy and rename files in your *OneDrive* folder on your computer, create a folder, move files, create a zipped folder, and rename a zipped folder.

Files Needed: ***[your initials] PP Intro-1a.pptx, [your initials] PP Intro-1b.xlsx, [your initials] PP Intro-2a.docx, [your initials] PP Intro-2b.docx***, and ***ARCC_Membership-Intro.accdb*** *(Student data files are available in the* Library *of your SIMnet account.)*
Completed Project File Names: ***[your initials] PP Intro-1a.pptx, [your initials] PP Intro-1b.xlsx, [your initials] PP Intro-2a.docx, [your initials] PP Intro-2b.docx, [your initials] PP Intro-3.accdb***, and ***ARCC Italy Tour-2020*** (zipped folder)

1. Copy and rename a file.
 a. Click the **File Explorer** on the *Taskbar* or click the **Start** button and select **File Explorer** to open a *File Explorer* window. If *File Explorer* is not available on the *Taskbar* or *Start* menu, use *Cortana* to find and open a *File Explorer* window.
 b. Browse the *File Explorer* window to locate your student data files.
 c. Select the ***ARCC_Membership-Intro*** file.
 d. Click the **Copy to** button [*Home* tab, *Organize* group] and select **Choose location** from the drop-down list to open the *Copy Items* dialog box.
 e. Browse to locate the *American River Cycling Club* folder you created in *Pause & Practice: Intro-1*.
 f. Select the ***American River Cycling Club*** folder and click the **Copy** button to copy the ***ARCC_Membership-Intro*** file to the *American River Cycling Club* folder (Figure Intro-105). The *Copy Items* dialog box closes and the copied file displays.

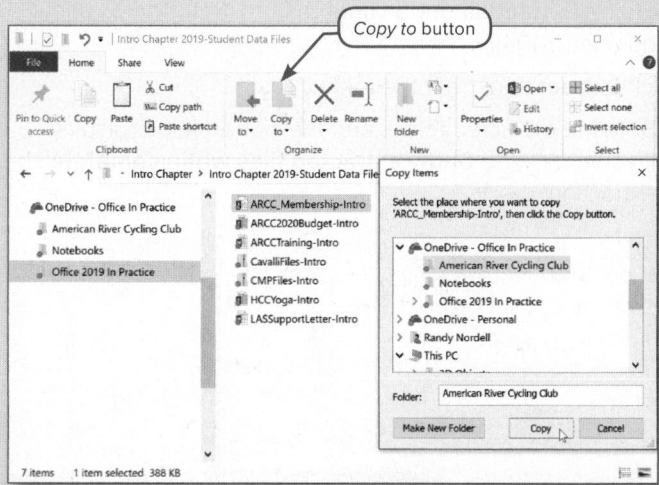

Figure Intro-105 *Copy Items* dialog box

 g. Use the *File Explorer* window to browse and locate the *American River Cycling Club* folder. Double-click the folder to open it.
 h. Click the ***ARCC_Membership-Intro*** file in the *American River Cycling Club* folder to select it.
 i. Click the **Rename** button [*Home* tab, *Organize* group], type [your initials] PP Intro-3 as the new file name, and press **Enter** (Figure Intro-106).

Figure Intro-106 Rename a file

2. Create a new folder and move files.
 a. With the *American River Cycling Club* folder still open, click the **New folder** button [*Home* tab, *New* group] (see Figure Intro-106).
 b. Type ARCC Italy Tour as the name of the new folder and press **Enter**.
 c. Select the ***[your initials] PP Intro-1a*** file.

d. Press the **Ctrl** key, select the *[your initials] PP Intro-1b*, *[your initials] PP Intro-2a*, *[your initials] PP Intro-2b*, and *[your initials] PP Intro-3* files, and release the **Ctrl** key. All five files should be selected.

e. Click the **Move to** button [*Home* tab, *Organize* group] and select **Choose location** to open the *Move Items* dialog box (Figure Intro-107).

f. Browse to locate the *ARCC Italy Tour* folder in the *Move Items* dialog box.

g. Select the **ARCC Italy Tour** folder and click the **Move** button to move the selected files to the *ARCC Italy Tour* folder.

h. Double-click the **ARCC Italy Tour** folder to open it and confirm the five files are moved.

i. Click the **Up** or **Back** arrow above the *Navigation* pane to return to the *American River Cycling Club* folder (see Figure Intro-107).

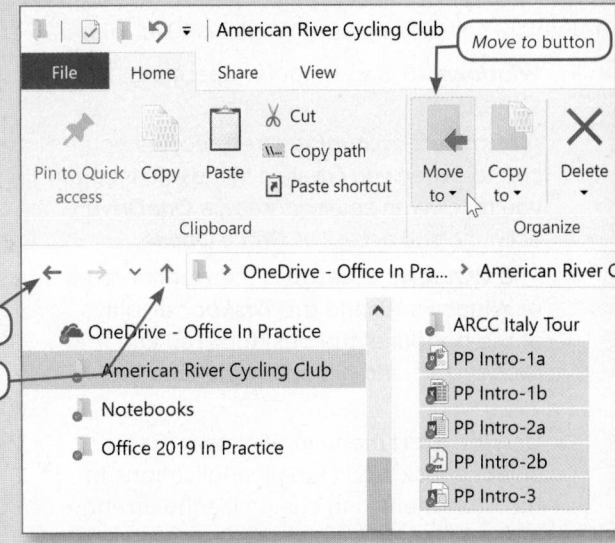

Figure Intro-107 Move selected files to a different folder

3. Create a zipped folder.
 a. Select the **ARCC Italy Tour** folder.
 b. Click the **Zip** button [*Share* tab, *Send* group]. A zipped (compressed) folder is created.
 c. Place the insertion point at the end of the zipped folder name, type *-2020*, and press **Enter** (Figure Intro-108).

4. Email the zipped folder to your instructor.
 a. Use your email account to create a new email to send to your instructor.
 b. Include an appropriate subject line and a brief message in the body.
 c. Attach the **ARCC Italy Tour-2020** zipped folder to the email message and send the email message.

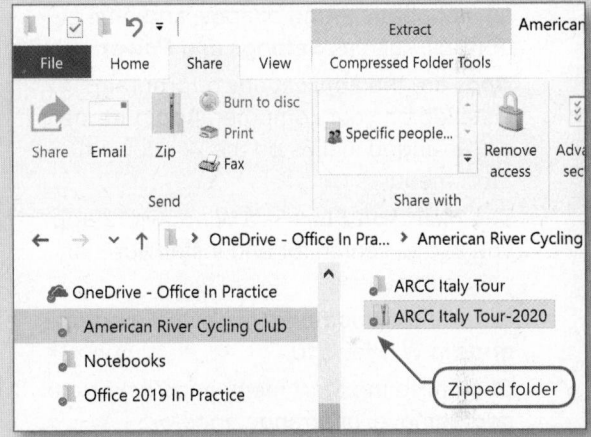

Figure Intro-108 Create a zipped folder

Chapter Summary

Intro. 1 Explore select features of Windows 10 (p. Intro-2).

- **Windows 10** is a computer operating system.
- A **Microsoft account** is a free account you create. When you create a Microsoft account, you receive an email address, a **OneDrive** account, and access to **Office Online**.
- The **Windows desktop** is the working area of Windows 10, and the **Taskbar** displays at the bottom of the desktop. You can rearrange icons and pin applications to the *Taskbar*.
- Use the **Start menu** in Windows 10 to select a task. You can pin applications to the *Start* menu and customize the arrangement of apps.
- The left side of the **Start menu** displays **Recently added** apps, **Most used** apps, an alphabetic listing of apps, and other buttons, such as **Settings** and **Power**.
- **Apps** are the applications or programs installed on your computer. App buttons are arranged in tiles on the Windows 10 *Start* menu.
- The **Microsoft Store** is a Windows 10 app you use to search for and install apps on your computer.
- Install both **traditional apps** and **modern apps** in Windows 10.
- Customize the *Start* menu and *Taskbar* to add, remove, or arrange apps.
- *File Explorer* is a window that displays files and folders on your computer.
- *OneDrive* is the cloud storage area where you can store files in a private and secure online location.
- The **OneDrive folder** in Windows 10 is one of your file storage location options.
- Access *OneDrive* folders and files using an internet browser window.
- **Cortana** is a search tool in Windows 10 used to locate information on your computer and the internet.
- **Task View** displays all open apps and windows as tiles on your desktop. Select an app or window to display or close.
- Use the **Settings** window to customize the Windows environment.
- The **Action Center** displays notifications and buttons to open many common Windows settings and features.

Intro. 2 Use basic features of Microsoft Office and navigate the Office working environment (p. Intro-12).

- **Office 2019/365** is application software that includes **Word**, **Excel**, **Access**, **PowerPoint**, **Outlook**, **OneNote**, and **Publisher**.
- **Office 2019** and **Office 365** include the same application products, but they differ in how you purchase them. Office 365 includes features that may not be available in Office 2019.
- **Office desktop apps** are the full-function Office 2019 or 365 products you install on your laptop or desktop computer.
- **Office universal apps** are a scaled-down version of Office applications installed on a tablet or mobile device.
- **Office Online** is free online software that works in conjunction with your online *Microsoft* account.
- A **Start page** displays when you open each of the Office applications. You can open an existing file or create a new file.
- The **Backstage view** in each of the Office applications performs many common tasks such as saving, opening an existing file, creating a new file, printing, and sharing.
- **Tell Me** is the Office help feature that displays Office commands related to specific topics.
- Use the mouse (or touchpad) on your computer to navigate the pointer on your computer screen. Use the pointer or click buttons to select text or objects.
- When using Office 2019/365 on a touch-screen computer, use the touch screen to perform actions. You can choose between **Touch Mode** and **Mouse Mode** in Office applications.

Intro. 3 Create, save, close, and open Office files (p. Intro-19).

- Create a new Office file from the *Start* page or *Backstage* view of the Office application.

- Assign a file name when you save a file for the first time.
- **AutoSave** is a new feature that automatically saves a file stored in *OneDrive*.
- Create folders to organize saved files, and you can save a file as a different file name.
- Office applications use a variety of different file types.
- Close an Office file when finished working on it. If the file has not been saved or changes have been made to the file, you are prompted to save the file before closing.
- Open an existing file from the *Start* page or from the *Open* area on *Backstage* view in each of the Office applications.

Intro. 4 Customize the view and display size in Office applications and work with multiple Office files (p. Intro-28).

- Each Office application has a variety of display views.
- Select an application view from the options on the **View tab** or the view buttons on the **Status bar**.
- The **Zoom** feature changes the display size of your file.
- **Minimize**, **restore down**, or **maximize** an open Office application window.
- Work with multiple Office files at the same time and switch between open files.
- **Snap Assist** enables you to arrange an open window on one side of your computer screen and select another window to fill the other side of the screen.

Intro. 5 Print, share, and customize Office files (p. Intro-32).

- Print a file in a variety of formats. The *Print* area on the *Backstage* view lists print options and displays a preview of your file.
- Export a file as a **PDF (portable document format)** file and save the PDF file to post to a web site or share with others.
- **Document properties** store information about a file.
- Share Office files in a variety of ways and enable others to view or edit shared files. To share a file with others, save the file in *OneDrive*.

- Program options are available on the *Backstage* view. Use program options to apply global changes to an Office application.

Intro. 6 Use the *Ribbon,* tabs, groups, dialog boxes, task panes, galleries, and the *Quick Access* toolbar (p. Intro-37).

- The **Ribbon** appears at the top of an Office window. It contains **tabs** and **groups** with commands to format and edit files.
- The **Ribbon Display Options** provides different ways to display the *Ribbon* in Office applications.
- A variety of **buttons**, **drop-down lists**, and **galleries** display within groups on each tab.
- **Dialog boxes** contain additional features not always displayed on the *Ribbon*.
- Click the **launcher** in the bottom-right corner of selected groups to open a dialog box.
- A **ScreenTip** displays information about commands on the *Ribbon*.
- Dialog boxes contain **radio buttons**, **check boxes**, **drop-down lists**, and **text boxes**.
- The **Quick Access toolbar** contains buttons that enable you to perform commands and displays in all Office applications. It is located in the upper left.
- Add or remove commands on the *Quick Access* toolbar.

Intro. 7 Use context menus, mini toolbar, keyboard shortcuts, and function keys in Office applications (p. Intro-41).

- A **context menu** displays when you right-click text or an object. A context menu contains different features depending on what you right-click.
- A **mini toolbar** is another context menu that displays formatting options.
- Use **keyboard shortcuts** to apply features or initiate commands.
- Numbered **function keys** perform commands in Office applications. On laptops, you may have to press the **Function key** (**Fn** or **fn**) to activate the numbered function keys.

Intro. 8 Organize and customize Windows folders and Office files (p. Intro-46).

- *Folders* store and organize files.
- Create, move, or copy files and folders. Files stored in a folder are moved or copied with that folder.
- Rename a file to change the file name.
- A deleted file or folder moves to the *Recycle Bin* on your computer by default. Alternatively, you can permanently delete files and folders.
- *Zip* files and/or folders into a *zipped (compressed) folder* to email or to share multiple files as a single file.
- *Extract* a zipped folder to create a regular Windows folder and to access its contents.

Check for Understanding

The SIMbook for this text (within your SIMnet account) provides the following resources for concept review:

- Multiple-choice questions
- Short answer questions
- Matching exercises

For these projects, you use your *OneDrive* to store files. If you don't already have a Microsoft account, see *SLO Intro.1: Using Windows 10* for information about creating a free personal Microsoft account.

Guided Project Intro-1

For this project, you organize and edit files for Emma Cavalli at Placer Hills Real Estate. You extract a zipped folder, rename files, manage multiple documents, apply formatting, and export as a PDF file.
[Student Learning Outcomes Intro.1, Intro.2, Intro.3, Intro.4, Intro.5, Intro.6, Intro.7, Intro.8]

Files Needed: *CavalliFiles-Intro* (zipped folder) *(Student data files are available in the* Library *of your* SIMnet *account.)*
Completed Project File Names: *PHRE* folder containing the following files: *BuyerEscrowChecklist-Intro*, *CavalliProspectingLetter-Intro*, *[your initials] Intro-1a.accdb*, *[your initials] Intro-1b.xlsx*, *[your initials] Intro-1c.docx*, *[your initials] Intro-1d.docx*, and *[your initials] Intro-1e.pdf*.

Skills Covered in This Project

- Copy and paste a zipped folder.
- Create a new folder in your *OneDrive* folder.
- Extract a zipped folder.
- Move a file.
- Rename a file.
- Open a Word document.

- Use *Task View* to switch between two open Word documents.
- Turn off *AutoSave*.
- Save a Word document with a different file name.
- Change display size.
- Use a mini toolbar, keyboard shortcut, context menu, and dialog box to apply formatting to selected text.
- Export a document as a PDF file.

1. Copy a zipped folder and create a new *OneDrive* folder.
 a. Click the Windows **Start** button and click **File Explorer** to open the *File Explorer* window. If *File Explorer* is not available on the *Start* menu, use *Cortana* to find and open the *File Explorer* window.
 b. Browse in the *File Explorer* window to locate your student data files.
 c. Select the **CavalliFiles-Intro** zipped folder from your student data files and press **Ctrl+C** or click the **Copy** button [*Home* tab, *Clipboard* group] to copy the folder.
 d. Select your **OneDrive** folder on the left of the *File Explorer* window, and click the **New folder** button [*Home* tab, *New* group] to create a new folder. If you don't have *OneDrive* available, create the new folder in a location where you store your files.
 e. Type PHRE and press **Enter**.
 f. Press **Enter** again to open the *PHRE* folder or double-click the folder to open it.
 g. Press **Ctrl+V** or click the **Paste** button [*Home* tab, *Clipboard* group] to paste the copied **CavalliFiles-Intro** zipped folder in the *PHRE* folder.

2. Extract a zipped folder.
 a. Select the **CavalliFiles-Intro** zipped folder.
 b. Click the **Compressed Folder Tools Extract** tab and click the **Extract all** button (Figure Intro-109). The *Extract Compressed (Zipped) Folders* dialog box opens.
 c. Uncheck the **Show extracted files when complete** box if it is checked.
 d. Click the **Extract** button. The zipped folder is extracted, and the *PHRE* folder now contains two *CavalliFiles-Intro* folders. One folder is zipped and the other is a regular folder.

e. Select the zipped **CavalliFiles-Intro** folder and click the **Delete** button [*Home* tab, *Organize* group] to delete the zipped folder.

3. Move and rename files.
 a. Double-click the **CavalliFiles-Intro** folder to open it.
 b. Click the first file, press and hold the **Shift** key, and click the last file to select all four files.
 c. Press **Ctrl+X** or click the **Cut** button [*Home* tab, *Clipboard* group] to cut the files from the current location (Figure Intro-110).
 d. Click the **Up** arrow to move up to the *PHRE* folder.
 e. Press **Ctrl+V** or click the **Paste** button [*Home* tab, *Clipboard* group] to paste and move the files.
 f. Select the **Cavalli files-Intro** folder and press **Delete** to delete the folder.
 g. Select the **CavalliPHRE-Intro** file and click the **Rename** button [*Home* tab, *Organize* group].
 h. Type [your initials] Intro-1a and press **Enter**.
 i. Right-click the **FixedMortgageRates-Intro** file and select **Rename** from the context menu.
 j. Type [your initials] Intro-1b and press **Enter**.

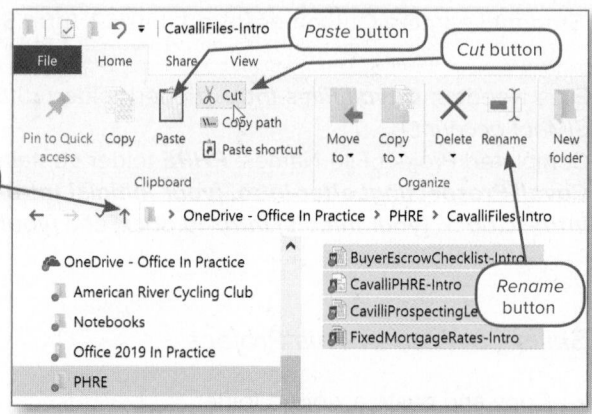

Figure Intro-109 **Extract a zipped folder**

Figure Intro-110 *Cut* **files to move from a folder**

4. Open two Word documents and rename a Word document.
 a. Click the **BuyerEscrowChecklist-Intro** file, press the **Ctrl** key, and click the **CavalliProspectingLetter-Intro** file to select both files.
 b. Press the **Enter** key to open both files in Word. If the files open in *Protected View*, click the **Enable Editing** button.
 c. Click the **Task View** button on your *Taskbar* (Figure Intro-111). All open windows display as tiles on your desktop.
 d. Select the **BuyerEscrowChecklist-Intro** document.
 e. Click the **AutoSave** button [*Quick Access* toolbar] to turn *AutoSave* off (if *AutoSave* is on).
 f. Click the **File** tab to open the *Backstage* view and select **Save As** on the left.
 g. Click the **Browse** button to open the *Save As* dialog box.
 h. Type [your initials] Intro-1c in the *File name* text box and click **Save**. The file is saved in the *PHRE* folder.
 i. Click the **X** in the upper-right corner of the Word window to close the document. The *CavalliProspectingLetter-Intro* document remains open.

Figure Intro-111 *Task View* **button on the** *Taskbar*

5. Change display size and edit and rename a Word document.
 a. Press the **Task View** button on your *Taskbar* and select the **CavalliProspectingLetter-Intro** document.

b. Click the **Zoom In** or **Zoom Out** button in the bottom right of the document window to change the display size to **120%** (Figure Intro-112).

Figure Intro-112 Use *Zoom* to change the display size to 120%

c. Select "**Placer Hills Real Estate**" in the first body paragraph of the letter. The mini toolbar displays (Figure Intro-113).

d. Click the **Bold** button on the mini toolbar to apply bold formatting to the selected text.

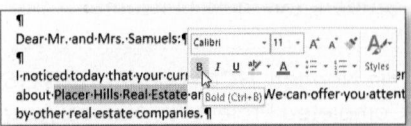

Figure Intro-113 Use the mini toolbar to apply formatting

e. Select "**Whitney Hills resident**" in the first sentence in the second body paragraph and press **Ctrl+I** to apply italic formatting to the selected text.

f. Select the text that reads "**Emma Cavalli**," below "Best regards,".

g. Right-click the selected text and select **Font** from the context menu to open the *Font* dialog box.

h. Check the **Small Caps** box in the *Effects* area and click **OK** to close the *Font* dialog box.

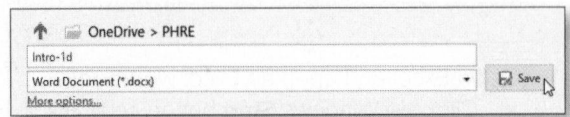

Figure Intro-114 *Save* area on the *Backstage* view.

i. Select "**Emma Cavalli**" (if necessary) and click the **Bold** button [*Home* tab, *Font* group].

j. Click the **File** tab and select **Save As** on the left. If the file is saved in *OneDrive* and *AutoSave* is turned on, select **Save a Copy**.

k. Type [your initials] Intro-1d in the *File name* text box and click **Save** (Figure Intro-114).

6. Export a Word document as a PDF file.

a. With the *[your initials] Intro-1d* still open, click the **File** tab to open the *Backstage* view.

b. Select **Export** on the left, select **Create PDF/XPS Document** in the *Export* area, and click the **Create PDF/XPS** button (Figure Intro-115). The *Publish as PDF or XPS* dialog box opens.

c. Deselect the **Open file after publishing** check box if it is checked.

d. Select the **Standard (publishing online and printing)** radio button in the *Optimize for* area.

e. Type [your initials] Intro-1e in the *File name* text box, select a location to save the file, and click **Publish**.

f. Click the **Save** button on the *Quick Access* toolbar or press **Ctrl+S** to save the document.

g. Click the **X** in the upper-right corner of the Word window to close the document and Word.

7. Your *PHRE* folder should contain the files shown in Figure Intro-116.

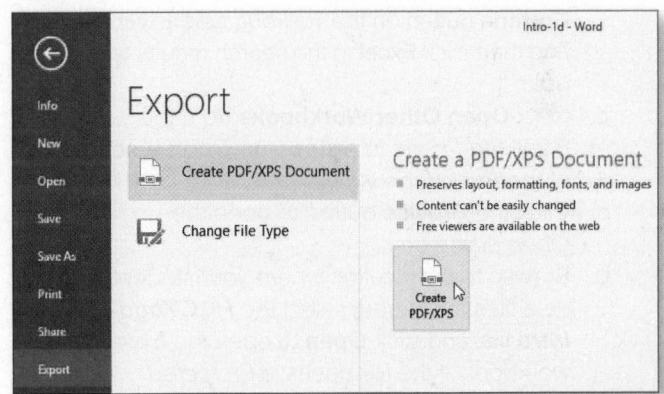

Figure Intro-115 Export as a PDF file

Figure Intro-116 Intro-1 completed

Guided Project Intro-2

For this project, you modify an Excel file for Hamilton Civic Center. You create a folder, rename a file, add document properties, use *Tell Me* to search for a topic, share the file, and export a file as a PDF file. [Student Learning Outcomes Intro.1, Intro.2, Intro.3, Intro.5, Intro.6, Intro.7, Intro.8]

File Needed: ***HCCYoga-Intro.xlsx*** *(Student data files are available in the* Library *of your SIMnet account.)*
Completed Project File Names: ***[your initials] Intro-2a.xlsx*** and ***[your initials] Intro-2b.pdf***

Skills Covered in This Project

- Open Excel and an Excel workbook.
- Create a new folder.
- Save an Excel workbook with a different file name.

- Add document properties to a file.
- Use *Tell Me* to search for a topic.
- Open a Word document.
- Share a file.
- Export a file as a PDF file.

1. Open Excel and open an Excel workbook.
 a. Click the Windows **Start** button and click **Excel** to open this application. If Excel 2019 is not available on the *Start* menu, click the **Cortana** button on the *Taskbar*, type Excel, and then click **Excel** in the search results to open it.
 b. Click **Open Other Workbooks** from the Excel *Start* page to display the *Open* area of the *Backstage* view.
 c. Click the **Browse** button to open the *Open* dialog box.
 d. Browse to the location where your student data files are stored, select the ***HCCYoga-Intro*** file, and click **Open** to open the Excel workbook. If the file opens in *Protected View,* click the **Enable Editing** button.

Figure Intro-117 Create a new folder from the *Save As* dialog box

2. Save a file as a different file name in your *OneDrive* folder.
 a. Click the **File** tab to open the *Backstage* view and select **Save As** (or **Save a Copy**) on the left.
 b. Click the **Browse** button to open the *Save As* dialog box.
 c. Select the **OneDrive** folder on the left and click the **New folder** button to create a new folder (Figure Intro-117). If *OneDrive* is not a storage option, select another location to create the new folder.
 d. Type HCC and press **Enter**.
 e. Double-click the **HCC** folder to open it.
 f. Type [your initials] Intro-2a in the *File name* area and click **Save** to close the dialog box and save the file.

3. Add document properties to the Excel workbook.
 a. Click the **File** button to open the *Backstage* view and select **Info** on the left if it is not already selected. The document properties display on the right.
 b. Place your insertion point in the *Title* text box ("Add a title") and type Yoga Classes as the worksheet title.
 c. Click the **Show All Properties** link at the bottom of the list of properties to display more properties (Figure Intro-118).

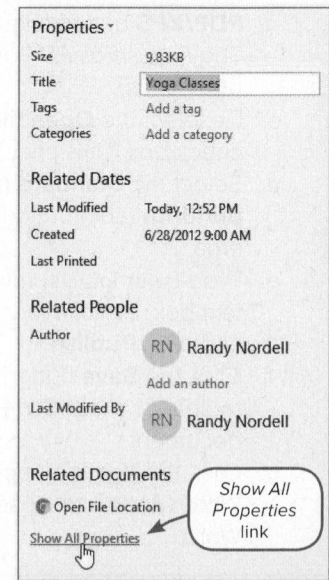

Figure Intro-118 Add document properties

d. Place your insertion point in the *Company* text box and type Hamilton Civic Center as the company name.

e. Click the **Back** arrow in the upper left of the *Backstage* window to return to the Excel workbook.

4. Use *Tell Me* to search for a topic.

a. Click the **Tell Me** search box at the top of the *Ribbon* and type Cell formatting (Figure Intro-119).

b. Select **Get Help on "Cell formatting"** and click **More Results for "Cell formatting"** to open the *Help* pane at the right.

c. Click the first result link to display information about the topic.

d. Click the **Back** arrow to return to the search list.

e. Click the **X** in the upper-right corner to close the *Help* pane.

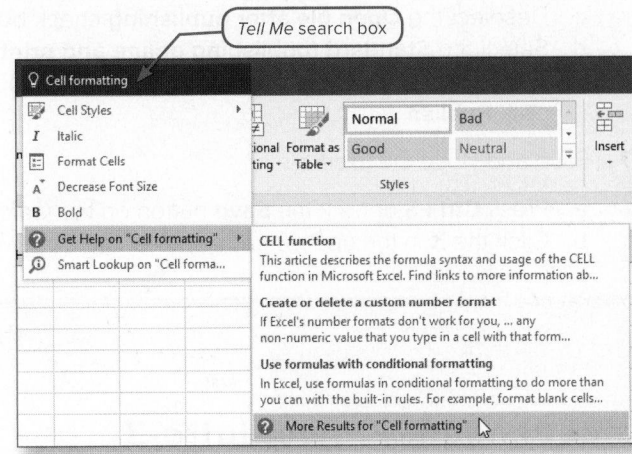

Figure Intro-119 Use *Tell Me* to search for a topic

5. Share an Excel workbook with your instructor. If your file is not saved on *OneDrive*, skip step 5.

a. Click the **Share** button in the upper-right corner of the Word window to open the *Send Link* window (Figure Intro-120). If you're using a personal Microsoft account, the *Share* pane displays at the right, and the sharing options differ slightly.

b. Click the **Link settings** button to open the *Link settings* window (Figure Intro-121).

c. Click the **Anyone** button and check the **Allow editing** box (if necessary).

d. Click **Apply** to close the *Link settings* window and return to the *Send Link* window.

e. Type your instructor's email address in the *Enter a name or email address* area (see Figure Intro-120).

f. Type a brief message to your instructor and click the **Send** button.

g. Click the **X** in the upper-right corner of the confirmation window to close it.

Figure Intro-120 *Send Link* window

Figure Intro-121 *Link settings* window

6. Export an Excel file as a PDF file.

a. Click the **File** tab to open the *Backstage* view.

b. Select **Export** on the left, select **Create PDF/XPS Document** in the *Export* area, and click the **Create PDF/XPS** button (Figure Intro-122). The *Publish as PDF or XPS* dialog box opens.

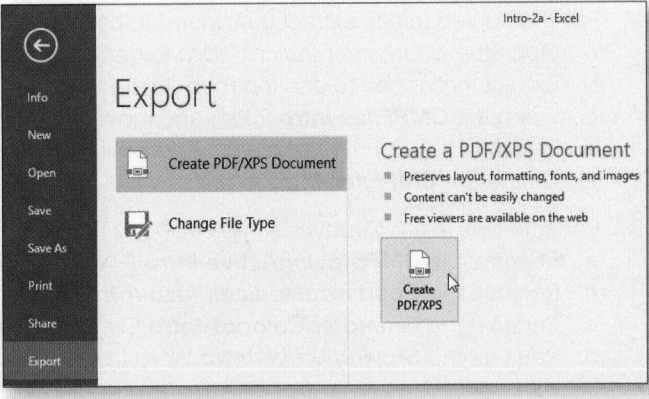

Figure Intro-122 Export as a PDF file

 c. Deselect the **Open file after publishing** check box if it is checked.

 d. Select the **Standard (publishing online and printing)** radio button in the *Optimize for* area.

 e. Type [your initials] Intro-2b in the *File name* text box, select a location to save the file, and click **Publish**.

7. Save and close the Excel file.

 a. Press **Ctrl+S** or click the **Save** button on the *Quick Access* toolbar to save the worksheet.

 b. Click the **X** in the upper-right corner of the Excel window to close the file and Excel.

Independent Project Intro-3

For this project, you organize and edit files for Courtyard Medical Plaza. You extract a zipped folder, delete a folder, move files, rename files, export a file as a PDF file, and share a file.
[Student Learning Outcomes Intro.1, Intro.2, Intro.3, Intro.5, Intro.8]

File Needed: **CMPFiles-Intro** (zipped folder) *(Student data files are available in the* Library *of your SIMnet account.)*

Completed Project File Names: **[your initials] Intro-3a.pptx, [your initials] Intro-3a-pdf.pdf, [your initials] Intro-3b.accdb, [your initials] Intro-3c.xlsx,** and **[your initials] Intro-3d.docx**

Skills Covered in This Project

- Copy and paste a zipped folder.
- Create a new folder in your *OneDrive* folder.
- Extract a zipped folder.
- Delete a folder.

- Move a file.
- Rename a file.
- Open a PowerPoint presentation.
- Export a file as a PDF file.
- Open a Word document.
- Share a file.

1. Copy a zipped folder and create a new *OneDrive* folder.

 a. Open a *File Explorer* window, browse to locate the **CMPFiles-Intro** zipped folder in your student data files and **Copy** the zipped folder.

 b. Go to your *OneDrive* folder and create a new folder named Courtyard Medical Plaza within the *OneDrive* folder. If *OneDrive* is not a storage option, select another location to create the new folder.

2. Paste a copied folder, extract the zipped folder, and move files.

 a. Open the *Courtyard Medical Plaza* folder and **Paste** the zipped folder.

 b. Extract the zipped folder and then delete the zipped folder.

 c. Open the **CMPFiles-Intro** folder and move all of the files to the *Courtyard Medical Plaza* folder.

 d. Return to the *Courtyard Medical Plaza* folder to confirm the four files were moved.

 e. Delete the **CMPFiles-Intro** folder.

3. Rename files in the *Courtyard Medical Plaza* folder.

 a. Rename the **CMPStayingActive-Intro** PowerPoint file as [your initials] Intro-3a.

 b. Rename the **CourtyardMedicalPlaza-Intro** Access file as [your initials] Intro-3b.

 c. Rename the **EstimatedCalories-Intro** Excel file as [your initials] Intro-3c.

 d. Rename the **StayingActive-Intro** Word file as [your initials] Intro-3d.

4. Export a PowerPoint file as a PDF file.
 a. Open the *[your initials] Intro-3a* file from the *Courtyard Medical Plaza* folder. The file opens in PowerPoint. If the file opens in *Protected View*, click the **Enable Editing** button.
 b. Export this file as a PDF file. Don't have the PDF file open after publishing and optimize for **Standard** format.
 c. Save the file as [your initials] Intro-3a-pdf and save in the *Courtyard Medical Plaza* folder.
 d. Close the PowerPoint file and exit PowerPoint.

5. Share a file with your instructor. If your files are not saved in *OneDrive*, skip step 5.
 a. Return to your *Courtyard Medical Plaza* folder and open the **Intro-3d** file. The file opens in Word. If the file opens in *Protected View*, click the **Enable Editing** button.
 b. Click the **Share** button in the upper-right corner of the Word window to open the *Send Link* window. If you're using a personal Microsoft account, the *Share* pane displays at the right, and the sharing options differ slightly.
 c. Click the **Link settings** button to open the *Link settings* window, click the **Anyone** button, check the **Allow editing** box (if necessary), and click **Apply** to close the *Link settings* window and return to the *Send Link* window.
 d. Type your instructor's email address in the *Enter a name or email address* area.
 e. Type a brief message to your instructor and click the **Send** button.
 f. Click the **X** in the upper-right corner of the confirmation window to close it.

6. Save and close the document and exit Word.

7. Close the *File Explorer* window containing the files for this project (Figure Intro-123).

Figure Intro-123 Intro-3 completed

Independent Project Intro-4

For this project, you modify a Word file for Life's Animal Shelter. You create a folder, rename a document, add document properties, modify a document, create a sharing link, export a document as a PDF file, and create a zipped folder.
[Student Learning Outcomes Intro.1, Intro.2, Intro.3, Intro.5, Intro.6, Intro.7, Intro.8]

File Needed: ***LASSupportLetter-Intro.docx*** *(Student data files are available in the* Library *of your SIMnet account.)*
Completed Project File Names: *[your initials] Intro-4a.docx*, *[your initials] Intro-4b.pdf*, and **LAS files** (zipped folder)

Skills Covered in This Project

- Open a Word document.
- Create a new folder.
- Save a file with a different file name.
- Apply formatting to selected text.
- Add document properties to the file.
- Create a sharing link.
- Export a file as a PDF file.
- Create a zipped folder.

1. Open a Word document, create a new folder, and save the document with a different file name.
 a. Open Word.
 b. Open the ***LASSupportLetter-Intro*** Word document from your student data files. If the file opens in *Protected View*, click the **Enable Editing** button.
 c. Open the **Save As** dialog box and create a new folder named LAS in your *OneDrive* folder. If *OneDrive* is not a storage option, select another location to create the new folder.
 d. Save this document in the *LAS* folder and use [your initials] Intro-4a as the file name.

2. Apply formatting changes to the document using a dialog box, keyboard shortcut, and mini toolbar.
 a. Select "**To:**" in the memo heading and use the launcher to open the *Font* dialog box.
 b. Apply **Bold** and **All caps** to the selected text.
 c. Repeat the formatting on the other three memo guide words "**From**:", "**Date**:", and "**Subject**:".
 d. Select "**Life's Animal Shelter**" in the first sentence of the first body paragraph and press **Ctrl+B** to apply bold formatting.
 e. Select the first sentence in the second body paragraph ("**Would you again consider** . . . ") and use the mini toolbar to apply *italic* formatting.

3. Add the following document properties to the document:
 Title: Support Letter
 Company: Life's Animal Shelter

4. Get a link to share this document with your instructor and email your instructor the sharing link. If your file is not saved on *OneDrive*, skip step 5.
 a. Click the **Share** button in the upper-right corner of the Word window. The *Send Link* window opens. If you are using a personal Microsoft account, the *Share* pane opens at the right, and the sharing options differ slightly.
 b. Click the **Link settings** button to open the *Link settings* window, click the **Anyone** button, check the **Allow editing** box (if necessary), and click **Apply** to return to the *Send Link* window.
 c. Click the **Copy Link** button to create sharing link.
 d. Click **Copy** to copy the sharing link and click the **X** in the upper-right corner to close the sharing link window.
 e. Use your email account to create a new email to your instructor. Include an appropriate subject line and a brief message in the body.
 f. Press **Ctrl+V** to paste the sharing link to your document in the body of the email and send the email message.
 g. Click the **Task View** button on the Windows *Taskbar* and select the ***Intro-4a*** document to display this document.
 h. Use the **Save** command on the *Quick Access* toolbar to save the file before continuing.

5. Export this document as a PDF file.
 a. Export this file as a PDF file. Don't have the PDF file open after publishing and optimize for **Standard** format.
 b. Save the file as [your initials] Intro-4b and save in the *LAS* folder.
 c. Save and close the document and exit Word.

6. Create a zipped folder.
 a. Use *File Explorer* to open the **LAS** folder in your *OneDrive* folder.
 b. Select the two files and create a zipped folder.
 c. Name the zipped folder LAS files.

7. Close the open *File Explorer* window (Figure Intro-124).

Figure Intro-124 Intro-4 completed

Challenge Project Intro-5

For this project, you create folders to organize your files for this class and share a file with your instructor.
[Student Learning Outcomes Intro.1, Intro.5, Intro.8]

Files Needed: Student data files for this course
Completed Project File Name: Share a file with your instructor

Using *File Explorer*, create *OneDrive* folders to contain all of the student data files for this class. Organize your files and folders according to the following guidelines:

- Create a *OneDrive* folder for this class.
- Create a *Student data files* folder inside the class folder.
- Copy and paste the student data files in the *Student data files* folder.
- Extract student data files and delete the zipped folder.
- Create a *Solution files* folder inside the class folder.
- Inside the *Solution files* folder, create a folder for each chapter.
- Create a folder to store miscellaneous class files such as the syllabus and other course handouts.
- Open one of the student data files and share the file with your instructor.

Challenge Project Intro-6

For this project, you save a file as a different file name, customize the *Quick Access* toolbar, share a file with your instructor, export a file as a PDF file, and create a zipped folder.
[Student Learning Outcomes Intro.1, Intro.2, Intro.3, Intro.5, Intro.6, Intro.8]

File Needed: Use an existing Office file
Completed Project File Names: *[your initials] Intro-6a* and *[your initials] Intro-6b*

Open an existing Word, Excel, or PowerPoint file. Save this file in a *OneDrive* folder and name it [your initials] Intro-6a. If you don't have any of these files, use one from your Pause & Practice projects or select a file from your student data files.

With your file open, perform the following actions:

- Create a new folder on *OneDrive* and save the file to this folder using a different file name.
- Customize the *Quick Access* toolbar to add command buttons. Add commands such as *New*, *Open*, *Quick Print*, and *Spelling* that you use regularly in the Office application.
- Share your file with your instructor. Enable your instructor to edit the file.
- Export the document as a PDF file. Save the file as [your initials] Intro-6b and save it in the same *OneDrive* folder as your open file.
- Zip the files in the folder.

Source of screenshots Microsoft Office 365 (2019): Word, Excel, Access, Powerpoint.

Microsoft® Office

IN PRACTICE

word

©Chris Ryan/Getty Images

Creating and Editing Documents

CHAPTER OVERVIEW

Microsoft Word (Word) has been and continues to be the leading word processing software in both the personal and business markets. Word improves with each new version and is used for creating and editing personal, business, and educational documents. Word enables you to create letters, memos, reports, flyers, brochures, and mailings without a vast amount of computer knowledge. This chapter covers the basics of creating and editing a Word document.

STUDENT LEARNING OUTCOMES (SLOs)

After completing this chapter, you will be able to:

SLO 1.1 Create, save, and open a Word document (p. 3).

SLO 1.2 Customize a document by entering and selecting text, using word wrap, and using *AutoComplete*, *AutoCorrect*, and *AutoFormat* features (p. 7).

SLO 1.3 Enhance a document using paragraph breaks, line breaks, spaces, and non-breaking spaces (p. 10).

SLO 1.4 Edit a document using cut, copy, paste, the *Clipboard*, and the undo, redo, and repeat features (p. 15).

SLO 1.5 Customize a document using different fonts, font sizes, and attributes (p. 18).

SLO 1.6 Enhance a document using text alignment and line and paragraph spacing (p. 28).

SLO 1.7 Finalize a document using Word's research, proofing, and learning tools (p. 32).

SLO 1.8 Apply custom document properties to a document (p. 38).

CASE STUDY

Throughout this book, you have the opportunity to practice the application features presented in each chapter. Each chapter begins with a case study that introduces you to the Pause & Practice projects in the chapter. Pause & Practice projects provide a chance to apply and practice key skills in a realistic and practical context. Each chapter contains three to five Pause & Practice projects.

Placer Hills Real Estate (PHRE) is a real estate company with regional offices throughout central California. PHRE encourages agents to use standard formats for their business documents. This ensures consistency in document appearance while also allowing agents to personalize their correspondence to customers and colleagues. In the Pause & Practice projects for this chapter, you create a business document related to the real estate business.

WORD

Pause & Practice 1-1: Create a business letter in block format with mixed punctuation.

Pause & Practice 1-2: Edit the business letter using copy, paste, and *Format Painter*. Modify the font, font size, color, style, and effects of selected text.

Pause & Practice 1-3: Finalize the business letter by modifying line spacing and paragraph spacing, changing paragraph alignment, translating text, using research and proofing tools, and adding document properties.

> **MORE INFO**
>
> *Appendix B: Business Document Formats* (online resource) contains examples of business documents.

SLO 1.1

Creating, Saving, and Opening Documents

In Microsoft Word, you can create a variety of document types. Your creativity and knowledge of Word enables you to create, edit, and customize high-quality and professional-looking documents. You can create Word documents from a new blank document, from existing Word templates, or from existing documents. Word enables you to save documents in a variety of formats.

Create a New Document

All new documents are based on the ***Normal template*** (*Normal.dotm*). When you create a Word document, a blank document displays in the Word window. This document has default fonts, font sizes, line and paragraph spacing, and margins—all of which are controlled by the *Normal* template.

> **HOW TO: Create a New Document**

1. Click the **File** tab to open the *Backstage* view.
 - When you first open Word, the *Start* page displays. You can open a new blank document from the *Start* page by clicking **Blank document**.
2. Click the **New** button (Figure 1-1).
3. Select **Blank document**. A new blank document opens in Word.

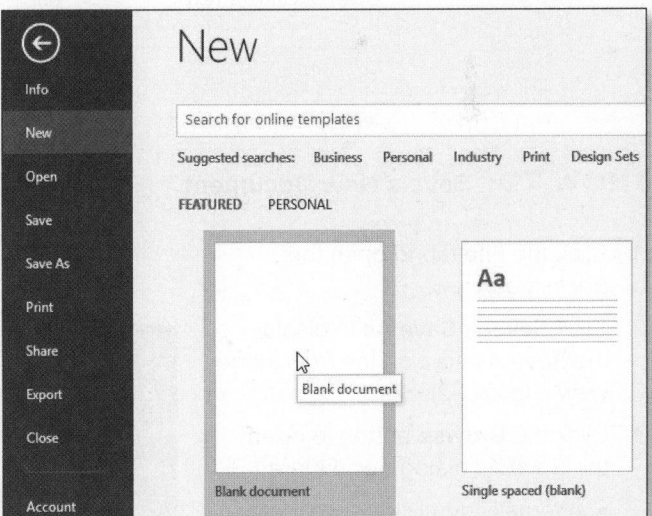

Figure 1-1 Open a new blank document

> **ANOTHER WAY**
>
> **Ctrl+N** opens a new blank document.

Save a Document

When you create a blank document, Word automatically assigns a generic file name to this document, such as *Document1*. Use the **Save As dialog box** to name and save a new document. You can save a Word document in a variety of file formats. By default, a Word document is saved as a *.docx* file. Other types of Word files are discussed throughout this text. Table 1-1 lists the more commonly used file formats.

Table 1-1: Save Formats

Type of File	File Extension	Uses
Word Document	.docx	Standard Word document.
Word Macro-Enabled Document	.docm	Word document with embedded macros.
Word 97-2003 Document	.doc	Word document that is compatible with previous versions of Microsoft Word.
Word Template	.dotx	Create a new document based upon a template.
Word Macro-Enabled Template	.dotm	Create a new document based upon a template with embedded macros.
Portable Document Format (PDF)	.pdf	Similar to a picture of a document that is used to preserve the formatting of a document.
Rich Text Format (RTF)	.rtf	Generic file format read by many different types of word processing programs while retaining the basic format of the document.
Plain Text	.txt	Files contain only text with no special formatting and open with most word processing programs.
Open Document Text	.odt	Format used in the Open Office word processing program.

▶HOW TO: Save a New Document

1. Click the **File** tab to open the *Backstage* view.

2. Click **Save** or **Save As** to display the *Save As* area on the *Backstage* view (Figure 1-2).

3. Click the **Browse** button to open the *Save As* dialog box (Figure 1-3).

 - Alternatively, click a save location (**OneDrive** or **This PC**), type the file name in the *Enter file name here* text box, and click **Save**. To change the save location, click the **More options** link to open the *Save As* dialog box (see Figure 1-2).

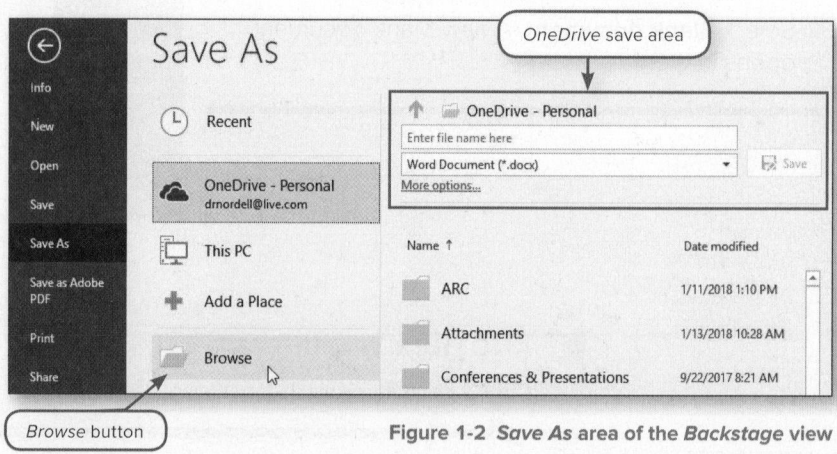

Figure 1-2 *Save As* area of the *Backstage* view

- You can also click the **Recent** button and select a recently used folder to open the *Save As* dialog box.

4. Use the folder list on the left side of the *Save As* dialog box to browse to a location to save the file (see Figure 1-3).

5. Type the file name in the *File name* area.

6. Click the **Save** button.

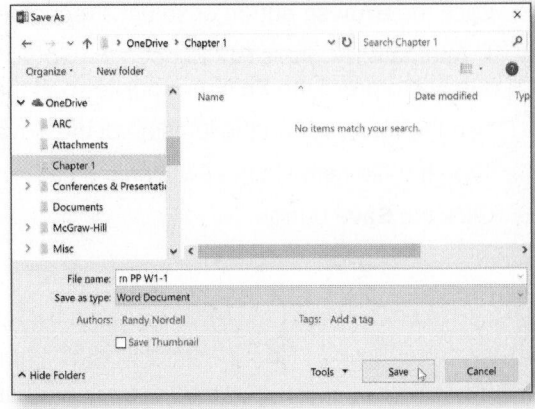

Figure 1-3 *Save As* dialog box

> **ANOTHER WAY**
>
> **F12** opens the *Save As* dialog box. When using a laptop computer, you might have to press the **Fn** (Function) key and the **F12** key to open the *Save As* dialog box.

After you have named and saved a document, you can save changes to the document without opening the *Save As* dialog box in the following ways:

- Press **Ctrl+S**.
- Click the **Save** button on the *Quick Access* toolbar.
- Select **Save** from the *Backstage* view.

AutoSave

Figure 1-4 *AutoSave* feature

AutoSave is a new feature that automatically saves a document that is stored on *OneDrive*, Microsoft's cloud storage area. The *AutoSave* feature turns on by default when you save a document to *OneDrive*, and the document is automatically saved as you change it.

This feature displays in the upper-left corner of the document (Figure 1-4). Click the **AutoSave** button to turn it on or off. When *AutoSave* is on, the save options on the *Backstage* view change from *Save* and *Save As* to **Save a Copy**.

Office 2019 Note: The *AutoSave* feature is not available in Office 2019.

Save As a Different File Name

You can save a document as a different name by opening the *Save As* dialog box and typing a new file name. When you save a file with a different file name, the original document is not changed and is still available. Saving with a different file name creates a new version of the original document, but the new document has a different file name.

▶HOW TO: Save As a Different File Name

1. Click the **File** tab to open the *Backstage* view.

2. Click the **Save As** button to display the *Save As* area.
 - If *AutoSave* is turned on, *Save a Copy* is the save option on the *Backstage* view rather than *Save* and *Save As*.

3. Click the **Browse** button or select a recent folder to open the *Save As* dialog box (see Figure 1-3).
 - Alternatively, press **F12** to open the *Save As* dialog box from within Word (not the *Backstage* view). You may have to press the **Fn** (Function) key and the **F12** key to open the *Save As* dialog box when using a laptop.
4. Use the folder list on the left side of the *Save As* dialog box to browse to a location to save the file.
5. Type the file name in the *File name* area.
6. Click the **Save** button.

> **MORE INFO**
>
> Avoid saving too many different versions of the same document. Rename only when you have a good reason to have multiple versions of a document.

Open a Document

You can open an existing document from your computer, *OneDrive*, other storage location, or an attachment from an email. After you open a document, edit the content and save the changes to the document.

▶ HOW TO: Open a Document

1. Click the **File** tab to open the *Backstage* view.
2. Click the **Open** button to display the *Open* area on the *Backstage* view.
3. Select the location where the document is stored.
 - The *Recent* area displays a list of recently used documents or folders.
 - You can also open a document from *OneDrive* or *This PC*.
4. Select a file or folder to open or click **Browse** to open the *Open* dialog box (Figure 1-5).
5. Select the file and click the **Open** button.
 - If the document opens in *Protected View*, click the **Enable Editing** button.

Figure 1-5 *Open* dialog box

> **ANOTHER WAY**
>
> **Ctrl+F12** opens the *Open* dialog box. Laptops may require **Fn+Ctrl+F12**.

Pin a Frequently Used Document

If you use a document frequently, pin it to the *Open* area on the *Backstage* view. Pinned documents appear at the top of the *Recent* documents list so you can quickly open the document.

In the *Open* area on the *Backstage* view, click **Recent** and then click the **pin** icon to the right of a file name to add the document to the *Pinned* area (Figure 1-6). Pinned files display in the *Pinned* area of the *Start* page and *Open* area of the *Backstage* view. Click the pinned file to open it.

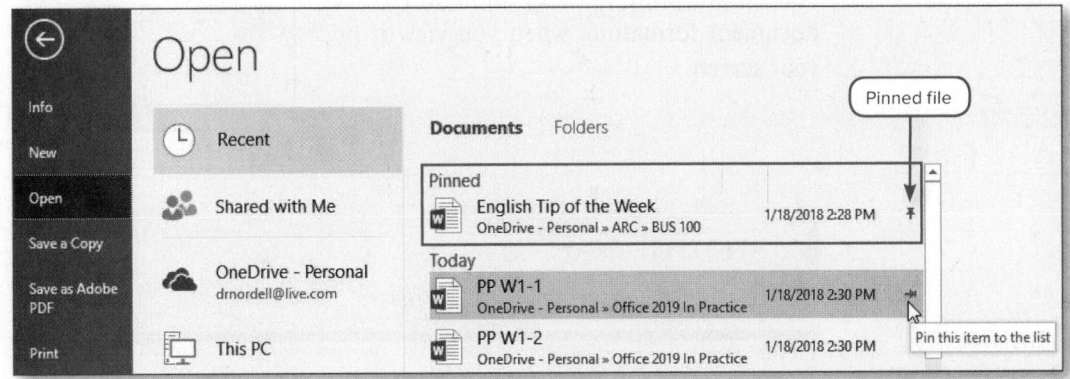

Figure 1-6 The *Pinned* area in the *Open* area on the *Backstage* view

Entering and Selecting Text

When creating or editing a document, you can type new text, insert text from another document, or copy text from a web page or another document. It is important to understand how to enter text, use word wrap, select text, show or hide formatting symbols, and use *AutoComplete* and *AutoCorrect* options to create professional-looking documents.

Type Text and Use Word Wrap

Word inserts text where the insertion point is flashing in the document. By default, text is aligned at the left margin and the text wraps to the next line when it reaches the right margin. This feature is called *word wrap*. Press **Enter** to begin a new paragraph or line of text.

Show/Hide Formatting Symbols

The *Show/Hide* feature displays or hides formatting symbols in your document. By default, *Show/Hide* is turned off and formatting symbols do not display in your document. When the *Show/Hide* feature is turned on, you can see paragraph breaks, line breaks, spaces, tabs, and other formatting symbols to help you create clean documents and to edit existing documents (Figure 1-7).

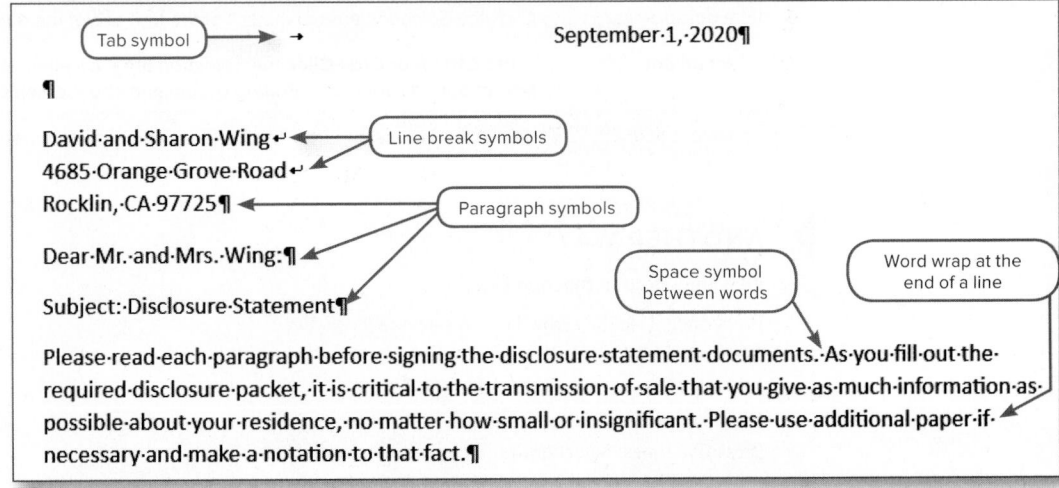

Figure 1-7 Document with *Show/Hide* turned on

Click the **Show/Hide** button in the *Paragraph* group on the *Home* tab to toggle on and off *Show/Hide* (Figure 1-8). These symbols do not print, but they allow you to see document formatting when you view it on your screen.

Show/Hide button

Figure 1-8 *Show/Hide* button

> **ANOTHER WAY**
>
> **Ctrl+Shift+8** turns on and off *Show/Hide*.

> **MORE INFO**
>
> When editing a document that has inconsistent formatting, begin by turning on **Show/Hide**.

Select Text

Word enables you to select words, lines, sentences, paragraphs, or the entire document. Select text to apply formatting, copy, move, or delete selected text. One way to select text is to click and drag the pointer over text. Word provides a variety of additional quick methods to select text. Table 1-2 lists ways to select text.

Table 1-2: Selecting Text

Select	Method
Word	Double-click the word.
Line	Click the *Selection* area, which is to the left of the left margin. Your pointer becomes a right-pointing arrow.
Multiple lines of text	Click the *Selection* area and drag up or down.
Sentence	Press **Ctrl+Click**. Hold down the **Ctrl** key and click the sentence.
Paragraph	Double-click the *Selection* area to the left of the paragraph.
Multiple paragraphs	Click the *Selection* area to the left of the first line of the paragraph and drag down.
Entire document	Press **Ctrl+A** or **Ctrl+Click** the *Selection* area. An alternative is to click the **Select** button [*Home* tab, *Editing* group] and choose **Select All**.
Non-adjacent text	Select text, press and hold the **Ctrl** key, and select non-adjacent text.

> **ANOTHER WAY**
>
> **F8** is the selection function key.
>
> Press once: Use the arrow keys to select text.
> Press twice: Select word.
> Press three times: Select sentence.
> Press four times: Select paragraph.
> Press five times: Select entire document.
>
> Press **Esc** to turn off **F8** selection.

AutoComplete

When you type a day, month, or date, Word uses the **AutoComplete** feature to automatically complete typing the date. AutoComplete saves you a few key strokes and enables you to be more efficient and accurate when entering dates. As you begin to type the date, Word displays the information in an **AutoComplete tag** (Figure 1-9). Press **Enter** to accept the *AutoComplete* entry. If you do not want this *AutoComplete* entry, keep typing and the *AutoComplete* entry disappears.

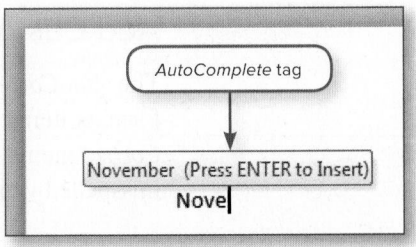

Figure 1-9 *AutoComplete* tag

AutoCorrect and AutoFormat

When you're typing, do you ever misspell a word by transposing letters or omitting a letter or adding a letter? Because we all regularly type errors, the **AutoCorrect** feature recognizes and corrects commonly misspelled words and grammatical errors. Word automatically inserts the following corrections:

- Eliminates two initial capitals in a word
- Capitalizes the first letter of a sentence
- Capitalizes the first letter of table cells
- Capitalizes the names of days
- Corrects accidental usage of the *Caps Lock* key
- Changes fractions such as 3/4 to ¾ and numbers such as 2nd to 2nd

Word's **AutoFormat** controls the formatting of items such as numbered and bulleted lists, fractions, ordinal numbers, hyphens and dashes, quotes, indents, and hyperlinks. For example, when you type 3/4 followed by a space, *AutoFormat* automatically changes the format of the fraction to ¾.

AutoCorrect Smart Tag

When Word automatically applies a correction or formatting change, you have the option to accept the change, undo the change, stop Word from making the change, or control *AutoCorrect* using the *AutoCorrect Options* dialog box. If you continue typing, the change is accepted. Often when Word automatically corrects a word, you don't even recognize that a change has been made.

If you do not want to accept a change, click the **AutoCorrect Options smart tag** on the changed word to open the *AutoCorrect Options* menu (Figure 1-10). For example, when you type reference initials at the end of a business letter, Word automatically capitalizes the first letter. Undo this automatic capitalization by clicking the *AutoCorrect Options* smart tag and selecting **Undo Automatic Capitalization**.

> **ANOTHER WAY**
>
> Press **Ctrl+Z** to reverse an automatic correction made by Word.

Figure 1-10 *AutoCorrect Options* smart tag

Add Custom AutoCorrect Entry

The *AutoCorrect* dialog box enables you to customize how Word automatically corrects and formats items in a document. In this dialog box, you can also add custom items to the *Auto-Correct* menu. For example, you can add a custom entry to the *AutoCorrect* menu to correct a misspelled word or type your name every time you type your initials.

> **HOW TO: Add a Custom AutoCorrect Entry**

1. Click the **File** tab to open the *Backstage* view.
2. Choose the **Options** button to open the *Word Options* dialog box.
3. Click the **Proofing** button on the left.
4. Select the **AutoCorrect Options** button. The *AutoCorrect* dialog box opens (Figure 1-11).
5. Type the text you want to replace in the *Replace* box.
6. Type the word(s) to replace the original text in the *With* box.
7. Choose **Add** to add this custom *AutoCorrect* entry.
 - Delete an *AutoCorrect* entry in the *AutoCorrect* dialog box by selecting the entry and clicking **Delete**.
 - Add exceptions to *AutoCorrect* by clicking the **Exceptions** button.
8. Click **OK** to close the *AutoCorrect* dialog box.
9. Click **OK** to close the *Word Options* dialog box.

Figure 1-11 *AutoCorrect* dialog box

SLO 1.3

Using Paragraph Breaks, Line Breaks, and Non-Breaking Spaces

Use paragraph and line breaks to organize a document into more readable groups of text. Several types of breaks are available to create attractive and readable documents.

Paragraph Breaks

The **Enter** key inserts a **paragraph break** and is marked by a **paragraph symbol** that displays at the end of each paragraph when *Show/Hide* is active (Figure 1-12). Use paragraph breaks to control the amount of white space between paragraphs of text within a document. Press **Enter** to create blank lines between paragraphs.

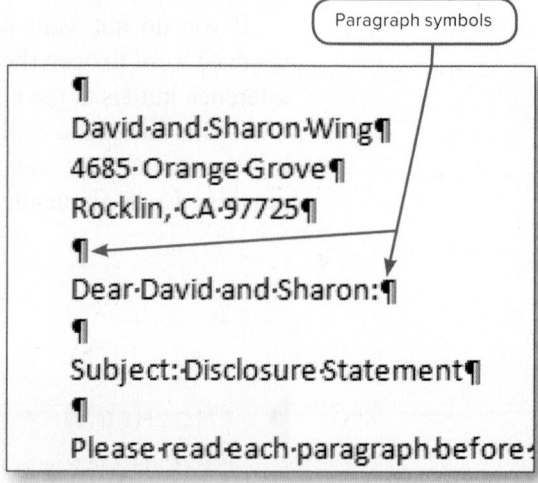

Figure 1-12 Paragraph breaks after and between lines

Many formatting features, such as indents, numbering, bullets, text alignment, line spacing, and paragraph spacing, apply to an entire paragraph. For example, if the insertion point is within a paragraph and you change the line spacing to double space, the entire paragraph is formatted with double spacing. It is not applied to the entire document or just the line where the insertion point is located. For more on line and paragraph spacing, see *SLO 1.6: Changing Text Alignment, Line Spacing, and Paragraph Spacing.*

Line Breaks

Use ***line breaks*** to control breaks between lines or sentences of text. The distinction between a paragraph break and a line break is that when line breaks are used, the text separated by line breaks is treated as one paragraph. Press **Shift+Enter** to insert a line break.

Use line breaks within a numbered or bulleted list to allow for multiple lines of text on separate lines or blank lines between the text without creating a new number or bullet (Figure 1-13). The line break symbol is different from the paragraph symbol.

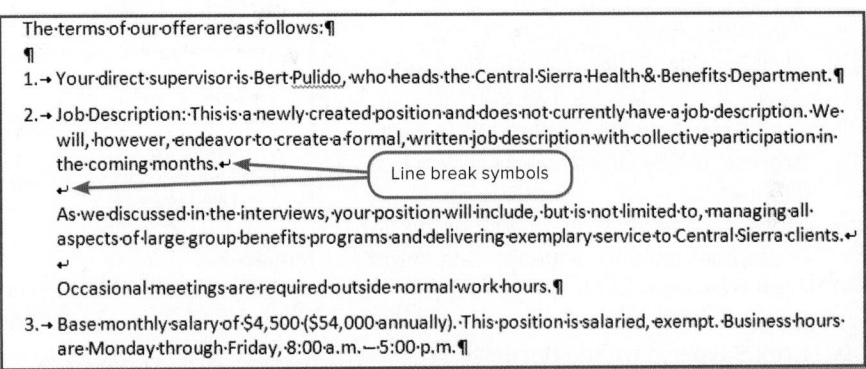

Figure 1-13 Line breaks used in a numbered list

Spaces and Non-Breaking Spaces

Use the *spacebar* to insert a space between words. Current practice now dictates one space after most punctuation marks, including periods, commas, semicolons, and ending quotation marks. Do not use spaces after a beginning quotation mark, before or after a hyphen in a hyphenated word, or when using a dash.

Occasionally, word wrap separates words that you may want to keep together. For example, you might want to keep a person's first and last name or a date together on the same line. In this case, use a ***non-breaking space*** to keep these words together. To insert a non-breaking space, press **Ctrl+Shift+Spacebar** between words rather than inserting a regular space. In Figure 1-14, a non-breaking space is used between 8:00 and a.m., which keeps this information together.

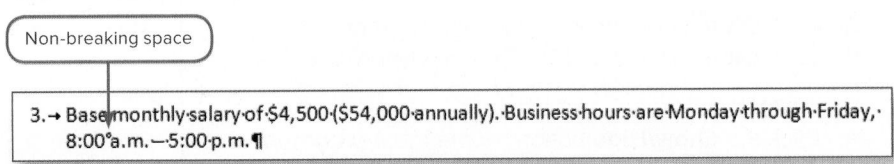

Figure 1-14 Non-breaking space used to keep text together

In this project, you create a block format business letter for Emma Cavalli, a realtor consultant for Placer Hills Real Estate. In a block format business letter, all lines begin at the left margin. For more examples of business documents, see *Appendix B* (online resource).

File Needed: None
Completed Project File Name: *[your initials] PP W1-1.docx*

1. Open a new document.
 a. Open Microsoft Word and click **Blank document** on the *Start* page. If Word is already open, click the **File** tab to open the *Backstage* view, click **New**, and click **Blank document**.

2. Save the document.
 a. Click the **File** tab to open the *Backstage* view.
 b. Click **Save As** on the left and then click **Browse** to open the *Save As* dialog box (Figure 1-15).
 c. Browse to the location on your computer or storage device to save the document.
 d. Type [your initials] PP W1-1 in the *File name* area.
 e. Click **Save** to save the document.

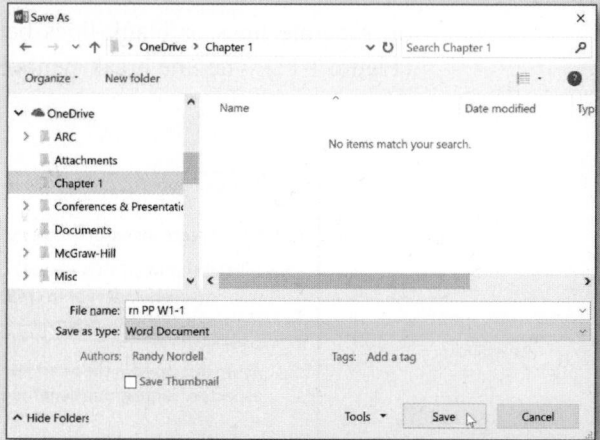

Figure 1-15 *Save As* dialog box

> ## ANOTHER WAY
>
> **F12** opens the *Save As* dialog box. When using a laptop computer, you might have to press the **Fn** (Function) key and the **F12** key to open the *Save As* dialog box.

3. Create an *AutoCorrect* entry.
 a. Click the **File** tab to open the *Backstage* view and select **Options** on the left to open the *Word Options* dialog box.
 b. Click the **Proofing** button on the left and select **AutoCorrect Options** to open the *AutoCorrect* dialog box (Figure 1-16).
 c. Click the **AutoCorrect** tab if it is not already selected.
 d. Type Cavali in the *Replace* area.
 e. Type Cavalli in the *With* area.
 f. Click the **Add** button to add the *AutoCorrect* entry.
 g. Click **OK** to close the *AutoCorrect* dialog box.
 h. Click **OK** to close the *Word Options* dialog box.

4. Use *AutoComplete* to insert a date.
 a. Click the **Show/Hide** button [*Home* tab, *Paragraph* group] to turn on the *Show/Hide* feature.

Figure 1-16 Add an *AutoCorrect* entry

b. Begin typing the current date on the first line of the document (use September 1, 2020 format) and press **Enter** when the *AutoComplete* tag appears. The month is automatically inserted (Figure 1-17).

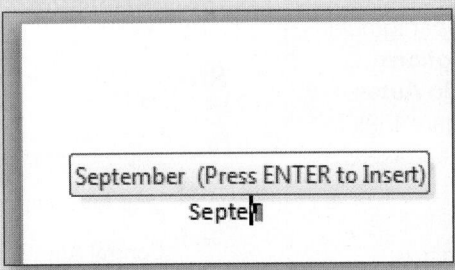

September (Press ENTER to Insert)
Septe|

Figure 1-17 *AutoComplete* tag

c. Continue typing the rest of the date; press **Enter** if the *AutoCorrect* tag displays the current date.
d. Press **Enter** two times after typing the date.

5. Type the inside address, salutation, and subject line of the letter.
 a. Type David and Sharon Wing and press **Shift+Enter** to insert a line break.
 b. Type 4685 Orange Grove Road and press **Shift+Enter** to insert a line break.
 c. Type Rocklin, CA 97725 and press **Enter** to insert a paragraph break.
 d. Type Dear Mr. and Mrs. Wing: as the salutation and press **Enter**.
 e. Type Subject: Disclosure Statement as the subject and press **Enter**.

> **MORE INFO**
>
> In the salutation of a business letter, use "Dear" followed by a courtesy title (Mr., Mrs., Ms., Miss, or Dr.) and the person's last name.

6. Type the body paragraphs of the business letter and insert a non-breaking space.
 a. Type the following paragraph and press **Enter** once at the end of the paragraph. You will not need to press *Enter* at the end of each line because word wrap automatically moves text to the next line as you reach the right margin.

 Please read each paragraph before signing the disclosure statement documents. As you fill out the required disclosure packet, it is critical to the transmission of sale that you give as much information as possible about your residence, no matter how small or insignificant. Please use additional paper if necessary and make a notation to that fact.

 b. Type the following second paragraph and press **Enter** once at the end of the paragraph.

 If there is information about the neighborhood or neighbors that you as a buyer would want to know about, be sure to reveal that information. Be sure to address those types of questions on the Real Estate Transfer Disclosure Statement, item #11 on page 2.

 c. Delete the space between the words "Real" and "Estate" in the second paragraph and press **Ctrl+Shift+Spacebar** to insert a non-breaking space between.

7. Type the closing lines of the business letter.
 a. Place your insertion point on the blank line below the second body paragraph, type Best regards, and then press **Enter** two times.
 b. Type Emma Cavalli and press **Shift+Enter** to insert a line break.
 c. Type Realtor Consultant and press **Shift+Enter** to insert a line break.
 d. Type Placer Hills Real Estate and press **Enter** to insert a paragraph break.

e. Type your initials in lowercase letters and press **Shift+Enter** to insert a line break. Word automatically capitalizes the first letter because it is the first letter in a new paragraph.

f. Click the **AutoCorrect Options** smart tag and select **Undo Automatic Capitalization** (Figure 1-18) or press **Ctrl+Z** to undo automatic capitalization.

g. Type Enclosure on the blank line below the reference initials. An enclosure notation indicates to the reader that something is enclosed with the letter.

Emma·Cavalli↵
Realtor·Consultant↵
Placer·Hills·Real·Estate¶

AutoCorrect Options smart tab

Rn↵

↶ <u>U</u>ndo Automatic Capitalization

<u>S</u>top Auto-capitalizing First Letter of Sentences

⚡ <u>C</u>ontrol AutoCorrect Options…

Figure 1-18 *AutoCorrect Options* smart tag

8. Press **Ctrl+S** to save the document (Figure 1-19). You can also save the document by clicking the **Save** button on the *Quick Access* toolbar or in the *Backstage* view.

9. Click the **File** tab and select **Close** (or press **Ctrl+W**) to close the document.

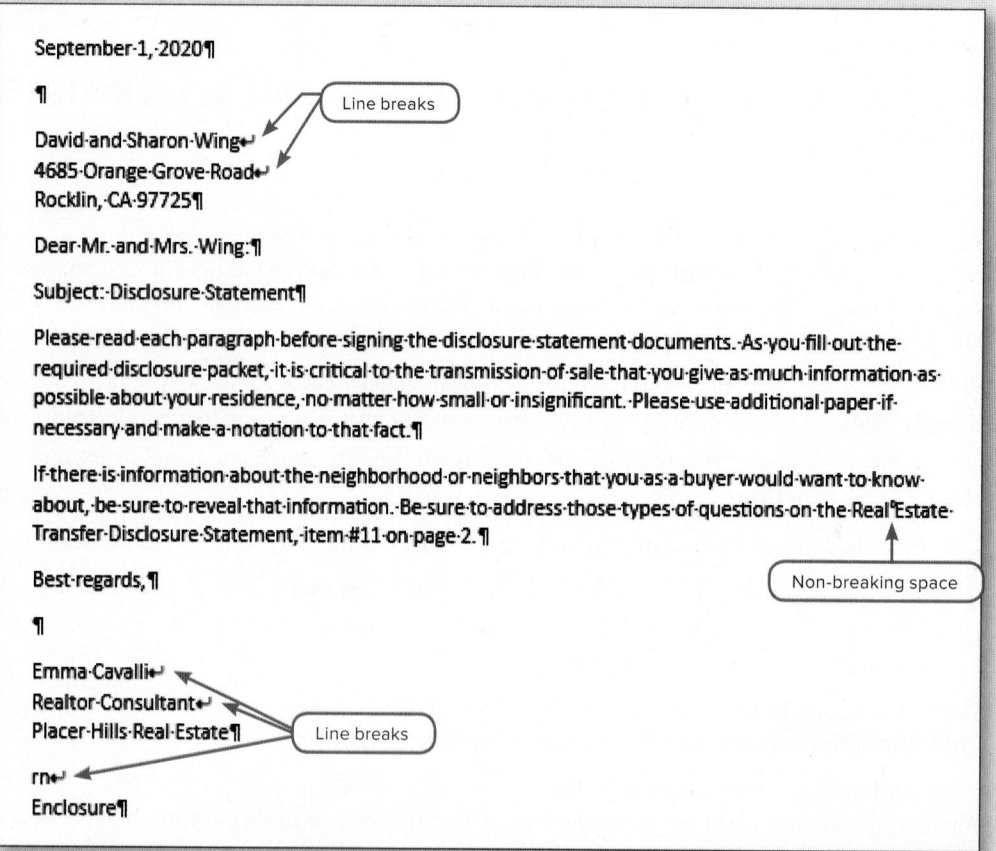

September·1,·2020¶

¶

David·and·Sharon·Wing↵ Line breaks
4685·Orange·Grove·Road↵
Rocklin,·CA·97725¶

Dear·Mr.·and·Mrs.·Wing:¶

Subject:·Disclosure·Statement¶

Please·read·each·paragraph·before·signing·the·disclosure·statement·documents.·As·you·fill·out·the·required·disclosure·packet,·it·is·critical·to·the·transmission·of·sale·that·you·give·as·much·information·as·possible·about·your·residence,·no·matter·how·small·or·insignificant.·Please·use·additional·paper·if·necessary·and·make·a·notation·to·that·fact.¶

If·there·is·information·about·the·neighborhood·or·neighbors·that·you·as·a·buyer·would·want·to·know·about,·be·sure·to·reveal·that·information.·Be·sure·to·address·those·types·of·questions·on·the·Real°Estate·Transfer·Disclosure·Statement,·item·#11·on·page·2.¶

Best·regards,¶ Non-breaking space

¶

Emma·Cavalli↵
Realtor·Consultant↵
Placer·Hills·Real·Estate¶ Line breaks

rn↵
Enclosure¶

Figure 1-19 PP W1-1 completed

Moving and Copying Text

Editing is an important phase in document creation. Editing involves not only proofreading and correcting grammar and spelling mistakes but also arranging text within a document, which can include cutting, copying, and pasting. Word provides tools to easily move and copy information within a document or between multiple documents.

Move Text

Moving text removes it from one location (cut) and places it in another location (paste). Two methods used to move text are *drag and drop* or *cut and paste*.

> **ANOTHER WAY**
>
> Press **Ctrl+C** to copy.
> Press **Ctrl+X** to cut.
> Press **Ctrl+V** to paste.

▶ HOW TO: Move Text Using Drag and Drop

1. Select the text you want to move.
 - Refer to the "Select Text" section in *SLO 1.2: Entering and Selecting Text* for methods of selecting text.
2. Click and hold the selected text with your pointer.
3. Drag the text to the desired new location and release the pointer (Figure 1-20).

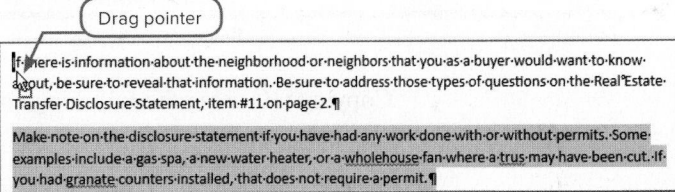

Figure 1-20 Move using drag and drop

The following are ways to move text using *Cut* and *Paste*:

- *Cut and Paste buttons*: Click the **Cut** and **Paste** buttons in the *Clipboard* group on the *Home* tab.
- *Shortcut commands*: Press **Ctrl+X** to cut and **Ctrl+V** to paste.
- *Context menu*: Right-click the selected text to display this menu.

▶ HOW TO: Move Text Using Cut and Paste

1. Select the text you want to move.
2. Click the **Cut** button [*Home* tab, *Clipboard* group].
 - You can also press **Ctrl+X** or right-click the selected text and choose **Cut** from the context menu.
3. Place your insertion point in the desired location.
4. Click the **Paste** button [*Home* tab, *Clipboard* group].
 - Alternatively, press **Ctrl+V** or right-click and choose from one of the *Paste Options* from the context menu. *Note:* See the "Paste Text and Paste Options" section below for the different paste options available.

Copy Text

An efficient method of inserting text into a document is to copy it from another location, such as a web page or a different document, and paste it into your document. Copying text leaves the text in its original location and places a copy of the text in a new location.

You can *copy* text by using the drag-and-drop method or the *Copy* and *Paste* buttons. Use the drag-and-drop method when copying text within the same document. The drag-and-drop method for copying is similar to the method for moving, except that you press the **Ctrl** key when dragging the text to be copied to another location.

▶**HOW TO:** Copy Text Using Drag and Drop

1. Select the text you want to copy.
2. Press the **Ctrl** key and click and hold the selected text with your pointer.
 - A **+** (plus sign) appears next to your pointer, indicating this text is being copied.
3. Drag to the desired new location and release the pointer (Figure 1-21). Release the **Ctrl** key after you have released the pointer.

Insert copied text

Make·note·on·the·disclosure·statement·if examples·include·a·gas·spa,·a·new·water· you·had·granate·counters·installed,·that·c

Please·complete·the·enclosed·statement· questions·or·concerns,·please·call·me·at·9 and·thank·you·for·you're·business.¶

Copy pointer

Figure 1-21 Copy using drag and drop

Copying text using the following copy and paste method is similar to moving text using the cut and paste method:

- *Copy and Paste buttons*: Press the **Copy** and **Paste** buttons in the *Clipboard* group on the *Home* tab.
- *Shortcut commands*: Press **Ctrl+C** to copy and **Ctrl+V** to paste.
- *Context menu*: Right-click the selected text to display this menu.

Paste Text and Paste Options

Word provides multiple paste options. You may want to paste plain text without formatting into a document or merge the format from the source document into the new document. You have three primary paste options when you use the *Paste* button in the *Clipboard* group (Figure 1-22) or from the context menu:

- *Keep Source Formatting*: Retains formatting from source document (the document where the text was copied)
- *Merge Formatting*: Merges formatting from source document and current document
- *Keep Text Only*: Pastes only unformatted text

The default paste option is *Keep Source Formatting*. In addition to these paste options, other contextual paste options are available when you paste information from lists, tables, or graphic objects.

Keep Source Formatting

Merge Formatting

File Home Inse

Cut

Copy

Paste Format Painter

Paste Options:

Paste Special...

Set Default Paste...

Figure 1-22 *Paste* options

Keep Text Only

▶ MORE INFO

If you have trouble with the format of pasted text, try pasting the text as plain text and formatting the text *after* you have pasted it into the document.

Clipboard Pane

When you copy or cut an item from a document, Word stores this information on the **Clipboard**. The *Clipboard* stores text, pictures, tables, lists, and graphics. When Word is open, the *Clipboard* stores multiple items copied from Word documents and also items from web pages or other applications. From the *Clipboard*, you can select a previously copied item and paste it into a document.

Figure 1-23 *Clipboard* launcher

The **Clipboard pane** displays all the items stored on *Clipboard*. To display the *Clipboard* pane, click the **Clipboard** launcher in the bottom-right corner of the *Clipboard* group on the *Home* tab (Figure 1-23). The *Clipboard* pane displays on the left side of the Word window and stores up to 24 copied items.

> **MORE INFO**
>
> The **launcher** (also referred to as the **dialog box launcher**) is referred to throughout this text. Click the launcher in the bottom-right corner of a group to open a dialog box or pane for additional options.

▶ HOW TO: Use the Clipboard Pane to Paste Text

1. Select the text you want to copy or cut and click the **Copy** or **Cut** button [*Home* tab, *Clipboard* group].
 - Alternatively, press **Ctrl+C** to copy or **Ctrl+X** to cut selected text.
2. Place the insertion point in the document where you want to paste the text.
3. Click the **Clipboard** launcher to open the *Clipboard* pane on the left side of the Word window (see Figure 1-23).
4. Click the item to paste or click the drop-down arrow to the right of the item and choose **Paste** (Figure 1-24). The selected content from the *Clipboard* is inserted in the document.
 - *Paste All* pastes all the items in the *Clipboard* at the insertion point in the document.
 - *Clear All* empties the contents of the *Clipboard*.
5. Click the **X** in the upper-right corner of the *Clipboard* pane to close it.

Figure 1-24 *Clipboard* pane

Undo Change

You can undo, redo, or repeat previous actions. All these commands are available on the **Quick Access toolbar**, which is above the *Ribbon* on the upper left.

When you click the **Undo** button, the last action you performed is reversed. Undo multiple actions by clicking the **Undo** drop-down arrow to the right of the button and selecting the actions to undo (Figure 1-25). For example, if you select the third item in the list to undo, the previous two items will also undo.

Figure 1-25 *Undo* button on the *Quick Access* toolbar

Redo and Repeat Change

The **Redo** and **Repeat** features are similar to the undo feature. The same button is used for both commands, and it is context sensitive. Depending on the previous action performed, the button is either *Redo* or *Repeat*.

Figure 1-26 *Redo* button on the *Quick Access* toolbar

When you use the *Undo* button, the *Redo* button is activated so you can redo the previous change (Figure 1-26).

When you perform an action or apply formatting in a document, the *Repeat* button is activated (the icon changes) so you can repeat the previous action or formatting (Figure 1-27). For example, if you need to copy the date or a name into a document in multiple places, use the *Repeat* feature to accomplish this task quickly and accurately.

Figure 1-27 *Repeat* button on the *Quick Access* toolbar

> **ANOTHER WAY**
>
> Press **Ctrl+Z** to undo.
> Press **Ctrl+Y** to redo or repeat.

SLO 1.5

Changing Fonts, Font Sizes, and Attributes

Word has many features to customize the appearance of text within a document. You can change the font and font size; add font styles such as bold, italic, and underlining; change the case of text; add font and text effects; adjust the scale, spacing, and position of text; and change the default font settings. You can use buttons in the *Font* group on the *Home* tab, the *Font* dialog box, and the mini toolbar to apply formatting to text.

Font and Font Size

The two main categories of fonts are serif and sans serif. **Serif fonts** have structural details (flair) at the top and bottom of most of the letters. Commonly used serif fonts include Cambria, Times New Roman, and Courier New. **Sans serif fonts** have no structural details on the letters. Commonly used sans serif fonts include Calibri, Arial, and Century Gothic.

Font size is measured in **points** (pt.); the larger the point, the larger the font. Most documents use between 10 and 12 pt. font sizes. Titles and headings generally are larger font sizes.

When creating a new document, choose a font and font size before you begin typing, and it applies to the entire document. If you want to change the font or font size of existing text, select the text before applying the change.

> **MORE INFO**
>
> The default font and font size in Microsoft Word are Calibri and 11 pt.

▶HOW TO: Change Font and Font Size

1. Select the text you want to format.
2. Click the **Font** drop-down list to display the list of available fonts (Figure 1-28).
 - The *Font* drop-down list has three sections: *Theme Fonts*, *Recently Used Fonts*, and *All Fonts*.
3. Select the font to apply to the selected text.
4. Click the **Font Size** drop-down list to display the list of available font sizes (Figure 1-29).

Figure 1-28 *Font* drop-down list

Figure 1-29 *Font size* drop-down list

5. Select a font size to apply to selected text.
 - You can also click the **Font Size** text box and type a size.
 - Click the **Increase Font Size** and **Decrease Font Size** buttons to increase or decrease the size of the font in small increments.

▶ **ANOTHER WAY**

Press **Ctrl+>** (Ctrl+Shift+.) to *Increase Font Size*.
Press **Ctrl+<** (Ctrl+Shift+,) to *Decrease Font Size*.

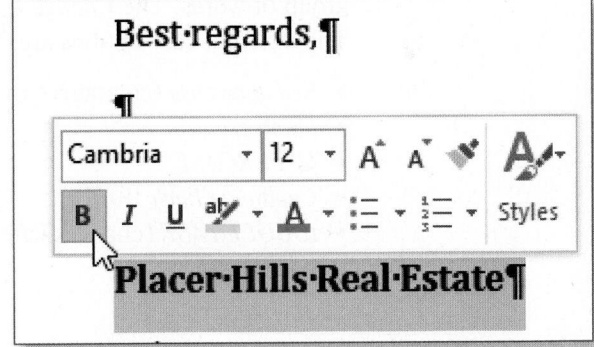

Figure 1-30 Select or right-click text to display the mini toolbar

The ***mini toolbar*** displays when you select or right-click text (Figure 1-30). Use the mini toolbar to apply text formatting. Similar to the context menu, the mini toolbar is contextual and displays different options depending on the selection.

Bold, Italic, and Underline Font Styles

Add ***font styles*** such as ***Bold***, ***Italic***, and ***Underline*** to fonts to improve their appearance or call attention to specific text. The font style buttons for *Bold*, *Italic*, and *Underline* are available in the *Font* group on the *Home* tab.

To apply a font style, select the desired text, and click the **Bold**, **Italic**, or **Underline** button in the *Font* group on the *Home* tab (Figure 1-31). You can also click a font style button to turn on a style, type the text, and click the font style button again to turn off the style.

Figure 1-31 *Font* group on the *Home* tab

> **ANOTHER WAY**
>
> **Ctrl+B** applies *Bold* formatting.
> **Ctrl+I** applies *Italic* formatting.
> **Ctrl+U** applies *Underline* formatting.

Other Font Style Buttons

The following are other font styles and effects in the *Font* group on the *Home* tab (see Figure 1-31). Several style and effect features display on the mini toolbar when you select or right-click text:

- *Strikethrough*
- *Subscript*
- *Superscript*
- *Text Effects and Typography*, which includes *Outline, Shadow, Reflection, Glow, Number Styles, Ligatures,* and *Stylistic Sets*
- *Text Highlight Color*
- *Font Color*

Change Case

The ***Change Case*** feature provides a quick and easy way to change the case of a single word or group of words. The *Change Case* button is in the *Font* group on the *Home* tab (Figure 1-32). The different case options are:

- *Sentence case* (capitalizes the first letter of the sentence)
- *lowercase*
- *UPPERCASE*
- *Capitalize Each Word*
- *tOGGLE cASE* (changes letters that are uppercase to lowercase and lowercase letters to uppercase)

Figure 1-32 *Change Case* options

Font Dialog Box

The *Font dialog box* combines many of the *font style* and *effect options* in one location for easy access. Click the **Font** launcher in the bottom-right corner of the *Font* group to open the *Font* dialog box (Figure 1-33).

In addition to the *Font*, *Font Style*, and *Size* commands on the *Font* tab, use the *Font* dialog box to change *Font Color*, *Underline Style*, *Underline Color*, and *Effects*. The *Preview* area displays a preview of selected changes, styles, and effects.

The *Advanced* tab lists *Character Spacing* options such as *Scale*, *Spacing*, *Position*, and *Kerning*. From this tab, you can also open the *Format Text Effects* dialog box.

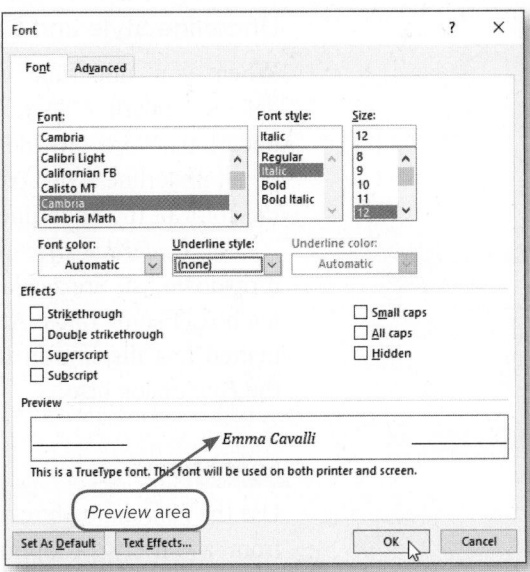

Figure 1-33 *Font* dialog box

ANOTHER WAY

Ctrl+D opens the *Font* dialog box.

Font Color

By default, the font color in a Word document is black. You can change the font color of selected text to add emphasis. The **Font Color** drop-down list in the *Font* dialog box displays a list of available font colors.

▶**HOW TO: Change Font Color**

1. Select the text you want to be a different color.
2. Click the **Font** launcher [*Home* tab, *Font* group]. The *Font* dialog box opens (Figure 1-34).
3. Click the **Font Color** drop-down arrow to display the list of font colors.
 - The drop-down list of font color options includes *Theme Colors*, *Standard Colors*, and *More Colors*. Theme colors are those colors associated with the theme of the document. For more on themes, see *SLO 2.7: Using Styles and Themes*.
4. Choose **OK** to close the *Font* dialog box.

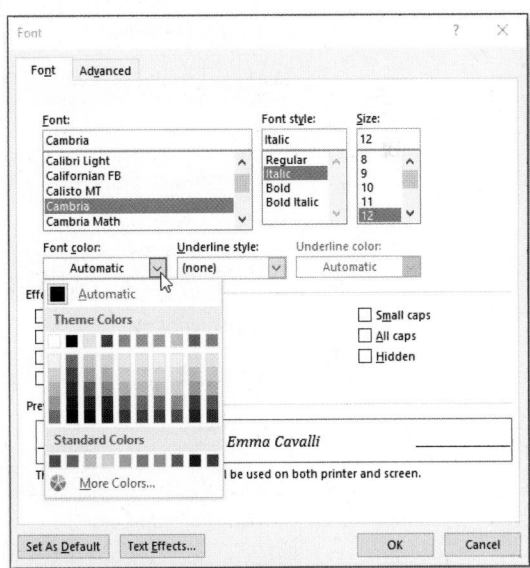

Figure 1-34 Change font color in the *Font* dialog box

ANOTHER WAY

Change the font color by clicking the **Font Color** button [*Home* tab, *Font* group].

Underline Style and Color

When you underline selected text, the default underline style is a solid black underline. Word provides a variety of additional underline styles. You can also change the color of the underline.

The *Underline style* and *Underline color* drop-down lists are available in the *Font* dialog box (Figure 1-35). A preview of the formatted text displays in the *Preview* area of the *Font* dialog box.

Font Effects

Use the *Font* dialog box to apply font effects from a variety of options in the *Effects* section. Several font effects are also available in the *Font* group on the *Home* tab. Table 1-3 lists the different font styles and effects.

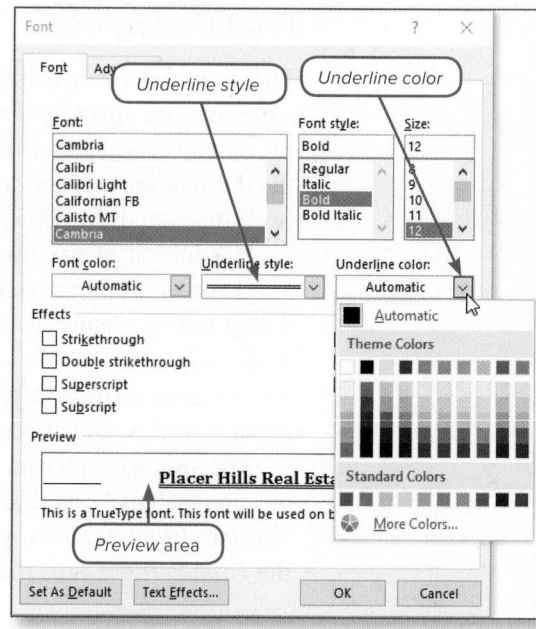

Figure 1-35 Change underline style and color

Table 1-3: Font Styles and Effects

Style/Effect	Example
Bold	This **word** is in bold.
Italic	This *word* is in italic.
Bold and Italic	This ***word*** is in bold and italic.
Underline	This sentence is underlined.
Double underline	This word is double underlined.
Underline Words only	This sentence is words only underlined.
Thick underline with color	This word has a thick, colored underline.
Strikethrough	This ~~word~~ has a strikethrough.
Double strikethrough	~~This sentence has a double strikethrough.~~
Subscript	H_2O uses a subscript number.
Superscript	Footnotes and endnotes use superscript numbers or letters.[1]
Small caps	MICROSOFT WORD is in small caps.
All caps	THIS SENTENCE IS IN ALL CAPS.
Hidden	
Text Highlight Color	This word has a highlight color.
Font Color	This sentence has a font color applied.

> **MORE INFO**
>
> *Hidden* text appears in your on-screen document, but it does not print or display in print preview.

Character Spacing

Character Spacing options allow you to add more or less space between letters and words. You can also vertically raise and lower letters and words (Figure 1-36).

- ***Scale***: Changes the horizontal spacing of a word or group of words by a percentage. Choose from preset percentages or type a custom percentage for scaling.
- ***Spacing***: Increases or decreases the space between letters. Choose from three options: *Normal*, *Expanded*, and *Condensed*. For *Expanded* and *Condensed*, choose the amount of points to expand or condense the selected text.
- ***Position***: Vertically raises or lowers text by a selected number of points.
- ***Kerning***: Adjusts the space between letters in a proportional font.

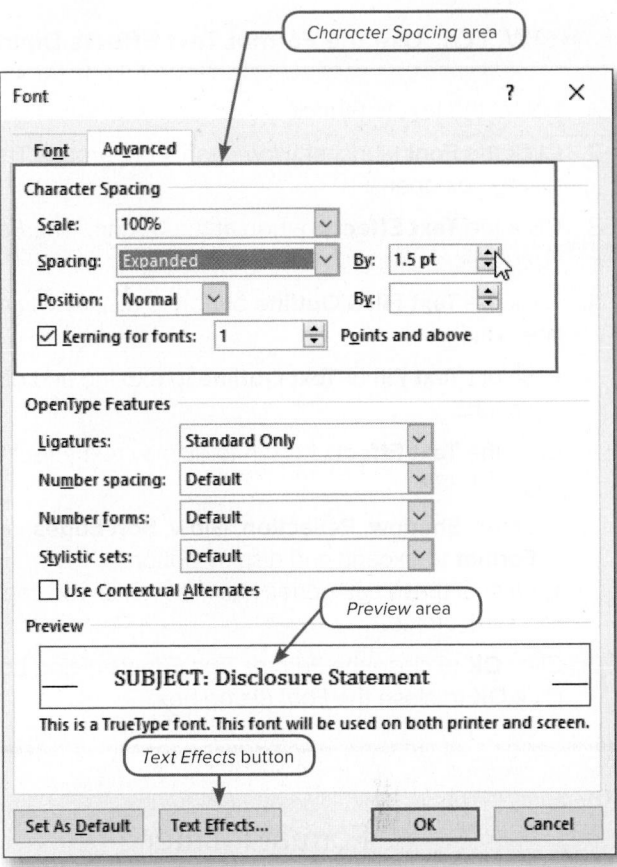

Figure 1-36 *Font* dialog box *Advanced* tab

Text Effects

Text Effects add special formatting features to selected text, such as *Outline*, *Shadow*, *Reflection*, and *Glow* (Figure 1-37). The *Text Effects* button is in the *Font* group on the *Home* tab. Many preset options are available for the different text effects, and more custom text effect options are available in the *Format Text Effects* pane.

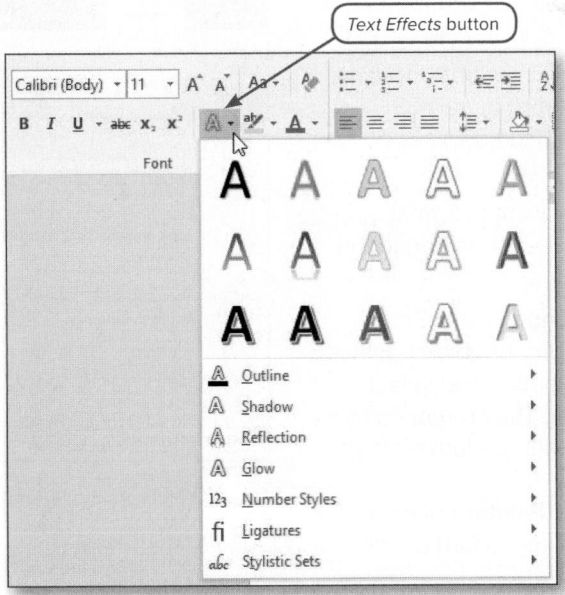

Figure 1-37 *Text Effects* button in the *Font* group

▶ HOW TO: Use the Format Text Effects Dialog Box

Figure 1-38 *Format Text Effects* dialog box

1. Select the text to format.
2. Click the **Font** launcher [*Home* tab, *Font* group]. The *Font* dialog box opens.
3. Click the **Text Effects** button at the bottom. The *Format Text Effects* dialog box opens.
4. Click the **Text Fill & Outline** button to display fill and outline options.
 - Select **Text Fill** or **Text Outline** to expand and display options.
5. Click the **Text Effects** button to display text effect options (Figure 1-38).
 - Select **Shadow**, **Reflection**, **Glow**, **Soft Edges**, or **3-D Format** to expand and display options.
 - Each of these categories has *Presets*, or you can customize the effect.
6. Click **OK** to close the *Format Text Effects* dialog box and click **OK** to close the *Font* dialog box.

Format Painter

The **Format Painter** copies text formatting from selected text and applies the same formatting to other text in the same document or a different document. The *Format Painter* copies font, font size, line spacing, indents, bullets, numbering, styles, and other formatting features in Word. This feature saves time in applying formats and ensures consistency in document format.

▶ HOW TO: Use the Format Painter

1. Select the formatted text you want to copy.
2. Click the **Format Painter** button [*Home* tab, *Clipboard* group] (Figure 1-39). The *Format Painter* icon displays (Figure 1-40).
3. Select the text you want to format, and Word applies the formatting to the selected text.
 - To apply formatting to multiple non-adjacent selections, double-click the **Format Painter** button and select the text to format. The *Format Painter* remains active until you turn off the feature.
 - Click the **Format Painter** button again or press the **Esc** key to turn off the *Format Painter*.

Figure 1-39 *Format Painter* button

Figure 1-40 *Format Painter* icon

Clear All Formatting

The *Clear All Formatting* feature removes all formatting for the selected text and returns it to plain text (Figure 1-41). For example, if you applied multiple formatting styles and effects to text, use the *Clear Formatting* feature rather than individually deselecting all the formatting options previously selected.

Figure 1-41 *Clear All Formatting* button in the *Font* group

> **MORE INFO**
>
> Be careful when using the *Clear Formatting* feature. It not only clears all text formatting but also clears line and paragraph spacing, numbering, bullets, and style formatting.

Change Default Font and Font Size

Recall that the default font in Microsoft Word is Calibri and the default font size is 11 pt. This *default* setting applies to each new blank document you create. Each new document is based on the *Normal.dotm* template. This template stores default settings for documents and controls document elements such as font, font size, line spacing, paragraph spacing, alignment, and styles.

You can change default settings on the current document only or change default settings in the *Normal* template. If you change the default settings for the *Normal* template, each new blank document uses the new default font and font size.

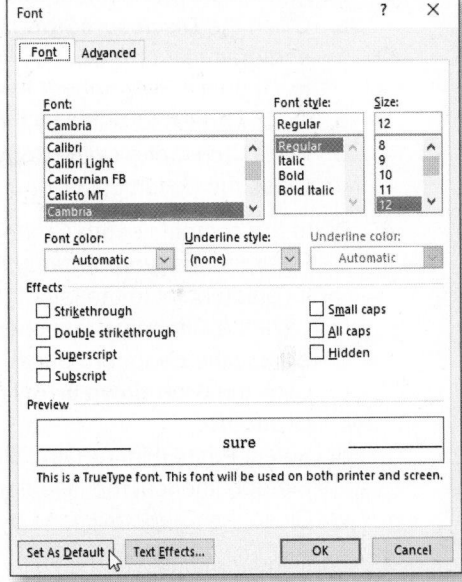

Figure 1-42 *Set As Default* button in the *Font* dialog box

> **HOW TO: Change the Default Font and Font Size**

1. Select the text you want to format.
2. Click the **Font** launcher [*Home* tab, *Font* group]. The *Font* dialog box opens (Figure 1-42).
3. Click the **Font** tab if it is not already selected.
4. Select the font and font size to set as the default.
5. Click the **Set As Default** button on the bottom left. A confirmation dialog box opens with two options (Figure 1-43):
 - *This document only?*
 - *All documents based on the Normal template?*
6. Select an option and click **OK** to close the dialog box.
7. Click **OK** to close the *Font* dialog box.

Figure 1-43 Change default settings confirmation options

> **MORE INFO**
>
> Be careful about changing default settings in the *Normal* template. Do this only when you are sure you want to change global default settings.

In this Pause & Practice project, you customize the content of the block format letter Emma created for Placer Hills Real Estate using cut, copy, paste, and the *Clipboard*. You also enhance your document by changing the font and applying font attributes.

Files Needed: ***[your initials] PP W1-1.docx*** and ***DisclosureStatement-01.docx*** *(Student data files are available in the* Library *of your SIMnet account.)*
Completed Project File Name: ***[your initials] PP W1-2.docx***

1. Open the ***[your initials] PP W1-1*** document completed in *Pause & Practice 1-1*.
 a. Click the **File** tab to open the *Backstage* view and click **Open** on the left.
 b. Click **Browse** to open the *Open* dialog box.
 c. Browse to locate the ***[your initials] PP W1-1*** document, select the document, and click **Open**.

2. Save this document as ***[your initials] PP W1-2***.
 a. Click the **File** tab to open the *Backstage* view and select **Save As** on the left. If the document is saved on *OneDrive* and *AutoSave* is on, select **Save a Copy**.
 b. Click **Browse** to open the *Save As* dialog box and select the desired location to save the file.
 c. Change the file name to [your initials] PP W1-2.
 d. Click **Save** to rename the document and close the *Save As* dialog box.

3. Copy text from a document to the *Clipboard*.
 a. Open the ***DisclosureStatement-01*** document from your student date files. Ignore any spelling and grammar errors in this document; you will correct these in *Pause & Practice 1-3*. If the document opens in *Protected View*, click the **Enable Editing** button.
 b. Press **Ctrl+A** to select all the text.
 c. Press **Ctrl+C** or click the **Copy** button [*Home* tab, *Clipboard* group].
 d. Close the document without saving.

4. Paste the contents of the *Clipboard*.
 a. Return to the ***[your initials] PP W1-2*** document and place your insertion point to the left of "Best regards,".
 b. Click the **Clipboard** launcher [*Home* tab, *Clipboard* group] to display the *Clipboard* pane.
 c. Click the **drop-down arrow** to the right of the copied text in the *Clipboard*.
 d. Select **Paste** (Figure 1-44). The paragraphs of text are pasted in the document at the insertion point.
 e. Close the *Clipboard* pane by clicking the **X** in the upper-right corner.

Figure 1-44 Paste text from the *Clipboard*

5. Copy the formatting of the first paragraph to the two new paragraphs.
 a. Place your insertion point in the first body paragraph of the letter.
 b. Click the **Show/Hide** button [*Home* tab, *Paragraph* group] to display formatting symbols if necessary.
 c. Click the **Format Painter** button [*Home* tab, *Clipboard* group].
 d. Select the last two paragraphs in the body of the letter (don't select "Best regards,"). Be sure to include the paragraph mark at the end of the last body paragraph (Figure 1-45). The *Format Painter* applies the formatting to the paragraphs.

Make note on the disclosure statement if you have had any work done with or without permits. Some examples include a gas spa, a new water heater, or a wholehouse fan where a trus may have been cut. If you had granate counters installed, that does not require a permit.¶
Please complete the enclosed statement by [date] and return it to me. As always, if you have any questions or concerns, please call me at 916-450-3334 or email me at ecavalli@phre.com. Best wishes and thank you for you're business.¶ ᴬ̄ᴵ ← *Format Painter* pointer
Best regards,¶

Figure 1-45 Use the *Format Painter* to apply formatting to selected text

6. Copy text using the drag-and-drop method.
 a. Double-click the word "**disclosure**" in the first sentence of the third body paragraph to select it.
 b. Press the **Ctrl** key and click and hold the selected text with your pointer.
 c. Drag and drop the text between the words "enclosed" and "statement" in the first sentence in the last body paragraph (Figure 1-46). Confirm one space displays before and after the copied word.

Figure 1-46 Copy text using drag and drop

7. Move a paragraph in the body of the letter.
 a. Select the entire third paragraph in the body of the letter ("**Make note . . .**"), including the paragraph mark at the end of the paragraph.
 b. Click the **Cut** button [*Home* tab, *Clipboard* group] or press **Ctrl+X**. The selected paragraph is cut from the document and stored on the *Clipboard*.
 c. Place your insertion point at the beginning of the second body paragraph ("**If there is . . .**").
 d. Click the top half of the **Paste** button [*Home* tab, *Clipboard* group] or press **Ctrl+V**.

8. Insert and format a date.
 a. Delete the placeholder "[date]" (including the brackets) in the last paragraph and type the date that is one week from today (use January 1, 2020 format).
 b. Select the date you just typed.
 c. Click the **Text Highlight Color** drop-down list button [*Home* tab, *Font* group or on the mini toolbar] and choose the **Yellow** text highlight color (Figure 1-47).

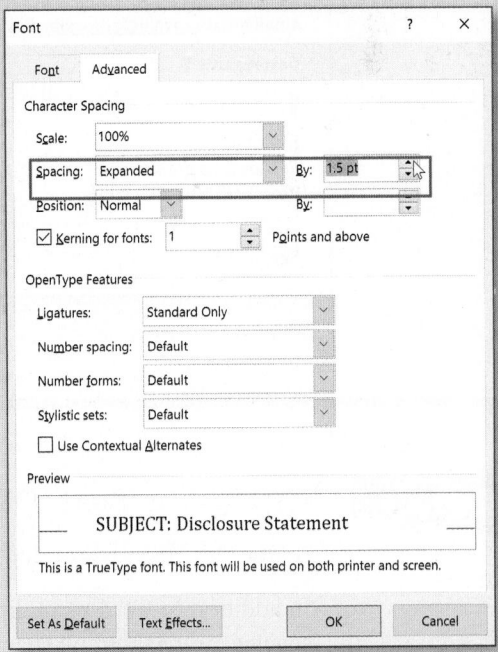

Figure 1-47 Apply text highlight color

9. Change the font and font size of the entire document.
 a. Press **Ctrl+A** to select all the text in the document.
 b. Click the **Font** drop-down list button [*Home* tab, *Font* group] and select **Cambria**.
 c. Click the **Font Size** drop-down list button [*Home* tab, *Font* group] and select **12**.

10. Change the case and spacing of selected text.
 a. Select the word "**Subject**" in the subject line of the document.
 b. Click the **Change Case** button [*Home* tab, *Font* group] and select **UPPERCASE**. Do not use the *Font* dialog box to change the case.
 c. Select the entire subject line.
 d. Click the **Font** launcher [*Home* tab, *Font* group] to open the *Font* dialog box. **Ctrl+D** also opens the *Font* dialog box.
 e. Click the **Advanced** tab.
 f. Click the **Spacing** drop-down list in the *Character Spacing* area and select **Expanded**.
 g. Click the up arrow in the *By* area to the right of *Spacing* to change the character spacing to expanded by **1.5 pt** (Figure 1-48).
 h. Click **OK** to close the *Font* dialog box.

Figure 1-48 Change character spacing

11. Apply font styles to selected text.
 a. Select the email address "**ecavalli@phre.com**" in the last body paragraph.
 b. Click the **Font Color** drop-down list button [*Home* tab, *Font* group] and select the **ninth color** (**Dark Blue**) in the *Standard Colors* area.
 c. Click the **Underline** button or press **Ctrl+U** to apply an underline to the selected email address.
 d. Select the writer's name "**Emma Cavalli**" (below "Best regards,").
 e. Click the **Font** launcher in the bottom-right corner of the *Font* group to open the *Font* dialog box.
 f. Click the **Font** tab and check the **Small caps** box in the *Effects* area.
 g. Click **OK** to close the *Font* dialog box.
 h. Select the writer's title "**Realtor Consultant**" and click the **Italic** button or press **Ctrl+I**.
 i. Select the company name "**Placer Hills Real Estate**" and click the **Bold** button or press **Ctrl+B**.

12. Save and close the document (Figure 1-49).

September·1,·2020¶

¶

David·and·Sharon·Wing↵
4685·Orange·Grove·Road↵
Rocklin,·CA·97725¶

Dear·Mr.·and·Mrs.·Wing:¶

SUBJECT:·Disclosure·Statement¶

Please·read·each·paragraph·before·signing·the·disclosure·statement·documents.·As·you·fill·out·the·required·disclosure·packet,·it·is·critical·to·the·transmission·of·sale·that·you·give·as·much·information·as·possible·about·your·residence,·no·matter·how·small·or·insignificant.·Please·use·additional·paper·if·necessary·and·make·a·notation·to·that·fact.¶

Make·note·on·the·disclosure·statement·if·you·have·had·any·work·done·with·or·without·permits.·Some·examples·include·a·gas·spa,·a·new·water·heater,·or·a·wholehouse·fan·where·a·trus·may·have·been·cut.·If·you·had·granate·counters·installed,·that·does·not·require·a·permit.¶

If·there·is·information·about·the·neighborhood·or·neighbors·that·you·as·a·buyer·would·want·to·know·about,·be·sure·to·reveal·that·information.·Be·sure·to·address·those·types·of·questions·on·the·Real·Estate·Transfer·Disclosure·Statement,·item·#11·on·page·2.¶

Please·complete·the·enclosed·disclosure·statement·by·September·8,·2020·and·return·it·to·me.·As·always,·if·you·have·any·questions·or·concerns,·please·call·me·at·916-450-3334·or·email·me·at·ecavalli@phre.com.·Best·wishes·and·thank·you·for·you're·business.¶

Best·regards,¶

¶

EMMA·CAVALLI↵
Realtor·Consultant↵
Placer·Hills·Real·Estate¶

rn↵
Enclosure¶

Figure 1-49 PP W1-2 completed

SLO 1.6

Changing Text Alignment, Line Spacing, and Paragraph Spacing

In addition to word wrap, line breaks, and paragraphs breaks, you can use text alignment, line spacing, and paragraph spacing to control the layout and white space between the parts of your document.

Default Settings

Just as font and font size have default settings, Word has default settings for paragraph alignment, line spacing, and paragraph spacing. These default settings are stored in the *Normal* template on which all new blank documents are based. Table 1-4 summarizes font, line spacing, and paragraph default settings:

Table 1-4: Normal Template Default Settings

Setting	Default Setting
Font	Calibri
Font Size	11 pt.
Horizontal Paragraph Alignment	Left
Line Spacing	1.08 lines
Paragraph Spacing—Before	0 pt.
Paragraph Spacing—After	8 pt.

Paragraph Alignment

Paragraph alignment controls the horizontal alignment of paragraphs. A paragraph is a single word, a group of words, a sentence, or multiple sentences. Paragraphs are separated by paragraph breaks. A group of words using word wrap and line breaks is considered one paragraph.

The four different paragraph alignment options are:

- *Left* (default): The paragraph is aligned on the left margin.
- *Center*: The paragraph is centered between the left and right margins.
- *Right*: The paragraph begins and is aligned on the right margin.
- *Justify*: The paragraph is aligned flush with both the left and right margins.

> **ANOTHER WAY**
>
> Press **Ctrl+L** to *Align Text Left*.
> Press **Ctrl+E** to *Center* text.
> Press **Ctrl+R** to *Align Text Right*.
> Press **Ctrl+J** to *Justify* text.

Change the alignment of a paragraph by clicking a paragraph alignment button in the *Paragraph* group on the *Home* tab (Figure 1-50). When changing the alignment of a single paragraph, the entire paragraph need not be selected; the insertion point only needs to be within the paragraph for the alignment to be applied. Text alignment can also be changed in the *Paragraph* dialog box.

Figure 1-50 Paragraph alignment options in the *Paragraph* group

Line Spacing

Line spacing refers to the amount of blank space between lines of text within a paragraph. The default setting in Word is 1.08 lines, which is slightly more than single spacing. Most documents you type are single-spaced or 1.08 line spacing, but you may want to use double-spacing (two lines) when needed, such as when typing an academic report.

As with paragraph alignment, you can apply line spacing to an individual paragraph, multiple paragraphs, or an entire document.

To change line spacing, click the **Line and Paragraph Spacing** button in the *Paragraph* group on the *Home* tab and select an option (Figure 1-51). Choose from the preset line spacing options or select **Line Spacing Options** to open the *Paragraph* dialog box and set custom line spacing.

Figure 1-51 *Line and Paragraph Spacing* button in the *Paragraph* group

▶ ANOTHER WAY

Ctrl+1 applies single-space (1 line).
Ctrl+5 applies 1.5 line spacing.
Ctrl+2 applies double-space (2 lines).

The *Paragraph* dialog box includes additional line spacing options (Figure 1-52). The *At Least* and *Exactly* options allow you to specify points of spacing, rather than lines of spacing, between lines of text. The *Multiple* option enables you to set a line spacing option that is not a whole number, such as 1.3 or 2.25 line spacing.

Figure 1-52 *Line spacing* options in the *Paragraph* dialog box

▶ MORE INFO

If a document has inconsistent line spacing, it looks unprofessional. Select the entire document and set the line spacing to enhance consistency and improve readability.

Paragraph Spacing

While line spacing controls the amount of space between lines of text in a paragraph, *paragraph spacing* controls the amount of spacing before and after paragraphs. For example, you might want the text of a document to be single-spaced but prefer to have more blank space before and after paragraphs. Use paragraph spacing to accomplish this task.

Before and *After* paragraph spacing is set in points. The default *After* paragraph spacing is 8 pt., which is a little less than one blank line. The default *Before* paragraph spacing is 0 pt.

Change *Before* and *After* paragraph spacing in the *Paragraph* group on the *Layout* tab (Figure 1-53). You can also change *Before* and *After* paragraph spacing in the *Paragraph* dialog box and from the *Line and Paragraph Spacing* button in the *Paragraph* group on the *Home* tab.

Use the *Line and Paragraph Spacing* button in the *Paragraph* group on the *Home* tab to **Add/ Remove Space Before Paragraph** or **Add/Remove Space After Paragraph** (Figure 1-54). These options are contextual and change depending on whether *Before* or *After* paragraph spacing is already applied on the text.

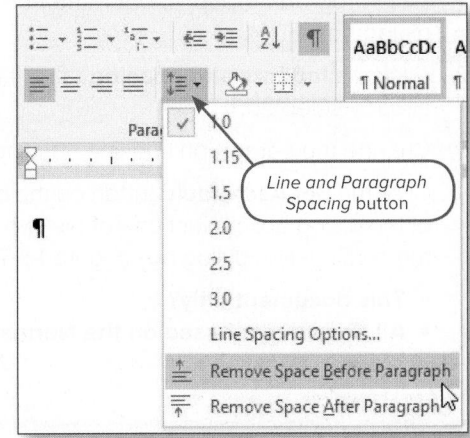

Figure 1-53 *Paragraph* group on the *Layout* tab

> ▶ **MORE INFO**
>
> Insert line breaks to keep lines of text as a single paragraph. *Before* and *After* paragraph spacing is not applied to individual lines of text when line breaks are used to create a paragraph.

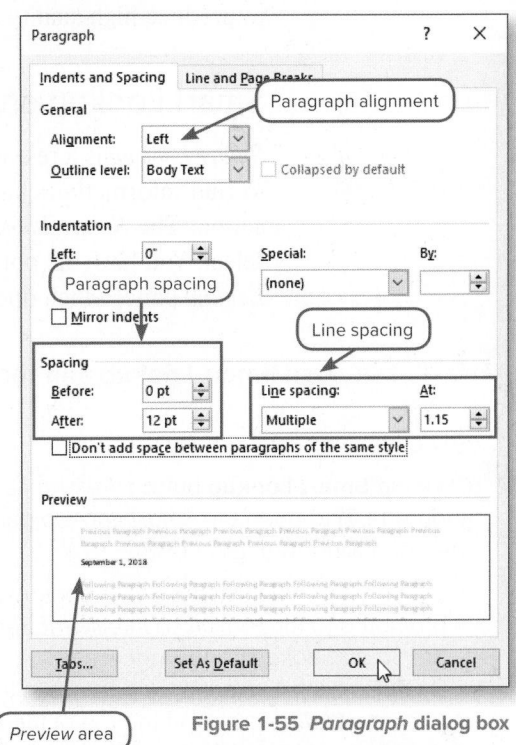

Figure 1-54 *Add/Remove* paragraph spacing options

Paragraph Dialog Box

The **Paragraph dialog box** combines many of the alignment and spacing options included in the *Paragraph* groups on the *Home* and *Layout* tabs.

▶**HOW TO:** Change Alignment and Spacing in the Paragraph Dialog Box

1. Select the text to format.
2. Click the **Paragraph** launcher [*Home* or *Layout* tab, *Paragraph* group] to open the *Paragraph* dialog box (Figure 1-55).
3. Click the **Alignment** drop-down list in the *General* area and select **Left**, **Centered**, **Right**, or **Justified**.
 - The *Indentation* section of this dialog box controls indents. Indents are covered in *SLO 2.3: Using Indents*.
4. Change **Before** and **After** paragraph spacing in the *Spacing* section.
 - Type the number of points of spacing or use the spinner (up and down) arrows.
 - The *Don't add space between paragraphs of the same style* check box controls paragraph spacing between paragraphs of the same style, which is primarily used with numbered and bulleted lists and outlines.
5. Click the **Line spacing** drop-down list to select a line spacing option.
 - Alternatively, type a custom line spacing in the **At** text box. The Line spacing changes to *Multiple*.
6. Notice the *Preview* area displays how your document will look with changes.
7. Click **OK** to close the *Paragraph* dialog box.

Figure 1-55 *Paragraph* dialog box

Change Default Line and Paragraph Spacing

Use the *Paragraph* dialog box to set default paragraph alignment and spacing. This process is similar to changing the default font and font size settings.

▶ **HOW TO:** Change the Default Paragraph Alignment and Spacing

1. Click the **Paragraph** launcher [*Home* or *Layout* tab, *Paragraph* group] to open the *Paragraph* dialog box.
2. Click the **Indents and Spacing** tab if it is not already selected.
3. Change the paragraph and line spacing settings.
4. Click the **Set As Default** button on the bottom left of the dialog box. Select one of the two options in the confirmation dialog box (Figure 1-56):
 - **This document only?**
 - **All documents based on the Normal template?**
5. Click **OK**.

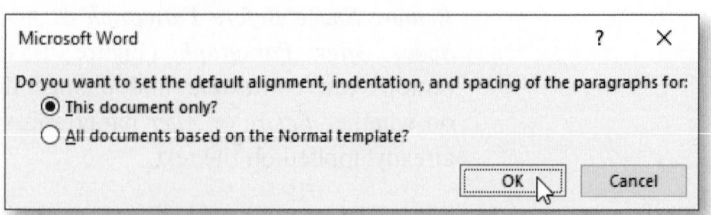

Figure 1-56 Change default setting confirmation options

Using Smart Lookup and Proofreading Tools

The words and grammar you use in a document reflect your professionalism and the reputation of your organization. Word provides many proofing and editing tools to improve the quality of the documents you produce. The *Smart Lookup* feature enables you to search for information on the internet without leaving Word. The spelling, grammar, and thesaurus features help you to produce high-quality and professional-looking documents.

Smart Lookup and the Smart Lookup Pane

Smart Lookup is a research feature in Word. This feature uses Bing, an internet search engine, to find information about a selected word or words in a document without leaving the application. The **Smart Lookup pane** displays information from the internet about the words you select. You have the option to find additional information by clicking a hyperlink in the *Smart Lookup* pane, which opens an internet browser displaying additional internet content.

▶ **HOW TO:** Use Smart Lookup and the Smart Lookup Pane

1. Select the word or words to research.
2. Click the **Smart Lookup** button [*References* tab, *Research* group] (Figure 1-57) to open the *Smart Lookup* pane on the right side of the Word window (Figure 1-58).
 - The first time you use the *Smart Lookup* feature, you may be prompted to turn on *Office Intelligent Services*. Click **Turn on** in the *Smart Lookup* pane if necessary.
 - By default, the *Explore* area displays in the *Smart Lookup* pane.
 - Click the **Define** button at the top of the *Smart Lookup* pane to display a definition of the selected word(s).
 - A privacy notice may appear in the *Smart Lookup* pane upon first time use.

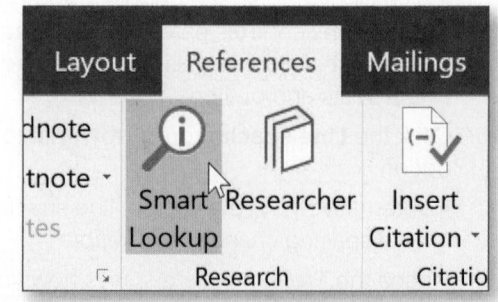

Figure 1-57 *Smart Lookup* button

3. View the research results in the *Smart Lookup* pane.

- To view additional information about a research result, click one of the results, which is a hyperlink that will open an internet browser window displaying additional information about the topic.
- To perform additional research on a different word, select the word in the document and click the **Smart Lookup** button again. The new results appear in the *Smart Lookup* pane.

4. Click the **X** in the upper-right corner of the *Smart Lookup* pane to close the pane.

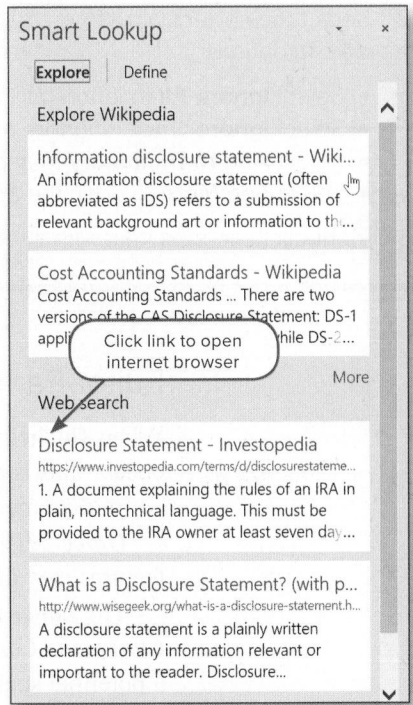

Figure 1-58 *Smart Lookup* pane

> **ANOTHER WAY**
>
> Right-click a word or selected words and choose **Smart Lookup** from the context menu to open the *Smart Lookup* pane.

Automatic Spelling and Grammar Notifications

Recall that Word uses *AutoCorrect* to automatically correct many commonly misspelled words. When typing a document, Word constantly compares the words you type with the words in its dictionary. When Word doesn't recognize a word, it marks the potential *spelling error* with a *red wavy underline*. Word also checks the grammar of your document and marks potential word choice or *grammatical errors* with a *blue double underline* and *clarity and conciseness errors* with a *light brown dotted line*.

> **MORE INFO**
>
> When Word marks a word as a possible spelling error, it does not necessarily mean that the word is misspelled. Many proper nouns are not included in the Word dictionary.

When you right-click a potential spelling or grammar error, the context menu displays options for correction and provides additional information, such as word definitions and a reason for grammatical errors.

▶ HOW TO: Correct Spelling and Grammatical Errors

1. Right-click a word that has a red wavy underline, blue double underline, or light brown dotted line.

- A context menu opens that provides editing options depending on the type of potential error (Figure 1-59).
- For potential spelling errors, a list of possible corrections displays. The definition of the word displays below some options.
- Click the arrow to the right of a word in the context menu to select *Read Aloud*, *Add to AutoCorrect*, or *AutoCorrect Options*.
- Potential grammar errors display possible corrections and a reason for the grammatical error. Click the arrow to the right of a correction in the context menu to *Read Aloud*.

Figure 1-59 Correct a spelling error

2. Select the correct word from the list to replace the misspelled word. You can also choose from the following editing options:
 - Select **Ignore All** to ignore all instances of this spelling throughout the document.
 - Select **Ignore Once** to ignore a potential grammar error.
 - Select **Add to Dictionary** to add the word to the Word dictionary.
 - Select **See More** to open the *Editor* pane at the right

3. Right-click the next item with a red or blue underline to repeat the editing process.

Editor Pane

When finalizing a document, proofread it one last time and use the spelling and grammar check. This is especially true with longer documents. You can use the *Editor pane* to check an entire document for potential spelling, grammatical, and clarity and conciseness errors.

Office 2019 Note: This pane is labeled ***Proofing*** rather than *Editor* in Office 2019 and some features may differ slightly.

The *Editor* pane is contextual. The label below the *Editor* pane title (*Spelling*, *Grammar*, or *Clarity and Conciseness*) and the available options change depending on whether Word detects a potential spelling or grammatical error.

▶**HOW TO:** Use the Editor Pane

1. Press **Ctrl+Home** to move to the beginning of your document. When checking a document for correct spelling and grammar, it is best to start at the beginning of the document.

2. Click the **Spelling & Grammar** button [*Review* tab, *Proofing* group] to open the *Editor* pane (Figure 1-60).
 - The first potential spelling or grammatical error displays in the *Editor* pane.
 - Click the **Read Aloud** button (speaker icon) to have Word read the sentence containing the error.

3. Select the correct word from the *Suggestions* list to replace the incorrect word.
 - A definition of each suggested word displays below each word in the list of suggestions.
 - Click the drop-down list to the right of a word and select **Change All** to change all instances of the misspelled word. Other options on the drop-down list include *Read Aloud*, *Spell Out*, *Add to AutoCorrect*, and *AutoCorrect Options*.
 - If no word options are available, retype the word in the body of the document.

4. Select **Ignore Once**, **Ignore All**, or **Add to Dictionary** if the word does not need to be changed.
 - If you select *Add to Dictionary*, the selected word is added to the dictionary, so it is not detected as a potential error in the future.

5. Click **OK** to finish when the dialog box opens indicating the spelling and grammar check is complete.

Figure 1-60 *Editor* pane

ANOTHER WAY

F7 opens the *Editor* pane.

Customize the Dictionary

When you spell check a document, you can easily add a word to the *Word Dictionary*. When you add a word to the dictionary, Word creates a custom dictionary. You can manually add or delete words from the custom dictionary. Many proper nouns are marked as a misspelled word during a spell check. You can add commonly used proper nouns to the dictionary so they won't be marked as a misspelled word each time you spell check a document.

▶HOW TO: Add Words to the Custom Dictionary

1. Click the **File** tab to open the *Backstage* view.
2. Click the **Options** button to open the *Word Options* dialog box.
3. Click the **Proofing** button.
4. Click the **Custom Dictionaries** button. The *Custom Dictionaries* dialog box opens (Figure 1-61).
5. Select the dictionary to edit in the *Dictionary List*.
 - The *RoamingCustom.dic* is typically the default custom dictionary.
6. Click the **Edit Word List** button. Your custom dictionary dialog box opens (Figure 1-62). Words previously added to your dictionary display in the *Dictionary* area.
7. Click the **Word(s)** text box, type a word to add to your dictionary, and click the **Add** button to add the word to your dictionary.
 - To delete a word from the dictionary, select the word and click the **Delete** button.
8. Click **OK** when finished to close the dialog box.
9. Click **OK** to close the *Custom Dictionaries* dialog box.
10. Click **OK** to close the *Word Options* dialog box.

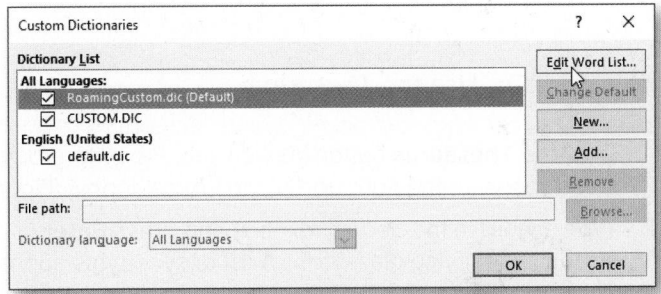

Figure 1-61 *Custom Dictionaries* dialog box

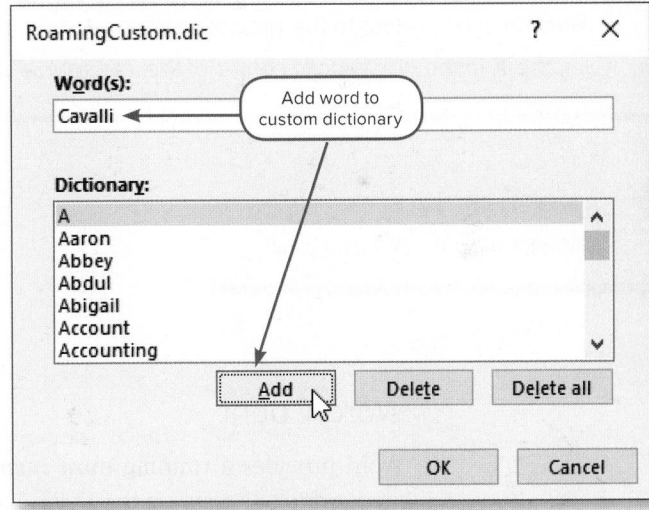

Figure 1-62 Add word to custom dictionary

The Thesaurus

Word provides a *Thesaurus* feature to help you find *synonyms* to add variety to your writing. A varied vocabulary indicates a more educated and professional writer.

Word provides two ways to use the *Thesaurus* to find synonyms. The first and quickest way is to select a word in the document and use the context menu (right-click) to replace a selected word with an appropriate synonym.

▶HOW TO: Find Synonyms Using the Context Menu

1. Right-click the word you want to replace with an appropriate synonym. The context menu displays.
2. Place your pointer on **Synonyms**. Another context menu appears with a list of synonym choices.
3. Select the synonym you prefer (Figure 1-63). The selected synonym replaces the selected word in the text and the menus close.

You can also use the *Thesaurus* feature in the *Thesaurus* pane. This method enables you to search for synonyms for any word, not just a selected word in your document.

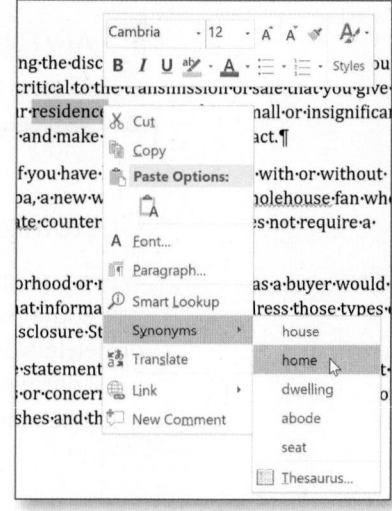

Figure 1-63 Use *Thesaurus* to find synonyms

▶HOW TO: Use the Thesaurus

1. Click the **Thesaurus** button [*Review* tab, *Proofing* group]. The *Thesaurus* pane opens on the right side of the Word window (Figure 1-64).
2. Type a word in the *Search* text box and press **Enter** or click the **Search** button (magnifying glass icon). A list of synonyms appears in the *Thesaurus* area.
3. Click the **drop-down arrow** to the right of the synonym and select **Insert** or **Copy**.
 - You can also click a synonym in the list to look up synonyms for that word. Click the **Back** arrow to return to the previous synonym list.
4. Click the **X** in the upper-right corner of the *Thesaurus* pane to close this pane.

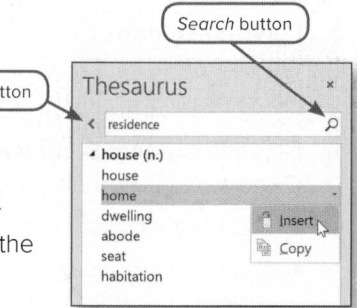

Figure 1-64 *Thesaurus* pane

> ▶ **ANOTHER WAY**
>
> **Shift+F7** opens the *Thesaurus* pane.

Figure 1-65 *Word Count* area on the *Status* bar

Word Count

Word provides a running ***word count*** in each document, which displays on the *Status* bar in the bottom-left corner of the Word window (Figure 1-65). Click the **Word Count** area to open the *Word Count* dialog box to display more detailed information: number of pages, words, characters (no spaces), characters (with spaces), paragraphs, and lines (Figure 1-66). You can also choose whether to have Word count words in textboxes, footnotes, and endnotes.

Word Count	? ✕
Statistics:	
Pages	1
Words	228
Characters (no spaces)	1,116
Characters (with spaces)	1,333
Paragraphs	11
Lines	28

☑ Include textboxes, footnotes and endnotes

Close

Figure 1-66 *Word Count* dialog box

Read Aloud

The ***Read Aloud*** feature increases accessibility and adds another proofreading tool to your Word documents. This feature reads a word, selected text, or an entire document. You can control the speed in which text is read and select a voice to read your text.

▶ HOW TO: Use the Read Aloud Feature

1. Select a word or group of words to read aloud.
 - Alternatively, place your insertion point at a location in your document where you want the reading to begin.
2. Click the **Read Aloud** button [*Review* tab, *Speech* group].
 - Word reads the selected word or words. If no words are selected, Word begins reading from the insertion point.
 - The *Read Aloud* controls appear in the upper-right corner (Figure 1-67).
3. Click the **Pause** button to pause the reading. Click the **Play** button to resume reading.
4. Click the **Settings** button to change *Reading speed* or *Voice Selection*.
5. Click the **Next** or **Previous** button to move to and read the next or previous paragraph.
6. Click the **X** in the upper-right corner of the *Read Aloud* controls to close the controls.

Figure 1-67 *Read Aloud controls*

Learning Tools

In addition to the *Read Aloud* feature, Word provides a set of ***Learning Tools***. These tools increase accessibility by enabling users to view a document at different widths, change the page color, change the text spacing, view spaces between syllables in words, and use the *Read Aloud* feature.

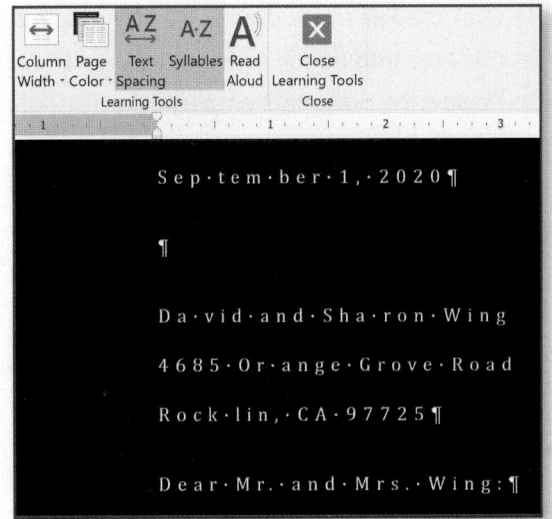

Figure 1-68 *Learning Tools*

▶ HOW TO: Use the Learning Tools

1. Click the **Learning Tools** button [*View* tab, *Immersive* group]. The *Immersive Learning Tools* contextual tab displays (Figure 1-68).
2. Click the **Column Width** button [*Immersive Learning Tools* tab, *Learning Tools* group] and select **Very Narrow**, **Narrow**, **Moderate**, or **Wide** to change the display width.

3. Click the **Page Color** button [*Immersive Learning Tools* tab, *Learning Tools* group] and select **None**, **Sepia**, or **Inverse** to change the display color.

4. Click the **Text Spacing** button [*Immersive Learning Tools* tab, *Learning Tools* group] to increase or decrease the spacing between letters and words.

5. Click the **Syllables** button [*Immersive Learning Tools* tab, *Learning Tools* group] to display a space between syllables in words. Click the **Syllables** button again to hide the space between syllables.

6. Click the **Read Aloud** button [*Immersive Learning Tools* tab, *Learning Tools* group] to read selected words or begin reading from the insertion point.

 - The *Read Aloud* controls appear in the upper-right corner.

7. Click the **Close** button [*Immersive Learning Tools* tab, *Close* group] to close the *Learning Tools* view and return to your document.

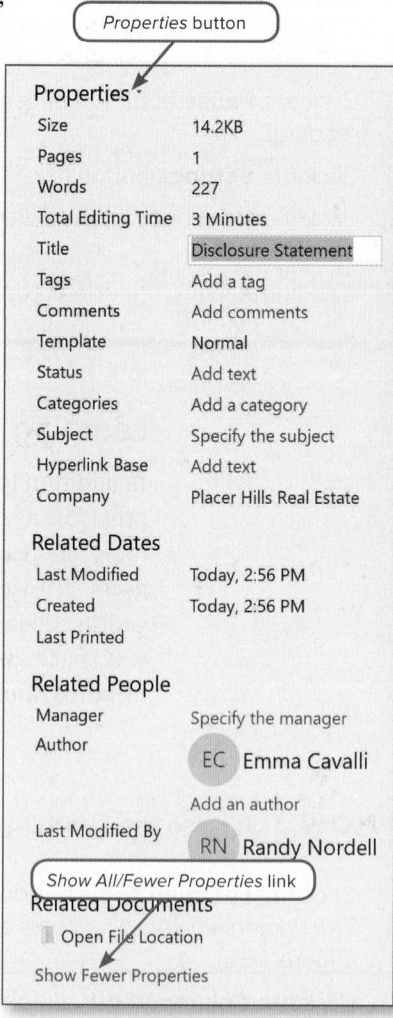

Figure 1-69 Document properties on the *Backstage* view

SLO 1.8 Customizing Document Properties

Document properties are details about a document. These details are not visible in the text of the document but are included as hidden information within the document. Document properties include fields such as *Title*, *Author*, *Comments*, *Subject*, *Company*, *Created*, and *Last Modified*. Several document properties are automatically generated, such as *Words*, *Total Editing Time*, and *Last Modified*, whereas other document property details are edited individually.

Document Properties

Document properties are viewed and edited in the *Info* area on the *Backstage* view. Document properties are saved within the document and can be viewed by others.

▶HOW TO: Add Document Properties

1. Click the **File** tab to display the *Backstage* view.

2. Click the **Info** button if it is not already selected.

3. Review the document properties on the right side of the window (Figure 1-69).

 - Document property field names are listed on the left, and the information in these fields displays on the right.

4. Click a field and type information to edit the document property.

 - Several properties cannot be changed because they are automatically generated by Word.

5. Click the **Show All/Fewer Properties** link at the bottom to display more or fewer document property fields.

6. Click the **Back** arrow in the upper-left corner of the *Backstage* view to return to the document when you finish entering and reviewing document properties.

Advanced Properties

In addition to viewing and editing the document properties on the *Backstage* view, you can also display document properties in the ***Properties dialog box*** (Figure 1-70). In the *Info* area on the *Backstage* view, click the **Properties** button (see Figure 1-69) and select **Advanced Properties** to open the *Properties* dialog box.

You can modify the document properties on the *Summary* tab. The title of the *Properties* dialog box is contextual. The file name displays before *Properties* in the title bar of the dialog box.

Print Document Properties

You can print document properties using the *Backstage* view. When you print document properties, only a page listing the document properties prints, not the document itself.

Figure 1-70 *Properties* dialog box

▶ **HOW TO: Print Document Properties**

1. Click the **File** tab to open the *Backstage* view.
2. Select **Print** on the left.
3. Click **Print All Pages** and select **Document Info** from the drop-down list (Figure 1-71).
4. Click the **Print** button to print the document properties.

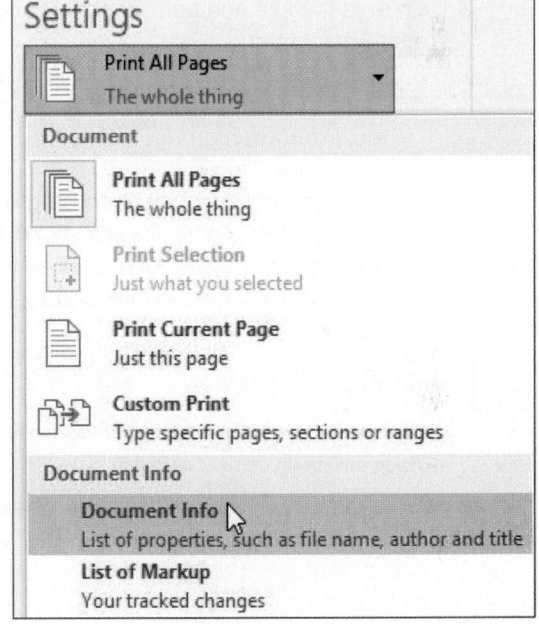

Figure 1-71 Print document properties

PAUSE & PRACTICE: WORD 1-3

In the final Pause & Practice project in this chapter, you add the finishing touches on a document for Placer Hills Real Estate. You customize paragraph and line spacing, change paragraph alignment, and use spelling and grammar checkers to produce an error-free document. You also modify the document properties.

File Needed: **[your initials] PP W1-2.docx**
Completed Project File Name: **[your initials] PP W1-3.docx**

1. Open the **[your initials] PP W1-2** document completed in *Pause & Practice 1-2*.
 a. Click the **File** tab to open the *Backstage* view and click **Open** on the left.
 b. Click **Browse** to open the *Open* dialog box.
 c. Browse to locate the **[your initials] PP W1-2** document, select the document, and click **Open**.

2. Save this document with a different file name.
 a. Click the **File** tab to open the *Backstage* view and select **Save As** on the left. If your document is saved on *OneDrive* and *AutoSave* is turned on, select **Save a Copy**.
 b. Click **Browse** to open the *Save As* dialog box and select the desired location to save the file.
 c. Change the file name to [your initials] PP W1-3.
 d. Click **Save** to save the document with a different file name and close the *Save As* dialog box.

3. Change the line and paragraph spacing for the entire document.
 a. Press **Ctrl+A** to select the entire document.
 b. Click the **Paragraph** launcher [*Home* or *Layout* tab, *Paragraph* group] to open the *Paragraph* dialog box (Figure 1-72).
 c. Change the *Line spacing* to **Single**.
 d. Change the *After* spacing to **12 pt**. Use the up arrow or type the amount of spacing.
 e. Click **OK** to close the dialog box.

Figure 1-72 Change *Line spacing* and *After* paragraph spacing in the *Paragraph* dialog box

> **ANOTHER WAY**
>
> Change line spacing in the *Paragraph* group on the *Home* tab. Change *Before* and *After* paragraph spacing in the *Paragraph* group on the *Layout* tab.

4. Add paragraph spacing before the date line of the business letter.
 a. Select or place your insertion point in the first line (date line) of the business letter.
 b. Click the **Layout** tab.
 c. Change the *Before* spacing to **72 pt**. (Figure 1-73). *Note:* 72 pt. is approximately 1", which is commonly used as the spacing before the date line on business letters.

Figure 1-73 Change *Before* paragraph spacing in the *Paragraph* group

5. Change the paragraph alignment of selected text.
 a. Select or place your insertion point in the subject line of the business letter.
 b. Click the **Center** button [*Home* tab, *Paragraph* group] or press **Ctrl+E**.

6. Use the *Thesaurus* to find synonyms for selected words.
 a. Select the word "**reveal**" in the third body paragraph.

b. Click the **Thesaurus** button [*Review* tab, *Proofing* group]. The *Thesaurus* pane opens on the right with a list of synonyms for the selected word (Figure 1-74).

c. Click the **drop-down arrow** to the right of the word "divulge" and choose **Insert**. The word "divulge" replaces "reveal."

d. Click the **X** in the upper-right corner of the *Thesaurus* pane to close the pane.

e. Right-click the word "**residence**" in the first body paragraph. A context menu opens.

f. Point to **Synonyms** and a list of synonyms appears.

g. Select "**home**" from the list of synonyms. The word "home" replaces "residence."

Figure 1-74 Insert a synonym from the *Thesaurus* pane

7. Add a word to the custom dictionary.
 a. Click the **File** tab to open the *Backstage* view.
 b. Click the **Options** button to open the *Word Options* dialog box.
 c. Click **Proofing** on the left.
 d. Click the **Custom Dictionaries** button in the *When correcting spelling in Microsoft Office programs* area. The *Custom Dictionaries* dialog box opens.
 e. Select **RoamingCustom.dic** in the *Dictionary List*. If this dictionary is not available, select the available custom dictionary.
 f. Click the **Edit Word List** button. The *RoamingCustom.dic* dialog box opens (Figure 1-75).
 g. Type your last name in the *Word(s)* area and click the **Add** button. If your last name is already in the dictionary, the *Add* button is shaded gray.
 h. Click **OK** to close the *RoamingCustom.dic* dialog box.
 i. Click **OK** to close the *Custom Dictionaries* dialog box.
 j. Click **OK** to close the *Word Options* dialog box.

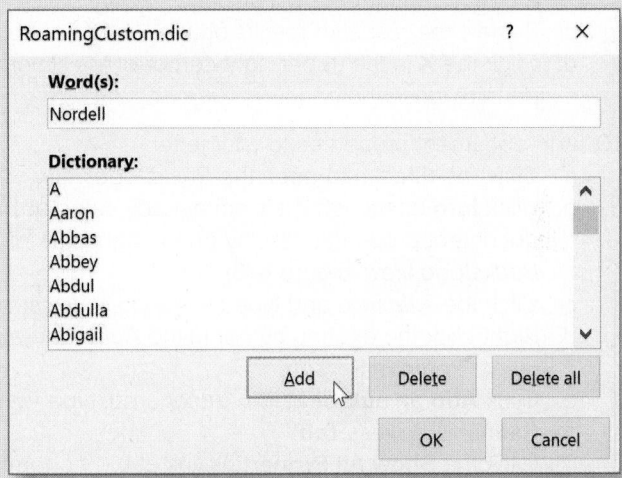

Figure 1-75 Add a word to the custom dictionary

8. Spell and grammar check the document.
 a. Right-click the word "**wholehouse**" in the second paragraph. A context list of words appears (Figure 1-76).
 b. Select "**whole house**." The correctly spelled word replaces the incorrectly spelled word.
 c. Place your insertion point at the beginning of the document or press **Ctrl+Home**.
 d. Click the **Spelling & Grammar** button [*Review* tab, *Proofing* group] or press **F7** to open the *Editor* pane on the right (Figure 1-77).
 Office 2019 Note: This pane is labeled **Proofing** rather than *Editor* in Office 2019 and some features may differ slightly.
 e. Click "**truss**" in the *Suggestions* area in *Editor* pane to replace the misspelled word.

Figure 1-76 Correct spelling using the context menu

f. Continue spell checking the remainder of the document. Change "granate" to **granite** and "you're" to **your**."

g. Click **Add to Dictionary** for "Cavalli" if it is marked as incorrect.

h. Click **Ignore Once** for your reference initials if it is marked as incorrect.

i. Click **OK** to close the dialog box that opens and informs you that the spelling and grammar check is complete. The *Editor* pane closes.

9. Use *Smart Lookup* to research selected words.

a. Select "**Transfer Disclosure Statement**" in the third body paragraph.

b. Click the **Smart Lookup** button [*References* tab, *Research*]. The *Smart Lookup* pane opens on the right. If you are using this feature for the first time, you may receive a message about privacy and must click the **Got it** button before data will display.

c. Review the research results on the *Smart Lookup* pane.

d. Click the **X** in the upper-right corner of the *Smart Lookup* pane to close the pane.

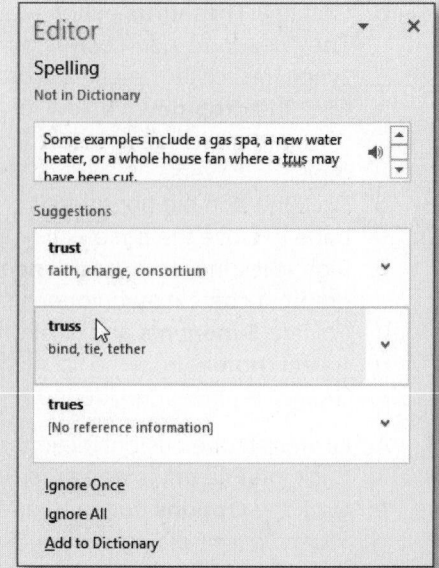

Figure 1-77 *Editor* pane

10. Add document properties to your letter.

a. Click the **File** tab to open the *Backstage* view.

b. Click **Info** on the left if it is not already selected. The document properties display on the right side of the *Backstage* view (Figure 1-78).

c. Click the *Title* field and type Disclosure Statement.

d. Right-click the existing author in the *Author* area and select **Remove Person**.

e. Click **Add an author** in the *Author* area, type Emma Cavalli, and press **Tab**.

f. Click the **Show All Properties** link at the bottom. Additional document properties display.

g. Click the *Company* area and type Placer Hills Real Estate.

h. Click the **Properties** drop-down list at the top of the *Properties* area and choose **Advanced Properties**. The document properties display in the *Summary* tab of the *Properties* dialog box.

i. Type Real Estate in the *Subject* text box.

j. Click **OK** to close the *Properties* dialog box and click the **Back** arrow to return to the document.

11. Use the *Read Aloud* feature.

a. Place your insertion point at the beginning of the first body paragraph ("Please read each paragraph. . .").

b. Click the **Read Aloud** button [*Review* tab, *Speech* group]. Word begins reading the first paragraph and the *Read Aloud* controls display at the left.

c. Click the **Pause** button in the *Read Aloud* controls.

d. Click the **Settings** button and change the **Reading speed** and **Voice Selection** as desired (Figure 1-79).

e. Press **Esc** to close the *Settings* menu.

f. Click the **Next** button to skip to the next paragraph.

g. Click the **Stop** button to stop the reading and close the *Read Aloud* controls.

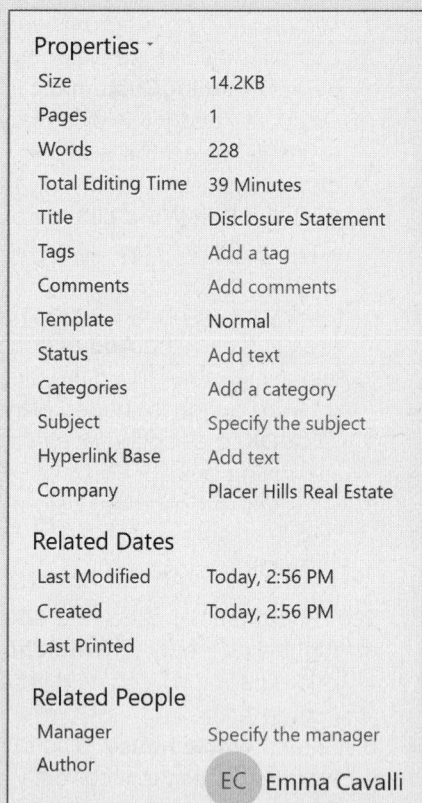

Figure 1-78 Document properties on the *Backstage* view

Play/Pause Next Settings Stop

Reading speed

Voice Selection

Microsoft Zira

Figure 1-79 *Read Aloud controls*

Figure 1-80 *Learning Tools*

12. Use the *Learning Tools*.
 a. Click the **Learning Tools** button [*View* tab, *Immersive* group]. The *Immersive Learning Tools* contextual tab displays.
 b. Click the **Column Width** button [*Immersive Learning Tools* tab, *Learning Tools* group] and select **Moderate** to change the display width.
 c. Click the **Page Color** button and select **Inverse**.
 d. Click the **Text Spacing** button if necessary to display wide spacing. This button toggles between wide and normal spacing.
 e. Click the **Syllables** button to display a space between syllables in words (Figure 1-80).
 f. Click the **Close Learning Tools** button [*Immersive Learning Tools* tab, *Close* group] to close the *Learning Tools* view and return to your document.
13. Save and close the document (Figure 1-81).

September·1,·2020¶

¶

David·and·Sharon·Wing ↵
4685·Orange·Grove·Road ↵
Rocklin,·CA·97725¶

Dear·Mr.·and·Mrs.·Wing:¶

SUBJECT:·Disclosure·Statement¶

Please·read·each·paragraph·before·signing·the·disclosure·statement·documents.·As·you·fill-out·the·required·disclosure·packet,·it·is·critical·to·the·transmission·of·sale·that·you·give·as·much·information·as·possible·about·your·home,·no·matter·how·small·or·insignificant.·Please·use·additional·paper·if·necessary·and·make·a·notation·to·that·fact.¶

Make·note·on·the·disclosure·statement·if·you·have·had·any·work·done·with·or·without·permits.·Some·examples·include·a·gas·spa,·a·new·water·heater,·or·a·whole·house·fan·where·a·truss·may·have·been·cut.·If·you·had·granite·counters·installed,·that·does·not·require·a·permit.¶

If·there·is·information·about·the·neighborhood·or·neighbors·that·you·as·a·buyer·would·want·to·know·about,·be·sure·to·divulge·that·information.·Be·sure·to·address·those·types·of·questions·on·the·Real·Estate·Transfer·Disclosure·Statement,·item·#11·on·page·2.¶

Please·complete·the·enclosed·disclosure·statement·by·September·8,·2020·and·return·it·to·me.·As·always,·if·you·have·any·questions·or·concerns,·please·call·me·at·916-450-3334·or·email·me·at·ecavalli@phre.com.·Best·wishes·and·thank·you·for·your·business.¶

Best·regards,¶

¶

EMMA·CAVALLI ↵
Realtor·Consultant ↵
Placer·Hills·Real·Estate¶

rn ↵
Enclosure¶

Figure 1-81 PP W1-3 completed

Chapter Summary

1.1 Create, save, and open a Word document (p. W1-3).

- New Word documents are based on the **Normal template** (*Normal.dotm*).
- Save documents with the existing file name or with a different file name.
- **AutoSave** automatically saves documents saved in *OneDrive*.
- A **Word document** (**.docx**) is the standard file format. Word documents can be saved in a variety of file formats.
- Open, edit, and save existing Word documents.

1.2 Customize a document by entering and selecting text, using word wrap, and using *AutoComplete*, *AutoCorrect*, and *AutoFormat* features (p. W1-7).

- **Word wrap** automatically wraps text to the next line as you reach the right margin of the document.
- The **Show/Hide** button displays formatting symbols in the document to enable properly and consistently formatted documents.
- Select text in a variety of ways: select individual words, an entire line, multiple lines of text, a sentence, a paragraph, multiple paragraphs, or the entire document.
- **AutoComplete** automatically completes a day, month, or date when entering text.
- **AutoCorrect** automatically corrects commonly misspelled words and capitalization errors.
- **AutoFormat** automatically controls the formatting of items such as numbered and bulleted lists.
- Add, delete, and edit *AutoCorrect* entries and customize *AutoCorrect* options in Word.

1.3 Enhance a document using paragraph breaks, line breaks, spaces, and non-breaking spaces (p. W1-10).

- The **Enter** key on the keyboard inserts a **paragraph break**. Click the *Show/Hide* button to display the **paragraph symbol**.
- **Line breaks** control breaks between lines or sentences to retain paragraph formatting between lines.
- **Non-breaking spaces** keep related words together.

1.4 Edit a document using cut, copy, paste, the *Clipboard*, and the undo, redo, and repeat features (p. W1-15).

- Word provides a variety of methods to **cut**, **copy**, and **paste** text in a document.
- The **Clipboard** stores cut or copied text. Use the *Clipboard* to paste text into a document.
- Use **Undo**, **Redo**, and **Repeat** when working on a document. These features are available on the **Quick Access toolbar**.

1.5 Customize a document using different fonts, font sizes, and attributes (p. W1-18).

- **Serif** and **sans serif** are the two main categories of **fonts**.
- Fonts are measured in **points** (pt.). Most documents use between 10 and 12 pt. font size.
- Change fonts and font size for specific text or the entire document.
- **Bold**, **Italic**, and **Underline** are font styles.
- Other font effects include **Strikethrough**, **Subscript**, **Superscript**, **Small caps**, and **All caps**.
- Change the case of text in Word using the **Change Case** button or the **Font** dialog box.
- The **Font dialog box** provides many **font**, **size**, **style**, and **effect options**.
- Modify the **scale**, **spacing**, **position**, and **kerning** of selected text using the **Advanced** tab in the *Font* dialog box.
- The **Format Painter** applies formatting from selected text to other text.
- The **Clear Formatting** feature removes all formatting applied to selected text.
- Change the **default** font and font size in Word by opening the *Font* dialog box.

1.6 Enhance a document using text alignment and line and paragraph spacing (p. W1-28).

- **Paragraph alignment** describes how text is aligned horizontally between the margins of a document: **Left**, **Center**, **Right**, or **Justified**.
- **Line spacing** refers to the amount of blank space between lines of text in a paragraph.
- **Paragraph spacing** is the amount of space between paragraphs. Paragraph spacing is measured in points.

- Modify alignment, line spacing, and paragraph spacing on the *Home* or *Layout* tab or in the **Paragraph dialog box**.
- Change the default line and paragraph spacing in Word by opening the *Paragraph* dialog box.

1.7 Finalize a document using Word's research, proofing, and learning tools (p. W1-32).

- **Smart Lookup** is used to research selected word(s) without leaving Word. Research results display in the **Smart Lookup pane**.
- Word automatically checks documents for **spelling** and **grammatical errors**.
- Word marks potential spelling, incorrect word, or grammatical errors with a colored line under the words. Correct errors by selecting options in the context menu.
- Manually spell and grammar check a document using the *Editor* pane.
- Customize the **Word dictionary** by adding, deleting, or modifying words in the word list.
- Use the **Thesaurus** to find synonyms for words in your document.

- Word includes a **Word Count** feature.
- The **Read Aloud** feature reads text in a document.
- **Learning Tools** enables users to change page width, page color, text spacing; view spaces between syllables in words; and use the *Read Aloud* feature.

1.8 Apply custom document properties to a document (p. W1-38).

- Add **document properties**, such as *Title*, *Author*, *Company*, *Subject*, *Created*, and *Last Modified*.
- Add document properties on the *Backstage* view or in the *Properties* dialog box.

Check for Understanding

The SIMbook for this text (within your SIMnet account) provides the following resources for concept review:

- Multiple-choice questions
- Short answer questions
- Matching exercises

Guided Project 1-1

In this project, Jennie Owings at Central Sierra Insurance writes a business letter to Hartford Specialty regarding the renewal of the insurance policy for Valley Custom Manufacturing. This business letter appears in block format and uses open punctuation. See *Appendix B* (online resource) for examples of business document formats and mixed and open punctuation.
[Student Learning Outcomes 1.1, 1.2, 1.3, 1.4, 1.5, 1.6, 1.7, 1.8]

File Needed: ***ValleyCustomManufacturing-01.docx*** *(Student data files are available in the* Library *of your* SIMnet *account.)*
Completed Project File Name: *[your initials]* **Word 1-1.docx**

Skills Covered in This Project

- Add document properties.
- Use block business letter format using open punctuation.
- Change line spacing.
- Change paragraph spacing.
- Use *AutoComplete*.
- Use paragraph breaks for proper spacing between the parts of a business letter.

- Copy and paste text from another document using the *Clipboard*.
- Use *Show/Hide*.
- Undo automatic capitalization.
- Change font size.
- Apply font styles.
- Use *Smart Lookup*.
- Use spelling and grammar checker.
- Add words to the dictionary.

1. Open a new Word document.
 a. Click the **File** tab to open the *Backstage* view.
 b. Click **New** on the left and click **Blank document**. You can also click **Blank document** from the *Start* page when you first open Word.

2. Save the document as *[your initials]* **Word 1-1**.
 a. Click the **File** tab to open the *Backstage* view and select **Save As** on the left.
 b. Click **Browse** to open the *Save As* dialog box and select the desired location to save the file.
 c. Change the file name to [your initials] Word 1-1.
 d. Click **Save** to rename the document and close the *Save As* dialog box.

3. Add document properties.
 a. Click the **File** tab to open *Backstage* view and click the **Info** button on the left if it is not already selected.
 b. Click the **Show All Properties** link at the bottom of the *Properties* area.
 c. Type Valley Custom Manufacturing in the *Title* field.
 d. Type Central Sierra Insurance in the *Company* field.
 e. Click the **Back** arrow in the upper left of the *Backstage* view to return to the document.

4. Change the line and paragraph spacing of the document.
 a. Click the **Paragraph** launcher [*Home* or *Layout* tab, *Paragraph* group] to open the *Paragraph* dialog box (Figure 1-82).
 b. Change the *Line spacing* to **Single**.
 c. Change the *After* paragraph spacing to **0 pt**.
 d. Choose **OK** to close the *Paragraph* dialog box.

5. Use *AutoComplete* to type a date.
 a. Turn on **Show/Hide** [*Home* tab, *Paragraph* group] if it is not already turned on.
 b. Type the current date using month, day, year format (September 1, 2020). As you begin typing the date, *AutoComplete* completes the month and current date. Press **Enter** to accept the *AutoComplete* date.
 c. Press **Enter** four times (quadruple space) after the date.

6. Type the inside address, salutation, and subject line.
 a. Type Mrs. Cammie Speckler and press **Enter** once at the end of the line.
 b. Type Hartford Specialty and press **Enter** once.
 c. Type 4788 Market Street, Suite A205 and press **Enter** once.
 d. Type San Francisco, CA 95644 and press **Enter** two times.
 e. Type Dear Mrs. Speckler as the salutation and press **Enter** two times. No colon is used after the salutation when using open punctuation.
 f. Type RE: Valley Custom Manufacturing as the subject line and press **Enter** two times.

Figure 1-82 *Paragraph* dialog box

7. Copy text from another document and paste it into the current document.
 a. Click the **File** to open the *Backstage* view and select **Open** at the left.
 b. Click the **Browse** button to open the *Open* dialog box.
 c. Locate and select the ***ValleyCustomManufacturing-01*** document from your student data files and click **Open**. If the document opens in *Protected View*, click the **Enable Editing** button.
 d. Press **Ctrl+A** to select the entire document.
 e. Click the **Copy** button [*Home* tab, *Clipboard* group] or press **Ctrl+C**.
 f. Close ***ValleyCustomManufacturing-01*** without saving the document.
 g. Return to the *[your initials] Word 1-1* document and place your insertion point on the last blank line of the document.
 h. Click the **Clipboard** launcher [*Home* tab, *Clipboard* group] to open the *Clipboard* pane (Figure 1-83).
 i. Click the **drop-down arrow** to the right of the copied text in the *Clipboard* and click **Paste**. The paragraphs of text are pasted in the body of the document.
 j. Click the **X** in the upper-right corner of the *Clipboard* pane to close it.

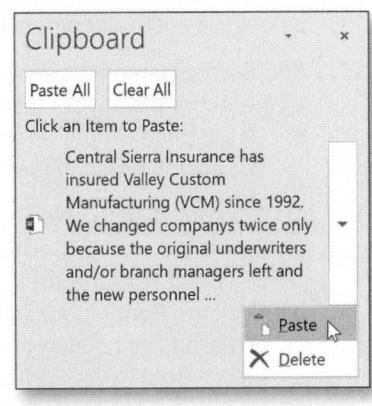

Figure 1-83 Paste from the *Clipboard*

8. Use the *Format Painter* to format the inserted paragraphs.
 a. Place your insertion point on the first line of the document (date line).
 b. Click the **Format Painter** button [*Home* tab, *Clipboard* group] to turn on the *Format Painter*.
 c. Select the five body paragraphs of the letter to apply the formatting (Figure 1-84).

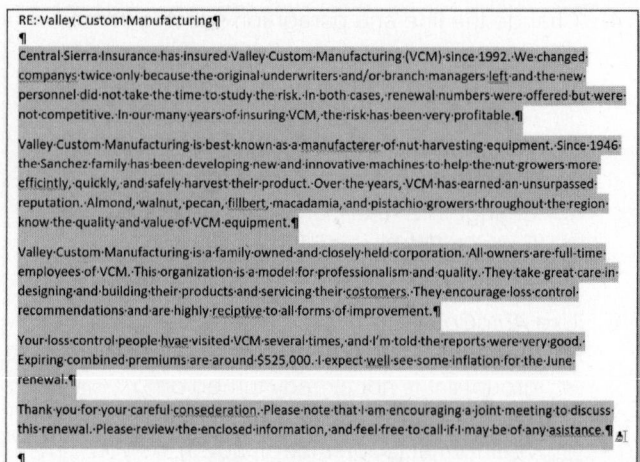

Figure 1-84 Use the *Format Painter* to copy formatting

9. Insert a blank line between each of the body paragraphs.
 a. Place your insertion point at the end of the first body paragraph and press **Enter**. A paragraph symbol marks the end of each paragraph.
 b. Press **Enter** after each of the remaining body paragraphs including the last body paragraph.

10. Enter the closing lines of the document.
 a. Place your insertion point on the last blank line below the body of the letter.
 b. Type Sincerely and press **Enter** four times. Type Jennie Owings, Vice President and press **Enter**.
 c. Type Central Sierra Insurance and press **Enter** two times.
 d. Type your reference initials (your first and last initials in lowercase letters with no punctuation).
 e. Press **Enter**. *AutoCorrect* automatically capitalizes the first letter of your reference initials.
 f. Click the **AutoCorrect Options** smart tag (Figure 1-85). The *AutoCorrect Options* smart tag appears when you place your pointer below your reference initials.

Figure 1-85 *AutoCorrect Options* smart tag

 g. Select **Undo Automatic Capitalization** to undo the automatic capitalization of your reference initials.
 h. Place your insertion point on the blank line below your reference initials and type Enclosure as an enclosure notation.

11. Select the entire document (**Ctrl+A**) and change the font size to **10 pt**. [*Home* tab, *Font* group].

12. Add *Before* paragraph spacing to the date line.
 a. Select or place your insertion point in the date line.
 b. Change the *Before* spacing to **72 pt**. [*Layout* tab, *Paragraph* group] (Figure 1-86).

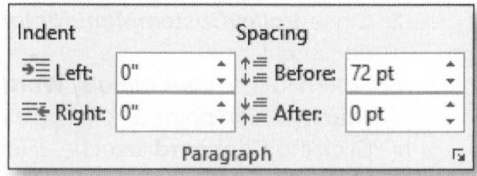

Figure 1-86 Change *Before* paragraph spacing on the date line

13. Apply a font style to selected text.
 a. Select the words "**Central Sierra Insurance**" in the first body paragraph.
 b. Click the **Font** launcher [*Home* tab, *Font* group] to open the *Font* dialog box.
 c. Select **Bold** in the *Font style* area, check the **Small caps** box in the **Effects** area, and click **OK** to close the *Font* dialog box.
 d. Select the words "**Valley Custom Manufacturing (VCM)**" in the first body paragraph.
 e. Click the **Bold** button [*Home* tab, *Font* group] or press **Ctrl+B**.

14. Use *Smart Lookup* to research selected words.
 a. Select "**harvesting equipment**" in the second body paragraph.
 b. Click the **Smart Lookup** button [*References* tab, *Research* group]. The *Smart Lookup* pane opens on the right.
 c. Review the research results on the *Smart Lookup* pane.
 d. Click the **X** in the upper-right corner of the *Smart Lookup* pane to close the pane.

15. Spell and grammar check the entire document.
 a. Place your insertion point at the top of the document (or press **Ctrl+Home**).
 b. Click the **Spelling & Grammar** button [*Review* tab, *Proofing* group]. The *Editor* pane opens at the right (Figure 1-87).

 Office 2019 Note: This pane is labeled ***Proofing*** rather than *Editor* in Office 2019 and some features may differ slightly.

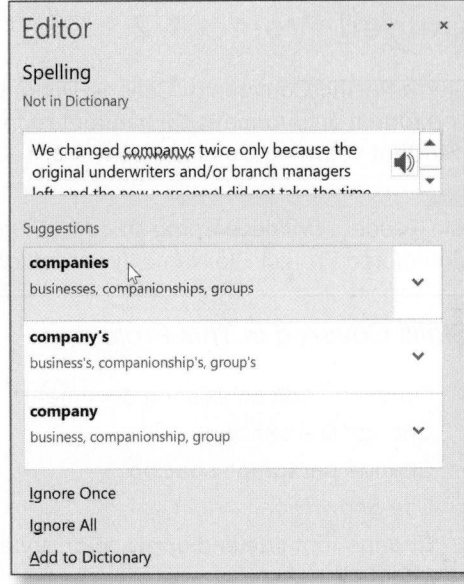

Figure 1-87 Select correct word from the *Editor* pane

 c. Add "Cammie" and "Speckler" to the dictionary if they are marked as potential spelling errors. Click **Add to Dictionary** to add each name.
 d. Select the correct word in the *Editor* pane for the remaining spelling and grammatical errors (see Figure 1-87).
 e. Continue checking the document from the beginning if prompted. Choose **Yes**.
 f. Click **Ignore Once** if your reference initials are marked as a potential spelling or grammatical error.
 g. Click **OK** to close the dialog box that informs you the spelling and grammar check is complete.

16. Save and close the document (Figure 1-88).

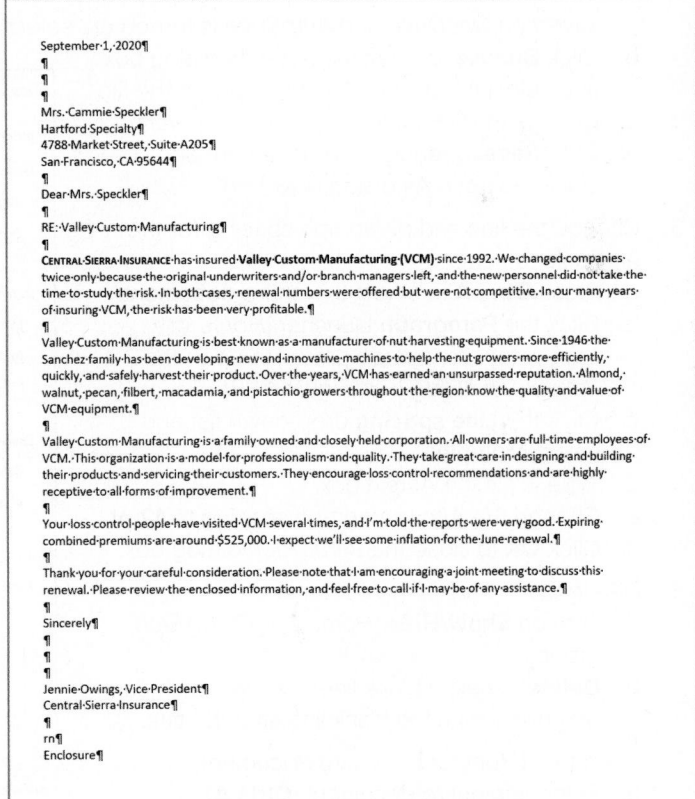

Figure 1-88 Word 1-1 completed

Guided Project 1-2

Sierra Pacific Community College District is a multi-campus community college district. In this project, you format an informational handout regarding online learning.
[Student Learning Outcomes 1.1, 1.2, 1.3, 1.4, 1.5, 1.6, 1.7, 1.8]

File Needed: ***OnlineLearning-01.docx*** *(Student data files are available in the* Library *of your SIMnet account.)*
Completed Project File Name: ***[your initials] Word 1-2.docx***

Skills Covered in This Project

- Open and edit an existing document.
- Change line spacing.
- Change paragraph spacing.
- Use *Show/Hide.*
- Change font size and apply color, styles, and effects.

- Cut and paste to move a paragraph.
- Use drag and drop to move a paragraph.
- Apply a shadow text effect.
- Use the *Format Painter.*
- Use spelling and grammar checker.
- Use *Read Aloud.*
- Add document properties.

1. Open the ***OnlineLearning-01*** document from your student data files.
 a. Click the **File** tab to open the *Backstage* view and click **Open** on the left.
 b. Click **Browse** to open the *Open* dialog box.
 c. Browse to locate the ***OnlineLearning-01*** document, select the document, and click **Open**. If the document opens in *Protected View*, click the **Enable Editing** button.

2. Save the document as *[your initials] Word 1-2.*
 a. Click the **File** tab to open the *Backstage* view and select **Save As** on the left. If your document is saved on *OneDrive* and *AutoSave* is turned on, select **Save a Copy**.
 b. Click **Browse** to open the *Save As* dialog box and select the desired location to save the file.
 c. Change the file name to [your initials] Word 1-2.
 d. Click **Save** to rename the document and close the *Save As* dialog box.

3. Change the line and paragraph spacing for the entire document.
 a. Press **Ctrl+A** to select the entire document.
 b. Click the **Paragraph** launcher [*Home* or *Layout* tab, *Paragraph* group] to open the *Paragraph* dialog box (Figure 1-89).
 c. Click the **Line spacing** drop-down list and select **Multiple**.
 d. Type 1.2 in the *At* text box.
 e. Change the *After* paragraph spacing to **12 pt**.
 f. Click **OK** to close the *Paragraph* dialog box.

4. Delete blank lines in the document.
 a. Turn on **Show/Hide** [*Home* tab, *Paragraph* group].
 b. **Delete** the extra blank line between each paragraph including the blank line after the title.

5. Change the font for the entire document.
 a. Select the entire document (**Ctrl+A**).
 b. Change the font to **Cambria** [*Home* tab, *Font* group].

Figure 1-89 Change *Line spacing* and *After* paragraph spacing

6. Change the paragraph spacing, alignment, font size, styles, effects, and color of the title.
 a. Select the title of the document ("**Online Learning Information**").
 b. Click the **Layout** tab.
 c. Change the *Before* spacing to **36 pt**. and the *After* spacing to **18 pt**. [*Paragraph* group].
 d. Click the **Center** button [*Home* tab, *Paragraph* group].
 e. Click the **Font** launcher [*Home* tab, *Font* group]. The *Font* dialog box opens (Figure 1-90).
 f. Change the *Font* style to **Bold** and change the *Font Size* to **24**.
 g. Click the **Small caps** check box in the *Effects* area.
 h. Click the **Font color** drop-down list and choose the **fourth color** in the **first row** of the *Theme Colors* (**Blue-Gray**, **Text 2**).
 i. Click the **Advanced** tab.
 j. Click the **Spacing** drop-down list and select **Expanded**. Change the *By* to **1.2 pt**.
 k. Click **OK** to close the *Font* dialog box.

Figure 1-90 Change font style, size, effects, and color

7. Move paragraphs in the document and insert a heading.
 a. Select the last paragraph in the document, including the paragraph mark at the end of the paragraph.
 b. Click the **Cut** button [*Home* tab, *Clipboard* group] or press **Ctrl+X**.
 c. Place your insertion point before the second line of the document ("Definition of Online Learning Modalities").
 d. Click the top half of the **Paste** button [*Home* tab, *Clipboard* group] or press **Ctrl+V**.
 e. Click at the beginning of the pasted paragraph and type Where Are We Now with Online Learning? and press **Enter**.
 f. Select the paragraph that begins "Hybrid Course:" including the paragraph mark at the end of the paragraph.
 g. Move this paragraph using the drag-and-drop method (click, hold, and drag) so it appears before the paragraph that begins with "Television or Tele-web Course:" (Figure 1-91).

Figure 1-91 Move paragraph using drag and drop

8. Format section headings in the document and use the *Format Painter*.
 a. Select the first section heading ("**Where Are We Now with Online Learning?**").
 b. Click the **Font** launcher [*Home* tab, *Font* group] to open the *Font* dialog box and click the **Font** tab if necessary (Figure 1-92).
 c. Change the font *Size* to **12 pt**.
 d. Change the *Font color* to the **fourth color** in the **first row** of the *Theme Colors* (**Blue-Gray, Text 2**).
 e. Change the *Underline style* to **Double underline**.
 f. Change the *Underline color* to the **fourth color** in the **first row** of the *Theme Colors* (**Blue-Gray, Text 2**).
 g. Click **OK** to close the *Font* dialog box.
 h. Confirm the formatted heading is still selected and click the **Text Effects and Typography** button [*Home* tab, *Font* group].
 i. Place your pointer on **Shadow** and select the **first option** in the *Outer* category (**Offset: Bottom Right**) (Figure 1-93).
 j. Confirm the formatted heading still selected and click the **Format Painter** button [*Home* tab, *Clipboard* group].
 k. Select the next heading ("**Definition of Online Learning Modalities**") to apply the formatting.

9. Format paragraph headings in the document.
 a. Select the first paragraph heading ("**Online Course:**"), including the colon.
 b. Click the **Font** launcher [*Home* tab, *Font* group] to open the *Font* dialog box.
 c. Change the *Font style* to **Bold**.
 d. Change the *Font color* to the **fourth color** in the **first row** of the *Theme Colors* (**Blue-Gray, Text 2**).
 e. Click the **Small caps** check box in the *Effects* area.
 f. Click **OK** to close the *Font* dialog box.

10. Use the *Format Painter* to copy formatting to the other paragraph headings.
 a. Select the "**Online Course:**" heading if necessary and double click the **Format Painter** button.
 b. Select the other paragraph headings ("**Hybrid Course:**", "**Television or Tele-web Course:**", and "**web-Enhanced Course:**") to apply the formatting.
 c. Click the **Format Painter** button again to turn off the *Format Painter*.

11. Correct spelling and grammar in the document using the context menu.
 a. Right-click the first misspelled word ("**managment**") and choose the correct spelling from the list of options.
 b. Repeat this process for "**potion**."
 c. Click **Ignore All** or **Ignore Once** if other words are marked as potentially incorrect.

Figure 1-92 Format heading using the *Font* dialog box

Figure 1-93 Apply *Shadow* text effect

12. Select the sentence in parentheses at the end of the document, including the parentheses, and click the **Italic** button [*Home* tab, *Font* group] or press **Ctrl+I**.

13. Use the *Read Aloud* feature.

a. Place your insertion point at the beginning of the first body paragraph ("SPCCD was a pioneer. . .").

b. Click the **Read Aloud** button [*Review* tab, *Speech* group]. Word begins reading the first paragraph and the *Read Aloud* controls display at the left.

c. Click the **Pause** button in the *Read Aloud* controls.

d. Click the **Settings** button and change the **Reading speed** and **Voice Selection** as desired (Figure 1-94).

e. Press **Esc** to close the *Settings* menu.

f. Click the **Next** button to skip to the next paragraph.

g. Click the **Stop** button to stop the reading and close the *Read Aloud* controls.

Figure 1-94 *Read Aloud* controls

14. Add document properties using the *Properties* dialog box.

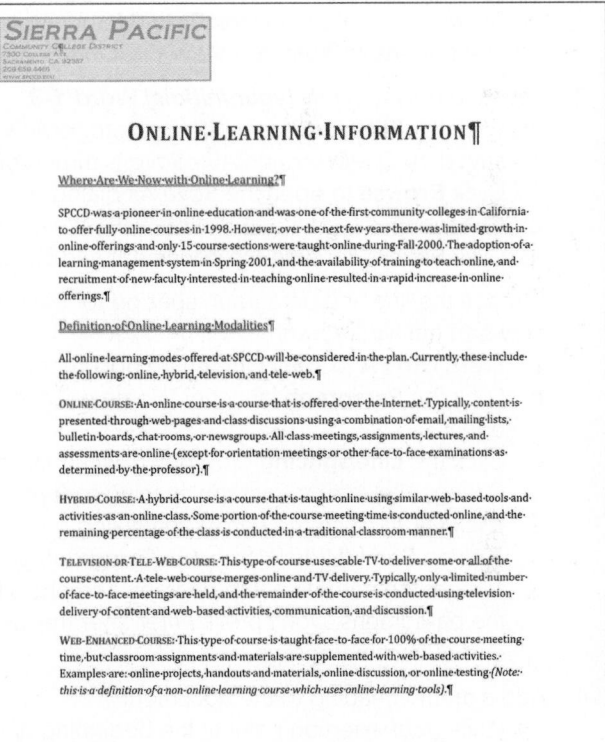

a. Click the **File** tab to open the *Backstage* view and click the **Info** button if it is not already selected.

b. Click the **Properties** button on the right and choose **Advanced Properties**. The *Properties* dialog box opens.

c. Click the **Summary** tab if necessary.

d. Type Online Learning Information in the *Title* text box.

e. Type Online Learning in the *Subject* text box.

f. Delete the existing author name in the *Author* area and type Tanesha Morris as the author.

g. Click **OK** to accept changes and close the *Properties* dialog box.

h. Click the **Back** arrow in the upper left of the *Backstage* view to return to the document.

15. Save and close the document (Figure 1-95).

Figure 1-95 Word 1-2 completed

Guided Project 1-3

In this project, you create a memo for American River Cycling Club about using heart rate to increase the effectiveness of training. See *Appendix B* (online resource) for examples of business document formats. [**Student Learning Outcomes 1.1, 1.2, 1.3, 1.5, 1.6, 1.7, 1.8**]

File Needed: ***HeartRate-01.docx*** *(Student data files are available in the* Library *of your SIMnet account.)*
Completed Project File Name: ***[your initials] Word 1-3.docx***

Skills Covered in This Project

- Open and edit an existing document.
- Change line spacing.
- Change paragraph spacing.
- Use *Show/Hide*.
- Add a memo heading to a document.
- Change paragraph alignment.

- Change font size and apply styles and effects.
- Use the *Format Painter*.
- Add text highlight color.
- Use non-breaking space.
- Use *Thesaurus*.
- Add words to the dictionary.
- Add document properties.

1. Open the ***HeartRate-01*** document from your student data files.
 a. Click the **File** tab to open the *Backstage* view and click **Open** on the left.
 b. Click **Browse** to open the *Open* dialog box.
 c. Browse to locate the ***HeartRate-01*** document, select the document, and click **Open**. If the document opens in *Protected View*, click the **Enable Editing** button.

2. Save the document as ***[your initials] Word 1-3.***
 a. Click the **File** tab to open the *Backstage* view and select **Save As** on the left. If your document is saved on *OneDrive* and *AutoSave* is turned on, select **Save a Copy**.
 b. Click **Browse** to open the *Save As* dialog box and select the desired location to save the file.
 c. Change the file name to [your initials] Word 1-3.
 d. Click **Save** to rename the document and close the *Save As* dialog box.

3. Change the line and paragraph spacing for the entire document and insert a paragraph break between each paragraph.
 a. Press **Ctrl+A** to select the entire document.
 b. Click the **Paragraph** launcher [*Home* or *Layout* tab, *Paragraph* group]. The *Paragraph* dialog box opens.
 c. Click the **Line spacing** drop-down list and select **Single**.
 d. Change the *After* paragraph spacing to **0 pt**.
 e. Click **OK** to close the *Paragraph* dialog box.
 f. Turn on **Show/Hide** [*Home* tab, *Paragraph* group] if it is not already on.
 g. Click at the end of each paragraph and press **Enter** once to add a blank line between each of the paragraphs. Don't press *Enter* after the last body paragraph. A paragraph symbol marks the end of each paragraph.

4. Add a memo heading to the document.
 a. Place your insertion point at the beginning of the first paragraph ("What is Maximum Heart Rate?") and press **Enter**.
 b. Place the insertion point on the blank line above the first paragraph.
 c. Type TO: and press **Tab** two times.
 d. Type All ARCC Club Members and press **Enter** two times.
 e. Type FROM: and press **Tab** two times.
 f. Type Taylor Mathos, ARCC Coach and press **Enter** two times.
 g. Type DATE: and press **Tab** two times.
 h. Type the current date in month, day, year format (January 1, 2020) and press **Enter** two times.
 i. Type SUBJECT: and press **Tab** once.
 j. Type Heart Rate Training and press **Enter** two times.

5. Change the paragraph alignment and font styles of selected text.
 a. Select the second and third paragraphs in the body of the memo (beginning with "**220 – Your Age . . .**" and ending with "**. . . heart rate is 180.)**"), including the paragraph mark at the end of the third paragraph.

b. Click the **Center** button [*Home* tab, *Paragraph* group] or press **Ctrl+E**.
c. Select the paragraph beginning "**220 – Your Age . . .**" and click the **Bold** button [*Home* tab, *Font* group] or press **Ctrl+B**.
d. Select the next paragraph and click the **Italic** button [*Home* tab, *Font* group] or press **Ctrl+I**.
e. **Delete** the blank line between the second and third paragraphs (Figure 1-96).

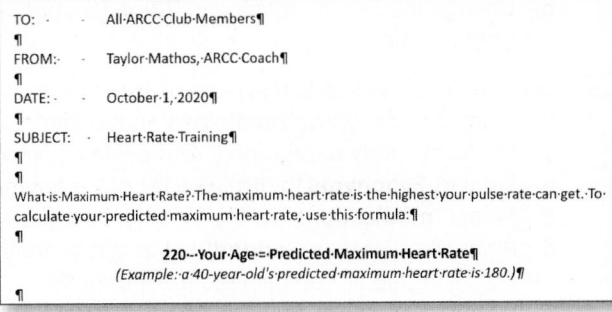

Figure 1-96 Memo heading added and paragraphs formatted

6. Change the font and style of selected text.
a. Press **Ctrl+A** to select the entire document.
b. Click the **Increase Font Size** button [*Home* tab, *Font* group] to increase the font size to 12 pt. (Figure 1-97).
c. Select the words "**What is Maximum Heart Rate?**" in the first sentence of the first body paragraph.

Figure 1-97 *Increase Font Size* button

d. Click the **Font** launcher [*Home* tab, *Font* group] to open the *Font* dialog box (Figure 1-98).
e. Change the *Font style* to **Bold**.
f. Change the *Underline style* to **Words only**.
g. Change the *Underline color* to the **tenth color** in the **first row** of the *Theme Colors* (**Green, Accent 6**).
h. Select the **Small caps** check box in the *Effects* area.
i. Click **OK** to close the *Font* dialog box.
j. Select the text if necessary and click the **Format Painter** button [*Home* tab, *Clipboard* group].
k. Select the words "**Target Heart Rate Zone**" in the first sentence of the fifth paragraph in the body ("You gain the most benefits . . ."). The *Format Painter* applies the formatting to the selected words.
l. Select the last sentence of the fifth body paragraph ("**Do not exercise above 85 percent . . .**") including the period at the end of the second sentence.
m. Click the **Text Highlight Color** drop-down arrow [*Home* tab, *Font* group] (Figure 1-99) and select the **fourth option** in the **third row** (**Gray-25%**).

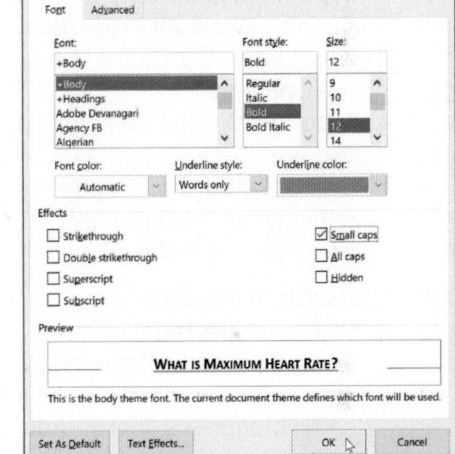

Figure 1-98 Change font style and effects

7. Use a non-breaking space to keep words together.
a. **Delete** the space between the words "Target" and "Heart" in the first sentence of the fifth paragraph in the body ("You gain the most benefits . . .").
b. Place your insertion point between these two words and press **Ctrl+Shift+Spacebar** to insert a non-breaking space. "Target" is wrapped to the next line so the words do not break between lines.
c. Delete the space between "80" and "percent" in the next sentence and press **Ctrl+Shift+Spacebar** to insert a non-breaking space.

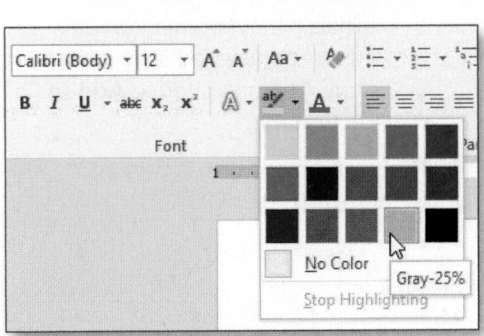

Figure 1-99 *Text Highlight Color* drop-down list

8. Add *Before* paragraph spacing to the first line of the memo heading.
a. Place the insertion point in the first line of the memo heading ("**TO: . . .**").

b. Change the *Before* spacing to **72 pt**. [*Layout* tab, *Paragraph* group].

9. Use the *Thesaurus* to find synonyms for selected words.
 a. Right-click the word "**medicines**" in the third sentence of the fourth body paragraph ("Your actual maximum . . .").
 b. Point to **Synonyms** to display a list of synonyms.
 c. Select "**medications**" as the synonym (Figure 1-100).
 d. Right-click the word "**added**" in the last sentence of the fifth paragraph ("You gain the most benefits . . .").
 e. Point to **Synonyms** and select "**additional**."

10. Add reference initials to the document.
 a. Click at the end of the last paragraph and press **Enter** two times.
 b. Type your reference initials in lowercase letters.

11. Add document properties.
 a. Click the **File** tab to open the *Backstage* view.
 b. Click the **Info** button if necessary to display the document properties on the right.
 c. Type Heart Rate Training in the *Title* text box.
 d. Right-click the existing author in the *Author* area and select **Remove Person**.
 e. Type Taylor Mathos in the *Author* text box.
 f. Click the **Show All Properties** link at the bottom of the document properties.
 g. Type ARCC in the *Company* text box.
 h. Click the **Back** arrow in the upper left of the *Backstage* view to return to the document.

12. Add words to the dictionary.
 a. Right-click "**Mathos**" in the second line of the memo heading if it is marked as a potential spelling error and choose **Add to Dictionary** from the context menu.
 b. Right-click your reference initials if they are marked as incorrectly spelled (red wavy underline) and choose **Add to Dictionary**.

13. Save and close the document (Figure 1-101).

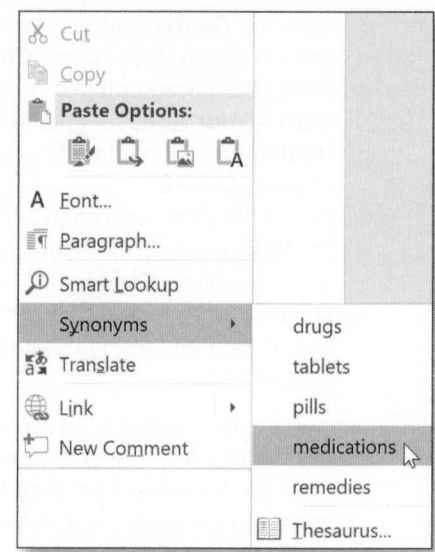

Figure 1-100 Select synonym from context menu

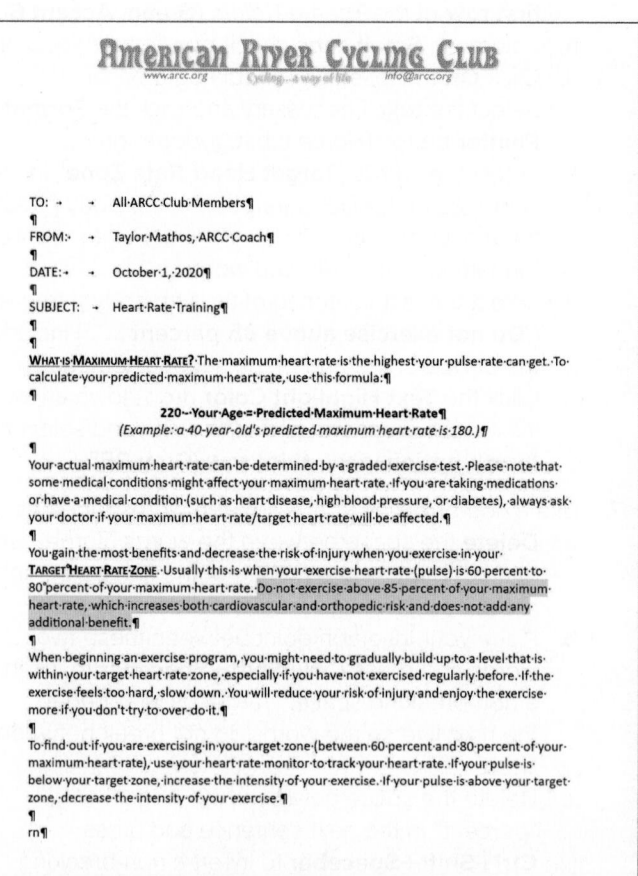

Figure 1-101 Word 1-3 completed

Independent Project 1-4

In this project, you format a business letter for Emma Cavalli to send to clients whose current home listings are expiring. See *Appendix B* (online resource) for examples of business document formats and mixed and open punctuation.
[Student Learning Outcomes 1.1, 1.2, 1.3, 1.4, 1.5, 1.6, 1.7, 1.8]

File Needed: ***ExpiredLetter-01.docx*** *(Student data files are available in the* Library *of your SIMnet account.)*
Completed Project File Name: ***[your initials] Word 1-4.docx***

Skills Covered in This Project

- Open and edit an existing document.
- Change line spacing.
- Change paragraph alignment and spacing.
- Change font and font size.
- Use *Show/Hide*.

- Format document as a block format business letter with mixed punctuation.
- Move text.
- Change font styles and effects.
- Use *Smart Lookup*.
- Use *Read Aloud*.
- Add document properties.
- Use spelling and grammar checker.

1. Open the ***ExpiredLetter-01*** document from your student data files. If the document opens in *Protected View*, click the **Enable Editing** button.

2. Save this document as ***[your initials] Word 1-4.***

3. Apply the following formatting changes to the entire document:
 a. Select the entire document.
 b. Change the *Before* and *After* paragraph spacing to **0 pt**.
 c. Change the line spacing to **Single**.
 d. Change the paragraph alignment to **Left**.
 e. Change the font and font size to **Calibri** and **11 pt**.

4. Turn on **Show/Hide** and press **Enter** at the end of each paragraph to add a blank line after each paragraph (including the last paragraph).

5. Type and format the opening lines of the business letter.
 a. Press **Ctrl+Home** or move your insertion point to the top of the document.
 b. Type the current date (use January 1, 2020 format) and press **Enter** four times.
 c. Type the following inside address and press **Enter** two times after the last line:

 Mr. Rick Hermann
 9035 Masi Drive
 Fair Oaks, CA 95528

 d. Type Dear Mr. Hermann: as the salutation and press **Enter** two times after the salutation. One blank line displays between the salutation and the body of the letter.
 e. Add **72 pt**. *Before* paragraph spacing to the date line.

6. Type the closing lines of the business letter.
 a. Place your insertion point on the blank line below the last body paragraph and press **Enter**.
 b. Type Best regards, and press **Enter** four times.
 c. Type the following closing lines:

 Emma Cavalli
 Realtor Consultant
 Placer Hills Real Estate

 d. Press **Enter** two times after the company name and type your reference initials in lowercase letters.

7. Move a paragraph and sentence.
 a. Move the third body paragraph so it appears before the second body paragraph. Confirm one blank line displays between each of the body paragraphs. If a blank space displays in front of the first word in the third paragraph, delete it.
 b. Move the last two sentences in the new second body paragraph ("A lot of detail . . .") to the beginning of the paragraph. Verify proper spacing displays between sentences.

8. Apply formatting to text in the business letter.
 a. Select "**Placer Hills Real Estate**" in the first body paragraph and apply **Bold** and **Small caps** formatting.
 b. Select the first sentence in the third paragraph including the period ("The service and experience . . .") and apply **Italic** formatting.
 c. Select the writer's name at the bottom and apply **Small caps** formatting.
 d. Select the writer's title and apply **Italic** formatting.
 e. Select the company name below the writer's title and apply **Bold** formatting.

9. Use *Smart Lookup* to research selected words.
 a. Select "**Fair Oaks**" in the first body paragraph.
 b. Click the **Smart Lookup** button [*References* tab, *Research* group]. The *Smart Lookup* pane opens on the right.
 c. Review the research results in the *Smart Lookup* pane.
 d. Click the **X** in the upper-right corner of the *Smart Lookup* pane to close the pane.

10. Use the **Read Aloud** feature [*Review* tab, *Speech* group] to read the first two body paragraphs.

11. Add the following document properties:
 a. *Title*: Expired Letter
 b. *Company*: Placer Hills Real Estate
 c. *Manager*: Kelsey Kroll
 d. *Author*: Emma Cavalli (right-click and choose **Remove Person** to remove existing author)

12. Spell and grammar check the entire document, apply changes where necessary, and ignore proper nouns.

13. Save and close the document (Figure 1-102).

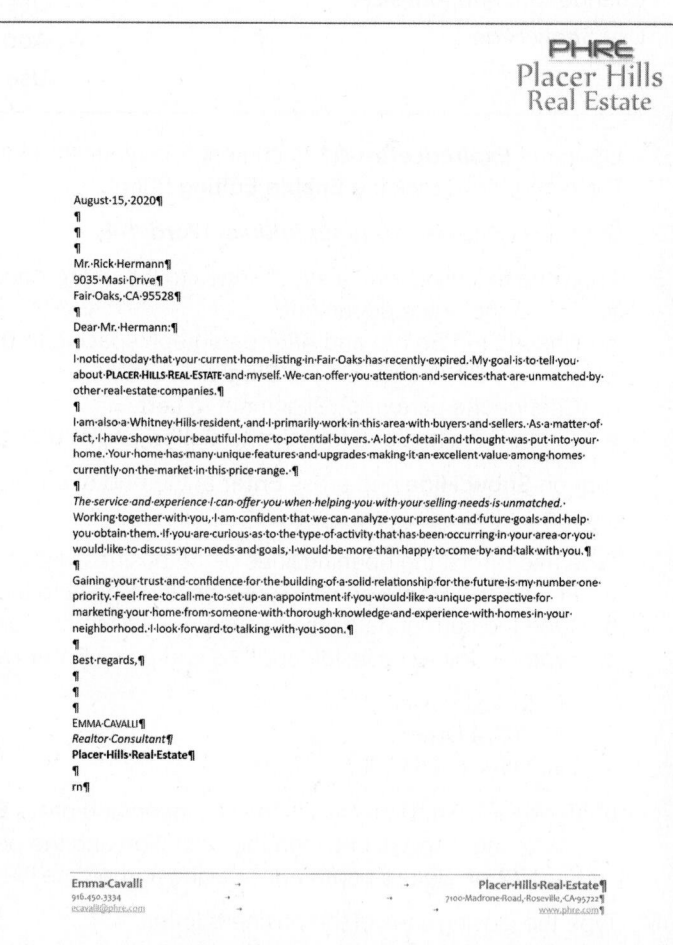

Figure 1-102 Word 1-4 completed

Independent Project 1-5

In this project, you combine information from different documents to create a memo for Sierra Pacific Community College District. This memo is a draft of the values statement for the district. See *Appendix B* (online resource) for examples of business document formats.
[Student Learning Outcomes 1.1, 1.2, 1.3, 1.4, 1.5, 1.6, 1.7, 1.8]

File Needed: ***ValuesStatement-01a.docx*** and ***ValuesStatement-01b.docx*** *(Student data files are available in the* Library *of your SIMnet account.)*
Completed Project File Name: *[your initials]* **Word 1-5.docx**

Skills Covered in This Project

- Open and edit an existing document.
- Change line spacing.
- Change paragraph spacing.
- Change font and font size.
- Use *Show/Hide*.

- Format a document as a memo.
- Use spelling and grammar checker.
- Change font styles and effects.
- Use the *Format Painter*.
- Move text.
- Add document properties.

1. Open the ***ValuesStatement-01a*** document from your student data files. If the document opens in *Protected View*, click the **Enable Editing** button.

2. Save this document as *[your initials]* **Word 1-5.**

3. Copy text from another document and paste it into the current document.
 a. Open the ***ValuesStatement-01b*** document from your student data files.
 b. Select and **copy** all the text in this document.
 c. Close the ***ValuesStatement-01b*** document without saving.
 d. Return to the *[your initials]* **Word 1-5** document.
 e. Place your insertion point at the end of the document and press **Enter**.
 f. **Paste** the copied text below the existing paragraphs.
 g. **Delete** the extra paragraph breaks between the first four paragraphs and at the end of the document.

4. Select the entire document and apply the following formatting changes:
 a. Change *After* paragraph spacing to **12 pt**.
 b. Change the line spacing to **1.15**.
 c. Change the font and font size to **Calibri** and **10 pt**.

5. Type and format the heading lines in the memorandum.
 a. Turn on **Show/Hide**.
 b. Place your insertion point at the beginning of the document and press **Enter**.
 c. Place your insertion point on the blank line at the beginning of the document and type the following memo information. Press **Tab** (once or twice) after the guidewords to align information at 1" and press **Enter** once at the end of each of the first three lines of the memo heading (don't press *Enter* after the SUBJECT line).

 TO: All SPCCD Faculty, Staff, and Managers
 FROM: Lanita Morrow, Chancellor
 DATE: type current date (use January 1, 2020 format)
 SUBJECT: Draft of SPCCD Values Statement

 d. Change the *Before* paragraph spacing on the "TO:" line of the memo heading to **24 pt**.
 e. Change the *After* paragraph spacing on the "SUBJECT:" line of the memo heading to **18 pt**.

6. Spell and grammar check the entire document.
 a. Add the chancellor's first and last names to the dictionary if they are marked as potential spelling errors.
 b. Correct other spelling and grammar errors as necessary.

7. Apply formatting to a paragraph heading and use the *Format Painter* to copy formatting.
 a. Select the first paragraph heading ("**Access**") in the body of the memo and apply the following formatting:

 > *Font style*: **Bold**
 > *Font color*: **Fourth color** in the **first row** of *Theme Colors* (**Blue-Gray, Text 2**)
 > *Underline*: **Double Underline**
 > *Underline color*: **Fourth color** in the **first row** of *Theme Colors* (**Blue-Gray, Text 2**)
 > *Effects*: **Small caps**

 b. Use the *Format Painter* to apply this formatting to each of the other paragraph headings in the body of the memo.

8. Move body paragraphs.
 a. Use cut and paste or drag and drop to move the body paragraphs so they are ordered alphabetically by paragraph heading. Exclude the first body paragraph ("Below is a draft . . ."). Be sure to include the paragraph symbol at the end of each paragraph when cutting or dragging.
 b. Verify that no extra *Enters* (paragraph marks) display after the last paragraph.
 c. Verify that no extra spaces display before the first word in each of the paragraphs.

9. Delete any extra blank lines at the end of the document so this document fits on one page if necessary.

10. Add the following document properties:
 a. *Title*: SPCCD Values Statement
 b. *Company*: Sierra Pacific Community College District
 c. *Author*: Yoon Soo Park (right-click and choose **Remove Person** to remove existing author)

11. Save and close the document (Figure 1-103).

Figure 1-103 Word 1-5 completed

Independent Project 1-6

In this project, you create a professional and appealing brochure for Emma Cavalli at Placer Hills Real Estate using formatting features in Word.
[Student Learning Outcomes 1.1, 1.2, 1.3, 1.4, 1.5, 1.6, 1.7, 1.8]

File Needed: ***Brochure-01.docx*** *(Student data files are available in the* Library *of your SIMnet account.)*
Completed Project File Name: *[your initials] **Word 1-6.docx***

Skills Covered in This Project

- Open and edit an existing document.
- Change font and font size.
- Change paragraph spacing.
- Change line spacing.
- Use *Show/Hide*.
- Change paragraph alignment.
- Change font styles and effects.
- Use the *Format Painter*.
- Move text.
- Use the thesaurus to find synonyms.
- Use *Smart Lookup*.
- Use *Read Aloud*.
- Add document properties.

1. Open the ***Brochure-01*** document from your student data files. If the document opens in *Protected View*, click the **Enable Editing** button.

2. Save this document as *[your initials] **Word 1-6.***

3. Select the entire document and apply the following formatting changes:
 a. Change the font and font size to **Cambria** and **10 pt**.
 b. Change the *After* paragraph spacing to **6 pt**.
 c. Change the line spacing to **Single**.

4. Apply formatting to the opening lines of the document.
 a. Select the first five lines of the document ("**Emma Cavalli**" to "**Email: ecavalli@phre.com**") and change the *After* paragraph spacing to **2 pt**.
 b. Select the first six lines of the document ("**Emma Cavalli**" to "**web: www.phre.com/ecavalli**") and **Center** these lines.
 c. Select the first line of the document ("**Emma Cavalli**") and apply the following changes:
 Font size: **12 pt**.
 Font style: **Bold**
 Font color: **tenth color** in the **last row** of *Theme Colors* (**Green, Accent 6, Darker 50%**)
 d. Select the second line of the document ("**Realtor Consultant**") and apply **Bold** formatting.
 e. Select the third line of the document ("**Putting Your Needs First**") and apply **Italic** formatting.

5. Apply formatting to a section heading and use the *Format Painter*.
 a. Select the first section heading, "**Personal Statement**," and apply **Bold**, **Underline**, and **Small Caps** formatting.
 b. Change the *Before* paragraph spacing to **12 pt**. and the *After* paragraph spacing to **3 pt**.
 c. Use the *Format Painter* to copy this formatting to the other section headings:

 "**Real Estate Experience**"
 "**Why I Am a Real Estate Agent**"
 "**What Clients are Saying**"
 "**Professional Credentials**"
 "**Education & Training**"

6. Turn on **Show/Hide** and combine the four sentences in the "Why I Am a Real Estate Agent" section into one paragraph. Delete paragraph marks and insert spaces as needed.

7. Apply the following changes in the "What Clients are Saying" section:
 a. Select the second paragraph ("It was a pleasure . . ."), apply **Italic**, and change the *After* spacing to **0 pt**.
 b. Select the source of the quote ("**-Rod & Luisa Ellisor, Rocklin, CA**") and right-align this text.
 c. Repeat the above two steps for the second quote ("Emma is conscientious . . .") and the source of the quote ("-Jon & Robin Anderson . . .").

8. Move the third section heading and the paragraph below it ("Why I Am a Real Estate Agent") so it appears before the second section ("Real Estate Experience").

9. Select the lines of text in the "Professional Credentials" section (don't include the heading) and change the *After* paragraph spacing to **3 pt**.

10. Use the *Format Painter* to repeat the above formatting to the lines of text (excluding the heading) in the "Education & Training" section.

11. Use the thesaurus to find an appropriate synonym for the following words:
 a. Replace "surpass" (in the "Personal Statement" section) with "**exceed**."
 b. Replace "emotions" (in the "Why I Am a Real Estate Agent" section) with "**sentiments**."

12. Use *Smart Lookup* to research selected words.
 a. Select "**University of Nevada, Reno**" in the "Education & Training" section.
 b. Click the **Smart Lookup** button [*References* tab, *Research* group]. The *Smart Lookup* pane opens on the right.
 c. Review the research results in the *Smart Lookup* pane.
 d. Click the **X** in the upper-right corner of the *Smart Lookup* pane to close the pane.

13. Use the *Read Aloud* feature [*Review* tab, *Speech* group] to read the first two body paragraphs.

14. Add the following document properties:
 a. *Title*: Brochure
 b. *Company*: Placer Hills Real Estate
 c. *Author*: Emma Cavalli (right-click and choose **Remove Person** to remove existing author)

15. Save and close the document (Figure 1-104).

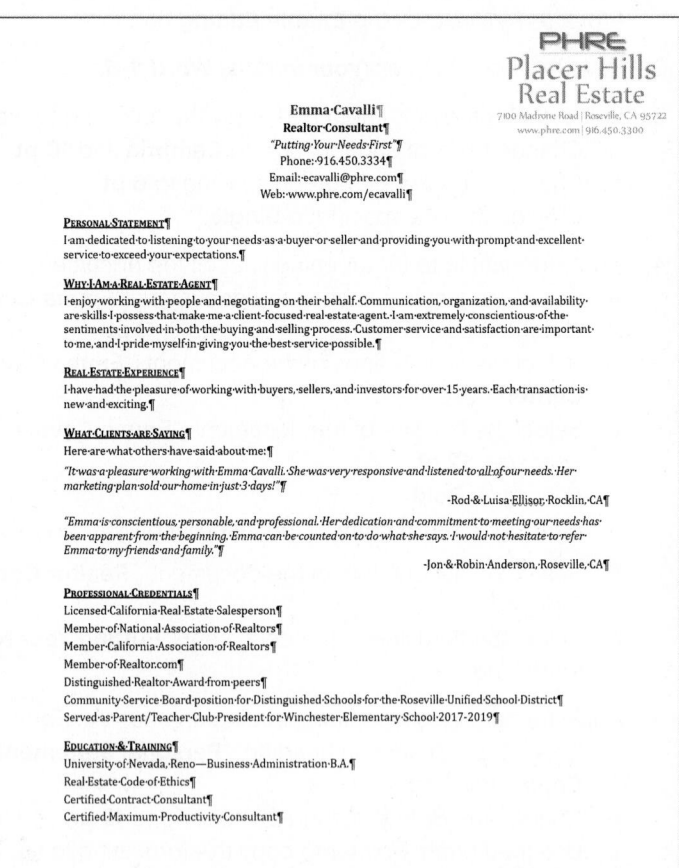

Figure 1-104 Word 1-6 completed

Improve It Project 1-7

In this project, you create a block format business letter for Margaret Jepson, an insurance agent at Central Sierra Insurance. You improve the formatting and text in this document and add opening and closing lines to create a properly formatted business letter. For more information on creating a correctly formatted block format business letter, see *Appendix B* (online resource).
[Student Learning Outcomes 1.1, 1.2, 1.3, 1.5, 1.6, 1.7, 1.8]

File Needed: ***RenewalLetter-01.docx*** *(Student data files are available in the* Library *of your SIMnet account.)*
Completed Project File Name: *[your initials]* **Word 1-7.docx**

Skills Covered in This Project

- Open and edit an existing document.
- Change font and font size.
- Change paragraph spacing.
- Change line spacing.

- Use spelling and grammar checker.
- Format a business letter.
- Change paragraph alignment.
- Change font styles and effects.
- Use the *Format Painter*.
- Add document properties.

1. Open the ***RenewalLetter-01*** document from your student data files. If the document opens in *Protected View*, click the **Enable Editing** button.

2. Save this document as *[your initials]* **Word 1-7**.

3. Select the entire document and apply the following formatting:
 a. *Line spacing*: **Single**
 b. *Before* and *After paragraph spacing*: **0 pt**.
 c. *Font*: **Calibri**
 d. *Font size*: **11 pt**.

4. Correct spelling and grammar as needed.

5. Type the opening lines of the business letter.
 a. Turn on **Show/Hide** if it is not already on.
 b. Place your insertion point at the top of the document and press **Enter**.
 c. Place your insertion point on the blank line at the beginning of the document, type the current date (use January 1, 2020 format), and press **Enter** four times.
 d. Type the following inside address and press **Enter** two times after the last line:

 Mr. Rick DePonte
 8364 Marshall Street
 Granite Bay, CA 95863

 e. Type Dear Mr. DePonte: as the salutation press **Enter** two times.
 f. Type Subject: Policy HO-2887-5546-B as the subject line and press **Enter** once.
 g. Apply **72 pt**. *Before* paragraph spacing on the date line.

6. Type the closing lines of the business letter.
 a. Place the insertion point on the last blank line of the document and type Best regards, as the complimentary close.
 b. Press **Enter** four times.
 c. Type the following information below as the writer's name, title, and company and press **Enter** two times after the last line:

 Margaret Jepson, ARM, CIC, CRM
 Insurance Agent
 Central Sierra Insurance

d. Type your initials in lowercase letters as the reference initials, press **Enter** once, and **Undo** the automatic capitalization of your reference initials.

e. Type Enclosure as the enclosure notation at the end of the business letter.

7. Apply formatting to the renewal premium information.
 a. **Center** the four lines of renewal premium information in the body of the letter.
 b. Apply **Bold** and **Small caps** formatting to the headings (including the colons) for each of these four lines of renewal premium information.
 c. Format the "Total Premium" dollar amount as **Bold**, **Italic**, and **Double Underline**.

8. Type Hartford Specialty to replace the "*[Company Name]*" placeholder (delete brackets also) in the second body paragraph.

9. Type Rick to replace the "*[First Name]*" placeholder in the last body paragraph.

10. Add the following document properties:
 a. *Title*: Renewal Letter
 b. *Company*: Central Sierra Insurance
 c. *Author*: Margaret Jepson (right-click and choose **Remove Person** to remove existing author)

11. Save and close the letter (Figure 1-105).

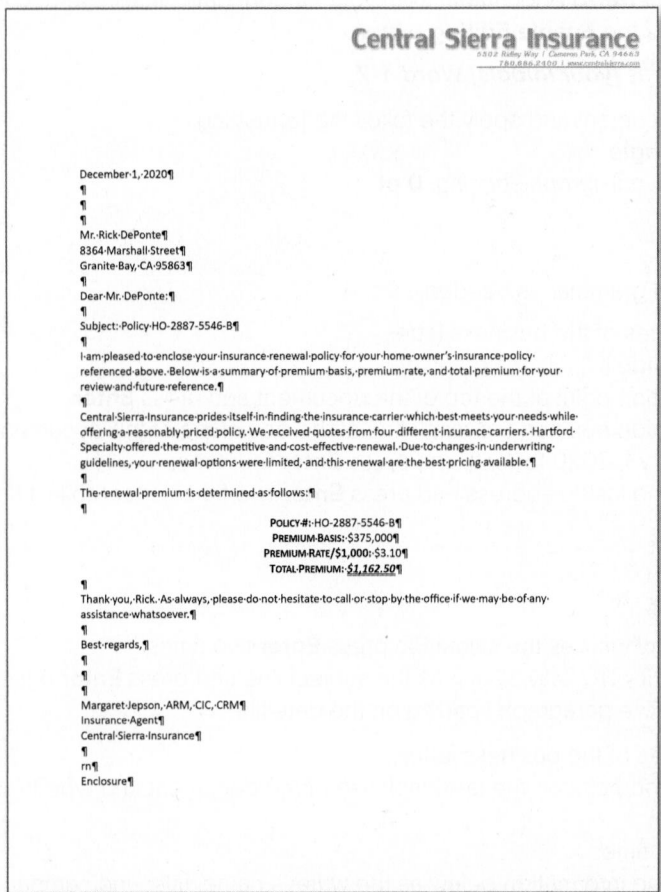

Figure 1-105 Word 1-7 completed

Challenge Project 1-8

Create a cover letter for a job application. A cover letter typically accompanies a resume to introduce an applicant to a prospective employer. You can use and modify an existing cover letter, or you can create a new one. It is important to customize each cover letter for each job for which you are applying.
[Student Learning Outcomes 1.1, 1.2, 1.3, 1.4, 1.5, 1.6, 1.7, 1.8]

File Needed: None
Completed Project File Name: *[your initials] Word 1-8.docx*

Open a new document and save this document as *[your initials] Word 1-8.*

Type this document as a personal business letter in block format. For more information on formatting a personal business letter, see *Appendix B* (online resource). Many online resources are available to help you with both content and format. One of the best online resources for writing is the Online Writing Lab (OWL) from Purdue University (http://owl.english.purdue.edu/owl/). Search this site for helpful information about cover letters.

Modify your document according to the following guidelines:

- Move sentences and paragraphs as needed to produce a well-organized cover letter.
- Add words to the dictionary as needed.
- Use the *Thesaurus* to find synonyms as needed.
- Include document properties, and spell and grammar check the document.

Challenge Project 1-9

Create a list of five places you would like to visit in the next five years. For each of the places you list, compose a short paragraph about that place and why it is interesting to you. Research each of the places you choose using the internet. Use your own words when composing the paragraphs about each place.
[Student Learning Outcomes 1.1, 1.2, 1.3, 1.4, 1.5, 1.6, 1.7, 1.8]

File Needed: None
Completed Project File Name: *[your initials] Word 1-9.docx*

Open a new document and save it as *[your initials] Word 1-9.*

Modify your document according to the following guidelines:

- Create and format a title for the document.
- Format each of the headings by modifying the font, style, and attributes.
- Change line and paragraph spacing as needed to create an attractive and readable document.
- Use consistent line and paragraph spacing throughout the document.
- Use the *Format Painter* to apply consistent formatting throughout the document.
- Move the paragraphs so the places are listed in priority order.
- Include document properties, and spell and grammar check the document.

Challenge Project 1-10

Create a flyer for an upcoming event for an organization to which you belong. Be sure to include all the relevant information for this event and arrange it attractively and professionally on the page.
[Student Learning Outcomes 1.1, 1.2, 1.3, 1.5, 1.6, 1.7, 1.8]

File Needed: None
Completed Project File Name: *[your initials] Word 1-10.docx*

Open a new document and save it as *[your initials] Word 1-10.*

Modify your document according to the following guidelines:

- Create and format a title for the document.
- Format the information by modifying the fonts, styles, and attributes.
- Change line and paragraph spacing as needed to create an attractive and readable document.
- Change the text alignment as desired.
- Use the *Format Painter* to keep formatting consistent throughout the document.
- Include document properties, and spell and grammar check the document.

Source of screenshots Microsoft Office 365 (2019): Word, Excel, Access, Powerpoint.

Formatting and Customizing Documents

CHAPTER OVERVIEW

In addition to creating common business documents, Microsoft Word provides formatting and editing tools to customize a variety of documents. Formatting features such as custom margins, tab stops, indents, page numbering, headers, footers, breaks, lists, styles, themes, borders, and shading help you produce readable and attractive professional and personal documents.

STUDENT LEARNING OUTCOMES (SLOs)

After completing this chapter, you will be able to:

SLO 2.1 Format a document by customizing margins, page orientation, paper size, vertical alignment, and page movement (p. W2-68).

SLO 2.2 Improve alignment and page layout by setting, using, and editing tab stops in a document (p. W2-72).

SLO 2.3 Apply indents to control text alignment (p. W2-76).

SLO 2.4 Enhance document layout by inserting page numbers, headers, and footers (p. W2-82).

SLO 2.5 Control pagination with page and section breaks (p. W2-89).

SLO 2.6 Use customized bulleted and numbered lists to effectively present information (p. W2-91).

SLO 2.7 Apply styles and themes to improve consistency in document format (p. W2-95).

SLO 2.8 Use find and replace to edit a document and use the *Resume Assistant* to customize a resume (p. W2-100).

SLO 2.9 Improve overall document design and format with borders, shading, horizontal lines, and hyperlinks (p. W2-103).

CASE STUDY

Courtyard Medical Plaza has a preschool for its employees' children. The preschool is currently looking for qualified applicants to fill a vacant teacher position. In the Pause & Practice projects, you modify a resume for Richelle Wilkinson. You apply features covered in this chapter to create an attractive and informative resume.

Pause & Practice 2-1: Edit a resume to change margins and set tab stops and indents.

Pause & Practice 2-2: Modify a resume to include a header with text and a page number.

Pause & Practice 2-3: Enhance a resume by using bulleted lists, a page break, and a theme.

Pause & Practice 2-4: Finalize a resume by using find and replace, borders, shading, horizontal line, hyperlinks, and *Resume Assistant*.

Customizing Margins and Page Layout

Use margins to create *white space* around the edges of a document. White space improves the readability of a document and prevents the document from appearing cluttered. The document type and content influence the margin settings you apply. Other ways to customize a document include changing the page orientation, page size, vertical alignment, or page movement.

Page Layout Settings

When you open a new Word document, the default settings control margins, page orientation, paper size, and vertical alignment. Table 2-1 lists the default page layout settings for a new document.

Table 2-1: Default Page Layout Settings

Page Layout Option	Default Setting
Margins	1" top, bottom, left, and right
Page Orientation	Portrait
Paper Size	8.5"×11" (Letter)
Vertical Alignment	Top

Page layout settings apply to the entire Word document, and you can easily change all of these settings using the *Layout* tab.

Margin Settings

Margin settings are measured in inches; the default margin settings for a new Word document are 1". Word provides a variety of *preset margin settings*. You can choose and change margins from the *Margins* drop-down list.

▶ HOW TO: Change Margin Settings

1. Click the **Layout** tab.
2. Click the **Margins** button [*Page Setup* group]. Preset margin options appear in the *Margins* drop-down list (Figure 2-1).
3. Select the desired margin settings from the drop-down list of options.

The *Margins* drop-down list provides preset margin options. You are not limited to these preset options; you can also create your own custom margin settings in the *Page Setup* dialog box.

> ▶ MORE INFO
>
> The top of the *Margins* list displays the *Last Custom Setting* option, which is the most recent custom margin settings applied.

Figure 2-1 *Margins* drop-down list

Page Setup Dialog Box

If you want to apply margin settings that are not listed in the preset margin settings in the *Margins* drop-down list, use the **Page Setup dialog box** (Figure 2-2) to change one or more of the margin settings and to create custom margins.

▶HOW TO: Set Custom Margins

1. Click the **Layout** tab.
2. Click the **Page Setup** launcher [*Page Setup* group] to open the *Page Setup* dialog box (see Figure 2-2).
 - Alternatively, click the **Margins** button and select **Custom Margins**.
3. Click the **Margins** tab if it is not already selected.
4. Change the *Top*, *Bottom*, *Left*, and *Right* margin settings using one of the following methods:
 - Click the **Top**, **Bottom**, **Left**, or **Right** margin box and type the desired margin setting.
 - Click the **up** or **down arrow** to increase or decrease the margin size. Each click of the up or down arrow increases or decreases the margins by 0.1".
 - Press **Tab** to move from one text box to another in the *Margins* area.
 - The *Preview* area displays a document thumbnail with the customized margin settings.
5. Click the **Apply to** drop-down list and select an option to apply margin settings: **Whole document**, **This point forward**, or **This section**.
6. Click **OK** to apply the custom margin settings.

Figure 2-2 *Page Setup* dialog box

> ▶ **MORE INFO**
>
> Margin settings apply to the entire document by default. However, you can apply different margin settings to different sections of a document. Sections and section breaks are covered later in this chapter.

Page Orientation

Page orientation refers to the direction of the page. The two different orientation options in Word are **Portrait** and **Landscape**. Portrait is the tall orientation (8.5"×11"), which is the default page orientation in Word. Landscape is the wide orientation (11"×8.5"). Change page orientation by clicking the **Orientation** button in the *Page Setup* group on the *Layout* tab (Figure 2-3).

> ▶ **ANOTHER WAY**
>
>
> Change page orientation in the *Page Setup* dialog box.

Figure 2-3 Page orientation settings

Paper Size

Paper size refers to the actual size of the paper of your final printed document. A new document in Word is standard letter size, which is 8.5"×11" by default. Word also provides other preset paper size settings, as shown in Figure 2-4.

Change paper size by clicking the **Size** button in the *Page Setup* group on the *Layout* tab. When a different paper size is set, the margins of the document do not change. You may need to adjust the margin setting when you change the paper size. You can also set a custom paper size in the *Page Setup* dialog box.

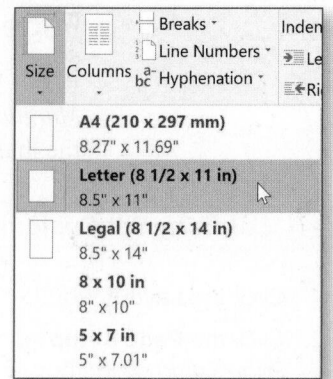

Figure 2-4 Paper size preset options

Vertical Alignment

If you are creating a flyer or a title page for a report, you might want to vertically center the information on the page. *Vertical alignment* controls the position of text between the top and bottom margins. Changing the vertical alignment of a page, section, or document is a much more effective method than using paragraph breaks (pressing *Enter* multiple times) to align information vertically. Word has four vertical alignment options.

- *Top*: Text begins at the top margin of the document, which is the default setting in Word.
- *Center*: Text is centered vertically between the top and bottom margins.
- *Justified*: Space is automatically added between lines to fill the entire vertical space between the top and bottom margins.
- *Bottom*: Text begins at the bottom margin of the document.

▶**HOW TO:** Change Vertical Alignment

1. Click the **Layout** tab.
2. Click the **Page Setup** launcher [*Page Setup* group]. The *Page Setup* dialog box opens.
3. Click the **Layout** tab.
4. Click the **Vertical alignment** drop-down list in the *Page* area (Figure 2-5).
5. Select a vertical alignment option and click **OK**.

Use the Ruler

Microsoft Word provides horizontal and vertical *rulers* that display both the horizontal typing line length and the vertical typing space available in a document. The rulers are divided into 1/8" increments. Half-inch markers are longer vertical or horizontal lines (depending on the ruler) and inch markers are numerical. The typing area on the rulers displays in white, while the margin area is shaded (Figure 2-6). To display rulers, check the **Ruler** box in the *Show* group on the *View* tab.

Figure 2-5 Change vertical alignment

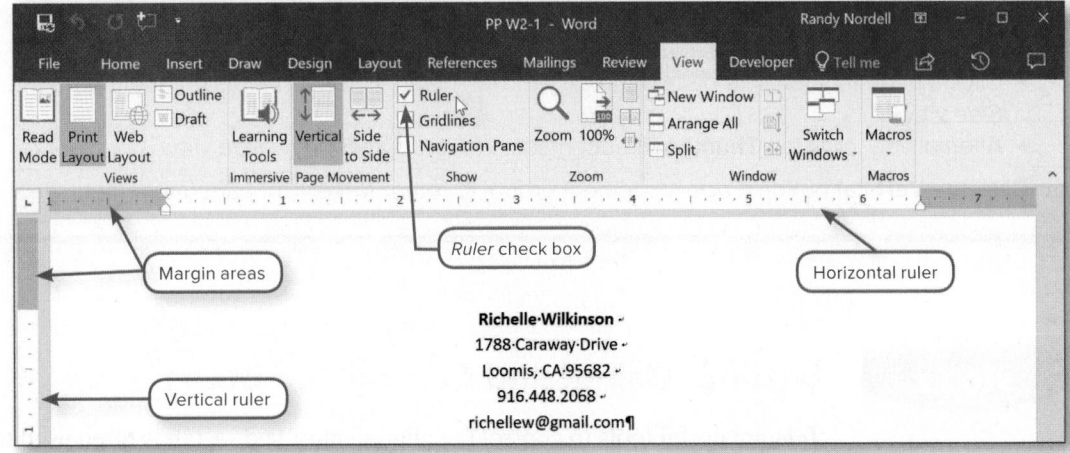

Figure 2-6 Horizontal and vertical rulers displayed

> ### MORE INFO
>
> The rulers are increasingly important and useful as you begin using tab stops, indents, columns, tables, and section breaks.

Page Movement

By default, you move vertically through a multi-page document. The ***Side to Side*** option enables you to scroll horizontally through a document with multiple pages. Scrolling horizontally resembles the look of a book and displays multiple pages on the screen. Additionally, the *Side to Side* page movement includes an option to view your document as ***Thumbnails***, which display multiple pages tiled on the screen. Click a thumbnail to navigate to a page in your document.

▶HOW TO: Use Side to Side Page Movement

1. Click the **View** tab.
2. Click the **Side to Side** button [*Page Movement* group]. The document displays pages horizontally on the screen (Figure 2-7).
3. Use the left and right arrow keys or the mouse scroll wheel to scroll horizontally through the pages.

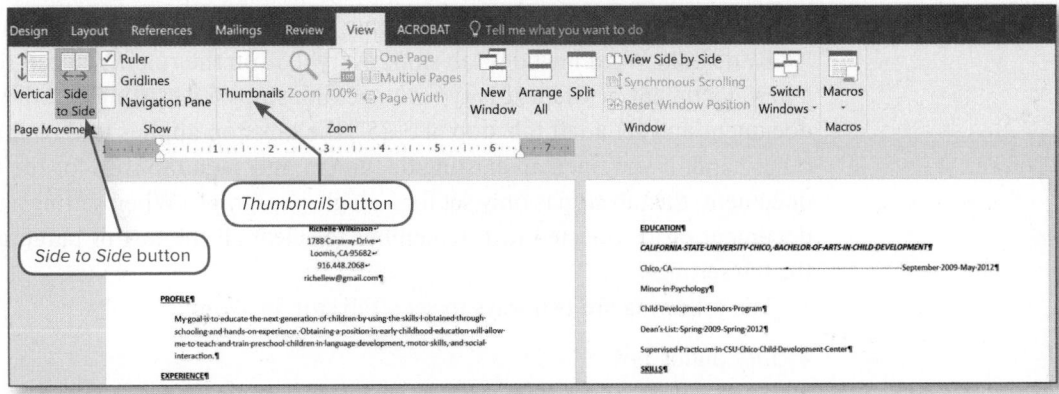

Figure 2-7 *Side to Side* page movement view

4. Click the **Thumbnails** button [*Zoom* group] to display all pages of the document as thumbnail icons.
 - A page number displays below each page thumbnail.
 - Click a page thumbnail to display the page. The *Thumbnail* option turns off and the page displays in *Side to Side* view.
 - Alternatively, click the **Thumbnail** button again to return to *Side to Side* view.
5. Click the **Vertical** button [*Page Movement* group] to return to *Vertical* page movement view.

Setting, Using, and Editing Tab Stops

Tabs are useful tools to control the alignment of text. A tab is often used to indent the first line of a paragraph. A *tab stop* is where your insertion point stops after you press the *Tab* key. Tabs can also be used to align text in columns or to begin the date at the horizontal midpoint on a modified block business letter. The five different types of tab stops are described in Table 2-2.

Table 2-2: Types of Tab Stops

Type of Tab Stop	Description	Tab Stop Indicator	Tab Stop in Use	
Left	Text is left-aligned at the tab stop.	∟	Left tab	
Center	Text is centered on the tab stop.	⊥	Center tab	
Right	Text is right-aligned at the tab stop.	⌐		Right tab
Decimal	Decimal point is aligned at the tab stop.	⊥	Decimal tab 620.50	8.375
Bar	A vertical bar (line) is inserted at the tab stop.	I	A bar tab between	displays these words

Set a Tab Stop

Tabs are different from margins because tab stops apply to a paragraph or selected paragraphs rather than an entire document or sections of a document. This is important to keep in mind when setting, using, and editing tab stops.

By default, Word includes tab stops every 0.5" on the ruler. You can set custom tab stops in a new document before text is typed or set tab stops for existing text. If you open a new blank document and set a left tab stop at 3.25", the tab stop applies to the entire document. On the other hand, if you open an existing document and set a tab stop for the first paragraph of the document, the tab stop is only set for a single paragraph. When setting a tab stop in an existing document or for selected text, remember to select all the text or paragraphs before you apply the tab settings.

The following are two ways to set a tab stop in Word.

- *Tabs* dialog box
- Ruler

Set a Tab Stop Using the Tabs Dialog Box

The ***Tabs dialog box*** is an effective and easy method to set single or multiple tab stops. Access the *Tabs* dialog box from the *Paragraph* dialog box. Open the *Paragraph* dialog box by clicking the **Paragraph** launcher from the *Paragraph* group on either the *Home* or *Layout* tabs.

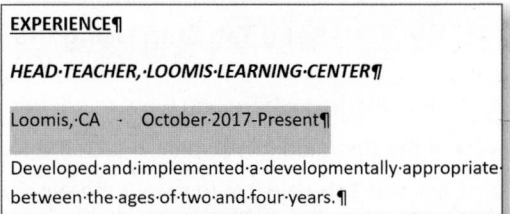

Figure 2-8 Select text before setting tab stops

Figure 2-9 *Tabs* button in *Paragraph* dialog box

> ▶ **HOW TO:** Set a Tab Stop Using the Tabs Dialog Box

1. Select the text where you want to set a tab stop (Figure 2-8).
2. Click the **Home** or **Layout** tab.
3. Click the **Paragraph** launcher to open the *Paragraph* dialog box.
4. Click the **Tabs** button (Figure 2-9) to open the *Tabs* dialog box.
5. Type the desired tab stop position in the **Tab stop position** text box.
6. Select the **Left**, **Center**, **Right**, **Decimal**, or **Bar** radio button in the *Alignment* area.
7. Click the **Set** button (Figure 2-10). The tab stop appears in the list of tab stops below the *Tab stop position* text box.
8. Click **OK** to close the *Tabs* dialog box.
 - The tab stop is applied to the selected text.
 - The tab stop is visible on the ruler.

Figure 2-10 Set a right tab stop in the *Tabs* dialog box

> ▶ **MORE INFO**
>
> Set and use tab stops to align and balance columns of text rather than pressing *Tab* multiple times between columns.

Set a Tab Stop Using the Ruler

Using the ruler to set tab stops is a quick way to add them to a document. You can also easily move or remove tab stops using the ruler. Use the ***Tab selector*** to select the type of tab stop you want to insert. The *Tab* selector is located at the top of the vertical ruler on the left side of the Word window (Figure 2-11). When setting tab stops in an existing document, it is very important to select the text or paragraphs where you want the tab stop to apply before setting the tab stop.

▶ HOW TO: Set a Tab Stop Using the Ruler

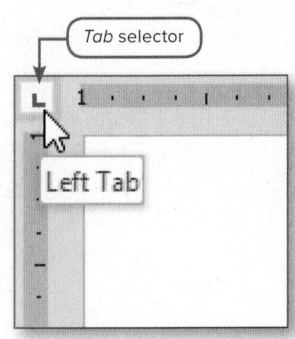

Figure 2-11 *Tab* selector

1. Select the text where you want to set the new tab stop(s).
 - If the rulers do not display, check the **Ruler** box [*View* tab, *Show* group].

2. Click the **Tab** selector to select the type of tab stop to set (see Figure 2-11).
 - The *Tab* selector toggles through the different types of tabs and indents: left, center, right, decimal, bar, first line indent, and hanging indent.

3. Click the ruler to set a tab stop.
 - When setting tab stops using the ruler, click the bottom edge of the ruler to set a tab stop (Figure 2-12).

Figure 2-12 Set a left tab stop at 2.5" on the ruler

Move a Tab Stop

It can be challenging to align text correctly and balance space between columns. As you practice setting tabs, you will become more comfortable selecting the correct type of tab stop to use, adjusting the settings of existing tab stops, and removing tab stops. When using multiple columns, adjust tab stops so you have the same amount of white space between columns.

The easiest way to move tab stops is by using the ruler. When using the ruler to adjust a tab stop, be sure to select the appropriate text before moving a tab stop.

▶ HOW TO: Move a Tab Stop

1. Select the text or paragraphs containing the tab stops you want to edit.

2. Left-click the **tab stop** on the ruler and drag it to the new location (Figure 2-13).
 - When you click the tab stop to be moved, a vertical alignment guide appears. This alignment guide displays the position of the tab stop.
 - Press the **Alt** key when you are moving a tab stop to display a vertical guide and horizontal ruler settings to assist in moving a tab stop to a specific measurement (Figure 2-14).

3. Release the pointer to set the tab stop in the new location.

4. Repeat this process until you are satisfied with the placement of your tab stops.

Figure 2-13 Move a tab stop using the ruler

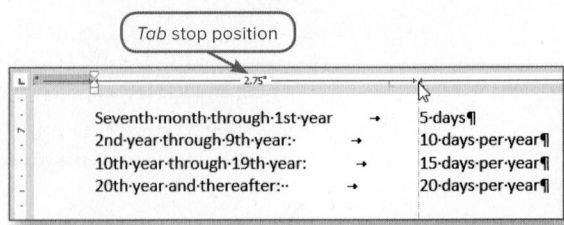

Figure 2-14 Use the *Alt* key to adjust a tab stop

W2-74

Remove a Tab Stop

When setting tab stops using the ruler, you may unintentionally add a tab stop. Or, you may want to remove unwanted tab stops. When removing tab stops from existing text, it is very important to select the text or paragraphs before deleting the tabs. When you remove or clear a tab stop, the tabbed text realigns to the default 0.5" tab stop or nearest remaining custom tab stop. Following are three different ways to remove tab stops:

- Drag a tab stop off (below) the ruler.
- Clear a single tab stop in the *Tabs* dialog box.
- Clear all tab stops in the *Tabs* dialog box.

To clear a single tab stop using the ruler, select the text or paragraphs, select the tab stop to remove, drag the tab stop down below the ruler, and release the pointer.

When using the *Tabs* dialog box to remove tab stops, you can clear a single tab stop or clear all existing tab stops on the selected text or paragraphs.

Figure 2-15 Clear a tab stop in the *Tabs* dialog box

> ▶ **HOW TO: Clear a Tab Stop Using the Tabs Dialog Box**

1. Select the text or paragraphs containing the tab stops to remove.
2. Click the **Paragraph** launcher [*Home* or *Layout* tab] to open the *Paragraph* dialog box.
3. Click the **Tabs** button to open the *Tabs* dialog box.
4. Select the tab stop to remove in the list of existing tab stops, and click the **Clear** button to remove a single tab stop (Figure 2-15). Repeat on any other tab stops you want to remove.
 - Click the **Clear All** button to clear all tab stops.
5. Click **OK** to close the *Tabs* dialog box.

Add a Tab Leader

Tab leaders insert dots or a line between text when using tab stops. The most common type of leader is the dot leader, which is regularly used in a table of contents. In a table of contents, a dot leader displays between the text and the right-aligned page number. You can also use leaders to insert a dashed line in the blank space between columns or to create a solid underline when creating a printed form.

Word has three different types of tab leaders. Examples of each type appear in Table 2-3.

Table 2-3: Types of Leaders

Leader	Example of Use
Dot	Chapter 1 ... 4
Dash	Vacation Days ------ 10 days per year
Solid underline	Name _____

Use the *Tabs* dialog box to add tab leaders to existing tabbed text or to set new tab stops.

1. Select the text or paragraphs where you want to add a tab leader.

2. Click the **Paragraph** launcher [*Home* or *Layout* tab] to open the *Paragraph* dialog box.

3. Click the **Tabs** button to open the *Tabs* dialog box.

4. Select an existing tab stop or type a number in the *Tab stop position* text box to set a new tab stop.

5. Select the type of leader to apply in the *Leader* area (see Figure 2-15).

6. Click **Set**. Figure 2-16 is an example of a dash leader.

7. Click **OK** to close the *Tabs* dialog box.

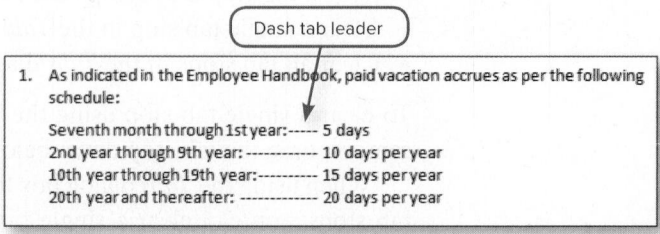

Dash tab leader

1. As indicated in the Employee Handbook, paid vacation accrues as per the following schedule:

 Seventh month through 1st year:----- 5 days
 2nd year through 9th year: ------------ 10 days per year
 10th year through 19th year:---------- 15 days per year
 20th year and thereafter: ------------- 20 days per year

Figure 2-16 Tab stop with a dash leader

Change Default Tab Stops

By default, new documents include a left tab stop every 0.5". When you set a tab stop in Word, the custom tab stop overrides all preceding default tab stop, but the default tab stops to the right of your custom tab stop remain. For example, if you set a left tab stop at the horizontal midpoint (typically 3.25") and press **Tab** to move to the horizontal midpoint, your insertion point will move to the midpoint, not 0.5". But if you press **Tab** again, your insertion point will stop at the next default tab stop, which is 3.5".

You can customize the half-inch interval for default tab stops. If you change the default tab stop setting, this change affects only the current document, not all new documents.

1. Click the **Paragraph** launcher [*Home* or *Layout* tab] to open the *Paragraph* dialog box.

2. Click the **Tabs** button to open the *Tabs* dialog box.

3. Type a value or use the up or down arrow to change the default tab stop setting in the *Default tab stops* area (Figure 2-17).

4. Click **OK** to close the *Tabs* dialog box.

Figure 2-17 Change default tab stops

SLO 2.3

Using Indents

Indents are another powerful tool to control how text aligns between the left and right margins. Consider indents to be temporary margins, which apply to selected paragraphs. Use indents to indent the first line of each paragraph, set off a long quote in a report, or indent the carry-over lines of bulleted or numbered lists.

Similar to setting tab stops, it is important to select the text where you want to apply indent settings. Set indents using the ruler, the *Paragraph* group on the *Layout* tab, or the *Paragraph* dialog box. Table 2-4 describes the four different types of indents.

Table 2-4: Types of Indents

Indent	Example of Use	Ruler Indent Marker
Left Indent	This paragraph has a left indent.	Left Indent
Right Indent	This paragraph has a right indent.	Right Indent
First Line Indent	This paragraph has a first line indent.	First Line Indent
Hanging Indent	This paragraph has a hanging indent.	Hanging Indent

Left and Right Indents

Indents apply to an entire paragraph or multiple paragraphs, not just lines of text within a paragraph. When setting an indent, select the paragraph(s) on which to apply the indent. If your insertion point is in a paragraph, the indent you set applies to that paragraph only.

▶ HOW TO: Set a Left and Right Indent

1. Select the text or paragraph where you want to apply the indent. If it is just one paragraph, place your insertion point in that paragraph.

2. Click the **Layout** tab.
 - Alternatively, click the **Paragraph** launcher to open the *Paragraph* dialog box.

3. Change the *Left* and *Right* indent settings [*Paragraph* group on the *Layout* tab or Indentation area in the *Paragraph* dialog box]. The change applies to the selected text (Figure 2-18).

 - When you apply an indent to a paragraph and press *Enter* at the end of the paragraph, the indent carries over to the next paragraph.

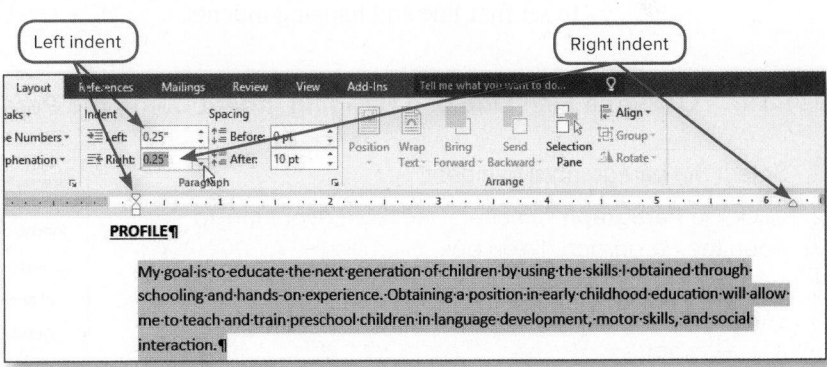

Figure 2-18 Change left and right indents

Indents can also be set using the ruler. Select the text to indent and drag the indent marker to the desired location. As you drag the indent marker, an alignment guide displays the location where your text aligns.

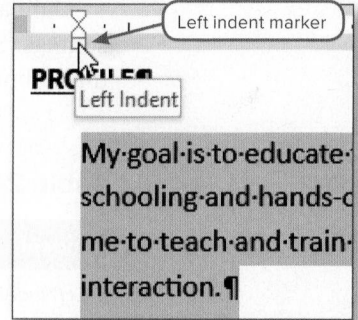

Figure 2-19 Change left indent using the ruler

▶ HOW TO: Set Indents Using the Ruler

1. Select the text or paragraph to indent. If it is just one paragraph, place your insertion point in that paragraph.
2. Left click the **left indent marker** (bottom square), drag to the desired location, and release the pointer. The left indent applies to the selected text (Figure 2-19).
3. Left click the **right indent marker**, drag to the desired location, and release the pointer. The right indent applies to the selected text (Figure 2-20).

Figure 2-20 Change right indent using the ruler

The *Decrease Indent* and *Increase Indent* buttons in the *Paragraph* group on the *Home* tab increase or decrease the left indent in increments of 0.5" (Figure 2-21). Remove a left indent by positioning the insertion point at the beginning of the paragraph and pressing **Backspace** or clicking the **Decrease Indent** button.

First Line and Hanging Indents

Add a *First line indent* to indent the first line of a paragraph instead of pressing *Tab*. A *Hanging indent* is typically used with bulleted and numbered lists but can be used effectively to indent text that wraps to a second or additional lines, such as entries on a references page. Use the *Paragraph* dialog box to set first line and hanging indents.

Figure 2-21 *Decrease Indent* and *Increase Indent* buttons

▶ HOW TO: Set a First Line or a Hanging Indent Using the Paragraph Dialog box

1. Select the paragraph(s) to indent.
2. Click the **Paragraph** launcher [*Home* or *Layout* tab] to open the *Paragraph* dialog box.
3. Click the **Special** drop-down list in the *Indentation* area and choose the type of indent: **First line** or **Hanging** (Figure 2-22).
4. Type the indent amount or use the up or down buttons in the *By* area to increase or decrease the amount of the indent.
 - The *Preview* area displays the text with the indent applied.
5. Click **OK** to close the *Paragraph* dialog box.

Figure 2-22 Set first line or hanging indent using the *Paragraph* dialog box

To set a first line indent using the ruler, select the paragraph(s) to indent and drag the first line indent marker (top triangle) to the desired location (Figure 2-23). The alignment guide displays where the first line of each paragraph aligns.

To set a hanging indent using the ruler, select the paragraph(s) to indent and drag the hanging indent marker (bottom triangle) to the desired location (Figure 2-24). The alignment guide displays where the carryover lines of the paragraph align.

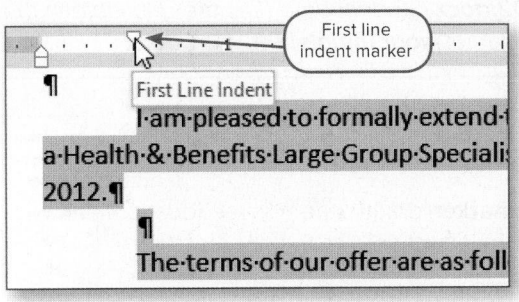

Figure 2-23 Set a first line indent using the ruler

Figure 2-24 Set a hanging indent using the ruler

An **outdent** aligns text outside the left or right margins. Outdents can be used to emphasize section headings so they display slightly to the left of the left margin. To apply an outdent, set a **negative value** (−0.25") in the indents area in the *Paragraph* dialog box or *Paragraph* group on the *Layout* tab or by dragging the indent marker outside of the left or right margins.

Remove Indents

Removing indents moves the indent markers back to either the left or right margin, so the margins control the alignment of text rather than the indents. Remember to select the paragraph or paragraphs before removing the indents. To remove an indent, set the indent value to **0"** using the *Paragraph* dialog box or the *Paragraph* group on the *Layout* tab (Figure 2-25).

The ruler can also be used to remove indents. When using this method, select the text or paragraphs on which to remove the indents and drag the indent marker(s) to the margin.

Figure 2-25 Remove indents using the *Paragraph* dialog box

In this Pause & Practice project, you format a resume for Richelle Wilkinson. This resume is a two-page document, and you change the margins, set tab stops and leaders, and use indents.

File Needed: ***Resume-02.docx*** *(Student data files are available in the* Library *of your SIMnet account.)*
Completed Project File Name: ***[your initials] PP W2-1.docx***

1. Open the ***Resume-02*** document from your student data files.

2. Save this document as [your initials] PP W2-1.

3. Change the margins of the resume.
 a. Click the **Layout** tab.
 b. Click the **Page Setup** launcher [*Page Setup* group] to open the *Page Setup* dialog box (Figure 2-26). Alternatively, click the **Margins** button and select **Custom Margins**.
 c. Type .75 in the **Top** text box in the *Margins* area and press **Tab** to move to the *Bottom* text box.
 d. Type .75 in the *Bottom* text box.
 e. Click the **down arrow** to the right of the *Left* text box to change the left margin to **1"**.
 f. Click the **down arrow** to the right of the *Right* text box to change the right margin to **1"**.
 g. Click the **Apply to** drop-down list at the bottom of the dialog box and select **Whole document** if it is not already selected.
 h. Click **OK** to apply the new margin settings and close the dialog box.

Figure 2-26 Change margins in the *Page Setup* dialog box

4. Set a right tab stop with a dash leader.
 a. Select the "**Loomis, CA October 2017 Present**" text below "*HEAD TEACHER, LOOMIS LEARNING CENTER.*"
 b. Click the **Paragraph** launcher [*Layout* or *Home* tab] to open the *Paragraph* dialog box.
 c. Click the **Tabs** button in the bottom-left corner of the *Paragraph* dialog box to open the *Tabs* dialog box (Figure 2-27).
 d. Type 6.5 in the *Tab stop position* area.
 e. Select the **Right** radio button in the *Alignment* area.
 f. Select the **3** (dash leader) radio button in the *Leader* area.
 g. Click the **Set** button to set this tab stop and leader.
 h. Click the **OK** button to close the dialog box.

5. Use the *Format Painter* to apply the tab setting to multiple areas of the resume.
 a. Place the insertion point in the line you just formatted.
 b. Double-click the **Format Painter** button [*Home* tab, *Clipboard* group].

Figure 2-27 Set a right tab stop with a dash leader

c. Click each of the city, state, and date lines in the "EXPERIENCE" and "EDUCATION" sections to apply the tab settings as shown in Figure 2-28.

d. Click the **Format Painter** button to turn off copy format.

6. Remove an existing tab stop and set a left tab stop.
 a. Select the lines of text below the "REFERENCES" heading on the second page.
 b. Click the **Paragraph** launcher [*Layout* or *Home* tab] to open the *Paragraph* dialog box.
 c. Click the **Tabs** button to open the *Tabs* dialog box.
 d. Select the existing tab stop (**2.5"**) in the *Tab stop position* area and click the **Clear** button to remove the existing tab.
 e. Type 3.75 in the *Tab stop position* area.
 f. Select the **Left** radio button in the *Alignment* area if it is not already selected.
 g. Select the **1 None** radio button in the *Leader* area if it is not already selected.
 h. Click the **Set** button to set the left tab stop (Figure 2-29).
 i. Click the **OK** button to close the dialog box.

7. Apply a left and right indent to selected text.
 a. Place the insertion point in the paragraph below the "PROFILE" heading on the first page.
 b. Click the **Layout** tab.
 c. Type .25 in the **Left** indent area [*Paragraph* group] and press **Tab**.
 d. Type .25 in the **Right** indent area [*Paragraph* group] and press **Enter**.

8. Save and close this document (Figure 2-30).

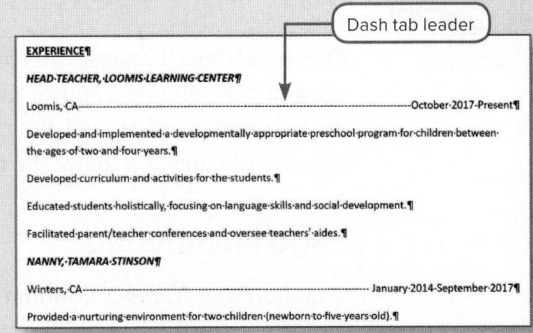

Figure 2-28 Use the *Format Painter* to apply tab settings

Figure 2-29 Set a left tab stop on selected text

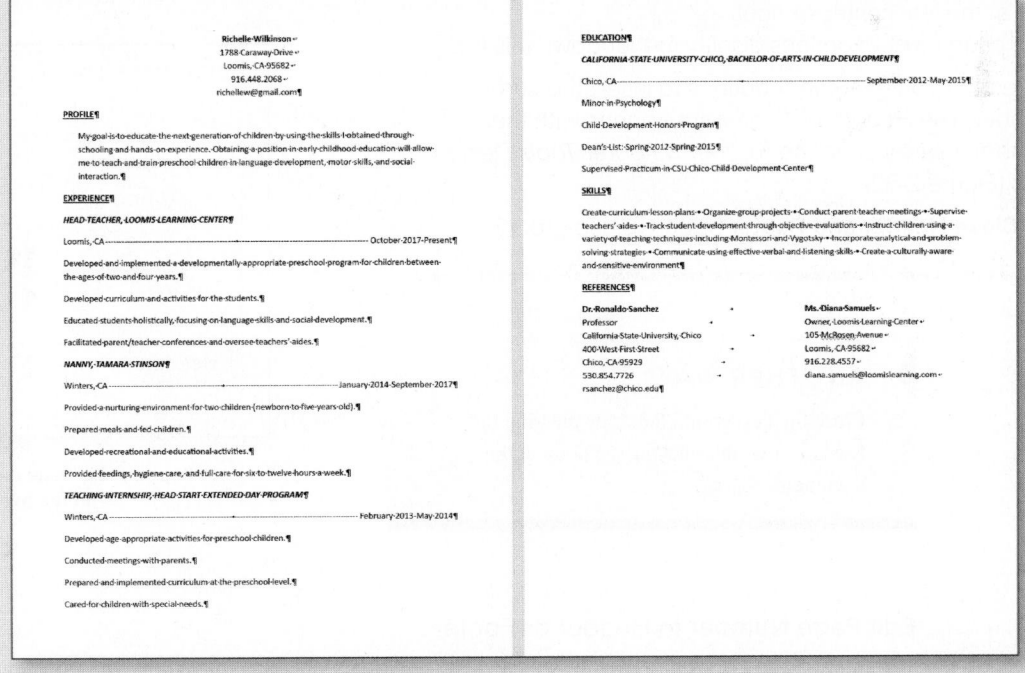

Figure 2-30 PP W2-1 completed

Inserting Page Numbers, Headers, and Footers

Page numbering, *headers*, and *footers* are regularly used in multiple-page documents. Headers, footers, and page numbers appear on each page of the document, which means you only have to type the information once, and Word repeats that information on each subsequent page. The header area of a document is above the top margin, and the footer area is below the bottom margin.

Page Numbering

Use the *Page Number* command in Word to insert a *page number field* in the header, footer, or current location in a document. The page number field displays the current page number. When inserting a page number, specify the page number location and the page number format.

Insert Page Number

Word provides a variety of page number locations, horizontal alignment options, and number format options. The following is a list of the basic page number placement options:

- *Top of Page*
- *Bottom of Page*
- *Page Margins*
- *Current Position*

▶ HOW TO: Insert a Page Number

1. Click the **Insert** tab.
2. Click the **Page Number** button [*Header & Footer* group]. A drop-down list of options appears (Figure 2-31).
3. Click either **Top of Page** or **Bottom of Page**. Another drop-down list of page number options appears.
 - The top three options in this list are simple page numbers aligned at the left, center, or right.
 - Custom page number options display further down this list.
4. Select one of the page number options to insert the current page number. The *Header* or *Footer* area opens with the page number inserted, and the *Header & Footer Tools Design* tab opens (Figure 2-32).
5. Click the **Close Header and Footer** button [*Close* group].

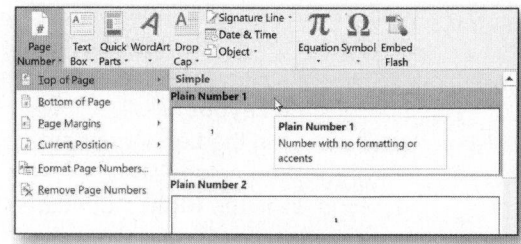

Figure 2-31 Insert page number

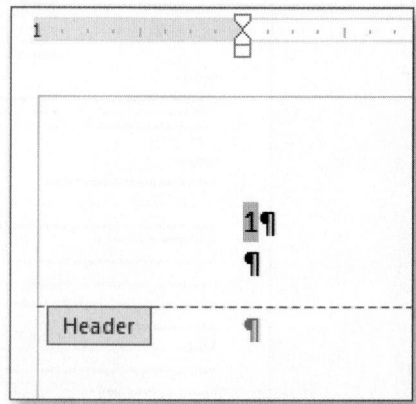

Figure 2-32 Page number inserted in the header on the left

▶ ANOTHER WAY

Close the header and footer by pressing the **Esc** key or double-clicking the body of the document.

Edit Page Number in Header or Footer

When you close the header or footer, the page number appears in gray rather than black like the text of the document. The header and footer areas are outside the boundaries of the margins.

If you want to edit the page number or contents of the header or footer, you must open the header or footer. The following are three ways to do this:

- Right-click the header or footer and select **Edit Header** or **Edit Footer**.
- Click the **Insert** tab, click the **Header** or **Footer** button in the *Header & Footer* group, and choose **Edit Header** or **Edit Footer**.
- Double-click the header or footer area of the document.

Different First Page

Occasionally, you may not want the page number, header, or footer to print on the first page of the document, but you want these page elements to appear on the second and continuing pages. For example, on both multiple-page business letters and reports, the page number typically does not display on the first page but displays on the second and subsequent pages. Use the *Different First Page* option to control the display of page numbers, headers, and footers on page one.

▶HOW TO: Set a Different First Page Header and Footer

1. Go to the first page of the document.
2. Open the header or footer if it is not already open. Use one of the following methods to open the header or footer if it is not already open:
 - Right-click the header or footer and select **Edit Header** or **Edit Footer**.
 - Click the **Insert** tab, click the **Header** or **Footer** button in the *Header & Footer* group, and choose **Edit Header** or **Edit Footer**.
 - Double-click the header or footer area of the document.
3. Click the **Different First Page** check box [*Header & Footer Tools Design* tab, *Options* group] (Figure 2-33).
4. Click the **Close Header and Footer** button [*Close* group]. The page number, header, and footer no longer display on the first page but display on the second and continuing pages.

Figure 2-33 *Different First Page* check box

Page Number Format

After adding page numbers, specify the page number format, select a different starting page number, or add a chapter number before the page number. The *Page Number Format* dialog box provides a variety of page numbering options (Figure 2-34).

Figure 2-34 *Page Number Format* dialog box

> **HOW TO:** Format Page Numbers

1. Click the **Page Number** button [*Insert* tab or *Header & Footer Tools Design, Header & Footer* group] and select **Format Page Numbers** to open the *Page Number Format* dialog box (see Figure 2-34).
2. Click the **Number format** drop-down list and select a page number format. Choose from six preset page numbering options.
3. Select **Continue from previous section** (default setting) or **Start at** a different page number in the *Page numbering* section.
 - Click the **Start at** radio button to set a different starting page number.
 - Type the starting page number or use the up or down arrow to set the starting page number.
4. Click **OK** to close the *Page Number Format* dialog box.
5. Click the **Close Header and Footer** button [*Close* group] if necessary.

Remove Page Number

To remove page numbering from a document, use one of the following options:

- Select **Remove Page Numbers** from the *Page Number* drop-down list (Figure 2-35).
- Open the header or footer and manually delete the page number.

Figure 2-35 Remove page numbers

Insert Header and Footer Content

In addition to inserting page numbers into the header or footer of a document, you might want to include the number of pages in the document, date or time, title of the document, company name, or other custom content. You can enter information manually into the header or footer, or insert document property fields.

> **HOW TO:** Insert Custom Header and Footer Content

1. Click the **Insert** tab.
2. Click the **Header** or **Footer** button [*Insert* tab, *Header & Footer* group] and select **Edit Header** or **Edit Footer**. The header or footer of the document opens and the *Header & Footer Tools Design* tab displays.
 - When you edit a header or footer, both the header and footer open and the *Header & Footer Tools Design* tab displays.
 - Use the **Go to Header** or **Go to Footer** buttons [*Navigation* group] to move to the header or footer (Figure 2-36).
3. Type information in the *Header* or *Footer* area (Figure 2-37).
 - Change the formatting and alignment as desired.
 - You can insert a page number with the header or footer open.
4. Click the **Close Header and Footer** button [*Close* group].

Figure 2-36 *Navigation* group on the *Header & Footer Tools Design* tab

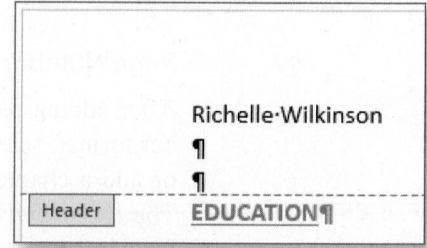

Figure 2-37 Enter custom information in the header

Microsoft Word 365 Chapter 2: Formatting and Customizing Documents

Number of Pages Field

In addition to inserting the current page number in a document, you can add a field code to automatically insert the total number of pages in a document (*NumPages* field).

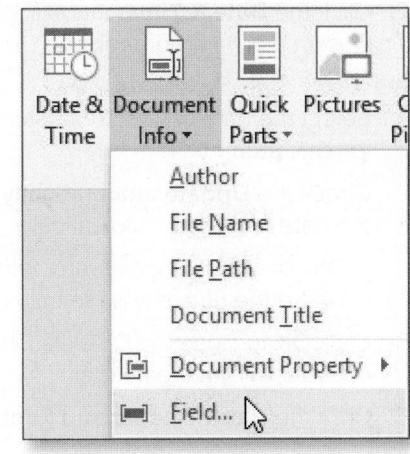

Figure 2-38 Insert field code

▶**HOW TO:** Insert the Number of Pages Field

1. Open the header or footer. The page number should already be inserted in the document.
2. Click before the page number, type Page, and press the **spacebar**.
3. Click after the page number, press the **spacebar**, type of, and press the **spacebar**.
4. Click the **Document Info** button [*Header & Footer Tools Design* tab, *Insert* group] (Figure 2-38).
 - Alternatively, click the **Quick Parts** button.
5. Select **Field** from the drop-down list. The *Field* dialog box opens (Figure 2-39).
6. Scroll down the *Field names* area and select **NumPages**. The field description displays in the *Description* area.
7. Select a page number format in the *Format* area.
8. Click **OK** to close the *Field* dialog box. The number of pages in the document displays (Figure 2-40).
9. Click the **Close Header and Footer** button [*Close* group].

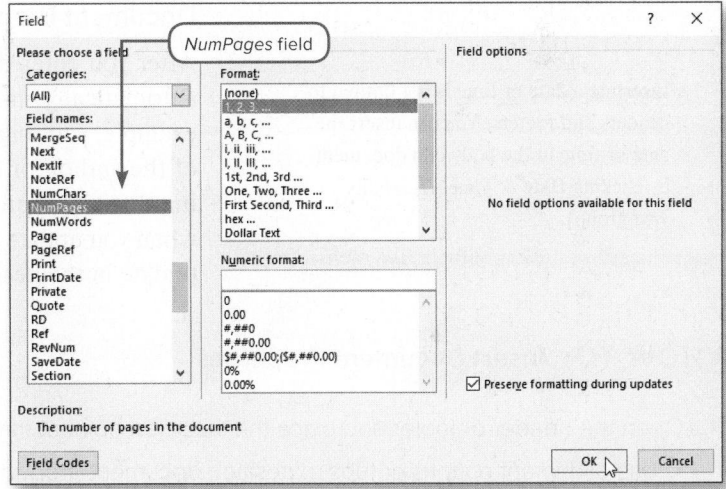

Figure 2-39 Insert *NumPages* field from the *Field* dialog box

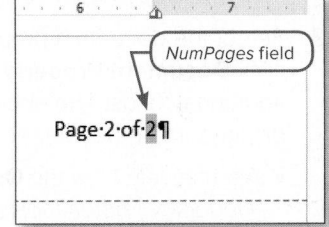

Figure 2-40 Page number and number of pages field inserted into the header

Date and Time

Word can automatically insert a date and/or time in your document. When you insert the date or time, choose from a variety of date and time formats. The date and time can be set to update automatically each time you open the document.

▶ HOW TO: Insert the Date and Time

1. Open the header or footer area and position the insertion point at the location to insert the date.

 • Use alignment buttons or tabs to position the date and/or time in the header or footer.

2. Click the **Date & Time** button [*Header & Footer Tools Design* tab, *Insert* group]. The *Date and Time* dialog box opens (Figure 2-41).

3. Select the date or time format to use in the *Available formats* area.

4. Check the **Update automatically** check box if you want the date to update automatically.

 • Do not check *Update automatically* on documents where the date should remain constant.

5. Click **OK** to close the *Date and Time* dialog box. The date displays in the header.

6. Click the **Close Header and Footer** button [*Close* group].

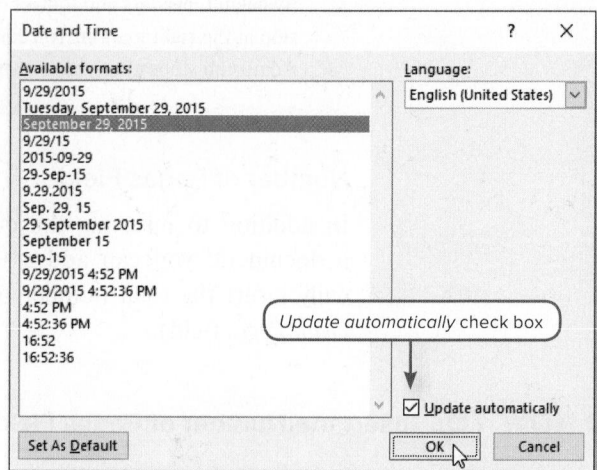

Figure 2-41 *Date and Time* dialog box

MORE INFO

Inserting a date or time is not limited to headers and footers. You can insert the date or time in the body of a document by clicking **Date & Time** [*Insert* tab, *Text* group].

Document Properties

After you enter document properties in a Word document, you can automatically insert this information in the header or footer. For example, you might want to include the title of the document, name of the author, or date last modified. One of the advantages of inserting document properties rather than typing this information is that when you update the document properties, these fields automatically update in the header or footer and throughout the document.

▶ HOW TO: Insert Document Properties

1. Open the header or footer and place the insertion point at the location to insert the document property.

 • Use alignment buttons or tabs to position document property fields in the header or footer.

2. Click the **Document Info** button [*Header & Footer Tools Design* tab, *Insert* group] (Figure 2-42).

3. Select the document property field or click **Document Property** to select from additional fields. The document property displays in the document (Figure 2-43).

 • Alternatively, click the **Quick Parts** button [*Header & Footer Tools Design* tab, *Insert* group] and select **Document Property**.
 • Press the **right arrow** key on your keyboard to deselect a document property field.

4. Click the **Close Header and Footer** button [*Close* group].

Figure 2-42 Insert document property field

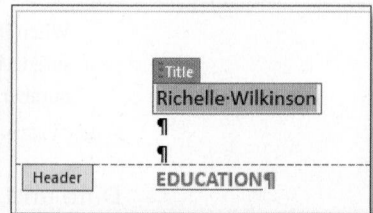

Figure 2-43 *Title* document property field inserted in the header

Built-In Headers, Footers, and Page Numbers

In addition to inserting basic page numbers, manually adding header or footer content, and inserting date and time, Word provides you with a variety of built-in custom header, footer, and page number format options. Many of the header and footer options include document properties that are automatically inserted and updated.

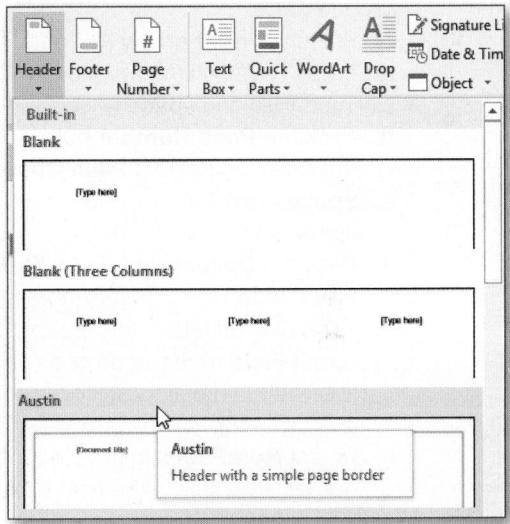

Figure 2-44 List of built-in headers

▶HOW TO: Insert a Built-In Header, Footer, or Page Number

1. Click the **Insert** tab.

2. Click the **Header**, **Footer**, or **Page Number** button [*Header & Footer* group] and select a built-in header, footer, or page number from the drop-down list (Figure 2-44).

 - Document property fields update automatically with document property information.
 - Some fields, such as *Pick the date,* require you to input or select information.

3. Click the **Close Header and Footer** button [*Close* group].

Some of Word's built-in headers, footers, and page numbers include tables, graphics, and advanced formatting. Editing the elements may be challenging without a thorough understanding of this type of content.

PAUSE & PRACTICE: WORD 2-2

In this Pause & Practice project, you modify the resume from *Pause & Practice 2-1*. You add a header that appears only on the second page of the document and insert a document property field, page number, and Word field into the header.

File Needed: ***[your initials] PP W2-1.docx***
Completed Project File Name: ***[your initials] PP W2-2.docx***

1. Open the ***[your initials] PP W2-1*** document completed in *Pause & Practice 2-1*.

2. Save this document as [your initials] PP W2-2.

3. Edit the document properties.
 a. Click the **File** tab to open the *Backstage* view and select **Info** if necessary.
 b. Type Richelle Wilkinson in the **Title** document property text box.
 c. Click the **Back** arrow to return to the resume.

4. Insert a document property field in the header of the resume.
 a. Place the insertion point at the beginning of the first page.
 b. Click the **Insert** tab.
 c. Click the **Header** button [*Header & Footer* group] and select **Edit Header** from the drop-down list. The header on the first page opens.
 d. Click the **Document Info** button [*Header & Footer Tools Design* tab, *Insert* group] and select **Document Title** from the drop-down list. The *Title* document property displays in the header.
 e. Leave the header open for the next instruction.

5. Insert a page number and number of pages field in the header and set it to display only on the second page.
 a. Press the **right arrow** key once to deselect the inserted document property field.
 b. Press **Tab** two times to move to the right margin.
 c. Type Page and **space** once.
 d. Click the **Page Number** button [*Header & Footer* group], select **Current Position** from the drop-down list, and select **Plain Number**. The page number displays in the header.
 e. **Space** once, type of, and **space** once.
 f. Click the **Document Info** (or **Quick Parts**) button [*Header & Footer Tools Design* tab, *Insert* group] and select **Field** from the drop-down list. The *Field* dialog box opens (Figure 2-45).
 g. Select **NumPages** in the *Field names* area (this is the field code to insert the total number of pages in the document).
 h. Select **1, 2, 3** in the *Format* area and click **OK** to insert the number of pages in the header.
 i. Press **Enter** two times to insert two blank lines after the header.
 j. Check to ensure proper spacing is used between each of the words and page numbers.

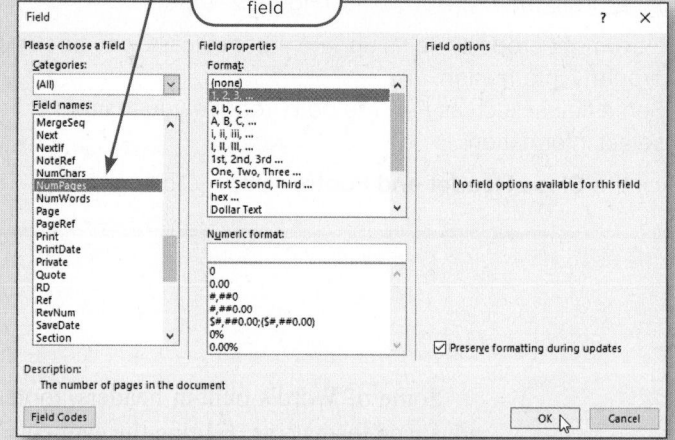

Figure 2-45 Insert *NumPages* field

 k. Check the **Different First Page** check box [*Header & Footer Tools Design* tab, *Options* group]. This removes the header content from the first page, but the header content displays on the second page (Figure 2-46).

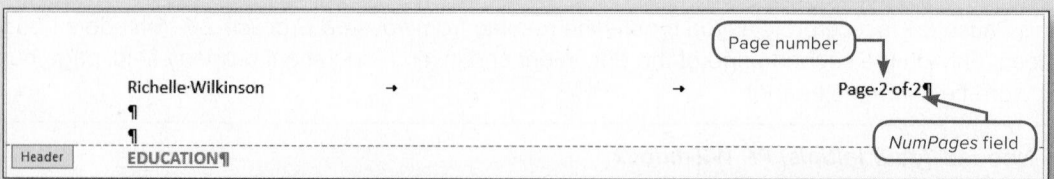

Figure 2-46 Header with document property field, page number, and number of pages field

 l. Click the **Close Header and Footer** button [*Close* group] to close the header and return to the document.

6. Save and close the document (Figure 2-47).

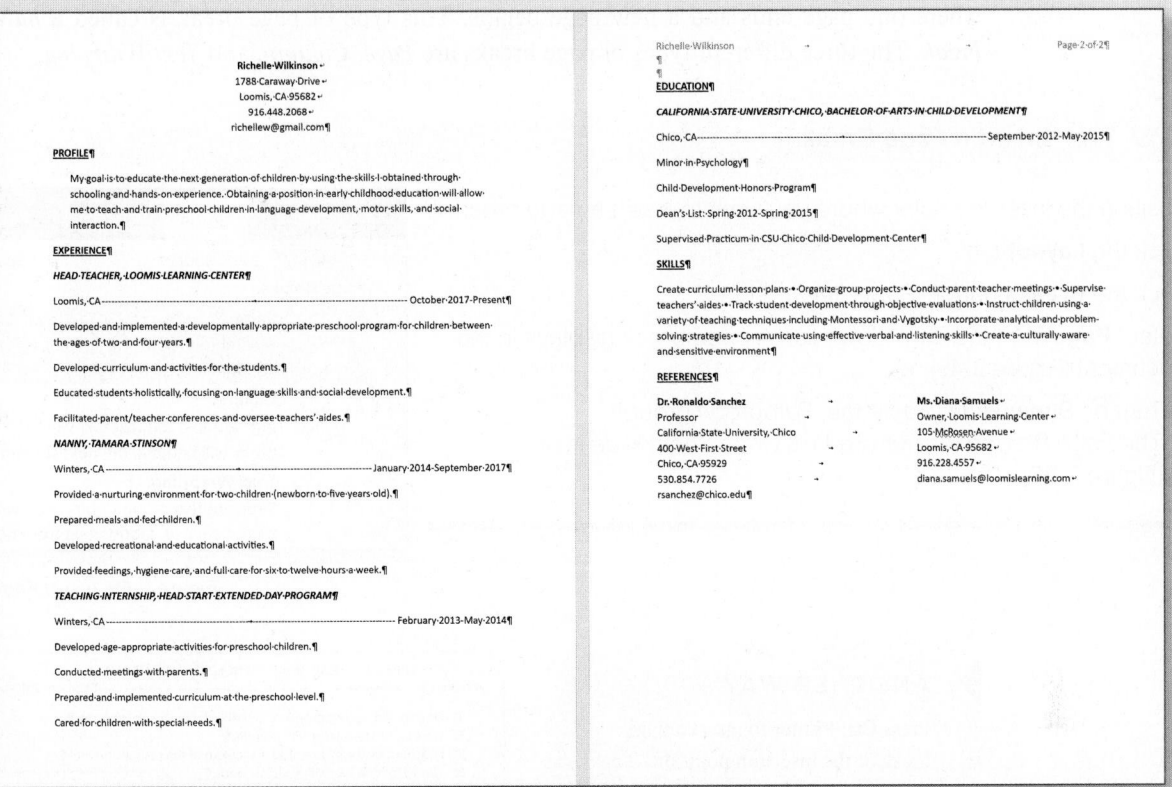

Figure 2-47 PP W2-2 completed

Using Page and Section Breaks

As you're typing a document and get to the bottom of the page, Word automatically moves to the top of the next page so you can continue typing; this is referred to as a *soft page break*. The document's content and margins determine how much information fits on a page and what information flows to a new page.

Occasionally, you may want to start a new page before you get to the bottom margin, or you may want different margins or page orientation in a different section of a document. Word provides options for page and section breaks to control page endings and formatting (Figure 2-48).

> **MORE INFO**
>
> Turn on **Show/Hide** [*Home* tab, *Paragraph* group] when working with page and section breaks, so you can view the placement of page and section breaks.

Figure 2-48 Page and section breaks

Page Breaks

Page breaks end one page and begin a new page. When you insert a *Page* break, you control where one page ends and a new page begins. This type of page break is called a ***hard page break***. The three different types of page breaks are *Page*, *Column*, and *Text Wrapping*.

▶HOW TO: Insert a Page Break

1. Position the insertion point where you want to insert a page break.
2. Click the **Layout** tab.
3. Click the **Breaks** button [*Page Setup* group].
4. Select **Page** from the drop-down list. A page break displays in the document (Figure 2-49).
 - Turn on **Show/Hide** [*Home* tab, *Paragraph* group].
 - The *Page Break* indicator displays when *Show/Hide* is on (Figure 2-50).

Figure 2-49 Insert *Page* break

▶ ANOTHER WAY

Press **Ctrl+Enter** to insert a page break at the insertion point or click the **Insert** tab and click **Page Break** in the *Pages* group.

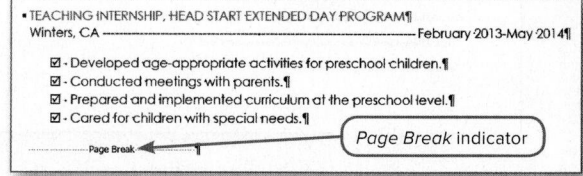

Figure 2-50 *Page* break inserted in a document

Section Breaks

Section breaks provide more formatting control over your document than page breaks. Insert a section break to control the format of an individual section of a document. Use section breaks to format different headers, footers, and page numbering. If you want one page in your document to be landscape orientation, insert a section break and change the orientation for that section. The following are the four different types of section breaks:

- *Next Page*: Insert a section break and start the new section on the next page.
- *Continuous*: Insert a section break and start the new section on the same page.
- *Even Page*: Insert a section break and start the new section on the next even-numbered page.
- *Odd Page*: Insert a section break and start the new section on the next odd-numbered page.

▶HOW TO: Insert a Next Page Section Break

1. Position the insertion point at the location in your document to end one page and begin a new section on a new page.
2. Click the **Layout** tab.
3. Click the **Breaks** button [*Page Setup* group].
4. Select **Next Page** from the drop-down list. A next page section break displays in the document.
 - Turn on **Show/Hide** [*Home* tab, *Paragraph* group].

- The *Section Break (Next Page)* indicator displays when *Show/Hide* is on (Figure 2-51).

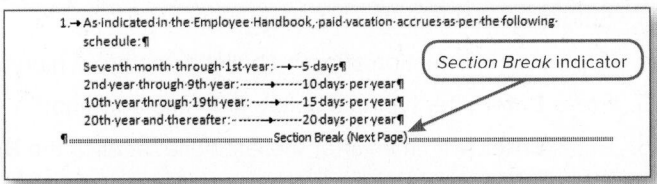

Figure 2-51 *Next Page* section break inserted in a document

Edit Page and Section Breaks

When finalizing a document, you may need to change the placement of a page or section break or remove a page or section break from the document. Delete and move breaks the same way you delete and move text from a document.

To delete a page or section break, select the break and press **Delete**.

To move a section or page break to a new location, first select the **Page Break** or **Section Break**, and then use **Cut** and **Paste** or the drag-and-drop method (Figure 2-52).

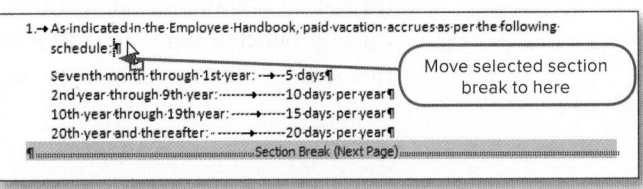

Figure 2-52 Move a section break using drag and drop

SLO 2.6

Using Bulleted, Numbered, and Multilevel Lists

Bulleted and *numbered lists* highlight important information. Generally, use bulleted lists when the order of information is not important, and use numbered lists for sequential information. A *Multilevel list* combines a variety of numbers, letters, and bullets. Word provides built-in bulleted, numbered, and multilevel lists, but you can customize how the information in the list displays and aligns.

> **MORE INFO**
>
> When using bulleted and numbered lists, do not use a period at the end of lists containing only words or short phrases. If you are using complete sentences in your list, use a period at the end of each sentence.

Create a Bulleted List

You can create a bulleted list from existing text or create a new bulleted list by typing text. Choose the type of bullet to use from the *Bullet Library* in the *Bullets* drop-down list.

▶ **HOW TO:** Create a Bulleted List

1. Place the insertion point at the location to begin the list or select the text to convert to a bulleted list.
2. Click the **Bullets** drop-down arrow [*Home* tab, *Paragraph* group] to display the library of bullet options (Figure 2-53).
 - If you click the *Bullets* button (not the *Bullets* drop-down arrow), the most recently used bullet is used for the bulleted list.

3. Select a bullet from the list of options.

4. Type your information after the bullet if you are typing a new bulleted list.

5. Press **Enter** after typing a bulleted item to add another bullet.

6. Press **Enter** two times after the last bullet or click the **Bullets** button to turn off bullets.

Figure 2-53 *Bullets* drop-down list

By default, bulleted lists are formatted with a hanging indent. The first line is indented 0.25" and the hanging indent is set at 0.5". Adjust the indent using the *Decrease Indent* or *Increase Indent* buttons, ruler, or *Paragraph* dialog box.

Add new bulleted items in the middle or at the end of the list by pressing **Enter** in front of or at the end of an existing bulleted item. To add a bulleted item before the first item in the list, click at the beginning of the first item and press **Enter**.

> MORE INFO
>
> To add a blank line between bulleted items, use a line break (**Shift+Enter**) at the end of a bulleted item.

Customize a Bulleted List

In addition to using the bullets listed in the *Bullets Library*, you can select and use a custom bullet. You have the option of using a symbol from one of the font groups or using a picture. If you use a picture, use *Bing Image Search* to find a picture or select a graphic file of your own.

Figure 2-54 *Define New Bullet* dialog box

▶HOW TO: Customize a Bulleted List

1. Select the bulleted list.

2. Click the **Bullets** drop-down arrow [*Home* tab, *Paragraph* group] and select **Define New Bullet**. The *Define New Bullet* dialog box opens (Figure 2-54).

3. Click the **Symbol**, **Picture**, or **Font** button to open a dialog box.

 - If you click **Symbol**, the *Symbol* dialog box opens (Figure 2-55). From the *Font* drop-down list, select a font set (the most common are *Symbol*, *Wingdings*, and *Webdings*) or *Recently used symbols*.
 - Each symbol has a character code to identify the symbol (see Figure 2-55).
 - If you click **Picture**, the *Insert Pictures* dialog box opens. Use *Bing Image Search* to find a picture or select a graphic file of your own.
 - If you click **Font**, the *Font* dialog box opens where you change the font size of the bullet. Changing the bullet font size does not change the size of the bulleted text.

Figure 2-55 *Symbol* dialog box

4. Select the bullet to use and click **OK** (or **Insert** or **Open** depending on the open dialog box) to close the dialog box.
5. Click **OK** to close the *Define New Bullet* dialog box.

You also have the option of formatting text with multiple levels of bullets with a different bullet for each level. Each subsequent bullet level is indented to distinguish it from the previous level. The following are methods to increase or decrease the bullet level.

- Click the **Bullets** drop-down arrow [*Home* tab, *Paragraph* group] and select a bullet list level from the **Change List Level** drop-down list (Figure 2-56).
- Select or click at the beginning of a bulleted item and press **Tab** to increase the bullet level.
- Select or click at the beginning of a bulleted item and click the **Increase Indent** button [*Home* tab, *Paragraph* group] to increase the bullet level.
- Press **Shift+Tab** or click the **Decrease Indent** button to decrease the bullet level.

Figure 2-56 Change bulleted list level

Create a Numbered List

Creating a numbered list is similar to creating a bulleted list. The *Numbering Library* in the *Numbering* drop-down list contains number format options.

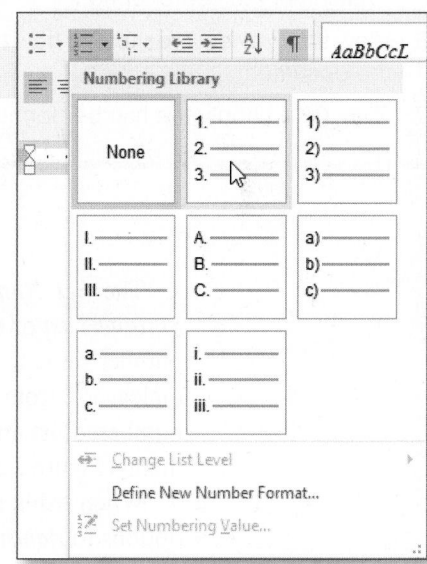

Figure 2-57 Numbering format options

> ▶ **HOW TO: Create a Numbered List**
>
> 1. Place the insertion point at the location to begin the list or select the text to convert to a numbered list.
> 2. Click the **Numbering** drop-down arrow [*Home* tab, *Paragraph* group] to display the library of numbering options (Figure 2-57).
> - If you click the *Numbering* button, the most recently used number format is applied to the numbered list.
> 3. Select a number style from the list of options.
> 4. Type your information after the number if you are typing a new numbered list.
> 5. Press **Enter** after a numbered item to add another numbered item.
> 6. Press **Enter** two times after the last numbered item or click the **Numbering** button to turn off numbering.

> ▶ **ANOTHER WAY**
>
> Both the *Numbering* and *Bullets* drop-down lists are available from the mini toolbar when you select or right-click text.

Customize a Numbered List

In addition to being able to select a format from the *Numbering Library*, you also have the options to *Change List Level*, *Define New Number Format*, and *Set Numbering Value*.

The ***Change List Level*** option in the *Numbering* drop-down list enables you to select the level of the list. The numbering of each subsequent level of the list is dependent upon the number format you select.

You are not limited to the numbering formats available in the *Numbering* drop-down list. The ***Define New Number Format*** option enables you to customize how the numbered list displays.

Figure 2-58 *Define New Number Format* dialog box

▶ **HOW TO:** Customize a Numbered List

1. Select the numbered list.
2. Click the **Numbering** drop-down arrow [*Home* tab, *Paragraph* group] and select **Define New Number Format**. The *Define New Number Format* dialog box opens (Figure 2-58).
3. Click the **Number style** drop-down list and select a number format.
 - Click the **Font** button to change the numbering font, size, or style.
4. Use the *Number format* area to customize how the numbers display.
 - Typically, a period follows the numbers, but you can change this to an ending parenthesis, hyphen, other character, or no punctuation.
5. Click the **Alignment** drop-down arrow to change number alignment.
 - Numbers align on the left by default, but you can change the number alignment to center or right.
6. View the *Preview* area to see how the number format will display in the document.
7. Click **OK** to apply the number format and close the dialog box.

The ***Set Numbering Value*** dialog box includes options to *Start new list* or *Continue from previous list*. You can also set the number value to begin a new list. Open the *Set Numbering Value* dialog box from the *Numbering* drop-down list or right-click a numbered list and select *Set Numbering Value* from the context menu (Figure 2-59).

When using numbering, the context menu (right-click) lists options to *Adjust List Indents*, *Restart at 1*, *Continue Numbering*, and *Set Numbering Value* (Figure 2-60).

Figure 2-59 *Set Numbering Value* dialog box

> **MORE INFO**
>
> Use the *Format Painter* to copy numbered or bulleted list formatting to other areas in a document.

Figure 2-60 Context menu numbering options

Multilevel Lists

Multilevel lists enable you to customize a list using a combination of numbers, letters, or bullets. Word provides a *List Library* from which to select a multilevel list. You can customize an existing multilevel list or define your own list.

As you define a new multilevel list, you have the following options to customize each level of the list:

- Number format including font and starting number
- Number style, which can be a number, letter, Roman numeral, or bullet
- Position of the number and the text that follows

▶ HOW TO: Define a New Multilevel List

1. Select the text or the beginning point on which to apply a multilevel list.

2. Click the **Multilevel List** drop-down arrow [*Home* tab, *Paragraph* group].

3. Select **Define New Multilevel list** from the drop-down list. The *Define new Multilevel list* dialog box opens (Figure 2-61).

4. Click the **More** button in the bottom left of the dialog box to display all formatting options.

5. Select the level to modify in the *Click level to modify* area.

6. Select the *Number format*, *Start at* number, and *Number style for this level* in the *Number format* area.

7. Set the *Number alignment*, the *Aligned at* measurement (which is the first line indent), and *Text indent at* measurement (which is the hanging indent) in the *Position* area.

8. Click the **Set for All Levels** button to open the *Set for All Levels* dialog box where you set the indents for all levels (Figure 2-62). Click **OK** to close the *Set for All Levels* dialog box.

9. Select the next level to modify in the *Click level to modify* area and change settings as described in the steps above.

10. Click **OK** to apply the multilevel list settings after customizing the levels.

Figure 2-61 *Define new Multilevel list* dialog box

Figure 2-62 *Set for All Levels* dialog box

SLO 2.7

Using Styles and Themes

Styles are a collection of preset formatting to apply to a paragraph or selected text. A style controls the font, font size, style, color, effects, indents, line spacing, paragraph spacing, and borders applied to text. Use styles to apply preset formatting to titles, section headings, paragraph headings, text, lists, and tables. *Themes* are a collection of fonts, colors, and effects to apply to an entire document. Use both styles and themes to maintain consistent formatting throughout a single document or multiple documents.

Style Gallery

The *Style gallery* in the *Styles* group on the *Home* tab provides numerous built-in styles to apply to selected text in a document (Figure 2-63). The *Style* gallery does not display all the available styles but rather displays the more commonly used styles.

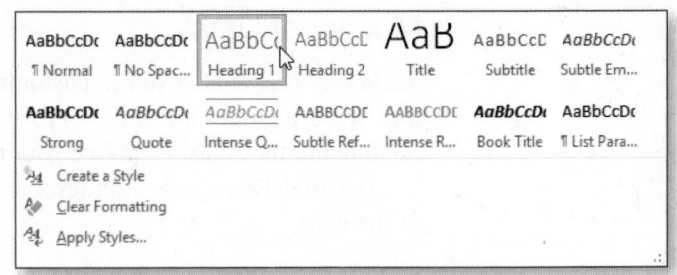

Figure 2-63 *Style* gallery

Apply a Built-In Style

You can quickly preview or apply styles to selected text or paragraphs. To preview a style, place the pointer on a style in the *Style* gallery. A live preview of the style displays on the selected text or paragraph. Apply a style to the text by choosing a style in the *Style* gallery.

▶HOW TO: Apply a Built-In Style from the Style Gallery

1. Select the text or paragraph where you want to apply the style.
2. Select a style from the *Style* gallery [*Home* tab, *Styles* group].
 - Click the **More** button to see all the styles in the *Style* gallery (Figure 2-64).
 - Click the **down arrow** on the right side of the gallery to see the next row of styles available in the *Style* gallery.

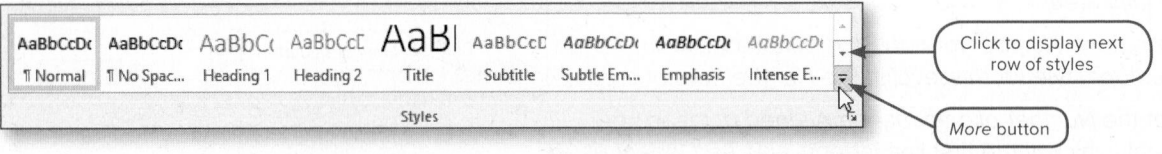

Figure 2-64 Click the *More* button to display additional styles

▶ ANOTHER WAY

Use the mini toolbar to apply a style to selected text by selecting or right-clicking text, choosing **Styles** from the mini toolbar, and selecting the style to apply.

Modify a Style

Once a style has been applied to text, the style can be modified. One way to do this is changing the font, font size, color, style, or effects on the selected text without actually changing the style.

The other option is to modify the style. The advantage of modifying a style is that the formatting will be consistent when the style is applied to other text in a document. When you modify a style, all other text with this style applied updates automatically. The following are two ways to modify a style:

- *Update [style name] to Match Selection*
- *Modify* style

▶ HOW TO: Update Style to Match Selection

1. Apply a style to selected text.
2. Apply formatting changes on the text where the style was applied.
3. Select the text you changed.
4. Right-click the style in the *Style* gallery and choose **Update [style name] to Match Selection** (Figure 2-65).
 - The style updates to match the selected text.
 - All other text with this style applied updates automatically.

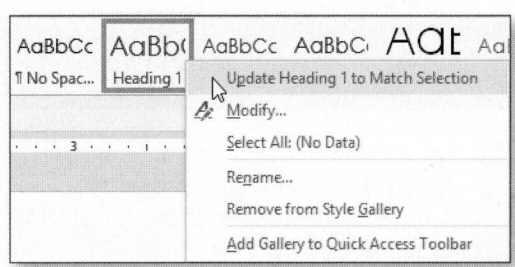

Figure 2-65 Update style to match selected text

You can also modify a style using the *Modify Style* dialog box.

▶ HOW TO: Modify an Existing Style

1. Right-click the style to modify in the *Style* gallery and select **Modify**. The *Modify Style* dialog box opens (Figure 2-66).
2. Make basic formatting changes in the *Formatting* area of the dialog box.
 - The updated style displays in the *Preview* area, and a summary of the style formatting displays below the *Preview* area.
3. Click the **Format** button at the bottom-left corner to open other dialog boxes, such as *Font*, *Paragraph*, *Tabs*, and *Borders*, for additional formatting changes.
 - Change the style formatting, and click **OK** to apply changes and to close the dialog box.
4. Click **OK** to apply the style change and to close the *Modify Style* dialog box.

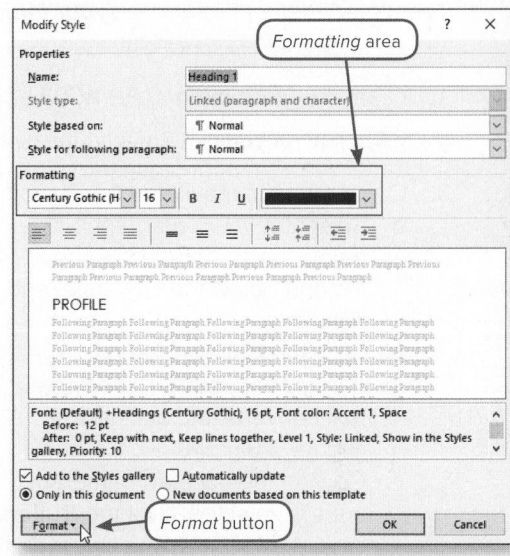

Figure 2-66 *Modify Style* dialog box

Apply a Theme

A theme is a collection of fonts, colors, and effects. Themes are similar to styles, but instead of applying a format to selected text, themes apply formatting to an entire document. All documents have a theme; the default theme for a new document is *Office*. You can change the theme of a document or individually change the *Theme Colors*, *Theme Fonts*, or *Theme Effects* in a document.

▶ HOW TO: Apply a Document Theme

1. Click the **Design** tab.
2. Click the **Themes** button [*Document Formatting* group].
3. Select the theme to apply from the *Themes* gallery (Figure 2-67).
4. Click the **Colors**, **Fonts**, or **Effects** buttons [*Design* tab, *Document Formatting* group] to change each of these options individually within the existing theme.

Figure 2-67 Change the *Theme* of a document

In this Pause & Practice project, you modify the resume you edited in *Pause & Practice 2-2*. You add a bulleted list, customize the bulleted list, insert a page break, apply and modify styles, and apply a document theme.

File Needed: ***[your initials] PP W2-2.docx***
Completed Project File Name: ***[your initials] PP W2-3.docx***

1. Open the ***[your initials] PP W2-2*** document completed in *Pause & Practice 2-2*.

2. Save this document as [your initials] PP W2-3.

3. Convert text to a bulleted list, customize the bullet, and use the *Format Painter*.

 a. Select the four paragraphs of text below the "EXPERIENCE" heading and below the city, state, and date line.

 b. Click the **Bullets** button [*Home* tab, *Paragraph* group]. The selected text converts to a bulleted list (Figure 2-68).

 c. Confirm the bulleted paragraphs are still selected, click the **Bullets** drop-down arrow, and select **Define New Bullet**. The *Define New Bullet* dialog box opens.

 d. Click the **Symbol** button. The *Symbol* dialog box opens (Figure 2-69).

 e. Click the **Font** drop-down list and scroll down to select **Wingdings**.

 f. Scroll down the list of symbols and select the **check box** symbol (*Character code* 254).

 g. Click **OK** to close the *Symbol* dialog box.

 h. Click **OK** to close the *Define New Bullet* dialog box.

 i. Double-click the **Format Painter** button and apply this bullet format to lines of text in the other "EXPERIENCE" sections and the "EDUCATION" section (see Figure 2-71). Don't apply bullet formatting to the city, state, and date lines where the tab stops and leaders display.

 j. Click the **Format Painter** button again to turn off this feature.

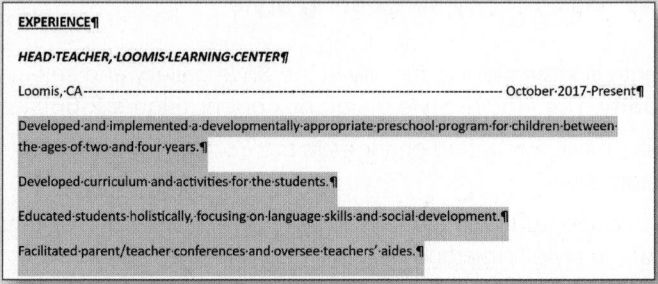

Figure 2-68 Apply bullets to selected text

Figure 2-69 *Symbol* dialog box

4. Insert a page break in the document.

 a. Turn on **Show/Hide** [*Home* tab, *Paragraph* group] if necessary.

 b. Place the insertion point in front of the "EDUCATION" heading.

 c. Select the **Layout** tab and click the **Breaks** button [*Page Setup* group].

 d. Select **Page** from the drop-down list. A page break displays at the bottom of the first page, and the "EDUCATION" section moves to the next page.

5. Change the theme and theme color of the document.
 a. Click the **Design** tab.
 b. Click the **Themes** button [*Document Formatting* group] and select **Ion** from the *Themes* gallery.
 c. Click the **Colors** button [*Document Formatting* group] and select **Red** from the *Theme Colors*.

6. Apply styles from the *Style* gallery to selected text.
 a. Select "**Richelle Wilkinson**" on the first page of the resume (don't select the line break character).
 b. Click the **Title** style in the *Style* gallery [*Home* tab].
 c. Change the font size to **20 pt**.
 d. Apply the **Heading 1** style to each of the underlined main headings ("PROFILE," "EXPERIENCE," "EDUCATION," "SKILLS," and "REFERENCES").
 e. Apply the **Heading 2** style to each of the bold and italicized subheadings in the "EXPERIENCE" and "EDUCATION" sections.

7. Modify a style.
 a. Select the "**PROFILE**" heading.
 b. Change the *Before* paragraph spacing to **16 pt**.
 c. Right-click the **Heading 1** style in the *Style* gallery [*Home* tab, *Styles* group] and select **Update Heading 1 to Match Selection** (Figure 2-70). This style change applies to all text with *Heading 1* style.
 d. Select "**CALIFORNIA STATE UNIVERSITY CHICO, BACHELOR OF ARTS IN CHILD DEVELOPMENT**" in the "EDUCATION" section (not "REFERENCES" section) on the second page and change the font size to **11 pt**.
 e. Right-click the **Heading 2** style in the *Style* gallery [*Home* tab, *Styles* group] and select **Update Heading 2 to Match Selection**.

8. Save and close the document (Figure 2-71).

Figure 2-70 Update style to match selection

Figure 2-71 PP W2-3 completed

Using Find and Replace and Resume Assistant

Find and *Replace* are two extremely useful and powerful tools in Word. The *Find* feature searches for and locates words and phrases in a document. The *Replace* feature searches for a word or phrase and replaces it with other text. You can also use *Find* and *Replace* to search for a specific type of formatting in a document and replace it with different formatting. These features are particularly useful in longer documents. When using *Find* or *Replace*, it is best to position your insertion point at the top of the document so Word searches from the beginning of your document. The **Resume Assistant** connects with *LinkedIn* and provides assistance in Word when working on a resume.

Find

When you use the **Find** feature, the **Navigation pane** opens on the left and displays all instances of text matching your search (Figure 2-72). Word also highlights in yellow each instance of the matching text in the document. Navigate through the document to view each instance and edit as desired.

> ▶ **HOW TO:** Use Find in the Navigation Pane

1. Place your insertion point at the beginning of the document.
2. Click the **Find** button [*Home* tab, *Editing* group]. The *Navigation* pane opens on the left.
3. Click the **Search document** text box at the top of the *Navigation* pane and type the text for which to search (see Figure 2-72).
 - The matching results display below the text box.
 - Word highlights the matching text in the document.

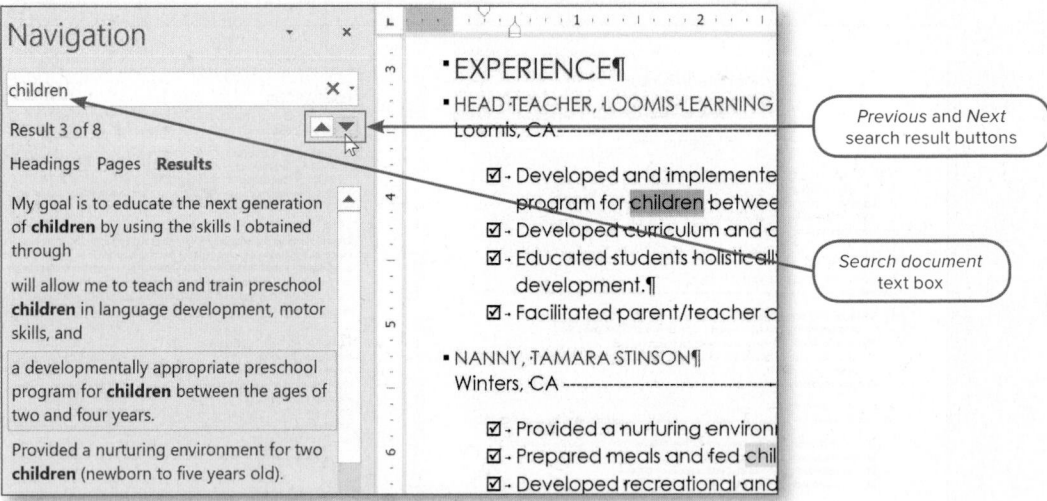

Figure 2-72 Use *Find* in the *Navigation* pane

4. Click the **Next** or **Previous** search result buttons to move through each matching instance in the document.
 - Alternatively, click the matching instances below the *Search document* text box to go to a specific occurrence of the matching text.
5. Edit the highlighted text in the document.
6. Click the **X** to the right of the *Search Document* text box to clear the current search.
7. Click the **X** in the upper-right corner of the *Navigation* pane to close the pane.

Find and Replace

The ***Find and Replace*** dialog box includes three different advanced options for searching your document: *Find*, *Replace*, and *Go To*. The *Find* tab of the *Find and Replace* dialog box not only searches for text in your document but also searches for specific formatting (such as font styles, line spacing, or paragraph spacing). For example, search for all text that is bold or italic, or that has 6 pt. *After* paragraph spacing.

Use the *Replace* feature to search for text, formatting, or a combination of text and formatting and to replace the matching text with other text, formatting, or formatted text. This feature is a quick and efficient way to find and replace text in a document.

▶ HOW TO: Use Replace

1. Place your insertion point at the beginning of the document.

2. Click the **Replace** button [*Home* tab, *Editing* group] or press **Ctrl+H**. The *Find and Replace* dialog box opens with the *Replace* tab displayed (Figure 2-73).

3. Click the **Find what** text box and type the text for which you are searching.

4. Click the **Replace with** text box and type the text to replace the found text.

5. Click the **More** button to display advanced find options. The *Less* button hides the advanced find options.

6. Click the **Format** or **Special** button to add formatting options or special characters to either the text for which you are searching or the replacement text.

 • Place the insertion point in the **Find what** or **Replace with** text box before selecting a format or special character.

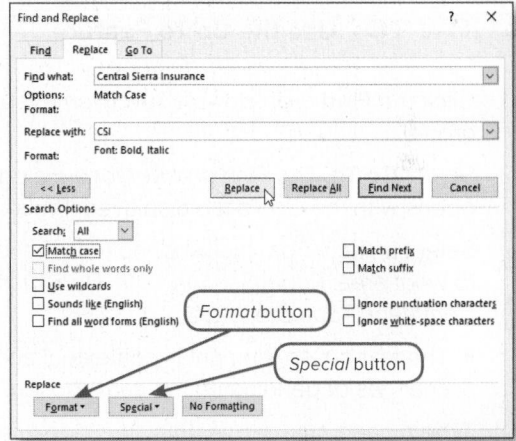

Figure 2-73 Replace text

7. Click the **Find Next** button to locate the first occurrence of the text (and formatting) for which you are searching.

 • It is best to click the **Less** button to collapse this dialog box when finding and replacing content in your document.

8. Select **Replace** (this occurrence), **Replace All** (all occurrences), or **Find Next** (skip this occurrence without replacing and move to the next) to apply an action on each occurrence.

 • When you select one of these options, Word moves to the next occurrence.
 • When you finish finding and replacing text in the document, a dialog box opens informing you that Word has finished searching the document. Click **OK** to close this dialog box.

9. Click the **X** in the upper-right corner to close the *Find and Replace* dialog box.

When using *Find* or *Replace*, wildcards are helpful to find information. You can use wildcards before, after, or between words.

• ***Question mark (?)***: A wildcard for a single character. For example, *w???* finds any words that begins with "w" and contains four letters (for example, when, with, warm, or wish).
• ***Asterisk (*)***: A wildcard for a string of characters. For example, **search*** finds any form of the word "search" (for example, searches, searching, or searched).

Go To

The ***Go To*** feature enables you to move quickly to specific items or locations in your document. This feature is different from *Find* because *Go To* moves to specific objects or locations in your document such as a page, section, or bookmark. This feature is available on the *Go To* tab in the *Find and Replace* dialog box.

▶ HOW TO: Use the Go To Feature

1. Click the **Find** drop-down arrow [*Home* tab, *Editing* group].
2. Select **Go To**. The *Find and Replace* dialog box opens with the *Go To* tab displayed (Figure 2-74).
3. Select an item from the list of options in the *Go to what* area: *Page, Section, Line, Bookmark, Comment, Footnote,* etc.
 - The text box to the right is contextual and changes depending on the item chosen.
4. Type a page number, section, line, bookmark, etc., in the text box.
5. Click the **Go To** button.
6. Click **Close** to close this dialog box.

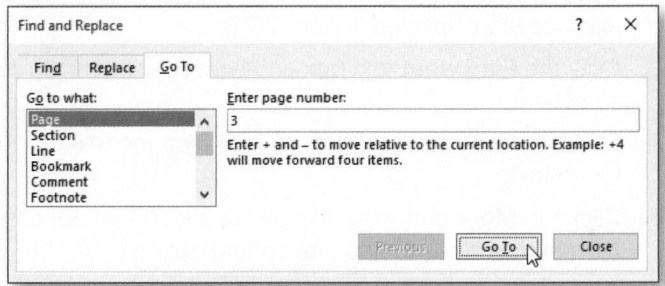

Figure 2-74 *Go To* in the *Find and Replace* dialog box

Resume Assistant

The new ***Resume Assistant*** feature connects with *LinkedIn* and provides assistance when working on a resume. When you open a document that Word believes is a resume, a notification opens and asks if you want to see resume suggestions (Figure 2-75). Based on the content of the resume, the *Resume Assistant* provides examples of resumes and other information to help you customize your resume.

Office 2019 Note: The *Resume Assistant* feature is not available in Office 2019 and some versions of Office 365.

Figure 2-75 *Resume Assistant* notification

▶ HOW TO: Use the Resume Assistant

1. Open an existing resume and click **See resume suggestions** to open the *Resume Assistant* pane on the right (Figure 2-76).

 - If this notification does not display, click the **Resume Assistant** button [*Review* tab, *Resume* group].
 - If the *Resume Assistant* button is not active, turn on the *LinkedIn Features*. Click the **File** tab to open the *Backstage* view, click **Options** to open the *Word Options* dialog box, and check the **Enable LinkedIn features in my Office applications** box in the *LinkedIn Features* area.

2. Click **Get started** if necessary. This menu may not display in the *Resume Assistant* pane if you've used the *Resume Assistant* previously.

3. Type a role and industry (optional) if necessary and click **See examples**. Resume examples display in the *Resume Assistant* pane (Figure 2-77). This menu may not display in the *Resume Assistant* pane if you've used the *Resume Assistant* previously.

 - The *Role* area may already be populated with text based upon your resume. You can change the role if necessary.
 - The *Resume Assistant* pane displays examples of resumes, top skills for the type of job, articles on resume writing, and suggested jobs.

4. Click the **Read more** link on an example resume to view detailed information.

 - Click the **Back** arrow to return to the main *Resume Assistant* pane.
 - Click the **Filter examples by top skills** drop-down list to filter resume examples.

5. Click the **X** in the upper-right corner of the *Resume Assistant* pane to close this pane.

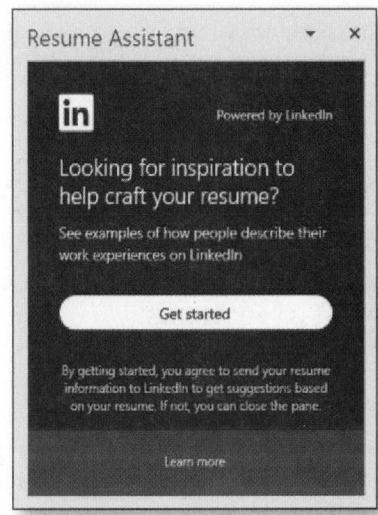

Figure 2-76 **Get started using the**
Resume Assistant

Using Borders, Shading, and Hyperlinks

Borders and *shading* are excellent ways to highlight or emphasize important information in a document. Word provides preset border options, as well as custom border and shading options.

A *hyperlink* functions like a button and is used to take a reader to a web page, open an existing or

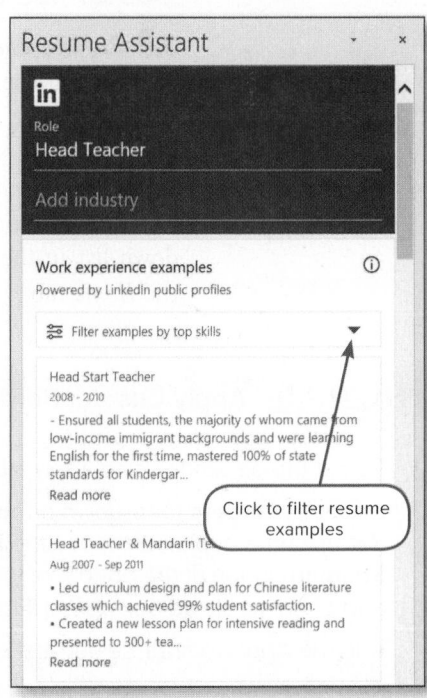

Figure 2-77 *Resume Assistant* pane

new document, open an email message, or move to another location in the current document. You can add a hyperlink to text or a graphic object.

Apply Built-In Borders

Use the *Borders drop-down list* in the *Paragraph* group on the *Home* tab to quickly apply borders to selected text. Borders are typically applied to paragraphs, but they can also be applied to selected text. Borders, by default, apply to the paragraph where your insertion point is located. Figure 2-78 shows the different types of built-in borders.

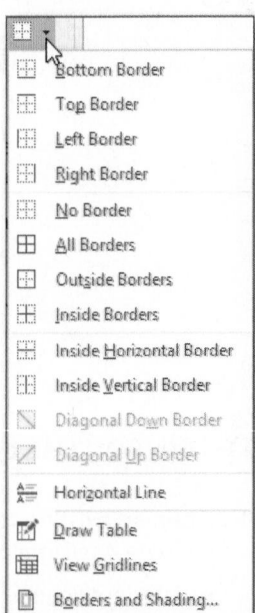

Figure 2-78 *Borders drop-down list*

▶ HOW TO: Apply Built-In Borders

1. Select the paragraph or place the insertion point in the paragraph to apply the border.
2. Click the **Home** tab.
3. Click the **Borders** drop-down arrow [*Paragraph* group] (see Figure 2-78).
4. Click the border option to apply to the selected paragraph.

> **MORE INFO**
>
> Remove borders by selecting the paragraph or text on which the borders are applied and clicking the **No Border** option in the *Borders* drop-down list.

Customize Borders

The *Borders and Shading dialog box* provides many more options to customize the type of borders you use. Not only can you customize the style, width, and color of a border line but also customize where the border is placed in relation to the selected text. The *Borders and Shading* dialog box is available from the *Borders* drop-down list in the *Paragraph* group on the *Home* tab.

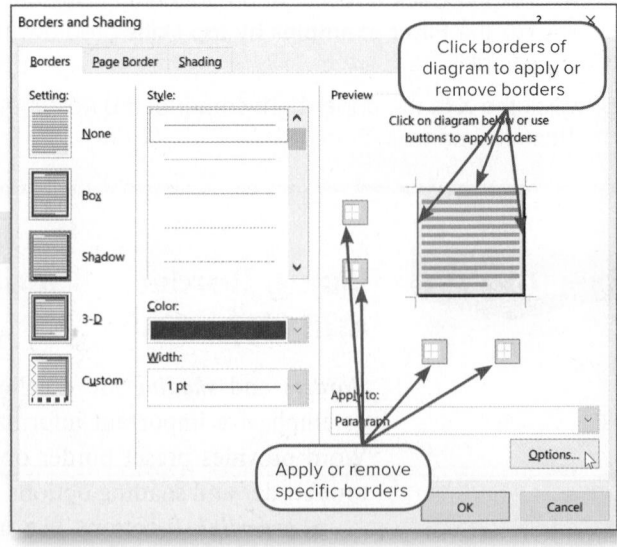

Figure 2-79 *Borders and Shading* **dialog box**

▶ HOW TO: Apply Custom Borders

1. Select the paragraph(s) to apply a border.
2. Click the **Borders** drop-down arrow [*Home* tab, *Paragraph* group] and choose the **Borders and Shading** option at the bottom of the list. The *Borders and Shading* dialog box opens (Figure 2-79).
 - In the *Apply to* area, select *Text* or *Paragraph*.
3. Select the type of border to use in the *Setting* area. Your options are *None, Box, Shadow, 3-D,* and *Custom*.

W2-104

4. Select a style of the line from the list of options in the *Style* area.

5. Click the **Color** drop-down arrow and select line color.

6. Click the **Width** drop-down arrow and select the width of the border line. The width of the line is measured in points.

7. View the *Preview* area to see how the border will appear in your document.

 - In the *Preview* area, customize how the borders appear by clicking the *Top*, *Bottom*, *Left*, or *Right* border buttons to turn a border on or off (see Figure 2-79).
 - Alternatively, click a border preview icon to turn a border on or off.

8. Click the **Options** button to open the *Border and Shading Options* dialog box (Figure 2-80).

 - This dialog box includes the option to add additional space (padding) between the border and the text at the *Top*, *Bottom*, *Left*, and *Right*.
 - The spacing is measured in points.
 - Click **OK** to close the *Border and Shading Options* dialog box.

9. Click **OK** to close the *Borders and Shading* dialog box.

Figure 2-80 *Border and Shading Options dialog box*

> **MORE INFO**
>
> When you click the *Borders* button [*Paragraph* group], the last border selected becomes the function of the *Borders* button. For example, if you last applied a bottom border, clicking the **Borders** button applies a bottom border again.

Apply Shading

Applying shading to a paragraph or text is similar to applying borders. *Shading* applies a background color to selected text. *Shading* color options are available from the *Shading* drop-down list in the *Paragraph* group on the *Home* tab or the *Shading* tab in the *Borders and Shading* dialog box.

The shading colors available are dependent upon the theme of the document. Click the **Shading** drop-down list and select from *Theme Colors* or *Standard Colors* (Figure 2-81). If you want a color that is not available in the menu, click *More Colors* to select from a color palette.

Figure 2-81 Shading color options from the *Shading* drop-down list

▶ **HOW TO: Apply Shading from the Borders and Shading Dialog Box**

1. Select the paragraph(s) to apply a shade.

2. Click the **Borders** drop-down arrow [*Home* tab, *Paragraph* group] and choose the **Borders and Shading** option at the bottom of the list. The *Borders and Shading* dialog box opens (Figure 2-82).

3. Click the **Shading** tab.

4. Click the **Fill** drop-down arrow and select a shading fill color.

 - Alternatively, select a shading *Style* or *Color* in the *Patterns* area.
 - From the *Style* drop-down list, select a gradient percent or a fill pattern as the shading style.

- From the *Color* drop-down list, select a fill color for the gradient or pattern you selected.
- You do not have to use a pattern style or color for shading. Usually just a fill color is sufficient.

5. Click **OK** to close the *Borders and Shading* dialog box.

Figure 2-82 Shading options in the *Borders and Shading* dialog box

Apply a Page Border

Page borders are different from paragraph or text borders. A page border surrounds the entire page rather than selected paragraphs or text. Page borders are useful and attractive when creating flyers or handouts. A page border consists of a line with varying styles, widths, and colors, or you can use art graphics as a page border.

HOW TO: Apply a Page Border

1. Click the **Design** tab.
2. Click the **Page Borders** button [*Page Background* group]. The *Borders and Shading* dialog box opens with the *Page Border* tab displayed (Figure 2-83).
3. Select the type of page border to apply in the *Setting* area.
4. Select a border style in the *Style* list.
 - Alternatively, select an art design to apply as the border from the **Art** drop-down list.
5. Select a border color and width from the **Color** and **Width** drop-down lists.
6. Customize page borders by clicking the **Top**, **Bottom**, **Left**, or **Right** border buttons in the *Preview* area to turn on or off borders if desired.
7. Click the **Apply to** drop-down list and select the page(s) to apply the page border. Your options are:
 - *Whole document*
 - *This section*
 - *This section – First page only*
 - *This section – All except first page*
8. Click **OK** to close the *Borders and Shading* dialog box.

Figure 2-83 Apply a page border

> **MORE INFO**
>
> When you apply a page border, the text in the document is not affected because the page border is placed outside the margin boundaries.

Insert a Horizontal Line

In addition to inserting top and bottom borders on selected text, you can also insert a *horizontal line* to use as a border to separate information on a page. A horizontal line is a graphic object inserted into the document. When you insert a horizontal line, the line is the width of the page. More information about using and customizing graphics is covered in *SLO 4.5: Working with Graphics*.

▶**HOW TO:** Insert a Horizontal Line

1. Place your insertion point at the location to insert a horizontal line.
2. Click the **Borders** drop-down arrow [*Home* tab, *Paragraph* group].
3. Select **Horizontal Line** from the drop-down list (Figure 2-84).
 - The horizontal line is treated as a separate paragraph and has a paragraph mark to the right.

Create a Hyperlink

A hyperlink is an excellent way to direct users to information on a web site, another document, or a location in the same document. Hyperlink can also be used for an email address,

Figure 2-84 Insert a horizontal line

which automatically opens a new Microsoft Outlook email message addressed to the recipient. When creating a hyperlink, you can also customize the *ScreenTip* and the target frame.

> **MORE INFO**
>
> Typically, hyperlinks are underlined and a different color to distinguish them from regular text in a document. In a Word document, Press **Ctrl+Click** to follow a hyperlink.

The *ScreenTip* is the text that displays when you place your pointer over a hyperlink in the document. The *target frame* is the window where the hyperlink document or web site opens. Word provides many different target frame options from which to choose. Usually, it is best to choose **New window** if the link is to a different document or a web page. An email hyperlink always opens in a new window.

▶**HOW TO:** Create a Hyperlink

1. Select the text or graphic to create a hyperlink.
 - If you are creating a hyperlink to a web page, copy (**Ctrl+C**) the web page address (URL) before selecting the text or graphic.
2. Click the top half of the **Link** button [*Insert* tab, *Links* group] to open the *Insert Hyperlink* dialog box (Figure 2-85).

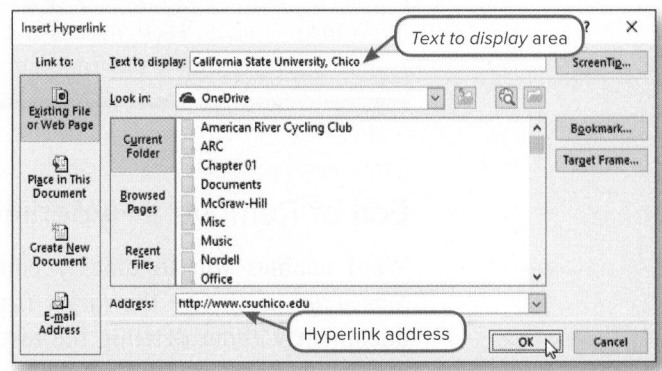

Figure 2-85 *Insert Hyperlink* dialog box

- The text you selected in the document displays as the hyperlink in the *Text to display* area. If you type other text in this text box, it will replace the text you selected in the document.
- Alternatively, click the **Link** drop-down list (bottom half) and select a copied URL to apply a hyperlink on the selected text without opening the *Insert Hyperlink* text box (Figure 2-86). To customize the hyperlink, open the *Insert Hyperlink* dialog box.

3. Select the type of hyperlink in the *Link to* area. Your options are *Existing File or web Page*, *Place in This Document*, *Create New Document*, or *E-mail Address*.

- If you are linking to a file, browse your computer in the *Look in* area to locate and select the file.
- If you are linking to a web page, type or paste (**Ctrl+V**) a web address in the *Address* area.
- If you are linking to a place in the document, a list of headings from which to choose displays.
- If you are inserting a link to create a new document, options for the new document display.
- If you are linking to an email address, type the email address, and create a subject line for the email (optional).

4. Click the **ScreenTip** button to insert text that displays when you place the pointer over the hyperlink (Figure 2-87).

- Type the *ScreenTip* text and click **OK** to close the *Set Hyperlink ScreenTip* dialog box.

5. Click the **Target Frame** button to open the *Set Target Frame* dialog box (Figure 2-88).

- From the drop-down list of options, select where the hyperlink destination will open.
- Check the **Set as default for all hyperlinks** box to make your target frame selection the default for all hyperlinks in your document.
- Click **OK** to close the *Set Target Frame* dialog box.

6. Click **OK** to insert the hyperlink and close the *Insert Hyperlink* dialog box.

Figure 2-86 Insert hyperlink from *Link* drop-down list

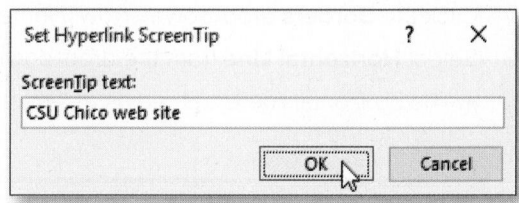

Figure 2-87 *Set Hyperlink ScreenTip* dialog box

Figure 2-88 *Set Target Frame* dialog box

▶ ANOTHER WAY

Ctrl+K opens the *Insert Hyperlink* dialog box. *Link* options are also available in the context menu when you right-click a word, selected text, or an object.

Edit or Remove a Hyperlink

Word enables you to quickly edit hyperlinks to change hyperlink information, add a *ScreenTip*, or change the target frame. Also, you can quickly remove a hyperlink from a document without deleting the text in the document. When you remove a hyperlink from existing text or an object, the text or object in your document is not deleted. Only the hyperlink is removed.

▶ HOW TO: Edit or Remove a Hyperlink

1. Select or click the hyperlink to edit.
2. Click the top half of the **Link** button [*Insert* tab, *Links* group]. The *Edit Hyperlink* dialog box opens.
 - Alternatively, press **Ctrl+K** to open the *Edit Hyperlink* dialog box.
3. Change hyperlink information or options as needed.
4. Click the **Remove Link** button to remove an existing hyperlink (Figure 2-89).
 - When you click **Remove Link**, the *Edit Hyperlink* dialog box closes automatically.
5. Click **OK** to close the *Edit Hyperlink* dialog box if necessary.

Figure 2-89 Edit or remove a hyperlink

ANOTHER WAY

Right-click a hyperlink and select **Edit Hyperlink** or **Remove Hyperlink**.

PAUSE & PRACTICE: WORD 2-4

In this Pause & Practice project, you finalize the resume you edited in *Pause & Practice 2-3*. You use *Find and Replace*, apply borders and shading to selected text, add hyperlinks to the document, and use the *Resume Assistant*.

File Needed: *[your initials] PP W2-3.docx*
Completed Project File Name: *[your initials] PP W2-4.docx*

1. Open the *[your initials] PP W2-3* document completed in *Pause & Practice 2-3*.
2. Save this document as [your initials] PP W2-4.
3. Use *Find and Replace* to replace the hyphen between dates with an en dash.
 a. Place your insertion point at the top of the document (or press **Ctrl+Home**).
 b. Click the **Replace** button [*Home* tab, *Editing* group] or press **Ctrl+H** to open the *Find and Replace* dialog box.
 c. Type **–** (hyphen) in the *Find what* text box.
 d. Place the insertion point in the *Replace with* text box.
 e. Click the **More** button if the *Search Options* are not already displayed.
 f. Click the **Special** button and select **En Dash** (Figure 2-90). The en dash is used between dates.

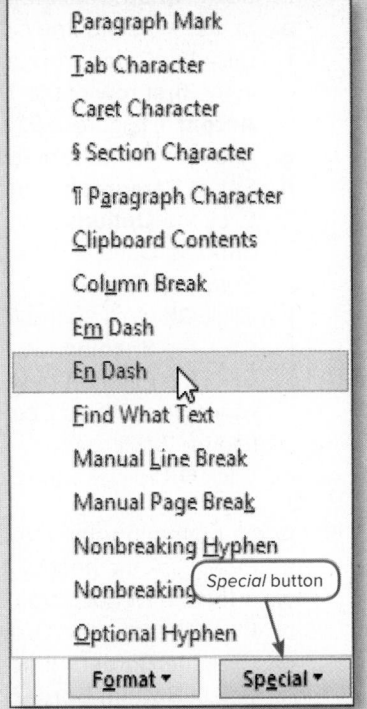

Figure 2-90 Select *En Dash* as the special character to replace a hyphen

g. Click the **Less** button to collapse the **Find and Replace** dialog box (Figure 2-91).
h. Click the **Find Next** button to locate the first instance of a hyphen.

Figure 2-91 Use *Find and Replace*

i. Choose **Find Next** to skip the hyphenated word in the first paragraph.
j. Click the **Replace** button to replace each occurrence of a hyphen between the dates with an en dash; choose **Find Next** to skip and not replace each occurrence of a hyphenated word.
k. Click **OK** when Word has finished searching the document.
l. Click **Close** to close the *Find and Replace* dialog box.

4. Add borders and shading to a paragraph.
 a. Turn on **Show/Hide** [*Home* tab, *Paragraph* group] if necessary.
 b. Select the paragraph after the "PROFILE" heading on the first page, including the paragraph mark at the end of the paragraph.
 c. Click the **Borders** drop-down arrow [*Home* tab, *Paragraph* group] and select **Borders and Shading** to open the *Borders and Shading* dialog box.
 d. Select **Shadow** in the *Setting* area.
 e. Select the **solid line** (first option) in the *Style* area.
 f. Click the **Color** drop-down list and select **fifth color** in the **first row** of the *Theme Colors* (**Dark Red, Accent 1**) (Figure 2-92).
 g. Click the **Width** drop-down list and select **1 pt**.
 h. Select **Paragraph** in the *Apply to* area if necessary.
 i. Click the **Options** button to open the *Border and Shading Options* dialog box and change *Top* and *Bottom* to **2 pt**.
 j. Click **OK** to close the *Border and Shading Options* dialog box.
 k. Click the **Shading** tab.
 l. Click the **Fill** drop-down list and select the **first color** in the **second row** of the *Theme Colors* (**White, Background 1, Darker 5%**) (Figure 2-93).
 m. Click **OK** to close the *Borders and Shading* dialog box.

Figure 2-92 Select border color in the *Borders and Shading* dialog box

5. Add a bottom border to the header.
 a. Right-click the header on the second page and select **Edit Header** to open the *Header* area on the second page.
 b. Place the insertion point in the first line of the header.
 c. Click the **Borders** drop-down arrow [*Home* tab, *Paragraph* group].
 d. Select **Bottom Border**. A 1 pt. red border displays because that is the last border setting you used.
 e. Click the **Close Header and Footer** button [*Header & Footer Tools Design* tab, *Close* group].

Figure 2-93 Apply shading to selected text

6. Insert a hyperlink to an email address.
 a. Select the email address in the heading information near the top of the first page.
 b. Click the top half of the **Link** button [*Insert* tab, *Links* group] or press **Ctrl+K** to open the *Insert Hyperlink* dialog box (Figure 2-94).
 c. Click the **E-mail Address** button in the *Link to* area.
 d. Type richellew@outlook.com in the *Text to display* area.
 e. Type richellew@outlook.com in the *E-mail address* area. Word automatically inserts "mailto:" before the email address.
 f. Click the **ScreenTip** button. The *Set Hyperlink ScreenTip* dialog box opens (Figure 2-95).
 g. Type Email Richelle in the *ScreenTip text* area and click **OK** to close the *Set Hyperlink ScreenTip* dialog box.
 h. Click **OK** to close the *Insert Hyperlink* dialog box.

Figure 2-94 **Insert hyperlink to an email address**

Figure 2-95 *Set Hyperlink ScreenTip* dialog box

7. Insert a hyperlink to a web site.
 a. Select "**California State University, Chico**" in the "REFERENCES" section on the second page. Don't select this text in the "EDUCATION" section.
 b. Click the top half of the **Link** button or press **Ctrl+K** to open the *Insert Hyperlink* dialog box (Figure 2-96).
 c. Select **Existing File or web Page** in the *Link to* area. The *Text to display* area has *California State University, Chico* already filled in.
 d. Type www.csuchico.edu in the *Address* text box of the dialog box. Word automatically inserts "http://" before the web address.
 e. Click the **ScreenTip** button, type CSU Chico web site, and click **OK** to close the *Set Hyperlink ScreenTip* dialog box.
 f. Click the **Target Frame** button in the *Insert Hyperlink* dialog box to open the *Set Target Frame* dialog box.
 g. Select **New window** from the drop-down list and check the **Set as default for all hyperlinks** box (Figure 2-97).
 h. Click **OK** to close the *Set Target Frame* dialog box and click **OK** to close the *Insert Hyperlink* dialog box.

Figure 2-96 **Insert hyperlink to a web page**

Figure 2-97 *Set Target Frame* dialog box

8. Add hyperlinks to email addresses.
 a. Place the insertion point after "rsanchez@chico.edu" in the "REFERENCES" section on the second page.
 b. Press the **spacebar** once to automatically convert the text to a hyperlink to the email address.
 c. Place the insertion point after "diana.samuels@loomislearning.com" in the "REFERENCES" section and press the **spacebar** once to convert it to a hyperlink.

9. Use the *Resume Assistant*.
 a. Click the **Resume Assistant** button [*Review* tab, *Resume* group]. If the *Resume Assistant* button is not active, turn on the *LinkedIn Features*. Click the **File** tab to open the *Backstage* view, click **Options** to open the *Word Options* dialog box, and check the **Enable LinkedIn features in my Office applications** box in the *LinkedIn Features* area.

 Office 2019 Note: The *Resume Assistant* feature is not available in Office 2019 and some versions of Office 365.

 b. Click **Get started** if necessary. This menu may not display in the *Resume Assistant* pane if you've used the *Resume Assistant* previously.
 c. Click **See examples** if necessary. This menu may not display in the *Resume Assistant* pane if you've used the *Resume Assistant* previously. Resume examples display in the *Resume Assistant* pane (Figure 2-98).
 d. Click the **Read more** link on an example resume to view detailed information.
 e. Click the **Back** arrow to return to the main *Resume Assistant* pane.
 f. Scroll down the *Resume Assistant* pane to view the other information in this pane.
 g. Click the **X** in the upper-right corner of the *Resume Assistant* pane to close this pane.

10. Save and close the document (Figure 2-99).

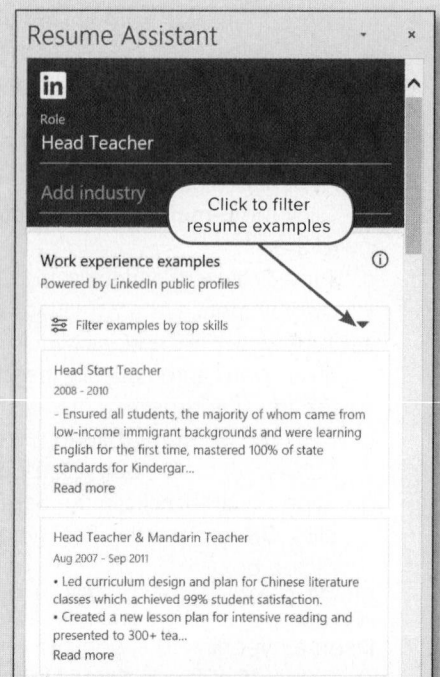

Figure 2-98 *Resume Assistant pane*

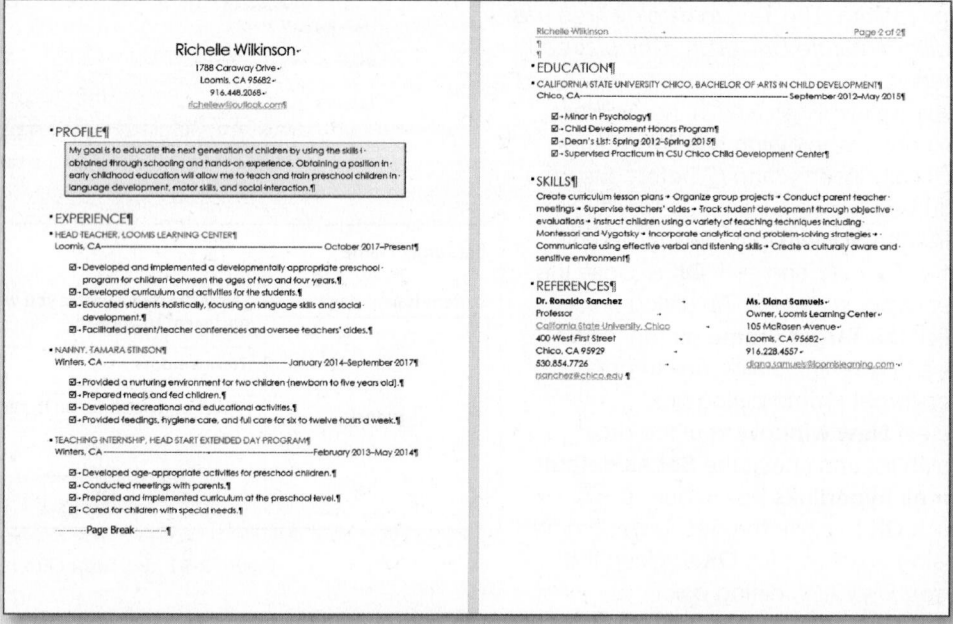

Figure 2-99 PP W2-4 completed

Chapter Summary

2.1 Format a document by customizing margins, page orientation, paper size, vertical alignment, and page movement (p. W2-68).

- Adjust the **margins** of a document to increase or decrease the **white space** surrounding the text. Adjust the top, bottom, left, and right margins of a document.
- **Landscape** and **Portrait** are the two **page orientation** options.
- A standard sheet of paper is 8½"×11". Select other paper sizes or create a custom paper size.
- **Vertical alignment** controls text alignment between the top and bottom margins. By default, text aligns vertically at the top of the document. Other vertical alignment options include center, justified, or bottom vertical alignment.
- Use horizontal and vertical **rulers** to display the typing area on a document.
- Change default page settings using the **Page Setup dialog box**.
- Change the page movement to **Side to Side** to view and scroll through your document horizontally rather than vertically.
- Use the **Thumbnails** feature to display your document as miniature page icons.

2.2 Improve alignment and page layout by setting, using, and editing tab stops in a document (p. W2-72).

- Five different types of **tab stops** are available: **Left**, **Center**, **Right**, **Decimal**, and **Bar**.
- Set, modify, or remove tab stops using the ruler or the **Tabs dialog box**.
- Use the **Tab selector** on the left side of the ruler to select a type of tab stop to set.
- Add **Leaders** with tab stops. Three different types of leaders are available: **Dot**, **Dash**, and **Solid underline**.
- In a Word document, default tab stops are set every 0.5". Customize default tab stops using the *Tabs* dialog box.

2.3 Apply indents to control text alignment (p. W2-76).

- **Indents** function as temporary margins and enable you to arrange paragraphs horizontally between the margins.
- Word provides four types of indents: *left*, *right*, *first line*, and *hanging*.

- Apply, modify, and remove indents with the ruler, *Layout* tab, or *Paragraph* dialog box.

2.4 Enhance document layout by inserting page numbers, headers, and footers (p. W2-82).

- Insert a **page number** into the header or footer in various locations or use default tab settings.
- **Headers** and **footers** are areas above and below a document's top and bottom margins.
- The **Different First Page** option enables you to remove or have different first page content in the header or footer.
- Header and footer content is typed once, and it appears on subsequent pages.
- Customize headers and footers with text, page numbers, the date, and other document property fields.
- A variety of built-in header, footer, and page numbering options are available.

2.5 Control pagination with page and section breaks (p. W2-89).

- Use **page breaks** to control the ending and beginning of pages in a document.
- Use **section breaks** for different page setup formatting in different sections of a document.
- Word provides four different section break options: **Next Page**, **Continuous**, **Even Page**, and **Odd Page**.
- Section breaks are visible in a document when the *Show/Hide* feature is turned on.

2.6 Use customized bulleted and numbered lists to effectively present information (p. W2-91).

- Use **bulleted** and **numbered lists** to emphasize important information.
- Customize lists by using different symbols or pictures as bullets.
- Use numbering to display an ordered list.
- Customize lists by changing number format and levels.
- Use **Multilevel lists** to customize a list using a combination of numbers, letters, or bullets.

2.7 Apply styles and themes to improve consistency in document format (p. W2-95).

- A **style** is a collection of preset formatting applied to selected text.
- The **Style gallery** is a collection of built-in styles.

- Existing styles can be modified.
- A **theme** is a collection of fonts, colors, and effects applied to a document.

2.8 Use find and replace to edit a document and use the *Resume Assistant* to customize a resume. (p. W2-100).

- The **Find** feature in Word searches for specific text or format in a document.
- The **Navigation pane** displays all occurrences of the text for which you are searching.
- The **Replace** feature searches for specific text in a document and replaces it with other text.
- Both *Find* and *Replace* search for and replace formatting in a document.
- Use the **Go To** feature to go directly to a page, section, line, or other area in your document.
- The **Resume Assistant** connects with *LinkedIn* and provides assistance in Word when working on a resume.

2.9 Improve overall document design and format with borders, shading, horizontal lines, and hyperlinks (p. W2-103).

- Apply **borders** and **shading** to text and paragraphs in a document.
- Word provides a variety of built-in border and shading options. Customize borders and shading using the **Borders and Shading dialog box**.
- Apply **page borders** to an individual page or all pages in a document.
- A **horizontal line** is a graphic object.
- A **hyperlink** takes readers to a web page, a different document, a different location in a document, or an email address. An email hyperlink opens Microsoft Outlook and places the recipient's email address in the email message.

Check for Understanding

The SIMbook for this text (within your SIMnet account) provides the following resources for concept review:

- Multiple-choice questions
- Short answer questions
- Matching exercises

Guided Project 2-1

In this project, you create a form for contractors seeking insurance coverage at Central Sierra Insurance. You apply a theme, styles, a multilevel list, tab stops, leaders, indents, borders and shading, a page break, and page numbering.
[Student Learning Outcomes 2.1, 2.2, 2.3, 2.4, 2.5, 2.6, 2.7, 2.9]

File Needed: *InsuranceQuestionnaire-02.docx* *(Student data files are available in the* Library *of your SIMnet account.)*
Completed Project File Name: *[your initials] Word 2-1.docx*

Skills Covered in This Project

- Modify an existing document.
- Change margins.
- Apply a document theme and theme color.
- Change font size, line spacing, and paragraph spacing.
- Apply a style to selected text.
- Modify an existing style.
- Apply borders and shading to selected text.
- Set and use a tab stop with an underline leader.
- Apply and modify a multilevel list.
- Insert a page break.
- Insert a built-in page number in the footer.
- View the document in *Side to Side* view.

1. Open the *InsuranceQuestionnaire-02* document from your student data files.

2. Save this document as [your initials] Word 2-1.

3. Change the margins of the document.
 a. Click the **Page Setup** launcher [*Layout* tab, *Page Setup* group] to open the *Page Setup* dialog box.
 b. Change the *Left* and *Right* margins to **0.75"**.
 c. Click **OK** to close the *Page Setup* dialog box.

4. Change the theme and theme color of the document.
 a. Click the **Themes** button [*Design* tab, *Document Formatting* group].
 b. Select **Integral** from the drop-down list.
 c. Click the **Colors** button [*Document Formatting* group] (Figure 2-100).
 d. Select **Aspect** from the drop-down list.

5. Change the font size, paragraph spacing, and line spacing of the entire document.
 a. Press **Ctrl+A** to select the entire document.
 b. Change the font size to **11 pt**.
 c. Change the line spacing to **Single** (**1.0**).
 d. Change the *After* paragraph spacing to **6 pt**.

6. Apply styles to selected text.
 a. Place the insertion point in the first line of text ("Contractor's Insurance Questionnaire").

Figure 2-100 *Theme Colors drop-down list*

b. Click the **Title** style [*Home* tab, *Styles* group] in the *Style* gallery.

c. Select the second line of the document ("**Please carefully . . .**").

d. Right-click the selected text, click **Styles** on the mini toolbar, and select **Book Title** from the *Style* gallery.

e. Click the **Change Case** button [*Home* tab, *Font* group] and select **UPPERCASE**.

f. Select "**Applicant's Instructions**" and apply the **Intense Quote** style from the *Style* gallery. If necessary, click the **More** button in the *Style* gallery (bottom-right corner) to display all styles.

g. Apply the **Strong** style to the three words in all caps ("**ALL**," "**NONE**," and "**NONE**") in the next paragraph ("Please answer ALL questions . . .").

h. Select "**Insurance Application Disclaimer**" on the second page of the document and apply the **Intense Quote** style.

7. Modify an existing style.

a. Click the **More** button [*Home* tab, *Styles* group] to display all the styles in the *Style* gallery.

b. Right-click the **Intense Quote** style in the *Style* gallery and select **Modify** (Figure 2-101). The *Modify Style* dialog box opens.

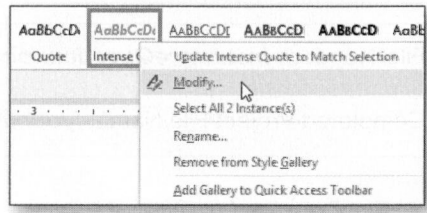

Figure 2-101 Modify an existing style

c. Change the font size to **12 pt**. in the *Formatting* area.

d. Click the **Format** button on the bottom-left corner and select **Paragraph**. The *Paragraph* dialog box opens.

e. Change the *Left* and *Right* indent to **0**.

f. Click **OK** to close the *Paragraph* dialog box.

g. Click the **Only in this document** radio button if it is not already selected to apply the style changes to only this document.

h. Click **OK** to close the *Modify Style* dialog box. The style changes apply to all text formatted with the *Intense Quote* style on both the first and second pages.

Figure 2-102 Apply a left and right border

8. Add borders and shading to selected text.

a. Select the first three paragraphs below "Insurance Application Disclaimer" on the second page.

b. Click the **Borders** drop-down arrow [*Home* tab, *Paragraph* group] and select **Borders and Shading** to open the *Borders and Shading* dialog box (Figure 2-102).

c. Select **Custom** in the *Setting* area.

d. Select the **solid line** border (first option) in the *Style* area.

e. Click the **Color** drop-down list and select the **fifth color** in the **first row** of the *Theme Colors* (**Orange, Accent 1**).

f. Click the **Width** drop-down list and select **1 pt**.

g. Click the **Left** and **Right** border buttons in the *Preview* area (see Figure 2-102).

h. Select **Paragraph** in the *Apply to* area if necessary.

i. Click the **Options** button to open the *Border and Shading Options* dialog box.

j. Change the *Left* and *Right* settings to **5 pt**. and click **OK** to close the *Border and Shading Options* dialog box.

k. Click the **Shading** tab (Figure 2-103), click the **Fill** drop-down list, and select **fifth color** in the **second row** of the *Theme Colors* (**Orange, Accent 1, Lighter 80%**).

l. Click **OK** to close the *Borders and Shading* dialog box.

Figure 2-103 Select shading *Fill* color

9. Change the paragraph spacing and add a tab stop with an underline leader to selected text.
 a. Select the last three lines of text on the second page.
 b. Click the **Paragraph** launcher [*Home* or *Layout* tab] to open the *Paragraph* dialog box.
 c. Change the *Before* paragraph spacing to **12 pt**.
 d. Click the **Tabs** button to open the *Tabs* dialog box (Figure 2-104).
 e. Type 7 in the *Tab stop position* text box.
 f. Click the **Right** radio button in the *Alignment* area.
 g. Click the **4** (solid underline) radio button in the *Leader* area.
 h. Click the **Set** button to set this tab stop and click **OK** to close the *Tabs* dialog box.
 i. Click at the end of the "Name and Title of the Insured" line and press **Tab**. A solid underline displays across the page to the right margin.
 j. Repeat step i on the next two lines.

Figure 2-104 Set a right tab stop with an underline leader

10. Add a multilevel list to selected text and modify lists settings.
 a. Select the lines of text beginning with "**Applicant**" on the first page and ending with the last "**If yes, please explain:**" on the second page.
 b. Click the **Multilevel List** button [*Home* tab, *Paragraph* group] and select the **1), a), i)** option.
 c. Click the **Multilevel List** button again and select **Define New Multilevel List**. The *Define new Multilevel list* dialog box opens.
 d. Click the **Set for All Levels** button to open the *Set for All Levels* dialog box (Figure 2-105).
 e. Set the *Bullet/Number position for first level* to **0"**.
 f. Set the *Text position for first level* to **0.3"**.
 g. Set the *Additional indent for each level* to **0.3"**.
 h. Click **OK** to close the *Set for All Levels* dialog box and click **OK** to close the *Define new Multi-level list* dialog box.

11. Increase indent on selected lines.
 a. Click anywhere in the list to deselect it.
 b. Place your insertion point in 13 in the numbered list ("If yes, . . .") and click the **Increase Indent** button [*Home* tab, *Paragraph* group]. This line is now letter *a)*.
 c. Repeat step b on each of the lines in the list that begin with "If yes, . . ." The list should display 28 numbered items when you finish this process.

Figure 2-105 Change settings for a multilevel list

12. Change paragraph spacing on the multilevel list and add a right tab stop with an underline leader.
 a. Select the entire multilevel list.
 b. Click the **Paragraph** launcher [*Home* or *Layout* tab] to open the *Paragraph* dialog box.
 c. Deselect the **Don't add space between paragraphs of the same style** check box (Figure 2-106).

Figure 2-106 Add spacing between lines of text with the same style

d. Click the **Tabs** button to open the *Tabs* dialog box.

e. Type 7 in the *Tab stop position* text box.

f. Click the **Right** radio button in the *Alignment* area.

g. Click the **4** (solid underline) radio button in the *Leader* area.

h. Click the **Set** button to set this tab stop and click **OK** to close the *Tabs* dialog box.

i. Click at the end of the first numbered item ("Applicant:") and press **Tab**. A solid underline displays across the page to the right margin.

j. Repeat step i on each of the numbered and lettered paragraphs.

13. Save the document.

14. Insert a page break in the document.

a. Place the insertion point before the text in number 22 in the multilevel list.

b. Press **Ctrl+Enter** to insert a page break.

15. Add a page number in the footer of the document.

a. Place your insertion point at the beginning of the document or press **Ctrl+Home**.

b. Click the **Page Number** button [*Insert* tab, *Header & Footer* group].

c. Select **Bottom of Page** to display the drop-down list.

d. Scroll down and choose **Bold Numbers 3** in the *Page X of Y* section. The page numbers display at the right of the footer.

e. Click the blank line below the page numbers in the footer and press **Backspace** to delete the blank line.

f. Click the **Close Header and Footer** button [*Header & Footer Tools Design* tab, *Close* group].

16. View the document in *Side to Side* page movement.

a. Click the **Side to Side** button [*View* tab, *Page Movement* group].

b. Click the **Vertical** button to return to your document [*View* tab, *Page Movement* group].

17. Save and close the document (Figure 2-107).

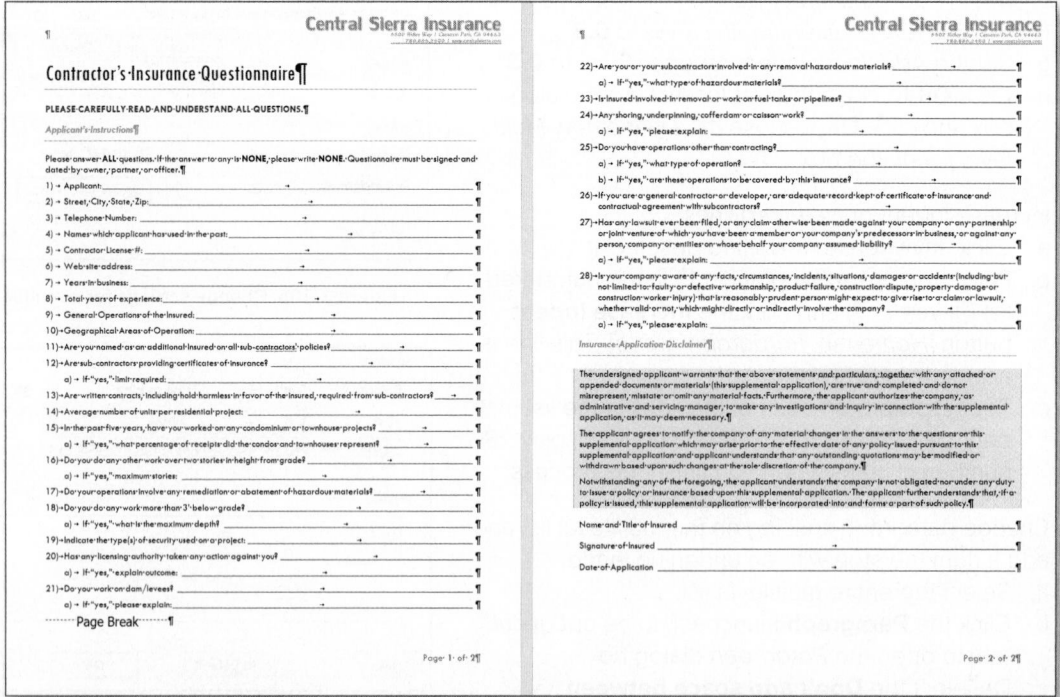

Figure 2-107 Word 2-1 completed

Guided Project 2-2

In this project, you create a checklist for employees at Placer Hills Real Estate to track the tasks they need to complete when a house enters escrow. You create a bulleted list, modify a bullet in a list, set and modify tab stops, apply and modify styles, and insert document properties in the footer.
[Student Learning Outcomes 2.1, 2.2, 2.3, 2.4, 2.6, 2.7, 2.9]

File Needed: **SellerEscrowChecklist-02.docx** (Student data files are available in the Library of your SIMnet account.)
Completed Project File Name: **[your initials] Word 2-2.docx**

Skills Covered in This Project

- Modify an existing document.
- Change margins, line spacing, font, and font size.
- Set a tab stop using the ruler.
- Set a tab stop with leader.
- Apply a style to selected text.

- Modify an existing style.
- Apply and customize a bulleted list.
- Use the *Format Painter*.
- Insert a document property field and date in the footer.
- Apply a border in the footer.

1. Open the **SellerEscrowChecklist-02** document from your student data files.

2. Save this document as [your initials] Word 2-2.

3. Change margins, vertical alignment, line spacing, font, and font size, and delete blank lines.
 a. Click the **Margins** button [*Layout* tab, *Page Setup* group] and select **Normal** from the drop-down list.
 b. Click the **Page Setup** launcher to open the *Page Setup* dialog box and click the **Layout** tab.
 c. Change *Vertical alignment* in the *Page* area to **Center** and click **OK** to close the dialog box.
 d. Press **Ctrl+A** to select the entire document.
 e. Change the font to **Calibri** and change the font size to **12 pt**.
 f. Change the line spacing to **2.0** (Double).
 g. Turn on **Show/Hide**.
 h. Delete all the blank lines between the lines of text.

4. Add text to the document.
 a. Place the insertion point after "Seller" in the second line of the document and press **Tab** once.
 b. Type Property Address.
 c. Place the insertion point after "Escrow Company" and press **Tab** once.
 d. Type Escrow #.
 e. Place the insertion point after "Tasks to be Completed" and press **Tab** once.
 f. Type Date Completed.

5. Set tab stops using the ruler to align information. If the ruler does not display, check the **Ruler** box [*View* tab, *Show* group].
 a. Select the second and third lines of text (beginning with "**Seller**" and ending with "**Escrow #**").
 b. Verify that the **Left Tab** is selected in the *Tab* selector area to the left of the horizontal ruler.
 c. Click the ruler at **3.5"** to set a left tab stop. If you click the wrong location on the ruler, drag the tab stop to the correct location (Figure 2-108).

Figure 2-108 Set left tab stop using the ruler

d. Select the fourth line of text (beginning with "Tasks").
e. Click the **Tab** selector to change to a **Center Tab** stop (Figure 2-109).
f. Click the ruler at **5.5"** to set a center tab stop.

Figure 2-109 Center tab stop

6. Set tab stops and add leaders to create lines for users to fill in information.
 a. Select the second and third lines of text (beginning with "**Seller**" and ending with "**Escrow #**").
 b. Click the **Paragraph** launcher to open the *Paragraph* dialog box.
 c. Click the **Tabs** button to open the *Tabs* dialog box.
 d. Type 3 in the *Tab stop position* area.
 e. Click the **Right** radio button in the *Alignment* area.
 f. Click the **4** (solid underline) radio button in the *Leader* area.
 g. Click the **Set** button to set this tab stop.
 h. Type 6.5 in the *Tab stop position* area.
 i. Click the **Right** radio button in the *Alignment* area.
 j. Click the **4** (solid underline) radio button in the *Leader* area.
 k. Click the **Set** button to set this tab stop.
 l. Click **OK** to close the *Tabs* dialog box.

7. Use tab stops to align text and insert underline leader.
 a. Place the insertion point before "Property Address" and press **Tab** once.
 b. Place the insertion point to the right of "Property Address" and press **Tab** once.
 c. Place the insertion point before "Escrow #" and press **Tab** once.
 d. Place the insertion point to the right of "Escrow #" and press **Tab** once.

8. Apply styles to selected text and update a style.
 a. Place the insertion point in the first line of text ("Seller Escrow Checklist").
 b. Select **Title** style in the *Style* gallery [*Home* tab, *Styles* group].
 c. Change the *After* paragraph spacing to **24 pt**. [*Layout* tab, *Paragraph* group].
 d. Click the **Center** alignment button [*Home* tab, *Paragraph* group] to center the title.
 e. Select "**Tasks to be Completed**" and apply the **Book Title** style from the *Style* gallery.
 f. Change the font size of the selected text to **14 pt**. and apply a **Double underline**.
 g. Right-click the **Book Title** style in the *Style* gallery and select **Update Book Title to Match Selection**. The *Book Title* style is updated.
 h. Select "**Date Completed**" and apply the **Book Title** style.

9. Create a bulleted list to selected text and apply a custom bullet.
 a. Select the lines of text beginning with "**Open Escrow . . .**" and ending with "**Disclosures Sent to Agent**."
 b. Click the **Bullets** drop-down arrow [*Home* tab, *Paragraph* group] and select **Define New Bullet**. The *Define New Bullet* dialog box opens.
 c. Click the **Symbol** button to open the *Symbol* dialog box (Figure 2-110).
 d. Click the **Font** drop-down arrow and select **Wingdings**.
 e. Locate and select the **open square** bullet with a shadow (Character code 113).
 f. Click **OK** to close the *Symbol* dialog box.
 g. Click the **Font** button in the *Define New Bullet* dialog box. The *Font* dialog box opens.
 h. Change the *Size* to **14 pt**.
 i. Click **OK** to close the *Font* dialog box and click **OK** to close the *Define New Bullet* dialog box.
 j. Confirm the bulleted list is still selected and click the **Decrease Indent** button [*Home* tab, *Paragraph* group] to align the bulleted list at the left margin.

Figure 2-110 Select a symbol for a custom bullet

10. Change the hanging indent and add tab stops.
 a. Select the bulleted list if it is not already selected.
 b. Click the **Paragraph** launcher to open the *Paragraph* dialog box.
 c. Change the *Hanging* indent to **0.3"**.
 d. Click the **Tabs** button to open the *Tabs* dialog box (Figure 2-111).
 e. Type 4.5 in the *Tab stop position* area.
 f. Click the **Left** radio button in the *Alignment* area, click the **1 None** radio button in the *Leader* area, and click the **Set** button to set this tab stop.
 g. Type 6.5 in the *Tab stop position* area.
 h. Click the **Right** radio button in the *Alignment* area, click the **4** (solid underline) radio button in the *Leader* area, and click the **Set** button to set this tab stop, and click **OK** to close the *Tabs* dialog box.
 i. Place the insertion point after "Open Escrow with Escrow Company" and press **Tab** two times. A solid underline displays between 4.5" and 6.5".
 j. Repeat step i on the remaining lines in the bulleted list.

Figure 2-111 *Tabs* dialog box

11. Add text to the document.
 a. Place the insertion point at the end of the document (after the solid underline in the last line of text) and press **Enter**.
 b. Click the **Bullets** button [*Home* tab, *Paragraph* group] to turn off the bullet format for this line.
 c. Type Fax/Email Clear Pest Report and press **Enter**.
 d. Type Title and press **Enter**.
 e. Type Lender and press **Enter**.
 f. Type Buyer's Agent.

12. Apply a style to selected text and use the *Format Painter*.
 a. Select "**Fax/Email Clear Pest Report**" and apply the **Book Title** style from the *Style* gallery or mini toolbar.
 b. Place the insertion point in one of the bulleted items.
 c. Click the **Format Painter** button [*Home* tab, *Clipboard* group] to copy the formatting of this bulleted item.
 d. Select the last three lines of text (beginning with "**Title . . .**"). The *Format Painter* copies the bullet formatting and tab settings to these lines of text.
 e. Press **Tab** two times after each of these last three lines to insert the tabs and leaders.

13. Insert a document property field, the date, and a border in the footer of the document.
 a. Click the **Footer** button [*Insert* tab, *Header & Footer* group] and select **Edit Footer** from the drop-down list to open the footer.
 b. Click the **Document Info** button [*Header & Footer Tools Design* tab, *Insert* group], click **Document Property**, and select **Company**. The *Company* document property field displays in the footer.
 c. Press the **right arrow** key once to deselect the *Company* field.
 d. Press **Tab** two times, type Last updated:, and **space** once. The text aligns at the right side of the footer.
 e. Click the **Date & Time** button [*Header & Footer Tools Design* tab, *Insert* group] to open the *Date and Time* dialog box.
 f. Select the spelled-out month, day, year option (January 1, 2020), check the **Update automatically** box, and click **OK** to insert the date and close the dialog box.
 g. Select all the text in the footer and change the font to **Calibri** and the font size to **10 pt**.

h. Click the **Borders** drop-down arrow [*Home* tab, *Paragraph* group] and select **Borders and Shading** to open the *Borders and Shading* dialog box.
i. Click the **Color** drop-down list and select **Automatic** (if it is not already selected).
j. Click the **Width** drop-down list and select **½ pt**.
k. Click the **Top** border button in the *Preview* area to apply a top border to the footer.
l. Click **OK** to close the *Borders and Shading* dialog box.
m. Click the **Close Header and Footer** button [*Header & Footer Tools Design* tab, *Close* group].

14. Save and close the document (Figure 2-112).

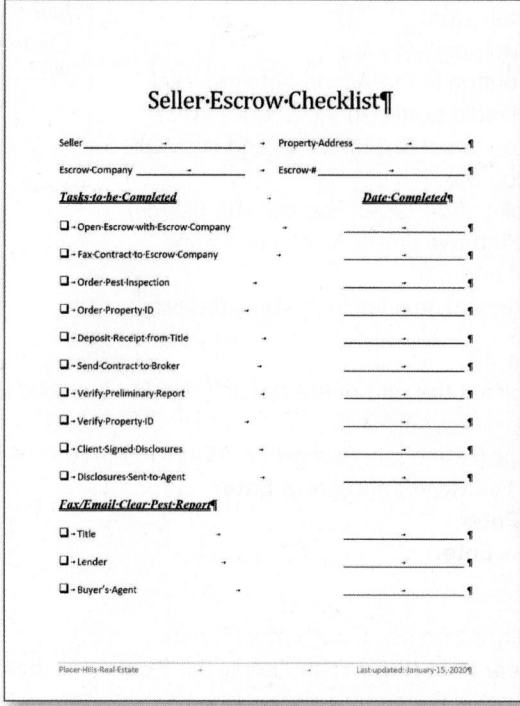

Figure 2-112 Word 2-2 completed

Guided Project 2-3

In this project, you edit and format the personal training guide for the American River Cycling Club to improve readability and effectiveness. You use find and replace, apply a document theme, modify styles, customize numbered and bulleted lists, apply borders and shading, and insert headers, footers, and document properties.
[Student Learning Outcomes 2.1, 2.3, 2.4, 2.6, 2.7, 2.8, 2.9]

File Needed: ***PersonalTrainingProgram-02.docx*** (*Student data files are available in the* Library *of your SIMnet account.*)
Completed Project File Name: *[your initials]* ***Word 2-3.docx***

Skills Covered in This Project

- Modify an existing document.
- Apply a document theme.
- Change margins.
- Change line spacing and paragraph spacing.
- Apply a style to selected text.
- Apply borders and shading to selected text.
- Update an existing style.
- Customize a multilevel bulleted list.
- Use *Find*.
- Use *Find* and *Replace*.
- Insert a hyperlink.
- Insert header, footer, page number, and document properties.
- Use *Side to Side* page movement and *Thumbnails*.

1. Open the ***PersonalTrainingProgram-02*** document from your student data files.

2. Save this document as [your initials] Word 2-3.

3. Apply a document theme and change the line and paragraph spacing.
 a. Click the **Themes** button [*Design* tab, *Document Formatting* group] and select **Slice** from the drop-down list of theme options.
 b. Click the **Page Setup** launcher [*Layout* tab, *Page Setup* group] to open the *Page Setup* dialog box.
 c. Change the *Left* and *Right* margins to **1"** and click **OK** to close the *Page Setup* dialog box.
 d. Press **Ctrl+A** to select the entire document.
 e. Change the line spacing to **1.15** using the *Line and Paragraph Spacing* drop-down list.
 f. Change the *After* paragraph spacing to **10 pt**. on the entire document.
 g. Turn on **Show/Hide**.

4. Apply styles to the title, subtitle, and section headings.
 a. Select the title (first line) of the document.
 b. Apply the **Title** style from the *Style* gallery [*Home* tab, *Styles* group].
 c. Change the font size to **20 pt**. and apply **bold** and **center** alignment.
 d. Select the subtitle (second line) of the document.
 e. Apply the **Subtitle** style from the *Style* gallery [*Home* tab, *Styles* group].
 f. Change the font size to **16 pt**. and apply **center** alignment.
 g. Select the first section heading ("**General Guidelines**").
 h. Apply the **Heading 1** style from the *Style* gallery.
 i. Apply the **Heading 1** style to the remaining bold section headings in the document ("**Personal Training Program Guidelines**," "**More About Long Rides**," "**Training Intensity and Heart Rate**," "**Tracking Training Miles or Hours**," and "**Using a Training Log**").

5. Update a style in the document.
 a. Select the first section heading ("**General Guidelines**") including the paragraph mark at the end of the line.
 b. Change the *Before* paragraph spacing to **12 pt**. and the *After* paragraph spacing to **6 pt**.
 c. Click the **Borders** drop-down arrow [*Home* tab, *Paragraph* group] and select **Borders and Shading** to open the *Borders and Shading* dialog box.
 d. Select **Shadow** in the *Setting* area.
 e. Select the **solid line** (first option) in the *Style* area.
 f. Click the **Color** drop-down list and select the **fifth color** in the **last row** of the *Theme Colors* (**Dark Blue, Accent 1, Darker 50%**) (Figure 2-113).
 g. Click the **Width** drop-down list and select **1 pt**.
 h. Click the **Apply to** drop-down list and select **Paragraph** if necessary.
 i. Click the **Shading** tab, click the **Fill** drop-down list, and select the **fifth color** in the **second row** of the *Theme Colors* (**Dark Blue, Accent 1, Lighter 80%**).

Figure 2-113 Select border line color

 j. Click the **Apply to** drop-down list and select **Paragraph** if necessary.

 k. Click **OK** to close the *Borders and Shading* dialog box. Confirm that "**General Guidelines**" is still selected.

 l. Right-click the **Heading 1** style in the *Style gallery*, and select **Update Heading 1 to Match Selection**. All the headings in the document with the *Heading 1* style applied update automatically.

Figure 2-114 Customize bulleted list

6. Customize the bullets and indents for the bulleted list.

 a. Right-click the first bulleted item on the first page and select **Adjust List Indents**. The *Define new Multilevel list* dialog box opens.

 b. Click **1** in the *Click level to modify* area.

 c. Click the **Number style for this level** drop-down list and select **New Bullet** (Figure 2-114) to open the *Symbol* dialog box.

 d. Click the **Font** drop-down list, select **Webdings**, click the **right pointing triangle** (Character code 52), and click **OK** to close the *Symbol* dialog box (Figure 2-115).

 e. Click **2** in the *Click level to modify* area in the *Define new Multilevel list* dialog box.

 f. Click the **Number style for this level** drop-down list and select **New Bullet** to open the *Symbol* dialog box.

Figure 2-115 Select bullet from *Webdings* font set

 g. Click the **Font** drop-down list, select **Webdings**, click the **double right pointing triangle** (Character code 56), and click **OK** to close the *Symbol* dialog box.

 h. Click the **Set for All Levels** button in the *Define new Multilevel list* dialog box. The *Set for All Levels* dialog box opens (Figure 2-116).

 i. Change the *Bullet/Number position for first level* to **0.25"**, change the *Text position for first level* to **0.5"**, and change *Additional indent for each level* to **0.25"**.

 j. Click **OK** to close the *Set for All Levels* dialog box and click **OK** to close the *Define new Multilevel list* dialog box. All the first and second level bullets and indents in the entire document are changed.

Figure 2-116 Set indents for all levels

7. Use the *Find* feature to find text in the document.

 a. Place your insertion point at the beginning of the document (or press **Ctrl+Home**).

 b. Click the **Find** button [*Home* tab, *Editing* group] or press **Ctrl+F** to open *Find* in the *Navigation* pane.

 c. Type personal training program in the *Search Document* area. All instances of this text appear in the *Navigation* pane and are highlighted in the document.

 d. Click after "personal training program" in the first body paragraph on the first page and type **(PTP)**. Verify one space displays before and after "(PTP)".

 e. Select "**PTP**" (not the parentheses) and apply **italic** format.

 f. Click the **X** in the upper-right corner of the *Navigation* pane to close this pane.

8. Use the replace feature to find and replace text in the document.

 a. Place your insertion point at the beginning of the document (or press **Ctrl+Home**).

 b. Click the **Replace** button [*Home* tab, *Editing* group] to open the *Find and Replace* dialog box with the *Replace* tab selected (Figure 2-117).

 c. Type personal training program in the *Find what* area.

d. Type **PTP** in the *Replace with* area.
e. Click the **More** button to display more search options.
f. Click the **Format** button and select **Font** to open the *Replace Font* dialog box.
g. Click **Italic** in the *Font style* area and click **OK** to close the *Replace Font* dialog box.
h. Click the **Less** button to collapse the *Find and Replace* dialog box.
i. Click the **Find Next** button to find the first occurrence of "personal training program" in the document.
j. Do not replace this text in the title, first body paragraph, or section heading. Replace all other occurrences of "personal training program" with "PTP". Click the **Replace** button to replace the highlighted occurrence or click the **Find Next** button to skip and not replace an occurrence.
k. Click **OK** when you are finished searching the document and click **Close** to close the *Find and Replace* dialog box.

Figure 2-117 Replace text with text and formatting

9. Add a hyperlink to the document.
 a. Select the subtitle of the document ("**American River Cycling Club**").
 b. Click the top half of the **Link** button [*Insert* tab, *Links* group] or press **Ctrl+K** to open the *Insert Hyperlink* dialog box.
 c. Click the **Existing File or web Page** button in the *Link to* area.
 d. Type www.arcc.org in the *Address* area. Word automatically inserts "http://" before the web address.
 e. Click the **ScreenTip** button to open the *Set Hyperlink ScreenTip* dialog box.
 f. Type American River Cycling Club and click **OK** to close the *Set Hyperlink ScreenTip* dialog box.
 g. Click the **Target Frame** button to open the *Set Target Frame* dialog box.
 h. Select **New window** from the drop-down list.
 i. Click **OK** to close the *Set Target Frame* dialog box and click **OK** to close the *Insert Hyperlink* dialog box.

10. Insert header and footer on the second and continuing pages.
 a. Place your insertion point at the beginning of the document (or press **Ctrl+Home**).
 b. Click the **Page Number** button [*Insert* tab, *Header & Footer* group].
 c. Click **Top of Page** and select **Accent Bar 2** from the drop-down list. The page number displays in the header area.
 d. Check the **Different First Page** check box [*Header & Footer Tools Design* tab, *Options* group] to remove the header from the first page so it only displays on the second and continuing pages.

11. Insert document property fields in the footer.
 a. Open the header (if necessary) and click the **Go to Footer** button [*Navigation* group].
 b. Click the **Next** button [*Navigation* group] to move to the footer on the second page.
 c. Click the **Document Info** button [*Insert* group], click **Document Property**, and select **Company** to insert the company document property field.
 d. Press the **right arrow** key once to deselect the property field.
 e. Press **Tab** two times to move the insertion point to the right margin in the footer.
 f. Click the **Document Info** button [*Insert* group] and select **Document Title** to insert the title document property field.
 g. Press **Ctrl+A** to select all the text in the footer.
 h. Apply **bold** and **italic** formatting and change the font size to **10 pt**.

i. Click the **Go to Header** button [*Header & Footer Tools Design* tab, *Navigation* group] to move to the header on the second page.

j. Press **Ctrl+A** to select all the text in the header and change the font size to **10 pt**.

k. Click the **Close Header and Footer** button [*Header & Footer Tools Design* tab, *Close* group]. The header and footer information should appear on the second and continuing pages in the document.

12. View the document in *Side to Side* page movement and view as *Thumbnails*.
 a. Click the **Side to Side** button [*View* tab, *Page Movement* group] to display your document horizontally.
 b. Scroll through the pages of your document using the left and right arrows keys or the scroll wheel on the mouse.
 c. Click the **Thumbnails** button [*View* tab, *Zoom* group] to display all pages as thumbnails.
 d. Select page **3** to view this page in *Side to Side* page movement view.
 e. Click the **Vertical** button [*View* tab, *Page Movement* group] to return to your document.

13. Save and close the document (Figure 2-118).

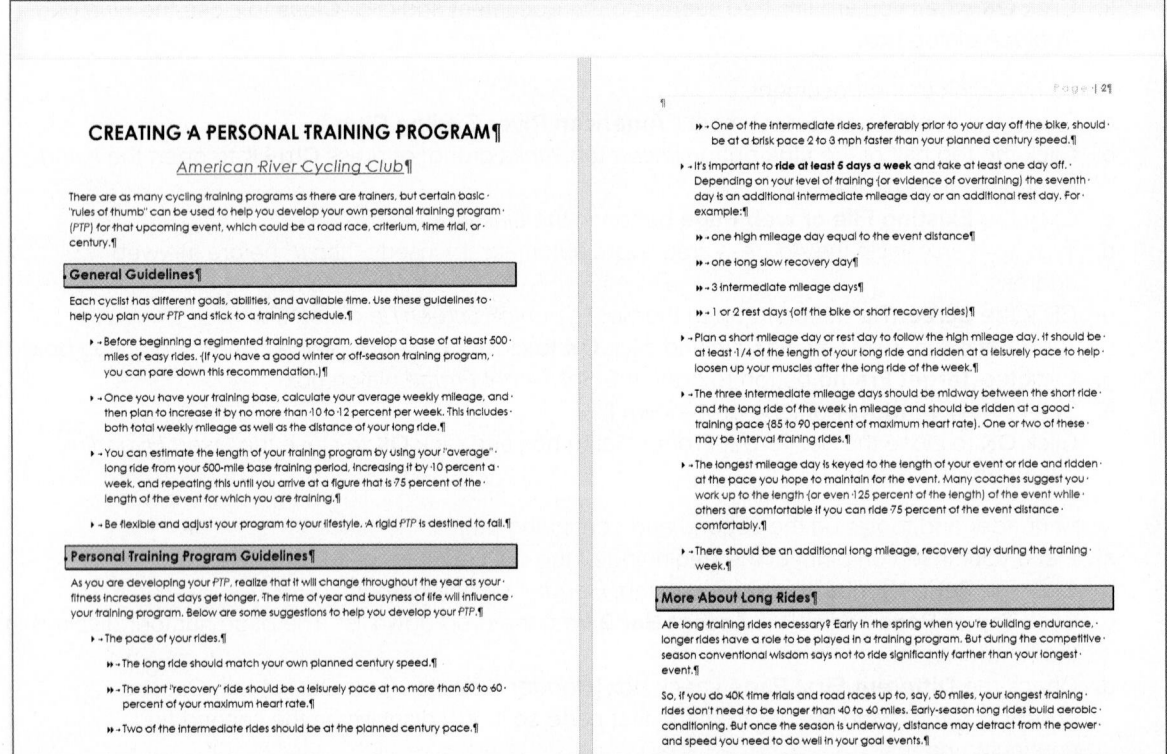

Figure 2-118 Word 2-3 completed (pages 1 and 2 of 5)

Independent Project 2-4

In this project, you use styles, indents, lists, tab stops, the replace feature, footers, and document properties to customize the Emergency Procedures document for Sierra Pacific Community College District.
[**Student Learning Outcomes 2.1, 2.2, 2.3, 2.4, 2.6, 2.7, 2.8, 2.9**]

File Needed: **EmergencyProcedures-02.docx** *(Student data files are available in the* Library *of your* SIMnet account.)
Completed Project File Name: ***[your initials] Word 2-4.docx***

Skills Covered in This Project

- Modify an existing document.
- Apply a document theme and theme color.
- Change margins and font size.
- Apply and modify a style.
- Apply a border to selected text.
- Apply and customize a numbered and bulleted list.

- Use the *Format Painter.*
- Set and modify tab stops.
- Use *Replace.*
- Insert a footer with document properties and current date.
- Insert a page border.
- Center text vertically.
- Use *Side to Side* page movement.

1. Open the **EmergencyProcedures-02** document from your student data files.

2. Save this document as [your initials] Word 2-4.

3. Change the theme to **Integral** and the theme color to **Red**.

4. Change the top, bottom, left, and right margins to **0.75"**.

5. Select the entire document and change the font size to **12 pt**.

6. Format the title of the document.
 a. Select the title of the document and apply **Heading 1** style.
 b. Open the *Font* dialog box, apply **All caps** effect, and change the font size to **16 pt**.
 c. Change the *Before* paragraph spacing to **0 pt**.
 d. Add a **bottom border** to the title using the **Borders** drop-down list.

7. Apply and modify the *Heading 2* style and delete blank lines.
 a. Apply the **Heading 2** style to each of the bold section headings.
 b. Select the first section heading ("**Emergency Telephones [Blue Phones]**").
 c. Change *Before* paragraph spacing to **12 pt**. and *After* paragraph spacing to **3 pt**.
 d. Apply **small caps** effect.
 e. Update **Heading 2** style to match selection. All the section headings are updated.
 f. Turn on **Show/Hide** and delete all the blank lines in the document.

8. Select the bulleted list in the first section and change it to a numbered list.

9. Apply numbering format and formatting changes, and use the *Format Painter*.
 a. Apply numbering to the text below the section headings in the following sections: "*Assaults, Fights, or Emotional Disturbances*"; "*Power Failure*"; "*Fire*"; "*Earthquake*"; and "*Bomb Threat*."
 b. Select the numbered list in the "Bomb Threat" section.
 c. Open the *Paragraph* dialog box, set *Before* and *After* paragraph spacing to **2 pt**., deselect the **Don't add space between paragraphs of the same style** check box, and click **OK** to close the dialog box.
 d. Use the *Format Painter* to copy this numbering format to each of the other numbered lists.
 e. Reset each numbered list so it begins with **1** (right-click the first item in each numbered list and select **Restart at 1** from the context menu).

10. Customize a bulleted list and use the *Format Painter*.
 a. Select the text in the "Accident or Medical Emergency" section.
 b. Create a custom bulleted list and use a **double right-pointing triangle** symbol (*Webdings,* Character code 56).

 c. Open the *Paragraph* dialog box and confirm the left indent is **0.25"** and hanging indent is **0.25"**. If not, change the settings.

 d. Set *Before* and *After* paragraph spacing to **2 pt**. and deselect the **Don't add space between paragraphs of the same style** check box.

 e. Use the *Format Painter* to apply this bulleted list format to the following text in the following sections: "*Tips to Professors and Staff*" and "*Response to Students*."

11. Change indent and paragraph spacing and apply a style.
 a. Select the text below the "Emergency Telephone Locations" heading.
 b. Set a **0.25"** left indent.
 c. Set *Before* and *After* paragraph spacing to **2 pt**.
 d. Confirm the **Don't add space between paragraphs of the same style** box is unchecked (*Paragraph* dialog box).
 e. Apply **Book Title** style to each of the telephone locations in the "Emergency Telephone Locations" section. Select only the location, not the text in parentheses or following text.

12. Change left indent and paragraph spacing and set a tab stop with a dot leader.
 a. Select the text below the "Emergency Phone Numbers" heading.
 b. Open the *Paragraph* dialog box and set a **0.25"** left indent for this text.
 c. Set *Before* and *After* paragraph spacing to **2 pt**. and confirm the **Don't add space between paragraphs of the same style** box is unchecked.
 d. Open the *Tabs* dialog box, set a right tab stop at **7"**, and use a **dot leader (2)**.
 e. Press **Tab** before the phone number (after the space) on each of these lines. The phone numbers align at the right margin with a dot leader between the text and phone number.

13. Apply the **Intense Reference** style to the paragraph headings in the "Accident or Medical Emergency" section ("*Life-Threating Emergencies*" and "*Minor Emergencies*"). Include the colon when selecting the paragraph headings.

14. Use the *Replace* feature to replace all instances of "Phone 911" with "CALL 911" with **bold** font style. *Note*: If previous *Find* or *Replace* criteria displays in the *Replace* dialog box, remove this content before performing this instruction.

15. Insert a footer with document property fields and the current date that appears on every page.
 a. Edit the footer on the first page and use the ruler to move the center tab stop to **3.5"** and the right tab stop to **7"**.
 b. Insert the **Title** document property field on the left. Use the **right arrow** key to deselect the document property field.
 c. **Tab** to the center tab stop and insert the **Company** document property field at center. Use the **right arrow** key to deselect the document property field.
 d. **Tab** to the right tab stop, insert (not type) the date (use January 1, 2020 format), and set it to update automatically.
 e. Change the font size of all the text in the footer to **10 pt**.
 f. Add a **top border** to the text in the footer using the **Borders** drop-down list and close the footer.

16. Use the *Borders and Shading* dialog box to insert a **Page Border** on the entire document. Use **Shadow** setting and **solid line** style. Select the **fifth color** in the **first row** of the *Theme Colors* (**Dark Red, Accent 1**) and **1 pt**. line width.

17. Center the entire document vertically. (Hint: Use the *Page Setup* dialog box.)

18. View the document in **Side to Side** page movement view [*View* tab, *Page Movement* group] and then return to **Vertical** page movement view.

19. Save and close the document (Figure 2-119).

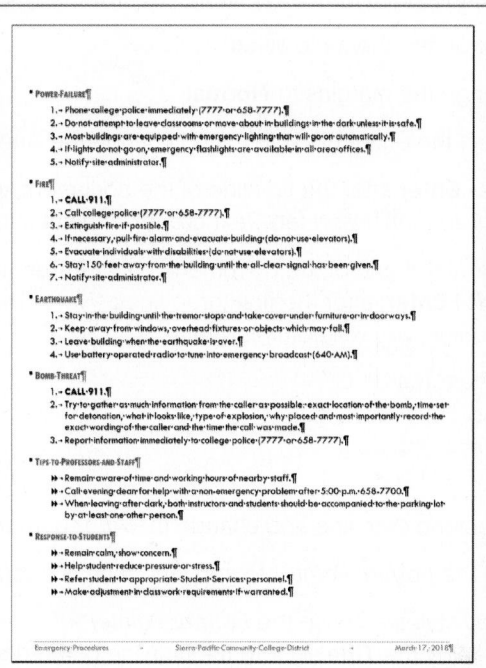

Figure 2-119 Word 2-4 completed

Independent Project 2-5

In this project, you format a bank authorization letter for Placer Hills Real Estate. You modify the formatting of an existing document, apply a theme, apply and modify styles, set tab stops, apply borders, and insert and edit hyperlinks.
[Student Learning Outcomes 2.1, 2.2, 2.7, 2.9]

File Needed: **BankAuthorization-02.docx** (Student data files are available in the Library of your SIMnet account.)
Completed Project File Name: **[your initials] Word 2-5.docx**

Skills Covered in This Project

- Modify an existing document.
- Apply a document theme.
- Change margins.
- Insert an automatically updated date.
- Apply and modify a style.

- Expand font spacing.
- Change paragraph spacing.
- Use the *Format Painter*.
- Set and use tab stops.
- Apply borders and shading to selected text.
- Insert a hyperlink.
- Edit a hyperlink.

1. Open the ***BankAuthorization-02*** document from your student data files.

2. Save this document as [your initials] Word 2-5.

3. Change the theme to **Wisp**.

4. Change the margins to **Normal**.

5. Select the entire document and change the *After* paragraph spacing to **18 pt**.

6. Press **Enter** after the first line of the document, insert (don't type) the current date (use January 1, 2020 format) [*Insert* tab, *Text* group], and set it to update automatically.

7. Click at the end of the document, press **Enter**, and type the following information. Use line breaks (**Shift+Enter**) after the first three lines. (*Note*: The email address is automatically converted to a hyperlink; you will edit this later.)

 Emma Cavalli
 Placer Hills Real Estate
 ecavalli@phre.com
 916-450-3334

8. Select the date line and change the *After* paragraph spacing to **30 pt**.

9. Use the *Format Painter* to copy the date line format to the "**Sincerely**," line.

10. Apply styles and use the *Format Painter*.
 a. Apply the **Title** style to the first line of the document and change the *Before* paragraph spacing to **36 pt**.
 b. Select "**Authorization Letter to Lender**," apply the **Intense Reference** style, and expand the font *Spacing* to **1 pt**.
 c. Select the five lines of text beginning with "**Bank/Financial Institution:**" and ending with "**Borrower Name(s):**" and apply the **Book Title** style.
 d. Use the *Format Painter* to copy the "Bank/Financial Institution" format to "**Seller/Borrower Signature(s)**".

11. Set a tab stop with a leader.
 a. Select the five lines of text beginning with "**Bank/Financial Institution:**" and ending with "**Borrower Name(s):.**"
 b. Set a right tab stop at **6.5"** with a **solid underline leader (4)**.
 c. Press **Tab** after each of these five lines to insert the solid underline leader to the right margin.

12. Apply a border and shading to the paragraph.
 a. Select the paragraph beginning "**Please consider . . .**".
 b. Apply a border with **Shadow** setting, **solid line** style.
 c. Select the **second color** in the **second row** in the *Theme Colors* (**Black, Text 1, Lighter 50%**) and **1½ pt**. line width.
 d. Change the border **Options** so there is **4 pt**. from text on the top, bottom, left, and right.
 e. Set the shading **Fill** color to the **first color** in the **second row** in the *Theme Colors* (**White, Background 1, Darker 5%**).

13. Select the "**Seller/Borrower Signature(s)**" line and apply a **Custom** border that is **solid line, Automatic** color, and **2¼ pt**. width, and apply it to the **top** of the selected paragraph.

14. Insert and customize a hyperlink.
 a. Select "**Placer Hills Real Estate**" in the closing lines and insert a hyperlink.
 b. Type www.phre.com as the web page address.
 c. Type Placer Hills Real Estate as the *ScreenTip*.
 d. Set the target frame to **New window** and make this the default for all hyperlinks.

15. Edit the "ecavalli@phre.com" email hyperlink and type **Email Emma Cavalli** as the *ScreenTip*.

16. Save and close the document (Figure 2-120).

Figure 2-120 Word 2-5 completed

Independent Project 2-6

In this project, you edit, format, and customize the conference registration form for Central Sierra Insurance's Agriculture Insurance Conference. You use a continuous section break, find and replace text, set tab stops and leaders, apply styles, bullets, indents, borders, shading, and hyperlinks.
[**Student Learning Outcomes 2.1, 2.2, 2.3, 2.4, 2.5, 2.6, 2.7, 2.8, 2.9**]

File Needed: ***ConferenceRegistrationForm-02.docx*** *(Student data files are available in the* Library *of your SIMnet account.)*
Completed Project File Name: ***[your initials] Word 2-6.docx***

Skills Covered in This Project

- Modify an existing document.
- Change margins, font, font size, line spacing, and paragraph spacing.
- Insert a header.
- Apply a style.
- Use *Find and Replace*.

- Insert a continuous section break.
- Insert a horizontal line.
- Set different margins for different sections.
- Customize a bulleted list and indents.
- Set and use tab stops and leaders.
- Apply borders and shading to selected text.
- Insert hyperlinks.

1. Open the **ConferenceRegistrationForm-02** document from your student data files.

2. Save this document as [your initials] Word 2-6.

3. Change the top and bottom margins to **0.5"**.

4. Select all the text in the document and change the font size to **10 pt.**, line spacing to **1** (Single), and *After* paragraph spacing to **6 pt**.

5. Apply styles to title and subtitle.
 a. Turn on **Show/Hide** if necessary.
 b. Select and **cut** the first line of the document (including the paragraph mark) and **paste** it in the header.
 c. Delete the blank line below the text in the header.
 d. Select the text in the header, apply **Title** style, align **center**, change the *After* paragraph spacing to **6 pt.**, and close the header.
 e. Select the first two lines in the body of the document (company name and date), apply **Subtitle** style, align **center**, and change the *After* paragraph spacing to **6 pt**.

6. Use *Find* and *Replace*.
 a. Use *Find* to locate all occurrences of "Agriculture Insurance Conference."
 b. Apply **italic** formatting to each occurrence except in the header and close the *Navigation* pane.
 c. Use *Replace* to find all occurrences of "Oct." (include the period) and replace with "**May**".
 d. Use *Replace* to find all occurrences of "Westfield Hotel & Spa" and replace with "***Northgate Resort***" with **Bold Italic** font style.

7. Click at the end of the second body paragraph ("Please help us to determine . . .") and insert a **continuous** section break [*Layout* tab, *Page Setup* group].

8. Click the blank line below the section break and insert a **Horizontal Line** from the **Borders** drop-down list (see "Insert a Horizontal Line" in *SLO 2.9: Using Borders, Shading, and Hyperlinks*).

9. Place the insertion point in the document below the section break and change the left and right margins to **1.25"** and *Apply to* **This section**.

10. Set a tab stop with a leader.
 a. Select the first two lines of text below the horizontal line.
 b. Set a **right** tab stop at **6"** with a **solid underline leader (4)**.
 c. Press **Tab** after each of these lines to insert the solid underline leader to the right margin.

11. Define a new multilevel list and customize bullets and indents.
 a. Press the **Ctrl** key and select the four different bulleted lists in the document. The *Ctrl* key enables you to select non-adjacent text in the document. Don't select the text between each of the bulleted lists, and confirm all bulleted items are selected.
 b. Open the **Define new Multilevel list** dialog box (in the *Multilevel List* drop-down list).
 c. Change the level **1** *Number style* to a **New Bullet** and select the **shaded open square bullet** (*Wingdings,* Character code 113).
 d. Change levels **2** and **3** to the same bullet used on level 1.
 e. Change the **Font** size of the bullets on each of the first three levels to **12 pt**.
 f. **Set for All Levels** the indents so the first level begins at **0"**, the text position for first level begins at **0.25"**, and the additional indent for each level is **0.25"**.

12. Set tab stops with a leader.
 a. Select the "**Flying—Arrival time:**" line.
 b. Set a **right** tab stop at **3"** with a **solid underline leader (4)**.
 c. Press **Tab** after this line to insert the leader.
 d. Select the "**I need directions to *Northgate Resort* from:**" line.
 e. Set a **right** tab stop at **5"** with a **solid underline leader (4)**.
 f. Press **Tab** after this line to insert the leader.

13. Change indents and apply custom borders and shading to selected text.
 a. Select the last two lines in the document, align **center**, and change the left and right indents to **1"**.
 b. Open the *Borders and Shading* dialog box and select **Custom** in the *Settings* area.
 c. Apply a **double line** border, select the **fourth color** in the **first row** of the *Theme Colors* (**Dark Blue, Text 2**), select **¾ pt**. width, and apply to the **top** and **bottom** borders in the *Preview* area.
 d. Select the **Shading** tab, apply a **Fill** color, and select the **fourth color** in the **second row** of the *Theme Colors* (**Dark Blue, Text 2, Lighter 80%**).

14. Insert and customize hyperlinks to email addresses.
 a. Use *Find* to locate the first occurrence of "apelandale@centralsierra.com."
 b. Select this email address and insert a hyperlink to an email address.
 c. Type apelandale@centralsierra.com as the *Text to display* and *E-mail address*. In the *E-mail address* text box, "mailto:" is automatically inserted in front of the email address.
 d. Type Email Asia Pelandale as the *ScreenTip*.
 e. Repeat steps b–d above on the second occurrence of this email address.

15. Save and close the document (Figure 2-121).

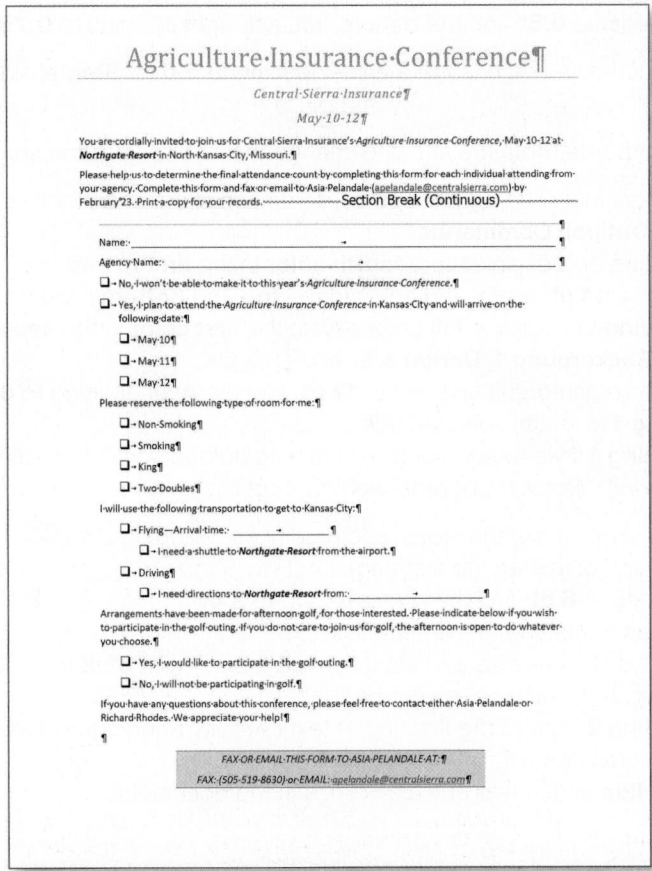

Figure 2-121 Word 2-6 completed

Improve It Project 2-7

In this project, you modify a document that contains shortcuts for Microsoft Outlook. Courtyard Medical Plaza wants to distribute the document to all of its employees. You use tab stops, styles, and many other page layout features that you have learned in this chapter to create a professional and attractive reference document.

[Student Learning Outcomes 2.1, 2.2, 2.4, 2.5, 2.7, 2.9]

File Needed: **OutlookShortcuts-02.docx** (Student data files are available in the Library of your SIMnet account.)

Completed Project File Name: **[your initials] Word 2-7.docx**

Skills Covered in this Project

- Modify an existing document.
- Change margins, line spacing, and paragraph spacing.
- Apply and modify a style.
- Apply borders and shading to selected text.
- Set and modify tab stops and leaders.
- Use the *Format Painter*.
- Insert a page break.
- Edit footer content and tab stops.

1. Open the **OutlookShortcuts-02** document from your student data files.

2. Save this document as [your initials] Word 2-7.

3. Change the page orientation to **Landscape**.

4. Change the top margin to **0.5"** and the bottom, left, and right margins to **0.75"**.

5. Select the entire document and change the line spacing to **1.0** (or **Single**) and the *After* paragraph spacing to **4 pt**.

6. Remove the bottom border from the title and change the *After* paragraph spacing to **0 pt**.

7. Apply custom borders and shading, change paragraph spacing, and modify the *Heading 1* style.
 a. Select "**Global Outlook Commands**."
 b. Apply a **single line** border, select the **fourth color** in the **first row** of the *Theme Colors* (**Dark Blue, Text 2**), select **1 pt**. width, and apply to the **top** and **bottom** borders in the *Preview* area.
 c. Select the **Shading** tab, apply a **Fill** color, select the **first color** in the **second row** of the *Theme Colors* (**White, Background 1, Darker 5%**), and click **OK**.
 d. Change the *Before* paragraph spacing to **12 pt**. and the *After* spacing to **0 pt**.
 e. Update **Heading 1** to match selected text.
 f. Apply the **Heading 1** style to each of the remaining bolded section headings ("*Mail,*" "*Calendar,*" "*Contacts,*" "*Tasks,*" "*Notes,*" "*Journal,*" and "*Formatting*").

8. Change paragraph spacing, set tab stops, and modify the *Heading 2* style.
 a. Select the third line of text on the first page ("Activity Shortcut . . .") and change the *Before* paragraph spacing to **6 pt**. and the *After* spacing to **3 pt**.
 b. Apply **Small caps** formatting to the selected text.
 c. Confirm the text is still selected and set three **left** tab stops at **3"**, **5"**, and **8.25"**.
 d. Update **Heading 2** to match selected text.
 e. Apply the **Heading 2** style to the first line of text ("Activity Shortcut . . .") after each section heading to create column headings.
 f. Turn on **Show/Hide** and delete any blank lines in the document.

9. Set tab stops and leaders to align text under the column headings and use the *Format Painter* to copy formatting.
 a. Select all the tabbed text in the first section ("Global Outlook Commands") below the column headings ("Activity Shortcut . . .") beginning with "**Go to Mail**" and ending with "**Delete selected item Ctrl+D**."
 b. Set the following tabs stops:
 3" left tab stop with **dot leader (2)**
 5" left tab stop with **no leader (1)**
 8.25" left tab stop with **dot leader (2)**
 c. Use the *Format Painter* to apply these tab settings to the remaining text below the column headings ("Activity Shortcut . . .") in all the other sections.

10. Remove the existing footer and insert a custom footer.
 a. Place your insertion point at the beginning of the document.
 b. Edit the footer and remove all content.
 c. Open the *Tabs* dialog box, **Clear All** existing tab stops, set a **center** tab stop at **4.75"**, and a **right** tab stop at **9.5"**.
 d. Insert the **Company** document property field on the left side of the footer.
 e. Press the **right arrow** key to deselect the document property field, **tab** to the center tab stop, and insert the **Title** (or **Document Title**) document property field.
 f. Press the **right arrow** key to deselect the document property field, **tab** to the right tab stop.
 g. Type Page, **space** once, insert a plain page number in the current position.
 h. **Space** once, type of, **space** once, and insert the **NumPages** field (use **1,2,3. . .** format).
 i. Apply a **single line** border, select the **fourth color** in the **first row** of the *Theme Colors* (**Dark Blue, Text 2**), select **1 pt**. width, and apply to the **top** border in the *Preview* area.
 j. Change the font size of all of the text in the footer to **10 pt**.
 k. Set the footer so it does not appear on the first page and close the footer.

11. Insert a **Page** break on the third page before the "Formatting" heading. This document fits on four pages.

12. Save and close the document (Figure 2-122).

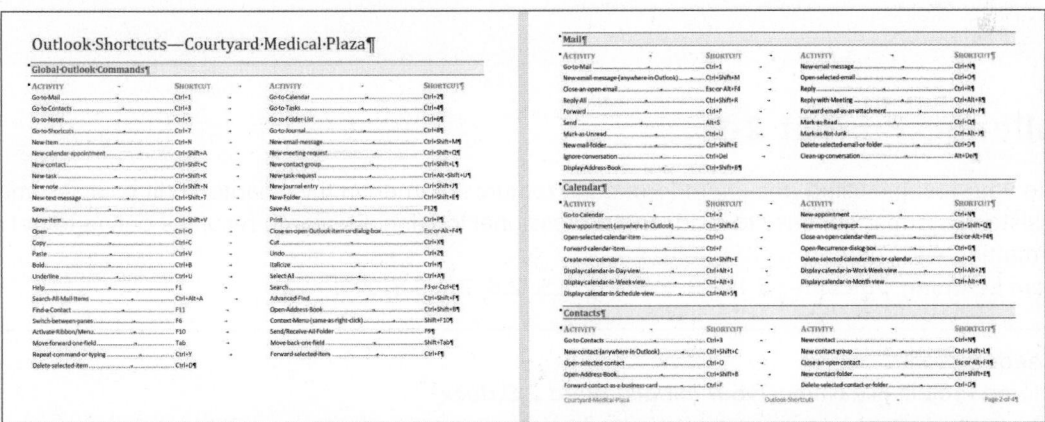

Figure 2-122 Word 2-7 completed (pages 1 and 2 of 4)

Challenge Project 2-8

Create an agenda for an upcoming meeting for an organization you are a member of, such as a club, church committee, volunteer organization, student group, or neighborhood association. Research online to find the common components of agendas. Robert's Rules of Order is a good source of information about meetings and guidelines for meeting protocol.
[Student Learning Outcomes 2.1, 2.2, 2.3, 2.6, 2.7, 2.9]

File Needed: None
Completed Project File Name: *[your initials] Word 2-8.docx*

Create a new document and save it as [your initials] Word 2-8. An agenda can include, but is not limited to, the following items:
- Organization name as the title
- Meeting date, start time, and end time
- Meeting location
- Meeting attendees
- Topic headings
- Topic subheadings (include details for each topic heading)
- The time each topic is expected to last

Modify your document according to the following guidelines:
- Apply styles.
- Use a multilevel list for the agenda items and subheadings.
- Customize number or bullet format and indents as needed.
- Use a right tab stop with a leader to align the amount of time allocated for each main topic heading.
- Apply borders, shading, and/or a horizontal line to create an attractive agenda.
- Adjust margins as needed.
- Include an appropriate header and/or footer.

Challenge Project 2-9

Update your resume using document formatting features learned in this chapter. Edit your resume so it is consistently formatted, easy to read, and professional looking. Research resumes online to get ideas for formatting and content.
[Student Learning Outcomes 2.1, 2.2, 2.3, 2.4, 2.5, 2.6, 2.7, 2.8, 2.9]

File Needed: None
Completed Project File Name: *[your initials] Word 2-9.docx*

Open an existing resume or create a new document and save it as [your initials] Word 2-9. Modify your document according to the following guidelines:
- Apply a document theme.
- Use the *Resume Assistant* (if available) to find examples of similar resumes.

- Apply styles to headings and subheadings to improve consistency in format.
- Adjust margins as needed.
- Use bulleted lists with customized bullets and indents to attractively arrange information.
- Set and use tab stops and indents as necessary to align information.
- Apply borders, shading, and/or a horizontal line to emphasize information in your resume.
- Use page or section breaks as needed.
- Use *Find and Replace* as needed.
- Insert hyperlinks for appropriate information (email address and company names).
- Include a header and/or footer on the second and continuing pages if your resume is more than one page.

Challenge Project 2-10

Format your favorite recipe using some of the formatting features learned in this chapter. Review online recipes using the Food Network, Epicurious, Simply Recipes, or other food web sites.
[Student Learning Outcomes 2.1, 2.2, 2.3, 2.6, 2.7, 2.9]

File Needed: None
Completed Project File Name: *[your initials] Word 2-10.docx*

Create a new document and save it as [your initials] Word 2-10. Your recipe should include, but is not limited to, the following:
- Recipe title
- Descriptive paragraph about the recipe
- Tab stops to arrange quantity and ingredients (and special instructions if needed)
- Numbered, step-by-step instructions
- Recipe source and/or additional information

Modify your document according to the following guidelines:
- Apply a document theme.
- Apply styles.
- Adjust margins as needed.
- Set and use a combination of tab stops (left, right, center, decimal, bar, and leaders) as necessary to attractively line up information.
- Use a numbered list for instructions.
- Use left, right, first line, and/or hanging indents as necessary.
- Apply borders, shading, page border, and/or a horizontal line to highlight or emphasize information in your recipe.
- Insert hyperlinks to appropriate information (link to online recipe).

CHAPTER

3

Collaborating with Others and Working with Reports

CHAPTER OVERVIEW

Creating a long report with a table of contents, citations, footnotes or endnotes, a reference page, and headers and footers can be a challenging task. Word includes numerous tools to automatically create components in a report or a multipage document. Using these tools not only saves you time, it also improves consistency within your documents. Word also provides a variety of collaboration tools to help you more efficiently and effectively work with others on documents.

STUDENT LEARNING OUTCOMES (SLOs)

After completing this chapter, you will be able to:

SLO 3.1 Insert, review, edit, and customize comments (p. 139).

SLO 3.2 Modify and review a document using *Track Changes* and share an online document (p. 142).

SLO 3.3 Insert and edit footnotes and endnotes in a document (p. 151).

SLO 3.4 Create a bibliography with properly formatted sources and insert citations into a document (p. 156).

SLO 3.5 Create and edit a table of contents based on headings (p. 168).

SLO 3.6 Insert a cover page and modify content and content control fields (p. 172).

SLO 3.7 Apply and customize headers and footers in a multipage document (p. 175).

CASE STUDY

American River Cycling Club (ARCC) is a community cycling club that promotes fitness for the entire region. ARCC members include recreational cyclists who enjoy the exercise and camaraderie, as well as competitive cyclists who compete in road, mountain, and cyclocross races throughout the cycling season.

For the Pause & Practice projects, you create a report for club members to describe how to develop a personal training program. In this report, you incorporate many of the report features covered in the chapter to produce a professional-looking and useful report.

Pause & Practice 3-1: Review a report that includes comments and edits marked with tracked changes.

Pause & Practice 3-2: Insert endnotes into the report, convert endnotes to footnotes, add reference sources, insert citations, and create a bibliography page.

Pause & Practice 3-3: Apply styles to headings, create a table of contents based on the headings in the document, modify the table of contents, insert a cover page, customize headers and footers, and share an online file.

Using Comments

When you are collaborating with others on a report or document, use *comments* to provide feedback in the document without making changes to the text of the document. For example, use comments to ask a question, include a suggestion, record notes to yourself, or provide additional information. You can also customize how comments appear in a document, review comments in a document, edit comments, and delete comments.

Change User Name

Each comment and tracked change in a document is attributed to the user name stored in Office. When you sign in to Word with your Microsoft Account, Word uses this information as the *user name*. Word uses your user name as the *author* of each new document created. Each person editing a document is referred to as a *reviewer*.

If you are using a public computer, such as in a computer lab on your college campus, the user name is a generic name assigned to Office for that computer. To make sure the comments you add in a document are attributed to you, change your user name and initials in Office.

> **HOW TO: Change User Name**

1. Click the **Tracking** launcher [*Review* tab, *Tracking* group] to open the *Track Changes Options* dialog box.

2. Click the **Change User Name** button to open the *Word Options* dialog box (Figure 3-1).

3. Type your name in the *User name* text box in the *Personalize your copy of Microsoft Office* area.

4. Type your initials in the *Initials* text box.

5. Check the **Always use these values regardless of sign in to Office** box.

6. Click **OK** to close the *Word Options* dialog box.

7. Click **OK** to close the *Track Changes Options* dialog box.

Figure 3-1 Change user name and initials in the *Word Options* dialog box

> **ANOTHER WAY**
>
> Click the **File** tab to open the *Backstage* view. Click **Options** to open the *Word Options* dialog box to change user name and initials.

Insert a Comment

When you insert a comment, the comment appears in a ***balloon*** in the ***Markup area***, which is the area to the right of a document. The *Markup* area opens when a document has comments or tracked changes (we discuss tracking changes in *SLO 3.2: Using Track Changes and Sharing*). Comments in a document are marked with the name of the author of the comment and the time or date the comment was created. The text of the comment appears below the author's name in the balloon.

▶HOW TO: Insert a Comment

1. Select the text at the location to insert a comment.
 - When you place your insertion point at the beginning of a word or within a word, the comment is attached to the entire word.
2. Click the **New Comment** button [*Review* tab, *Comments* group] (Figure 3-2).

Figure 3-2 *New Comment button*

 - Alternatively, right-click text in the document and select **New Comment** from the context menu.
 - Additionally, in Office 365, click the **Comments** icon in the upper-right corner of the Word window and select **New Comment** (Figure 3-3). This button is not available in Office 2019.
 - The comment balloon appears in the *Markup* area to the right of the Word window.
 - The comment time or date displays as either minutes or hours ago (for example, *4 minutes ago*), or if it was created more than 24 hours ago, the date displays.
 - The word or words in the document with the comment attached are highlighted.

Figure 3-3 Insert *New Comment*

3. Type comment text in the balloon (Figure 3-4).

Figure 3-4 Comment in a balloon in the *Markup* area

4. Click within the document to leave the *Markup* area.

> ▶ MORE INFO
>
> The *Display for Review* view [*Review* tab, *Tracking* group] determines how comments display in the document. *Display for Review* views are covered in the next section, *SLO 3.2: Using Track Changes and Sharing*.

Ink Comments

Another option to insert a comment is to use *Ink Comment*. **Ink Comment** is used to hand write a comment or note using a stylus or your finger on a touch-screen computer. Ink comments function similarly to comments except they display larger in the *Markup* area, and an eraser is used to remove text from the comment. This feature is not available on computers without a touch screen.

▶HOW TO: Use Ink Comments

1. Select the text at the location to insert a comment.
2. Click the **Ink Comment** button [*Review* tab, *Comments* group] (Figure 3-5).
 - The comment balloon appears in the *Markup* area to the right of the Word window.

Figure 3-5 *Ink Comment* in the *Markup* area

3. Use your finger or stylus to write a comment in the *Ink Comment* area.
 - To remove text in an ink comment, click the **Eraser** button [*Review* tab, *Comments* group] and use your finger, stylus, or pointer to erase the text in the comment.
4. Click within the document to return to the document.

Review Comments

Each comment in a document is attributed to the reviewer who made the comment. When you place your pointer on text in a document where a comment is attached, a tag displays with the reviewer's name, the date and time of the comment, and the comment text (Figure 3-6).

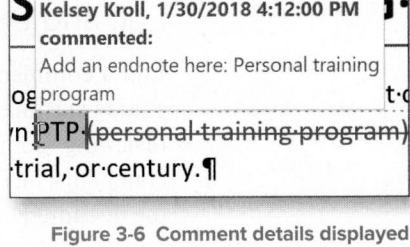

Figure 3-6 Comment details displayed in a tag

If you are working on a long document with multiple comments, Word provides navigation tools to move to the next or previous comment in the document. Click the **Next** or **Previous** button in the *Comments* group on the *Review* tab (Figure 3-7) to move to the next or previous comment in your document.

Figure 3-7 Move to the next or previous comment

> **ANOTHER WAY**
>
> Click the **Comments** icon in the upper-right corner of the Word window and select **Previous** or **Next**.

Reply to a Comment

To reply to a comment, click the **Reply** button on the right side of the comment in the *Markup* area (Figure 3-8). A reply area opens within the existing comment. Type a reply below the original comment.

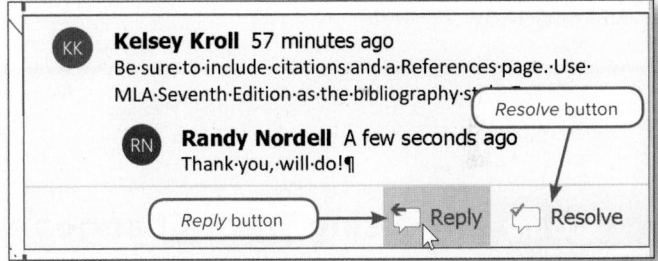

Figure 3-8 Reply to a comment

> **ANOTHER WAY**
>
> Right-click an existing comment in the *Markup* area or the highlighted text in a document with a comment attached. Select **Reply To Comment** from the context menu.

Resolve Comment

You can also resolve a comment after you take action on the comment and when you don't want the comment deleted. When a comment is resolved, the text of the comment changes to a light gray color, and the highlighted text in the document where the comment is attached is a lighter shade of the comment color.

To resolve a comment, click the **Resolve** button on the comment (see Figure 3-8). Alternatively, right-click a comment in the *Markup* area and select **Resolve Comment** from the context menu (Figure 3-9). Reopen a resolved comment by clicking the **Reopen** button on the comment or right-clicking the comment and selecting **Reopen Comment**.

Edit and Delete Comments

Edit a comment by clicking the comment balloon and editing existing text or typing new text. Once you finish reviewing comments, you can delete them. Delete comments individually or delete all the comments in the document at once.

Figure 3-9 *Resolve Comment* from the context menu

▶ HOW TO: Delete Comments

1. Click the comment balloon in the *Markup* area.
 - Alternatively, click **Next** or **Previous** [*Review* tab, *Comments* group] to select a comment (see Figure 3-7).
2. Click the top half of the **Delete** button [*Review* tab, *Comments* group] to delete the selected comment.
 - Alternatively, right-click a comment and select **Delete Comment** from the context menu.
3. Click the bottom half of the **Delete** button and select **Delete All Comments in Document** to delete all the comments in the document (Figure 3-10).

Figure 3-10 Delete all comments in the document

SLO 3.2

Using Track Changes and Sharing

Track Changes is a valuable editing tool in Word that marks changes in a document. All reviewers can see changes to the document. This feature is very useful when working with a group on a report or project. As you review tracked changes in a document, accept, reject, or skip the marked changes. Different options are available for viewing how tracked changes display in the document. Word also provides the ability to share online documents with others and use real-time collaboration.

Track Changes

To mark editing changes in a document, you must first turn on *Track Changes*. Once *Track Changes* is turned on, all editing and formatting changes are marked in the document. Tracked changes display in the body of the document and in balloons in the *Markup* area. Each line in the document that has a change is marked with a vertical gray or red line (depending on *Display for Review* view, which is covered in the next section) to the left of the line. Reviewers can easily see where changes have been made.

▶HOW TO: Use Track Changes

1. Click the top half of the **Track Changes** button [*Review* tab, *Tracking* group] (Figure 3-11).
 - When *Track Changes* is turned on, the button is highlighted.
 - Alternatively, click the bottom half of the **Track Changes** button and select **Track Changes** to turn on *Track Changes*.
2. Edit, delete, insert, or format text in the document.
 - The *Display for Review* view determines how editing changes appear in the document. The *Display for Review* views are covered in the next section.
3. Click the top half of the **Track Changes** button to turn off *Track Changes*.

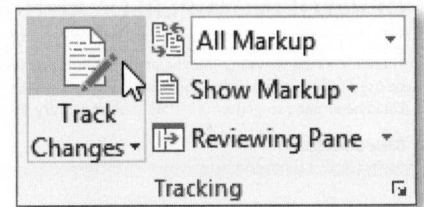

Figure 3-11 Turn on *Track Changes*

> **ANOTHER WAY**
>
> **Ctrl+Shift+E** toggles *Track Changes* on and off.

Display for Review Views

The ***Display for Review*** view determines the appearance of editing changes in a document when using *Track Changes*. Click the **Display for Review** drop-down list in the *Tracking* group on the *Review* tab to select a *Display for Review* view (Figure 3-12). Table 3-1 lists and describes each of these different views.

Figure 3.12 *Display for Review* views

Table 3-1: Display for Review Views

Display for Review View	Description
Simple Markup	Displays a final version of the document with the proposed changes incorporated. A red line to the left of a line marks changed lines in the document. Click the **Show Comments** button [*Review* tab, *Comments* group] to display or hide comments in the document.
All Markup	Displays added, deleted, and edited text in the body of the document. Formatting changes and comments display in balloons on the right. A gray line to the left of a line marks changed lines in the document.
No Markup	Displays a final version of the document with the proposed changes incorporated. All editing changes and comments are hidden.
Original	Displays the original document with proposed changes not incorporated. All editing changes and comments are hidden.

All Markup view is typically used when reviewing a document with changes tracked (Figure 3-13). When using ***Simple Markup***, ***No Markup***, or ***Original*** view, the tracked changes are still in the document, but they are hidden so you can view the final or original version without markup displayed. It is important to understand these different views when using *Track Changes* to edit a document.

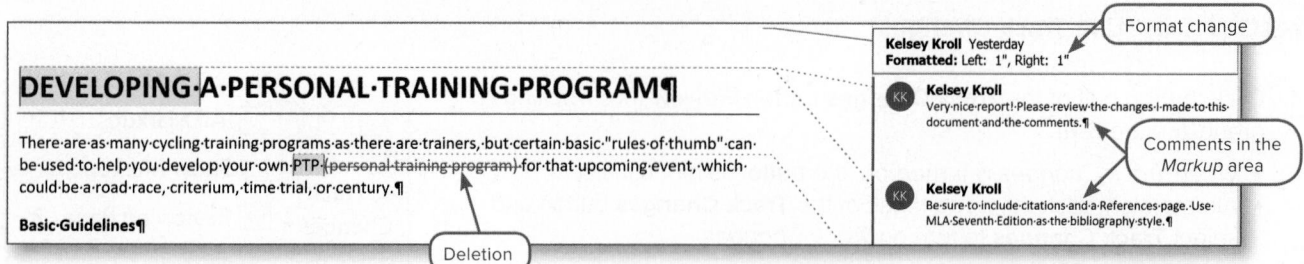

Figure 3-13 Changes tracked in a document displayed in *All Markup* view

Accept and Reject Changes

After a document has been marked with editing changes, you can review each proposed change and either accept or reject the change. It's best to work in *All Markup* view when reviewing a document with changes tracked. When you accept an editing or formatting change, the change is applied to the document, and the inline markup and/or balloon is removed. When you reject an editing or formatting change, the text and formatting revert back to their original form.

Similar to comments, each editing change is attributed to a reviewer. Place your pointer on a change in the body of the text or on a balloon to display a tag containing the reviewer's name, the date and time of the change, and a description of the change (Figure 3-14).

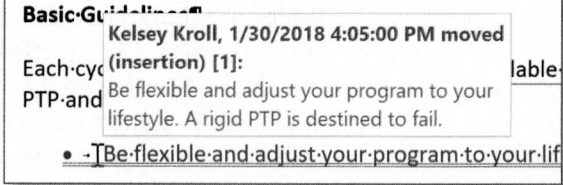

Figure 3-14 Tracked changes details displayed in a tag

▶ HOW TO: Accept and Reject Changes

1. Place the insertion point at the beginning of the document (**Ctrl+Home**).
2. Click the **Display for Review** drop-down list [*Review* tab, *Tracking* group] and select **All Markup** if this is not the current view.
3. Click the **Next** button [*Review* tab, *Changes* group] to select the next change made to the document (Figure 3-15).
 - Click the **Previous** button to select the previous revision.
 - If you are in *No Markup* or *Original* view and click the *Next* or *Previous* button, the view automatically changes to *All Markup*.

Figure 3-15 Move to the next revision in the document

4. Click the **Accept** or **Reject** button [*Review* tab, *Changes* group] to accept or reject the change and move to the next revision.
 - Click the bottom half of the **Accept** button to display additional options: *Accept and Move to Next, Accept This Change, Accept All Changes Shown, Accept All Changes*, and *Accept All Changes and Stop Tracking* (Figure 3-16).

Figure 3-16 *Accept All Changes and Stop Tracking* option

- Click the bottom half of the **Reject** button to display additional options: *Reject and Move to Next*, *Reject Change*, *Reject All Changes Shown*, *Reject All Changes*, and *Reject All Changes and Stop Tracking*.
- When accepting and rejecting changes, Word also stops on comments. Click **Accept** to leave the comment in the document or **Reject** to delete the comment.
- Click **Next** to skip a comment or revision in the document.

5. Continue accepting or rejecting changes in the document.

6. Click **OK** in the dialog box that confirms no more comments or tracked changes are in the document. (Figure 3-17).

- When all changes have been accepted or rejected, no vertical lines display to the left of the text in the body of the document.

Figure 3-17 Dialog box that appears after reviewing the document

> ANOTHER WAY

Right-click a change and select **Accept "*description of change*"** or **Reject "*description of change*"** from the context menu.

Reviewing Pane

When working with a document that has many tracked changes or comments, the ***Reviewing pane*** is a useful tool. The *Reviewing* pane is a separate pane that includes all tracked changes and comments. It can be displayed vertically on the left side of the Word window or horizontally at the bottom of the Word window (Figure 3-18). If many changes and comments display in a document and all the balloons cannot fit in the *Markup* area, the *Reviewing* pane automatically opens.

To open the *Reviewing* pane, click the **Reviewing Pane** button in the *Tracking* group on the *Review* tab and select either **Reviewing Pane Vertical** or **Reviewing Pane Horizontal**.

> MORE INFO

When the *Reviewing* pane opens, the title of the pane is *Revisions*. This book refers to this pane as the *Reviewing* pane.

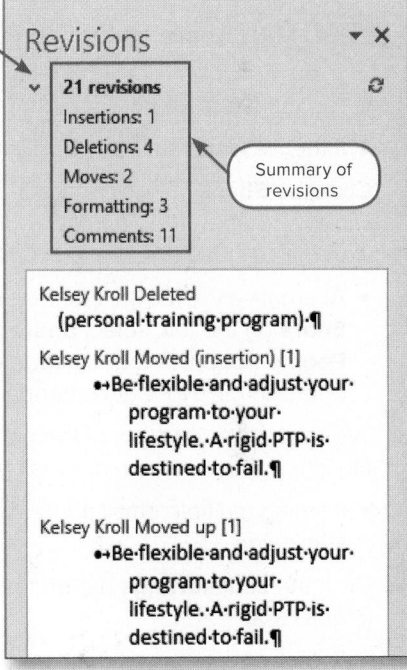

Figure 3-18 *Reviewing* pane displayed vertically

At the top of the *Reviewing* pane, a summary displays the number of revisions in the document. Click the arrow to the left of the revision summary to display the number of insertions, deletions, moves, formatting changes, and comments in the document. Right-click any of the revisions in the *Reviewing* pane and select **Accept** or **Reject** from the context menu.

Share an Online File

In addition to collaborating with others on a document using *Comments* and *Track Changes*, Word also provides you with the option of sharing an online file with others. Sharing an online

file gives you the ability to work with others on the same file at the same time, which is called *real-time collaboration*.

To share a file, it must first be saved in *OneDrive*. If you try to share a file that is not saved in *OneDrive*, Word prompts you to save your document to *OneDrive* before sharing it. Depending on the type of Microsoft account you're using, the sharing options display in a ***Send Link*** window (education and business Microsoft accounts) (Figure 3-19) or the ***Share*** pane (personal Microsoft account). The *Send Link* window or *Share* pane provides options to type or select recipients, set the permission level of the shared file, type a message recipients receive through email, or get a sharing link.

Figure 3-19 *Send Link* window

▶HOW TO: Share an Online File (Education and Business Microsoft Accounts)

1. Open the file to share.
 - If the file is not saved in *OneDrive*, save the file to *OneDrive*.
2. Click the **Share** button (Figure 3-20) in the upper-right corner of the Word window to open the *Send Link* window (see Figure 3-19). The *Share* button icon may display differently in Office 2019.

Figure 3-20 *Share* button

 - Alternatively, click the **File** button to open the *Backstage* view, click **Share** on the left, select **Share with People**, and click the **Share with People** button. The *Backstage* view closes and the *Send Link* window opens in the Word document.
3. Type the email address of the person with whom you are sharing the file in the *Enter a name or email address* area.
 - If typing multiple email addresses, separate each with a semicolon.
4. Click the **Link settings** button to open the *Link settings* window (Figure 3-21).
 - Select who can use the sharing link.
 - Check the **Allow editing** box to enable recipients to edit the shared file. Deselect the **Allow editing** box to enable recipients to open and view the shared file, but restrict them from editing it.
 - Set an expiration date for the sharing link if desired (optional).
5. Click **Apply** to set the sharing link options and to return to the *Send Link* window.
6. Type a message to recipient(s) in the *Add a message* area. This is optional.
7. Click the **Send** button. An email is sent to people you invited.
8. Click the **X** to close the confirmation window.

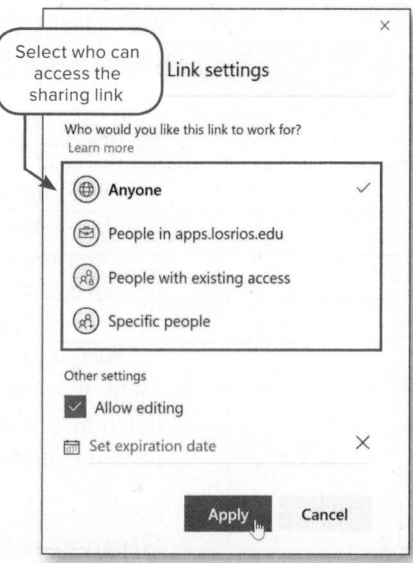

Figure 3-21 *Link settings* window

If you're using a personal Microsoft account, the *Share* pane opens at the right after you click the *Share* button.

▶ HOW TO: Share an Online File (Personal Microsoft Account)

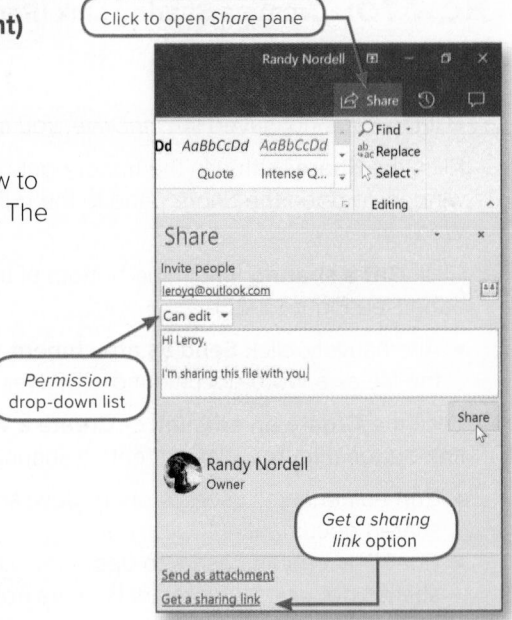

1. Open the file to share.
 - If the file is not saved in *OneDrive*, save the file to *OneDrive*.
2. Click the **Share** button in the upper-right corner of the Word window to open the *Share* pane to the right of the Word window (Figure 3-22). The *Share* button icon may display differently in Office 2019.
3. Type or select the email address of the person with whom you are sharing the file in the *Invite people* area.
4. Select **Can edit** or **Can view** from the *Permission* drop-down list.
 - *Can edit* enables users to edit a shared document.
 - *Can view* enables users to open and view a shared document but restricts users from editing the document.
5. Type a message to recipient(s) in the *Message* area.
6. Click the **Share** button. An email is sent to people you invited.
7. Click the **X** to close the *Share* pane.

Figure 3-22 Share a *OneDrive* file using the *Share* pane

Create a Sharing Link

Creating a sharing link (hyperlink) is another way to share a file with others rather than sending an email through Word. You can create and copy a sharing link and email the sharing link to others. You have the option of creating an *Edit link* or a *View-only link*.

▶ HOW TO: Create a Sharing Link (Education and Business Microsoft Accounts)

1. Open the file to share.
 - If the file is not saved in *OneDrive*, you are prompted to save the file to *OneDrive*.
2. Click the **Share** button in the upper right of the Word window to open the *Send Link* window.
3. Click the **Link settings** button to open the *Link settings* window (see Figure 3-21).
 - Select who can use the sharing link.
 - Check the **Allow editing** box to enable recipients to edit the shared file. Deselect the **Allow editing** box to enable recipients to open and view the shared file, but restrict them from editing it.
 - Set an expiration date for the sharing link if desired (optional).
4. Click **Apply** to set the sharing link options and to return to the *Send Link* window.
5. Click the **Copy Link** button to open the window that displays the sharing link (Figure 3-23).
6. Click the **Copy** button to copy the sharing link.
7. Click the **X** to close the confirmation window.
8. Paste the copied sharing link in an email, Word document, or other online location.

Figure 3-23 Copy sharing link

If you're using a personal Microsoft account, the *Share* pane opens at the right after you click the *Share* button.

▶HOW TO: Create a Sharing Link (Personal Microsoft Account)

1. Open the file to share.
 - If the file is not saved in *OneDrive*, you are prompted to save the file to *OneDrive*.
2. Click the **Share** button in the upper right of the Word window to open the *Share* pane to the right of the Word window.
3. Click **Get a sharing link** at the bottom of the *Share* pane (see Figure 3-22).
 - Alternatively, click **Send as attachment** to email the file as a Word document or PDF file.
4. Click the **Create an edit link** or **Create a view-only link** button (Figure 3-24) to create a sharing link.
 - *Can edit* enables users to open, view, and edit a shared document.
 - *Can view* enables users to open and view a shared document but restricts users from editing the document.
5. Click the **Copy** button to copy the sharing link (Figure 3-25).
6. Click the **Back** arrow to the left of *Get a sharing link* at the top of the *Share* pane to return to the main *Share* pane, or click the **X** to close the *Share* pane.
7. Paste the copied sharing link in an email, Word document, or other online location.

Figure 3-24 Create a sharing link Figure 3-25 Copy a sharing link

PAUSE & PRACTICE: WORD 3-1

For this Pause & Practice project, you modify the *Developing a Personal Training Program* report for American River Cycling Club using comments and *Track Changes*.

Files Needed: **PersonalTrainingProgram-03.docx** *(Student data files are available in the* Library *of your* SIMnet *account.)*
Completed Project File Names: ***[your initials] PP W3-1.docx***

1. Open the **PersonalTrainingProgram-03** document from your student data files.
2. Save the document as [your initials] PP W3-1.
3. Change user name and initials.
 a. Click the **Tracking** launcher [*Review* tab, *Tracking* group] to open the *Track Changes Options* dialog box.
 b. Click the **Change User Name** button to open the *Word Options* dialog box.
 c. Type your first and last name in the *User name* text box in the *Personalize your copy of Microsoft Office* area.
 d. Type your first and last initials in lowercase letters in the *Initials* text box.
 e. Check the **Always use these values regardless of sign in to Office** box.

f. Click **OK** to close the *Word Options* dialog box.

g. Click **OK** to close the *Track Changes Options* dialog box.

4. Change *Display for Review* view.

a. Click the **Display for Review** drop-down list [*Review* tab, *Tracking* group] and select **Original** to view the original document without changes (Figure 3-26).

b. Click the **Display for Review** drop-down list again and select **No Markup** to view the final document with proposed changes applied.

Figure 3-26 Change *Display for Review* view

c. Click the **Display for Review** drop-down list again and select **Simple Markup** to view the document with proposed changes applied. A red line on the left indicates changes in the document.

d. Click the **Show Comments** button [*Review* tab, *Comments* group] to hide comment text if the text displays in the balloons. Only comment balloons display.

e. Click the **Display for Review** drop-down list again and select **All Markup** to view the final document with proposed changes visible inline and comments in balloons in the *Markup* area.

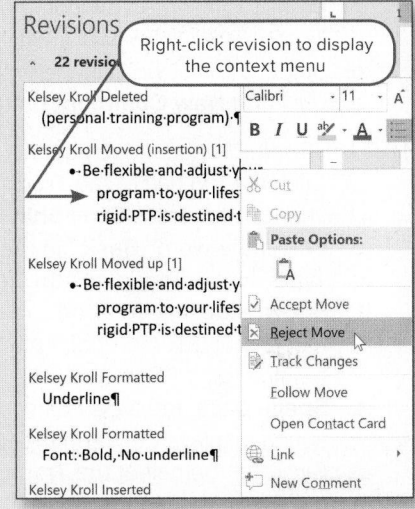

5. Display the *Reviewing* pane and reject changes.

a. Click the **Reviewing Pane** drop-down arrow [*Review* tab, *Tracking* group] and select **Reviewing Pane Vertical**. The *Reviewing* pane displays on the left side of the Word window.

b. Find the moved bulleted item ("Kelsey Kroll Moved (insertion) [1]") in the *Reviewing* pane.

c. Right-click "**Kelsey Kroll Moved (insertion) [1]**" and select **Reject Move** from the context menu (Figure 3-27).

d. Click the **X** in the upper-right corner of the *Reviewing* pane to close it.

Figure 3-27 Reject moved text in the *Reviewing* pane

6. Accept changes in the document.

a. Place your insertion point at the beginning of the document (or **Ctrl+Home**).

b. Click the **Next** button [*Review* tab, *Changes* group] to select the first change (left and right margins changed).

c. Click the top half of the **Accept** button [*Review* tab, *Changes* group] to accept the change. Word automatically moves to the next item, which is a comment.

d. Click the **Next** button [*Review* tab, *Changes* group] three times to skip the first three comments and to locate the next tracked change ("personal training program" deleted).

e. Click the top half of the **Accept** button to accept the change.

f. Click the bottom half of the **Accept** button and select **Accept All Changes** from the drop-down list (Figure 3-28). All of the remaining changes in the document are accepted and disappear from view. Only comments remain in the *Markup* area.

Figure 3-28 Accept all changes in the document

7. Resolve a comment and reply to a comment.

a. Place your insertion point at the beginning of the document.

b. Click the **Next** button [*Review* tab, *Comments* group] to move to the first comment.

c. Click the **Resolve** button on the comment in the *Markup* area or right-click the comment and select **Resolve Comment** from the context menu (Figure 3-29). A resolved comment becomes grayed out text.

d. Click the **Next** button to move to the next comment ("Be sure to include . . .").

e. Click the **Reply** button on the comment in the *Markup* area (see Figure 3-29).

f. Type Thank you, will do!

8. Delete selected comments in the document.
 a. Click the **Next** button [*Review* tab, *Comments* group] to move to the next (third) comment.
 b. Click the top half of the **Delete** button [*Review* tab, *Comments* group] to delete the comment.
 c. Continue clicking **Next** and **Delete** to delete the remaining comments. Don't delete the first two comments on the first page.

9. Add comments to the document.
 a. Place the insertion point at the top of the document (**Ctrl+Home**).
 b. Click the **New Comment** button [*Review* tab, *Comments* group] to insert a new comment.
 c. Type Insert a cover page and table of contents in the new comment.
 d. Select the first word in the first body paragraph ("**There**").
 e. Click the **New Comment** button and type Proofread this report one more time in the new comment.

10. Use *Track Changes* to revise the document.
 a. Click the top half of the **Track Changes** button [*Review* tab, *Tracking* group] to turn on track changes (or press **Ctrl+Shift+E**).
 b. Select the word "**Basic**" in the first section heading below the first body paragraph.
 c. Type General to replace the selected word. Verify one space displays after the word (turn on **Show/Hide** if necessary).
 d. Place your insertion point after "Training" (and before the space) in the second section heading on the first page ("Personal Training Guidelines").
 e. **Space** once and type Program to insert the word between "Training" and "Guidelines." Verify one space displays between the words.
 f. Click the top half of the **Track Changes** button to turn off *Track Changes*.

11. Save and close the document (Figure 3-30).

Figure 3-29 Resolve and reply to comments

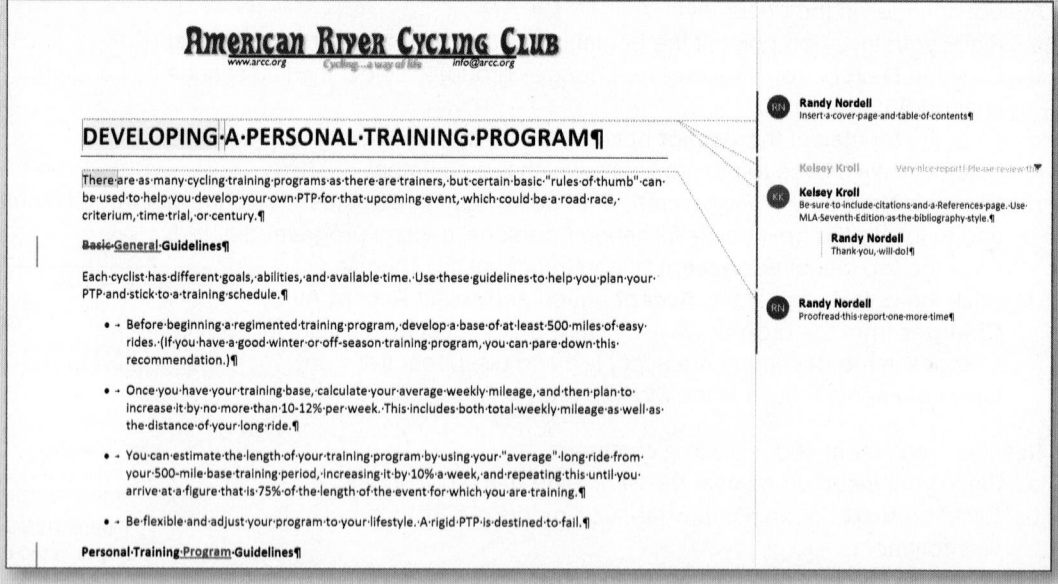

Figure 3-30 PP W3-1 completed

Using Footnotes and Endnotes

Footnotes and *endnotes* cite reference sources used in a document. Footnotes and endnotes can also be used to include additional information. Footnotes display at the bottom of each page, while endnotes display at the end of the document.

As you insert footnotes and endnotes, Word numbers them consecutively. If you insert a footnote or endnote before or between existing notes, Word automatically reorders notes. You can customize the number format and convert footnotes to endnotes or endnotes to footnotes.

Insert a Footnote

When you insert a footnote into a document, a *reference marker*, which is a number or letter in superscript format (smaller font size and slightly raised above the typed line), displays directly after the word. Word then places the insertion point at the bottom of the page where you type the text of the footnote. A thin top border above the note separates the note from the text in the body of the document.

Footnotes display in the body of the document at the bottom of the page, not in the footer area, and the text on a page with a footnote adjusts to allow space for the footnote.

▶ HOW TO: Insert a Footnote

1. Position the insertion point directly after the word where the footnote is to be inserted.
2. Click the **References** tab.
3. Click the **Insert Footnote** button [*Footnotes* group] (Figure 3-31).
 A reference marker displays in the body of the document (Figure 3-32), and the insertion point is positioned after the corresponding reference marker in the footnote area near the bottom of the page.
4. Type the footnote text in the footnote area of the page (Figure 3-33).

Figure 3-31 *Insert Footnote* button

Figure 3-32 **Footnote reference marker in the body of the document**

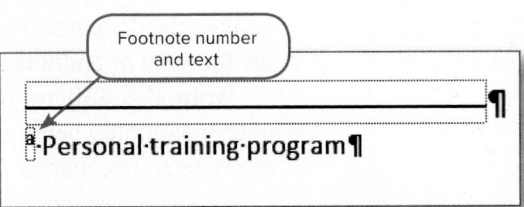

Figure 3-33 **Footnote text at the bottom of the page**

5. Click the body of the document to leave the footnote area and to return to the document.

Insert an Endnote

Inserting endnotes is similar to inserting footnotes. The main difference is the text for the endnote displays after the text at the end of the document rather than at the bottom of the page where the note appears.

1. Position the insertion point directly after the word where the endnote is to be inserted.
2. Click the **References** tab.
3. Click the **Insert Endnote** button [*Footnotes* group] (Figure 3-34). The reference marker displays in the body of the document, and the insertion point is positioned after the corresponding reference marker at the end of the document.
4. Type the endnote text.
5. Click the body of the document to leave the endnote area and to return to the document.

Figure 3-34 *Insert Endnote* button

> **ANOTHER WAY**
>
> **Alt+Ctrl+F** inserts a footnote. **Alt+Ctrl+D** inserts an endnote.

View Footnotes and Endnotes

Once you insert footnotes or endnotes in your document, it is easy to see the footnote or endnote text at the bottom of a page or at the end of the document. However, you might have a difficult time locating the reference markers in the body of the document. Word provides you with a tool to easily locate footnote reference markers in your document.

Click the **Next Footnote** button in the *Footnotes* group on the *References* tab to move to the next footnote (Figure 3-35). Click the **Next Footnote** drop-down arrow to display a list of options to move to the next or previous footnote or endnote. Click the **Show Notes** button in the *Footnotes* group to toggle between the note reference markers (in the body of the document) and the note text (in the footnote or endnote area).

Word also displays the text of the footnote or endnote when you place your pointer over a reference marker (Figure 3-36).

Figure 3-35 *Next Footnote* drop-down list

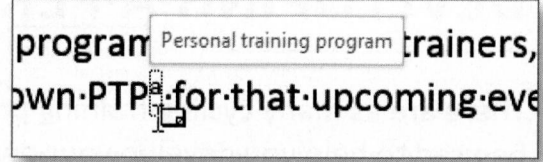

Figure 3-36 Footnote text displayed as a tag

> **ANOTHER WAY**
>
> Use the *Go To* feature in the *Find and Replace* dialog box to go to a specific note. Press **Ctrl+G** to open the *Find and Replace* dialog box with the *Go To* tab displayed.

Customize Footnotes and Endnotes

By default, footnotes are numbered consecutively with numbers (1, 2, 3) and endnotes are numbered with lowercase Roman numerals (i, ii, iii). Letters or symbols such as an asterisk (*), section mark (§), or number symbol (#) are other reference marker options. You can customize how notes are numbered and where they display in a document.

▶ HOW TO: Customize Footnotes and Endnotes

1. Click the **Footnotes** launcher [*Reference* tab, *Footnotes* group] to open the *Footnote and Endnote* dialog box (Figure 3-37).

2. Select the **Footnotes** or **Endnotes** radio button in the *Location* area.
 - In the drop-down list for *Footnotes*, you have the option to position the footnote text at the *Bottom of page* (default) or *Below text*.
 - In the drop-down list for *Endnotes*, you have the option to position the endnote text at the *End of document* (default) or *End of section*.

3. Customize *Number format*, *Custom mark*, *Start at*, or *Numbering* in the *Format* area.

4. Click the **Apply changes to** drop-down list and select where to apply changes: *Whole document* or *This section* (if multiple sections exist in your document).

5. Click **Apply** to close the dialog box and apply the changes. Do not click *Insert*, which inserts a footnote or endnote in the document.

Figure 3-37 *Footnote and Endnote* dialog box

▶ **MORE INFO**

Use the *Footnote and Endnote* dialog box to insert a footnote or endnote.

Modify Footnote and Endnote Format

In addition to customizing note placement and format, you can also change the format of footnote and endnote text. Apply formatting to footnote or endnote text the same way you format regular text in the document.

Select the footnote or endnote text and apply formatting changes such as font, font size, style, line or paragraph spacing, or text effects (Figure 3-38). Use the buttons on the *Home* or *Layout* tab, the context menu (right-click selected text), the mini toolbar, or keyboard shortcuts to apply formatting changes.

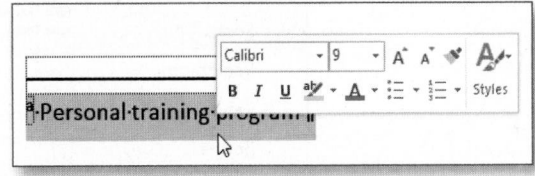

Figure 3-38 Apply formatting to footnote text

Modify Footnote and Endnote Styles

Styles determine the appearance of the footnotes and endnotes in your document. Styles include the font, font size, text styles and effects, and paragraph formatting. When you insert a footnote, Word applies the *Footnote Text* style.

Modify the *Footnote Text* or *Endnote Text* style to automatically update all of your footnote or endnote text.

1. Right-click the footnote or endnote text and select **Style** from the context menu. The *Style* dialog box opens, and the name of the style displays in the *Styles* area (Figure 3-39).

2. Click the **Modify** button to open the *Modify Style* dialog box (Figure 3-40).

3. Change the font formatting in the *Formatting* area.

4. Click the **Format** button to display a list of other formatting options (see Figure 3-40).

 • When you select a format option, another dialog box opens.
 • Apply formatting changes and click **OK** to close the dialog box.

5. Click **OK** to close the *Modify Style* dialog box.

6. Click **Apply** to apply changes to the style and close the *Style* dialog box.

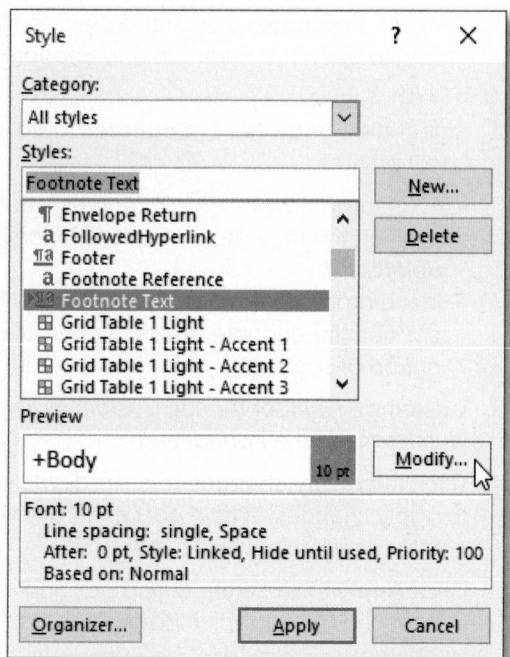

Figure 3-39 *Style* dialog box

Figure 3-40 *Modify Style* dialog box

Convert Footnotes and Endnotes

At times, you may want to convert footnotes to endnotes or endnotes to footnotes. Rather than deleting and re-creating the notes, Use the *Convert Notes* feature. When you convert notes, Word automatically renumbers the reference markers and moves the note text to the correct location in the document.

▶HOW TO: Convert Footnotes and Endnotes

1. Click the **Footnotes** launcher [*References* tab, *Footnotes* group] to open the *Footnote and Endnote* dialog box.
2. Click the **Convert** button in the *Location* area. The *Convert Notes* dialog box opens (Figure 3-41).
3. Select from one of the three convert options: **Convert all footnotes to endnotes**, **Convert all endnotes to footnotes**, or **Swap footnotes and endnotes**.
4. Click **OK** to close the *Convert Notes* dialog box.
5. Click **Close** to close the *Footnote and Endnote* dialog box.
 - Do not click *Insert* or Word will insert a footnote or endnote.

Figure 3-41 *Convert Notes* dialog box

> **MORE INFO**
>
> All three of the convert options are active *only* if you have both footnotes and endnotes in your document. Otherwise, only one option is active.

Convert individual notes using the context menu. Right-click a footnote or endnote (*not* the reference marker in the text of the document) and select **Convert to Endnote** or **Convert to Footnote** (Figure 3-42).

Figure 3-42 Convert individual note

Move Footnotes and Endnotes

Move footnotes and endnotes in the same way you move text in a document. To move a note, select the **reference marker** in the body of the document (Figure 3-43) and use one of the following methods:

- Drag and drop
- **Ctrl+X** to cut and **Ctrl+V** to paste
- *Cut* and *Paste* buttons [*Home* tab, *Clipboard* group]
- *Cut* and *Paste* options in the context menu

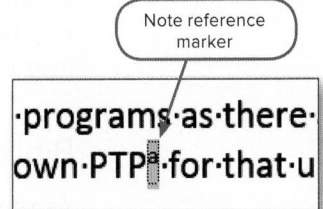

Figure 3-43 Select note reference marker to move

> **MORE INFO**
>
> When moving a note, select the note carefully to ensure that you are only moving the note and not any spaces, text, or paragraph marks.

Delete Footnotes and Endnotes

When you delete a note, Word removes the reference marker and the text of the note. Your remaining notes renumber and remain in consecutive order. To delete a note, always delete the note reference marker in the body of the document, which also deletes the note text in the footnote or endnote area.

▶ HOW TO: Delete a Note

1. Select the **reference marker** in the body of the document (*not* the text of the footnote or endnote at the bottom of the page or end of the document).
2. Press **Delete** on the keyboard. Both the note marker and the note in the footnote or endnote area are deleted.
 - Deleting footnote or endnote text in the footnote or endnote area will not delete the note reference marker in the body of the document.
3. Check to ensure proper spacing around text where the note was deleted.

Creating a Bibliography and Inserting Citations

Typically, the most tedious and time-consuming aspect of writing a research paper is compiling sources, creating a bibliography page, and citing sources in the body of the report. A *source* is the complete bibliographic reference for a book, journal article, or web page. A *citation* is the abbreviated source information that you place in the body of the report to credit the source of the information you use. A *bibliography* or *works cited* page lists the sources used in the report. Word includes tools to create sources, insert citations, and create a bibliography or works cited page at the end of your report.

Report Styles

A variety of report styles exist, and each differs not only in the overall format of the report but also in the format for sources and citations. The most common report styles are the following:

- *APA* (American Psychological Association)
- *Chicago* (*The Chicago Manual of Style*)
- *MLA* (Modern Language Association)
- *Turabian* (*Manual for Writers of Research Papers, Theses, and Dissertations*)

MLA and APA are the two most common report formats. Table 3-2 lists the general characteristics of each of these two report styles. Within each of these report formats, the format can vary depending on the preference of your college or instructor. Always follow the formatting instructions your instructor provides.

Bibliography Styles

As you begin compiling the sources for your report, the first step is to select the *bibliography style* of the report. The bibliography style determines how citations display in the body of the report and how references appear on a references, bibliography, or works cited page.

Table 3-2: Common Report Styles

Report Features	APA	MLA
Font	11 or 12 pt.	11 or 12 pt.
Line Spacing	Academic APA is double-spaced and business APA is single spaced.	Double-space.
Margins	For an unbound report, use 1" for all margins. For a left-bound report, use 1.5" left margin and 1" top, bottom, and right margins.	Use 1" margins.
Heading Information	Heading information is typically typed on a title page.	Left align at the top of the first page and include author's name, instructor's name, class, and date on separate lines.
Title	The title is either on the title page or horizontally centered on the first page of the report.	Center on the first page of the report.
Header	Include report title and page number on the right.	Include author's last name and page number on the right.
Uses	Typically used in social and behavioral sciences, business, and nursing.	Typically used in humanities.

▶ **HOW TO:** Select the Bibliography Style of the Report

1. Click the **Reference** tab.
2. Click the **Style** drop-down arrow [*Citations & Bibliography* group].
3. Select the style of the report from the drop-down list of report styles (Figure 3-44).

> **MORE INFO**
>
> The report style you select controls the formatting of sources and citations; it does not control the overall formatting of your report. Apply the correct character, paragraph, and page formatting to the body of your report.

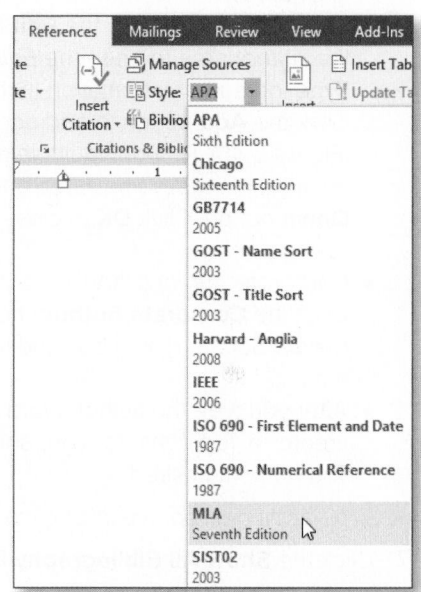

Figure 3-44 Select bibliography style

Add a New Source

When writing a report, gather bibliographic information about sources used in your report (author; title of book, journal, or article; publication date and edition; publisher or online location). When you use the *Add New Source* feature, Word inserts a citation in your report at the insertion point and stores this source information. Use stored sources to insert additional citations and to create a bibliography page.

▶HOW TO: Add a New Source

1. Position the insertion point at the location to insert a citation.

2. Click the **Insert Citation** button [*References* tab, *Citations & Bibliography* group].

3. Select **Add New Source**. The *Create Source* dialog box opens (Figure 3-45).

4. Click the **Type of Source** drop-down list and select the type of source.

 • The fields for the source change depending on the type of source you choose.

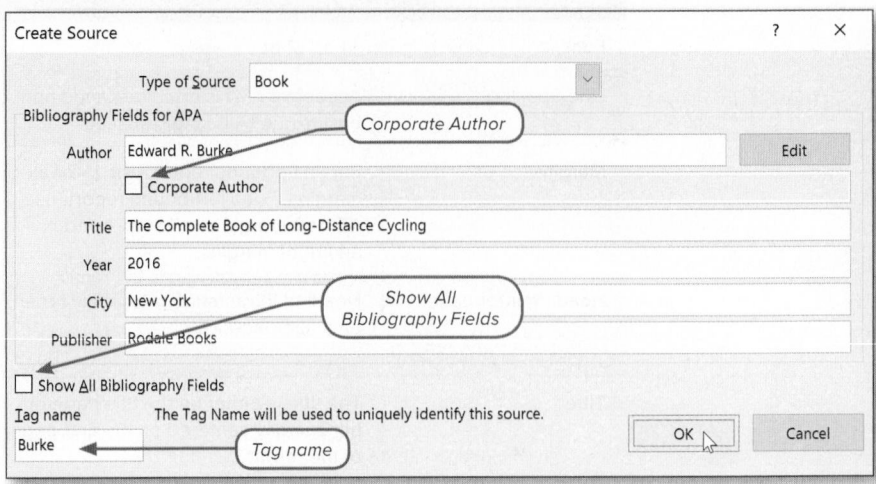

Figure 3-45 *Create Source* dialog box

5. Type the author information in the *Author* area. Enter this information differently depending on the author(s) of the source.

 • *Individual Author*: Type first name, middle initial, and last name (with no commas) in the *Author* field.
 • *Multiple Authors*: Click the **Edit** button to the right of the *Author* area to open the *Edit Name* dialog box. Type the author information in the *Add name* fields. Click the **Add** button to add additional authors (Figure 3-46). Reorder multiple authors by selecting an author in the *Names* area and clicking the **Up** or **Down** button. Click **OK** to close the *Edit Name* dialog box.
 • *Corporate Author* (USA Cycling or Velo News): Click the **Corporate Author** check box in the *Create Source* dialog box and type the corporate author.
 • After you type the author, Word automatically creates a *Tag name* for your source. Edit the *Tag name* if desired.

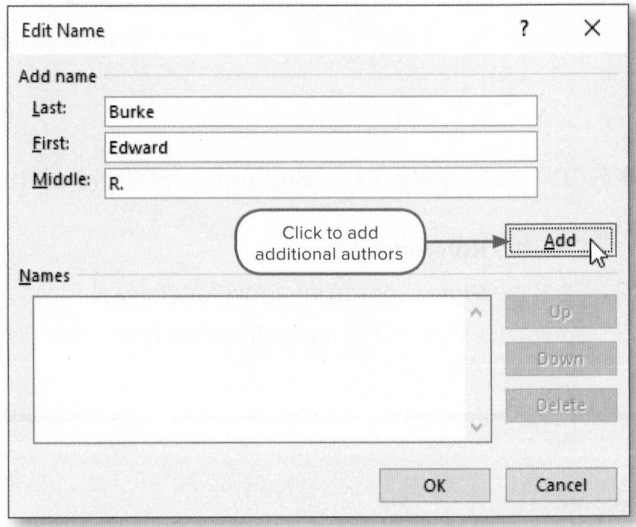

Figure 3-46 *Edit Name* dialog box

6. Type additional source information as needed (see Figure 3-45).

7. Click the **Show All Bibliography Fields** check box to display more fields, such as the edition of the book.

8. Click **OK** to close the *Create Source* dialog box.

 • The citation displays in the document in the report style you selected (Figure 3-47).
 • The *Researcher* pane may open on the right. If necessary, click the **X** in the upper-right corner to close the pane. The *Researcher* is discussed later in this section.

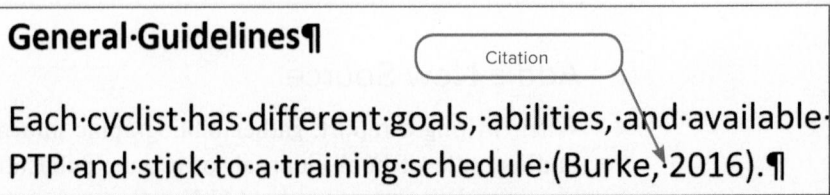

Figure 3-47 Citation inserted in text

Insert a Citation

Often, you cite a source more than once in a report. Once a source is added to your document, insert the same citation without re-entering the source information. When inserting a citation, choose from citations you have previously created.

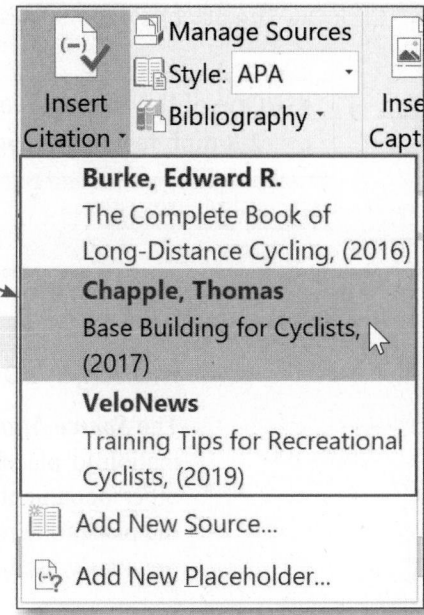

Citations available in the document

▶ HOW TO: Insert a Citation

1. Position the insertion point at the location to insert a citation.
2. Click the **Insert Citation** button [*References* tab, *Citations & Bibliography* group].
 - A list of previously used or created sources displays in the drop-down list (Figure 3-48).
3. Select from your list of sources.
 - The citation is inserted in the document.
 - When you insert a citation, Word automatically inserts a space between the citation and the preceding word.

Figure 3-48 Insert citation from a previously created source

> **MORE INFO**
>
> When inserting citations, the citation typically is placed one space after the preceding word and directly before the punctuation mark. Always check your document to ensure proper spacing.

Insert a Placeholder

Occasionally, you may need to insert a citation but do not have all the bibliographic information to create the source. A ***placeholder*** temporarily marks a spot where a citation needs to be completed. Later, you can add bibliographic source information for any placeholders inserted in the document.

▶ HOW TO: Insert a Placeholder

1. Position the insertion point at the location to insert a placeholder.
2. Click the **Insert Citation** button [*References* tab, *Citations & Bibliography* group].
3. Select **Add New Placeholder**. The *Placeholder Name* dialog box opens (Figure 3-49).
4. Type the name of the placeholder.
 - Do not use spaces between words in the placeholder text because the placeholder name is the tag name of the source.
 - If necessary, use an underscore between words when naming a placeholder.

Figure 3-49 Insert a placeholder

5. Click **OK**. The placeholder displays in the document and looks similar to a citation (Figure 3-50).

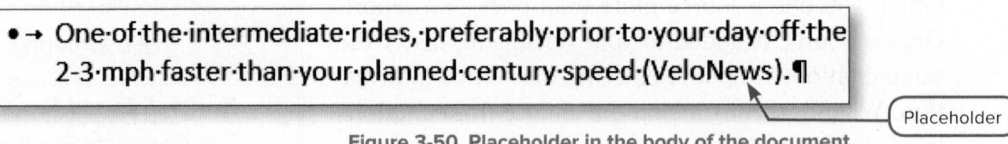

• → One-of-the-intermediate-rides,·preferably·prior·to·your·day·off·the
2-3·mph·faster·than·your·planned·century·speed·(VeloNews).¶

Placeholder

Figure 3-50 Placeholder in the body of the document

Manage Sources

The ***Source Manager*** dialog box enables you to edit existing sources, add bibliographic information to placeholders, create new sources, and copy sources that were created and used in other documents. The *Source Manager* dialog box displays the sources used in your report, the placeholders that need bibliographic information, and a master list of all sources you have previously used.

▶ **HOW TO: Manage Sources**

1. Click the **Manage Sources** button [*References* tab, *Citations & Bibliography* group]. The *Source Manager* dialog box opens (Figure 3-51).

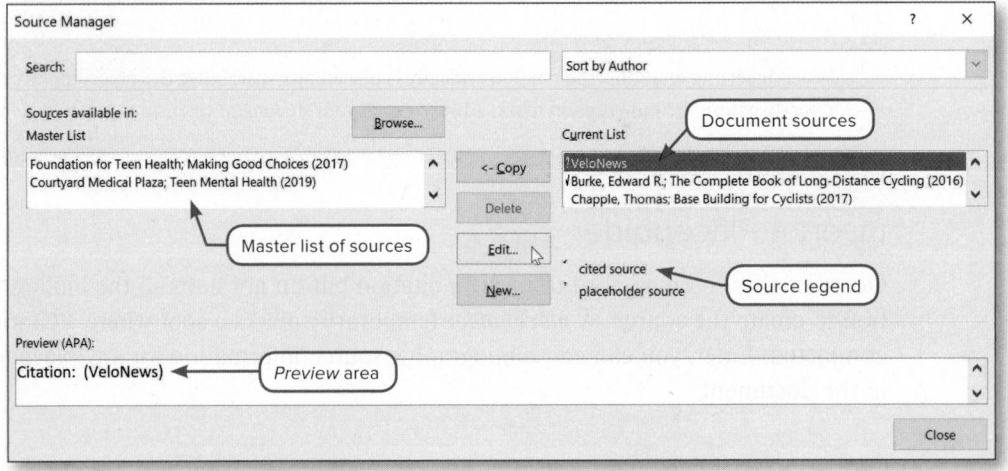

Figure 3-51 *Source Manager* dialog box

* The *Master List* of sources on the left displays *all* available sources. Some of these may have been created in other Word documents.
* The *Current List* displays the sources available in your current document.
* Sources that are cited in the document have a checkmark next to them.
* Sources that are placeholders have a question mark next to them and require additional information.
* The *Preview* area displays the contents of your source.

2. Copy a source from the *Master List* to the *Current List* by selecting the source on the left and clicking the **Copy** button. The copied source remains in the *Master List*.

3. Edit a source from either list by selecting a source and clicking the **Edit** button (see Figure 3-51). The *Edit Source* dialog box opens.

 * Edit the source and click **OK**.
 * Word automatically updates citations in your document after changes to the source are completed.

4. Add bibliographic information to a placeholder by selecting the placeholder and clicking the **Edit** button. The *Edit Source* dialog box opens.

- Add bibliographic information to the placeholder and click **OK**.
- When bibliographic information is added to a placeholder, it becomes a complete source, and the question mark next to it changes to a check.
- Word automatically replaces the placeholder with a citation in your document when you add bibliographic information.

5. Create a new source by clicking the **New** button. The *Create Source* dialog box opens.

- Type the bibliographic information and click **OK**.
- This source is now available as a citation to insert in your document.
- This source is also added to the *Master List*.

6. Delete a source from either list by selecting the source and clicking the **Delete** button.

- You cannot delete a source from the *Current List* if it is cited in the document. You must first delete the citation in the document before deleting a source in the *Source Manager* dialog box.
- If a source is in both lists and you delete it from one list, it is not deleted from the other list.

7. Click **Close** to close the *Source Manager* dialog box and apply any changes made.

Edit Citations and Sources

After citations and placeholders are inserted into the document, edit the citation or source without using the *Source Manager* dialog box. When you click a citation or placeholder in your document, a drop-down list of editing options displays (Figure 3-52):

Figure 3-52 Edit citation and source options

- ***Edit Citation***: Opens the *Edit Citation* dialog box and enables you to add a page number to the citation or suppress any currently displayed information.
- ***Edit Source***: Opens the *Edit Source* dialog box and enables you to update source bibliographic information.
- ***Convert citation to static text***: Changes the citation from a Word field that is automatically generated and updated to static text that is not updated.
- ***Update Citations and Bibliography***: Updates your bibliography page to reflect any changes to citations or sources.

> **MORE INFO**
>
> Edit citations and placeholders using either the drop-down list or the context menu.

You can move or delete a citation or placeholder in the body of the text by clicking the citation or placeholder handle on the left and dragging it to a new location (to move) or by pressing **Delete** (to delete) on your keyboard (Figure 3-53).

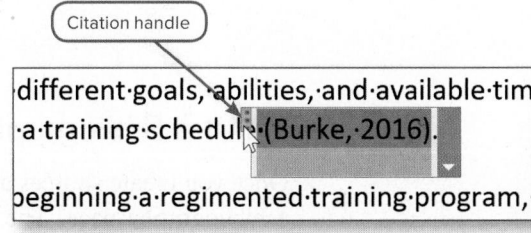

Figure 3-53 Select a citation to move or delete

Use the Researcher

The *Researcher* enables you to search for quotes, citable sources, and images about a topic in your report and displays information from journals and web sites in the *Researcher* pane on the right side of the Word window. From the results in the *Researcher* pane, you can review topics to gather information, add citations to the report, and add topic headings to the report. When you add a citation to the report, the complete bibliographic information is saved as a source in the *Source Manager*, and this source is saved in the *My Research* area of the *Researcher* pane for future reference.

Office 2019 Note: The *Researcher* feature is not available in Office 2019.

▶HOW TO: Use the Researcher and Research Pane

1. Click the **Researcher** button [*References* tab, *Research* group]. The *Researcher* pane opens on the right side of the Word window (Figure 3-54).

2. Type key words of the search topic in the search text box and press **Enter**. Search results display in the *Researcher* pane (Figure 3-55).

 • *Relevant topics* and *Top sources for [search topic]* display in the *Researcher* pane.

3. Click a topic or source to view detailed information.

 • Click the **Back** arrow to return to search results in the *Researcher* pane.

4. Click the plus sign (**+**) in the upper-right corner of a *topic* result to add a heading to the report.

 • A heading is added to the report and a comment is attached to the heading.
 • The heading is formatting in *Heading 1* style.
 • The comment includes a link to the topic.

5. Click the plus sign (**+**) in the upper-right corner of a *source* result to add a citation to the report.

 • A dialog box may open in the *Researcher* pane asking if you want to "*Create a bibliography?*" Select **Create** or **No thanks**.
 • When a citation is added to a report from the *Researcher* pane, the complete bibliographic information is saved as a source in the *Source Manager*.
 • Click the **My Research** tab in the *Researcher* pane to view topics and sources you have added to reports.

6. Click the **X** in the upper-right corner of the *Researcher* pane to close the pane.

Figure 3-54 *Researcher pane*

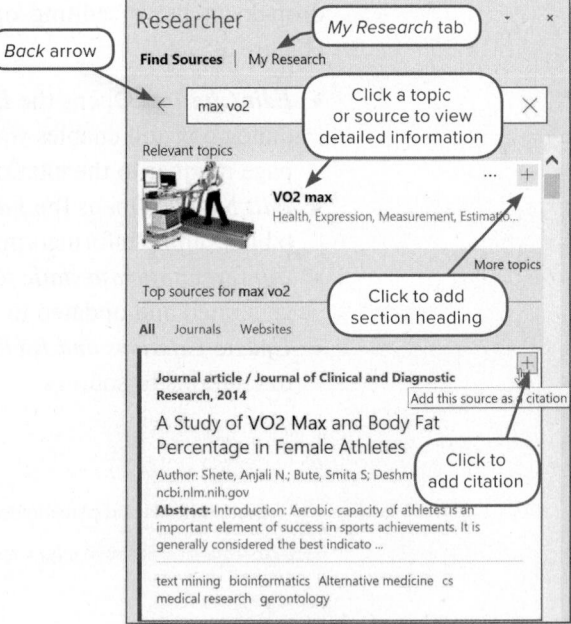

Figure 3-55 Search results in the *Researcher* pane

Insert a Bibliography

Once you create sources and insert citations in the body of the report, you are ready to create a bibliography page. The bibliography page is automatically generated from the sources in

your document and is formatted according to the selected *Bibliography Style*. Word provides a variety of bibliography options.

The *Bibliography*, *References*, and *Works Cited* built-in options insert a page title above the list of sources. The *Insert Bibliography* option inserts only the sources; you can add a title of your choice. If you plan to include a table of contents in your report, it is best to use one of the built-in options. Word applies a style to the bibliography title and automatically includes the bibliography page in the table of contents.

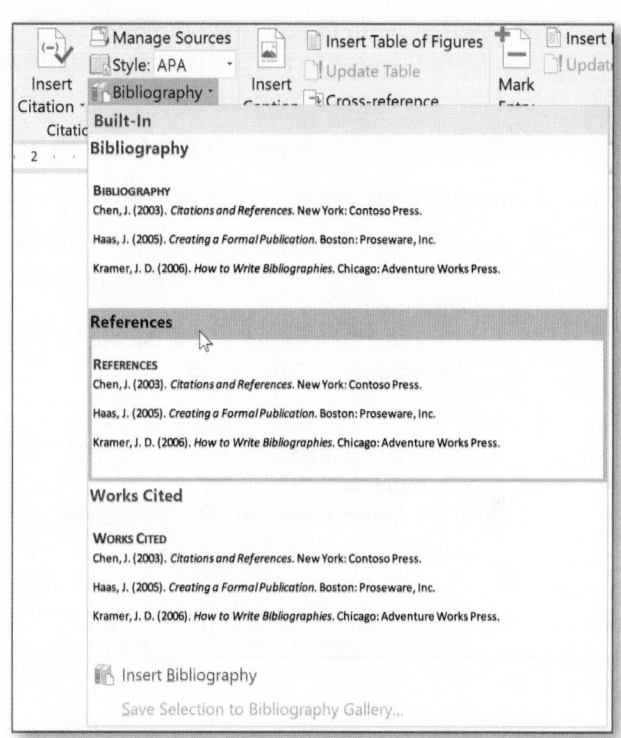

▶HOW TO: Insert a Bibliography

1. Position the insertion point at the location to insert the bibliography.

 - It is usually best to insert a page break (**Ctrl+Enter**) at the end of the document and begin the bibliography on a new page.

2. Click the **Bibliography** button [*References* tab, *Citations & Bibliography* group] to display the list of options (Figure 3-56).

3. Select a bibliography option. The bibliography displays in the document.

Figure 3-56 Insert *References* page

If changes are made to sources after the bibliography page has been inserted, you must update the bibliography. Click one of the references on the bibliography page to select the entire bibliography and click **Update Citations and Bibliography** (Figure 3-57).

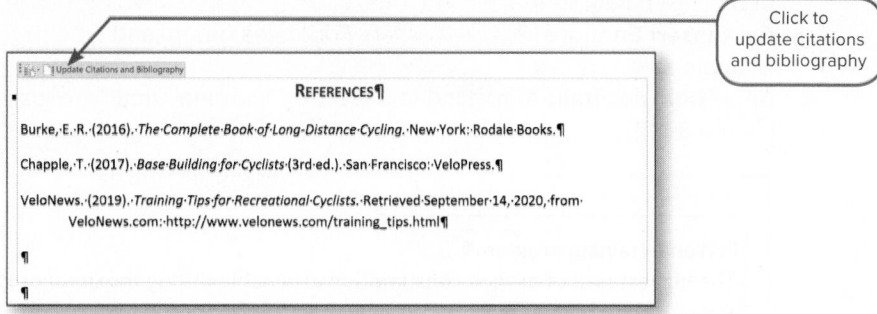

Figure 3-57 *References* page inserted into the document

▶ ANOTHER WAY

Right-click the bibliography and choose **Update Field** or press **F9** to update the bibliography.

For this Pause & Practice project, you modify the *Developing a Personal Training Program* report for American River Cycling Club. You accept tracked changes, delete comments, add and modify notes, select the report style, add sources and citations, use the *Researcher*, and insert a bibliography page.

File Needed: *[your initials] PP W3-1.docx*
Completed Project File Name: *[your initials] PP W3-2.docx*

1. Open the *[your initials] PP W3-1* document completed in *Pause & Practice 3-1*.

2. Save this document as [your initials] PP W3-2.

3. Accept tracked changes and delete all comments in the document.
 a. Click the bottom half of the **Accept** button [*Review* tab, *Changes* group] and select **Accept All Changes**.
 b. Click the bottom half of the **Delete** button [*Review* tab, *Comments* group] and select **Delete All Comments in Document**.

4. Insert endnotes into the report.
 a. Position the insertion point after "PTP" and before the space (page 1, first body paragraph). Turn on **Show/Hide** if necessary.
 b. Click **Insert Endnote** [*References* tab, *Footnotes* group]. Word moves the insertion point to the endnote area on the last page.
 c. Type Personal training program in the endnote area.
 d. Position the insertion point after the first instance of "Max VO2" and before the space (page 3, "Training Intensity and Heart Rate" section, second sentence).

 MORE INFO

 Use the *Find* feature in the *Navigation* pane to locate specific words.

 e. Click **Insert Endnote** [*References* tab, *Footnotes* group] and type The highest rate of oxygen consumption attainable during maximal or exhaustive exercise in the endnote area.
 f. Position the insertion point after "RPM" and before the period (page 3, "Sample Session" section, end of last paragraph).
 g. Click **Insert Endnote** [*References* tab, *Footnotes* group] and type Revolutions per minute in the endnote area.
 h. Apply **bold** and **italic** formatting to the words "maximal" and "exhaustive" in the second endnote (Figure 3-58).

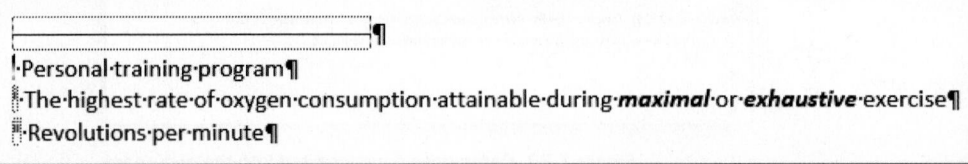

Figure 3-58 Endnotes added to report

5. Convert endnotes to footnotes and change numbering.
 a. Click the **Footnotes** launcher [*References* tab, *Footnotes* group]. The *Footnote and Endnote* dialog box opens.

b. Click the **Convert** button to open the *Convert Notes* dialog box (Figure 3-59).

c. Select **Convert all endnotes to footnotes** if necessary and click **OK**.

d. Click **Close** to close the *Footnote and Endnote* dialog box.

e. Click the **Footnotes** launcher again to open the *Footnote and Endnote* dialog box.

f. Click the **Footnotes** radio button if necessary.

g. Click the **Number format** drop-down arrow and select **a, b, c . . .** (Figure 3-60). Don't change any of the other *Format* settings.

h. Choose **Apply** to close the *Footnote and Endnote* dialog box and apply the changes.

i. Check your document to confirm that endnotes have been converted to footnotes and that the number format has been changed.

6. Change the style of the footnotes.

a. Right-click the footnote text at the bottom of the first page.

b. Select **Style** from the context menu (not mini toolbar). The *Style* dialog box opens.

c. Click the **Modify** button to open the *Modify Style* dialog box (Figure 3-61).

d. Change the font size to **9 pt**.

e. Change line spacing to **1.5** (see Figure 3-61).

f. Click **OK** to close the *Modify Style* dialog box.

g. Choose **Apply** to close the *Style* dialog box.

7. Select the report style for sources and citations.

a. Click the **Style** drop-down list [*References* tab, *Citations & Bibliography* group].

b. Select **MLA Seventh Edition**.

Figure 3-59 Convert endnotes to footnotes

Figure 3-60 Change the number format of footnotes

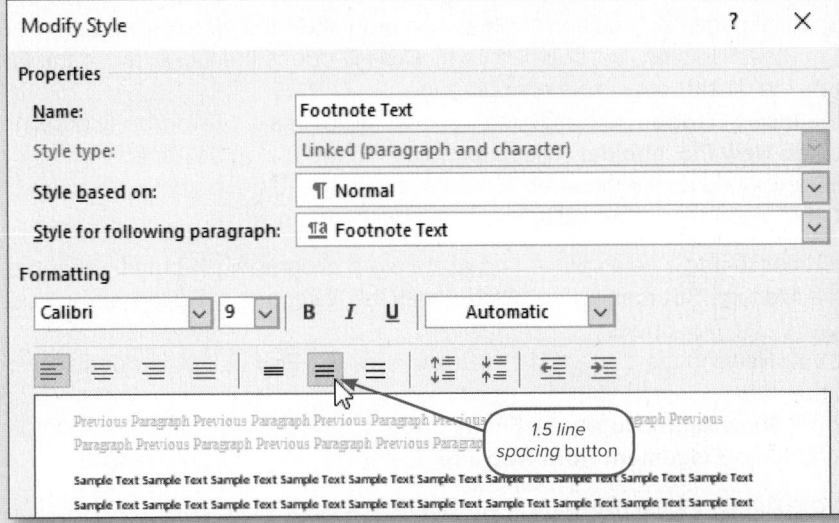

Figure 3-61 Modify *Footnote Text* style

8. Add a new source and insert a citation.
 a. Position the insertion point after the word "schedule" and before the period (page 1, "General Guidelines" section, end of first paragraph).
 b. Click the **Insert Citation** button [*References* tab, *Citations & Bibliography* group].
 c. Select **Add New Source**. The *Create Source* dialog box opens (Figure 3-62).

Figure 3-62 *Create Source* dialog box

 d. Select **Book** as the type of source.
 e. Type Edward R. Burke in the *Author* field.
 f. Type the following source information in the *Create Source* dialog box:

 Title: The Complete Book of Long-Distance Cycling
 Year: 2016
 City: New York
 Publisher: Rodale Books
 Tag name: Burke

 g. Click **OK** to add the source, insert the citation, and close the dialog box.

9. Add a placeholder to the report.
 a. Go to the first page and position the insertion point after the word "speed" and before the period ("Pace of Rides" section, last bulleted item). **Ctrl+G** opens the *Go To* tab in the *Find and Replace* dialog box to quickly move to a specific page.
 b. Click the **Insert Citation** button [*References* tab, *Citations & Bibliography* group].
 c. Select **Add New Placeholder**. The *Placeholder Name* dialog box opens.
 d. Type VeloNews (no space between words) as the placeholder text.
 e. Click **OK** to insert the placeholder and close the dialog box.

10. Manage sources to add a new source and complete bibliographic information for the placeholder.
 a. Click the **Manage Sources** button [*References* tab, *Citations & Bibliography* group]. The *Source Manager* dialog box opens.
 b. Select **VeloNews** in the *Current List* area and click the **Edit** button to open the *Edit Source* dialog box.
 c. Check the **Show All Bibliography Fields** box and type the following source information:
 Type of Source: **Document from web site**

 Corporate Author (check **Corporate Author** check box): VeloNews
 Name of web Page: Training Tips for Recreational Cyclists
 Name of web Site: VeloNews.com

Year: 2019
Year Accessed: 2020
Month Accessed: September
Day Accessed: 14
URL: http://www.velonews.com/training_tips.html

d. Click **OK** to close the *Edit Source* dialog box. The placeholder is updated as a complete source.
e. Click the **New** button in the *Source Manager* dialog box to create a new source.
f. Check the **Show All Bibliography Fields** box and type the following source information:

Type of Source: **Book**
Author: Thomas Chapple
Title: Base Building for Cyclists
Year: 2017
City: San Francisco
Publisher: VeloPress
Edition: 3rd
Tag name: Chapple

g. Click **OK** to close the *Create Source* dialog box.
h. Click **Close** to close the *Source Manager* dialog box.

11. Insert citations into the report.
 a. Go to the top of the second page and position the insertion point after "rest day" and before the period (second sentence of first paragraph).
 b. Click the **Insert Citation** button [*References* tab, *Citations & Bibliography* group] (Figure 3-63).
 c. Select the **Chapple, Thomas** source. The citation displays in the report.
 d. Use the **Insert Citation** button to insert the following citations:
 Burke, Edward, R.: after "training week" and before the period (page 2, "Duration of Rides" section, last bulleted item).
 VeloNews: after "overtraining" and before the period (page 3, "Other Heart Rate Factors" section, end of the paragraph).

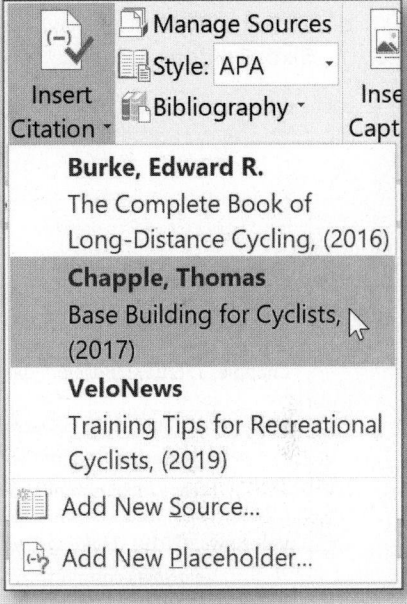

Figure 3-63 Insert a citation

12. Use the *Researcher* to insert a citation. If you are using Office 2019, skip all of step 12 because the *Researcher* is not available in Office 2019.
 a. Place your insertion point after "maximum heart rate" and before the period (page 3, "Training Intensity and Heart Rate" section, first paragraph).
 b. Click the **Researcher** button [*References* tab, *Research* group] to open the *Researcher* pane.
 c. Type max vo2 in the search text box and press **Enter**.
 d. Review the results in the *Top sources for max vo2* area (Figure 3-64).
 e. Click the plus sign (+) in the upper-right corner of one of the *Top sources* (not *Relevant topics*) to insert a citation at the insertion point in the report. If a dialog box opens and asks to "*Update a bibliography?*" click **No thanks**.

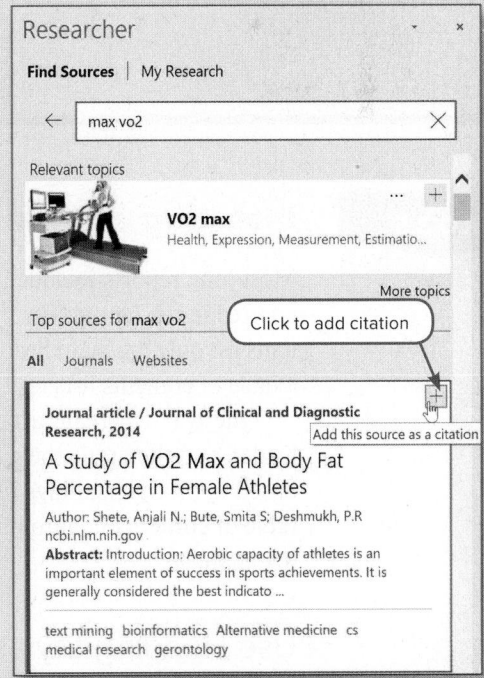

Figure 3-64 Add a citation from the *Researcher* pane

f. Review the citation you inserted in the report. The bibliographic information for this citation was also added as a source in the *Source Manager*.

g. Click the **X** in the upper-right corner of *Researcher* pane to close it.

13. Insert a bibliography and change report style.

a. Position the insertion point on the blank line at the end of the document and press **Ctrl+Enter** to insert a page break.

b. Click the **Bibliography** button [*References* tab, *Citations & Bibliography* group] and select **References** from the drop-down list. The *Reference* page displays on the blank page at the end of the document.

c. **Center** the "*References*" title and apply **10 pt** after paragraph spacing.

d. Click the **Style** drop-down list [*References* tab, *Citations & Bibliography* group] and select **APA Sixth Edition**.

14. Save and close the document (Figure 3-65). Your *References* page may be different depending on the citation you added using the *Researcher*.

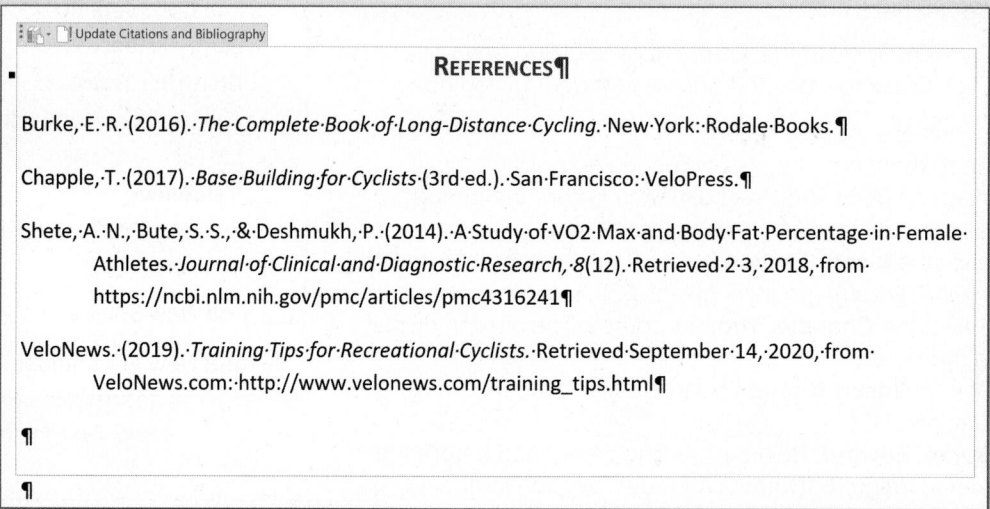

Figure 3-65 PP W3-2 References page

REFERENCES¶

Burke, E. R. (2016). *The Complete Book of Long-Distance Cycling.* New York: Rodale Books.¶

Chapple, T. (2017). *Base Building for Cyclists* (3rd ed.). San Francisco: VeloPress.¶

Shete, A. N., Bute, S. S., & Deshmukh, P. (2014). A Study of VO2 Max and Body Fat Percentage in Female Athletes. *Journal of Clinical and Diagnostic Research, 8*(12). Retrieved 2-3, 2018, from https://ncbi.nlm.nih.gov/pmc/articles/pmc4316241¶

VeloNews. (2019). *Training Tips for Recreational Cyclists.* Retrieved September 14, 2020, from VeloNews.com: http://www.velonews.com/training_tips.html¶

SLO 3.5 Inserting a Table of Contents

Most long reports include a ***table of contents*** to provide readers with an overview of the material covered in the report. The table of contents reflects the headings in the report; some tables of contents list only the main headings, while others might list second- and third-level headings. Typically, a table of contents lists headings on the left and page numbers on the right with a dot leader.

One way to create a table of contents is to manually type headings, set a tab with a dot leader, and then type the page number. But Word can automatically generate a table of contents based upon the headings in your report, which saves you time. When using Word to generate a table of contents, it automatically updates if headings are changed or moved or if page numbering changes.

Use Heading Styles for a Table of Contents

Word automatically generates a table of contents listing the headings in your report if you apply ***heading styles*** to each heading. Styles control the appearance of text by applying a specific font,

font size, color, font styles and effects, and spacing to the text on which a style is applied. The document *theme* determines the appearance of the styles. The *Style* gallery displays commonly used styles.

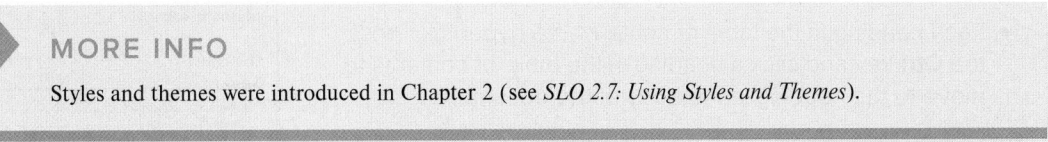

MORE INFO

Styles and themes were introduced in Chapter 2 (see *SLO 2.7: Using Styles and Themes*).

The first step in automatically generating a table of contents in a report is to apply a heading style to each heading in the document. Word provides multiple levels of heading styles (*Heading 1*, *Heading 2*, etc.).

▶ HOW TO: Apply Heading Styles

1. Select the heading where you want to apply a style.
2. Click the heading style to apply [*Home* tab, *Styles* group] (Figure 3-66). The style is applied to the heading.

Figure 3-66 Document styles displayed in the *Style* gallery

- Apply *Heading 1* to main headings, *Heading 2* to second level headings, and other heading styles as needed.
- When you place the insertion point on a style, Word displays a live preview of the style and temporarily applies the style to the selected text.
- Click the **More** button to expand the *Style* gallery to display additional styles.

3. Continue to select headings and apply styles. Apply a heading style to every heading you want to display in the table of contents.

- When a heading style has been applied to text, an *Expand/Collapse* button displays to the left of the heading (Figure 3-67). Click the **Expand/ Collapse** button to expand or collapse the text below the heading.

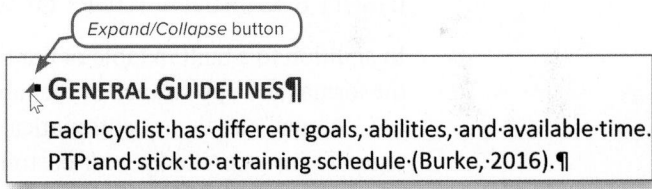

Figure 3-67 Expand or collapse text below a heading

Insert a Built-In Table of Contents

Word inserts the table of contents where you position the insertion point in the report. Therefore, it is a good idea to insert a blank page before the first page of your report and to position your insertion point on the blank page. Use a page break to insert the blank page at the top of your document.

▶ HOW TO: Insert a Built-In Table of Contents

1. Place the insertion point before the first line of the report and press **Ctrl+Enter** to insert a page break.
2. Position the insertion point at the top of the new first page.
3. Click the **References** tab.

4. Click the **Table of Contents** button [*Table of Contents* group] (Figure 3-68).

5. Select a built-in table of contents to insert. The table of contents displays in your report (Figure 3-69).

- Each heading in the table of contents is a hyperlink. Press the **Ctrl** key and click a heading in the table of contents to move to the heading in the body of the document.

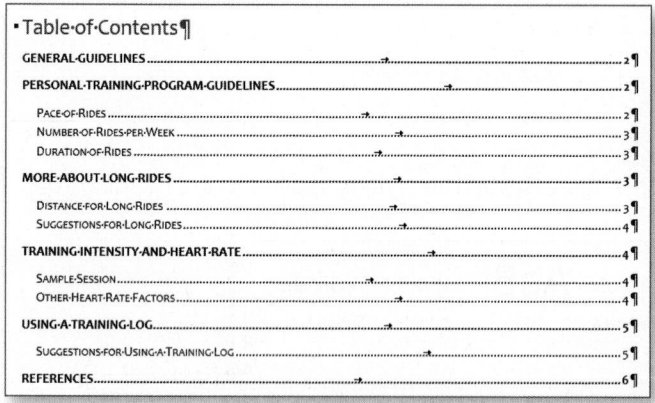

Figure 3-69 Table of contents inserted into the report

Figure 3-68 Insert built-in table of contents

Insert a Custom Table of Contents

In addition to a built-in table of contents, you can insert a custom table of contents and modify the format and appearance of the table. When you insert a custom table of contents, the "Table of Contents" title is not automatically inserted as it is when you insert a built-in table of contents. To insert a title on your custom table of contents page, type it before inserting your table of contents.

> **MORE INFO**
>
> It is usually best to apply font formatting (not a heading style) to the table of contents title. If you apply a heading style to the table of contents title, the table of contents title displays as an item in the table of contents when it is updated.

▶ HOW TO: Insert a Custom Table of Contents

1. Place the insertion point before the first line of your report and press **Ctrl+Enter** to insert a page break.
2. Position the insertion point at the top of the new first page.
 - If desired, type a title for the table of contents and press **Enter**.
 - Do not apply a heading style to the table of contents title.

3. Click the **Table of Contents** button [*References* tab, *Table of Contents* group].

4. Select **Custom Table of Contents**. The *Table of Contents* dialog box opens (Figure 3-70).

 • A preview of the table of contents appears in the *Print Preview* area.

5. Click the **Formats** drop-down list in the *General* area and select a table of contents format.

6. Select the number of heading levels to display in the *Show levels* area.

7. Customize the table of contents using the options below the *Print Preview* area where you can choose to not show page numbers, choose to not right align page numbers, and choose the type of tab leader to use with right-aligned page numbers.

8. Click **OK** to insert the table of contents.

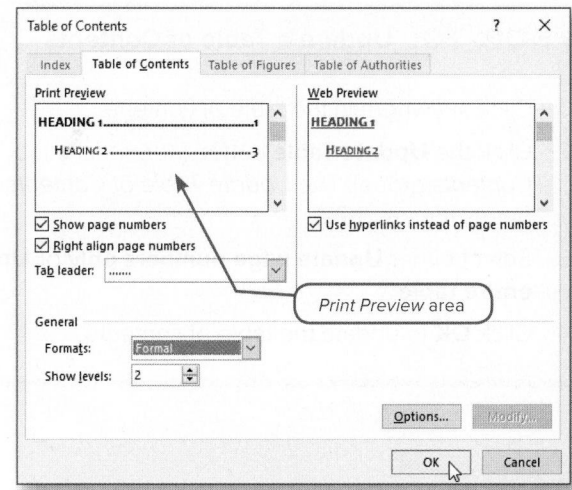

Figure 3-70 *Table of Contents* dialog box

Modify a Table of Contents

After inserting a table of contents, you may decide to use a different format or change the levels of headings that display. When you update a table of contents, you are actually replacing the old table of contents with a new one.

▶**HOW TO:** Modify a Table of Contents

1. Click anywhere in the table of contents.

2. Click the **Table of Contents** button [*References* tab, *Table of Contents* group].

3. Select **Custom Table of Contents**. The *Table of Contents* dialog box opens.

4. Customize the table of contents.

5. Click **OK**. A dialog box opens, confirming you want to replace the existing table of contents (Figure 3-71).

6. Click **Yes** to replace the table of contents.

Figure 3-71 Replace an existing table of contents

Update a Table of Contents

When you change your report, such as adding or modifying headings, content, or page breaks, the content and page numbers in the table of contents may no longer be accurate. You must update the table of contents to reflect these changes. You have the option of updating only page numbers or updating the entire table of contents, which includes both headings and page numbers.

1. Click anywhere in the table of contents.
2. Click the **Update Table** button [*References* tab, *Table of Contents* group]. The *Update Table of Contents* dialog box opens (Figure 3-72).
3. Select either **Update page numbers only** or **Update entire table**.
4. Click **OK** to update the table of contents.

Figure 3-72 Update a table of contents

▶ **ANOTHER WAY**

Press **F9** or right-click the table of contents and select **Update Field** to update the table of contents.

Remove a Table of Contents

If you no longer want a table of contents in your report, you can easily remove it. Click the **Table of Contents** button in the *Table of Contents* group on the *References* tab and select **Remove Table of Contents**. The table of contents is removed from your document (Figure 3-73).

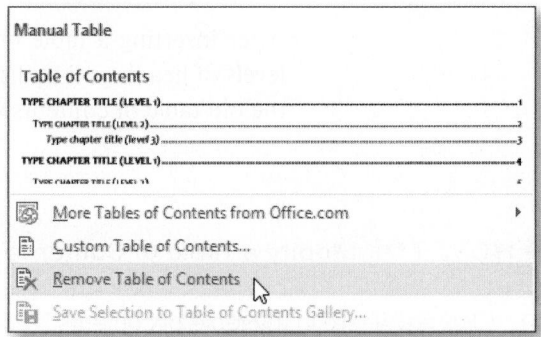

Figure 3-73 Remove a table of contents

SLO 3.6

Inserting a Cover Page

Reports frequently include a title page as the cover or introduction. If you're writing a formal report in APA style, the title page includes specific content and format. But if you're presenting a market analysis or product feasibility report, you may choose to include a *cover page* to introduce the report with professional appeal. Word provides a variety of cover page options.

Insert a Built-In Cover Page

When you insert a cover page into a document, Word automatically inserts it at the beginning of the document and inserts a page break to move the existing first page content to the second page.

To insert a cover page, click the **Cover Page** button in the *Pages* group on the *Insert* tab and select one of the built-in cover pages from the drop-down list (Figure 3-74). Additional custom cover pages are available on Office.com. Select **More Cover Pages from Office.com** to display a list of additional cover pages.

Customize Cover Page Content

The built-in cover pages in Word include graphics, text boxes, and Word fields. Some of the fields are *document property fields* and others are *content control fields*, fields where you type custom information. Customize the content of the fields, delete unwanted fields, and modify the graphics and text boxes on the cover page. The theme of your document controls the format of cover pages. Colors and fonts in a cover page change based on the selected theme.

Customize Document Property Content

If you add information to the document properties of your document, Word automatically populates the document properties fields in the cover page. When you type information into a document property field on the cover page, Word adds this information to your document properties.

Figure 3-74 Insert a built-in cover page

▶ HOW TO: Customize Document Properties

1. Click the **File** tab to open the *Backstage* view and select **Info** to display document properties (Figure 3-75).
2. Click the **Show All Properties** link at the bottom to display additional document property fields.
 - This link toggles between *Show All Properties* and *Show Fewer Properties*.
3. Add or modify document property content.
 - Fields, such as *Last Modified* and *Created*, cannot be modified.
 - To remove the *Author*, right-click the author and select **Remove Person**.
4. Click the **Back** arrow to return to the document. Word updates the document property fields on the cover page.

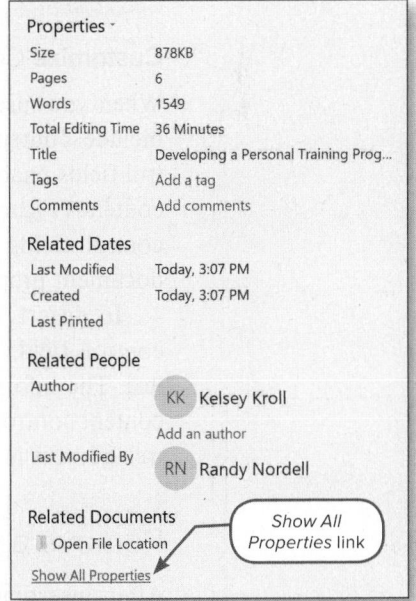

Figure 3-75 Document properties in the *Backstage* view

Add or Remove Document Property Fields

You can also add document property fields to the cover page or remove them. When you add a document property field to a cover page, the content of the field is automatically populated with the information from your document properties.

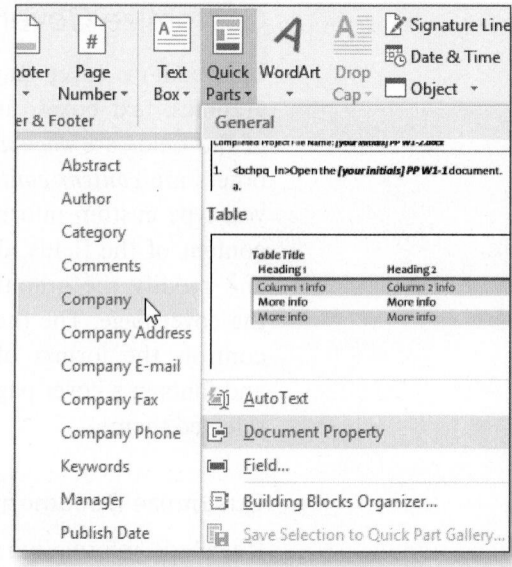

▶**HOW TO:** Add Document Property Fields

1. Position the insertion point at the place where you want to insert the document property field.
2. Click the **Insert** tab.
3. Click the **Quick Parts** button [*Text* group] (Figure 3-76).
4. Choose **Document Property**.
5. Select a document property field from the drop-down list. The document property field displays in the document.

> **MORE INFO**
>
> You can insert document property fields anywhere in a document.

Figure 3-76 Insert a document property field

To remove a document property field, click the **field handle** to select the field and press **Delete** (Figure 3-77). Check for proper spacing and paragraph breaks when you delete a document property field.

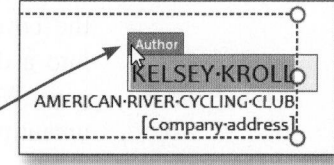

Field handle

Figure 3-77 Select and delete a document property field

> **MORE INFO**
>
> Deleting the contents of a document property or content control field does not delete the field. To remove a field, click the **field handle** to select the field and press **Delete**.

Customize Content Control Fields

When you insert a cover page, the page may include content control fields. Content control fields enable you to type or select custom content (Figure 3-78). Remove Word content control fields the same way you remove a document property field (see Figure 3-77).

Figure 3-78 Type text into a content control field

To insert custom content in a content control field, click the field and type the text. The information you type is not restricted by the content control field label. For example, you can type a web address in an *Address* field (see Figure 3-78).

Remove a Cover Page

After inserting a cover page, you may decide that you no longer need one or you want a different one. Removing a cover page is similar to removing a table of contents. Click the **Cover Page** button on the *Insert* tab and select **Remove Current Cover Page** (Figure 3-79).

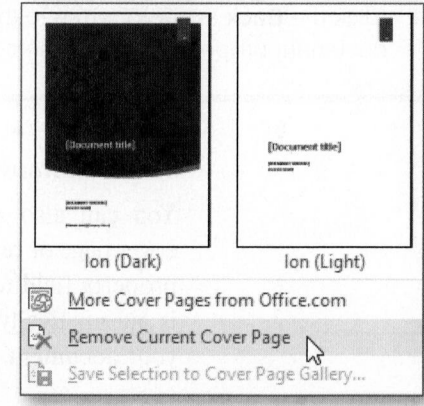

Figure 3-79 Remove a cover page

When you remove a cover page, Word deletes the entire contents of the cover page and removes the page break.

Using Advanced Headers and Footers

Headers and footers are used to include page numbers and document information at the top or bottom of each page in a report or multipage document. Headers appear at the top of the page, and footers appear at the bottom. Type headers and footers just once, and they automatically display on subsequent pages. You can automatically insert page numbers in the header or footer, and add custom content such as text, document property fields, the date, or borders.

Page and Section Breaks

For multipage documents, it is a good idea to insert page or section breaks to control page endings or special formatting in different sections. A *Page* break controls where one page ends and another begins. Use a *Next Page* section break when special document layout formatting is applied to a whole page or multiple pages of a document, such as landscape orientation to one page of the document. Use a *Continuous* section break when you apply special formatting to a section of the document, such as the two-column format to specific text on one page.

> **MORE INFO**
>
> Do not use a section break to control page endings.

▶**HOW TO: Insert a Page or Section Break**

1. Place the insertion point in the document at the location to insert a *Page* break or *Next Page* section break.
 - When inserting a *Continuous* section break, select the text on which to apply the section break.
 - When you insert a *Continuous* section break for selected text, Word inserts a *Continuous* section break before and after the selected text.
2. Click the **Breaks** button [*Layout* tab, *Page Setup* group] (Figure 3-80).
3. Select the type of break from the drop-down list.

> **ANOTHER WAY**
>
> **Ctrl+Enter** inserts a page break.

When working with page and section breaks, it is best to have the *Show/Hide* feature turned on to display breaks in a document. To delete a page or section break, select the break and press **Delete**.

Figure 3-80 Insert a page or section break

Built-In Headers, Footers, and Page Numbers

Word provides a variety of built-in headers, footers, and page numbering options to insert and customize. Insert built-in header and footer content with the header or footer open or while you are in the main document.

▶ HOW TO: Insert a Built-In Header, Footer, or Page Number

1. Click the **Insert** tab.

2. Click the **Header**, **Footer**, or **Page Number** button [*Header & Footer* group].

3. Select a built-in header, footer, or page number from the drop-down list (Figure 3-81). The content displays and the header or footer area opens.

 • When inserting a page number, select the position (*Top of Page*, *Bottom of Page*, *Page Margins*, or *Current Position*) to insert the page number.

 • Additional built-in headers, footers, and page numbers display when you place your pointer on *More Headers (Footer or Page Numbers) from Office.com.*

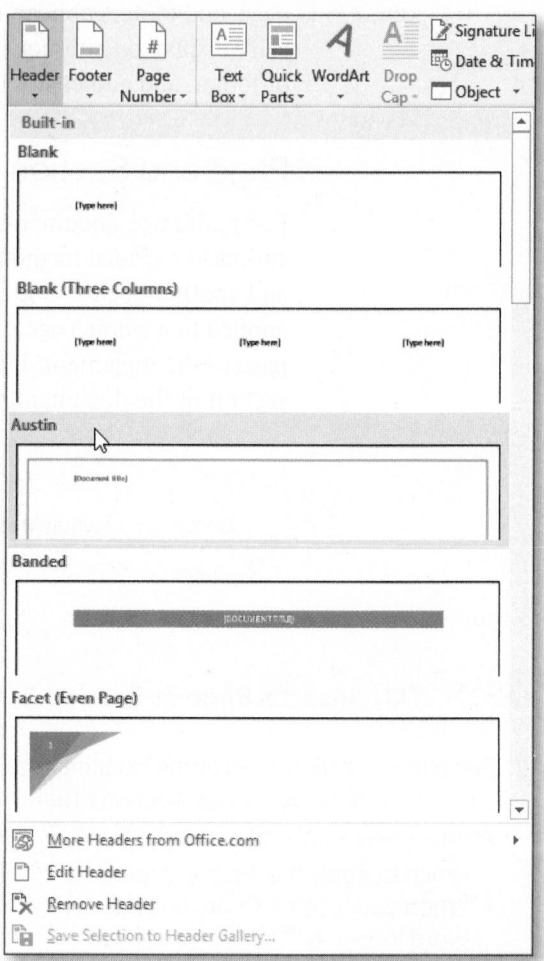

Many of Word's built-in headers and footers contain document property fields or content control fields. When you enter information in the document property area, these fields update automatically. For content control fields such as *Date* or *Address*, select or type the content to display (see Figure 3-78).

Figure 3-81 Insert a built-in header

Customize Header and Footer Content

In addition to the built-in header and footer content, you can type text or insert or delete content control fields. Format header and footer text as you would other text in your document by applying font formatting and borders, inserting graphics, and modifying or setting tabs for alignment.

Edit a header or footer in the following ways:

• Right-click the header or footer area and select **Edit Header** or **Edit Footer**.

• Click the **Header** or **Footer** button [*Insert* tab, *Header & Footer* group] and select **Edit Header** or **Edit Footer**.

• Double-click the header or footer area of the document.

▶ HOW TO: Insert Custom Content in the Header or Footer

1. Edit the header or footer. See above for different ways to edit the header or footer. The *Header & Footer Tools Design* tab opens (Figure 3-82).

Figure 3-82 Insert content from the *Header & Footer Tools Design* tab

2. Insert content from the *Header & Footer Tools Design* tab.
3. Type content, insert a document property field, insert the date, or insert built-in header, footer, or page number content to display in the header or footer (Figure 3-83).

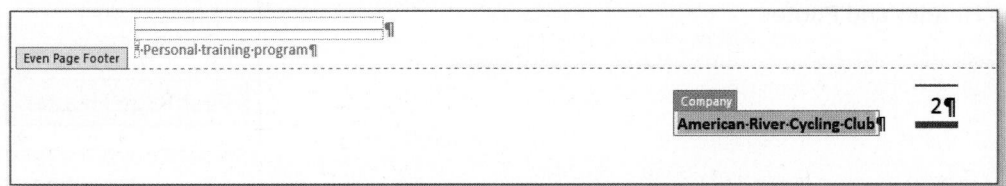

Figure 3-83 A built-in footer and document property field inserted in the footer

4. Align information in the header or footer by using horizontal alignment buttons (*Center* or *Align Right*) or tabs.

 - By default, a center tab stop is set at the horizontal midpoint, and a right tab stop is set at the right margin.
 - Insert a tab stop by clicking the **Insert Alignment Tab** button [*Header & Footer Tools Design* tab, *Position* group] (Figure 3-84).
 - Alternatively, modify, add, or remove tabs on the *Ruler* or in the *Tabs* dialog box [*Paragraph* dialog box, *Tabs* button].

Figure 3-84 Header and footer position options

5. Apply formatting to header and footer content.
6. Change the position of the header and footer in the *Position* group.

 - By default, the header and footer are positioned 0.5" from the top and bottom of the page (see Figure 3-84).
 - Alternatively, change these settings in the *Page Setup* dialog box on the *Layout* tab.

7. Click **Close Header and Footer** to return to the main document.

Different First Page Header and Footer

For many reports, the page number or header and footer content should not display on the first page, but it does display on subsequent pages. When you select the ***Different First Page*** option, Word removes existing content from the header and footer on the first page. You can choose to leave the first page header and footer blank or insert content that is different from the header and footer on second and subsequent pages.

▶ HOW TO: Insert a Different First Page Header and Footer

1. Edit the header or footer on the first page of the document.

2. Check the **Different First Page** check box [*Header & Footer Tools Design* tab, *Options* group] (Figure 3-85).

 • When the *Different First Page* check box is checked, the header (or footer) label displays ***First Page Header*** (or ***First Page Footer***) to distinguish it from other headers and footers in the document, which are labeled *Header* (or *Footer)* (Figure 3-86).

 • The header (or footer) label changes when you apply other header and footer formatting such as odd and even pages or have different headers for different sections of your document.

3. Click **Close Header and Footer**.

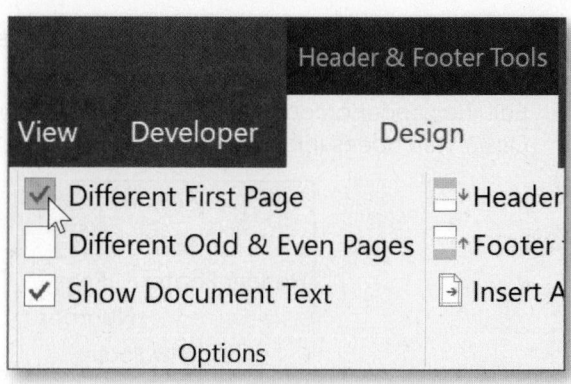

Figure 3-85 Apply *Different First Page* header and footer

Figure 3-86 First page header

Different Odd and Even Pages

Just as you can have different header and footer content on the first page, Word provides the option of having ***different odd and even pages*** header and footer content on a multipage document. For example, you may want the title of the report to appear on all even pages in the footer and the page number and a company name to appear on odd pages.

> ▶ **MORE INFO**
>
> It is best to insert header and footer content on the first page of your document and then make any desired header and footer option changes.

▶ HOW TO: Insert Different Odd and Even Headers and Footers

1. Edit the header or footer on the first page of the document.

2. Check the **Different Odd & Even Pages** check box [*Header & Footer Tools Design* tab, *Options* group] (see Figure 3-85).

 • When the *Different Odd & Even Pages* check box is checked, the header (or footer) label displays *Odd* (or *Even*) *Page Header* (or *Footer*) to distinguish it from other headers and footers in the document (Figure 3-87).

3. Click **Close Header and Footer**.

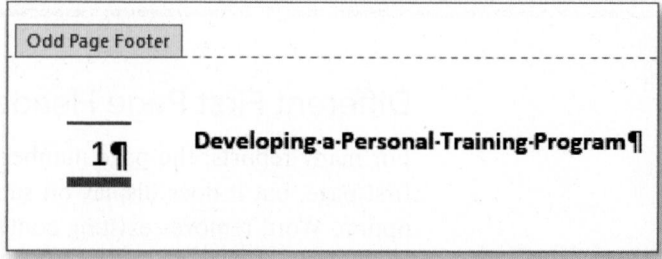

Figure 3-87 Odd page footer

Link to Previous Header or Footer

Section breaks separate your document into different sections. When you have different sections in your document, the headers and footers are by default linked to previous headers and footers. For example, a page number that appears in the footer of the first section of a document will also appear in the same position in the next section footer because it is linked to the previous footer. Break this link to format header and footer content in one section independently of the header or footer in another section. To break the link, click the **Link to Previous** button.

> ▶ **HOW TO:** Link or Unlink a Header or Footer

1. Edit the header or footer to be unlinked from the previous section.
 - By default, the *Link to Previous* button is on (shaded).
 - The *Same as Previous* label displays on the right of the header or footer.
2. Click the **Link to Previous** button [*Header & Footer Tools Design* tab, *Navigation* group] to unlink it from the previous section (Figure 3-88).

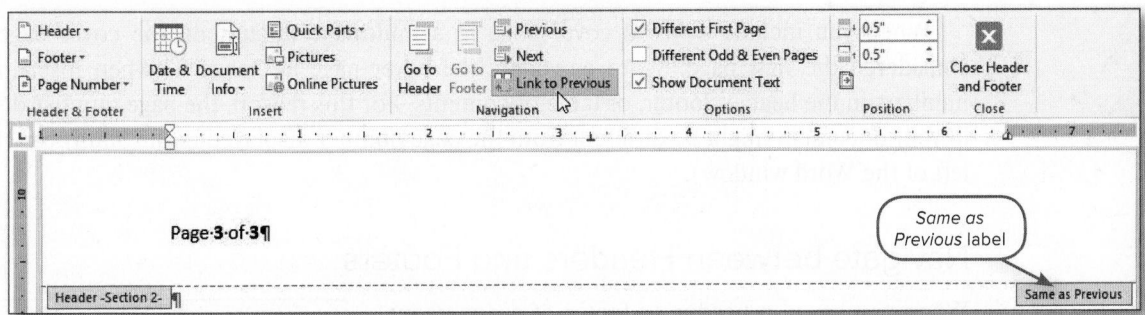

Figure 3-88 *Link to Previous* button

 - The *Same as Previous* label no longer displays.
 - The header or footer content still displays, but you can edit it without it changing the header or footer content in the previous section.
3. Click the **Link to Previous** button to link header or footer content to a previous section after it has been unlinked.
 - Click **Yes** in the dialog box that opens asking if you want to link the header or footer to the previous section (Figure 3-89).
4. Click the **Close Header and Footer** button.

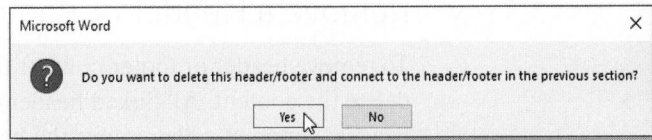

Figure 3-89 Link header or footer content to the previous section

Format Page Numbers

When using page numbers in your document, you can change the page number format and the starting page number. For example, reports typically use Roman numerals on the front matter pages (title page, table of contents, executive summary) and regular numbers on the body pages. If you are using different numbering for different sections of a document, insert a next page section break between sections. This allows you to format the page numbering of each section differently.

1. Select the page number to format in the header or footer.

2. Click the **Page Number** button [*Header & Footer Tools Design* tab, *Header & Footer* group].

3. Select **Format Page Numbers** from the drop-down list. The *Page Number Format* dialog box opens (Figure 3-90).

4. Click the **Number format** drop-down list and select the number format.

5. Select either the **Continue from previous section** or **Start at** radio button in the *Page numbering* area.

 - If you select *Continue from previous section*, the numbering continues consecutively from the previous section.
 - If you select *Start at*, select the starting page number for the section.

6. Click **OK** to close the *Page Number Format* dialog box.

Figure 3-90 *Page Number Format* dialog box

When you include a Word cover page in a multipage document, the cover page is *not* considered the first page. Word considers the cover page as "page 0" when inserting page numbers in the header, footer, or table of contents. For this reason, the page number displayed in your document might be different from the page number displayed in the *Status* bar (bottom left of the Word window).

Navigate between Headers and Footers

When you are in a header or footer of a document, Word provides a variety of buttons to navigate the header or footer areas: *Go to Header*, *Go to Footer*, *Previous*, and *Next*. These navigation buttons are in the *Navigation* group on the *Header & Footer Tools Design* tab (Figure 3-91).

Figure 3-91 Header and footer navigation buttons

Remove a Header or Footer

To remove header or footer content from a document, open the header or footer and manually delete the content. All linked header or footer content is also removed when you do this. Word can also automatically remove the header or footer from a document.

1. Click the **Insert** button.

2. Click the **Header or Footer** button [*Header & Footer* group].

3. Select **Remove Header** or **Remove Footer** from the drop-down list (Figure 3-92). The header or footer content is removed.

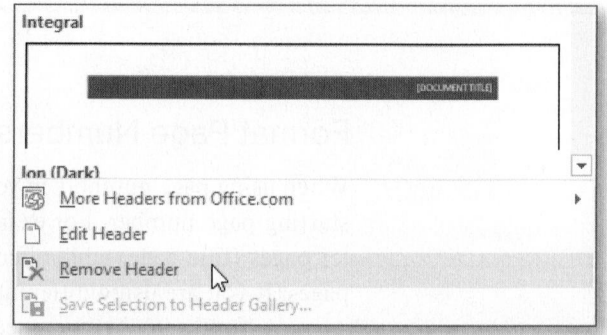

Figure 3-92 Remove header

For this Pause & Practice project, you continue to modify the *Personal Training Program* report for the American River Cycling Club. You apply styles to headings in the report, insert and modify a table of contents, insert and modify a cover page, and insert customized footers.

File Needed: *[your initials] PP W3-2.docx*
Completed Project File Name: *[your initials] PP W3-3.docx*

1. Open the *[your initials] PP W3-2* document completed in *Pause & Practice 3-2*.

2. Save this document as [your initials] PP W3-3.

3. Apply styles to the headings in the report.
 a. Select the "**General Guidelines**" heading on the first page.
 b. Click the **Heading 1** style [*Home* tab, *Styles* group] to apply this style to the selected heading (Figure 3-93). If the *Heading 1* style is not visible, click the **More** button to display the entire *Styles* gallery.

 Figure 3-93 Apply *Heading 1* style

 c. Apply the **Heading 1** style to the following headings (bolded headings in the document):

 Personal Training Program Guidelines
 More about Long Rides
 Training Intensity and Heart Rate
 Using a Training Log

 d. Apply the **Heading 2** style to the following subheadings (underlined headings in the document):

 Pace of Rides
 Number of Rides per Week
 Duration of Rides
 Distance for Long Rides
 Suggestions for Long Rides
 Sample Session
 Other Heart Rate Factors
 Suggestions for Using a Training Log

4. Add a table of contents at the beginning of the report.
 a. Turn on **Show/Hide** [*Home* tab, *Paragraph* group] if necessary.
 b. Position the insertion point at the beginning of the document before the title ("Developing a Personal Training Program").
 c. Click the **Breaks** button [*Layout* tab, *Page Setup* group] and select **Page** or press **Ctrl+Enter** to insert a page break.
 d. Position the insertion point before the page break on the new first page.
 e. Click the **Table of Contents** button [*References* tab, *Table of Contents* group] (Figure 3-94).

 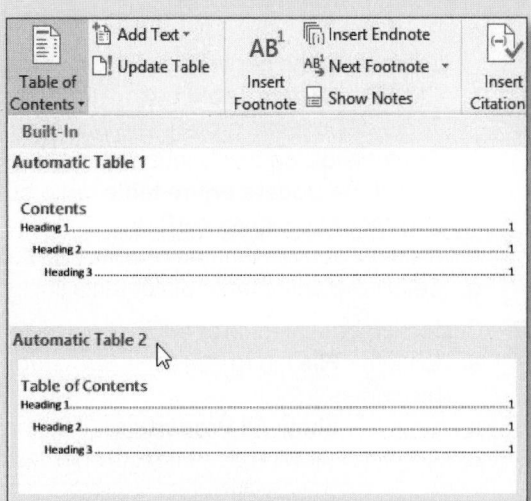

 Figure 3-94 Insert table of contents

f. Select **Automatic Table 2** from the drop-down list. The table of contents displays on the first page of the report.

5. Customize the table of contents.
 a. Position the insertion point in the body of the table of contents.
 b. Click the **Table of Contents** button [*References* tab, *Table of Contents* group].
 c. Select **Custom Table of Contents** to open the *Table of Contents* dialog box (Figure 3-95).
 d. Click the **Formats** drop-down list and select **Formal**.
 e. Set the number of levels to **2** in the *Show levels* area.
 f. Check the **Show page numbers** and **Right align page numbers** boxes if they are not already checked.
 g. Select the dot leader option from the *Tab leader* drop-down list if it is not already selected.
 h. Click **OK** to close the dialog box. A dialog box opens, confirming you want to replace the existing table of contents (Figure 3-96).
 i. Click **OK** to replace the existing table of contents.

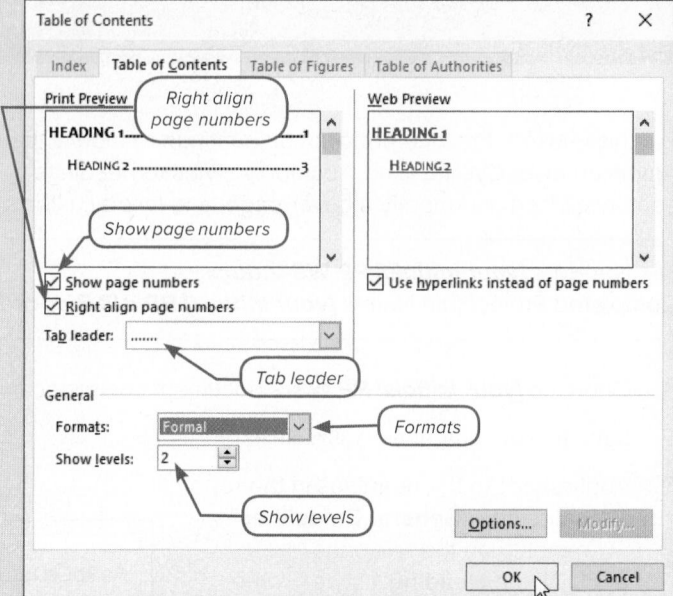

Figure 3-95 Customize table of contents

6. Insert page breaks and update the table of contents.
 a. Position the insertion point in front of the "Number of Rides per Week" heading on the second page.
 b. Click the **Breaks** button [*Layout* tab, *Page Setup* group] and select **Page** to insert a page break (or press **Ctrl+Enter**).
 c. Repeat this process on the following headings:
 Suggestions for Long Rides
 Using a Training Log
 d. Place the insertion point in the table of contents at the beginning of the document.
 e. Click the **Update Table** button [*References* tab, *Table of Contents* group]. The *Update Table of Contents* dialog box opens.
 f. Select the **Update entire table** radio button and click **OK** (Figure 3-97). If a blank line displays above the table of contents, select the **paragraph mark** and press **Delete**.
 g. Select the entire table of contents (including the heading) and change the font to **Calibri**.

Figure 3-96 Replace existing table of contents

Figure 3-97 Update entire table of contents

7. Customize document properties.
 a. Click the **File** tab to open the *Backstage* view and select **Info** (if necessary) to display document properties.
 b. Click the **Show All Properties** link in the document properties area.
 c. Add the following document properties:

 Title: Developing a Personal Training Program
 Company: American River Cycling Club
 Manager: Olesia Sokol

d. Right-click the author's name in the *Author* area and select **Remove Person**.
 e. Click the **Back** arrow to return to the report.

8. Add a cover page and customize fields.
 a. Click the **Cover Page** button [*Insert* tab, *Pages* group] and select **Semaphore**. The cover page displays on the page before the table of contents.
 b. Click the **Date** field, click the **Date** drop-down arrow, and select the current date.
 c. Click the **Author** document property field near the bottom of the cover page, select the field handle (Figure 3-98), and press **Delete** to delete the field. The insertion point is on the blank line where the *Author* field was removed, although it may not be visible.

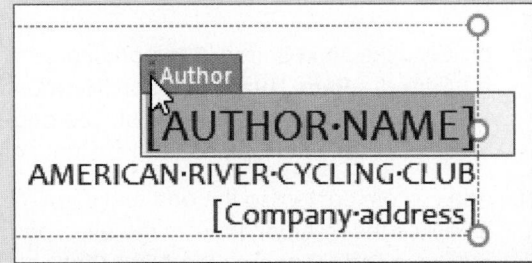

Figure 3-98 Select and delete the document property field

 d. Click the **Quick Parts** button [*Insert* tab, *Text* group], select **Document Property**, and select **Manager** from the drop-down list to insert the *Manager* field above the company name.
 e. Click the **Company Address** field and type www.arcc.org in the field.
 f. Right-click the **Subtitle** field ("[Document Subtitle]") and select **Remove Content Control** from the context menu.
 g. Click the **Title** field and apply **bold** format. Bold formatting applies to the entire *Title* field.
 h. Save the document.

9. Insert odd page and even page footers.
 a. Place your insertion point at the beginning of the document (cover page).
 b. Click the **Footer** button [*Insert* tab, *Header & Footer* group] and select **Edit Footer** to open the footer area.
 c. Check the **Different First Page** box (if it is not already checked) and check the **Different Odd & Even Pages** box [*Header & Footer Tools Design* tab, *Options* group].
 d. Click the **Next** button [*Navigation* group] (Figure 3-99) to move to the odd page footer on the second page (table of contents).
 e. Click the **Page Number** button [*Header & Footer* group].
 f. Select **Bottom of Page** and select **Two Bars 1** from the drop-down list (Figure 3-100). The page number "1" displays on the second page.

Figure 3-100 Select a built-in page number

 g. Click the **Next** button [*Navigation* group] to move to the even page footer on the next page.

 h. Click the **Page Number** button [*Header & Footer* group], select **Bottom of Page**, and select **Two Bars 2** from the drop-down list. The page number "2" displays on the right.

 i. Leave the footer open to add custom content in the next step.

10. Add custom content to the odd and even footers.

 a. Place the insertion point in the even page footer.

 b. Press **Ctrl+R** or click the **Align Right** button [*Home* tab, *Paragraph* group] to position the insertion point on the right.

 c. Click the **Document Info** button [*Header & Footer Tools Design* tab, *Insert* group] (Figure 3-101).

 d. Select **Document Property** and choose **Company** from the drop-down list. The *Company* document property field displays on the right side of the footer area.

 e. Select the **Company** document property field, change the font size to **10 pt**, and apply **bold** formatting.

 f. Click the **Previous** button [*Header & Footer Tools Design* tab, *Navigation* group] to move to the odd page footer on the previous page. The insertion point should be on the left after the page number "1."

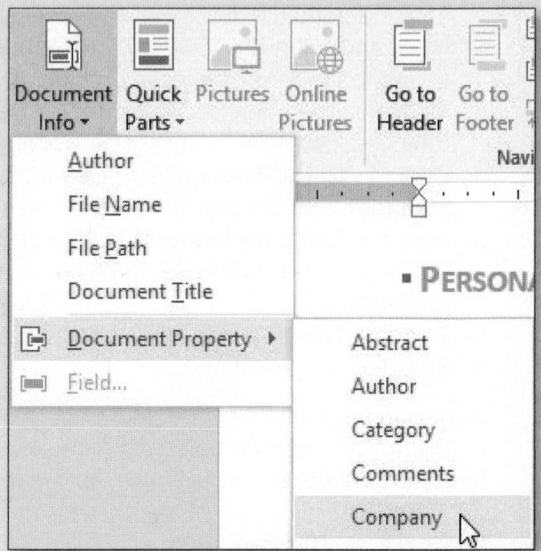

Figure 3-101 Insert a document property field

 g. Click the **Document Info** button [*Header & Footer Tools Design* tab, *Insert* group] and select **Document Title** from the drop-down list. The *Title* document property field displays in the footer.

 h. Select the **Title** document property field, change the font size to **10 pt**, and apply **bold** formatting.

 i. Click the **Close Header and Footer** button [*Header & Footer Tools Design* tab, *Close* group].

 j. Review the document to ensure correct page numbering. No footer displays on the cover page of the document. The table of contents footer displays page "1" and the title of the report at the left. The first body page footer displays page "2" and the company name at the right. Each subsequent page should be numbered consecutively with odd and even footers.

11. Create a sharing link to share this file with your instructor.

 a. Save this document on *OneDrive* if you haven't already. If you don't have the ability to save to *OneDrive*, skip all of step 11.

 b. Click the **Share** button in the upper-right corner of the Word window. The *Send Link* window opens (Figure 3-102). If you are using a personal Microsoft account, the *Share* pane opens at the right, and the sharing options differ slightly.

 c. Click the **Link settings** button to open the *Link settings* window.

 d. Click the **Anyone** button and check the **Allow editing** box (if necessary) (Figure 3-103).

 e. Click **Apply** to return to the *Send Link* window.

 f. Click the **Copy Link** button to create a sharing link.

 g. Click **Copy** to copy the sharing link and click the **X** in the upper-right corner to close the sharing link window (Figure 3-104).

Figure 3-102 *Send Link* window

h. Use your email account to create a new email to your instructor. Include an appropriate subject line and a brief message in the body.

i. Press **Ctrl+V** to paste the sharing link to your document in the body of the email and send the email message.

12. Save and close the document (Figure 3-105).

Figure 3-103 *Link settings* window

Figure 3-104 Copy sharing link

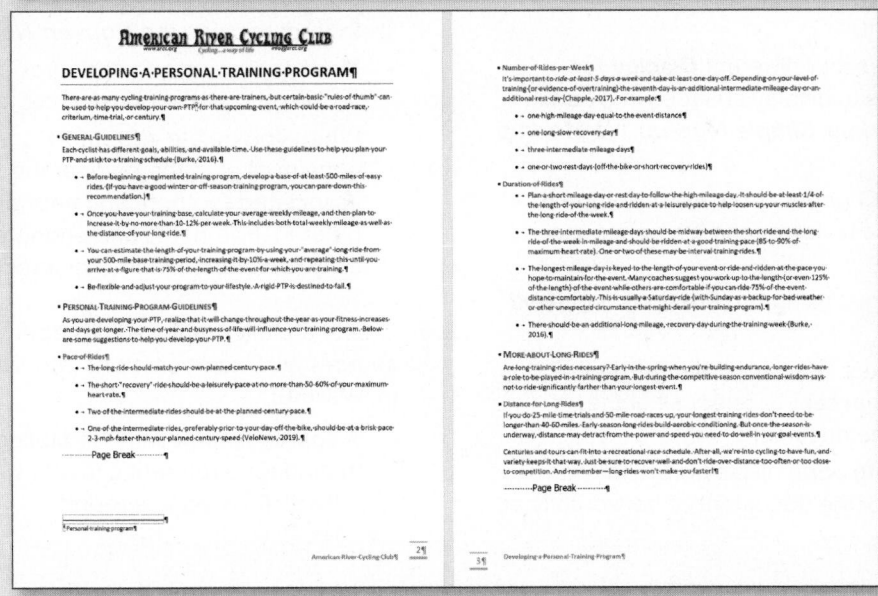

Figure 3-105 PP W3-3 completed (pages 1–4 of 7)

Chapter Summary

3.1 Insert, review, edit, and customize comments (p. W3-139).

- Use **comments** to insert a note or provide feedback in a document. The content and format of the document does not change.
- Use **Ink Comment** to insert a handwritten comment using a stylus or finger on a touch-screen computer.
- Users can add, edit, or delete comments. Comments appear to the right of the document in the **Markup area**.
- Comments are numbered sequentially in a document and are associated with a Microsoft Office **user name** and **initials**, which is customized in the *Word Options* dialog box.
- Multiple reviewers can add comments to a document.
- Use the **Next** and **Previous** buttons to review the comments in the document.
- When you place your pointer on a comment, a tag provides details about the user name and date and time of the comment.
- **Reply** to a comment or **Resolve** a comment to mark it as resolved.
- Delete comments individually or delete all comments in the document.

3.2 Modify and review a document using *Track Changes* and share an online document (p. W3-142).

- **Track Changes** is a collaboration tool that enables reviewers to make and track changes in a document.
- Word provides four different **Display for Review views** to display changes in a document: **All Markup**, **Simple Markup**, **No Markup**, and **Original**.
- When *Track Changes* is on, each change is attributed to a reviewer and his or her user name.
- Review changes using the **Previous** and **Next** buttons.
- Accept or reject individual changes in the document, or accept or reject all of the changes in the document.
- The **Reviewing pane** displays vertically on the left side of the document or horizontally at the bottom of the document and shows all the changes in the document.
- Customize which markup displays in the document.
- Use the *Track Changes Options* dialog box to customize how tracked changes appear in a document.
- Share online files with others. More than one user can edit an online file at the same time, which enables **real-time collaboration** on documents.
- The **Send Link** or **Share pane** provides different options for sharing an online document.

3.3 Insert and edit footnotes and endnotes in a document (p. W3-151).

- Add **footnotes** and **endnotes** to include additional information or reference sources.
- Footnotes appear at the bottom of the page, and endnotes appear at the end of the document.
- A **reference marker** is a number, letter, or symbol that indicates a footnote or endnote in the body of the document.
- Change the location, number format, and starting number for footnotes and endnotes in the *Footnote and Endnote* dialog box.
- Word styles control the format of footnotes and endnotes. Edit styles to modify how your footnote and endnote text appears in the document.
- Convert footnotes to endnotes or endnotes to footnotes using the **Convert Notes** dialog box.
- Move footnotes and endnotes using the drag and drop method or using cut and paste.
- When you delete a footnote or endnote reference marker in the body of the document, the associated footnote and endnote text is also deleted. Footnotes and endnotes automatically renumber if one is deleted or inserted.

3.4 Create a bibliography with properly formatted sources and insert citations into a document (p. W3-156).

- A **source** is the complete bibliographic information for a reference (book, web page, journal article) used in a report.

- A *citation* is the abbreviated source information used in the body of a report.
- The *bibliography style* controls the format of the sources on the bibliography page and citations in the body of the document.
- Add a *placeholder* to temporarily mark a citation in the body of a report.
- Use the *Source Manager* dialog box to create and edit sources, edit placeholders, and view available sources.
- Use the *Researcher* to search for quotes, citable sources, and images about a topic and to display information from journals and web sites in the *Researcher* pane.
- Insert a *bibliography* or *works cited* page to list the sources in your document.

3.5 Create and edit a table of contents based on headings in a document (p. W3-168).

- Word can automatically generate a *table of contents* for a document.
- *Heading styles* (Heading 1, Heading 2, etc.) determine the content for a table of contents.
- Use built-in table of contents formats or customize the format of the table of contents.
- Use the *Table of Contents* dialog box to customize the format and the number of levels displayed in the table of contents.
- When document headings or pagination change, update the table of contents to reflect the changes.

3.6 Insert a cover page and modify content and content control fields (p. W3-172).

- Word provides a variety of built-in *cover pages* available to add to your documents.
- A cover page has graphics, colors, text boxes, and Word fields that you can customize. The document theme controls the colors and fonts on the cover page.
- Use *document property* and *content control fields* to display information on the cover page. Customize or delete this content.

3.7 Apply and customize headers and footers in a multipage document (p. W3-175).

- *Headers* and *footers* provide information and page numbers in a document. Headers are located at the top, and footers are located at the bottom of a document.
- *Page* and *section breaks* control pagination and page numbering in a document.
- Insert a variety of built-in headers, footers, and page numbers into a document.
- Customize content and page numbering in headers and footers.
- *Different first page* headers and footers enable you to include different information on the first page of a document.
- Use *odd and even page* headers and footers to display different information on odd and even pages in a document.
- Change the page number format and starting page number in the *Page Number Format* dialog box.

Check for Understanding

The SIMbook for this text (within your SIMnet account) provides the following resources for concept review:

- Multiple-choice questions
- Short answer questions
- Matching exercises

Guided Project 3-1

For this project, you customize the *Online Learning Plan* for Sierra Pacific Community College District. You review comments and tracked changes, add document properties, apply styles, create a table of contents, insert and modify footnotes, insert headers and footers, and add a customized cover page. [Student Learning Outcomes 3.1, 3.2, 3.3, 3.5, 3.6, 3.7]

File Needed: ***OnlineLearningPlan-03.docx*** *(Student data files are available in the* Library *of your SIMnet account.)*
Completed Project File Name: *[your initials]* ***Word 3-1.docx***

Skills Covered in This Project

- Modify user name and initials.
- Reject and accept tracked changes.
- Reply to a comment and resolve a comment.
- Customize document properties.
- Apply styles to selected text.
- Insert page breaks.

- Insert a table of contents.
- Insert footnotes.
- Modify footnote number format.
- Insert built-in page numbers and document property fields in the footer.
- Insert a cover page and remove and add document property fields.
- Update a table of contents.

1. Open the ***OnlineLearningPlan-03*** document from your student data files.

2. Save this document as [your initials] Word 3-1.

3. Change user name and initials.
 a. Click the **Tracking** launcher [*Review* tab, *Tracking* group] to open the *Track Changes Options* dialog box.
 b. Click the **Change User Name** button to open the *Word Options* dialog box.
 c. Type your first and last name in the *User name* text box in the *Personalize your copy of Microsoft Office* area.
 d. Type your first and last initials in lowercase letters in the *Initials* text box.
 e. Check the **Always use these values regardless of sign in to Office** box.
 f. Click **OK** to close the *Word Options* dialog box and click **OK** to close the *Track Changes Options* dialog box.

4. Display the *Reviewing* pane and reject changes.
 a. Click the **Display for Review** drop-down list [*Review* tab, *Tracking* group] and select **All Markup** to view the document with comments and proposed changes visible.
 b. Click the **Reviewing Pane** drop-down arrow [*Review* tab, *Tracking* group] and select **Reviewing Pane Vertical**. The *Reviewing* pane displays on the left side of the Word window.
 c. Find where "Hasmik Kumar Deleted **Television or Tele-Web course—**" in the *Reviewing* pane.
 d. Right-click this deletion and select **Reject Deletion** from the context menu (Figure 3-106).
 e. Click the **X** in the upper-right corner of the *Reviewing* pane to close it.

Right-click revision to display the context menu

Figure 3-106 Reject a deletion in the *Reviewing* pane

5. Accept changes in the document.
 a. Place your insertion point at the top of the document.
 b. Click the **Next** button [*Review* tab, *Changes* group] to select the first change (Left: 1").

 c. Click the top half of the **Accept** button [*Review* tab, *Changes* group] to accept the change and move to the next change.
 d. Click the top half of the **Accept** button again to accept the change (delete CCD).
 e. Click the bottom half of the **Accept** button and select **Accept All Changes** from the drop-down list (Figure 3-107). All of the remaining changes in the document are accepted. Only comments remain in the *Markup* area.

 Figure 3-107 Accept all changes in the document

6. Reply to a comment, resolve a comment, and delete a comment.
 a. Place your insertion point at the top of the document and click the **Next** button [*Review* tab, *Comments* group] to move to the first comment.
 b. Click the **Reply** button in the *Markup* area.
 c. Type Done!
 d. Click the **Resolve** button on the comment in the *Markup* area (Figure 3-108). The comment and reply become grayed out.
 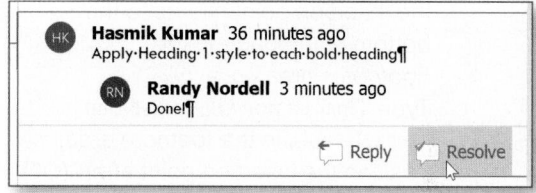
 e. Click the **Next** button [*Review* tab, *Comments* group] to move to the second comment (not the reply to the first comment).
 f. Click the top half of the **Delete** button [*Review* tab, *Comments* group] to delete the comment.

 Figure 3-108 *Resolve* button on a comment

 g. Click the **Display for Review** drop-down list [*Review* tab, *Tracking* group] and select **No Markup** so comments are not visible.

7. Add document properties.
 a. Click the **File** tab to open the *Backstage* view.
 b. Click **Show All Properties** in the *Properties* area.
 c. Add the following document properties:

 Title: Online Learning Plan
 Company: Sierra Pacific Community College District
 Manager: Hasmik Kumar

 d. Click the **Back** arrow to return to the document.

8. Apply styles to the document.
 a. Go to the first page of the document, select the title ("**Online Learning Plan**"), and apply the **Title** style.
 b. Select the subtitle ("**Sierra Pacific Community College District**") and apply the **Subtitle** style.
 c. Apply the **Heading 1** style to all the main headings (all caps and bold) in the document.
 d. Apply the **Heading 2** style to all subheadings (underlined) in the document.

9. Insert a table of contents into the report.
 a. Place your insertion point in front of the first main heading in the document ("Purpose of this Plan") and press **Ctrl+Enter** to insert a page break.
 b. Go to the new first page of the document, place the insertion point directly after the subtitle and press **Enter**.
 c. Click the **Table of Contents** button [*References* tab, *Table of Contents* group] (Figure 3-109).
 d. Select **Automatic Table 2**. The table of contents displays below the subtitle.

e. Select the words "**Table of Contents**" in the table of contents, click the **Font Color** drop-down list, and select **Automatic**. If a blank line displays between the subtitle and "Table of Contents," **delete** it. Turn on **Show/Hide** if necessary.

10. Insert footnotes into the document.
 a. Go to the second page of the document and position the insertion point after "web-Enhanced course" and before the dash.
 b. Click the **Insert Footnote** button [*References* tab, *Footnotes* group]. A footnote reference marker appears after the text and the insertion point moves to the bottom of the page in the *Footnotes* area.
 c. Type This is a non-OL course that uses OL tools. in the footnote area.
 d. Position the insertion point after "(OL)" and before the space (page 2, "Purpose of This Plan" section, second sentence).
 e. Click the **Insert Footnote** button and type Online learning is referred to as OL throughout this report. in the footnote area. This footnote becomes footnote 1, and the other footnote automatically becomes number 2.

11. Modify footnote number format.
 a. Click the **Footnotes** launcher to open the *Footnote and Endnote* dialog box (Figure 3-110).
 b. Click the **Number format** drop-down list and select **i, ii, iii, . . .**.
 c. Click **Apply** to close the dialog box and apply the number format change.

12. Insert and modify content in the footer.
 a. Place your insertion point at the beginning of the document.
 b. Click the **Footer** button [*Insert* tab, *Header & Footer* group] and select **Edit Footer**.
 c. Click the **Document Info** button [*Header & Footer Tools Design* tab, *Insert* group] and select **Document Title** from the drop-down list to insert the *Title* document property field.
 d. Press the **right arrow** once to deselect the document property field and press **Tab** to move to the center preset tab stop.
 e. Click the **Document Info** button, select **Document Property**, and select **Company** from the drop-down list.
 f. Press the **right arrow** once to deselect the document property field and press **Tab** to move to the right preset tab stop.

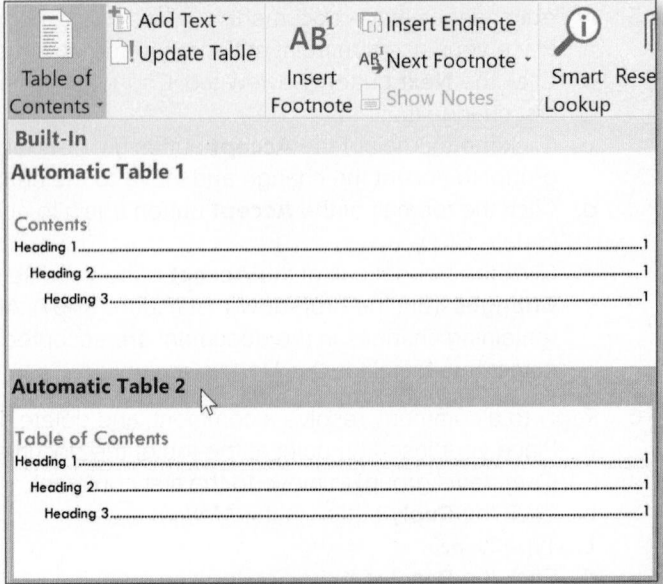

Figure 3-109 Insert a table of contents

Figure 3-110 Modify the footnote number format

g. Click the **Page Number** button [*Insert* tab, *Header & Footer* group], select **Current Position**, and select **Bold Numbers** from the drop-down list.

h. Select all of the text in the footer and change the font size to **10 pt** (Figure 3-111).

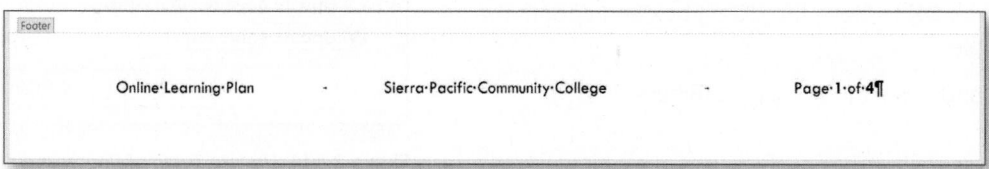

Figure 3-111 Document properties and built-in page number inserted into the footer

i. Click the **Close Header and Footer** button [*Header & Footer Tools Design* tab, *Close* group].

13. Insert a page break.
 a. Position the insertion point before the last subheading ("How are Courses and Programs Selected for Online Learning Delivery?") on page 2 of the report.
 b. Press **Ctrl+Enter** to insert a page break.

14. Insert a cover page and modify content control fields.
 a. Place your insertion point at the top of the document.
 b. Click the **Cover Page** button [*Insert* tab, *Pages* group].
 c. Select the **Retrospect** built-in cover page from the drop-down list. The cover page displays before the first page of the document.
 d. Click the **Subtitle** ("Document Subtitle") content control field handle and press **Delete** (Figure 3-112) to delete the entire content control field.

Figure 3-112 Select and delete a content control field

 e. Click the **Author** content control field handle and press **Delete**.
 f. Confirm the insertion point is on the blank line where the *Author* field was deleted.
 g. Click the **Quick Parts** button [*Insert* tab, *Text* group], select **Document Property**, and select **Manager** from the drop-down list.
 h. Apply **bold** formatting to the *Company* document property field.
 i. Type www.spccd.edu in the *Address* ("Company Address") field. The web address displays in all caps; you will fix this in the next step.
 j. Select the **Address** document property field, open the *Font* dialog box, deselect the **All caps** check box, and click **OK**. The web address changes to lowercase (Figure 3-113).

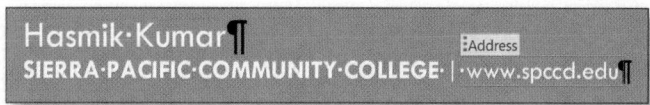

Figure 3-113 Document property fields modified on the cover page

15. Update the table of contents.
 a. Click the table of contents.

b. Click the **Update Table** button [*References* tab, *Table of Contents* group]. The *Update Table of Contents* dialog box opens (Figure 3-114).

c. Select the **Update entire table** radio button.

d. Click **OK** to close the dialog box and update the table.

16. Save and close the document (Figure 3-115).

Figure 3-114 *Update Table of Contents* dialog box

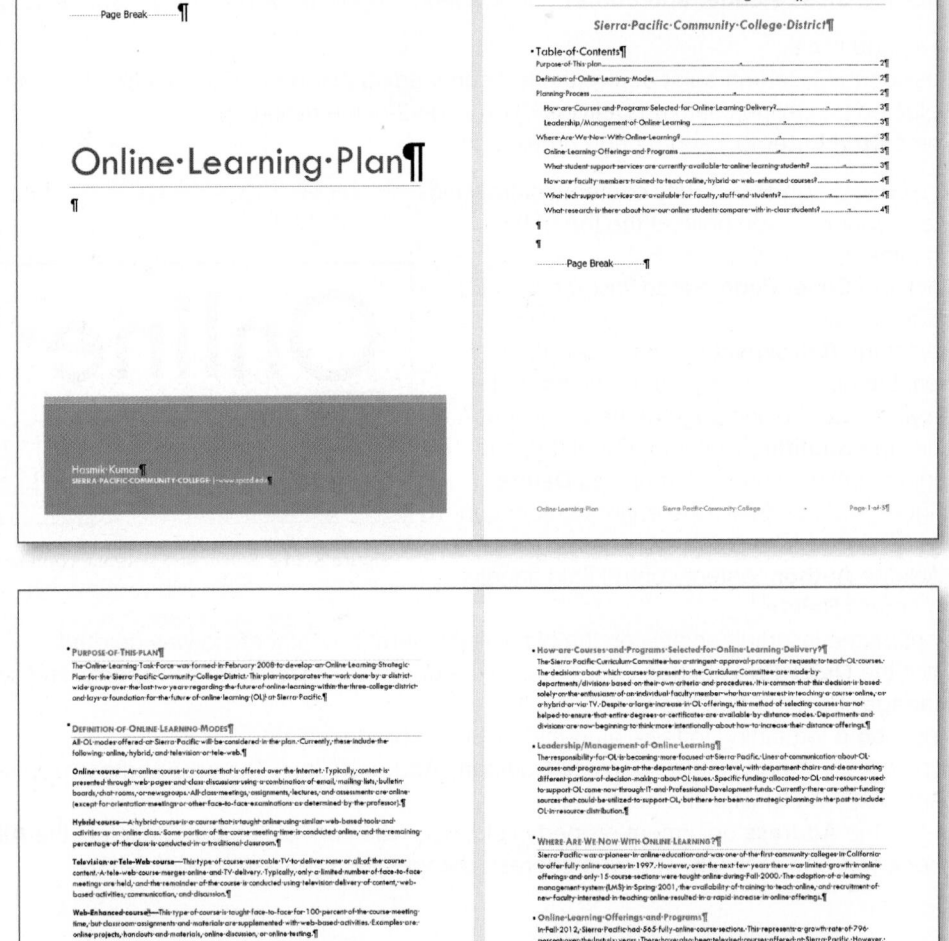

Figure 3-115 Word 3-1 completed (first four of six pages)

Guided Project 3-2

For this project, you create a multipage insurance renewal letter that Central Sierra Insurance will send on behalf of Valley Custom Manufacturing. You review comments and tracked changes, use *Track Changes*, format the document as a business letter, insert a document property field, insert and customize header content, use footnotes and endnotes, and insert a page and section break.
[Student Learning Outcomes 3.1, 3.2, 3.3, 3.7]

File Needed: *ValleyCustomManufacturing-03.docx (Student data files are available in the Library of your SIMnet account.)*
Completed Project File Name: *[your initials] Word 3-2.docx*

Skills Covered in This Project

- Review tracked changes and comments.
- Use *Track Changes*.
- Change *Display for Review* view.
- Format the document as a block format business letter.
- Insert a next page section break.
- Change margins and header location on a section of a document.
- Use a different first page header.

- Insert a document property, date, and page number in the header.
- Format the page number in the header.
- Apply a bottom border.
- Insert footnotes.
- Convert footnotes to endnotes and change number format.
- Insert a page break to control pagination.
- Accept tracked changes.
- Share a document.

1. Open the **ValleyCustomManufacturing-03** document from your student data files.

2. Save this document as [your initials] Word 3-2.

3. Review a comment, accept tracked changes, and delete a comment.
 a. Click the **Display for Review** drop-down list [*Review* tab, *Tracking* group] and select **All Markup**.
 b. Read the comment in the *Markup* area at the top of the document and review the tracked changes in the document.
 c. Click the **Next** button [*Review* tab, *Changes* group] to move to the first tracked change (not comment).
 d. Click the bottom half of the **Accept** button [*Review* tab, *Changes* group] and select **Accept and Move to Next**.
 e. Click the bottom half of the **Accept** button and select **Accept All Changes**.
 f. Click the bottom half of the **Delete** button [*Review* tab, *Comments* group] and select **Delete All Comments in Document**.

4. Change user name and initials.
 a. Click the **Tracking** launcher [*Review* tab, *Tracking* group] to open the *Track Changes Options* dialog box.
 b. Click the **Change User Name** button to open the *Word Options* dialog box.
 c. Type your first and last name in the *User name* text box in the *Personalize your copy of Microsoft Office* area.
 d. Type your first and last initials in lowercase letters in the *Initials* text box.
 e. Check the **Always use these values regardless of sign in to Office** box.
 f. Click **OK** to close the *Word Options* dialog box and click **OK** to close the *Track Changes Options* dialog box.

5. Turn on *Track Changes* and format the first page of the document as a block format business letter.
 a. Click the top half of the **Track Changes** button [*Review* tab, *Tracking* group] to turn on *Track Changes* and turn on **Show/Hide**. All changes will be tracked.
 b. Place your insertion point in front of "LIABILITY" on the first page.
 c. Click the **Breaks** button [*Layout* tab, *Page Setup* group] and select **Next Page** in the *Section Breaks* area.
 d. Move to the last blank line on the first page (in front of the paragraph mark and section break), type Sincerely, and press **Enter** four times.
 e. Type Jennie Owings, Vice President and press **Enter** once.
 f. Type Central Sierra Insurance and press **Enter** two times.
 g. Type your initials in lowercase letters with no spaces or punctuation and press **Enter**. Word automatically capitalizes the first letter of your initials. Use the **smart tag** to undo automatic capitalization (Figure 3-116).

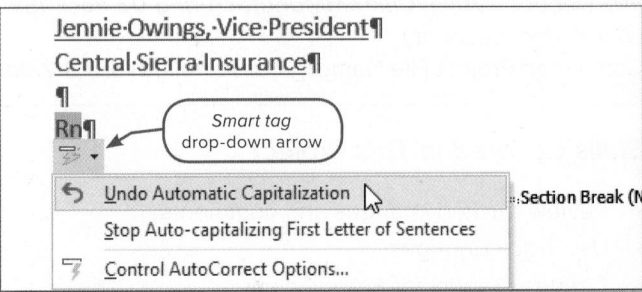

Figure 3-116 Use the smart tag to undo automatic capitalization

 h. Type Enclosure on the line after your reference initials.
 i. Place your insertion point at the top of the document and press **Enter** four times.
 j. Place the insertion point on the first blank line at the top and click the **Date & Time** button [*Insert* tab, *Text* group]. The *Date and Time* dialog box opens.
 k. Select the *January 1, 2020* date format, check the **Update automatically** box, and click **OK** to close the dialog box and insert the date.
 l. Select the dateline and apply **24 pt** *Before* paragraph spacing.

6. Modify the margins and header position in the second section of the document.
 a. Place your insertion point in the second section of the document (page 2 or 3).
 b. Click the **Page Setup** launcher [*Layout* tab, *Page Setup* group] to open the *Page Setup* dialog box.
 c. Change the *Top* margin to **1.5"** and the *Left* and *Right* margins to **1.25"**.
 d. Click the **Layout** tab.
 e. Change the *From edge: Header* setting to **1"** in the *Headers and footers* area.
 f. Click the **Apply to** drop-down list and select **This section** (if not already selected) (Figure 3-117).
 g. Click **OK** to close the dialog box and apply the settings.

7. Insert header content on the second and continuing pages.
 a. Place your insertion point at the top of the document.

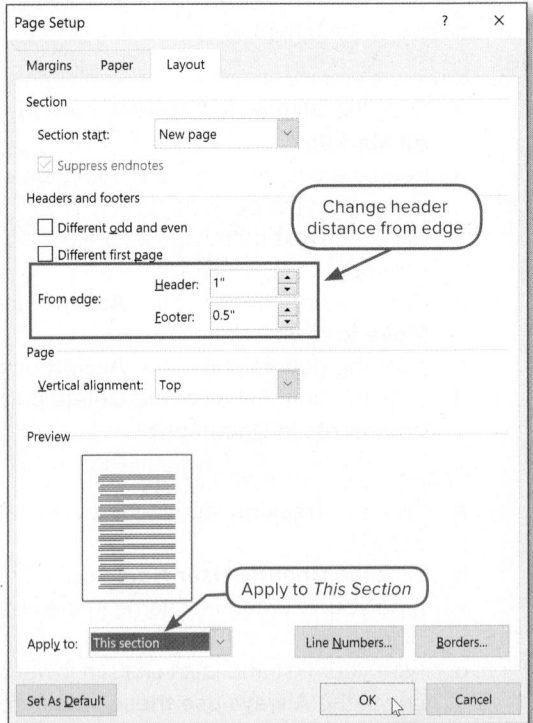

Figure 3-117 Change the header position in this section of the document

b. Click the **Header** button [*Insert* tab, *Header & Footer* group] and select **Edit Header** from the drop-down list.

c. Check the **Different First Page** box [*Header & Footer Tools Design* tab, *Options* group].

d. Click the **Next** button [*Header & Footer Tools Design* tab, *Navigation* group] to move to the header in section 2.

e. Click the **Document Info** button [*Header & Footer Tools Design* tab, *Insert* group] and select **Document Title**.

f. Press the **right arrow** on the keyboard to deselect the document property field and press **Enter**.

g. Click the **Date & Time** button [*Header & Footer Tools Design* tab, *Insert* group]. The *Date and Time* dialog box opens.

h. Select the *January 1, 2020* date format, check the **Update automatically** check box, and click **OK** to close the dialog box and insert the date.

i. Leave the header open for the next instructions.

8. Insert the page number in the header and format the page number.

a. Press **Enter** after the date in the header.

b. Type Page and **space** once.

c. Click the **Page Number** button [*Header & Footer Tools Design* tab, *Header & Footer* group], click **Current Position**, and select **Plain Number** from the drop-down list.

d. Click the **Page Number** button and select **Format Page Numbers** to open the *Page Number Format* dialog box (Figure 3-118).

e. Click the **Start at** radio button in the *Page numbering* area and change the page number to **2**.

f. Click **OK** to close the dialog box.

g. Place the insertion point after the page number and press **Enter** two times.

h. Select the page number line, click the **Borders** drop-down arrow [*Home* tab, *Paragraph* group], and select **Bottom Border**.

i. Click the **Close Header and Footer** button [*Header & Footer Tools Design* tab, *Close* group]. The header appears on the second and continuing pages.

Figure 3-118 Change the *Start at* page number

9. Insert footnotes.

a. Go to page 4 and place the insertion point after the period at the end of the last line of text (after "reports are included.").

b. Click the **Insert Footnote** button [*References* tab, *Footnotes* group].

c. Type A list of drivers was faxed as a separate attachment. in the footnotes area.

d. Go to the first page and place the insertion point after the period at the end of the fourth body paragraph (after "2020 renewal.").

e. Click the **Insert Footnote** button and type Inflation is anticipated to be 2 percent. in the footnotes area.

10. Convert footnotes to endnotes and change number format.

a. Click the **Footnotes** launcher to open the *Footnote and Endnote* dialog box.

b. Click the **Convert** button. The *Convert Notes* dialog box opens (Figure 3-119).

Figure 3-119 Convert footnotes to endnotes

c. Select the **Convert all footnotes to endnotes** radio button and click **OK** to close the *Convert Notes* dialog box.

d. Click **Close** to close the *Footnote and Endnote* dialog box.

e. Click the **Footnotes** launcher again to open the *Footnote and Endnote* dialog box (Figure 3-120).

f. Select the **Endnotes** radio button if it is not selected.

g. Click the **Number format** drop-down list and select **a, b, c, . . .**.

h. Click the **Apply changes to** drop-down list and select **Whole document**.

i. Click **Apply** to close the dialog box and apply the changes.

11. Insert a page break.
 a. Go to page 2 and place the insertion point in front of the "PROPERTY" heading.
 b. Click the **Breaks** button [*Layout* tab, *Page Setup* group] and select **Page** in the *Page Breaks* area. A page break is inserted, and the "PROPERTY" heading and following text move to page 3.

12. Change *Display for Review* view and accept all tracked changes.
 a. Click the **Display for Review** drop-down list [*Review* tab, *Tracking* group] and select **Simple Markup**. A red line on the left indicates where changes were made.
 b. Scroll through the four pages to review the document.
 c. Click the bottom half of the **Accept** button [*Review* tab, *Tracking* group] and select **Accept All Changes and Stop Tracking**.

13. Save the document.

14. Share the document with your instructor.
 a. Save this document on *OneDrive* if you haven't already. If you don't have the ability to save to *OneDrive*, skip all of step 14.
 b. Click the **Share** button in the upper-right corner of the Word window to open the *Send Link* window (Figure 3-121). If you're using a personal Microsoft account, the *Share* pane displays at the right, and the sharing options differ slightly.
 c. Click the **Link settings** button to open the *Link settings* window (Figure 3-122).

Figure 3-120 Change endnote number format

Figure 3-121 *Send Link* window

Figure 3-122 *Link settings* window

d. Click the **Anyone** button and check the **Allow editing** box (if necessary).

e. Click **Apply** to close the *Link settings* window and return to the *Send Link* window.

f. Type your instructor's email address in the *Enter a name or email address* area (see Figure 3-121).

g. Type a brief message to your instructor and click the **Send** button.

h. Click the **X** in the upper-right corner of the confirmation window to close it.

15. Save and close the document (Figure 3-123).

Figure 3-123 Word 3-2 completed

Guided Project 3-3

For this project, you customize the *Teen Substance Abuse* report for Courtyard Medical Plaza. You use *Comments* and *Track Changes*, and you add citations, a bibliography page, table of contents, headers and footers, and a cover page.
[Student Learning Outcomes 3.1, 3.2, 3.4, 3.5, 3.6, 3.7]

File Needed: ***TeenSubstanceAbuse-03.docx*** *(Student data files are available in the* Library *of your SIM-net account.)*
Completed Project File Name: *[your initials]* **Word 3-3.docx**

Skills Covered in This Project

- Turn on *Track Changes* and change *Display for Review* view.
- Set the bibliography style.
- Insert a placeholder for a citation.
- Create a source and insert a citation.
- Use the *Source Manager* to edit a placeholder and create a new source.
- Insert a bibliography page.

- Use styles to format the title and headings.
- Create a table of contents.
- Insert built-in odd and even headers.
- Insert a document property field into a header.
- Update a table of contents.
- Insert and customize a cover page.
- Accept tracked changes and resolve a comment.
- Share a document.

1. Open the ***TeenSubstanceAbuse-03*** document from your student data files.

2. Save this document as [your initials] Word 3-3.

3. Change the user name and initials.
 a. Click the **Tracking** launcher [*Review* tab, *Tracking* group] to open the *Track Changes Options* dialog box.
 b. Click the **Change User Name** button to open the *Word Options* dialog box.
 c. Type your first and last name in the *User name* text box in the *Personalize your copy of Microsoft Office* area.
 d. Type your first and last initials in lowercase letters in the *Initials* text box.
 e. Check the **Always use these values regardless of sign in to Office** box.
 f. Click **OK** to close the *Word Options* dialog box and click **OK** to close the *Track Changes Options* dialog box.

4. Turn on *Track Changes* and change the *Display for Review* view.
 a. Click the top half of the **Track Changes** button [*Review* tab, *Tracking* group] to turn on *Track Changes* and turn on **Show/Hide**. All changes will be tracked.
 b. Click the **Display for Review** drop-down list [*Review* tab, *Tracking* group] and select **Simple Markup**. A red line on the left indicates tracked changes.

5. Select the report style and insert placeholders for a citation.
 a. Click the **Style** drop-down list [*References* tab, *Citations & Bibliography* group].
 b. Select **Chicago Sixteenth Edition**.
 c. Go to the "What Problems Can Teen Substance Abuse Cause?" section on page 1 and place the insertion point at the end of the last sentence in the second paragraph ("unsafe substances") and before the period.
 d. Click the **Insert Citation** button [*References* tab, *Citations & Bibliography* group] and select **Add New Placeholder**. The *Placeholder Name* dialog box opens.
 e. Type Foundation and click **OK**. The placeholder for the citation displays in the report.
 f. Go to the "Can Teen Substance Use and Abuse Be Prevented?" section on page 2 and place the insertion point at the end of the last sentence in the first paragraph ("and drugs") and before the period.

g. Click the **Insert Citation** button and select the **Foundation** placeholder from the drop-down list (Figure 3-124).

6. Insert a citation into the report.

a. Go to the "What Is Teen Substance Abuse?" section on page 1 and place the insertion point at the end of the last sentence in the second paragraph ("most often") and before the period.

b. Click the **Insert Citation** button [*References* tab, *Citations & Bibliography* group] and select **Add New Source**. The *Create Source* dialog box opens (Figure 3-125).

c. Check the **Show All Bibliography Fields** box and create a new source with the following information:

Figure 3-124 Insert a placeholder for a citation

Type of Source: **Journal Article**
Author: Kelly L. Sanchez
Title: Examining High School Drug Use
Journal Name: Journal of Secondary Education
Year: 2018
Pages: 22-26
Volume: XXI
Issue: 2
Tag Name: Sanchez

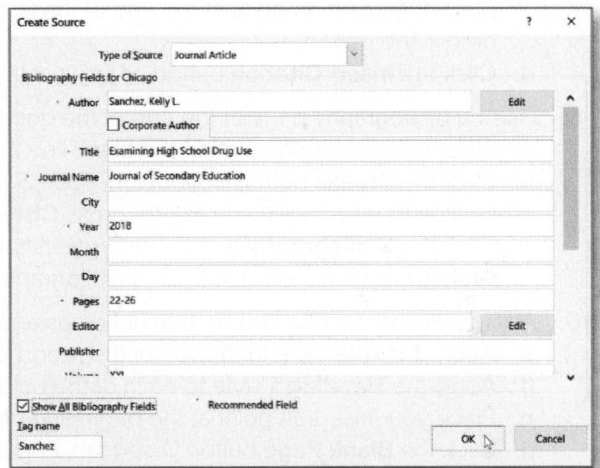

d. Click **OK** to close the dialog box and insert the citation. The citation displays in the report.

7. Use the *Source Manager* to create a new source and provide source information for a placeholder.

Figure 3-125 *Create Source dialog box*

a. Click the **Manage Sources** button [*References* tab, *Citations & Bibliography* group] to open the *Source Manager* dialog box.

b. Select the **Foundation** placeholder in the *Current List* area and click **Edit**. The *Edit Source* dialog box opens.

c. Use the following information to edit the placeholder source:

Type of Source: **web site**
Corporate Author: Foundation for Teen Health
Name of web Page: Making Good Choices
Year: 2017
Year Accessed: 2020
Month Accessed: June
Day Accessed: 25
URL: http://www.foundationforteenhealth.org/choices.htm

d. Click **OK** to close the dialog box and update the placeholders. The placeholders in the report are updated with the proper citation from the source information. Leave the *Source Manager* dialog box open.

e. Click the **New** button in the *Source Manager* dialog box. The *Create Source* dialog box opens.

f. Create a new source with the following information:

Type of Source: **Document From web site**
Corporate Author: Courtyard Medical Plaza
Name of web Page: Teen Mental Health
Name of web Site: Courtyard Medical Plaza
Year: 2019

Month: March
Day: 6
URL: http://www.cmp.com/Teen_Mental_Health.pdf
Tag Name: CMP

 g. Click **OK** to close the dialog box and click **Close** to close the *Source Manager* dialog box.

8. Insert citations into the report.
 a. Go to the "Why Do Teens Abuse Drugs and Alcohol?" section on page 1 and place the insertion point at the end of the last sentence in the second paragraph ("increased risk") and before the period.
 b. Click the **Insert Citation** button [*References* tab, *Citations & Bibliography* group] and select the **Courtyard Medical Plaza** citation from the drop-down list.
 c. Go to the "What Should You Do if You Discover Your Teen Is Using?" section on page 2 and place the insertion point at the end of the last sentence in the second paragraph ("or both") and before the period.
 d. Click the **Insert Citation** button and select the **Sanchez, Kelly L.** citation from the drop-down list.

9. Insert a bibliography page at the end of the document.
 a. Place your insertion point on the blank line at the end of the document.
 b. Click the **Breaks** button [*Layout* tab, *Page Setup* group] and select **Page** in the *Page Breaks* section to insert a page break (or press **Ctrl+Enter**).
 c. Click the **Bibliography** button [*References* tab, *Citations & Bibliography* group] and select **Bibliography** to insert the built-in bibliography into the document.

10. Apply styles to the title and section headings and insert a table of contents.
 a. Apply the **Title** style to the title of the report on the first page.
 b. Apply the **Heading 1** style to each of the bold section headings in the report.
 c. Place your insertion point at the beginning of the report.
 d. Click the **Blank Page** button [*Insert* tab, *Pages* group] to insert a blank page before the first page of the report.
 e. Place your insertion point at the top of the new first page, type Teen Substance Abuse, and press **Enter**. The text should be formatted as *Title* style. If it's not, apply the **Title** style.
 f. Click the **Table of Contents** button [*References* tab, *Table of Contents* group] and select **Automatic Table 1** from the drop-down list. The table of contents is inserted below the title.

11. Insert odd and even page headers and customize content.
 a. Confirm the insertion point is on the first page, click the **Header** button [*Insert* tab, *Header & Footer* group], and select **Edit Header** from the drop-down list.
 b. Check the **Different Odd & Even Pages** check box [*Header & Footer Tools Design* tab, *Options* group].
 c. Select **Motion (Odd Page)** from the drop-down list of built-in headers [*Header & Footer* group].
 d. Delete the existing text in the text box to the left of the page number. Don't delete the text box.
 e. Click the **Document Info** button [*Header & Footer Tools Design* tab, *Insert* group], click **Document Property**, and select **Company** from the drop-down list (Figure 3-126).

Figure 3-126 Odd page header inserted and content customized

 f. Click the **Next** button to move to the *Even Page Header*.

g. Click the **Header** button [*Header & Footer Tools Design* tab, *Header & Footer* group] and select **Motion (Even Page)** from the drop-down list.

h. Click the **Close Header and Footer** button [*Close* group].

12. Insert page breaks to control page endings.
 a. Go to the second page, click in front of the last section heading ("What Are the Signs of Substance Abuse"), and insert a **Page** break.
 b. Go to the third page, click in front of the last section heading ("Can Teen Substance Use and Abuse Be Prevented"), and insert a **Page** break.

13. Update the table of contents.
 a. Click the table of contents on the first page.
 b. Click the **Update Table** button at the top of the content control field. The *Update Table of Contents* dialog box opens (Figure 3-127).
 c. Select the **Update entire table** radio button and click **OK**.

Figure 3-127 Update the table of contents

14. Insert and customize a cover page.
 a. Place your insertion point at the beginning of the document.
 b. Click the **Cover Page** button [*Insert* tab, *Pages* group].
 c. Select the **Slice (Dark)** built-in cover page from the drop-down list. The cover page displays on a new page before the table of contents.
 d. Select the **Title** document property field, apply **Bold** formatting, and change the font size to **40 pt**.
 e. Click the **Subtitle** content control field handle and press **Delete**.
 f. Press **Ctrl+Home** to move the insertion point to the top of the cover page.
 g. Click the **Quick Parts** button [*Insert* tab, *Text* group], select **Document Property**, and select **Company** from the drop-down list.
 h. Select the **Company** document property field, apply **Bold** and **Small Caps** formatting, and change the font size to **36 pt**.

15. Review comments and track changes.
 a. Click the **Display for Review** drop-down list [*Review* tab, *Tracking* group] and select **All Markup**.
 b. Right-click the comment in the *Markup* area at the top of the third page and select **Resolve Comment**.
 c. Click the bottom half of the **Accept** button [*Changes* group] and select **Accept All Changes and Stop Tracking**.
 d. Click the **Display for Review** drop-down list [*Review* tab, *Tracking* group] and select **No Markup**.
 e. Save the document.

16. Share the document with your instructor.
 a. Save this document on *OneDrive* if you haven't already. If you don't have the ability to save to *OneDrive*, skip all of step 16.
 b. Click the **Share** button in the upper-right corner of the Word window to open the *Send Link* window (Figure 3-128). If you're using a personal Microsoft account, the *Share* pane displays at the right, and the sharing options differ slightly.

c. Click the **Link settings** button to open the *Link settings* window (Figure 3-129).

d. Click the **Anyone** button and check the **Allow editing** box (if necessary).

e. Click **Apply** to close the *Link settings* window and return to the *Send Link* window.

f. Type your instructor's email address in the *Enter a name or email address* area (see Figure 3-128).

g. Type a brief message to your instructor and click the **Send** button.

h. Click the **X** in the upper-right corner of the confirmation window to close it.

17. Save and close the document (Figure 3-130).

Figure 3-128 *Send Link* window

Figure 3-129 *Link settings* window

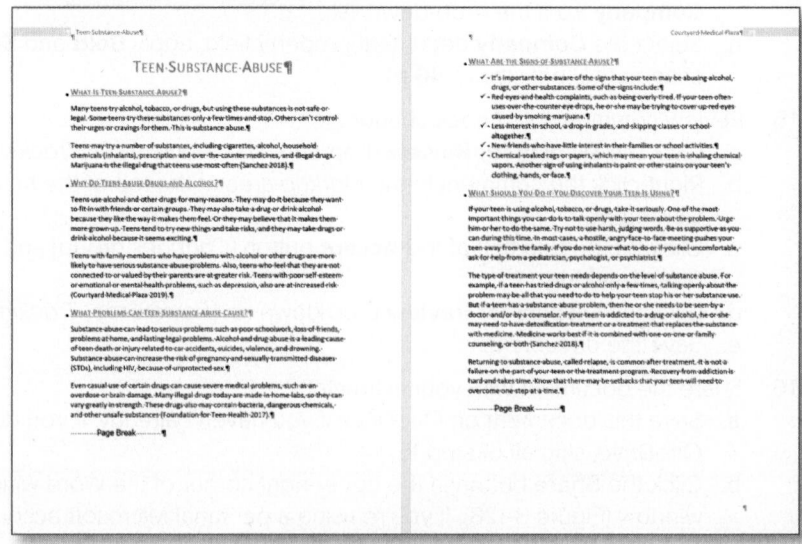

Figure 3-130 Word 3-3 completed (first four of six pages)

Independent Project 3-4

For this project, you modify the *Tips for Better Heart Rate Monitor Training* document from the American River Cycling Club. You use *Track Changes* and comments, insert and modify endnotes, insert placeholders, create sources, insert a bibliography page, insert a table of contents and cover page, and use custom headers and footers.
[Student Learning Outcomes 3.1, 3.2, 3.3, 3.4, 3.5, 3.6, 3.7]

File Needed: ***HeartRateMonitorTraining-03.docx*** *(Student data files are available in the* Library *of your SIMnet account.)*
Completed Project File Name: ***[your initials] Word 3-4.docx***

Skills Covered in This Project

- Use comments and *Track Changes*.
- Insert endnotes.
- Insert a placeholder for a citation.
- Use the *Source Manager* to edit placeholders and create a new source.
- Change the bibliography style.
- Insert a bibliography page.

- Convert endnotes to footnotes.
- Insert a table of contents.
- Insert and modify a cover page.
- Insert custom headers and footers.
- Insert a document property field.
- Insert page breaks.
- Change the footnote number format.
- Resolve a comment.
- Accept tracked changes.

1. Open the ***HeartRateMonitorTraining-03*** document from your student data files.
2. Save this document as [your initials] Word 3-4.
3. Change user name and initials.
 a. Open the *Track Changes Options* dialog box (**Tracking** launcher) and click the **Change User Name** button to open the *Word Options* dialog box.
 b. Type your first and last name in the *User name* text box and your first and last initials in lowercase letters in the *Initials* text box.
 c. Check the **Always use these values regardless of sign in to Office** box, click **OK** to close the *Word Options* dialog box, and click **OK** to close the *Track Changes Options* dialog box.
4. Turn on *Track Changes* and insert a comment.
 a. Turn on **Track Changes** and change the *Display for Review* view to **Simple Markup**.
 b. Select the title, insert a **New Comment**, and type Insert endnotes, citations, a references page, a table of contents, and a cover page in the new comment.
 c. Click the **Show Comments** button (if necessary) to close the *Markup* area on the right and display only the comment balloon and not the comment text.
5. Insert endnotes.
 a. Insert an endnote at the end of the first body paragraph on the first page (after the period after "your training rides.").
 b. Type See the References page for related book and articles. in the endnote area.
 c. Go to the "Analyze Your Heart Rate Data" section on page 1 and insert an endnote at the end of the body paragraph (after the period after "and duration.").
 d. Type See the ARCC web site (www.arcc.org) for information about specific heart rate monitors. in the endnote area.
 e. Go to the "Comparing Heart Rate Values with Others" section on page 2 and insert an endnote at the end of the second body paragraph (after the period after "predict performance.").
 f. Type 220-age is an estimate of maximum heart rate. in the endnote area.
6. Insert placeholders for citations.
 a. Go to the "Know Your Resting Heart Rate" section on page 1, place the insertion point at the end of the second body paragraph and before the period ("psychological stress"), and insert a placeholder named **RoadCycling**.

 b. Go to the "Perform a Threshold Test" section on page 1, place the insertion point at the end of the second body paragraph and before the period ("threshold test"), and insert a placeholder named **Segura**.

 c. Go to the "Not Analyzing Heart Rate Data" section on page 2, place the insertion point at the end of the body paragraph and before the period ("cycling training"), and insert a placeholder named **Wallace**.

7. Use the *Source Manager* dialog box to provide source information for the three placeholders. Check the **Show All Bibliography Fields** box, if necessary to display additional fields.

 a. **Edit** the **RoadCycling** placeholder to include the following information.

 Type of Source: **Document from web site**
 Corporate Author: Road Cycling
 Name of web Page: Training with a Heart Rate Monitor
 Name of web Site: RoadCycling.com
 Year: 2018
 Year Accessed: 2020
 Month Accessed: January
 Day Accessed: 25
 URL: http://www.roadcycling.com/heart_rate.html

 b. **Edit** the **Segura** placeholder to include the following information.

 Type of Source: **Article in a Periodical**
 Author: Manuel A. Segura
 Title: Maximizing Threshold Training
 Periodical Title: Cycling Weekly
 Year: 2019
 Month: March
 Day: 1
 Pages: 35-41

 c. **Edit** the **Wallace** placeholder to include the following information.

 Type of Source: **Book**
 Author: Ingrid L. Wallace
 Title: Understanding Heart Rate
 Year: 2017
 City: Chicago
 Publisher: Penguin Books

8. Convert all endnotes to footnotes.

9. Change the bibliography style and insert a references page at the end of the document.

 a. Change the bibliography style of the report to **APA**.

 b. Place your insertion point on the blank line at the end of the document and insert a **page break**.

 c. Insert a **References** bibliography on the last page.

 d. **Center** the *References* heading and apply **10 pt** *After* paragraph spacing.

10. Insert a table of contents.

 a. Place the insertion point at the top of the document and insert a **page break**.

 b. Place the insertion point in front of the page break at the top of the new first page.

 c. Type Table of Contents and press **Enter** two times.

 d. Select text you just typed, change the font size to **14 pt**, apply **bold** and **small caps** formatting.

 e. Place your insertion point on the blank line below "Table of Contents."

 f. Insert a **Custom Table of Contents** and use **Simple** format, show **2** levels of headings, show page numbers, right align page numbers, and use a dot tab leader.

11. Insert a cover page.

 a. Insert the **Ion (Dark)** built-in cover page.

 b. Select the **Year** field and choose the current date.

c. Select the **Title** field, change the font size to **44 pt**, apply **bold** formatting, and align **center**.

d. Delete the **Subtitle** and **Author** fields. Be sure to delete the entire fields, not just the text.

e. Select the **Company** field, change the font size to **12 pt**, and apply **bold** formatting.

f. Select the **Company Address** field and type www.arcc.org.

12. Insert a header and footer.

a. Place the insertion point in the table of contents on the second page.

b. Edit the header, type Page, **space** once, and insert a plain page number in the current position.

c. **Align Right** the header information (use **Align Right**, not a tab).

d. Go to the footer on the second page and insert the **Company** document property field.

e. Press the right arrow key to deselect the field and press **Tab** two times.

f. Type www.arcc.org on the right.

g. Use the *Borders and Shading* dialog box to apply a **solid line**, **Automatic** color, **¾ pt** width, **top** and **bottom border** to the information in the footer.

h. Change the font size of the information in the header and footer to **10 pt**.

i. Close the header and footer. No header or footer should appear on the cover page.

13. Insert a **page break** before the "Analyze Your Heart Rate Data" and "Not Being Aware of Factors Affecting Heart Rate" headings.

14. Change the footnote number format to **A, B, C**.

15. Resolve a comment and accept all tracked changes.

a. Click the **Show Comments** button to display comments.

b. **Resolve** the comment near the top of the third page.

c. Accept all changes in the document and stop tracking changes.

d. Click the **Show Comments** button again so the text of the comment does not display.

16. **Update** the entire table of contents.

17. Save and close the document (Figure 3-131).

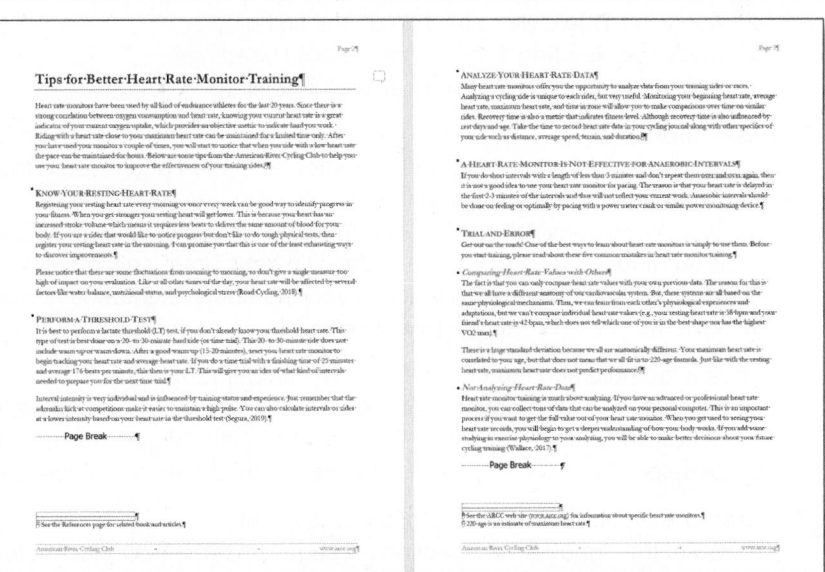

Figure 3-131 Word 3-4 completed (first four of six pages)

Independent Project 3-5

Sierra Pacific Community College District gives incoming college students a *Student Success Tips* document. For this project, you review comments and tracked changes, apply heading styles, and insert footnotes, placeholders, and a works cited page, table of contents, and cover page.
[Student Learning Outcomes 3.1, 3.2, 3.3, 3.4, 3.5, 3.6, 3.7]

File Needed: ***StudentSuccess-03.docx*** *(Student data files are available in the* Library *of your SIMnet account.)*
Completed Project File Name: ***[your initials] Word 3-5.docx***

Skills Covered in This Project

- Review and delete a comment.
- Reject and accept tracked changes.
- Apply title and heading styles.
- Insert and modify footnotes.
- Insert a placeholder.
- Use the *Source Manager* to update a reference.
- Change the bibliography style.

- Insert a works cited page.
- Insert a table of contents.
- Use different odd and even page footers.
- Insert page numbers and a document property field into the footer.
- Insert and customize a cover page.
- Insert a page break.
- Update a table of contents.
- Share a document.

1. Open the **StudentSuccess-03** document from your student data files.

2. Save this document as [your initials] Word 3-5.

3. Review and delete selected comments and tracked changes.
 a. Change the *Display for Review* view to **All Markup**.
 b. Read the comment at the top of the document and then **delete** the comment.
 c. Find the first tracked change in the document (left, right, and top margin changed) and **Reject Format Change**.
 d. Review the changes in the document and then **Accept All Changes** in the document.

4. Apply styles to the title and headings.
 a. Apply the **Title** style to the title on the first page.
 b. Apply the **Heading 1** style to all the bold headings
 c. Apply the **Heading 2** style to all the underlined headings.

5. Insert footnotes.
 a. Go to the "Schedule Your Time" section on page 1 and insert a footnote after "Weekly Schedules" in the first sentence.
 b. Type Weekly Schedules are available from your counselor or in the college bookstore. as the footnote text.
 c. Insert another footnote in the "Schedule Your Time" section at the end of the "Be sure to schedule your time for all these in your 119 hours." sentence and after the period.
 d. Type Be sure to schedule recreational time in your 119 hours. as the footnote text.

6. Move a footnote and modify the footnote number format.
 a. Select the first footnote reference marker (in the body) and move it so it appears after "Weekly Schedule" in the "Track Your Time" section (use drag and drop or cut and paste).
 b. Deselect the moved footnote and change the footnote number format to **a, b, c**.

7. Insert placeholders in the body of the document.
 a. Go to the "Introduction" section on page 1, insert a new placeholder named Navarro at the end of the body paragraph (after "your advantage" and before the period).

b. Go to the "Test Anxiety" section on page 2 and insert a new placeholder named Sierra at the end of the body paragraph (after "become a problem" and before the period).

c. Go to the "Goal Setting" section on page 4 and insert the Navarro placeholder (not a new placeholder) at the end of the intro paragraph (after "your goals" and before the period).

8. Use the *Source Manager* dialog box to provide source information for the two placeholders. Check the **Show All Bibliography Fields** box if necessary.

a. **Edit** the **Navarro** placeholder to include the following information.

Type of Source: **Book**
Author: Tessa C. Navarro
Title: Study Skills for College Students
Year: 2018
City: Chicago
Publisher: McGraw-Hill

b. **Edit** the **Sierra** placeholder to include the following information.

Type of Source: **Document from web site**
Corporate Author: Sierra Pacific Community College District
Name of web Page: Tips for Student Success
Name of web Site: spccd.edu
Year: 2019
Year Accessed: 2020
Month Accessed: February
Day Accessed: 2
URL: http://www.spccd.edu/tips4success.pdf

9. Use the *Researcher* to insert a citation.

a. Go to the "Procrastination" section on page 1 and place your insertion point at the end of the third sentence and before the period ("a million disguises").

b. Open the *Researcher* pane, type procrastination in the search box, and press **Enter**.

c. Review the *Top sources for procrastination*.

d. Locate one of the journal articles and click the plus sign (+) in the upper-right corner to add a citation to your document. The source is also added to the *Source Manager*. Click **No thanks** if a dialog box opens and asks if you want to update your bibliography.

e. Close the *Researcher* pane.

10. Change bibliography style and insert a works cited page.

a. Change the bibliography style to **MLA**.

b. Place your insertion point on the blank line at the end of the document and insert a **page break**.

c. Insert a **Works Cited** bibliography.

11. Insert a table of contents.

a. Place your insertion point at the beginning of the document and insert a **page break**.

b. Place your insertion point before the page break on the new first page.

c. Type Student Success Tips and press **Enter**.

d. Insert the **Automatic Table 1** table of contents.

e. Apply the **Title** style to "**Student Success Tips**" on the new first page.

12. Insert a footer and add custom content.

a. Edit the footer on the first page of the document (table of contents).

b. Check the **Different Odd & Even Pages** box. The insertion point displays in the odd page footer.

c. Insert the **Accent Bar 2** from the *Page Number*, *Current Position* drop-down list.

d. Press **Tab** two times and insert the **Document Title** (or **Title**) document property field.

e. Go to the even page footer and insert the **Accent Bar 2** from the *Page Number*, *Current Position* drop-down list.

 f. Press **Tab** two times and insert the **Company** document property field.

 g. Change the font size to **10 pt** and apply **bold** formatting to all footer content in both the even and odd page footers.

 h. Close the footer.

13. Insert and customize a cover page.

 a. Insert the **Slice (Light)** cover page.

 b. Delete the **Subtitle** ("Document subtitle") and **Course** ("Course title") document property fields.

 c. Change the font size of the title on the cover page to **40 pt** and apply **bold** formatting.

14. Insert a **page break** before the "Physical Signs of Test Anxiety" heading.

15. Update the entire table of contents and save your document.

16. Share the document with your instructor.

 a. Save this document on *OneDrive* if you haven't already. If you don't have the ability to save to *OneDrive*, skip all of step 16.

 b. Click the **Share** button in the upper-right corner of the Word window to open the *Send Link* window. If you are using a personal Microsoft account, the *Share* pane opens at the right, and the sharing options differ slightly.

 c. Edit the **Link settings** to **Allow editing** to **Anyone** and **Apply** these link settings.

 d. Type your instructor's email address in the email area.

 e. Type a brief message to your instructor and **Send** the sharing link.

 f. Click the **X** in the upper-right corner of the confirmation window to close it.

17. Save and close the document (Figure 3-132).

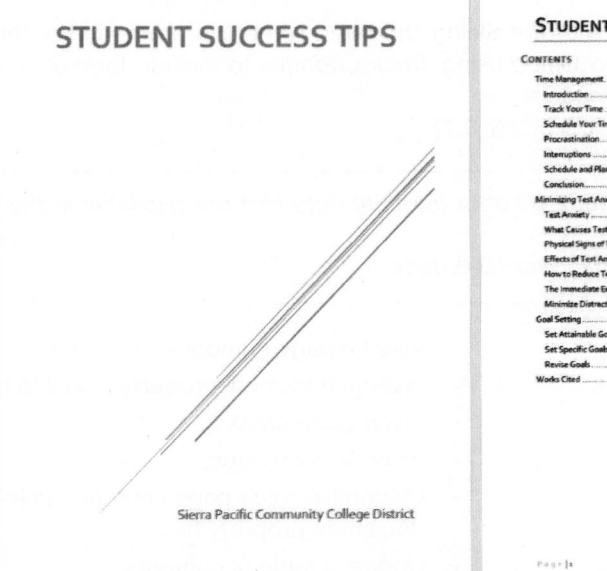

STUDENT SUCCESS TIPS

Sierra Pacific Community College District

STUDENT SUCCESS TIPS

CONTENTS

Page | a — Student Success Tips

STUDENT SUCCESS TIPS

TIME MANAGEMENT

Introduction
There's no such thing as time management! So why should you read the rest of this handout? Because there is such a thing as self-management and that's the key to making time your ally rather than your enemy. There are only 24 hours in your day, just the same as everybody else's. So how do you end up frustrated, angry, behind in your work, and dead on your feet? Maybe because you don't know how to use those 24 hours to your advantage (Navaro).

Track Your Time
If using your time wisely is a problem for you, you probably don't have a very good idea of where it all goes. It just seems to go! A good place to start, then, is to keep track of how you use your time. Get a Weekly Schedule and faithfully keep track of how you use your waking hours for one week. The results will probably surprise you.

Schedule Your Time
The next step is to pick up several more of these Weekly Schedules and do some planning. You'll discover, among other things, that if you get seven hours sleep a night, you have 119 hours per week to do everything you need to do. That, of course, includes going to class, eating, athletic events, social activities, personal hygiene, time-in-transit, studying, student organizations, telephone and TV time, etc. Be sure to schedule time for all these in your 119 hours.* Then try sticking to your schedule for a week. This should give you a good idea of where your real priorities are!

Procrastination
If you have trouble, chances are there's a culprit lurking somewhere. Chances are this culprit's name is "Procrastination." Procrastination masquerades in a million disguises (O'Donoghue and Rabin). Among the more common of these are:

- "One more day won't make any difference; I'll just put that off until tomorrow."
- "It won't matter if I'm a few minutes late; no one else will be on time."
- "I work best under pressure."
- "I'll watch just 15 more minutes of TV."

Interruptions
Learn to say NO once your priorities are set. Turning down an invitation doesn't mean you'll never be asked to do something again. Weigh the consequences. Making a decision based on what you know is best for you at the time leads to greater respect from your friends, not to a reputation as a party-pooper.

- Stay away from the telephone when you're trying to get work done.
- Turn off your cell phone or pager. If it's important, they'll call back.
- Stay away from email and instant messaging. Limit how often you check these things.

* Weekly Schedules are available from your counselor or in the college bookstore.
* Be sure to schedule recreational time in your 119 hours.

Page | 2 — Sierra Pacific Community College District

Schedule and Plan Ahead
- Use a monthly calendar to help you allocate your study time on the Weekly Schedule. At the beginning of each quarter, spend an hour with your calendar to enter all important dates. As you receive course syllabi, enter the dates for quizzes, papers, etc., on your calendar. Then estimate the time needed to prepare for each of these. The rule-of-thumb is "Plan ahead by working backwards."
- By counting backwards like this, you'll be surprised how well you're using your time and how much better your grade will be when you're not under pressure. And, by being honest with yourself and taking account of all your priorities, you'll be able to go to the football game and not feel guilty.
- At the start of each week, transfer important items from your calendar to your Weekly Schedule. This helps you to avoid things that might otherwise sneak up on you.
- An alternative to a paper calendar is to use an electronic calendar. You could use the one on your desktop computer (e.g., Microsoft Outlook) or smart phone.
- Be sure to schedule time for your fitness routine and for study breaks. Your brain works best when it has sufficient oxygen. Your concentration is enhanced when you go hard at a task until you feel yourself fading. Then Break! A good rule-of-thumb is to work for 45 minutes and then break for 15. But watch yourself! More than 15 minutes is more than a break!

Conclusion
Suggestions such as these don't lead to enslavement by a calendar. But, it leads to a greater sense of freedom and accomplishment because you're in control. That's all self-management is—managing your life more effectively. By following these suggestions, you'll be happier, more satisfied, and more productive.

MINIMIZING TEST ANXIETY

Test Anxiety
Most students experience some level of anxiety during an exam. However, when anxiety begins to affect exam performance it has become a problem (Sierra Pacific Community College District).

What Causes Test Anxiety
- Lack of preparation as indicated by:
 - Cramming the night before the exam
 - Poor time management
 - Failure to organize text information
 - Poor study habits
- Worrying about the following:
 - Past performance on exams
 - How friends and other students are doing
 - The negative consequences of failure

Page | 3 — Student Success Tips

Figure 3-132 Word 3-5 completed (first four of seven pages)

Independent Project 3-6

Courtyard Medical Plaza works closely with the Skiing Unlimited winter ski program. For this project, you modify the *Skiing Unlimited Training Guide* using *Track Changes* to include footnotes, a table of contents, cover page, and headers and footers.
[Student Learning Outcomes 3.1, 3.2, 3.3, 3.5, 3.6, 3.7]

File Needed: ***SkiingUnlimitedTrainingGuide-03.docx*** *(Student data files are available in the Library of your SIMnet account.)*
Completed Project File Name: ***[your initials] Word 3-6.docx***

Skills Covered in This Project

- Review and delete a comment.
- Change the *Display for Review* view.
- Review and accept tracked changes.
- Change margins.
- Apply title and heading styles.
- Insert a custom table of contents.

- Insert a page number in the header.
- Insert a document property field into the footer.
- Insert page breaks.
- Insert a cover page.
- Customize cover page content and insert a document property field.
- Update a table of contents.

1. Open the ***SkiingUnlimitedTrainingGuide-03*** document from your student data files.

2. Save this document as [your initials] Word 3-6.

3. Change user name and initials.
 a. Open the *Track Changes Options* dialog box (**Tracking** launcher) and click the **Change User Name** button to open the *Word Options* dialog box.
 b. Type your first and last name in the *User name* text box and your first and last initials in lowercase letters in the *Initials* text box.
 c. Check the **Always use these values regardless of sign in to Office** box, click **OK** to close the *Word Options* dialog box, and click **OK** to close the *Track Changes Options* dialog box.

4. Change *Display for Review* view, review and delete a comment, and accept *Tracked Changes*.
 a. Change the *Display for Review* view to **All Markup** and review tracked changes in the document.
 b. Read the comment on the first page and then **delete** the comment.
 c. **Accept All Changes** in the document.

5. Change the left and right margins to **1"**.

6. Apply styles to the title and headings.
 a. Apply the **Title** style to the title on the first page.
 b. Apply the **Heading 1** style to all the bold headings.
 c. Apply the **Heading 2** style to all the underlined headings.
 d. Apply the **Heading 3** style to all the italicized headings.

7. Insert and customize footnotes.
 a. Insert a footnote after the "Skiing Procedures" heading on the first page.
 b. Type Skiing procedures vary depending on the clients' needs. as the footnote text.
 c. Insert a footnote after the "Guiding Techniques" heading on the second page.
 d. Type A minimum of two guides is required for all clients. as the footnote text.
 e. Change the footnote *Number format* to **A, B, C** and change *Numbering* to **Continuous**.

8. Insert a custom table of contents.
 a. Place your insertion point at the beginning of the document and insert a **page break**.
 b. Type Table of Contents at the beginning of the first line (before the page break) on the new first page and press **Enter**.
 c. Insert a **Custom Table of Contents**, use **Fancy** format, show **2** levels of headings, show page numbers, right align page numbers, and do not include a tab leader.
 d. Apply the **Title** style to the "**Table of Contents**" heading on the table of contents page.

9. Insert header and footer.
 a. Edit the header on the first page (table of contents) and insert the **Bold Numbers 3** built-in page number at the **Top of Page**.
 b. Remove the blank line below the page numbers.
 c. Go to the footer on the same page and insert the **Title** document property field on the left. Use the right arrow key to deselect the document property field.
 d. Press **Tab** two times and insert the **Company** field on the right.
 e. **Bold** the text in the footer and close the footer.

10. Insert page breaks to keep headings with the text below.
 a. Insert a **page break** before the "Beginning Wedge Christie Turns" heading (page 4).
 b. Insert a **page break** before the "Introduction to Equipment" heading (page 5).

11. Insert and modify a cover page.
 a. Insert the **Grid** cover page.
 b. Delete the **Subtitle** field.
 c. Place the insertion point on the blank line between the *Title* and *Abstract* fields and insert the **Company** document property field.
 d. Delete the **Abstract** field.
 e. Select the **Company** document property field, change the font size to **20 pt**, apply **bold** formatting, and change the text color to the **fourth color** in the **first row** of the *Theme Colors* (**Blue-Gray, Text 2**).

12. Update the entire table of contents.

13. Save and close the document (Figure 3-133).

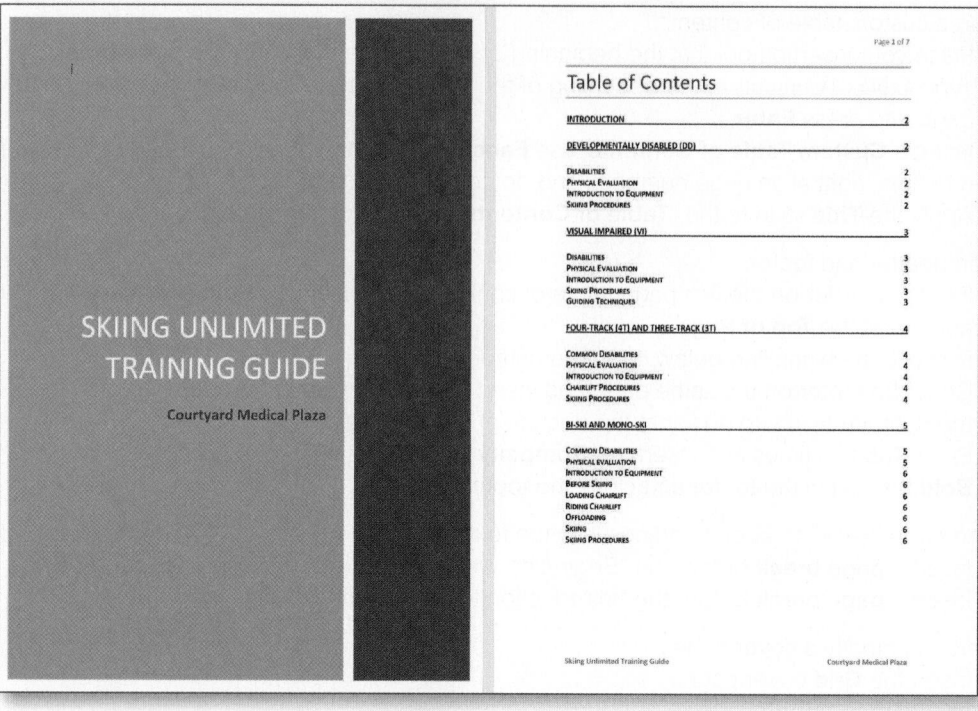

Figure 3-133 Word 3-6 completed (first four of eight pages)

Improve It Project 3-7

American River Cycling Club is working with a cycling tour company to arrange a trip to cycle through the Tuscany region of Italy. The original document from the cycling tour company needs to be improved and updated. Modify the document to remove content and add a cover page, table of contents, footnotes, and a footer.
[Student Learning Outcomes 3.1, 3.2, 3.3, 3.5, 3.6, 3.7]

File Needed: ***ItalyTourItinerary-03.docx*** *(Student data files are available in the* Library *of your SIMnet account.)*
Completed Project File Name: ***[your initials] Word 3-7.docx***

1. Open the ***ItalyTourItinerary-03*** document from your student data files.

Skills Covered in This Project

- Delete a comment and review tracked changes.
- Change the *Display for Review* view.
- Edit a document using *Track Changes.*
- Remove the existing cover page, table of contents, and header and footer.
- Apply a style and update a style.
- Insert page breaks.

- Move and delete an endnote.
- Convert endnotes to footnotes.
- Insert and customize footnotes.
- Insert a custom table of contents.
- Edit document properties.
- Insert and modify a cover page.
- Insert custom footer content.
- Review and accept tracked changes.
- Share a document.

2. Save this document as [your initials] Word 3-7.

3. Change user name and initials.
 a. Open the *Track Changes Options* dialog box (**Tracking** launcher) and click the **Change User Name** button to open the *Word Options* dialog box.
 b. Type your first and last name in the *User name* text box and your first and last initials in lower-case letters in the *Initials* text box.
 c. Check the **Always use these values regardless of sign in to Office** box, click **OK** to close the *Word Options* dialog box, and click **OK** to close the *Track Changes Options* dialog box.

4. Change *Display for Review* view, review and delete a comment, and turn on *Track Changes.*
 a. Change the *Display for Review* view to **All Markup** and review the changes in the document.
 b. Read the comment on the first page and then delete the comment.
 c. Turn on **Track Changes** and change the *Display for Review* view to **Simple Markup**.

5. Remove the existing cover page, table of contents, and header and footer content.
 a. Click the **Cover Page** button [*Insert* tab, *Pages* group] and select **Remove Current Cover Page**.
 b. Click the **Table of Contents** button [*References* tab, *Table of Contents* group] and select **Remove Table of Contents**.
 c. Use **Remove Header** and **Remove Footer** to remove all header and footer content.

6. Change the page orientation to **Landscape**.

7. Apply a heading style and update a style.
 a. Apply the **Day** style to the "Day 1: . . ." heading on the first page.
 b. Place your insertion point in the "Day 1" heading and **Update Heading 1 to Match Selection**. The new *Heading 1* style applies to all day headings in the document.

8. Insert page breaks.
 a. Click in front of "Day 3" and insert a **page break**.
 b. Insert a **page break** for each of the odd-numbered days so only two days appear on each page.

9. Add text and apply style.
 a. Place your insertion point on the blank line after "*Distance*:" in the "Day 2" section.
 b. Press **Enter** and type Notes and Questions at the insertion point.
 c. Apply the **Day** style to the text you just typed.
 d. Repeat steps b and c to insert this information at the end of the "Day 4" and "Day 6" sections.
 e. Go to the "Day 8" section, place your insertion point on the blank line below the "Kilometers to Miles Conversion" information and above the endnotes.
 f. Press **Enter**, type Notes and Questions, and apply the **Day** style to the text you just typed.

10. Move and delete endnotes and convert endnotes to footnotes.
 a. Move the first endnote marker (after the distance on "Day 3") to appear in the "Day 2" section after "*Distance*: 83 km".
 b. Change the text to Day 2 is the longest day of the tour. in the endnote text area.
 c. Delete the endnote reference marker after "Day 4." The endnote text is removed when you delete the reference marker.
 d. Convert all endnotes to footnotes.

11. Insert and customize footnotes.
 a. Place your insertion point after "*Distance*: 0-26 km" in the "Day 4" section, insert a footnote, and type Day 4 is an optional riding day. in the footnote text area. *Note*: The footnote number may not be consecutive until you accept tracked changes, which you will do later.
 b. Place your insertion point after "*Distance*: 42-58 km" in the "Day 5" section, insert a footnote, and type Day 5 has two routes from which to choose. in the footnote text area.
 c. Place your insertion point after "*Distance*: 52-68 km" in the "Day 6" section, insert a footnote, and type Day 6 has three routes from which to choose. in the footnote text area.
 d. Change the footnote *Number format* to **a, b, c** and change *Numbering* to **Continuous** if it is not already selected. *Note*: The footnote number may not be consecutive until you accept tracked changes, which you will do later.

12. Insert a custom table of contents.
 a. Place your insertion point at the beginning of the document and insert a **page break**.
 b. Type Contents on the first line on the new first page (before the page break) and press **Enter**.
 c. Insert a **Custom Table of Contents**, use **Distinctive** format, show **1** level of headings, show page numbers, right align page numbers, and include a solid line tab leader.
 d. Select the "Day 1" through "Day 8" lines of text in the table of contents and apply **12 pt** *After* paragraph spacing.

13. Edit the following document properties.

 Title: Cycling Classic Tuscany: Tour Itinerary
 Company: American River Cycling Club

14. Insert and modify a cover page.
 a. Insert the **Semaphore** cover page.
 b. Select the current date in the **Publish Date** field.
 c. Change the font size of the *Title* field to **48 pt** and apply **bold** format.
 d. Delete the **Subtitle** (*Document Subtitle*) and **Author** fields.
 e. Change the font size of the *Company* field to **14 pt** and apply **bold** format.
 f. Select the *Address* field and type www.arcc.org in the field.

15. Insert footers on the second and continuing pages.
 a. Go to the second page of the document (table of contents) and edit the footer.
 b. Change the alignment to **right**, insert the **Company** document property field, deselect the field (right arrow key), and **space** once.

 c. Type | (press **Shift+** to type a vertical line) and **space** once.

 d. Type Page and **space** once.

 e. Insert a plain page number in the current position.

 f. **Bold** all the text in the footer and close the footer.

16. Change *Display for Review* view, accept tracked changes, and turn off *Track Changes*.

 a. Change the *Display for Review* view to **All Markup**.

 b. Review the tracked changes in the document.

 c. Turn off **Track Changes** and **Accept All Changes** in the document.

 d. Save the document.

17. Share the document with your instructor.

 a. Save this document on *OneDrive* if you haven't already. If you don't have the ability to save to *OneDrive*, skip all of step 17.

 b. Click the **Share** button in the upper-right corner of the Word window to open the *Send Link* window. If you are using a personal Microsoft account, the *Share* pane opens at the right, and the sharing options differ slightly.

 c. Edit the **Link settings** to **Allow editing** to **Anyone** and **Apply** these link settings.

 d. Type your instructor's email address in the email area.

 e. Type a brief message to your instructor and **Send** the sharing link.

 f. Click the **X** in the upper-right corner of the confirmation window to close it.

18. Save and close the document (Figure 3-134).

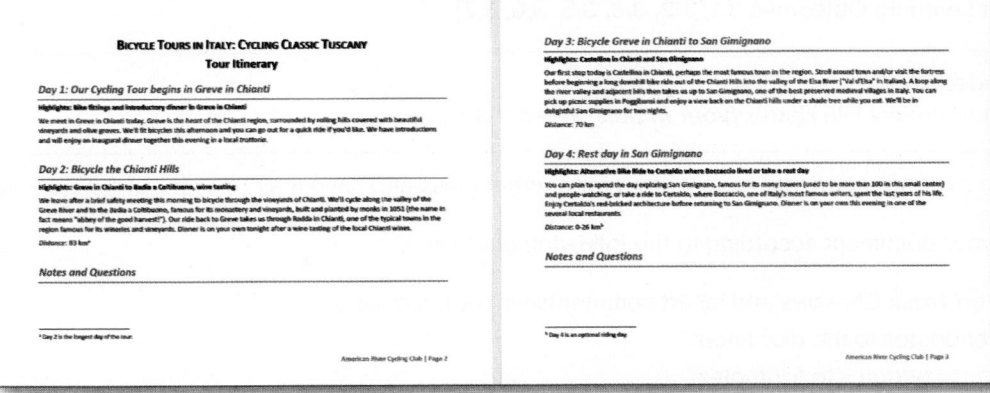

Figure 3-134 Word 3-7 completed (first four of six pages)

Challenge Project 3-8

Modify a report you have written for another class to include citations, a bibliography or works cited page, a table of contents, a cover page, and headers and footers. Use comments and *Track Changes*.
[Student Learning Outcomes 3.1, 3.2, 3.4, 3.5, 3.6, 3.7]

File Needed: None
Completed Project File Name: *[your initials] Word 3-8.docx*

Open an existing report you have created and save it as [your initials] Word 3-8.

Modify your document according to the following guidelines:

- Turn on *Track Changes* and insert comments where necessary.
- Select the citation style to use for your report (APA, MLA, Chicago).
- Add citations to the body of your report and create sources.
- Add placeholders for citations in the body of your report.
- Use the *Researcher* to find sources of information and insert citations.
- Insert a bibliography or works cited page at the end of your report.
- Use the *Source Manager* to edit placeholders and sources and add new sources if necessary.
- Insert other citations in the body as necessary.
- Update the bibliography page.
- Apply headings styles and insert a table of contents.
- Insert a cover page and customize content.
- Insert a header, footer, and page number from the built-in list of options.
- Use different first page headers and footers.
- Insert page breaks to control pagination as necessary.

Challenge Project 3-9

Add footnotes and endnotes, heading styles, a table of contents, a cover page, and headers and footers to a multipage document that you have written. Use comments and *Track Changes*.
[Student Learning Outcomes 3.1, 3.2, 3.3, 3.5, 3.6, 3.7]

File Needed: None
Completed Project File Name: *[your initials] Word 3-9.docx*

Open an existing report you have written for another class and save it as [your initials] Word 3-9.

Modify your document according to the following guidelines:

- Turn on *Track Changes* and insert comments where necessary.
- Add endnotes to the document.
- Convert endnotes to footnotes.
- Change the number format for footnotes.
- Move a footnote to a new location and delete a footnote.

- Insert a custom header or footer in your document.
- Add a page number in the header or footer of the document.
- Insert page breaks to control pagination as necessary.
- Apply headings styles and insert a table of contents.
- Insert a cover page and customize content.
- Insert custom header and footer content.
- Use different first page or odd and even page headers and footers.
- Accept all tracked change and turn off *Track Changes*.
- Insert page breaks to control pagination as necessary.

Challenge Project 3-10

Modify a report or multipage document you have written for another class to include a table of contents, a cover page, and headers and footers. Use comments and *Track Changes*.
[Student Learning Outcomes 3.1, 3.2, 3.5, 3.6, 3.7]

File Needed: None
Completed Project File Name: *[your initials] Word 3-10.docx*

Open an existing report or multipage document and save it as [your initials] Word 3-10.

Modify your document according to the following guidelines:

- Turn on *Track Changes* and insert comments where necessary.
- Apply *Heading 1* and *Heading 2* styles to the headings of your document. If the document does not have headings, add two levels of headings to the document.
- Insert a built-in or custom table of contents as the first page of your document.
- Include two levels of headings in the table of contents.
- Customize the *Title*, *Company*, and *Author* document property fields.
- Insert a cover page of your choice.
- Customize the cover page by adding or removing a document property or content control fields.
- Add custom information to content control fields.
- Insert a header, footer, and page number from the built-in list of options.
- Use different first page or odd and even page headers and footers.
- Insert page breaks to control pagination as necessary.
- Update the table of contents.

Source of screenshots Microsoft Office 365 (2019): Word, Excel, Access, Powerpoint.

Using Tables, Columns, and Graphics

CHAPTER OVERVIEW

Tables, columns, and graphics enhance the appearance and readability of your Word documents. For example, use tables to attractively arrange and align information in column and row format. Format documents with columns to improve readability and provide additional white space. You can also insert and manipulate graphics to add attention-grabbing visual elements to your documents. This chapter introduces you to the Word tools used to add and customize tables, columns, and graphics.

STUDENT LEARNING OUTCOMES (SLOs)

After completing this chapter, you will be able to:

SLO 4.1 Improve the design and readability of a document by using tables to present and arrange information (p. W4-219).

SLO 4.2 Modify a table by changing the column and row size, aligning text, using the *Table Properties* dialog box, sorting data, and using *AutoFit* (p. W4-223).

SLO 4.3 Enhance the appearance and function of a table by applying borders and shading, using table styles, inserting formulas, and converting text into a table (p. W4-229).

SLO 4.4 Modify the layout and design of a document using columns to present information (p. W4-236).

SLO 4.5 Improve a document by adding, modifying, and arranging pictures (p. W4-240).

SLO 4.6 Enrich a document by adding and customizing graphic objects such as shapes, *SmartArt*, *WordArt*, symbols, icons, 3D models, and online video (p. W4-248).

WORD

CASE STUDY

For the Pause & Practice projects in this chapter, you modify a brochure for Emma Cavalli, a realtor consultant with Placer Hills Real Estate (PHRE). In the past, Emma distributed brochures that were poorly designed and negatively impacted the effectiveness of her message. You modify one of Emma's brochures to include tables, columns, and graphics to improve the overall layout and effectiveness of the document.

Pause & Practice 4-1: Modify an existing brochure to include a table that presents information attractively.

Pause & Practice 4-2: Enhance the table in the brochure by using borders, shading, and table styles.

Pause & Practice 4-3: Improve the readability of the brochure by arranging text in columns.

Pause & Practice 4-4: Add visual elements to the brochure to improve the overall design of the document.

Creating and Editing Tables

SLO 4.1

In chapter 2, you learned to align information into column and row format using tab stops. *Tables* are another tool to organize information into column and row format. In addition to aligning data, tables enable you to apply additional formatting options.

> **MORE INFO**
>
> Most web pages organize information into table and row format even though you might not see the table borders or structure.

Tables

A table consists of individual *cells* where you enter information. Cells are grouped into *columns* and *rows*. When using tables, it is important to distinguish between cells, columns, and rows (Figure 4-1).

- *Cell*: The area where a column and row intersect
- *Column*: A vertical grouping of cells (think of vertical columns that support a building)
- *Row*: A horizontal grouping of cells (think of horizontal rows of seating in a stadium or auditorium)

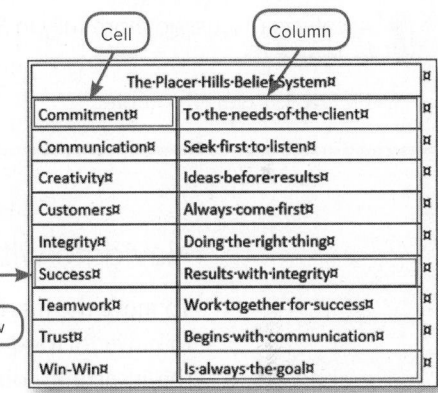

Figure 4-1 Table

▶ HOW TO: Insert a Table

1. Place your insertion point at the location to insert a table.
2. Click the **Insert** tab.
3. Click the **Table** button [*Tables* group] to open the drop-down list.
4. Click and drag across the *Insert Table* grid to select the number of columns and rows you want in the table (Figure 4-2). The table is inserted into your document.

 - As you drag across the grid, the *Insert Table* label changes to display the size of the table (*3×7 Table*).

> **MORE INFO**
>
> Word lists table dimensions in column and row format. For example, a three-column and seven-row table is a 3 × 7 table.

Figure 4-2 *Insert Table* drop-down list

Another way to insert a table is to use the ***Insert Table*** dialog box.

> **HOW TO: Insert a Table Using the Insert Table Dialog Box**

1. Place your insertion point at the location to insert a table.
2. Click the **Table** button [*Insert* tab, *Tables* group] to open the drop-down list.
3. Select **Insert Table** to open the *Insert Table* dialog box (Figure 4-3).
4. Type or select the desired number of columns and rows in the *Table size* area.
5. Select how the table is distributed horizontally between the left and right margins in the *AutoFit behavior* area.
 - *AutoFit* is discussed more fully in *SLO 4.2: Arranging Text in Tables*.
6. Click **OK** to insert the table.

Figure 4-3 *Insert Table* dialog box

Navigate within a Table

To move the insertion point within a table, press **Tab** (or the **right arrow** key on your keyboard) to move forward one cell in the current row. When you get to the end of a row and press *Tab*, the insertion point moves to the first cell in the next row. **Shift+Tab** (or the **left arrow** key) moves you back one cell at a time. You can also use your pointer to click a cell.

Table Tools Layout Tab

When you insert a table into a document, the contextual ***Table Tools tabs*** display on the *Ribbon*. Word provides two *Table Tools* tabs: ***Design*** and ***Layout***. These contextual toolbars display whenever you place the insertion point in the table or select a region of the table. The *Table Tools Layout* tab provides a variety of formatting options (Figure 4-4). For more on the *Table Tools Design* tab, see *SLO 4.3: Formatting and Editing Tables*.

Figure 4-4 *Table Tools Layout* tab

Select Table and Text

When working with tables, you can select the entire table; a cell, column, or row; or multiple cells, columns, or rows to apply formatting changes. Word provides a variety of table selection tools.

- ***Table selector handle***: This handle appears above the upper-left corner of the table when the pointer is on the table (Figure 4-5). Click the **table selector** to select the entire table.
- ***Row selector***: The row selector is the right-pointing arrow when your pointer is just to the

Figure 4-5 Table selector handle

left of the table row (Figure 4-6). When the pointer becomes the row selector, click to select a single row. To select multiple rows, click and drag up or down.

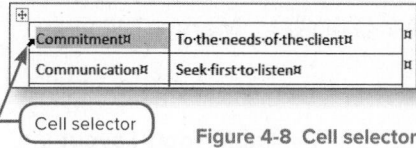

Figure 4-6 **Row selector**

- *Column selector*: The column selector is the thick, black down arrow when your pointer is on the top border of a column (Figure 4-7). When the pointer becomes the column selector, click to select a single column. To select multiple columns, click and drag left or right.

Figure 4-7 **Column selector**

- *Cell selector*: The cell selector is the thick, black right-pointing arrow when your pointer is just inside the left border of a cell (Figure 4-8). When the pointer becomes the cell selector, click to select a single cell. To select multiple cells, click and drag left, right, up, or down. When the cell selector displays, double-click to select the entire row.

Figure 4-8 **Cell selector**

- *Select button*: The *Select* button is located on the *Table Tools Layout* tab in the *Table* group. Click the **Select** button to access a drop-down list of table selection options (Figure 4-9).

Add Rows and Columns

When you insert a table into a document, you are not limited to your original table dimensions. The following are methods to insert columns and rows in a table.

Figure 4-9 *Select drop-down list*

- *Insert Control*: Place your pointer on the left outside edge of a row or top outside edge of a column to display the insert row or column control (plus sign). Click the **insert control** to add a row or column (Figure 4-10). Select multiple rows or columns and click the insert control to add the number or rows or columns selected.

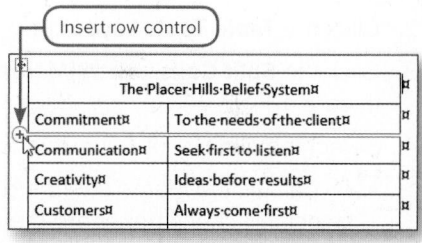

- *Table Tools Layout tab*: In the *Rows & Columns* group, you can insert a row above or below the current row or a column to the left or right of the current column (see Figure 4-10).

Figure 4-10 **Insert row control**

- *Mini toolbar*: Select a cell, row, column, or table to display the mini toolbar. You can also right-click the table to display the mini toolbar. Click the **Insert** button to display a list of insert options (Figure 4-11).
- *Insert Cells dialog box*: Open this dialog box by clicking the **Rows & Columns** launcher on the *Table Tools Layout* tab (Figure 4-12).
- *Tab*: When your insertion point is in the last cell in the last row, press **Tab** to insert a new row below the last row.

Figure 4-11 Use the mini toolbar to insert a row

Figure 4-12 *Insert Cells* dialog box

Merge and Split Cells

Many times when you use tables you want information to span across multiple columns, such as when you are inserting a title or subtitle in a table. Use the ***Merge Cells*** feature to combine multiple columns, rows, and cells into one cell.

▶ HOW TO: Merge Cells

Figure 4-13 *Merge Cells* button

1. Select the cells to merge.
2. Click the **Table Tools Layout** tab.
3. Click the **Merge Cells** button [*Merge* group] (Figure 4-13). The cells merge into one cell.

Word also enables you to split a cell into multiple cells. Split cells that were previously merged or split a single cell into multiple columns and rows. When splitting cells, the *Split Cells* dialog box prompts you to specify the number of columns and rows.

▶ HOW TO: Split Cells

Figure 4-14 *Split Cells* dialog box

1. Select the cell(s) to split.
2. Click the **Table Tools Layout** tab.
3. Click the **Split Cells** button [*Merge* group]. The *Split Cells* dialog box opens (Figure 4-14).
4. Select the number of columns and rows.
 - By default, the *Merge cells before split* check box is selected. When you select this check box, Word merges the selected cells before splitting them into the desired number of columns and rows.
5. Click **OK** to split the cells.

Copy or Move Columns and Rows

Copying or moving columns and rows in a table is similar to how you copy or move text in a document. Select the column or row to copy or move, and use one of the following methods:

- ***Keyboard Shortcuts***: **Ctrl+C** (copy), **Ctrl+X** (cut), and **Ctrl+V** (paste).
- ***Context menu***: Right-click the selected column or row and select **Cut**, **Copy**, or **Paste**.

- **Drag and drop**: Drag and drop the column or row to the new location to move it. Hold the **Ctrl** key while dragging and dropping to copy a column or row.
- **Clipboard group on the Home tab**: Use the **Cut**, **Copy**, and **Paste** buttons in this group.

Delete Columns and Rows

At times, you may need to remove columns or rows from your table. Click the **Delete** button in the *Rows & Columns* group on the *Table Tools Layout* tab or the mini toolbar to remove cells, columns, rows, or an entire table. You have the following options (Figure 4-15):

- *Delete Cells. . .* (opens the *Delete Cells* dialog box)
- *Delete Columns*
- *Delete Rows*
- *Delete Table*

Figure 4-15 *Delete* options

Delete a Table

If you select an entire table and press *Delete* on your keyboard, only the information in the table is deleted; the blank table remains in your document. To delete a table, select the **Delete Table** option from the *Delete* drop-down on the *Table Tool Layout* tab or mini toolbar (see Figure 4-15). The **Delete Table** option is also available on the context menu when you select and right-click a table.

SLO 4.2

Arranging Text in Tables

You can adjust the width of columns and the height of rows and control how text is aligned within the cells of a table. Word provides a variety of table resizing and text alignment options. You also can sort information automatically within a table.

Resize Columns and Rows

When you insert a table into a document, the default size for the table is the width of the document. You can manually adjust the width of columns and the height of rows.

Drag the column or row borders to increase or decrease the size of a column or row. When you place your pointer on the vertical border of a column, the pointer changes to a *resizing pointer* (Figure 4-16). Drag the column border to the left or right to adjust the size of the column. Use the same method to adjust the height of a row by dragging the top or bottom border of a row up or down.

Figure 4-16 Manually adjust column width

> **MORE INFO**
>
> When you manually adjust the height of a row, it adjusts the height of the selected row only. Usually, it is best to keep the height of rows consistent.

Word also enables you to set a specific size for columns and rows. Adjust the size of columns and rows before merging cells. When adjusting the size of columns or rows after merging cells, be very careful when selecting cells.

▶ HOW TO: Resize Columns and Rows

1. Select the cells, columns, or rows to resize.
2. Click the **Table Tools Layout** tab.
3. Change the height or width to the desired size [*Cell Size* group] (Figure 4-17).
 - Manually type the specific size or use the up or down arrows (spinner box) to resize.

Figure 4-17 Set cell *Height* and *Width*

AutoFit a Table

When you insert a table into a document, the table is automatically set to the width of the typing line (inside the left and right margins). Word has three different *AutoFit* options to adjust the column width of the table. Click the **AutoFit** button in the *Cell Size* group on the *Table Tools Layout* tab to display the *AutoFit* options (Figure 4-18).

Figure 4-18 *AutoFit* options

- *AutoFit Contents*: Adjusts column widths to fit the contents of the table.
- *AutoFit Window*: Distributes the column widths so the table fits across the width of the page. (This is the default setting when you insert a table into a document.)
- *Fixed Column Width*: Adjusts columns to a fixed column width.

> ### MORE INFO
>
> When you insert a table, the table has the same formatting as the text in the document. If your rows seem too tall, the text in the table may contain *Before* or *After* paragraph spacing that controls the height of the rows in your table.

Distribute Rows and Columns

Word provides features to evenly distribute rows and columns, which is useful when the sizes of columns and rows in a table are uneven. *Distribute Rows* and *Distribute Columns* are on the *Table Tools Layout* tab in the *Cell Size* group (Figure 4-19).

- *Distribute Rows*: This feature evenly distributes the rows based on the height of the existing table, adjusting all rows to a consistent height.
- *Distribute Columns*: This feature evenly distributes the columns based on the width of the existing table, adjusting all columns to the same width.

Figure 4-19 Distribute rows and columns

> ### ANOTHER WAY
>
> *AutoFit* and *Distribute* options are available from the context menu when a table is selected.

Text Alignment

In chapter 1, you learned paragraph alignment and how to left align, right align, center, or justify text. In chapter 2, you learned how to change the vertical alignment of a page or section. Similarly, when using tables, you have both horizontal and vertical alignment options. Align all text in the table or select individual cells, columns, or rows. Table 4-1 displays nine alignment options that are available in the *Alignment* group on the *Table Tools Layout* tab (Figure 4-20).

Figure 4-20 Text alignment options within a table

Table 4-1: Alignment Options

Align Top Left	Align Top Center	Align Top Right
Align Center Left	Align Center	Align Center Right
Align Bottom Left	Align Bottom Center	Align Bottom Right

> **MORE INFO**
>
> For horizontal alignment, text in the table is usually aligned on the left and numbers are aligned on the right. If you increase row height, it's generally best to vertically center text within a cell.

Cell Margins

In addition to being able to change alignment in cells, you can also adjust *cell margins*. Just like the margins on a Word document, the cells of a table have top, bottom, left, and right margins. Cell margins add space around text within a cell. The default cell margins are 0" top and bottom, and 0.08" left and right.

▶ HOW TO: Change Cell Margins

1. Select the entire table to change the cell margins for all cells in the table.
 - Click the table selector handle to select the entire table or click the **Select** button [*Table Tools Layout* tab, *Table* group] and click **Select Table**.
 - You can also change cell margins on individual cells.
2. Click the **Table Tools Layout** tab.
3. Click the **Cell Margins** button [*Alignment* group]. The *Table Options* dialog box opens (Figure 4-21).
4. Enter the desired changes to the *Top, Bottom, Left,* and *Right* cell margins.
 - You can also add spacing between cells in the *Default cell spacing* area. This puts padding (space) around the outside of the cells.
 - If you don't want the size of your table to be automatically adjusted, deselect the **Automatically resize to fit contents** check box.
5. Click **OK** to apply the cell margin settings.

Figure 4-21 *Table Options* dialog box

Table Properties Dialog Box

The **Table Properties** dialog box consolidates many table sizing and alignment options in one location. The *Table Properties* dialog box includes separate tabs for *Table, Row, Column, Cell,* and *Alt Text.* To open the *Table Properties* dialog box, click the **Properties** button in the *Table* group on the *Table Tools Layout* tab (Figure 4-22). You can also open the *Table Properties* dialog box from the context menu.

- **Table tab**: Adjusts the size of the table, alignment, text wrapping, positioning, borders and shading, and cell margins.
- **Row tab**: Adjusts the height of rows and controls how rows break between pages.
- **Column tab**: Adjusts the width of columns.
- **Cell tab**: Adjusts the width of cells, vertical alignment of information in cells, and cell margins.
- **Alt Text tab**: Alternative text (alt text) is an information tag that displays when you place your pointer on the table. Screen readers use alt text in tables to accommodate those with visual impairments. Alt text is very common on web pages.

Figure 4-22 *Table Properties* dialog box

Sort Data in Tables

Word also provides the ability to sort information within a table. For example, use the **Sort** feature to arrange the text in the first column of a table alphabetically or sort numbers in descending order. When using the *Sort* feature on a table, rows of information rearrange according to how you specify the sort.

▶**HOW TO: Sort Data in a Table**

1. Place your insertion point in the table.
2. Select the **Table Tools Layout** tab.
3. Click the **Sort** button [*Data* group]. The entire table is selected and the *Sort* dialog box opens (Figure 4-23).
4. Click the **Sort by** drop-down list and select the column to use to sort the table.
 - Sort using any of the columns in the table.
5. Click the **Type** drop-down list and select the type of sort to perform: *Text, Number,* or *Date.*
6. Click the **Using** drop-down list and select the cell information to use in the sort.
 - *Paragraphs* is the default option, and usually, this is the only option available.

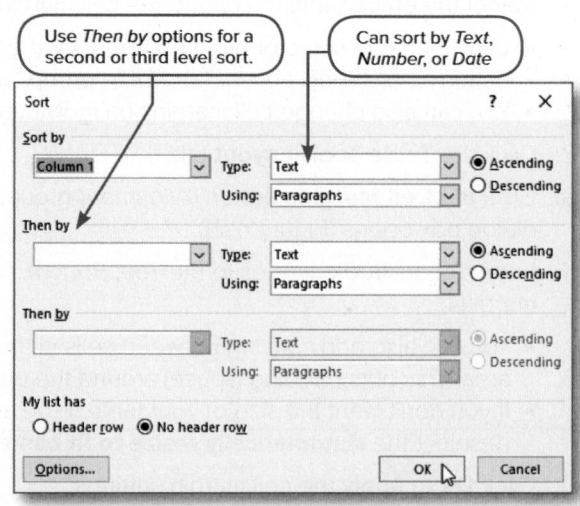

Figure 4-23 *Sort* dialog box

7. Select **Ascending** (A to Z or 1 to 10) or **Descending** (Z to A or 10 to 1) for the sort order.
 - To add a second- or third-level sort on different columns, click the **Then by** drop-down list and add additional sorts.
 - If your table has a header row (title or column headings), click the **Header row** radio button to omit this row from the sort.
8. Click **OK** to perform the sort. The table sorts according to the settings in the *Sort* dialog box.

> **MORE INFO**
>
> If your table has both a title and column headings, select the rows of the table to be sorted before clicking the **Sort** button so that only the data in the table is sorted.

> **ANOTHER WAY**
>
> Manually sort or arrange rows using copy (**Ctrl+C**), cut (**Ctrl+X**), and paste (**Ctrl+V**), or the drag and drop method.

PAUSE & PRACTICE: WORD 4-1

For this Pause & Practice project, you begin modifying Emma Cavalli's brochure. You add a table to the end of this document and then modify the table.

File Needed: ***Brochure-04.docx*** *(Student data files are available in the* Library *of your SIMnet account.)*
Completed Project File Name: ***[your initials] PP W4-1.docx***

1. Open the ***Brochure-04*** document from your student data files.
2. Save this document as [your initials] PP W4-1.
3. Move to the end of the document and insert a table.
 a. Place the insertion on the blank line at the end of the document (or press **Ctrl+End**).
 b. Click the **Insert** tab.
 c. Click the **Table** button [*Tables* group] and select a **3×7 Table** using the table grid. The table displays in the document.
4. Type the following information in Table 4-2. Press **Tab** to move from one cell to the next cell in the row. Leave the third column blank. *Note*: Table 4-2 is formatted for readability and will display differently in Word.

Table 4-2

Commitment	To the needs of the client	
Communication	Seek first to listen	
Integrity	Doing the right thing	
Customers	Always come first	
Teamwork	Work together for success	
Success	Results with integrity	
Creativity	Ideas before results	

5. Delete a column and insert rows.
 a. Place the insertion point in any cell in the last column.
 b. Click the Delete button [*Table Tools Layout* tab, *Rows & Columns* group] and select Delete Columns.
 c. Place the insertion point in the second row and click the Insert Below button [*Table Tools Layout* tab, *Rows & Columns* group]. A blank row is inserted below the second row.
 d. Type the following information in the new third row:

Trust	Begins with communication

 e. Click the last cell of the table (bottom right cell) and press **Tab** to insert a new row at the bottom of the table.
 f. Type the following information in the new last row:

Win-Win	Is always the goal

6. *AutoFit* the table and adjust the column and row size.
 a. Place your insertion point in the table.
 b. Click the **AutoFit** button [*Table Tools Layout* tab, *Cell Size* group] and select **AutoFit Contents**. The column widths adjust to fit the contents of the table.
 c. Place the insertion point in the first column.
 d. Change the *Width* to **1.2"** [*Table Tool Layout* tab, *Cell Size* group]
 e. Place the insertion point in the second column.
 f. Change the *Width* to **2"**.
 g. Use the table selector handle (upper-left corner) to select the entire table.
 h. Click the **Properties** button [*Table Tool Layout* tab, *Table* group] to open the *Table Properties* dialog box (Figure 4-24).
 i. Click the **Row** tab and check the **Specify height** box.
 j. Type .25 in the *Specify height* field and select **Exactly** from the *Row height is* drop-down list.
 k. Click **OK** to close the *Tables Properties* dialog box and apply these settings.

Figure 4-24 Change row height on the selected table

7. Insert a row and merge cells.
 a. Click anywhere in the table so the entire table is no longer selected.
 b. Select the first row of the table. The mini toolbar displays.
 c. Click the **Insert** button on the mini toolbar and select **Insert Above** to insert a new row at the top of the table.
 d. Select the new first row (if it is not already selected) and click the **Merge Cells** button [*Table Tools Layout* tab, *Merge* group]. The cells in the first row merge into one cell.
 e. Type The Placer Hills Belief System in the merged first row.

8. Sort the table by text in the first column.
 a. Select the **second through tenth (last) rows** of the table. Don't select the first merged row.
 b. Click the **Sort** button [*Table Tools Layout* tab, *Data* group]. The *Sort* dialog box opens (Figure 4-25).

Figure 4-25 Sort the table by the first column in ascending order

W4-228

 c. Click the **Sort by** drop-down list and select **Column 1**.
 d. Click the **Ascending** radio button if necessary. Leave *Type* as **Text** and *Using* as **Paragraphs**.
 e. Click **OK** to sort the rows below the title in alphabetical order.

9. Change cell margins and text alignment.
 a. Select the entire table.

> **▶ MORE INFO**
>
> Click the **table selector** handle in the upper left of the table or click the **Select** button in the *Table* group on the *Table Tool Layout* tab and choose **Select Table**.

 b. Click the **Cell Margins** button [*Table Tools Layout* tab, *Alignment* group]. The *Table Options* dialog box opens (Figure 4-26).
 c. Change the *Left* and *Right* cell margins **0.05"**.
 d. Check the **Automatically resize to fit contents** box (if it is not already checked) and click **OK**. Keep the table selected for the next instruction.
 e. Click the **Align Center Left** button (**first alignment button** in the **second row**) [*Table Tools Layout* tab, *Alignment* group] to align text left horizontally and center vertically within each cell.
 f. Place the insertion point in the first row of the table to deselect the table.
 g. Click the **Align Center** button (**second alignment button** in the **second row**) [*Table Tools Layout* tab, *Alignment* group] to center the title horizontally and vertically.

10. Save and close this document (Figure 4-27).

Figure 4-26 Change cell margins

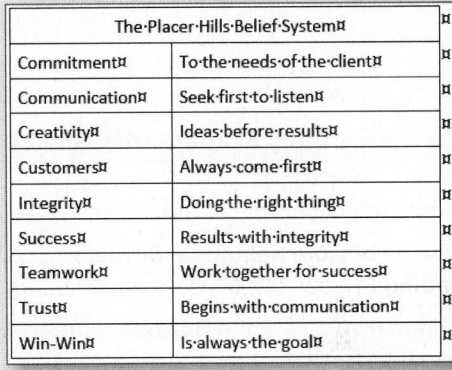

Figure 4-27 PP W4-1 completed (table only displayed)

Formatting and Editing Tables

In addition to the ability to adjust the structure of tables, Word provides you with many tools to enhance the appearance of tables. For example, add custom borders, shading, and table styles to tables. You can also add formulas to tables and convert text into tables.

Table Tools Design Tab

Word provides two *Table Tools* tabs when working with tables: *Design* and *Layout*. Both tabs are contextual and only display when the table or a portion of the table is selected or when the insertion point is in the table. The **Table Tools Design tab** enables you to apply table style options, table styles, and borders (Figure 4-28).

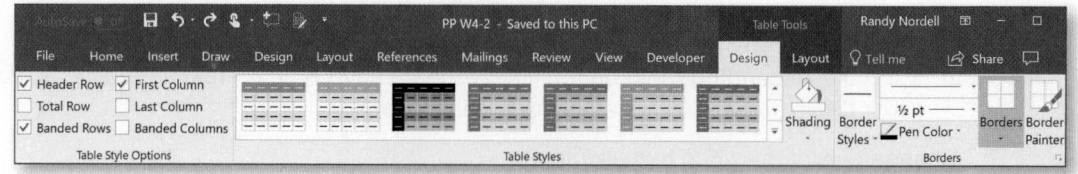

Figure 4-28 *Table Tools Design* tab

Table Borders

By default, when you insert a table, Word formats the table with borders around each cell. You can apply borders to an individual cell, a group of cells, or an entire table. When applying borders, it is important to be very precise when selecting the area of the table to apply borders.

The *Borders* button is located in the *Borders* group on the *Table Tools Design* tab, in the *Paragraph* group on the *Home* tab, or on the mini toolbar. The *Borders* drop-down list displays a variety of border options (Figure 4-29). You can also apply borders using the *Borders and Shading* dialog box.

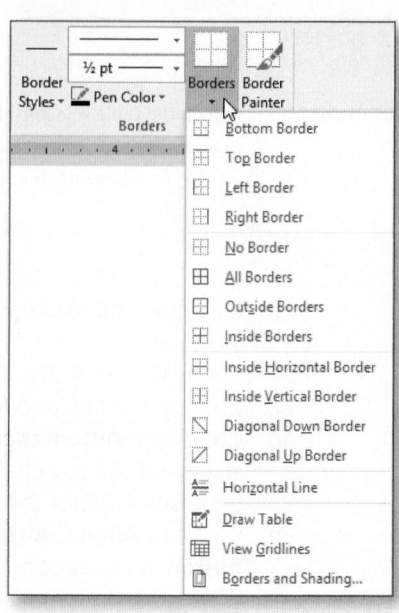

Figure 4-29 *Borders* drop-down list

▶ **HOW TO:** Apply Borders to a Table Using the Borders and Shading Dialog Box

1. Select the entire table or the desired area of the table to apply borders.

2. Click the **bottom half** of the **Borders** button [*Table Tools Design* tab, *Borders* group] and select **Borders and Shading** to open the *Borders and Shading* dialog box (Figure 4-30).

 • Alternatively, click the **Borders** drop-down list [*Home* tab, *Paragraph* group] or the **Borders** drop-down list on the mini toolbar.
 • The selection in the *Apply to* area depends on whether you are applying borders to the entire table or selected cells or rows.

3. Select the type of border from the list of options in the *Setting* area.

 • Remove all borders by selecting **None**.

4. Select the *Style* of the border from the list of options.

5. Click the **Color** drop-down list and select the color of the border.

6. Click the **Width** drop-down list and select the width of the border.

7. View the *Preview* area to see how borders display.

 • Click the border buttons in the *Preview* area or click the diagram borders to turn borders on or off.

8. Click **OK** to apply the border settings and close the *Borders and Shading* dialog box.

Figure 4-30 *Borders and Shading* dialog box

View Gridlines

When borders are removed from a table, it is difficult to see the column and row structure of your table. When a table format does not include borders, click the **View Gridlines** button [*Table Tools Layout* tab, *Table* group] to display cell boundaries. Gridlines display in the document only; they do not print (Figure 4-31).

THE·PLACER·HILLS·BELIEF·SYSTEM¤	
COMMITMENT¤	To·the·needs·of·the·client¤
COMMUNICATION¤	Seek·first·to·listen¤
CREATIVITY¤	Ideas·before·results¤
CUSTOMERS¤	Always·come·first¤
INTEGRITY¤	Doing·the·right·thing¤
SUCCESS¤	Results·with·integrity¤
TEAMWORK¤	Work·together·for·success¤
TRUST¤	Begins·with·communication¤
WIN-WIN¤	Is·always·the·goal¤

Figure 4-31 Table displayed with *View Gridlines* and no borders

Table Shading

You can apply shading to specific cells or to an entire table. Click the **bottom half** of the **Shading** button in the *Table Styles* group on the *Table Tools Design* tab to display a color palette. Choose from *Theme Colors* or *Standard Colors* (Figure 4-32). Theme colors change depending on the theme of your document. Choose a custom color by selecting **More Colors**, which opens the *Colors* dialog box. Remove shading by selecting **No Color**.

You can also apply, change, or remove shading using the *Shading* tab in the *Borders and Shading* dialog box.

Figure 4-32 Table *Shading* options

> **ANOTHER WAY**
>
> Apply borders and shading from the mini toolbar by right-clicking the table or a portion of the table.

Table Styles

Table Styles are built-in styles for tables and are similar to text styles (see *SLO 2.7: Using Styles and Themes*). Table styles include a variety of borders, shading, alignment, and formatting options. Word provides a wide variety of built-in table styles in the *Table Styles* group on the *Table Tools Design* tab. Click the **More** button on the bottom right to display the *Table Styles* gallery (Figure 4-33).

After you apply a table style, you can customize all aspects of

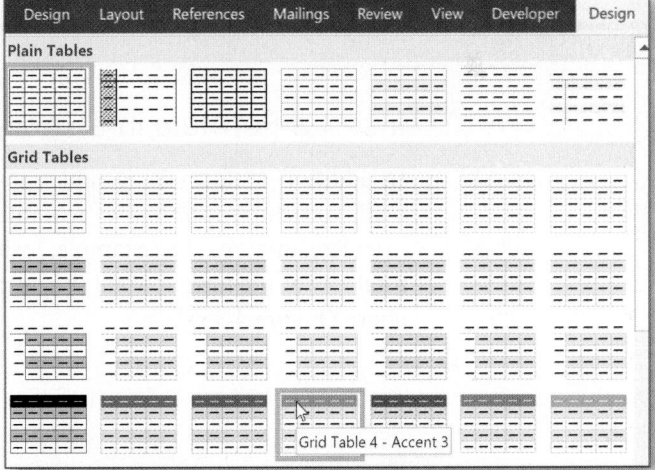

Figure 4-33 *Table Styles* gallery

the table. Remove all formatting of a table by selecting the **Clear** option at the bottom of the *Table Styles* gallery.

Table Style Options

Word offers a variety of *Table Style Options* to customize tables (Figure 4-34). For example, many tables have a header row or column, or a total or last row, where you may want to apply special formatting for emphasis. When you select one or more of the *Table Style Options*, Word applies special formatting to the table style you select. Select your table style options before applying a table style.

☑ Header Row	☑ First Column
☐ Total Row	☐ Last Column
☑ Banded Rows	☐ Banded Columns
Table Style Options	

Figure 4-34 *Table Style Options* group

> **MORE INFO**
>
> *Banded Rows* apply shading to every other row. *Banded Columns* apply shading to every other column.

▶ HOW TO: Apply a Table Style and Table Style Options

1. Place your insertion point in the table.
2. Click the **Table Tools Design** tab.
3. Select the *Table Style Options* to apply to the table [*Table Style Options* group] (see Figure 4-34).
 - Consider the content of your table when deciding the table style options to apply.
 - When you select or deselect table style options, the thumbnails of the table styles in the *Table Styles* gallery change to reflect the options you have chosen.
4. Click the **More** button to display the *Table Styles* gallery.
 - Scroll down the *Table Styles* gallery to view additional table styles.
5. Choose a table style. Word applies the style and options to your table.
 - When you point to a table style in the *Table Styles* gallery, Word temporarily displays the table style on your table to preview your table with the style applied.

Insert a Formula in a Table

In addition to formatting tables to be more attractive and easier to read, you can add *formulas* to tables. Add formulas to automatically calculate amounts. For example, insert a formula in a total row of the table to total the numbers in the rows above (Figure 4-35).

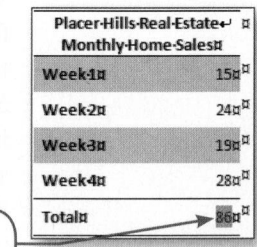

Formula that adds the numbers above

Figure 4-35 Formula in a table

> **MORE INFO**
>
> Remember, it's best to align amount figures on the right in a table.

Most formulas used in tables in Word are simple formulas that calculate numbers in a column or row. When you insert a formula, Word, by default, inserts the *SUM* formula, which adds the range of numbers in the column or row. Word also enables you to insert more complex formulas.

HOW TO: Insert a Formula in a Table

1. Place the insertion point in the cell to insert the formula.

2. Click the **Formula** button [*Table Tools Layout* tab, *Data* group]. The *Formula* dialog box opens, and the formula displays in the *Formula* text box (Figure 4-36).

3. Adjust the formula and the range as necessary.

 • Select different formula functions from the **Paste function** drop-down list.

4. Click the **Number format** drop-down list and select a number format.

5. Click **OK** to insert the formula.

Figure 4-36 *Formula* dialog box

Update a Formula

A formula performs calculations on values in a table. If values in the table change, update the formula. Update a formula in one of two ways:

• Right-click the formula and select **Update Field**.
• Select the formula and press the **F9** function key (you might have to press **Fn+F9** if using a laptop).

Convert Text to a Table

Occasionally, you may want to create a table from existing text. For example, you may want to convert text that is arranged using tabs into a table or convert an existing table into text. Word provides *Convert Text to Table* or *Convert Table to Text* options.

When converting text into a table, the selected text must be separated by tabs, commas, paragraph breaks, or other characters. Word uses these characters to separate text into individual cells in the table.

HOW TO: Convert Text to a Table

1. Select the text to be converted to a table.

2. Click the **Insert** tab.

3. Click **Tables** [*Tables* group] and select **Convert Text to Table**. The *Convert Text to Table* dialog box opens (Figure 4-37).

4. Select the number of columns or rows in the *Table size* area.

 • Word automatically detects the size of the table you need.
 • You may not be able to change one or both values, depending on the text you selected.

5. Select an *AutoFit* option in the *AutoFit behavior* area.

 • The default setting is *Fixed column width*.

6. Select how you want Word to separate columns and rows in the *Separate text at* area.

 • Word automatically picks an option based on the selected text.

7. Click **OK** to convert the text to a table.

Figure 4-37 *Convert Text to Table* dialog box

PAUSE & PRACTICE: WORD 4-2

For this Pause & Practice project, you continue to modify Emma's brochure. You apply a table style and table style options to the table you created in the previous Pause & Practice project. You also convert text to a table and apply borders and shading.

File Needed: *[your initials] PP W4-1.docx*
Completed Project File Name: *[your initials] PP W4-2.docx*

1. Open the *[your initials] PP W4-1* document completed in *Pause & Practice 4-1*.

2. Save this document as [your initials] PP W4-2.

3. Apply table style options and a table style.
 a. Place your insertion point in the table at the end of the document.
 b. Click the **Table Tools Design** tab.
 c. Select **Header Row**, **Banded Rows**, and **First Column** [*Table Style Options* group] if they are not already selected. The other check boxes should not be selected.
 d. Click the **More** button in the *Table Styles* group to open the *Table Styles* gallery.
 e. Select the **Grid Table 5 Dark – Accent 3** style (Figure 4-38) to apply the style to the table.

Figure 4-38 Select table style

4. Apply a custom top and bottom border to the table.
 a. Select the **first row** (title) of the table.
 b. Click the **Borders** drop-down arrow [*Table Tools Design* tab, *Borders* group] and select **Borders and Shading**. The *Borders and Shading* dialog box opens.
 c. Select **Custom** in the *Setting* area.
 d. Click the **Color** drop-down list and select the **second option** in the **first row** of *Theme Colors* (**Black, Text 1**).
 e. Click the **Width** drop-down list and select **1½ pt**.
 f. Select the **solid line** (first line style in the list) in the *Style* area if it is not already selected.
 g. Click the **top boundary** of the example cell in the *Preview* area to add a modified top border (Figure 4-39).

Figure 4-39 Apply custom borders

h. Click **OK** to close the dialog box and add the border.
 i. Select the entire **bottom row** of the table.
 j. Open the *Borders and Shading* dialog box and apply the same custom border to the **bottom boundary** of the selected row (**Black, Text 1**; **1½ pt**; **solid line**).
 k. Click **OK** to add the border and close the dialog box.

5. Vertically align text in cells.
 a. Select the entire table and click the **Properties** button [*Table Tools Layout* tab, *Table* group] to open the *Table Properties* dialog box.
 b. Click the **Cell** tab and select **Center** in the *Vertical alignment* area.
 c. Click **OK** to close the dialog box.

6. Apply formatting changes to the text in the table.
 a. Select the first row (title).
 b. Open the *Font* dialog box, change *Size* to **12** and *Font color* to the **second option** in the **first row** of *Theme Colors* (**Black, Text 1**), and check **All caps** in the *Effects* area.
 c. Click **OK** to close the *Font* dialog box.
 d. Select the text in the first column, not including the title.
 e. Open the *Font* dialog box and check **Small caps** in the *Effects* area.
 f. Click **OK** to close the *Font* dialog box.

7. Convert text to a table.
 a. Go to the first page and select the three lines of text after "Realtor Consultant" ("**Phone**" through "**www.phre.com/ecavalli**"). Be sure to include the paragraph mark at the end of the third line, but don't select the blank line below the three lines of text.
 b. Click the **Insert** tab.
 c. Click the **Table** button [*Tables* group] and select **Convert Text to Table**. The *Convert Text to Table* dialog box opens (Figure 4-40).
 d. Change the *AutoFit behavior* to **AutoFit to contents**.
 e. Click **OK** to convert selected text to a table.

Figure 4-40 *Convert Text to Table* dialog box

8. Remove all borders, add custom borders and shading, and display table gridlines.
 a. Select the table if necessary, click the **Borders** drop-down arrow [*Table Tools Design* tab, *Borders* group], and select **No Border** to remove all borders.
 b. Click the **Borders** drop-down arrow again and select **Top Border**.
 c. Click the **Borders** drop-down arrow again and select **Bottom Border**.
 d. Select the table if necessary, click the **Shading** drop-down arrow [*Table Tools Design* tab, *Table Styles* group], and select the **seventh option** in the **second row** of *Theme Colors* (**Olive Green, Accent 3, Lighter 80%**) (Figure 4-41).
 e. Click the **View Gridlines** button [*Table Tools Layout* tab, *Table* group] to display non-printing gridlines on the table.

Figure 4-41 Select *Shading* color

9. Save and close the document (Figure 4-42).

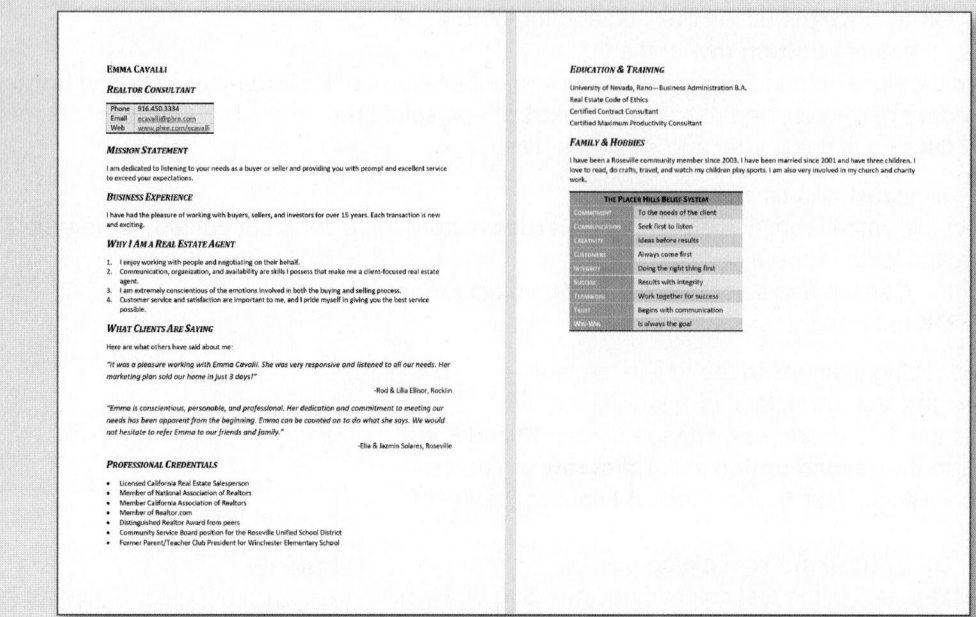

Figure 4-42 PP W4-2 completed

Using Columns

Columns are used to arrange text and tables to improve the readability, layout, and design of a document. By default, Word documents display text in a single column. You can apply columns to an entire document or to selected sections of a document. Word includes preset column setting options, or you can customize column settings to control the number of columns, column width, and space between columns. Use column and section breaks to control column endings and to balance columns.

Preset Column Settings

Apply column settings to a new document or to an existing document. To apply preset column settings, click the **Columns** button on the *Layout* tab in the *Page Setup* group (Figure 4-43). The *Two* and *Three* column options set columns with equal width, while the *Left* and *Right* column options format documents in two columns of unequal width.

When you apply columns to a document, the column settings apply only to that section of the document. If your document contains no section breaks, columns apply to the entire document.

Figure 4-43 Preset column options

Customize Columns

Use the *Columns dialog box* to apply column settings or to customize current column settings. In the *Columns* dialog box, select the number of columns, adjust the column width and space between columns, insert a line between columns, and select the portion of the document to apply the column settings.

▶HOW TO: Customize Columns Using the Columns Dialog Box

1. Click the **Layout** tab.
2. Click the **Columns** button [*Page Setup* group].
3. Select **More Columns**. The *Columns* dialog box opens (Figure 4-44).
4. Select column settings from the *Presets* options or *Number of columns* box.
 - Based on the number of columns you choose, Word automatically sets the column width and spacing.
 - The default spacing between columns is 0.5".
 - You can choose to have more than three columns in the *Number of columns* area.
5. Adjust the column widths and spacing as desired in the *Width and spacing* area.
 - Deselect the **Equal column widths** check box to apply unequal column widths.
 - When *Equal column width* is deselected, adjust the width and spacing of each column individually.
 - When *Equal column width* is selected, adjust the width and spacing to apply to all columns.
6. Click the **Apply to** drop-down list and select the portion of the document where you want to apply column settings: **Whole document** or **This point forward**.
 - When *This point forward* is selected, Word inserts a continuous section break at the insertion point in the document and applies column settings to the text after the continuous section break.
 - If you selected text before opening the *Columns* dialog box, *Selected text* is the default selection in the *Apply to* drop-down list.
7. Check the **Line between** check box to insert a vertical line between columns if desired.
8. View the *Preview* area to see a diagram of how your columns will display.
9. Click **OK** to apply column settings.

Figure 4-44 *Columns* dialog box

Convert Text to Columns

Apply column settings to the *Whole document*, from *This point forward*, or to *Selected text*. Depending on the portion of the document where you are applying column settings, Word applies the column settings and inserts any needed section breaks. Use the *Apply to* drop-down list in the *Columns* dialog box to select an option (see Figure 4-44). Table 4-3 describes how Word handles each of the options.

Table 4-3: Apply to Column Options

Columns Applied to	Actions
Whole Document	Word applies column settings to the entire document. No section breaks are added.
This point forward	Word inserts a continuous section break before the insertion point in the document and applies the column setting beginning at the insertion point, which becomes a new section of the document.
Selected text	When text is selected and column settings are applied, Word inserts a continuous section break before and after the selected text. The column settings apply only to that section.

Insert a Column Break

Column widths control the horizontal text wrapping, while the top and bottom margins or section breaks control where a column ends and wraps to the next column. Insert *column breaks* to end a column and move subsequent text to the next column.

▶ **HOW TO:** Insert a Column Break

1. Place the insertion point at the location to end a column or begin the next column.
2. Click the **Layout** tab.
3. Click the **Breaks** button [*Page Setup* group].
4. Select **Column** in the *Page Breaks* options (Figure 4-45).
 - A column break indicator displays when *Show/Hide* is on (Figure 4-46).

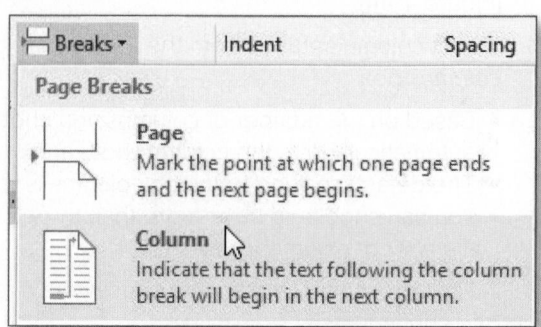

Figure 4-45 Insert *Column* break

▶ **ANOTHER WAY**

Ctrl+Shift+Enter inserts a column break. The *Columns* dialog box also includes an option to start a new column.

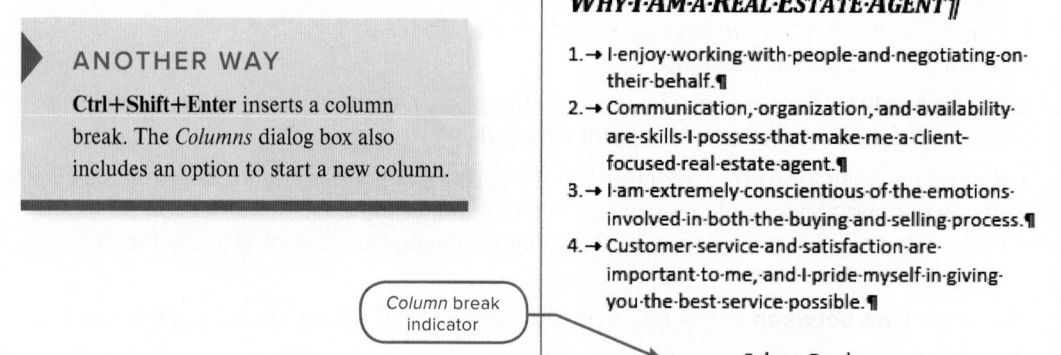

Figure 4-46 *Column* break inserted

▶ **MORE INFO**

Always turn on **Show/Hide** (**Ctrl+Shift+8**) when using page, section, or column breaks to help you see these elements in your document.

Balance Columns

Column breaks are one way to balance columns on a page. Another way is to use a *continuous section break*. To format columns with equal length on a page, insert a continuous section break at the end of the last column on the page. Word automatically adjusts columns so they are approximately the same length.

▶ **HOW TO:** Balance Columns Using a Continuous Section Break

1. Place the insertion point at the end of the last column in your document.
2. Click the **Layout** tab.

3. Click the **Breaks** button [*Page Setup* group].
4. Select **Continuous** in the *Section Breaks* options.
 - A continuous section break indicator displays when *Show/Hide* is turned on.

MORE INFO

Balancing columns using a continuous section break works only if no other column breaks control column endings on that page.

PAUSE & PRACTICE: WORD 4-3

For this Pause & Practice project, you apply columns to Emma's brochure. With the use of columns and column breaks, you arrange the columns and format the document to fit on one page.

File Needed: *[your initials] PP W4-2.docx*
Completed Project File Name: *[your initials] PP W4-3.docx*

1. Open the *[your initials] PP W4-2* document completed in *Pause & Practice 4-2*.

2. Save this document as [your initials]

3. Change the page orientation and margins.
 a. Click the **Orientation** button [*Layout* tab, *Page Setup* group] and select **Landscape**.
 b. Click the **Page Setup** launcher to open the Page Setup dialog box.
 c. Change the *Top* margin to **1.2"**, and the *Bottom*, *Left*, and *Right* margins to **0.5"**.
 d. Click **OK** to close the dialog box and apply the margin settings. If a dialog box opens informing you that the margins are outside the printable area, click **Ignore**.

4. Arrange the text in columns and customize columns.
 a. Place your insertion point at the top of the document.
 b. Click the **Columns** button [*Layout* tab, *Page Setup* group] and select **Two**. The text displays in two columns.
 c. Click the **Columns** button again [*Layout* tab, *Page Setup* group] and select **More Columns**. The *Columns* dialog box opens (Figure 4-47).
 d. Select **Three** in the *Presets* area.
 e. Change the *Spacing* to **0.6"** in the *Width and spacing* area.
 f. Click the **Apply to** drop-down list and select **Whole document** if necessary.
 g. Click **OK** to apply custom column settings.

5. Use column breaks to control column endings.
 a. Place the insertion point in front of "What Clients Are Saying."
 b. Click the **Breaks** button [*Layout* tab, *Page Setup* group] and select **Column** to insert a column break.

Figure 4-47 Customize column settings

c. Place the insertion point in front of "Education & Training."

d. Press **Ctrl+Shift+Enter** to insert a column break.

6. Save and close the document (Figure 4-48).

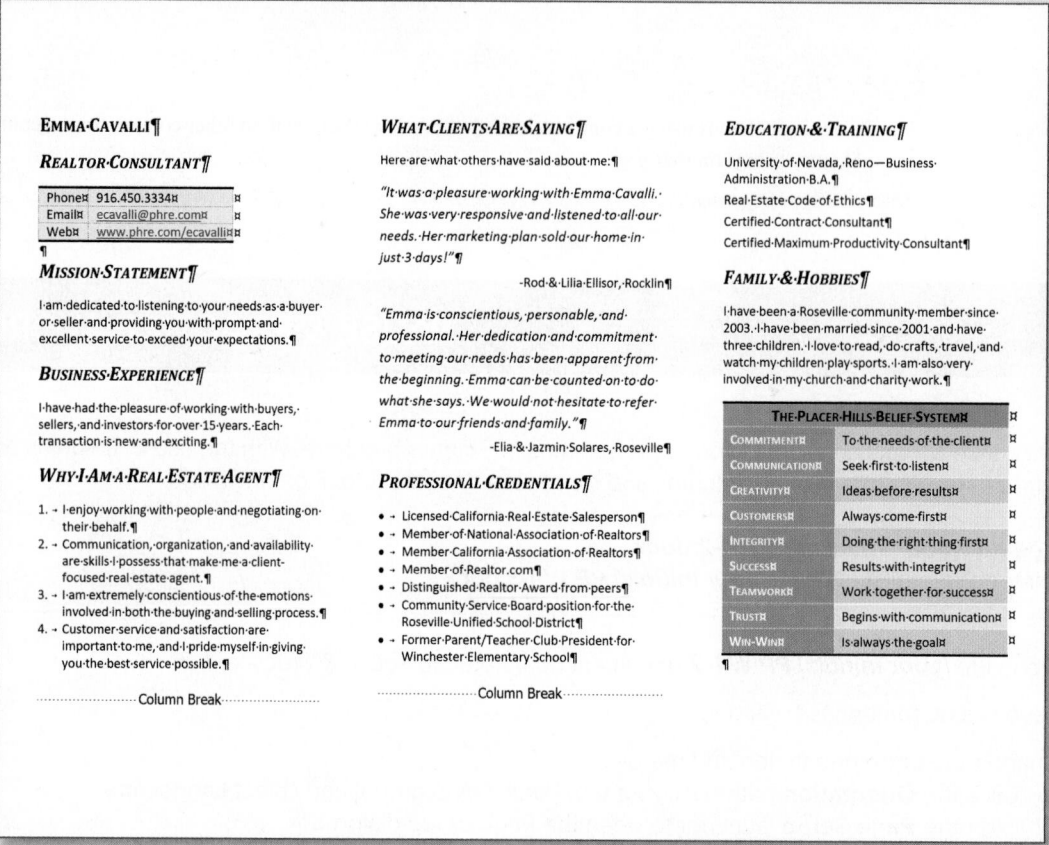

Figure 4-48 PP W4-3 completed

Working with Graphics

Use graphics to visually present information and to enhance a document. Graphics include pictures stored on your computer, online pictures, shapes, *SmartArt*, and *WordArt*. This section describes how to insert and arrange picture graphics. *SLO 4.6: Working with Other Graphics* introduces other types of graphic objects available in Word.

Pictures and Online Pictures

Use pictures and graphics to add visual elements to your documents. Add your own pictures and graphics to Word documents or use Bing images to find a wide variety of online pictures. Word uses the term *picture* generically to refer to any type of visual image that is saved as a graphic file. Table 4-4 describes common types of graphic formats.

Table 4-4: Types of Graphics

Format	Full Name	Extension	Details
PNG	Portable Network Graphics	.png	Used with pictures and editing pictures; high-quality resolution
JPEG	Joint Photographic Experts Group	.jpeg or .jpg	Relatively small file size; many pictures are saved and distributed in JPEG format
TIFF	Tagged Image File Format	.tiff	Used with high-quality digital photos and has a larger file size than JPEG or PNG
GIF	Graphics Interchange Format	.gif	Used with graphics with fewer colors
WMF	Windows Metafile	.wmf	Windows format used with many graphic images
BMP	Windows Bitmap	.bmp	Proprietary Windows format used with many Microsoft graphic images

Insert a Picture

To enhance a document, insert your own picture or a picture you have saved. See the steps below to insert a picture into a document.

▶ HOW TO: Insert a Picture

1. Place the insertion point in the document where you want the picture inserted.
2. Click the **Insert** tab.
3. Click the **Pictures** button [*Illustrations* group]. The *Insert Picture* dialog box opens (Figure 4-49).

Figure 4-49 *Insert Picture* dialog box

4. Browse to the location on your computer and select a picture.
5. Click the **Insert** button to insert the picture and close the *Insert Picture* dialog box.

When you find a picture on the internet you want to include in a document, you can either save the picture and insert it, or copy and paste the picture into your document. Press **Ctrl+C** to copy the picture and **Ctrl+V** to paste the picture.

Include pictures obtained from the web only if you have permission from the image owner to avoid copyright infringement. For academic purposes, you may include images if you reference their sources as you would any other research citation.

> **ANOTHER WAY**
>
> Use the context menu (right-click) to both copy a picture and paste it into a document.

Use Alt Text

Alternative text, referred to as *alt text*, is text used to describe a picture, table, or graphic object. In Word documents, alt text is used by screen readers to provide an audio description of the graphic for those with visual impairments.

Depending on the type of picture you insert, Word may automatically generate alt text based upon the content of the picture and temporarily display the alt text at the bottom of the picture (Figure 4-50). Customize the alt text description

Figure 4-50 Alt text temporarily displays at the bottom of a picture

tion in the *Alt Text* pane. Alt text does not permanently display on the graphic or in your document; it is hidden text attached to the graphic, similar to document properties.

▶HOW TO: Edit Alt Text

1. Insert a picture into your document.
 - Alt text may temporarily display at the bottom of the picture (see Figure 4-50).
 - Some versions of Word automatically generate alt text based on the content of the picture.
2. Click the **Alt Text** button [*Picture Tools Format* tab, *Accessibility* group]. The *Alt Text* pane opens on the right (Figure 4-51).
 - Alternatively, right-click the picture and select **Edit Alt Text** from the context menu or click the alt text that temporarily displays at the bottom of the picture to open the *Alt Text* pane.
3. Edit the alt text as desired.
4. Click the **X** in the upper-right corner to close the *Alt Text* pane.

Figure 4-51 *Alt Text* pane

Insert an Online Picture

Word provides a variety of online picture choices using *Bing Image Search*. When using an image from *Bing Image Search*, make sure you have the permission of the image owner to avoid copyright infringement.

1. Place the insertion point in the document where you want the picture inserted.
2. Click the **Insert** tab.
3. Click the **Online Pictures** button [*Illustrations* group] to open the *Insert Pictures* dialog box.
4. Click the *Bing* text box, type keywords for the image you want to find, and press **Enter**.

- Thumbnails of pictures appear below the search box (Figure 4-52).
- By default, the *Creative Commons only* box is checked, which displays only those pictures that require no license or fee. Deselect this check box to display all pictures that match the search keywords.
- Click the **Filter** drop-down lists to refine your search.

5. Select the picture to insert into your document.

- Click the link below a picture to view a larger picture in a browser window. Close the browser window and return to the Word document.

6. Click the **Insert** button to insert the picture into your document.

- Pictures may include a caption below the inserted picture.
- Click the border of the caption text box to select it and press **Delete** to remove the caption if desired.

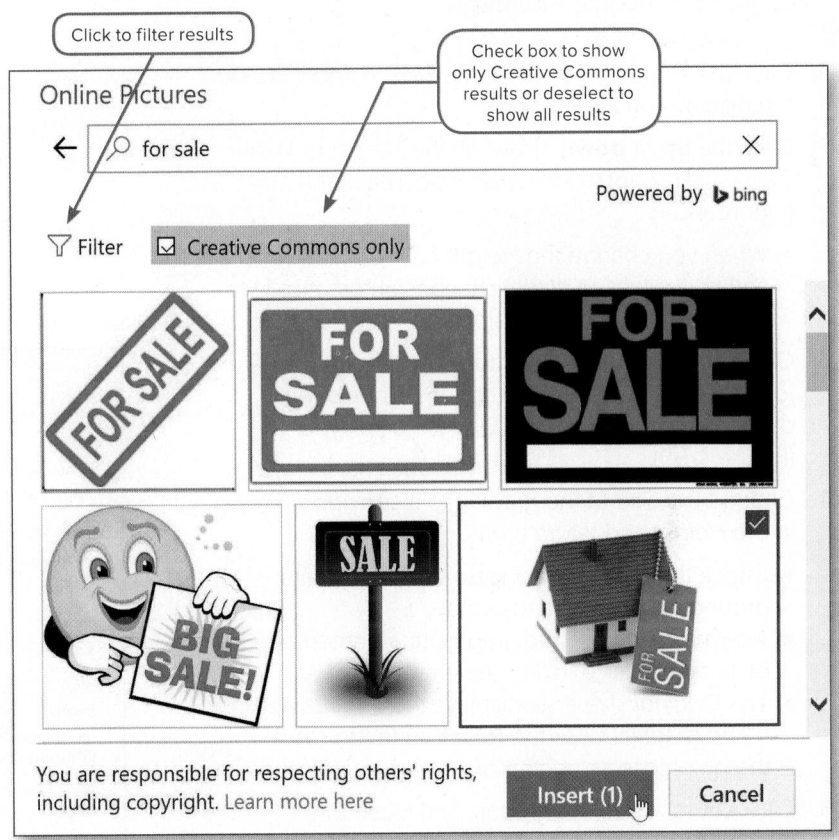

Figure 4-52 Insert an online picture

Resize a Graphic

In most cases, you will need to resize a graphic to fit properly in your document. Manually change the size of a graphic by dragging the top, bottom, side, or corner handles. Alternatively, enter a precise measurement in the *Layout* dialog box or the *Height* and *Width* text boxes in the *Size* group on the *Picture Tools Format* tab.

When you select (click) a graphic, *sizing handles* appear on each side and in each corner (Figure 4-53). To resize the graphic, click and hold one of the handles and drag in or out to decrease or increase the

Figure 4-53 Resize a graphic using the sizing handles

size of the graphic. Use the corner handles to maintain the horizontal and vertical proportion of the image. If you use the side, top, or bottom handles to resize, the proportions of the image may become distorted.

You can also resize the image to a specific size or to a percentage of its original size.

▶HOW TO: Resize an Image

1. Click the image to select it. The *Picture Tools Format* tab displays on the *Ribbon*.

2. Click the **up** or **down** arrows in the *Height* or *Width* area [*Size* group] to increase or decrease the size (Figure 4-54).

 - When you change the *Height* or *Width*, the other setting (*Height* or *Width*) changes automatically to keep the graphic proportional.

Figure 4-54 *Size* group on the *Picture Tools Format* tab

3. Click the **Size** launcher [*Picture Tools Format* tab] to display additional sizing options. The *Layout* dialog box opens with the *Size* tab displayed (Figure 4-55).

4. Change the size of the graphic to a specific size in the *Height* and *Width* areas.

 - Check the **Lock aspect ratio** box to maintain proportional height and width.
 - Alternatively, scale the graphic to a percentage of its original size in the *Scale* area.
 - The *Original size* area displays the original size of the graphic. Click the **Reset** button to reset the graphic to its original size.

5. Click **OK** to resize the graphic and close the dialog box.

Figure 4-55 *Size* options in the *Layout* dialog box

> ▶ **ANOTHER WAY**
>
> Open the *Layout* dialog box by right-clicking the graphic and selecting **Size and Position**.

Wrap Text around a Graphic

Use the ***text wrapping*** options to control how the text aligns or wraps around a graphic. You can also choose to position the graphic in front of or behind text.

▶HOW TO: Wrap Text around a Graphic

1. Click the graphic to select it.
2. Click the **Wrap Text** button [*Picture Tools Format* tab, *Arrange* group] (Figure 4-56).
3. Select a text wrapping option.

- Select **More Layout Options** to display additional text wrapping options. The *Layout* dialog box opens with the *Text Wrapping* tab displayed (Figure 4-57).
- Use the *Layout* dialog box to customize text wrapping [*Text Wrapping* tab], specify the position of the graphic [*Position* tab], and resize the graphic [*Size* tab].
- In the *Wrap text* area, choose *Both sides*, *Left only*, *Right only*, or *Largest only*.
- In the *Distance from text* area, set a specific distance from the graphic to wrap text.
- Click **OK** to close the *Layout* dialog box.

Figure 4-56 *Wrap Text* options

Figure 4-57 *Text Wrapping* tab in the *Layout* dialog box

You can also click the **Layout Options** button to the right of a selected graphic and select a text wrapping option (Figure 4-58). Click the **See more** link to open the *Layout* dialog box.

> **MORE INFO**
>
> *In Line with Text* is the default option when you insert a graphic into a document.

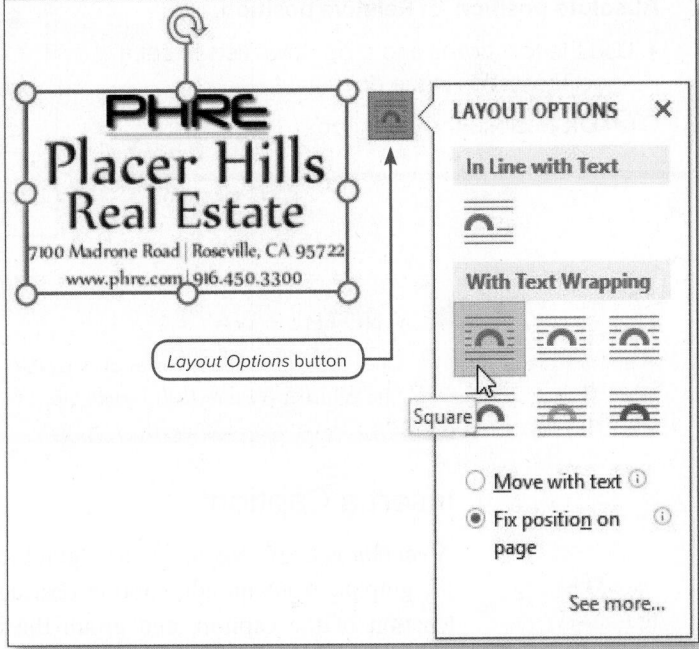

Figure 4-58 *Layout Options* menu

Position a Graphic

In addition to adjusting the size of a graphic and specifying how text wraps around a graphic, you can also control the position of the graphic in your document. Select the graphic, click the **Align** button in the *Arrange* group on the *Picture Tools Format* tab, and select an alignment option from the drop-down list (Figure 4-59).

Position a graphic by dragging the graphic to the desired location or specifying the exact location relative to the margins, page, or column. For example, you can position a graphic 5" from the left margin and 6" from the top margin of the document. The *Position* tab in the *Layout* dialog box offers customization options (Figure 4-60).

Figure 4-59 *Align* options

▶**HOW TO:** Position a Graphic

1. Click the graphic to select it.
2. Click the **Picture Tools Format** tab.
3. Click the **Position** button [*Arrange* group] and select **More Layout Options**. The *Layout* dialog box opens with the *Position* tab selected (see Figure 4-60).
4. Select a *Horizontal* position radio button: **Alignment**, **Book layout**, **Absolute position**, or **Relative position**.
 - Use the text boxes and drop-down lists to set a specific location in the document.
5. Select a *Vertical* position radio button: **Alignment**, **Absolute position**, or **Relative position**.
 - Use the text boxes and drop-down lists to set a specific location in the document.
6. Click **OK** to close the dialog box.

Figure 4-60 *Position* tab in the *Layout* dialog box

▶ **ANOTHER WAY**

Open the *Layout* dialog box by clicking the **Size** launcher [*Picture Tools Format* tab].

Insert a Caption

A *caption* is a text box added to a graphic to describe the graphic. You can edit caption text, customize the location of the caption, and group the caption and graphic to create a single graphic object (Figure 4-61). Grouping graphic objects is covered in the next section.

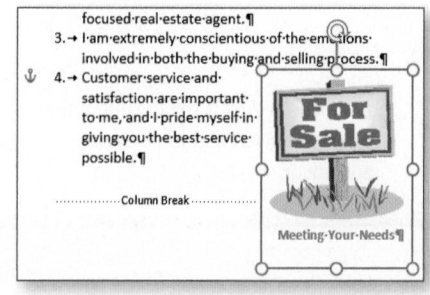

Figure 4-61 Graphic with caption below

▶ HOW TO: Insert a Caption

1. Right-click the graphic and select **Insert Caption** from the context menu. The *Caption* dialog box opens (Figure 4-62).

 - Alternatively, click the **Insert Caption** button [*References* tab, *Captions* group] to open the *Caption* dialog box.
 - Word automatically creates a caption for the selected object. Add a description after the label in the *Caption* text box. You cannot delete the label in the *Caption* text box.
 - After adding a caption to a graphic, you can edit or delete the caption text within the document.

2. Click the **Label** drop-down list and choose **Equation**, **Figure**, or **Table**.

 - Add a custom label by clicking the **New Label** button and typing a custom label.
 - Check the **Exclude label from caption** box to remove the label (but not the number).

3. Click the **Position** drop-down list and select the location of the caption.

4. Click **OK** to insert the caption.

5. Edit the caption in the text box after it is added to the graphic (Figure 4-63).

 - Customize the size and color of the caption text and adjust the size and position of the text box.

Figure 4-62 *Caption dialog box*

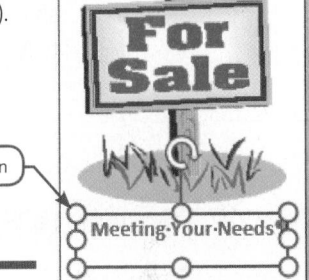

Figure 4-63 **Caption added to graphic**

Group Graphic Objects

When you work with graphics, you can *group* related graphics and objects. For example, group a picture and its caption or group the graphic objects that comprise a company logo. The advantage of grouping graphics is to create one object that can be resized and positioned.

▶ HOW TO: Group and Ungroup Graphics

1. Press the **Ctrl** key and click the graphics to be grouped (Figure 4-64).

2. Click the **Group** button [*Picture Tools Format* tab, *Arrange* group].

3. Select **Group**. The selected objects become one grouped object (Figure 4-65).

 - Notice that the number of sizing handles changes from 16 handles for two separate objects to 8 handles on the grouped object.
 - To ungroup grouped items, select the grouped object, click the **Group** button in the *Arrange* group on the *Picture Tools Format* tab, and select **Ungroup**.

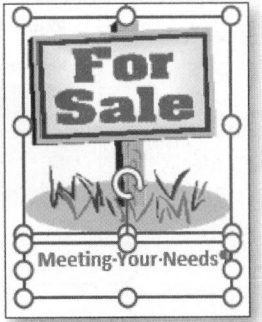

Figure 4-64 **Multiple objects selected to be grouped together**

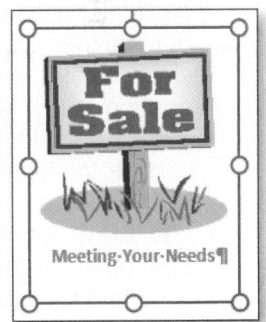

Figure 4-65 **Grouped objects**

> **ANOTHER WAY**
>
> *Group* and *Ungroup* options are available in the context menu by right-clicking selected graphics or a grouped object.

Working with Other Graphic Objects

In addition to inserting and customizing pictures, Word provides a variety of other graphic objects. Add shapes, *SmartArt*, *WordArt*, symbols, icons, 3D models, and videos as visual elements. Each of these graphic objects include design and format options to customize the appearance and position of the objects.

Insert and Customize a Shape

Word provides a variety of **shapes** to insert into your document. Word's *Shapes* gallery groups shapes into eight categories (Figure 4-66). The *Recently Used Shapes* categories collects shapes you recently selected. When inserting a shape or line, you actually draw the object in your document. After drawing a shape, you can edit the size, position, alignment, and text wrapping.

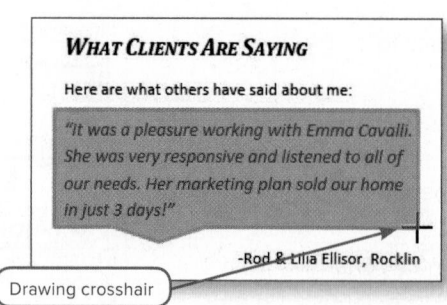

Figure 4-66 *Shapes* drop-down list

▶ HOW TO: Insert a Shape

1. Click the **Insert** tab.
2. Click the **Shapes** button [*Illustrations* group] to display the gallery of shape options.
3. Select the shape to use. The pointer becomes a drawing crosshair (large, dark plus sign) when you position the pointer in the document.
4. Click and drag to create the shape (Figure 4-67). When you release the pointer, the shape displays in the document.
 - You don't have to be perfectly accurate when drawing the shape because you can easily resize and position it.
 - The document theme controls the format of the shape.
 - Use text wrapping to position the shape on top or behind text or wrap text around a shape.

Figure 4-67 Draw a shape

> ### MORE INFO
> To create an exact square or circle or to draw a straight line, press the **Shift** key while drawing.

After a shape has been inserted, it can be moved or resized. You can customize the shape fill color, outline color and weight, or shape effect. See Figure 4-68 and its callouts for examples of the available selection and sizing handles. The following is a list of those options:

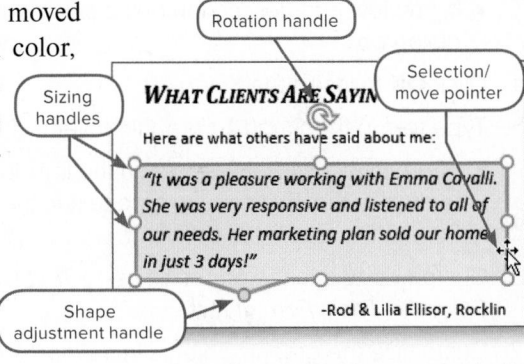

Figure 4-68 Shape selected with handles displayed

- **Selection/move pointer**: This pointer (four-pointed arrow) enables you to select and move objects. Select multiple objects by pressing the **Ctrl** key and selecting the objects.
- **Sizing handles**: Eight sizing handles are located on corners and sides of the shape. When you point to a handle, the pointer becomes a sizing pointer (two-pointed arrow).
- **Rotation handle**: The rotation handle is the circular arrow at the top of the selected shape. Rotate a shape by clicking and dragging this handle to the left or right.
- **Shape adjustment handle**: This handle is the yellow circle and is not available for all shapes. Use this handle to change the shape of an object. Also, use this handle to change the size or location of a callout, corner roundness, and other shape elements.

When you select a shape, the *Drawing Tools Format* tab displays on the *Ribbon* with options to format the shape (Figure 4-69).

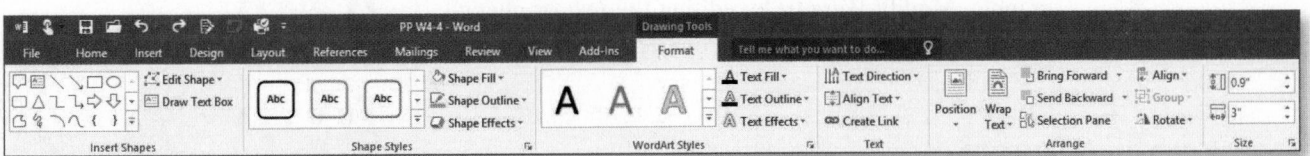

Figure 4-69 *Drawing Tools Format* tab

Insert and Customize SmartArt

SmartArt graphics are a combination of shapes and text boxes. *SmartArt* includes a variety of categories, and within each category, numerous options are available (Figure 4-70). After inserting a *SmartArt* graphic, use **SmartArt Tools Design** and **SmartArt Tools Format** tabs to customize the text content and the graphic's structure.

▶ **HOW TO: Insert and Customize SmartArt**

1. Position your insertion point at the location to insert the *SmartArt*.
2. Click the **SmartArt** button [*Insert* tab, *Illustrations* group]. The *Choose a SmartArt Graphic* dialog box opens (see Figure 4-70).
3. Select a *SmartArt* graphic.
 - *SmartArt* categories display on the left side of the dialog box.

Figure 4-70 *Choose a SmartArt Graphic* dialog box

- A preview and description of the selected *SmartArt* displays on the right of the dialog box.

4. Click **OK** to insert the *SmartArt*.

5. Type text in the *SmartArt* graphic objects (Figure 4-71).

 - Alternatively, click the arrow on the left side of the *SmartArt* graphic to display the *Text* pane to type text in the *SmartArt* graphic.
 - Format the text in the *SmartArt*.

6. Customize text in the *SmartArt* using *Text Fill*, *Text Outline*, and *Text Effects* on the *SmartArt Tools Format* tab.

7. Customize the graphic objects in a *SmartArt* graphic using the *SmartArt Tools Design* and *Format* tabs.

 - The *SmartArt Tools Design* tab controls the overall design and colors of the *SmartArt* objects.
 - The *SmartArt Tools Format* tab provides options to customize the shape of objects, colors, borders, fill, and effects.

Figure 4-71 *SmartArt* with text inserted

Insert and Customize WordArt

Use **WordArt** to create special effects with text. Select text in a document or type text to create the *WordArt* object. When you insert *WordArt*, you are actually inserting a text box that can be manipulated as a graphic. Modify *WordArt* by editing the text or changing the size, position, color, fill, or effects of this object.

Figure 4-72 *WordArt* gallery

▶**HOW TO: Insert WordArt**

1. Position your insertion point at the location to insert the *WordArt*.

 - Alternatively, select text in the document to convert text to a *WordArt* object.

2. Click the **WordArt** button [*Insert* tab, *Text* group] and select a *WordArt* style from the gallery of options (Figure 4-72). The *WordArt* text box displays in your document.

3. Type text in the *WordArt* text box.

 - The placeholder text (*Your text here*) is selected when you insert the *WordArt* (Figure 4-73). Type to replace the placeholder text. If the placeholder text is not selected, select it before typing text.

4. Click anywhere in your document away from the text box to deselect the *WordArt* graphic.

Figure 4-73 *WordArt* inserted into a document

Customizing *WordArt* is similar to customizing other graphic objects in Word. When you select the *WordArt* text box, the **Drawing Tools Format** tab displays (Figure 4-74). The following are ways to customize a *WordArt* graphic:

Figure 4-74 *Drawing Tools Format* tab

- Use the **Drawing Tools Format** tab to change the *WordArt* style, add a border, and change the fill, outline, and effects of the *WordArt* text.

- Resize the *WordArt* graphic using the sizing handles on the corners and sides.
- Rotate the *WordArt* text box using the rotation handle.
- Change the position and text wrapping of the *WordArt* in the same way you manipulate other graphics.

Modify Graphics with Styles

You can apply a variety of styles, fills, outlines, and effects to each of the different types of graphic objects. Contextual tabs display when you select a graphic object, and each tab includes a variety of *style galleries* (Figure 4-75).

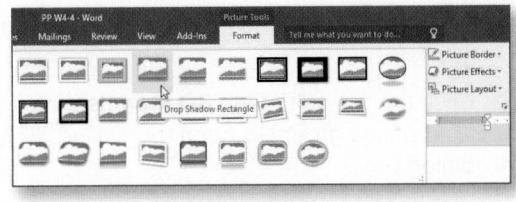

Figure 4-75 *Picture Styles* gallery

When applying styles to graphics, Word provides a *live preview*. When you place the pointer on a style from one of the style galleries, Word temporarily applies the style to the selected graphic to preview how it will appear in the document.

Insert Icons and 3D Models

In addition to inserting pictures, shapes, and other graphic objects, Word provides a variety of icons and 3D models. *Icons* are small images you insert into a document and can be resized and positioned similar to other graphic objects.

Figure 4-76 *Insert Icons* dialog box

▶ **HOW TO:** Insert an Icon

1. Position the insertion point at the location to insert an icon.
2. Click the **Icon** button [*Insert* tab, *Illustrations* group] to open the *Insert Icons* dialog box (Figure 4-76).
 - Categories of icons display on the left.
3. Select an **icon** and click the **Insert** button to insert the icon and close the *Insert Icons* dialog box.
 - The contextual *Graphic Tools Format* tab displays.
4. Use options in the *Graphics Styles* group [*Graphic Tools Format* tab] to apply **Graphics Styles**, **Graphics Fill**, **Graphics Outline**, or **Graphics Effects**.
5. Use the options in the *Arrange* and *Size* groups [*Graphic Tools Format* tab] to position, wrap text, or resize the icon.
 - Alternatively, click the **Layout Options** button to display the *Layout Options* menu and select a text wrapping option (Figure 4-77). Or, use the resizing handles to resize the icon.
 - Click the **See more** link near the bottom of the *Layout Options* menu to open the *Layout* dialog box for additional position, text wrapping, and size options.

Figure 4-77 Icon with *Layout Options* menu displayed

A *3D model* is a graphic object similar to a picture, but it can be rotated on its center axis to display the object at different angles and tilt. Insert and customize 3D models similar to other graphic objects.

▶ **HOW TO: Insert a 3D Model from Online Sources**

1. Position the insertion point at the location to insert a 3D model.

2. Click the top half of the **3D Models** button [*Insert* tab, *Illustrations* group] to open the *Online 3D Models* dialog box.

 - Categories of 3D models display in the dialog box. Select a category to display 3D models.
 - Alternatively, type keywords in the *Type a keyword here* text box and press **Enter** or click the **search** icon (magnifying glass) to display 3D models (Figure 4-78).

3. Select a **3D model** and click the **Insert** button to insert the 3D model and to close the *Online 3D Models* dialog box.

 - The contextual *3D Model Tools Format* tab displays.

4. Click the **More** button in the *3D Model Views* group [*3D Model Tools Format* tab] to display and select a 3D model view.

 - Alternatively, click the **rotation** handle in the middle of the 3D model and rotate the object on its center axis (Figure 4-79).

5. Use the options in the *Arrange* and *Size* groups [*3D Model Tools Format* tab] to position, wrap text, or resize the 3D model.

 - Alternatively, click the **Layout Options** button to display the *Layout Options* menu and select a text wrapping option. Or, use the resizing handles to resize the 3D model.
 - Click the **See more** link near the bottom of the *Layout Options* menu to open the *Layout* dialog box for additional position, text wrapping, and size options.
 - To reset a 3D model to its original view and/or position, click the **Reset 3D Model** button [*3D Model Tools Format* tab, *Adjust* group] and select **Reset 3D Model** (resets view) or **Reset 3D Model and Size** (resets view and size).

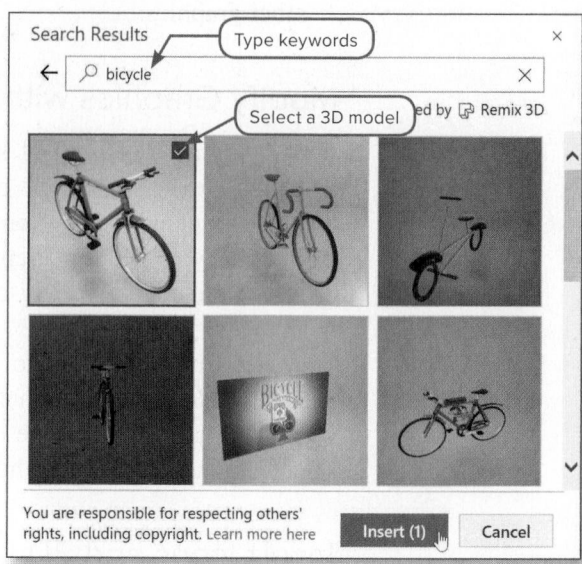

Figure 4-78 Search results in the *Online 3D Models* dialog box

Figure 4-79 3D model

▶ **ANOTHER WAY**

To insert a 3D model that is already saved as a file, click the **3D Models** button [*Insert* tab, *Illustrations* group] and select **From a File**.

Insert Online Video

Word also provides the ability to insert videos. Although, inserting videos is much more common when using Microsoft PowerPoint or developing web sites, you may have a document where a video clip would be appropriate and useful. An *online video* in a Word document is a graphic object that links to an online video and is played from within Word.

▶ HOW TO: Insert an Online Video

1. Position the insertion point at the location to insert a video.
2. Click the **Online Video** button [*Insert* tab, *Media* group] to open the *Insert Video* dialog box (Figure 4-80).
3. Type keywords in the **YouTube** text box.
 - Alternatively, if you have already copied a video embed code, paste the code (**Ctrl+V**) in the *From a Video Embed Code* text box and press **Enter**. The video displays in the document.
4. Select a video in the search results and click **Insert**. The video displays in the document (Figure 4-81) and the contextual *Picture Tools Format* tab displays.

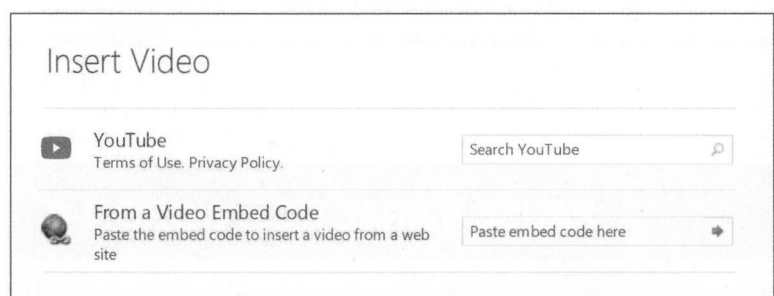

Figure 4-80 *Insert Video* dialog box

Figure 4-81 Video inserted into a document

5. Use the options on the *Picture Tools Format* tab to apply a style or border, position the video in the document, apply text wrapping, or resize the video.
 - Alternatively, click the **Layout Options** button to display the *Layout Options* menu and select a text wrapping option. Or, use the resizing handles to resize the video.
 - Click the **See more** link near the bottom of the *Layout Options* menu to open the *Layout* dialog box for additional position, text wrapping, and size options.
6. Click the **Play** button in the middle of the video to open the video in a new window.
 - Click the **Play** button again to begin the video.

Insert Symbols and Special Characters

Word also has a variety of symbols and other special characters to insert into a document (Figure 4-82). The *Symbols*, *Wingdings*, and *Webdings* font sets have an assortment of symbols and small graphics to insert into a document. Additional special characters are available, such as the em dash, en dash, and copyright symbols.

Figure 4-82 *Symbol* button on the *Insert* tab

▶ HOW TO: Insert a Symbol

1. Position the insertion point at the location to insert a symbol.
2. Click the **Symbol** button [*Insert* tab, *Symbols* group] to display a drop-down list of recently used symbols.

3. Select **More Symbols** (see Figure 4-82) to open the *Symbol* dialog box (Figure 4-83).

4. Click the **Font** drop-down list on the *Symbols* tab to select the font set.
 - Alternatively, click the **Special Character** tab to display the list of available special characters.

5. Select a symbol or special character to insert.
 - Each character has a numerical code for identification. The *Character code* area displays the code.

6. Click **Insert** to insert the symbol.

7. Click **Close** to close the dialog box.

Figure 4-83 *Symbol* dialog box

PAUSE & PRACTICE: WORD 4-4

For this Pause & Practice project, you finalize Emma's brochure by inserting a picture, shapes, and *Word-Art*. You format and arrange these graphic objects attractively in the document.

Files Needed: **[your initials] PP W4-3.docx**, **PHRElogo-04.png**, and **ForSale-04.png** *(Student data files are available in the Library of your SIMnet account.)*
Completed Project File Name: **[your initials] PP W4-4.docx**

1. Open the **[your initials] PP W4-3** document completed in *Pause & Practice 4-3*.

2. Save this document as [your initials] PP W4-4.

3. Insert the Placer Hills Real Estate logo at the bottom-right corner of the document.
 a. Position the insertion point below the table in the third column.
 b. Click the **Pictures** button [*Insert* tab, *Illustrations* group]. The *Insert Picture* dialog box opens.
 c. Select the **PHRElogo-04** file from the student data files and click **Insert**. Word may automatically insert alt text. You will edit alt text later in this project.

Figure 4-84 Adjust size of graphic

4. Arrange and format the logo.
 a. Select the logo (if necessary), click the **Wrap Text** button [*Picture Tools Format* tab, *Arrange* group], and choose **In Front of Text**.
 b. Type 1.2 in the *Height* box [*Size* group] and press **Enter** (Figure 4-84). The width automatically adjusts to keep the picture proportional.
 c. Click the middle of the picture and drag the graphic near the bottom-right corner of the document.
 d. Click the **Picture Border** button [*Picture Styles* group] and select the **seventh option** in the **first row** of the *Theme Colors* (**Olive Green, Accent 3**) (Figure 4-85).

Figure 4-85 Select *Picture Border* color

e. Click the **Picture Border** again, click **Weight**, and select **1½ pt**.

f. Click the **Position** button [*Arrange* group] and select **More Layout Options**. The *Layout* dialog box opens with the *Position* tab displayed (Figure 4-86).

g. Select the **Absolute position** radio button in the *Horizontal* area, type 8.6, click the **to the right of** drop-down list, and select **Page**.

h. Select the **Absolute position** radio button in the *Vertical* area, type 7, click the **below** drop-down list, and select **Page**.

i. Click **OK** to close the dialog box.

Figure 4-86 Customize position of the logo

5. Add a picture near the bottom of the first column.

a. Place the insertion point at the end of the fourth numbered item in the first column.

b. Click the **Pictures** button [*Insert* tab, *Illustrations* group]. The *Insert Picture* dialog box opens.

c. Select the ***ForSale-04*** picture from the student data files and click **Insert**.

d. Change the *Height* [*Picture Tools Format* tab, *Size* group] to **1.2"** and press **Enter**.

e. Right-click the picture, choose **Wrap Text**, and select **Square**.

f. Click the middle of the picture and drag it to the right of the fourth numbered item in the first column (Figure 4-87).

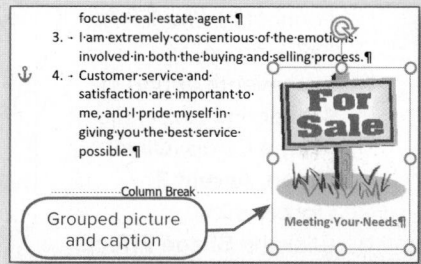

Figure 4-87 Picture and caption grouped

6. Insert a caption for the picture.

a. Right-click the picture and choose **Insert Caption** to open the *Caption* dialog box.

b. Click **OK** to insert a caption and close the *Caption* dialog box. Word inserts the default caption that serves as placeholder text.

c. Delete the placeholder text in the caption text box and type Meeting Your Needs as the caption. If the caption covers the bottom of the graphic, select the border of the caption and use the down keyboard arrow to move it down slightly.

d. Press **Ctrl+E** or click the **Center** button [*Home* tab, *Paragraph* group] to center the text in the caption.

e. With the caption still selected, press the **Ctrl** key and click the picture to select it also. Both the picture and the caption should be selected.

f. Click the **Group** button [*Picture Tools Format* tab, *Arrange* group] and choose **Group**. The two objects are grouped into one object (see Figure 4-87).

7. Change the paragraph spacing on the two quotes in the second column.

a. Place your insertion point in the first quoted paragraph in the second column (beginning with "It was a pleasure . . .").

b. Change the *After* paragraph spacing to **12 pt**.

c. Place your insertion point in the second quoted paragraph in the second column (beginning with "Emma is conscientious . . .").

d. Change the *After* paragraph spacing to **12 pt**.

8. Add and format a shape to the quoted text.
 a. Click the **Shapes** button [*Insert* tab, *Illustration* group] and select the **first option** in the **first row** in the *Callouts* area (**Speech Bubble: Rectangle**) (Figure 4-88). Your pointer becomes a drawing crosshair (dark plus sign).
 b. Place the drawing crosshair near the upper left of the first quote in the second column and click and drag to the lower right to draw the shape over the quoted text (Figure 4-89).
 c. Select the shape (if necessary), click the **Send Backward** drop-down arrow [*Drawing Tools Format* tab, *Arrange* group], and select **Send Behind Text** (Figure 4-90). The text displays on top of the shape.
 d. Click the *Shape Styles* **More** button [*Drawing Tools Format* tab, *Shape Styles* group] to display the gallery of shape styles.
 e. Select the **fourth option** in the **first row** of the *Theme Styles* (**Colored Outline – Olive Green, Accent 3**) (Figure 4-91).
 f. Click the **Shape Fill** button [*Drawing Tools Format* tab, *Shape Styles* group] and select the **seventh option** in the **second row** of the *Theme Colors* (**Olive Green, Accent 3, Lighter 80%**).
 g. Click the **Shape Effects** button [*Drawing Tools Format* tab, *Shape Styles* group], select **Shadow**, and choose the first option in the first row of the *Outer* category (**Offset: Bottom Right**) (Figure 4-92).
 h. Change the *Shape Height* to **1"** and the *Shape Width* to **3.1"** [*Drawing Tools Format* tab, *Size* group].
 i. Drag the shape to position it evenly behind the text. You can also use the keyboard arrow keys to position a selected shape.

9. Replicate and align the callout shape.
 a. Select the shape (if necessary), press **Ctrl+C** to copy it, and **Ctrl+V** to paste the copy of the shape into the document.
 b. Drag the new shape over the second quote.
 c. Change the *Shape Height* to **1.4"** [*Drawing Tools Format* tab, *Size* group].
 d. Drag the shape to position it evenly behind the text.
 e. Select the second shape (if necessary), press the **Shift** key, and click the right edge of the first shape to select both shapes (Figure 4-93).

Figure 4-88 Select shape

Figure 4-89 Draw rectangular shape

Figure 4-90 *Send Behind Text*

Figure 4-91 Apply a shape style

Figure 4-92 Select a shape *Shadow* option

Figure 4-93 Shapes positioned behind text

W4-256

f. Click the **Align** button [*Drawing Tools Format* tab, *Arrange* group] and select **Align Center**.

g. Use the up or down arrow keys to adjust the vertical position of the selected shape if necessary.

10. Add *WordArt* to the brochure and customize it.

a. Select the text "**Emma Cavalli**" including the paragraph mark at the top of the first column (turn on **Show/Hide** if necessary).

b. Click the **WordArt** button [*Insert* tab, *Text* group].

c. Select the **first option** in the **second row** to convert the selected text to *WordArt* (Figure 4-94).

d. Select the *WordArt* (if necessary) and change the *Shape Height* to **0.8"** and the *Shape Width* to **3.6"** [*Drawing Tools Format* tab, *Size* group]. Document content is temporarily adjusted and will be corrected in the following steps.

Figure 4-94 Select *WordArt* style

e. Click the **Text Effects** button [*Drawing Tools Format* tab, *WordArt Styles* group], click **Reflection**, and select the **first option** in the **first row** of the *Reflection Variations* category (**Tight Reflection: Touching**) (Figure 4-95).

f. Click the **Position** button [*Drawing Tools Format* tab, *Arrange* group] and select **More Layout Options**. The *Layout* dialog box opens.

g. Change the **Absolute position** in the *Horizontal* area to **0.2"** *to the right of* **Page**.

h. Change the **Absolute position** in the *Vertical* area to **0.2"** *below* **Page**.

i. Click **OK** to close the *Layout* dialog box.

Figure 4-95 Apply a *Reflection* text effect

11. Insert, resize, and position an icon.

a. Place the insertion point at the beginning of the second column.

b. Click the **Icons** button [*Insert* tab, *Illustrations* group] to open the *Insert Icons* dialog box.

c. Click the **Buildings** category on the left, select the **fourth option** in the **first row**, and click **Insert** (Figure 4-96). You may have to scroll down the categories on the left to locate the *Buildings* category.

d. Change the *Height* [*Graphic Tools Format* tab, *Size* group] to **0.8"**. The width adjusts automatically.

e. Click the **Wrap Text** button [*Graphic Tools Format* tab, *Arrange* group] and select **In Front of Text**.

f. Click the **Position** button [*Graphic Tools Format* tab, *Arrange* group] and select **More Layout Options**. The *Layout* dialog box opens.

g. Change the **Absolute position** in the *Horizontal* area to **3.7"** *to the right of* **Page**.

h. Change the **Absolute position** in the *Vertical* area to **0.2"** *below* **Page**.

i. Click **OK** to close the *Layout* dialog box.

Figure 4-96 *Insert Icons* dialog box

12. Edit the alt text on all three images in the document.
 a. Select the home icon near the top of the document and click the **Alt Text** button [*Graphic Tools Format* tab, *Accessibility* group]. The *Alt Text* pane opens.
 b. Type Icon of a home in the text box in the *Alt Text* pane.
 c. Select the "**For Sale**" graphic and type For Sale sign in the text box in the *Alt Text* pane.
 d. Select the *PHRE logo*, delete existing alt text if necessary, type PHRE logo in the text box, and close the *Alt Text* pane.

13. Save and close the document (Figure 4-97).

Emma Cavalli

REALTOR CONSULTANT

Phone	916.450.3334
Email	ecavalli@phre.com
Web	www.phre.com/ecavalli

MISSION STATEMENT

I am dedicated to listening to your needs as a buyer or seller and providing you with prompt and excellent service to exceed your expectations.

BUSINESS EXPERIENCE

I have had the pleasure of working with buyers, sellers, and investors for over 15 years. Each transaction is new and exciting.

WHY I AM A REAL ESTATE AGENT

1. I enjoy working with people and negotiating on their behalf.
2. Communication, organization, and availability are skills I possess that make me a client-focused real estate agent.
3. I am extremely conscientious of the emotions involved in both the buying and selling process.
4. Customer service and satisfaction are important to me, and I pride myself in giving you the best service possible.

Meeting Your Needs

WHAT CLIENTS ARE SAYING

Here are what others have said about me:

"It was a pleasure working with Emma Cavalli. She was very responsive and listened to all our needs. Her marketing plan sold our home in just 3 days!"

-Rod & Lilia Ellisor, Rocklin

"Emma is conscientious, personable, and professional. Her dedication and commitment to meeting our needs has been apparent from the beginning. Emma can be counted on to do what she says. We would not hesitate to refer Emma to our friends and family."

-Elia & Jazmin Solares, Roseville

PROFESSIONAL CREDENTIALS

- Licensed California Real Estate Salesperson
- Member of National Association of Realtors
- Member California Association of Realtors
- Member of Realtor.com
- Distinguished Realtor Award from peers
- Community Service Board position for the Roseville Unified School District
- Former Parent/Teacher Club President for Winchester Elementary School

EDUCATION & TRAINING

University of Nevada, Reno—Business Administration B.A.

Real Estate Code of Ethics

Certified Contract Consultant

Certified Maximum Productivity Consultant

FAMILY & HOBBIES

I have been a Roseville community member since 2003. I have been married since 2001 and have three children. I love to read, do crafts, travel, and watch my children play sports. I am also very involved in my church and charity work.

THE PLACER HILLS BELIEF SYSTEM	
COMMITMENT	To the needs of the client
COMMUNICATION	Seek first to listen
CREATIVITY	Ideas before results
CUSTOMERS	Always come first
INTEGRITY	Doing the right thing first
SUCCESS	Results with integrity
TEAMWORK	Work together for success
TRUST	Begins with communication
WIN-WIN	Is always the goal

PHRE
Placer Hills
Real Estate
7100 Madrone Road | Roseville, CA 95722
www.phre.com | 916.450.3300

Figure 4-97 PP W4-4 completed

Chapter Summary

4.1 Improve the design and readability of a document by using tables to present and arrange information (p. W4-219).

- *Tables* organize information in column and row format. A *column* is a vertical grouping of cells, and a *row* is a horizontal grouping of cells.
- A *cell* is the intersection of a column and row.
- Press **Tab** to move forward to the next cell and **Shift+Tab** to move to the previous cell.
- *Table Tools Layout* and *Table Tools Design* tabs provide many table formatting features.
- Copy or move columns or rows in a table.
- Add or delete columns and rows in tables.
- When working with tables, select individual cells, a range of cells, rows, columns, or an entire table.
- Merge a group of cells to create one cell. Cells can also be split into multiple cells.

4.2 Modify a table by changing the column and row size, aligning text, using the *Table Properties* dialog box, sorting data, and using *AutoFit* (p. W4-223).

- Resize columns and rows in a table.
- Use the *AutoFit* feature to automatically resize the table to fit the contents of the table, the window, or a fixed width.
- Align text in a cell both horizontally and vertically.
- *Cell margins* control the amount of spacing around the text within a cell.
- The *Table Properties* dialog box provides size and alignment options for cells, rows, columns, or an entire table.
- Sort table information in ascending or descending order.

4.3 Enhance the appearance and function of a table by applying borders and shading, using table styles, inserting formulas, and converting text into a table (p. W4-229).

- Apply borders and shading to parts of a table or to the entire table.
- *Table Styles* are collections of borders, shading, and formatting applied to a table. Word provides a gallery of table styles.
- Apply *Table Style Options* to a header row, total row, banded rows, first column, last column, or banded columns.

- *Formulas* in a table perform mathematical calculations.
- Convert existing text into a table or convert an existing table to text.

4.4 Modify the layout and design of a document using columns to present information (p. W4-236).

- Arrange text in a document in columns.
- Choose from preset column settings or customize column settings and space between columns using the *Columns dialog box*.
- *Column breaks* control column endings.
- Balance columns with column breaks or a *continuous section break*.

4.5 Improve a document by adding, modifying, and arranging pictures (p. W4-240).

- Pictures and graphics add visual appeal to a document. Insert a variety of graphic file types.
- *Alt text* is used by screen readers to provide an audio description of a graphic to assist individuals who are visually impaired.
- Resize a graphic and position it at a specific location in a document.
- *Text wrapping* controls how text wraps around graphics.
- The *Layout* dialog box includes options to change the position, text wrapping, and size of graphic objects.
- Add a *caption* to a graphic object.
- *Group* graphic objects together to create one graphic object, for easier resizing and positioning.

4.6 Enrich a document by adding and customizing graphic objects such as shapes, *SmartArt*, *WordArt*, symbols, icons, 3D models, and online video (p. W4-248).

- Insert shapes using the *Shapes* gallery. Customize shapes by changing size, position, fill color, outline color and width, and shape effects.
- *SmartArt* graphically presents information in a document.
- *WordArt* is special text formatting.
- Word provides a variety of formatting options and styles for *SmartArt*, *WordArt*, and other graphic objects.

- Use the *Symbols* dialog box to insert a variety of symbols and special characters.
- Use **icons** and **3D models** to visually enhance a document.
- An **online video** is a graphic object that links to an online video and can be played from within Word.

Check for Understanding

The SIMbook for this text (within your SIMnet account) provides the following resources for concept review:

- Multiple-choice questions
- Short answer questions
- Matching exercises

Guided Project 4-1

For this project, you modify the values statement document for Sierra Pacific Community College District to arrange text in columns, insert the company logo, and insert shapes.
[Student Learning Outcomes 4.4, 4.5, 4.6]

Files Needed: *ValuesStatement-04.docx* and *SPCCDlogo-04.png* (Student data files are available in the Library of your SIMnet account.)
Completed Project File Name: *[your initials] Word 4-1.docx*

Skills Covered in This Project

- Change page orientation.
- Change margins.
- Apply columns to text.
- Modify column settings.
- Insert a column break.

- Insert a picture.
- Change picture color.
- Modify picture size and position.
- Insert a shape.
- Modify shape size and position.
- Modify shape fill and outline.
- Edit alt text.

1. Open the **ValuesStatement-04** document from your student data files.

2. Save this document as [your initials] Word 4–1.

3. Change the orientation and margins of the document.
 a. Change the orientation of the document to **Landscape**.
 b. Change the top and bottom margins to **0.5"**.
 c. Change the left and right margins to **0.75"**.

4. Apply column formatting to the text in the body of the document.
 a. Place the insertion point in front of the first paragraph heading ("Access").
 b. Click the **Columns** button [*Layout* tab, *Page Setup* group] and select **More Columns**. The *Columns* dialog box opens (Figure 4-98).
 c. Select **Three** in the *Presets* area.
 d. Change the *Spacing* to **0.4"** in the *Width and spacing* area.
 e. Click the **Apply to** drop-down list and select **This point forward**.
 f. Click **OK** to close the *Columns* dialog box.

Figure 4-98 *Columns* dialog box

5. Insert a column break to balance the columns on the page.
 a. Place the insertion point in front of the "Student Learning Outcomes" paragraph heading in the first column.
 b. Click the **Breaks** button [*Layout* tab, *Page Setup* group] and select **Column**.

6. Insert, resize, and position the company logo on the bottom left of the document.
 a. Place the insertion point at the end of the last paragraph in the first column.
 b. Click the **Pictures** button [*Insert* tab, *Illustrations* group].
 c. Select the ***SPCCDlogo-04*** file from the student data files and click **Insert**.
 d. Click the **Wrap Text** button [*Picture Tools Format* tab, *Arrange* group] and select **Behind Text**.
 e. Right-click the logo and choose **Size and Position**. The *Layout* dialog box opens (Figure 4-99).
 f. Change the *Height* to **120%** in the *Scale* area on the *Size* tab and press **Tab**. The width automatically adjusts to keep the logo proportional.
 g. Click the **Position** tab.
 h. Change the **Absolute position** in the *Horizontal* area to **0.3"** *to the right of* **Page**.
 i. Change the **Absolute position** in the *Vertical* area to **7.2"** *below* **Page**.
 j. Click **OK** to close the *Layout* dialog box.

Figure 4-99 Resize logo as a percentage of its original size

7. Change the color of the logo.
 a. Select the logo (if necessary) and click the **Color** button [*Picture Tools Format* tab, *Adjust* group].
 b. Select the **first option** in the *Color Saturation* area (**Saturation: 0%**) (Figure 4-100).

8. Add a shape around the title, resize the shape, and modify the outline and fill.
 a. Click the **Shapes** button [*Insert* tab, *Illustrations* group] and select the **third option** in the *Rectangles* area (**Rectangle: Single Corner Snipped**). Your pointer becomes a crosshair (dark plus sign) (Figure 4-101).
 b. Click and drag the crosshair over the title and then release the pointer (Figure 4-102).
 c. Click the **Shape Fill** button [*Drawing Tools Format* tab, *Shape Styles* group] and select the **first color** in the **third row** of the *Theme Colors* (**White, Background 1, Darker 15%**).
 d. Click the **Shape Outline** button [*Drawing Tools Format* tab, *Shape Styles* group] and select the **first color** in the **last row** of the *Theme Colors* (**White, Background 1, Darker 50%**).
 e. Click the **Shape Outline** button again, select **Weight**, and select **1½ pt**.
 f. Click the **Send Backward** drop-down arrow [*Drawing Tools Format* tab, *Arrange* group] and select **Send Behind Text** from the drop-down list.
 g. Change the *Shape Height* [*Drawing Tools Format* tab, *Size* group] to **0.4"** and the *Shape Width* to **6.3"**.

Figure 4-100 Change *Color Saturation*

Figure 4-101 Select shape

SIERRA·PACIFIC·COMMUNITY·COLLEGE·DISTRICT·VALUES¶

Figure 4-102 Draw shape around the title

h. Click the **Align** button [*Drawing Tools Format* tab, *Arrange* group] and select **Align Center**.

i. Use the up and down keyboard arrow keys to vertically center the shape behind the title.

9. Edit the alt text on the shape and graphic in the document.

a. Select the border of the shape at the top of the document and click **Alt Text** button [*Drawing Tools Format* tab, *Accessibility* group]. The *Alt Text* pane opens.

b. Type Shape around the title in the text box in the *Alt Text* pane.

c. Select the *Sierra Pacific logo*, type Sierra Pacific logo in the text box in the *Alt Text* pane, and close the *Alt Text* pane.

10. Save and close the document (Figure 4-103).

SIERRA PACIFIC COMMUNITY COLLEGE DISTRICT VALUES

ACCESS

Students are the reason we exist, and their education is our primary purpose. We recognize that residents of the region are entitled to an opportunity to attend and to be successful in college.

BENEFITS OF EDUCATION

Individuals and society benefit from citizens who achieve the full extent of their personal, intellectual, and physical ability; engage in critical and creative thinking; exhibit responsible citizenship; succeed in a competitive global work environment; and participate in lifelong learning.

EXCELLENCE

Excellence in instruction and student services is essential to develop the full potential of each student.

LEADERSHIP

Responsible leadership and service among all Sierra Pacific Community College District faculty, staff, and students are nurtured and encouraged so the college will be a leader for positive change, growth, and transformation in student-oriented educational practices.

STUDENT LEARNING OUTCOMES

Identification and assessment of student learning outcomes promotes and improves student success and the effective use of SPCCD resources to create innovative and flexible learning opportunities.

DIVERSITY

We are a community enriched by the experience of students, faculty, staff, and administrators from a variety of cultures, ethnic and economic backgrounds, age is and abilities. We are committed to providing and nurturing a safe environment for the free exchanges of ideas.

COMMUNITY DEVELOPMENT

The curricular and co-curricular programs and services of the college benefit the region served through enhanced intellectual and physical growth, economic development, and exposure to the arts, sciences, and humanities.

HUMAN RESOURCES

Faculty and staff members are our most important resources and are entitled to a supportive, collegial work environment that recognizes excellence, provides opportunities for professional development, service and leadership, and encourages meaningful involvement in an interest-based decision-making process.

COMMUNICATION

Achievement of the Sierra Pacific Community College District mission and vision requires an effective system of communication with internal and external constituencies that is based on honesty, trust, civility, and mutual respect.

INNOVATION AND RISK TAKING

Addressing challenges and change requires creativity, assessment, flexibility, and responsible risk-taking to achieve our vision, mission and goals.

FISCAL RESPONSIBILITY

It is necessary to maintain a fiscally sound, efficient, and effective operation that achieves our mission within the resources available.

EVALUATION

Efficient and effective accomplishment of the ARC mission, vision, and student learning outcomes requires regular and ongoing data-based evaluation.

SIERRA PACIFIC
COMMUNITY COLLEGE DISTRICT
7300 COLLEGE AVE
SACRAMENTO, CA 92387
209.658.4466
WWW.SPCCD.EDU

Figure 4-103 Word 4-1 completed

Guided Project 4-2

For this project, you modify a document about maximum and target heart rate for the American River Cycling Club. You arrange text in a table and insert and modify *SmartArt* and a picture.
[Student Learning Outcomes 4.1, 4.2, 4.3, 4.5, 4.6]

File Needed: ***MaximumHeartRate-04.docx*** and ***HeartRate-04.png*** *(Student data files are available in the Library of your SIMnet account.)*
Completed Project File Name: *[your initials] **Word 4-2.docx***

Skills Covered in This Project

- Insert and resize *WordArt*.
- Position and modify *WordArt*.
- Convert text to a table.
- Apply a table style.
- Modify table and text alignment.

- Change cell margins in a table.
- Insert and add text to a *SmartArt* graphic.
- Resize, position, and format *SmartArt*.
- Insert, resize, and position a picture.
- Insert a caption.
- Align and group graphic objects.
- Edit alt text.

1. Open the ***MaximumHeartRate-04*** document from your student data files.

2. Save this document as [your initials] Word 4–2.

3. Insert *WordArt* as the title of the document and modify the *WordArt* object.
 a. Select the title of the document, "**American River Cycling Club**" (including the paragraph mark).
 b. Click the **WordArt** button [*Insert* tab, *Text* group].
 c. Select the **third option** in the **first row** from the *WordArt* gallery (Figure 4-104).
 d. Change the *Shape Width* [*Drawing Tools Format* tab, *Size* group] to **6.5"**.
 e. Click the **Position** button [*Drawing Tools Format* tab, *Arrange* group] and select **More Layout Options**. The *Layout* dialog box opens (Figure 4-105).
 f. Change **Alignment** in the *Horizontal* area to **Centered** *relative to* **Margin**.
 g. Change **Absolute position** in the *Vertical* area to **0.2"** *below* **Page**.
 h. Click **OK** to close the *Layout* dialog box.
 i. Click the **Text Effects** button [*Drawing Tools Format* tab, *WordArt Styles* group], select **Reflection**, and select the **first option** in the **first row** of the *Reflection Variations* area (**Tight Reflection: Touching**) (Figure 4-106).

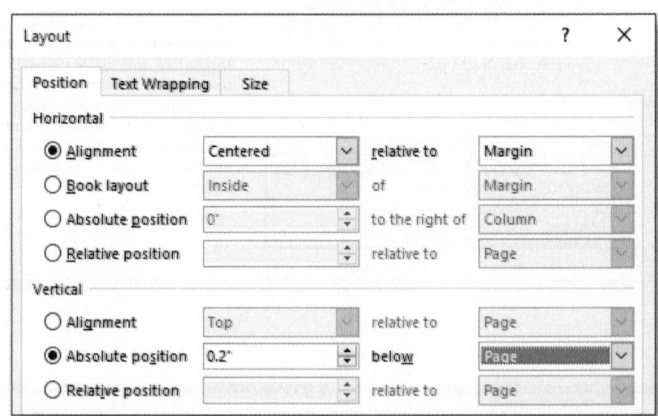

Figure 4-104 Insert *WordArt*

Figure 4-105 Adjust position of *WordArt*

4. Convert text into a table and format the table.
 a. Select all the tabbed text at the bottom of the document (including the last paragraph mark).
 b. Click the **Table** button [*Insert* tab, *Tables* group] and select **Convert Text to Table**. The *Convert Text to Table* dialog box opens.
 c. Click the **AutoFit to contents** radio button in the *AutoFit behavior* area.
 d. Click **OK** to close the dialog box.
 e. Click the **Table Tools Design** tab.
 f. Check the **Header Row** and **Banded Rows** boxes [*Table Style Options* group] (if necessary) and deselect the other check boxes.
 g. Click the **More** button in the *Table Styles* group to display the *Table Styles* gallery.
 h. Select **Grid Table 4 – Accent 2** in the *Grid Tables* section (Figure 4-107).
 i. Place the insertion point before "Zone" in the second column in the first row, press **Backspace** to delete the space between words, and press **Enter**.
 j. Place the insertion point before "Heart" in the third column in the first row, press **Backspace** to delete the space between words, and press **Enter**.

Figure 4-106 Apply *Reflection* option

Figure 4-107 *Table Styles* gallery

5. Adjust the size and alignment of the table.
 a. Use the table selector handle to select the entire table.
 b. Click the **Align Center** button [*Table Tool Layout* tab, *Alignment* group] (Figure 4-108). All text in the table is centered vertically and horizontally.
 c. Click the **Properties** button [*Table Tools Layout* tab, *Table* group].
 d. Click the **Table** tab, select **Center** in the *Alignment* area, and click **OK** to close the dialog box. The entire table is centered horizontally on the page.
 e. Click the **Cell Margins** button [*Table Tools Layout* tab, *Alignment* group]. The *Table Options* dialog box opens.
 f. Change the *Top* and *Bottom* cell margins to **0.03"** and the *Left* and *Right* cell margins to **0.1"**.
 g. Click **OK** to close the *Table Options* dialog box.

Figure 4-108 *Align Center* the text in the table

6. Insert and modify a *SmartArt* graphic.
 a. Place the insertion point at the end of the second body paragraph, "(*Example*: . . .)," in the first section.
 b. Click the **SmartArt** button [*Insert* tab, *Illustrations* group]. The *Choose a SmartArt Graphic* dialog box opens (Figure 4-109).

Figure 4-109 *Choose a SmartArt Graphic* dialog box

c. Click **Process** in the list of *SmartArt* types.

d. Select **Continuous Block Process** and click **OK** to insert the *SmartArt*. If the *Text* pane displays on the left of the *SmartArt* graphic, click the **X** in the upper-right corner to close it.

e. Click the placeholder text (*[Text]*) in the first rectangle graphic, type 220, **space** once, and type - (hyphen or minus).

f. Click the next placeholder text, type Your Age, **space** once, and type =.

g. Click the last placeholder text, type Predicted Maximum Heart Rate.

7. Format, resize, and position the *SmartArt*.

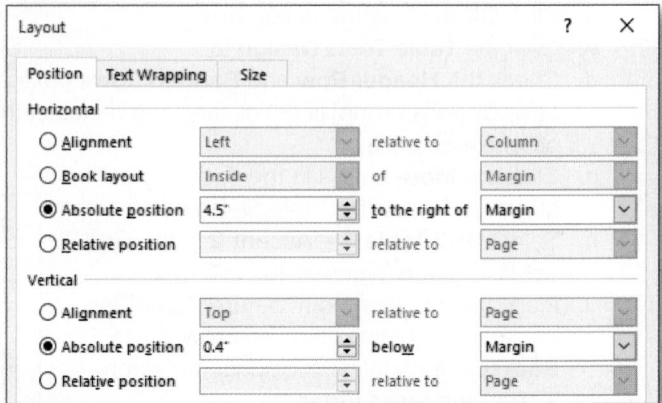

Figure 4-110 Adjust *SmartArt* position

a. Click the outside frame of the *SmartArt* graphic to select the entire *SmartArt* graphic. *Note*: Select the entire *SmartArt* and not an object within the graphic.

b. Change the *Shape Height* to **1.5"** and the *Shape Width* to **2.6"** in the *Size* group [*SmartArt Tools Format* tab].

c. Click the **Wrap Text** button [*SmartArt Tools Format* tab, *Arrange* group] and select **Square**.

d. Click the **Position** button [*SmartArt Tools Format* tab, *Arrange* group] and select **More Layout Options**. The *Layout* dialog box opens (Figure 4-110).

e. Change the **Absolute position** in the *Horizontal* area to **4.5"** *to the right of* **Margin**.

f. Change **Absolute position** in the *Vertical* area to **0.4"** *below* **Margin**.

g. Click **OK** to close the *Layout* dialog box.

h. Select the *SmartArt* (if necessary), select **Intense Effect** from the *SmartArt Styles* gallery [*SmartArt Tools Design* tab, *SmartArt Styles* group] (Figure 4-111).

Figure 4-111 Apply *SmartArt* style

i. Click the edge of the first text box ("220 -") to select it and press **Ctrl+B** to apply bold format. Repeat this format on the other two text boxes.

j. Select the last text box (if it is not already selected) and click the **SmartArt Tools Format** tab.

k. Click the **Shape Fill** button and select **sixth color** in the **first row** of the *Theme Colors* (**Red, Accent 2**) as the fill color (Figure 4-112).

Figure 4-112 Change *Shape Fill* color

8. Insert a picture and resize and position the graphic.

a. Place the insertion point at the end of the second section heading ("Target Heart Rate").

b. Click the **Pictures** button [*Insert* tab, *Illustrations* group] to open the *Insert Picture* dialog box.

 c. Locate the **HeartRate-04** picture from your student data files and click **Insert**.

 d. Change the *Height* [*Picture Tools Format* tab, *Size* group] to **1"** (the width adjusts automatically).

 e. Click the **Wrap Text** button [*Picture Tools Format* tab, *Arrange* group] and select **Tight**.

 f. Click the **Align** button [*Picture Tools Format* tab, *Arrange* group] and select **Align Right**.

9. Format the picture and insert a caption.

 a. Select the picture (if necessary), click the **More** button in the *Pictures Styles* group [*Picture Tools Format* tab] to display the gallery of styles.

 b. Select the **Bevel Rectangle** picture style (Figure 4-113).

 c. Right-click the picture and select **Insert Caption** from the context menu. The *Insert Caption* dialog box opens.

 d. Click **OK** to insert the caption.

 e. Select and delete the caption placeholder text, and type Know your target heart rate as the caption text.

Figure 4-113 Apply *Picture Style*

 f. Select the caption text, click the **Text Fill** button [*Drawing Tools Format* tab, *WordArt Styles* group], and select the **sixth color** in the **first row** of the *Theme Colors* (**Red, Accent 2**) as the text color.

 g. Change the caption *Height* to **0.2"** and the *Width* to **1.5"** in the *Size* group [*Drawing Tools Format* tab].

 h. Press the **Ctrl** key and click the picture. Both the caption and picture should be selected.

 i. Click the **Align** button [*Drawing Tools Format* tab, *Arrange* group] and select **Align Center**.

 j. Click the **Group** button [*Arrange* group] and select **Group**. The picture and caption are grouped into one object.

10. Edit the alt text on the graphics in the document.

 a. Select the border of the *SmartArt* to select the entire *SmartArt* graphic.

 b. Right-click the *SmartArt* graphic and select **Edit Alt Text** from the context menu. The *Alt Text* pane opens.

 c. Type Graphic of predicted maximum heart rate in the text box in the *Alt Text* pane.

 d. Select the picture of a heart, type Picture of a heart in the text box in the *Alt Text* pane, and close the *Alt Text* pane.

11. Save and close the document (Figure 4-114).

American River Cycling Club

WHAT IS MAXIMUM HEART RATE?

The maximum heart rate is the highest your pulse rate can get. To calculate your **predicted maximum heart rate**, use this formula:

(Example: a 40-year-old's predicted maximum heart rate is 180.)

Your actual maximum heart rate can be determined by a graded exercise test. Please note that some medicines and medical conditions might affect your maximum heart rate. If you are taking medicines or have a medical condition (such as heart disease, high blood pressure, or diabetes), always ask your doctor if your maximum heart rate/target heart rate will be affected.

TARGET HEART RATE

You gain the most benefits and decrease the risk of injury when you exercise in your target heart rate zone. Usually this is when your exercise heart rate (pulse) is 60 percent to 80 percent of your maximum heart rate. Do not exercise above 85 percent of your maximum heart rate. This increases both cardiovascular and orthopedic risk and does not add any extra benefit.

Know your target heart rate

When beginning an exercise program, you might need to gradually build up to a level that is within your target heart rate zone, especially if you have not exercised regularly before. If the exercise feels too hard, slow down. You will reduce your risk of injury and enjoy the exercise more if you don't try to over-do it.

To find out if you are exercising in your target zone (between 60 percent and 80 percent of your maximum heart rate), use your heart rate monitor to track your heart rate. If your pulse is below your target zone (see the chart below), increase your rate of exercise. If your pulse is above your target zone, decrease your rate of exercise.

Age	Target Heart Rate (HR) Zone (60-85%)	Predicted Maximum Heart Rate
20	120-170	200
25	117-166	195
30	114-162	190
35	111-157	185
40	108-153	180
45	105-149	175
50	102-145	170
55	99-140	165
60	96-136	160
65	93-132	155
70	90-128	150

Figure 4-114 Word 4-2 completed

Guided Project 4-3

For this project, you format a buyer escrow checklist for Placer Hills Real Estate. You convert text to a table, format the table, and insert a picture.
[**Student Learning Outcomes 4.1, 4.2, 4.3, 4.5, 4.6**]

Files Needed: ***BuyerEscrowChecklist-04.docx***, ***Check-04.png***, and ***PHRElogo-04.png*** *(Student data files are available in the* Library *of your SIMnet account.)*
Completed Project File Name: *[your initials] **Word 4-3.docx***

Skills Covered in This Project

- Convert text to a table.
- Add columns to a table.
- Apply bullets and modify alignment.
- *AutoFit* a table.
- Apply table styles and borders.
- Modify row width and column height.
- Center text vertically in a table.
- Insert, resize, and position a picture.
- Change picture color.
- Use absolute position and text wrapping.
- Apply border and effects to a picture.
- Edit alt text.

1. Open the ***BuyerEscrowChecklist-04*** document from your student data files.

2. Save this document as [your initials] Word 4-3.

3. Convert text to a table.
 a. Select the text beginning with "**Task**" through "**Verify Preliminary Report with Lender**" (including the last paragraph mark).
 b. Click the **Table** button [*Insert* tab, *Tables* group].
 c. Click the **Convert Text to Table** button. The *Convert Text to Table* dialog box opens.
 d. Click **OK** to accept the default settings. The text converts to a table with 1 column and 14 rows.

4. Add columns and column headings to the table.
 a. Select the entire table (if necessary), click the **Table Tools Layout** tab.
 b. Click the **Insert Right** button [*Rows & Columns* group] to insert a blank column to the right of the existing column.
 c. Click the **Insert Right** button two more times to insert two more columns. Your table should now have four columns.
 d. Type the following column headings in the first row:
 Column 2: Date Completed
 Column 3: Initials
 Column 4: Notes

5. Add bullets to selected text.
 a. Select all of the text in the first column below "Task."
 b. Apply an **open square bullet** to these items (*Wingdings*, Character code 111).
 c. Click the **Decrease Indent** button once so the first line indent is 0" and the hanging indent is 0.25".

6. Apply table style and apply formatting.
 a. Place your insertion point in the first cell in the first column.
 b. Click the **AutoFit** button [*Table Tools Layout* tab, *Cell Size* group] and select **AutoFit Contents**.
 c. Click the **Table Tools Design** tab.
 d. Check the **Header Row** and **Banded Rows** boxes in the *Table Style Options* group. The other options should be unchecked.
 e. Click the **More** button in the *Table Styles* group to open the *Table Styles* gallery.
 f. Select **Grid Table 5 Dark** style (Figure 4-115).
 g. Select the column headings (first row of the table).
 h. **Bold** and **center** the column headings. You might have to click the **Bold** button more than once to bold all column headings.

Figure 4-115 Apply table style

7. Modify cell size and alignment.
 a. Use the table selector handle to select the entire table or use the **Select** button [*Table Tools Layout* tab, *Table* group] and click **Select Table**.
 b. Change the *Height* [*Table Tools Layout* tab, *Cell Size* group] to **0.35"**. The row height changes on the entire table.

c. Click the **Properties** button [*Table Tools Layout* tab, *Table* group]. The *Table Properties* dialog box opens.

d. Click the **Cell** tab, select **Center** in the *Vertical alignment* area, and click **OK** to close the *Table Properties* dialog box.

e. Place your insertion point in the fourth column and change the *Width* [*Table Tools Layout* tab, *Cell Size* group] to **1.5"**.

8. Insert a picture, customize it, and position it in the document.

a. Place your insertion point at the end of the "Buyer(s):" line after the solid underline tab leader.

b. Click the **Pictures** button [*Insert* tab, *Illustrations* group]. The *Insert Pictures* dialog box opens.

c. Locate the **Check-04** file from your student data files and click **Insert**.

d. Change the *Height* to **1.5"** [*Picture Tools Format* tab, *Size* group] (the width adjusts automatically).

e. Click the **Wrap Text** button [*Picture Tools Format* tab, *Arrange* group] and select **Tight**.

f. Click the **Color** button [*Picture Tools Format* tab, *Adjust* group] and select the **third option** in the **second row** in the *Recolor* area (**Olive Green, Accent color 2 Dark**) (Figure 4-116).

Figure 4-116 Change picture color

g. Click the **Position** button [*Picture Tools Format* tab, *Arrange* group] and select **More Layout Options** to open the *Layout* dialog box (Figure 4-117).

h. Change the **Absolute position** in the *Horizontal* area to **5.5"** *to the right of* **Margin**.

i. Change the **Absolute position** in the *Vertical* area to **0.7"** *below* **Margin**.

j. Click **OK** to close the *Layout* dialog box.

9. Insert a picture, position it in the document, and customize it.

Figure 4-117 Position picture

a. Place your insertion point at the end of the title.

b. Click the **Pictures** button [*Insert* tab, *Illustrations* group]. The *Insert Picture* dialog box opens.

c. Select the **PHRElogo-04** file from the student data files and click **Insert**.

d. Right-click the picture, select **Wrap Text**, and choose **In Front of Text**.

e. Click the **Position** button [*Picture Tools Format* tab, *Arrange* group] and select **More Layout Options** to open the *Layout* dialog box.

f. Change the **Absolute position** in the *Horizontal* area to **6.2"** *to the right of* **Page**.

g. Change the **Absolute position** in the *Vertical* area to **0.2"** *below* **Page**.

h. Click **OK** to close the *Layout* dialog box.

i. Click the **Picture Border** button [*Picture Tools Format* tab, *Picture Styles* group] and select the **sixth color** in the **first row** of the *Theme Colors* (**Olive Green, Accent 2**) (Figure 4-118).

Figure 4-118 Apply *Picture Border* color

j. Click the **Picture Border** button again, click **Weight**, and select **1½ pt**.

k. Click the **Picture Effects** button [*Picture Tools Format* tab, *Picture Styles* group], select **Shadow**, and select **second option** in the **first row** of the *Outer* category (**Offset: Bottom**).

10. Edit the alt text on the graphics in the document.

 a. Select the *PHRE* logo near the top and click **Alt Text** button [*Picture Tools Format* tab, *Accessibility* group]. The *Alt Text* pane opens.

 b. Type PHRE logo in the text box in the *Alt Text* pane.

 c. Select the checkmark picture, type Picture of a checkmark in the text box in the *Alt Text* pane, and close the *Alt Text* pane.

11. Save and close the document (Figure 4-119).

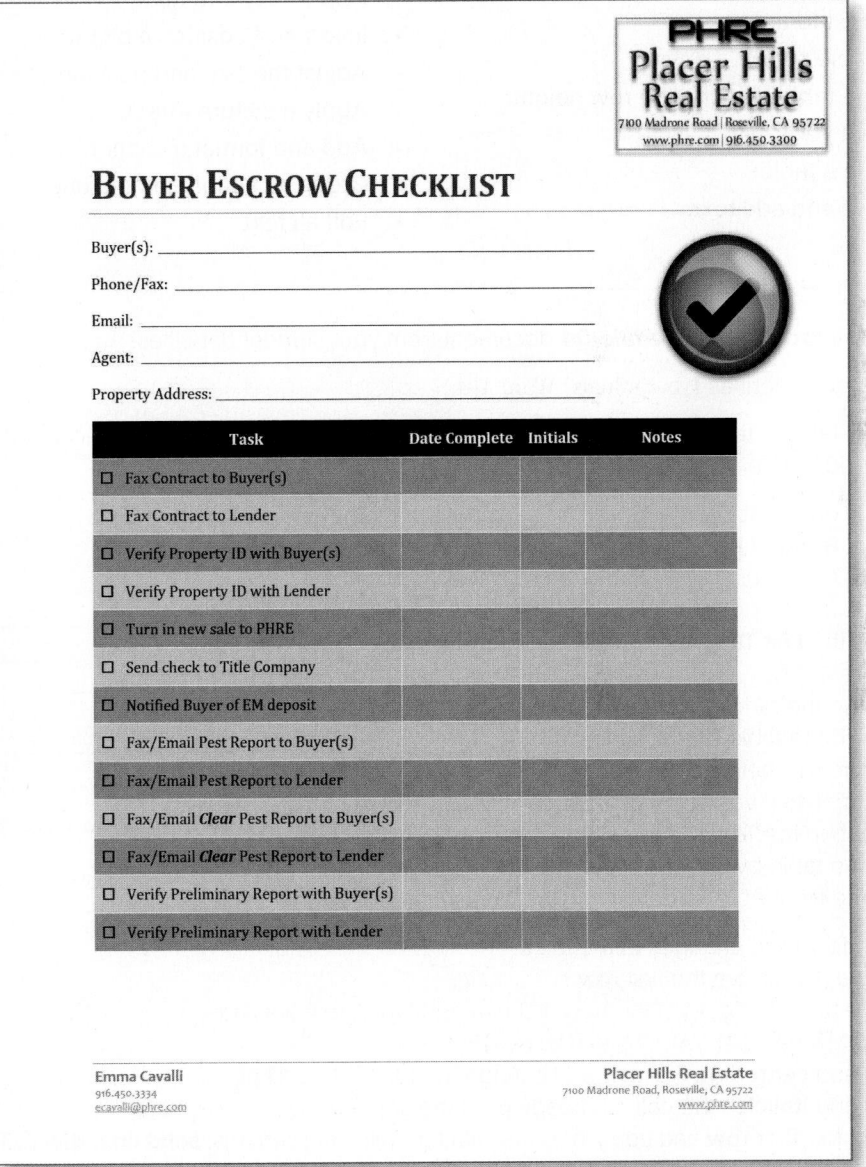

Figure 4-119 Word 4-3 completed

Independent Project 4-4

For this project, you format a vaccination schedule for Courtyard Medical Plaza by converting text to a table, formatting the table, and inserting a picture.
[Student Learning Outcomes 4.1, 4.2, 4.3, 4.5, 4.6]

Files Needed: ***VaccinationSchedule-04.docx***, ***CMPLogo-04.png***, and ***Vaccination-04.png*** (*Student data files are available in the* Library *of your SIMnet account.*)
Completed Project File Name: ***[your initials] Word 4-4.docx***

Skills Covered in This Project

- Convert text to a table.
- Apply a table style.
- *AutoFit* the table and change row height.
- Center text vertically.
- Sort text in a table.
- Insert rows and add text.
- Merge cells.

- Apply custom borders.
- Apply a style to text.
- Insert and position a picture.
- Adjust the size and position of a picture.
- Apply a picture effect.
- Add and format a caption.
- Group a caption and picture.
- Edit alt text.

1. Open the ***VaccinationSchedule-04*** document from your student data files.

2. Save this document as [your initials] Word 4-4.

3. Select the tabbed text in the middle of the document and convert it to a table (accept default settings). Don't include the blank line below the tabbed text.

4. Select the entire table and apply the following changes:
 a. Select **Banded Rows** in the *Table Style Options* group [*Table Tools Design* tab] and deselect all other check boxes.
 b. Apply the **List Table 1 Light – Accent 2** table style (Figure 4-120).
 c. Change the font size on all the text in the table to **10 pt**.
 d. **AutoFit** the table and choose **AutoFit Window**.
 e. Change row height to **0.25"**.
 f. Center all text vertically within each cell. (*Hint*: Use the *Cell* tab in the *Table Properties* dialog box.)
 g. Sort the table by **Name of Vaccine** in **Ascending** order. Be sure to select **Header row** in the *My list has* area of the *Sort* dialog box.

Figure 4-120 Apply a table style

5. Make the following changes to the table:
 a. Insert a row above the first row.
 b. Merge the three cells in the new first row and type the following:

 RECOMMENDED VACCINATION SCHEDULE
 c. **Bold** and **center** the first row and change the font size to **11 pt**.
 d. **Bold** and **italicize** the column headings in the second row.
 e. Select the **first row** and apply borders with the following settings: **solid line, Black, Text 1** color (**second color** in the **first row** of Theme Colors), **1½ pt**. width, and apply a **top** and **bottom** border.
 f. Select the second row and apply a border with the following settings: **solid line, Black, Text 1** color, **1½ pt**. width, and apply a **bottom** border. Do not remove the top border applied in the previous step.

g. Select the last row and apply a border with the following settings: **solid line**, **Black, Text 1** color, **1½ pt.** width, and apply a **bottom** border.

h. **Align Center** [*Table Tools Layout* tab, *Alignment* group] the column headings.

i. **Align Center** the text in the third column.

6. Insert the Table 4-5 information alphabetically into the table. Insert rows where needed.

Table 4-5

Meningococcal conjugate (MCV)	At 11-12 years	1
Hepatitis B (HepB)	At birth, 1-2 months, and 6 months	3

7. Modify the title of the document ("Vaccination Schedule").

a. Apply the **Title** style to the title of the document.

b. Change the *After* paragraph spacing to **8 pt**.

c. **Center** the title horizontally.

d. Apply **small caps** and **bold** formatting to the title.

8. Insert and modify a picture.

a. Place the insertion point after the title and insert the ***CMPLogo-04*** picture from your student data files. Use the *Insert Picture* dialog box.

b. Change text wrapping to **Top and Bottom**.

c. Change the height of the logo to **1"**. Verify the logo remains proportional.

d. Apply the **Offset: Bottom Right** shadow picture effect (*Outer* category).

e. Set the *Horizontal* **Absolute position** to **0.2"** *to the right of* **Page**.

f. Set the *Vertical* **Absolute position** to **0.2"** *below* **Page**.

9. Insert a picture and add a caption.

a. Place the insertion point at the end of the first body paragraph and insert the ***Vaccination-04*** picture from your student data files. Use the *Insert Picture* dialog box.

b. Change the text wrapping to **Square**.

c. Change the height of the picture to **1.3"**. Verify the graphic remains proportional.

d. Drag the picture to the right of the first and second paragraphs.

e. Insert a caption, delete the caption placeholder text, and type Don't neglect your vaccinations! as the caption text.

f. **Center** the caption text, change the font color to **Red, Accent 2** (**sixth color** in the **first row** of *Theme Colors*), and turn off italics if it is applied to the text.

g. Select the caption and the picture and **Align Center**.

h. **Group** the caption and the picture.

i. Set the *Horizontal* **Absolute position** to **6"** *to the right of* **Margin**.

j. Set the *Vertical* **Absolute position** to **0.8"** *below* **Margin**.

10. Edit the alt text of the graphic objects.

a. Edit the alt text of the CMP logo and type Courtyard Medical Plaza logo as the alt text.

b. Edit the alt text of the graphic of a doctor, type Graphic of a doctor as the alt text, and close the *Alt Text* pane.

11. Save and close the document (Figure 4-121).

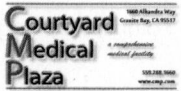

VACCINATION SCHEDULE

Think of vaccines as a coat of armor for your child. To keep it shiny and strong, you have to make sure your child's immunizations are up to date. Timely vaccinations help to prevent disease and keep your family and the community healthy. Some immunizations are given in a single shot, while others require a series of shots over a period of time.

Vaccines for children and teenagers are listed alphabetically below with their routinely recommended ages. Missed doses will be assessed by your child's physician and given if necessary. Keep a personal record of all immunizations and bring it with you to each office visit.

Don't neglect your vaccinations!

RECOMMENDED VACCINATION SCHEDULE

Name of Vaccine	When It's Recommended	Total Doses
Chickenpox (varicella)	At 12 months and 4-6 years	2
Diphtheria, tetanus, and pertussis (DTaP)	At 2, 4, 6 and 12-15 months, and 4-6 years	5
Haemophilus influenzae type b (Hib)	At 2, 4, 6, and 12 months	4
Hepatitis A (HepA)	At 12 and 18 months	3
Hepatitis B (HepB)	At birth, 1-2 months, and 6 months	3
Human papillomavirus (HPV)	3-dose series for girls at age 11-12 years	3
Inactivated influenza (flu shot)	Annually starting at age 6 months	Annually
Inactivated poliovirus (IPV)	At 2, 4, 6 months, and 4-6 years	4
Live intranasal influenza	Annually starting at age 2 years	Annually
Measles, mumps, and rubella (MMR)	At 12 months and 4-6 years	2
Meningococcal conjugate (MCV)	At 11-12 years	1
Pneumococcal conjugate (PCV)	At 2, 4, 6, and 12 months	4
Pneumococcal polysaccharide (PPSV)	At 2, 4, 6, and 12 months	4
Rotavirus (RV)	At 2, 4, and 6 months	3
Tetanus and diphtheria (Td)	At 11-12 years	1

These recommendations are for generally healthy children and teenagers and are for information only. If your child has ongoing health problems, special health needs or risks, or if certain conditions run in your family, talk with your child's physician. He or she may recommend additional vaccinations or schedules based on earlier immunizations and special health needs.

Figure 4-121 Word 4-4 completed

Independent Project 4-5

For this project, you create an emergency telephone information sheet for Sierra Pacific Community College District (SPCCD). You add and modify a *SmartArt* graphic, convert text to a table, insert a new table, format the tables, and insert the company logo.
[Student Learning Outcomes 4.1, 4.2, 4.3, 4.5, 4.6]

Files Needed: ***EmergencyTelephones-04.docx*** and ***SPCCDlogo.png*** *(Student data files are available in the* Library *of your SIMnet account.)*
Completed Project File Name: *[your initials]* **Word 4-5.docx**

Skills Covered in This Project

- Modify an existing document.
- Insert a *SmartArt* graphic.
- Add text to a *SmartArt* graphic.
- Resize, change the color of, and apply a style to *SmartArt*.
- Convert text to a table and *AutoFit*.
- Sort text in a table.
- Insert a row, merge cells, and add information.

- Apply a table style.
- Change cell margins and alignment.
- Apply a style to text.
- Insert a table and type text.
- Insert a picture.
- Adjust a picture size and position.
- Insert, modify, and position an icon.
- Insert a symbol and the current date.
- Edit alt text.

1. Open the **EmergencyTelephones-04** document from your student data files.

2. Save this document as [your initials] Word 4–5.

3. Insert a *SmartArt* graphic and add text.

 a. Place your insertion point in front of the second section heading ("Emergency Telephone Locations").
 b. Insert the **Vertical Chevron List** *SmartArt* graphic from the *List* category (Figure 4-122).
 c. Type 1 in the graphic text box in the upper-left corner of the *SmartArt* graphic (first chevron shape).
 d. Type 2 in the second graphic text box in the first column of the graphic.
 e. Type 3 in the third graphic text box in the first column of the graphic.

 Figure 4-122 Insert *SmartArt* graphic

 f. Type the following text in the bulleted text boxes in the second column. You do not need to add bullets because bullets are already included in the *SmartArt*.

 - Press the "Help" button
 - Speak when the light comes on

 - Stay on the line
 - You will be connected with the college police

 - State clearly the nature of the emergency and your location

 g. Use **Backspace** to remove the extra bullet in the last graphic in the second column.

4. Resize and format the *SmartArt* graphic.

 a. Select the frame of the graphic to select the entire graphic.
 b. Change the height to **2.5"** and the width to **4.2"**.
 c. Change the text wrapping to **Top and Bottom**.
 d. **Change Colors** [*SmartArt Tools Design* tab] of the entire *SmartArt* graphic to **Dark 2 Fill** (Figure 4-123).
 e. Apply the **Intense Effect** *SmartArt* style.

 Figure 4-123 Change *SmartArt* colors

5. Convert text to a table.
 a. Select the tabbed text below the second section heading ("Emergency Telephone Locations"). Do not select the paragraph mark below the last row.
 b. **Convert Text to Table** and select **AutoFit to contents**.

6. Sort the table text by **Column 1** in **Ascending** order.

7. Add a title row and insert text.
 a. Add a row above the first row.
 b. Merge the cells in this row.
 c. Type Blue Emergency Telephones in the merged first row.

8. Format the table.
 a. Select **Header Row**, **First Column**, and **Banded Rows** in the *Table Style Options* group (if necessary). Deselect all other options.
 b. Apply the **List Table 2** table style.
 c. Select the entire table and change the top and bottom cell margins to **0.04"** and the left and right cell margins to **0.1"**.
 d. Vertically **center** all text in the table. (*Hint*: Use the *Cell* tab in the *Table Properties* dialog box.)
 e. Select the first row and horizontally **center** the text. This text should be centered vertically and horizontally.

9. Insert, resize, and position the SPCCD logo.
 a. Place your insertion point at the beginning of the document and insert the ***SPCCDlogo_04*** picture (from your student data files). Use the *Insert Picture* dialog box.
 b. Change the width to **3"** and keep the size proportional.
 c. Change the text wrapping to **Top and Bottom** and drag the logo above the title.
 d. Set the *Horizontal* **Absolute position** to **0.3"** *to the right of* **Page**.
 e. Set the *Vertical* **Absolute position** to **0.3"** *below* **Page**.
 f. Change the **Color** [*Picture Tools Format* tab, *Adjust* group] to **Saturation: 0%**.

10. Insert, modify, and position an icon.
 a. Place your insertion point at the end of the title.
 b. Insert an icon and select the phone in the *Communications* section (Figure 4-124).
 c. Change the width to **2"** and keep the size proportional.
 d. Change the text wrapping to **Tight**.
 e. Set the *Horizontal* **Alignment** to **Right** *relative to* **Margin**.
 f. Set the *Vertical* **Absolute position** to **1.1"** *below* **Margin**.
 g. Change the **Graphics Fill** color to **Dark Blue, Text 2** (**fourth color** in the **first row** of *Theme Colors*).

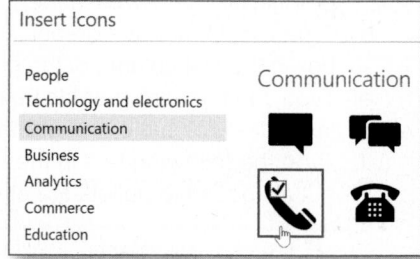

Figure 4-124 Insert an icon

11. Modify the footer to include a symbol and the current date.
 a. Edit the footer and **space** once at the end of the text on the right side of the footer.
 b. Insert a **solid circle** symbol from the *Symbol* font set (Character code 183) and **space** once after it.
 c. Type Revised: and **space** once.
 d. Insert the current date in MM/DD/YY format, set it so that it does not update automatically, and close the footer.

12. Edit the alt text of the graphic objects.
 a. Edit the alt text of the Sierra Pacific logo, type Sierra Pacific logo as the alt text.
 b. Select the entire *SmartArt* graphic, type Graphic of emergency telephone instructions as the alt text.
 c. Edit the alt text of the phone icon, type Icon of a blue phone as the alt text, and close the *Alt Text* pane.

13. Save and close the document (Figure 4-125).

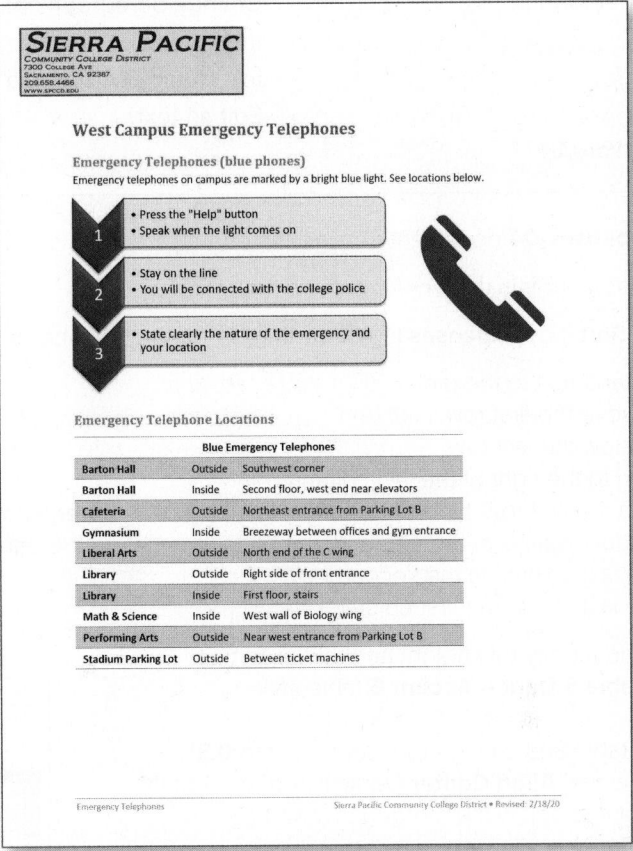

Figure 4-125 Word 4-5 completed

Independent Project 4-6

For this project, you modify a memo for Life's Animal Shelter. You edit an existing table, add rows and a column, format the table, insert formulas into the table, and insert and modify *WordArt* and a 3D model. [Student Learning Outcomes 4.1, 4.2, 4.3, 4.6]

File Needed: **WeeklyExpenses-04.docx** *(Student data files are available in the* Library *of your SIMnet account.)*
Completed Project File Name: **[your initials] Word 4-6.docx**

Skills Covered in This Project

- Modify an existing document.
- Modify a table row height.
- Change cell alignment.

- Add rows and a column to a table.
- Merge table rows.
- Modify the borders and shading of a table.
- Insert formulas into a table.

- Set the formula number format.
- Update formulas.
- Format selected text.
- Insert *WordArt*.
- Modify and position *WordArt*.

- Change paragraph spacing.
- Insert a date.
- Insert and customize a 3D model.
- Edit alt text.

1. Open the **WeeklyExpenses-04** document from your student data files.

2. Save this document as [your initials] Word 4–6.

3. Select the table and **Sort** it by **Expenses** in **Ascending** order (the table has a header row).

4. Add rows, a column, and text to the table.
 a. Insert one row above the first row.
 b. Insert one row below the last row.
 c. Insert one column to the right of the last column.
 d. Merge the cells in the first row, type Life's Animal Shelter, press **Enter**, and type Weekly Expenses. If a paragraph symbol displays at the end of the subtitle text, delete the paragraph symbol.
 e. Type Totals in the last column in the second row.
 f. Type Totals in the last row in the first column.

5. Apply a table style and modify row height and text alignment.
 a. Apply the **Grid Table 5 Dark – Accent 6** table style (Figure 4-126).
 b. Select the entire table and change the row height to **0.3"**.
 c. Select the first row and **Align Center** (vertical and horizontal).
 d. Select the first column below the merged row and **Align Center Left**.
 e. Select columns 2–9 (including blank cells) below the merged row and **Align Center Right**.
 f. Select the column headings in the second row (beginning with "**Mon**" and ending with "**Totals**") and apply **Bold** formatting.

Figure 4-126 Apply a table style.

6. Insert formulas into the table.
 a. Place your insertion point in the last row of the second column, insert a **Formula** [*Table Tools Layout* tab, *Data* group] to add the figures above. The formula should be **=SUM(ABOVE)**. Use the **$#,##0.00;($#,##0.00)** number format (Figure 4-127).
 b. Insert the same formula and number format in remaining cells in the last row, except for the last column.
 c. Place your insertion point in the last column of the third row, insert a **Formula** to add the figures to the left. The formula should be **=SUM(LEFT)**. Use the **$#,##0.00;($#,##0.00)** number format.
 d. Insert the same formula and number format in remaining rows in the last column. Verify the correct formula, **=SUM(LEFT)**, has been inserted in each of these cells. Replace "ABOVE" with "LEFT" in the formula, if needed.

Figure 4-127 Insert a formula into the table

7. Change expense data and update formulas.
 a. Change the "Wages" for "Wednesday" to 592.75.
 b. Right-click the total amount in this column and select **Update Field** from the context menu to update the total.
 c. Update the totals formulas in the last two rows in the last column. The total in the last cell in the last row should be $12,536.34.

8. Format text in the table and *AutoFit* the table.
 a. Apply **small caps**, and **12 pt.** font size to the text in the first row.
 b. **Bold** the total amounts in the last row.
 c. **Bold** the total amounts in the last column.
 d. AutoFit the table and select **AutoFit Window**.

9. Insert and customize *WordArt* for the company logo.
 a. Place the insertion point at the beginning of the document.
 b. Insert **WordArt** and select the **third option** in the **first row** (Figure 4-128).
 c. Type Life's Animal Shelter as the text for the *WordArt*.
 d. Select the text in the *WordArt* and change the text to **small caps** and **40 pt**.
 e. Change the **Text Fill** to **Orange, Accent 6** (**last color** in the **first row** of *Theme Colors*).
 f. Change the **Shadow** text effect to **Offset: Right** (**first option** in the **second row** of the *Outer* category).
 g. Set the *Horizontal* **Alignment** to **Left** *relative to* **Margin**.
 h. Set the *Vertical* **Absolute position** to **0.2"** *below* **Page**.

Figure 4-128 Insert *WordArt*

10. Modify the heading lines of the memo.
 a. Add **36 pt.** before paragraph spacing on the first line of the memo heading ("TO: . . .").
 b. Insert the current date on the date line in the memo heading to replace the placeholder text and set it to update automatically (use January 1, 2020 format).

11. Insert, rotate, resize, and position a 3D model.
 a. Place your insertion point before "TO:" in the memo heading lines.
 b. Click the bottom half of the **3D Models** button and select **From Online Sources**.
 c. Type dog in the search text box and press **Enter**.
 d. Select and insert a 3D model of your choice.
 e. Select and drag the 3D model near the right margin.
 f. Use the rotation handle in the middle of the 3D model to rotate the model to an angle of your choice
 g. Change the *Width* to **1.5"**.
 h. Click the **Position** button and select **Position in Top Right with Square Text Wrapping**.

12. Edit the alt text of the graphic objects.
 a. Edit the alt text of the Word Art near the top of the document and type Life's Animal Shelter Word Art as the alt text.
 b. Edit the alt text of the 3D model dog, type 3D model of a dog as the alt text, and close the *Alt Text* pane.

13. Save and close the document (Figure 4-129).

LIFE'S ANIMAL SHELTER

TO: Life's Animal Shelter Staff and Volunteers

FROM: Kelly Sung, Director of Services

DATE: April 3, 2020

SUBJECT: Weekly Expenses

Thank you for the time you have spent volunteering at Life's Animal Shelter. Our staff and volunteers have contributed countless hours making this shelter a safe environment for animals and providing adoption services for families in our community. You have been a part of hundreds of animal rescues and adoptions over the past year. Families throughout our region are enjoying their new pets thanks to your dedication and work at Life's Animal Shelter.

I'm providing you with our expenses update for the last week. Our operating funds come through donations and pet adoption fees. Thank you for your help in keeping our expenses at a moderate level. Because of you, we are able to offer reasonable adoption fees to animal lovers in our community.

Again, thank you for all of your hard work. Because of you, Life's Animal Shelter valuably serves our community providing shelter and adoption services.

LIFE'S ANIMAL SHELTER WEEKLY EXPENSES								
Expenses	Mon	Tue	Wed	Thurs	Fri	Sat	Sun	Totals
Electricity	19.45	20.09	21.75	19.02	19.99	23.56	19.45	$ 143.31
Equipment	199.03	209.25	198.90	229.05	245.09	351.98	205.55	$1,638.85
Food	340.45	344.05	350.51	340.01	341.48	359.75	340.02	$2,416.27
Heat	25.75	26.01	28.05	25.03	25.99	31.04	24.99	$ 186.86
Medicine	525.33	529.31	535.25	524.59	527.99	543.39	540.01	$3,725.87
Wages	675.21	580.91	592.75	579.55	680.81	750.05	565.90	$4,425.18
Totals	$1,785.22	$1,709.62	$1,727.21	$1,717.25	$1,841.35	$2,059.77	$1,695.92	$12,536.34

Life's Animal Shelter Weekly Expenses

Figure 4-129 Word 4-6 completed

Improve It Project 4-7

For this project, you edit a document for Courtyard Medical Plaza. You arrange text in columns, position the company logo, and apply formatting to improve the overall layout of the document.
[Student Learning Outcomes 4.4, 4.5]

Files Needed: *StayingActive-04.docx* and *CMPlogo.png* (Student data files are available in the Library of your SIMnet account.)
Completed Project File Name: *[your initials] Word 4-7.docx*

Skills Covered in This Project

- Modify an existing document.
- Apply style formatting to the title and headings.
- Change font size and alignment.
- Change paragraph spacing.
- Use the *Format Painter*.
- Arrange text in columns.
- Change spacing between columns.
- Use a column break to balance columns.
- Insert a picture.
- Resize and position a picture.
- Edit alt text.

1. Open the **StayingActive-04** document from your student data files.

2. Save this document as [your initials] Word 4-7.

3. Modify the title of the document.
 a. Apply **Intense Reference** style to the title ("Tips for Staying Active").
 b. Change to **18 pt.** font size.
 c. Align **center**.
 d. Change the *Before* paragraph spacing to **36 pt.** and *After* paragraph spacing to **12**.

4. Modify section headings of the document.
 a. Apply **Subtle Reference** style to the first section heading ("**Try Some of the Following Suggestions**").
 b. Change the font size to **14 pt.** and **center** the section heading.
 c. Change *Before* paragraph spacing to **12 pt.** and *After* paragraph spacing to **6 pt**.
 d. Use the **Format Painter** to apply the formatting of the first section heading to the second section heading ("**To Keep Exercise Fun and Interesting**").

5. Format the last line of the document to make it part of the bulleted list that precedes it and format it consistently with the other bulleted items.

6. Apply column format to the multilevel list following the first section heading.
 a. Select the multilevel list in the first section and apply two-column format. Do not include the section heading. If the section break above the list has a number, turn off numbering on this line.
 b. Customize the space between columns to **0.75"**.

7. Apply column format to the bulleted list following the second section heading.
 a. Select the bulleted list in the second section and apply two-column format. Do not include the section heading. If the section break above the list has a bullet, turn off bullets on this line.
 b. Customize the space between columns to **0.75"**.
 c. Insert a **column break** before the third bulleted item to balance the columns.

8. Place the insertion point at the end of the first section heading ("Try Some of the Following Suggestions") and **delete** the paragraph mark.

9. Place the insertion point at the end of the second section heading ("To Keep Exercise Fun and Interesting") and **delete** the paragraph mark.

10. Insert, resize, and position a picture.
 a. Place your insertion point at the top of the document and insert the **CMPlogo-04** picture. Use the *Insert Picture* dialog box.
 b. Change the width to **2.5"** and keep the size proportional.
 c. Change the text wrapping to **In Front of Text**.
 d. Set the *Horizontal* **Absolute position** to **0.2"** *to the right of* **Page**.
 e. Set the *Vertical* **Absolute position** to **0.2"** *below* **Page**.
 f. Edit the alt text of the CMP logo, type Courtyard Medical Plaza logo as the alt text, and close the *Alt Text* pane.

11. Save and close the document (Figure 4-130).

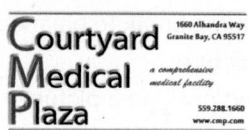

TIPS FOR STAYING ACTIVE

Almost any activity that gets you moving and strengthens your muscles is good for your health and can help you meet your fitness and weight goal. If you haven't been exercising regularly, start out slowly and gradually increase duration, frequency, and intensity. If you have been exercising regularly, keep it up!

TRY SOME OF THE FOLLOWING SUGGESTIONS:

1) AIM FOR AT LEAST 30 TO 60 MINUTES OF MODERATE INTENSITY ACTIVITY ON MOST DAYS.
 a) You can get your exercise all at once or spread it out during the day.
 i) For example, exercising for three 10-minute periods is just as effective as exercising for 30 minutes at a time.
 b) The more physical activity you do, the more calories you burn and the greater the health benefit.

2) IF YOU DON'T LIKE COUNTING CALORIES, TRY COUNTING YOUR STEPS! WALKING 10,000 STEPS A DAY CAN HELP YOU MANAGE YOUR WEIGHT.
 a) Use a pedometer (an easy-to-wear device that senses your body's motion) to count your steps and motivate you to increase your activity.
 b) Use a journal to track your walking.

3) USE BOTH AEROBIC AND STRENGTHENING ACTIVITIES ARE IMPORTANT TO LOSING WEIGHT AND KEEPING IT OFF.
 a) As you grow older, your body slows down and your metabolism—the rate at which your body burns calories—naturally decreases.
 b) Taking a brisk walk will boost your metabolism and keep you burning calories for hours afterward.

4) REMEMBER THAT ANY FORM OF EXERCISE IS GOOD FOR YOU.
 a) Household chores
 i) Cleaning windows
 ii) Vacuuming
 iii) Folding clothes
 b) Yard work and gardening
 c) Using stairs rather than an elevator
 d) Getting up and moving regularly at work

TO KEEP EXERCISE FUN AND INTERESTING:

✓ PICK ONE OR MORE ACTIVITIES YOU ENJOY. Regular exercise is more likely to become a healthy habit when it's fun as well as rewarding. Varying your activities can help prevent boredom.

✓ EXERCISE WITH A FRIEND. The support and companionship will help keep you going.

✓ THINK ABOUT THE PAYOFFS. Exercise not only helps control weight, it is beneficial to the body and mind in a number of ways. It improves health, boosts your immune system, helps control appetite, helps you feel more energetic and relaxed, and raises your self-confidence!

✓ SET REALISTIC EXERCISE GOALS. Reward yourself in healthy ways when you achieve them.

Figure 4-130 Word 4-7 completed

Challenge Project 4-8

A budget tracks actual or anticipated spending and compares the amount you spend with your earnings. For this project, use skills learned in this chapter to create a weekly or monthly budget.
[Student Learning Outcomes 4.1, 4.2, 4.3, 4.5, 4.6]

File Needed: None
Completed Project File Name: *[your initials] Word 4-8.docx*

Create a new document and save it as [your initials] Word 4-8.

A budget can include, but is not limited to, the following elements:

- Document title
- Time frame of the budget
- Expenditure categories
- Days in the week or weeks in the month
- Row and column totals

Modify your document according to the following guidelines:

- Format your budget in a table.
- Use column headings for days or weeks.
- Use row headings for expense categories.
- Use formulas to total rows and columns.
- Sort table by expenditure amounts.
- Apply table style formatting.
- Adjust shading and borders as needed.
- Adjust column width and row height.
- Modify cell margins.
- Format row and column totals.
- Insert a picture, icon, 3D model, or other graphic.
- Format, resize, and position a graphic.
- Edit alt text.
- Adjust document margins as needed.
- Include an appropriate header and/or footer.

Challenge Project 4-9

Newspapers and magazines arrange text in column format to improve readability and overall attractiveness of the publication. For this project, you arrange an existing document you have written (an essay, blog entry, article for a newspaper, or posting for Craigslist) in column format.
[Student Learning Outcomes 4.4, 4.5, 4.6]

File Needed: None
Completed Project File Name: *[your initials] Word 4-9.docx*

Open an existing document you have created and save it as [your initials] Word 4-9.

A document in column format can include, but is not limited to, the following elements:

- Document title
- Byline (Author name)
- Section headings
- Graphics

Modify your document according to the following guidelines:

- Format your article in column format. Don't include the title as part of the columns.
- Change spacing between columns and/or add a vertical line between columns.
- Use a column or continuous section break to balance the columns.
- Insert a graphic.
- Adjust size, wrapping, and position of the graphic.
- Add a caption to the graphic.
- Edit alt text.
- Adjust margins as needed.
- Include an appropriate header and/or footer.

Challenge Project 4-10

A weekly schedule helps you organize and manage work, school, family, and personal time more effectively. For this project, use a table to create a weekly schedule and calculate the time you spend on each daily activity.
[Student Learning Outcomes 4.1, 4.2, 4.3, 4.5, 4.6]

File Needed: None
Completed Project File Name: *[your initials] Word 4-10.docx*

Create a new document and save it as [your initials] Word 4–10.

A weekly schedule can include, but is not limited to, the following elements:

- Document title
- Days of the week
- Time commitment categories
- Row and column totals

Modify your document according to the following guidelines:

- Format your weekly schedule as a table.
- Use column headings for days of the week.
- Use row headings for time commitment categories.
- Use formulas to total rows and columns.
- Apply table style formatting.
- Adjust shading and borders as needed.
- Adjust column width and row height.
- Adjust cell margins as needed.
- Format row and column totals.
- Insert a graphic.
- Format, resize, and position a graphic.
- Edit alt text.
- Adjust document margins as needed.
- Include an appropriate header and/or footer.

Source of screenshots Microsoft Office 365 (2019): Word, Excel, Access, Powerpoint.

Microsoft® Office

IN PRACTICE

excel

©Chris Ryan/Getty Images

CHAPTER 1

Creating and Editing Workbooks

CHAPTER OVERVIEW

Microsoft Excel (Excel) is spreadsheet software for creating an electronic workbook. A workbook consists of rows and columns to organize data, perform calculations, print reports, and build charts. With Excel, you can create simple to complex personal or business workbooks. This chapter presents basic procedures for creating and editing an Excel workbook.

STUDENT LEARNING OUTCOMES (SLOs)

After completing this chapter, you will be able to:

SLO 1.1 Create, save, and open an Excel workbook (p. E1-3).

SLO 1.2 Enter and edit labels and values in a worksheet (p. E1-7).

SLO 1.3 Use the SUM function to build a simple formula (p. E1-19).

SLO 1.4 Format a worksheet with font attributes, borders, fill, cell styles, and themes (p. E1-22).

SLO 1.5 Modify columns and rows in a worksheet (p. E1-30).

SLO 1.6 Insert, delete, and move worksheets in a workbook (p. E1-36).

SLO 1.7 Modify the appearance of a workbook by adjusting zoom size, changing views, and freezing panes (p. E1-41).

SLO 1.8 Review and prepare a workbook for final distribution by spell checking, setting properties, and adjusting page setup options (p. E1-47).

CASE STUDY

Paradise Lakes Resort (PLR) is a vacation company with properties located throughout northern Minnesota. PLR staff use Excel to track revenue, monitor expenses, maintain employee records, and perform similar tasks. In the Pause & Practice projects for Chapter 1, you create, edit, and format a workbook that displays categories of revenue for one week.

Pause & Practice 1-1: Open, edit, and save a workbook.

Pause & Practice 1-2: Use *SUM* and format data in a worksheet.

Pause & Practice 1-3: Edit columns, rows, and sheets in a workbook.

Pause & Practice 1-4: Finalize a workbook for distribution.

Creating, Saving, and Opening a Workbook

In Microsoft Excel, the file that you open, edit, and save is a **workbook**. Each workbook contains **worksheets**, which are comparable to individual pages in a Word document. A worksheet is also referred to as a **spreadsheet** or a **sheet**, and you can use these terms interchangeably. This text also uses the terms "workbook" and "file" interchangeably.

Create a New Workbook

By default, a new workbook includes one worksheet, but a workbook can include multiple sheets. The worksheet **tab** is located near the bottom left of the workbook window and is labeled *Sheet1*.

When you first open Excel, the **Excel Home page** displays and you can create a new blank workbook, open a recently saved workbook, or create a workbook from an Excel template (a model workbook). Click **Blank workbook** to start a new blank workbook. You can also select *Blank workbook* from the *New* area in the *Backstage* view.

> **ANOTHER WAY**
>
> Press **Esc** to leave the Excel *Home* page and open a blank workbook.

> **HOW TO: Create a New Workbook from the Backstage View**

1. Click the **File** tab to display the *Backstage* view.
2. Select **New** on the left to display the *New* area in the *Backstage* view (Figure 1-1).

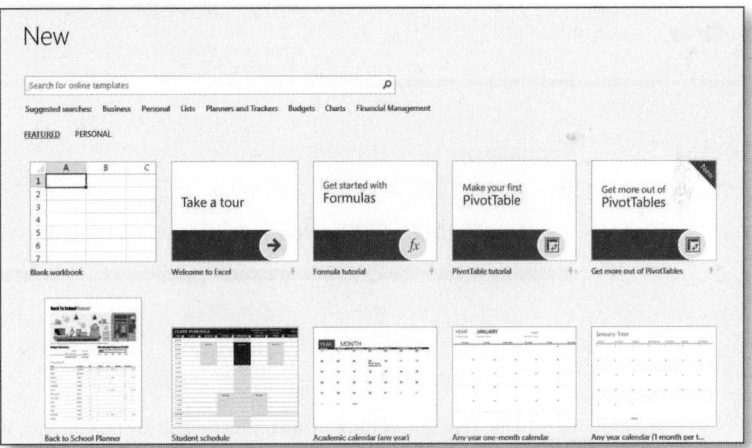

Figure 1-1 *Backstage* view for creating new workbooks

- Templates display with a thumbnail preview and name.
- Available templates update regularly so your screen may not match the figure.

3. Click **Blank workbook** to create a new blank workbook.

> **ANOTHER WAY**
>
> Press **Ctrl+N** to open a new workbook.

Save and Close a Workbook

When you open a blank workbook, Excel automatically assigns a file name, such as *Book1*, but you should type a descriptive file name for the workbook in the *Save As* area. Save a workbook on your computer, in a *OneDrive* folder, or on external media.

▶HOW TO: Save a New Workbook

1. Click the **File** tab to display the *Backstage* view.
2. Select **Save As** on the left to display the *Save As* area.
 - Press **Ctrl+S** to open the *Save As* area in the *Backstage* view for a workbook that has not yet been saved.
3. Select the location to save your workbook.
 - Click **Recent** to display a list of recently used folders.
 - Click **OneDrive** to see your cloud folder names.
 - Click **This PC** to save the file to the *Documents* or another folder on the computer.
 - Click **Add a Place** to select a commonly used cloud location.
 - Click **Browse** to open the *Save As* dialog box for further navigation (Figure 1-2).
4. Click a folder name to open it and type the file name in the file name box.
5. Click **Save**.

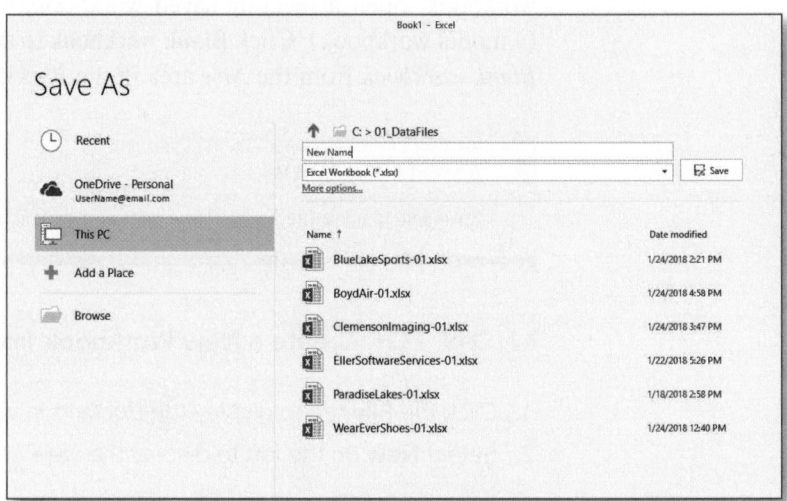

Figure 1-2 *Save As* area in *Backstage* view

▶ ANOTHER WAY

Press **F12 (FN+F12)** to open the *Save As* dialog box.

▶ MORE INFO

The *AutoSave* feature turns on by default when you save a file to *OneDrive*, and changes made to the file are automatically saved as you work. *AutoSave* displays in the upper-left corner of the title bar.

You can re-save a workbook with the same file name by pressing **Ctrl+S** or by clicking the **Save** button in the *Quick Access toolbar*.

To close a workbook, click the **File** tab and choose **Close**. Press **Ctrl+W** or **Ctrl+F4** to close a workbook, too. These commands leave Excel running with a blank screen so that you can open another file or start a new workbook.

Click the **X** (*Close* button) in the upper-right corner of the window to close a workbook. If the workbook is the only one open, this command closes the file and exits Excel. If multiple workbooks are open, clicking the *Close* button closes only the active workbook.

Open a Workbook

A workbook can be opened from the *Home* page, the *Open* area in the *Backstage* view, or the *Open* dialog box. When a workbook is opened from an internet or unrecognized source, it opens in *Protected View*. Click **Enable Editing** when you know that it is safe to work with the file.

> **HOW TO: Open a Workbook**

1. Click the **File** tab to open the *Backstage* view.
2. Click **Open** to display the *Open* area.
 - Recently used workbook names are listed on the right.
 - Click *Folders* to display a list of recently used folders (Figure 1-3).
 - *Shared with Me* lists workbooks that others have shared with you.
 - *OneDrive* lists your cloud folder names.
 - The *This PC* option lists recently used folder names on the computer.
 - Click **Add a Place** to identify a new cloud location or click **Browse** to locate a folder.
3. Select the location and folder where the workbook is stored.
4. Locate and click the workbook name.
 - The workbook opens.

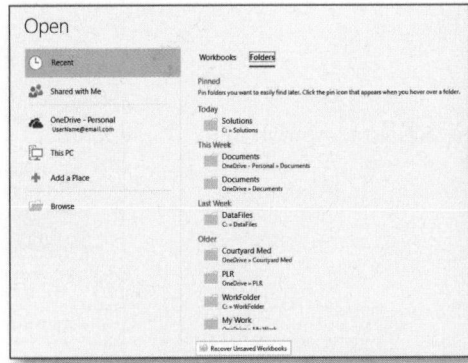

Figure 1-3 *Open* area in *Folders* view

> **ANOTHER WAY**
>
> **Ctrl+O** displays the *Open* area in the *Backstage* view. **Ctrl+F12** displays the *Open* dialog box.

> **MORE INFO**
>
> From an *Explorer* window, double-click a workbook file name to launch Excel and open the workbook.

Save a Workbook with a Different File Name

To preserve an existing workbook, open and save it with a different file name, creating a copy of the original file with a new name. Follow the same steps that you would when saving a new workbook.

> **HOW TO: Save a Workbook with a Different File Name**

1. Click the **File** tab to open the *Backstage* view.
2. Click **Save As** to display the *Save As* area.
 - When *AutoSave* is active, click **Save a Copy** to open the *Save As* area.
 - The current folder name displays.
3. Navigate to and select the folder name.
4. Type or edit the workbook name in the file name area.
5. Click **Save** to save the file and return to the workbook.

Workbook File Formats

Excel workbooks are saved as *.xlsx* files, indicated as *Excel Workbook* in the *Save As* area and dialog box. You can save a workbook in other formats for ease in sharing data. For example, save a workbook in *Excel 97-2003* format so that a coworker with an earlier version of Excel can use the data, or create a PDF file to display data for users who do not have Excel.

The *Save As* area and the *Save As* dialog box list available formats (Figure 1-4). Table 1-1 lists common formats for saving an Excel workbook.

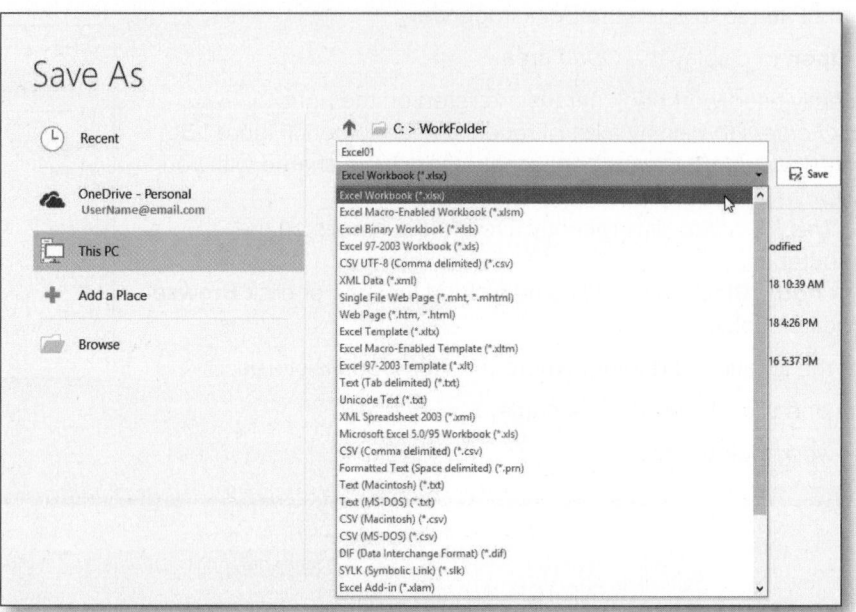

Figure 1-4 Workbook file formats

Table 1-1: Common Save Formats

Type of Document	File Name Extension	Uses of This Format
Excel Workbook	.xlsx	Excel workbook compatible with versions 2010 and later.
Excel Macro-Enabled Workbook	.xlsm	Excel workbook with embedded macros.
Excel 97-2003 Workbook	.xls	Excel workbook compatible with older versions of Microsoft Excel.
Excel Template	.xltx	Model or sample Excel workbook stored in the Custom Office Templates folder.
Excel Macro-Enabled Template	.xltm	Model or sample Excel workbook with embedded macros stored in the Custom Office Templates folder.
Portable Document Format (PDF)	.pdf	An image of the workbook for viewing that can be opened with free software.
Text (tab-delimited)	.txt	Data only with columns separated by a tab character. File can be opened by many applications.
Comma Separated Values (CSV)	.csv	Data only with columns separated by a comma. File can be opened by many applications.
OpenDocument Spreadsheet	.ods	Workbook for the Open Office suite as well as Google Docs.
Web Page	.htm, .html	Excel workbook formatted for posting on a web site that includes data, graphics, and linked objects.

SLO 1.2

Entering and Editing Data

A worksheet consists of columns and rows. Column labels are letters and row labels are numbers. Enter data in a *cell*, which is the intersection of a column and a row. Each cell is identified with a *cell reference* (or *cell address*), the column letter and row number that represents the location of the cell. Cell A1 is the intersection of column A and row 1. A rectangular group of cells is a *range*. The range address **A1:B3** identifies six cells in two columns and three rows.

A worksheet displays column and row headings as well as gridlines to help you identify the location of data. You can change the gridlines and headings options from the *View* tab if you prefer to see a cleaner background for your work. The *Gridlines* and *Headings* settings in the *Show* group are toggles that display or hide these features.

> **MORE INFO**
>
> From the *View* tab, you can also display or hide the formula bar and the ruler.

Enter Labels and Values

Data in a worksheet cell is text, a number, or a formula. A *label* is text that displays a name, a title, or similar descriptive information. Labels are not included in calculations. A *value* is a number that can be used in a calculation or is the result of a calculation. A *formula* is a calculation or expression that displays a result.

When you type data that includes alphabetic characters and numbers, Excel treats that data as a label. Examples include a street address or an ID such as ABC123. When you type data with numbers that are not used in calculations, enter the data as a label by typing an apostrophe (') before the data. Examples of this type of data include a telephone or Social Security number without hyphens.

> **MORE INFO**
>
> If you type a Social Security number *with* hyphens, Excel identifies it as a label.

When a label in a cell is longer or wider than the cell, the label spills into an empty adjacent cell. If adjacent cells are not empty, the label is truncated or cut off in the cell, but the entire entry is visible in the *Formula bar*. The *Formula* bar appears below the *Ribbon* and displays the contents of the selected cell. When a value is too large for the width of the cell, the cell displays a series of # symbols or shows the value in exponential notation (part of the number with E+n as in 1235E+4). To see all cell contents, simply widen the column.

To enter data, click the cell with the pointer to select and activate the cell. The pointer appears as a solid, white cross (a thick plus sign) when selecting data in the worksheet. The *active cell* displays a solid border, and its address appears in the *Name box* (Figure 1-5).

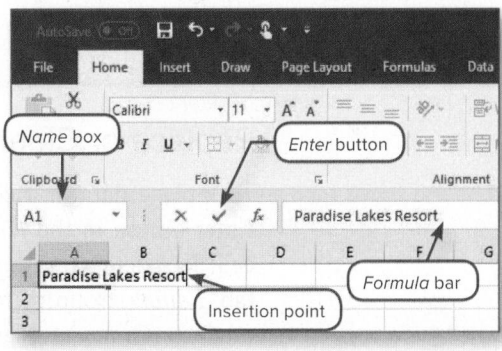

Figure 1-5 Entering data

1. Select the cell and type the data. When you type, an insertion point displays.
 - The label or value appears in the cell and in the *Formula* bar.
2. Press **Enter** to complete the entry and activate the cell below.
 - Press **Tab** to complete the entry and activate the cell to the right.
 - Press any keyboard directional arrow key to complete the entry and activate the cell in the direction of the arrow.
 - Press **Ctrl+Enter** to complete the entry and keep the current cell active.
 - Click the **Enter** button in the *Formula* bar to complete the entry and keep the cell active.

Edit Cell Contents

You can edit cell data as you type or after the entry is complete. To edit as you type, press the **Backspace** key to delete characters to the left of the insertion point, or use arrow keys to move the insertion point and press the **Delete** key to erase characters to the right of the insertion point. To edit a completed entry, start *Edit* mode by double-clicking the cell or by pressing **F2 (FN+F2)**. The word "Edit" appears in the *Status* bar to alert you that data entry is in progress. Position the insertion point either in the cell or in the *Formula* bar, edit the entry, and press any completion key.

When using keyboard function keys, you may need to press the **FN** key with the function key to access the command. This depends on the type of computer as well as the keyboard. This text will show a shortcut like this **F2 (FN+F2)** as a reminder to note your keyboard layout.

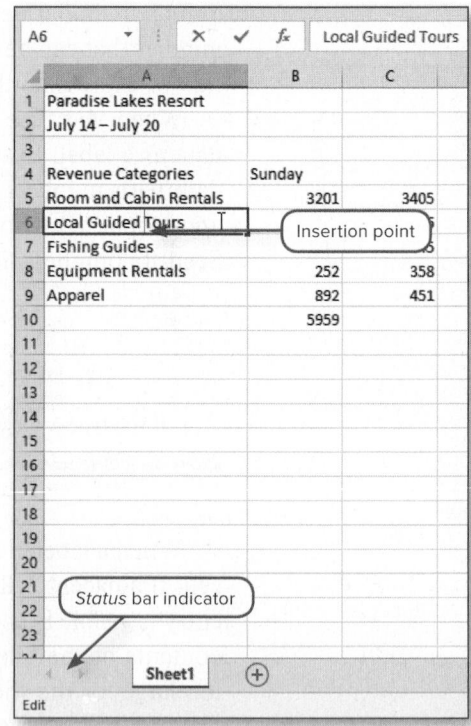

Figure 1-6 *Edit* mode

1. Double-click the cell to be edited.
 - You can also click the cell and press **F2 (FN+F2)** to start *Edit* mode.
2. Position the insertion point in the cell or the *Formula* bar (Figure 1-6).
3. Edit the data.
4. Press **Enter**.

Replace or Clear Cell Contents

To replace data in a cell, select the cell and type the new data. Then press **Enter**, click the **Enter** button in the *Formula* bar, or press any completion key. The new data displays in the cell. To delete data from a cell, select the cell and press **Delete** or click the **Clear** button [*Home* tab, *Editing* group]. From the *Clear* button options, you can choose *Clear All, Clear Formats*, or *Clear Contents* (Figure 1-7). Pressing the **Delete** key removes the contents and preserves formatting.

▶ HOW TO: Clear Cell Contents

1. Select the cell or cells.
2. Press **Delete** on the keyboard.
 - Click the **Clear** button [*Home* tab, *Editing* group] and choose an option.
 - *Clear All* removes formatting and content.
 - *Clear Formats* only clears formatting and keeps data.
 - *Clear Contents* deletes content but keeps formatting.

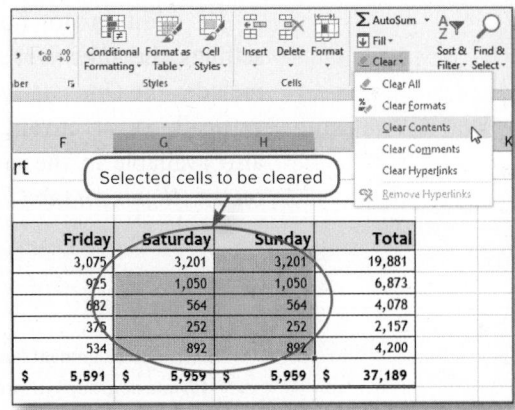

Figure 1-7 *Clear* button options

Align and Indent Cell Contents

Excel recognizes a combination of letters, numbers, spaces, and other characters as a label. Labels are aligned on the bottom left of the cell. When you type only numbers into a cell, Excel identifies the entry as a value. Values are aligned on the right and bottom of the cell.

You can change the vertical and horizontal *alignment* of data in a cell from the *Alignment* group on the *Home* tab (Figure 1-8). Horizontal alignment choices are *Align Left, Center,* and *Align Right*. Vertical alignment options are *Top Align, Middle Align,* and *Bottom Align*.

An *indent* moves cell contents away from the left edge of the cell. In Figure 1-8, labels in rows 5:9 are offset from the label in row 4. The *Increase Indent* button [*Home* tab, *Alignment* group] moves cell contents one space to the right if the data is left-aligned. Remove an indent by clicking the *Decrease Indent* button [*Home* tab, *Alignment* group].

▶ HOW TO: Align and Indent Text

1. Select the cell.
2. Click a horizontal text alignment button [*Home* tab, *Alignment* group].
 - *Center* positions a label midway between the left and right boundaries of the cell.
 - *Align Left* starts a label at the left boundary of the cell.
 - *Right Align* positions a label at the right cell boundary.
3. Click a vertical text alignment button [*Home* tab, *Alignment* group].

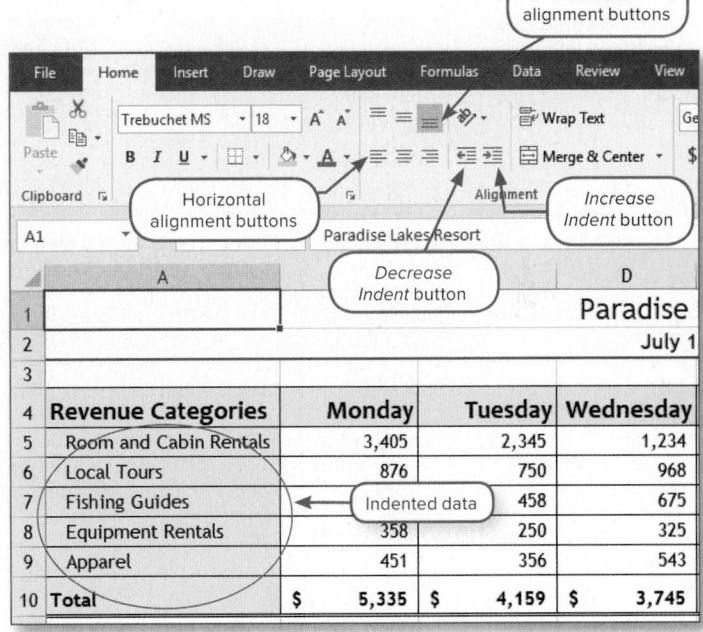

Figure 1-8 Alignment and indent options

 - *Middle Align* positions data midway between the top and bottom cell boundaries.
 - *Top Align* places data at the top cell boundary.
 - *Bottom Align* aligns data at the bottom boundary of the cell.
4. Click an indent button [*Home* tab, *Alignment* group].
 - The *Increase Indent* button moves data toward the right cell boundary.
 - The *Decrease Indent* button moves data toward the left cell boundary.

In addition to horizontal and vertical settings, the *Alignment* group on the *Home* tab includes the *Orientation* button to display data vertically or at an angle. These settings are also available in the *Format Cells* dialog box on the *Alignment* tab (Figure 1-9).

> **MORE INFO**
>
> Click the **Alignment** launcher [*Home* tab, *Alignment* group] or press **Ctrl+1** to open the *Format Cells* dialog box.

Figure 1-9 *Alignment* tab, *Format Cells* dialog box

Select Cells

As you format or edit a worksheet, the first step is to select the cell or cells to be edited. Select a single cell by clicking it. Select a range by clicking the first cell and dragging the pointer in any direction to select adjacent cells. Table 1-2 outlines basic selection methods.

Table 1-2: Selection Methods

Selection	Instructions
Entire Column or Row	Point to and click the column heading. Point to and click the row heading.
All Worksheet Cells	Press **Ctrl+A** or click the **Select All** button (above the row 1 heading and to the left of the column A heading).
Adjacent Cells by Dragging the Pointer	Click the first cell and drag the selection pointer over the cells to be included. Release the pointer.
Adjacent Cells Using the Shift Key and the Pointer	Click the first cell, press **Shift**, and click the last cell in the range.
Adjacent Cells Using the Shift and Arrow Keys	Click the first cell, press **Shift**, and press any arrow key.
Nonadjacent Cells	Click a cell or select the first range, press **Ctrl**, and select the next cell or range. Release the pointer first; then release the **Ctrl** key.
Single Cell or Range Using the *Name Box*	Type a cell or range address in the *Name* box and press **Enter**.

You can see selected cell ranges in Figure 1-10.

To deselect a range of cells, click a cell that is not in the selection. To remove a selected cell from a selected range, press **Ctrl** and click the cell to be deselected.

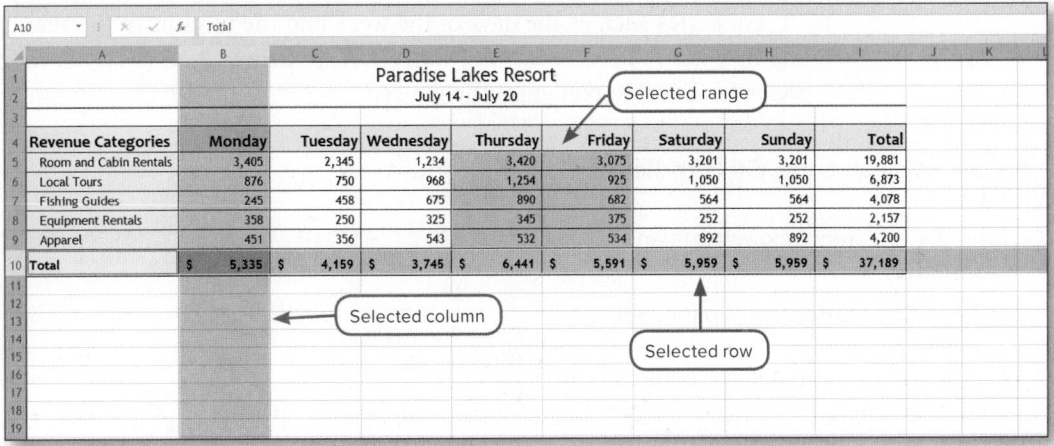

Figure 1-10 Selected cells in a worksheet

▶ MORE INFO

To enter data column by column, select the entire cell range, type the first entry, and press **Enter**.
Continue to type each entry and press **Enter**. The insertion point moves down each column and to the
top of the next column based on the selected range.

The pointer changes shape depending on the current task or mode. Table 1-3 describes the
shapes and indicates when they appear.

Table 1-3: Pointer Shapes

Pointer Icon	Pointer Use
✚	**Selection pointer** (thick, white cross or plus sign) selects a cell or range; the selection pointer appears when you move the pointer over a cell.
┼	**Fill pointer** (crosshair or thin, black plus sign) copies cell contents or completes a series; it appears when you place the pointer on the *Fill Handle*, the tiny square in the bottom-right corner of a selected cell or range.
↕	**Move pointer** (solid, white arrow with a black four-pointed arrow) moves data; it appears when you place the pointer on the border of a selected cell or range.
45↘	**Resize pointer** (two-pointed arrow) adjusts a formula cell range or an object; it appears when you place the pointer on a selection handle in a formula range or on a sizing handle for a selected object.

The Fill Handle

A *series* is a list of labels or values that follows a pattern. An example of a label series is the
days of the week or the months of the year. A series of values is 1, 3, 5, 7, 9. Excel recognizes
patterns and can complete most series with the ***Fill Handle***. If no recognizable series exists, the
Fill Handle copies the data.

The *Fill Handle* is a small square in the lower-right corner of the cell or selected range. Drag
this handle across the cell range for the series or to copy data. When you release the pointer,
the data is completed, and the *Auto Fill Options* button displays near the end of the series. This
button provides choices for how to complete the series, but you usually do not need to make
any changes.

For series such as the days of the week and the months of the year, you only need to enter the first item in the series. For other series, such as 2, 4, 6, 8, you need to enter at least two items for Excel to recognize the pattern.

> **HOW TO: Use the Fill Handle to Create a Series**

1. Type the first item in the series and press **Enter**.
 - Press **Ctrl+Enter** to keep the cell active.
 - Type two or three entries to identify a custom series.
2. Select the cell with the entry.
 - Select all cells with data that identify the pattern.
3. Point to the *Fill Handle* to display the *Fill* pointer (thin, black plus sign) (Figure 1-11).
4. Click and drag the *Fill* pointer through the last cell for the series.
 - A series can be horizontal or vertical.
 - You can double-click the *Fill* pointer to complete data down a column if other columns are already completed to the last row.
5. Release the pointer.
 - The series is complete and the *Auto Fill Options* button appears.
6. Click the **Auto Fill Options** button.
 - Choose an option as desired (Figure 1-12).
 - *Auto Fill* options depend on the data type.
7. Continue to the next task.
 - The *Auto Fill Options* button disappears when you enter data in a cell or give a command.

Figure 1-11 Use the *Fill Handle* to complete a series

Figure 1-12 Completed series with *Auto Fill Options* button

AutoComplete

AutoComplete is an Excel feature that displays a suggested label in a column when the first character or two that you type matches a label already in the column. *AutoComplete* enables you to quickly and accurately complete repetitive data. It works only for data that is alphanumeric, not for a column of values.

In a column that lists city names, for example, a particular city name might be repeated many times. The first time it appears, you type it as usual. For the second and succeeding occurrences of the name, Excel completes the label as soon as you type the first character. If the *AutoComplete* suggestion is correct, press **Enter**. If the suggestion is not correct, continue typing the label as needed.

Excel usually makes a suggestion after you type a single character in a cell in the column. If the column has more than one entry that begins with that character, type a second character and *AutoComplete* displays another suggestion. Press **Enter** to accept.

E1-12

▶HOW TO: Use AutoComplete

1. Type the first character in a label.
 - A suggested label appears in the cell.
 - Type a second and third character when many labels begin with the same letter.
 - Type uppercase or lowercase characters to display an *AutoComplete* suggestion.
2. Press **Enter** to accept the *AutoComplete* suggestion (Figure 1-13).
 - Continue typing to ignore an *AutoComplete* suggestion.
 - Press **Enter** to complete a new label.

Figure 1-13 *AutoComplete* suggestion

Cut, Copy, and Paste Cell Contents

Excel has the same *Cut*, *Copy*, and *Paste* commands as other Windows applications. Use the **Cut** command to move data from one location to another. The **Copy** command duplicates cell contents to a different location. The **Paste** command places cut or copied data in the selected location. Data is cut or copied from a *source cell* or range and is pasted in a *destination cell* or range. When you cut or copy data, it is stored on the Windows *Clipboard* as well as the *Office Clipboard*.

Move or Cut Cell Contents

Move data using drag and drop, keyboard shortcuts, or *Cut* and *Paste* commands in the *Clipboard* group on the *Home* tab. Drag and drop is quick when you want to move or copy cells within a visible range on the worksheet. When you use the drag-and-drop method, the source data is not stored on either clipboard.

▶HOW TO: Move Data Using Drag and Drop

1. Select the cell(s) to be moved. Point to a border of the selection to display a move pointer (black four-pointed arrow with white arrow).
2. Click and drag the selection to the new location (Figure 1-14).
 - A preview selection shows the destination address.
 - The pointer displays a white arrow as you drag.
3. Release the pointer.

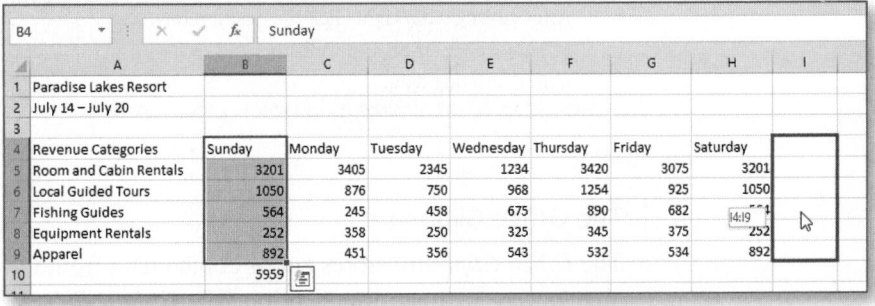

Figure 1-14 Drag and drop to move data

When you use the *Cut* command from the *Ribbon* or the keyboard shortcut, the selected data is placed on both clipboards. You can paste once from the Windows *Clipboard*. You can paste multiple times from the *Office Clipboard*. Use one of three methods to cut data:

- *Ribbon* commands: **Cut** and **Paste** buttons [*Home* tab, *Clipboard* group]
- Shortcut commands: **Ctrl+X** to cut and **Ctrl+V** to paste
- Context menu: Right-click and select **Cut**; right-click and select **Paste**

▶ HOW TO: Move Data Using Cut and Paste

1. Select the cell or range to be moved.
2. Click the **Cut** button [*Home* tab, *Clipboard* group].
 - A moving border surrounds the source cell(s) (Figure 1-15).
3. Select the destination cell for data that was cut.
 - Select the top-left cell in a destination range.
4. Click the **Paste** button [*Home* tab, *Clipboard* group].
 - If the destination cell(s) are not empty, pasted data overwrites existing data.

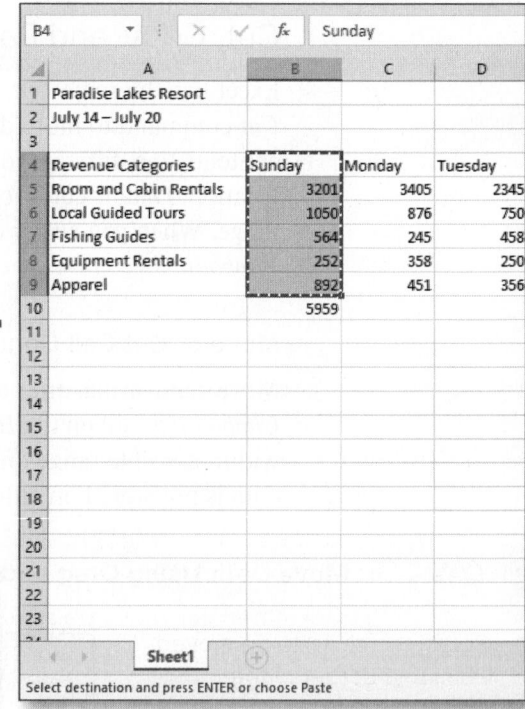

Figure 1-15 Cut data has moving border

The Office Clipboard

The *Office Clipboard* stores cut or copied data from Office applications and the data are available for pasting in any application. The *Office Clipboard* holds up to 24 items with each cut or copied item appearing, in turn, at the top of the pane. Click the **Clipboard** launcher to open the *Clipboard* task pane.

▶ HOW TO: Use the Office Clipboard

1. Click the **Home** tab.

2. Click the **Clipboard** launcher to open the *Clipboard* pane (Figure 1-16).

3. Click **Clear All** to empty the *Clipboard*.

 - The button is gray if the clipboard is empty.

4. Select data to be cut or copied.

5. Click the **Copy** or **Cut** button [*Home* tab, *Clipboard* group].

 - Use any *Cut* or *Copy* command from the *Ribbon* or keyboard.
 - Each item moves to the first position in the *Clipboard* pane.

6. Select a destination cell.

7. Click the item icon in the *Clipboard* to paste it.

 - You can paste an item multiple times in different locations.

8. Click the **Close** button to hide the *Clipboard*.

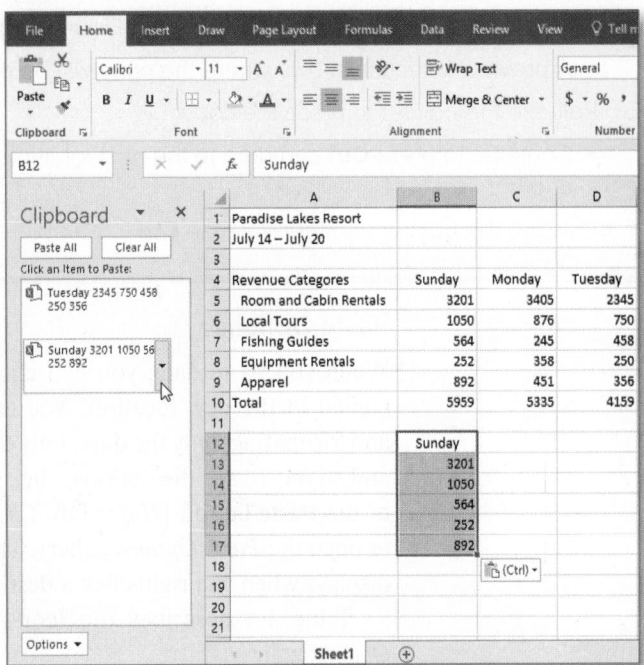

Figure 1-16 *Clipboard* pane

MORE INFO

To remove an item from the *Clipboard* task pane, click its drop-down arrow and choose **Delete**.

Copy Cell Contents

Copying data places a duplicate on the *Clipboard* so that it can be pasted in another location. When you use a *Ribbon*, keyboard, or context menu command, you can paste the data multiple times. You can copy data using the drag-and-drop method and paste it multiple times, even though the copied data is not placed on the *Clipboard*.

The *Copy* command stores data on the *Clipboard*, and the *Paste* command duplicates *Clipboard* contents in the worksheet.

- *Ribbon* commands: **Copy** and **Paste** buttons [*Home* tab, *Clipboard* group]
- Shortcut commands: **Ctrl+C** to copy and **Ctrl+V** to paste
- Context menu: Right-click and choose **Copy**; right-click and choose **Paste**

▶ HOW TO: Copy Data Using Drag and Drop

1. Select the cell(s) to be copied.

2. Point to a border of the selection to display the move pointer.

3. Press **Ctrl** to display the copy pointer.

 - The copy pointer is a white arrow with a tiny plus sign.

4. Drag the selection to the desired location (Figure 1-17).
 - A preview selection shows where the copy will be pasted.
5. Release the pointer to place the copy.
 - Continue to press **Ctrl** and drag to the next location for another copy.
6. Release the pointer and then release **Ctrl** to complete the task.

Figure 1-17 Copy data using drag and drop

Paste Options

When you paste data, you can choose how it is copied in the new location. You can paste data and formatting, only the data, only the formatting, and so on. To see the options, click the lower half of the **Paste** button [*Home* tab, *Clipboard* group] to open the *Paste Options* gallery. The gallery also displays when you right-click a destination cell.

Table 1-4 describes the icons in the *Paste Options* gallery:

Table 1-4: Paste Options

Group	Paste Icon	Paste Option	Description
Paste		Paste	Copies all data and formatting; this is the default option.
		Formulas	Copies all data and formulas, but no formatting.
		Formulas & Number Formatting	Copies all data and formulas with formatting.
		Keep Source Formatting	Copies all data and formatting; same as *Paste.*
		Match Destination Formatting	Copies data and applies formatting used in the destination.
		No Borders	Copies all data, formulas, and formatting except for borders.
		Keep Source Column Widths	Copies all data, formulas, and formatting and sets destination column widths to the same width as the source columns.
		Transpose	Copies data and formatting and reverses data orientation so that rows are pasted as columns and columns are pasted as rows.
		Merge Conditional Formatting	Copies data and *Conditional Formatting* rules. This option is available only if the copied data has conditional formatting.
Paste Values		Values	Copies only formula results (not the formulas) without formatting.
		Values & Number Formatting	Copies only formula results (not the formulas) with formatting.
		Values & Source Formatting	Copies only formula results (not the formulas) with all source formatting.

Other Paste Options		Formatting	Copies only formatting, no data.
		Paste Link	Pastes a 3-D reference to data or a formula.
		Picture	Pastes a picture object of the data. Data is static, but the object can be formatted like any object.
		Linked Picture	Pastes a picture object of the data. The copied data is dynamic and reflects edits made in the source data. Format the picture like any object.

> **MORE INFO**
>
> The *Paste Special* command opens a dialog box with additional options to paste comments, data validation, themes, and arithmetic operations.

PAUSE & PRACTICE: EXCEL 1-1

In this project, you open an Excel workbook that tracks revenue for one week at Paradise Lakes Resort. You add labels and values to complete the report; align labels; and edit, cut, and paste data. Your worksheet will have deliberate spelling errors for checking in a later Pause & Practice exercise.

File Needed: **ParadiseLakes-01.xlsx**
Completed Project File Name: **[your initials] PP E1-1.xlsx**

1. Open a workbook.
 a. Click the **File** tab and click **Open**.
 b. Navigate to the folder where your data files are stored.
 c. Click the name of the folder to open it.
 d. Locate the file name **ParadiseLakes-01** and click to open it.
 e. Click **Enable Editing** if the workbook has opened in *Protected View* (Figure 1-18).

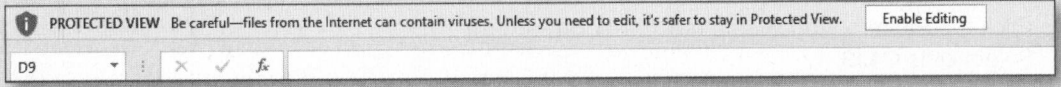

Figure 1-18 Workbook opened in *Protected View*

2. Save the workbook with a different name.
 a. Click the **File** tab and choose **Save As**.
 b. Click **Browse** to open the *Save As* dialog box.
 c. Navigate to and select a location to save the workbook.
 d. Change the file name to [your initials] PP E1-1 in the *File name* area.
 e. Click **Save** to save the file and close the *Save As* dialog box.

3. Enter data.
 a. Click cell **A1** and type Paradise Lakes Resort.
 b. Press **Enter**.
 c. Click cell **A10**, type Total, and press **Enter**.
 d. Type the values shown below in cells **G5:H9**.

	G	H
5	3075	3201
6	925	1050
7	682	564
8	375	252
9	534	892

4. Use the *Fill Handle* to complete a series.
 a. Click cell **B4**.
 b. Point to the *Fill Handle* (small square in the lower-right corner) until the *Fill* pointer (thin, black plus sign) appears.
 c. Click and drag the *Fill* pointer to reach cell **H4**.
 d. Release the pointer.

5. Edit worksheet data.
 a. Click cell **B10**.
 b. Press **Delete** to remove the contents.
 c. Double-click cell **A4** to start *Edit* mode.
 d. Click to position the insertion point and delete the "i" in "Categories" to create a deliberate spelling error.
 e. Press **Enter** to accept the edit.
 f. Click cell **A9** and type Aparel with the error. You will correct errors in *Pause & Practice 1-4*.
 g. Press **Enter** to replace the entry.

6. Indent and align text.
 a. Select cells **A5:A9**.
 b. Click the **Increase Indent** button twice [*Home* tab, *Alignment* group].
 c. Select cells **B4:H4**.
 d. Click the **Center** button [*Home* tab, *Alignment* group].

7. Cut and paste data.
 a. Select cells **B4:B9**.
 b. Click the **Cut** button [*Home* tab, *Clipboard* group].
 c. Click cell **I4**.
 d. Click the **Paste** button [*Home* tab, *Clipboard* group].
 e. Select cells **C4:I9**.
 f. Point to any border of the selected range to display a black, four-pointed arrow with a white arrow.
 g. Drag the range to start in cell **B4** and release the pointer.
 h. Click cell **A1**.

8. Save and close the workbook (Figure 1-19).

 a. Press **Ctrl+S** to save the workbook with the same file name.
 b. Click the **Close** button in the upper-right corner to exit Excel.

▲	A	B	C	D	E	F	G	H
1	Paradise Lakes Resort							
2	July 14 – July 20							
3								
4	Revenue Categores	Monday	Tuesday	Wednesday	Thursday	Friday	Saturday	Sunday
5	Room and Cabin Rentals	3405	2345	1234	3420	3075	3201	3201
6	Local Tours	876	750	968	1254	925	1050	1050
7	Fishing Guides	245	458	675	890	682	564	564
8	Equipment Rentals	358	250	325	345	375	252	252
9	Aparel	451	356	543	532	534	892	892
10	Total							

Figure 1-19 PP E1-1 completed

Using the SUM Function

A *formula* calculates a result for numeric data in a cell. A *function* is a built-in formula. *SUM* is a function that adds the values in a cell range. The terms "formula" and "function" are used interchangeably.

To use the *SUM* function, click the cell where you want to show a total. Then click the **AutoSum** button [*Home* tab, *Editing* group]. Excel inserts the function =SUM() with a suggested range of cells to be added between the parentheses. If that range is correct, press **Enter**, **Ctrl+Enter**, or click the **Enter** button in the *Formula* bar to complete the function. If the suggested range is not correct, select a different range or choose cells individually and then press a completion key. The sum is shown in the cell, and the function is visible in the *Formula* bar.

> **ANOTHER WAY**
>
> The *Function Library* group on the *Formulas* tab has an *AutoSum* button. You can also enter =SUM() in a cell by pressing **Alt** and the **+/=** key on the top keyboard row.

▶ HOW TO: Use the SUM Function

1. Click the cell for the total.

2. Click the **AutoSum** button [*Home* tab, *Editing* group] (Figure 1-20).

3. Press **Enter** to accept the range and complete the function.
 - Drag the pointer to select a different range before pressing **Enter**.
 - If the row or column of values to be added is adjacent to the formula cell as shown in Figure 1-20, you can double-click the **AutoSum** button to insert and accept the function.

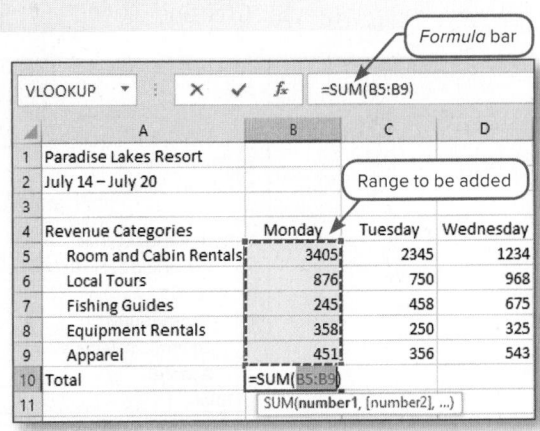

Figure 1-20 *SUM* function

Function Syntax

An Excel function has *syntax*, the required elements and the order of those elements for the function to work. Every function starts with the equals sign [=] followed by the name of the function and a set of parentheses. Within the parentheses, you enter the argument(s). An *argument* is the cell reference or value required to complete the function. A function can have a single argument or multiple arguments. In =SUM(B5:B9), the argument is the range B5:B9. Multiple arguments in a function are separated by commas. This function includes three arguments: =SUM(B5, B10, B15).

SUM(B5:B9)

SUM(B5, B10, B15)

Copy the SUM Function

Copy the *SUM* function using regular copy and paste commands, as well as the *Fill Handle*. When *SUM* is used to total data in rows or columns, enter the formula in the first column or row and copy it to the other locations. In Figure 1-21, for example, the same function is used in cells B10 through H10, each with its own argument. The formula in cell B10 is =SUM(B5:B9), the formula for cell C10 is =SUM(C5:C9) and so on. When a function is copied into adjacent cells, use the *Fill Handle*. Excel copies the formula and adjusts each argument based on the location in the worksheet.

▶ **HOW TO: Use the Fill Handle to Copy a Function**

1. Click the cell with the function to be copied.
2. Point to the *Fill Handle* in the lower-right corner.
3. Click and drag the *Fill* pointer across the cells where the function should be pasted (Figure 1-21).

B10	▾	:	× ✓	fx	=SUM(B5:B9)				
◢	A	B	C	D	E	F	G	H	I
1	Paradise Lakes Resort								
2	July 14 – July 20								
3									
4	Revenue Categories	Monday	Tuesday	Wednesday	Thursday	Friday	Saturday	Sunday	
5	Room and Cabin Rentals	3405	2345	1234	3420	3075	3201	3201	
6	Local Tours	876	750	968	1254	925	1050	1050	
7	Fishing Guides	245	458	675	890	682	564	564	
8	Equipment Rentals	358	250	325	345	375	252	252	
9	Apparel	451	356	543	532	534	892	892	
10	Total	5335	4159	3745	6441	5591	5959	5959	
11									
12									

Figure 1-21 Use the *Fill Handle* to copy a function

Edit the Function Argument

If you edit a value in a cell that is referenced in a formula or function, the results are automatically recalculated. If you must change a cell or range argument in a function, however, you use *Edit* mode to enter new references. In *Edit* mode, you can make a change in the *Formula* bar or in the cell. You can often use the **Range Finder** to drag or select a new range, too. The *Range Finder* is an Excel feature that highlights and color-codes formula cells as you enter or edit a formula or function.

▶ HOW TO: Edit an Argument Range in the Formula Bar

1. Select the cell with the function.
2. Click the argument cell range in the *Formula* bar.
 - The *Range Finder* highlights the argument range in the worksheet.
 - The range is color-coded in the *Formula* bar to match the highlighted range (Figure 1-22).
3. Type the new cell references in the *Formula* bar.
4. Press **Enter**.
 - Click the **Enter** button in the *Formula* bar to complete the edit.

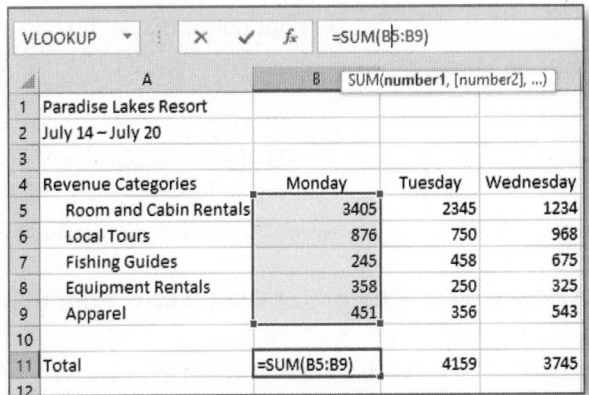

Figure 1-22 Argument range is color-coded

You can drag a *Range Finder* handle to select a different argument range, expanding or shrinking the number of included cells. This is easy to do when the formula cell is not adjacent to the range.

▶ HOW TO: Edit an Argument Range by Dragging

1. Double-click the cell with the function.
 - *Edit* mode starts (Figure 1-23).
2. Drag the selection handle down to expand the argument range.
 - Drag the selection handle up to shrink the argument range.
3. Press **Enter** to complete the change.
 - Click the **Enter** button in the *Formula* bar.

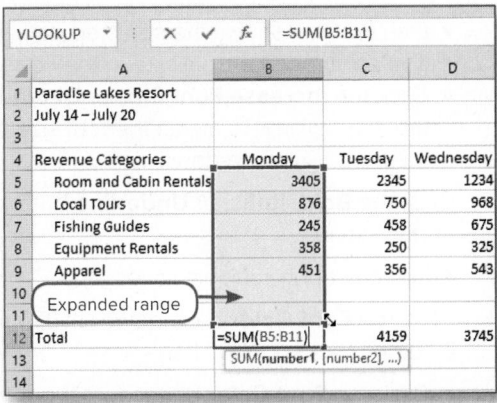

Figure 1-23 Edit an argument range by dragging

SLO 1.4

Formatting a Worksheet

A new workbook uses a default *theme* named *Office* which is a collection of fonts, colors, and special effects. The default theme applies the 11 point Calibri font and the *General* number format to all cells. You can change the theme as well as individual font attributes, or you can add fill and borders to highlight or emphasize data.

Font Face, Size, Style, and Color

A *font* is a type design for alphanumeric characters, punctuation, and keyboard symbols. *Font size* specifies the size of the character, measured in *points* (pt.). A point is equal to 1/72 of an inch. The *font style* refers to the thickness or angle of the characters and includes settings such as **bold**, underline, or *italic*. *Font color* is the hue of the characters in the cell. Apply any of these font attributes to a single cell, a range of cells, or selected characters in a cell.

Default font attributes for Excel workbooks are:

- Font: Calibri
- Font size: 11 point
- Font color: Black, Text 1

> **MORE INFO**
>
> The font list displayed on your computer depends on your Windows installation and other installed applications.

▶**HOW TO:** Customize Font, Style, Font Size, and Font Color

1. Select the cell or range to be formatted.
 - You can format cells before any data is entered.
 - You can select a range of characters in the *Formula* bar.
2. Click the **Font** drop-down list [*Home* tab, *Font* group].
 - A list of available fonts displays.
3. Point to a font name.
 - *Live Preview* shows the selected data with the new font applied (Figure 1-24).
4. Click the **Font Size** drop-down list [*Home* tab, *Font* group] and select a size.
 - *Live Preview* shows the selected data in the new size.
 - You can type a custom size in the *Font Size* area.
 - Click the **Increase Font Size** or **Decrease Font Size** button [*Home* tab, *Font* group] to adjust the font size to the next or previous size in the *Font Size* drop-down list.
5. Click the **Bold**, **Italic**, or **Underline** button [*Home* tab, *Font* group] to apply a style.
 - You can apply multiple styles.
6. Click the **Font Color** drop-down list [*Home* tab, *Font* group] and select a color.
 - Click the **Font Color** button (not the arrow) to apply the most recent font color shown on the button.

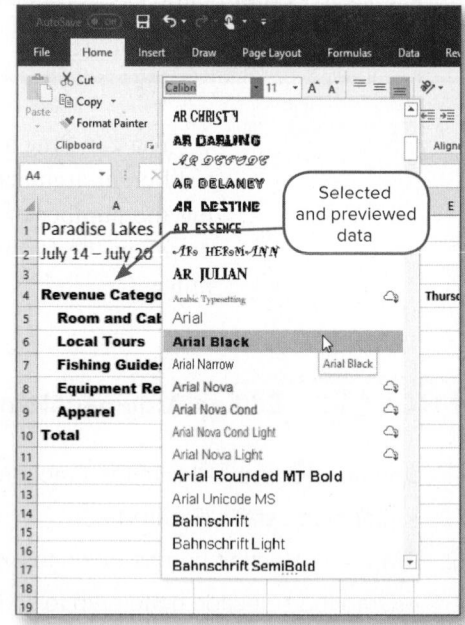

Figure 1-24 *Live Preview* when selecting a font name

The *mini toolbar* includes common commands from the *Font*, *Alignment*, and *Number* groups. It appears when you right-click a cell or selected range (Figure 1-25).

Figure 1-25 Mini toolbar

The *Format Cells* dialog box includes basic format settings and more. It has six tabs: *Number*, *Alignment*, *Font*, *Border*, *Fill*, and *Protection*.

- Mini toolbar: Right-click a cell or selected range.
- *Format Cells* dialog box: Click the **Font** launcher in the *Font* group, press **Ctrl+1**, or right-click a selected cell and choose **Format Cells** (Figure 1-26).

The Format Painter

The **Format Painter** copies formatting attributes and styles from one cell to another cell or range. You can apply your custom formats without having to redefine each attribute, saving time and ensuring consistency in format.

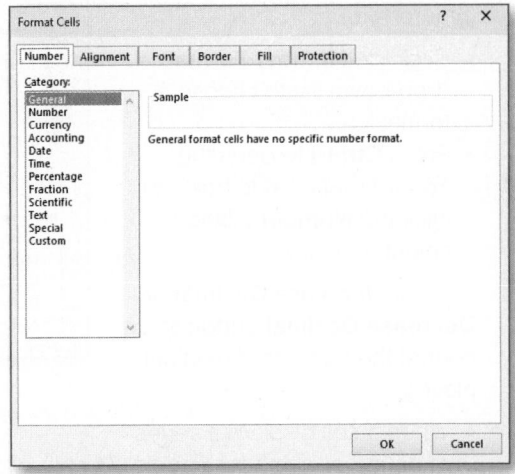

Figure 1-26 *Format Cells* dialog box

▶**HOW TO:** Use the Format Painter

1. Select a cell that contains the formatting you want to copy.
2. Click the **Format Painter** button [*Home* tab, *Clipboard* group].
 - The pointer changes to a thick, white cross with a tiny paint brush.
 - Double-click the **Format Painter** button to lock it for painting formats to multiple areas in the worksheet.
3. Click the cell or drag across the range to be formatted (Figure 1-27).
4. Release the pointer.
 - The *Format Painter* is no longer active.
 - If the *Format Painter* command is locked, click the **Format Painter** button or press **Esc** to turn off the command.

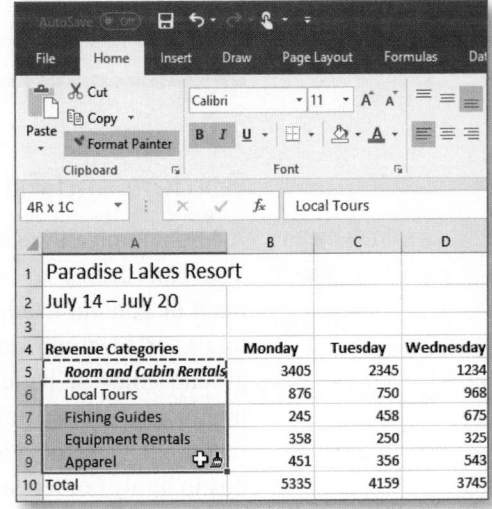

Figure 1-27 Copy formats to a range using *Format Painter*

Number Formats

You can format values with currency symbols, decimal points, commas, percent signs, and more so that data are quickly recognized and understood. The *Number* group on the *Home* tab includes command buttons for *Accounting*, *Percent*, and *Comma* styles, as well as command buttons to *Increase Decimal* or *Decrease Decimal*. Dates and times are values, and *Date* and *Time* formats are included in the *Number* group. From the *Format Cells* dialog box, you can apply and customize these number formats or create your own format.

▶HOW TO: Format Numbers

1. Select the cell or range of values.

2. Click a command button [*Home* tab, *Number* group] (Figure 1-28).

 - Click the **Number Format** drop-down list to choose a format.
 - Press **Ctrl+1** to open the *Format Cells* dialog box and click the **Number** tab to select a format.

3. Click the **Increase Decimal** or **Decrease Decimal** button to control the number of decimal places.

 - When a cell displays a series of pound or number symbols (#####), widen the column to see the value.

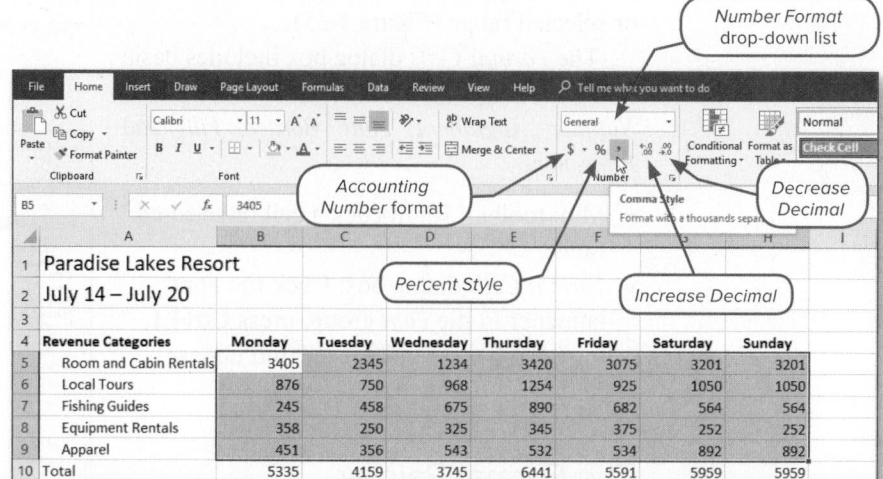

Figure 1-28 *Number* group on the *Home* tab

▶ ANOTHER WAY

Click the **Number** launcher [*Home* tab] to open the *Format Cells* dialog box.

Borders and Fill

A *border* is an outline for a cell or a range. You can design a border to separate main or column headings, to emphasize totals, or to group data. *Fill* is a background color or pattern and is used to highlight or draw attention to data. Use the *Ribbon* or the *Format Cells* dialog box to apply borders and fill color.

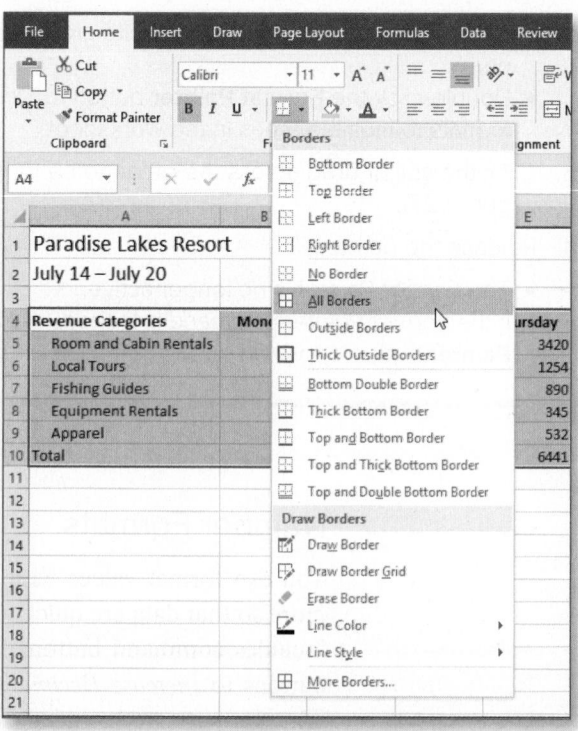

Figure 1-29 *Borders* drop-down list

▶HOW TO: Add Borders and Fill Using the Ribbon

1. Select the cell or range.

2. Click the arrow next to the **Borders** button [*Home* tab, *Font* group].

 - The **Borders** button shows the most recently used border style.

3. Select a border option from the list (Figure 1-29).

 - To remove a border, choose **No Border**.

E1-24

4. Click the arrow for the **Fill Color** button [*Home* tab, *Font* group].

- Click the **Fill Color** button to apply the most recently selected color.
- To remove a fill, choose **No Fill**.

5. Select a color tile in the palette (Figure 1-30).

- *Live Preview* displays the cell or range with the color applied.
- Click **More Colors** to build a custom color.

Figure 1-30 *Fill Color* palette

The *Format Cells* dialog box has a *Border* tab and a *Fill* tab. From the *Border* tab, choose a different line style, a different color, or different positions for the border. From the *Fill* tab, you can design patterned or gradient fills. A ***pattern*** fill uses crosshatches, dots, or stripes. A ***gradient*** is a blend of two or more colors. Use fill choices carefully, because they affect the readability of your data.

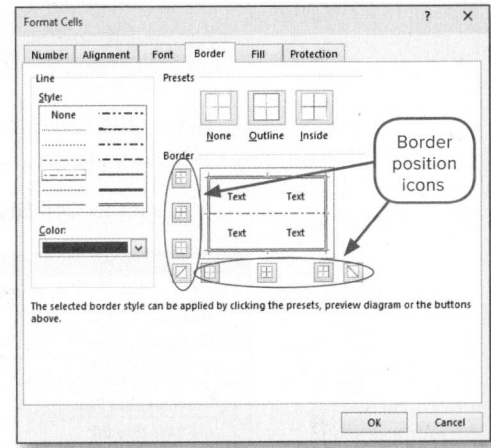

▶ HOW TO: Add Borders and Fill Using the Format Cells Dialog Box

1. Select the cell or range.

2. Click the **Font** launcher [*Home* tab, *Font* group] to open the *Format Cells* dialog box.

- Press **Ctrl+1** to open the *Format Cells* dialog box.
- Right-click a cell in the range and select **Format Cells**.

3. Click the **Border** tab (Figure 1-31).

- Click **None** to remove all borders.

4. Choose a color from the *Color* drop-down list.

- Select the color before choosing a line style or location.

5. Select a line style in the *Style* area.

6. Click **Outline** in the *Presets* area to apply an outside border.

- The *Preview* area shows the border.
- Build a custom border by clicking the desired icons in the *Border* area or by clicking the desired position in the *Preview* area.

7. Click the **Fill** tab (Figure 1-32).

Figure 1-31 **Build a custom border in the *Format Cells* dialog box**

Figure 1-32 *Fill* tab in the *Format Cells* dialog box and *Fill Effects* dialog box

8. Select a color tile in the *Background Color* area.
 - Select a color from the *Pattern Color* list and select a pattern from the *Pattern Style* list.
 - Click **Fill Effects** to apply a gradient. Choose two colors, a shading style, and a variant.
9. Click **OK** to close the *Format Cells* dialog box.

Cell Styles

A *cell style* is a set of formatting elements that includes font style, size, color, alignment, borders, and fill, as well as number formats. Like other formatting, you select the cell or range and then apply a cell style. When you apply a cell style, the style format overwrites individual formatting already applied. After a cell style is applied, however, you can individually change any of the attributes. The *Cell Styles* gallery is located in the *Styles* group on the *Home* tab.

> ### MORE INFO
>
> Your screen size and settings determine if you see part of the *Cell Styles* gallery in the *Ribbon* or only the *Cell Styles* button.

▶ HOW TO: Apply Cell Styles

1. Select the cell or range.
2. Click the **More** button in the *Cell Styles* gallery.
 - Click the **Cell Styles** button [*Home* tab, *Styles* group] to open the gallery (Figure 1-33).

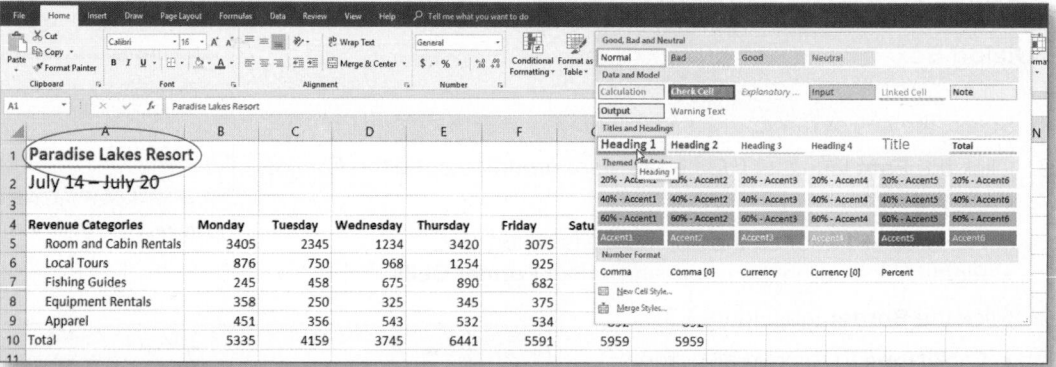

Figure 1-33 *Cell Styles* gallery and *Live Preview* for selected cells

3. Point to a style name to see a *Live Preview* in the worksheet.
4. Click a style name to apply it.

Workbook Themes

A workbook *theme* is a professionally designed set of fonts, colors, and effects. When you change the workbook theme, data formatted with theme settings are reformatted with the new theme fonts, colors, and effects. Change the theme to quickly restyle a worksheet without having to individually edit cell formats throughout the sheet.

A theme includes a font name for headings and one for body text. You can see the names of *Theme Fonts* at the top of the *Font* list. *Theme Colors* are identified in the color palettes for

the **Fill** and **Font Color** buttons [*Home* tab, *Font* group]. Cell styles use font and color settings from the theme.

The *Themes* gallery lists built-in themes, and additional themes are available online. You can also create and save your own theme.

> **HOW TO:** Change the Workbook Theme

1. Click the **Theme** button [*Page Layout* tab, *Themes* group].
 - The *Themes* gallery opens.
2. Point to a theme name.
 - *Live Preview* displays the worksheet with new format settings (Figure 1-34).
3. Click a theme icon to apply a different theme.
 - Display the **Font** button list [*Home* tab, *Font* group] to see the theme font names at the top of the list.
 - Display the **Font Color** and **Fill Color** button galleries [*Home* tab, *Font* group] to see new theme colors.

Figure 1-34 *Themes* gallery and a *Live Preview* in the worksheet

> **MORE INFO**
>
> Rest the pointer on the **Themes** button [*Page Layout* tab, *Themes* group] to see the name of the current theme. Rest the pointer on the **Fonts** button [*Page Layout* tab, *Themes* group] to see font defaults for the theme.

PAUSE & PRACTICE: EXCEL 1-2

In this project, you open the workbook you created in *Pause & Practice 1-1*. You add totals using *SUM* and copy the function using *AutoFill*. Your format changes result in truncated or cutoff data; you learn how to adjust column widths in the next learning objective and repair this problem in the next Pause & Practice project.

File Needed: ***[your initials] PP E1-1.xlsx***
Completed Project File Name: ***[your initials] PP E1-2.xlsx***

1. Open a workbook and save it as a different name.
 a. Click the **File** tab and choose **Open**. Locate the folder where your file is stored.
 c. Open ***[your initials] PP E1-1***. (Click **Enable Editing** if the workbook has opened in *Protected View*.)

 b. Press **F12 (FN+F12)** to open the *Save As* dialog box.

 c. Locate the folder where your files are saved.

 d. Edit the file name to [your initials] PP E1-2 and click **Save**.

2. Calculate daily totals using *SUM*.

 a. Click cell **B10**.

 b. Click the **AutoSum** button [*Home* tab, *Editing* group].

 c. Press **Enter** to accept the suggested range and to complete the formula.

3. Copy a function using the *Fill Handle*.

 a. Click cell **B10**.

 b. Point to the *Fill Handle* in the lower-right corner of the cell.

 c. Click and drag the *Fill* pointer to cell **H10** (Figure 1-35). Release the pointer.

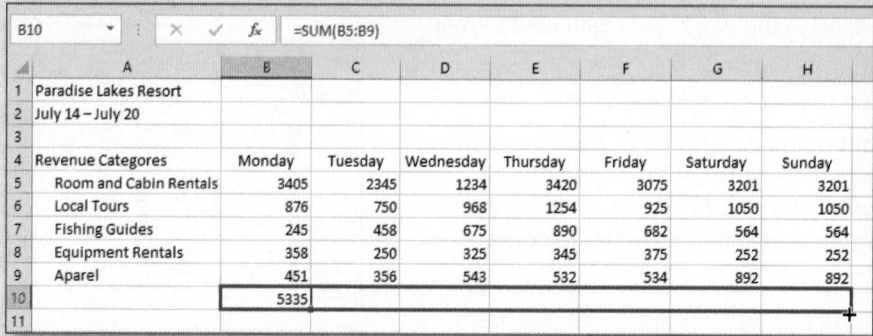

Figure 1-35 Copy a function with the *Fill* pointer

4. Calculate sales category totals.

 a. Click the empty cell **J5**.

 b. Double-click the **AutoSum** button [*Home* tab, *Editing* group] to accept and complete the formula.

5. Edit the argument cell range.

 a. Click cell **J5**.

 b. Click the *Formula* bar showing the range **B5:I5**.

 c. Change the range to display **B5:h5**. When you type the "h," you will see a *Formula AutoComplete* list. Ignore the list (Figure 1-36).

 d. Press **Enter** to accept the new range.

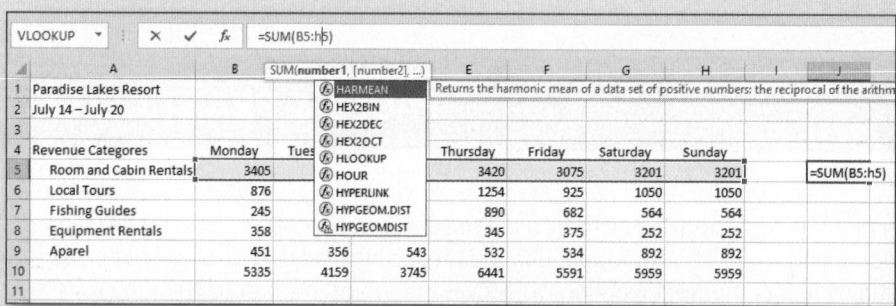

Figure 1-36 Edit the cell reference in the *Formula* bar

6. Copy a function using the *Fill Handle*.

 a. Select cell **J5** and point to the *Fill Handle*.

 b. Click and drag the *Fill* pointer to cell **J10**. Release the pointer.

7. Drag and drop to move a cell range.

 a. Select cells **J5:J10**.

 b. Point to any border of the selected range to display the move pointer.

c. Drag the range to cells **I5:I10**.

d. Type Total in cell **I4**.

8. Apply cell styles.

 a. Select cell **A1** and click the **Cell Styles** button or the **More** button [*Home* tab, *Styles* group] to open the *Cell Styles* gallery.

 b. Click **Title** in the *Titles and Headings* group.

 c. Select cell **A2** and click the **Cell Styles** button or the **More** button [*Home* tab, *Styles* group].

 d. Select **Heading 2** in the *Titles and Headings* group.

 e. Select cells **A10:I10** and open the *Cell Styles* gallery [*Home* tab, *Styles* group].

 f. Select **Total** in the *Titles and Headings* group.

 g. Select cells **A4:A10**, press **Ctrl**, and select cells **B4:I4** to add them to the selection.

 h. Open the *Cells Style* gallery and select **Light Blue, 20% - Accent1** in the *Themed Cell Styles* category.

 i. Click cell **F1** to deselect cells and view the styles.

9. Change the theme and apply font attributes.

 a. Click the **Themes** button [*Page Layout* tab, *Themes* group] and choose **Facet** from the gallery.

 b. Select cell **A4** and click the **Home** tab.

 c. Click the **Font** drop-down list [*Font* group] and select **Candara** in the *All Fonts* section.

 d. Click the **Font Size** drop-down list and select **16 pt**.

 e. Click the **Bold** button [*Font* group].

 f. Select cells **A5:I10**.

 g. Click the **Font Size** drop-down list and choose **12 pt**.

10. Use the *Format Painter*.

 a. Click cell **A4**.

 b. Click the **Format Painter** button [*Home* tab, *Clipboard* group].

 c. Drag to paint cells **B4:I4** and release the pointer (Figure 1-37).

	A	B	C	D	E	F	G	H	I
1	Paradise Lakes Resort								
2	July 14 - July 20								
3									
4	Revenue Categores	Monday	Tuesday	Wednesday	Thursday	Friday	Saturday	Sunday	Total
5	Room and Cabin Rental	3405	2345	1234	3420	3075	3201	3201	19881
6	Local Tours	876	750	968	1254	925	1050	1050	6873
7	Fishing Guides	245	458	675	890	682	564	564	4078
8	Equipment Rentals	358	250	325	345	375	252	252	2157
9	Aparel	451	356	543	532	534	892	892	4200
10	Total	5335	4159	3745	6441	5591	5959	5959	37189

Figure 1-37 Paint the format from cell A4

11. Apply number formats and align text.

 a. Select cells **B5:I9**.

 b. Click the **Comma Style** button [*Home* tab, *Number* group] and leave cells B5:I9 selected.

 c. Click the **Decrease Decimal** button [*Home* tab, *Number* group] two times while cells B5:I9 are selected.

 d. Select cells **B10:I10**.

 e. Click the **Accounting Number Format** button [*Home* tab, *Number* group]. You may see a series of # symbols in the cells.

 f. Click the **Decrease Decimal** button [*Home* tab, *Number* group] two times.

 g. Select cells **B4:I4**.

 h. Click the **Align Right** button [*Home* tab, *Alignment* group]. Not all labels are visible with this alignment setting.

 i. Apply **Bold** to cell **A10**.

12. Add borders.
 a. Select cells **A4:I10** and click the **Border** button arrow [*Home* tab, *Font* group].
 b. Select **All Borders**. The border format from the *Total* cell style in row 10 is overwritten with the *All Borders* format.
 c. Select cells **A10:I10** and press **Ctrl+1** to open the *Format Cells* dialog box.
 d. Click the **Border** tab.
 e. Click the bottom border icon in the *Border* preview area to remove the border (Figure 1-38).
 f. Click the double solid line style (second column, seventh style).
 g. Click the bottom border position in the preview area to reset the border (Figure 1-39).
 h. Click **OK** to close the *Format Cells* dialog box and to apply the new border.
 i. Select cells **A2:I2** and open the *Format Cells* dialog box.
 j. Click the **Border** tab and click the bottom border position two times to remove the bottom border.
 k. Click the **Color** drop-down list, and select **Dark Green, Accent2, Darker 25%** (sixth column).
 l. Select the thick, solid line style (second column, fifth style).
 m. Click the bottom border location in the preview area to reset the border.
 n. Click **OK** and then click cell **A1**.

13. Click the **Save** button in the *Quick Access* toolbar.

14. Click the **File** tab and click **Close**, or press **Ctrl+W** to close the workbook (Figure 1-40).

Figure 1-38 Remove the bottom border

Figure 1-39 Reset the bottom border

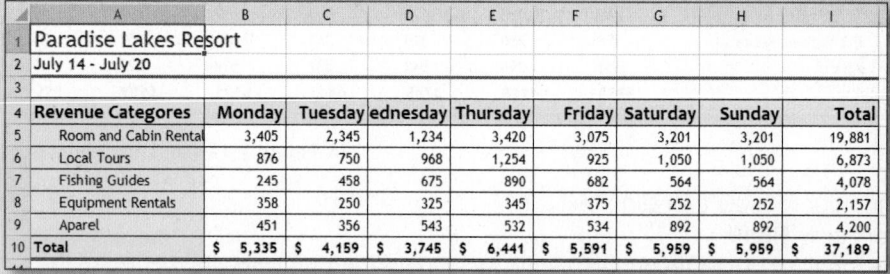

	A	B	C	D	E	F	G	H	I
1	Paradise Lakes Resort								
2	July 14 - July 20								
3									
4	**Revenue Categores**	**Monday**	**Tuesday**	**Wednesday**	**Thursday**	**Friday**	**Saturday**	**Sunday**	**Total**
5	Room and Cabin Rental	3,405	2,345	1,234	3,420	3,075	3,201	3,201	19,881
6	Local Tours	876	750	968	1,254	925	1,050	1,050	6,873
7	Fishing Guides	245	458	675	890	682	564	564	4,078
8	Equipment Rentals	358	250	325	345	375	252	252	2,157
9	Aparel	451	356	543	532	534	892	892	4,200
10	**Total**	$ 5,335	$ 4,159	$ 3,745	$ 6,441	$ 5,591	$ 5,959	$ 5,959	$ 37,189

Figure 1-40 PP E1-2 completed

SLO 1.5

Modifying Columns and Rows

A worksheet includes a default number of rows and columns, each in the default width and height for the workbook theme. Over 1 million rows and more than 16,000 columns are available for use. You can modify the width of a column, insert columns, change the height of a row, delete a column, and apply other changes to the worksheet.

Adjust Column Width and Row Height

The default width for a column in a worksheet using the Office theme is 8.43 characters (64 pixels) in the default font. Change column width to any value between 0 and 255 characters. The default height of each row is 15 points (20 pixels). A *pixel* measures one screen dot. You can change column width or row height by dragging the border between column or row headings, by using the context menu or by selecting a command from the **Format** button list [*Home* tab, *Cells* group]. You can adjust one or more columns or rows at the same time.

▶ HOW TO: Change Column Width or Row Height

1. Select one or more cells in the same column.
 - The cells need not be in adjacent rows.
2. Click the **Format** button [*Home* tab, *Cells* group].
3. Select **Row Height**.
 - The *Row Height* dialog box opens.
4. Enter a height in points and click **OK**.
 - The row height adjusts for the rows in which you selected cells.
5. Select one or more cells in the same row.
 - The cells need not be in adjacent columns.
6. Click the **Format** button [*Home* tab, *Cells* group].
7. Select **Column Width**.
 - The *Column Width* dialog box opens.
8. Enter a new width in characters and click **OK** (Figure 1-41).

	B6	▼ : × ✓ fx	876						
	A	B	C	D	E	F	G	H	I
1	Paradise Lakes Resort								
2	July 14 - July 20								
3									
4	**Revenue Categories**	**Monday**	**Tuesday**	**ednesday**	**Thursday**	**Friday**	**Saturday**	**Sunday**	**Total**
5	Room and Cabin Rentals	3,405	2,345	1,234	3,420	3,075	3,201	3,201	19,881
6	Local Tours	876	750	968	1,254	925	1,050	1,050	6,873
7	Fishing Guides	245	458		682		564	564	4,078
8	Equipment Rentals	358	250			375	252	252	2,157
9	Apparel	451	356			534	892	892	4,200
10	**Total**	$ 5,335	$ 4,159	$		5,591	$ 5,959	$ 5,959	$ 37,189
11									

Column Width dialog box: Column width: 12 [OK] [Cancel]

Figure 1-41 Change the column width for columns B:F

You can quickly change column widths and row heights using the worksheet headings. Point to the border between two column or row headings and click and drag to set a new width or height. When you point to a border, the pointer changes to a resize arrow, and you will see a *ScreenTip* with the setting as you drag. You can use this method with multiple columns or rows, too. Drag across the headings to select the number of columns or rows to adjust, and then click and drag any border in the selected group.

AutoFit Columns and Rows

The *AutoFit* feature resizes column width or row height to fit the width or height of the longest or tallest entry. The quickest way to *AutoFit* a column is to double-click the right border of the column heading (Figure 1-42). To *AutoFit* a row, double-click the bottom border of the row heading. You can *AutoFit* multiple columns or rows by first selecting them and double-clicking any border within the selection. You can also use the *AutoFit Column Width* or the *AutoFit Row Height* commands on the **Format** button in the *Cells* group on the *Home* tab.

> ▶ **HOW TO:** AutoFit Column Width or Row Height
>
> 1. Point to the border to the right of the column heading or below the row heading.
> - Drag to select more than one column or row.
> 2. Double-click the resize arrow.
> - All selected columns and rows adjust to the longest or tallest entry.

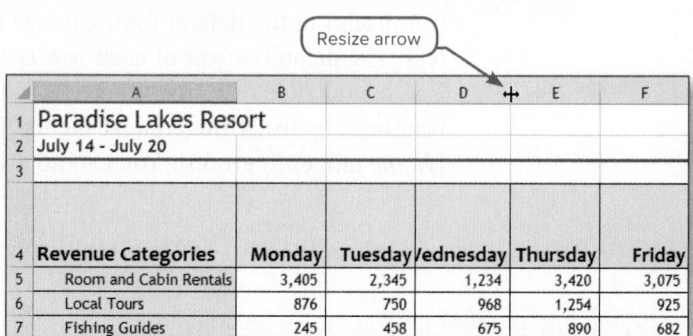

Figure 1-42 Double-click a column border to *AutoFit* its width to the longest item

Wrap Text, Merge Cells, and Center Across Selection

When a label is too long for the column width, it spills into an empty adjacent cell. If the adjacent cell is not empty, a long label may be cut off within the cell. You can widen the column or wrap text. Wrapped text is often used to show lengthy column titles on more than one line (Figure 1-43).

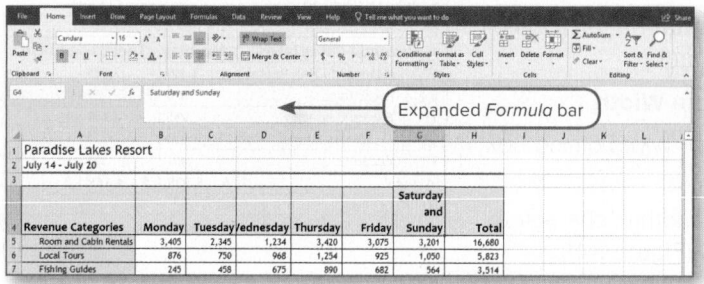

Figure 1-43 Label in cell G4 wraps to two lines; *Formula* bar expanded

The *Wrap Text* command displays a label on multiple lines within the cell, splitting the label between words to fit the width of the column. You control where the label splits by inserting a manual *line break*. Press **Alt+Enter** after the word where you want a new line to start. When using multi-line labels, expand the *Formula* bar by clicking the expand or collapse button at the right edge of the *Formula* bar.

> ▶ MORE INFO
>
> After using the *Wrap Text* command, you may need to adjust the column width or row height to better display the label.

▶ HOW TO: Wrap Text in a Cell

1. Select the cell with the label.
2. Click the **Home** tab.
3. Click the **Wrap Text** button in the *Alignment* group.
 - To control the split, edit the cell and click at the desired location. Press **Alt+Enter** to insert a manual line break and then press **Enter** to finish.
4. Adjust the column width and row height as desired.

> ▶ **ANOTHER WAY**
>
> As you type a label, press **Alt+Enter** at the point where a new line should start, finish the label, and press **Enter**. The *Wrap Text* command is automatically enabled.

The *Merge & Center* command combines two or more cells into one cell and centers the data within the combined cell. This command is a quick way to center a main label over multiple columns. Because the result is one large cell, you can format the area with special fill effects. When you use *Merge & Center*, the data must be in the upper-left cell of the selection.

The *Merge & Center* button [*Home* tab, *Alignment* group] includes options to merge cells without centering and to unmerge cells.

▶ HOW TO: Merge and Center

1. Select the cells to be merged and centered.
 - You can merge and center the cells first and then enter the data.
2. Click the **Home** tab.
3. Click the **Merge & Center** button [*Alignment* group] (Figure 1-44).

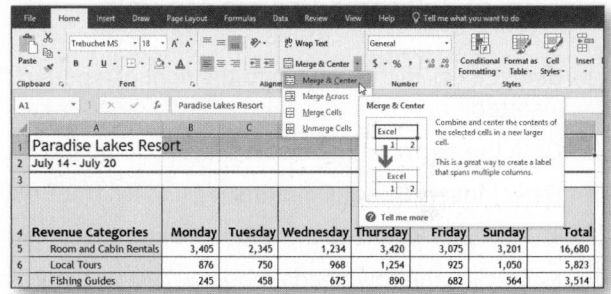

Figure 1-44 Select cells to merge and center

The *Center Across Selection* command horizontally centers multiple rows across multiple columns. When you have two or three rows of labels to center, select the entire range and center them with one command. This command does not merge cells, and you can still insert and delete rows and columns in the centered area.

The *Center Across Selection* command is on the *Alignment* tab in the *Format Cells* dialog box.

Insert and Delete Columns and Rows

You can insert or delete rows or columns in a worksheet. When you do, Excel moves existing data to make room for new data or to fill the gap left by deleted data. Functions or formulas are automatically updated to include an inserted row or column, and they reflect deleted rows or columns in the argument or range.

▶HOW TO: Center Across a Selection

1. Select the cell range that includes the data to be centered.
 - Select all rows with data to be centered.
 - Select columns to identify the range over which the labels should be centered.
2. Click the **Alignment** launcher [*Home* tab, *Alignment* group].
3. Click the *Horizontal* drop-down arrow and choose **Center Across Selection** (Figure 1-45).
4. Click **OK**.

Figure 1-45 Selection A1:I2 identifies area for centering

You can insert rows and columns from options on the *Insert* button [*Home* tab, *Cells* group]. A second way is to right-click a column or row heading and choose *Insert* from the context menu. To insert multiple columns or rows, first select the number of columns or rows that you want to insert. For example, if you want to insert two columns to the left of column A, select columns A:B. Then use any *Insert* command to insert two new columns.

▶HOW TO: Insert a Column or a Row

1. Select a cell in the column to the right of where a new column is to be inserted.
2. Click the arrow on the **Insert** button [*Home* tab, *Cells* group].
3. Select **Insert Sheet Columns**.
 - A column inserts to the left of the current column.
4. Right-click the row heading below the row where a new row should appear.
5. Choose **Insert** from the context menu (Figure 1-46).
 - A row appears above the selected row.

Figure 1-46 Insert a row above row 9

> ## ANOTHER WAY
> Select a cell and press **Ctrl+plus sign (+)** in the numeric keypad. Choose **Entire Column** or **Entire Row** and press **Enter**. Press **Ctrl+minus sign (−)** in the numeric keypad to delete a column or row.

When you delete a column or row, data are deleted and the remaining columns and rows shift to the left or up. Most functions or formulas are updated if you delete a row or column that is within the argument range.

Delete rows and columns using the **Delete** button [*Home* tab, *Cells* group] or from the context menu. To delete multiple columns or rows, select them and use the **Delete** command.

▶ HOW TO: Delete Columns or Rows

1. Select a cell in the column to be deleted.
2. Click the arrow on the **Delete** button [*Home* tab, *Cells* group].
3. Select **Delete Sheet Columns**.
 - The entire column is deleted.
 - Remaining columns shift to the left.
4. Right-click the row heading for the row to be deleted.
 - The context menu opens.
5. Choose **Delete**.
 - The entire row is deleted.
 - Remaining rows shift up.

Hide and Unhide Columns and Rows

If a worksheet has more data than necessary for your current task, hide data to optimize screen space. In a checkbook register with data for several years, you might want to hide rows from two years ago so that you only see the current year's data. You should not delete the old data because it is necessary for record-keeping.

Hidden rows and columns are available and included in calculations and can be shown whenever necessary. The *Hide* and *Unhide* commands apply to columns or rows; you cannot hide cells. When a column or row is hidden, a tiny gap displays between the column or row headings. In addition, column or row headings are not consecutive, so you can quickly identify what is hidden.

▶ HOW TO: Hide and Unhide Columns or Rows

1. Click the row or column heading of the row or column to be hidden.
 - Select multiple row or column headings as desired.
 - Rows or columns need not be adjacent.

2. Right-click one of the selected row or column headings.

- The context menu opens.

3. Select **Hide** (Figure 1-47).

- The entire row or column is hidden.
- Formula references to hidden cells are maintained.

4. Drag across the column or row headings for the hidden columns or rows.

- Drag from the column to the left of a hidden column to one column to the right of a hidden column.
- Drag from the row above hidden rows to one row below hidden rows.

5. Right-click one of the selected row or column headings.

- The context menu opens.

6. Select **Unhide**.

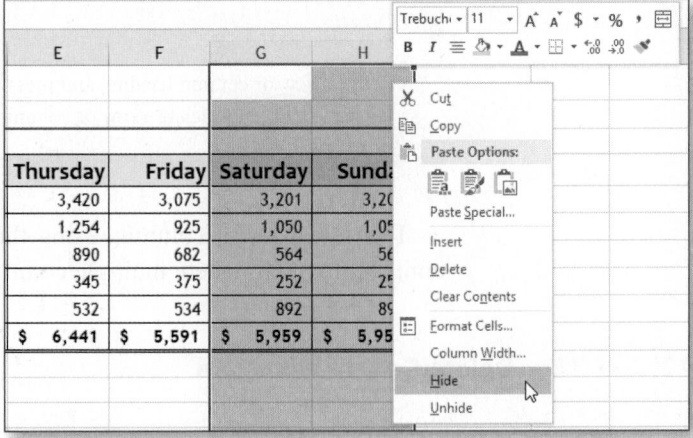

Figure 1-47 Hide two columns

ANOTHER WAY

To hide or unhide columns or rows, select the column or row headings, click the **Format** button [*Home* tab, *Cells* group], choose **Hide & Unhide**, and select the desired command.

SLO 1.6

Inserting, Deleting, and Moving Worksheets

Each worksheet in an Excel workbook has a worksheet tab near the bottom left of the Excel window that displays the name of the sheet. A new workbook starts with one sheet, but the number of worksheets is limited only by the size of memory on the computer. You can insert and delete sheets, rename them, and change the tab color. You can also hide, copy, or move sheets.

Insert and Delete Worksheets

You can keep related worksheets in a single workbook for ease in managing your files and tasks. For example, a monthly workbook could include revenue and expense, payroll, and customer data sheets. When a workbook includes multiple worksheets, activate a sheet by clicking its tab name.

Insert worksheets using the **Insert** button [*Home* tab, *Cells* group] or by simply clicking the **New Sheet** button to the right of the tab names. You can also right-click an existing sheet tab and choose **Insert** to open an *Insert* dialog box. Inserted worksheets are named *SheetN*, where *N* is the next available number.

To delete the active worksheet, right-click the sheet tab and select **Delete**. You can also click the arrow on the **Delete** button [*Home* tab, *Cells* group] and select **Delete Sheet**.

MORE INFO

Press **Ctrl+Page Down** to move to the next worksheet in the tab order. Press **Ctrl+Page Up** to move to the previous sheet.

▶ HOW TO: Insert and Delete Worksheets

1. Click the **New Sheet** button (plus sign) to the right of the worksheet tabs (Figure 1-48).
 - A new sheet inserts to the right of the active sheet.
2. Click the arrow on the **Insert** button [*Home* tab, *Cells* group].
3. Select **Insert Sheet**.
 - A new sheet inserts to the left of the active sheet.
4. Right-click a tab and select **Insert**.
 - The *Insert* dialog box opens.
5. Select **Worksheet** and click **OK**.
 - The new sheet inserts to the left of the active sheet.
6. Right-click a sheet tab and choose **Delete**.
 - The sheet is deleted.
7. Click the arrow on the **Delete** button [*Home* tab, *Cells* group] and select **Delete Sheet**.
 - The sheet is deleted.

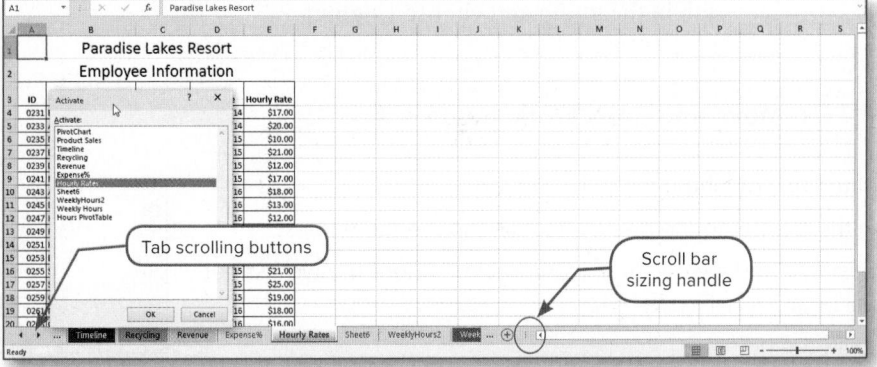

Figure 1-48 *New Sheet* button

▶ **ANOTHER WAY**
Press **Shift+F11** to insert a worksheet to the left of the active sheet.

▶ **MORE INFO**
To delete or insert multiple sheets, select multiple tabs. Then right-click one of the selected tabs and choose **Delete** or **Insert**.

Rename Worksheets and Change Tab Color

New worksheets are named *Sheet1*, *Sheet2*, and so on, but you can rename a worksheet to identify its contents and purpose. The tab width adjusts to display the name, so if you use lengthy names, you limit the number of tabs visible at the same time. When you cannot see all the tabs, use the *tab scrolling buttons* located to the left of the leftmost tab name. Move forward and backward through the tabs, or right-click a tab scrolling button to display the *Activate* dialog box with a list of existing worksheet names (Figure 1-49). The tab scrolling buttons are enabled when needed.

Figure 1-49 *Activate* dialog box and tab scrolling buttons

Apply a *tab color* to further distinguish a particular sheet. The color palette includes tiles for theme and standard colors, as well as an option to build a custom color.

▶ HOW TO: Rename a Worksheet and Apply a Tab Color

1. Double-click the worksheet tab.
 - Right-click the tab and select **Rename**.
2. Type the new name on the tab and press **Enter**.
 - Click the **Format** button [*Home* tab, *Cells* group] and select **Rename Sheet**.
3. Right-click the worksheet tab.
4. Choose **Tab Color** from the context menu to open the palette (Figure 1-50).
 - Click the **Format** button [*Home* tab, *Cells* group] and select **Tab Color**.
5. Select a color.
6. Click another tab to better see the tab color.

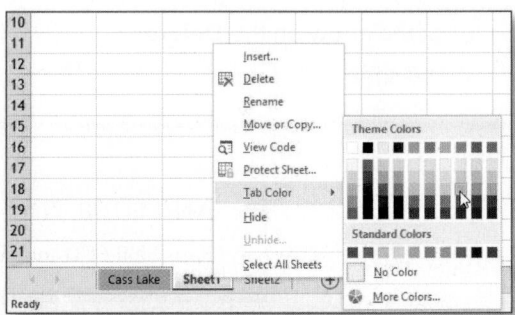

Figure 1-50 Change the tab

Move and Copy Worksheets

Rearrange (move) tabs to display the worksheets in your preferred left-to-right order. You can also move worksheets to another workbook.

Copy a worksheet to create an exact duplicate of the data and formatting. When you copy a worksheet, the copy is named with the same name as the original followed by a number in parentheses (for example: *January (2)*).

When moving sheets within a workbook, simply drag the tab to the desired location. When moving or copying to another workbook, however, use the *Move or Copy* dialog box.

You can move or copy multiple sheets. Select sheet names using **Ctrl** or **Shift**. The word *[Group]* displays in the title bar. After you complete the move or copy command, right-click any tab in the group and choose **Ungroup**.

▶ HOW TO: Move and Copy Worksheets

1. Point to the worksheet tab to be moved.
2. Drag the pointer to the desired location in the tab names.
 - A triangle and a worksheet icon preview where the worksheet will be moved (Figure 1-51).
3. Release the pointer.
4. Right-click the worksheet tab to be copied.

Figure 1-51 Drag a sheet tab to a position

5. Select **Move or Copy**.
 - The *Move or Copy* dialog box opens.
 - Click the **Format** button [*Home* tab, *Cells* group] to select **Move or Copy Sheet**.
6. Click the **To book** drop-down arrow and choose a workbook name.
 - To copy the sheet in the same workbook, choose its name.
 - To copy the worksheet into a different workbook, choose its name; the workbook must be open.
7. Choose a sheet name in the *Before sheet* list.
 - Choose **(move to end)** to place the copied sheet as the last tab.
8. Select the **Create a copy** box (Figure 1-52).
9. Click **OK** to close the dialog box.
 - The copied worksheet has the same name as the original followed by *(2)*.
10. Rename the copied sheet as desired.

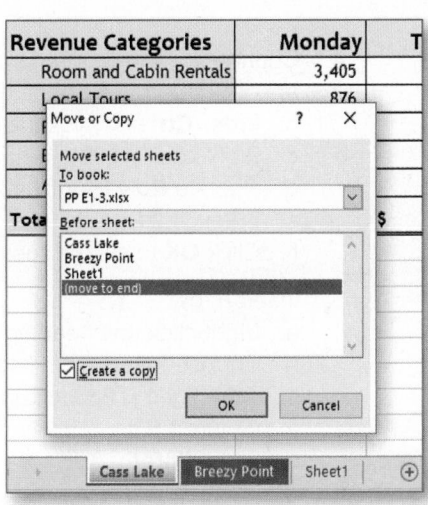

Figure 1-52 *Move or Copy* dialog box

> **ANOTHER WAY**
>
> To copy a worksheet by dragging, press **Ctrl** and drag the tab to the desired location for the copy.

PAUSE & PRACTICE: EXCEL 1-3

In this project, you open *[your initials] PP E1-2* and adjust column heights and row widths, insert a row, merge and center cells, and add borders. You also copy and rename sheets, apply tab colors, and delete worksheets.

File Needed: *[your initials] PP E1-2.xlsx*
Completed Project File Name: *[your initials] PP E1-3.xlsx*

1. Open the *[your initials] PP E1-2* workbook completed in *Pause & Practice 1-2*.

2. Save the file as [your initials] PP E1-3. (If your file is saved in *OneDrive* and *AutoSave* is on, select **Save a Copy**.)

3. Change the width of columns B through I.
 a. Point to the column **B** heading to display a down-pointing arrow.
 b. Click and drag to reach column I.
 c. Click the **Format** button [*Home* tab, *Cells* group].
 d. Select **Column Width** from the menu.
 e. Enter 14 in the *Column Width* dialog box.
 f. Click **OK** to set the new width for the selected columns.

4. Change the row height for rows 4 and 10.
 a. Click the row **4** heading.
 b. Press **Ctrl** and click the row **10** heading. Two rows are selected.
 c. Right-click the row **4** heading.
 d. Choose **Row Height** from the context menu.
 e. Enter 24 as the new height.
 f. Click **OK** to set the row height for both rows.

5. Insert a row.
 a. Right-click row heading **9**.
 b. Choose **Insert**. The inserted row is row 9, and the remaining rows have shifted down.
 c. Type Food & Beverage in cell **A9**. The format of the other rows applies to the new row. (Figure 1-53).
 d. Press **Enter**.

	A	B	C	D	E	F	G	H	I
1	Paradise Lakes Resort								
2	July 14 - July 20								
3									
4	Revenue Categores	Monday	Tuesday	Wednesday	Thursday	Friday	Saturday	Sunday	Total
5	Room and Cabin Rental	3,405	2,345	1,234	3,420	3,075	3,201	3,201	19,881
6	Local Tours	876	750	968	1,254	925	1,050	1,050	6,873
7	Fishing Guides	245	458	675	890	682	564	564	4,078
8	Equipment Rentals	358	250	325	345	375	252	252	2,157
9	Food & Beverage								
10	Aparel	451	356	543	532	534	892	892	4,200
11	Total	$ 5,335	$ 4,159	$ 3,745	$ 6,441	$ 5,591	$ 5,959	$ 5,959	$ 37,189

Figure 1-53 New row and label

6. Hide a row.
 a. Select cell **A9**.
 b. Click the **Format** button [*Home* tab, *Cells* group].
 c. Select **Hide & Unhide** in the *Visibility* category.
 d. Select **Hide Rows**. The selected row is hidden.

7. Center titles across a selection.
 a. Select cells **A1:I2**.
 b. Click the **Alignment** launcher [*Home* tab, *Alignment* group].
 c. Click the *Horizontal* drop-down arrow and choose **Center Across Selection**.
 d. Click **OK**.

8. Rename a worksheet and change the tab color.
 a. Double-click the **Sheet1** tab name.
 b. Type Cass Lake.
 c. Press **Enter**.
 d. Right-click the **Cass Lake** tab name and select **Tab Color**.
 e. Select **Green, Accent1, Darker 50%** (fifth column).

9. Copy and rename a worksheet to create a formatted worksheet for the Breezy Point data.
 a. Right-click the **Cass Lake** tab.
 b. Choose **Move or Copy**. The *Move or Copy* dialog box opens.
 c. Choose **(move to end)** in the *Before sheet* list.
 d. Select the **Create a copy** box.
 e. Click **OK**. The copied sheet is named *Cass Lake (2)*.
 f. Double-click the **Cass Lake (2)** tab, type Breezy Point, and press **Enter**.
 g. Right-click the **Breezy Point** tab and choose **Tab Color**.

h. Format the tab color to **Orange, Accent4, Darker 25%** (eighth column).
i. Select cells **B5:H10** and press **Delete** (Figure 1-54).
j. Press **Ctrl+Home**.

	A	B	C	D	E	F	G	H	I
1				Paradise Lakes Resort					
2				July 14 - July 20					
3									
4	Revenue Categores	Monday	Tuesday	Wednesday	Thursday	Friday	Saturday	Sunday	Total
5	Room and Cabin Rentals								
6	Local Tours								
7	Fishing Guides								
8	Equipment Rentals								
10	Aparel								
11	Total	$ -	$ -	$ -	$ -	$ -	$ -	$ -	$ -

Figure 1-54 Data deleted on copied sheet

10. Click the **Cass Lake** tab and press **Ctrl+Home**.

11. Press **Ctrl+S** to save the workbook.

12. Click the **File** tab and click **Close** to close the workbook (Figure 1-55).

	A	B	C	D	E	F	G	H	I
1				Paradise Lakes Resort					
2				July 14 - July 20					
3									
4	Revenue Categores	Monday	Tuesday	Wednesday	Thursday	Friday	Saturday	Sunday	Total
5	Room and Cabin Rental	3,405	2,345	1,234	3,420	3,075	3,201	3,201	19,881
6	Local Tours	876	750	968	1,254	925	1,050	1,050	6,873
7	Fishing Guides	245	458	675	890	682	564	564	4,078
8	Equipment Rentals	358	250	325	345	375	252	252	2,157
10	Aparel	451	356	543	532	534	892	892	4,200
11	Total	$ 5,335	$ 4,159	$ 3,745	$ 6,441	$ 5,591	$ 5,959	$ 5,959	$ 37,189

Figure 1-55 PP E1-3 completed

SLO 1.7

Modifying the Appearance of a Workbook

You can adjust how you view data in a worksheet. You can select a view, zoom in or out on the data, freeze parts of the screen, split the worksheet into two panes, and switch between multiple open windows.

Workbook Views

The *View* tab has a *Workbook Views* group with three main views or layouts for working in an Excel worksheet. The views are ***Normal***, ***Page Break Preview***, and ***Page Layout***. You can also create ***Custom Views***.

- *Normal* view is the default and is used to create and modify a worksheet.
- *Page Break Preview* displays printed pages with dashed or dotted lines to mark where new pages start.
- *Page Layout* view opens the header and footer areas, indicates margin areas, and shows rulers.
- *Customs Views* enable you to name and save display and print settings, such as hidden columns or selected cells.

Buttons for *Normal* view, *Page Layout* view, and *Page Break Preview* appear on the right side of the *Status* bar.

▶**HOW TO:** Switch Workbook Views Using the Status Bar

1. Click the **View** tab.
 - The *Normal* button is activated in the *Workbook Views* group.
2. Click the **Page Layout** button in the *Status* bar.
 - This view displays the header, the footer, and margin areas (Figure 1-56).

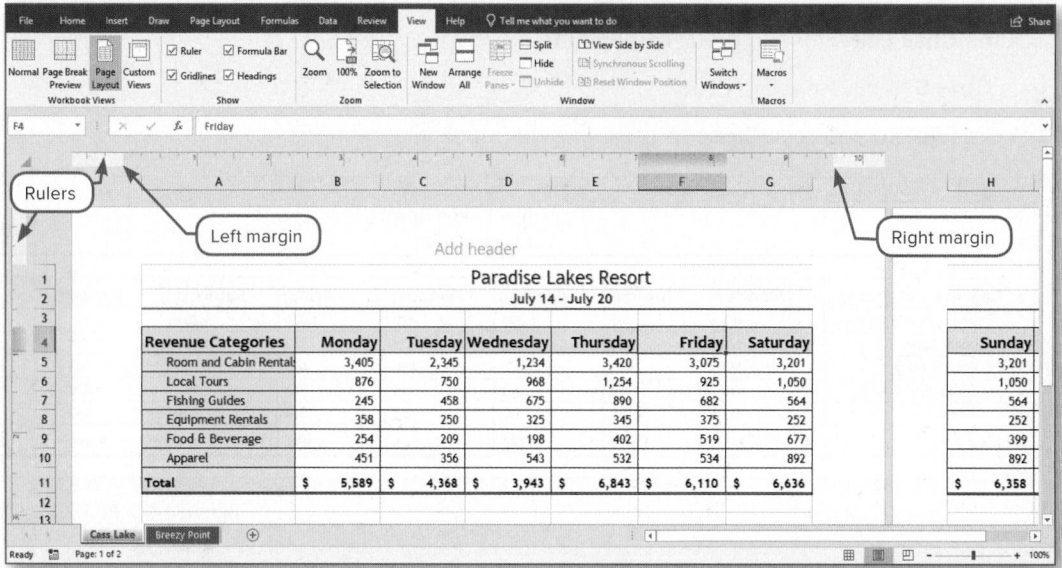

Figure 1-56 *Page Layout* view

3. Click the **Page Break Preview** button in the *Status* bar.
 - If the data does not fit on a single page, a dashed line indicates where the second page will start (Figure 1-57).

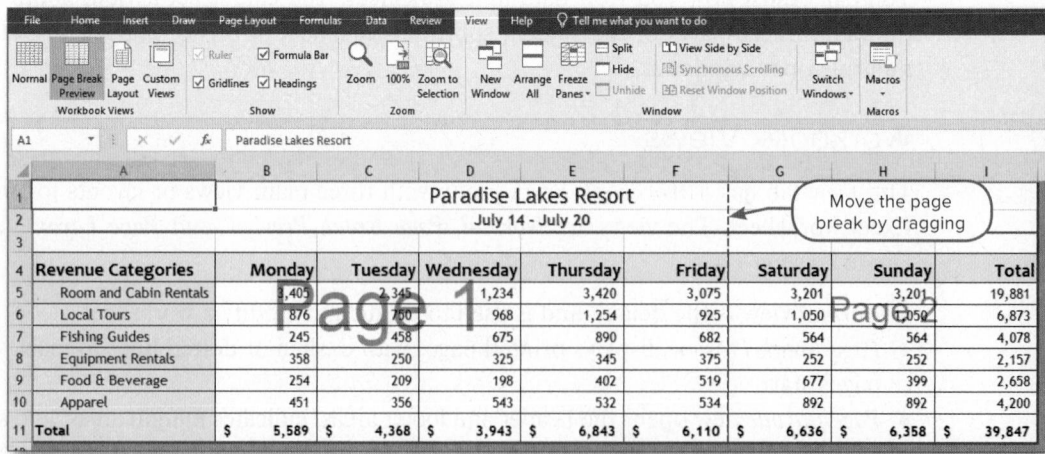

Figure 1-57 *Page Break Preview*

4. Click the **Normal** button in the *Status* bar.

Zoom Options

You can change a sheet's magnification to see more of the data at once (zoom out) or to scrutinize content more carefully (zoom in). Use the *Zoom* group on the *View* tab or the *Zoom* controls in the *Status* bar.

The *Status* bar controls include a **Zoom In** button, a **Zoom Out** button, and the **Zoom** slider. The slider is the vertical bar in the middle of the horizontal line which you drag to change the magnification level.

▶ HOW TO: Change Zoom Levels

1. Click the **Zoom In** button in the *Status* bar.
 - The magnification increases in 10% increments with each click.
2. Click the **Zoom Out** button in the *Status* bar.
 - The magnification decreases in 10% increments with each click.
3. Drag the **Zoom** slider in the middle of the horizontal line to the left or right to set a value (Figure 1-58).
 - The magnification percentage displays to the right of the line.

Figure 1-58 Zoom slider

4. Click the **Zoom** button [*View* tab, *Zoom* group].
 - The *Zoom* dialog box includes preset values.
5. Click a radio button to choose a *Magnification* level.
 - Select **Fit selection** for a selected range to fill the screen.
 - Choose **Custom** to enter any magnification value.
6. Click **OK**.

> ▶ **ANOTHER WAY**
> The *Zoom* group [*View* tab] has *100%* and *Zoom to Selection* buttons.

Freeze Panes

In a worksheet with many rows and columns of information, it is not possible to see all the data at once. As you scroll to see information on the right, related labels or values on the left scroll out of view. The *Freeze Panes* command locks rows or columns in view so that you can position data for easy review. The worksheet is divided into two or four panes (sections) with a thin, black border to indicate the divisions.

The active cell becomes the top-left corner of the moving pane. For example, if you select cell B5 and select the *Freeze Panes* command, column A and rows 1:4 are stationary.

▶ HOW TO: Freeze and Unfreeze Panes

1. Select a cell in the worksheet.
 - Click a cell one row below the last row to be frozen.
 - Click a cell one column to the right of the last column to be locked.
2. Click the **Freeze Panes** button [*View* tab, *Window* group].
 - Select **Freeze Top Row** to lock row 1 in view, regardless of the active cell.
 - Choose **Freeze First Column** to keep the first column in view, regardless of the active cell.

3. Select **Freeze Panes**.
 - All rows above and all columns to the left of the active cell are locked in position.
 - A thin, black border identifies frozen rows and columns.
4. Scroll the data in any direction (Figure 1-59).
5. Click the **Freeze Panes** button [*View* tab, *Window* group].
6. Select **Unfreeze Panes**.
 - The black border is removed.

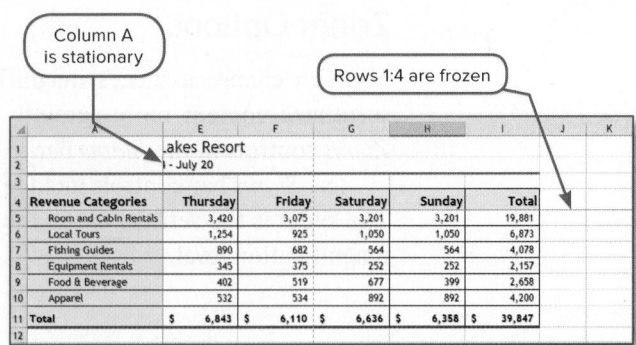

Figure 1-59 *Freeze Panes* results when cell B5 is selected and columns B:D are scrolled left

Split a Worksheet into Panes

The *Split* command divides a worksheet into two or four display panes. Each pane shows the same sheet, but you can arrange each pane to show different rows and columns or the same rows and columns. Only one active cell displays, and you may not see it in all the panes. Because it is one worksheet, an edit can be made in any pane.

The panes are split based on the position of the active cell when you select the command. A *splitter bar* is a light gray bar that spans the window, either horizontally, vertically, or both. You can drag a splitter bar to resize the panes.

▶HOW TO: Split a Worksheet

1. Select the cell for the location of a split.
 - Click a cell in column A (except cell A1) to split the worksheet into two horizontal panes.
 - Click a cell in row 1 (but not cell A1) to split the worksheet into two vertical panes.
 - Click a cell to split the worksheet into four panes.
2. Click the **Split** button [*View* tab, *Window* group].
3. Drag a splitter bar to resize a pane (Figure 1-60).
4. Click the **Split** button [*View* tab, *Window* group] to remove the split.

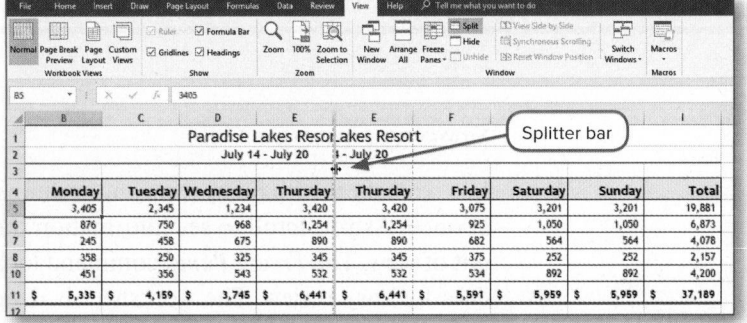

Figure 1-60 Split worksheet

> ### ANOTHER WAY
> Remove a window split by double-clicking the splitter bar.

Hide or Unhide Worksheets

A *hidden worksheet* is a worksheet whose tab does not display. It is part of the workbook and can be referenced in calculations. A worksheet might be hidden to prevent accidental changes to it, or it might hold data that should not be easily visible. Hide a worksheet using the **Format**

button [*Home* tab] or by right-clicking the sheet tab. You cannot hide a worksheet if it is the only sheet in the workbook.

 MORE INFO

The command to print an *Entire Workbook* does not print a hidden worksheet.

▶**HOW TO:** Hide and Unhide Worksheets

1. Right-click the sheet tab to hide.
 - Press **Ctrl** to select multiple sheets, then right-click any one of the selected tabs.
2. Select **Hide**.
 - The worksheet tab is hidden.
3. Right-click any worksheet tab.
4. Select **Unhide**.
 - The *Unhide* dialog box opens.
5. Select the tab name to unhide (Figure 1-61).
6. Click **OK**.

Figure 1-61 *Unhide* dialog box

 MORE INFO

The *Hide* command on the *View* tab hides a workbook. A hidden workbook can be used to store programming routines such as macros or external reference data that should be protected from viewing or accidental editing.

Switch Windows Command

The **Switch Windows** command changes or cycles through open workbooks. You can switch windows from the *Ribbon*, from the Windows taskbar, or with the keyboard shortcut **Ctrl+F6**. When you click the **Switch Windows** button [*View* tab, *Window* group], a menu lists the names of open workbooks. To use the Windows taskbar, point to the Excel icon to see a thumbnail with the file name of each open workbook, and click the one to be edited. The keyboard shortcut toggles between the last two viewed workbooks.

When only two workbooks are open, you can view them side by side. The *View Side by Side* button is grayed out when only one workbook is open. For side-by-side viewing, you can scroll the windows together or separately. *Synchronous Scrolling* moves both workbooks in the same direction at the same time. This is especially helpful when worksheets have the same types of data in the same locations. Synchronous scrolling is automatically enabled when you choose the *View Side by Side* command.

▶ MORE INFO

If three or more workbooks are open when you select the *View Side by Side* command, the *Compare Side by Side* dialog box opens with the names of open workbooks. The one you select displays side by side with the active workbook.

1. Open two or more workbooks.
2. Click the **Switch Windows** button [*View* tab, *Window* group].
 - The names of open workbooks display.
3. Click the name of the workbook to view.

View Multiple Worksheets

The *New Window* command opens a new separate window with the same workbook. The new window displays the workbook name in the title bar followed by a colon and number. Combined with the *Arrange All* command, you can position different parts of the workbook to make comparisons or monitor changes as you work. Figure 1-62 shows different sheets in the same workbook.

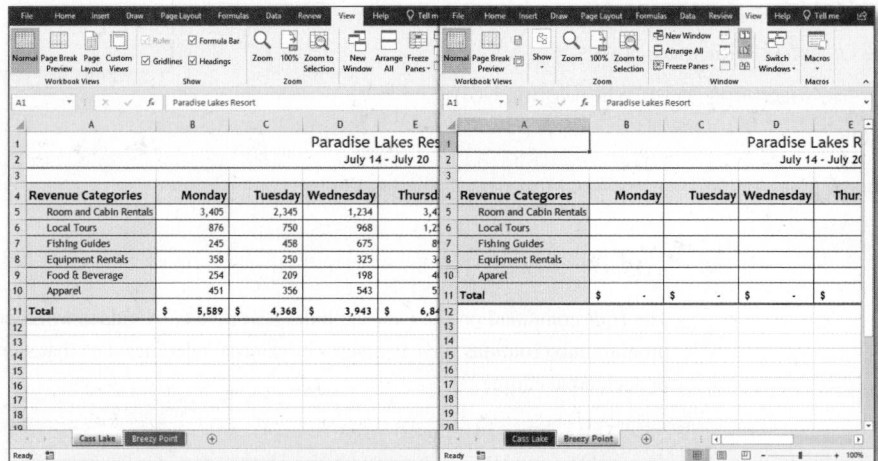

Figure 1-62 Two windows for a workbook

> MORE INFO
>
> Open as many windows as needed and arrange them all.

▶HOW TO: View Multiple Worksheets at the Same Time

1. Click the **View** tab and click the **New Window** button [*Window* group].
 - A second window opens for the same workbook and is active.
 - Both windows are maximized.
2. Click the **Arrange All** button [*View* tab, *Window* group].
 - The *Arrange Windows* dialog box opens.
3. Choose an option for arranging the windows.
 - The active window displays on the left (vertically tiled) or at the top (horizontally tiled).
 - If several workbooks are open but only the active workbook has multiple windows, choose **Windows of active workbook** so that only those windows display.

4. Click **OK**.
 - The active window is arranged on the left or at the top.
5. Click the **Maximize** button in either title bar.
 - The window is full size.
6. Click the **Close** button (**X**) in the title bar to close the window.
 - The other window displays at its tiled size.
7. Click the **Maximize** button.

Finalizing a Workbook

Before you distribute your work to others, make sure that it is ready for sharing. A quick spell check can help locate and correct misspelled labels. Enter document properties or insert headers and footers to help identify your work. You can control how your worksheet prints by setting margins, changing the orientation, or adjusting page breaks.

Check Spelling

The *Spelling* command scans a worksheet and locates words that do not match entries in the main Office dictionary; it also finds duplicate words. The dictionary is shared among all Office applications, and you can add labels to it, such as unusual or technical words. You can spell check the entire worksheet or a selected range.

The *Spelling* dialog box includes options for handling an error, as shown in Table 1-5.

Table 1-5: Spelling Dialog Box Options

Option	Action
Ignore Once	Skips the occurrence of the label.
Ignore All	Skips all occurrences of the same spelling of the label.
Add to Dictionary	Adds the label to the default dictionary.
Change	Changes the label to the highlighted entry in the *Suggestions* box.
Change All	Same as *Change*, but changes the same label throughout the worksheet.
Delete	Appears for *Repeated Word*. Click to delete one occurrence of the label.
AutoCorrect	Adds the label to the *AutoCorrect* list.
Options	Opens the *Excel Options* dialog box to the *Proofing* tab for changing default settings.
Undo Last	Reverses the most recent correction.
Cancel	Discontinues spell checking.

▶**HOW TO:** Spell Check a Worksheet

1. Press **Ctrl+Home** to move to cell **A1**.
 - Start at the beginning of the worksheet.
 - Select a range to limit spell checking to that group of cells.

2. Click the **Review** tab and click the **Spelling** button [*Proofing* group].

 - The first error is located.
 - A list of suggested corrections displays.

3. Select the correct spelling in the list.

 - If no acceptable suggestions display, click the **Not in Dictionary** box and type the correct spelling of the label.

4. Click **Change** to replace the misspelled label (Figure 1-63).

5. Click **OK** when spelling is complete.

Figure 1-63 *Spelling* dialog box

Document Properties

A *document property* or *metadata* is a field of information. Metadata are settings and content including the author name, the date the file was created, the type and size of file, and more. Certain properties cannot be edited such as dates and file size; these settings are automatically updated. You can edit other document properties, including *Title*, *Author*, and *Subject*. A partial list of properties is available in the *Backstage* view on the right in the *Info* pane.

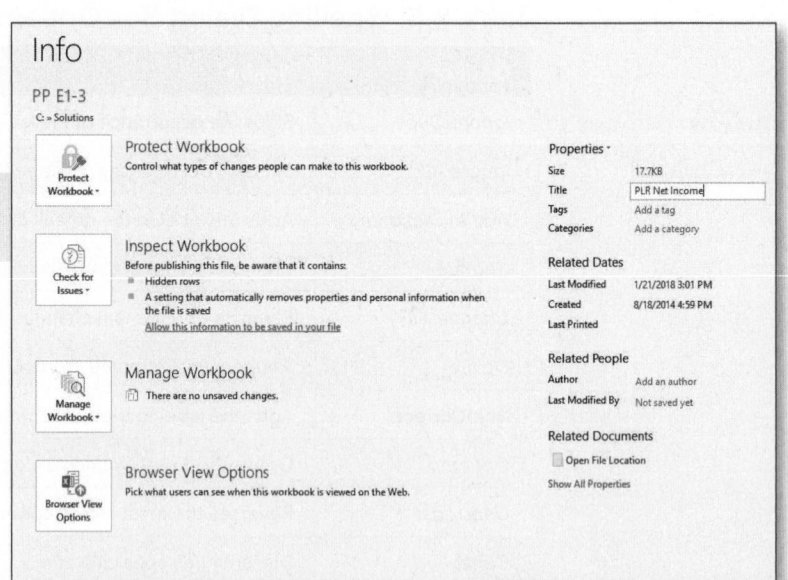

Figure 1-64 Workbook properties

> **HOW TO: Add Document Properties in Backstage View**

1. Click the **File** tab to display the *Backstage* view.

2. Select **Info** if it is not already selected.

 - Property field names are listed.

3. Click an entry box to enter or edit an item (Figure 1-64).

4. Return to the workbook and save the file.

The Properties Dialog Box

You can review all properties in the *Properties* dialog box. The *General*, *Statistics*, and *Contents* tabs list metadata. The *Summary* tab includes properties such as the title, subject, and keywords. Keywords are used in file search commands. On the *Custom* tab, choose additional properties and type default values.

▶ HOW TO: Open the Properties Dialog Box

1. Display the *Backstage* view and click **Info**.
2. Click the **Properties** button.
3. Select **Advanced Properties**.
 * The *Properties* dialog box opens (Figure 1-65).
4. Click a tab to view or edit a property.
5. Click **OK** to close the dialog box.

Figure 1-65 *Properties* dialog box

The Page Setup Dialog Box

The *Page Setup* dialog box offers several command groups for controlling how a worksheet prints. The commands are from the *Sheet Options*, *Scale to Fit*, and *Page Setup* groups on the *Page Layout* tab, as well as commands for setting headers and footers. The **Page Setup** launcher [*Page Layout* tab, *Page Setup* group] opens the dialog box.

Figure 1-66 *Page* tab in the *Page Setup* dialog box

▶ ANOTHER WAY

Open the *Page Setup* dialog box by clicking the launcher in the *Scale to Fit* or the *Sheet Options* group on the *Page Layout* tab.

Each tab in the *Page Setup* dialog box includes a *Print*, a *Print Preview*, and an *Options* button (Figure 1-66). The *Options* button opens the *Printer Properties* dialog box. Table 1-6 summarizes commands on each tab in the *Page Setup* dialog box:

Table 1-6: Page Setup Dialog Box Options

Tab	Available Settings
Page	Set the *Orientation* to *Portrait* or *Landscape*. Use *Scaling* to shrink or enlarge the printed worksheet to the paper size. Choose a *Paper size* or set *Print quality*. Define the *First page number*.
Margins	Adjust *Top*, *Bottom*, *Left*, and *Right* worksheet margins. Set *Header* and *Footer* top and bottom margins. *Center on page* horizontally and/or vertically.
Header/Footer	Choose a preset header or footer layout. Create a custom header or footer. Specify first and other page headers. Set header and footers to scale with worksheet and to align with margins.
Sheet	Identify a *Print area* other than the entire worksheet. Identify *Print titles* to repeat on each page. Print *Gridlines*, *Row and column headings*, *Comments*, and *Error messages*.

Margins, Page Orientation, and Paper Size

A new Excel workbook uses the following default settings:

- Top and bottom margins: 0.75"
- Left and right margins: 0.7"
- Header and footer margins: 0.3"
- Portrait orientation
- Letter size paper

The **Margins** button [*Page Layout* tab, *Page Setup* group] lists *Normal*, *Wide*, and *Narrow* for margin settings as well as *Custom Margins*. When you select **Custom Margins**, the *Page Setup* dialog box opens to the *Margins* tab. Here you set any value for any margin area, including the header and the footer. You can also center the page horizontally or vertically from this tab.

The *Orientation* button [*Page Setup* group, *Page Layout* tab] has two choices, *Portrait* or *Landscape*. A portrait page is taller than it is wide. A landscape page is wider than it is tall. The *Size* button lists paper sizes, but your printer must be able to accommodate the size.

You can modify settings for one worksheet or for several worksheets at a time. To format multiple worksheets, you need to group the worksheet tabs. Do this by clicking the first tab name, holding **Shift**, and clicking the last tab name to select all sheets between those two names. You can also click the first tab name, press **Ctrl**, and click nonadjacent sheet names to create a group.

▶ HOW TO: Set Margins, Page Orientation, and Paper Size

1. Click the **Margins** button [*Page Layout* tab, *Page Setup* group].
2. Select **Custom Margins** to open the *Page Setup* dialog box (Figure 1-67).
 - The dialog box opens to the *Margins* tab.
3. Type each margin setting as desired.
 - Use the spinner buttons to change the margin value.
4. Select the **Horizontally** box in the *Center on page* area.
 - This command centers the data between the left and right margins.
 - You can also vertically center the data on the page.

Figure 1-67 *Margins* tab in the *Page Setup* dialog box

5. Click the **Page** tab in the *Page Layout* dialog box.
6. Select the radio button for **Portrait** or **Landscape**.
7. Click the **Paper size** arrow and select a paper size.
 - The default paper size is 8½ × 11" (called *Letter*).
8. Click **OK** to close the dialog box.

> **MORE INFO**
>
> Top and bottom margins must be greater than header and footer margins. If they are not, worksheet data prints over header and footer text.

> **ANOTHER WAY**
>
> In *Page Layout* view, you can set margins using the ruler. Display the rulers by clicking the *View* tab and selecting the *Ruler* box [*Show* group]. Point to a margin boundary to display a two-pointed arrow and drag the pointer to a new setting.

Headers and Footers

A *header* is information that prints at the top of each page. A *footer* is data that prints at the bottom of each page. Use a header or a footer to display identifying information such as a company name or logo, page numbers, the date, or the file name.

Each header or footer has left, middle, and right sections. Information in the left section is left aligned, data in the middle section is centered, and material in the right section is right aligned. You can select a predefined header and footer, or create your own.

> **MORE INFO**
>
> Predefined headers and footers include one, two, or three elements, separated by commas. One element prints in the center section. Two elements print in the center and right sections. Three elements use all three sections.

Headers and footers are not visible in *Normal* view, but they can be viewed in *Page Layout* view or *Print Preview*. Insert and edit headers and footers in *Page Layout* view.

▶ HOW TO: Insert a Header and Footer Using the Ribbon

1. Select the worksheet.
 - Select more than one worksheet to apply the same header or footer.
2. Click the **Insert** tab.
3. Click the **Header & Footer** button [*Text* group].
 - The view changes to *Page Layout* view.
 - Three header sections display at the top of the worksheet.
 - The *Header & Footer Tools Design* tab is active.
4. Click a header section.

5. Click an element name in the *Header & Footer Elements* group [*Header & Footer Tools Design* tab].

 - A code is inserted with an ampersand (&) and the element name enclosed in square brackets (Figure 1-68).
 - You can type your own label in a section.
 - You can select and delete codes and text in a section.

6. Click the **Go To Footer** button [*Header & Footer Tools Design* tab, *Navigation* group].

7. Click a footer section.

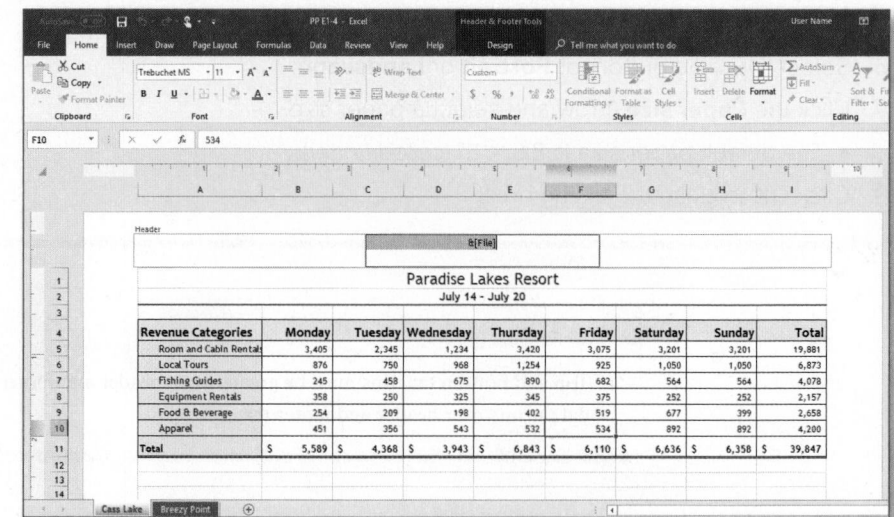

Figure 1-68 *Header* section in *Page Layout* view

8. Click an element name in the *Header & Footer Elements* group [*Header & Footer Tools Design* tab].

 - The related code is inserted.
 - You can type your own label in a footer section.
 - You can select and delete codes and text in a section.

9. Click any worksheet cell.

 - The header and footer appear as they will print.
 - The *Header & Footer Tools Design* tab no longer displays.

10. Click the **Normal** button in the *Status* bar.

 - The header and footer are not visible in *Normal* view.

> **ANOTHER WAY**
>
> To insert a built-in header or footer, click the **Header or Footer** button [*Header & Footer Tools Design* tab, *Header & Footer* group] and select an option.

> **MORE INFO**
>
> In a typed header or footer label such as "Research & Development," type two ampersands in the section like this: Research && Development. This distinguishes the required ampersand from the one used in an element code such as &[Date].

You can also use the *Page Setup* dialog box to insert a header or a footer. A *Header & Footer* tab includes the preset headers and footers, as well as a *Custom Header* or *Custom Footer* option.

▶HOW TO: Insert Headers or Footers on Multiple Sheets

1. Select a single tab or multiple worksheet tabs.

 - Click the first worksheet tab for the group, press **Shift**, and click the last tab.
 - Click a worksheet tab, press **Ctrl**, and click a nonadjacent tab.
 - Right-click any tab and click **Select All Sheets**.

2. Click the **Page Setup** launcher [*Page Layout* tab, *Page Setup* group.

- The *Page Setup* dialog box opens.

3. Click the **Header/Footer** tab.

4. Click the arrow for the *Header* or the *Footer* text box (Figure 1-69).

- A list of built-in header or footer layouts opens.
- Choose **(none)** to remove a header or footer.

5. Choose a predefined header or footer.

- The header or footer displays in the preview area.

6. Click **Custom Header** or **Custom Footer** to open the *Header* or *Footer* dialog box (Figure 1-70).

7. Click a section.

8. Click a button to insert an element.

- Point to a button to see its *ScreenTip*.
- The text or code appears in the section.

9. Click **OK** to close the *Header* or *Footer* dialog box.

- The custom header or footer displays in the preview area.

10. Click **OK** to close the *Page Setup* dialog box.

11. Right-click a sheet tab and choose **Ungroup Sheets**.

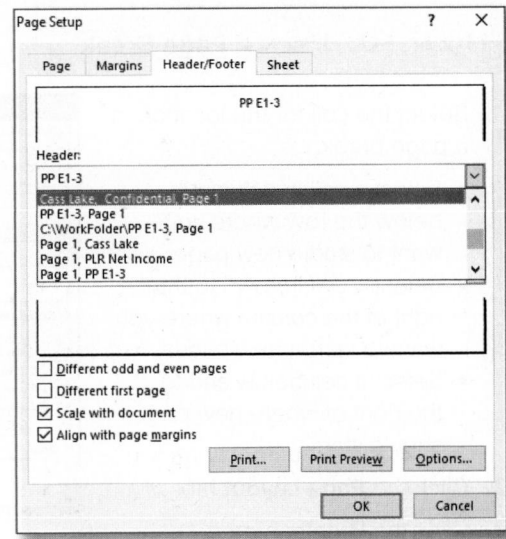

Figure 1-69 Select a built-in header or footer in the *Page Setup* dialog box

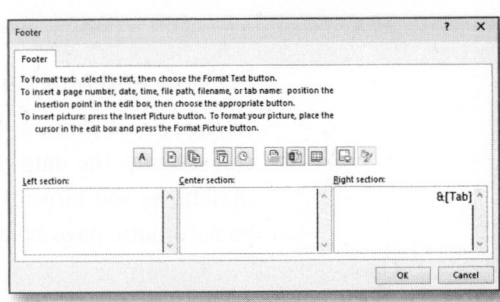

Figure 1-70 Custom *Footer* dialog box

Remove a header or footer in *Page Layout* view or from the *Page Setup* dialog box. To remove headers and footers from multiple worksheets, select the sheet tabs so that they are grouped. In *Page Layout* view, click the header or footer section and delete labels and codes. From the *Page Setup* dialog box, simply select *(none)* from the *Header* or *Footer* drop-down list.

▶**HOW TO: Remove Headers and Footers**

1. Select the worksheet(s).

2. Click the **Page Setup** launcher [*Page Layout* tab, *Page Setup* group].

3. Click the **Header/Footer** tab.

4. Click the **Header** or **Footer** drop-down list and select **(none)**.

5. Click **OK** to close the *Page Setup* dialog box.

6. Ungroup sheets if needed.

Page Breaks

A *page break* is a printer code that starts a new page. When worksheet data spans more than one printed page, automatic page breaks are inserted based on the paper size, the margins, and scaling. Automatic page breaks readjust as you add or delete data. You can insert manual page breaks, too. Manual page breaks do not adjust as you edit worksheet data.

In *Page Break Preview*, an automatic page break displays as a dotted or dashed blue line. A manual page break appears as a solid, blue line.

▶HOW TO: Insert a Page Break

1. Select the cell for the location of a page break.

 - Select a cell in column A below the row where you want to start a new page.
 - Select a cell in row 1 to the right of the column where you want to start a new page.
 - Select a cell below and to the right of where new pages should start.

2. Click the **Page Layout** tab.

3. Click the **Breaks** button.

4. Select **Insert Page Break** (Figure 1-71).

 - A manual page break displays as a thin, solid line in the worksheet in *Normal* view.

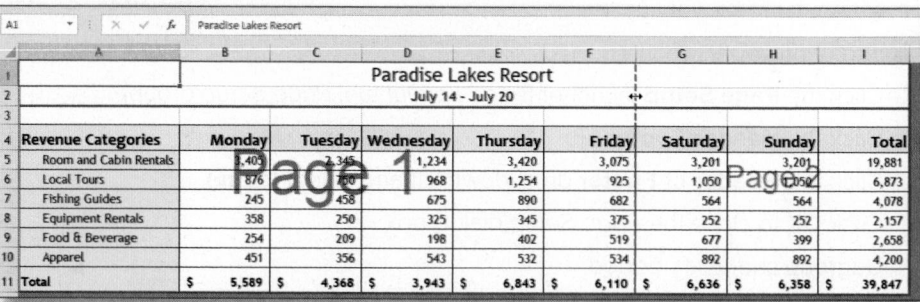

Figure 1-71 Page break inserted after Column D

Preview and Move a Page Break

In *Page Break Preview*, move an automatic or a manual page break by dragging its blue line. You can see how the data displays and evaluate the new printed pages. Depending on the amount of data, as you move a page break, another automatic break may be inserted. When you move an automatic page break, it becomes a manual page break.

> ▶ **MORE INFO**
>
> To move a page break in *Normal* view, you must delete the existing break and insert a new one; you cannot drag the line.

▶HOW TO: Preview and Move a Page Break

1. Click the **Page Break Preview** button in the *Status* bar.

 - Adjust the zoom size in *Page Break Preview*.

2. Point to the page break (dashed or solid, blue line) to display a two-pointed arrow.

Figure 1-72 Drag a page break line to a new position

3. Drag the pointer to a new location (Figure 1-72).

 - If you drag an automatic page break, it converts to a manual break.

4. Release the pointer.

 - A manual page break appears as a solid, blue line.
 - Another automatic page break may be inserted if the data requires it.

5. Click the **Normal** button in the *Status* bar.

Remove a Manual Page Break

You can remove a manual page break in *Normal* view or *Page Break Preview*. Click a cell immediately to the right of or below the break and then click the **Remove Page Break** button [*Page Layout* tab, *Page Setup* group]. When you delete a manual page break, Excel may insert a new automatic page break.

> **MORE INFO**
>
> Insert a manual page break before an automatic page break to "delete" the automatic break.

▶ HOW TO: Remove a Manual Page Break

1. Click the **Page Break Preview** button in the *Status* bar.
2. Click a cell immediately to the right of or below the page break to be removed.
3. Click the **Breaks** button [*Page Layout* tab, *Page Setup* group].
 - Select **Reset All Page Breaks** to remove all manual page breaks.
4. Click **Remove Page Break** (Figure 1-73).
 - An automatic page break is inserted if required.

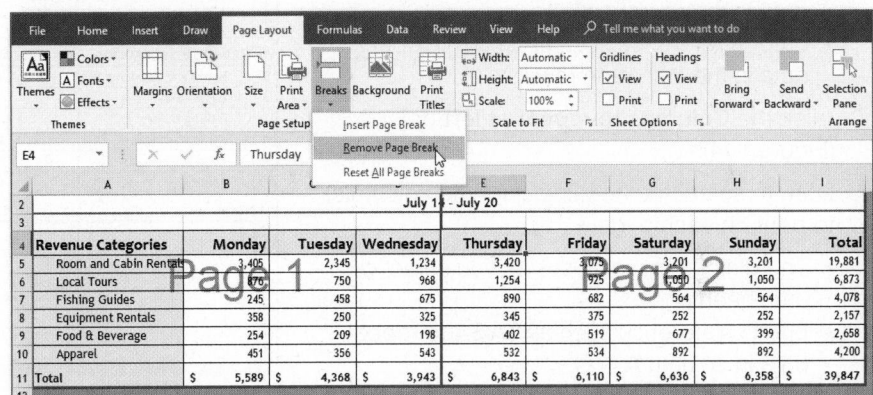

Figure 1-73 Remove a manual page break

> **ANOTHER WAY**
>
> In *Page Break Preview*, drag a manual page break off the page to the right. Excel inserts an automatic page break if required by the margins and other settings.

Customize Print Settings

You can print the entire workbook, the current worksheet, or a selected cell range by making a choice in the *Settings* area in the *Backstage* view for the *Print* command. The *Sheet Options* and *Page Setup* groups on the *Page Layout* command tab include additional options for repeating titles, displaying a background image, and printing gridlines, column letters, and row numbers.

Gridlines, the vertical and horizontal lines that form the columns and rows, are a visual guide to your working on the sheet. Row and column headings serve a similar purpose—to help you navigate in a worksheet. By default, the gridlines and headings do not print, but you can print them using an option on the *Page Layout* tab.

A ***print title*** is a row or column of data that is repeated on each printed page. For example, print main labels from rows 1:3 and from column A on each printed page of a 20-page worksheet.

►HOW TO: Print Gridlines, Print Titles, and Column and Row Headings

1. Click the **Page Layout** tab.
2. Select the **Print** box under *Gridlines* in the *Sheet Options* group.
3. Select the **Print** box under *Headings* in the *Sheet Options* group.
4. Click the **Print Titles** button [*Page Layout* tab, *Page Setup* group].
 - The *Page Setup* dialog box opens to the *Sheet* tab.
5. Click the **Rows to repeat at top** box.
6. Drag to select the heading(s) for the row(s) to print on each page.
 - The row reference(s) displays in the text box.
 - The **$** symbol is an identifier to include all data in the row(s).
 - Enter a reference such as $1:$3 to repeat data in the first three rows.
7. Click the **Columns to repeat at left** box (Figure 1-74).
8. Drag to select the heading(s) for the column(s) to print on each page.
 - The dialog box collapses as you select column headings.
 - Enter a reference such as $A:$A to repeat data in column A.
9. Click **OK**.

Figure 1-74 *Sheet* tab in the *Page Setup* dialog box

> ►ANOTHER WAY
>
> Print *Gridlines* and *Row and column headings* by selecting an option in the *Page Setup* dialog box.

Scale to Fit

The **Scale to Fit** command enlarges or shrinks printed data to fit a specific number of pages or a particular paper size. You can scale printed data as a percentage of normal size or by setting the number of pages. Normal size is how the data would print in the current font size and is shown as *Automatic* in the *Scale to Fit* group [*Page Layout* tab].

►HOW TO: Scale to Fit

1. Click the **Page Layout** tab.
2. Click the **Width** drop-down list [*Scale to Fit* group] and select an option.
3. Click the **Height** drop-down list [*Scale to Fit* group] and select an option (Figure 1-75).
 - Click the **Scale** button spinner arrows to set a percentage of the normal size.

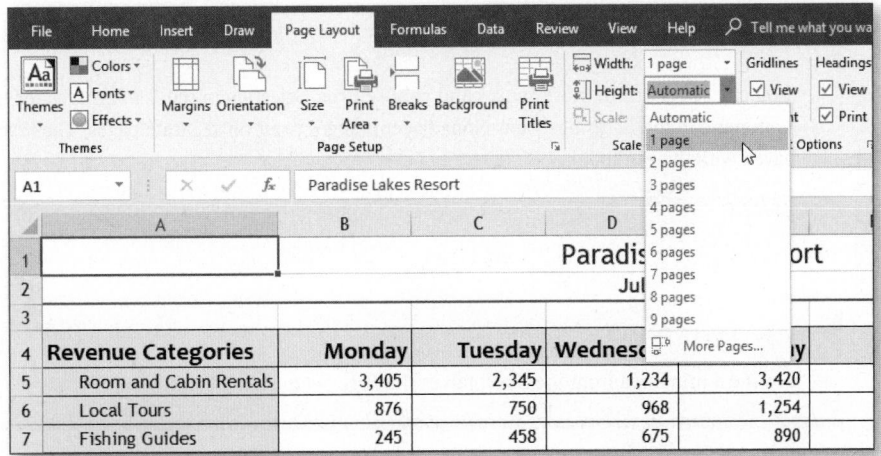

Figure 1-75 *Scale to Fit* options

ANOTHER WAY

Click the **Scale to Fit** launcher [*Page Layout* tab, *Scale to Fit group*] to open the *Page Setup* dialog box and set options in the *Scaling* area.

Print Area

A **print area** is the data that prints from a *Print* command. The default print area is the entire worksheet, but you can identify any range of cells as a print area. You can add adjacent data to a print area, and you can clear a print area to return to the default.

▶HOW TO: Set and Clear a Print Area

1. Select the cells to print.
 - You can select nonadjacent ranges but they print on separate pages.
2. Click the **Page Layout** tab.
3. Click the **Print Area** button [*Page Setup* group] (Figure 1-76).
4. Select **Set Print Area**.
 - You can see the print area in the *Backstage* view for the *Print* command and in *Page Break Preview*.
 - A print area is saved with the workbook.
5. Click the **Print Area** button [*Page Layout* tab, *Page Setup* group].
6. Select **Clear Print Area**.
 - All print areas are cleared.
 - The default print area is reset to print the entire sheet.

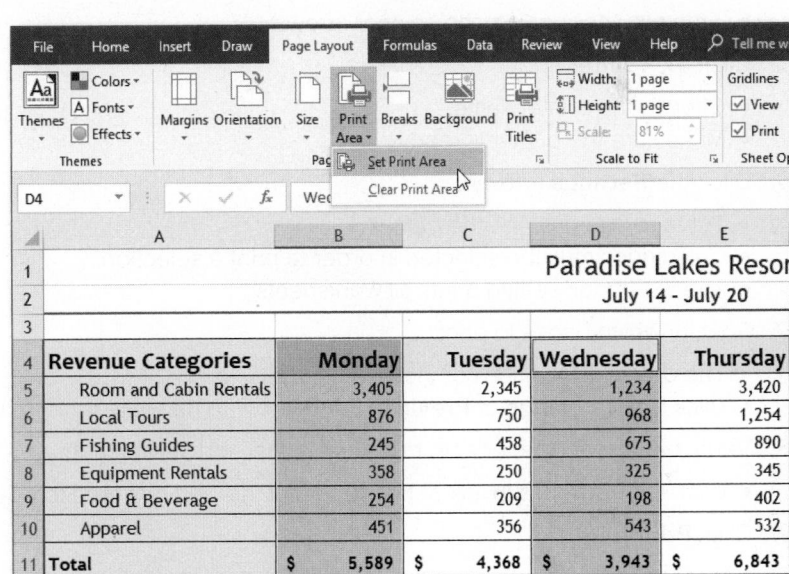

Figure 1-76 Nonadjacent print areas

Print a Worksheet or Workbook

The *Print* command in the *Backstage* view provides a preview so that you can make changes before actual printing. The *Show Margins* button toggles the display of margin and column markers. Drag the column and margin markers to new settings. The *Zoom to Page* button toggles between two zoom settings for the preview.

▶HOW TO: Preview and Print a Worksheet

1. Click the **File** tab and select **Print**.
 - Click **Print Preview** in the *Page Setup* dialog box to open the *Print* command in the *Backstage* view.
2. Click **Show Margins** to display margin and column markers.
3. Click **Zoom to Page** to toggle between zoom sizes.
4. Set the number of *Copies*.
 - Type a number or use the spinner arrows.
5. Click the **Printer** arrow.
 - Choose the printer name.
 - Make sure the printer is ready.
6. Click the **Settings** arrow.
 - The active sheets are the default.
 - Cell ranges must be selected in order to print a selection.
 - The workbook setting prints all worksheets.
7. Specify which pages to print.
 - The default is all pages of the worksheet.
 - Click the **Next Page** or **Previous Page** arrow to navigate through multiple pages.
8. Verify orientation, paper size, margin settings, and scaling (Figure 1-77).
 - Click the **Page Setup** link at the bottom of the *Settings* area to open the *Page Setup* dialog box.
9. Click **Print**.
 - The data is sent to the printer.
 - The *Backstage* view closes.

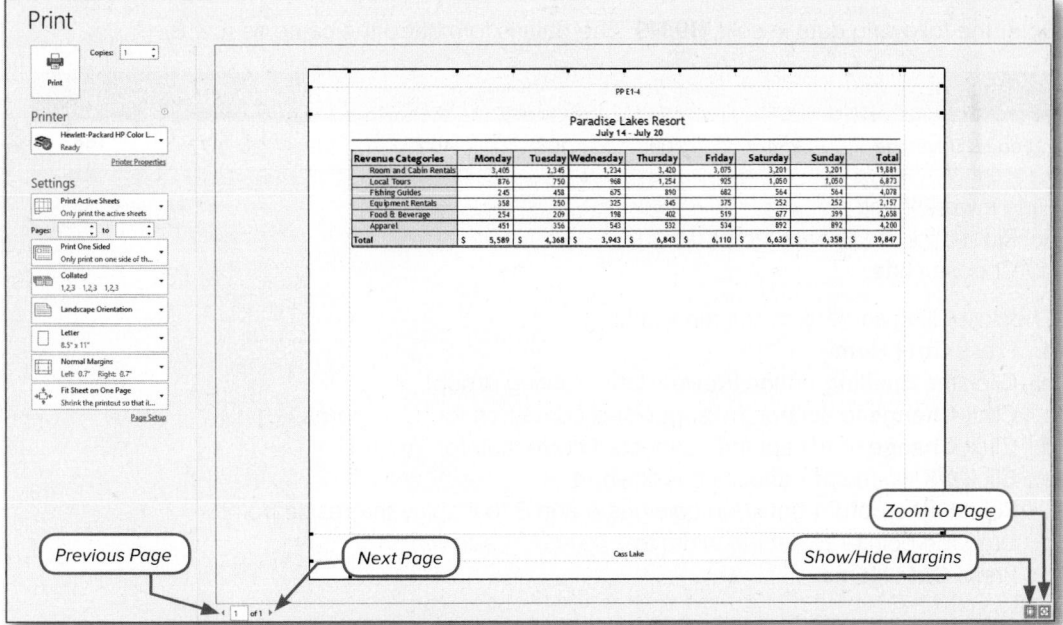

Figure 1-77 *Backstage* view for *Print*

ANOTHER WAY

Press **Ctrl+P** to open the *Print* command in the *Backstage* view.

PAUSE & PRACTICE: EXCEL 1-4

In this project, you open *[your initials] PP E1-3.xlsx* to unhide a row, add data, and hide a sheet. You also spell check a worksheet, set document properties, and finalize the workbook for distribution.

File Needed: *[your initials] PP E1-3.xlsx*
Completed Project File Name: *[your initials] PP E1-4.xlsx*

1. Open *[your initials] PP E1-3* completed in *Pause & Practice 1-3*.

2. Save the workbook as [your initials] PP E1-4. (If your file is saved in *OneDrive* and *AutoSave* is on, select **Save a Copy**.)

3. Select the **Cass Lake** worksheet.

4. Unhide row 9.
 a. Click and drag to select row headings **8:10**.
 b. Right-click either of the selected row headings.
 c. Choose **Unhide** from the context menu.

5. Enter the following data in cells **B9:H9**. The data is formatted the same as row 8.

	B	C	D	E	F	G	H
Food & Beverage	254	209	198	402	519	677	399

6. Hide a worksheet.
 a. Right-click the **Breezy Point** tab.
 b. Choose **Hide**.

7. Check spelling and adjust column width.
 a. Press **Ctrl+Home**.
 b. Click the **Spelling** button [*Review* tab, *Proofing* group].
 c. Click **Change** to accept the suggested correction for "Categores."
 d. Click **Change** to accept the suggested correction for "Aparel."
 e. Click **OK** when spell checking is finished.
 f. Point to the border between columns A and B to display the resize pointer.
 g. Drag the pointer to set the width to 25.63 (210 pixels).
 h. Press **Ctrl+Home**.

8. Enter document properties.
 a. Click the **File** tab to display the *Backstage* view.
 b. Click the **Show All Properties** link at the bottom of the properties list.
 c. Click the *Title* text box and type PP Excel 1-4.
 d. Type Draft in the *Status* text box.
 e. Click the *Subject* text box and type Weekly Revenue (Figure 1-78).
 f. Click the **Show Fewer Properties** link at the bottom of the properties list.
 g. Return to the worksheet.

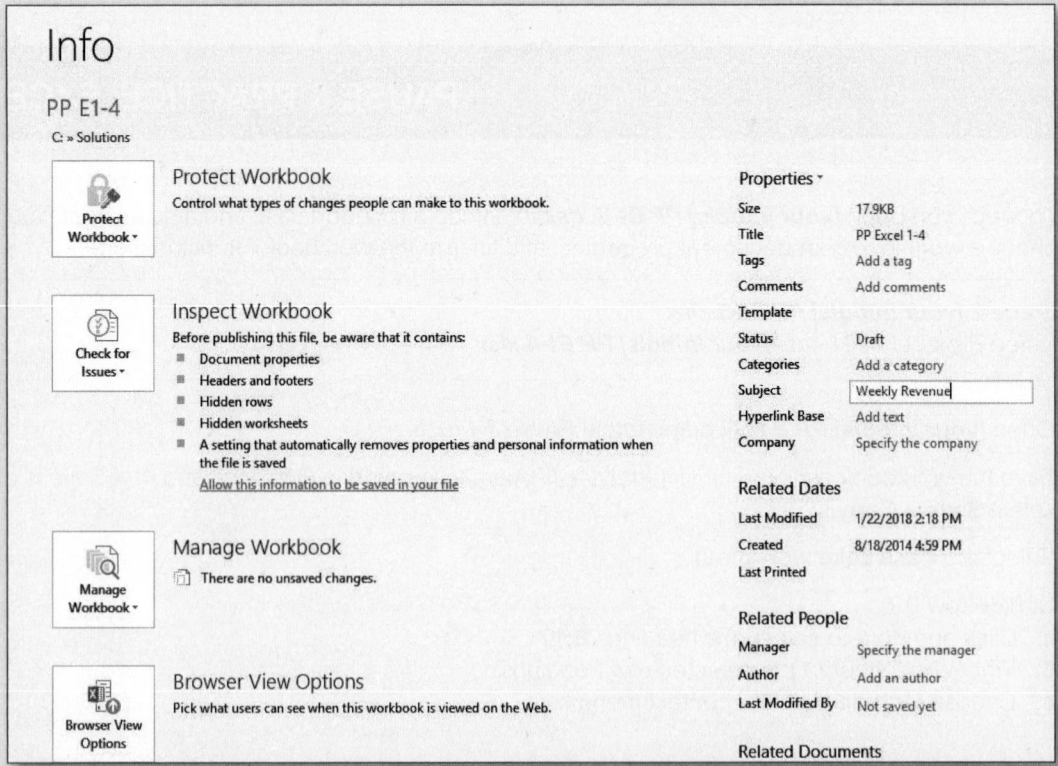

Figure 1-78 Properties in *Backstage* view

9. Change page setup options.
 a. Click the **Page Layout** tab.
 b. Click the **Orientation** button and select **Landscape**.
 c. Click the **Page Setup** launcher to open the *Page Setup* dialog box.
 d. Click the **Fit to** button on the **Page** tab.
 e. Set **1** page wide and **1** page tall.
 f. Click the **Margins** tab.
 g. Select the **Horizontally** box in the *Center on page* area.
 h. Do not close the dialog box.

10. Add a header and footer.
 a. Click the **Header/Footer** tab.
 b. Click the **Header** drop-down list and select *[your initials] PP E1-4*. The file name displays in the preview center section.
 c. Click the **Footer** drop-down list and select **Cass Lake** to insert the sheet name in the center section of the footer.
 d. Click **OK** to close the *Page Setup* dialog box.

11. Preview and print the worksheet.
 a. Click the **File** tab and select **Print**. *Print Preview* displays how the worksheet will print.
 b. Return to the worksheet, or select the printer and click **Print** if you are instructed to do so.

12. Save and close the workbook (Figure 1-79).

PP E1-4

Paradise Lakes Resort
July 14 - July 20

Revenue Categories	Monday	Tuesday	Wednesday	Thursday	Friday	Saturday	Sunday	Total
Room and Cabin Rentals	3,405	2,345	1,234	3,420	3,075	3,201	3,201	19,881
Local Tours	876	750	968	1,254	925	1,050	1,050	6,873
Fishing Guides	245	458	675	890	682	564	564	4,078
Equipment Rentals	358	250	325	345	375	252	252	2,157
Food & Beverage	254	209	198	402	519	677	399	2,658
Apparel	451	356	543	532	534	892	892	4,200
Total	$ 5,589	$ 4,368	$ 3,943	$ 6,843	$ 6,110	$ 6,636	$ 6,358	$ 39,847

Cass Lake

Figure 1-79 PP E1-4 completed

Chapter Summary

1.1 Create, save, and open an Excel workbook (p. E1-3).

- A new Excel workbook has one worksheet and is named *BookN,* with numbers assigned in order throughout a work session.
- Save a workbook with a descriptive name that identifies the contents and purpose.
- Create a new workbook from the *Excel Start* page or from the *New* command on the *File* tab.
- A workbook opened or copied from an online source opens in **Protected View**.
- An Excel workbook is an *.xlsx* file, but it can be saved in other formats for easy sharing of data.

1.2 Enter and edit labels and values in a worksheet (p. E1-7).

- Data is entered in a **cell** which is the intersection of a column and a row. Each cell has an address or reference.
- Data is recognized as a label or a value. Labels are not used in calculations. A label is left-aligned in the cell; a value is right-aligned.
- A **formula** is a calculation that displays a value as its result in the worksheet.
- Press **F2** (**FN+F2**) or double-click a cell to start *Edit* mode. After making the change, press **Enter** to complete the edit.
- Horizontal alignment options for cell data include *Align Left, Center,* and *Align Right.* Data can also be indented from the cell border. Vertical alignment choices are *Top Align, Middle Align,* and *Bottom Align.*
- A group or selection of cells is a **range**. Use the pointer and keyboard shortcuts to select a range.
- Use the **Fill Handle** to create a series that follows a pattern. The *Fill Handle* copies data when no pattern exists.
- **AutoComplete** supplies a suggestion for a column entry that begins with the same character as a label already in the column.
- Cut, copy, and paste commands include drag and drop, as well as regular Windows **Cut, Copy**, and **Paste** buttons on the *Home* tab, context menus, and keyboard shortcuts.

1.3 Use the *SUM* function to build a simple formula (p. E1-19).

- A **function** is a built-in formula. Results appear in the worksheet cell, but the function displays in the *Formula* bar.
- The **AutoSum** button [*Home* tab, *Editing* group] inserts the *SUM* function in a cell to add the values in a selected range.
- Each function has **syntax** which is its required parts in the required order. A function begins with an equals sign (=), followed by the name of the function. After the name, the function **argument** is shown in parentheses.
- Change a function argument by entering new cell references in the *Formula* bar or by dragging the range border in the worksheet.
- When you copy a function, Excel adjusts cell references to match their locations in the worksheet.

1.4 Format a worksheet with font attributes, borders, fill, cell styles, and themes (p. E1-22).

- Apply font attributes from the *Font* group on the *Ribbon* or from the *Format Cells* dialog box.
- Font attributes include the **font** name or face, the **font size**, font styles such as bold, italic, and underline, and the **font color**.
- Number formats include decimals, commas, currency symbols, and percent signs. They also determine how negative values appear in the worksheet.
- Apply number formats from the *Ribbon* or the *Format Cells* dialog box.
- The **Format Painter** copies formatting from one cell to another.
- Add borders or fill color to cells for easy identification, clarification, and emphasis.
- A **cell style** is a preset collection of font, font size, alignment, color, borders, and fill color and is based on the theme.
- A **theme** is a collection of fonts, colors, and special effects for a workbook.
- Use themes and cell styles to quickly format a worksheet with consistent, professionally designed elements.

1.5 Modify columns and rows in a worksheet (p. E1-30).

- The default column width and row height depend on the font size defined by the workbook theme.
- Change the width of a column or the height of a row by dragging the border between the headings.
- *AutoFit* a column or row by double-clicking the border between the headings.
- The *Format* button [*Home* tab, *Cells* group] includes commands to change **row height** and **column width**.
- Insert or delete a column or a row by right-clicking the column or row heading and choosing *Insert* or *Delete*.
- The *Insert* and *Delete* buttons [*Home* tab, *Cells* group] include commands for inserting and deleting rows and columns.
- Display a label on multiple lines in a cell using the *Wrap Text* command to split the label.
- The *Merge & Center* command combines two or more cells into one and centers the data within that new cell.
- Use the *Center Across Selection* command to center multiple rows of data across the same range.
- Hide one or multiple rows or columns, but they are still available for use in a formula.

1.6 Insert, delete, and move worksheets in a workbook (p. E1-36).

- The number of worksheets in a workbook is limited only by the amount of computer memory.
- Click the *New Sheet* button next to the worksheet tabs to insert a new sheet in a workbook.
- The *Insert* and *Delete* buttons [*Home* tab, *Cells* group] include options to insert and delete worksheets.
- Double-click a worksheet tab, type a name, and press **Enter** to rename a sheet.
- Apply a *tab color* to distinguish a particular sheet by changing the background color.
- Move a worksheet tab to another location in the list of tabs by dragging it to that location.
- Create an exact duplicate of a worksheet in the same or another workbook with the *Move or Copy* command or the context menu.

1.7 Modify the appearance of a workbook by adjusting zoom size, changing views, and freezing panes (p. E1-41).

- View a workbook in three ways: *Normal*, *Page Layout*, and *Page Break Preview*.
- Switch views using the *Status* bar buttons or from the *Workbook Views* group on the *View* tab.
- Adjust the zoom size to display more or less data on screen. Zoom controls are available in the *Status* bar and from the *View* tab.
- Use the *Freeze Panes* command to lock selected rows or columns on screen to scroll data while keeping important data in view.
- Use the *Split* command to divide the screen into multiple sections to see different areas of a large worksheet at once.
- Hide a worksheet from view and unintended editing.
- When multiple workbooks are open, the *Switch Windows* command lists the open workbook names.
- Switch among open workbooks using the Windows taskbar.
- The *New Window* command displays the same workbook in a second window. Use this command with the *Arrange All* command to view different areas or sheets of a workbook at the same time.

1.8 Review and prepare a workbook for final distribution by spell checking, setting properties, and adjusting page setup options (p. E1-47).

- Spell checking a workbook follows the same steps as other Office applications.
- A *document property* is *metadata* stored with the file.
- Several properties are supplied by Excel and cannot be edited. Other document properties are added or edited by the user.
- Several properties are visible and are edited in the *Info* area in the *Backstage* view.
- Open the *Properties* dialog box to build or edit properties.
- The *Page Layout* tab includes commands to set page margins and orientation.
- Add *headers* and *footers* to print at the top and bottom of each page.

- Excel inserts automatic page breaks when a worksheet fills more than one printed page.
- Insert manual **page breaks** to change where a new page starts.
- Print **gridlines** as well as row and column headings from commands on the *Page Layout* tab or in the *Page Setup* dialog box.
- Use the **Print** area in the *Backstage* view to make additional changes to the printed worksheet. Changes include choosing to print only a selection or the entire workbook.

Check for Understanding

The **Online Learning Center** for this text (within your SIMnet account) provides the following resources for concept review.

- Multiple-choice questions
- Short answer questions
- Matching exercises

Guided Project 1-1

Life's Animal Shelter (LAS) maintains data in an Excel workbook to track daily expenses for categories that include supplies, animal food, and wages. You will create a new workbook for the current week, enter and format the data, and prepare the workbook for distribution.
[Student Learning Outcomes 1.1, 1.2, 1.3, 1.4, 1.5, 1.6, 1.7, 1.8]

File Needed: None
Completed Project File Name: *[your initials] Excel 1-1.xlsx*

Skills Covered in This Project

- Create and save a workbook.
- Enter labels and values.
- Use the *Fill Handle*.
- Set column widths and row heights.
- Merge and center labels.
- Apply a workbook theme and cell styles.

- Apply font attributes and insert borders.
- Use *SUM* and set number formatting.
- Copy and rename worksheets.
- Set worksheet tab color.
- Change page setup options.
- Use spell check.
- Adjust zoom size and freeze panes.

1. Create and save a workbook.
 a. Create a new **Blank workbook**.
 b. Click the **Save** button on the *Quick Access* toolbar to open the *Save As* area.
 c. Navigate to and select the folder to save the workbook.
 d. Name the workbook [your initials] Excel 1-1 and click **Save**.

2. Rename the sheet and set the tab color.
 a. Double-click the **Sheet1** tab name.
 b. Type Week 1 and press **Enter**.
 c. Click the **Format** button [*Home* tab, *Cells* group].
 d. Select **Tab Color** in the *Organize Sheets* category.
 e. Select **Blue Accent1, Darker 50%** (fifth column).

3. Enter data with deliberate errors.
 a. Type Life's Aminal Shelter with the spelling error in cell **A1**, and press **Enter**.
 b. Type Setember 1 through 7 with the spelling error in cell **A2**, and press **Enter**.
 c. Type Expens Categories in cell **A4**, and press **Enter**.
 d. Type Monday in cell **B4**, and press **Enter**.

4. Adjust column width.
 a. Point to the border between the column **A** and column **B** headings to display a two-pointed arrow.
 b. Double-click to *AutoFit* column **A**.

5. Enter labels and values into the worksheet.
 a. Type *Pet nutrition* information in row 5 as shown in Figure 1-80.
 b. Type *Veterinary supplies* information in row 6 as shown in Figure 1-80.
 c. Type *Shelter supplies* information in row 7 as shown in Figure 1-80.
 d. Type *Salaries and wages* and *Utilities (prorated)* information in rows 8 and 9 as shown in Figure 1-80.

6. Use the *Fill Handle* to fill a series and copy data.
 a. Select cell **B4**.
 b. Click and drag the *Fill* pointer to cell **H4**.
 c. Select cells **B8:B9**. One *Fill Handle* displays in cell B9.
 d. Click and drag the *Fill* pointer to cell **H9**. When no discernible pattern exists, the *Fill Handle* copies data.
 e. Point to the border between the column **D** and column **E** headings to display a two-pointed arrow.
 f. Double-click to *AutoFit* column **D**.

	A	B	C	D	E	F	G	H
1	Life's Aminal Shelter							
2	Setember 1 through 7							
3								
4	Expens Categories	Monday						
5	Pet nutrition	55.25	47.5	38.55	27.45	42.5	35.25	51.75
6	Veterinary supplies	27.85	32.35	35	25	28.5	38.75	44.85
7	Shelter supplies	78	56.45	65.35	55	70	60.25	45.35
8	Salaries and wages	475						
9	Utilities (prorated)	45						
10								

Figure 1-80 Labels and values to be entered with errors in cells A1:A2 and A4

7. Merge and center labels.
 a. Select cells **A1:H1** and click the **Merge & Center** button [*Home* tab, *Alignment* group].
 b. Select cells **A2:H2** and click the **Merge & Center** button [*Home* tab, *Alignment* group].
 c. Select cells **B4:H4**.
 d. Click the **Center** button [*Home* tab, *Alignment* group].

8. Choose a workbook theme.
 a. Click the **Themes** button [*Page Layout* tab, *Themes* group].
 b. Choose **Integral** from the gallery.
 c. Click the **Home** tab. All labels and values are set in the **Tw Cen MT** font.

9. Apply cell styles.
 a. Select cell **A1** and click the **Cells Styles** button or the **More** button [*Home* tab, *Styles* group].
 b. Select **Title** in the *Titles and Headings* category. For the *Integral* theme, a title is formatted in the *Tw Cen MT Condensed* font, 18 points.
 c. Select cell **A2** and click the **Cells Styles** or the **More** button [*Home* tab, *Styles* group].
 d. Select **Heading 2** in the *Titles and Headings* category. The second level heading uses *Tw Cen MT* bold, 13 points. Both styles use a dark blue color.
 e. Select cells **A4:A9**.
 f. Press **Ctrl** and select cells **B4:H4**. Two ranges are selected.
 g. Click the **Cells Styles** or the **More** button [*Home* tab, *Styles* group].
 h. Select **Light Turquoise, 40% - Accent1** in the *Themed Cell Styles* category.
 i. Click the **Bold** button [*Home* tab, *Font* group].
 j. Select cell **A10**.
 k. Type Total and press **Enter**. The format from the column is automatically applied.

10. Apply font attributes.
 a. Select cells **A4:H10**.
 b. Click the **Font size** drop-down list [*Home* tab, *Font* group] and select **12**.
 c. Change the font size for cell **A2** to **14**.
 d. Select cells **A5:A9**.
 e. Click the **Increase Indent** button [*Home* tab, *Alignment* group] two times.
 f. Select cell **A10** and click the **Align Right** button [*Home* tab, *Alignment* group].

11. Use the *SUM* function and copy a formula.
 a. Select cell **B10**.
 b. Click the **AutoSum** button [*Home* tab, *Editing* group] and press **Enter** to accept the suggested range.
 c. Select cell **B10** and drag the *Fill* pointer to cell **H10**.

12. Apply number formatting.
 a. Select cells **B5:H10**.
 b. Click the **Accounting Number Format** button [*Home* tab, *Number* group]. Column widths are adjusted to accommodate the values.
 c. Click the **Decrease Decimal** button [*Home* tab, *Number* group] two times. Column widths do not adjust.

13. Change row heights.
 a. Click the heading for row **4**.
 b. Press **Ctrl** and click the row **10** heading. Two rows are selected.
 c. Right-click the row **4** heading.
 d. Choose **Row Height** and type 25 as the new height.
 e. Click **OK**.
 f. Click the heading for row **5** and drag down to select rows **5:9**.
 g. Point to the bottom border of the row **9** heading to display the resize arrow.
 h. Drag the pointer down to reach a height of **21.00 (28 pixels)** and release the pointer (Figure 1-81).

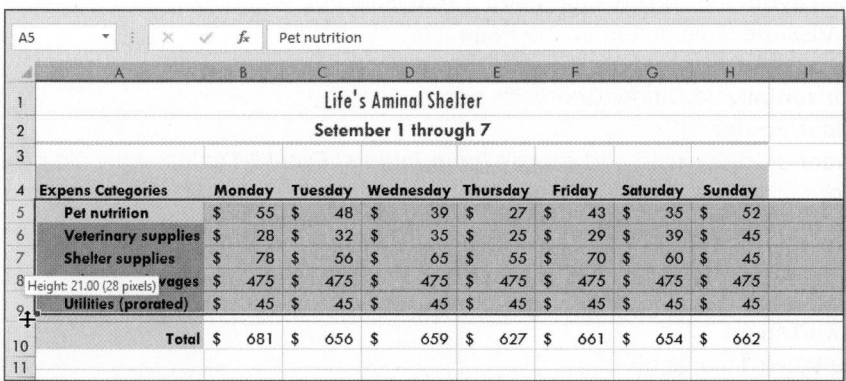

Figure 1-81 Change row heights for rows 5:9

14. Insert a row and change column width.
 a. Select cell **A9** and then right-click row heading **9**.
 b. Choose **Insert** from the context menu. The new row is located above the selected row; other rows shift down.
 c. Enter Cages and equipment in cell **A9**.
 d. Point to the border between columns **A** and **B** to display the resize arrow.
 e. Drag the pointer to a width of **22.50 (185 pixels)** and release the pointer.

15. Enter the following data in row **9**. A zero (0) displays as a small dash.

	B	C	D	E	F	G	H
Cages and equipment	35	35	25	0	0	35	40

16. Insert borders and change the font size.
 a. Select cells **A4:H11**.
 b. Click the **Borders** button drop-down list and choose **All Borders**.
 c. Select cell **A2** and press **Ctrl+1** to open the *Format Cells* dialog box.
 d. Click the **Border** tab.
 e. Click the blue bottom border in the preview area to remove it.
 f. Click the **Color** drop-down arrow and select **Black, Text 1** (second column).
 g. Click to select the solid, thick line (second column, sixth style) in the *Style* group.

h. Click the bottom border in the preview area (Figure 1-82).
i. Click **OK**.
j. Select cell **A1** and change the font size to **24**.

17. Spell check a worksheet.
 a. Press **Ctrl+Home** to go to cell **A1**.
 b. Click the **Spelling** button [*Review* tab, *Proofing* group].
 c. Type Animal in the *Not in Dictionary* box and click **Change**.
 d. Choose "September" in the *Suggestions* list and click **Change**.
 e. Correct "Expens" when the error is located.
 f. Click **OK**.
 g. Press **Ctrl+Home**.

18. Change page setup options.
 a. Click the **Page Layout** tab and click the **Page Setup** launcher.
 b. Select the **Landscape** radio button on the **Page** tab.
 c. Click the **Margins** tab.
 d. Select the **Horizontally** box under *Center on page*.
 e. Click the **Header/Footer** tab.
 f. Click the **Header** drop-down list and choose *[your initials] Excel 1-1* to insert the file name in the center section.
 g. Click **OK**.
 h. Press **Ctrl+F2** to preview the worksheet.
 i. Press **Esc** to close the *Backstage* view.

Figure 1-82 Create a custom border

19. Copy and edit a worksheet.
 a. Right-click the **Week 1** tab name.
 b. Select **Move or Copy** from the menu.
 c. Select **(move to end)** in the *Before sheet* list.
 d. Select the **Create a copy** box and click **OK**.
 e. Select cells **B5:H10** on the copied worksheet, and delete the data.
 f. Double-click cell **A2** to start *Edit* mode.
 g. Change "September 1 through 7" to September 8 through 14.
 h. Double-click the **Week 1 (2)** tab name.
 i. Type Week 2 and press **Enter**.
 j. Right-click the **Week 2** tab name and choose **Tab Color**.
 k. Select **Green, Accent4, Darker 50%** (eighth column).

20. Click the **Week 1** sheet tab.

21. Preview a worksheet.
 a. Click the **File** tab and select **Print**.
 b. Press **Esc** to return to the worksheet.

22. Change the zoom size and freeze panes.
 a. Select cell **B5**.
 b. Click the **Zoom In** button in the *Status* bar five times.
 c. Click the **Freeze Panes** button [*View* tab, *Window* group].
 d. Choose **Freeze Panes**.
 e. Scroll the window on the right so that column **F** is immediately to the right of column **A** (Figure 1-83). (Increase or decrease the zoom size as needed.)
 f. Select cell **A1**.

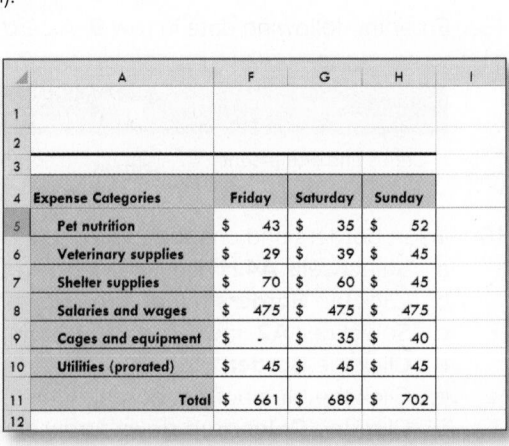

Figure 1-83 Panes frozen and positioned

23. Save and close the workbook (Figure 1-84).

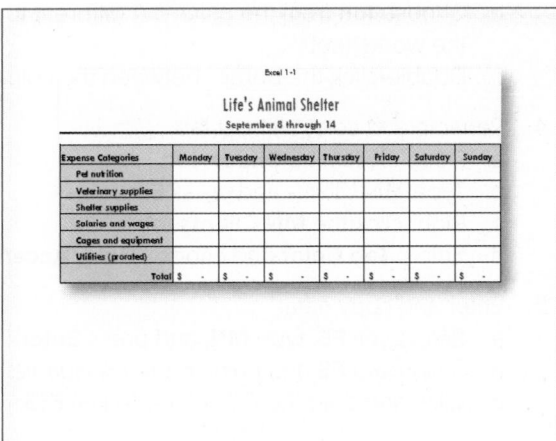

Figure 1-84 Excel 1-1 completed

Guided Project 1-2

In this project, you edit a worksheet for Eller Software Services representative Adam White. He maintains client data with sales revenue and specific products or services. You plan to format the data, complete the calculation, and prepare the worksheet for sharing with management.
[Student Learning Outcomes 1.1, 1.2, 1.3, 1.4, 1.5, 1.6, 1.7, 1.8]

File Needed: **EllerSoftwareServices-01.xlsx** [Student data files are available in the Library of your SIMnet account.]
Completed Project File Name: **[your initials] Excel 1-2.xlsx**

Skills Covered in This Project

- Open and save a workbook.
- Choose a workbook theme.
- Rename and apply color to sheet tabs.
- Enter and copy labels using the *Fill Handle*.
- Set font attributes and number formats.

- Use *SUM*.
- Center labels across a selection.
- Change page orientation and scale a worksheet for printing.
- Design borders.
- Insert a row.
- Adjust page setup options.

1. Open the workbook **EllerSoftwareServices-01.xlsx** from your student data files. If the workbook opens in *Protected View*, click **Enable Editing** in the security bar.

2. Save the workbook with a new file name.
 a. Press **F12** (**FN+F12**) to open the *Save As* dialog box.
 b. Navigate to the folder where your files are stored.
 c. Rename the file [your initials] Excel 1-2.
 d. Click **Save**.

3. Choose a workbook theme.
 a. Click the **Themes** button [*Page Layout* tab, *Themes* group].
 b. Choose **Ion** from the gallery. A different font, *Century Gothic*, is used for all data in the worksheet.
 c. Double-click the border between the column **C** and column **D** headings to *AutoFit* column **C**.

4. Rename and color a sheet tab.
 a. Double-click the **Sheet1** tab.
 b. Type MN Clients and press **Enter**.
 c. Right-click the **MN Clients** tab.
 d. Select **Tab Color** and choose **Gold, Accent3** (seventh column).

5. Enter and copy data.
 a. Select cell **F5**, type **MN**, and press **Enter**.
 b. Select cell **F5** and point to the *Fill Handle*.
 c. Click and drag the *Fill* pointer to cell **F13**.

6. Format data.
 a. Select cells **D5:D13**.
 b. Press **Ctrl+1** to open the *Format Cells* dialog box.
 c. Click the **Number** tab.
 d. Click **Special** in the *Category* list.
 e. Select **Phone Number** in the *Type* list and click **OK** (Figure 1-85).
 f. Select cells **I6:I13**.
 g. Click the **Comma Style** button [*Home* tab, *Number* group].
 h. Select cell **I5**.
 i. Click the **Accounting Number Format** button [*Home* tab, *Number* group]. A series of # symbols, when they appear, means the column is not wide enough to display the data (Figure 1-86).
 j. Double-click the border between the column **I** and column **J** headings to *AutoFit* column **I**.

Figure 1-85 Special number format

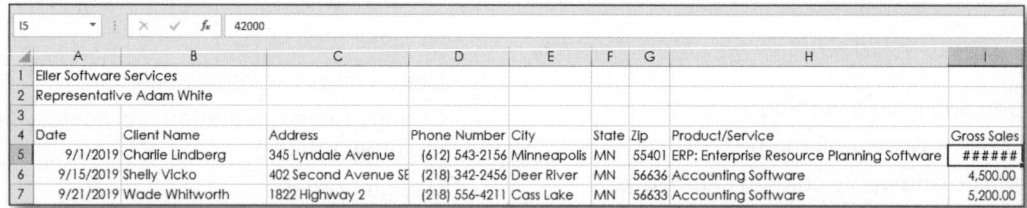

Figure 1-86 Column I is not wide enough

7. Enter and edit the reference range for the *SUM* function.
 a. Click cell **A15**, type Total, and press **Enter**.
 b. Select cell **I15**.
 c. Click the **AutoSum** button [*Home* tab, *Editing* group]. The suggested range includes an empty row.
 d. Click cell **I5** and drag to select cells **I5:I13**. Your selected range is highlighted and shown in the *Formula* bar and in the cell (Figure 1-87).
 e. Press **Enter** to accept the range. The *Accounting Number* format is applied.

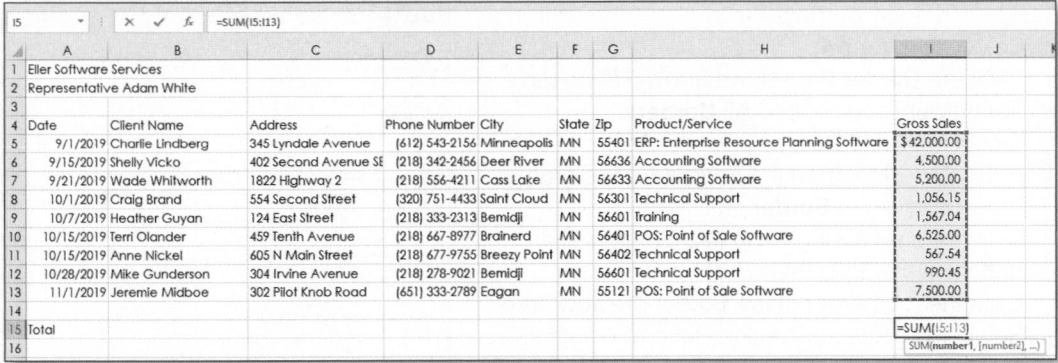

Figure 1-87 New range selected for *SUM*

8. Center labels across a selection.
 a. Select cells **A1:I2** and click the **Alignment** launcher [*Home* tab, *Alignment* group].
 b. Click the *Horizontal* arrow and select **Center Across Selection**.
 c. Click **OK**.

9. Apply font attributes and cell styles.
 a. Select cell **A1**, click the **Font Size** drop-down list [*Home* tab, *Font* group], and select **24**.
 b. Select cell **A2** and change the font size to **18**.
 c. Select cells **A4:A15**, press **Ctrl**, and then select cells **B4:I4**.
 d. Click the **Cell Styles** button or the **More** button and select **Light Yellow, 40% - Accent3** (third column) in the *Themed Cell Styles* category.
 e. Click the **Bold** button [*Home* tab, *Font* group] while the cells are selected.
 f. Select cell **I15** and apply the **Total** cell style.
 g. Select cells **A4:I4**.
 h. Click the **Font Size** drop-down list [*Home* tab, *Font* group] and select **12**.
 i. Click the **Center** button [*Home* tab, *Alignment* group].
 j. *AutoFit* column **D**.
 k. Select cell **A15** and click the **Align Right** button [*Home* tab, *Alignment* group].

10. Edit a label.
 a. Double-click cell **H9** to start *Edit* mode.
 b. Press **Home** to position the insertion point before the word "Training."
 c. Type **ERP** and press **Spacebar**.
 d. Press **Enter**.

11. Insert a row.
 a. Right-click row heading **10**.
 b. Choose **Insert** from the context menu.
 c. In cell **A10**, type 10/10/19 and press **Tab**.
 d. Complete the data as shown here. For the phone number, do not type any spaces; it is automatically formatted when you press **Tab** to move to the next cell. For the city, state, and product/service columns, press **Tab** to accept the *AutoComplete* suggestion.

 B10 Hillary Marschke
 C10 245 West Third Avenue
 D10 3203555443 (press **Tab**)
 E10 sa (press **Tab**)
 F10 m (press **Tab**)
 G10 56301
 H10 t (press **Tab**)
 I10 750

12. Design and apply borders.
 a. Select cells **A4:I14**.
 b. Click the **Border** drop-down arrow [*Home* tab, *Font* group] and choose **All Borders**.
 c. Select cells **A16:I16**.
 d. Press **Ctrl+1** to open the *Format Cells* dialog box and click the **Border** tab.
 e. Select the solid, single line (first column, sixth option) in the *Style* list.
 f. Click the top border in the *Border* preview area.
 g. Select the solid, double line (second column, seventh option) in the *Style* list.
 h. Click the bottom border in the *Border* preview area (Figure 1-88).
 i. Click **OK**.
 j. Select cells **A15:I16**.
 k. Click the **Border** arrow [*Home* tab, *Font* group] and choose **Left Border**.
 l. Click the **Border** arrow [*Home* tab, *Font* group] and choose **Right Border**.

Figure 1-88 Design a double border

13. Hide a column.
 a. Right-click the column **E** heading.
 b. Select **Hide**.
 c. Press **Ctrl+Home**.

14. Change page setup options.
 a. Click the **Page Layout** tab.
 b. Click the **Orientation** button [*Page Setup* group] and choose **Landscape**.
 c. In the *Scale to Fit* group, click the **Width** arrow and choose **1 page**.
 d. Click the **Insert** tab.
 e. Click the **Header & Footer** button In the *Text* group. The view switches to *Page Layout* with the insertion point in the center header section. The *Header & Footer Tools Design* toolbar displays.
 f. Click the **Go to Footer** button in the *Navigation* group.
 g. Click the **Footer** button in the *Header & Footer* group (Figure 1-89).

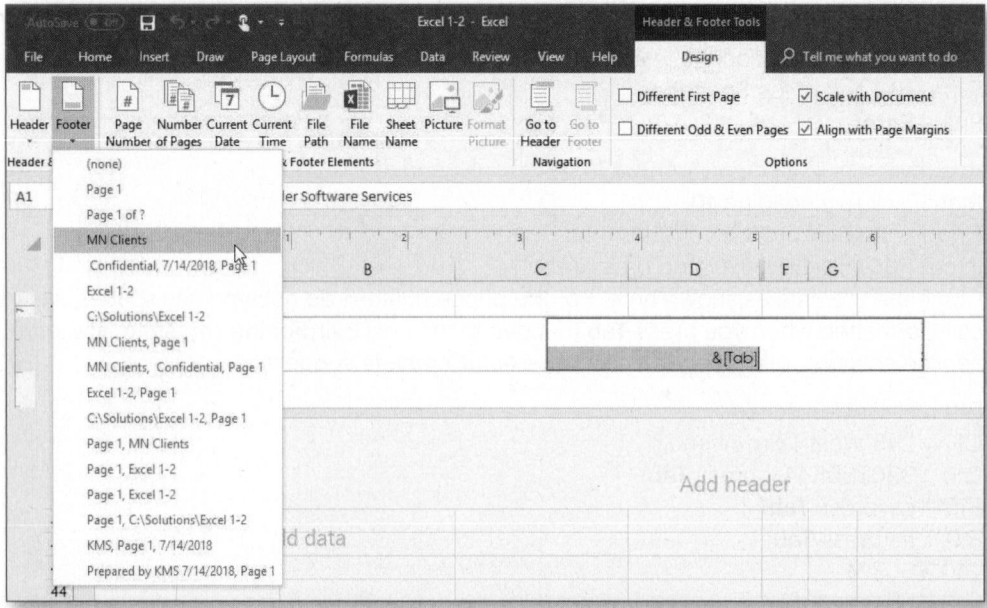

Figure 1-89 Select a built-in footer

h. Choose **MN Clients** to insert the sheet name in the footer. The *Header & Footer Tools Design* toolbar closes.

i. Click the **Normal** button in the *Status* bar. The footer is not visible in this view.

15. Preview and print the worksheet.
 a. Select **Print** from the *File* tab.
 b. Review the worksheet layout.
 c. Click **Print** or press **Esc** to return to the workbook.

16. Save and close the workbook (Figure 1-90).

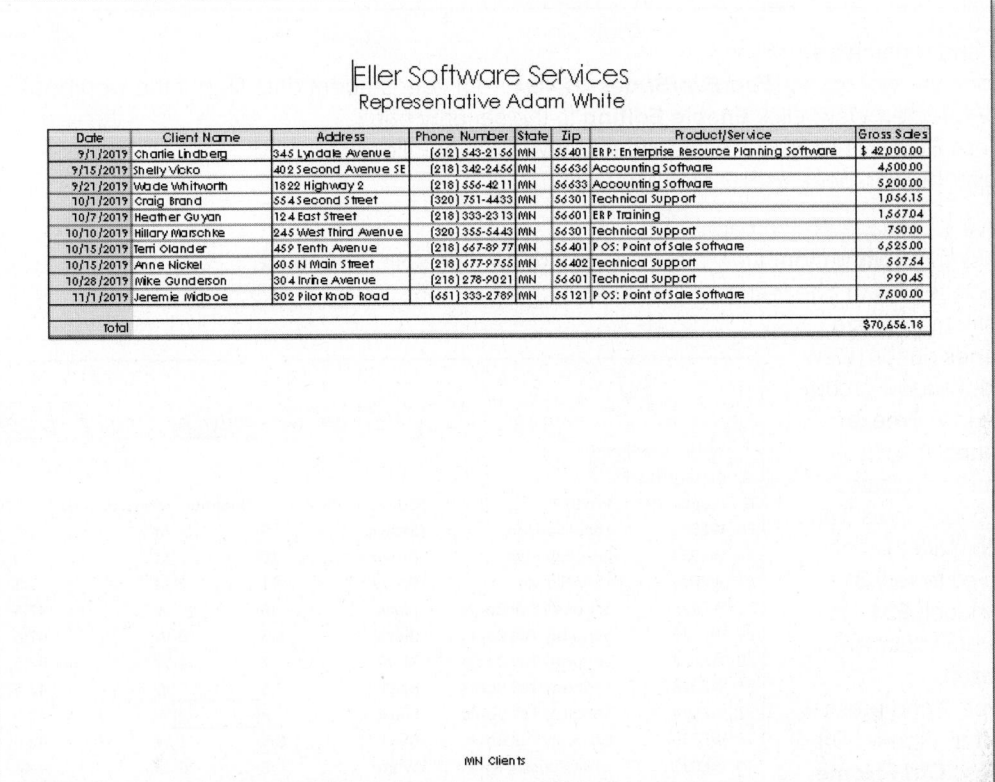

Figure 1-90 Excel 1-2 completed

Guided Project 1-3

In this project, you edit a worksheet for Wear-Ever Shoes that tracks their product inventory. You change the zoom size, reset the panes, and format data. You copy an existing formula to calculate the value of the current stock and insert a column for new data. After adjusting print options, you set a print area for a specific product line.

[Student Learning Outcomes 1.1, 1.2, 1.4, 1.5, 1.6, 1.7, 1.8]

File Needed: **WearEverShoes-01.xlsx** [*Student data files are available in the* Library *of your SIMnet account.*]
Completed Project File Name: **[your initials] Excel 1-3.xlsx**

Skills Covered in This Project

- Open and save a workbook.
- Change zoom size and remove a split.
- Freeze panes.
- Format labels and values.
- Use the *Fill Handle* to copy a formula and fill a series.
- Check spelling.

- Apply a workbook theme, cell styles, and font attributes.
- Merge and center labels.
- Insert a column and adjust column widths and row heights.
- Adjust alignment, indents, and borders.
- Rename the sheet tab.
- Use *Page Layout* view to insert a footer.

1. Open and rename a workbook.
 a. Open the workbook **WearEverShoes-01.xlsx** from your student data files. If the workbook opens in *Protected View,* click **Enable Editing** in the security bar.
 b. Press **F12** (**FN+F12**) and locate the folder where your files are saved.
 c. Save the workbook as [your initials] Excel 1-3.

2. Remove a split and freeze panes.
 a. Click the **Split** button [*View* tab, *Window* group]. The split is removed.
 b. Click cell **A4** to freeze the column titles at this position.
 c. Click the **Freeze Panes** button [*View* tab, *Window* group].
 d. Choose **Freeze Panes**. A solid border appears between rows 3 and 4 to mark the pane.
 e. Scroll to row **31** and click cell **E31**. The column titles are frozen.
 f. Type 3 and press **Enter** (Figure 1-91).
 g. Press **Ctrl+Home**. The insertion point returns to cell **A4**.

	A	B	C	D	E	F	G	H
1	Wear-Ever Shoes							
2	Current Stock							
3	Product ID	Product	Color	Size	Quantity	Men's or V	Cost	Value
25	WE022	Lazy Flip-Flops	Brown	9	4	M	7.5	
26	WE023	Lazy Flip-Flops	Brown	10	2	M	7.5	
27	WE024	Lazy Flip-Flops	Brown	11	2	M	7.5	
28	WE025	Seriously Tall Boots	Black	6	0	W	42.5	
29	WE026	Seriously Tall Boots	Black	6.5	0	W	42.5	
30	WE027	Seriously Tall Boots	Black	7	1	W	42.5	
31	WE028	Seriously Tall Boots	Black	7.5	3	W	42.5	
32	WE029	Seriously Tall Boots	Black	8	2	W	42.5	
33	WE030	Seriously Tall Boots	Black	8.5	1	W	42.5	
34	WE031	Glide Running Shoes	White	8	6	M	48	

Figure 1-91 Panes frozen at cell A4

3. Change zoom size and unfreeze the pane.
 a. Click the **100%** button [*View* tab, *Zoom* group].
 b. Click the **Freeze Panes** button [*View* tab, *Window* group].
 c. Choose **Unfreeze Panes**.
 d. Click cell **A1**.

4. Check spelling in the worksheet.
 a. Click the **Spelling** button [*Review* tab, *Proofing* group]. The first occurrence of "Hikin" is found as misspelled.
 b. Select **Hiking** in the *Suggestions* list.
 c. Click **Change All** to correct all occurrences of the misspelled word (Figure 1-92).
 d. Click **OK**.

5. Use the *Fill Handle* to copy a formula.
 a. Click **H4**. The formula displays in the *Formula* bar. The formula multiplies the quantity by the cost to calculate the value of the current stock.

b. Point to the *Fill Handle* for cell **H4** (Figure 1-93).

c. Double-click the *Fill* pointer. The formula is copied down the entire column.

d. Press **Ctrl+Home**.

6. Click the **Themes** button [*Page Layout* tab, *Themes* group] and choose **Ion** from the gallery.

Figure 1-92 Change all occurrences of a misspelled word

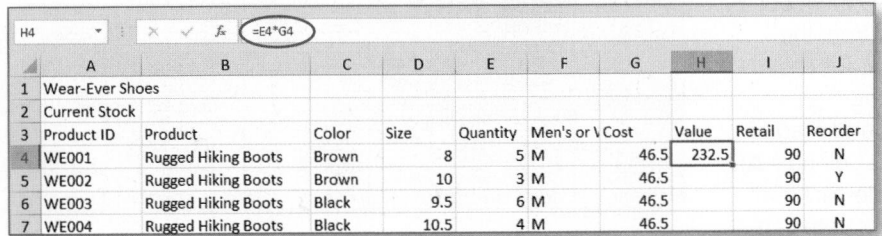

Figure 1-93 Formula to be copied

7. Merge and center the titles.
 a. Select cells **A1:J1** and click the **Merge & Center** button [*Home* tab, *Alignment* group].
 b. Merge and center cells **A2:J2**.

8. Apply cell styles and adjust row height.
 a. Select cell **A1**, click the **Cell Styles** button or the **More** button [*Home* tab, *Styles* group], and select **Title** in the *Titles and Headings* category.
 b. Select cell **A2** and apply the **Heading 4** style.
 c. Click the **Font Size** arrow [*Home* tab, *Font* group] and select **14 pt**. The font size change overwrites the font size of the cell style.
 d. Point to the row **1** heading and drag to select row headings **1:2**.
 e. Click the **Format** button [*Home* tab, *Cells* group] and choose **Row Height**.
 f. Type 22 as the new row height and press **Enter**.
 g. Select cells **A3:J3**.
 h. From the *Cell Styles* gallery [*Home* tab], select **Light Yellow, 40% - Accent3**.
 i. Apply **bold** to the selected cells.
 j. Click the row **3** heading.
 k. Point to the bottom border of the row heading to display the resize arrow.
 l. Drag the resize arrow to **21.00** (**28 pixels**) as the new row height and release the pointer (Figure 1-94).
 m. Click the **Zoom Out** button in the *Status* bar if necessary so that you can see all rows (1:39).

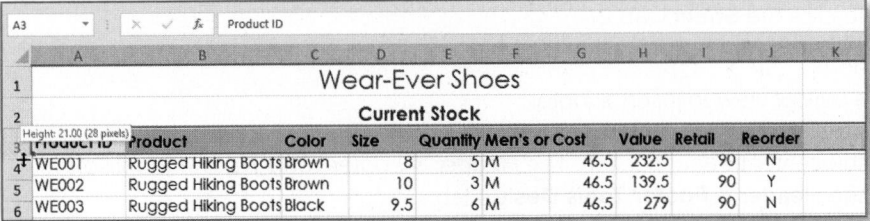

Figure 1-94 Adjust row height from the row heading

9. Change alignment, format values, apply borders, and increase the indent.
 a. Select cells **D4:F39**.
 b. Click the **Center** button [*Home* tab, *Alignment* group].
 c. Select cells **G4:H39**.
 d. Click the **Accounting Number Format** button [*Home* tab, *Alignment* group].
 e. Click cells **A3:J39**.
 f. Click the **Borders** drop-down arrow [*Home* tab, *Font* group] and select **All Borders**.
 g. Click the **Font size** drop-down arrow [*Home* tab, *Font* group] and choose **12** while the cells are selected.
 h. Select cells **B4:C39** and click the **Increase Indent** button [*Home* tab, *Alignment* group] one time. This moves the label away from the border for easier reading.
 i. Click and drag to select columns **A:J**.
 j. Double-click the border between columns J and K to *AutoFit* the selected columns (Figure 1-95).

Figure 1-95 Select column headings to *AutoFit*

 k. Select and **center** align the labels in row **3**.

10. Insert a column and create a pattern to fill data.
 a. Right-click column heading **B**.
 b. Choose **Insert** from the context menu.
 c. In cell **B3**, type Disc? and press **Enter**.
 d. In cell **B4**, type No and press **Enter**.
 e. In cell **B5**, type No and press **Enter**.
 f. In cell **B6**, type Yes and press **Enter**. The pattern is two occurrences of *No* and one occurrence of *Yes*.
 g. Select cells **B4:B6** and increase the indent twice.
 h. Select cells **B4:B6** and double-click the *Fill* pointer (Figure 1-96).
 i. Select cells **A4:A39** and increase the indent one time.
 j. Press **Ctrl+Home**.

Figure 1-96 Double-click the *Fill* pointer to complete a series

11. Rename the sheet tab.
 a. Double-click the **Sheet1** tab.
 b. Type Inventory and press **Enter**.

12. Use *Page Layout* view to insert a footer.
 a. Click the **Page Layout** button in the *Status* bar.
 b. Click the center header section. The *Header & Footer Tools Design* tab displays.
 c. Click the **Header & Footer Tools Design** tab.

d. Click the **Go to Footer** button [*Header & Footer Tools Design* tab, *Navigation* group].

e. Click the middle section if necessary.

f. Click the **File Name** button in the *Header & Footer Elements* group. The code is &[File].

g. Click a worksheet cell to see the file name.

h. Switch to *Normal* view and press **Ctrl+Home**.

13. Change page setup options.

a. Click the **Page Layout** tab and click the **Page Setup** launcher.

b. Display the *Page* tab and select the **Landscape** radio button under *Orientation*.

c. Select the **Fit to** radio button and enter 1 page wide by 1 tall.

d. Click **OK**.

14. Set a print area.

a. Select cells **A1:K11**.

b. Click the **Page Layout** tab.

c. Click the **Print Area** button [*Page Setup* group] and select **Set Print Area**.

d. Press **Ctrl+Home**.

e. Click the **File** tab and select **Print** to preview the worksheet print area.

f. Return to the worksheet.

15. Click the **Save** button in the *Quick Access* toolbar to save the workbook changes. The print area is saved.

16. Close the workbook (Figure 1-97).

Wear-Ever Shoes
Current Stock

Product ID	Disc?	Product	Color	Size	Quantity	Men's or Women's	Cost	Value	Retail	Reorder
WE001	No	Rugged Hiking Boots	Brown	8	5	M	$ 46.50	$ 232.50	90	N
WE002	No	Rugged Hiking Boots	Brown	10	3	M	$ 46.50	$ 139.50	90	Y
WE003	Yes	Rugged Hiking Boots	Black	9.5	6	M	$ 46.50	$ 279.00	90	N
WE004	No	Rugged Hiking Boots	Black	10.5	4	M	$ 46.50	$ 186.00	90	N
WE005	No	Rugged Hiking Boots	Black	7.5	4	W	$ 53.50	$ 214.00	98	N
WE006	Yes	Rugged Hiking Boots	Black	8	2	W	$ 53.50	$ 107.00	98	Y
WE007	No	Rugged Hiking Boots	Brown	9	3	W	$ 53.50	$ 160.50	98	N
WE008	No	Rugged Hiking Boots	Brown	8.5	2	W	$ 53.50	$ 107.00	98	Y
WE009	Yes	Comfy Walking Shoes	Brown	8.5	4	M	$ 47.50	$ 190.00	65	N
WE010	No	Comfy Walking Shoes	Black	9	1	M	$ 47.50	$ 47.50	65	Y
WE011	No	Comfy Walking Shoes	Navy	7.5	4	W	$ 47.50	$ 190.00	65	N
WE012	Yes	Comfy Walking Shoes	Black	8	1	W	$ 47.50	$ 47.50	65	Y
WE013	No	Comfy Walking Shoes	Taupe	7.5	2	W	$ 47.50	$ 95.00	65	N
WE014	No	Comfy Walking Shoes	Brown	8	3	W	$ 47.50	$ 142.50	65	Y
WE015	Yes	Lazy Flip-Flops	Pink	6	4	W	$ 7.50	$ 30.00	14	N
WE016	No	Lazy Flip-Flops	Pink	7	0	W	$ 7.50	$ -	14	N
WE017	No	Lazy Flip-Flops	Pink	8	2	W	$ 7.50	$ 15.00	14	Y
WE018	Yes	Lazy Flip-Flops	White	6	3	W	$ 7.50	$ 22.50	14	N
WE019	No	Lazy Flip-Flops	White	7	1	W	$ 7.50	$ 7.50	14	N
WE020	No	Lazy Flip-Flops	White	8	2	W	$ 7.50	$ 15.00	14	Y
WE021	Yes	Lazy Flip-Flops	Brown	8	2	M	$ 7.50	$ 15.00	14	Y
WE022	No	Lazy Flip-Flops	Brown	9	4	M	$ 7.50	$ 30.00	14	N
WE023	No	Lazy Flip-Flops	Brown	10	2	M	$ 7.50	$ 15.00	14	Y
WE024	Yes	Lazy Flip-Flops	Brown	11	2	M	$ 7.50	$ 15.00	14	Y
WE025	No	Seriously Tall Boots	Black	6	0	W	$ 42.50	$ -	80	Y
WE026	No	Seriously Tall Boots	Black	6.5	0	W	$ 42.50	$ -	80	Y
WE027	Yes	Seriously Tall Boots	Black	7	1	W	$ 42.50	$ 42.50	80	Y
WE028	No	Seriously Tall Boots	Black	7.5	3	W	$ 42.50	$ 127.50	80	Y
WE029	No	Seriously Tall Boots	Black	8	2	W	$ 42.50	$ 85.00	80	Y
WE030	Yes	Seriously Tall Boots	Black	8.5	1	W	$ 42.50	$ 42.50	80	Y
WE031	No	Glide Running Shoes	White	8	6	M	$ 48.00	$ 288.00	75	N
WE032	No	Glide Running Shoes	White	9	6	M	$ 48.00	$ 288.00	75	N
WE033	Yes	Glide Running Shoes	White	10	6	M	$ 48.00	$ 288.00	75	N
WE034	No	Glide Running Shoes	Black	8	2	M	$ 48.00	$ 96.00	75	N
WE035	No	Glide Running Shoes	Black	9	3	M	$ 48.00	$ 144.00	75	N
WE036	Yes	Glide Running Shoes	Black	10	1	M	$ 48.00	$ 48.00	75	Y

Excel 1-3

Figure 1-97 Excel 1-3 completed

Independent Project 1-4

As a staff member at Blue Lake Sports Company, you are expected to prepare the monthly sales worksheet. You edit and format data, complete calculations, and prepare the workbook for distribution. You also copy the sheet for next month's data.
[Student Learning Outcomes 1.1, 1.2, 1.3, 1.4, 1.5, 1.6, 1.8]

File Needed: ***BlueLakeSports-1.xlsx*** [*Student data files are available in the* Library *of your SIMnet account.*]
Completed Project File Name: ***[your initials] Excel 1-4.xlsx***

Skills Covered in This Project

- Open and save a workbook.
- Choose a workbook theme.
- Edit and format data.
- Center labels across a selection.

- Use *SUM* and the *Fill Handle.*
- Adjust column width and row height.
- Insert a header and a footer.
- Adjust page layout options.
- Copy and rename a worksheet.

1. Open ***BlueLakeSports-01.xlsx*** from your student data files. If the workbook opens in *Protected View*, click **Enable Editing** in the security bar.

2. Save the workbook as [your initials] Excel 1-4 in your usual location.

3. Apply the **Slice** theme to the worksheet.

4. Edit worksheet data.
 a. Edit the title in cell **A2** to display Monthly Sales by Department.
 b. Edit cell **D6** to 1950.

5. Select cells **A1:F2** and click the **Alignment** launcher [*Home* tab]. Click the *Horizontal* arrow, choose **Center Across Selection**, and click **OK**.

6. Select and delete row **8**.

7. Use the *Fill Handle* to complete a series.
 a. Select cell **B3**.
 b. Use the *Fill Handle* to complete the series to **Week 4** in column **E**.
 c. *AutoFit* columns **C:E** to display the complete label.

8. Use *SUM* and the *Fill Handle* to calculate totals.
 a. Use the **AutoSum** button to build a *SUM* function in cell **F4**.
 b. Use the *Fill Handle* to copy the formula in cell **F4** to cells **F5:F16**.
 c. Delete the contents of cell **F17** if you copied the formula to that cell.
 d. Select cells **B17:F17** and click the **AutoSum** button. The *SUM* formula is inserted, and a **Quick Analysis** options button appears (Figure 1-98).
 e. Press **Esc** to ignore the *Quick Analysis* options.

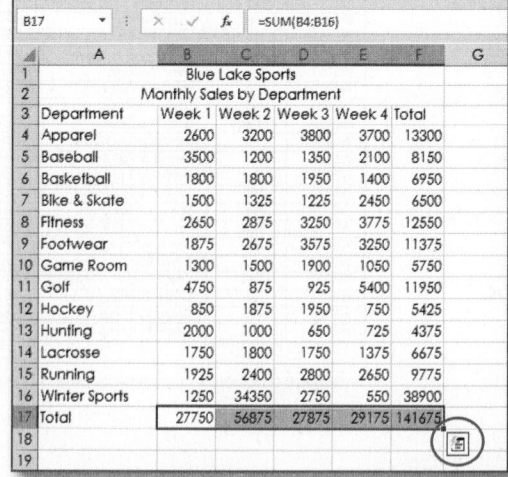

Figure 1-98 *AutoSum* complete with *Quick Analysis* button

9. Format labels and values.
 a. Select cells **A1:A2** and increase the font size to **18**.
 b. Increase the row height of rows **1:2** to **24 (32 pixels)**.
 c. Format cells **A3:F3** as **Bold** and increase the row height to **18 (24 pixels)**.
 d. Center the data in cells **B3:F3**.
 e. Format cells **B4:F16** with **Comma Style** and decrease the decimal two times.
 f. Select cells **B17:F17** and apply the **Accounting Number Format** with no decimal places.
 g. Apply the **All Borders** format to cells **A3:F17**.
 h. *AutoFit* columns **B:F**.

10. Finalize the worksheet.
 a. Click the **Insert** tab and click the **Header & Footer** button [*Text* group].
 b. In the right header section, insert the **Sheet Name** field.
 c. Go to the footer and click the right section.
 d. Type [your first and last name] (Figure 1-99).

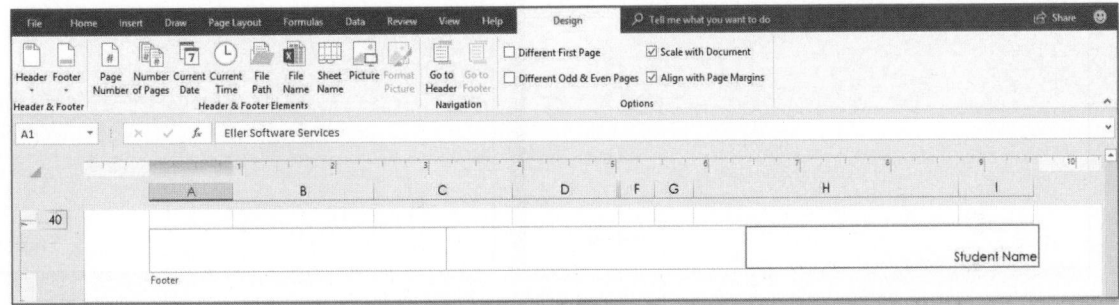

Figure 1-99 Add a footer in *Page Layout* view

 e. Click a cell in the worksheet and then return to *Normal* view.
 f. Center the worksheet horizontally on the page.

11. Copy and rename a worksheet.
 a. Right-click the *January* sheet tab and choose **Move or Copy**.
 b. Make a copy of the sheet at the end.
 c. Rename the copied sheet February.
 d. Format the *February* sheet tab color to **Dark Blue, Accent1** (fifth column).
 e. Delete the values in cells **B4:E16** and press **Ctrl+Home**.
 f. Return to the *January* sheet and press **Ctrl+Home**.

12. Preview the *January* sheet.

13. Save and close the workbook (Figure 1-100).

January

Blue Lake Sports
Monthly Sales by Department

Department	Week 1	Week 2	Week 3	Week 4	Total
Apparel	2,600	3,200	3,800	3,700	13,300
Baseball	3,500	1,200	1,350	2,100	8,150
Basketball	1,800	1,800	1,950	1,400	6,950
Bike & Skate	1,500	1,325	1,225	2,450	6,500
Fitness	2,650	2,875	3,250	3,775	12,550
Footwear	1,875	2,675	3,575	3,250	11,375
Game Room	1,300	1,500	1,900	1,050	5,750
Golf	4,750	875	925	5,400	11,950
Hockey	850	1,875	1,950	750	5,425
Hunting	2,000	1,000	650	725	4,375
Lacrosse	1,750	1,800	1,750	1,375	6,675
Running	1,925	2,400	2,800	2,650	9,775
Winter Sports	1,250	34,350	2,750	550	38,900
Total	$27,750	$56,875	$27,875	$29,175	$141,675

Student Name

February

Blue Lake Sports
Monthly Sales by Department

Department	Week 1	Week 2	Week 3	Week 4	Total
Apparel					-
Baseball					-
Basketball					-
Bike & Skate					-
Fitness					-
Footwear					-
Game Room					-
Golf					-
Hockey					-
Hunting					-
Lacrosse					-
Running					-
Winter Sports					-
Total	$ -	$ -	$ -	$ -	$ -

Student Name

Figure 1-100 Excel 1-4 completed

Independent Project 1-5

Clemenson Imaging employs certified staff to perform mobile medical imaging at several hospitals statewide. Your worksheet maintains a log of which hospitals were visited and what images were made. You need to format the data and finalize the worksheet.
[Student Learning Outcomes 1.1, 1.2, 1.3, 1.4, 1.5, 1.6, 1.7, 1.8]

File Needed: **ClemensonImaging-01.xlsx** [Student data files are available in the Library of your SIMnet account.]
Completed Project File Name: **[your initials] Excel 1-5.xlsx**

Skills Covered in This Project

- Open and save a workbook.
- Use *SUM*.
- Unfreeze panes and change the zoom size.
- Format data.
- Merge and center labels.
- Adjust column width and row height.
- Apply borders.
- Copy a sheet and rename a tab.
- Add document properties.
- Change page layout options.

1. Open ***ClemensonImaging-01**.xlsx* from your student data files and save it as [your initials] Excel 1-5. If the workbook opens in *Protected View*, click **Enable Editing** in the security bar.

2. Edit the label in cell **A1** to insert LLC after "Clemenson Imaging." Edit the label in cell **A2** to show "Second Quarter . . ." instead of "First Quarter."

3. Merge and center the label in cell **A1** across the worksheet data and then do the same for the label in cell **A2**.

4. Scroll to and select cell **A41**. Type Total. Right-align this label and apply bold format.

5. Use *SUM* in cell **F41** to add the values in cells **F5:F40**.

6. Unfreeze the panes and set a zoom size to display rows 1:30.

7. *AutoFit* columns **D:G**.

8. Format data.
 a. Click cell **A1** and set the font size to **18**.
 b. Change the label in cell **A2** to a font size of **14**.
 c. Select cells **A4:H4** and apply bold and center alignment.
 d. Format cells **A4:H4** to use the **White, Background 1, Darker 15%** fill color (first column).
 e. Format the row height for row **4** to **21.00 (28 pixels)**.
 f. Select cells **A4:H41** and apply **All Borders**.
 g. Select cells **A41:H41** and apply the fill color **White, Background 1, Darker 15%** (first column).
 h. Bold the value in cell **F41**.

9. Set page layout options.
 a. Change the page orientation to **Landscape**.
 b. Center the worksheet horizontally.
 c. Scale the sheet to fit on a single page.
 d. Add a footer that displays the current date in the left section and your first and last name in the right section.

10. Add document properties.
 a. Click the **File** tab and select **Info**.
 b. Click the **Properties** drop-down arrow and select **Advanced Properties**.
 c. Click the **Summary** tab, click the **Title** box, and type Procedures.
 d. Click the **Author** box and type your first and last name (Figure 1-101).
 e. Click **OK** and return to the worksheet.

11. Rename *Sheet1* as Second Qtr.

12. Copy the *Second Qtr* sheet and place it at the end. Name the copy Third Qtr. Set this tab color to **Blue, Accent1, Darker 50%** (fifth column).

13. Select the *Third Qtr* sheet, and edit the label in cell **A2** to show "Third Quarter. . .".

14. Delete the contents of cells **A5:H40** on the *Third Qtr* sheet.

15. Select cell **A5** and return to the *Second Qtr* sheet.

16. Press **Ctrl+Home** and preview the entire workbook (Figure 1-102).

17. Save and close the workbook (Figure 1-103).

Figure 1-101 *Properties* dialog box

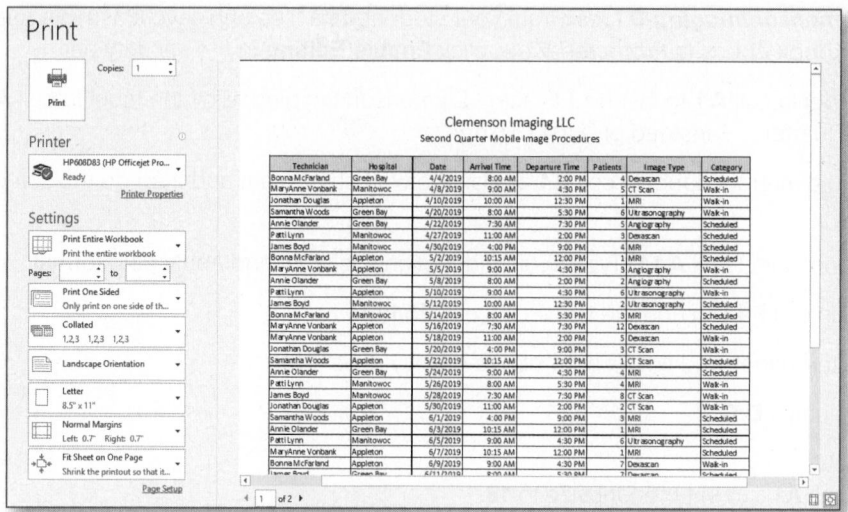

Figure 1-102 Entire workbook selected for preview and print

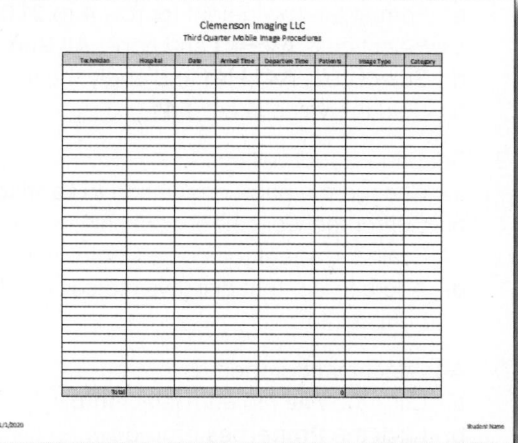

Figure 1-103 Excel 1-5 completed

Independent Project 1-6

As accounts receivable clerk for Livingood Income Tax and Accounting, you track daily payments from clients in an Excel worksheet. After entering the data, you format the worksheet and prepare it for distribution to coworkers.

[Student Learning Outcomes 1.1, 1.2, 1.4, 1.5, 1.6, 1.8]

File Needed: None
Completed Project File Name: *[your initials] Excel 1-6.xlsx*

Skills Covered in This Project

- Create and save a workbook.
- Enter labels, dates, and values.
- Use the *Fill Handle* to build series.
- Change font size and attributes.

- Adjust column width and row height.
- Choose a theme and cell styles.
- Choose page layout options.
- Rename and apply color to sheet tabs.

1. Create a new workbook and save it as [your initials] Excel 1-6.

2. Apply the **Organic** theme for the workbook.

3. Type Livingood Income Tax and Accounting in cell **A1** and press **Enter**.

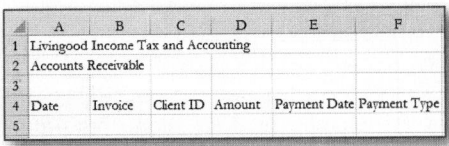

4. Type Accounts Receivable in cell **A2** and press **Enter**.

5. Type the labels in row **4** as shown here in Figure 1-104:

Figure 1-104 Data to be entered

6. *AutoFit* columns **E:F** to display each label in row 4.

7. Type 8/18/19 in cell **A5** to enter the date. In cell **A6**, type 8/20/19 to set a pattern for the dates.

8. Select cells **A5:A6** and use the *Fill Handle* to fill in dates to cell A15.

9. Select cell **B5** and type 1001 for the first invoice number. In cell **B6**, type 1002 to set a pattern for the invoice numbers.

10. Select cells **B5:B6** and use the *Fill Handle* to fill in invoice numbers to reach cell B15.

11. Type LITA001 in cell **C5** as the first client ID. In cell **C6**, type LITA002 to set a pattern.

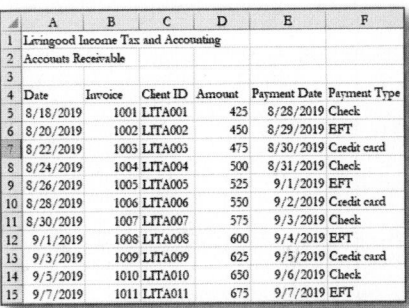

12. Use the *Fill Handle* to complete the client ID numbers.

13. Type 425 in cell **D5**. In cell **D6**, type 450 to set the pattern and fill in the amounts.

14. Type the first two payment dates in column **E** and fill the cells (Figure 1-105).

Figure 1-105 All columns filled

15. Type the first three payment types in cells **F5:F7** and then use the *Fill Handle* to complete the cells in column F.

16. Format data.
 a. Select cells **C5:C15**, increase the indent one time, and *AutoFit* the column. Do the same for the payment type data.
 b. Format the values in column **D** as **Accounting Number Format**.
 c. Select cells **A1:F2** and click the **Alignment** launcher [*File* tab]. Click the *Horizontal* arrow, choose **Center Across Selection**, and click **OK**. Change the font size to **18**.
 d. Select the labels in row **4** and apply bold and center alignment.
 e. *AutoFit* columns that do not show all the data.
 f. Apply **All Borders** to cells **A4:F15**. Apply an **Outside Border** for cells **A1:F2**.
 g. Apply the **Green, Accent1, Lighter 60%** fill color (fifth column) to cells **A1:F2** and **A4:F4**.
 h. Apply the **Green, Accent1, Lighter 60%** fill color (fifth column) to cells **A6:F6**.
 i. Use the **Ctrl** key to select the data in rows **8**, **10**, **12**, and **14** and apply the same fill color.

17. Rename *Sheet1* as AR and set the tab color to **Green, Accent1** (fifth column).

18. Define page layout and add document properties.
 a. Center the worksheet horizontally on the page.
 b. Create a header with the sheet name in the left section and your name in the right section.
 c. Delete an existing author name and key your first and last name as *Author* in the *Properties* dialog box.
 d. Type Receivables in the *Title* box (Figure 1-106).
 e. Preview your worksheet.

19. Save and close the workbook (Figure 1-107).

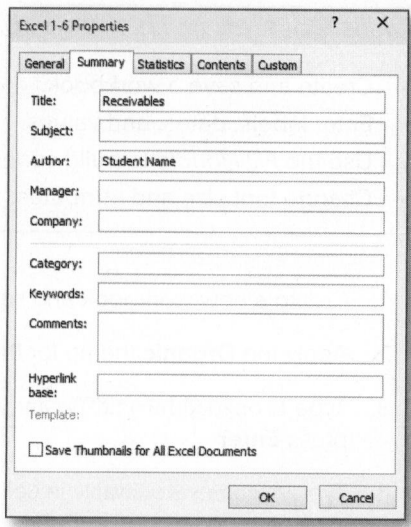

Figure 1-106 Properties entered in dialog box

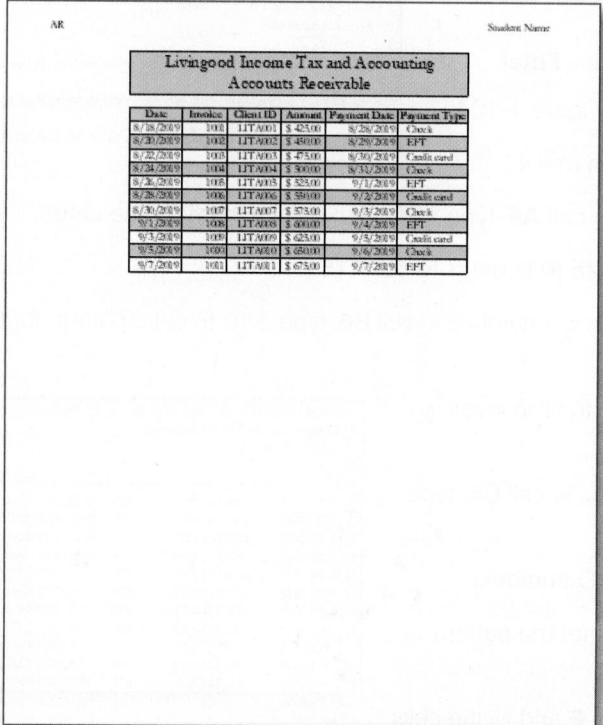

Figure 1-107 Excel 1-6 completed

Improve It Project 1-7

In this project, you complete a worksheet that maintains flight statistics for Boyd Air. The data has been imported from the reservation system, and you now need to add finishing touches.
[Student Learning Outcomes 1.1, 1.2, 1.3, 1.4, 1.5, 1.6, 1.7, 1.8]

File Needed: ***BoydAir-01.xlsx*** [*Student data files are available in the* Library *of your SIMnet account.*]
Completed Project File Name: ***[your initials] Excel 1-7.xlsx***

Skills Covered in This Project

- Open and save a workbook.
- Change the zoom level and remove a split.
- Enter and merge and center labels.
- Insert a row and set column width.

- Format data.
- Use *SUM*.
- Apply cell styles.
- Rename and color the sheet tab.
- Adjust page layout options.
- Add document properties.

1. Open the workbook ***BoydAir-01.xlsx*** from your student data files. If the workbook opens in *Protected View*, click **Enable Editing** in the security bar.

2. Save the workbook as [your initials] Excel 1-7.

3. Remove the split from the window.

4. Type Boyd Air in cell **A1** and Flight Statistics in cell **A2**.

5. Merge and center the labels in cells **A1** and **A2**. Change the font size for both labels to **16**.

6. Insert a row at row **3**.

7. Center and bold the labels in row **4**. *AutoFit* columns to show each label in row 4.

8. Change the zoom size to **100%**.

9. Select cells **B5:D18**, press **Ctrl**, and select cells **G5:G18**. Increase the indent one time.

10. Apply **All Borders** for cells **A4:H19**.

11. Calculate the total number of passengers in cell **H19**.

12. Apply the **Orange, Accent2** cell style to cells **A3:H3** and cells **A20:H20**.

13. Select cells **A3:H3** and **A20:H20** and apply **Outside Borders**.

14. Modify page layout options.
 a. Change the orientation to **Landscape**.
 b. Center the worksheet horizontally on the page.
 c. Show the file name in the left header section.
 d. Type your first and last name in the right header section.

15. Name the sheet tab Feb-Mar and format the tab color as **Orange, Accent2** (sixth column).

16. Set the document properties to show your first and last name as the *Author*. In the *Title* field, type Flight Stats.

17. Preview your worksheet.

18. Save and close the workbook (Figure 1-108).

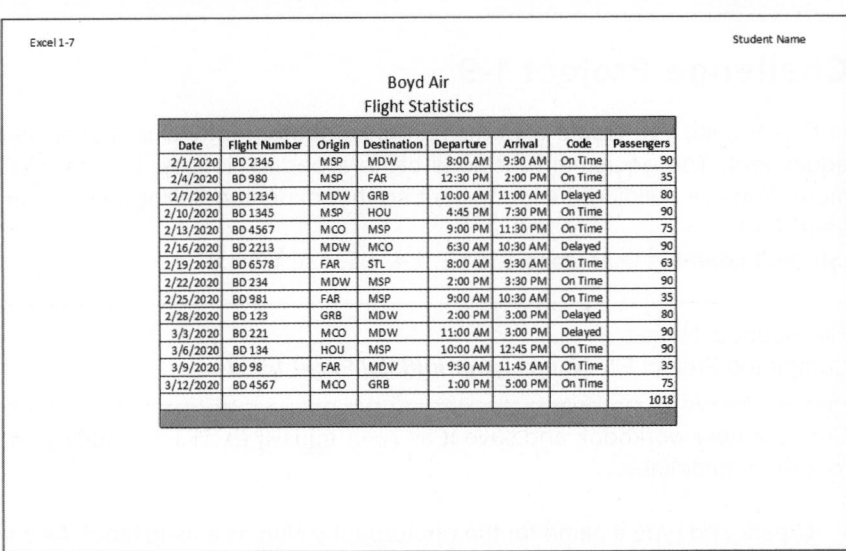

Figure 1-108 Excel 1-7 completed

Challenge Project 1-8

In this project, you create a workbook that lists and tracks candy and beverage sales at a gourmet chocolate store for selected holidays or special events. You enter and format the data and then finalize the workbook for distribution.
[Student Learning Outcomes 1.1, 1.2, 1.3, 1.4, 1.5, 1.6, 1.8]

File Needed: None
Completed Project File Name: *[your initials] Excel 1-8.xlsx*

Create a new workbook and save it as [your initials] Excel 1-8. Modify your workbook according to the following guidelines:

- Choose a workbook theme.
- Determine and type a name for the store in cell **A1**. In cell **A2**, type Sales by Holiday.
- Starting in cell **B3**, type the names of four chocolate candies and one chocolate beverage (cells B3:F3).
- Type the names of five holidays, celebrations, or special events in cells **A4:A8**.
- Fill in values to reflect dollar or unit sales, and format these values appropriately.
- Calculate a total for each holiday and a total for each candy or beverage. Add labels for these totals.
- Use cell styles, borders, fill color, or other formatting to design your worksheet.
- *AutoFit* columns and adjust row heights as needed.
- Insert a footer that includes your name in one section and the date in another section.
- Use portrait orientation and fit the worksheet to a single page. Center it horizontally.
- Name the sheet tab and set a tab color.
- Enter the company name in the *Title* field in the document properties.

Challenge Project 1-9

In this project, you create a worksheet for a photography club that rents retail space for selling used equipment. The equipment includes camera bodies, lenses, tripods, cases, accessories, books, and more. You are building the worksheet so that expected selling prices can be entered each month for each item.
[Student Learning Outcomes 1.1, 1.2, 1.4, 1.5, 1.6, 1.7, 1.8]

File Needed: None
Completed Project File Name: *[your initials] Excel 1-9.xlsx*

Create a new workbook and save it as [your initials] Excel 1-9. Modify your workbook according to the following guidelines:

- Create and type a name for the photography club as a main label. As a second label, type a label that specifies the purpose of the worksheet.
- Type Jan in cell **B3**. Fill the months to **Dec** in column **M**.

- In cells **A4:A13**, type the names of ten items related to any type of photography equipment. Research a web site that sells similar items.
- As the January price for the first item, type a realistic value as a resale price. For the February price, type a value that is a few dollars more than the January price. Select these two cells to identify a pattern and fill prices for the remaining months.
- Repeat the tasks in the previous step for each of the ten items to fill in values for all the items.
- Use cell styles, borders, fill color, or other formatting to design the worksheet.
- Adjust column widths and row heights.
- Insert a header that includes your name in the right section.
- Use landscape orientation and fit the worksheet to a single page.
- Enter the club's name in the *Author* field in the document properties pane.
- Name the worksheet tab and choose a tab color.
- Split the sheet at cell **G1**. Arrange the data so that you see cell **A1** in each window.

Challenge Project 1-10

In this project, you create a spreadsheet that details your expected monthly income and expenses.
[Student Learning Outcomes 1.1, 1.2, 1.3, 1.4, 1.5, 1.6, 1.8]

File Needed: None
Completed Project File Name: *[your initials] Excel 1-10.xlsx*

Create a new workbook and save it as [your initials] Excel 1-10. Modify your workbook according to the following guidelines:

- Type the main label Expected Monthly Income and Estimated Expenses. Type your name as a second label.
- Type Income in cell **A3**. In cells **A4:A7**, enter labels for four categories of income. For example, you may have regular wages from one or more jobs, interest from a certificate of deposit, rent from property that you own, income from internet sales, etc. Include descriptive labels, enter values in cells **B4:B7**, and include an income calculation using *SUM* in cell **B8**.
- Type Expenses in cell **D3**. In cells **D4:D9**, enter labels for six categories of expenses. These include rent, a mortgage payment, insurance, loan payments, food, clothing, entertainment, transportation, and so on. Complete labels, enter values in cells **E4:E9**, and use *SUM* to calculate total expenses in cell **E10**.
- Format the data with borders, fill color, font styles, and number formats. Adjust page layout options so that the sheet fits on a single portrait page.
- Spell check the sheet.
- Name the sheet Jan and choose a tab color.
- Copy the sheet and name the copy Feb. Choose a different tab color.
- Delete the expense amounts on the *Feb* sheet.
- Copy the *Feb* sheet to create a worksheet for March.
- Add document properties to identify the workbook.

Source of screenshots Microsoft Office 365 (2019): Word, Excel, Access, Powerpoint.

CHAPTER 2

Working with Formulas and Functions

CHAPTER OVERVIEW

With its capabilities in mathematical, scientific, engineering, and other calculations, Excel is a valuable tool for business, government, education, and you. Use Excel to create a simple addition formula or a sophisticated calculation with layers of arithmetic. In this chapter, you learn how to build a basic formula and how to use mathematical rules. You also explore Excel function categories.

STUDENT LEARNING OUTCOMES (SLOs)

After completing this chapter, you will be able to:

SLO 2.1 Build and edit basic formulas (p. E2-89).

SLO 2.2 Set the mathematical order of operations in a formula (p. E2-91).

SLO 2.3 Use absolute, mixed, relative, and 3D references in a formula (p. E2-93).

SLO 2.4 Use formula auditing tools in a worksheet (p. E2-99).

SLO 2.5 Work with *Statistical* and *Date & Time* functions (p. E2-106).

SLO 2.6 Work with functions from the *Financial*, *Logical*, and *Lookup & Reference* categories (p. E2-114).

SLO 2.7 Build functions from the *Math & Trig* category (p. E2-122).

CASE STUDY

In the Pause & Practice projects in this chapter, you work with a multi-sheet workbook for Paradise Lakes Resort (PLR), the northern Minnesota chain of resorts. You build formulas to complete a simple income statement, to calculate data for the boutique division, and to track information about the youth camp.

Pause & Practice 2-1: Build and audit formulas in a worksheet.

Pause & Practice 2-2: Insert *Statistical* and *Date & Time* functions in a workbook.

Pause & Practice 2-3: Use *Financial*, *Logical*, *Lookup*, and *Math & Trig* functions in a workbook.

Building and Editing a Formula

An Excel *formula* is an expression or statement that uses common arithmetic operations to perform a calculation. Basic arithmetic operations are addition, subtraction, multiplication, and division. The formula is entered in a cell and refers to other cells or ranges in the worksheet or workbook. The formula appears in the *Formula* bar, but the results appear in the cell.

You learned in Chapter 1 that a function is a built-in formula. Like a function, a formula begins with an equals sign (=). After the equals sign, you enter the address of the first cell, followed by the arithmetic operator, followed by the next cell in the calculation. An example of a simple addition formula is **=B5 +B6** which adds the values in cells B5 and B6.

Basic arithmetic operators are listed in Table 2-1. Enter arithmetic operators using the numeric keypad or the symbols on the number keys at the top of the keyboard.

In the multiplication formula **=C5*C6**, the value in cell C5 is multiplied by the value in cell C6. Use cell references in a formula or a value known as a *constant*. In the formula **=D5*85%**, the constant is 85%.

Table 2-1: Arithmetic Operators

Character	Operation
+	Addition
−	Subtraction
*	Multiplication
/	Division

Type a Formula

For a simple formula, type it. Click the cell, type the equals sign, type the first cell address, type the operator, type the next cell address, and so on. Press any completion key when the formula is finished. Formulas are not case sensitive, so you can type cell addresses in lowercase letters. Excel automatically converts cell references to uppercase when the formula is completed. If you press **Esc** before completing a formula, it is canceled and nothing is entered in the cell.

As you type a cell address after the equals sign, *Formula AutoComplete* displays a list of functions and range names that match the character that you typed. You can ignore the list and continue typing. In addition, the *Range Finder* highlights and color codes each cell as you type its address.

▶HOW TO: Type a Formula

1. Click the cell for the formula.
2. Type an equals sign (=) to begin the formula.
3. Type the column letter for the first cell reference (Figure 2-1).
 - *Formula AutoComplete* displays a list of functions and range names.
 - You can type a lowercase or uppercase character.
4. Type the row number for the cell reference.
 - The *Range Finder* color codes the cell and its reference.
5. Type the arithmetic operator.
6. Type the cell address for the next reference.

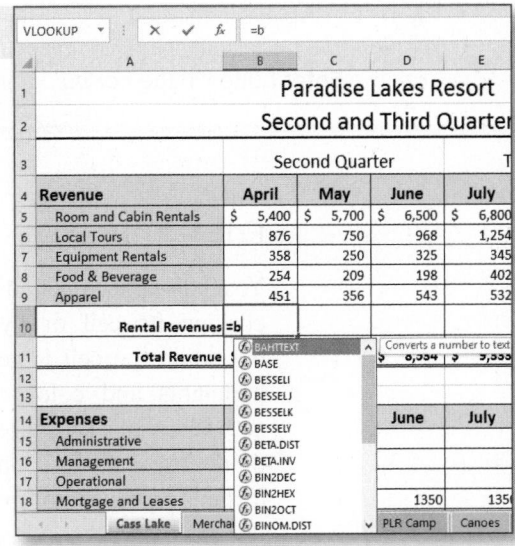

Figure 2-1 *Formula AutoComplete* while typing a formula

7. Press **Enter**.
 - The result displays in the cell where the formula is located (Figure 2-2).
 - The *Formula* bar displays the formula.
 - One way to complete a formula is to click the **Enter** button (the check mark) in the *Formula* bar.
 - Press **Ctrl+Enter** to complete a formula.

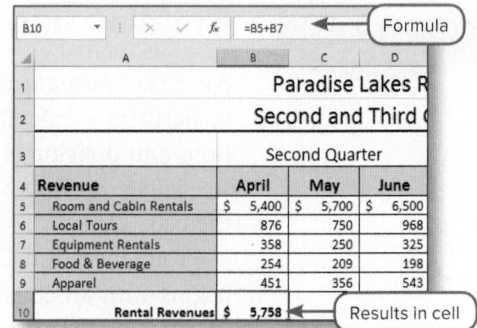

Figure 2-2 Formula and result

Point and Click to Build a Formula

Instead of typing a cell address, you can point to and click the cell to enter its address in a formula. This method guards against your typing the wrong address. You will not see a *Formula AutoComplete* list, but the *Range Finder* will highlight and color code the cells.

▶ **HOW TO:** Point and Click to Build a Formula

1. Click the cell for the formula.
2. Type an equals sign (=) to start the formula.
3. Point to and click the first cell for the formula.
 - The reference is entered in the cell and in the *Formula* bar.
 - The *Range Finder* highlights and color codes the reference.
 - If you click the wrong cell, click the correct cell to replace the address.
4. Type the arithmetic operator.
5. Point to and click the next cell for the formula (Figure 2-3).
 - The reference is entered in the cell and in the *Formula* bar.
 - The *Range Finder* highlights and color codes the reference.
6. Press **Enter**.
 - The result displays in the cell.
 - The *Formula* bar displays the formula.
 - Click the **Enter** button in the *Formula* bar or press **Ctrl+Enter** to complete a formula.

Figure 2-3 Point and click to build a formula

Edit a Formula

You edit a formula in *Edit* mode by double-clicking its cell or by clicking the *Formula* bar while the cell is active. The *Range Finder* highlights and color codes the formula cell as well as the cells used in the formula. Add or remove cells and operators to build a new formula in the cell or in the *Formula* bar.

> **ANOTHER WAY**
> Click the cell and press **F2 (FN+F2)** to start *Edit* mode.

▶HOW TO: Edit a Formula

1. Double-click the formula cell.
 - The *Range Finder* highlights and color codes the cells.
2. Edit the formula in the cell (Figure 2-4).
 - Edit the cell address or type a different operator.
 - Select a cell address and click a different cell to replace the reference.
 - Use the *Formula* bar to edit a formula.
3. Press **Enter**.
 - Click the **Enter** button in the *Formula* bar or press **Ctrl+Enter** to complete a formula.

Figure 2-4 Edit a formula in the cell

SLO 2.2

Setting Mathematical Order of Operations

A formula can have more than one operator, such as a combination of addition and multiplication. Figure 2-5 illustrates two formulas a restaurant might use to calculate a bill for a couple who ordered the same items. The formula in cell B6 lists the additions first and multiplies by 2; the total of $24 is incorrect. The formula in cell B8 is the same except for the parentheses; the correct amount is $42.

	A	B	C	D	E	F	G
1	Appetizer	$4					
2	Entrée	$10					
3	Dessert	$4					
4	Beverage	$3					
5							
6	2 people	$24	⬅ Formula is =B1+B2+B3+B4*2				
7							
8		$42	⬅ Formula is =(B1+B2+B3+B4)*2				
9							

Figure 2-5 Formulas with multiple operators

Excel follows *mathematical order of operations*, which is the sequence of arithmetic calculations. The order in which the mathematics in a formula is carried out depends on the operator, as well as left-to-right order. The basic sequence is left to right, but multiplication and division are done before addition and subtraction. This concept is also known as *order of precedence* or *math hierarchy*.

You control the order of operations with parentheses. The formula in cell B8 (see Figure 2-5) uses parentheses to reorder the calculation. The parentheses group the addition ($4+$10+$4+$3 = 21) and multiply the result by 2 ($21*2 = $42).

In a formula with multiple operators, references enclosed in parentheses are calculated first. If a value with an exponent exists, it is calculated next. Multiplication and division follow, and finally addition and subtraction. When two operators have the same precedence, Excel calculates them from left to right.

Table 2-2: Mathematical Order of Precedence

Operator	Operation	Order of Precedence
()	**P**arentheses	First
^	**E**xponent	Second
*	**M**ultiplication	Third
/	**D**ivision	Third
+	**A**ddition	Fourth
−	**S**ubtraction	Fourth

Exponents raise a number to a power. The formula **3^3** multiplies 3 * 3 * 3, 27. Use the
caret symbol (**^**) to build a formula with an exponent.

Multiple Operators in a Formula

When different operators are used in a formula, you must determine how the calculation should
be completed and if parentheses are necessary to set the proper order. Here are formulas with
two operators. Because addition and subtraction are equal in priority, Excel calculates from
left to right.

$$5 + 1 - 3 = 3 \qquad 5 - 1 + 3 = 7$$

Below are formulas with two operators with different priority. Excel calculates the multiplica-
tion first and then follows left to right order.

$$2 + 5 * 3 = 17 \qquad 2 * 5 + 3 = 13$$

Consider this formula with three different operators. Because multiplication and division
are equal priority but are higher than addition, the multiplication is first, followed by the
division (left to right). The result of those calculations is added to 5.

$$= 2 * 5/2 + 5 = 10$$

▶HOW TO: Use Multiple Operators in a formula

1. Type = to start the formula.

2. Type ((left parenthesis) to start the calculation that should
 have priority.

 • The calculation in parentheses can occur anywhere in the
 formula.

3. Click the first cell for the calculation to be enclosed in
 parentheses.

4. Type the arithmetic operator.

5. Click the next cell for the calculation to be enclosed in
 parentheses.

6. Type) (right parenthesis) to end the calculation with priority
 (Figure 2-6).

 • You must have matching parentheses.

7. Complete the formula.

8. Press **Enter**.

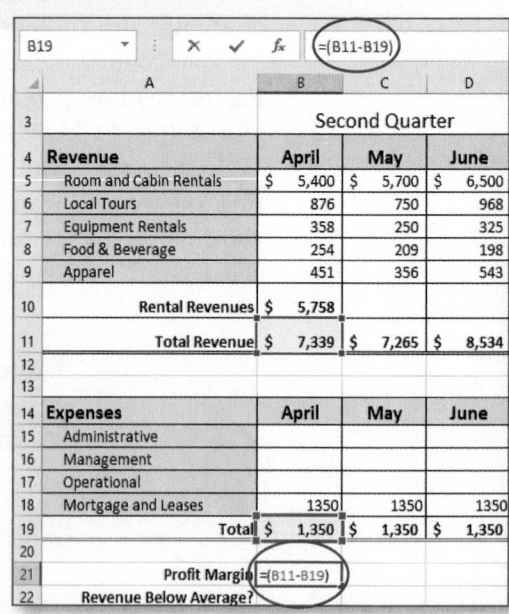

Figure 2-6 Set the order of operations with parentheses

Using Absolute, Mixed, Relative, and 3D References

Cell references in a formula are identified in different ways. How a cell reference is identified affects how the formula is adjusted when it is copied.

- A *relative cell reference* is the location of a cell, such as cell **B2**. In column B, the formula is =**B5+B7**, but when copied to column C, it is =**C5+C7**. When you copy a formula with relative references, copied references are updated to the new locations.
- An **absolute cell reference** is indicated with dollar signs as in cell **B2**. When an absolute reference is copied, it does not change. In the formula =**B6−C7**, B6 would not change when copied anywhere in the workbook. C7, on the other hand, would reflect where the copy is located. You can type the dollar signs in an absolute reference, but it is easier to use the **F4 (FN+F4)** function key. When building a formula, enter the cell address and then press **F4 (FN+F4)**.
- A *mixed cell reference* has one relative and one absolute reference. Cell **$B2** is a mixed reference. When it is copied, it always refers to column B, but the row number updates to the row where the copy is located. The formula =**$B5+C$6** has two mixed references. When copied, this formula will always show column B for the first address and row 6 for the second address.
- A *3D cell reference* is a cell located in another worksheet in the same workbook. It can be absolute, mixed, or relative. A 3D reference includes the name of the sheet as in **Sheet2!B2** or **Inventory!$B2**. The sheet name is followed by an exclamation point. When you point and click to build a 3D reference, the sheet name and the exclamation point are automatically entered. When the sheet name includes special characters (@, #, &, etc.), the name is enclosed in single quotes as in **'Inventory#'!$B2**. When you type a 3D reference, you must spell the sheet name correctly and include the exclamation point and single quotes.

Table 2-3 illustrates each cell reference type:

Table 2-3: Cell Reference Types

Cell Reference	Reference Type	Behavior When Copied
B2	Relative	Cell address updates to new location(s).
B2	Absolute	Cell address does not change.
$B2	Mixed	Column does not change; row updates to new location(s).
B$2	Mixed	Row does not change; column updates to new location(s).
Sheet2!B2	3D Relative	Cell address updates to new location(s).

> **MORE INFO**
>
> When used in a reference, the dollar sign ($) and the exclamation point (!) are identifiers. The dollar sign is not treated as a currency symbol, and the exclamation point is not considered punctuation.

Copy a Formula with a Relative Reference

When a formula with relative references is copied, the copied formulas use cell addresses that reflect their locations in the worksheet. In the Paradise Lakes worksheet shown in Figure 2-7, the formula to calculate rental revenue in cell B10 is **=B5+B7**. The formula for cell C10 is **=C5+C7**. The formula in cell B10 can be copied to cells C10:G10 and will automatically adjust for each column.

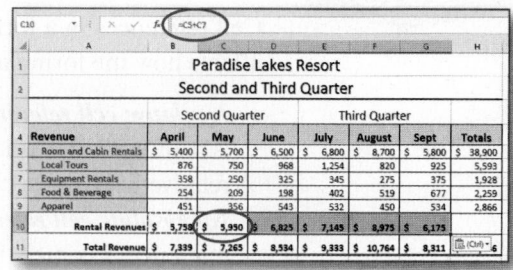

Figure 2-7 Copy a formula with a relative reference

▶**HOW TO:** Copy a Formula with a Relative Reference

1. Select the cell with the formula.
 - Select multiple adjacent cells.
2. Press **Ctrl+C** to copy the formula(s).
 - Click and drag the *Fill* pointer if the copies are adjacent to the original formula(s).
 - Use the **Copy** button on the *Home* tab if you prefer.
3. Select the destination cell or range.
 - Click the first cell in a destination range when pasting multiple cells.
4. Press **Ctrl+V** to paste the formula (see Figure 2-7).
 - The pasted formula reflects its location on the worksheet.
 - Ignore the **Paste Options** button.
 - Use the **Paste** button on the *Home* tab if you prefer.
5. Press **Esc** to cancel the **Paste** command.

Build and Copy a Formula with an Absolute Reference

An absolute reference in a formula maintains that address when copied. An example is a worksheet in which expenses are calculated as a percentage of revenue. You type the percentage once in a worksheet cell, use an absolute reference to that cell in the first occurrence of the formula, and copy the formula.

To change a cell address to an absolute reference, press the **F4 (FN+F4)** function key while keying or editing the formula. The first press of the key inserts dollar signs for the row and column reference. Another press of the **F4 (FN+F4)** key changes to a mixed reference, and each press of the key cycles to the next option.

▶**HOW TO:** Build and Copy a Formula with an Absolute Reference

1. Click the cell for the formula.
2. Type an equals sign (=) to begin the formula.
3. Click the cell to be referenced in the formula.
4. Press **F4 (FN+F4)**.
 - The reference becomes absolute (Figure 2-8).
5. Complete the formula and press **Enter**.

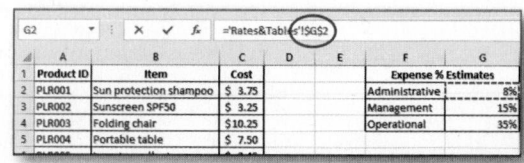

Figure 2-8 Make a reference absolute

6. Select the cell with the formula.
7. Press **Ctrl+C** to copy the formula(s).
 - Use the **Copy** button on the *Home* tab if you prefer.
 - Click and drag the *Fill* pointer if the copies are adjacent to the original formula.
8. Select the destination cell or range.
9. Press **Ctrl+V** to paste the formula.
 - The pasted formula uses the same cell reference as the original.
 - Use the **Paste** button on the *Home* tab if you prefer.
 - Ignore the **Paste Options** button.

> **MORE INFO**
>
> When you type a constant in a formula, such as **=B7*12**, the constant (12) is treated as an absolute value.

Build and Copy a Formula with a Mixed Reference

A mixed cell reference has one relative and one absolute reference in the cell address. Part of the copied formula is unchanged and part is updated. A mixed reference has one dollar sign. You still use the **F4 (FN+F4)** function key, because each press of the function key cycles through different combinations for displaying the dollar signs.

▶**HOW TO:** Build and Copy a Formula with a Mixed Reference

1. Click the cell for the formula.
2. Type an equals sign (=) to begin the formula.
3. Click the cell to be referenced in the formula.
4. Press **F4 (FN+F4)**.
 - The reference is absolute.
5. Press **F4 (FN+F4)** again.
 - The column reference is relative and the row reference is absolute.
6. Press **F4 (FN+F4)** again (Figure 2-9).
 - The row reference is relative and the column reference is absolute.
7. Complete the formula and press **Enter**.
8. Select the formula cell.
9. Press **Ctrl+C** to copy the formula(s).
 - You can use the **Copy** button on the *Home* tab.
 - Drag the *Fill* pointer if copies are adjacent to the original formula.
10. Click the destination cell or range.
11. Press **Ctrl+V** to paste the formula.
 - The pasted formula does not change the absolute part of the reference but updates the relative part.
 - Use the **Paste** button on the *Home* tab if you prefer.

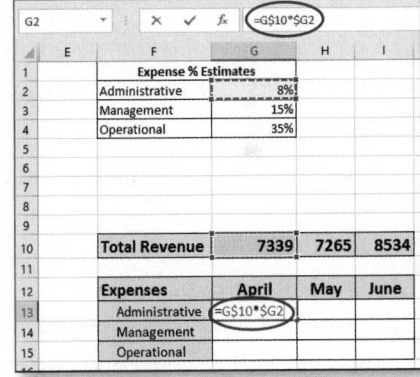

Figure 2-9 Formula with mixed references

Create a Formula with a 3D Reference

An important feature of an Excel workbook is being able to refer to data on any sheet in a formula. This type of formula is called a *3D reference*, because it uses more than one sheet or surface to calculate a result.

A 3D reference includes the name of the worksheet and can be absolute, mixed, or relative.

Table 2-4: Sample 3D References

Cell on Sheet1	Formula on Sheet1	Results
B4	=B3+Sheet2!B3+Sheet3!B3	Adds the values in cell B3 on Sheet1, Sheet2, and Sheet3.
B7	=SUM(B4:B6)+Sheet2!A12	Adds the values in cells B4:B6 on Sheet1 to the value in cell A12 on Sheet2.
C8	=C7*Sheet2!D4	Multiplies the value in cell C7 by the value in cell D4 on Sheet2.
D10	=Sheet2!B2/Sheet3!B2	Divides the value in cell B2 on Sheet2 by the value in cell B2 on Sheet3.

> **MORE INFO**
>
> An external reference formula refers to a cell in another workbook. It can be absolute, mixed, or relative. An external reference includes the name of the workbook in square brackets as in **[PLRSales]Sheet!B$2**.

▶ HOW TO: Create a Formula with a 3D Reference

1. Click the cell for the formula and type =.
2. Click the first cell for the formula.
3. Type the operator.
4. Select the sheet tab with the cell to be used in the formula.
5. Click the cell required in the formula.
 - Press **F4** (**FN+F4**) to make the reference absolute or mixed as needed (Figure 2-10).
6. Type the next operator and complete the formula as needed.
 - The next cell can be on the same or another sheet.
7. Press **Enter** or any completion key.

Figure 2-10 3D cell reference

Range Names and Formula AutoComplete

A *range name* is a label assigned to a single cell or a group of cells. You can use range names instead of cell references in a formula. Instead of **=B11*10%**, name cell B11 as "Revenue" to build the formula **=Revenue*10%**. Descriptive range names help you interpret a formula.

In addition, named cell ranges appear in the *Formula AutoComplete* list for ease in building formulas. A named cell range is an absolute reference in a formula.

You create a range name using the *Name* box or from the *Defined Names* group on the *Formulas* tab. The *Name Manager* command in this group enables you to create, edit, and delete range names. If you alter a range name, Excel automatically updates formulas that use that range name. The *Apply Names* command (*Define Name* button) enables you to assign a name to existing formulas that refer to the cells identified in the range name.

Follow these basic rules for naming a cell range:

- Begin a range name with a letter.
- Use a short, descriptive name.
- Do not use spaces or special characters in a range name.
- Separate words in a range name with an underscore as in "First_Qtr," or use initial caps for each word such as "FirstQtr."
- Do not name a range with a single character such as "N."
- Do not name a range with a cell reference such as "B2."

To use the name in a formula, type the first character of the name to display the *Formula AutoComplete* list. You may need to type a second character to see the name in a workbook that includes many range names. Select the range name in the list and press **Tab**, or double-click the name to enter it in the formula. Range names are automatically substituted in formulas when you select the named cell range in the worksheet while building a formula.

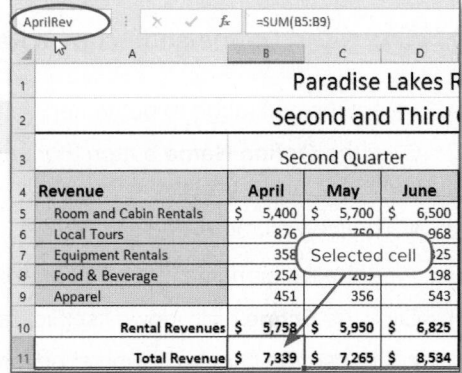

Figure 2-11 Name a range in the *Name* box

▶ HOW TO: Name a Range and Use Formula AutoComplete

1. Select the cell or range to be named.
2. Click the **Name** box at the left of the *Formula* bar.
3. Type the name and press **Enter** (Figure 2-11).
4. Click the cell for the formula.
5. Type = to start the formula.
6. Type the first one or two letters of the range name.
 - The *Formula AutoComplete* list shows range and function names.
 - The list is alphabetical, and function names are uppercase.
7. Find the range name and double-click it (Figure 2-12).
 - The name is inserted in the formula.
 - You can also click the name in the list to highlight it and press **Tab**.
8. Complete the formula.
9. Press **Enter** when the formula is complete.

Expenses	April	May
Administrative	=to	
Management	TODAY	
Operational	Total_Revenue	
Mortgage and Leases	1350	1350
Total	$ 1,350	$ 1,350

Figure 2-12 Use *Formula AutoComplete* with a range name

In addition to selecting cell ranges to name them, use row and column labels to create range names. The *Create from Selection* button on the *Formulas* tab automatically assigns range names based on labels in the top row, the left column, or both.

▶ HOW TO: Create Names from a Selection

1. Select the range including row or column labels (or both) (Figure 2-13).
 - Values and related labels must be adjacent.
2. Click the **Create from Selection** button [*Formulas* tab, *Defined Names* group].
 - The *Create Names from Selection* dialog box opens.
3. Select the **Top row** or **Left column** box.
 - Choose both options if appropriate for the data.
 - Other options include bottom row and right column.
4. Click **OK**.
5. Click the **Name box** arrow in the *Formula* bar.
 - All range names are listed.

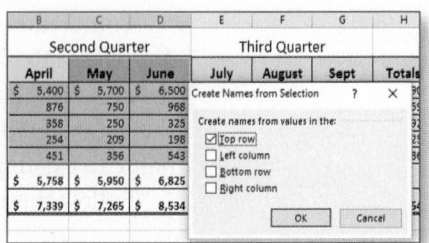

Figure 2-13 *Create Names from Selection* dialog box

The **Define Name** button [*Formulas* tab, *Defined Names* group] opens the *New Name* dialog box. Type the name, enter a comment, select the cells, and specify a *scope*. The scope determines if the range applies to a particular sheet or to the entire workbook. By default, a range name applies to the workbook. If you use the name "JanSales" on Sheet1, you cannot use it again on Sheet2, unless you scope each name to a particular sheet. When you scope names to a worksheet, you can use the name multiple times in the workbook.

▶ HOW TO: Define and Scope a Range Name

1. Select the cell range to be named.
2. Click the **Define Name** button [*Formulas* tab, *Defined Names* group].
 - The *New Name* dialog box opens.
3. Type the range name in the *Name* box.
4. Click the **Scope** drop-down list (Figure 2-14).
 - Choose the name of a worksheet as desired.
5. Select or edit the *Refers to* entry.
 - The selected cell range address displays.
 - If no cells are selected, type or select the range address.
6. Click **OK**.

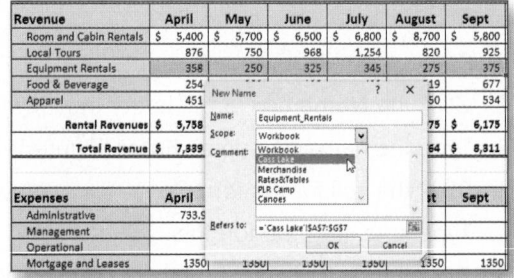

Figure 2-14 *New Name* dialog box and the *Scope* list

The *Use in Formula* button [*Formulas* tab, *Defined Names* group] displays a list of range names for insertion in a formula. You can also display a list of range names using the *Paste Name* dialog box. Press the **F3** (**FN+F3**) function key to open the *Paste Name* dialog box.

▶ HOW TO: Paste a Range Name in a Formula and Paste a List

1. Click the formula cell and type =.
2. Press **F3** (**FN+F3**) to open the *Paste Name* dialog box.
 - Range names appear in alphabetical order.

3. Find the range name and double-click it (Figure 2-15).

- Select the range name and press **Enter** or click **OK**.
- The range name displays in the formula.
- The worksheet displays the highlighted range.

4. Complete the formula and press **Enter**.

5. Click a blank cell in an unused area of the worksheet.

- Select a cell on another worksheet.

6. Click the **Use in Formula** button [*Formulas* tab, *Defined Names* group].

7. Select **Paste Names**.

- The *Paste Name* dialog box opens.

8. Click **Paste List**.

- A list of range names and cell references is pasted.
- You can edit and format the list of range names.

Figure 2-15 Choose a range name for the formula

SLO 2.4

Using Formula Auditing Tools

Formula auditing is the process of reviewing formulas for accuracy. Excel automatically audits formulas as you enter them and when you open a workbook based on its error checking rules [*File* tab, *Options*, *Formulas* pane]. Excel recognizes many errors, but not all of them. For example, if you type a formula that multiplies the values in two cells when it should add the values, you must find that error on your own. You may encounter circumstances when Excel identifies an error but the formula is correct.

> **MORE INFO**
>
> Open the Excel *Options* dialog box to set whether automatic error checking is enabled and to select which rules are used.

When Excel finds an error in a formula, it displays a small green error triangle in the top-left corner of the cell. Click the cell to see the *Trace Error* button and point to the button to see a *ScreenTip* about the error. The *Trace Error* button has a drop-down list with options for dealing with the error.

▶HOW TO: Trace an Error

1. Click the cell with the triangle error.

- The *Trace Error* button appears.

2. Point to the **Trace Error** button to display a *ScreenTip*.

3. Click the **Trace Error** drop-down list (Figure 2-16).

- Options for handling the error display.

4. Choose an option for the error.

- The options depend on the type of error.
- Select **Ignore Error** if the formula is correct.

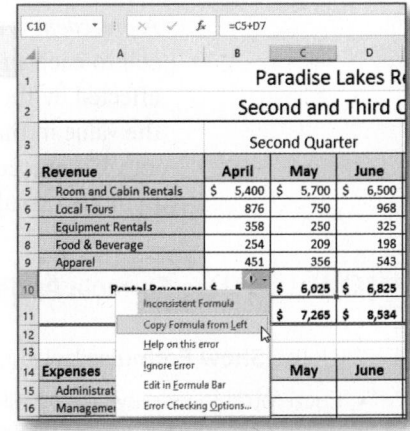

Figure 2-16 *Trace Error* button and its drop-down list

In addition to the green triangle error, Excel functions can result in a standard error message in the cell. For example, if you create a division formula that divides by a blank cell, the result is #DIV/0!. When you click the *Trace Error* button, it is identified as a division by zero error. Excel error messages occur for a syntax error, such as spelling a function name incorrectly, using an incorrect operator or symbol, having the wrong number of arguments, and so on. A standard error message starts with the number sign (#) and ends with an exclamation point (!).

> **MORE INFO**
>
> Use the *Go to Special* dialog box [*Find & Select* button, *Home* tab, *Editing* group] to highlight cells with formula errors, blank cells, and cells with precedents and dependents. This command helps identify potential problems in a workbook.

The Formula Auditing Group

The *Formula Auditing* group on the *Formulas* tab includes tools to check formulas for logic, consistency, and accuracy. These commands enable you to examine what contributes to a formula and to analyze if the formula is correct. The tools are helpful, but they do require that you correct the problem.

Table 2-5: Formula Auditing Buttons

Button	Description
Trace Precedents	Displays lines with arrows to identify all cells referenced in the formula in the active cell
Trace Dependents	Displays lines with arrows to all cells that use the active cell directly or indirectly in a formula
Remove Arrows	Removes all lines and arrows from the *Trace Precedents* or *Trace Dependents* buttons
Show Formulas	Displays formulas in the cells
Error Checking	Checks data against the error rules in Excel *Options*
Evaluate Formula	Steps through each part of a formula and displays an outcome for each part so that an error can be isolated
Watch Window	Opens a floating window that displays selected cells and values for monitoring

Trace Precedents and Dependents

A *precedent* is a cell that contributes to the formula results. Excel displays lines from the formula cell to each precedent cell for an easy way to audit your formula. A *dependent* is a cell that is affected by the active cell. Excel displays lines from the active cell to each cell that depends on the value in that cell. The lines may be blue or red, depending on the type of error identified, if any. If a precedent or dependent cell is located on a different worksheet, a black line and arrow point to a small worksheet icon, but this does not identify the actual error cell address.

▶HOW TO: Use Formula Auditing Tools

1. Click the **Show Formulas** button [*Formulas* tab, *Formula Auditing* group].
 - Each formula displays in its cell.
 - Show or hide formulas by pressing **Ctrl+`** (grave accent next to the 1 key at the top of the keyboard).
2. Select the formula cell.

3. Click the **Trace Precedents** button [*Formulas* tab, *Formula Auditing* group].

 - Lines and arrows identify cells that contribute to the formula results (Figure 2-17).
 - You can trace precedents and dependents with formulas shown or hidden.

4. Click the **Remove Arrows** button [*Formulas* tab, *Formula Auditing* group].

 - Clicking the button removes all arrows.
 - Click the **Remove Arrows** drop-down list to specify the type of arrow to remove.

5. Click a cell that is referenced in a formula.

 - The cell need not have a formula.

6. Click the **Trace Dependents** button [*Formulas* tab, *Formula Auditing* group].

 - Lines and arrows trace to cells that are affected by the active cell.

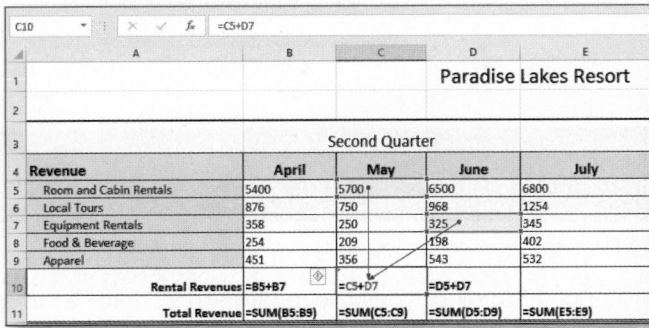

Figure 2-17 *Trace Precedents* arrows with formulas shown

7. Click the **Remove Arrows** button [*Formulas* tab, *Formula Auditing* group].

8. Click the **Show Formulas** button [*Formulas* tab, *Formula Auditing* group].

 - Formulas are hidden.
 - Show or hide formulas by pressing **Ctrl+`**.

> **MORE INFO**
>
> In a complex worksheet with sophisticated formulas, click the **Trace Precedents** button [*Formulas* tab, *Formula Auditing* group] once to trace the first layer of precedents. Then click the button again to trace the precedents of the precedents.

The Formula Correction Message Window

As you complete a formula with a minor error (for example, typing "5c" as a cell address), Excel displays a message box with information about the error (Figure 2-18). For many of these types of errors, review the suggested correction and select **Yes**. For an error that Excel finds but to which it cannot offer a solution, a message box opens with suggestions. However, you need to solve the problem on your own.

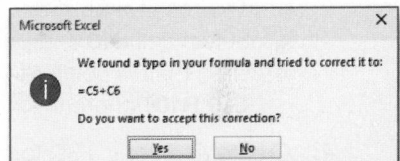

Figure 2-18 Formula correction message window

Circular Reference

A *circular reference* is an error that occurs when a formula includes the cell address of the formula. For example, if the formula in cell **B10** is **=B5+B10**, the reference is circular. When you try to complete such a formula, a message box opens as shown in Figure 2-19. The *Status* bar displays the location of circular references, but Excel does not correct this type of error. You can keep a circular reference in a worksheet, but the formula results are inaccurate.

Figure 2-19 Circular reference and its message window

PAUSE & PRACTICE: EXCEL 2-1

For this project, you build formulas in a Paradise Lakes Resort worksheet. You use mixed and absolute references, a 3D reference, and set an order of precedence. You also name cell ranges and use auditing tools.

File Needed: ***ParadiseLakes-02.xlsx*** *(Student data files are available in the Library of your SIMnet account.)*
Completed Project File Name: ***[your initials] PP E2-1.xlsx***

1. Open the ***ParadiseLakes-02.xlsx*** workbook from your student data files. (If the workbook opens in *Protected View*, click **Enable Editing**.)

2. Save the workbook as [your initials] PP E2-1.

3. Enter and copy an addition formula.
 a. Click cell **B10** on the **Cass Lake** sheet.
 b. Type = to start a formula.
 c. Click cell **B5** to insert the first rental item in the formula.
 d. Type + as the mathematical operator.
 e. Click cell **B7** to add the second rental item. The formula is =**B5+B7** (Figure 2-20).
 f. Press **Enter** or click the **Enter** button in the *Formula* bar. The result is $5,758.
 g. Select cell **B10** and point to the *Fill* handle.
 h. Drag the *Fill* pointer to copy the formula to cells **C10:H10**. Ignore the *Auto Fill Options* button.

Figure 2-20 Point and click to build a formula

4. Create and copy a 3D formula with absolute cell references.
 a. Select cell **B15**. Administrative expense is calculated by multiplying the total revenue for the month by a set percentage.
 b. Type = to start the formula.
 c. Click cell **B11**, the total revenue for April.
 d. Type * to indicate multiplication.
 e. Click the **Rates&Tables** sheet tab. The sheet name is inserted in the *Formula* bar with single quotes and an exclamation point.
 f. Click cell **G2**, the percentage for administrative expenses. The cell address is added to the formula.
 g. Press **F4** (**FN+F4**) to make the reference absolute (Figure 2-21).
 h. Press **Enter**. The formula is complete and the *Cass Lake* sheet is active.
 i. Select cell **B15** and drag the *Fill* pointer to copy the formula to cells **C15:G15**. The reference to cell G2 remains for each copied formula (Figure 2-22).

Figure 2-21 Absolute 3D reference in the formula

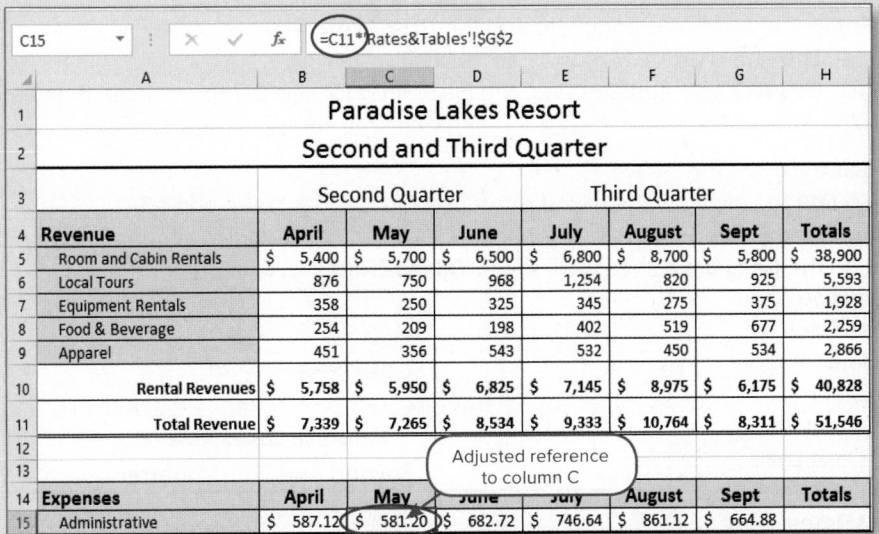

Figure 2-22 Copied formula with absolute reference

5. Create and copy a 3D formula with mixed references.
 a. Select cell **B16**. Management expense is calculated by multiplying the total revenue for the month by the set percentage.
 b. Type = to start the formula.
 c. Click cell **B11**, the total revenue for April.
 d. Press **F4** (**FN+F4**) to make the reference absolute (B11).
 e. Press **F4** (**FN+F4**) to make the reference mixed with the row reference absolute (B$11). When the formula is copied to row 17, it will remain B$11 (Figure 2-23). When copied to column C, the relative reference will be C$11.
 f. Type * for multiplication.
 g. Click the **Rates&Tables** sheet tab. The sheet name is inserted in the *Formula* bar.
 h. Click cell **G3**, the percentage for management expenses.
 i. Press **F4** (**FN+F4**) to make the reference absolute (G3).
 j. Press **F4** (**FN+F4**) to make the reference mixed with the row reference absolute (G$3).
 k. Press **F4** (**FN+F4**) to make the column reference absolute ($G3) (Figure 2-24). When copied to row 17 in the **Cass Lake** sheet, the relative reference will be $G4.

Figure 2-23 Mixed cell reference

G3 ▼ : × ✓ *fx*	=B$11*'Rates&Tables'!$G3						
	A	B	C	D	E	F	G

▲	A	B	C	D	E	F	G
1	Product ID	Item	Cost			Expense % Estimates	
2	PLR001	Sun protection shampoo	$ 3.75			Administrative	8%
3	PLR002	Sunscreen SPF50	$ 3.25			Management	15%
4	PLR003	Folding chair	$10.25			Operational	35%
5	PLR004	Portable table	$ 7.50				

Figure 2-24 Absolute reference to column G

l. Press **Enter**. The formula is complete and the *Cass Lake* sheet is active.

m. Select cell **B16** and drag its *Fill* pointer to cell **B17**.

n. Keep cells **B16:B17** selected and drag the *Fill* pointer for cell B17 to copy the formulas to cells **C16:G17**.

6. Use *Formula Auditing* tools.

a. Click cell **D17** to view how the mixed reference formula has been copied.

b. Click the **Trace Precedents** button [*Formulas* tab, *Formula Auditing* group]. The formula refers to cell D11 on the **Cass Lake** sheet and to the **Tables&Rates** sheet.

c. Click cell **E16** and click the **Trace Precedents** button. The formula refers to cell E11 on the **Cass Lake** sheet and to the **Tables&Rates** sheet (Figure 2-25).

d. Click the **Remove Arrows** button [*Formulas* tab, *Formula Auditing* group].

e. Click the **Show Formulas** [*Formulas* tab, *Formula Auditing* group] to see all formulas. This view does not display number formatting (Figure 2-26).

E16		fx	=E$11*'Rates&Tables'!$G3					
	A	B	C	D	E	F	G	H
1			Paradise Lakes Resort					
2			Second and Third Quarter					
3			Second Quarter			Third Quarter		
4	Revenue	April	May	June	July	August	Sept	Totals
5	Room and Cabin Rentals	$ 5,400	$ 5,700	$ 6,500	$ 6,800	$ 8,700	$ 5,800	$ 38,900
6	Local Tours	876	750	968	1,254	820	925	5,593
7	Equipment Rentals	358	250	325	345	275	375	1,928
8	Food & Beverage	254	209	198	402	519	677	2,259
9	Apparel	451	356	543	532	450	534	2,866
10	Rental Revenues	$ 5,758	$ 5,950	$ 6,825	$ 7,145	$ 8,975	$ 6,175	$ 40,828
11		$ 7,339	$ 7,265	$ 8,534	$ 9,333	$ 10,764	$ 8,311	$ 51,546
12		Another sheet icon						
13								
14	Expenses	April	May	June	July	August	Sept	Totals
15	Administrative	$ 587.1	$ 581.20	$ 682.72	$ 746.64	$ 861.12	$ 664.88	
16	Management	$ 1,100.85	$ 1,089.75	$ 1,280.10	$ 1,399.95	$ 1,614.60	$ 1,246.65	
17	Operational	$ 2,568.65	$ 2,542.75	$ 2,986.90	$ 3,266.55	$ 3,767.40	$ 2,908.85	
18	Mortgage and Leases	1350	1350	1350	1350	1350	1350	
19	Total	$ 5,607	$ 5,564	$ 6,300	$ 6,763	$ 7,593	$ 6,170	$ -

Figure 2-25 Formula precedents

E16		fx	=E$11*'Rates&Tables'!$G3					
	A	B	C	D	E	F	G	
1			Paradise Lakes Resort					
2			Second and Third Quarter					
3			Second Quarter			Third Quarter		
4	Revenue	April	May	June	July	August	Sept	To
5	Room and Cabin Rentals	5400	5700	6500	6800	8700	5800	=SUM(B5:G5
6	Local Tours	876	750	968	1254	820	925	=SUM(B6:G6
7	Equipment Rentals	358	250	325	345	275	375	=SUM(B7:G
8	Food & Beverage	254	209	198	402	519	677	=SUM(B8:G8
9	Apparel	451	356	543	532	450	534	=SUM(B9:G5
10	Rental Revenues	=B5+B7	=C5+C7	=D5+D7	=E5+E7	=F5+F7	=G5+G7	=H5+H7
11	Total Revenue	=SUM(B5:B9)	=SUM(C5:C9)	=SUM(D5:D9)	=SUM(E5:E9)	=SUM(F5:F9)	=SUM(G5:G9)	=SUM(H5:H
12								
13								
14	Expenses	April	May	June	July	August	Sept	To
15	Administrative	=B11*'Rates&Tables'!$G	=C11*'Rates&Tables'!$G	=D11*'Rates&Tables'!$G	=E11*'Rates&Tables'!$G	=F11*'Rates&Tables'!$G	=G11*'Rates&Tables'!$G	
16	Management	=B$11*'Rates&Tables'!$(=C$11*'Rates&Tables'!$(=D$11*'Rates&Tables'!$(=E$11*'Rates&Tables'!$(=F$11*'Rates&Tables'!$(=G$11*'Rates&Tables'!$(
17	Operational	=B$11*'Rates&Tables'!$(=C$11*'Rates&Tables'!$(=D$11*'Rates&Tables'!$(=E$11*'Rates&Tables'!$(=F$11*'Rates&Tables'!$(=G$11*'Rates&Tables'!$(
18	Mortgage and Leases	1350	1350	1350	1350	1350	1350	
19	Total	=SUM(B15:B18)	=SUM(C14:C18)	=SUM(D14:D18)	=SUM(E14:E18)	=SUM(F14:F18)	=SUM(G14:G18)	=SUM(H15:
20								

Cass Lake | Merchandise | Rates&Tables | PLR Camp | Canoes

Figure 2-26 Formulas displayed in worksheet

f. Click the **Show Formulas** [*Formulas* tab, *Formula Auditing* group] to hide the formulas.

7. Edit a formula and correct an error.
 a. Select cells **H15:H18** and click the **AutoSum** button [*Home* tab, *Editing* group]. The *SUM* function displays in each cell.
 b. Widen column **H** to display all data.
 c. Double-click cell **H16** to start *Edit* mode.
 d. Edit the cell range in the *SUM* formula to display **B15:G16** and press **Enter** to create a deliberate error. The green error triangle appears in the upper-left corner of the cell.
 e. Click cell **H16** to display the **Trace Error** button and then click the button. This formula is now inconsistent with others in the column (Figure 2-27).

H16	▼	:	×	✓	*fx*	=SUM(B15:G16)				
⊿	A		B	C	D	E	F	G	H	
1				Paradise Lakes Resort						
2				Second and Third Quarter						
3				Second Quarter			Third Quarter			
4	**Revenue**		**April**	**May**	**June**	**July**	**August**	**Sept**	**Totals**	
5	Room and Cabin Rentals		$ 5,400	$ 5,700	$ 6,500	$ 6,800	$ 8,700	$ 5,800	$ 38,900	
6	Local Tours		876	750	968	1,254	820	925	5,593	
7	Equipment Rentals		358	250	325	345	275	375	1,928	
8	Food & Beverage		254	209	198	402	519	677	2,259	
9	Apparel		451	356	543				2,866	
10	Rental Revenues		$ 5,758	$ 5,950	$ 6,825	$	Inconsistent Formula		$ 40,828	
11	Total Revenue		$ 7,339	$ 7,265	$ 8,534	$	Copy Formula from Above		$ 51,546	
12							Help on this error			
13							Ignore Error			
14	**Expenses**		**April**	**May**	**June**		Edit in Formula Bar		**Totals**	
15	Administrative		$ 587.12	$ 581.20	$ 682.72	$	Error Checking Options...		$ 4,123.68	
16	Management		$ 1,100.85	$ 1,089.75	$ 1,280.10	$ 1,399.95	$ 1,614.60	$ 1,24 ! ▾	$ 11,855.58	
17	Operational		$ 2,568.65	$ 2,542.75	$ 2,986.90	$ 3,266.55	$ 3,767.40	$ 2,908.85	$ 18,041.10	

Figure 2-27 *Trace Error* button and options

 f. Select **Copy Formula from Above** to correct the error.
 g. Click cell **H16** and click the **Trace Precedents** button [*Formulas* tab, *Formula Auditing* group]. The formula refers to the correct cells in row 16.
 h. Click the **Remove Arrows** button [*Formulas* tab, *Formula Auditing* group].

8. Set mathematical order of operations.
 a. Select cell **B21**. Profit margin, as a percentage, is revenue minus expenses divided by revenue. The formula is **=(B11—B19)/B11**; the parentheses are necessary so that the subtraction is done before the division.
 b. Type **=(** to start the formula and insert the opening parenthesis.
 c. Click cell **B11**, the total revenue for April.
 d. Type **—** for subtraction.
 e. Click cell **B19**, total expenses for April.
 f. Type **)** to set the precedence with the closing parenthesis.
 g. Type **/** for division and click cell **B11** (Figure 2-28).
 h. Press **Enter**. The result is formatted as *Accounting Number* format to match the source cells.

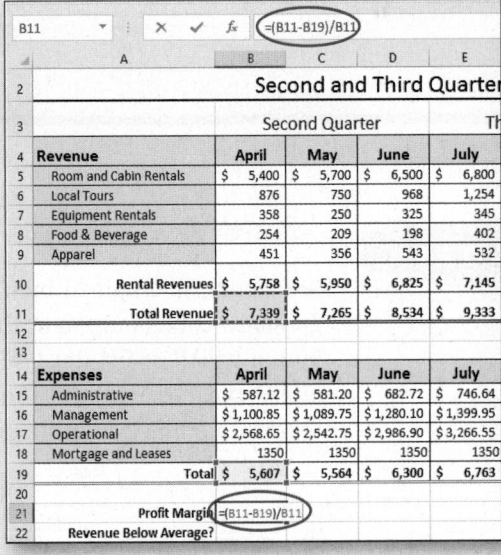

B11	▼	:	×	✓	*fx*	=(B11-B19)/B11		
⊿	A		B	C	D	E		
2			Second and Third Quarter					
3			Second Quarter			Th		
4	**Revenue**		**April**	**May**	**June**	**July**		
5	Room and Cabin Rentals		$ 5,400	$ 5,700	$ 6,500	$ 6,800		
6	Local Tours		876	750	968	1,254		
7	Equipment Rentals		358	250	325	345		
8	Food & Beverage		254	209	198	402		
9	Apparel		451	356	543	532		
10	Rental Revenues		$ 5,758	$ 5,950	$ 6,825	$ 7,145		
11	Total Revenue		$ 7,339	$ 7,265	$ 8,534	$ 9,333		
12								
13								
14	**Expenses**		**April**	**May**	**June**	**July**		
15	Administrative		$ 587.12	$ 581.20	$ 682.72	$ 746.64		
16	Management		$ 1,100.85	$ 1,089.75	$ 1,280.10	$ 1,399.95		
17	Operational		$ 2,568.65	$ 2,542.75	$ 2,986.90	$ 3,266.55		
18	Mortgage and Leases		1350	1350	1350	1350		
19	Total		$ 5,607	$ 5,564	$ 6,300	$ 6,763		
20								
21	Profit Margin		=(B11-B19)/B11					
22	Revenue Below Average?							

Figure 2-28 Set arithmetic order

i. Click cell **B21** and click the **Percent Style** button [*Home* tab, *Number* group].
j. Copy the formula in cell **B21** to cells **C21:G21**.

9. Name a cell range.
 a. Select cell **H11** and click the **Name** box.
 b. Type TotalRevenue in the *Name* box and press **Enter**.
 c. Select cells **B11:G11**.
 d. Click the **Define Name** button [*Formulas* tab, *Defined Names* group].
 e. Type Monthly_Rev in the *Name* box and click **OK** (Figure 2-29).
 f. Click cell **A1**.
 g. Click the **Name box** arrow and choose **TotalRevenue**. Cell H11 is selected.
 h. Click the **Name box** arrow and choose **Monthly_Rev**. Cells B11:G11 are selected.

10. Format cells **B16:H18** as **Comma Style**. Decrease the decimal two times.

11. Select cells **B15:H15** and decrease the decimal two times.

12. Press **Ctrl+Home**. Save and close the workbook (Figure 2-30).

New Name		?	X
Name:	Monthly_Rev		
Scope:	Workbook	⌄	
Comment:			
Refers to:	='Cass Lake'!B11:G11		
		OK	Cancel

Figure 2-29 Use the *New Name* dialog box to name a range

Paradise Lakes Resort
Second and Third Quarter

	Second Quarter			Third Quarter			
Revenue	**April**	**May**	**June**	**July**	**August**	**Sept**	**Totals**
Room and Cabin Rentals	$ 5,400	$ 5,700	$ 6,500	$ 6,800	$ 8,700	$ 5,800	$ 38,900
Local Tours	876	750	968	1,254	820	925	5,593
Equipment Rentals	358	250	325	345	275	375	1,928
Food & Beverage	254	209	198	402	519	677	2,259
Apparel	451	356	543	532	450	534	2,866
Rental Revenues	$ 5,758	$ 5,950	$ 6,825	$ 7,145	$ 8,975	$ 6,175	$ 40,828
Total Revenue	$ 7,339	$ 7,265	$ 8,534	$ 9,333	$ 10,764	$ 8,311	$ 51,546
Expenses	**April**	**May**	**June**	**July**	**August**	**Sept**	**Totals**
Administrative	$ 587	$ 581	$ 683	$ 747	$ 861	$ 665	$ 4,124
Management	1,101	1,090	1,280	1,400	1,615	1,247	7,732
Operational	2,569	2,543	2,987	3,267	3,767	2,909	18,041
Mortgage and Leases	1,350	1,350	1,350	1,350	1,350	1,350	8,100
Total	$ 5,607	$ 5,564	$ 6,300	$ 6,763	$ 7,593	$ 6,170	$ 37,997
Profit Margin	24%	23%	26%	28%	29%	26%	
Revenue Below Average?							

Figure 2-30 PP E2-1 completed

Working with Statistical and Date & Time Functions

A function is a named built-in formula. Excel functions are grouped into categories on the *Formulas* command tab in the *Function Library* group. This group also has an *Insert Function* button which opens the *Insert Function* dialog box. From this dialog box, you can display an alphabetical list of all functions, a list by category, or a recently used list. Use this dialog box to search for a function by name.

> **MORE INFO**
>
> A formula such as =B2+B3−B6 is usually not called a function because it has no function name.

The *Statistical* function category includes calculations that determine an average, a maximum, a minimum, and a count. These common functions are options on the *AutoSum* button on the *Home* tab. The *Formulas* tab also has an *AutoSum* button with the same options.

AVERAGE Function

The *AVERAGE* function calculates the arithmetic **mean** of a range of cells. The mean is determined by adding all the values and dividing the result by the number of values. The *AVERAGE* function ignores empty cells or cells that include labels. When calculating an average, do not include total values in the range to be averaged.

The *AVERAGE* function has one argument, *numberN*. A number argument can be a range such as B11:G11. You can average up to 255 numbers (or ranges). The proper syntax for an *AVERAGE* function is:

=AVERAGE(number1, [number2], [number3], . . .)

The *number1* argument is required and others are optional.

When you choose a function from the *AutoSum* button, you will see the function name, an assumed range within parentheses, and an **Argument ScreenTip** below the cell that displays the syntax. When you choose to type a function, the *ScreenTip* shows the next argument in bold type as a guideline.

▶**HOW TO:** Use the **AVERAGE** Function

1. Click the cell for the function.
2. Click the **AutoSum** button arrow [*Formulas* tab, *Function Library* group].
3. Select **Average**.
 - The function and an assumed argument range display in the *Formula* bar and in the cell.
4. Select the correct cell range (Figure 2-31).
 - You can type cell addresses rather than selecting cells.
 - When the selected cells have been named, the range name is substituted in the formula.

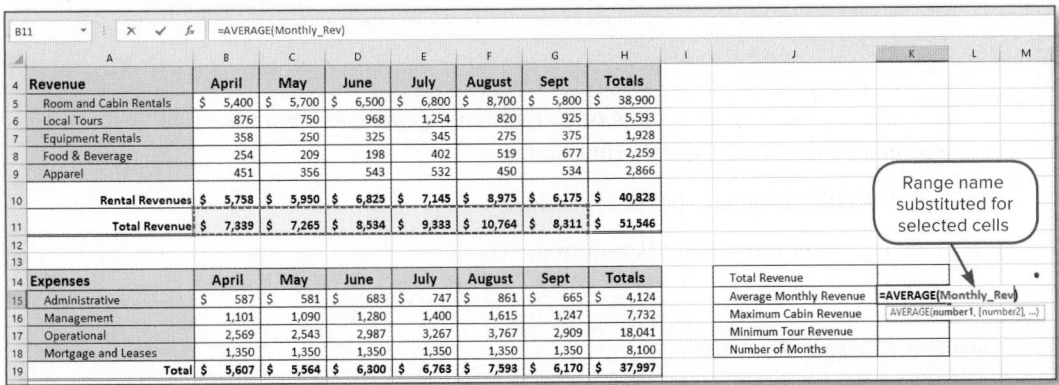

Figure 2-31 *AVERAGE* function

5. Press **Enter**.
 - Use any completion key.

COUNT Functions

Five functions in the *Statistical* category are *COUNT* functions. Count functions tally the number of items in a range. The basic *COUNT* function is an option on the *AutoSum* button, but it appears in the list as *Count Numbers*. The *COUNT* function includes only cells with values in its result.

From the *Statistical* group, choose *COUNTA* to include cells with values and labels. The *COUNTBLANK* function counts cells that are empty. Table 2-6 describes the *Statistical COUNT* functions.

Table 2-6: Statistical COUNT Functions

Count Functions	Description	Example Syntax
COUNT (Count Numbers)	Counts the cells that contain values within a range	=COUNT(A1:A15)
COUNTA	Counts the cells that contain any data type within a range	=COUNTA(A1:A15)
COUNTBLANK	Counts empty cells in a range	=COUNTBLANK(A1:A15)
COUNTIF	Counts the cells that meet the criteria argument within a range	=COUNTIF(A1:A15, "Services")
COUNTIFS	Counts the cells in one or more criteria ranges that meet respective criteria arguments	=COUNTIFS(B2:B5,"=A", C2:C5,"=21")

The *COUNT* function has one argument, *valueN*, and counts up to 255 cells or ranges. The proper syntax for a *COUNT* function is:

=COUNT(value1, [value2], [value3], . . .)

The *Value1* argument is required.

▶ HOW TO: Use the COUNT Function

1. Click the cell for the function.
2. Click the **AutoSum** button arrow [*Formulas* tab, *Function Library* group].
3. Select **Count Numbers**.
 - The *COUNT* function is inserted with an assumed range.
 - The function appears in the cell and in the *Formula* bar (Figure 2-32).

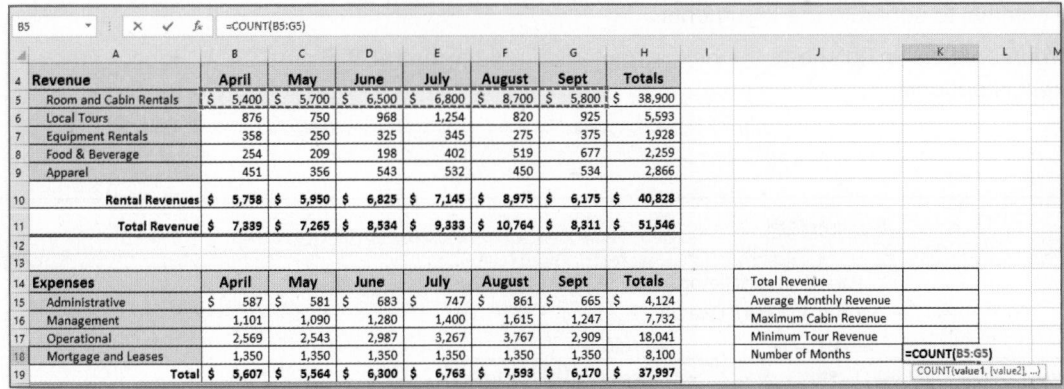

Figure 2-32 *COUNT* function

4. Select the correct cell range.
 - Type cell addresses rather than selecting cells.
5. Press **Enter** or any completion key.

> **MORE INFO**
>
> If you use *COUNT* with a range of labels, the result is zero (0).

MAX and MIN Functions

The *MAX* function finds the largest value in a range, and the *MIN* function finds the smallest value. Both functions are options on the *AutoSum* button. Each has one argument: the cells to be evaluated.

The proper syntax for *MAX* and *MIN* functions is:

=MAX(number1, [number2], [number3], . . .)
=MIN(number1, [number2], [number3], . . .)

In many worksheets, an argument range is a group of adjacent cells such as B11:G11, but the cells need not be next to each other. You can select individual cells anywhere in the worksheet for an argument, and they are separated by commas as in =MAX(B11, B15, B18).

▶ **HOW TO: Use the MAX Function with Nonadjacent Cells**

1. Click the cell for the function.
2. Click the **AutoSum** button arrow [*Formulas* tab, *Function Library* group].
3. Select **Max**.
 - The function displays in the cell and in the *Formula* bar.
 - The *Argument ScreenTip* shows the next argument in bold **number1**.
4. Click the first cell to be evaluated.

5. Type , (a comma) to separate the arguments.

- The *Argument ScreenTip* shows the next argument in bold **[number2]** (Figure 2-33). Square brackets mean the argument is optional.

Figure 2-33 Use nonadjacent cells for *MAX*

6. Click the next cell to be evaluated.
7. Type a comma , to add additional cells to the argument.
8. Press **Enter** when all the cells are listed.

AutoCalculate

The *AutoCalculate* feature is located on the right side of the *Status* bar where statistical and mathematical results display for selected cells. The calculations are *Average, Count, Numerical Count, Maximum, Minimum,* and *Sum.* The *Count* calculation is the equivalent of *COUNTA,* and *Numerical Count* is the same as *COUNT. AutoCalculate* enables you to see results without inserting a function in the worksheet. You can see and change which calculations are visible by right-clicking the *Status* bar to open the *Customize Status Bar* menu.

▶ **HOW TO: Use AutoCalculate**

1. Select the cell range or individual cells in the worksheet.
2. View the results on the *Status* bar.
 - Selected options appear on the *Status* bar when appropriate; no *SUM* displays when you select labels.
3. Right-click the right side of the *Status* bar (Figure 2-34).
 - The *Customize Status Bar* menu opens.
 - If a function name has a check mark to the left, it is active.

Figure 2-34 *AutoCalculate* results and other status bar options

4. Select a calculation name to activate it and show it on the *Status* bar.

5. Select a calculation name with a check mark to hide it from the *Status* bar.

TODAY and NOW Functions

The *Date & Time* category includes many functions for date and time arithmetic, for converting dates and times to values, and for controlling how dates and times display.

The *TODAY* function inserts the current date in the cell and updates each time the workbook opens. It uses the computer's clock, and the syntax is =TODAY(). The parentheses are necessary, but no arguments are required. The *NOW* function uses the syntax =NOW() and has no arguments. These two functions are *volatile* which means that the result depends on the current date, time, and computer.

After either function is inserted, you can format results to show both the date and the time. The *Format Cells* dialog box has a *Date* category and a *Time* category with many preset styles. Two date formats are available from the *Number Format* list [*Home* tab, *Number* group], *Short Date*, and *Long Date*.

Excel treats each date as a *serial number*, a unique value assigned to each date. Excel starts by setting January 1, 1900, as number 1; January 2, 1900 is number 2, and so on. January 1, 2020, is number 43831. You can see the serial number for any date by applying the *General* format to the cell.

> **MORE INFO**
>
> Display the Excel *Options* dialog box [*File* tab] and select the *Advanced* pane to set a 1904 date system which matches the date system in the Macintosh operating system.

Select **TODAY** or **NOW** from the *Date & Time* function category. Because they are widely used and have no arguments, you may prefer to type either with the help of *Formula AutoComplete*.

> **HOW TO:** Insert TODAY with Formula AutoComplete

1. Click the cell.

2. Type **=to** to display a filtered *Formula AutoComplete* list (Figure 2-35).

 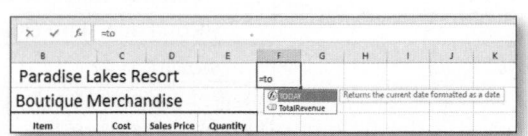

 Figure 2-35 *Formula Autocomplete* list

 - The list appears as soon as you type a character.
 - Each additional character further limits the list of names.

3. Point to the **TODAY** function name and double-click the name.

 - Alternatively, point and click to select the function name and then press **Tab**.
 - The name and parentheses are inserted.
 - If you accidentally press **Enter** to select a name and see an error in the cell, delete the cell contents and try again.

 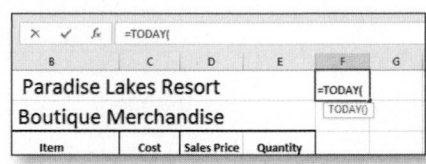

4. Press **Enter** to complete the function (Figure 2-36).

 Figure 2-36 *TODAY* inserted in cell

 - Excel supplies the closing parenthesis.
 - The current date is shown in the cell.
 - The *TODAY* function has no arguments.

PAUSE & PRACTICE: EXCEL 2-2

For this project, you open your Pause & Practice file and insert Excel functions to complete more of the worksheet. You insert functions from the *AutoSum* button and by typing. You also use *AutoCalculate* to check results.

File Needed: *[your initials] PP E2-1.xlsx*
Completed Project File Name: *[your initials] PP E2-2.xlsx*

1. Open the *[your initials] PP E2-1.xlsx* workbook completed in *Pause & Practice 2-1* and save it as [your initials] PP E2-2.

2. Enter functions using the *AutoSum* button.
 a. Click the **Cass Lake** worksheet tab and select cell **K14**.
 b. Click the **AutoSum** button arrow [*Formulas* tab, *Function Library* group].
 c. Choose **Sum**. The function name and parentheses are inserted, and a *Function ScreenTip* is visible.
 d. Select cells **B11:G11**. The range is highlighted on screen, and Excel has substituted the defined name that you set in *Pause & Practice 2-1* (Figure 2-37).
 e. Press **Enter**.
 f. Select cell **K15** and click the **AutoSum** button arrow [*Formulas* tab, *Function Library* group].
 g. Choose **Average**. The name and parentheses are inserted.
 h. Select cells **B11:G11**. The range is highlighted, but the range name is substituted.
 i. Press **Enter**. Average sales are $8,591.

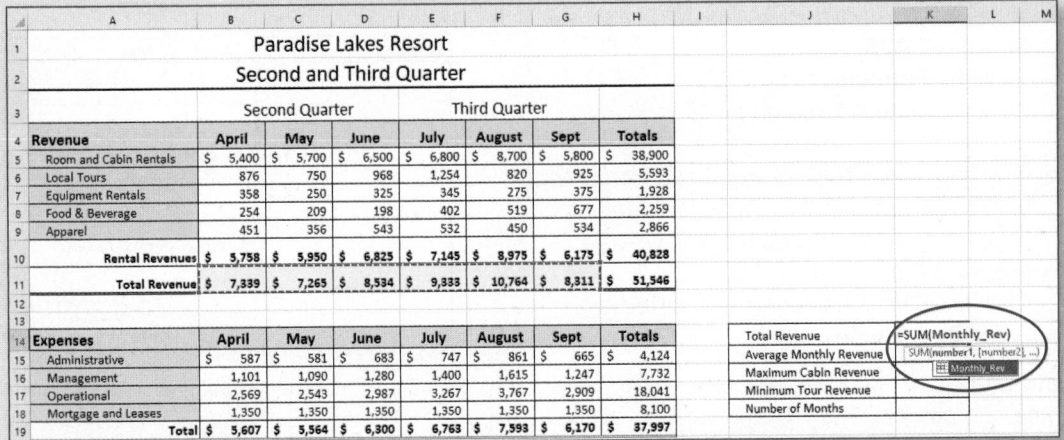

	A	B	C	D	E	F	G	H	I	J	K	L	M
1				Paradise Lakes Resort									
2				Second and Third Quarter									
3			Second Quarter			Third Quarter							
4	Revenue	April	May	June	July	August	Sept	Totals					
5	Room and Cabin Rentals	$ 5,400	$ 5,700	$ 6,500	$ 6,800	$ 8,700	$ 5,800	$ 38,900					
6	Local Tours	876	750	968	1,254	820	925	5,593					
7	Equipment Rentals	358	250	325	345	275	375	1,928					
8	Food & Beverage	254	209	198	402	519	677	2,259					
9	Apparel	451	356	543	532	450	534	2,866					
10	Rental Revenues	$ 5,758	$ 5,950	$ 6,825	$ 7,145	$ 8,975	$ 6,175	$ 40,828					
11	Total Revenue	$ 7,339	$ 7,265	$ 8,534	$ 9,333	$ 10,764	$ 8,311	$ 51,546					
12													
13													
14	Expenses	April	May	June	July	August	Sept	Totals		Total Revenue	=SUM(Monthly_Rev)		
15	Administrative	$ 587	$ 581	$ 683	$ 747	$ 861	$ 665	$ 4,124		Average Monthly Revenue	SUM(number1, [number2], ...)		
16	Management	1,101	1,090	1,280	1,400	1,615	1,247	7,732		Maximum Cabin Revenue	Monthly_Rev		
17	Operational	2,569	2,543	2,987	3,267	3,767	2,909	18,041		Minimum Tour Revenue			
18	Mortgage and Leases	1,350	1,350	1,350	1,350	1,350	1,350	8,100		Number of Months			
19	Total	$ 5,607	$ 5,564	$ 6,300	$ 6,763	$ 7,593	$ 6,170	$ 37,997					

Figure 2-37 Range name substituted in formula

3. Enter the *MAX* function by typing.
 a. Select cell **K16**.
 b. Type =ma to display the *Formula AutoComplete* list. You only need type as many characters as necessary to see the function name.
 c. Point to **MAX** in the list, click to select it, and press **Tab** (Figure 2-38).

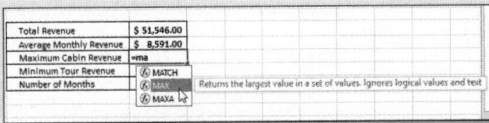

 d. Select cells **B5:G5** for the *number1* argument. This range is not named.
 e. Press **Enter**. Excel supplies the closing parenthesis.

Figure 2-38 Choose *MAX* from *Formula AutoComplete* list

4. Copy and edit a function.
 a. Select cell **K16** and use the *Fill* pointer to copy the formula to cell **K17**.

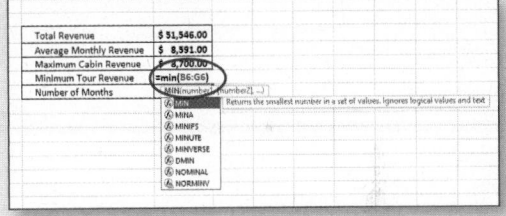

 b. Double-click cell **K17**. Note that the argument cell range was updated because it was a relative reference.
 c. Replace the function name *MAX* in the cell with **min** (Figure 2-39).
 d. Press **Enter**. The minimum tour value is $750.

Figure 2-39 Edit a function name

5. Type the *COUNT* function.
 a. Select cell **K18**.
 b. Type =cou to display the *Formula AutoComplete* list.
 c. Double-click **COUNTA** in the list. This function counts cells with labels and values. The *ScreenTip* shows the first argument as *value1*.
 d. Select cells **B4:G4** to count the months. The formula is =COUNTA(B4:G4).
 e. Press **Enter**. The final parenthesis is supplied and the result is 6.00.
 f. Select cells **K14:K18** and decrease the decimal two times.
 g. Apply the **General** format to cell **K18** [*Home* tab, *Number* group, *Number Format* drop-down list].

6. Check results with *AutoCalculate*.
 a. Select cells **B11:G11**.
 b. Right-click near the middle of the *Status* bar to display the options.
 c. Verify that **Average**, **Count**, and **Sum** are checked.
 d. Left-click anywhere in the *Status* bar to close the menu.
 e. Compare the values shown in the *Status* bar with the results in column K.

7. Insert the *TODAY* function.
 a. Select cell **A25**.
 b. Click the **Formulas** tab.
 c. Click the **Date & Time** button [*Function Library* group].
 d. Find and select **TODAY**. A *Function Arguments* dialog box notes that this function does not have any arguments and that it is volatile (Figure 2-40).
 e. Click **OK**. The current date is inserted.
 f. Press **Ctrl+Home**.

8. Save and close the workbook (Figure 2-41).

Expenses	April	May	June	July
Administrative	$ 587	$ 581	$ 683	$ 747
Management	1,101	1,090	1,280	1,400
Operational	2,569	2,543	2,987	3,267
Mortgage and Leases	1,350	1,350	1,350	1,350
Total	$ 5,607	$ 5,564	$ 6,300	$ 6,763

Function Arguments
Returns the current date formatted as a date.
This function takes no arguments.

=TODAY()

Formula result = Volatile

Help on this function OK Cancel

Figure 2-40 *Function Arguments* dialog box for *TODAY*

Paradise Lakes Resort
Second and Third Quarter

Revenue		Second Quarter			Third Quarter			
	April	May	June	July	August	Sept	Totals	
Room and Cabin Rentals	$ 5,400	$ 5,700	$ 6,500	$ 6,800	$ 8,700	$ 5,800	$ 38,900	
Local Tours	876	750	968	1,254	820	925	5,593	
Equipment Rentals	358	250	325	345	275	375	1,928	
Food & Beverage	254	209	198	402	519	677	2,259	
Apparel	451	356	543	532	450	534	2,866	
Rental Revenues	$ 5,758	$ 5,950	$ 6,825	$ 7,145	$ 8,975	$ 6,175	$ 40,828	
Total Revenue	$ 7,339	$ 7,265	$ 8,534	$ 9,333	$ 10,764	$ 8,311	$ 51,546	

Expenses	April	May	June	July	August	Sept	Totals			
Administrative	$ 587	$ 581	$ 683	$ 747	$ 861	$ 665	$ 4,124	Total Revenue	$	51,546
Management	1,101	1,090	1,280	1,400	1,615	1,247	7,732	Average Monthly Revenue	$	8,591
Operational	2,569	2,543	2,987	3,267	3,767	2,909	18,041	Maximum Cabin Revenue	$	8,700
Mortgage and Leases	1,350	1,350	1,350	1,350	1,350	1,350	8,100	Minimum Tour Revenue	$	750
Total	$ 5,607	$ 5,564	$ 6,300	$ 6,763	$ 7,593	$ 6,170	$ 37,997	Number of Months		6
Profit Margin	24%	23%	26%	28%	29%	26%				
Revenue Below Average?										
Current Date										

Figure 2-41 PP E2-2 completed

Working with Financial, Logical, and Lookup Functions

The *Financial* category includes functions that determine loan payments, the amount of interest earned, the rate of return on an investment, and more. Most of the functions in the *Logical* category display TRUE or FALSE as the result, but the *IF* function in this group returns results that you specify. An *IF* function can test if monthly revenue is above or below average and display "Yes" or "No" in the cell. The *Lookup & Reference* category is used to find and display information from a list in the workbook. For example, you might use a *Lookup* function to insert a price from a price list.

The Function Arguments Dialog Box

Functions require arguments in a particular order. They are easy to learn and build when you use the *Function Arguments* dialog box. This dialog box opens when you choose a function name from a category on the *Formulas* tab or when you use the *Insert Function* dialog box.

The *Function Arguments* dialog box shows each argument with an entry box and an explanation (Figure 2-42). You can select cells to enter an address, or type directly in the entry box. In addition to doing the work for you, the *Function Arguments* dialog box helps you learn the proper syntax for a function.

Function arguments may be required or optional. Optional arguments generally add a level of refinement to the calculation. In the *Function Arguments* dialog box and the *ScreenTip*, a required argument name is shown in bold. When you use *Formula AutoComplete* to build a function, the *ScreenTip* shows optional arguments in square brackets (example: [type]).

When you are not sure about a function's name or category, search for it in the *Insert Function* dialog box. Open this dialog box by clicking the **Insert Function** button on the *Formulas* tab [*Function Library* group] or the same button to the left of the *Formula* bar. In the search area, type the name of the function or a brief description of what you want the function to do. For example, type "rate of return" to list *Financial* functions that calculate a rate of return for an investment.

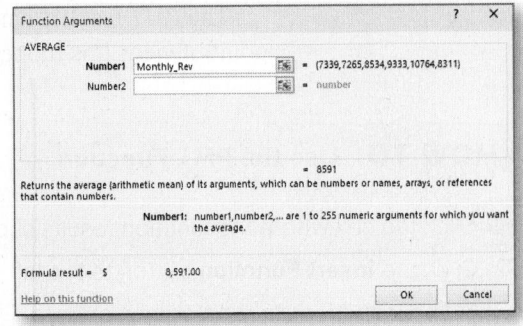

Figure 2-42 *Function Arguments* dialog box for *AVERAGE*

> **ANOTHER WAY**
>
> **Shift+F3** opens the *Insert Function* dialog box.

PMT Function

The *PMT* function is in the *Financial* category. It calculates a constant loan payment amount for a period of time at a stated interest rate. When you borrow money for tuition or to buy a car, use the *PMT* function to determine your monthly payment for a selected payback time.

The *PMT* function has five arguments. Three of them are required: *rate*, *nper*, and *pv*. The other arguments are optional: *fv* and *type*. The proper syntax for a *PMT* formula is:

=PMT(rate, nper, pv, [fv], [type])

- *Rate* is the interest rate, a percentage of the amount borrowed. Most rates are set at a yearly rate. To determine monthly payments, you must divide the rate by 12.
- *Nper* is the total number of periods for repayment. If you make monthly payments for five years, the *nper* argument is 60.
- *Pv* is the present value, the amount borrowed.
- *Fv* is any future value after the last payment, an amount still owed at the end of the loan. When the *fv* argument is omitted, it means zero or that you have paid back the entire amount.
- *Type* indicates if payments are made at the beginning or the end of the period. Most loan payments are at the beginning of the period, because the interest amount is less. The number *1* is used to set payment at the beginning of the period.

Figure 2-43 shows a *PMT* function in cell B7 **=PMT(B6/12,B5*12,B4,,1)**. In the *Formula* bar, arguments are separated by commas. Where two commas display with nothing between them, an argument has been omitted. In this case, it is the *fv* argument.

B6/12 is the interest *rate* divided by 12 to determine a monthly payment.
B5*12 is the *nper* argument, the number of years times 12, to determine the total number of payments.
B4 is the *pv* argument, the amount of money borrowed.
1 is the *type* argument and indicates that payment occurs at the beginning of the period.

Figure 2-43 *PMT* function is in cell B7

The *PMT* result is a negative number, because the function is calculated from the borrower's point of view. It is money paid out.

▶HOW TO: Use the PMT Function

1. Click the cell where the function results should display.
2. Click the **Insert Function** button to the left of the *Formula* bar.
 - The *Insert Function* dialog box opens.
3. Type payment in the *Search for a function* box.
4. Click **Go**.
 - A list of functions that include a type of payment displays (Figure 2-44).
5. Select **PMT** and click **OK**.
 - The *Function Arguments* dialog box opens.
 - The dialog box includes a description of the function.
6. Click the **Rate** box and click the cell with the interest rate.
 - You can type the rate in the entry box with the percent sign.
 - An explanation of the argument displays.
7. Type /12 immediately after the address in the *Rate* box.
 - Divide by 12 for monthly payments.
 - If payments are quarterly, divide by 4.
8. Click the **Nper** box and click the cell that contains the loan term.
9. Type *12 immediately after the address in the *Nper* box.
 - If the loan term is years and payments are quarterly, multiply by 4.
 - If the cell already displays the total number of payments, just click to enter the address.
10. Click the **Pv** box and click the cell that contains the amount of the loan.
11. Click the **Type** box.
 - The *Fv* argument is usually omitted, because loans require a zero balance at the end.
12. Type 1 in the *Type* box to set a payment at the beginning of the period (Figure 2-45).
 - Most loan payments are at the beginning, because the payment is less than if it were at the end of the period.
13. Click **OK**.

Figure 2-44 *Insert Function* dialog box

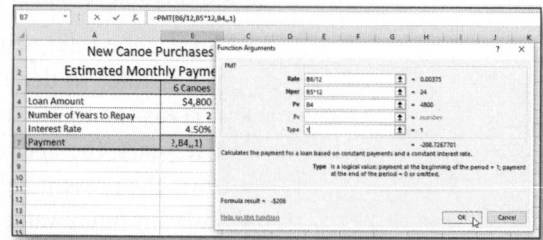

Figure 2-45 *Function Arguments* dialog box for *PMT*

> ### MORE INFO
>
> To show the payment as a positive value, type a minus sign (−) before the loan amount in the worksheet or before its cell address in the *Function Arguments* dialog box.

> ### ANOTHER WAY
>
> Choose the *PMT* function from the **Financial** button [*Formulas* tab, *Function Library* group].

IF Function

The *IF* function tests a condition or statement; if it is true, a specified result displays; if it is false, an alternative result displays. In the Paradise Lakes revenue worksheet, you can use an *IF* formula to determine if each month's revenue is above average. If it is, you can display "Yes," in the cell, and if it is not, you can display "No."

> **MORE INFO**
>
> An *IF* function is similar to an *IF* statement in many programming languages.

An *IF* function has three arguments, and its syntax is:

=IF (logical_test, value_if_true, value_if_false)

- The *logical_test* is the value or statement to be evaluated.
- The *value_if_true* is the result displayed in the cell when the *logical_test* is true. You can select a cell, enter text, or use a formula for this argument.
- The *value_if_false* is the result displayed in the cell when the *logical_test* is false. You can select a cell, enter text, or use a formula for this argument.

An *IF* function can use comparison or logical operators in its arguments. Table 2-7 describes the comparison operators:

Table 2-7: Comparison Operators

Operator	Description
=	Equal to
<>	Not equal to
>	Greater than
>=	Greater than or equal to
<	Less than
<=	Less than or equal to

Figure 2-46 has an *IF* function in cell D5 **=IF(B5>=4,18,20)**. When you use the *Function Arguments* dialog box to build a function, the commas to separate arguments are entered automatically.

B5>=4 is the *logical_test*. It determines if the value in cell B5 is equal to or greater than 4. Cell B5 is a relative reference so when the formula is copied, it will update to show the new row. The *value_if_true* argument is **18**. If the age is 4 or higher, the fee is $18. This value is a constant. It does not change when the formula is copied. The *value_if_false* argument is **20**, another constant. If the age is not 4 or higher, it must be lower and the fee is $20. The constant does not change when the formula is copied.

Figure 2-46 *IF* function in cell D5

Insert the *IF* function from the *Logical* category on the *Formulas* tab, from the *Insert Function* button, or by typing it. When you type an *IF* function, you must type the commas to separate arguments, and you must enclose text arguments within quotation marks.

▶HOW TO: Build an IF Function

1. Click the cell for the function.
2. Click the **Logical** button [*Formulas* tab, *Function Library* group].
 - The list of *Logical* functions opens.
3. Select **IF** in the list.
 - The *Function Arguments* dialog box for *IF* opens.
4. Click the **Logical_test** box.
5. Click the cell that will be evaluated.
 - Make the reference absolute if you know that the formula will be copied and that the reference should not change.
6. Type a comparison operator immediately after the cell address.
7. Type a value or click a cell to complete the expression to be tested.
 - Build a statement such as B11=K15 or B11<10000.
 - Make a cell reference absolute or mixed if necessary.
8. Click the **Value_if_true** box.
9. Type the label or click a cell that contains data that should display if the *logical_test* is true.
 - Type a value in the text box.
10. Click the **Value_if_false** box.
11. Type the label or click a cell that contains data that should display if the *logical_test* is false (Figure 2-47).
 - Results for the current cell display in the *Function Arguments* dialog box.
 - The *Function Arguments* dialog box provides quotation marks for text entries.

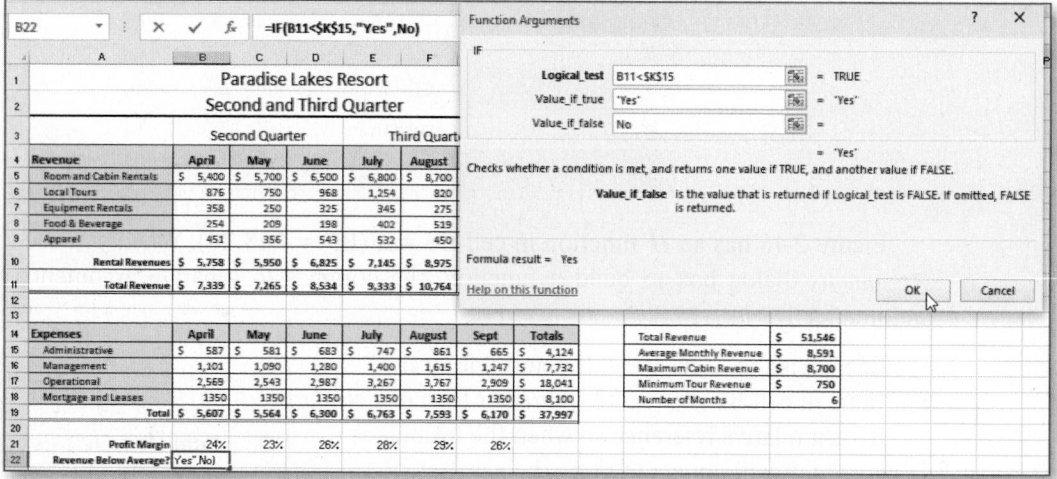

Figure 2-47 *Function Arguments* dialog box for *IF*

12. Click **OK**.

> **MORE INFO**
>
> The *value_if_false* argument for the *logical_test* can be another *IF* function which enables you to test for more than one possibility.

Lookup Functions

A *Lookup* function displays a piece of data from a range of cells in another part of the workbook. Two *Lookup* functions, *VLOOKUP* (vertical) and *HLOOKUP* (horizontal), are available. These two functions have the same syntax and similar arguments. *VLOOKUP* uses a lookup table that is organized in columns, and *HLOOKUP* uses a lookup range that is arranged in rows.

A *VLOOKUP* function has four arguments, and the syntax is:

=VLOOKUP (lookup_value, table_array, col_index_num, [range_lookup])

- The *lookup_value* is the data to be found or matched. It is usually a cell address, but you can type a value or a text string. The function locates this *lookup_value* in the first column of the table array. It then displays data from the designated column in the same row as the *lookup_value*.
- The *table_array* is a range of cells, sorted in ascending order by the first column. The range can be located on a different worksheet or in a different workbook. It is good practice to name the range so that its reference is absolute.
- The *col_index_num* sets which column in the *table_array* contains the data to display in the result. The columns are counted from left to right.
- The *[range lookup]* argument is either TRUE or FALSE. TRUE means that Excel finds the closest match to the *lookup_value*, which can return unexpected results. If the data in the table array is sorted, however, TRUE will generally return the correct match. When you set this argument to FALSE, Excel finds an exact match and the data can be in any order.

Figure 2-48 shows a *VLOOKUP* function in cell D3 in the worksheet on the left. The result (250) is from the third column in row 6 in the table array in the worksheet on the right. Both sheets are in the same workbook.

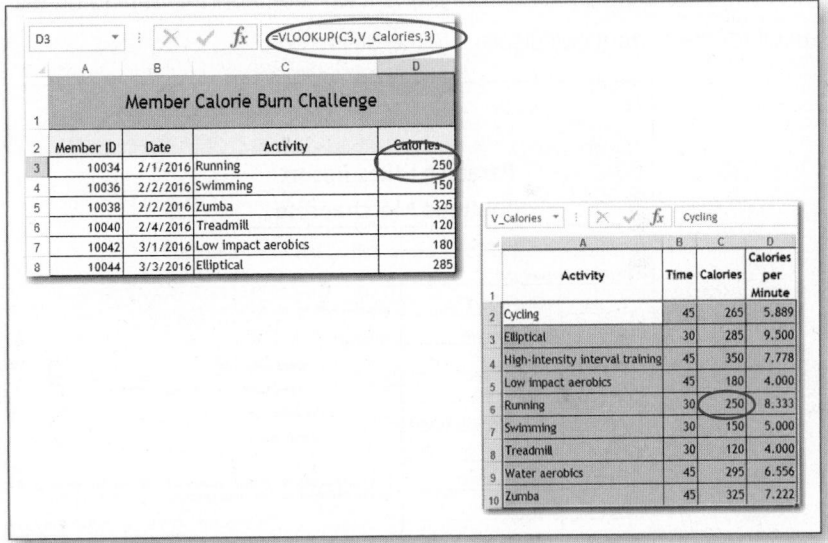

Figure 2-48 *VLOOKUP* function in cell D3 on the left

=VLOOKUP(C3,V_Calories,3)

- The *lookup_value* argument is cell C3 ("Running").
- The *table_array* argument is a named cell range, *V_Calories*. The "V" is a reminder that this range is a vertical lookup table. The *V_Calories* range is cells A2:D10 in the sheet on the right.
- The *col_index_num* argument is *3*, so the result is from the third column, the "Calories" column, in the *V_Calories* range.
- The *range_lookup* argument is omitted or TRUE. The data in the table array (on the right) is sorted so TRUE is acceptable for this argument.

Insert the *VLOOKUP* function from the *Lookup & Reference* category on the *Formulas* tab or by searching for it in the *Insert Function* dialog box. When you are experienced using the function, type it in the cell and use *Formula AutoComplete*.

▶**HOW TO:** Enter the VLOOKUP Function

1. Click the cell for the function.
2. Click the **Lookup & Reference** button [*Formulas* tab].
3. Select **VLOOKUP**.
 - The *Function Arguments* dialog box opens.
 - Move the dialog box if it covers data that you need to see or select.
4. Click the **Lookup_value** box.
5. Click the cell to be matched.
 - The *lookup_value* is typically a cell in the same row as the function.
 - This reference is usually relative.
6. Click the **Table_array** box.
7. Select the cell range with the lookup data.
 - When the lookup table is named, the range name is substituted.
 - The *Function Arguments* dialog box collapses while you select cells.
8. Press **F4** (**FN+F4**) to make the reference absolute if cell addresses are used.
 - When a range name has been substituted, you need not do this.
9. Click the **Col_index_num** box.
10. Type the column number, counting from the left, that contains the data to be displayed (Figure 2-49).
 - The result for the current cell displays in the dialog box.

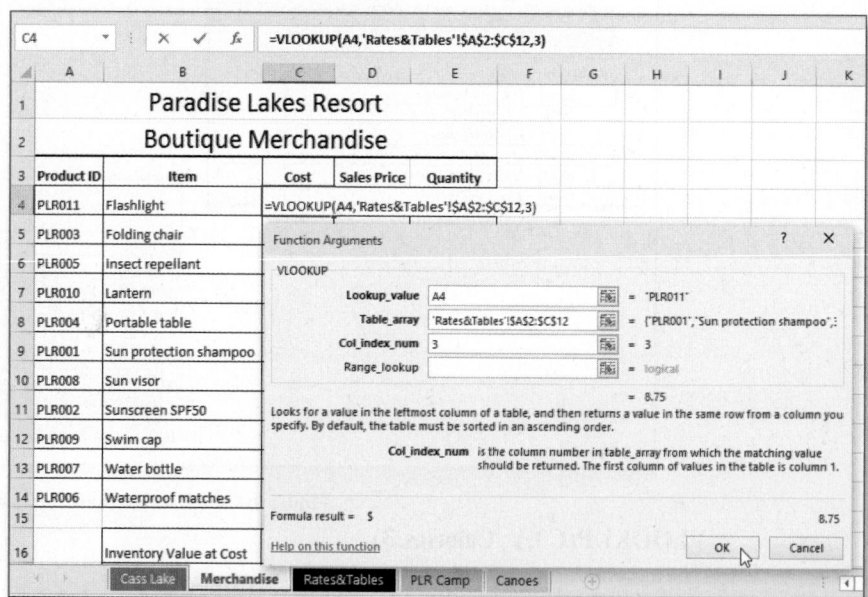

Figure 2-49 *Function Arguments* dialog box for *VLOOKUP*

11. Leave the *Range_lookup* argument box empty if the data in the table array is sorted in ascending order.
 - Type FALSE in the entry box to find an exact match when the data is not sorted.
12. Click **OK**.

The *HLOOKUP* function has a *row_index_num* argument instead of the *col_index_num* argument. The *table_array* is set up horizontally as seen in Figure 2-50, and the first row is arranged in alphabetical order from left to right. The *HLOOKUP* function is in cell C6 in the sheet on the left. The lookup table is named *H_Fees*, shown in the sheet on the right.

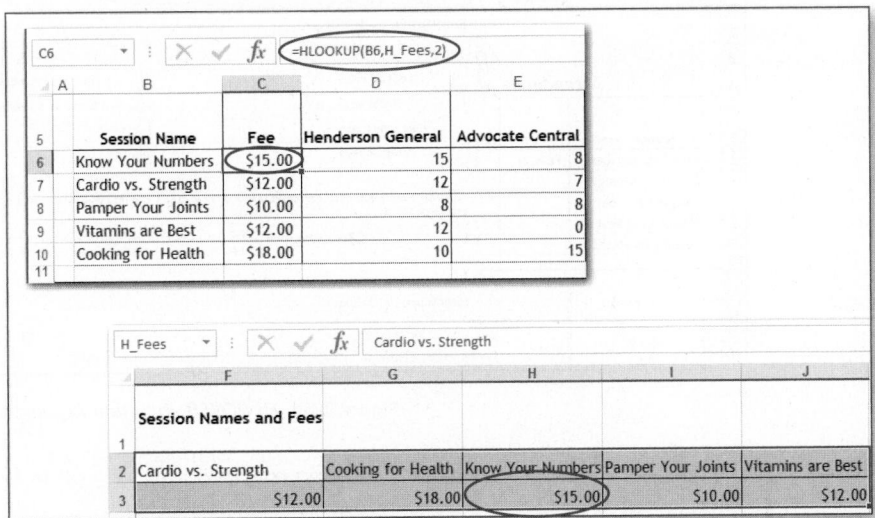

Figure 2-50 *HLOOKUP* in cell C6

=HLOOKUP(B6,H_Fees,2)

- The *lookup_value* argument is cell B6 ("Know Your Numbers").
- The *table_array* argument is a named cell range, *H_Fees*. The "H" is a visual cue for a horizontal lookup table. The *H_Fees* range is cells F2:J3 on the right.
- The *row_index_num* argument is *2*, so the data shown in cell C6 is from the second row of the *H_Fees* range.
- The *range_lookup* argument is omitted, because the first row in the data range is sorted alphabetically from left to right.

▶ **HOW TO:** Use The HLOOKUP Function

1. Click the cell for the function.
2. Click the **Lookup & Reference** button [*Formulas* tab].
3. Select **HLOOKUP**.
 - The *Function Arguments* dialog box opens.
4. Click the **Lookup_value** box.
5. Click the cell to be matched.
 - The *lookup_value* is typically a cell in the same row as the function.
 - This reference is usually relative.
6. Click the **Table_array** box.
7. Select the cell range with the lookup data.
 - When the lookup table is named, the range name is substituted.
 - The *Function Arguments* dialog box collapses while you select cells.
8. Press **F4** (**FN+F4**) to make the reference absolute when cell addresses are used.
9. Click the **Row_index_num** box.

10. Type the row number, counting the first row of the *table_array* as 1 (Figure 2-51).
 - The result for the current cell displays in the dialog box.

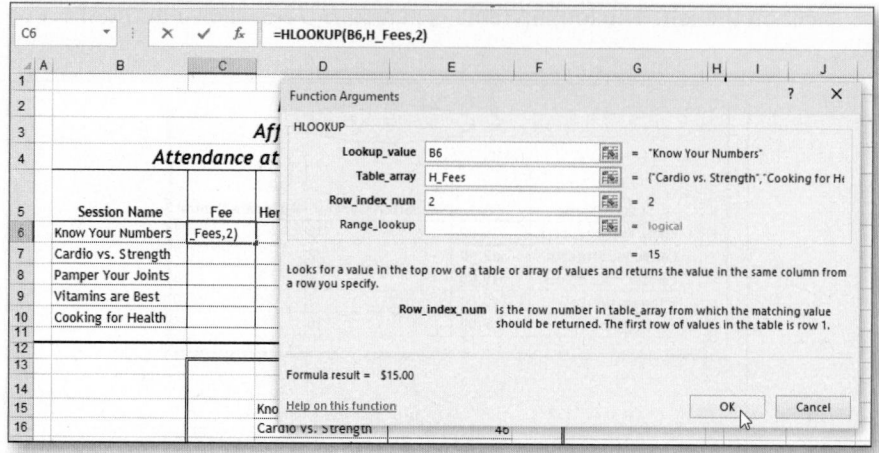

Figure 2-51 *HLOOKUP Function Arguments* dialog box

11. Leave the *Range_lookup* argument box empty if the first row of data in the table array is arranged alphabetically from left to right.

12. Click **OK**.

Using Math & Trig Functions

You have already used *SUM* from the *Math & Trig* function category. This category includes functions to display the absolute value of data, to calculate the cosine of an angle, or to return the power of a number. You might recognize the function *PI* or π from a math class. Three *Math & Trig* functions that are often used in business or personal calculations are *ROUND*, *SUMIF*, and *SUMPRODUCT*.

Round Function

Rounding means that a value is adjusted to display a specified number of decimal places or a whole number. You can round the numbers on your tax return in the United States, which means that you need not show any cents, just dollars.

The *ROUND* function has two arguments: *number* and *num_digits*.

=ROUND(number, num_digits)

- The **number** is the cell or the value to be adjusted.
- The **num_digits** sets the number of decimal places for rounding. When this argument is zero (0), the value displays as the nearest whole number. When the *num_digits* argument is greater than zero, the value is rounded to that number of decimal places. You can use a negative number for the *num_digits* argument, which rounds the value to the left of the decimal point. Make sure you understand the results when you round to the left of the decimal point.

When a value used in rounding is 5 or greater, results round up to the next digit. If you round 5.523 to show zero (0) decimal places, it rounds up to display as 6 because the value after the decimal point is 5. If you round 5.423 to two places, it rounds to 5.42 because the

value used for rounding is 3. The *Increase Decimal* and *Decrease Decimal* buttons follow these rounding principles for displaying values in the cell, as do the *Accounting Number* and *Currency* formats. These formats, however, keep the full unrounded value in the cell and use that value in calculations.

MORE INFO

When a value is rounded, the rounded value is used in calculations, not the full unrounded number.

▶ HOW TO: Use the ROUND Function

1. Click the cell for the function.

2. Type =rou and press **Tab**.
 - *Formula AutoComplete* inserts the function in the cell.
 - The *number* argument is bold in the *ScreenTip*.

3. Select the cell to be rounded.
 - The cell address appears in the cell and in the *Formula* bar.
 - You can type a value as the *number* argument.

4. Type , (a comma) to separate the arguments.
 - The *num_digits* argument is bold in the *ScreenTip*.

5. Type a number to set the number of decimal places (Figure 2-52).

6. Press **Enter**.

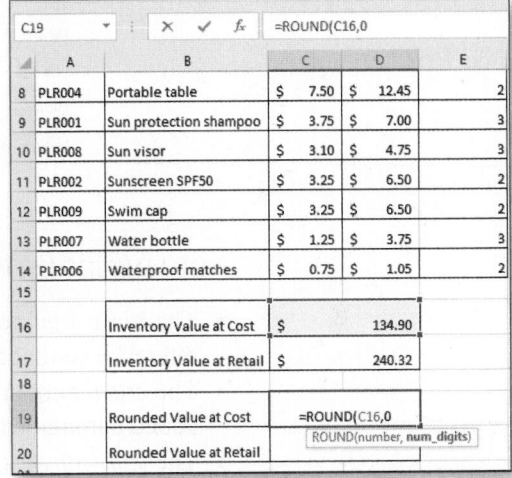

Figure 2-52 Type the *ROUND* function

MORE INFO

Excel has a *ROUNDDOWN* function that always rounds a number down or toward zero. The *ROUNDUP* function rounds a value up, away from zero.

SUMIF Function

The *SUMIF* function controls which data in a range are included in the total. It enables you to eliminate cells from the calculation by criteria that you set. **Criteria** are restrictions, conditions, or rules that must be met. In a *SUMIF* function, cell values are included in the sum only if they match the criteria.

The *SUMIF* function has three arguments.

=SUMIF (range, criteria, [sum_range])

- The **range** is the range of cells to be evaluated or searched, the values that are compared to the criteria.
- The **criteria** argument defines which cells from the range should be included in the sum. You can use comparison operators, cell references, a value, or text. When you use text or a comparison operator, the criteria must be enclosed in quotation marks.

- The *[sum_range]* is the cell range to be summed. This argument is optional, because it is omitted when the range to be summed is the same as the *range* argument.

Figure 2-53 illustrates a *SUMIF* function in cell I5 that totals sales for products that have a price greater than $10.

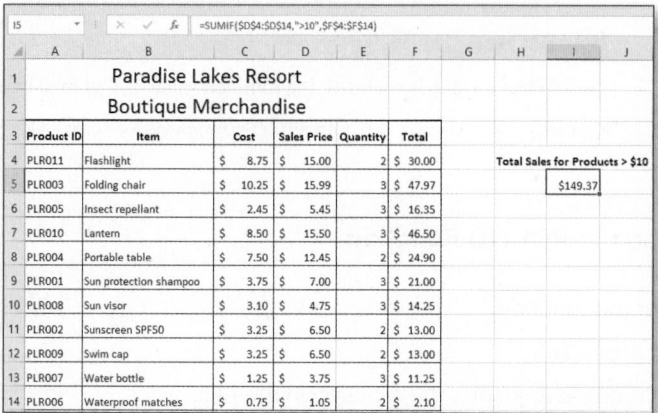

Figure 2-53 *SUMIF* function in cell I5

=SUMIF(D4:D14,">10",$F4:$F14)

- The *range* argument is the sales price column, cells D4:D14. It is an absolute reference so that the formula can be copied.
- The *criteria* argument is >10, shown in quotation marks. The quotation marks are added automatically when you use the *Function Arguments* dialog box.
- The *sum_range* argument is cells F4:F14, the cells to be added if the price is greater than 10.

MORE INFO

You can use wildcards (* or ?) in a criteria argument. For example, to sum sales for all items that begin with the letter S, use **s*** as the criteria. Criteria are not case-sensitive.

▶ HOW TO: Build a SUMIF Function

1. Click the cell for the function.
2. Click the **Math & Trig** button [*Formulas* tab, *Function Library* group].
3. Select **SUMIF**.
4. Click the **Range** box.
5. Select the cell range to be compared against the criteria.
 - Make the reference absolute if the formula might be copied.
 - Press **F3** (**FN+F3**) to paste a range name rather than selecting the range.
6. Click the **Criteria** box.
 - Type text to be compared or a value to be matched.
 - Type an expression with operators to be evaluated.
 - Quotation marks are automatically supplied.

7. Click the **Sum_range** box (Figure 2-54).
 - Select the cells to be added.
 - If the cells to be added are the same as those in the *range* argument, leave the entry blank.

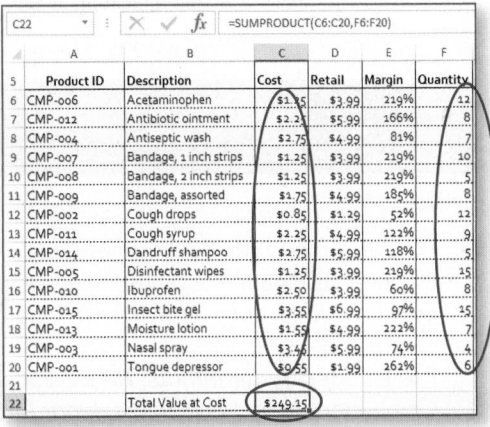

Figure 2-54 *Function Arguments* dialog box for *SUMIF*

8. Click **OK**.

SUMPRODUCT Function

The *SUMPRODUCT* function calculates the sum of the product of several ranges. It multiplies the cells identified in its *array* arguments and then it totals those individual products. A *product* is the result of a multiplication problem; 4 is the product of 2 times 2. An *array* is a range of cells in a row or a column. An array has a *dimension*, which is the number of columns or rows. The arrays A1:A5 and C1:C5 have the same dimension, five rows and one column.

The *SUMPRODUCT* function has the following syntax.

=SUMPRODUCT(array1, array2, [arrayN])

- The *array1* argument is the first range of cells for the multiplication.
- The *array2* argument is the range that is multiplied by the corresponding cells in the *array1* range. These two ranges must have the same number of cells, the same dimension.

It is possible to use more than two arrays so that you could have an *array3* argument or even more.

In Figure 2-55, the *SUMPRODUCT* function in cell C22 multiplies the first array C6:C20 by the corresponding values in cells F6:F20 and totals those products.

=SUMPRODUCT(C6:C20,F6:F20)

The value in cell C6 is multiplied by cell F6, cell C7 is multiplied by cell F7, and so on. Those individual products are summed, and the result is $249.15.

Figure 2-55 *SUMPRODUCT* in cell C22

▶ HOW TO: Build a SUMPRODUCT Function

1. Click the cell for the function.
2. Click the **Math & Trig** button [*Formulas* tab, *Function Library* group].
3. Select **SUMPRODUCT**.
 - The *Function Arguments* dialog box opens.
4. Click the **Array1** box.
5. Select the first cell range to be multiplied.
6. Click the **Array2** box.
7. Select the next cell range to be multiplied (Figure 2-56).
 - All arrays must have the same number of cells and rows.
 - Use as many arrays as required for the calculation.

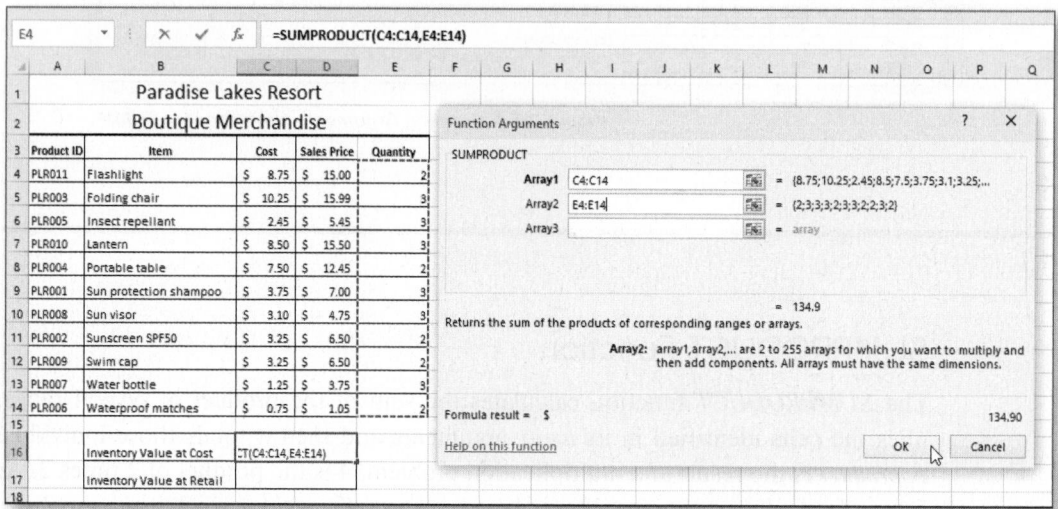

Figure 2-56 *Function Arguments* dialog box for *SUMPRODUCT*

8. Click **OK**.

> **MORE INFO**
>
> If an array in a *SUMPRODUCT* formula includes an empty cell, Excel treats that value as 0, but the multiplication by zero does not affect the sum.

PAUSE & PRACTICE: EXCEL 2-3

For this project, you continue working on the workbook for Paradise Lakes. You calculate totals related to camp attendance and merchandise inventory using functions from the *Math & Trig*, *Financial*, *Logical*, *Lookup & Reference*, and *Date & Time* categories.

File Needed: *[your initials] PP E2-2.xlsx*
Completed Project File Name: *[your initials] PP E2-3.xlsx*

1. Open the *[your initials] PP E2-2.xlsx* workbook completed in *Pause & Practice 2-2* and save it as [your initials] PP E2-3.

2. Click the **Cass Lake** worksheet tab.

3. Enter an *IF* function to determine if a month's revenue was below average.
 a. Click cell **B22** and click the **Formulas** tab.
 b. Click the **Logical** button In the *Function Library* group and select **IF**. The *Function Arguments* dialog box opens.
 c. Click the **Logical_test** text box and click cell **B11**.
 d. Type < for a less than operator after "B11" in the *Logical_test* box.
 e. Click cell **K15** and press **F4** (**FN+F4**) to make this an absolute reference.
 f. Click the **Value_if_true** box and type Yes. You need not type quotation marks when you use the *Function Arguments* dialog box.
 g. Press **Tab** to move to the *Value_if_false* box. Excel supplies the quotation marks for "Yes."
 h. Type No (Figure 2-57).
 i. Click **OK**. For April, the result is *Yes*.
 j. Click cell **B22** and click the **Center** button [*Home* tab, *Alignment* group].
 k. Use the *Fill* pointer to copy the formula in cell **B22** to cells **C22:G22**.
 l. Press **Ctrl+Home**.

Figure 2-57 Build an *IF* function

4. Use *SUMIF* to calculate results.
 a. Click the **PLR Camp** worksheet tab. The number of attendees is tracked with the camper's ID, gender, and age.
 b. Select cell **H4** and click the **Formulas** tab.
 c. Click the **Math & Trig** button in the *Function Library* group and select **SUMIF**.
 d. Click the **Range** text box and select cells **B4:B38**.
 e. Press **F4** (**FN+F4**) to make the reference absolute.
 f. Press **Tab** and type f in the *Criteria* box. Criteria are not case-sensitive. The cells in column B will be checked to determine if they show "F."
 g. Click the **Sum_range** box, select cells **C4:C38**, and press **F4** (**FN+F4**). The values in this range will be summed for those rows in which the gender is F (Figure 2-58).
 h. Click **OK**. Female camp days are 117.
 i. Click cell **H4** and use the *Fill* pointer to copy the formula to cell **H5**.
 j. Edit the formula in cell **H5** to show m instead of "f."

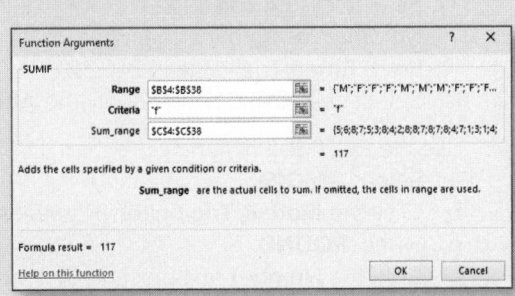

Figure 2-58 Build a *SUMIF* function

5. Use *VLOOKUP* to display costs.
 a. Click the **Merchandise** sheet tab and select cell **C4**. Individual costs are missing, but they are listed on the **Rates&Tables** sheet.
 b. Click the **Lookup & Reference** button [*Formulas* tab, *Function Library* group].
 c. Select **VLOOKUP**.
 d. Click the **Lookup_value** box and select cell **A4**.
 e. Click the **Table_array** box. The table with the costs is on the **Rates&Tables** sheet.
 f. Click the **Rates&Tables** worksheet tab and select cells **A2:C12**. This array or range includes the ID, the name, and the cost. The costs are in column C, the third column from the left.

g. Press **F4** (**FN+F4**) to make the array an absolute reference.
h. Click the **Col_index_num** box and type 3. The ID in cell A4 will be located in cells A2:C12 on the **Rates&Tables** sheet, and the cost in the third column will be displayed.
i. Click the **Range_lookup** box and type false (Figure 2-59).
j. Click **OK**. The cost for the first item is $8.75.
k. Copy the formula in cell **C4** to cells **C5:C14**.

Figure 2-59 Build a *VLOOKUP* function

6. Use *SUMPRODUCT* to calculate inventory values.
a. Click cell **C16**. This is a merged and centered cell.
b. Click the **Formulas** tab.
c. Click the **Math & Trig** button in the *Function Library* group and select **SUMPRODUCT**.
d. Click the **Array1** box and select cells **C4:C14**. The range includes 11 values.
e. Click the **Array2** box and select cells **E4:E14**. The range includes 11 values, and each one will be multiplied by the corresponding value in the same row in column C.
f. Click **OK**. The value of the inventory at cost is 134.9.
g. Click cell **C17**, type =sump, and press **Tab**. The function is inserted and the *ScreenTip* shows the next argument, *array1*.
h. Select cells **D4:D14** and type , (a comma) to separate the first argument from the second.
i. Select cells **E4:E14** (Figure 2-60). You need not type the closing parenthesis.
j. Press **Enter**. The value is 240.32.
k. Select cells **C16:C17** and apply the **Accounting Number** format.

Figure 2-60 Type a *SUMPRODUCT* function

7. Use the *ROUND* function.
a. Select cell **C19**.
b. Click the **Math & Trig** button [*Formulas* tab, *Function Library* group].
c. Select **ROUND**.
d. Click the **Number** text box and click cell **C16**.
e. Type 0 in the *Num_digits* text box.
f. Press **Enter**. The value is rounded up to $135.00.
g. Copy the formula in cell **C19** to cell **C20**. The value from cell C17 is rounded down to $240.00.

8. Use the *PMT* function to determine payments for new canoe purchases.
a. Click the **Canoes** sheet tab and click cell **B7**.
b. Click the **Formulas** tab and the **Financial** button [*Function Library* group].
c. Select **PMT**.
d. Click the **Rate** box and click cell **B6**.
e. Type /12 immediately after "B6," to divide the rate by 12 for monthly payments.
f. Click the **Nper** box and click cell **B5**. Type *12 to multiply by 12 for 12 months per year.
g. Click the **Pv** box and click cell **B4**. This is the amount of the loan.
h. Click the **Fv** box. Leave this blank to indicate no balance due at the end of the loan term.

i. Click the **Type** box and type 1. The payment will be made at the beginning of the month (Figure 2-61).

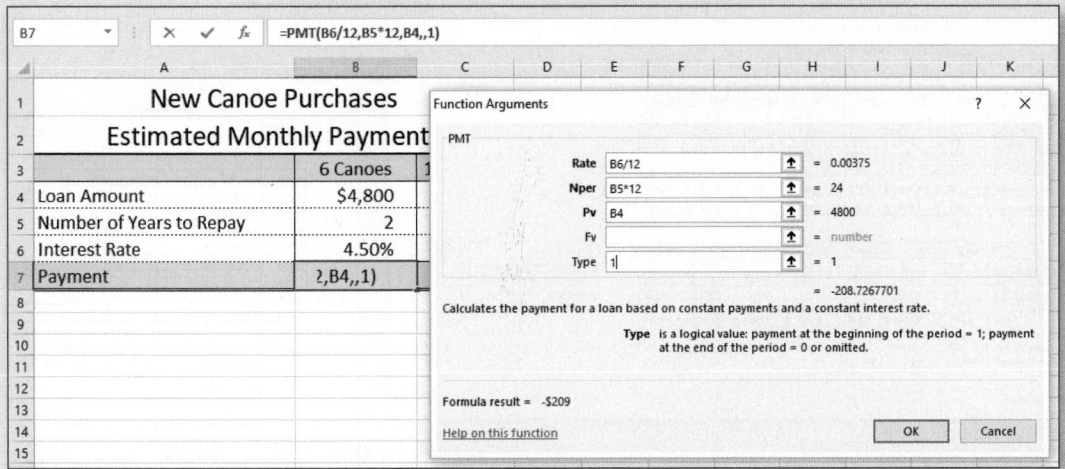

Figure 2-61 *PMT* function for payment at the beginning of the period

j. Click **OK**. The payment is −$209, a negative value because it is money paid out. This cell was formatted to show no decimal places.

9. Type the *PMT* function.

a. Click cell **C7**.

b. Type =pm, and press **Tab**. The *ScreenTip* shows the first argument, *rate*.

c. Click cell **C6** and type /12 and then type , (a comma). This divides the rate by 12 and enters a comma to separate the arguments (Figure 2-62).

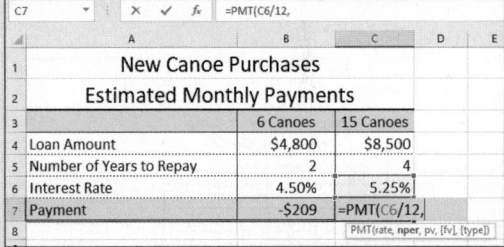

Figure 2-62 Type a *PMT* function

d. Click cell **C5** and type *12 and then type , (a comma) to multiply the number of years by 12 and move to the next argument.

e. Click cell **C4** for the *pv* argument, the amount of the loan.

f. Type , (a comma) to move to the *fv* argument.

g. Type , (another comma) to move to the *type* argument. *Formula AutoComplete* lists two options for the argument (Figure 2-63).

h. Double-click **1 - beginning of the period** in the *ScreenTip*.

i. Press **Enter**. The payment is −$196.

j. Press **Ctrl+Home**.

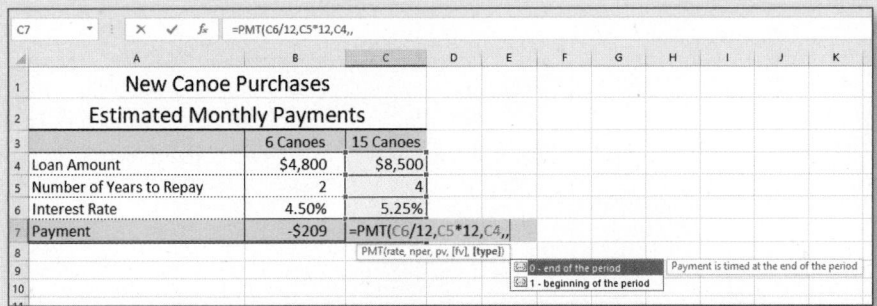

Figure 2-63 *Formula AutoComplete* for argument choices

10. Save and close the workbook (Figure 2-64).

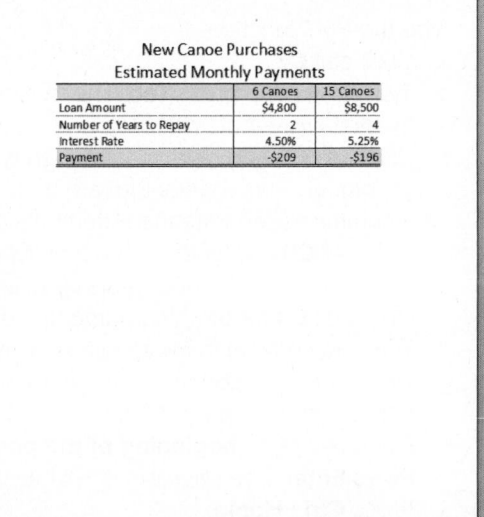

Figure 2-64 PP E2-3 completed

Chapter Summary

2.1 Build and edit basic formulas (p. E2-89).

- A *formula* is a calculation that uses arithmetic operators, worksheet cells, and constant values. Basic arithmetic operations are addition, subtraction, multiplication, and division.
- Type a formula in the cell or point and click to select cells.
- When you type a formula, *Formula AutoComplete* displays suggestions for completing the formula.
- Formulas are edited in the *Formula* bar or in the cell to change cell addresses, use a different operator, or add cells to the calculation.

2.2 Set mathematical order of operations in a formula (p. E2-91).

- Excel follows mathematics rules for the order in which operations are carried out when a formula has more than one operator.
- Control the sequence of calculations by placing operations that should be done first within parentheses.
- Use the following acronym to help remember the order of arithmetic operations: **P**lease **E**xcuse **M**y **D**ear **A**unt **S**ally (**P**arentheses, **E**xponentiation, **M**ultiplication, **D**ivision, **A**ddition, **S**ubtraction).

2.3 Use absolute, mixed, relative, and 3D references in a formula (p. E2-93).

- A *relative cell reference* in a formula is the cell address which, when copied, updates to the address of the copy.
- An *absolute cell reference* is the cell address with dollar signs, as in A5. This reference does not change when the formula is copied.
- A *mixed cell reference* contains one relative and one absolute address, as in $B5 or B$5. When copied, the absolute part of the reference does not change.
- A *3D cell reference* is a cell in another worksheet in the same workbook. It includes the name of the worksheet followed by an exclamation point, as in *Inventory!B2*.
- Name a single cell or a group of cells with a defined *range name*.
- Use range names in formulas instead of cell addresses.

- *Formula AutoComplete* displays range names so that you can paste them in a formula.
- A named range is an absolute reference.

2.4 Use formula auditing tools in a worksheet (p. E2-99).

- Excel highlights several types of formula errors as you work, but you still need to review errors and make corrections.
- Excel automatically error-checks formulas based on its internal rules. A potential error is marked in the upper-left corner of the cell with a small triangle.
- *Formula auditing* tools include several commands to aid your review of workbook formulas and functions.
- The *Formula Auditing* group on the *Formulas* tab includes the *Trace Precedents* and *Trace Dependents* buttons.
- A *circular reference* is an error that occurs when a formula includes the address of the formula.
- Occasionally, errors are noted as you press a completion key and can be quickly corrected by accepting the suggested correction in the message window.

2.5 Work with *Statistical* and *Date & Time* functions (p. E2-106).

- The *AVERAGE* function calculates the arithmetic mean by adding values and dividing by the number of values.
- The *COUNT* function tallies the number of cells in a range. Different *COUNT* functions are available based on whether cell contents are labels, values, or blank.
- *MAX* and *MIN* functions find the largest and the smallest values, respectively, in a range.
- Commonly used statistical functions are options on the *AutoSum* button.
- The *AutoCalculate* feature displays numerical results such as *Sum*, *Average*, and *Count* on the *Status* bar for selected cells.
- The *Date & Time* category includes a *TODAY* function and a *NOW* function that display the current date and time.

2.6 Work with functions from the *Financial*, *Logical*, and *Lookup & Reference* categories (p. E2-114).

- Use the *Function Arguments* dialog box for help in completing an Excel function.

- The *Function Arguments* dialog box includes a description of the function and an explanation of each argument.
- The *PMT* function from the *Financial* category calculates a constant payment amount for a loan.
- The *Logical* function *IF* evaluates a statement or condition and displays a particular result when the statement is true and another result when the condition is false.
- A *Lookup* function displays data from a cell located in another part of the workbook.
- Two widely used *Lookup* functions are *VLOOKUP* (vertical) and *HLOOKUP* (horizontal).

2.7 Build functions from the *Math & Trig* category (p. E2-122).

- The *ROUND* function adjusts a value up or down based on the number of decimal places.

- The *SUMIF* function includes cells in a total only if they meet a set criteria or condition.
- The *SUMPRODUCT* function multiplies corresponding cells from an **array** and then totals the results of each multiplication.

Check for Understanding

The SIMbook for this text (within your SIMnet account) provides the following resources for concept review:

- Multiple-choice questions
- Short answer questions
- Matching exercises

Guided Project 2-1

Courtyard Medical Plaza (CMP) has doctor offices, a pharmacy, x-ray and lab services, insurance and billing support, optometry and dental facilities, and on-site dining. You will complete an inventory worksheet for the pharmacy as well as insurance and payment data for the optometry group.
[Student Learning Outcomes 2.1, 2.2, 2.3, 2.4, 2.5, 2.6, 2.7]

File Needed: **CourtyardMedical-02.xlsx** (Student data files are available in the Library of your SIMnet account.)
Completed Project File Name: **[your initials] Excel 2-1.xlsx**

Skills Covered in This Project

- Build and copy formulas.
- Name cell ranges.
- Set the mathematical order of operations.
- Use relative, mixed, and absolute cell references in formulas.
- Use AVERAGE, MAX, and MIN.
- Use SUMIF.
- Check results with AutoCalculate.
- Use the VLOOKUP function.
- Use formula auditing tools.
- Use the PMT and SUMPRODUCT functions.
- Insert the TODAY function.

1. Open the **CourtyardMedical-02.xlsx** workbook from your student data files and save it as [your initials] Excel 2-1.

2. Enter and copy subtraction formulas.
 a. Click cell **E2** on the **Lookup_Data** worksheet. To calculate the dollar amount of the margin, subtract the cost from the retail price.
 b. Type an equals sign (=) to start the formula.
 c. Click cell **D2**, the retail price.
 d. Type a minus sign or hyphen (−) to subtract and click cell **C2**, the cost.
 e. Click the **Enter** button (check mark) in the Formula bar. The pointer stays in the formula cell. The margin for acetaminophen is $1.49.
 f. Drag the Fill pointer to copy the formula in cell **E2** to cells **E3:E16**. The Auto Fill Options button appears near cell E16.
 g. Click the **Auto Fill Options** button and choose **Fill Without Formatting** (Figure 2-65). This option copies the formula without the top border from cell E2.
 h. Format cells **E3:E16** as **Currency**.
 i. Click the **Optometry** sheet tab and select cell **G5**.
 j. Type = to start the formula to subtract the patient's share from the billed amount.
 k. Click cell **E5**, the billed amount.

Figure 2-65 Copy without formatting to preserve borders

l. Type −, click cell **F5**, and press **Enter**.
 m. Copy the formula in cell **G5** to cells **G6:G24** without formatting to maintain the fill color.

3. Name cell ranges.
 a. Select cells **E5:E24**. This named range will refer to the billable amounts.
 b. Click the **Name** box.
 c. Type Billables in the *Name* box and press **Enter**.
 d. Click the **Lookup_Data** worksheet tab.
 e. Select cells **A2:D16**. This named range will not include the calculated margin.
 f. Click the **Name** box.
 g. Type Costs in the *Name* box and press **Enter**.
 h. Select cells **H2:I5** and name the range Insurers.
 i. Click cell **A1** and click the **Name** box arrow to see the range names in the workbook (Figure 2-66).

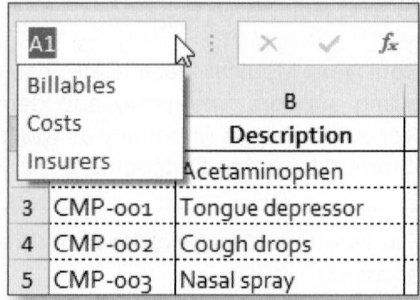

Figure 2-66 Range names in the worksheet

4. Use range names with *AVERAGE*, *MIN*, and *MAX*.
 a. Click the **Optometry** sheet tab and select cell **D27**.
 b. Type =aver and press **Tab**.
 c. Select cells **E5:E24** and press **Enter**. The range name is substituted in the formula when you select the cells in the worksheet.
 d. Select cell **D28**, click the **AutoSum** button arrow [*Home* tab, *Editing* group], and select **Max**.
 e. Select cells **E5:E24** and press **Enter**.
 f. Use *MIN* in cell **D29** with the same cell range.
 g. Apply the **Currency** format to cells **D27:D29**.

5. Unhide a column and set the order of operations in a formula.
 a. Click the **Insurance** sheet tab. Column D is hidden.
 b. Point to the column **C** heading and click and drag to select columns **C:E**.
 c. Right-click either column heading and choose **Unhide**. Column D has a *VLOOKUP* formula to display the service fee from the Insurers range on the **Lookup_Data** sheet.
 d. Select cell **E5**. The total with service charge is calculated by multiplying 1 plus the service fee times the billed amount.
 e. Type = and click cell **C5**.
 f. Type *(immediately after **C5**.
 g. Type 1+ immediately after the left parenthesis.
 h. Click cell **D5**. This part of the formula will be calculated first (Figure 2-67).
 i. Press **Enter**. Because the formula refers to a range name, the missing parenthesis is not automatically supplied (Figure 2-68).
 j. Click **Yes** to accept the suggested correction.
 k. Copy the formula to cells **E5:E24**.

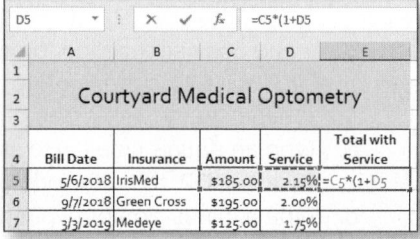

Figure 2-67 Set the order of the calculations in a formula

6. Format cells **E5:E24** as **Currency** from the *Number Format* drop-down list. The values are rounded to two decimal places (Figure 2-69).

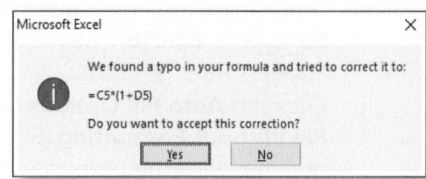

Figure 2-68 Formula correction message window

7. Use the *SUMIF* function to calculate billable amounts by insurance company.
 a. Click the **Optometry** worksheet tab and select cell **D31**.
 b. Click the **Math & Trig** button [*Formulas* tab, *Function Library* group].
 c. Select **SUMIF**.
 d. Click the **Range** box, select cells **C5:C24**, and press **F4 (FN+F4)** to make the reference absolute.

e. Click the **Criteria** box and select cell **C31** to use a relative reference to the company name.

f. Click the **Sum_range** text box and select cells **E5:E24**. The range name is substituted and is an absolute reference (Figure 2-70).

g. Click **OK**. The result is 1030, the total amount billed to Green Cross.

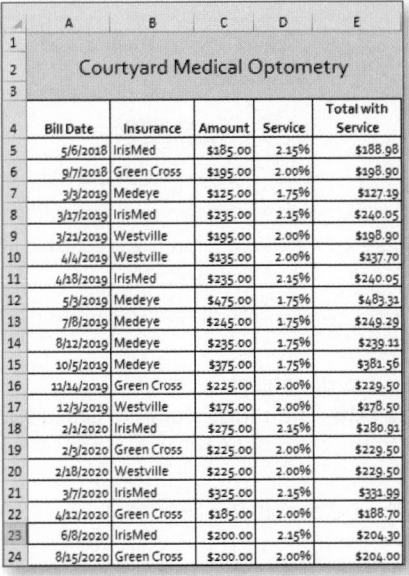

Figure 2-69 Results are rounded by the Currency format

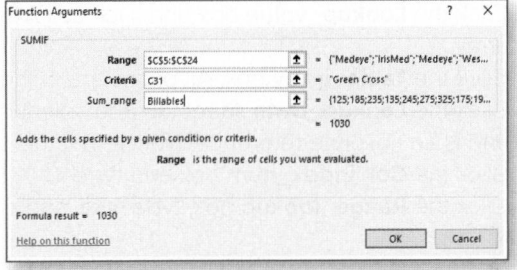

Figure 2-70 Absolute and relative reference arguments for *SUMIF*

8. Verify results with *AutoCalculate*.
 a. Select cells **E13:E15**.
 b. Press **Ctrl** and select cells **E20:E21**. These are the billable amounts for the Green Cross insurance company.
 c. Compare the *SUM* in the *Status* bar with the result in cell **D31** (Figure 2-71).

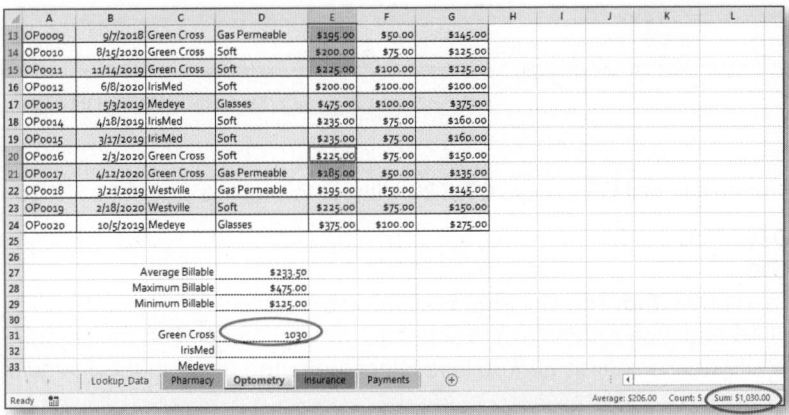

Figure 2-71 *AutoCalculate* results in *Status* bar

9. Copy the *SUMIF* function with a relative reference.
 a. Select cell **D31**.
 b. Drag the *Fill* pointer to copy the formula in cell **D31** to cells **D32:D34**. The *Auto Fill Options* button appears near cell D34.

c. Select cell **D32**. The reference to cell C31 in the original formula is updated to cell C32 in the copied formula (Figure 2-72).

10. Format cells **D31:D34** as **Currency** from the *Number Format* drop-down list. Press **Ctrl+Home**.

11. Use *VLOOKUP* with a range name to display costs.
 a. Click the **Pharmacy** worksheet tab and select cell **C6**. Cost and retail prices are missing.
 b. Click the **Lookup & Reference** button [*Formulas* tab, *Function Library* group] and select **VLOOKUP**.
 c. Click the **Lookup_value** box and click cell **A6**. The ID in column A will be located in the table array.
 d. Click the **Table_array** box. All prices are in the *Lookup_Data* sheet.
 e. Click the **Lookup_Data** sheet tab and select cells **A2:D16**. The range name *Costs* is substituted and is an absolute reference. Notice that the cost is in the third column.
 f. Click the **Col_index_num** box and type **3**.
 g. Click the **Range_lookup** box, type false, and click **OK**. The cost is 2.5 (Figure 2-73).

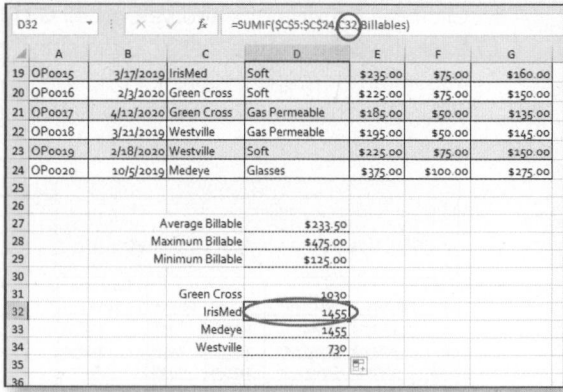

Figure 2-72 Relative reference is adjusted after copying

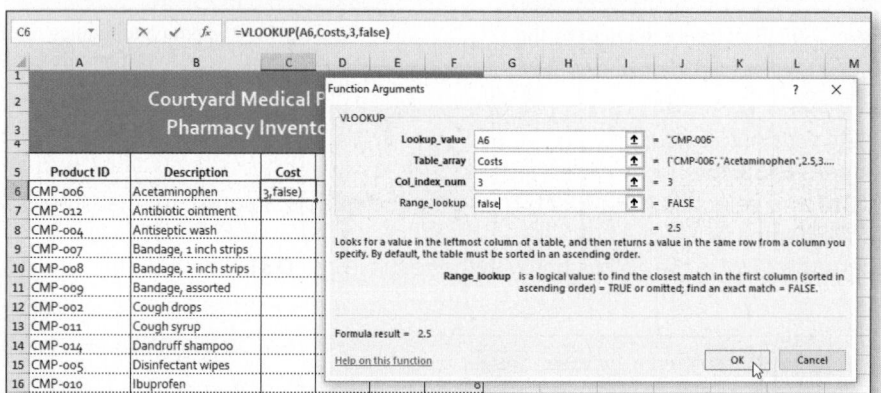

Figure 2-73 *VLOOKUP* and its arguments

 h. Copy the formula in cell **C6** to cells **C7:C20** without formatting. Format cells **C6:C20** as **Currency**.

12. Type the *VLOOKUP* function.
 a. Click cell **D6**.
 b. Type **=vl** and press **Tab**. The first argument is *lookup_value*.
 c. Select cell **A6** and type a comma (,) to separate the arguments. The next argument is *table_array*.
 d. Type costs and type a comma (,). (You can select the range name in the *Formula AutoComplete* list.)
 e. Type 4 for the *Col_index_num* argument and type a comma (,). The retail price is in the fourth column of the *Costs* range.
 f. Double-click **FALSE – Exact match** in the *ScreenTip* and press **Enter**. The closing parenthesis is supplied, and the retail price for acetaminophen is 3.99 (Figure 2-74).
 g. Copy the formula in cell **D6** to cells **D7:D20** without formatting to keep the borders and then format the cells as **Currency**.

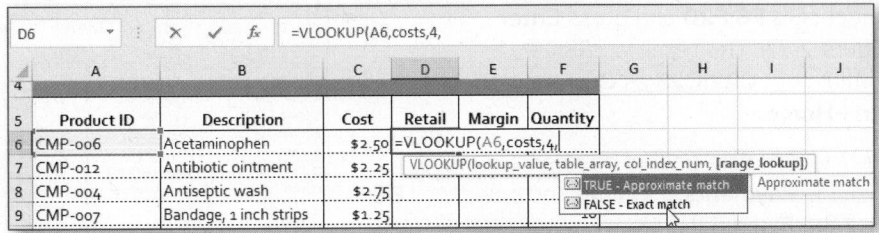

Figure 2-74 Double-click an option in the *ScreenTip*

13. Set the order of precedence in a formula.
 a. Click cell **E6**. The formula to calculate the margin subtracts the cost from the retail price and then divides by the cost. The margin is shown as a markup percentage.
 b. Type =(to start the formula and enter the opening parenthesis.
 c. Click cell **D6** for the retail price.
 d. Type − and click cell **C6** to subtract the cost from the retail price.
 e. Type) for the closing parenthesis. This forces the subtraction to be carried out first.
 f. Type / for division and click cell **C6** to divide the results by the cost (Figure 2-75).
 g. Press **Enter**. The results are formatted as currency.
 h. Apply **Percent Style** to cell **E6**. A margin of 60% means that the retail price is about 1.6 times the cost.
 i. Copy the formula in cell **E6** to cells **E7:E20** without formatting; then apply **Percent Style** to cells **E7:E20**.

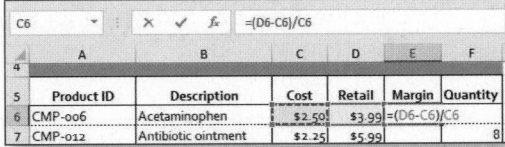

Figure 2-75 Formula to calculate profit margin

14. Trace precedents and dependents for formulas.
 a. Select cell **C6**.
 b. Click the **Trace Precedents** button [*Formulas* tab, *Formula Auditing* group]. The formula uses data from another worksheet and from cell **A6**.
 c. Select cell **E6** and click the **Trace Precedents** button.
 d. Select cell **D7** and click the **Trace Dependents** button. The arrow points to cell **E7**.
 e. Click the **Remove Arrows** button [*Formulas* tab, *Formula Auditing* group].

15. Enter a *SUMPRODUCT* function to calculate inventory values.
 a. Click cell **C22**.
 b. Click the **Math & Trig** button [*Formulas* tab, *Function Library* group] and select **SUMPRODUCT**.
 c. Click the **Array1** box and select cells **C6:C20**.
 d. Click the **Array2** box and select cells **F6:F20**. Both arrays have the same dimension (Figure 2-76).
 e. Click **OK**. The result in cell C22 is 264.15. Each value in column C is multiplied by its corresponding value in column E, and those results are summed.

Figure 2-76 Two arrays for *SUMPRODUCT*

16. Type the *SUMPRODUCT* function.
 a. Click cell **C23**.
 b. Type =sump and press **Tab**. The first argument is *array1*.
 c. Select cells **D6:D20** and type a comma (,) to separate the arguments. The next argument is *array2*.

d. Select cells **F6:F20** and press **Enter** (Figure 2-77). The result is 588.29.

e. Format cells **C22:C23** as **Currency**. Press **Ctrl+Home**.

17. Use *PMT* to calculate patient payments.
 a. Click the **Payments** sheet tab and select cell **B6**.
 b. Click the **Financial** button [*Formulas* tab, *Function Library* group] and select **PMT**.
 c. Click the **Rate** box and type 2.75%/12. You can type the rate when it is not shown in a cell. Yearly rates are divided by 12 for monthly payments.
 d. Click the **Nper** box and type 24. The length of the loan is indicated in the label in cell A4. Two-year financing means 24 monthly payments.
 e. Click the **Pv** box and click cell **A6**, the amount of a loan.
 f. Click the **Type** box and type 1 for payment at the beginning of the month. The *Fv* argument is blank (Figure 2-78).

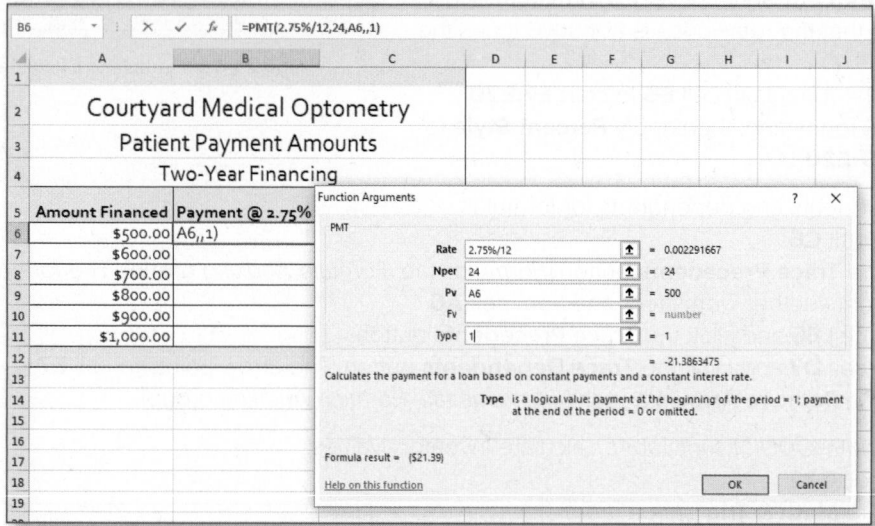

Figure 2-77 Both arrays have the same dimension

Figure 2-78 *PMT* arguments

g. Click **OK**. The payment for financing $500 is ($21.39).
h. Copy the formula to cells **B7:B11**. The reference to cell A6 is relative, and the *rate* and *nper* values that you typed are absolute.

18. Copy and edit a *PMT* function.
 a. Copy the formula in cell **B6** to cell **C6**.
 b. Select cell **C6** and click the **Insert Function** button in the *Formula* bar. The *Function Arguments* dialog box opens with the formula.
 c. Click the **Rate** text box and edit the calculation to 3.25%/12.
 d. Click the **Pv** box and set cell **A6** as the argument.
 e. Click **OK**. The payment for financing $500 at 3.25% is ($21.49).
 f. Copy the formula to cells **C7:C11**.

19. Enter the *TODAY* function.
 a. Select cell **A14**.
 b. Type =to, press **Tab**, and press **Enter**.
 c. Press **Ctrl+Home**.

20. Save and close the workbook (Figure 2-79).

Courtyard Medical Optometry

Patient ID	Initial Visit	Insurance	Prescription	Billed	Patient Share	Insurance Share
OP0001	3/3/2019	Medeye	Gas Permeable	$125.00	$50.00	$75.00
OP0002	5/6/2018	IrisMed	Soft	$185.00	$50.00	$135.00
OP0003	8/12/2019	Medeye	Glasses	$235.00	$75.00	$160.00
OP0004	4/4/2019	Westville	Glasses	$135.00	$75.00	$60.00
OP0005	7/8/2019	Medeye	Soft	$245.00	$50.00	$195.00
OP0006	2/1/2020	IrisMed	Soft	$275.00	$100.00	$175.00
OP0007	3/7/2020	IrisMed	Soft	$325.00	$100.00	$225.00
OP0008	12/3/2019	Westville	Gas Permeable	$175.00	$75.00	$100.00
OP0009	9/7/2018	Green Cross	Gas Permeable	$195.00	$50.00	$145.00
OP0010	8/15/2020	Green Cross	Soft	$200.00	$75.00	$125.00
OP0011	11/14/2019	Green Cross	Soft	$225.00	$100.00	$125.00
OP0012	6/8/2020	IrisMed	Soft	$200.00	$100.00	$100.00
OP0013	5/3/2019	Medeye	Glasses	$475.00	$100.00	$375.00
OP0014	4/18/2019	IrisMed	Soft	$235.00	$75.00	$160.00
OP0015	3/17/2019	IrisMed	Soft	$235.00	$75.00	$160.00
OP0016	2/3/2020	Green Cross	Soft	$225.00	$75.00	$150.00
OP0017	4/12/2020	Green Cross	Gas Permeable	$185.00	$50.00	$135.00
OP0018	3/21/2019	Westville	Gas Permeable	$195.00	$50.00	$145.00
OP0019	2/18/2020	Westville	Soft	$225.00	$75.00	$150.00
OP0020	10/5/2019	Medeye	Glasses	$375.00	$100.00	$275.00

Average Billable	$233.50
Maximum Billable	$475.00
Minimum Billable	$125.00

Green Cross	$1,030.00
IrisMed	$1,455.00
Medeye	$1,455.00
Westville	$730.00

Courtyard Medical Plaza Pharmacy Inventory

Product ID	Description	Cost	Retail	Margin	Quantity
CMP-006	Acetaminophen	$2.50	$3.99	60%	12
CMP-012	Antibiotic ointment	$2.25	$5.99	166%	8
CMP-004	Antiseptic wash	$2.75	$4.99	81%	7
CMP-007	Bandage, 1 inch strips	$1.25	$3.99	219%	10
CMP-008	Bandage, 2 inch strips	$1.25	$3.99	219%	5
CMP-009	Bandage, assorted	$1.75	$4.99	185%	8
CMP-002	Cough drops	$0.85	$1.29	52%	12
CMP-011	Cough syrup	$2.25	$4.99	122%	9
CMP-014	Dandruff shampoo	$2.75	$5.99	118%	5
CMP-005	Disinfectant wipes	$1.25	$3.99	219%	15
CMP-010	Ibuprofen	$2.50	$3.99	60%	8
CMP-015	Insect bite gel	$3.55	$6.99	97%	15
CMP-013	Moisture lotion	$1.55	$4.99	222%	7
CMP-003	Nasal spray	$3.45	$5.99	74%	4
CMP-001	Tongue depressor	$0.55	$1.99	262%	6

Total Value at Cost	$264.15
Total Value at Retail	$588.29

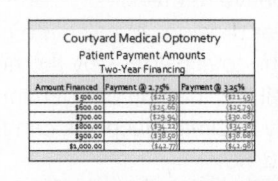

Figure 2-79 Excel 2-1 completed

Guided Project 2-2

Hamilton Civic Center (HCC) is a nonprofit community fitness center with an indoor pool, sauna, indoor track, project room, racquetball courts, meeting rooms, and a boutique. In this workbook, you complete tasks related to health seminars, a member challenge, and the daycare program.
[Student Learning Outcomes 2.1, 2.2, 2.3, 2.4, 2.5, 2.6, 2.7]

File Needed: ***HamiltonCivic-02.xlsx*** *(Student data files are available in the Library of your SIMnet account.)*
Completed Project File Name: *[your initials] Excel 2-2.xlsx*

Skills Covered in This Project

- Create and copy formulas.
- Name cell ranges.
- Use relative and absolute references.
- Set mathematical order of operations.

- Use *AutoCalculate* and formula auditing tools.
- Use *VLOOKUP* and *HLOOKUP*.
- Create an *IF* function.
- Create a *SUMIF* function.
- Use the *TODAY* function.

1. Open the ***HamiltonCivic-02.xlsx*** workbook from your student data files and save it as [your initials] Excel 2-2.

2. Name cell ranges.
 a. Select the **Seminars** sheet, select cells **B6:B10**, and click the **Name** box.
 b. Type Seminars in the *Name* box and press **Enter**.
 c. Click the **Data** sheet tab. You will name the cell ranges used in the *Lookup* functions.
 d. Select cells **A2:D10** and click the **Name** box.
 e. Type V_Calories in the *Name* box and press **Enter**. This will remind you that this range is a vertical table array. Note that the first column in the array is sorted in ascending order.
 f. Select cells **F2:J3** and click the **Name** box.
 g. Type H_Fees and press **Enter**. This range is a horizontal table array, arranged in alphabetical order from left to right.

3. Enter and copy a division formula.
 a. Select cell **D2** on the **Data** worksheet.
 b. Type an equals sign (=) to start the formula.
 c. Click cell **C2**, the total number of calories. This formula uses relative references.
 d. Type / for division. To calculate calories per minute, divide the total calories by the number of minutes.
 e. Click cell **B2**, the number of minutes, and press **Enter**. As many decimal places as can fit in the cell display (Figure 2-80).
 f. Drag the *Fill* pointer to copy the formula in cell **D2** to cells **D3:D10**. Ignore the *Auto Fill Options* button.
 g. Select cells **D2:D10** if necessary, and click the **Decrease Decimal** button [*Home* tab, *Number* group] two times. This applies the same number of decimal positions for all results.

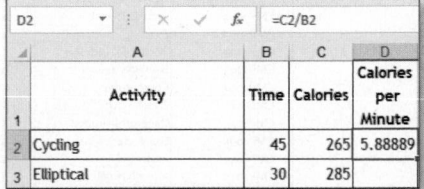

Figure 2-80 Decimal positions fill the cell

4. Use *HLOOKUP* with a range name to display fees.
 a. Click the **Seminars** worksheet tab and select cell **C6**. Fees are in the *H_Fees* range.
 b. Click the **Lookup & Reference** button [*Formulas* tab, *Function Library* group] and select **HLOOKUP**.
 c. Click the **Lookup_value** box and click cell **B6**.

d. Click the **Table_array** box.

e. Type h_fees the name of the range. It is not case sensitive, and quotation marks are not necessary.

f. Click the **Row_index_num** box and type 2 because the fees are in the second row of the *H_Fees* range. The **Range_lookup** box is empty (Figure 2-81).

g. Click **OK**. The fee is $15.00.

h. Copy the formula in cell **C6** to cells **C7:C10**.

Figure 2-81 Arguments for *HLOOKUP*

5. Enter and copy an addition formula.

a. Click cell **E15** and type an equals sign (=) to start the formula.

b. Click cell **D6**, the number of attendees for the seminar in Hendersonville.

c. Type + for addition.

d. Click cell **E6** to add the number of attendees for Advocate Central.

e. Type +, click cell **F6**, type +, and click cell **G6** (Figure 2-82).

f. Press **Enter**.

g. Drag the *Fill* pointer to copy the formula in cell **E15** to cells **E16:E19**. Ignore the *Auto Fill Options* button.

h. Click cell **E20**, click the **AutoSum** button [*Home* tab, *Editing* group], and press **Enter**. The total is 209 attendees.

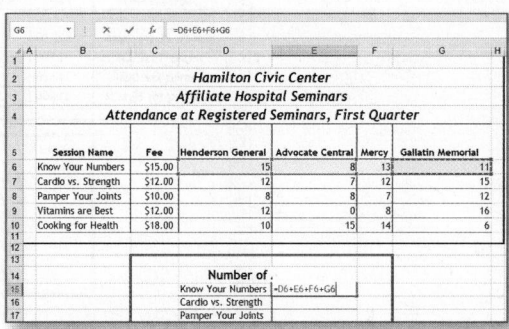

Figure 2-82 Simple addition formula

6. Set the order of operations in a formula.

a. Select cell **E24**.

b. Type = to start the formula and click cell **C6**.

c. Type * to multiply. The fee is multiplied by the sum of the attendees at each hospital.

d. Type (for the opening parenthesis. This forces the addition to be carried out first.

e. Click cell **D6**, type +, click cell **E6**, type +, click cell **F6**, type +, and click cell **G6**. Cells D6:G6 must be added first and that result is multiplied by cell C6.

f. Type) for the closing parenthesis (Figure 2-83).

g. Press **Enter**. The result is 705.

h. Format cell **E24** as **Currency** and copy the formula to cells **E25:E28**.

i. Click cell **E29**, click the **AutoSum** button [*Home* tab, *Editing* group], and press **Enter**.

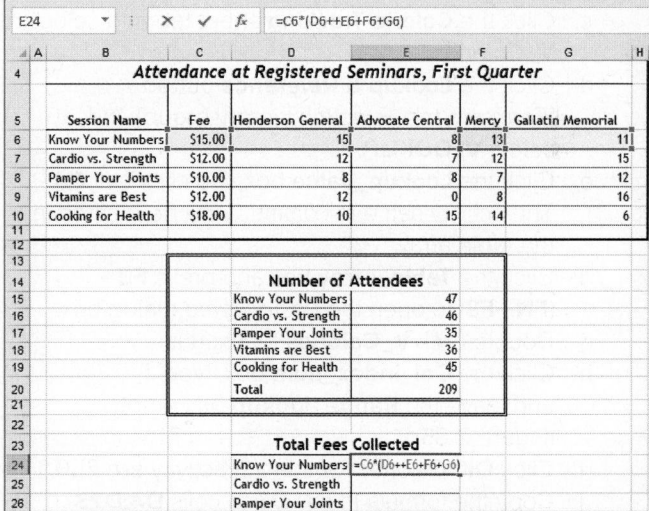

Figure 2-83 Addition done before multiplication

7. Use *AutoCalculate* and formula auditing tools.

a. Select cells **E24:E28**.

b. Compare the *SUM* in the *Status* bar with the result in cell E29.

c. Select cell **E15**.

d. Click the **Trace Precedents** button [*Formulas* tab, *Formula Auditing* group].

e. Click the **Trace Dependents** button. The formula in cell E15 has both precedent and dependent cells (Figure 2-84).

f. Click the **Remove Arrows** button [*Formulas* tab, *Formula Auditing* group].

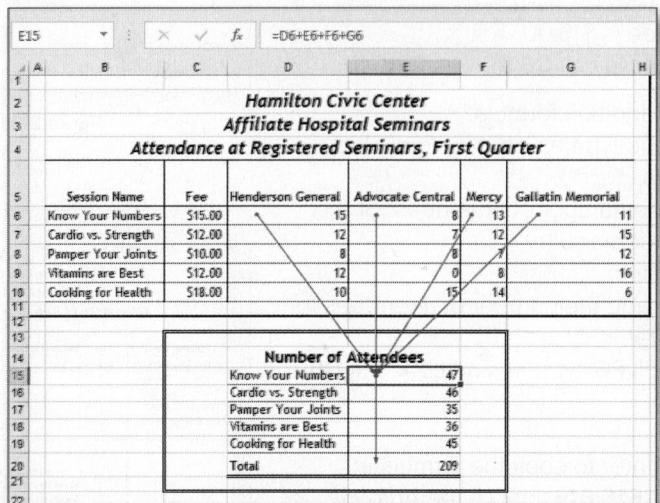

Figure 2-84 Precedent and dependent cells

8. Use *VLOOKUP* with a range name to display calories expended.

a. Click the **Data** sheet tab.

b. Click the **Name** box arrow and select **V_Calories**. Notice that total calories are in the third column.

c. Click the **Calorie Tracking** sheet tab and select cell **D3**. Calories by activity are within the range *V_Calories*.

d. Click the **Lookup & Reference** button [*Formulas* tab, *Function Library* group] and select **VLOOKUP**.

e. Click the **Lookup_value** box and click cell **C3**. The activity name in column C will be located in the table array.

f. Click the **Table_array** box and press **F3** (**FN+F3**) to open the *Paste Name* dialog box.

g. Double-click **V_Calories** to insert it.

h. Click the **Col_index_num** box, type 3, and leave the **Range_lookup** box empty (Figure 2-85).

Figure 2-85 Arguments for the *VLOOKUP* function

i. Click **OK**. Calories for the first activity are 250.

j. Copy the formula in cell **D3** to cells **D4:D23**.

9. Build a *SUMIF* formula with absolute and relative references.

a. Select cell **D28** on the **Calorie Tracking** sheet.

b. Click the **Recently Used** button [*Formulas* tab, *Function Library* group].

c. Look for and choose **SUMIF**. (If you do not see *SUMIF* in the list, click the **Math & Trig** button to find and select **SUMIF**.)

d. Click the **Range** box and select cells **C3:C23**, the range that will be evaluated.

e. Press **F4** (**FN+F4**) to make the cell references absolute.

f. Click the **Criteria** box and select cell **C28** to find rows with "cycling" as the activity. This is a relative reference.

g. Click the **Sum_range** box and select cells **D3:D23**, the values to be summed if the activity is cycling.

h. Press **F4** (**FN+F4**) to make the references absolute (Figure 2-86).

i. Click **OK**. The result is 795 calories.

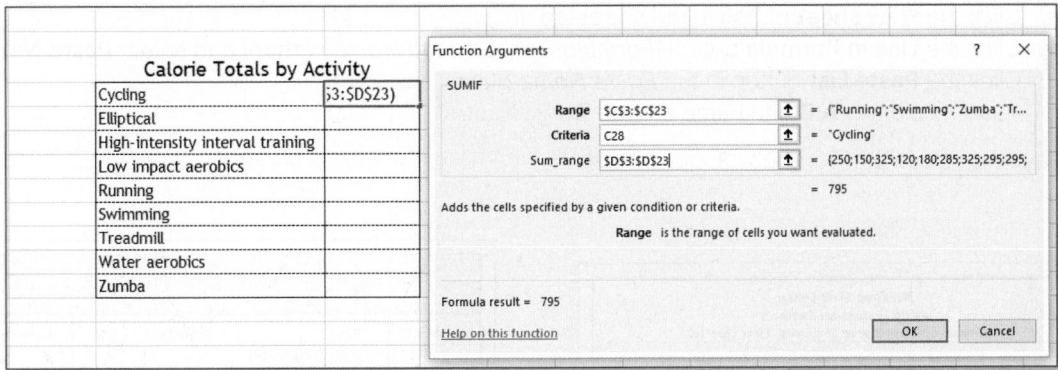

Figure 2-86 *SUMIF* function for cycling

10. Copy the formula in cell **D28** to cells **D29:D36** without formatting (Figure 2-87).

11. Create an *IF* function to calculate a fee based on age.

a. Click the **Day Care** sheet tab and select cell **D5**.

b. Click the **Logical** button [*Formulas* tab, *Function Library* group] and select **IF**.

c. Click the **Logical_test** box and click cell **B5**.

d. Type **>=4** to test if the child is 4 years old or greater.

e. Click the **Value_if_true** box and click cell **I9**. The fee for a child 4 years old or greater is $18.

f. Press **F4** (**FN+F4**) to make the reference absolute.

g. Click the **Value_if_false** box and click cell **I8**. If the child is not 4 years old or greater, the higher fee applies.

h. Press **F4** (**FN+F4**) to make the reference absolute (Figure 2-88).

i. Click **OK**. The fee for Mary is 18.

j. Format the result as **Currency**.

k. Copy the formula in cell **D5** to cells **D6:D14** without formatting to preserve the borders.

Figure 2-87 Copy the formula without formatting

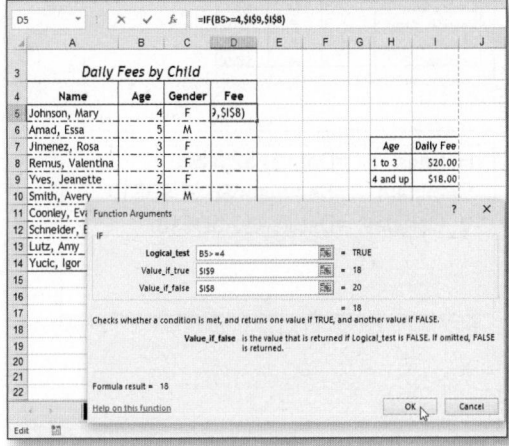

Figure 2-88 *IF* function to determine the fee

12. Insert the current date as a function.
 a. Click the **Data** sheet tab and click cell **A12**.
 b. Type =to and press **Tab** to select the function.
 c. Press **Enter**.
 d. Press **Ctrl+Home**.

13. Paste range names.
 a. Click the **New sheet** button in the sheet tab area.
 b. Click the **Use in Formula** button [*Formulas* tab, *Defined Names* group] and select **Paste Names**.
 c. Click the **Paste List** button in the *Paste Name* dialog box.
 d. *AutoFit* columns **A:B** and name the tab Range Names.

14. Save and close the workbook (Figure 2-89).

Hamilton Civic Center
Affiliate Hospital Seminars
Attendance at Registered Seminars, First Quarter

Session Name	Fee	Henderson	General	Advocate Central	Mercy	Gallatin	Memorial
Know Your Numbers	$15.00	15	8	13			11
Cardio vs. Strength	$12.00	12	7	12			15
Pamper Your Joints	$10.00	8	8	7			12
Vitamins are Best	$12.00	12	0	8			16
Cooking for Health	$18.00	10	15	14			6

Number of Attendees

Know Your Numbers	47
Cardio vs. Strength	46
Pamper Your Joints	35
Vitamins are Best	36
Cooking for Health	45
Total	209

Total Fees Collected

Know Your Numbers	$705.00
Cardio vs. Strength	$552.00
Pamper Your Joints	$350.00
Vitamins are Best	$432.00
Cooking for Health	$810.00
Total	$2,849.00

Hamilton Civic Center

Summer Day Care

Daily Fees by Child

Name	Age	Gender	Fee
Johnson, Mary	4	F	$18.00
Amed, Essa	5	M	$18.00
Jimenez, Rosa	3	F	$20.00
Remus, Valentina	3	F	$20.00
Yves, Jeanette	2	F	$20.00
Smith, Avery	2	M	$20.00
Coonley, Evan	5	M	$18.00
Schneider, Ellery	1	F	$20.00
Lutz, Amy	4	F	$18.00
Yuzio, Igor	3	M	$20.00

Age	Daily Fee
1 to 3	$20.00
4 and up	$18.00

H_Fees	=Data!F2:J3
Seminars	=Seminars!B6:B10
V_Calories	=Data!A2:D10

Member Calorie Burn Challenge

Member ID	Date	Activity	Calories
100 34	2/1/2020	Running	250
100 36	2/2/2020	Swimming	150
100 38	2/2/2020	Zumba	325
100 40	2/4/2020	Treadmill	120
100 42	3/1/2020	Low impact aerobics	180
100 44	3/3/2020	Elliptical	285
100 46	3/5/2020	Zumba	325
100 48	3/7/2020	Water aerobics	295
100 50	3/9/2020	Water aerobics	295
100 34	3/11/2020	Low impact aerobics	180
100 36	3/13/2020	Cycling	265
100 38	3/15/2020	Cycling	265
100 40	3/17/2020	Water aerobics	295
100 42	3/19/2020	High-intensity interval training	350
100 44	3/21/2020	High-intensity interval training	350
100 46	3/23/2020	Cycling	265
100 48	3/25/2020	Treadmill	120
100 50	3/27/2020	Zumba	325
100 36	3/29/2020	High-intensity interval training	350
100 34	3/31/2020	Treadmill	120
100 42	4/2/2020	Running	250

Calorie Totals by Activity

Cycling	795
Elliptical	285
High-intensity interval training	1050
Low impact aerobics	360
Running	500
Swimming	150
Treadmill	360
Water aerobics	885
Zumba	975

Activity	Time	Calories	Calories per Minute
Cycling	45	265	5.889
Elliptical	30	285	9.500
High-Intensity Interval training	45	350	7.778
Low Impact aerobics	45	180	4.000
Running	30	250	8.333
Swimming	30	150	5.000
Treadmill	30	120	4.000
Water aerobics	45	295	6.556
Zumba	45	325	7.222

Session Names and Fees

Cardio vs. Strength	Cooking for Health	Know Your Numbers	Pamper Your Joints	Vitamins are Best
$12.00	$18.00	$15.00	$10.00	$12.00

Figure 2-89 Excel 2-2 completed

Guided Project 2-3

Sierra Pacific Community College District (SPCCD) consists of four individual community colleges. The workbook for this project includes an amortization schedule for student loans and a fee and credit hour summary for several departments.

[Student Learning Outcomes 2.1, 2.2, 2.3, 2.4, 2.5, 2.6, 2.7]

File Needed: ***SierraPacific-02.xlsx*** *(Student data files are available in the* Library *of your SIMnet account.)*
Completed Project File Name: ***[your initials] Excel 2-3.xlsx***

Skills Covered in This Project

- Name cell ranges.
- Create and copy formulas.
- Set mathematical order of operations.
- Use absolute references in formulas.

- Insert the current date as a function.
- Use the *PMT* function.
- Audit formulas.
- Use *SUMIF* and *SUMPRODUCT*.

1. Open the ***SierraPacific-02.xlsx*** workbook from your student data files and save it as [your initials] Excel 2-3.

2. Set range names for the workbook.
 a. Select the **Student Loan** sheet and select cells **B5:C8**.
 b. Click the **Create from Selection** button [*Formulas* tab, *Defined Names* group].
 c. Verify that the **Left column** box in the *Create Names from Selection* dialog box is selected.
 d. Deselect the **Top row** box if it is checked and click **OK**.
 e. Select cells **E5:F7**. Repeat steps a–d to create range names.
 f. Click the **Name Manager** button [*Formulas* tab, *Defined Names* group] to view the names in the *Name Manager* dialog box (Figure 2-90). Notice that the cell references are absolute.
 g. Click **Close**.

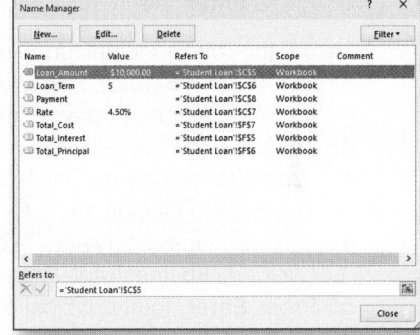

Figure 2-90 *Name Manager* dialog box

3. Enter a *PMT* function.
 a. Select **C8**.
 b. Click the **Financial** button [*Formulas* tab, *Function Library* group] and select **PMT**.
 c. Click the **Rate** box and click cell **C7**. The range name *Rate* is substituted and is an absolute reference.
 d. Type /12 immediately after **Rate** to divide by 12 for monthly payments.
 e. Click the **Nper** box and click cell **C6**. The substituted range name is *Loan_Term*.
 f. Type *12 after **Loan_Term** to multiply by 12.
 g. Click the **Pv** box and type a minus sign (−) to set the argument as a negative amount.
 h. Click cell **C5** (*Loan_Amount*) for the *pv* argument. A negative loan amount reflects the lender's perspective, because the money is paid out now (Figure 2-91).
 i. Leave the *Fv* and *Type* boxes empty.

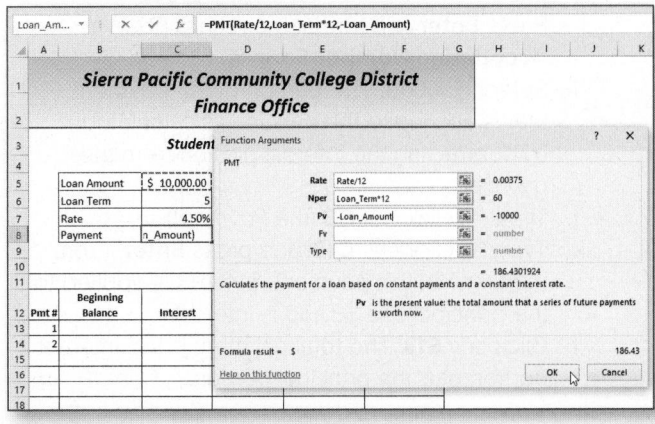

Figure 2-91 *Pv* argument is negative in the *PMT* function

j. Click **OK**. The payment for a loan at this rate is $186.43, shown as a positive value.

k. Verify or format cell **C8** as **Accounting Number Format** to match cell **C5**.

4. Create a total interest formula.

 a. Click cell **F5** (*Total_Interest*). This value is calculated by multiplying the monthly payment by the total number of payments to determine total outlay. From this amount, you subtract the loan amount.

 b. Type = and click cell **C8** (the *Payment*).

 c. Type * to multiply and click cell **C6** (*Loan_Term*).

 d. Type *12 to multiply by 12 for monthly payments. Values typed in a formula are constants and are absolute references.

 e. Type − immediately after *12 to subtract.

 f. Click cell **C5** (the *Loan_Amount*). The formula is *Payment * Loan_Term * 12 − Loan_Amount*. Parentheses are not required, because the multiplications are done from left to right, followed by the subtraction (Figure 2-92).

 g. Press **Enter**. The result is $1,185.81.

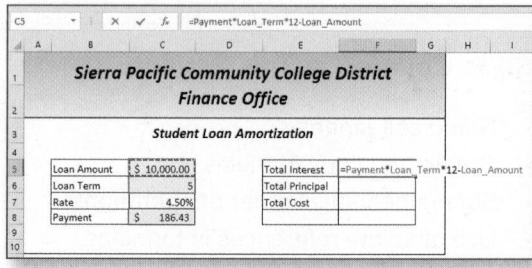

Figure 2-92 Left-to-right operations

5. Create the total principal formula and the total loan cost.

 a. Select cell **F6** (*Total_Principal*). This value is calculated by multiplying the monthly payment by the total number of payments. From this amount, subtract the total interest.

 b. Type = and click cell **C8** (the *Payment*).

 c. Type * to multiply and click cell **C6** (*Loan_Term*).

 d. Type *12 to multiply by 12 for monthly payments.

 e. Type − immediately after *12 to subtract.

 f. Click cell **F5** (the *Total_Interest*). The formula is *Payment * Loan_Term * 12 − Total_Interest*.

 g. Press **Enter**. Total principal is the amount of the loan.

 h. Click cell **F7**, the *Total_Cost* of the loan. This is the total principal plus the total interest.

 i. Type =, click cell **F5**, type +, click cell **F6**, and then press **Enter**.

6. Set order of mathematical operations to build an amortization schedule.

 a. Click cell **B13**. The beginning balance is the loan amount.

 b. Type =, click cell **C5**, and press **Enter**.

 c. Format the value as **Accounting Number Format**.

 d. Select cell **C13**. The interest for each payment is calculated by multiplying the balance in column B by the rate divided by 12.

 e. Type = and click cell **B13**.

 f. Type *(and click cell **C7**.

 g. Type /12). Parentheses are necessary so that the division is done first (Figure 2-93).

 h. Press **Enter** and format the results (37.5) as **Accounting Number Format**.

 i. Select cell **D13**. The portion of the payment that is applied to the principal is calculated by subtracting the interest portion from the payment.

 j. Type =, click cell **C8** (the *Payment*).

 k. Type −, click cell **C13**, and press **Enter**. From the first month's payment, $148.93 is applied to the principal and $37.50 is interest.

 l. Click cell **E13**. The total payment is the interest portion plus the principal portion.

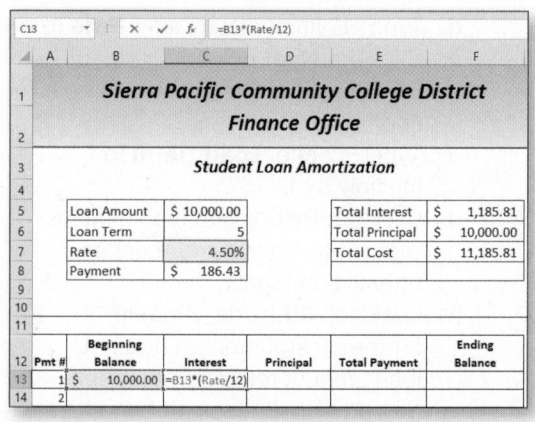

Figure 2-93 The interest formula

E2-146

m. Type =, click cell **C13**, type +, click cell **D13**, and then press **Enter**. The value matches the amount in cell **C8**.

n. Select cell **F13**. The ending balance is the beginning balance minus the principal payment. The interest is part of the cost of the loan.

o. Type =, click cell **B13**, type−, click cell **D13**, and then press **Enter**. The ending balance is $9,851.07.

B13	=Loan_Amount
C13	=B13*(Rate/12)
D13	=Payment−C13
E13	=C13+D13
F13	=B13−D13

7. Fill data and copy formulas.

a. Select cells **A13:A14**. This is a series with an increment of 1.

b. Drag the *Fill* pointer to reach cell **A72**. This sets 60 payments for a five-year loan term.

c. Select cell **B14**. The beginning balance for the second payment is the ending balance for the first payment.

d. Type =, click cell **F13**, and press **Enter**.

e. Double-click the *Fill* pointer for cell **B14** to fill the formula down to row **72**. The results are zero (displayed as a hyphen in Accounting Number Format) until the rest of the schedule is complete.

f. Select cells **C13:F13**.

g. Double-click the *Fill* pointer at cell **F13**. All of the formulas are filled (copied) to row **72** (Figure 2-94).

h. Scroll to see the values in row **72**. The loan balance reaches 0.

i. Press **Ctrl+Home**.

	Pmt #	Beginning Balance	Interest	Principal	Total Payment	Ending Balance
12						
13	1	$ 10,000.00	$ 37.50	$ 148.93	$ 186.43	$ 9,851.07
14	2	$ 9,851.07	$ 36.94	$ 149.49	$ 186.43	$ 9,701.58
15	3	$ 9,701.58	$ 36.38	$ 150.05	$ 186.43	$ 9,551.53
16	4	$ 9,551.53	$ 35.82	$ 150.61	$ 186.43	$ 9,400.92
17	5	$ 9,400.92	$ 35.25	$ 151.18	$ 186.43	$ 9,249.74
18	6	$ 9,249.74	$ 34.69	$ 151.74	$ 186.43	$ 9,098.00
19	7	$ 9,098.00	$ 34.12	$ 152.31	$ 186.43	$ 8,945.69
20	8	$ 8,945.69	$ 33.55	$ 152.88	$ 186.43	$ 8,792.80
21	9	$ 8,792.80	$ 32.97	$ 153.46	$ 186.43	$ 8,639.35
22	10	$ 8,639.35	$ 32.40	$ 154.03	$ 186.43	$ 8,485.31
23	11	$ 8,485.31	$ 31.82	$ 154.61	$ 186.43	$ 8,330.70
24	12	$ 8,330.70	$ 31.24	$ 155.19	$ 186.43	$ 8,175.51
25	13	$ 8,175.51	$ 30.66	$ 155.77	$ 186.43	$ 8,019.74
26	14	$ 8,019.74	$ 30.07	$ 156.36	$ 186.43	$ 7,863.38
27	15	$ 7,863.38	$ 29.49	$ 156.94	$ 186.43	$ 7,706.44
28	16	$ 7,706.44	$ 28.90	$ 157.53	$ 186.43	$ 7,548.91

60	48	$ 2,361.15	$ 8.85	$ 177.58	$ 186.43	$ 2,183.57
61	49	$ 2,183.57	$ 8.19	$ 178.24	$ 186.43	$ 2,005.33
62	50	$ 2,005.33	$ 7.52	$ 178.91	$ 186.43	$ 1,826.42
63	51	$ 1,826.42	$ 6.85	$ 179.58	$ 186.43	$ 1,646.84
64	52	$ 1,646.84	$ 6.18	$ 180.25	$ 186.43	$ 1,466.58
65	53	$ 1,466.58	$ 5.50	$ 180.93	$ 186.43	$ 1,285.65
66	54	$ 1,285.65	$ 4.82	$ 181.61	$ 186.43	$ 1,104.05
67	55	$ 1,104.05	$ 4.14	$ 182.29	$ 186.43	$ 921.76
68	56	$ 921.76	$ 3.46	$ 182.97	$ 186.43	$ 738.78
69	57	$ 738.78	$ 2.77	$ 183.66	$ 186.43	$ 555.12
70	58	$ 555.12	$ 2.08	$ 184.35	$ 186.43	$ 370.77
71	59	$ 370.77	$ 1.39	$ 185.04	$ 186.43	$ 185.73
72	60	$ 185.73	$ 0.70	$ 185.73	$ 186.43	$ 0.00

Figure 2-94 Formulas copied down columns

8. Build a multiplication formula.

a. Click the **Fees & Credit** sheet tab and select cell **F7**. Credit hours times number of sections times the fee calculates the total fees from a course.

b. Type =, click cell **C7**, type *, click cell **D7**, type *, click cell **E7**, and then press **Enter**. No parentheses are necessary because multiplication is done in left to right order (Figure 2-95).

c. Double-click the *Fill* pointer for cell **F7** to copy the formula.

d. Verify that cells **F7:F18** are **Currency** format. Set a single bottom border for cell **F18**.

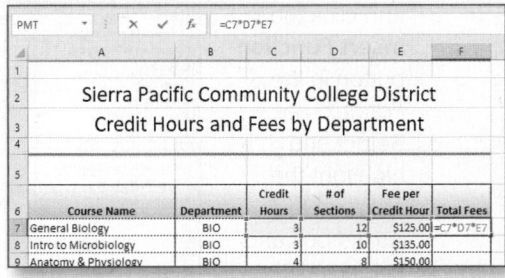

Figure 2-95 Formula to calculate total fees per course

9. Use *SUMIF* to calculate fees by department.
 a. Select cell **C26**.
 b. Click the **Math & Trig** button [*Formulas* tab, *Function Library* group] and select **SUMIF**.
 c. Click the **Range** box and select cells **B7:B18**. This range will be matched against the criteria.
 d. Press **F4** (**FN+F4**) to make the reference absolute.
 e. Click the **Criteria** box and select cell **B26**.
 f. Click the **Sum_range** box, select cells **F7:F18**, and press **F4** (**FN+F4**).
 g. Click **OK**. Total fees for the Biology department are 13350 (Figure 2-96).

Figure 2-96 *Function Arguments* dialog box for *SUMIF*

10. Copy a *SUMIF* function.
 a. Click cell **C26** and drag its *Fill* pointer to copy the formula to cells **C27:C29** without formatting to preserve the borders (Figure 2-97).
 b. Format cells **C26:C29** as **Currency**.

11. Use *SUMPRODUCT* and trace an error.
 a. Select cell **D26** and click the **Formulas** tab.
 b. Click the **Math & Trig** button in the *Function Library* group and select **SUMPRODUCT**.
 c. Click the **Array1** box and select cells **C7:C9**, credit hours for courses in the Biology Department.
 d. Click the **Array2** box and select cells **D7:D9**, the number of sections for the Biology Department.
 e. Click **OK**. The Biology Department offered 98 total credit hours.
 f. Click cell **D26** and point to its **Trace Error** button. The formula omits adjacent cells in the worksheet but it is correct.
 g. Click the **Trace Error** button and select **Ignore Error**.

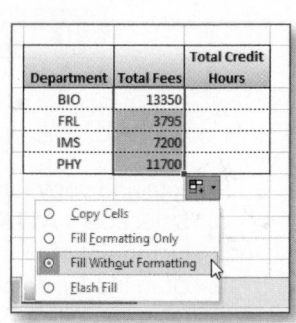

Figure 2-97 Formula is copied without formatting

12. Copy and edit *SUMPRODUCT*.
 a. Click cell **D26** and drag its *Fill* pointer to copy the formula to cells **D27:D29** without formatting to preserve the borders.
 b. Click cell **D27** and click the **Insert Function** button in the *Formula* bar.
 c. Select and highlight the range in the *Array1* box and select cells **C10:C12**. The range you select replaces the range in the dialog box (Figure 2-98).

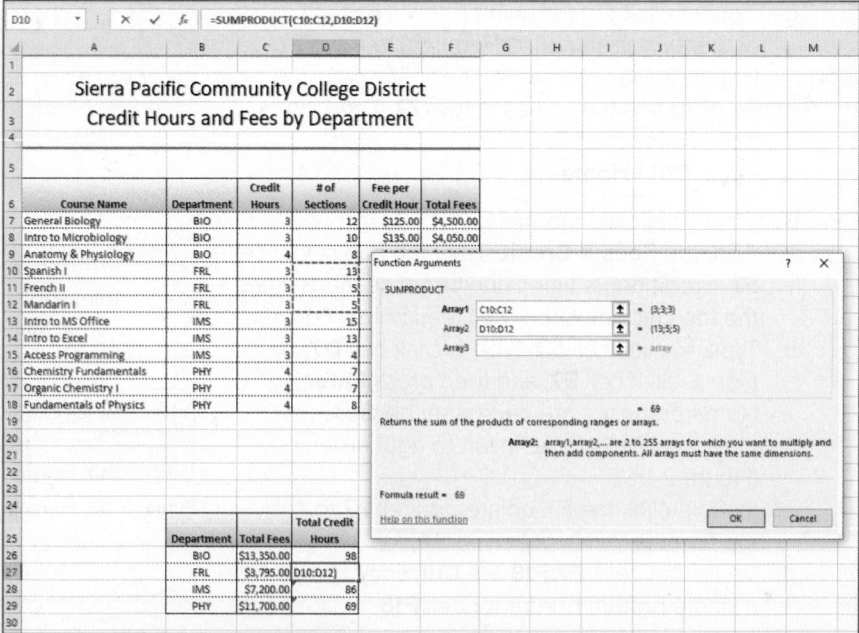

Figure 2-98 Replace the *ArrayN* arguments

d. Select the range in the *Array2* box and select cells **D10:D12**.

e. Click **OK**.

f. Edit and complete the formulas in cells **D28:D29** and ignore errors.

13. Insert the current date as a function.

 a. Select cell **F20**.

 b. Type =to and press **Tab** to select the function.

 c. Press **Enter**.

 d. Press **Ctrl+Home**.

14. Paste range names.

 a. Click the **New sheet** button in the sheet tab area.

 b. Name the new sheet **Range Names**.

 c. Press **F3** (**FN+F3**) to open the *Paste Name* dialog box.

 d. Click the **Paste List** button.

 e. *AutoFit* columns **A:B**.

15. Save and close the workbook (Figure 2-99).

Sierra Pacific Community College District
Finance Office

Student Loan Amortization

Loan Amount	$ 10,000.00		Total Interest	$	1,185.81
Loan Term	5		Total Principal	$	10,000.00
Rate	4.50%		Total Cost	$	11,185.81
Payment	$ 186.43				

Pmt #	Beginning Balance		Interest		Principal		Total Payment		Ending Balance
1	$	10,000.00	$	37.50	$	148.93	$	186.43	9,851.07
2	$	9,851.07	$	36.94	$	149.49	$	186.43	9,701.58
3	$	9,701.58	$	36.38	$	150.05	$	186.43	9,551.53
4	$	9,551.53	$	35.82	$	150.61	$	186.43	9,400.92
5	$	9,400.92	$	35.25	$	151.18	$	186.43	9,249.74
6	$	9,249.74	$	34.69	$	151.74	$	186.43	9,098.00
7	$	9,098.00	$	34.12	$	152.31	$	186.43	8,945.69
8	$	8,945.69	$	33.55	$	152.88	$	186.43	8,792.80
9	$	8,792.80	$	32.97	$	153.46	$	186.43	8,639.35
10	$	8,639.35	$	32.40	$	154.03	$	186.43	8,485.31
11	$	8,485.31	$	31.82	$	154.61	$	186.43	8,330.70
12	$	8,330.70	$	31.24	$	155.19	$	186.43	8,175.51
13	$	8,175.51	$	30.66	$	155.77	$	186.43	8,019.74
14	$	8,019.74	$	30.07	$	156.36	$	186.43	7,863.38
15	$	7,863.38	$	29.49	$	156.94	$	186.43	7,706.44
16	$	7,706.44	$	28.90	$	157.53	$	186.43	7,548.91
17	$	7,548.91	$	28.31	$	158.12	$	186.43	7,390.79
18	$	7,390.79	$	27.72	$	158.71	$	186.43	7,232.07
19	$	7,232.07	$	27.12	$	159.31	$	186.43	7,072.76
20	$	7,072.76	$	26.52	$	159.91	$	186.43	6,912.86
21	$	6,912.86	$	25.92	$	160.51	$	186.43	6,752.35
22	$	6,752.35	$	25.32	$	161.11	$	186.43	6,591.24
23	$	6,591.24	$	24.72	$	161.71	$	186.43	6,429.53
24	$	6,429.53	$	24.11	$	162.32	$	186.43	6,267.21
25	$	6,267.21	$	23.50	$	162.93	$	186.43	6,104.28
26	$	6,104.28	$	22.89	$	163.54	$	186.43	5,940.74
27	$	5,940.74	$	22.28	$	164.15	$	186.43	5,776.59
28	$	5,776.59	$	21.66	$	164.77	$	186.43	5,611.82
29	$	5,611.82	$	21.04	$	165.39	$	186.43	5,446.44
30	$	5,446.44	$	20.42	$	166.01	$	186.43	5,280.43

Sierra Pacific Community College District
Credit Hours and Fees by Department

Course Name	Department	Credit Hours	# of Sections	Fee per Credit Hour	Total Fees
General Biology	BIO	3	12	$125.00	$4,500.00
Intro to Microbiology	BIO	3	10	$135.00	$4,050.00
Anatomy & Physiology	BIO	4	8	$150.00	$4,800.00
Spanish I	FRL	3	13	$55.00	$2,145.00
French II	FRL	3	5	$55.00	$825.00
Mandarin I	FRL	3	5	$55.00	$825.00
Intro to MS Office	IMS	3	15	$75.00	$3,375.00
Intro to Excel	IMS	3	13	$75.00	$2,925.00
Access Programming	IMS	3	4	$75.00	$900.00
Chemistry Fundamentals	PHY	4	7	$125.00	$3,500.00
Organic Chemistry I	PHY	4	7	$150.00	$4,200.00
Fundamentals of Physics	PHY	4	8	$125.00	$4,000.00

Today

Department	Total Fees	Total Credit Hours
BIO	$13,350.00	98
FRL	$3,795.00	69
IMS	$7,200.00	96
PHY	$11,700.00	88

Loan_Amount	='Student Loan'!C5
Loan_Term	='Student Loan'!C6
Payment	='Student Loan'!C8
Rate	='Student Loan'!C7
Total_Cost	='Student Loan'!F7
Total_Interest	='Student Loan'!F5
Total_Principal	='Student Loan'!F6

	Beginning Balance	Interest	Principal	Total Payment	Ending Balance
31	$ 5,280.43	$ 19.80	$ 166.63	$ 186.43	$ 5,113.80
32	$ 5,113.80	$ 19.18	$ 167.25	$ 186.43	$ 4,946.55
33	$ 4,946.55	$ 18.55	$ 167.88	$ 186.43	$ 4,778.67
34	$ 4,778.67	$ 17.92	$ 168.51	$ 186.43	$ 4,610.16
35	$ 4,610.16	$ 17.29	$ 169.14	$ 186.43	$ 4,441.01
36	$ 4,441.01	$ 16.65	$ 169.78	$ 186.43	$ 4,271.24
37	$ 4,271.24	$ 16.02	$ 170.41	$ 186.43	$ 4,100.82
38	$ 4,100.82	$ 15.38	$ 171.05	$ 186.43	$ 3,929.77
39	$ 3,929.77	$ 14.74	$ 171.69	$ 186.43	$ 3,758.08
40	$ 3,758.08	$ 14.09	$ 172.34	$ 186.43	$ 3,585.74
41	$ 3,585.74	$ 13.45	$ 172.98	$ 186.43	$ 3,412.76
42	$ 3,412.76	$ 12.80	$ 173.63	$ 186.43	$ 3,239.13
43	$ 3,239.13	$ 12.15	$ 174.28	$ 186.43	$ 3,064.84
44	$ 3,064.84	$ 11.49	$ 174.94	$ 186.43	$ 2,889.91
45	$ 2,889.91	$ 10.84	$ 175.59	$ 186.43	$ 2,714.31
46	$ 2,714.31	$ 10.18	$ 176.25	$ 186.43	$ 2,538.06
47	$ 2,538.06	$ 9.52	$ 176.91	$ 186.43	$ 2,361.15
48	$ 2,361.15	$ 8.85	$ 177.58	$ 186.43	$ 2,183.57
49	$ 2,183.57	$ 8.19	$ 178.24	$ 186.43	$ 2,005.33
50	$ 2,005.33	$ 7.52	$ 178.91	$ 186.43	$ 1,826.42
51	$ 1,826.42	$ 6.85	$ 179.58	$ 186.43	$ 1,646.84
52	$ 1,646.84	$ 6.18	$ 180.25	$ 186.43	$ 1,466.58
53	$ 1,466.58	$ 5.50	$ 180.93	$ 186.43	$ 1,285.65
54	$ 1,285.65	$ 4.82	$ 181.61	$ 186.43	$ 1,104.05
55	$ 1,104.05	$ 4.14	$ 182.29	$ 186.43	$ 921.76
56	$ 921.76	$ 3.46	$ 182.97	$ 186.43	$ 738.78
57	$ 738.78	$ 2.77	$ 183.66	$ 186.43	$ 555.12
58	$ 555.12	$ 2.08	$ 184.35	$ 186.43	$ 370.77
59	$ 370.77	$ 1.39	$ 185.04	$ 186.43	$ 185.73
60	$ 185.73	$ 0.70	$ 185.73	$ 186.43	$ 0.00

Figure 2-99 Excel 2-3 completed

Independent Project 2-4

Central Sierra Insurance (CSI) sets bonus percentages based on commissions earned by each agent and calculates totals by branch office. This workbook also tracks fundraising efforts of employees for a community event.
[Student Learning Outcomes 2.1, 2.2, 2.3, 2.5, 2.6, 2.7]

File Needed: ***CentralSierra-02.xlsx*** *(Student data files are available in the* Library *of your SIMnet account.)*
Completed Project File Name: *[your initials]* **Excel 2-4.xlsx**

Skills Covered in This Project

- Create, copy, and edit formulas.
- Name cell ranges.
- Set mathematical order of operations.

- Set cell references to be absolute.
- Use the *NOW* function.
- Use *HLOOKUP* and *VLOOKUP* functions.
- Use the *SUMIF* function.
- Build an *IF* function.

1. Open the **CentralSierra-02.xlsx** workbook from your student data files and save it as [your initials] Excel 2-4. Review the data on each sheet.

2. Select the **Tables** sheet, select cells **A6:B10**, and create range names using the **Create from Selection** button [*Formulas* tab, *Defined Names* group].

3. Select cells **B1:F2** and click the **Name** box. Name the selection H_Rates. Note that the first row is arranged in ascending order.

4. Create an *HLOOKUP* function to display the bonus rate.
 a. Click the **Commissions** sheet tab and select cell **F5**.
 b. Start the *HLOOKUP* function and use cell **E5** as the *lookup_value*.
 c. For the *table_array* argument, use the **H_Rates** range.
 d. Use the second row for the *row_index_num* argument (Figure 2-100).

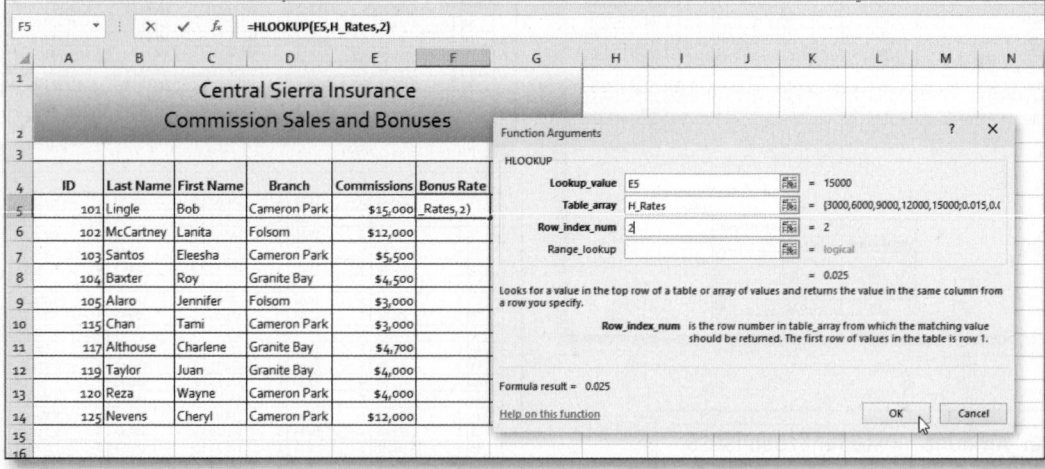

Figure 2-100 *HLOOKUP* function to display bonus rate

5. Format the results as **Percent Style** with two decimal places.

6. Copy the formula in cell **F5** to cells **F6:F14**.

7. Set order of operations to calculate total earnings.
 a. Select cell **G5**.
 b. Build a formula to add the commissions amount (E5) to the commissions amount times the rate (F5*E5).
 c. Copy the formula in cell **G5** to cells **G6:G14**.

8. Create and copy a *SUMIF* function to calculate total earnings by branch office.
 a. Select cell **E18**.
 b. Start the *SUMIF* function with cells **D5:D14** as the *Range* argument.
 c. Set the *Criteria* argument as a relative reference to cell **C18**.
 d. Select cells **G5:G14** for the *Sum_range* argument and make the references absolute.
 e. Copy the formula in cell **E18** to cells **E19:E20** without formatting to preserve borders.
 f. Format cells **E18:E21** as **Currency**.

9. Total the earnings in cell **E21**.

10. Create and format the current date.
 a. Select cell **G23** and insert the *NOW* function.
 b. Select cell **G23** and click the **Number** group launcher [*Home* tab]. On the *Number* tab, select the **Date** category.
 c. Scroll the *Type* list to find the date that displays the month spelled out, the date, a comma, and a four-digit year (Figure 2-101).
 d. Click **OK**. Press **Ctrl+Home**.

Figure 2-101 Date format selected

11. Create and copy a *VLOOKUP* function to display goals for each funding source.
 a. Click the **Family Day** sheet tab and select cell **F6**.
 b. Start the *VLOOKUP* function and use cell **E6** as the *lookup_value*.
 c. Click the **Tables** sheet tab for the *table_array* argument and use cells **A6:B10**. The data is sorted by the first column in ascending order.
 d. Use the second column as the *col_index_num* argument. The *range_lookup* argument is empty.
 e. Copy the formula in cell **F6** to cells **F7:F20** without formatting to preserve the fill color.
 f. Format cells **F6:F20** as **Currency** with no decimal places.

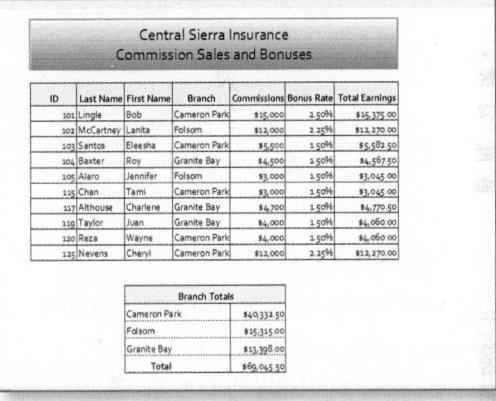

12. Create and copy an *IF* function.
 a. Select cell **H6** and start an *IF* function.
 b. Type a *logical_argument* to determine if cell **G6** is greater than or equal to (>=) cell **F6**.
 c. Type Yes as the *Value_if_true* argument and No as the *Value_if_false* argument.
 d. Copy the formula in cell **H6** to cells **H7:H20** without formatting to maintain the fill color.
 e. Center align cells **H6:H20**.
 f. Press **Ctrl+Home**.

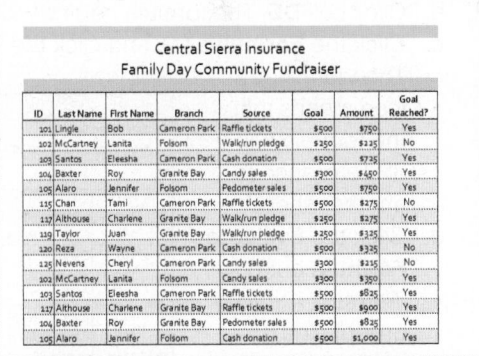

13. Insert a new sheet at the end of the tab names and paste the range names starting in cell A1. *AutoFit* columns **A:B** and name the worksheet as Range Names.

14. Save and close the workbook (Figure 2-102).

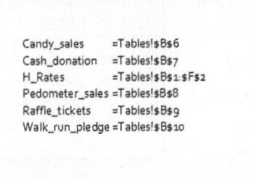

Figure 2-102 Excel 2-4 completed

Independent Project 2-5

San Diego Sailing keeps data about its fleet of rental and charter boats. One of the sheets is missing a piece of data and another sheet has circular reference errors. You will complete work on these sheets, calculate projected rates for each boat, and build basic statistics about past rentals.
[Student Learning Outcomes 2.1, 2.2, 2.3, 2.4, 2.5, 2.6, 2.7]

File Needed: **SanDiegoSailing-02.xlsx** (Student data files are available in the Library of your SIMnet account.)
Completed Project File Name: **[your initials] Excel 2-5.xlsx**

Skills Covered in This Project

- Create and copy formulas.
- Use formula auditing tools.
- Set mathematical order of operations.

- Use relative, mixed, and 3D cell references.
- Use COUNTIF and SUMIF functions.
- Build an IF formula.
- Insert the TODAY function.

1. Open the **SanDiegoSailing-02.xlsx** workbook from your student data files. When a workbook has a circular reference, a message box appears immediately as you open it (Figure 2-103).

> **Microsoft Excel** ✕
>
> ⚠ There are one or more circular references where a formula refers to its own cell either directly or indirectly. This might cause them to calculate incorrectly.
>
> Try removing or changing these references, or moving the formulas to different cells.
>
> [OK] [Help]

Figure 2-103 Circular reference message

2. Click **OK** in the message box. The *Status* bar indicates the workbook contains *Circular References*.

3. Save the workbook as [your initials] Excel 2-5. Review the data on each sheet.

4. Use formula auditing tools.
 a. Click the **New Prices** sheet tab. The *Status* bar identifies a cell that has a circular reference. The cells in column D include circular references.
 b. Click cell **D5**. The formula begins with 1 plus the value in cell D5, the circular reference.
 c. Click the **Formulas** tab and click the **Trace Precedents** button in the *Formula Auditing* group. The worksheet icon means that the formula has a 3D reference to another sheet.
 d. Click the **Evaluate Formula** button [*Formula Auditing* group]. The circular reference is identified as cell D5 (Figure 2-104).
 e. Click **Close** and click the **Remove Arrows** button [*Formula Auditing* group].

▲	A	B	C	D	E	F	G	H	I	J	K	L
1	San Diego Sailing											
2	New Prices at 5% and 10% Increases											
3					Half-Day		Full Day					
4	Boat ID	Make and Model	Length	5%	10%	5%	10%					
5	1010	Catalina Wave	28'4"	$0.00								
6	1015	Catalina Sky	28'4"	$0.00								
7	1146	Hunter Ray	33'6"	$0.00								
8	1150	Capri MKZ	24'8"	$0.00								
9	1152	Capri 22 Mk II	24'8"	$0.00								
10	1164	Capri 22 Mk II	24'8"	$0.00								
11	1168	Hunter 33	33'6"	$0.00								
12	1175	Beneteau 40	39'10"	$0.00								
13	1180	Beneteau 373	36'11"	$0.00								
14	1185	Hunter Sea	35'6"	$0.00								
15	1190	Beneteau 373	36'11"	$0.00								
16	1200	Beneteau 373	36'11"	$0.00								
17	1205	Beneteau 40	39'10"	$0.00								
18	1225	Hunter Sea	35'6"	$0.00								
19	1230	Catalina Wave	28'4"	$0.00								
20												

> **Evaluate Formula** ? ✕
>
> Reference: Evaluation:
> 'New Prices'!D5 = (1+D5)*Fleet!$H5
>
> This is a circular reference and may not evaluate to a result you expect.
>
> [Evaluate] [Step In] [Step Out] [Close]

Figure 2-104 Evaluate Formula dialog box

5. Edit and copy a formula with mixed references.
 a. Edit the formula in cell **D5** to show D$4 instead of "D5." The formula should multiply one plus the percentage value in cell D4 by the current rate on the **Fleet** sheet ($H5). With an absolute reference to row 4 and column H on the **Fleet** sheet, you can copy the formula down the column (Figure 2-105).

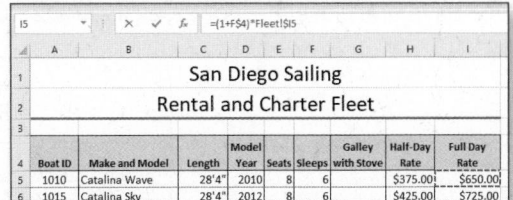

Figure 2-105 Mixed reference in the edited formula

 b. Copy the formula in cell **D5** to cells **D6:D19** without formatting to preserve the border. When the circular reference message box opens, click **OK**.
 c. Select cells **D5:D19** and drag the *Fill* pointer to copy the formulas to cells **E5:E19**.
 d. Click cell **E6**. The formula is adjusted to use the percentage value in cell E4 in place of cell D4. Note also that the reference on the **Fleet** sheet ($H6) is adjusted to show the correct row.

6. Build a formula with mixed references.
 a. Click cell **F5** and type =(1+ to start the formula.
 b. Select cell **F4** and make it an absolute reference to the row but not the column.
 c. Type)* for the closing parenthesis and multiplication.
 d. Click cell **I5** on the **Fleet** sheet, and make the reference absolute for the column but not the row (Figure 2-106).

Figure 2-106 Mixed references in the new formula

 e. Copy the formula down column **F** without formatting to preserve the border.
 f. Format cells **F5:F19** as **Currency** and then copy cells **F5:F19** to cells **G5:G19**.

7. Build an *IF* function formula.
 a. Click the **Fleet** sheet tab and select cell **G5**. Rental boats with a stove in the galley must seat 8 or more people.
 b. Create an *IF* function in which the *logical_test* argument determines if there are 8 or more seats.
 c. Use Yes for the *value_if_true* argument. Use No for the *value_if_false* argument. (If you type the formula, enclose the text arguments within quotation marks.)
 d. Copy the formula to cells **G6:G19** without formatting and then center the data in column G.

8. Insert the *TODAY* function in cell **B21**. Format the date to show the month spelled out, the date, and four digits for the year (January 1, 2020).

9. Create a division formula.
 a. Click the **Bookings** sheet tab and select cell **F5**. Calculate average revenue per passenger by dividing the fee by the number of passengers.
 b. Build the division formula.
 c. Copy the formula in cell **F5** to cells **F6:F19**.

10. Create and copy a *COUNTIF* function to count bookings by boat manufacturer.
 a. Select cell **D27**.
 b. Start the *COUNTIF* function from the *Statistical* category by clicking the **More Functions** button in the *Function Library* group.
 c. Use cells **C5:C19** as the *Range* argument.
 d. Set a *Criteria* argument that will select all boats in the "Beneteau" group. The criteria is **ben***. If you type the formula, include quotation marks.
 e. Copy the formula in cell **D27** to cells **D28:D30**.
 f. Edit the criteria in each copied formula in cells **D28:D30** to reflect the boat make.

11. Create and copy a *SUMIF* function to calculate total revenue by boat make.
 a. Select cell **E27**.
 b. Start the *SUMIF* function with cells **C5:C19** as the *Range*.

c. Set the *Criteria* argument to ben*.
d. Set the *Sum_range* argument to cells **E5:E19**.
e. Copy the formula in cell **E27** to cells **E28:E30**.
f. Edit the criteria in each copied formula in cells **E28:E30** as needed.

12. Complete formatting.
 a. Apply the **Currency** format to all values that represent money.
 b. Format the labels in cells **A1:A2** as **18** point.
 c. Select cells **A1:F2** and click the **Alignment** launcher [*Home* tab, *Alignment* group]. Center the labels across the selection.
 d. Merge and center the label in cell **C25** over cells **C25:E25** and format it at **16** points.
 e. Bold and center the labels in rows **4** and **26**.
 f. Select cells **A4:F19** and apply **All Borders**. Do the same for cells **C25:E30**.
 g. Center the page horizontally.

13. Save and close the workbook (Figure 2-107).

San Diego Sailing Bookings
Revenue per Passenger

Date	Boat ID	Make and Model	# of Passengers	Total Fees	Revenue per Passenger
4/5/2020	1010	Catalina Wave	4	$525.00	$131.25
4/8/2020	1015	Catalina Sky	6	$850.00	$141.67
4/11/2020	1146	Hunter Ray	6	$500.00	$83.33
4/14/2020	1150	Capri MKZ	6	$525.00	$87.50
4/17/2020	1152	Capri 22 Mk II	4	$325.00	$81.25
4/20/2020	1164	Capri 22 Mk II	3	$475.00	$158.33
4/23/2020	1168	Hunter 33	6	$725.00	$120.83
4/26/2020	1175	Beneteau 40	10	$850.00	$85.00
4/29/2020	1180	Beneteau 373	8	$350.00	$43.75
5/2/2020	1185	Hunter Sea	8	$650.00	$81.25
5/5/2020	1190	Beneteau 373	10	$625.00	$62.50
5/8/2020	1200	Beneteau 373	8	$725.00	$90.63
5/11/2020	1205	Beneteau 40	12	$850.00	$70.83
5/14/2020	1225	Hunter Sea	8	$725.00	$90.63
5/17/2020	1230	Catalina Wave	6	$675.00	$112.50

Bookings by Make

	Count	Total Revenue
Beneteau	5	$3,400.00
Capri	3	$1,325.00
Catalina	3	$2,050.00
Hunter	4	$2,600.00

San Diego Sailing
Rental and Charter Fleet

Boat ID	Make and Model	Length	Model Year	Seats	Sleeps	Galley with Stove	Half-Day Rate	Full Day Rate
1010	Catalina Wave	28'4"	2010	8	6	Yes	$375.00	$650.00
1015	Catalina Sky	28'4"	2012	8	6	Yes	$425.00	$725.00
1146	Hunter Ray	33'6"	2014	10	6	Yes	$350.00	$500.00
1150	Capri MKZ	24'8"	2011	6	4	No	$325.00	$500.00
1152	Capri 22 Mk II	24'8"	2016	6	4	No	$325.00	$500.00
1164	Capri 22 Mk II	24'8"	2016	6	4	No	$325.00	$500.00
1168	Hunter 33	33'6"	2018	10	6	Yes	$425.00	$725.00
1175	Beneteau 40	39'10"	2018	12	6	Yes	$489.00	$750.00
1180	Beneteau 373	36'11"	2017	10	6	Yes	$369.00	$725.00
1185	Hunter Sea	35'6"	2009	10	6	Yes	$349.00	$550.00
1190	Beneteau 373	36'11"	2017	10	6	Yes	$369.00	$625.00
1200	Beneteau 373	36'11"	2017	10	6	Yes	$369.00	$625.00
1205	Beneteau 40	39'10"	2018	12	6	Yes	$489.00	$750.00
1225	Hunter Sea	35'6"	2012	10	6	Yes	$349.00	$725.00
1230	Catalina Wave	28'4"	2019	8	6	Yes	$439.00	$675.00

January 1, 2020

San Diego Sailing
New Prices at 5% and 10% Increases

Boat ID	Make and Model	Length	Half-Day 5%	Half-Day 10%	Full Day 5%	Full Day 10%
1010	Catalina Wave	28'4"	$393.75	$412.50	$682.50	$715.00
1015	Catalina Sky	28'4"	$446.25	$467.50	$761.25	$797.50
1146	Hunter Ray	33'6"	$367.50	$385.00	$525.00	$550.00
1150	Capri MKZ	24'8"	$341.25	$357.50	$525.00	$550.00
1152	Capri 22 Mk II	24'8"	$341.25	$357.50	$525.00	$550.00
1164	Capri 22 Mk II	24'8"	$341.25	$357.50	$525.00	$550.00
1168	Hunter 33	33'6"	$446.25	$467.50	$761.25	$797.50
1175	Beneteau 40	39'10"	$513.45	$537.90	$787.50	$825.00
1180	Beneteau 373	36'11"	$387.45	$405.90	$761.25	$797.50
1185	Hunter Sea	35'6"	$366.45	$383.90	$577.50	$605.00
1190	Beneteau 373	36'11"	$387.45	$405.90	$656.25	$687.50
1200	Beneteau 373	36'11"	$387.45	$405.90	$656.25	$687.50
1205	Beneteau 40	39'10"	$513.45	$537.90	$787.50	$825.00
1225	Hunter Sea	35'6"	$366.45	$383.90	$761.25	$797.50
1230	Catalina Wave	28'4"	$460.95	$482.90	$708.75	$742.50

Figure 2-107 Excel 2-5 completed

Independent Project 2-6

Placer Hills Real Estate has regional offices throughout central California, and each office tracks its listings and sales data. In the workbook, you need to insert agent names, calculate market days, and determine sale price as a percentage of list price. You also calculate summary statistics.
[Student Learning Outcomes 2.1, 2.3, 2.5, 2.6]

File Needed: **PlacerHills-02.xlsx** [Student data files are available in the Library of your SIMnet account.]
Completed Project File Name: **[your initials] Excel 2-6.xlsx**

Skills Covered in This Project

- Use the *VLOOKUP* function.
- Create and copy formulas.
- Use dates in a subtraction formula.
- Name cell ranges.
- Use relative and 3D cell references in formulas.
- Use *AVERAGE*, *MAX*, *MIN*, and *COUNT*.
- Use *COUNTIF*.

1. Open the **PlacerHills-02.xlsx** workbook from your student data files and save it as [your initials] Excel 2-6. Review the data on each sheet.

2. Use the *VLOOKUP* function to insert the agent's last name in a new column on the **Listings** sheet.
 a. Insert a column at column **D**.
 b. Type Name in cell **D3** and click cell **D4**.
 c. Start a *VLOOKUP* function and set the agent ID (C4) as the *lookup_value* argument.
 d. Use an absolute reference to cells A2:B7 on the **Agents** sheet for the *table_array* argument. Do not include column titles in a table array, and note that the array is sorted in ascending order by the first column.
 e. Enter 2 for the *col_index_num* argument to display the agent's last name and leave the *range_lookup* argument blank.
 f. Copy the formula without formatting to preserve borders and display each agent's name. *AutoFit* column **D**.

3. Build a subtraction formula with dates.
 a. Select cell **O4** on the **Listings** sheet. Subtract the older date from the later date to determine the number of days on the market.
 b. Type = and click cell **N4**, the sold date.
 c. Type − for subtraction and click cell **B4**, the listing date.
 d. Press **Enter**. The result is formatted as a date (Figure 2-108).

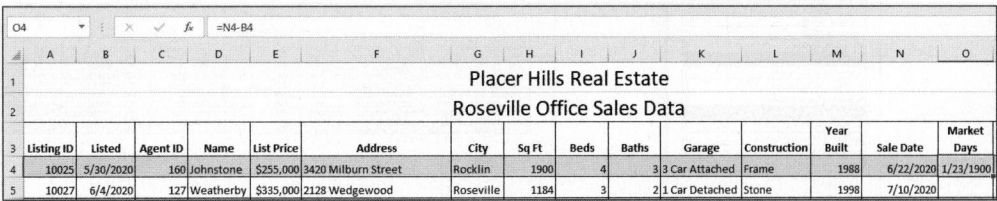

Figure 2-108 Result is formatted as a date

 e. Copy the formula in cell **O4** to cells **O5:O12** without formatting to preserve the fill color.
 f. Format cells **O4:O12** as **General**.

4. Calculate the sold price as a percentage of the list price.
 a. Select cell **Q4** and type =.
 b. Build a formula to divide the selling price by the list price.
 c. Copy the formula without formatting to preserve fill and format the column as **Percent Style** with **two** decimal places.

5. Name cell ranges.
 a. Select cells **E3:E12**.
 b. Press **Ctrl** and select cells **G3:G12**, **L3:L12**, and **P3:P12**.
 c. Click the **Create from Selection** button [*Formulas* tab, *Defined Names* group] and use the **Top row** to create range names.
 d. Press **Ctrl+Home**.
 e. Format this sheet to fit one page, landscape orientation.
 f. Insert a footer that displays the file name in the right section.

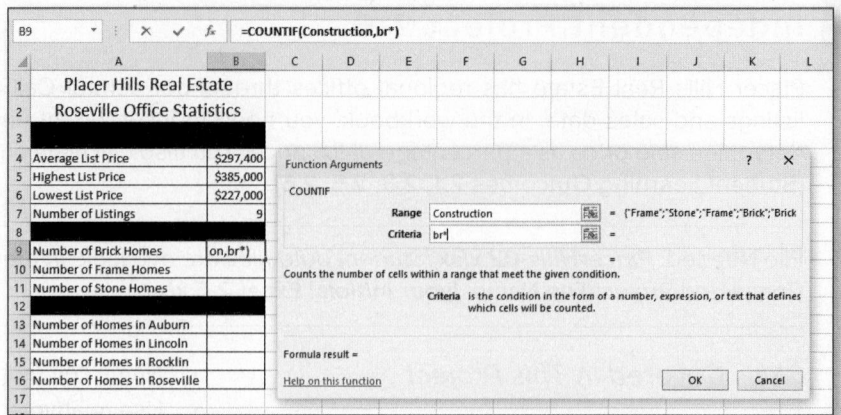

Figure 2-109 Arguments for *COUNTIF*

6. Calculate statistics for the agency.
 a. Click the **Statistics** sheet tab and select cell **B4**.
 b. Click the **AutoSum** button arrow and choose *Average*. No assumed range displays.
 c. Press **F3** (**FN+F3**) to open the *Paste Name* dialog box.
 d. Choose **List_Price** and click **OK**. Press **Enter**.
 e. Continue on this sheet to calculate the highest and lowest list prices as well as the number of listings. Be careful to select the correct range name, and remove **Currency** format as needed.

7. Use *COUNTIF* to calculate statistics.
 a. Select cell **B9**.
 b. Click the **More Functions** button in the *Function Library* group, choose **Statistical**, and select **COUNTIF**.
 c. Use the range name **Construction** for the *Range* argument (Figure 2-109).
 d. Type br* for the *Criteria* and click **OK**.
 e. Copy the formula and edit the criteria for cells **B10:B11**.
 f. Start a new *COUNTIF* function in cell **B13** with the **City** range name and wildcard criteria to locate Auburn. Then copy and edit the formula for cells **B14:B16**. Be sure to use criteria that will distinguish between city names that begin with "ro."

8. Center the sheet horizontally. Add a footer with the file name in the center section.

9. Save and close the workbook (Figure 2-110).

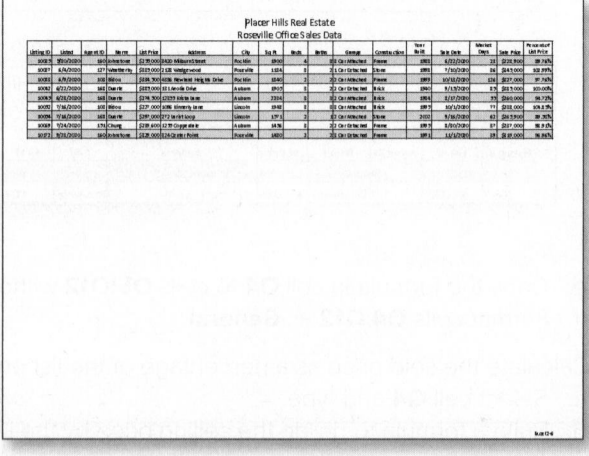

Figure 2-110 Excel 2-6 completed

Improve It Project 2-7

Mary's Rentals serves the light-to-heavy equipment rental needs of contractors, as well as the general public. Data has been imported from an Access database and needs to be handled for better management in Excel. Once that is done, you can calculate several statistics for the company.
[Student Learning Outcomes 2.1, 2.3, 2.4, 2.5, 2.7]

File Needed: ***MarysRentals-02.xlsx*** *(Student data files are available in the* Library *of your SIMnet account.)*
Completed Project File Name: ***[your initials] Excel 2-7.xlsx***

Skills Covered in This Project

- Use formula auditing tools.
- Name cell ranges.
- Create, copy, and edit formulas.

- Use relative references and range names in formulas.
- Use *Statistical* functions.
- Use functions from the *Math & Trig* category.

1. Open the ***MarysRentals-02.xlsx*** workbook from your student data files and save it as [your initials] Excel 2-7. The *Equipment* sheet is an inventory of equipment available for rental.

2. Correct errors on the *Rentals* sheet.
 a. Click the **Rentals** tab. This data was imported from an Access database, and error triangles display in many cells.
 b. Select cells **A2:A47** and click the **Trace Error** button near cell A2 (Figure 2-111). This data was imported as text (labels) but should be set as values.
 c. Select **Convert to Number**. The data are formatted as values and are right-aligned.
 d. Repeat for cells **B2:C47**.
 e. Center align cells **E2:E47**. This column specifies whether the rental was daily, weekly, or monthly.
 f. Press **Ctrl+Home**.

3. Name cell ranges.
 a. Select cells **B1:B47**, press **Ctrl**, and select cells **E1:E47** and cells **I1:I47**.
 b. Create names from the selection [*Formulas* tab, *Defined Names* group].
 c. Press **Ctrl+Home**.

Figure 2-111 *Trace Error* button for a selected range

4. Create and copy a *SUMIF* function with a relative reference.
 a. Click the **Generators** sheet tab and select cell **C5**.
 b. Start the *SUMIF* function with *Equipment_ID* as the *Range* argument.
 c. The *Criteria* argument is cell **A5**.
 d. The *Sum_range* argument is the *Total_Cost* range.
 e. Copy the formula in cell **C5** to cells **C6:C7**. The relative cell reference to cell A5 is adjusted.
 f. Format cells **C5:C7** as **Currency** with no decimal places.

5. Build a custom border.
 a. Select cells **A4:C7**.
 b. Press **Ctrl+1** to open the *Format Cells* dialog box and click the **Border** tab.
 c. Click the **Outline** button in the *Presets* section.
 d. Click the dotted line style (second option, first column, just below *None*) in the *Style* section.

e. Click the middle horizontal position in the *Border* preview area.

f. Click the single solid line style (last option, first column) in the *Style* section.

g. Click the middle vertical position in the *Border* preview area (Figure 2-112).

h. Click **OK**.

6. Complete formatting.
 a. Apply bold and centering to cells **A4:C4**.
 b. Format cells **A1:A2** to **16** points.
 c. Select cells **A1:C2** and use **Center Across Selection**.
 d. Center the sheet horizontally.
 e. Insert a header with the file name in the right section.

Figure 2-112 Build a custom border in the *Format Cells* dialog box

7. Use *SUMIF* to calculate daily, weekly, and monthly income rentals.
 a. Click the **Income Data** sheet tab and select cell **B4**.
 b. Start the *SUMIF* function with **Type** as the *Range* argument.
 c. Type d for daily income as the *Criteria* argument. If you type the formula, remember to enclose the criteria within quotation marks.
 d. Use the **Total_Cost** range for the *Sum_range* argument.
 e. Enter *SUMIF* formulas in cells **B5:B6**, or copy and edit the formula in cell B4.
 f. Use *SUM* in cell **B7**.
 g. Format cells **B4:B7** as **Currency** with no decimal places.

8. Use *COUNTIF* to count rentals by type.
 a. Select cell **B9** and start the *COUNTIF* function from the *Statistical* category.
 b. Use the range name **Type** as the *Range* argument. The *Criteria* is d.
 c. Create a separate formula in cells **B10:B11**, or copy and edit the formula in cell B9.

9. Add a border and fill.
 a. Select cells **A3:B12**.
 b. Click the **Font** group launcher [*Home* tab] and click the **Border** tab.
 c. Click the **Outline** button in the *Presets* section.
 d. Click the single solid line style (last option, first column) in the *Style* section.
 e. Click the middle vertical position in the *Border* preview area.
 f. Click the dotted line style (second option, first column) in the *Style* section.
 g. Click the middle horizontal position in the *Border* preview area.
 h. Click **OK**.
 i. Select cells **A3:B3**, **A8:B8**, and **A12:B12**.
 j. Click the arrow with the **Fill Color** button and choose **Black, Text 1, Lighter 50%** (second column).
 k. Select cells **A1:B2** and use **Center Across Selection**.
 l. Increase the font size for cells **A1:B2** to **16**.
 m. Center the sheet horizontally.
 n. Insert a footer with the file name in the right section.

10. Save and close the workbook (Figure 2-113).

Mary's Rentals
Income Statistics

Daily Rental Income	$4,990
Weekly Rental Income	$4,745
Monthly Rental Income	$1,440
Total	$11,175
Number of Daily Rentals	33
Number of Weekly Rentals	11
Number of Monthly Rentals	2

Rental ID	Equipment ID	Customer ID	Date Out	Type	# of Units
2512	9863	27	04 Jan 20	D	1
2513	10235	30	04 Jan 20	D	3
2513	10389	30	04 Jan 20	D	3
2514	10236	102	05 Jan 20	D	1
2514	10237	102	05 Jan 20	D	1
2515	10283	83	05 Jan 20	W	1
2516	10047	15	06 Jan 20	D	4
2517	10103	21	06 Jan 20	W	1
2518	9863	102	07 Jan 20	W	1
2519	10015	44	07 Jan 20	D	3
2520	10368	71	07 Jan 20	D	2
2521	10426	17	08 Jan 20	D	4
2522	10237	56	09 Jan 20	W	1
2522	10425	56	09 Jan 20	W	1
2523	10428	8	09 Jan 20	D	2
2524	10015	31	10 Jan 20	D	1
2525	10368	124	10 Jan 20	D	3
2526	10235	111	10 Jan 20	D	1
2527	10015	30	12 Jan 20	D	3
2527	10047	30	12 Jan 20	D	3
2527	10235	30	12 Jan 20	D	3
2527	10283	30	12 Jan 20	D	3
2528	10236	39	12 Jan 20	W	1
2529	10389	27	13 Jan 20	D	2
2530	10235	94	13 Jan 20	D	1
2530	10427	94	13 Jan 20	D	1
2531	10283	15	15 Jan 20	W	1
2532	9863	75	15 Jan 20	D	1
2533	10103	62	15 Jan 20	M	1
2534	10426	88	15 Jan 20	D	1
2535	10428	91	16 Jan 20	D	1
2536	10047	46	17 Jan 20	W	1
2537	10235	102	17 Jan 20	D	1
2538	10237	83	17 Jan 20	D	3
2538	10389	83	17 Jan 20	D	3
2539	10368	51	17 Jan 20	D	1
2540	10426	21	17 Jan 20	D	1
2541	9863	58	17 Jan 20	D	1
2542	10015	31	19 Jan 20	M	1
2543	9863	44	19 Jan 20	W	1
2544	10368	124	19 Jan 20	W	1
2545	10235	27	19 Jan 20	D	2
2546	10425	111	20 Jan 20	D	3
2547	10426	30	20 Jan 20	W	1
2548	10427	115	20 Jan 20	D	2
2549	10236	94	20 Jan 20	D	2

Excel 2-7

Date Due	Rate	Total Cost
05 Jan 20	$160.00	$160.00
07 Jan 20	$10.00	$30.00
07 Jan 20	$60.00	$180.00
06 Jan 20	$35.00	$35.00
06 Jan 20	$200.00	$200.00
12 Jan 20	$480.00	$480.00
10 Jan 20	$225.00	$900.00
13 Jan 20	$360.00	$360.00
14 Jan 20	$640.00	$640.00
10 Jan 20	$30.00	$90.00
09 Jan 20	$15.00	$30.00
12 Jan 20	$35.00	$140.00
16 Jan 20	$800.00	$800.00
16 Jan 20	$120.00	$120.00
11 Jan 20	$40.00	$80.00
12 Jan 20	$30.00	$30.00
13 Jan 20	$15.00	$45.00
11 Jan 20	$10.00	$10.00
15 Jan 20	$30.00	$90.00
15 Jan 20	$225.00	$675.00
15 Jan 20	$10.00	$30.00
15 Jan 20	$120.00	$360.00
19 Jan 20	$140.00	$140.00
15 Jan 20	$60.00	$120.00
14 Jan 20	$10.00	$10.00
14 Jan 20	$120.00	$120.00
22 Jan 20	$480.00	$480.00
16 Jan 20	$160.00	$160.00
15 Feb 20	$1,080.00	$1,080.00
16 Jan 20	$35.00	$35.00
17 Jan 20	$40.00	$40.00
24 Jan 20	$900.00	$900.00
18 Jan 20	$10.00	$10.00
20 Jan 20	$200.00	$600.00
20 Jan 20	$60.00	$180.00
18 Jan 20	$15.00	$15.00
18 Jan 20	$35.00	$35.00
18 Jan 20	$160.00	$160.00
19 Feb 20	$360.00	$360.00
26 Jan 20	$640.00	$640.00
26 Jan 20	$45.00	$45.00
21 Jan 20	$10.00	$20.00
23 Jan 20	$30.00	$90.00
27 Jan 20	$140.00	$140.00
22 Jan 20	$120.00	$240.00
22 Jan 20	$35.00	$70.00

Excel 2-7

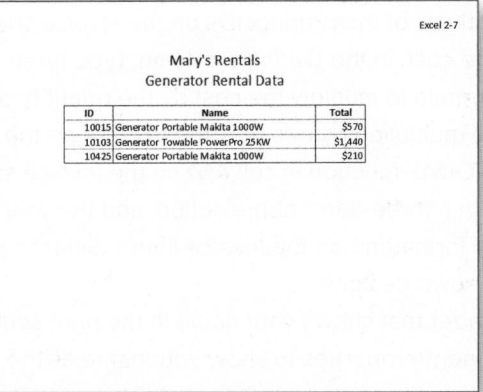

Mary's Rentals
Generator Rental Data

ID	Name	Total
10015	Generator Portable Makita 1000W	$570
10103	Generator Towable PowerPro 25KW	$1,440
10425	Generator Portable Makita 1000W	$210

Figure 2-113 Excel 2-7 completed

Challenge Project 2-8

For this project, you create a workbook for a hair products company that includes an inventory list and an invoice form. You use *VLOOKUP* to enter the cost of the product on the invoice and then calculate a total with taxes for each product.
[Student Learning Outcomes 2.1, 2.2, 2.3, 2.5, 2.6]

File Needed: None
Completed Project File Name: *[your initials] Excel 2-8.xlsx*

Create and save a workbook as [your initials] Excel 2-8. Modify your workbook according to the following guidelines:

- Type a name for the hair products company in cell **A1**. In cell **A2**, type Customer Invoice. In cells **A4:D4**, enter these labels: Product ID, Cost, Quantity, and Total with Tax. Do not include a comma or a period. Name the sheet tab Invoice.
- Insert a new sheet and name it Stock. In cells **A1:C1**, enter labels for Product ID, Name, and Cost with no punctuation.
- In cells **A2:C11**, enter data for ten products that can be purchased from your company. Use *AutoFill* to create a series for the *Product ID*. Because this range will be used as the table array in a *VLOOKUP* function, the product IDs must be in ascending order, either A to Z or low value to high value. Name the cell range Stock (without the labels in row 1).
- Enter Tax Rate as a label below the *Stock* range. In a cell either to the right or below the label, enter 3.75% as the rate.
- Type any three of the product IDs on the *Invoice* sheet in cells **A5:A7**. Use *VLOOKUP* in column B to display the cost. In the *Quantity* column, type three values to indicate the number ordered.
- Build a formula to multiply the cost by the quantity ordered in the *Total with Tax* column. This result should be multiplied by one plus the tax rate on the *Stock* sheet. Show a grand total in row 8.
- Use the *TODAY* function in cell **A10** on the *Invoice* sheet and format the date to show the date, the month with a three-letter abbreviation, and the year as two digits.
- Complete formatting on the *Invoice* sheet. Select a workbook theme if desired, use cell styles, or build your own designs.
- Add a header that shows your name in the right section.
- Set document properties to show your name as the author and the company name as the title. Spell check the workbook if necessary.

Challenge Project 2-9

For this project, you create a workbook for a mobile services provider to calculate revenue from purchased mobile apps. You enter and format data and use *SUMPRODUCT* to determine revenue by category.
[Student Learning Outcomes 2.1, 2.3, 2.5, 2.7]

File Needed: None
Completed Project File Name: *[your initials] Excel 2-9.xlsx*

Create and save a workbook as [your initials] Excel 2-9. Modify your workbook according to the following guidelines:

- Enter a name for your mobile services company in cell **A1**.
- Type Last Month's Activity in cell **A2**.
- Enter the labels App Name, Times Downloaded, and Cost in cells **B3:D3**.
- Type Books as the first category in cell **A4**. In cells **A7**, **A10**, and **A13**, type the names of three other categories of mobile applications. Examples might be "Travel," "Entertainment," "Games," "Health," "Sports," and so on.
- Complete data for two apps in the *Books* category in cells **B5:D6**. Then do the same for the other categories.
- Create a section that calculates revenue from each app category using the *SUMPRODUCT* function starting in row **18**.
- Use the *TODAY* function in a cell below the data and format the date to show a short date.
- Select a workbook theme if desired, use cell styles, or set your own formatting.
- Add a footer that shows the current date in the left section and your name in the right section.
- Set document properties to show your name as the author and a title of your choice. Spell check the workbook if necessary.

Challenge Project 2-10

In this project, you create a workbook that calculates monthly payments for a major purchase at four possible interest rates and different payback times.
[**Student Learning Outcomes 2.1, 2.3, 2.5, 2.6**]

File Needed: None
Completed Project File Name: *[your initials] Excel 2-10.xlsx*

Create and save a workbook as [your initials] Excel 2-10. Modify your workbook according to the following guidelines:

- Enter main labels that identify the worksheet and your proposed purchase.
- Build the first section for a *PMT* formula with the labels Loan, Rate, Term, and Payment. Because you plan to copy the section to show other possibilities, do not use range names.
- Fill in values for the loan amount, an interest rate, and the term. Include the percent sign when you type the interest rate. For the term, use the number of years or the number of months.
- Use *PMT* to calculate the payment made at the beginning of the month (*Type* argument). If you set months for the term, do not multiply the *Nper* argument by 12.
- Copy the entire section once below the current location with a blank row or two between. Then copy these two groupings one or two columns to the right. You should have four possible payment scenarios on the sheet.
- Edit the interest rate and term for each of the copied sections. Be consistent in how you indicate the term of the loan (years or months). Assume that the loan amount is the same.
- Use the *TODAY* function in a row below the data, and format the date to show a short date.
- Apply formatting choices to build an easy-to-read report.
- Add a footer with your name in the right section.
- Set document properties to show your name as the author, and spell check the workbook if necessary.

Source of screenshots Microsoft Office 365 (2019): Word, Excel, Access, Powerpoint.

CHAPTER 3

Creating and Editing Charts

CHAPTER OVERVIEW

In addition to building formulas and functions in a worksheet, use Excel to graph or chart data. After selecting values and labels, you can quickly create a professional looking chart with a few clicks of the mouse. This chapter introduces you to the basics of creating, editing, and formatting Excel charts.

STUDENT LEARNING OUTCOMES (SLOs)

After completing this chapter, you will be able to:

SLO 3.1 Create Excel chart objects and chart sheets (p. E3-163).

SLO 3.2 Use quick layouts and chart styles to design a chart (p. E3-167).

SLO 3.3 Edit chart elements including titles, data labels, and source data (p. E3-172).

SLO 3.4 Format chart elements with shape styles, fills, outlines, and special effects (p. E3-179).

SLO 3.5 Use pictures, shapes, and *WordArt* in a chart (p. E3-183).

SLO 3.6 Build pie charts and combination charts (p. E3-188).

SLO 3.7 Create sunburst and waterfall charts (p. E3-191).

SLO 3.8 Insert and format sparklines in a worksheet (p. E3-194).

CASE STUDY

In the Pause & Practice projects in this chapter, you use data in a Paradise Lakes Resort workbook to build charts that compare revenue categories for two quarters. You build column and pie charts as objects and separate sheets. You also add trendlines and sparklines to illustrate aspects of the data.

Pause & Practice 3-1: Create and edit column and bar charts.

Pause & Practice 3-2: Edit and format charts and chart elements.

Pause & Practice 3-3: Create and format pie, combo, and sunburst charts and insert sparklines.

Creating a Chart Object and a Chart Sheet

An Excel *chart* is a visual representation of numeric data in a worksheet. A chart helps you identify trends, make comparisons, and recognize patterns in the numbers. Charts are dynamic and linked to the data, so when values in the worksheet change, the chart is automatically redrawn. You can display a chart in the worksheet with its data, or place a chart on its own sheet.

Excel includes different kinds of charts and can recommend the best chart type based on your selected data. It is essential, however, that you select appropriate data for a chart, because it is possible to build charts that illustrate nothing of any consequence. With experience and practice, you will learn how to create charts for your work that have meaning.

Create a Chart Object

A *chart object* is a distinct item surrounded by a square border that is separate from worksheet data. A chart object contains chart elements such as titles, axes, and gridlines that can be selected for editing. You can size and position a chart object in a worksheet, as well as size and position each chart element on the chart.

Source data are the cells that contain values and labels to be graphed in a chart. When you select data for a chart, you usually do not include sums, averages, or similar calculations. In Figure 3-1, the source data include the series names in column A, the category names in row 4,

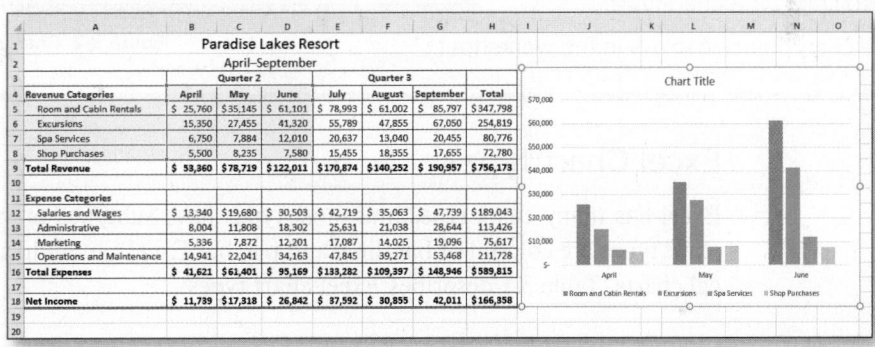

Figure 3-1 Chart object and its source data

and four values for each of three months. Each of the values is a *data point*, a cell containing a value. Each group of data points or values is a *data series*. This example includes four data series, one for each revenue category. Each data series has a name or label.

The text label that describes a data series is a *category label*. In Figure 3.1, the category labels are the month names.

> ### ANOTHER WAY
> Create a default chart object by selecting the data and pressing **Alt+F1**.

Data for a chart is best arranged with labels and values in adjacent cells and no empty rows. If you do not include labels for the source data, the chart does not include labels to describe the data. An empty row within the source data is graphed as a data point with a value of zero (0) and will distort the chart's ability to illustrate a comparison or trend.

When you select contiguous source data (all cells are next to each other), the *Quick Analysis* button appears in the lower-right corner of the selection. The *Quick Analysis* tool

lists command groups you would be likely to use for the selected data, such as *Formatting*, *Charts*, or *Totals*. When you select the *Charts* command, Excel shows recommended chart types. As you point to each type, you see a preview of the chart. Click the preferred type to create the chart object in the worksheet.

▶ **HOW TO: Create a Chart Object from the Quick Analysis Tool**

1. Select the source data range with labels and values.
 - The *Quick Analysis* button appears in the lower-right corner of the range.
2. Click the **Quick Analysis** button.
 - A dialog box with command categories opens (Figure 3-2).
3. Select **Charts**.
 - Possible chart types are listed.
4. Point to a chart type.
 - A preview of the chart object displays.
5. Click to select the chart type.
 - The chart object displays in the worksheet.

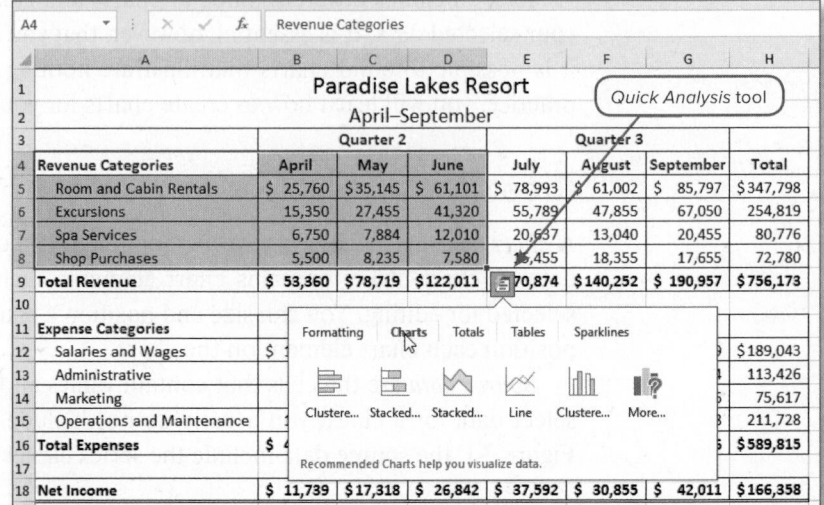

Figure 3-2 Chart preview from *Quick Analysis* choice

Excel Chart Types

Excel has many chart types and most types have subtypes or variations. The most common chart types are column or bar, line, and pie, but Excel can build powerful scientific and statistical charts. Table 3-1 describes Excel chart types:

Table 3-1: Excel Chart Types

Chart Type	Purpose	Data Example	Categories (Labels)	Values (Numbers)
Column	Illustrates data changes over a period of time or shows comparisons among items	Monthly sales data for three automobile models	Horizontal axis	Vertical axis
Bar	Displays comparisons among individual items or values at a specific period of time	Number of pairs sold for eight shoe styles	Vertical axis	Horizontal axis
Pie	Uses one data series to display each value as a percentage of the whole	Expenses or revenue by department for one quarter		One data series shown by slice size
Line	Displays trends in data over time, emphasizing the rate of change	Number of weekly web site views over a ten-week period	Horizontal axis	Vertical axis
Area	Displays the magnitude of change over time and shows the rate of change	Yearly consumption of apples, bananas, and pears over a ten-year period	Horizontal axis	Vertical axis
XY (Scatter) or Bubble	Displays relationships among numeric values in two or more data series; these charts do not have a category	Number of times a patient visits a doctor, amount billed to insurance, and cost billed to patient	Horizontal axis (value 1-x)	Vertical axis (value 2-y)

Continued

Chart Type	Purpose	Data Example	Categories (Labels)	Values (Numbers)
Stock	Displays three series of data to show fluctuations in stock prices from high to low to close	Opening, closing, and high price for Microsoft stock each day for 30 days	Horizontal axis	Vertical axis
Surface	Displays results for combinations of two sets of values on a surface	Windchill factor based on wind speed and outdoor temperature	NA	NA
Radar	Displays the frequency of multiple data series relative to a center point. There is an axis for each category	Style, comfort, and value ratings for three snow boot styles	NA	NA
TreeMap	Displays a hierarchical view of data with different sized and colored rectangles and sub-rectangles to compare the sizes of groups	Soda sales by product name, continent, country, and city	NA	NA
Sunburst	Displays a hierarchical view of data with concentric rings. The top hierarchy is the inner ring and each outer ring is related to its adjacent inner ring	Tablet sales by screen size, continent, country, and city	NA	NA
Histogram	Column-style chart that shows frequencies within a distribution	Number of students in each of five grade categories for an exam	Horizontal axis	Vertical axis
Box & Whisker	Displays the distribution of data with minimum, mean, maximum, and outlier values	Sales prices of homes in five suburbs during a three-week period	Horizontal axis	Vertical axis
Waterfall	Plots each element in a running total and displays negative and positive effects of each on the totals	Banking or savings account register	Horizontal axis	Vertical axis
Funnel	Plots values that progressively decrease from one stage or process to the next	Job applications received, applications selected, online interviews, team interviews	Vertical axis	Horizontal axis
Combo Chart	Uses two types of charts to graph values that are widely different	Line chart for number of monthly web site visits and a column chart for monthly sales of a selected product	Either	Either
Map Chart	Compares and plots values across geographical regions such as countries, states, counties, or postal codes	Tax revenue from all counties in a state or province	Either	Either

Size and Position a Chart Object

When you select a chart object, it is active and surrounded by eight selection handles. A *selection handle* is a small circle shape on each corner and in the middle of each side. To select the chart object, point to its border and click. When you select a chart object, the *Range Finder* highlights the source data in the worksheet. When you point to a selection handle, you will see a two-pointed resize arrow. Drag a corner handle to size the height and width proportionally.

To move a chart object, point to the chart border to display a four-pointed move pointer. Then drag the chart object to the desired location.

When a chart is active or selected, the contextual *Chart Tools Design* and *Format* tabs are available in the *Ribbon* and three *Quick Chart Tools* are available in the top-right corner of the object: *Chart Elements*, *Chart Styles*, and *Chart Filters*.

> **MORE INFO**
>
> You can select individual elements or parts of the chart, and each element has its own selection handles.

▶HOW TO: Move and Size a Chart Object

1. Select the chart object.
 - Point to the border of the chart and click.
2. Point to the outside border of the chart to display a move pointer.
 - Point anywhere along the border.
3. Drag the chart object to a new location and release the pointer button (Figure 3-3).
4. Point to a corner selection handle to display a resize arrow.
5. Drag the pointer to resize the chart proportionally.

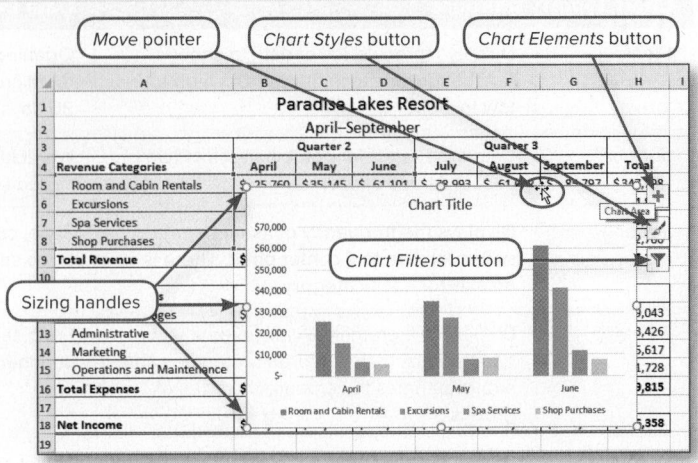

Figure 3-3 Selected chart object and move pointer

Create a Chart Sheet

A *chart sheet* is an Excel chart that displays on its own sheet in the workbook. A chart sheet does not have rows, columns, and cells, but the chart is linked to its data on the source worksheet.

From the *Quick Analysis* tool or the *Insert* tab, Excel creates a chart object. You must move the chart object to its own sheet with the *Move Chart* button on the *Chart Tools Design* tab. Excel uses default sheet names *Chart1, Chart2,* and so on, but you can type a descriptive name in the *Move Chart* dialog box. You can also rename the sheet at any time.

Create an automatic column chart sheet by selecting the data and pressing the **F11** (**FN+F11**) function key.

> ▶ MORE INFO
>
> When the *Recommended Charts* button does not recommend a chart type, select the source data again in a left-to-right order. If no suggestions display, click the **All Charts** tab and choose a type.

Source data for a chart need not be contiguous. The *Quick Analysis* tool does not appear for noncontiguous data, but you can click the **Recommended Charts** button in the *Charts* group on the *Insert* tab. The *Insert Chart* dialog box opens and recommends chart types.

▶HOW TO: Create a Chart Sheet for Noncontiguous Cells

1. Select the values and labels for the chart.
 - Select the first range, press the **Ctrl** key, and select each range (Figure 3-4).
2. Click the **Recommended Charts** button [*Insert* tab, *Charts* group].
 - The *Insert Chart* dialog box opens.
 - Click the **All Charts** tab to select any chart type.
3. Click the thumbnail for a chart type to preview the results.

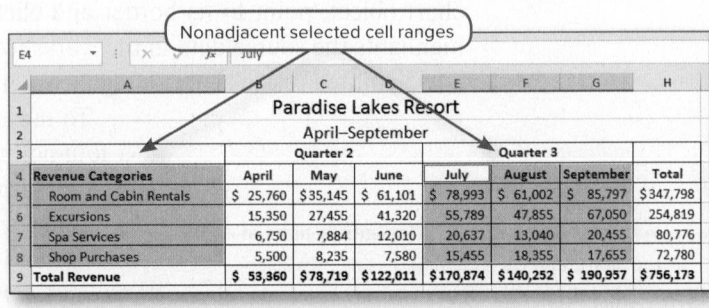

Figure 3-4 Source data ranges that are not next to each other

4. Click the preferred chart type and click **OK**.
 - The chart object is active.
 - The *Chart Tools* tabs are available.
5. Click the **Move Chart** button [*Chart Tools Design* tab, *Location* group].
6. Click the **New sheet** radio button (Figure 3-5).
7. Type a descriptive name for the chart sheet.
8. Click **OK**.

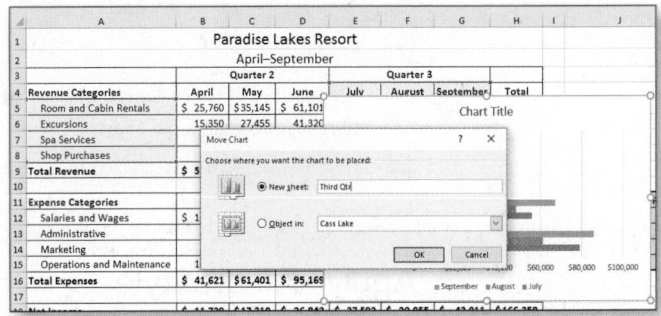

Figure 3-5 *Move Chart* dialog box

Using Quick Layouts and Chart Styles

A newly created chart has a default layout, color, and style. Excel has various tools to help you enhance the appearance of your chart for originality, readability, and appeal. The *Chart Tools Design* tab includes commands for selecting a chart layout, choosing a chart style, or changing the color scheme.

Apply a Quick Layout

A *chart layout* is a set of elements and the location of those elements. Elements are individual parts of a chart such as a main title, a legend, and axes titles. The *Quick Layout* button [*Chart Tools Design* tab, *Chart Layouts* group] opens a gallery of predefined layouts (Figure 3-6). As you point to an option in the gallery, *Live Preview* redraws the chart. When a chart layout adds an

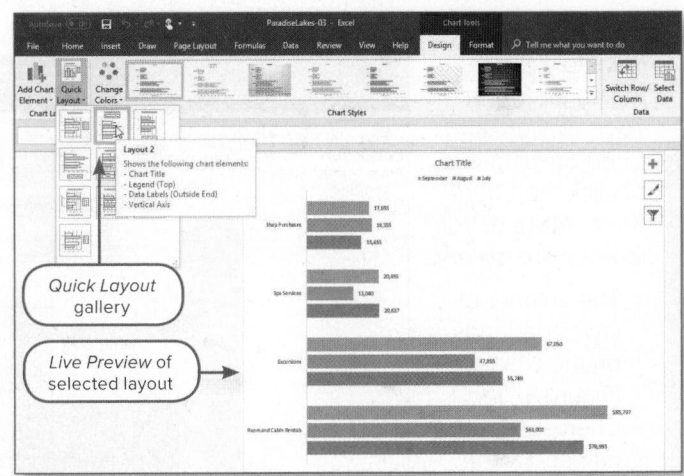

Figure 3-6 *Quick Layout* gallery

element such as a title, the element displays a generic label like "Chart Title." You can add or remove individual elements, as well as edit placeholder text.

▶ **HOW TO: Apply a Quick Layout to a Chart**

1. Select the chart object or the chart sheet tab.
2. Click the **Quick Layout** button [*Chart Tools Design* tab, *Chart Layouts* group].
 - The gallery displays a list of elements for each layout when you point to a thumbnail image.
 - Quick layouts are named *Layout 1* through the last number.
3. Point to a layout thumbnail to preview it in the chart.
4. Click a thumbnail to select it.
 - The chart is reformatted with the *Quick Layout* elements.

Apply a Chart Style

A ***chart style*** is a preset combination of colors and effects for a chart, its background, and its elements. The chart styles available for a chart are based on the current workbook theme. If you change the theme, the chart style colors are updated, and your chart reflects the new color palette. You can find chart styles in the *Chart Styles* group on the *Chart Tools Design* tab. Like a chart layout, you can preview the effects of a chart style as you point to each style in the gallery.

▶ HOW TO: Apply a Chart Style

1. Select the chart object or the chart sheet tab.

2. Point to a *Style* thumbnail [*Chart Tools Design* tab, *Chart Styles* group] or click the *Chart Styles* **More** button to open the gallery.

 - The number of styles depends on the chart type (Figure 3-7).
 - Chart styles are named *Style 1* through the last number.

3. Point to a style thumbnail to see a *Live Preview* in the chart.

4. Click to select a style.

 - The chart is redrawn with the selected style.

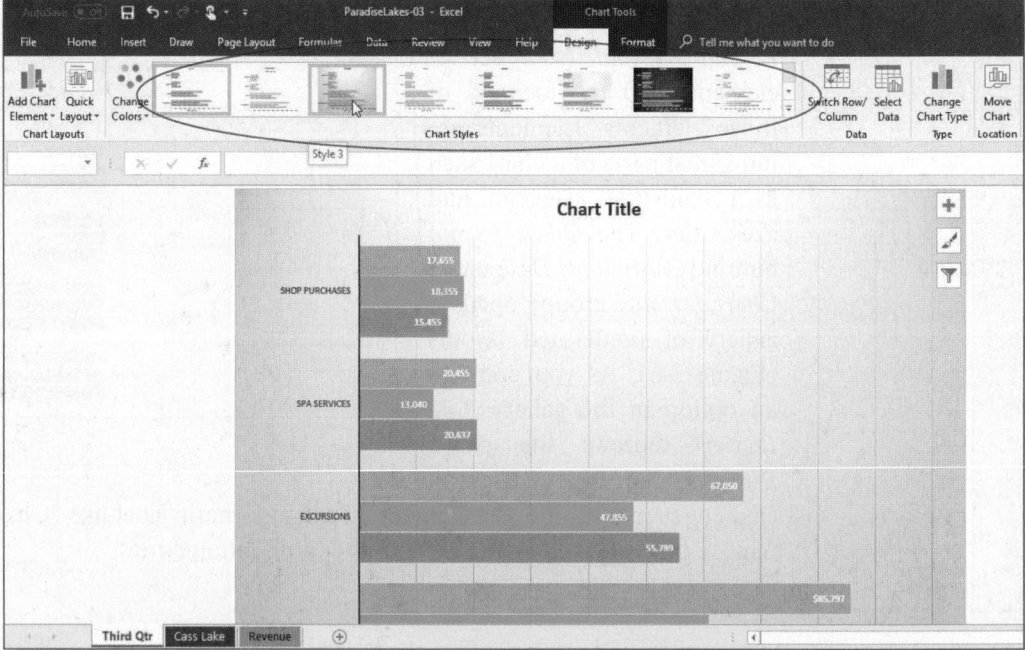

Figure 3-7 *Chart Styles* gallery and preview of selected style

Change Chart Colors

The workbook theme and the chart style form the basis for a chart's color scheme. The *Chart Styles* group [*Chart Tools Design* tab] includes a *Change Colors* button with optional color palettes. These palettes are divided into *Colorful* and *Monochromatic* groups.

▶ **HOW TO: Change Chart Colors**

1. Select the chart object or the chart sheet tab.
2. Click the **Change Colors** button [*Chart Tools Design* tab, *Chart Styles* group].
 - A gallery of color palettes opens (Figure 3-8).
 - Color schemes are named with the category (*Colorful* or *Monochromatic*) and a number.
3. Point to a palette to see a *Live Preview* in the chart.
4. Click to select a palette.
 - The chart is formatted with new colors.

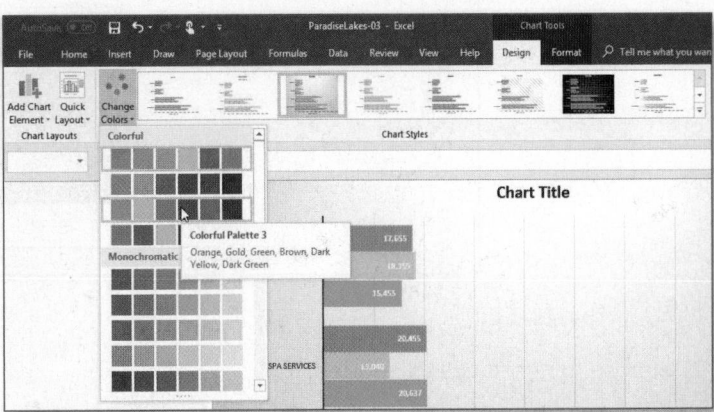

Figure 3-8 *Change Colors* gallery

Print a Chart

A chart object can be printed on the page with worksheet data, or it can be printed separately. To print a chart with the data, deselect the chart object by clicking a worksheet cell. Size and position the chart and scale the sheet to fit a printed page. Then use regular *Page Setup* commands to complete the print task, such as choosing the orientation or inserting headers or footers.

▶ **MORE INFO**

When you insert a header or footer in a selected chart object, that header or footer is not inserted on the worksheet.

To print only the chart object on its own sheet, select it and use regular *Print* and *Page Setup* options. A selected chart object, by default, prints scaled to fit a landscape page. A chart sheet also prints in landscape orientation and fits the page.

▶ **HOW TO: Print a Chart with Its Source Data**

1. Click any cell in the worksheet.
 - Size and position the chart object as needed.
2. Click the **File** tab to open the *Backstage* view (Figure 3-9).
3. Select **Print**.

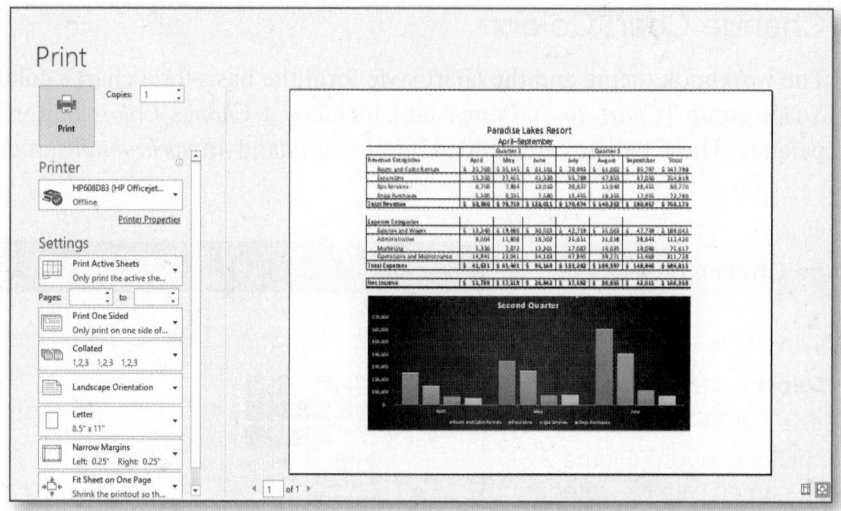

Figure 3-9 Print a chart with the data

4. Choose print settings as needed.
 • Set margins and scale the sheet to fit.
5. Click **Print**.

In this project, you insert a clustered column chart object in a worksheet that tracks revenue and expenses for Paradise Lakes Resort. You also insert a clustered bar chart sheet to highlight second quarter results.

File Needed: **ParadiseLakes-03.xlsx** *(Student data files are available in the* Library *of your SIMnet account.)*
Completed Project File Name: ***[your initials] PP E3-1.xlsx***

1. Open the **ParadiseLakes-03** workbook from your student data files and save it as [your initials] PP E3-1.

2. Create a chart object.
 a. Select cells **A4:D8** on the **Cass Lake** sheet. The cells include labels and values for the chart.
 b. Click the **Quick Analysis** button and select **Charts**.
 c. Click the **Clustered Column** icon.

3. Position and size the chart object.
 a. Click the chart object if it is not selected.
 b. Point to the chart border to display a move pointer.
 c. Drag the chart object so that its top-left corner is at cell **A20**.
 d. Point to the lower-right selection handle to display a resize arrow.
 e. Drag the pointer to reach cell **H35**.

4. Choose a quick layout.
 a. Select the chart object if necessary.
 b. Click the **Quick Layout** button [*Chart Tools Design* tab, *Chart Layouts* group].
 c. Click **Layout 3** (Figure 3-10).

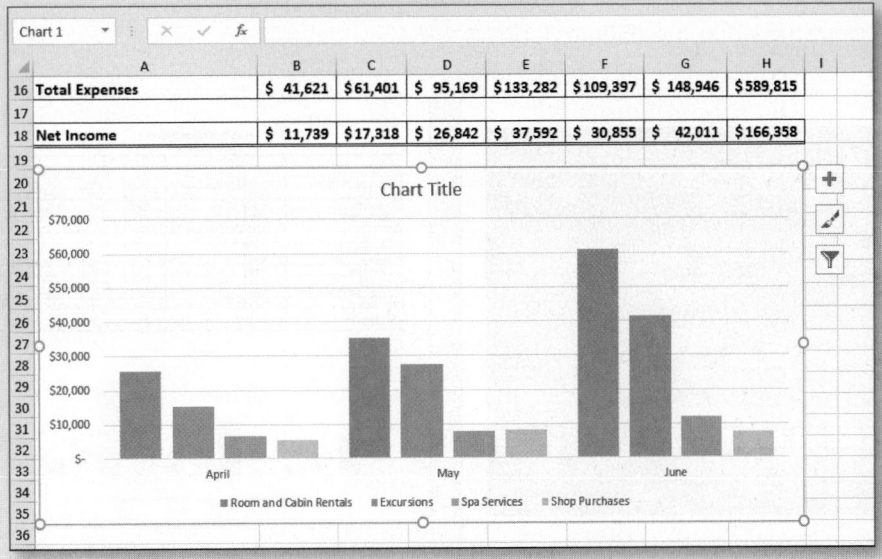

Figure 3-10 Chart object sized and positioned

5. Create a chart sheet.
 a. Select cells **A4:A8**.
 b. Press **Ctrl** and select cells **E4:G8**.
 c. Click the **Recommended Charts** button [*Insert* tab, *Charts* group].
 d. Select **Clustered Bar**.
 e. Click **OK**. The chart object is inserted and selected.
 f. Click the **Move Chart** button [*Chart Tools Design* tab, *Location* group].
 g. Click the **New sheet** radio button.
 h. Type Third Qtr as the sheet name.
 i. Click **OK**. The chart sheet tab is active.

6. Choose a chart style.
 a. Click the **More** button to open the *Chart Styles* gallery [*Chart Tools Design* tab, *Chart Styles* group].
 b. Select **Style 7**.

7. Preview the charts.
 a. Select the **Third Qtr** sheet if necessary.
 b. Click the **File** tab to open the *Backstage* view.
 c. Choose **Print** to preview the chart sheet (Figure 3-11).
 d. Click the **Back** arrow to return to the worksheet.
 e. Click the **Cass Lake** worksheet tab and select cell **A1**.
 f. Click the **File** tab and select **Print**. The worksheet and chart are previewed on a single page.
 g. Click the **Back** arrow to return to the worksheet.

Figure 3-11 Print preview for chart sheet

8. Save and close the workbook (Figure 3-12).

Figure 3-12 PP E3-1 completed chart object and chart sheet

Editing Chart Elements and Data

A *chart element* is a separate object. The chart layout and style affect which elements are initially displayed, but you can add, remove, format, size, and position elements as you design a chart. Table 3-2 describes common chart elements:

Table 3-2: Excel Chart Elements

Element	Description
Axis	Horizontal or vertical boundary that identifies what is plotted.
Axis title	Optional description for the categories or values.
Chart area	Background for the chart; can be filled with a color, gradient, or pattern.
Chart floor	Base or bottom for a 3D chart.
Chart title	Optional description or name for the chart.
Chart wall	Vertical background for a 3D chart.
Data label	Optional element that displays values with the marker for each data series.
Data marker	Element that represents individual values. The marker is a bar, a column, a slice, or a point on a line.
Data point	A single value or piece of data from a data series.
Data series	Group of related values that are in the same column or row and translate into the columns, lines, pie slices, and other markers.
Gridline	Horizontal or vertical line that extends across the plot area to help identify values.
Horizontal (category) axis	Describes what is shown in the chart and is created from row or column headings. In a bar chart, the category axis is the vertical axis; the category axis is the horizontal axis in a column chart.

Continued

Element	Description
Legend	Element that explains symbols, textures, or colors used to differentiate data series.
Plot area	Rectangular area bounded by the horizontal and vertical axes.
Tick mark	Small line or marker on an axis to guide in reading values
Trendline	Line or curve that displays averages in the data and can be used to forecast future averages.
Vertical (value) axis	Shows the numbers on the chart. In a bar chart, the vertical axis is along the bottom; in a column chart, the vertical axis is along the side.

> **MORE INFO**
>
> Not all charts have all elements. For example, a pie chart does not have any axes or axes titles.

Add and Remove Chart Elements

When you point to a chart element, a *ScreenTip* describes it. When you click the element, it is active and surrounded by selection handles, as shown for the legend in Figure 3-13. In addition to clicking, you can select an element from the *Chart Elements* drop-down list on the *Chart Tools Format* tab. The name of the selected element appears in the *Chart Elements* box.

Show or hide chart elements using the *Chart Elements* button in the top-right corner of a chart. When you click the button, the *Chart Elements* pane opens with a list of available elements for the chart type. In this pane, select or deselect the box to show or remove an element. To hide the pane, click the **Chart Elements** button again.

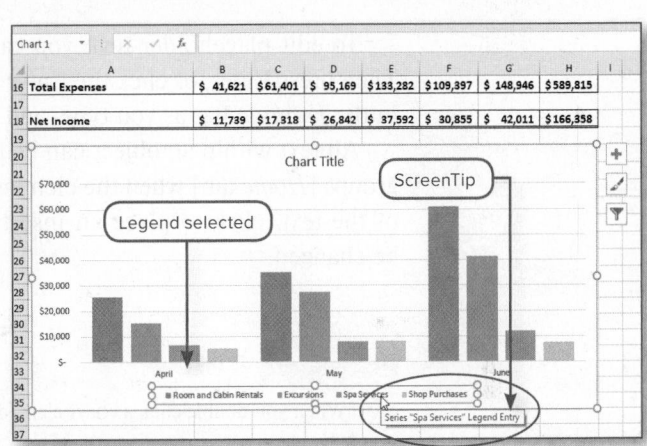

Figure 3-13 Selected legend and *ScreenTip* for a data series

> **ANOTHER WAY**
>
> Click the **Add Chart Element** button [*Chart Tools Design* tab, *Chart Layouts* group] to show a chart element.

Chart and Axes Titles

Chart layouts may include placeholders for a main chart title and for axes titles. If the quick layout does not include titles, you can add them. In either case, you must edit the placeholder text.

A main chart title is usually positioned above the chart, but within the chart area. Once you insert a title text box, you can select it and move it anywhere on the chart. You might use an axis title to clarify the categories or values represented in the chart. If the chart graphs the data well, axes titles are often not necessary.

▶HOW TO: Insert a Chart Title

1. Click the chart object or the chart sheet tab.

2. Click the **Chart Elements** button in the top-right corner of the chart.

3. Select the **Chart Title** box.

 - The *Chart Title* placeholder displays above the chart.

4. Click the **Chart Title** arrow in the *Chart Elements* pane to select a position for the title.

5. Select the *Chart Title* placeholder text (Figure 3-14).

 - The mini toolbar opens.
 - Triple-click the placeholder text or drag to select it.

6. Type a title to replace the placeholder text.

7. Click the chart border.

 - The title object is deselected.
 - If you press **Enter** while typing in the text box, you insert a new line in the title. Press **Backspace** to remove it, and then click the chart border.

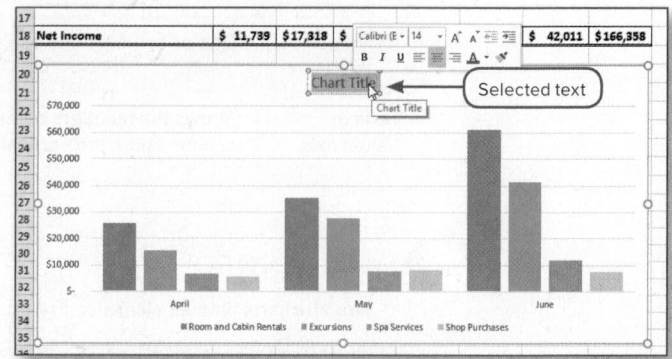

Figure 3-14 Placeholder text to be edited

To edit placeholder text, you can also select the object and type text in the *Formula* bar. Then press **Enter**, or click the **Enter** button in the *Formula* bar to complete it. The label appears in the *Formula* bar as you type, and you will not see it on the chart until you press **Enter**.

All text within an object can be formatted with font attributes from the *Font* and *Alignment* groups [*Home* tab] when the element is selected. When you want to apply a format to a portion of the text, click to place an insertion point inside the element and select the characters to be changed.

> ▶ **MORE INFO**
>
> When you double-click a chart element, the *Format* pane opens with format and design choices for that element.

Removing a chart element creates more room for the actual chart. In Figure 3-15, for example, the vertical axis title "Dollars" is probably not necessary. By removing it, the chart resizes to fit the chart area. You can always show the element again if you change your mind.

To delete a chart element, select it and press **Delete**. You can confirm which element is selected in the *Chart Elements* box on the *Chart Tools Format* tab [*Current Selection* group].

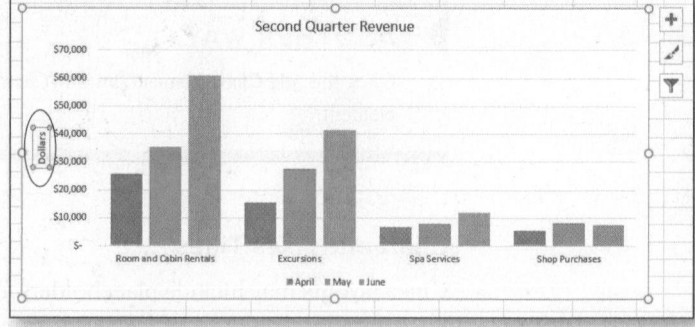

Figure 3-15 Delete an axis title to make more room for the chart

▶HOW TO: Delete a Chart Element

1. Click the chart element.
 - The element displays selection handles.
 - Confirm which element is selected in the *Chart Elements* list box [*Chart Tools Format* tab, *Current Selection* group].
2. Press **Delete**.
 - The chart resizes to fit the area.
 - Right-click the chart element and choose **Delete**.

▶ **ANOTHER WAY**

To remove an element, click the **Chart Elements** button in the top-right corner of the chart and deselect the box for that element.

Data Labels

Data labels display the number represented by a column, bar, pie slice, or other marker on the chart. Because the value axis uses a scale, it cannot show a precise value, but a data label can display that number. Data labels should be used when the chart does not have too many data series because they can clutter a chart. Or you can select just one or two of the data points (the individual bars or columns) and show labels for only that data.

Display data labels using the *Chart Elements* button on the chart or from the same button on the *Chart Tools Design* tab [*Chart Layouts* group].

▶HOW TO: Add Data Labels

1. Select the chart object or the chart sheet tab.
2. Click the **Chart Elements** button in the top-right corner of the chart.
3. Select the **Data Labels** box.
 - *Live Preview* shows data labels for each data point in the data series.
4. Point to **Data Labels** in the pane and point to its arrow (Figure 3-16).
 - Position choices for the labels are listed.
 - *Live Preview* updates as you point to each option.
5. Choose a location for the data labels.

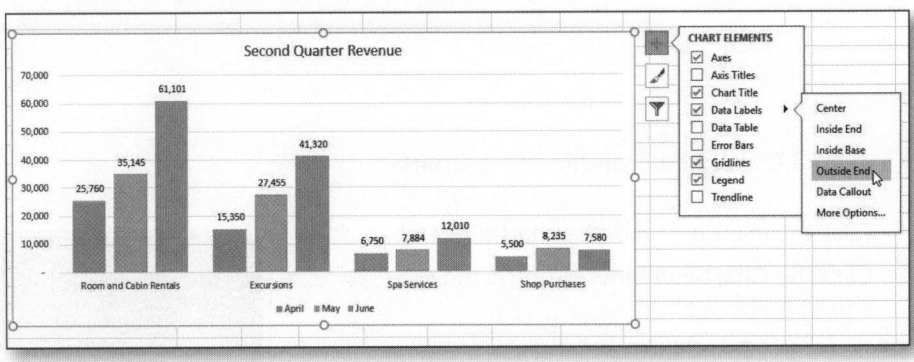

Figure 3-16 Data labels shown outside column markers

Data Table

A chart ***data table*** is a columnar display of the values for each data series in a chart, located just below the chart. When your readers do not have access to the source data for a chart, a data table can supply valuable information.

To include a data table below your chart, you can use the *Add Chart Element* button on the *Chart Tools Design* tab in the *Chart Layouts* group or the *Chart Elements* button on the chart.

You can show a data table with or without legend markers, a mini legend to the left of the table (Figure 3-17).

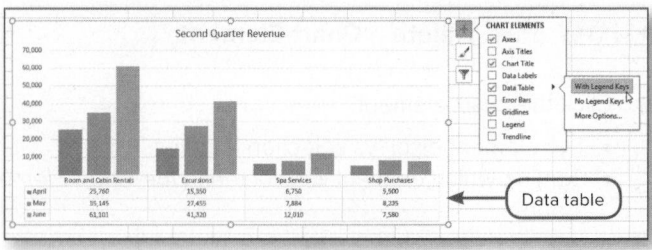

Figure 3-17 Data table element for a chart

Trendlines

A *trendline* is a chart element that plots patterns using a moving average of the current data. It uses a straight or curved line and can extend past the data to predict future averages. Not all chart types are suitable for trendlines, such as a pie or a treemap chart. A basic linear trendline is appropriate for values that tend to increase or decrease as time passes. A trendline traces data for one data series, as seen in Figure 3-18. If you have multiple data series, as in a typical column chart, add a trendline for each series.

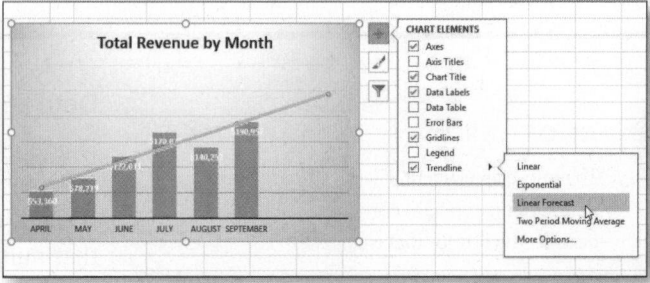

Figure 3-18 Column chart with "Total Revenue" linear trendline

> **ANOTHER WAY**
>
> Right-click a data series marker (its column) and choose **Add Trendline** to open the *Format Trendline* task pane and build a trendline.

HOW TO: Add a Trendline to a Chart

1. Click the chart object or the chart sheet tab.
2. Click the **Chart Elements** button in the top-right corner of the chart.
3. Select the **Trendline** box in the *Chart Elements* pane.
 - The *Add Trendline* dialog box lists the names of the data series.
 - When the chart has only one data series, the trendline is added to the chart.
4. Choose a data series for the trendline and click **OK** (Figure 3-19).
5. Point to the **Trendline** arrow in the *Chart Elements* pane.
 - Choose **Linear** to show a line for existing data.
 - Choose **Linear Forecast** to build a line for current and future data.

Figure 3-19 *Add Trendline* dialog box for chart with multiple data series

Switch Row and Column Data

Excel plots the data series based on the number of rows and columns selected in the worksheet and the chart type. Based on your choices, Excel determines if the labels are along the bottom or the side of the chart. When necessary, you can change which data series is plotted on the x-axis and which is plotted on the y-axis. In a column chart, the x-axis is along the bottom of the chart; the y-axis is along the left.

▶HOW TO: Switch Row and Column Data

1. Click the chart object or the chart sheet tab.
2. Click the **Switch Row/Column** button [*Chart Tools Design* tab, *Data* group] (Figure 3-20).
 - The data series becomes the categories.
 - Switch between how columns and rows are plotted as desired.

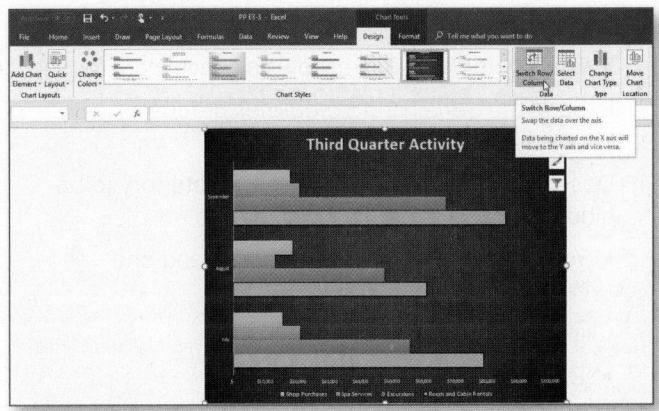

ANOTHER WAY

Click the **Chart Filters** button in the top-right corner of the chart and choose **Select Data** at the bottom of the pane to open the *Select Data Source* dialog box and click the **Switch Row/Column** button.

Figure 3-20 Column and row data switched

Change the Chart Type

When a chart does not depict what you intended, or you need a variety of chart types for a project, or you simply prefer a different chart, change the chart type. Changing the chart type assumes that the source data are the same and that they can be graphed in the new chart. You should not, for example, change a column chart with three data series into a pie chart, because a pie chart has only one series. The resulting chart would not represent the data as expected.

The **Change Chart Type** button is on the *Chart Tools Design* tab in the *Type* group. For a selected chart object or sheet, you can also right-click and choose **Change Chart Type** from the context menu. The *Change Chart Type* dialog box includes *Recommended Charts* and *All Charts* tabs like the *Insert Chart* dialog box.

▶HOW TO: Change the Chart Type

1. Click the chart object or chart sheet.
2. Click the **Change Chart Type** button [*Chart Tools Design* tab, *Type* group].
 - The *Change Chart Type* dialog box opens.
3. Click the **Recommended Charts** tab.
 - Click the **All Charts** tab if the recommended charts are not adequate.

4. Click a thumbnail image to preview the chart in the dialog box.

5. Select a chart type and click **OK**.

Filter Source Data

A chart displays all the categories and all the data series for the selected cells. You can, however, filter or refine which data displays by hiding categories or series. A *filter* is a requirement or condition that identifies which data are shown and which data are hidden. Chart filters do not change the underlying cell range for a chart, but they enable you to focus on particular data.

Filter chart data from the *Chart Filters* button in the top-right corner of the chart or in the *Select Data Source* dialog box [*Chart Tools Design* tab, *Data* group].

▶ HOW TO: Filter Source Data

1. Select the chart object or chart sheet tab.

2. Click the **Chart Filters** button in the top-right corner.

 • The *Chart Filters* pane shows a check mark for selected series and categories.

3. Expand the *Series* and *Categories* groups if needed.

4. Deselect the box for each series or category to be hidden.

 • You must select at least one series and one category.

5. Click **Apply** (Figure 3-21).

 • The chart is redrawn.

6. Click the **Chart Filters** button to close the pane.

 • Display the *Chart Filter* pane to show the hidden data when desired.

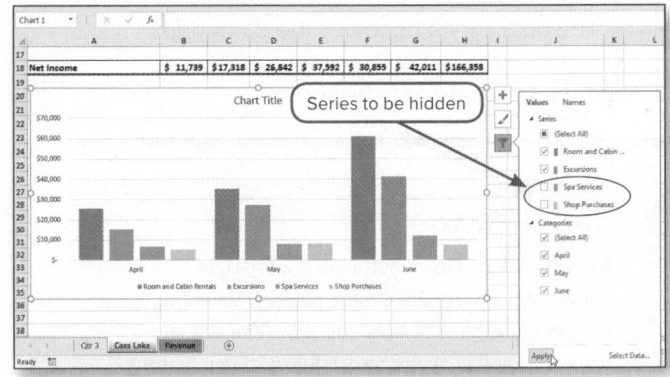

Figure 3-21 *Chart Filters* pane

Edit Source Data

The cells used to build a chart are its source data. Edit this data to change, add, or remove cells. In a column chart, for example, you can add a data series, or another column. To add or delete a data series in a chart object, select the chart and drag the sizing arrow in the lower-right corner of the highlighted cell range to expand or shrink the data range, as shown in Figure 3-22. Removing cells from the data range deletes that data series from the chart.

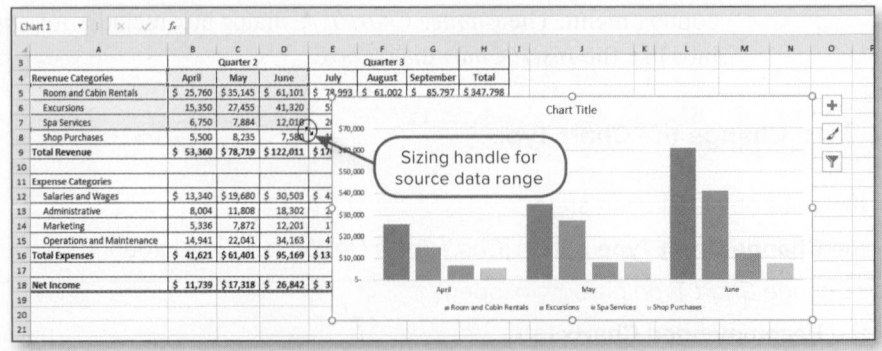

Figure 3-22 The "Shop Purchases" column will be removed from the chart

To edit the source data for a chart sheet, click the **Select Data** button on the *Chart Tools Design* tab [*Data* group] to open the *Select Data Source* dialog box.

▶**HOW TO: Add a Data Series in a Chart Sheet**

1. Click the chart sheet tab.

2. Click the **Select Data** button [*Chart Tools Design* tab, *Data* group].

 - The *Select Data Source* dialog box opens.
 - The worksheet is active, and the source cells are highlighted.

3. Select the new cell range in the worksheet (Figure 3-23).

 - If the cell ranges are not adjacent, select the first one, type a comma, and select the next range.
 - You can type cell addresses in the *Chart data range* box rather than selecting cells.

4. Click **OK**.

 - The chart sheet is active and redrawn with the edited source data range.

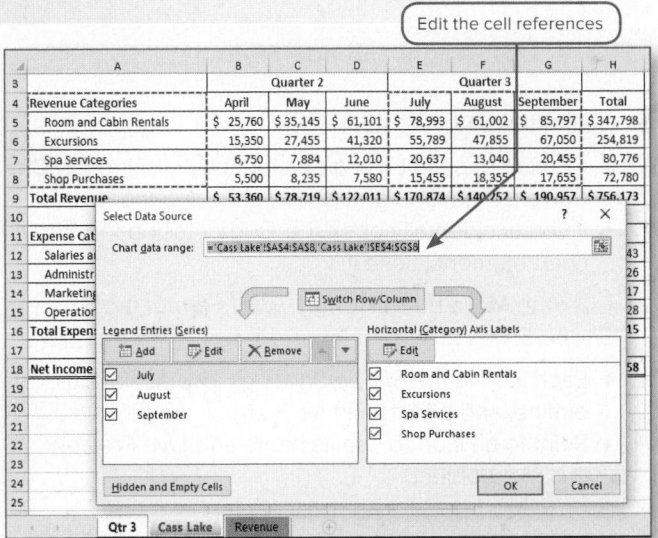

Figure 3-23 *Select Data Source* dialog box for a chart sheet

▶ **ANOTHER WAY**

Open the *Select Data Source* dialog box by clicking **Select Data** at the bottom of the *Chart Filters* pane. Define filters from this dialog box by selecting or deselecting a series or category name box.

SLO 3.4

Formatting Chart Elements

Quick Layout and *Chart Styles* apply formatting, but you can change most attributes to personalize your work. Applying your own format choices enables you to distinguish your charts from those of other Excel users. You can also use company, association, or school colors and images to further differentiate your charts.

Chart elements may consist of a group of related elements. A data series, for example, is the group of values for a particular item. Each data series includes data points. You can format the entire data series or an individual data point.

When you select a chart element, certain options on the *Chart Tools Design* tab apply to only that element. When the chart area (background) is selected, for example, you can change only its fill or border color.

Apply a Shape Style

A *shape style* is a predesigned set of borders, fill colors, and effects for a chart element. *Shape fill* is the background color, and *shape outline* is the border around the element. *Shape effects* include shadows, glows, bevels, or soft edges. All of these commands are available in the *Shape Styles* group on the *Chart Tools Format* tab.

Shape styles are shown in a gallery and are grouped as *Theme Styles* or *Presets*. Point to an icon to see a *ScreenTip* with a descriptive name and click an icon to apply it to the selected element. *Live Preview* is available for a chart object but not for a chart sheet.

▶ HOW TO: Apply a Shape Style

1. Select the chart element.
 - Confirm or select a chart element by clicking the **Chart Elements** drop-down arrow [*Chart Tools Format* tab, *Current Selection* group] and choosing the name.
 - If you accidentally open the *Format* task pane for a chart element, close it.
2. Click the **More** button [*Chart Tools Format* tab, *Shape Styles* group].
 - Each icon in the *Shape Styles* gallery displays fill, outline, and effects (Figure 3-24).
 - Point to an icon to see its name and *Live Preview* in a chart object.
3. Click a shape style icon.
 - The chart element is reformatted.

Figure 3-24 *Shape Style* gallery for the chart area

Apply Shape Fill, Outline, and Effects

Fill color, outline width and color, and special effects are available separately, and your choices override shape style settings already applied.

For fill color, you choose from the gallery, standard colors, or a custom color. After you choose a color, you can format it to use a gradient, a variegated blend of the color.

▶ HOW TO: Apply Gradient Fill to a Chart Element

1. Select the chart element.
 - Confirm or select a chart element from the **Chart Elements** list [*Chart Tools Format* tab, *Current Selection* group].
2. Click the **Shape Fill** button [*Chart Tools Format* tab, *Shape Styles* group].
 - The gallery and menu options display.
3. Point to a color tile to see its name in a *ScreenTip*.
 - *Live Preview* applies the color to an element in a chart object.
4. Select a color tile to apply the color.
5. Click the **Shape Fill** [*Chart Tools Format* tab, *Shape Styles* group].
6. Choose **Gradient** to open the gallery (Figure 3-25).
7. Point to a tile to see its description.
8. Click the preferred gradient.

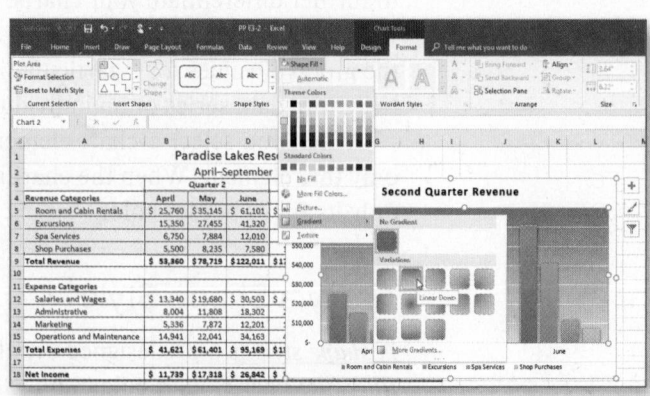

Figure 3-25 *Shape Fill* and *Gradient* galleries

The outline for a shape is a border that surrounds or encircles the element. Not all chart elements are suited to an outline, but elements such as the chart or plot area often benefit from the use of an outline. When you add an outline to a chart element, you can select a weight or thickness for the line, as well as a color. The thickness of an outline is measured in points, like fonts. Excel provides a gallery of weights to help you visualize the width. After you apply an outline, it is easier to see the effect if you deselect the chart object.

▶ HOW TO: Apply an Outline to a Chart Element

1. Select the chart element.
2. Click the **Shape Outline** button [*Chart Tools Format* tab, *Shape Styles* group].
 - The gallery and menu options display.
3. Choose a color.
4. Click the **Shape Outline** button [*Chart Tools Format* tab, *Shape Styles* group].
5. Click **Weight** to open its gallery.
6. Choose a width for the outline (Figure 3-26).
7. Click a worksheet cell or another chart element to see the outline.

Figure 3-26 *Outline color and Weight galleries*

Special effects commonly used are bevels and shadows, because they create a realistic, three-dimensional look. These effects are best used on larger elements, such as the chart area, because they can overwhelm smaller elements.

To remove an effect, select the element and click the **Shape Effects** button. Choose the effect group to select the first option such as *No Shadow* or *No Bevel*.

▶ HOW TO: Apply an Effect to a Chart Element

1. Select the chart element.
2. Click the **Shape Effects** button [*Chart Tools Format* tab, *Shape Styles* group].
 - The gallery lists effect groups and then variations for each group.
3. Select a group for the effect (Figure 3-27).
 - If a group name is grayed out, it is not available for the selected element.
4. Point to an icon to see its name.
5. Click to choose an effect.
6. Click a worksheet cell or another chart element to see the effect.

Figure 3-27 *Shape Effects gallery for the plot area*

The Format Task Pane

Every chart element has a *Format* task pane that consolidates shape, fill, and color options and provides custom commands for the element. To open the *Format* pane for a chart element, double-click the element or right-click it and choose *Format [Element Name]* from the menu. The *Format* pane opens to the right of the workbook window and automatically updates to reflect the selected element.

> **ANOTHER WAY**
>
> Open a *Format* task pane for a selected object by clicking the **Format Selection** button [*Chart Tools Format* tab, *Selection* group].

A task pane lists command options at the top of the pane. In Figure 3-28, *Title Options* and *Text Options* are available because the selected element is a chart title. The small triangle next to the first *Options* name enables you to choose a different chart element.

For each options group, the *Format* task panes have at least two buttons. The *Fill & Line*, *Effects*, and *Options* buttons are common, but other buttons are available for selected elements. Point to a button to see its *Screen-Tip*. When you click a button, the pane displays relevant commands.

Figure 3-28 *Format Chart Title* pane

> **MORE INFO**
>
> Expand or collapse a command group in the *Format* task pane by clicking the command name.

▶HOW TO: Use the Format Task Pane to Change Shape Fill

1. Double-click the chart element.
 - The *Format* task pane for the element opens on the right.
 - Select another element in the chart to see its task pane.
 - Select an element and click the **Format Selection** button [*Chart Tools Format* tab, *Current Selection* group] to open the task pane.

2. Click the name of the *Options* group at the top of the task pane.
 - For some chart elements, only one group displays.

3. Click the **Fill & Line** button in the *Format* task pane.

4. Click **Fill** to expand the group.

5. Click the **Color** button to open the gallery (Figure 3-29).

6. Choose the desired color.

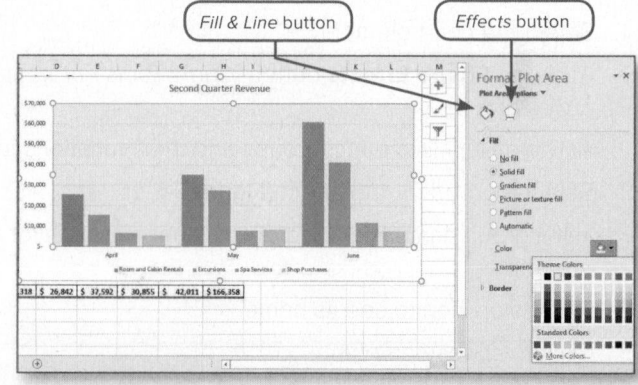

Figure 3-29 *Fill & Line* command in the *Format Plot Area* task pane

While the *Fill & Line* and *Effects* buttons offer similar commands for all elements, the *Options* button in a *Format* task pane is specific to the element. For a data series in a column chart, for example, these commands determine whether numbers are shown to the right or left of the chart (secondary or primary axis), or whether the columns overlap. A pie chart, on the other hand, has options that enable you to rotate the pie or explode slices.

▶HOW TO: Use the Format Task Pane to Format Data Labels

1. Double-click a data label element in the chart.
 - Right-click an element and choose **Format Data Labels**.
 - All data labels for one series are selected.
2. Choose **Label Options** at the top of the task pane.
 - Point to a button to see a *ScreenTip*.
 - *Text Options* are also available.
3. Click **Label Options** or **Number** to expand the command group.
4. Select format options for the labels (Figure 3-30).
 - Formats are applied as you select them.
5. Close the task pane.

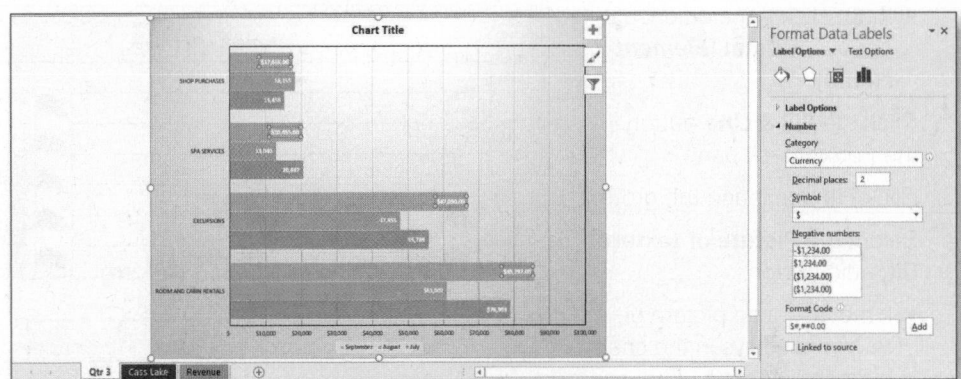

Figure 3-30 *Format Data Labels* pane with *Number* group expanded

Using Pictures, Shapes, and WordArt in a Chart

Enhance a chart with pictures, shapes, or *WordArt*. Insert pictures as separate design objects on the chart, or use them as fill for a chart element. You can draw a shape such as an arrow or a lightning bolt to highlight a particular data point on a chart. *WordArt* is often applied to a chart title for a distinctive look.

Use a Picture as Shape Fill

An image can be used to fill the chart area, the plot area, or a marker, especially bars, columns, or pie slices. You have probably seen bar charts with stick figures to illustrate population numbers or column charts with tiny automobile images to show auto sales. You can use an image file from your computer, from external media, or from an online source. Always verify that you have permission to use an image in your work.

The size and design of the picture is important, and you should guard against making the chart appear busy. You may be able to edit attributes of a picture in Excel, but this depends on the picture format.

Insert a picture using the *Fill* command on the *Format* task pane for the element. After you insert a picture, the task pane displays *Stretch* and *Stack* options. *Stretch* enlarges and elongates a single copy of a picture to fill the element. The *Stack* choice sizes and repeats the image to fill the area. Use the *Stack and Scale* setting for precise matching of the number of images used per unit of value.

▶ HOW TO: Use a Picture as Fill

1. Double-click the chart element for the fill.
 - The *Format* task pane opens.
 - Right-click the element and choose **Format [*Element Name*]**.

2. Click the **Fill & Line** button in the *Format* task pane.

3. Click **Fill** to expand the group.

4. Select the **Picture or texture fill** radio button.
 - If the last-used picture or texture displays in the chart element, ignore it. It will be replaced.

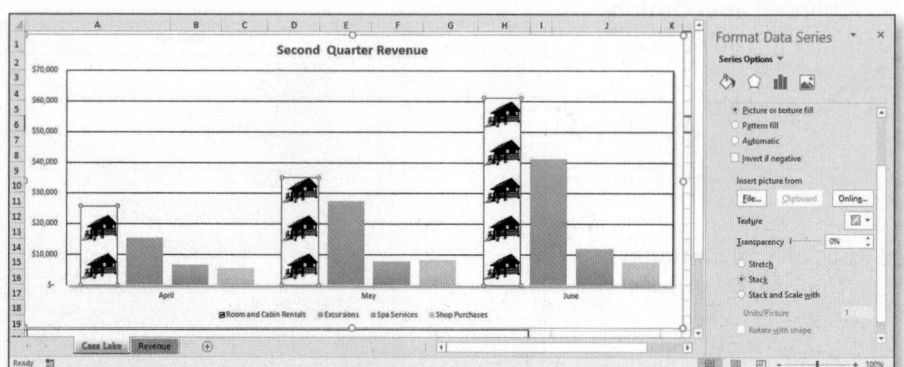

Figure 3-31 Image used as fill for data series

5. Click **Online** to search for an image or click **File** to choose a stored image.

6. Find and insert the image.
 - The picture fills the chart element.

7. Click the **Stack** button in the task pane (Figure 3-31).
 - Copies of the picture fill the element.

Insert Shapes

The *Shapes* gallery is located in the *Insert Shapes* group on the *Chart Tools Format* tab. These predefined shapes include arrows, lines, circles, and other basic figures. Shapes can be used to highlight or emphasize a point in the chart. They can be drawn anywhere on the chart, but are usually placed on the background or the plot area so they do not obscure any data. A shape, once drawn, is an object. When it is selected, the *Picture Tools Format* tab is available with commands for altering the appearance of the shape, as well as the *Format Shape* task pane.

▶ HOW TO: Insert a Shape in a Chart

1. Select the chart object or the chart sheet tab.

2. Click the **More** button [*Chart Tools Format* tab, *Insert Shapes* group].

3. Select a shape.

4. Click and drag to draw the shape on the chart.
 - The shape is selected.
5. Type text for the shape (Figure 3-32).
 - Text is optional.
 - Not all shapes can display text.
6. Click the **Drawing Tools Format** tab to format the shape.
 - Apply formatting from the *Format Shape* task pane.
7. Click a worksheet cell or another chart element to deselect the shape.

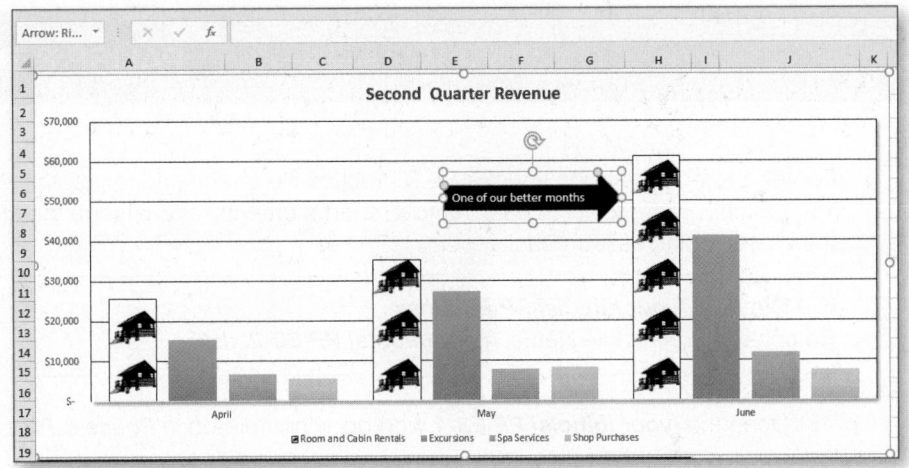

Figure 3-32 Shape inserted in chart

ANOTHER WAY

Insert a shape from the *Shapes* button on the *Insert* tab [*Illustrations* group].

Use WordArt in a Chart

WordArt is a text box with preset font style, fill, and effects. *WordArt* is best used for main titles, because smaller elements may be unreadable. You apply a *WordArt* style from the *Chart Tools Format* tab, *WordArt Styles* group. Format a *WordArt* style by individually changing its fill, outline, and effects.

MORE INFO

Insert a *WordArt* text box from the *Insert* tab [*Text* group] and position it on the chart.

▶ HOW TO: Use WordArt in a Chart

1. Select the chart title object.
 - You can also apply *WordArt* to an axis title, a data label, or the legend.
2. Click the **More** button to open the *WordArt Styles* gallery [*Chart Tools Format* tab, *WordArt Styles* group].
3. Point to a style icon to see a *ScreenTip* with a description.
 - The styles use colors and effects from the workbook theme.
 - *Live Preview* works in a chart object but not on a chart sheet.
4. Click the preferred style (Figure 3-33).

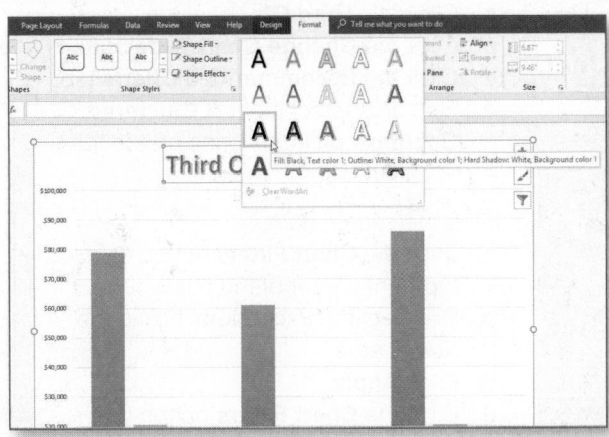

Figure 3-33 *WordArt Style* gallery for selected chart title

For this project, you open your Pause & Practice file to edit and format the Paradise Lakes Resort charts. You switch row and column data, remove chart elements, and change the chart type. Finally, you format the charts for increased visual appeal.

File Needed: *[your initials] PP E3-1.xlsx*
Completed Project File Name: *[your initials] PP E3-2.xlsx*

1. Open the *[your initials] PP E3-1* workbook completed in *Pause & Practice 3-1* and save it as [your initials] PP E3-2.

2. Switch the row and column data in the chart object.
 a. Click the **Cass Lake** worksheet tab.
 b. Point to the border or edge of the chart object and click to select it.
 c. Click the **Switch/Row Column** button [*Chart Tools Design* tab, *Data* group].

3. Edit, add, and remove chart elements.
 a. Click to select the chart title box.
 b. Point to the placeholder text and triple-click to select all of it.
 c. Type Second Quarter Activity.
 d. Click the chart border to deselect the title.
 e. Click the **Chart Elements** button in the top-right corner of the chart.
 f. Select the **Axis Titles** box.
 g. Select the horizontal *Axis Title* placeholder below the columns and press **Delete**.
 h. Select the vertical *Axis Title* placeholder.
 i. Click the *Formula* bar, type Monthly Revenue, and press **Enter** (Figure 3-34).
 j. Click a worksheet cell to deselect the chart object.

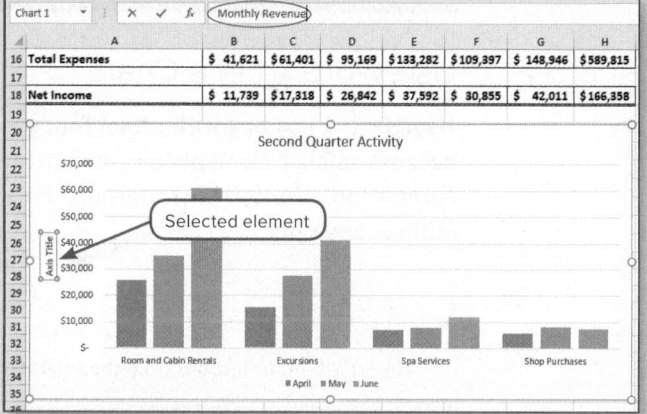

Figure 3-34 Edit placeholder text in the *Formula* bar

4. Change the chart type.
 a. Click the **Third Qtr** sheet tab.
 b. Click the **Change Chart Type** button [*Chart Tools Design* tab, *Type* group].
 c. Click the **Recommended Charts** tab.
 d. Find and select the first **Clustered Column** icon in the pane on the left.
 e. Click **OK**.

5. Filter the source data.
 a. Click the **Chart Filters** button at the top-right corner of the chart.
 b. Deselect the **Excursions** box in the *Series* area.
 c. Click **Apply**.
 d. Click the **Chart Filters** button to close the pane (Figure 3-35).

Figure 3-35 Filtered data in chart

6. Apply shape styles and outlines to chart elements.
 a. Click the **Cass Lake** tab and select the chart object.
 b. Click the **Chart Tools Format** tab and then click the **Chart Elements** drop-down arrow [*Current Selection* group].
 c. Choose **Plot Area** to select the plot area of the chart.
 d. Click the **More** button [*Chart Tools Format* tab, *Shape Styles* group].
 e. Click **Subtle Effect – Gold, Accent 4** in the fourth row in the *Theme Styles* group.
 f. Click the drop-down arrow for the **Shape Outline** button [*Chart Tools Format* tab, *Shape Styles* group].
 g. Choose **Black, Text 1** in the top row of the *Theme Colors*.
 h. Click the **Chart Elements** drop-down arrow [*Chart Tools Format* tab, *Current Selection* group].
 i. Choose **Vertical (Value) Axis Major Gridlines** to select the major gridlines in the plot area.
 j. Click the icon with the **Shape Outline** button [*Chart Tools Format* tab, *Shape Styles* group] to apply the last-used color (**Black, Text 1**).
 k. Click the **Chart Elements** drop-down arrow [*Chart Tools Format* tab, *Current Selection* group] and choose **Chart Area**.
 l. Apply **Black, Text 1** for the outline (Figure 3-36).
 m. Click a worksheet cell to deselect the chart object.

Figure 3-36 Plot area formatted

7. Use a picture as fill.
 a. Click the **Third Qtr** tab.
 b. Double-click one of the "Room and Cabin Rentals" columns to open the *Format Data Series* task pane.
 c. Click the **Fill & Line** button.
 d. Click **Fill** to expand the command group.
 e. Select the **Picture or texture fill** button.
 f. Click **Online**, type log cabin in the search box, and press **Enter**.
 g. Choose an image and insert it (Figure 3-37). If you choose an image that cannot be used as fill, a message appears in the columns; just select a different picture.
 h. Select the **Stack** radio button in the *Format Data Series* task pane.

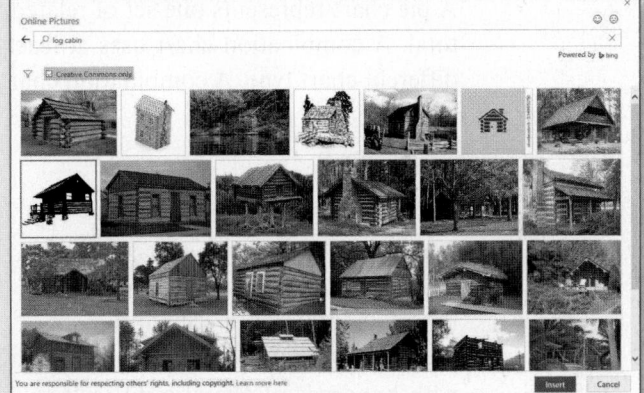

Figure 3-37 Online search for a picture as fill

 i. Click **Fill** to collapse the command group and click **Border** to expand its group.
 j. Select the **Solid line** radio button.
 k. Click the **Color** button and choose **Black, Text 1**.
 l. Close the task pane.

8. Use *WordArt* in a chart.
 a. Triple-click the **Chart Title** placeholder text to select the text.
 b. Type Third Quarter Activity.
 c. Triple-click the new label and change the font size to **32 pt**.
 d. Click the border area of the chart title to display the selection handles for the text box.
 e. Click the **More** button [*Chart Tools Format* tab, *WordArt Styles* group].
 f. Choose **Fill: Light Gray, Background color 2; Inner Shadow** (third row).

9. Format the legend.
 a. Click to select the legend.
 b. Click the **Home** tab and change the font size to **12 pt**.
 c. Click the chart border to deselect the legend.

10. Save and close the workbook (Figure 3-38).

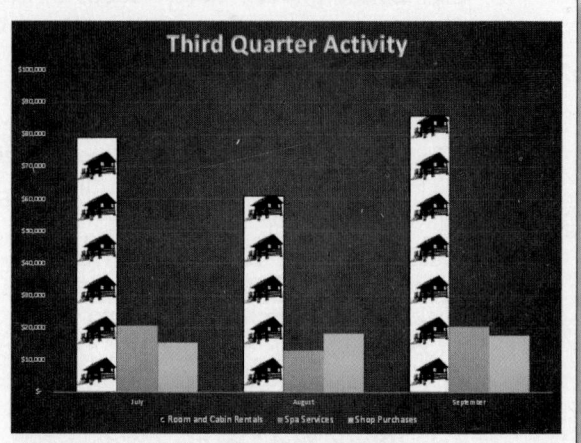

Figure 3-38 PP E3-2 completed worksheet and chart sheet

SLO 3.6

Building Pie and Combination Charts

A pie chart represents one set of related values and shows the proportion of each value to the total. A combination chart uses at least two sets of values and plots each data series with a different chart type. A combination chart can also have two value axes, one on the left and one on the right.

Create a 3-D Pie Chart

A pie chart graphs one data series and illustrates how each number relates to the whole. Be cautious about the number of categories, because a pie chart with hundreds of slices is difficult to interpret and does not depict the relationship among the values.

From the *Insert Pie or Doughnut Chart* button on the *Insert* tab, you can select from a gallery of 2-D or 3-D pie

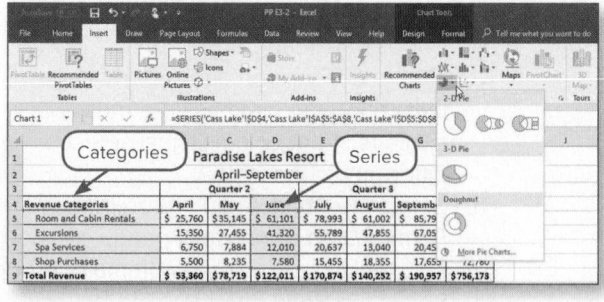

Figure 3-39 Selected data series and categories for a pie chart

types, as well as a doughnut shape (Figure 3-39). You can also select options for a pie chart with a bar or another pie chart. As you point to each subtype, *Live Preview* previews the chart.

▶ **HOW TO:** Create a 3-D Pie Chart Sheet

1. Select the cells that include the values and the category labels.
 - The labels and values need not be adjacent.

E3-188

2. Click the **Insert Pie or Doughnut Chart** button [*Insert* tab, *Charts* group].

3. Choose **3-D Pie**.

 - A pie chart object displays in the worksheet.

4. Click the **Move Chart** button [*Chart Tools Design* tab, *Location* group].

5. Click the **New sheet** button.

6. Type a name for the chart sheet.

7. Click **OK**.

Pie Chart Elements and Options

In a pie chart, the data series is represented by the whole pie. A data point is a slice of the pie. You can format the data series as a whole or as individual slices.

A pie chart can display a legend and a title. It does not, however, have axes and does not use axes titles. Use data labels in place of a legend, because they show the same information.

Custom commands for a pie chart are the angle of the first slice and the percent of explosion. These commands are available on the *Format* task pane for the data series (the whole pie) or for a selected data point (one slice). The angle of the first slice enables you to rotate the pie. The first slice starts at the top of the chart at 0° (zero degrees). As you increase that value, the slice arcs to the right. *Live Preview* displays the results, too.

Exploding a pie slice emphasizes that slice, because it moves the slice away from the rest of the pie. This uses more white space in the chart, and the pie gets smaller. You set explosion as a percentage.

▶ HOW TO: Rotate a Pie Chart and Explode a Slice

1. Double-click the pie shape.

 - The *Format Data Series* task pane opens.
 - Right-click the pie shape and choose **Format Data Series**.

2. Click the **Series Options** button.

3. Drag the vertical slider to set the *Angle of first slice*.

 - The percentage is shown in the entry box.
 - Type a percentage or use the spinner arrows to set a value.

4. Click the data point (slice) to explode.

 - The *Format Data Point* task pane opens.

5. Drag the vertical slider to set the *Pie Explosion* (Figure 3-40).

 - The percentage is shown in the entry box.
 - The larger the percentage, the farther the slice is from the rest of the pie.
 - Type a percentage or use the spinner arrows to set a value.

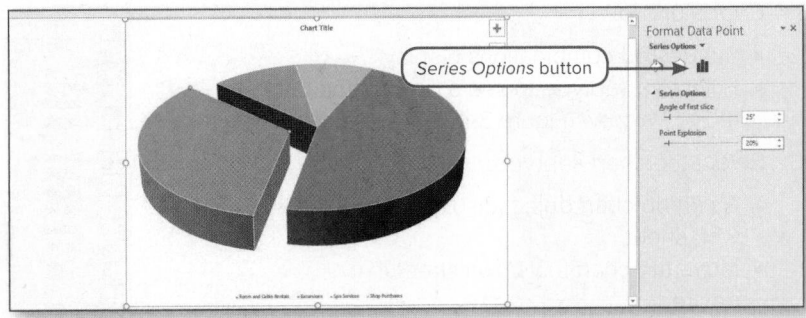

Figure 3-40 Exploded pie slice with angle of first slice changed

Create a Combination Chart

A combination chart includes at least two chart types such as a line chart and a column chart. Paradise Lakes Resort can use a combination chart to compare revenue from cabin and room rentals to total revenue. These two values require a wide range of numbers, so showing one series as a line and the other as a column focuses the comparison (Figure 3-41).

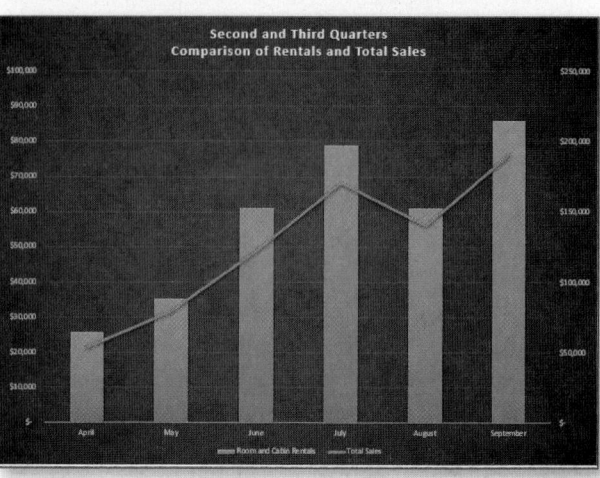

Figure 3-41 Line-Column combination chart

> **MORE INFO**
>
> A line and column combination chart resembles a column chart with a trendline, but the combination chart uses actual values. The trendline predicts values.

> **MORE INFO**
>
> Not all chart types can be combined. If you try to build an unacceptable combination, Excel opens a message box to inform you.

The most common combination of chart types is line and column, but you can also use a line and area combination. Excel offers an option to create a custom combination, but it is best to use this only after you have experience charting your data.

Create a combination chart from the *Insert Combo Chart* button in the *Charts* group on the *Insert* tab, as well as from the *All Charts* tab in the *Insert Chart* dialog box.

▶ HOW TO: Create a Combination Chart

1. Select the cell ranges for the chart.
 - The cell ranges need not be contiguous.
2. Click the **Insert Combo Chart** button [*Insert* tab, *Charts* group].
 - Suggested combinations display.
 - Point to a subtype to see a description and a *Live Preview* (Figure 3-42).
3. Select the chart subtype.
 - A combo chart object displays in the worksheet.
 - Move the chart to its own sheet if desired.

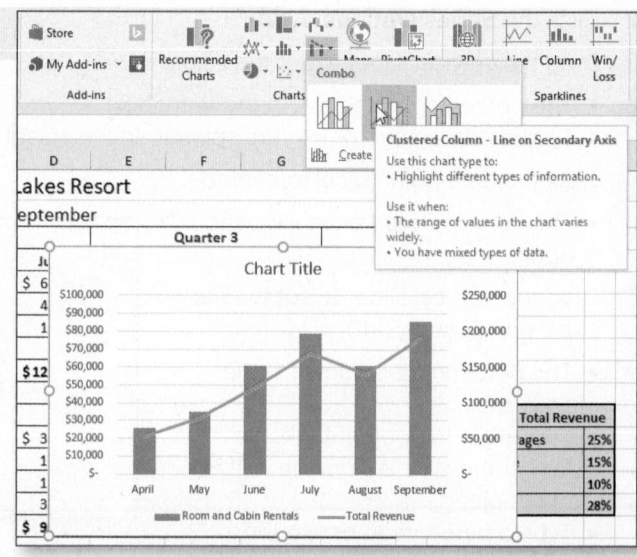

Figure 3-42 *Insert Combo Chart* button options

Combination Chart Elements and Options

A combination chart has at least two data series, each graphed in its own chart type. Keep this type of chart relatively simple, because its purpose is to compare unlike items and too many data series complicate what viewers see.

In a combination chart, you can display values on two vertical axes. The axis on the left is the primary

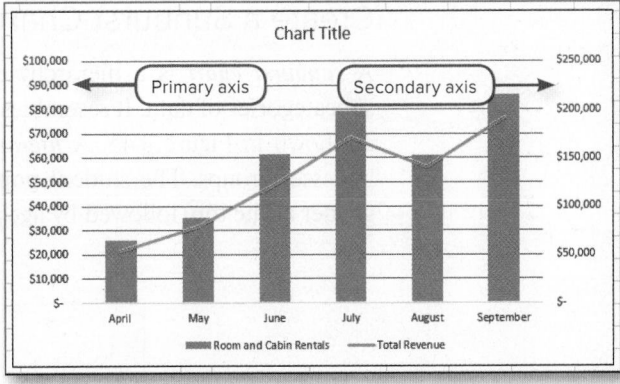

Figure 3-43 Secondary axis for a combo chart

axis; the one on the right is secondary (Figure 3-43). This option is best when the values are very different or use a different scale.

For the secondary axis, Excel builds the number scale based on the data. Select the data series to be plotted on the secondary axis and choose the option from the *Series Options* command group in the *Format* task pane. You can also define a secondary axis in the *Insert Chart* or the *Change Chart Type* dialog boxes.

A combination chart has the same elements and commands as a regular column or line chart. Apply chart styles and layouts, as well as shape fill, outline, effects, pictures, shapes, and *WordArt*.

▶**HOW TO:** Display a Secondary Axis on a Combination Chart

1. Select the chart object or the chart sheet tab.
2. Select the data series to be shown on the secondary axis.
 - Select the line or any column in a line-column combo chart.
 - You can also choose the data series from the *Chart Elements* box [*Chart Tools Format* tab, *Current Selection* group].
3. Click the **Format Selection** button [*Chart Tools Format* tab, *Current Selection* group].
4. Click the **Series Options** button in the task pane (Figure 3-44).
5. Click the **Secondary Axis** radio button.
 - Additional options for the axis depend on the chart type.
6. Close the *Format Data Series* task pane.

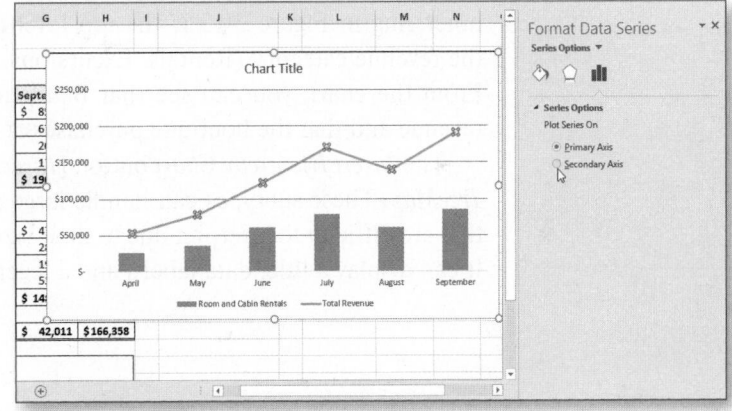

Figure 3-44 *Format Data Series* task pane to define a secondary axis

Creating Sunburst and Waterfall Charts

Specialty chart types in Excel visualize data in ways that previously required engineering, mapping, or other expert software. The *Charts* group on the *Insert* tab includes buttons for *Hierarchy*, *Statistic*, and *Map* charts. These charts have characteristics of standard Excel charts, as well as their own requirements or limitations. For example, to create a map chart, you must have high-detail geographical data and access to the *Bing Map* service.

Create a Sunburst Chart

A *sunburst chart* is a hierarchy chart that illustrates the relationship among categories and subcategories of data. It resembles a doughnut chart with concentric rings for each layer of data, as shown in Figure 3-45. A *hierarchy* is a division of data that identifies a top group followed by lesser groups. The student population at your college can be illustrated in a hierarchy with gender at the top, followed by age group, then home city, followed by area of study, and so on.

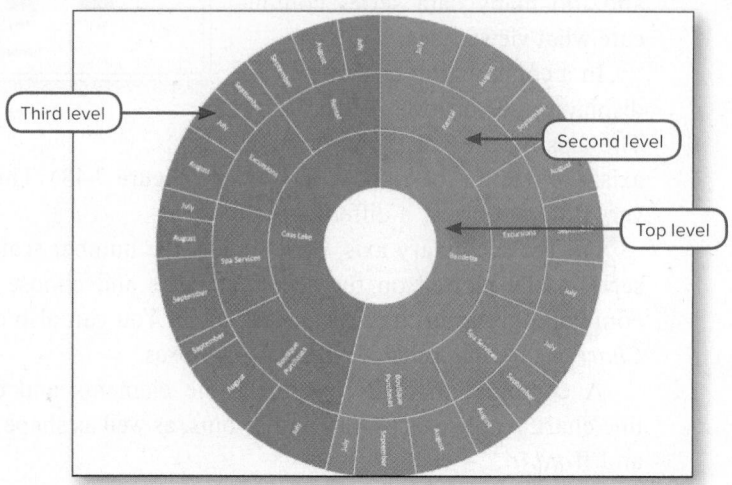

Figure 3-45 Sunburst chart for third quarter revenue for two locations

Paradise Lakes Resort keeps a record of revenue by location, category, and month. The inner ring in Figure 3-45 is the top level of the hierarchy, the location. The second level is the revenue category (Rentals, Excursions, etc.), and the outside ring is the month's revenue. From the chart, you can see that Baudette contributed slightly more than half of the total revenue and that the boutique purchases at Cass Lake were high.

The *Insert Hierarchy Chart* button [*Insert* tab, *Charts* group] has two subtypes, *Sunburst* and *TreeMap*. These subtypes can handle large amounts of data, but be careful not to build charts that are difficult to interpret due to their size. A sunburst chart has one data series and no axes. It can display a title, data labels, and a legend.

> **MORE INFO**
>
> A *TreeMap* chart illustrates hierarchical data using rectangles of various sizes and colors to represent the divisions and subdivisions.

▶ HOW TO: Create a Sunburst Chart

1. Select the source data with labels and values.
2. Click the **Insert Hierarchy Chart** button [*Insert* tab, *Charts* group].
 - A menu lists the subtypes.
 - From the *Quick Analysis* button, select **Charts**, **More**, and then click the **All Charts** tab.

3. Point to **Sunburst** to see a *Live Preview*.

4. Click **Sunburst** to select it.

 - A chart object displays in the worksheet.

5. Click the **Move Chart** button [*Chart Tools Design* tab, *Location* group].

6. Select **New sheet**.

7. Type a name for the chart sheet and click **OK**.

 - The *Chart Tools Design* and *Format* tabs are available.

8. Click the sunburst shape to select the circle.

9. Point to a category name in the inner ring and click to select the data point.

 - The category and its related items are selected (Figure 3-46).

Figure 3-46 Sunburst chart sheet with selected data point

10. Format the data point as desired.

 - If the *Format Data Point* task pane is not open, click the **Format Selection** button [*Chart Tools Format* tab, *Current Selection* group].

11. Click outside the chart background to deselect the chart.

Create a Waterfall Chart

A ***waterfall chart*** is a financial chart that displays a moving total for positive and negative values. A waterfall chart graphs how each expense or outlay affects the account. You might, for example, build a waterfall chart to visualize your monthly income sources (inflows) and expenditures (outlays) to watch how you spend your resources.

In Figure 3-47, it is obvious that payroll consumes most of the cash account for Paradise Lakes Resort. In a waterfall chart, the depth or height of the marker indicates the value. In the figure, the beginning balance and ending total markers rest on the bottom axis. The other amounts are described as floating.

A waterfall chart plots one data series and has a legend that clarifies the increase, decrease, and total colors. A waterfall chart also includes axes, titles, gridlines, and data labels.

The *Insert Waterfall or Stock Chart* button is in the *Chart* group on the *Insert* tab.

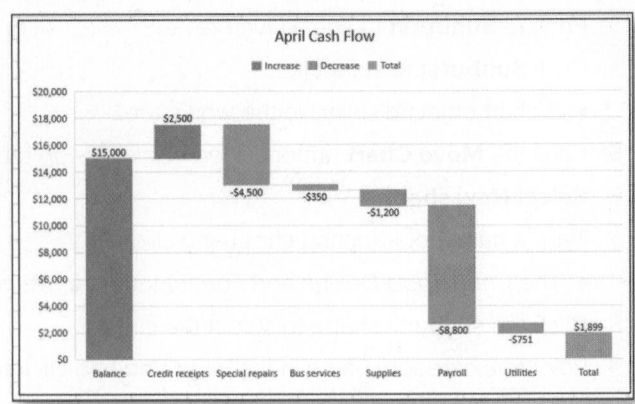

Figure 3-47 Waterfall chart for cash flow

▶ **HOW TO: Create a Waterfall Chart Sheet**

1. Select the source data with labels and values.
2. Click the **Insert Waterfall, Funnel, Stock, Surface, or Radar Chart** button [*Insert* tab, *Charts* group].
 - A menu lists the subtypes.
3. Click **Waterfall**.
 - A chart object is placed in the worksheet.
4. Click the **Move Chart** button [*Chart Tools Design* tab, *Location* group].
5. Select **New sheet**.
6. Type a name for the chart sheet and click **OK**.
 - The *Chart Tools Design* and *Format* tabs are available.
7. Click a column marker to select the data series.
8. Click the ending marker to select only that marker.
9. Click the **Format Selection** button [*Chart Tools Format* tab, *Current Selection* group].

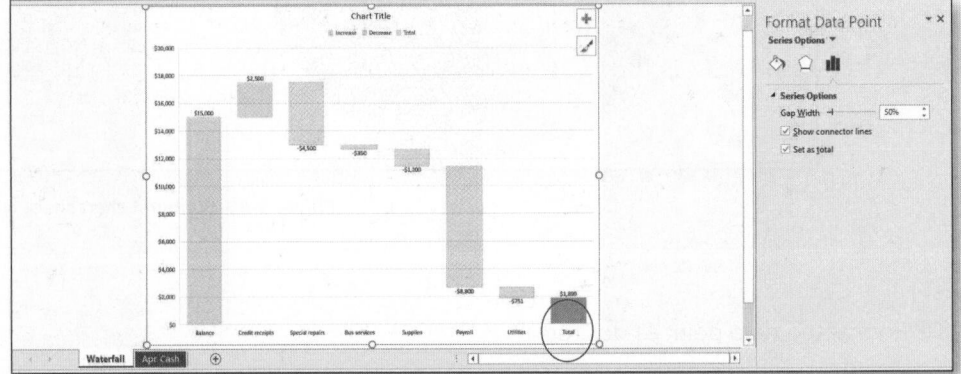

Figure 3-48 Set a marker as a total

10. Click the **Series Options** button in the task pane.
11. Expand the *Series Options* group.
12. Select the **Set as total** box (Figure 3-48).
 - The marker rests on the bottom axis and is no longer floating.
13. Close the task pane and click outside the chart to deselect it.

SLO 3.8

Inserting and Formatting Sparklines

Sparklines are miniature charts in a cell or cell range. Sparklines illustrate trends and patterns without adding a separate chart object or sheet. They do not have the same characteristics as an Excel chart.

Sparklines are created from a selected data range and placed in a location range, usually next to the data (Figure 3-49). They are embedded in the cell, almost like a background. If you enter a label or value in a cell with a sparkline, that data appears on top of the sparkline.

Sales Categories	April	May	June	July	August	September		Total
		Quarter 2			Quarter 3			
Room and Cabin Rentals	$ 25,760	$ 35,145	$ 61,101	$ 78,993	$ 61,002	$ 85,797		$ 347,798
Excursions	15,350	27,455	41,320	55,789	47,855	67,050		254,819
Spa Services	6,750	7,884	12,010	20,637	13,040	20,455		80,776
Shop Purchases	5,500	8,235	7,580	15,455	18,355	17,655		72,780
Total Sales	$ 53,360	$ 78,719	$ 122,011	$ 170,874	$ 140,252	$ 190,957		$ 756,173

Figure 3-49 Column sparklines in a worksheet

Insert Sparklines

Three sparkline types are available: *Line*, *Column*, and *Win/Loss*. The *Sparklines* commands are located on the *Insert* tab of the worksheet. The *Data Range* is the range of cells to be graphed, and the *Location Range* is the cell or range for the sparklines. The **Sparkline Tools Design** tab opens when you select the sparkline group.

▶ **HOW TO: Insert Column Sparklines in a Worksheet**

1. Select the cell range of data to be graphed.

2. Click the **Column Sparkline** button [*Insert* tab, *Sparklines* group].
 - The selected range address is shown in the *Data Range* entry box.
 - Select or edit the data range.

3. Click the *Location Range* box.

4. Select the cell or range for the sparklines (Figure 3-50).
 - The range address displays as an absolute reference.

5. Click **OK**.

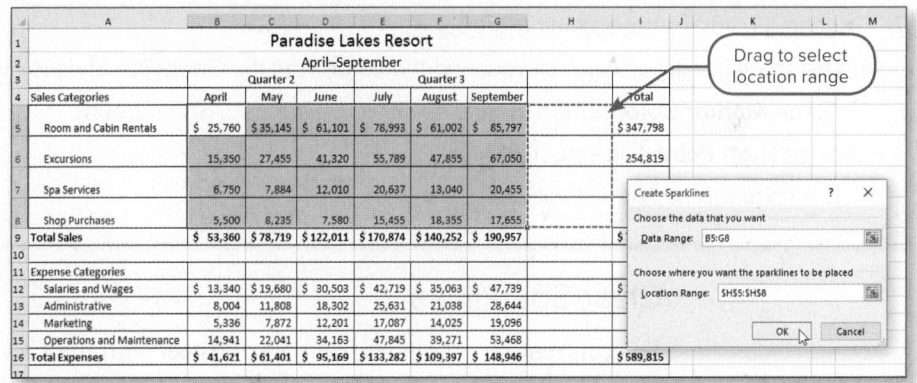

Figure 3-50 *Create Sparklines* dialog box

Sparkline Design Tools

When sparklines are selected, the *Sparkline Tools Design* tab opens. This contextual tab includes several options for changing the appearance of the sparklines. A *Sparkline Style* option changes the color scheme for the sparkline group, but you can also change colors with the *Sparkline Color* command. The *Marker Color* command enables you to choose a different color for identified values. A **marker** for a sparkline represents a data point value. You can use different colors to highlight the high, low, first, or last value, as well as negative values.

When you define a location range for sparklines, they are embedded as a group. If you select any cell in the sparkline range, the entire group is selected. Subsequent commands affect all sparklines in the group. From the *Group* section on the *Sparkline Tools Design* tab, you can ungroup the sparklines to format them individually.

From the *Sparkline Tools Design* tab, change the type of sparkline, such as making a column sparkline into a line sparkline. The *Show* group lists marker values that can be highlighted. When you select an option in the *Show* group, that individual marker is formatted with a different color.

▶ HOW TO: Format Sparklines

1. Click a cell with a sparkline.
 - The sparkline group is selected.
2. Click the **Sparkline Tools Design** tab.
3. Click the **More** button [*Sparkline Tools Design* tab, *Style* group].
4. Choose a sparkline style.
 - The sparkline group is recolored.
5. Select the **High Point** box in the *Show* group (Figure 3-51).
 - A default color based on the sparkline style is applied to the highest value in the sparkline for each row.
6. Click the **Sparkline Color** button [*Sparkline Tools Design* tab, *Style* group].
7. Choose a color for the sparkline group.
 - The sparkline group is recolored, and the color from the *Sparkline Style* is overridden.
8. Click the **Marker Color** button [*Sparkline Tools Design* tab, *Style* group].
9. Choose **High Point** and select a color.
 - The color for the highest value is reset.

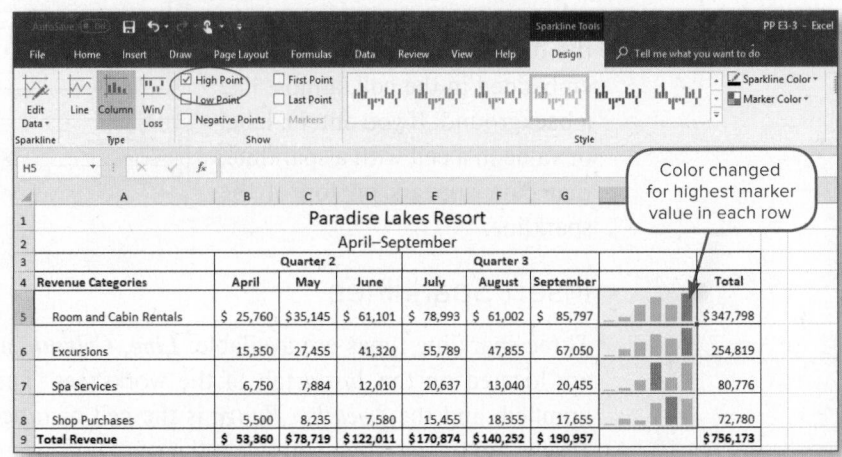

Figure 3-51 *High Point* marker selected for sparklines

Clear Sparklines

You can remove sparklines from a worksheet with the *Clear* command in the *Group* group on the *Sparkline Tools Design* tab. After sparklines are cleared, you may also need to delete the column where they were located or reset row heights and column widths.

▶ HOW TO: Clear Sparklines

1. Select any cell in the sparklines range.
2. Click the arrow with the **Clear Selected Sparklines** button [*Sparkline Tools Design* tab, *Group* group].
 - If you click the button and not its arrow, the selected sparkline cell is cleared.
3. Choose **Clear Selected Sparklines Groups**.

> **MORE INFO**
>
> Ungroup sparklines to create individual sparklines in each cell.

PAUSE & PRACTICE: EXCEL 3-3

For this project, you complete Paradise Lakes' revenue report by inserting a pie chart that shows the proportion of each revenue category. You also insert a combination chart sheet to compare rentals with total revenue and a sunburst chart to analyze third quarter revenue. Finally, you insert sparklines in the worksheet.

File Needed: *[your initials] PP E3-2.xlsx*
Completed Project File Name: *[your initials] PP E3-3.xlsx*

1. Open the *[your initials] PP E3-2* workbook completed in *Pause & Practice 3-2* and save it as [your initials] PP E3-3.

2. Create a pie chart for total sales revenue.
 a. Select the **Cass Lake** tab.
 b. Select cells **A5:A8** as the category.
 c. Press **Ctrl** and select cells **H5:H8** as the data series.
 d. Click the **Insert Pie or Doughnut Chart** button [*Insert* tab, *Charts* group].
 e. Choose **3-D Pie**.
 f. Click the **Move Chart** button [*Chart Tools Design* tab, *Location* group].
 g. Click the **New sheet** button and type Pie Chart as the sheet name.
 h. Click **OK**.

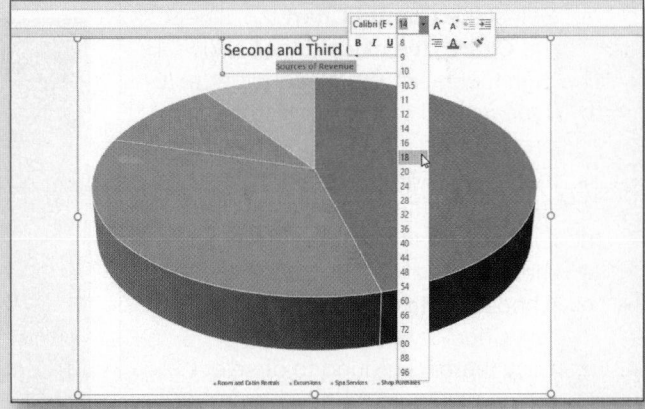

Figure 3-52 Chart titles typed and font size changed

3. Format a pie chart.
 a. Select the **Pie Chart** tab.
 b. Click the **Chart Title** placeholder to select it and then triple-click the **Chart Title** placeholder text.
 c. Type Second and Third Quarters and press **Enter**.
 d. Type Sources of Revenue on the second line.
 e. Drag to select the first line of the title.
 f. Use the mini toolbar to change the font size to **24 pt**.
 g. Drag to select the second line of the title.
 h. Use the mini toolbar to change the font size to **18 pt** (Figure 3-52).
 i. Click the chart border to deselect the title.
 j. Double-click the pie to open the *Format Data Series* task pane.
 k. Click the **Series Options** button in the *Format Data Series* task pane.
 l. Double-click the **Room and Cabin Rentals** slice to change to the *Format Data Point* task pane.

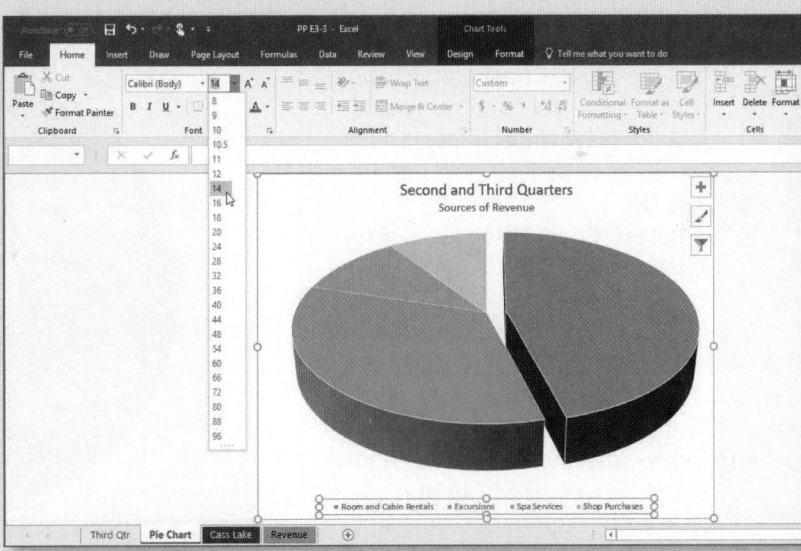

Figure 3-53 Change the font size from the *Home* tab

 m. Set the pie explosion percentage at **10%**.
 n. Close the task pane.
 o. Select the legend at the bottom of the chart to display selection handles.
 p. Click the **Home** tab and change the font size to **14 pt** (Figure 3-53).

4. Create a combination chart for total sales revenue and room and cabin rentals.
 a. Select the **Cass Lake** tab.
 b. Select cells **A4:G5** as one data series and category.

c. Press **Ctrl** and select cells **A9:G9** as another data series and category.
d. Click the **Insert Combo Chart** button [*Insert* tab, *Charts* group].
e. Choose **Clustered Column – Line on Secondary Axis**.
f. Click the **Move Chart** button [*Chart Tools Design* tab, *Location* group].
g. Click the **New sheet** button and type Combo Chart as the sheet name.
h. Click **OK**.

5. Format a combination chart.
 a. Select the **Combo Chart** tab, select the **Chart Title** placeholder, and then triple-click the placeholder text.
 b. Type Second and Third Quarters and press **Enter**.
 c. Type Comparison of Rentals and Total Revenue on the second line.
 d. Click the chart border to deselect the chart title.
 e. Choose **Style 6** [*Chart Tools Design* tab, *Chart Styles* group].
 f. Click the background to deselect the chart (Figure 3-54).

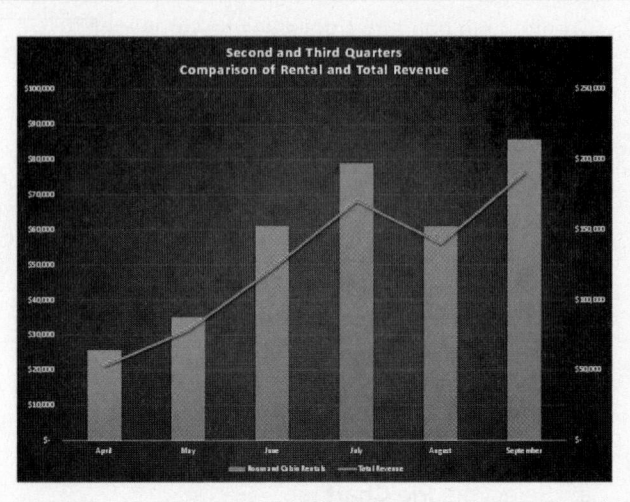

Figure 3-54 Combo chart with Style 6

6. Create a sunburst chart for third quarter revenue analysis.
 a. Select the **Revenue** tab.
 b. Select cells **A5:D28** as the data series and categories. This chart will illustrate revenue for Cass Lake and Baudette.
 c. Click the **Insert Hierarchy Chart** button [*Insert* tab, *Charts* group].
 d. Choose **Sunburst**.
 e. Click the **Move Chart** button [*Chart Tools Design* tab, *Location* group].
 f. Click the **New sheet** button and type Sunburst as the sheet name.
 g. Click **OK**.
 h. Select the **Chart Title** placeholder and type Third Quarter Revenue.
 i. Press **Enter** and type Cass Lake and Baudette on the second line (Figure 3-55).
 j. Click the chart border to deselect the title object.
 k. Click to select the title object and change its font size to **16 pt**.
 l. Click the background to deselect the chart.

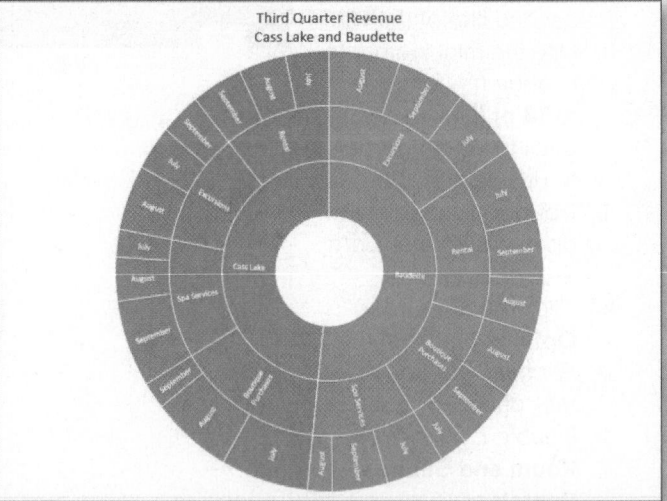

Figure 3-55 Sunburst chart with edited title

7. Insert sparklines in a worksheet.
 a. Select the **Cass Lake** tab.
 b. Right-click the column **H** heading and choose **Insert** to insert a new column.
 c. Select the cell range **B5:G8** as the data to be charted with sparklines.
 d. Click the **Column Sparkline** button [*Insert* tab, *Sparklines* group].
 e. Click the **Location Range** box and select cells **H5:H8**.
 f. Click **OK**.

8. Format sparklines.
 a. Click the **Sparkline Color** button [*Sparkline Tools Design* tab, *Style* group] and select **Green, Accent 6, Darker 25%** (last column).
 b. Select the sparkline group if necessary, click the **Format** button [*Home* tab, *Cells* group], and change the **Row Height** to **30 (40 pixels)**.
 c. Format column **H** to a width of **16.00 (117 pixels)**.
 d. Press **Ctrl+Home**.

9. Save and close the workbook (Figure 3-56).

Paradise Lakes Resort									
April–September									
		Quarter 2			Quarter 3				
Revenue Categories	April	May	June	July	August	September		Total	
Room and Cabin Rentals	$ 25,760	$35,145	$ 61,101	$ 78,993	$ 61,002	$ 85,797		$347,798	
Excursions	15,350	27,455	41,320	55,789	47,855	67,050		254,819	
Spa Services	6,750	7,884	12,010	20,637	13,040	20,455		80,776	
Shop Purchases	5,500	8,235	7,580	15,455	18,355	17,655		72,780	
Total Revenue	$ 53,360	$78,719	$122,011	$170,874	$140,252	$ 190,957		$756,173	
Expense Categories									
Salaries and Wages	$ 13,340	$19,680	$ 30,503	$ 42,719	$ 35,063	$ 47,739		$189,043	
Administrative	8,004	11,808	18,302	25,631	21,038	28,644		113,426	
Marketing	5,336	7,872	12,201	17,087	14,025	19,096		75,617	
Operations and Maintenance	14,941	22,041	34,163	47,845	39,271	53,468		211,728	
Total Expenses	$ 41,621	$61,401	$ 95,169	$133,282	$109,397	$ 148,946		$589,815	

Figure 3-56 PP E3-3 completed worksheet

Chapter Summary

3.1 Create Excel chart objects and chart sheets (p. E3-163).

- A **chart** is a visual representation of worksheet data.
- A **chart object** is an item or element in a worksheet.
- A **chart sheet** is an Excel chart on its own tab in the workbook.
- The cells with values and labels used to build a chart are its **source data**.
- Chart objects and sheets are linked to their source data and contain chart elements such as data labels or a chart title.
- Commonly used chart types are *Column*, *Line*, *Pie*, and *Bar*, and Excel can build statistical, financial, geographical, and scientific charts.
- Size and position a chart object in a worksheet, or move it to its own sheet using the *Move Chart* button in the *Location* group on the *Chart Tools Design* tab.
- The *Quick Analysis* tool includes a command group for charts, and it appears when the selected source data are contiguous.

3.2 Use quick layouts and chart styles to design a chart (p. E3-167).

- A **chart layout** is a set of elements and their locations in a chart.
- The *Quick Layout* button [*Chart Tools Design* tab, *Chart Layouts* group] includes predefined layouts for the current chart type.
- A **chart style** is a predefined combination of colors and effects for chart elements.
- Chart styles are based on the current workbook theme.
- The *Change Colors* command [*Chart Tools Design* tab, *Chart Styles* group] provides color palettes for customizing a chart.
- Print a chart object with its worksheet data or on its own sheet.
- A chart sheet prints on its own page in landscape orientation.

3.3 Edit chart elements including titles, data labels, and source data (p. E3-172).

- Select a **chart element** for editing.

- Chart elements include chart and axes titles, data labels, legends, gridlines, and more, depending on the type of chart.
- Excel plots data based on the number of rows and columns selected and the chart type, but row and column data can be switched.
- Use the *Change Chart Type* button on the *Chart Tools Design* tab to change selected chart types into another type.
- Filter chart data to hide and display values or categories without changing the source data.
- Edit source data for a chart to use a different cell range or to add or remove a data series.

3.4 Format chart elements with shape styles, fill, outlines, and special effects (p. E3-179).

- A **shape style** is a predesigned set of fill colors, borders, and effects.
- Apply **shape**, **fill**, **outline**, and **effects** to a chart element from the *Chart Tools Format* tab.
- A chart element has a *Format* task pane that includes fill, outline, and effects commands, as well as specific options for the element.
- Most formats can also be applied to a selected chart element from the *Home* tab.

3.5 Use pictures, shapes, and *WordArt* in a chart (p. E3-183).

- For chart shapes that have a fill color, you can use a picture as fill.
- Images used as fill can be from your own or online sources, but not all pictures work well as fill.
- Shapes are predefined outline drawings available from the *Insert Shapes* group on the *Chart Tools Format* tab or from the *Illustrations* group on the *Insert* tab.
- Place shapes on a chart to highlight or draw attention to a particular element.
- **WordArt** is a text box with a preset design, often used to format a chart title.

3.6 Build pie charts and combination charts (p. E3-188).

- A pie chart has one data series and shows each data point as a slice of the pie.
- A pie chart does not have axes, but it does have options to rotate or explode slices.

- A combination chart uses at least two chart types to highlight, compare, or contrast differences in data or values.
- Format a combination chart to show a secondary axis when values are widely different or use different scales.

3.7 Create sunburst and waterfall charts (p. E3-191).

- A *sunburst chart* has one data series that is grouped in a *hierarchy*.
- A sunburst chart illustrates the relationship among the hierarchies in a pie-like chart with concentric rings.
- A *waterfall chart* depicts a running total for positive and negative values.
- A waterfall chart is used for financial or other data that shows inflows and outlays of resources.
- A waterfall chart resembles a column chart and has category and value axes.
- Place a sunburst chart or a waterfall chart as an object or on a separate sheet.

3.8 Insert and format sparklines in a worksheet (p. E3-194).

- A *sparkline* is a miniature chart in a cell or range of cells in the worksheet.
- Three sparkline types are available: *Line*, *Column*, and *Win/Loss*.
- When inserted in a range of cells, sparklines are grouped and can be ungrouped.
- The *Sparkline Tools Design* tab is visible when a sparkline is selected and includes formatting options such as setting the color or identifying high and low values.

Check for Understanding

The SIMbook for this text (within your SIMnet account) provides the following resources for concept review:

- Multiple-choice questions
- Short answer questions
- Matching exercises

Guided Project 3-1

Life's Animal Shelter (LAS) is an animal care and adoption agency that accepts unwanted and abandoned domestic animals. For this project, you create expense charts and insert sparklines to help the agency track expenses for the first six months of the year. You also build a waterfall chart to graph cash flow for a month.
[Student Learning Outcomes 3.1, 3.2, 3.3, 3.4, 3.5, 3.6, 3.7, 3.8]

File Needed: **LAS-03.xlsx** *(Student data files are available in the* Library *of your SIMnet account.)*
Completed Project File Name: *[your initials] Excel 3-1.xlsx*

Skills Covered in This Project

- Create a chart object.
- Create a chart sheet.
- Apply *Quick Layout* and chart styles.
- Add and format chart elements.
- Change the chart type.

- Filter the data series.
- Insert a shape in a chart.
- Create and format a combination chart.
- Insert and format sparklines in a worksheet.
- Create and format a waterfall chart.

1. Open the **LAS-03** workbook from your student data files and save it as [your initials] Excel 3-1.

2. Create a pie chart object.
 a. Select the **Jan-June** sheet and select cells **A5:A10**. Press **Ctrl** and select cells **I5:I10**.
 b. Click the **Insert Pie or Doughnut Chart** button [*Insert* tab, *Charts* group].
 c. Select the **2D-Pie** chart subtype.

3. Create a chart sheet.
 a. Select the pie chart object.
 b. Click the **Move Chart** button [*Chart Tools Design* tab, *Location* group].
 c. Click the **New sheet** button.
 d. Type Pie Chart in the text box.
 e. Click **OK**.

4. Apply a chart style.
 a. Click the **More** button [*Chart Tools Design* tab, *Chart Styles* group].
 b. Select **Style 12**.

5. Edit and format chart elements.
 a. Click the chart title element.
 b. Click the *Formula* bar, type January through June Expenses, and press **Enter**.
 c. Triple-click the new label in the chart and change the font size to **28 pt**.
 d. Click the legend element to select it and to deselect the title element.
 e. Click the **Font Size** arrow [*Home* tab, *Font* group] and change the legend size to **12 pt**.
 f. Select the chart area. (You can confirm the selected chart object on the *Chart Tools Format* tab, *Current Selection* group.)
 g. Click the **Shape Outline** button [*Chart Tools Format* tab, *Shape Styles* group].
 h. Choose **Black, Text 1** (second column) as the color.
 i. Click the **Shape Outline** button again.

j. Choose **Weight** and select **1 pt**.
k. Click outside the chart background to see the outline (Figure 3-57).

6. Create a bar chart object.
 a. Click the **Jan-June** sheet tab.
 b. Select cells **A4:G9** as source data, omitting the *Rent* expense.
 c. Click the **Quick Analysis** button and select **Charts**.
 d. Select the clustered bar icon (fifth tile in *Quick Analysis* group).
 e. Point to the chart border to display a move pointer.
 f. Drag the chart object so that its top-left corner is at cell **A13**.
 g. Point to the bottom-right selection handle to display a resize arrow.
 h. Drag the pointer to reach cell **I30** (Figure 3-58).

7. Change the chart type.
 a. Click the bar chart object.
 b. Click the **Change Chart Type** button [*Chart Tools Design* tab, *Type* group].
 c. Click the **Recommended Charts** tab.
 d. Find and choose the **Clustered Column** icon in the left pane that displays the months on the horizontal axis.
 e. Click **OK**.

8. Filter the source data.
 a. Click the column chart object.
 b. Click the **Chart Filters** button in the top-right corner of the chart.
 c. Deselect the **January**, **February**, and **March** boxes.
 d. Click **Apply** in the *Chart Filters* pane (Figure 3-59).
 e. Click the **Chart Filters** button to close the pane.

9. Edit, format, and add chart elements.
 a. Click the chart title object.
 b. Click the *Formula* bar.
 c. Type Second Quarter Variable Expenses and press **Enter**.
 d. Click the **Chart Elements** arrow [*Chart Tools Format* tab, *Current Selection* group] and choose **Chart Area**.
 e. Click the **Shape Outline** button [*Chart Tools Format* tab, *Shape Styles* group].
 f. Choose **Black, Text 1** (second column) as the color.
 g. Click the **Shape Outline** button again and choose **Weight** and **1 pt**.

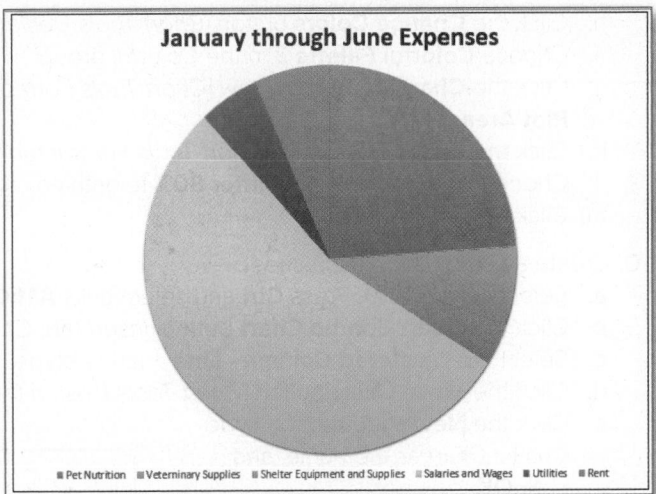

Figure 3-57 Pie chart sheet with format changes

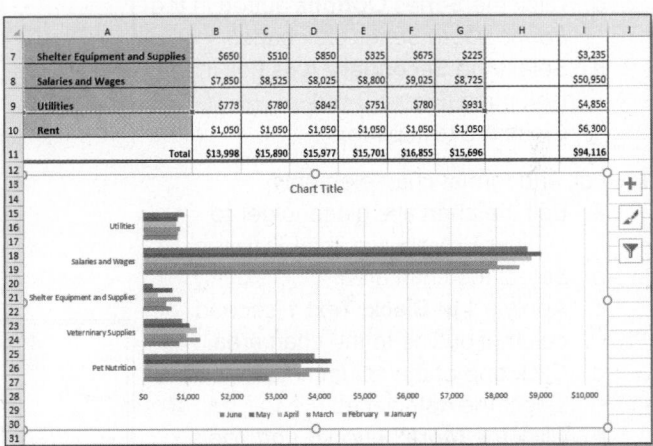

Figure 3-58 Bar chart object sized and positioned

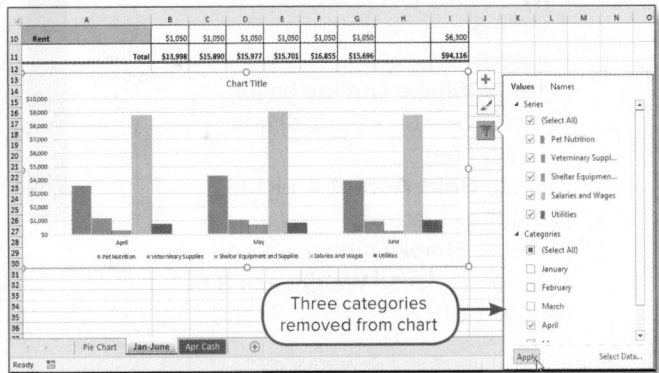

Figure 3-59 Chart filters applied

E3-203

h. Click the **Change Colors** button [*Chart Tools Design* tab, *Chart Styles* group].
 i. Choose **Colorful Palette 3** in the *Colorful* group.
 j. Click the **Chart Elements** arrow [*Chart Tools Format* tab, *Current Selection* group] and choose **Plot Area**.
 k. Click the **Shape Fill** button [*Chart Tools Format* tab, *Shape Styles* group].
 l. Choose **Gold, Accent 4, Lighter 80%** (eighth column) as the color.
 m. Click a worksheet cell.

10. Create a combination chart sheet.
 a. Select cells **A9:G9**. Press **Ctrl** and select cells **A11:G11**.
 b. Click the **Insert Combo Chart** button [*Insert* tab, *Charts* group].
 c. Select the **Clustered Column - Line** chart subtype.
 d. Click the **Move Chart** button [*Chart Tools Design* tab, *Location* group].
 e. Click the **New sheet** button, type Combo Chart as the name, and click **OK**.
 f. Double-click the line marker in the chart.
 g. Click the **Series Options** button in the *Format Data Series* task pane.
 h. Select the **Secondary Axis** box in the task pane (Figure 3-60).
 i. Close the task pane.

Figure 3-60 Combo chart and a secondary axis

11. Edit and format chart elements.
 a. Edit the chart title placeholder to Utilities Expense and Total Expenses.
 b. Select the chart area.
 c. Apply a **1 pt Black, Text 1** (second column) outline to the chart area.
 d. Click one of the column markers to select the data series.
 e. Click the **More** button [*Chart Tools Format* tab, *Shape Styles* group].
 f. Select **Moderate Effect – Black, Dark 1** (first column, fifth row) in the *Theme Styles* group.
 g. Click the line marker.
 h. Click the **Shape Outline** button [*Chart Tools Format* tab, *Shape Styles* group].
 i. Choose **Gold, Accent 4** (eighth column) as the color.
 j. Click the **Shape Outline** button again and choose **Weight** and **3 pt** (Figure 3-61).

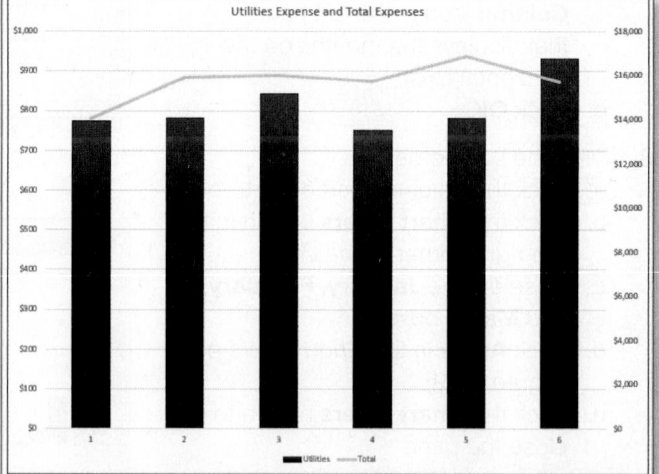

Figure 3-61 Line and column formatted in combo chart

12. Insert sparklines in the worksheet.
 a. Click the **Jan-June** sheet tab.
 b. Select cells **B5:G9** as the data range.
 c. Click the **Column Sparkline** button [*Insert* tab, *Sparklines* group].
 d. Select cells **H5:H9** for the *Location Range* and click **OK**.
 e. Click the **Sparkline Color** button [*Sparkline Tools Design* tab, *Style* group].
 f. Choose **White, Background 1, Darker 50%** (first column).

13. Insert a shape in a chart.
 a. Select the column chart object.
 b. Click the **More** button [*Chart Tools Format* tab, *Insert Shapes* group].
 c. Select the **Text Box** shape [*Basic Shapes* group].
 d. Draw a text box like the one shown in Figure 3-62.
 e. Type Utilities are to be removed from an updated chart per management request.
 f. Drag a selection handle to size the text box shape if necessary.
 g. Point to a border of the *Text Box* shape to display a four-pointed arrow and position it if needed.

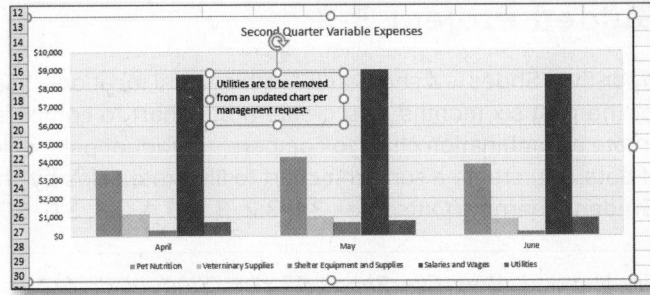

Figure 3-62 Text box shape inserted in chart

14. Click a worksheet cell and press **Ctrl+Home**.

15. Create a waterfall chart object.
 a. Select the **Apr Cash** sheet tab.
 b. Select cells **A5:B14**. These data represent cash coming in and going out for April.
 c. Click the **Insert Waterfall, Funnel, Stock, Surface, or Radar Chart** button [*Insert* tab, *Charts* group].
 d. Select **Waterfall**.

16. Size and position a chart object.
 a. Point to the chart border to display the move pointer.
 b. Drag the chart object so that its top-left corner is at cell **D1**.
 c. Point to the bottom-right selection handle to display the resize arrow.
 d. Drag the pointer to cell **M20**.

17. Format chart elements.
 a. Double-click the **Net Cash** column marker and then click the marker again to open the *Format Data Point* pane.
 b. Click the **Series Options** button in the task pane and expand the *Series Options* group.
 c. Select the **Set as total** box.
 d. Select the chart title placeholder, triple-click to select the text, and type April Cash Flow.
 e. Select the chart area and apply a **1 pt Text, Black 1** (second column) outline.
 f. Click a worksheet cell and press **Ctrl+Home**.

18. Save and close the workbook (Figure 3-63).

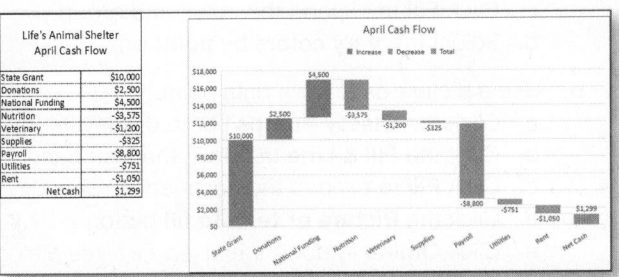

Figure 3-63 Excel 3-1 completed worksheets and charts

Guided Project 3-2

Wear-Ever Shoes is a shoe outlet with several locations. In a worksheet that tracks sales of popular items for the past six months, you create a bar chart to compare the number of pairs sold by style. You also create a combination chart to compare number of pairs sold and unit cost for each style. For another set of data, you create a sunburst chart to illustrate sales by shoe style, gender, and color.
[Student Learning Outcomes 3.1, 3.2, 3.3, 3.4, 3.5, 3.6, 3.7]

File Needed: **WearEverShoes-03.xlsx** *(Student data files are available in the* Library *of your SIMnet account.)*
Completed Project File Name: **[your initials] Excel 3-2.xlsx**

Skills Covered in This Project

- Create a chart sheet.
- Change the chart type.
- Apply a chart style.

- Add and format chart elements.
- Use a picture as fill.
- Create and format a combination chart.
- Use *WordArt* in a chart.
- Create and format a sunburst chart.

1. Open the **WearEverShoes-03** workbook from your student data files and save it as [your initials] Excel 3-2.

2. Create a column chart sheet.
 a. Select cells **A5:B16** on the **Unit Sales** sheet.
 b. Click the **Quick Analysis** button and choose **Charts**.
 c. Click the **Clustered Column** icon.
 d. Click the **Move Chart** button [*Chart Tools Design* tab, *Location* group].
 e. Click the **New sheet** button.
 f. Type Sales Chart and click **OK**.

3. Change the chart type.
 a. Click the **Sales Chart** sheet tab if necessary.
 b. Click the **Change Chart Type** button [*Chart Tools Design* tab, *Type* group].
 c. Click the **Recommended Charts** tab.
 d. Choose **Clustered Bar** in the left pane and click **OK**.

4. Apply a chart style.
 a. Click the **Chart Styles** button in the top-right corner of the chart.
 b. Select **Style 7**.
 c. Click the **Chart Styles** button to close the pane.

5. Add fill color to a data series.
 a. Double-click one of the bars to open the *Format Data Series* task pane.
 b. Click the **Fill & Line** button in the task pane.
 c. Click **Fill** to expand the command group.
 d. Select the **Vary colors by point** box.

6. Use a picture as fill for a data point.
 a. Click the **Classy Pumps** bar to display its *Format Data Point* task pane.
 b. Click the **Fill & Line** button in the task pane.
 c. Click **Fill** to expand the command group.
 d. Click the **Picture or texture fill** button.
 e. Click **Online** to open the *Insert Pictures* dialog box.
 f. Type heels in the *Bing* search box and press **Enter** (Figure 3-64).

g. Select an image and click **Insert**.

h. Click the **Stack** radio button in the task pane.

i. Close the task pane and click the chart border.

Figure 3-64 Online image search for fill in a data point

7. Create a combination chart sheet.

 a. Click the **Unit Sales** sheet tab.

 b. Select cells **A5:A16**. Press **Ctrl** and select cells **E5:F16**.

 c. Click the **Insert Combo Chart** button [*Insert* tab, *Charts* group].

 d. Select the **Clustered Column - Line on Secondary Axis** chart subtype.

 e. Click the **Move Chart** button [*Chart Tools Design* tab, *Location* group].

 f. Click the **New sheet** button.

 g. Type Cost&Retail and click **OK**.

8. Edit chart elements.

 a. Click the chart title placeholder.

 b. Type Cost and Selling Price Comparison in the *Formula* bar and press **Enter**.

 c. Select the chart title box.

 d. Click the **Home** tab and change the font size to **20 pt**.

 e. Select the chart area and apply a **1 pt Black, Text 1** outline.

 f. Click one of the column shapes to select the *Cost* series.

 g. Click the **More** button [*Chart Tools Format* tab, *Shapes Styles* group].

 h. Choose **Intense Effect - Blue, Accent 1** in the bottom row of the *Theme Styles* gallery.

 i. Select the line marker to select the *Retail Price* series.

 j. Click the **Shape Outline** button [*Chart Tools Format* tab, *Shape Styles* group] and choose **Black, Text 1** as the color.

 k. Change the weight of the line to **3 pt**.

9. Use *WordArt* in a chart.

 a. Click the chart title.

 b. Click the **More** button [*Chart Tools Format* tab, *WordArt Styles* group].

 c. Choose **Fill: Black, Text color 1; Shadow** in the first row of the gallery.

 d. Click the chart border to deselect the title.

10. Create a sunburst chart.

 a. Click the **Grouped Sales** sheet tab.

 b. Select cells **A5:D24**.

 c. Click the **Insert Hierarchy Chart** button [*Insert* tab, *Charts* group].

 d. Click **Sunburst** to select it.

 e. Click the **Move Chart** button [*Chart Tools Design* tab, *Location* group].

 f. Select **New sheet**, type Sunburst, and click **OK**.

11. Format a sunburst chart.

 a. Click the chart title element.

 b. Triple-click the placeholder text to select it.

 c. Type Sales by Style, Color, and Gender.

 d. Click the sunburst shape to select the circle and confirm that "Series" is the active element in the *Current Selection* group [*Chart Tools Format* tab].

e. Point to either side of the data label in the **Comfy Walking Shoes** arc in the inner ring and click to select the data point. The data point is the wedge that represents two colors of the style, men's and women's. Confirm your selection using the *Chart Tools Format* tab in the *Current Selection* group. It should display "Branch Comfy Walking."

f. Click the **Format Selection** button [*Chart Tools Format* tab, *Current Selection* group] to open the *Format Data Point* task pane.

g. Click the **Fill & Line** button.

h. Click **Fill** to expand the command group.

i. Choose **Solid fill** and click the **Color** button.

j. Choose **Orange, Accent 6, Lighter 40%** (last column)

k. Close the task pane.

l. Click outside the chart background to deselect the chart.

12. Save and close the workbook (Figure 3-65).

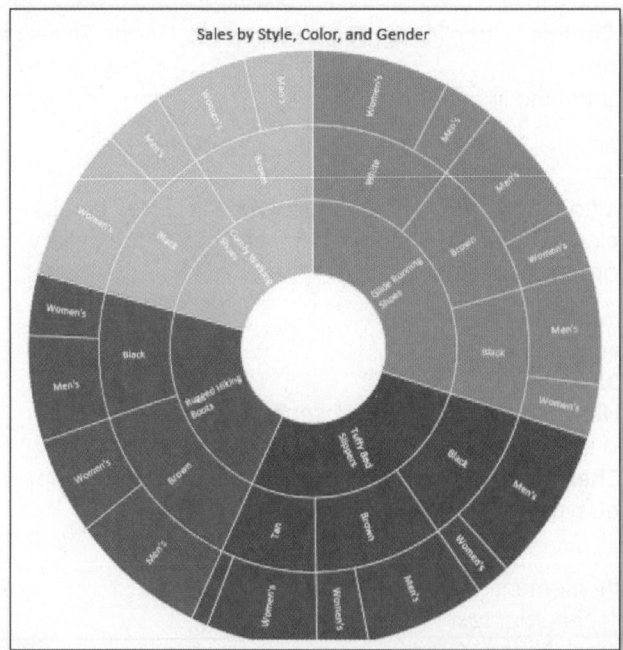

Figure 3-65 Excel 3-2 completed chart sheets

Guided Project 3-3

Blue Lake Sports has locations in several major cities and tracks sales by department in each store. For this project, you create a pie chart that shows each store's share of golf-related sales for the first quarter. You also create a line chart to illustrate week-to-week sales for specific departments in one of the stores and insert sparklines in the data.
[Student Learning Outcomes 3.1, 3.2, 3.3, 3.4, 3.6, 3.8]

File Needed: **BlueLakeSports-03.xlsx** (Student data files are available in the Library of your SIMnet account.)
Completed Project File Name: **[your initials] Excel 3-3.xlsx**

Skills Covered in This Project

- Create, size, and position a pie chart object.
- Apply a chart style.
- Change the chart type.
- Add and format chart elements.
- Create a line chart sheet.
- Apply a chart layout.
- Insert and format sparklines in a worksheet.

1. Open the **BlueLakeSports-03** workbook from your student data files and save it as [your initials] Excel 3-3.

2. Create a pie chart object.
 a. Select the **Revenue by Department** sheet, select cells **A4:F4**, press **Ctrl**, and select cells **A13:F13**.
 b. Click the **Recommended Charts** button [*Insert* tab, *Charts* group].
 c. Choose **Pie** and click **OK**.

3. Apply a chart style.
 a. Select the chart object.
 b. Click the **More** button [*Chart Tools Design* tab, *Chart Styles* group].
 c. Select **Style 12**.

4. Size and position a chart object.
 a. Point to the chart object border to display the move pointer.
 b. Drag the chart object so its top-left corner is at cell **A21**.
 c. Point to the bottom-right selection handle to display the resize arrow.
 d. Drag the pointer to cell **G36**.

5. Change the chart type.
 a. Select the pie chart object and click the **Change Chart Type** button [*Chart Tools Design* tab, *Type* group].
 b. Select the **All Charts** tab and choose **Pie** in the left pane.
 c. Choose **3-D Pie** and click **OK**.

6. Format pie chart elements.
 a. Double-click the pie to open its *Format Data Series* task pane.
 b. Click the **Atlanta** slice to update the pane to the *Format Data Point* task pane. (Rest the pointer on a slice to see its identifying *ScreenTip*.)
 c. Click the **Series Options** button in the *Format Data Series* task pane.
 d. Set the pie explosion percentage at **10%**.
 e. Close the task pane.
 f. Click the chart object border to deselect the **Atlanta** slice.

7. Add and format chart elements in a pie chart.
 a. Click the **Chart Elements** button in the top-right corner of the chart.
 b. Select the **Data Labels** box.

c. Click the **Data Labels** arrow to open its submenu and choose **More Options**.
d. Click the **Label Options** button In the *Format Data Labels* pane.
e. Click **Label Options** to expand the group.
f. Select the **Percentage** box.

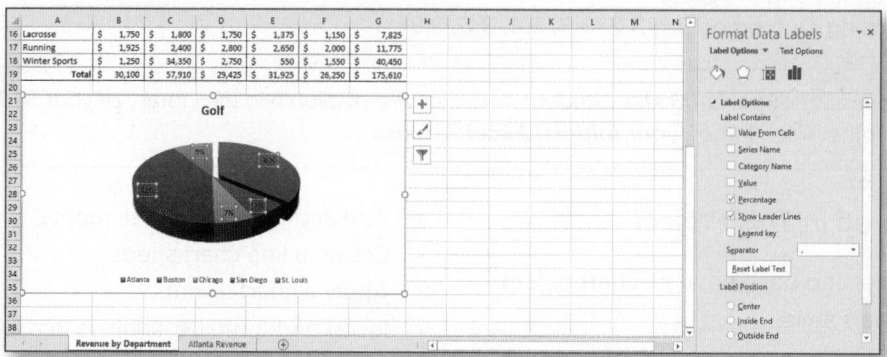

Figure 3-66 *Format Data* task pane for data labels

g. Deselect the **Value** box (Figure 3-66).
h. Press **Ctrl+B** to apply bold.
i. Change the font size to **12 pt** [*Home* tab, *Font* group].
j. Click the chart object border to select it.
k. Click the **Shape Outline** button [*Chart Tools Format* tab, *Shape Styles* group] and choose **Purple, Accent 4, Darker 50%** (eighth column).
l. Click the **Shape Outline** button and choose **Weight** and **1 pt**.
m. Click a worksheet cell.

8. Create a line chart sheet.
a. Select the **Atlanta Revenue** sheet tab.
b. Select cells **A4:E7**.
c. Click the **Quick Analysis** button and choose **Charts**.
d. Select **Line**.
e. Click the **Move Chart** button [*Chart Tools Design* tab, *Location* group].
f. Click the **New sheet** button.
g. Type Promo Depts and click **OK**.

9. Apply a chart layout.
a. Click the **Quick Layout** button [*Chart Tools Design* tab, *Chart Layouts* group].
b. Select **Layout 5** to add a data table to the chart sheet (Figure 3-67).

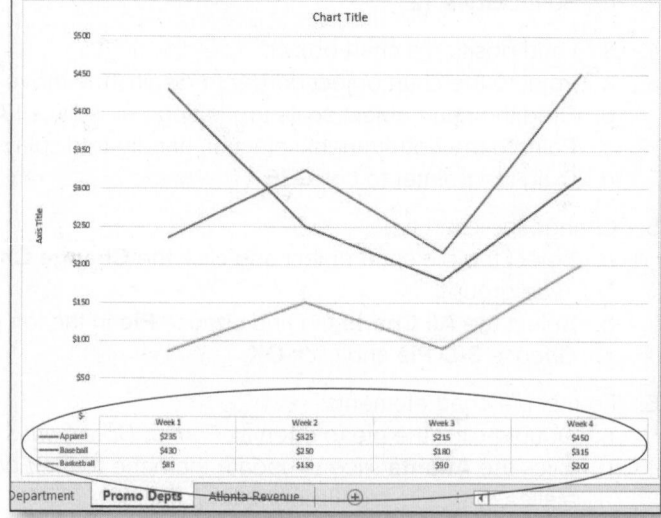

Figure 3-67 Data table added by *Quick Layout*

10. Change the chart type.
a. Click the **Change Chart Type** button [*Chart Tools Design* tab, *Type* group].
b. Select the **All Charts** tab and choose **Line with Markers** in the *Line* category.
c. Click **OK**.

11. Edit chart elements in a line chart.
 a. Click the chart title placeholder.
 b. Type Special Promotion Departments in the *Formula* bar and press **Enter**.
 c. Click the vertical axis title placeholder.
 d. Type Dollar Sales in the *Formula* bar and press **Enter**.
 e. Click the **Chart Elements** drop-down arrow [*Chart Tools Format* tab, *Current Selection* group].

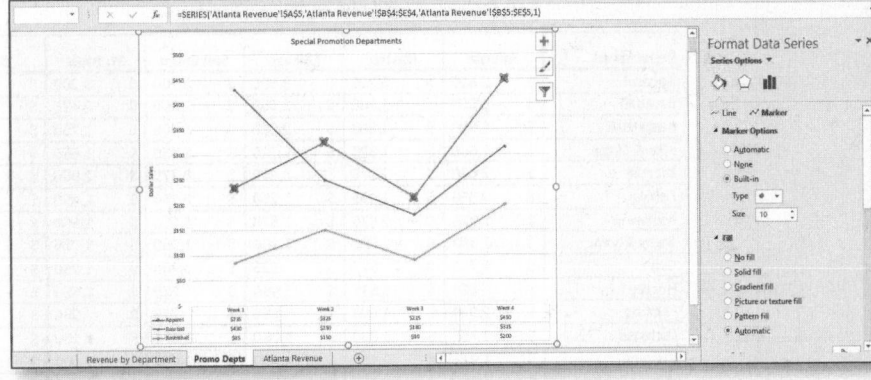

Figure 3-68 Marker options for the data series

 f. Choose **Series "Apparel"** to select the line in the chart.
 g. Click the **Format Selection** button [*Chart Tools Format* tab, *Current Selection* group].
 h. Click the **Fill & Line** button in the *Format Data Series* task pane.
 i. Click **Marker** and then click **Marker Options** to expand the group (Figure 3-68).
 j. Choose **Built-in** and set the **Size** to **10**.
 k. Click the *Series Options* triangle at the top of the task pane and choose **Series "Baseball"** (Figure 3-69).
 l. Apply the same marker changes for the baseball series.
 m. Select the **Basketball** series and apply the same marker changes.
 n. Close the task pane and click outside the chart.

12. Insert sparklines in the worksheet.
 a. Click the **Atlanta Revenue** tab.
 b. Right-click the column **F** heading and choose **Insert**.
 c. Select cells **B5:E18** as the data range.
 d. Click the **Line Sparkline** button [*Insert* tab, *Sparklines* group].
 e. Select cells **F5:F18** in the *Location Range* box.
 f. Click **OK**.

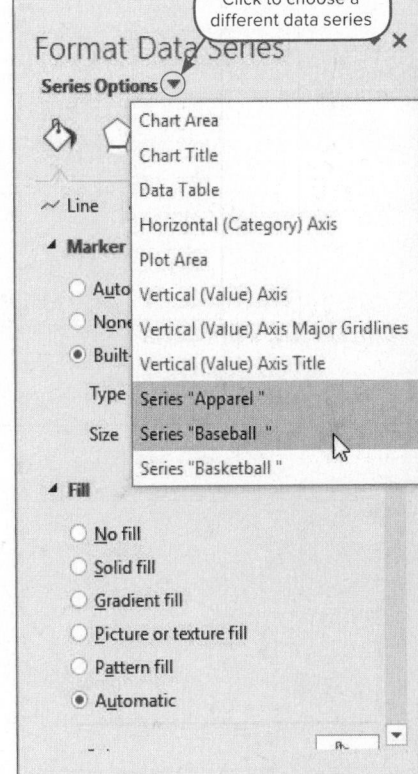

Figure 3-69 New data series selected

13. Format sparklines in worksheet.
 a. Click the **Format** button [*Home* tab, *Cells* group] and change the **Row Height** to **24**.
 b. Click the **Format** button [*Home* tab, *Cells* group] and set the **Column Width** to **35**.
 c. Select the **Markers** box in the *Show* group in the *Sparkline Tools Design* tab.
 d. Click the **Sparkline Color** button [*Sparkline Tools Design* tab, *Style* group].
 e. Choose **Black, Text 1** (second column) for the line color.
 f. Click cell **A1**.

14. Change the page orientation to landscape.

15. Save and close the workbook (Figure 3-70).

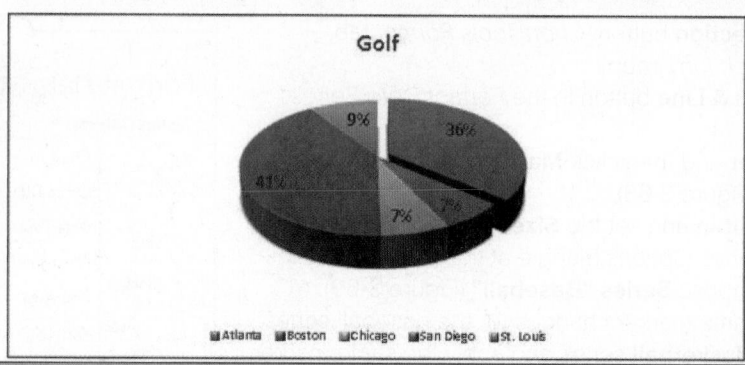

Blue Lake Sports
First Quarter Sales by City

Department	Atlanta	Boston	Chicago	San Diego	St. Louis	Total
Apparel	$ 2,600	$ 3,200	$ 3,800	$ 3,700	$ 3,200	$ 16,500
Baseball	$ 3,500	$ 1,200	$ 1,350	$ 2,100	$ 2,475	$ 10,625
Basketball	$ 1,800	$ 1,800	$ 2,250	$ 1,400	$ 1,750	$ 9,000
Bike & Skate	$ 1,500	$ 1,325	$ 1,225	$ 2,450	$ 1,650	$ 8,150
Exercise	$ 2,650	$ 2,875	$ 3,250	$ 3,775	$ 2,950	$ 15,500
Fishing	$ 2,350	$ 1,035	$ 1,250	$ 2,750	$ 1,450	$ 8,835
Footwear	$ 1,875	$ 2,675	$ 3,575	$ 3,250	$ 2,950	$ 14,325
Game Room	$ 1,300	$ 1,500	$ 1,900	$ 1,050	$ 1,275	$ 7,025
Golf	$ 4,750	$ 875	$ 925	$ 5,400	$ 1,250	$ 13,200
Hockey	$ 850	$ 1,875	$ 1,950	$ 750	$ 1,650	$ 7,075
Hunting	$ 2,000	$ 1,000	$ 650	$ 725	$ 950	$ 5,325
Lacrosse	$ 1,750	$ 1,800	$ 1,750	$ 1,375	$ 1,150	$ 7,825
Running	$ 1,925	$ 2,400	$ 2,800	$ 2,650	$ 2,000	$ 11,775
Winter Sports	$ 1,250	$ 34,350	$ 2,750	$ 550	$ 1,550	$ 40,450
Total	$ 30,100	$ 57,910	$ 29,425	$ 31,925	$ 26,250	$ 175,610

Golf

9% 36% 41% 7% 7%

Atlanta Boston Chicago San Diego St. Louis

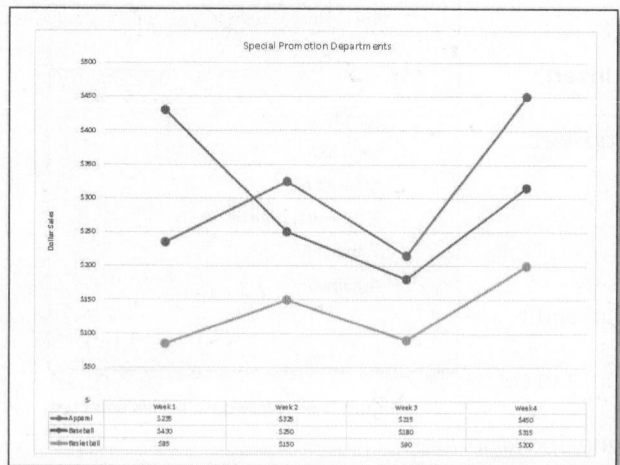

Special Promotion Departments

	Week 1	Week 2	Week 3	Week 4
Apparel	$235	$325	$335	$460
Baseball	$430	$250	$180	$315
Basketball	$85	$150	$90	$200

Blue Lake Sports
January Sales in Atlanta

Department	Week 1	Week 2	Week 3	Week 4		Total
Apparel	$ 235	$ 325	$ 215	$ 450		$ 1,225
Baseball	$ 430	$ 250	$ 180	$ 315		$ 1,175
Basketball	$ 85	$ 150	$ 90	$ 200		$ 525
Bike & Skate	$ 200	$ 325	$ 75	$ 175		$ 775
Exercise	$ 150	$ 160	$ 180	$ 170		$ 660
Fishing	$ 75	$ 150	$ 85	$ 200		$ 510
Footwear	$ 500	$ 350	$ 275	$ 330		$ 1,455
Game Room	$ 45	$ 75	$ 35	$ 15		$ 170
Golf	$ 175	$ 350	$ 580	$ 200		$ 1,305
Hockey	$ 85	$ 125	$ 50	$ 35		$ 295
Hunting	$ 125	$ 350	$ 475	$ 450		$ 1,400
Lacrosse	$ 200	$ 50	$ 65	$ 75		$ 390
Running	$ 165	$ 235	$ 325	$ 180		$ 905
Winter Sports	$ 75	$ 15	$ -	$ 15		$ 105
Total	$ 2,545	$ 2,910	$ 2,630	$ 2,810		$ 10,895

Figure 3-70 Excel 3-3 completed worksheet and charts

Independent Project 3-4

For this project, you create a column chart to illustrate April–September revenue for Classic Gardens and Landscapes. You also build a pie chart sheet to graph the proportion that each category contributes to total revenue.
[Student Learning Outcomes 3.1, 3.2, 3.3, 3.4, 3.5, 3.6]

File Needed: ***ClassicGardens-03.xlsx*** *(Student data files are available in the Library of your SIMnet account.)*
Completed Project File Name: *[your initials] Excel 3-4.xlsx*

Skills Covered in This Project

- Create a chart object.
- Size and position a chart object.
- Edit and format chart elements.

- Edit the source data for a chart.
- Build a pie chart sheet.
- Use texture as fill.
- Add and format data labels in a chart.

1. Open the **ClassicGardens-03** workbook from your student data files and save it as [your initials] Excel 3-4.

2. Create a **Clustered Column** chart object for cells **A4:G9**.

3. Move the chart object so that its top-left corner is at cell **A12**. Size the bottom of the chart to reach cell **H30**.

4. Edit the chart title to display CGL Major Sales Revenue and press **Enter**. On the second line, type Second and Third Quarters. (In the *Formula* bar, press **Alt+Enter** to start a new line.)

5. Apply chart **Style 14** to the chart.

6. Format the first line of the chart title to a font size of **20 pt**. Format the second title line as **18 pt**.

7. Apply a **1 pt Black, Text 1** (second column) outline to the chart area.

8. Verify that the chart is still selected. In the highlighted range in the worksheet, drag the resize pointer to remove the *Design Consulting* data series from the chart (Figure 3-71).

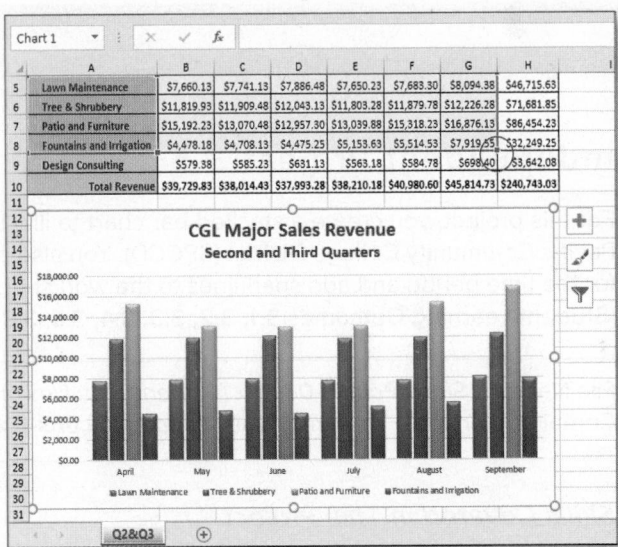

Figure 3-71 Resize the chart by dragging the resize pointer

9. Create a *3-D Pie* chart sheet for cells **A4:A9** and cells **H4:H9**. Move the chart to its own sheet named Revenue Breakdown.

10. Edit the chart title to display Revenue by Category. Change the font size to **32**.

11. Select the legend and change the font size to **12**.

12. Apply the **Woven mat** texture fill (first row, fourth column) to the *Patio and Furniture* slice.

13. Select the pie shape and add data labels to display in the center of each slice.
 a. Display the *Format Data Labels* task pane, choose the **Accounting** format [*Label Options* button, *Number* group], and set **0** decimal places.
 b. Change the data label font size to **14 pt** and apply **bold** [*Home* tab, *Font* group].

14. Deselect the chart.

15. Save and close the workbook (Figure 3-72).

Classic Gardens and Landscapes (CGL)
Revenue for Quarters 2 and 3

Revenue Categories	April	May	June	July	August	September	Total
Lawn Maintenance	$7,660.13	$7,741.13	$7,886.48	$7,650.23	$7,683.30	$8,094.38	$46,715.63
Tree & Shrubbery	$11,819.93	$11,909.48	$12,043.13	$11,803.28	$11,879.78	$12,226.28	$71,681.85
Patio and Furniture	$15,192.23	$13,070.48	$12,957.30	$13,039.88	$15,318.23	$16,876.13	$86,454.23
Fountains and Irrigation	$4,478.18	$4,708.13	$4,475.25	$5,153.63	$5,514.53	$7,919.55	$32,249.25
Design Consulting	$579.38	$585.23	$831.13	$563.18	$584.78	$698.40	$3,642.08
Total Revenue	$39,729.83	$38,014.43	$37,993.28	$38,210.18	$40,980.60	$45,814.73	$240,743.03

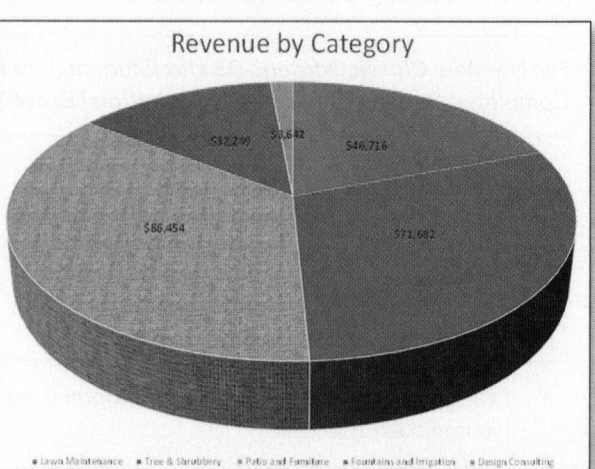

Figure 3-72 Excel 3-4 completed worksheet and chart

Independent Project 3-5

For this project, you create a stacked bar chart to illustrate projected tuition and fee amounts for Sierra Pacific Community College District (SPCCD). You also create a pie chart to show total projected revenue for the time period and add sparklines to the worksheet.
[Student Learning Outcomes 3.1, 3.2, 3.3, 3.4, 3.6, 3.8]

File Needed: ***SierraPacific-03.xlsx*** *(Student data files are available in the* Library *of your SIMnet account.)*
Completed Project File Name: ***[your initials] Excel 3-5.xlsx***

Skills Covered in This Project

- Create a chart object.
- Size and position a chart object.
- Apply a chart style.
- Switch row and column data.
- Edit chart source data.
- Create a pie chart sheet.
- Edit and format chart elements.
- Insert and format sparklines in a sheet.

1. Open the ***SierraPacific-03*** workbook from your student data files and save it as [your initials] Excel 3-5.

2. Select cells **A3:E7** and use the *Quick Analysis* tool to create a stacked bar chart object.

3. Size and position the chart below the worksheet data in cells **A10:G28**.

4. Apply **Style 6**.

5. Edit the chart title to display Tuition Revenue Projection.

6. Apply a ½ pt **Dark Blue, Text 2** outline (fourth column) to the chart object.

7. Edit the source data to remove the *Utilization and Facilities* fees from the chart.

8. Switch the row and column data for the chart so that semester names are shown on the vertical axis.

9. Create a 3-D pie chart sheet for cells **A4:A7** and cells **F4:F7**. Move the chart to a new sheet named Total Revenue.

10. Apply **Style 3** and a **Black, Text 1** (second column) ½ **pt** outline.

11. Edit the chart title to Projected Revenue Sources.

12. Format the legend font size to **12 pt**.

13. Select the **Tuition & Fees** sheet, and create a column sparkline with cell **G8** as the location range for cells **B8:E8**. Format cell **G8** with **Outside Borders** [*Home* tab, *Font* group].

14. Save and close the workbook (Figure 3-73).

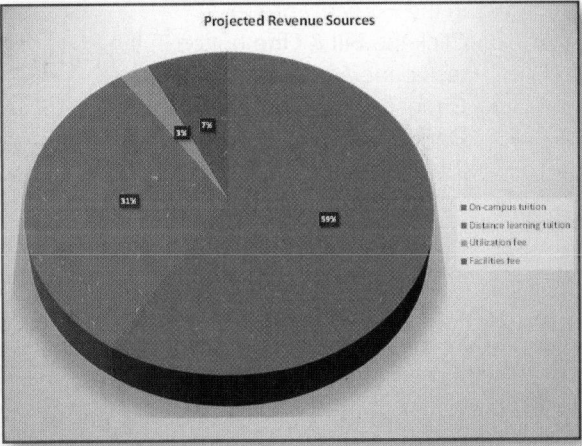

Figure 3-73 Excel 3-5 completed worksheet and chart

Independent Project 3-6

For this project, you create charts to illustrate data about the number of procedures performed at Courtyard Medical Plaza (CMP), as well as how patients came to the facility. You also prepare a waterfall chart for the operations account.
[Student Learning Outcomes 3.1, 3.2, 3.3, 3.4, 3.5, 3.7]

File Needed: **CourtyardMedical-03.xlsx** (Student data files are available in the Library of your SIMnet account.)
Completed Project File Name: **[your initials] Excel 3-6.xlsx**

Skills Covered in This Project

- Create a column chart sheet.
- Add and edit chart elements.
- Add and format a trendline in a chart.
- Insert a text box shape in a chart.
- Display gridlines in a chart.
- Create a waterfall chart.

1. Open the **CourtyardMedical-03** workbook from your student data files and save it as [your initials] Excel 3-6.

2. Select the **Patient Arrivals** worksheet. Create a clustered column chart for cells **A5:M5** and cells **A7:M7**. Move the chart to its own sheet named Immed Care.

3. Edit the chart title to display Immediate Care Patient Count.

4. Click the **Chart Elements** button and select **Trendline**.

5. Click the options arrow next to **Trendline** and select **More Options** to open the *Format Trendline* task pane.
 a. Verify that the line is **Linear**.
 b. Set the **Forward** value to **12** in the *Forecast* group.
 c. Click the **Fill & Line** button in the task pane and select **Solid line**.
 d. Choose **Olive Green, Accent 3, Darker 50%** (seventh column) for the line color.
 e. Set the **Width** of the trendline to **4 pt**.
 f. Click the **Dash type** arrow and select the fourth option, **Dash**.

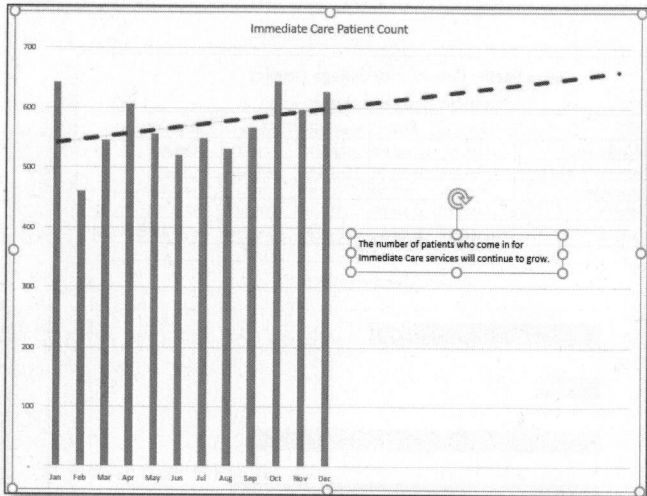

Figure 3-74 Text box shape in a chart

6. Draw a *Text Box* shape between the 300 and 400 gridlines and type The number of patients who come in for Immediate Care services will continue to grow. (Figure 3-74).

7. Select the **Procedures Count** worksheet and use the *Quick Analysis* tool to create a clustered column chart for cells **A5:D16**. Move the chart to its own sheet named Procedures Chart.

8. Edit the chart title to Number of Procedures on the first line and Three-Month Period on the second line.

9. Change the chart type to a clustered bar chart.

10. Click the **Chart Elements** button. Show **Primary Major Vertical**, **Primary Major Horizontal**, and **Primary Minor Vertical** gridlines.

11. Use the *Format* task pane to format each gridline group to use **Black, Text 1, Lighter 50%** (second column) as the line color.

12. Select the *Plot Area* and use the **Shape Fill** button to apply **Tan, Background 2** (third column).

13. Select the **Operations** sheet tab and create a waterfall chart object for cells **A3:B9**.

14. Position the waterfall chart object so that its top-left corner is at cell **A11**. Size the object to reach cell **I28**.

15. Select the ending balance marker and set it as a total.

16. Edit the chart title placeholder to CMP Operations Account.

17. Select the chart area and apply a **1 pt Black, Text 1** (second column) outline.

18. Click a worksheet cell and press **Ctrl+Home**.

19. Save and close the workbook (Figure 3-75).

 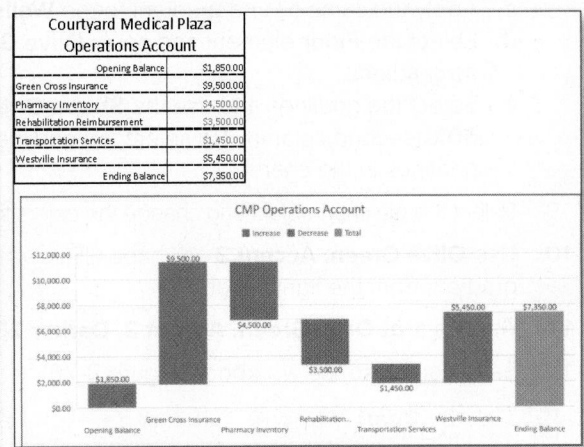

Figure 3-75 Excel 3-6 completed worksheet and charts

Improve It Project 3-7

Central Sierra Insurance is a multi-office company that handles commercial and personal insurance products. In this project, you add missing data and verify that the charts are updated.
[**Student Learning Outcomes 3.2, 3.3, 3.4**]

File Needed: ***CentralSierra-03.xlsx*** *(Student data files are available in the* Library *of your SIMnet account.)*
Completed Project File Name: ***[your initials] Excel 3-7.xlsx***

Skills Covered in This Project

- Edit source data.
- Switch row and column data.
- Change chart colors.

- Apply a chart style.
- Add and format elements in a chart.
- Use gradient fill for a chart object.
- Change the chart type.

1. Open the ***CentralSierra-03*** workbook from your student data files and save it as [your initials] Excel 3-7. Two chart objects display on the worksheet.

2. Insert a new row at row 8.

3. Type Motorcycle in cell **A8**. In cells **B8:D8**, type these values: 15, 82, and 24.

4. Change the pie chart object to a **3-D Pie** and apply **Style 3**. Notice that a data series for "Motorcycle" has been added.

5. Switch the row and column data for the column chart. The data series for "Motorcycle" is not included.

6. Click the **Select Data** button [*Chart Tools Design* tab, *Data* group] and reset the source data to show cells **A5:D10**.

7. Change the column chart color scheme to **Monochromatic Palette 7** in the *Monochromatic* list.

8. Format chart elements.
 a. Select the **Side Wall** of the column chart and apply **Olive Green, Accent 3** shape fill (seventh column).
 b. Use the **Shape Fill** button to apply the **Linear Down** gradient in the *Light Variations* group to the side wall.

c. Apply the same fill and gradient to the **Walls** element.

d. Select the **Floor** element and apply **Olive Green, Accent 3, Lighter 60%** (seventh column) with no gradient.

e. Select the gridlines and use the **Shape Outline** button to format them with **Black, Text 1, Lighter 50%** (second column). (To select the gridlines, select the *Plot Area* and then click one of the gridlines in the chart.)

9. Select the pie chart object and change the colors to **Monochromatic Palette 7** in the *Monochromatic* group.

10. Use **Olive Green, Accent 3** as shape fill (seventh column) for the pie chart area with a **Linear Down** gradient from the light variations.

11. Apply a **1 pt Olive Green, Accent 3, Darker 25%** outline (seventh column) to both chart objects.

12. Save and close the workbook (Figure 3-76).

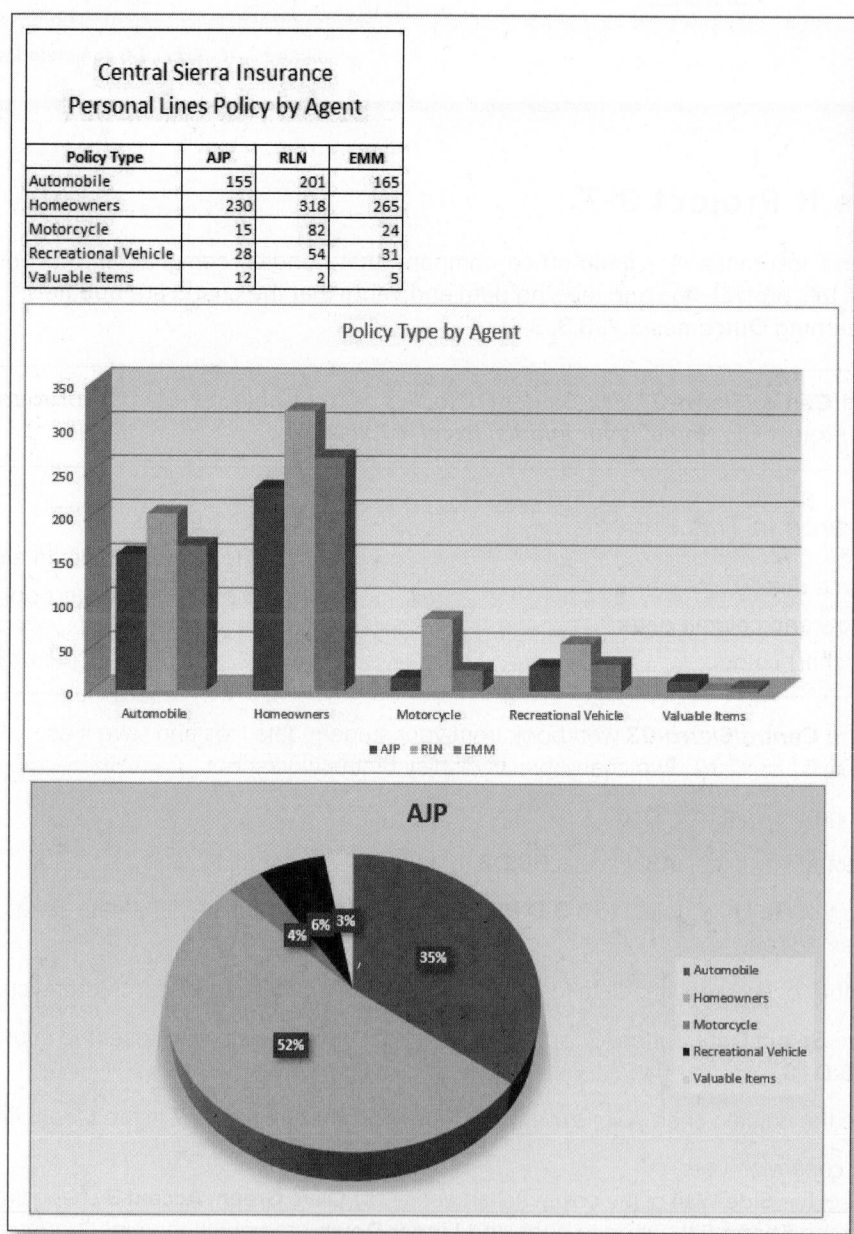

Central Sierra Insurance Personal Lines Policy by Agent

Policy Type	AJP	RLN	EMM
Automobile	155	201	165
Homeowners	230	318	265
Motorcycle	15	82	24
Recreational Vehicle	28	54	31
Valuable Items	12	2	5

Figure 3-76 Excel 3-7 completed worksheet with charts

Challenge Project 3-8

For this project, you build a worksheet that displays data from three departments in a supermarket. Each department has one or more subgroups, and each subgroup lists one or more items. From this hierarchical data, you create a TreeMap chart.
[Student Learning Outcomes 3.1, 3.2, 3.3, 3.4, 3.7]

File Needed: None
Completed Project File Name: *[your initials] Excel 3-8.xlsx*

Create a new workbook and save it as [your initials] Excel 3-8. Modify your workbook according to the following guidelines:

- Type Grocery in cell **A2** as a general category in the supermarket. In cell **B2**, type Coffee as a product subgroup. In cells **C2:C3**, type Ground and Whole Bean as further divisions of the coffee subgroup.
- Type Pasta in cell **B4**. In cells **C4:C5**, type the names of two types of pasta (spaghetti, rotini, vermicelli, bucatini, rigatoni, etc.).
- Type the name of another category of items in the supermarket in cell **B6**. Then in cells **C6:C7**, type the names of two products in the category.
- Select cell **A8** and type Produce. In cell **B8**, type Apples. In cells **C8:C9**, type the names of two varieties of apples.
- Complete another subgroup for the *Produce* category in cells **B10:C11**.
- Type a value for each item in column **D** that represents the number of items or dollars.
- Select the data and create a *TreeMap* hierarchy chart on its own sheet.
- Edit the chart title and apply a chart style.
- Insert two rows at row **8** and create a "Dairy" grouping for the supermarket and note how the *TreeMap* is adjusted.

Challenge Project 3-9

For this project, you create a worksheet and accompanying charts to track daily usage of your smartphone, tablet, or other device.
[Student Learning Outcomes 3.1, 3.2, 3.3, 3.4, 3.5]

File Needed: None
Completed Project File Name: *[your initials] Excel 3-9.xlsx*

Create a new workbook and save it as [your initials] Excel 3-9. Modify your workbook according to the following guidelines:

- Enter the days of the week as column headings, starting in cell **B2**.
- Create row headings starting in cell **A3** by typing the names of five daily tasks or activities for your device. Examples are "Send text," "Receive phone call," "Use GPS," "View video," or similar tasks.
- Enter a value for the number of times you perform each task on each day.

- Type a main title for your data in row 1. Format your data.
- Create a column chart object that compares the number of times for each task on Monday.
- Size and position the chart object below the worksheet data.
- Change the layout or apply a chart style.
- Edit the chart title placeholder to display an appropriate title.
- Format chart elements to create an attractive, easy-to-understand chart of your data.
- Determine the task with the greatest Monday value, and create another column chart that displays daily numbers for that one task.
- Size and position this chart object below the first chart.
- Format the second chart to complement the first chart.

Challenge Project 3-10

For this project, you create a worksheet with a column/line combo chart that compares air temperature and humidity level in your city or town for 10 days. You also insert a single sparkline in the data.
[Student Learning Outcomes 3.1, 3.2, 3.3, 3.4, 3.6, 3.8]

File Needed: None
Completed Project File Name: *[your initials] Excel 3-10.xlsx*

Create a new workbook and save it as [your initials] Excel 3-10. Modify your workbook according to the following guidelines:

- Enter dates in cells **A4:A13** for each of the last 10 days or each of the next 10 days.
- Enter a recorded or predicted temperature in degrees for each date at 12 noon in column **B**. Use an online weather reference or a weather app.
- Enter corresponding humidity levels as percentages in column **C**. Use the same weather reference or make an estimate.
- Type a main title for the data, as well as column labels.
- Create a clustered column/line combo chart with a secondary axis for the percentages. Move the chart to its own sheet.
- Change the layout or apply a chart style.
- Edit and format the chart elements as needed.
- Select the range of temperature values in the worksheet as the data range for a line sparkline. As the location range, select cell **D14**. Format column **D** as **32.00 (229 pixels)** wide.
- Format the sparkline and adjust row heights to better display the data and the sparkline.

Formatting, Organizing, and Getting Data

CHAPTER OVERVIEW

Excel can use data from many sources, as well as provide data to other programs. When data are shared among applications, the data are usually in a list or table layout similar to a database. This chapter covers how to format data as an Excel table, how to sort and filter data, how to import data from other sources, and how to build a *PivotTable*.

STUDENT LEARNING OUTCOMES (SLOs)

After completing this chapter, you will be able to:

SLO 4.1 Create and format a list as an Excel table (p. E4–222).

SLO 4.2 Apply *Conditional Formatting* rules, as well as *Color Scales*, *Icon Sets*, and *Data Bars* (p. E4–228).

SLO 4.3 Sort data by one or more columns or by attribute (p. E4–235).

SLO 4.4 Filter data by using *AutoFilters* and by creating an *Advanced Filter* (p. E4–238).

SLO 4.5 Use subtotals, groups, and outlines for tabular data in a worksheet (p. E4–242).

SLO 4.6 Import data into an Excel worksheet from a text file, a database file, and other sources (p. E4–248).

SLO 4.7 Export Excel data as a text file and into a Word document (p. E4–254).

SLO 4.8 Build and format a *PivotTable* (p. E4–259).

CASE STUDY

For the Pause & Practice projects in this chapter, you create worksheets for Paradise Lakes Resort. To complete the work, you format a list as an Excel table, sort and filter data, import and clean data, and create a PivotTable.

Pause & Practice 4-1: Format data as an Excel table and set conditional formatting.

Pause & Practice 4-2: Sort, filter, and subtotal data.

Pause & Practice 4-3: Import and *Flash Fill* data in a workbook.

Pause & Practice 4-4: Create and format a *PivotTable* and a *PivotChart*.

Creating and Formatting an Excel Table

An Excel *table* is a list of related pieces of information that is formatted with a title row followed by rows of data (Figure 4-1). When data are in a table format, you can organize, sort, filter, and calculate results easily and quickly, much like a database.

The *header row* is the first row of a table with descriptive titles or labels. Each row of data is a *record* and each column is a *field*. The label in the header row is sometimes referred to as the *field name*. When you format Excel data as a table, follow these guidelines to optimize your tables for use of Excel commands:

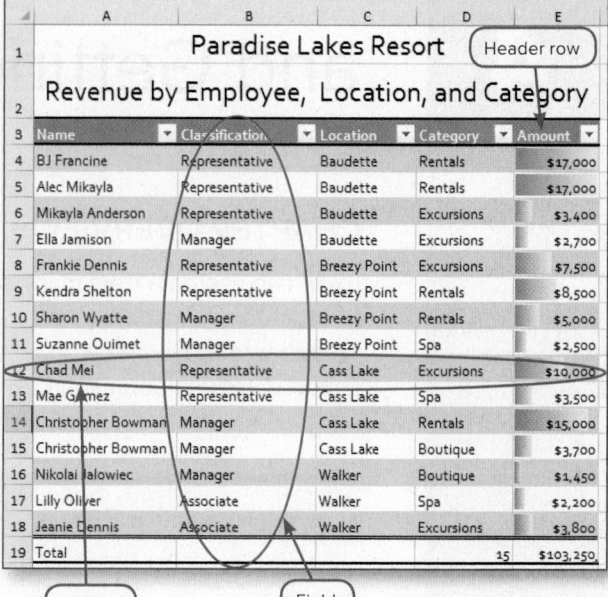

Figure 4-1 Excel table

- Type descriptive labels in the first row and begin each label with a letter, not a number.
- Assign each header a unique label; do not repeat any of the descriptive labels.
- Keep the same type of data within each column (text or values).
- Do not leave blank rows within the data.
- Keep the table separate from other data on the worksheet.

Create an Excel Table

When data are arranged as a list and conform to the guidelines just described, a simple format command creates an Excel table. Select the data and click the **Format as Table** button in the *Styles* group on the *Home* tab to open the *Table Styles* gallery. Choose a style and click **OK** in the *Format as Table* dialog box. A second way to create an Excel table is to select the data and click the **Table** button in the *Tables* group on the *Insert* tab. The *Format as Table* dialog box opens and creates the table with a default style.

After your data are formatted as a table, each label in the header row displays an *AutoFilter* arrow, and the contextual *Table Tools Design* tab opens with command groups for modifying the table. Recall from chapter 3 that a filter is criteria that determine which data are shown and which are hidden. From *AutoFilter* arrows, you can show records for employees in a particular location or display revenue from certain months.

> **MORE INFO**
>
> *AutoFilter* arrows replace the worksheet column headings (A, B, C, and so on) when you scroll down in a table with many records. *AutoFilter* arrows do not print.

▶ HOW TO: Create an Excel Table

1. Select the cells to be formatted as a table.
 - Include the header row with column titles.
2. Click the **Format as Table** button [*Home* tab, *Styles* group] to open the table gallery.
 - Table styles are organized in light, medium, and dark categories.

3. Click a table style.
 - Apply a different style after the table is created (Figure 4-2).

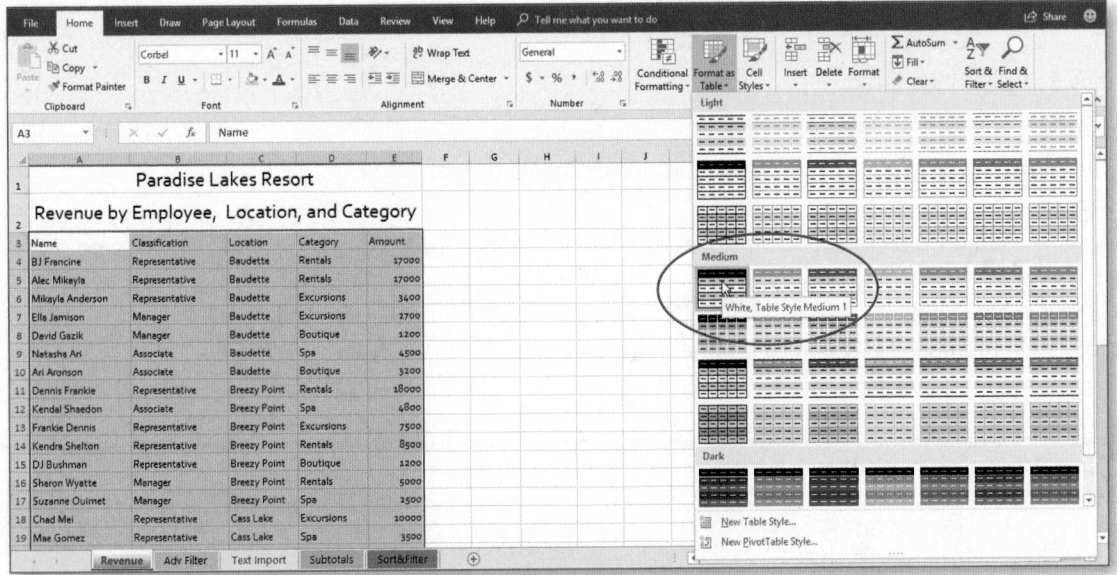

Figure 4-2 *Table Styles* gallery and selected data

4. Confirm the cell range in the *Format As Table* dialog box.
 - Drag to select a different range if necessary.
5. Select the **My table has headers** box in the *Format As Table* dialog box.
 - When the selected range does not have column titles, Excel inserts a row above the data with the labels *Column1, Column2,* and so on. You can edit these names.
6. Click **OK**.
 - When the selected range includes data from an outside source, you will see a message box asking to remove the data connection. Click **Yes** to create the table (Figure 4-3).

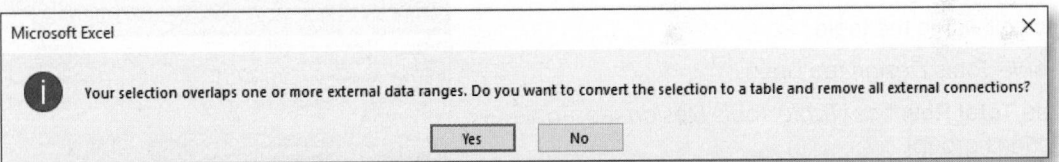

Figure 4-3 Message box for data from an outside source

> **ANOTHER WAY**
>
> Select the header and data rows, click the **Quick Analysis** tool, and choose **Tables**. Then, click the **Table** button to format the data in a default table style. This method is not available for data from an outside source.

Table Styles and Options

A *table style* is a predesigned set of format settings with a color scheme, alternating fill for rows and columns, vertical and horizontal borders, and more. You select a style when you create a table from the **Format as Table** button, or apply a different style at any time. Predefined table

styles are classified as *Light*, *Medium*, and *Dark* and use colors based on the workbook theme. Remove a style by selecting *None* in the *Light* group.

▶HOW TO: Apply a Table Style

1. Click any cell within the table.
 - The *Table Tools Design* tab displays.
2. Click the **More** button [*Table Tools Design* tab, *Table Styles* group].
 - The *Table Styles* gallery opens.
 - Styles are named *ColorName, Table Style Light 1*; *ColorName, Table Style Medium 4*; *ColorName, Table Style Dark 8*, and so on.
 - The *None* style is the first icon in the *Light* group when an existing style is already applied.
3. Point to a style thumbnail to see a *Live Preview* in the table.
4. Click to select and apply a style.

 MORE INFO

Create and save a custom table style by clicking the **More** button in the *Table Styles* group [*Table Tools Design* tab] and choosing **New Table Style**.

The *Table Style Options* group on the *Table Tools Design* tab includes commands for showing or hiding various parts of the table such as the header row or a total row. When you select a total row, a blank row inserts as the last row, and you can choose which calculation displays in each column. Other options are banded columns or rows, which alternate fills or borders. A command to apply bold to data in the first or last column or both is available. You can also hide the *AutoFilter* arrows.

▶HOW TO: Display a Total Row in a Table

1. Click any cell within the table.
 - The *Table Tools Design* tab opens.
2. Select the **Total Row** box [*Table Tools Design* tab, *Table Style Options* group].
 - The total row displays as the last row in the table.
3. Click a cell in the total row and click its arrow to open the calculation list.
 - The default calculation is *Sum* for numeric data.
4. Choose the calculation for the column (Figure 4-4).
 - Use *Count* for alphanumeric columns.

Figure 4-4 Table with total row

 MORE INFO

Custom Views [*View* tab, *Workbook Views* group] are not available in an Excel table.

E4-224

The Table Tools and Properties Groups

The *Tools* group on the *Table Tools Design* tab includes commands to remove duplicate records and to convert the table to a regular cell range. The *Insert Slicer* command opens a filter window for hiding or showing records in the table. The *Properties* group includes the table name and a command to resize the table.

A **duplicate row** is a record in a table that has exactly the same information in one or more columns. The *Remove Duplicates* command scans a table to locate and delete rows with repeated data in the specified columns. In the *Remove Duplicates* dialog box, you set which columns might have duplicate data. If you check all the columns, a row must have the same data in every column as another row.

▶ HOW TO: Remove Duplicates

1. Click any cell within the table.
2. Click the **Remove Duplicates** button [*Table Tools Design* tab, *Tools* group] (Figure 4-5).
3. Select the box for each column that might have duplicate data.
 - Click **Unselect All** to remove all checkmarks and select a single label.
 - Excel recognizes headers and does not scan them for duplicate content.
4. Click **OK**.
 - A message box indicates how many duplicate values were removed and how many unique values remain.
5. Click **OK**.
 - The rows are removed from the table.
 - The command does not preview which rows are deleted.
 - **Undo** this command if needed.

Figure 4-5 *Remove Duplicates* dialog box

The *Insert Slicer* command opens a floating window that is used as a visual filter, enabling you to work with smaller pieces of large datasets. If a table has 10,000 records but you are concerned with one location or category, insert a slicer to control which records display in the table. A *Slicer* window is an object that can be sized and positioned, and it displays selection handles like other objects. The contextual *Slicer Tools Options* tab is available when a slicer object is active with settings to customize the floating window.

▶ HOW TO: Insert a Slicer

1. Click any cell within the table.
2. Click the **Insert Slicer** button [*Table Tools Design* tab, *Tools* group].
 - The *Insert Slicers* dialog box lists all field names in the table.
3. Select the box for the field to be used for filtering (Figure 4-6).
 - You can select more than one field to open multiple slicers.

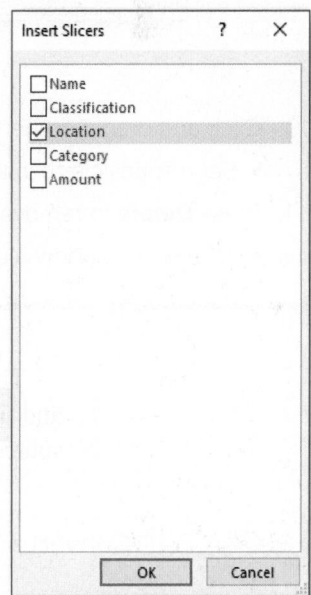

Figure 4-6 *Insert Slicers* dialog box

4. Click **OK**.
 - The *Slicer* window is a graphic object and can be selected.
 - All records display in the table.
5. Click an item name to filter the data.
 - The records are filtered.
 - You can press **Ctrl** and click another item to apply more than one filter.
 - You can toggle the **Multi-Select** button in the *Slicer* title bar and then click to turn off multiple items for filtering.
6. Click the **Clear Filter** button in the *Slicer* title bar.
 - All the records display.
7. Click the **More** button [*Slicer Tools Options* tab, *Slicer Styles* group].
8. Select a style for the *Slicer*.
9. Click the **Columns** spinner button [*Slicer Tools Options* tab, *Buttons* group] to set the number of columns in the *Slicer* (Figure 4-7).

Figure 4-7 *Slicer* window for a table

10. Click and drag a corner selection handle to resize the *Slicer*.
 - Set a specific size in the *Size* group [*Slicer Tools Options* tab].
11. Press **Delete** to remove the *Slicer* window.
 - The *Slicer* window must be selected to be deleted.

The *Convert to Range* command removes table formatting and options except for font style and fill colors. You may need to convert a table to a range when combining data from different sources or when sharing data with applications that require unformatted data.

▶HOW TO: Convert a Table to a Range

1. Click any cell within the table.
2. Click the **Convert to Range** button [*Table Tools Design* tab, *Tools* group] (Figure 4-8).

3. Click **Yes** in the message box.
 - The data display as a regular range of cells.
 - Font size, font style, and colors remain.
 - Format the data as needed.

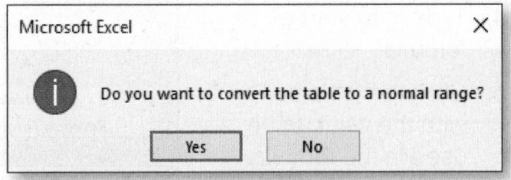

Figure 4-8 *Convert to Normal Range* message box

> **MORE INFO**
>
> If a normal data range has a header row, show *AutoFilter* arrows by clicking the **Filter** button on the *Data* tab.

Tables are named automatically as *TableN* where *N* is a number. To change the name to a more descriptive label, click the *Table Name* box in the *Properties* group on the *Table Tools Design* tab and type the name. Do not use spaces in a table name, and table names in a workbook must be unique. From the *Properties* group, you can also open the *Resize Table* dialog box to select an expanded or reduced cell range for the table. A table also has a resize arrow in its bottom right cell that you drag to grow or shrink the table. Tables grow automatically when you press **Tab** after the last item in the last row to start a new record.

Structured References and Table Formulas

In addition to the table name, each column is assigned a name using the label in its header row. The column name with its table name is known as a ***structured reference***. An example is *Table1[Category]* as the reference for the category column in *Table1*. Column names are enclosed in square brackets. In addition to column names, specific table item names are *#All*, *#Data*, *#Headers*, *#This Row*, and *#Totals*, each preceded by the **#** symbol as an identifier.

Structured references are supplied automatically in formulas, making it easy to identify what is being calculated. When you point to build a formula, you will see [*@ColumnName*] as the reference, with **@** inserted as an identifier (Figure 4-9). The table name and structured reference names appear in *Formula AutoComplete* lists, and you can refer to those ranges in formulas outside the table. As you work with structured references, expand the *Formula* bar to better see a lengthy formula. The *Expand/Collapse Formula Bar* button is on the right edge of the *Formula* bar.

> **MORE INFO**
>
> To enter cell references in a table formula instead of structured references, disable **Use table names in formulas** in Excel *Options* [*File* tab, *Options*, *Formulas* pane].

Tables are automatically expanded to include a new column when you type a label adjacent to the last row heading. As part of its *Table AutoExpansion* feature, Excel copies a formula to complete a column with a calculation.

▶HOW TO: Add a Calculation Column in a Table

1. Select the cell to the right of the last column heading in the table.
 - The data must be formatted as an Excel table.
2. Type the new column label and press **Enter**.
 - A column is added to the table.
3. Select the cell below the new label.

4. Type = to start a formula.

5. Click the table cell with the value to be used in the formula.

 - The column name in square brackets preceded by an **@** symbol is inserted.

6. Complete the formula (Figure 4-9).

 - You can refer to non-table cells in the worksheet or type a constant.

7. Press **Enter**.

 - The formula is copied down the entire column.
 - Enter the formula in any row in the column for it to be copied.

Figure 4-9 Structured references in a table

MORE INFO

Disable automatic copying of table formulas in the *AutoCorrect Options, AutoFormat As You Type* tab [*File* tab, *Options, Proofing* pane].

SLO 4.2

Applying Conditional Formatting

Conditional formatting commands apply formats to cells only when the cells meet the criteria. For example, use conditional formatting to display revenue amounts below a certain level in a bold red font. Conditional formatting is dynamic; the formatting adapts if the data change.

Basic conditional formatting commands are *Highlight Cells Rules* and *Top/Bottom Rules*. For these commands, you set the rule or criteria in a dialog box and choose the format. Another type of conditional formatting is *data visualization*, in which the cell displays a fill color, a horizontal bar, or an icon.

Highlight Cells Rules

Highlight Cells Rules use relational or comparison operators to determine if the value or label should be formatted. *Highlight Cells Rules* include common operators such as *Equal To* and *Greater Than*. You can also create your own rule using other operators or a formula.

Access all of the conditional formatting options from the *Conditional Formatting* button in the *Styles* group on the *Home* tab (Figure 4-10). You can also choose a default conditional formatting rule from the *Quick Analysis* tool options.

Figure 4-10 *Highlight Cells Rules* menu

HOW TO: Create a "Less Than" Highlight Cells Rule

1. Select the cell range.
2. Click the **Conditional Formatting** button [*Home* tab, *Styles* group].
3. Select **Highlight Cells Rules** and select **Less Than**.
 - The *Less Than* dialog box opens.
4. Type a value in the *Format cells that are LESS THAN* box.
 - *Live Preview* applies the default format to cells that meet the criteria.
5. Click the arrow for the *with* box.
 - A list of preset formats displays.
6. Choose a format (Figure 4-11).
 - Choose *Custom Format* to open the *Format Cells* dialog box and build a format.
7. Click **OK**.
 - Formatting is applied to cells that meet the criteria.
 - Click a cell away from the range to better see the formatting.

Figure 4-11 Less Than dialog box

Top/Bottom Rules

Top/Bottom Rules use ranking to format the highest (top) or lowest (bottom) items, either by number or percentage. You set the number or percentage in the dialog box as well as the format. You can also set a rule to format values that are above or below average (Figure 4-12).

For a selected range, the *Formatting* group in the *Quick Analysis* tool provides the most likely conditional formatting choices.

Figure 4-12 Top/Bottom Rules

HOW TO: Create a Top 10% Rule

1. Select the cell range.
 - The *Quick Analysis* button appears in the bottom right cell of the range.
2. Click the **Quick Analysis** button.
3. Choose **Formatting**.
 - Commonly used conditional format choices are listed.
4. Choose **Top 10%** (Figure 4-13).
 - The number of cells equal to the *Top 10%* of the number of cells in the column are formatted with a default format.
 - Edit the format to use different attributes.

Figure 4-13 Quick Analysis options for conditional formatting

Use a Formula for a Rule

In addition to the *Highlight Cells* or *Top/Bottom* rules, you can create a conditional formatting formula using operators, criteria, and settings in the *New Formatting Rule* dialog box. For example, build a rule to format cells in the amount column if the location is Baudette. A formula must result in either TRUE or FALSE (a Yes or No question) to be used as criteria.

▶ HOW TO: Use a Formula in a Conditional Formatting Rule

1. Select the cell range.
2. Click the **Conditional Formatting** button [*Home* tab, *Styles* group].
3. Select **New Rule**.
 - The *New Formatting Rule* dialog box opens.
 - The choices in the dialog box update based on the rule type.
4. Choose **Use a formula to determine which cells to format** in the *Select a Rule Type* list.
5. Type = in the *Edit the Rule Description* area in the *Format values where this formula is true* box.
 - You must start the formula with an equals sign (**=**).
 - The formula must be built so that the result is either TRUE or FALSE.
6. Type the formula.
 - Use relative cell references to the first row of data (Figure 4-14).
 - When you click to enter the cell reference, it is absolute; press **F4 (FN+F4)** to change it to relative.
 - Text in the formula must be enclosed in quotation marks.
7. Click **Format** to open the *Format Cells* dialog box.
8. Build the format and click **OK**.
9. Click **OK** to close the *New Formatting Rule* dialog box.
 - Cells that meet the formula condition are formatted.

Figure 4-14 *New Formatting Rule* and *Format Cells* dialog boxes

Data Bars, Color Scales, and Icon Sets

Data visualization formats cells with icons, fill color, or shaded bars to distinguish values. Visualization formats highlight low, middle, or top values or compare the values to each other. Data visualization commands are *Data Bars, Color Scales,* and *Icon Sets.*

These three commands are part of the conditional formatting group, because they apply a rule for determining what displays in the cell. You can choose which colors or icons are applied from the *Conditional Formatting* button [*Home* tab, *Styles* group]. When you select an option from the *Quick Analysis* button, however, a default choice is applied.

▶HOW TO: Format Data with Data Bars

1. Select the cell range.
2. Click the **Quick Analysis** button.
3. Choose **Formatting**.
 - *Data Bars* compare the value in each cell to the other values in the range by the length of the bar.
 - *Color Scales* use a variation of two or three colors to indicate low, middle, and high values.
 - *Icon Sets* insert icons that represent the upper, middle, or lower values of the cell range.
4. Choose **Data Bars** (Figure 4-15).
 - A default data bar style and color is applied.

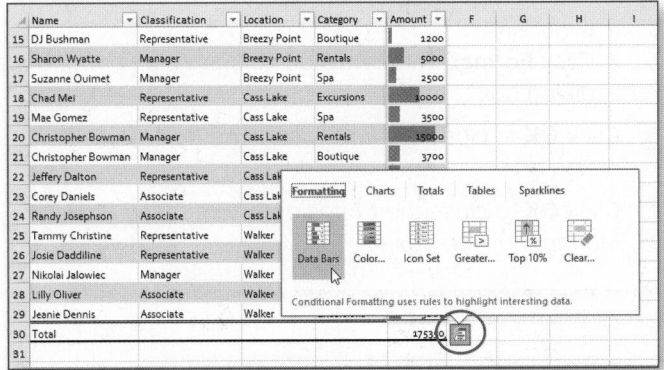

Figure 4-15 Setting *Data Bars* from the *Quick Analysis* button

Manage Conditional Formatting Rules

You can edit any conditional formatting rule, including data visualization commands, from the *Conditional Formatting Rules Manager* dialog box. From this dialog box, you can reset the range to be formatted, change the actual format, change the rule, or delete the rule.

Figure 4-16 *Conditional Formatting Rules Manager* dialog box

If you select the formatted range before you start the *Manage Rules* command, the rule for that selection displays in the *Conditional Formatting Rules Manager* dialog box. You can also show all the rules in the current sheet or another one (Figure 4-16).

When you click **Edit Rule**, the *Edit Formatting Rule* dialog box opens. This dialog box is similar to the *New Formatting Rule* dialog box, and you set options the same way.

▶HOW TO: Manage Conditional Formatting Rules

1. Select the formatted cell range.
2. Click the **Conditional Formatting** button [*Home* tab, *Styles* group].
3. Choose **Manage Rules**.
 - *Current Selection* is listed in the *Show formatting rules for* box.
 - Choose **This Worksheet** to list all rules in the worksheet.
4. Select the rule name to be modified.
5. Select **Edit Rule**.
 - The *Edit Formatting Rule* dialog box opens.
 - The current *Rule Description* displays.
 - You can select another rule type in the top half of the dialog box.

6. Select options to change the rule in the *Edit the Rule Description* area.

- The options depend on the rule type (Figure 4-17).
 - Click **Format** when available to open the *Format Cells* dialog box.

7. Click **OK** to close the *Edit Formatting Rule* dialog box.

8. Click **OK** to close the *Conditional Formatting Rules Manager* dialog box.

Figure 4-17 *Edit Formatting Rule* dialog box for data bars

You can clear conditional formatting from a selected range or from the entire sheet. For a selected range, click the **Quick Analysis** button and choose **Clear...** You can also choose **Clear Rules** from the **Conditional Formatting** button menu.

PAUSE & PRACTICE: EXCEL 4-1

For this project, you format data as a table, add a total row, and remove duplicate records. As you complete formulas on the sheet, you see structured references. You also set conditional formatting with data bars.

File Needed: ***ParadiseLakes-04.xlsx*** *(Student data files are available in the* Library *of your SIMnet account.)*
Completed Project File Name: ***[your initials] PP E4-1.xlsx***

1. Open the ***ParadiseLakes-04*** workbook from your student data files and save it as [your initials] PP E4-1.

2. Click the **Revenue** sheet tab.

3. Format data as an Excel table.
 a. Select cells **A3:E30**.
 b. Click the **Format as Table** button [*Home* tab, *Styles* group].
 c. Select **Periwinkle, Table Style Medium 20** from the gallery (third row in the group).
 d. Verify that the **My table has headers** box is selected in the *Format As Table* dialog box.
 e. Click **OK**.

4. Add a total row to a table.
 a. Click a cell within the table.
 b. Select the **Total Row** box [*Table Tools Design* tab, *Table Style Options* group].
 c. Click cell **D31** and choose **Count** from the drop-down list.
 d. Select the amounts in cells **E4:E31** and format them as **Currency**. Decrease the decimal two times to show zero decimal places (Figure 4-18).

5. Remove duplicate rows in a table.
 a. Click a cell within the table.
 b. Click the **Remove Duplicates** button [*Table Tools Design* tab, *Tools* group].
 c. Click **Unselect All** to deselect all the boxes.
 d. Select the **Name** box and the **Amount** box. When you look for duplicate data in specific columns, you can speed up search activities.
 e. Click **OK** in the *Remove Duplicates* dialog box. One record will be removed, the one for Josie Daddiline. The records for Christopher Bowman are not duplicated in the selected columns.
 f. Click **OK** in the message box.

6. Apply conditional formatting using data bars.
 a. Select cells **E4:E29**.
 b. Click the **Conditional Formatting** button [*Home* tab, *Styles* group].
 c. Point to **Data Bars** to see its menu.
 d. Select **Blue Data Bar** in the *Gradient Fill* group (Figure 4-19).

	A	B	C	D	E
1	Paradise Lakes Resort				
2	Revenue by Employee, Location, and Category				
3	Name	Classification	Location	Category	Amount
4	BJ Francine	Representative	Baudette	Rentals	$17,000
5	Alec Mikayla	Representative	Baudette	Rentals	$17,000
6	Mikayla Anderson	Representative	Baudette	Excursions	$3,400
7	Ella Jamison	Manager	Baudette	Excursions	$2,700
8	David Gazik	Manager	Baudette	Boutique	$1,200
9	Natasha Ari	Associate	Baudette	Spa	$4,500
10	Ari Aronson	Associate	Baudette	Boutique	$3,200
11	Dennis Frankie	Representative	Breezy Point	Rentals	$18,000
12	Kendal Shaedon	Associate	Breezy Point	Spa	$4,800
13	Frankie Dennis	Representative	Breezy Point	Excursions	$7,500
14	Kendra Shelton	Representative	Breezy Point	Rentals	$8,500
15	DJ Bushman	Representative	Breezy Point	Boutique	$1,200
16	Sharon Wyatte	Manager	Breezy Point	Rentals	$5,000
17	Suzanne Ouimet	Manager	Breezy Point	Spa	$2,500
18	Chad Mei	Representative	Cass Lake	Excursions	$10,000
19	Mae Gomez	Representative	Cass Lake	Spa	$3,500
20	Christopher Bowman	Manager	Cass Lake	Rentals	$15,000
21	Christopher Bowman	Manager	Cass Lake	Boutique	$3,700
22	Jeffery Dalton	Representative	Cass Lake	Rentals	$3,700
23	Corey Daniels	Associate	Cass Lake	Excursions	$4,500
24	Randy Josephson	Associate	Cass Lake	Boutique	$1,500
25	Tammy Christine	Representative	Walker	Rentals	$17,500
26	Josie Daddiline	Representative	Walker	Rentals	$12,000
27	Nikolai Jalowiec	Manager	Walker	Boutique	$1,450
28	Josie Daddiline	Representative	Walker	Rentals	$12,000
29	Lilly Oliver	Associate	Walker	Spa	$2,200
30	Jeanie Dennis	Associate	Walker	Excursions	$3,800
31	Total			27	$187,350

Figure 4-18 Data formatted as a table

Figure 4-19 Choose a gradient fill for data bars

7. Manage conditional formatting rules.
 a. Select cells **E4:E29**.
 b. Click the **Conditional Formatting** button [*Home* tab, *Styles* group].
 c. Choose **Manage Rules**.
 d. Click **Edit Rule**.
 e. Click the **Color** arrow for **Fill** in the *Bar Appearance* area.
 f. Choose **Gold, Accent 3** (seventh column).
 g. Click the arrow for **Border** in the *Bar Appearance* area.
 h. Choose **No Border** (Figure 4-20).
 i. Click **OK** to close the *Edit Formatting Rule* dialog box.
 j. Click **OK** to close the *Conditional Formatting Rules Manager* dialog box.

8. Refer to a structured reference in a formula.
 a. Select cell **H4** and type = to start a formula.
 b. Click cell **E30** to insert a structured reference to the total in the Amount column.
 c. Type *(1+, click cell **G4**, and type) to calculate a new total that reflects a 2% increase (Figure 4-21).
 d. Press **Enter**. The target total is $178,857.
 e. Copy the formula to cells **H5:H6**. The structured reference is absolute.

Figure 4-20 Edit the rule for data bars

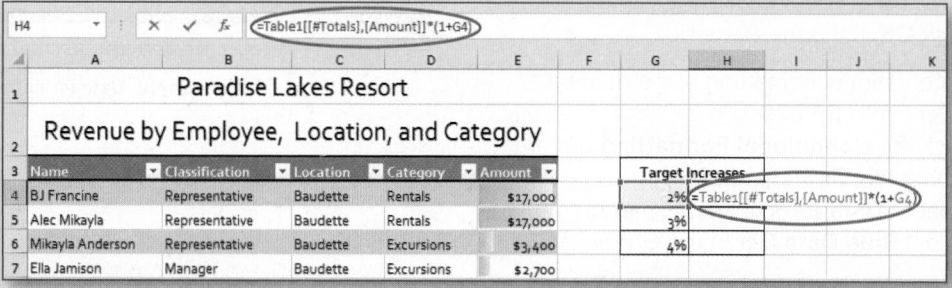

Figure 4-21 Structured reference in a formula

9. Save and close the workbook (Figure 4-22).

Figure 4-22 PP E4-1 completed

Sorting Data

Sorting is the process of arranging rows of data in an identified order. For Paradise Lakes Resort, you can arrange the revenue table by classification to compare results for a particular job title or by highest to lowest amount.

Ascending order sorts data alphabetically from A to Z or numerically from the smallest to the largest value. In a ***descending*** sort, data are arranged alphabetically Z to A or numerically from the largest to the smallest value.

Sort Options

To be sorted, data must be organized in rows and columns like an Excel table, but it need not be formatted as a table. In addition to text or number sorting, you can sort data by fill color, font color, or cell icon from *Conditional Formatting*.

The *Sort & Filter* button on the *Home* tab in the *Editing* group lists *A to Z* sort, *Z to A* sort, and *Custom Sort* (multiple columns) commands. The same commands are available in the *Sort & Filter* group on the *Data* tab as separate buttons.

Sort Data by One Column

When data have a header row followed by rows of data with at least one empty row above and below the data, click any cell in the column you want to sort and choose a sort command. Excel recognizes and sorts the entire dataset.

Data to be sorted include text, numbers, or dates. Dates are treated as values. An ascending sort (smallest to largest) arranges dates so that the earliest date is first. A descending date sort organizes the data so that the most current date is first.

Undo a sort task by clicking the **Undo** button [*Quick Access* toolbar]. You can also sort data many times to arrange it in your preferred order.

▶**HOW TO: Sort Data by a Single Column**

1. Select a cell in the column to be used for sorting.
 - Click a cell with data, not the column header.

2. Click the **Sort A to Z** button [*Data* tab, *Sort & Filter* group] (Figure 4-23).
 - The records are arranged in alphabetical or smallest-to-largest order based on the first character in each cell in the column.
 - If the first character in an alphanumeric column is a value or special character, that record is sorted at the top.

3. Click the **Sort Z to A** button [*Data* tab, *Sort & Filter* group].
 - The records are arranged in reverse alphabetical or largest-to-smallest order based on the first character.
 - If the first character in an alphanumeric column is a value or special character, that record is sorted at the bottom.

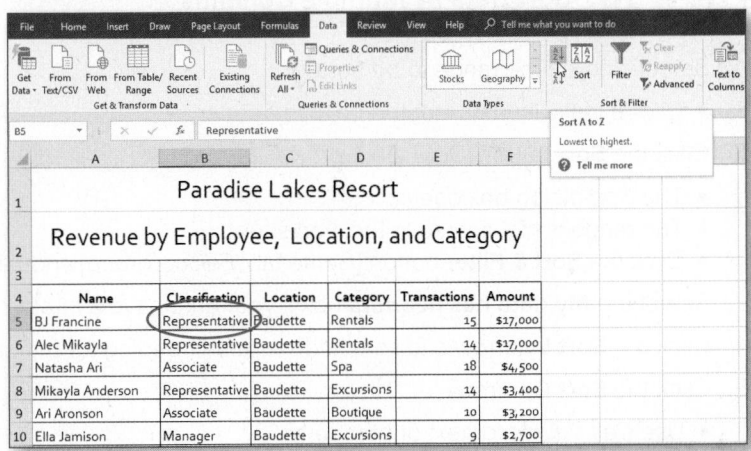

Figure 4-23 Cell B5 selected to sort by classification

Sort Data by Multiple Columns

You can sort data by more than one column. An example of data that are often sorted by two columns is a list with cities in one column and states or provinces in another. Data can be sorted by state so that Alabama is before Arizona, and within Arizona, Phoenix is before Tuscon. When you use the *Sort & Filter* button [*Home* tab, *Editing* group] or a sort button on the *Data* tab, you sort first by the least important field. The least important field in a city and state sort is the city. Use the *Sort* dialog box which opens when you click the **Sort** button [*Data* tab, *Sort & Filter* group] or when you choose **Custom Sort** from the *Sort & Filter* button options.

The data in Figure 4-24 are sorted by two columns: classification and amount. *Classification* is the top or first sort level and *Amount* is second. When you use the *Sort* dialog box, sort by *Classification* first and then by *Amount*. When you use the *Sort & Filter* button, sort first by *Amount* and then by *Classification*.

	A	B	C	D	E	F
2	Revenue by Employee, Location, and Category					
3						
4	Name	Classification	Location	Category	Transactions	Amount
5	Randy Josephson	Associate	Cass Lake	Boutique	12	$1,500
6	Lilly Oliver	Associate	Walker	Spa	10	$2,200
7	Ari Aronson	Associate	Baudette	Boutique	10	$3,200
8	Jeanie Dennis	Associate	Walker	Excursions	8	$3,800
9	Natasha Ari	Associate	Baudette	Spa	18	$4,500
10	Corey Daniels	Associate	Cass Lake	Excursions	22	$4,500
11	Kendal Shaedon	Associate	Breezy Point	Spa	20	$4,800
12	David Gazik	Manager	Baudette	Boutique	6	$1,200
13	Nikolai Jalowiec	Manager	Walker	Boutique	6	$1,450
14	Suzanne Ouimet	Manager	Breezy Point	Spa	4	$2,500
15	Ella Jamison	Manager	Baudette	Excursions	9	$2,700
16	Christopher Bowman	Manager	Cass Lake	Boutique	15	$3,700
17	Sharon Wyatte	Manager	Breezy Point	Rentals	7	$5,000
18	Christopher Bowman	Manager	Cass Lake	Rentals	14	$15,000
19	DJ Bushman	Representative	Breezy Point	Boutique	5	$1,200
20	Mikayla Anderson	Representative	Baudette	Excursions	14	$3,400
21	Mae Gomez	Representative	Cass Lake	Spa	12	$3,500
22	Jeffery Dalton	Representative	Cass Lake	Rentals	5	$3,700
23	Frankie Dennis	Representative	Breezy Point	Excursions	16	$7,500
24	Kendra Shelton	Representative	Breezy Point	Rentals	10	$8,500

Figure 4-24 Data sorted by "Classification" and "Amount"

▶HOW TO: Sort Data by Multiple Columns

1. Select a cell in the range to be sorted.
 - Click a cell with data, not the column header.
2. Click the **Sort** button [*Data* tab, *Sort & Filter* group].
 - The *Sort* dialog box opens.
 - The range is highlighted in the worksheet.
 - Click the **Sort & Filter** button [*Home* tab, *Editing* group] and select **Custom Sort**.
3. Select the **My data has headers** box if your data have a header row.
4. Click the **Sort by** arrow and select the column heading for the first sort level.
5. Click the **Sort On** arrow.
 - Use *Cell Values* for text or numbers.
 - If the data have a cell attribute such as a font color, select the name of the attribute.
6. Click the **Order** arrow and choose a sort option.
 - For columns with numbers or dates, the options are *Smallest to Largest* and *Largest to Smallest*.
 - The *Custom List* option provides special sorting orders for days of the week and months of the year so that data are sorted chronologically.

7. Click **Add Level** to add a second sort column.

8. Click the **Then by** arrow and select the second column heading.

9. Click the **Sort On** arrow and choose **Cell Values** or an attribute.

10. Click the **Order** arrow and choose a sort order (Figure 4-25).

 - Click the **Options** button in the *Sort* dialog box to specify case-sensitive sorting or to change the orientation of ascending and descending sorts.

11. Click **OK**.

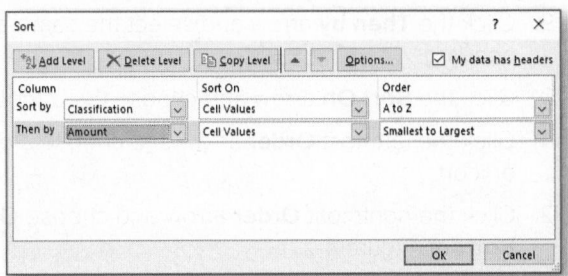

Figure 4-25 *Sort* dialog box

Sort Data by Cell Attribute

An ***attribute*** is a setting or property. Cell attributes used for sorting are font color, cell fill color, and the conditional formatting icon. These choices are options for the *Sort On* choice in the *Sort* dialog box, and they are available when you choose **Sort** from a cell's context menu.

When you sort by font or fill color, the *Order* choices are the colors used in the column. You choose a color and set its position in the sorted column. Column E in Figure 4-26 is sorted by the icon set with the green checkmark icon on the top.

	A	B	C	D	E	F
4	Name	Classification	Location	Category	Transactions	Amount
5	Christopher Bowman	Manager	Cass Lake	Rentals	14	$15,000
6	Chad Mei	Representative	Cass Lake	Excursions	24	$10,000
7	Josie Daddiline	Representative	Walker	Rentals	10	$12,000
8	Josie Daddiline	Representative	Walker	Rentals	12	$12,000
9	BJ Francine	Representative	Baudette	Rentals	15	$17,000
10	Alec Mikayla	Representative	Baudette	Rentals	14	$17,000
11	Tammy Christine	Representative	Walker	Rentals	16	$17,500
12	Dennis Frankie	Representative	Breezy Point	Rentals	16	$18,000
13	Sharon Wyatte	Manager	Breezy Point	Rentals	7	$5,000
14	Frankie Dennis	Representative	Breezy Point	Excursions	16	$7,500
15	Kendra Shelton	Representative	Breezy Point	Rentals	10	$8,500
16	Randy Josephson	Associate	Cass Lake	Boutique	12	$1,500
17	Lilly Oliver	Associate	Walker	Spa	10	$2,200
18	Ari Aronson	Associate	Baudette	Boutique	10	$3,200
19	Jeanie Dennis	Associate	Walker	Excursions	8	$3,800
20	Natasha Ari	Associate	Baudette	Spa	18	$4,500
21	Corey Daniels	Associate	Cass Lake	Excursions	22	$4,500
22	Kendal Shaedon	Associate	Breezy Point	Spa	20	$4,800
23	David Gazik	Manager	Baudette	Boutique	6	$1,200

Figure 4-26 Data sorted by icon in "Amount" column

▶ HOW TO: Sort Data by Cell Attribute

1. Select a cell in the column to sort.

2. Click the **Sort** button [*Data* tab, *Sort & Filter* group].

 - The *Sort* dialog box opens.
 - Click the **Sort & Filter** button [*Home* tab, *Editing* group] and select **Custom Sort**.

3. Select the **My data has headers** box if the data have a header row.

4. Click the **Sort by** arrow and select the column heading.

5. Click the **Sort On** arrow and choose the attribute.

 - The column must have data with different font colors, cells with different fill colors, or conditional formatting icons.

6. Click the leftmost **Order** arrow and choose a color or icon.

7. Click the rightmost **Order** arrow and choose **On Top** or **On Bottom**.

8. Click **Add Level**.

9. Click the **Then by** arrow and select the same column heading.

10. Click the **Sort On** arrow and choose the attribute.

11. Click the leftmost **Order** arrow and choose a color or icon.

12. Click the rightmost **Order** arrow and choose **On Top** or **On Bottom** (Figure 4-27).

 • Add and define as many sort levels as needed.

13. Click **OK**.

Figure 4-27 Conditional formatting icon order in the *Sort* dialog box

> **MORE INFO**
>
> To sort by icon sets, right-click a cell with the icon that you want first and select **Sort** and then **Put Selected Formatting Icon on Top**.

Sort Data in an Excel Table

When data are formatted as a table, you can sort from the *AutoFilter* arrows with each label in the header row. Sort choices are listed at the top of the pane that opens when you click an *AutoFilter* arrow.

▶**HOW TO: Sort Data in an Excel Table**

1. Click the **AutoFilter** arrow for the column heading that represents the lowest sort level.

 • The *AutoFilter* pane lists sort choices at the top.

2. Choose **Sort A to Z** or **Sort Smallest to Largest** (Figure 4-28).

 • The table is sorted by the column.
 • *Sort Smallest to Largest* appears for numeric data.

3. Click the **AutoFilter** arrow for the column heading that represents the top sort level.

4. Choose **Sort A to Z** or **Sort Smallest to Largest**.

 • The table maintains the sort order from the first selected column within the sorted data for the top-level column.

Figure 4-28 *AutoFilter* arrow sort choices

SLO 4.4

Filtering Data

You can usually work more efficiently when you filter large amounts of data to show only rows of importance to your task. For example, filter data to show records for the year, the month, the individual, the product, or a similar grouping. When you filter data, information that does

not meet the requirements is temporarily hidden. A filter specifies which data are shown and which are hidden.

AutoFilters

In list-type data or an Excel table, the *Filter* button [*Data* tab, *Sort & Filter* group] displays or hides the *AutoFilter* arrow for each label in the header row. When you click an *AutoFilter* arrow, a pane displays sort options, filter types based on the data type, and check boxes for every piece of data. You can select boxes to mark which records display, or build a filter.

▶**HOW TO:** Display and Use AutoFilters

1. Select a cell in the list.
2. Click the **Filter** button [*Data* tab, *Sort & Filter* group].
 - *AutoFilter* arrows appear in the header row with each label.
 - *AutoFilter* arrows display by default in an Excel table.
3. Click the **AutoFilter** arrow for the column used for filtering.
 - All items are selected and displayed in the data.
 - Filter options depend on the type of data in the column.
4. Click the **(Select All)** box to remove all checkmarks.
5. Select the box for each item to be shown (Figure 4-29).
6. Click **OK**.
 - Records that meet the criteria display with row headings in blue.
 - Records that do not meet the criteria and their row numbers are hidden.
 - A filter symbol appears with the column *AutoFilter* arrow.

Figure 4-29 *AutoFilter* for "Category" column

To remove a filter and display the complete list, click the **AutoFilter** arrow for the column and choose **Clear Filter From (ColumnName)**. You can also click the **Clear** button in the *Sort & Filter* group on the *Data* tab.

> **ANOTHER WAY**
>
> An *AutoFilter* arrow and a *Slicer* window display the same results.

Custom AutoFilter

A ***custom AutoFilter*** is criteria that you build in a dialog box. A custom *AutoFilter* provides more options for how rows display, because you can use multiple criteria with *AND* and *OR*. For a column with alphanumeric data, *Text Filters* are available, or use *Number Filters* and *Date Filters* for columns with those types of data. Operators use common words such as *Equals*, *Begins With*, or *Contains* (Figure 4-30).

▶ HOW TO: Create a Custom Text AutoFilter

1. Select a cell in the data to filter.
2. Click the **Filter** button [*Data* tab, *Sort & Filter* group] to display *AutoFilter* arrows for the header row.
3. Click the **AutoFilter** arrow for the column used for filtering.
4. Select **Text Filters** and choose an operator.
 - The *Custom AutoFilter* dialog box opens.
5. Type criteria for the first operator in the box on the right.
 - You can also select a value from the drop-down list.
 - You can use wildcard characters.
6. Click the **And** or **Or** radio button.
 - *Or* conditions include rows that match either criteria.
 - *And* conditions are more restrictive and require that both criteria be met.
7. Click the arrow to choose a second operator.
 - A second operator is optional.
8. Type or select criteria for the second operator (Figure 4-31).
9. Click **OK**.
 - Rows in the data are filtered.

Figure 4-30 Text filters for a custom *AutoFilter*

Figure 4-31 *Custom AutoFilter* dialog box

Advanced Filter

For an *Advanced Filter*, you build a criteria range separate from the data and type the conditions within that range. You can show the results in the data range, or you can display filtered data in another location on the sheet. Using another location for results enables you to create separate reports with filtered rows while the main list displays all data. An *Advanced Filter* requires more setup work, but it enables you to apply more complex filters. You can even use a formula in the criteria.

A *criteria range* is at least two rows in which the first row must use the same column names as the data; the second row is where criteria are entered. You need not use all column names, and you can use more than one row for criteria. Create a criteria range in empty rows anywhere on the worksheet or on another sheet. In Figure 4-32, the criteria range is cells G5:K6.

Multiple rows below the header row in the criteria range set *AND* or *OR* conditions. If you enter criteria on the same row, they are treated as *AND* conditions. In Figure 4-32, "assoc*" in cell H6 and ">2500" in cell K6 are criteria. Both criteria must be met for a record to be displayed. For an *OR* condition, use a second (or third) row in the criteria range. An *OR* filter displays a record if any one of the requirements is met.

To show filtered results in another location, create an *output* or *extract range*. You specify one row for this range, and it should include the same column headings as the data.

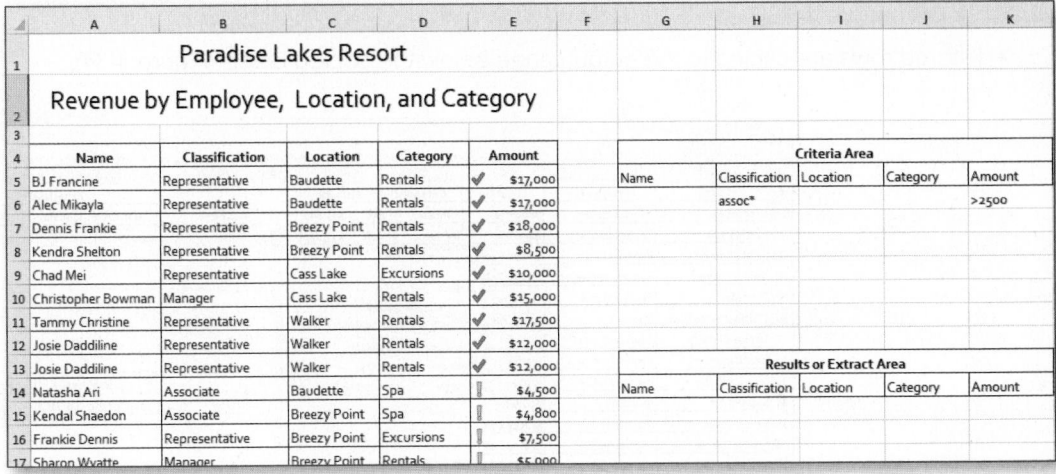

Paradise Lakes Resort
Revenue by Employee, Location, and Category

	Name	Classification	Location	Category	Amount				Criteria Area			
5	BJ Francine	Representative	Baudette	Rentals	✓ $17,000		Name	Classification	Location	Category	Amount	
6	Alec Mikayla	Representative	Baudette	Rentals	✓ $17,000			assoc*			>2500	
7	Dennis Frankie	Representative	Breezy Point	Rentals	✓ $18,000							
8	Kendra Shelton	Representative	Breezy Point	Rentals	✓ $8,500							
9	Chad Mei	Representative	Cass Lake	Excursions	✓ $10,000							
10	Christopher Bowman	Manager	Cass Lake	Rentals	✓ $15,000							
11	Tammy Christine	Representative	Walker	Rentals	✓ $17,500							
12	Josie Daddiline	Representative	Walker	Rentals	✓ $12,000				Results or Extract Area			
13	Josie Daddiline	Representative	Walker	Rentals	✓ $12,000		Name	Classification	Location	Category	Amount	
14	Natasha Ari	Associate	Baudette	Spa	$4,500							
15	Kendal Shaedon	Associate	Breezy Point	Spa	$4,800							
16	Frankie Dennis	Representative	Breezy Point	Excursions	$7,500							
17	Sharon Wyatte	Manager	Breezy Point	Rentals	$5,000							

Figure 4-32 *Advanced Filter* setup

In Figure 4-32, the extract range is cells G14:K14. Filtered rows are copied below these headings and take up as many rows as necessary. The output range must be on the same worksheet as the data, but you can copy the results to another sheet or another workbook.

▶ HOW TO: Create an Advanced Filter

1. Select labels in the header row for fields that will be used for filtering.
 - Copy all the labels in the header row if preferred.
2. Copy the labels to a *Criteria* area.
 - The criteria area can be on the same sheet or another sheet in the workbook.
 - If the criteria range is above the data, leave at least one blank row between it and the data.
3. Copy the labels again to an *Extract* area.
 - The output or extract area must be on the same sheet as the data.
 - Leave blank rows below the labels for the filtered results.
4. Type criteria in the criteria range.
 - Criteria is not case sensitive.
 - Use wildcard characters in the criteria.
5. Click a cell in the data range.
6. Click the **Advanced** button [*Data* tab, *Sort & Filter* group].
 - The *Advanced Filter* dialog box opens.
7. Select **Copy to another location** In the *Action* group.
8. Verify or select the range (including the header row) in the *List range* box.
 - If the data range is named, press **F3 (FN+F3)** and select the name.
9. Select the criteria cell range with its header row in the *Criteria range* box.
 - If the criteria range is named, press **F3 (FN+F3)** and select the name.
 - Type cell references to identify the criteria range.
10. Select the extract range in the *Copy to* box.
 - This range is the row of labels.

11. Click **OK** (Figure 4-33).

 • Filtered rows are copied to the output range below the copied labels (Figure 4-34).

Figure 4-33 *Advanced Filter* dialog box

	Name	Classification	Location	Category	Amount			Criteria Area			
5	BJ Francine	Representative	Baudette	Rentals	✔ $17,000		Name	Classification	Location	Category	Amount
6	Alec Mikayla	Representative	Baudette	Rentals	✔ $17,000			assoc*			>2500
7	Dennis Frankie	Representative	Breezy Point	Rentals	✔ $18,000						
8	Kendra Shelton	Representative	Breezy Point	Rentals	✔ $8,500						
9	Chad Mei	Representative	Cass Lake	Excursions	✔ $10,000						
10	Christopher Bowman	Manager	Cass Lake	Rentals	✔ $15,000						
11	Tammy Christine	Representative	Walker	Rentals	✔ $17,500						
12	Josie Daddiline	Representative	Walker	Rentals	✔ $12,000						
13	Josie Daddiline	Representative	Walker	Rentals	✔ $12,000			Results or Extract Area			
14	Natasha Ari	Associate	Baudette	Spa	⫿ $4,500		Name	Classification	Location	Category	Amount
15	Kendal Shaedon	Associate	Breezy Point	Spa	⫿ $4,800		Natasha Ari	Associate	Baudette	Spa	$4,500
16	Frankie Dennis	Representative	Breezy Point	Excursions	⫿ $7,500		Kendal Shaedon	Associate	Breezy Point	Spa	$4,800
17	Sharon Wyatte	Manager	Breezy Point	Rentals	⫿ $5,000		Corey Daniels	Associate	Cass Lake	Excursions	$4,500
18	Corey Daniels	Associate	Cass Lake	Excursions	⫿ $4,500		Ari Aronson	Associate	Baudette	Boutique	$3,200
19	Mikayla Anderson	Representative	Baudette	Excursions	✖ $3,400		Jeanie Dennis	Associate	Walker	Excursions	$3,800
20	Ella Jamison	Manager	Baudette	Excursions	✖ $2,700						

Figure 4-34 *Advanced Filter* results copied to another location

> **MORE INFO**
>
> Enter < > as criteria to display records that have any entry in the column. Enter = as criteria to show rows that have no entry in the column.

SLO 4.5

Using Subtotals, Groups, and Outlines

A *subtotal* is a summary row for data that are grouped. A *group* is a set of data that have the same entry in one or more columns. Figure 4-35 shows groups by "Location" with subtotals in the "Transactions" and "Amount" columns. An *outline* is a summary that groups records so that individual groups can be displayed or hidden from view. Use these three features to organize and calculate results for worksheets with large sets of data.

The Subtotal Command

The **Subtotal** command in the *Outline* group on the *Data* tab inserts summary rows for a sorted list and formats the data as an *outline*. The *Subtotal* command is available for a normal range of cells, not an Excel table. The *Subtotal* command includes *SUM*, *AVERAGE*, *MAX*, or *MIN*, as well as other *Statistical* functions.

To use the *Subtotal* command, the data should have a header row with data rows following, and you must sort the rows by the main field (column) to be summarized or totaled. To display revenue numbers by location, for example, sort the data by location. The *Subtotal* command groups the rows by this field but can show subtotals for any column.

	A	B	C	D	E	F
1	Paradise Lakes Resort					
2	Revenue by Employee, Location, and Category					
3						
4	Name	Classification	Location	Category	Transactions	Amount
5	BJ Francine	Representative	Baudette	Rentals	15	$17,000
6	Alec Mikayla	Representative	Baudette	Rentals	14	$17,000
7	Natasha Ari	Associate	Baudette	Spa	18	$4,500
8	Mikayla Anderson	Representative	Baudette	Excursions	14	$3,400
9	Ari Aronson	Associate	Baudette	Boutique	10	$3,200
10	Ella Jamison	Manager	Baudette	Excursions	9	$2,700
11	David Gazik	Manager	Baudette	Boutique	6	$1,200
12			Baudette Total		86	$49,000
13	Dennis Frankie	Representative	Breezy Point	Rentals	16	$18,000
14	Kendra Shelton	Representative	Breezy Point	Rentals	10	$8,500
15	Frankie Dennis	Representative	Breezy Point	Excursions	16	$7,500
16	Sharon Wyatte	Manager	Breezy Point	Rentals	7	$5,000
17	Kendal Shaedon	Associate	Breezy Point	Spa	20	$4,800
18	Suzanne Ouimet	Manager	Breezy Point	Spa	4	$2,500
19	DJ Bushman	Representative	Breezy Point	Boutique	5	$1,200
20			Breezy Point Total		78	$47,500

Figure 4-35 Grouped rows with subtotals in two columns

> **MORE INFO**
>
> If data are formatted as an Excel table, convert it to a normal cell range [*Table Tools Design* tab, *Tools* group] to use the *Subtotal* command.

▶ HOW TO: Display Subtotals

1. Sort the data by the column for which subtotals will be calculated.
2. Click a cell in the data range.
3. Click the **Subtotal** button [*Data* tab, *Outline* group].
 - When data have a header row followed by data rows, the range is selected.
4. Click the **At each change in** arrow.
5. Choose the column heading name that was used for sorting.
 - Subtotals need not be shown for this column.
6. Click the **Use function** arrow and select the function.
7. Select each field that should display a subtotal in the **Add subtotal to** list.
 - Verify the function applies to the column data type; for example, do not use *Sum* for a text column.
8. Choose **Replace current subtotals**.
 - If the range already has subtotals, they are replaced.
9. Choose **Summary below data** (Figure 4-36).
 - The "Summary" row can be placed above the data if you prefer.
 - Choose the option to split a group across pages.
 - Use this dialog box to remove subtotals.

Figure 4-36 *Subtotal* dialog box

10. Click **OK** (Figure 4-37).
 - A subtotal row appears below each group.
 - A grand total appears after the last row of data.
 - Outline buttons appear to the left of the column and row headings.
 - The outline is expanded, showing all details.

		A	B	C	D	E	F
	4	Name	Classification	Location	Category	Transactions	Amount
	5	Ari Aronson	Associate	Baudette	Boutique	10	$3,200
	6	David Gazik	Manager	Baudette	Boutique	6	$1,200
	7	DJ Bushman	Representative	Breezy Point	Boutique	5	$1,200
	8	Christopher Bowm	Manager	Cass Lake	Boutique	15	$3,700
	9	Randy Josephson	Associate	Cass Lake	Boutique	12	$1,500
	10	Nikolai Jalowiec	Manager	Walker	Boutique	6	$1,450
	11				**Boutique Total**		$12,250
	12	Mikayla Anderson	Representative	Baudette	Excursions	14	$3,400
	13	Ella Jamison	Manager	Baudette	Excursions	9	$2,700
	14	Frankie Dennis	Representative	Breezy Point	Excursions	16	$7,500
	15	Chad Mei	Representative	Cass Lake	Excursions	24	$10,000
	16	Corey Daniels	Associate	Cass Lake	Excursions	22	$4,500
	17	Jeanie Dennis	Associate	Walker	Excursions	8	$3,800
	18				**Excursions Total**		$31,900
	19	BJ Francine	Representative	Baudette	Rentals	15	$17,000
	20	Alec Mikayla	Representative	Baudette	Rentals	14	$17,000
	21	Dennis Frankie	Representative	Breezy Point	Rentals	16	$18,000
	22	Kendra Shelton	Representative	Breezy Point	Rentals	10	$8,500
	23	Sharon Wyatte	Manager	Breezy Point	Rentals	7	$5,000
	24	Christopher Bowm	Manager	Cass Lake	Rentals	14	$15,000
	25	Jeffery Dalton	Representative	Cass Lake	Rentals	5	$3,700
	26	Tammy Christine	Representative	Walker	Rentals	16	$17,500
	27	Josie Daddiline	Representative	Walker	Rentals	10	$12,000
	28	Josie Daddiline	Representative	Walker	Rentals	12	$12,000
	29				**Rentals Total**		$125,700
	30	Natasha Ari	Associate	Baudette	Spa	18	$4,500
	31	Kendal Shaedon	Associate	Breezy Point	Spa	20	$4,800
	32	Suzanne Ouimet	Manager	Breezy Point	Spa	4	$2,500
	33	Mae Gomez	Representative	Cass Lake	Spa	12	$3,500
	34	Lilly Oliver	Associate	Walker	Spa	10	$2,200
	35				**Spa Total**		$17,500
	36				**Grand Total**		$187,350

Figure 4-37 "Amount" subtotals for each category

The *Subtotal* command inserts the *SUBTOTAL* function in each cell with a result. Its arguments are *Function_num*, and *RefN*. *Function_num* is a number from 1 through 11 that specifies which calculation was selected in the *Subtotal* dialog box. *Ref1* is the range to be summed. If you chose *Sum*, for example, the function is =SUBTOTAL(9,F5:F11) in which "9" represents the *SUM* function, and the range is cells F5:F11.

> **MORE INFO**
>
> The *Function_num* arguments are in alphabetical order, so that *AVERAGE* is 1, *COUNT* is 2, and so on. See the argument list in Excel *Help* for this function.

Outline Buttons

An outline groups and summarizes data. A worksheet can have only one outline; the outline includes all of the worksheet data or a portion of the data. Outlines have levels, indicated by the numbered buttons to the left of the column headings. Each *Outline Level* button shows an increasing level of detail. An outline can have up to eight levels. The worksheet in Figure 4-37 has three levels: a grand total (1), a category total for each group (2), and all the rows (3).

Each group has an *Expand/Collapse* button, shown to the left of the row headings. This button is a toggle and shows a minus sign (−) or a plus sign (+). When an individual group is collapsed, you do not see details for that group, only the subtotal.

1. Click a collapse button (−) to hide details for a group.
 • Only the subtotal row displays.
2. Click an expand button (+) to display details for a group.
3. Click the **Level 1** button (1) to reveal the grand total.
4. Click the **Level 2** button (2) to see the second outline level details (Figure 4-38).
5. Click the **Level 3** button (3) to display all details.

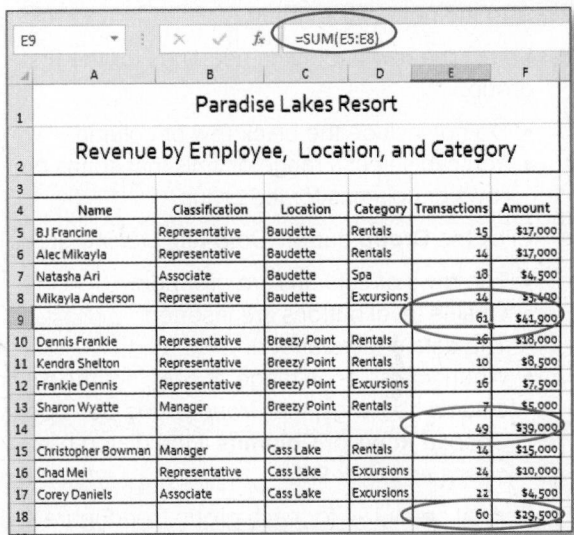

Figure 4-38 Level 2 outline results

Create an Auto Outline

An *Auto Outline* inserts groups based on where formulas are located. Consistent data and formulas that follow a pattern are necessary. The data in Figure 4-39 are grouped by location, and *SUM* formulas display after each group in columns E and F.

If data are not properly formatted, Excel displays a message that an *Auto Outline* cannot be created.

Figure 4-39 Data sorted by location with formulas for each group

▶HOW TO: Create an Auto Outline

1. Click a cell within the data range.
2. Click the **Group** button arrow [*Data* tab, *Outline* group].
3. Select **Auto Outline**.
 • Outline level buttons are inserted.
 • The outline is expanded.
4. Click each collapse button to hide details (Figure 4-40).

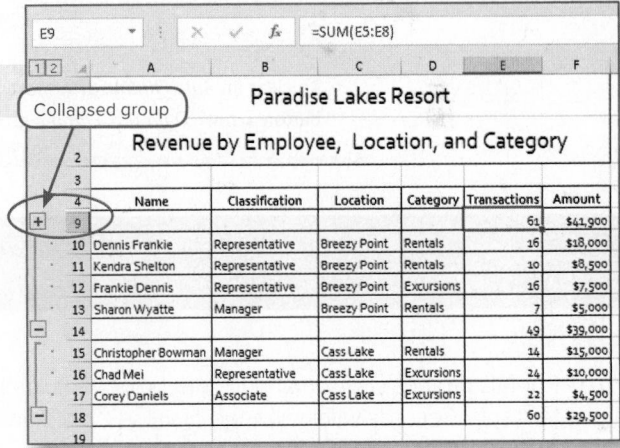

Figure 4-40 *Auto Outline* with two levels; "Baudette" group is collapsed

Define Groups

You can create a group, by rows or columns, for data that does not have totals or formulas. This can be a time-consuming task for a large set of records, but you can use groups to hide irrelevant records and concentrate on groups that require editing.

To define groups, data must be sorted or arranged so that you can select a range of cells to indicate the group. In addition, you must insert a blank summary row either above or below the

group (or a blank column to the left or right of the group). Use blank rows to enter subtitles for the data before or after grouping.

The data in Figure 4-41 are sorted by the "Classification" column, so that groups can be created for each job title. Note that a blank row has been inserted after each group.

▶ **HOW TO:** Define a Group

1. Sort the data (or arrange columns) based on the preferred grouping.

2. Insert a blank row at the end of each sort group (or at the start of each group).

 - Insert the blank row above the group if you want to label each group.
 - For column data, the summary column is usually to the right of the group.

3. Select the row or column headings for the first group.

 - Do not include the blank row or column.
 - You can select a range of cells that spans the rows or columns for the group.

4. Click the **Group** button [*Data* tab, *Outline* group].

 - The rows or columns are grouped.
 - Outline level buttons are inserted.
 - The data are expanded.
 - When you select a range of cells, not the row or column headings, the *Group* dialog box opens. Choose **Rows** or **Columns** if the dialog box opens and click **OK**.

5. Repeat steps 1–4 for each group (see Figure 4-41).

Figure 4-41 Data sorted by "Classification"; blank rows inserted after each title

> ▶ MORE INFO
>
> To clear an *Auto Outline* or remove all groups, click a cell within the group. Then, click the **Ungroup** button arrow [*Data* tab, *Outline* group] and select **Clear Outline**.

PAUSE & PRACTICE: EXCEL 4-2

For this project, you sort and filter data for Paradise Lakes Resort based on location. You use a *Number Filter* to display records within a range of values, build an advanced filter, and include subtotals in the workbook.

File Needed: *[your initials] PP E4-1.xlsx*
Completed Project File Name: *[your initials] PP E4-2.xlsx*

1. Open the *[your initials] PP E4-1* workbook completed in *Pause & Practice 4-1* and save it as [your initials] PP E4-2.

2. Click the **Sort&Filter** sheet tab.

3. Sort data in a worksheet.
 a. Click cell **A5**.
 b. Click the **Sort** button [*Data* tab, *Sort & Filter* group].
 c. Select the **My data has headers** box if necessary.
 d. Click the **Sort by** arrow and select **Location**.
 e. Choose **Cell Values** for *Sort On* and **A to Z** for *Order*.
 f. Click **Add Level**.
 g. Click the **Then by** arrow and select **Amount**.
 h. Choose **Cell Values** for *Sort On* and **Largest to Smallest** for *Order* (Figure 4-42).
 i. Click **OK**. The data sort alphabetically by location and then by amount in descending order.

Figure 4-42 Multiple column sort with text and numeric data

4. Use a *Number AutoFilter*.
 a. Click cell **A5**.
 b. Click the **Filter** button [*Data* tab, *Sort & Filter* group] to display *AutoFilter* arrows.
 c. Click the *AutoFilter* arrow for "Amount."
 d. Point to **Number Filters** and select **Between**.
 e. Type 5000 in the **is greater than or equal to** box.
 f. Type 10000 in the **is less than or equal to** box (Figure 4-43).
 g. Click **OK**.

5. Click the **Adv Filter** sheet tab.

Figure 4-43 *Custom AutoFilter* dialog box for "Amount" between $5,000 and $10,000

6. Set a criteria range.
 a. Type assoc* in cell **H6**.
 b. Type >1500 in cell **K6**.

7. Run an *Advanced Filter*.
 a. Click cell **A5**.
 b. Click the **Advanced** button [*Data* tab, *Sort & Filter* group].
 c. Select the **Copy to another location** radio button.
 d. Verify that cells **A4:E31** are identified in the **List range** box.
 e. Click the **Criteria range** box and select cells **G5:K6**.
 f. Click the **Copy to** box and select cells **G14:K14** (Figure 4-44).
 g. Click **OK**. Six records are extracted and displayed.
 h. Widen column **G** to display the names.

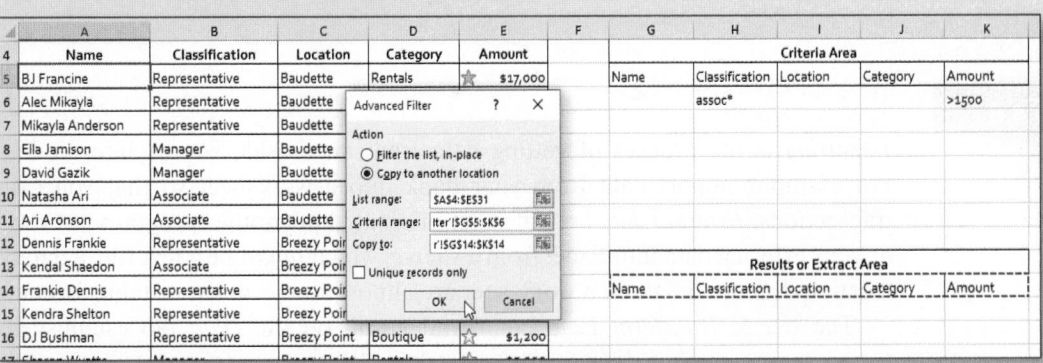

Figure 4-44 Criteria and extract ranges; *Advanced Filter* dialog box

8. Click the **Subtotals** sheet tab.

9. Show subtotals in a list.
 a. Click a cell in the **Location** column. The records are sorted by this column.
 b. Click the **Subtotal** button [*Data* tab, *Outline* group].
 c. Click the **At each change in** arrow and choose **Location**.
 d. Click the **Use function** arrow and choose **Sum**.
 e. Select **Transactions** and **Amount** in the **Add subtotal to list** box.
 f. Click **OK** (Figure 4-45).

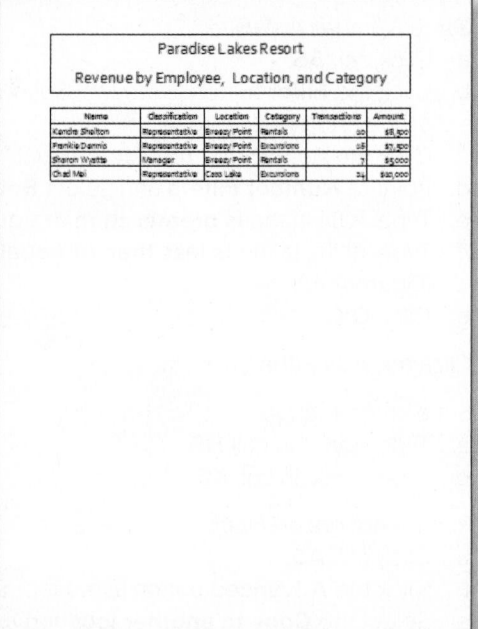

Figure 4-45 PP E4-2 completed

10. Save and close the workbook.

SLO 4.6

Importing Data

Importing is the process of getting data from an outside source into an Excel worksheet. For example, import data from your bank into a worksheet so that you can analyze your transactions. *External data* are data that originated in another program or format. You import or copy external data into Excel from a *source*, which might be a text file, a database, or a cloud location. Imported data in a worksheet are almost always in list or table format.

The *Get & Transform Data* command group on the *Data* tab establishes a connection to the source so that data can be refreshed. When you copy data into a worksheet using *Copy* and *Paste* command, no connection to the source is established. Data connections are discussed later in this section.

Text Files

A *text file* is a document that includes raw data with no formatting. Text files are .txt (text) documents such as those created in NotePad or WordPad. Another widely used text format is .csv (comma separated values); you might see this type of file when you download a bank statement.

Text files separate data into *fields*. In one method, a character such as a comma or a tab separates the fields, and the file is described as *delimited* (tab-delimited file). A *delimiter* is the character used to separate the data. Common delimiters are the tab, space, and comma characters.

A second way to separate fields in a text file is by *fixed width*. Each field is a specified number of characters followed by a space. If the first name field is set at 25 characters, the name "Tom," is imported as 3 characters plus 22 spaces. The second field always starts at position 26.

When you click the **From Text/CSV** button in the *Get & Transform Data* group on the *Data* tab, the *Import Data* dialog box opens (Figure 4-46). The data preview with the recognized delimiter and data types and display in the worksheet. Text files are imported through a query. A *query* is a combination of definitions and filters that connects to and extracts the data. Manage imported text data as an Excel table, or use Excel's *Query Editor*.

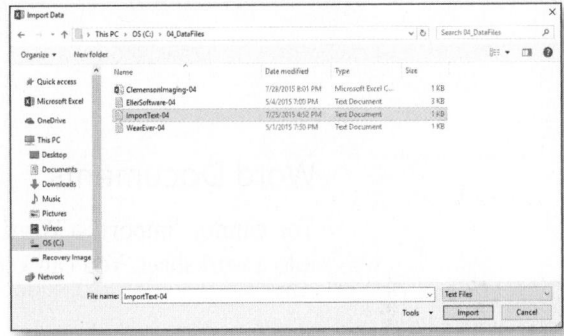

Figure 4-46 *Import Data* dialog box

> **MORE INFO**
>
> Many legacy or mainframe computer systems use fixed width files for data.

▶ HOW TO: Import a Tab-Delimited Text File into a Worksheet

1. Select the cell in which imported data should begin.
2. Click the **From Text/CSV** button [*Data* tab, *Get & Transform Data* group].
3. Navigate to and select the text file name in the *Import Data* dialog box.
4. Click **Import**.
 - A simple query dialog box shows how the data will be separated into columns.
 - The delimiter character is identified.
 - The data type is identified based on the first rows of data.
5. Click the **Load** arrow and select **Load To** so that you can specify where the text displays (Figure 4-47).
 - A second *Import Data* dialog box opens.
6. Select **Existing worksheet**.
 - The active cell displays as the location.
 - Select another cell as needed.

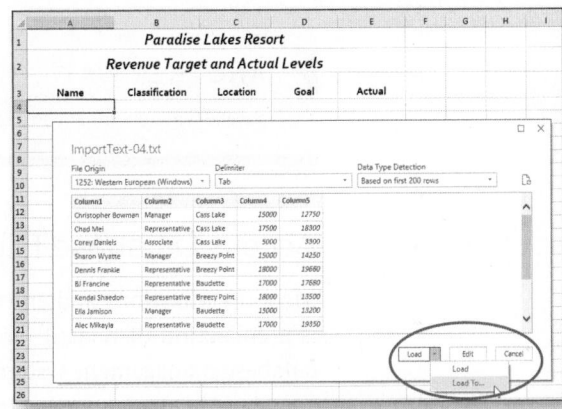

Figure 4-47 Query preview for imported text file

7. Click **OK**.

- The data are available in the worksheet in an Excel table.
- The *Queries & Connections* pane displays at the right and can be dragged to another location.
- The *Table Tools* and *Query Tools* command tabs display (Figure 4-48).

8. Close the *Queries & Connections* pane.

- Open the *Queries & Connections* pane from the *Data* tab.
- Refresh data from the *Data* tab or the *Query Tools* tab.

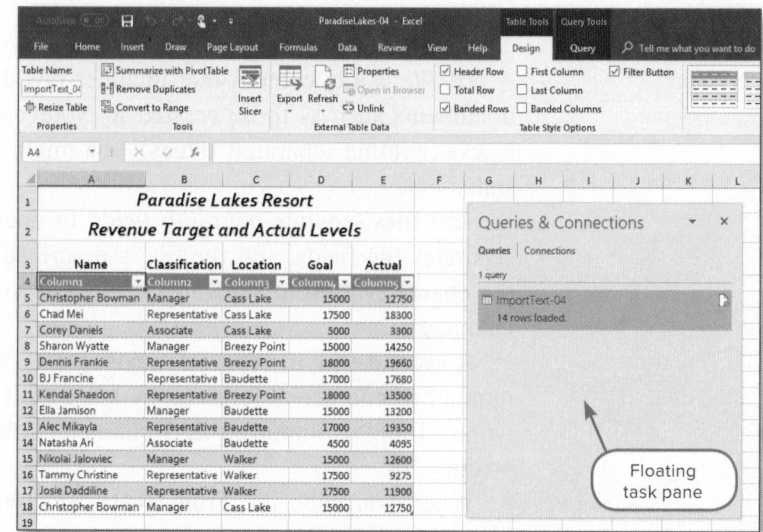

Figure 4-48 Imported text file

Word Documents

You cannot "import" a Word document into Excel, but you can copy and paste data from Word into a worksheet. You can keep the Word formatting, or choose the current worksheet format.

▶ **HOW TO:** Copy Data from a Word Document

1. Select the cell in which imported data should begin.
2. Start Word and open the document.
3. Select the data to be copied.
4. Click the **Copy** button [*Home* tab, *Clipboard* group].
5. Switch to the Excel worksheet.
6. Click the arrow with the **Paste** button [*Home* tab, *Clipboard* group].
7. Choose **Match Destination Formatting** from the *Paste* gallery.

- The data are pasted in the worksheet.
- If you click the **Paste** button, data are pasted with the Word formatting.

> ▶ **ANOTHER WAY**
> Save a Word document as a text file (.txt) and import the text file into Excel.

Access Database Files

Most organizations and enterprises maintain large amounts of data in a database. A *database* is a collection of related tables, queries, forms, and reports. *Microsoft Access* is a relational database management system that is part of the Office suite. You can import a table or a query from an Access database into an Excel worksheet. In Access, a table is a data list, and a query is a subset of the list.

Because a database includes many tables and queries, the *Navigator* dialog box opens so that you can choose the table or query to import. Access data are imported as an Excel table, a *PivotTable*, or a *PivotChart*.

>
> MORE INFO
>
> Load imported data directly into the *Query Editor* for further management before loading into the worksheet.

▶**HOW TO:** Import an Access Table into a Worksheet

1. Select the cell in which imported data should begin.

2. Click the **Get Data** button [*Data* tab, *Get & Transform Data* group].

3. Select **From Database** and then choose **From Microsoft Access Database**.

4. Navigate to and select the database name in the *Import Data* dialog box.

5. Click **Import**.
 - The *Navigator* window displays the names of queries and tables in the database.

6. Select the name of the table or query.
 - The data display in the preview window (Figure 4-49).

Figure 4-49 *Navigator* preview for table to be imported

7. Click the **Load** arrow and select **Load To**.
 - The *Import Data* dialog box opens.
 - You can import data as a *PivotTable*, a *PivotChart*, or as a connection for later use.

8. Select **Existing worksheet**.
 - The active cell displays as the location.
 - You can select another cell.

9. Click **OK**.
 - The data are available in the worksheet in an Excel table.
 - The *Queries & Connections* pane displays at the right.
 - Field names from the Access table or query are column headings in the Excel table.

10. Click the *Table Tools Design* tab.

11. Click the **Properties** button [*External Table Data* group].
 - The *External Data Properties* dialog box opens.
 - Adjust formatting and refresh options.

12. Click the **Query Properties** button (to the right of the *Name* box).

- The *Query Properties* dialog box opens (Figure 4-50).
- Type a description for the query.
- Set how the data are refreshed or updated.
- The *Definition* tab identifies the source of the imported data.

13. Click **Cancel** to close the *Query Properties* dialog box.

14. Click **Cancel** to close the *External Data Properties* dialog box.

Figure 4-50 *External Data Properties* and *Query Properties* dialog boxes

> **MORE INFO**
>
> Import tables and queries from relational databases with the *Get Data* button, *From Other Sources* command [*Data* tab, *Get & Transform Data* group].

Web Site Data

The typical web site has protected multimedia content with images, video, and audio, not list-type data for importing into Excel. Web sites that deal with research, statistics, demographics, and similar data, however, usually have downloadable text or Excel files (Figure 4-51). From the web site, you simply click the link to download the data.

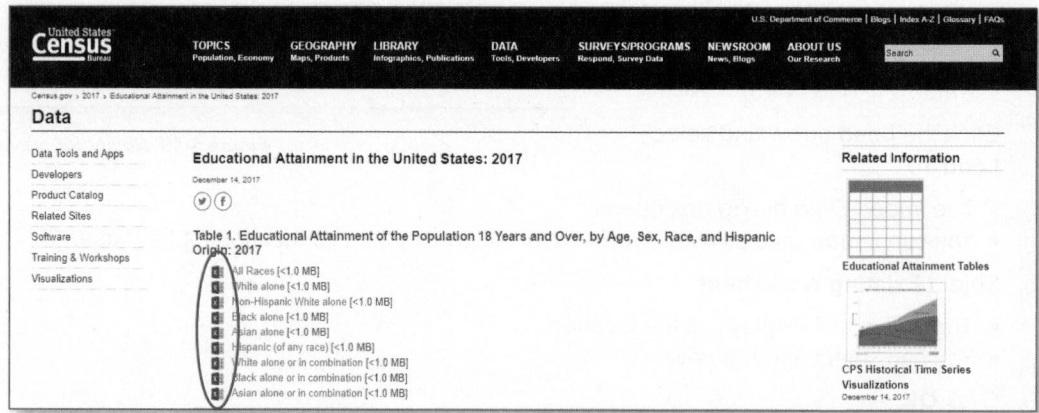

Figure 4-51 Web page with data in Excel format

Use the *From web* command on the *Data* tab to import data that are formatted as an HTML table. You navigate to the page with data, copy the URL for the web page, and paste the URL into the *From web* dialog box. This command builds an underlying query to display the data in the worksheet and uses the *Navigator* window to preview the data.

Workbook Queries and Connections

When you use the *Get & Transform Data* group on the *Data* tab, Excel builds a query that you can edit, refresh, name, or remove. The query includes a **connection**, an identifier and a link for data that originates outside the workbook.

When you open a workbook that has data connections, you will usually see a security warning bar at the top of the worksheet. When you are sure that the connection is safe, click **Enable Content** to work with the data.

▶ HOW TO: Manage External Data

1. Click a cell within the imported data.
2. Click the **Properties** button [*Data* tab, *Queries & Connections* group].
 - The *External Data Properties* dialog box displays.
 - The dialog box lists format and refresh options for imported data.
3. Close the *External Data Properties* dialog box.
4. Click the **Queries & Connections** button [*Data* tab, *Queries & Connections* group] to display or hide the *Queries & Connections* pane.
 - The button toggles the display of the pane.
 - Existing queries and connections are listed.
5. Point to a table or query name in the *Queries & Connections* pane.
 - A pop-up window displays with information about the data.
6. Click the ellipsis (. . .) near the bottom of the window and select **Properties** (Figure 4-52).
 - The *Query Properties* dialog box opens.
 - Rename the query or table, add a description, or set how data are refreshed.
 - Click the *Definition* tab to edit a query in the *Query Editor*.
7. Click **Cancel** to close the *Query Properties* dialog box.

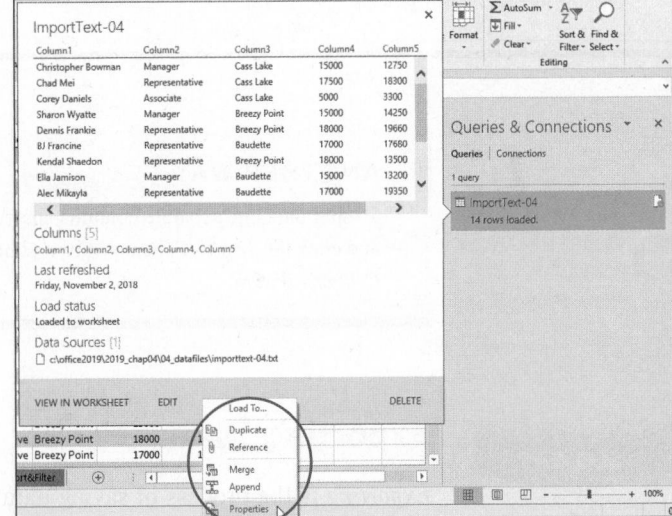

Figure 4-52 Pop-up window for imported data

Flash Fill

Imported data often need to be "cleaned" because they may not be in the correct sort order, they may have missing or incorrect data, and so on. *Flash Fill* is a feature that recognizes a pattern in the first cell and suggests data for the remaining rows in a column. For example, imagine that imported data lists first and last names in a single column, but you want first and last names in separate columns. Type the first person's name in an empty column next to the original column. As you start to type a second name below the first one, *Flash Fill* previews the completed column. Just press **Enter** to complete the column. The *Flash Fill Options* button appears after you press **Enter** so that you can undo the fill if necessary or accept all the suggestions.

▶HOW TO: Flash Fill Data in a Worksheet

1. Click the first cell in an empty column next to the original data.

 - The first *Flash Fill* column must be adjacent to the original data.
 - Use an empty column or insert a column.

2. Type the data as you want it to appear.

3. Press **Enter** and type data in the cell below the first cell.

 - The suggested list is previewed.
 - If the suggestion list does not appear, try typing a third item in the column (Figure 4-53).
 - The data must be consistent and follow a recognizable pattern.

4. Press **Enter** to complete the *Flash Fill*.

 - If no *Flash Fill* suggestion list displays, click the **Flash Fill** button [*Data* tab, *Data Tools* group] with the insertion point in the column.

	A	B	C	D
1		*Paradise Lakes Resort*		
2		*Revenue Target and Actual Levels*		
3	**Name**	**Email Address**	**Classification**	**Location**
4	Christopher Bowman	c.bowman@123.com	Manager	Cass Lake
5	Chad Mei	c.mei@123.com	Representative	Cass Lake
6	Corey Daniels	c.daniels@123.com	Associate	Cass Lake
7	Sharon Wyatte	s.wyatte@123.com	Manager	Breezy Point
8	Dennis Frankie	d.frankie@123.com	Representative	Breezy Point
9	BJ Francine	bj.francine@123.com	Representative	Baudette
10	Kendal Shaedon	k.shaedon@123.com	Representative	Breezy Point
11	Ella Jamison	e.jamison@123.com	Manager	Baudette
12	Alec Mikayla	a.mikayla@123.com	Representative	Baudette
13	Natasha Ari	n.ari@123.com	Associate	Baudette
14	Nikolai Jalowiec	n.jalowiec@123.com	Manager	Walker
15	Tammy Christine	t.christine@123.com	Representative	Walker
16	Josie Daddiline	j.daddiline@123.com	Representative	Walker
17	Christopher Bowman	c.bowman@123.com	Manager	Cass Lake

Figure 4-53 *Flash Fill* suggestion list

ANOTHER WAY

To split data into separate columns, insert blank columns to the right. Select the column to be split and click the **Text to Columns** button [*Data* tab, *Data Tools* group]. Complete the *Convert Text to Columns Wizard*.

SLO 4.7

Exporting Data

Exporting is the process of saving data in a format to be used by another program or application. This can be as simple as providing a PDF file for viewing, copying data into Word, or saving worksheet data as a text file.

Export Data as a Text File

Most software applications can read a text file, a common way to transfer or share data. You can save Excel data as a tab-delimited, space-delimited, or comma-delimited file. When you save worksheet data as a text file, Excel renames the sheet with the same file name that you type for the text file. You can save only one worksheet in a text file. If a workbook has multiple sheets, a message box will alert you that only the current sheet will be saved.

▶HOW TO: Save Excel Data as a Tab-Delimited File

1. Click the worksheet tab with data to export.

 - The insertion point can be in any cell.

2. Click the **File** tab and select **Export**.

3. Select **Change File Type**.

4. Select **Text (Tab delimited)** as the file type (Figure 4-54).

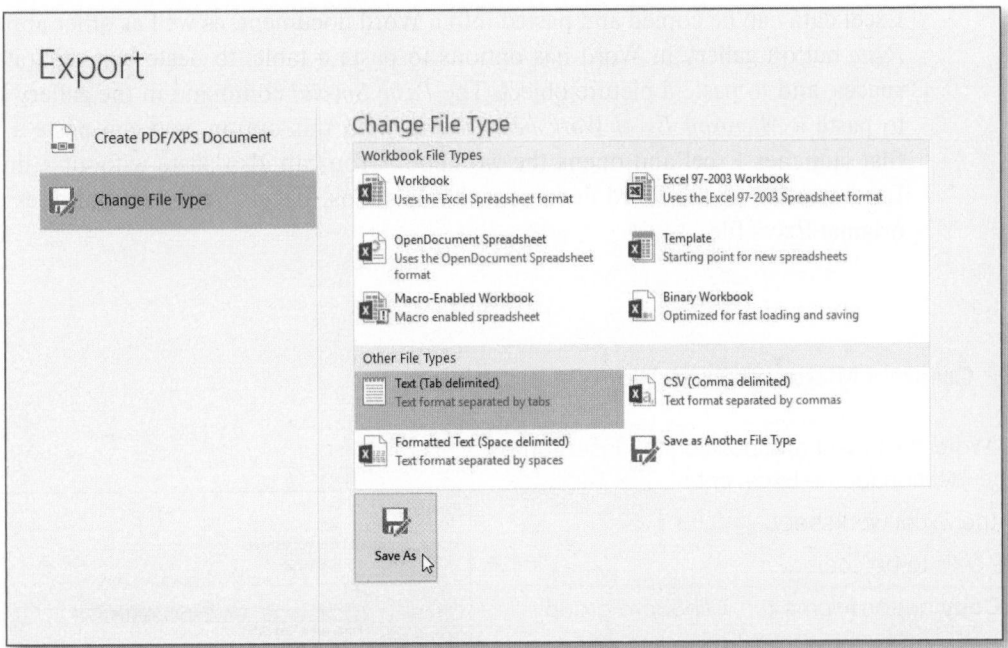

Figure 4-54 *Export* command in *Backstage* view

5. Click **Save As**.
 - The *Save As* dialog box opens with *Text (Tab-delimited)* as the *Save as type*.
6. Navigate to the location for the exported data.
7. Type a file name for the text file in the *File name* box.
8. Click **Save**.
 - If a workbook has more than one sheet, a message box reminds you that only one sheet can be exported. Click **OK** in this message box.
9. Click **Yes** to acknowledge that Excel features may be lost if the message box appears.
 - The worksheet tab has the same name as the exported file.
10. Rename the sheet tab as desired.
11. Click the **File** tab and choose **Save As**.
12. Select **Excel Workbook** as the *Save as type* in the *Save As* dialog box.
13. Navigate to the folder for saved work.
14. Select or type the original workbook file name and click **Save**.
15. Click **Yes** to replace the file.
16. Close the workbook.
 - The exported text file is available in the folder selected for saving.
 - The original workbook is unchanged and resaved.

> **MORE INFO**
> To use Excel data in an Access table, export the data as a text file. You can then import the text file into an Access table.

Export Data via the Clipboard

Excel data can be copied and pasted into a Word document, as well as other applications. The *Paste* button gallery in Word has options to paste a table, to paste text separated by tabs or spaces, and to paste a picture object. The *Paste Special* command in the gallery has an option to paste a *Microsoft Excel Worksheet Object*. With this option, you can paste a link in Word that launches Excel and opens the workbook. You can also paste without a link to open an Excel window in the Word document that has most Excel commands but does not affect the original Excel file.

▶HOW TO: Create a Microsoft Excel Worksheet Object

1. Open the Word document and position the insertion point at the location for the Excel data.

2. Switch to the Excel worksheet.

3. Select the cells to be copied.

4. Click the **Copy** button [*Home* tab, *Clipboard* group].
 - The data can be formatted as a table or a normal range.
 - You can also press **Ctrl+C** to copy.

5. Switch to the Word document.

6. Click the arrow with the **Paste** button [*Home* tab, *Clipboard* group] and choose **Paste Special**.

7. Select **Microsoft Excel Worksheet Object** in the *Paste Special* dialog box.

8. Select **Paste link** in the *Paste Special* dialog box (Figure 4-55).

9. Click **OK**.
 - The data are pasted as a worksheet object.

10. Complete work in the Word document.
 - Use horizontal alignment commands to position the object if necessary.
 - Double-click anywhere in the object to launch Excel and open the source workbook.

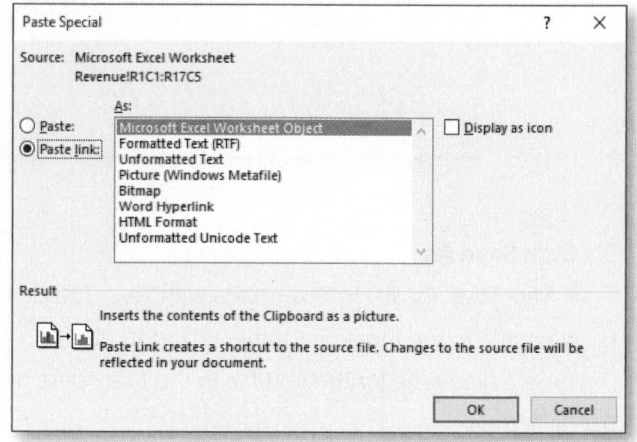

Figure 4-55 *Paste Special* dialog box

SharePoint Lists

SharePoint Server and ***SharePoint Online*** are a family of products that enables collaboration and simultaneous work by co-workers and team members. You can export data in an Excel table to a *SharePoint* list so that others in your work circle have access to the data. The *Export* button is in the *External Table Data* group on the *Table Tools Design* tab, and it launches the *Export Table to SharePoint List Wizard*. To work with *SharePoint*, you must have access and permission from the service administrator.

For this project, you import data from a text file into an Excel worksheet, format the data as an Excel table, copy data from a Word document, and use *Flash Fill* to complete the worksheet for Paradise Lakes Resort.

Files Needed: *[your initials] PP E4-2.xlsx*, *ImportText-04.txt*, and **CopyWord-04.docx** *(Student data files are available in the* Library *of your SIMnet account.)*
Completed Project File Name: *[your initials] PP E4-3.xlsx*

1. Open the *[your initials] PP E4-2* workbook completed in *Pause & Practice 4-2* and save it as [your initials] PP E4-3.

2. Import data from a text file.
 a. Select cell **A4** on the **Text Import** tab.
 b. Click the **From Text/CVS** button [*Data* tab, *Get & Transform Data* group].
 c. Navigate to and select *ImportText-04.txt* from your student data files in the *Import Data* dialog box.
 d. Click **Import**.
 e. Click the **Load** arrow and select **Load To**.
 f. Select **Existing worksheet**.
 g. Confirm or select cell **A4** as the location.
 h. Click **OK** in the *Import Data* dialog box.
 i. Close the *Queries & Connections* pane.
 j. Select cells **A3:E3** and drag and drop (or cut and paste) the cells to cells **A4:E4** and replace the column labels.

3. Copy data from a Word document.
 a. Select cell **A19**.
 b. Open Microsoft Word and open the **CopyWord-04** document from your student data files. Enable editing if necessary.
 c. Select all the data and click the **Copy** button [*Home* tab, *Clipboard* group].
 d. Switch to the Excel window.
 e. Click the arrow on the **Paste** button [*Home* tab, *Clipboard* group] and choose **Match Destination Formatting** (Figure 4-56).
 f. Select cells **D5:E28** and apply the **Currency** number format with zero decimals.
 g. Adjust the widths of columns **C:E** to **11.43 (85 pixels)**.

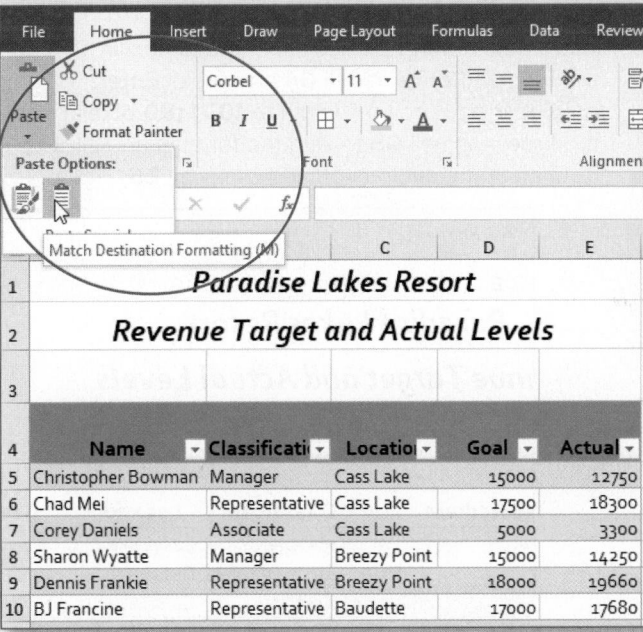

Figure 4-56 *Paste Options* for copied data

4. Use *Flash Fill* to create an email address column.
 a. Insert a column between columns **A** and **B**.
 b. Type Email Address in cell **B4**.

c. Increase the width of the "Email Address" column to **31.00 (222 pixels)**.

d. In cell **B5**, type c.bowman@somewhere .com and press **Enter**.

e. Select cell **B6** and type c.m to start the second address and display the *Flash Fill* suggested list.

f. Press **Enter**. If the *Flash Fill* suggestion list did not appear, click the **Flash Fill** button [*Data* tab, *Data Tools* group].

5. Format data as an Excel table.

a. Select cells **A4:F28**. Because the data were imported from different sources, you must select the range.

b. Click the **Format as Table** button [*Home* tab, *Styles* group].

c. Choose **White, Table Style Light 1** (first row in the group) (Figure 4-57).

Name	Email Address	Classification	Location	Goal	Actual
Christopher Bowman	c.bowman@somewhere.com	Manager	Cass Lake	$15,000	$12,750
Chad Mei	c.mei@somewhere.com	Representative	Cass Lake	$17,500	$18,300
Corey Daniels	c.daniels@somewhere.com	Associate	Cass Lake	$5,000	$3,300
Sharon Wyatte	s.wyatte@somewhere.com	Manager	Breezy Point	$15,000	$14,250
Dennis Frankie	d.frankie@somewhere.com	Representative	Breezy Point	$18,000	$19,660
BJ Francine	bj.francine@somewhere.com	Representative	Baudette	$17,000	$17,680
Kendal Shaedon	k.shaedon@somewhere.com	Representative	Breezy Point	$18,000	$13,500
Ella Jamison	e.jamison@somewhere.com	Manager	Baudette	$15,000	$13,200
Alec Mikayla	a.mikayla@somewhere.com	Representative	Baudette	$17,000	$19,350
Natasha Ari	n.ari@somewhere.com	Associate	Baudette	$4,500	$4,095
Nikolai Jalowiec	n.jalowiec@somewhere.com	Manager	Walker	$15,000	$12,600
Tammy Christine	t.christine@somewhere.com	Representative	Walker	$17,500	$9,275
Josie Daddiline	j.daddiline@somewhere.com	Representative	Walker	$17,500	$11,900
Christopher Bowman	c.bowman@somewhere.com	Manager	Cass Lake	$15,000	$12,750
Jeffery Dalton	j.dalton@somewhere.com	Manager	Cass Lake	$15,000	$12,750
Mae Gomez	m.gomez@somewhere.com	Representative	Cass Lake	$17,500	$13,300
Randy Josephson	r.josephson@somewhere.com	Associate	Cass Lake	$5,000	$3,300
Suzanne Ouimet	s.ouimet@somewhere.com	Manager	Breezy Point	$15,000	$14,250
Frankie Dennis	f.dennis@somewhere.com	Representative	Breezy Point	$18,000	$15,660
DJ Bushman	dj.bushman@somewhere.com	Representative	Breezy Point	$17,000	$17,680
Kendra Shelton	k.shelton@somewhere.com	Representative	Breezy Point	$18,000	$13,500
David Gazik	d.gazik@somewhere.com	Manager	Baudette	$15,000	$13,200
Mikayla Anderson	m.anderson@somewhere.com	Representative	Baudette	$17,000	$9,350
Ari Aronson	a.aronson@somewhere.com	Associate	Baudette	$4,500	$4,095

Figure 4-57 Imported data formatted with new table style

6. Add a column with a calculation to a table.

a. Type Difference in cell **G4** and press **Enter**.

b. Change the column width to **10.71 (80 pixels)** and set a black bottom border for cell **G4**.

c. Type = in cell **G5** to start the formula and click cell **F5**.

d. Type − for subtraction and click cell **E5** (Figure 4-58).

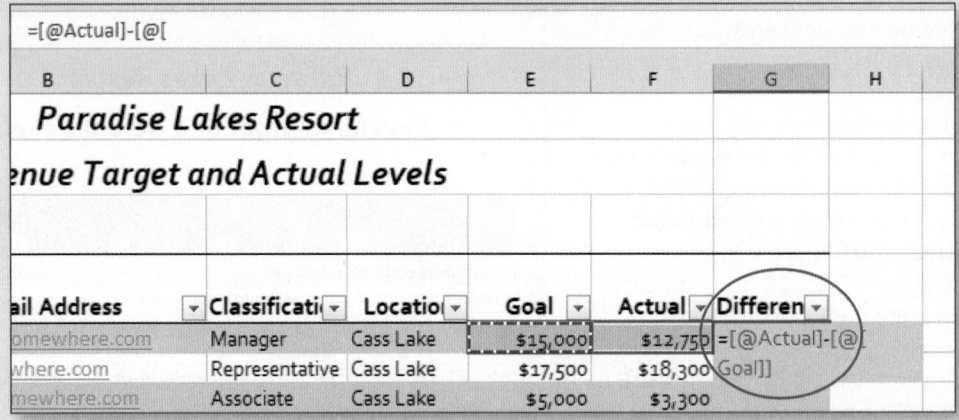

Figure 4-58 Structured references in a table formula

e. Press **Enter** to copy the formula in the column.

f. Select cells **G5:G28** and press **Ctrl+1** to open the *Format Cells* dialog box.

g. Select the *Number* tab, choose **Currency** with zero decimal places and negative numbers in red (no parentheses), and close the dialog box.

h. Select cell **G4** and apply a black **Bottom Border**.

i. Select cells **A1:G1** and click the **Merge & Center** button [*Home* tab, *Alignment* group] to remove the centering. Then, click the **Merge & Center** button again to re-center the cells over the new range.

j. Unmerge and then re-merge and center cells **A2:G2**.
k. Format row **3** with a height of **15.00 (20 pixels)** and row **4** at **22.50 (30 pixels)**.
l. Change the page orientation to **Landscape**.

7. Save and close the workbook. Close the Word document (Figure 4-59).

Paradise Lakes Resort
Revenue Target and Actual Levels

Name	Email Address	Classification	Location	Goal	Actual	Difference
Christopher Bowman	c.bowman@somewhere.com	Manager	Cass Lake	$15,000	$12,750	$2,250
Chad Mei	c.mei@somewhere.com	Representative	Cass Lake	$17,500	$18,300	$800
Corey Daniels	c.daniels@somewhere.com	Associate	Cass Lake	$5,000	$3,300	$1,700
Sharon Wyatte	s.wyatte@somewhere.com	Manager	Breezy Point	$15,000	$14,250	$750
Dennis Frankie	d.frankie@somewhere.com	Representative	Breezy Point	$18,000	$19,660	$1,660
BJ Francine	bj.francine@somewhere.com	Representative	Baudette	$17,000	$17,680	$680
Kendal Shaedon	k.shaedon@somewhere.com	Representative	Breezy Point	$18,000	$13,500	$4,500
Ella Jamison	e.jamison@somewhere.com	Manager	Baudette	$15,000	$13,200	$1,800
Alec Mikayla	a.mikayla@somewhere.com	Representative	Baudette	$17,000	$19,350	$2,350
Natasha Ari	n.ari@somewhere.com	Associate	Baudette	$4,500	$4,095	$405
Nikolai Jalowiec	n.jalowiec@somewhere.com	Manager	Walker	$15,000	$12,600	$2,400
Tammy Christine	t.christine@somewhere.com	Representative	Walker	$17,500	$9,275	$8,225
Josie Daddiline	j.daddiline@somewhere.com	Representative	Walker	$17,500	$11,900	$5,600
Christopher Bowman	c.bowman@somewhere.com	Manager	Cass Lake	$15,000	$12,750	$2,250
Jeffery Dalton	j.dalton@somewhere.com	Manager	Cass Lake	$15,000	$12,750	$2,250
Mae Gomez	m.gomez@somewhere.com	Representative	Cass Lake	$17,500	$13,300	$4,200
Randy Josephson	r.josephson@somewhere.com	Associate	Cass Lake	$5,000	$3,300	$1,700
Suzanne Ouimet	s.ouimet@somewhere.com	Manager	Breezy Point	$15,000	$14,250	$750
Frankie Dennis	f.dennis@somewhere.com	Representative	Breezy Point	$18,000	$15,660	$2,340
DJ Bushman	dj.bushman@somewhere.com	Representative	Breezy Point	$17,000	$17,680	$680
Kendra Shelton	k.shelton@somewhere.com	Representative	Breezy Point	$18,000	$13,500	$4,500
David Gazik	d.gazik@somewhere.com	Manager	Baudette	$15,000	$13,200	$1,800
Mikayla Anderson	m.anderson@somewhere.com	Representative	Baudette	$17,000	$9,350	$7,650
Ari Aronson	a.aronson@somewhere.com	Associate	Baudette	$4,500	$4,095	$405

Figure 4-59 PP E4-3 completed

SLO 4.8

Building and Formatting PivotTables

A **PivotTable** is a cross tabulation report based on list-type data. It is a separate worksheet in which you sort, filter, and calculate large amounts of data. *PivotTables* are analysis tools, an important part of **Business Intelligence (BI)**. Business intelligence is a combination of applications and processes that enable you to "drill-down" into data and assess various types of results or changes. In a table or list with thousands of records, build a *PivotTable* to quickly show average revenue by state, by city, or other criteria, and, just as quickly, return to the entire list (Figure 4-60).

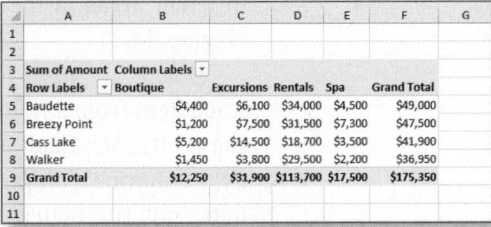

Figure 4-60 An Excel *PivotTable*

PivotTables are interactive, because you rearrange the report for analysis by clicking or dragging. Rearranging data is *pivoting* the data so that you look at it from a different perspective. It takes time and practice to create and understand all the features of a *PivotTable*, but it is easy to experiment with placing fields, sorting data, or filtering results.

Create a PivotTable

Data for a *PivotTable* should follow the same guidelines as those recommended for an Excel table in the beginning of this chapter. Data can be formatted as a table or as a list. A *PivotTable* is placed on its own sheet in the workbook.

The *Tables* group on the *Insert* tab includes the *PivotTable* button, as well as the *Recommended PivotTables* button. When you are first learning about *PivotTables*, the *Recommended PivotTables* button may help you gain experience building these reports.

After you create a *PivotTable*, the contextual *PivotTable Tools Analyze* and *Design* tabs are available for additional format choices and data commands.

▶ HOW TO: Create a PivotTable

1. Click a cell in the data range.
 - The data range must have a header row.
2. Click the **Recommended PivotTables** button [*Insert* tab, *Tables* group] (Figure 4-61).
 - A data range is assumed and highlighted in the worksheet.
3. Point to a preview tile on the left to see a *ScreenTip* for the proposed *PivotTable*.
4. Select the preferred *PivotTable* and click **OK**.
 - The *PivotTable* report is created on a separate sheet.

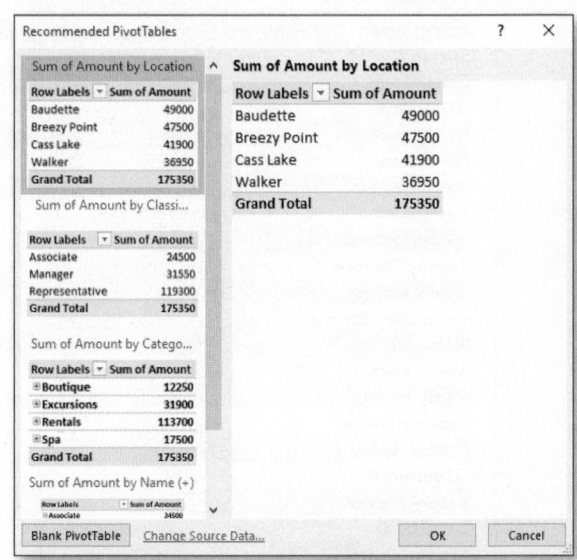

Figure 4-61 *Recommended PivotTables* for a data range

The PivotTable Fields Pane

A *PivotTable* is created on a new sheet in the workbook, and the *PivotTable Fields* pane opens at the right. From this pane, add and remove fields from the report and drag field names into different areas in the pane to reset how the data are organized (Figure 4-62).

Filters, *Columns*, *Rows*, and *Values* areas display in the pane. Each item from a field in the *Rows* area appears in its own row in the *PivotTable*. Each item in a field in the *Columns* area displays as a column. Columns and rows are usually the categories of data, not the actual values. Fields in the *Values* area are the ones that are summed, averaged, counted, or otherwise used in a calculation. *Filters* are fields placed as separate buttons above the *PivotTable* which act like *AutoFilter* arrows. Row and column labels include a filter arrow in the body of the *PivotTable*, and row data have collapse/expand buttons for certain field layouts. You can filter data from the filter arrows with a field, or insert a *Slicer* window.

Figure 4-62 *PivotTable Fields* pane

Float the *PivotTable Fields* pane by pointing to its title bar and dragging it into the work-sheet area.

1. Click a cell in the body of the *PivotTable*.
2. Drag a field name from the *Choose fields to add to report* area into the *Columns* area in the *PivotTable Fields* pane and release the pointer button.
 - Columns for the field items are added to the report.
 - A grand total column is added.
3. Drag a field name into the *Filters* area and release the pointer button (Figure 4-63).
 - The field is added as a filter button in row 1 of the *PivotTable*.
 - No filter is applied.

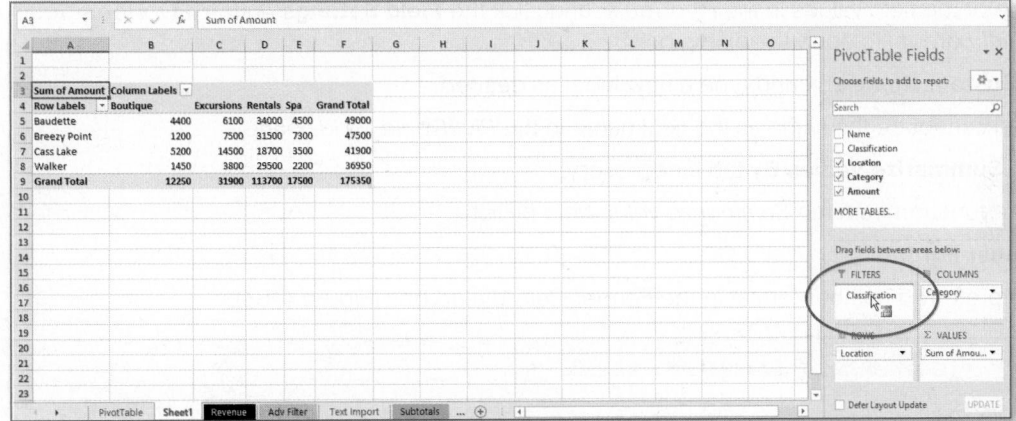

Figure 4-63 Drag fields in the *PivotTable Fields* pane

4. Drag a field name from the *Rows* area to the left and into the worksheet area.
 - The field is removed from the *PivotTable*.
5. Drag a field name from one area in the *PivotTable Fields* pane to another area.
 - The *PivotTable* is updated after each change.

Field Settings

Fields in a *PivotTable* include settings or attributes that depend on the type of data. **Field Settings** for a text field include layout and print options, as well as subtotal and filter choices. The *Layout* group on the *PivotTable Tools Design* tab includes many of the same commands as the *Field Settings* dialog box.

The **Value Field Settings** for a *PivotTable Values* field determine how data are summarized. The default function is *SUM*, but you can change the function or select a custom percentage, difference, or ranking. From the *Value Field Settings* dialog box, edit the label that appears in the *PivotTable*, choose a function, and set how numbers are formatted. To select a field in a *PivotTable*, click the field name in the *Row Labels* row or any cell in the column.

▶ HOW TO: Change Value Field Settings in a PivotTable

1. Click the arrow for *Sum of [Field Name]* in the *Values* area in the *PivotTable Fields* pane.
2. Select **Value Field Settings** from the menu.
 - The *Value Field Settings* dialog box opens.
 - Click one of the field values in the *PivotTable*, and click the **Field Settings** button [*PivotTable Tools Analyze* tab, *Active Field* group] to open the dialog box.
3. Click the **Custom Name** box and type a new label as desired.
 - The label cannot be the same as the field name in the *PivotTable Fields* pane.
4. Select the **Summarize Values By** tab if necessary.
5. Choose the function from the *Summarize value field by* list.
6. Click **Number Format**.
7. Select the preferred number format in the *Format Cells* dialog box (Figure 4-64).

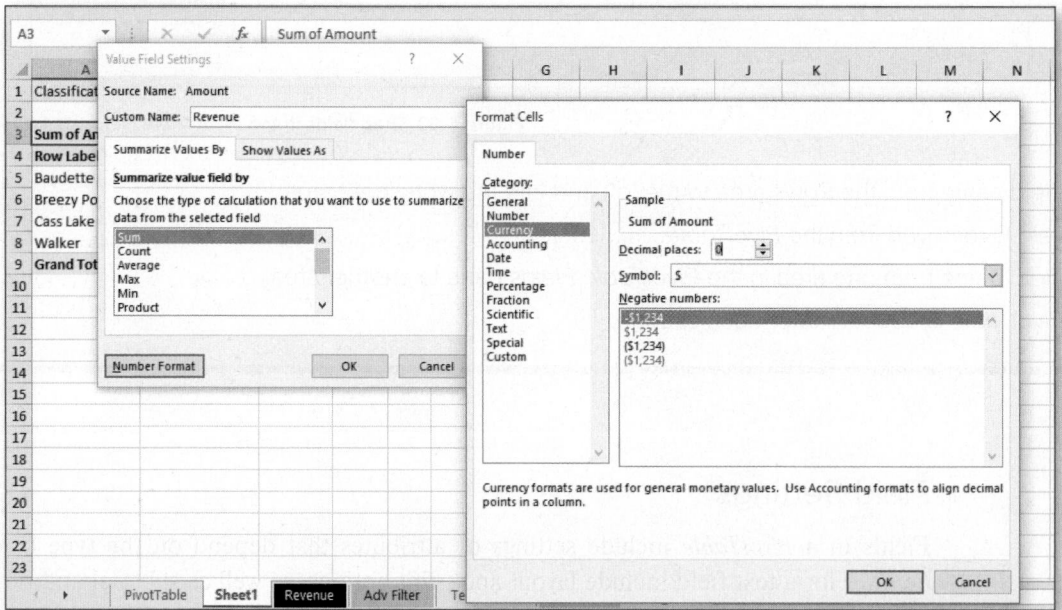

Figure 4-64 *Value Field Settings* dialog box and *Number Format* options

8. Click **OK** to close the *Format Cells* dialog box.
9. Click **OK** to close the *Value Field Settings* dialog box.
 - A new label, if entered, displays in the *PivotTable* and in the task pane.
 - The entire field is formatted.

Format a PivotTable

A *PivotTable* is formatted from the *PivotTable Tools Design* tab or from the *Home* tab. The *PivotTable Tools Design* contextual tab includes *PivotTable* styles which are similar to Excel table styles. Changes made from the *PivotTable Tools Design* tab affect the entire table.

From the *PivotTable Style Options* group, choose whether row and column headings are bold and filled and whether columns and rows are banded with fill or borders. These options depend on the *PivotTable* style. From the *Home* tab, change the font size and style, set alignment, and more. When you apply changes from the *Home* tab, the format is applied to the selected cell or cells.

▶HOW TO: Format a PivotTable

1. Click a cell in the *PivotTable*.
2. Click the **More** button for the *PivotTable Styles* group [*PivotTable Tools Design* tab].
 - The style gallery is categorized by light, medium, and dark colors.
3. Point to a style thumbnail to see a *Live Preview*.
 - The styles are named *(Color), Pivot Style Light 1, (Color), Pivot Style Light 2,* and so on.
 - You can design your own style.
4. Click to select a style.
5. Select the box for **Banded Rows** in the *PivotTable Styles Options* group [*PivotTable Tools Design* tab].
 - The rows are filled or a border is applied, based on the selected *PivotTable* style.
6. Select the box for **Banded Columns** in the *PivotTable Styles Options* group [*PivotTable Tools Design* tab].
 - The columns are filled or a border is applied.

PivotTable Layout

The *Layout* group commands on the *PivotTable Tools Design* tab alter the appearance of a *PivotTable*. You can hide or display subtotals and grand totals, insert a blank row after items, or repeat row labels. The *Report Layout* command offers choices for the report design and selections for repeated labels.

▶HOW TO: Adjust Layout and PivotTable Options

1. Click a cell in the *PivotTable*.
2. Click the **Subtotals** button [*PivotTable Tools Design* tab, *Layout* group].
 - Subtotals can be hidden or shown.
 - Subtotals can be placed at the top or the bottom of each item.
3. Select an option for subtotals.
4. Click the **Grand Totals** button [*PivotTable Tools Design* tab, *Layout* group].
 - Grand totals display at the right for columns and at the bottom for rows.
5. Choose an option for grand totals (Figure 4-65).
6. Click the **Report Layout** button [*PivotTable Tools Design* tab, *Layout* group].
 - A *Compact* format places row data in one column and occupies the least amount of horizontal space.
 - An *Outline* form places row data in separate columns (Figure 4-66).

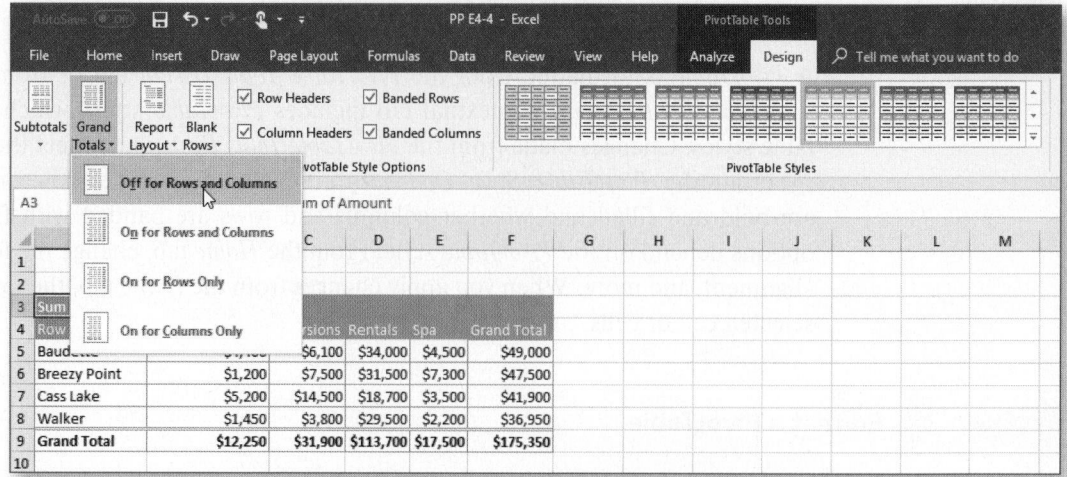

Figure 4-65 Display or hide total column and row

- *Tabular* form starts row data in the same row but in separate columns.
- *Repeat Item Labels* displays the row data in each row like an Excel table.

7. Click the **Blank Rows** button [*PivotTable Tools Design* tab, *Layout* group].

- You can display a blank row before or after each item.

8. Click the **Options** button [*PivotTable Tools Analyze* tab, *PivotTable* group] (Figure 4-67).

- The *PivotTable Options* dialog box has six tabs.
- Some options are also available in the *Layout* group on the *PivotTable Tools Design* tab.

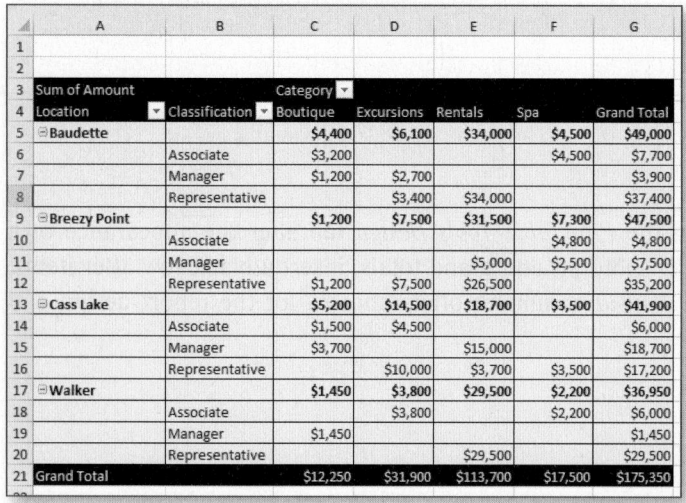

Figure 4-66 *Outline* report layout

Figure 4-67 *PivotTable Options* dialog box

Refresh a PivotTable

Although a *PivotTable* is based on worksheet data, the *PivotTable* is not automatically updated when data are edited. This is a security measure because a *PivotTable* can be associated with data in a different workbook or an external source such as a database. Use the context-sensitive menu for any cell in the *PivotTable* and choose **Refresh**, or click the **Refresh** button in the *Data* group on the *PivotTable Tools Analyze* tab.

▶ HOW TO: Refresh Data in a PivotTable

1. Click any cell in the *PivotTable*.
2. Click the **Refresh** button [*PivotTable Tools Analyze* tab, *Data* group].
 - *PivotTable* data updates.
 - Refresh all data connections in the workbook by clicking the arrow for the **Refresh** button and selecting **Refresh All**.

Calculated Fields

A **calculated field** is a field in the *PivotTable* that is not a field in the source data. A calculated field uses a value field from the *PivotTable*'s underlying data in a formula. When you insert a calculated field, it displays as the rightmost field in the *PivotTable*, but you can move it and edit its *Value Field Settings*.

▶ HOW TO: Insert a Calculated Field

1. Click a cell in the *PivotTable*.
2. Click the **Fields, Items, and Sets** button [*PivotTable Tools Analyze* tab, *Calculations* group].
3. Select **Calculated Field**.
4. Click the **Name** box in the *Insert Calculated Field* dialog box.
5. Type a name for the calculated field.
 - The name must be unique.
6. Click the **Formula** box and delete the zero and the space after the equals sign.
7. Enter the formula (Figure 4-68).
 - Double-click a field name in the *Fields* list to insert it in the formula.
 - Select a field name and click **Insert Field**.
 - Type an operator or a constant value to build the formula.
8. Click **OK**.
 - The calculated field is added at the right in the *PivotTable* (Figure 4-69).
 - The field name is included in the *PivotTable Fields* pane.
 - An associated *PivotChart* is updated to include the new field.

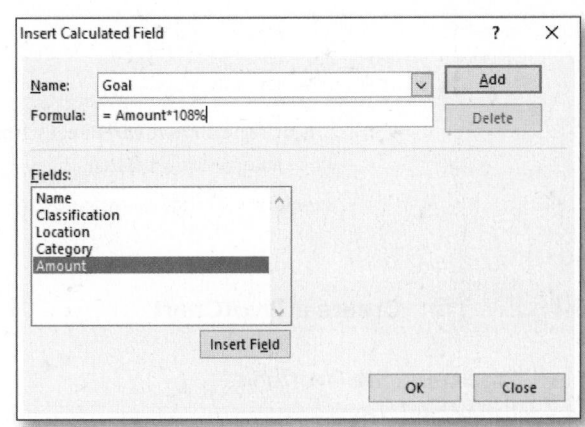

Figure 4-68 A calculated field uses a *PivotTable* field in a formula

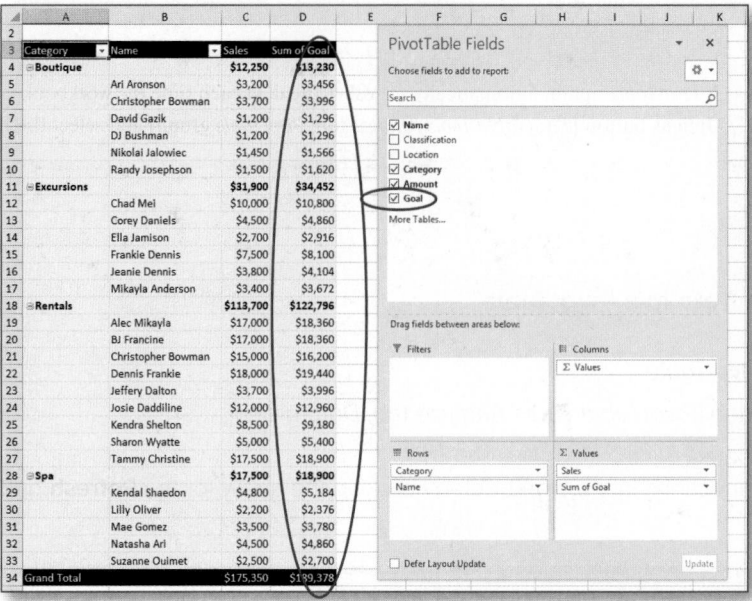

Figure 4-69 Calculated field inserted in the *PivotTable*

> **MORE INFO**
>
> Delete a calculated field by right-clicking a cell in the column and choosing *Remove "Field Name."*

Create a PivotChart

A *PivotChart* contains charted data that updates with the *PivotTable* and has the same field buttons and filter options. The *PivotChart* button is on the *PivotTable Tools Analyze* tab.

Format a *PivotChart* like an Excel chart from its *PivotChart Tools Design* and *Format* tabs. Select a style, switch row and column data, change the chart type, and so on. When the chart object is selected, you will see the *PivotChart Tools Analyze* tab with the same commands as the *PivotTable Tools Analyze* tab and the *PivotChart Fields* task pane. A *PivotChart* and its *PivotTable* are linked, and you make changes from command tabs for the table or the chart.

> **MORE INFO**
>
> Create a *PivotChart* directly from a list in the worksheet; its underlying *PivotTable* is automatically created.

▶ HOW TO: Create a PivotChart

1. Click a cell in the *PivotTable*.
2. Click the **PivotChart** button [*PivotTable Tools Analyze* tab, *Tools* group].
 - The *Insert Chart* dialog box opens.
3. Select a chart type from the list on the left.

E4-266

4. Select a subtype for the chart.
5. Click **OK** (Figure 4-70).
 - The chart displays as a chart object.
 - The *PivotChart Tools Analyze, Design,* and *Format* tabs are available.
 - The *PivotChart Fields* pane is similar to the *PivotTable Fields* pane.

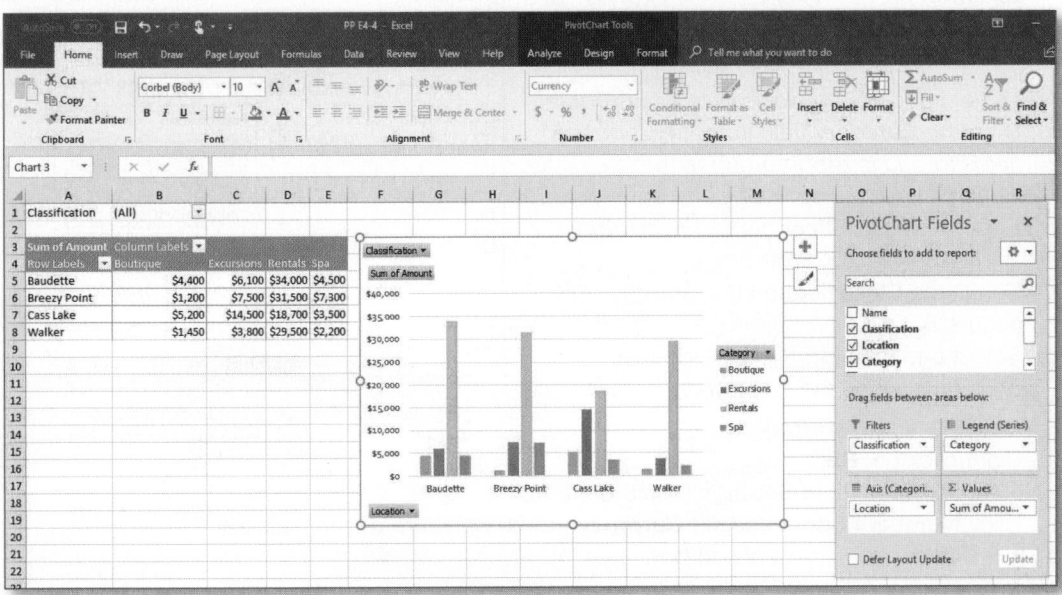

Figure 4-70 *PivotChart* inserted as object

For this project, you create a *PivotTable* for Paradise Lakes Resort using the Excel table as its source. You also create a *PivotChart* and add a slicer to the worksheet. Your workbook now has data connections, so you may see a security warning when you open the file, depending on the settings on your computer.

File Needed: *[your initials] PP E4-3.xlsx*
Completed Project File Name: *[your initials] PP E4-4.xlsx*

1. Open the *[your initials] PP E4-3* workbook completed in *Pause & Practice 4-3*. The security bar informs you that the data connections have been disabled (Figure 4-71).

2. Click **Enable Content**. (If you did not see the security bar, continue to step 3.)

3. Save the workbook as [your initials] PP E4-4.

Figure 4-71 Security warning for a workbook with data connections

4. Create a *PivotTable*.
 a. Click cell **A4** on the **Revenue** sheet tab.
 b. Click the **Recommended PivotTables** button [*Insert* tab, *Tables* group].
 c. Locate and click the **Sum of Amount by Location** preview tile.
 d. Click **OK**.
 e. Name the worksheet tab PivotTable.

5. Add a field and a *Slicer* window in a *PivotTable*.
 a. Drag the **Category** field from the *Choose fields to add to report* group to the *Columns* area in the *PivotTable Fields* pane.
 b. Click the **Insert Slicer** button [*PivotTable Tools Analyze* tab, *Filter* group].
 c. Select the **Classification** box and click **OK** (Figure 4-72).
 d. Select and drag the *Slicer* window to position it below the *PivotTable*.

6. Format fields in a *PivotTable*.
 a. Right-click cell **B5**.
 b. Choose **Value Field Settings** from the menu.
 c. Click **Number Format** and set **Currency** format with zero decimal places.
 d. Click **OK** to close each dialog box.

7. Create a *PivotChart*.
 a. Click the **PivotChart** button [*PivotTable Tools Analyze* tab, *Tools* group].
 b. Select **Clustered Column** from the *Column* group and click **OK**.
 c. Click the **Quick Layout** button [*PivotChart Tools Design* tab, *Chart Layouts* group].
 d. Select **Layout 3**.
 e. Click to select the **Chart Title** placeholder.
 f. Click the *Formula* bar, type Revenue by Category, and press **Enter**.
 g. Position the chart object so that its top-left corner is at cell **H3**.

8. Adjust fields in a *PivotTable* and *PivotChart*.
 a. Click **Representative** in the *Slicer* window. The data are filtered in the *PivotTable* and in the *PivotChart*.
 b. Click the **Category** button in the chart.
 c. Deselect **(Select All)** to remove all the checkmarks (Figure 4-73).
 d. Select the **Excursions** and **Rentals** boxes and click **OK**.

Figure 4-72 *Category* field added as column and *Slicer* window displayed

Figure 4-73 Data will be filtered in the chart and the table

9. Click cell **A1**.

10. Save and close the workbook (Figure 4-74).

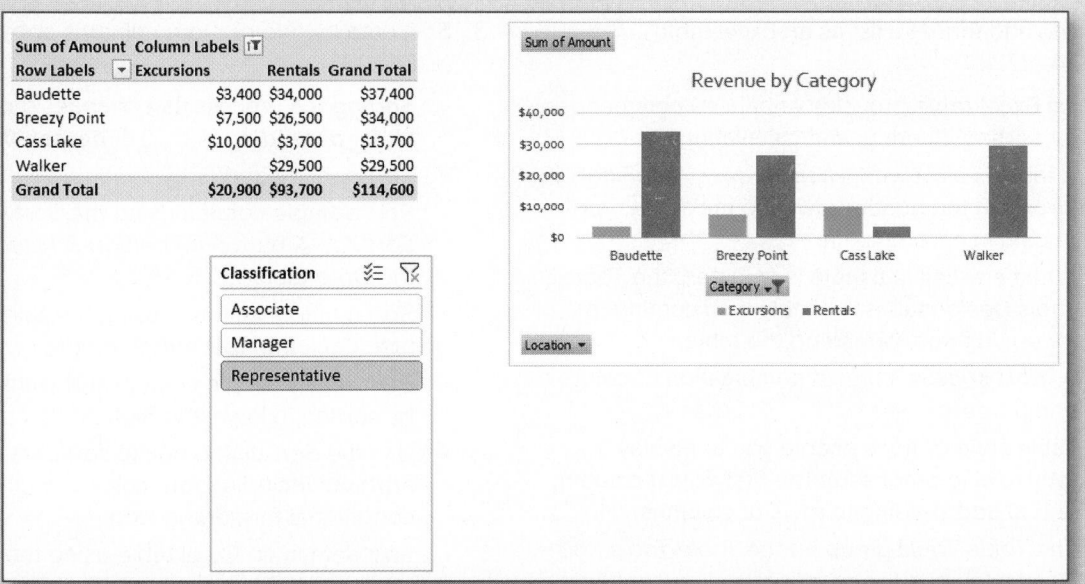

Figure 4-74 PP E4-4 completed

Chapter Summary

4.1 Create and format a list as an Excel table (p. E4–222).

- An Excel *table* provides enhanced commands for sorting, filtering, and calculating data.
- A table is a list with a *header row*, *AutoFilter* arrows in the header row, and the same type of data in each column.
- When any cell in a table is selected, the *Table Tools Design* tab is available with commands for editing and formatting the table.
- A *table style* is a preset combination of colors and borders.
- Table style options enable you to display a total row, to emphasize the first or last column, and to add shading to rows or columns.
- The *Table Tools* group on the *Table Tools Design* tab has commands to remove duplicate rows, to convert a table to a normal cell range, or to insert a *slicer* window for filtering the data.
- The automatic name for a table and several of its parts are *structured references*.
- Structured references appear in *Formula AutoComplete* lists and are substituted automatically in formulas that refer to certain cell ranges in the table.

4.2 Apply *Conditional Formatting* rules as well as *Color Scales, Icon Sets,* and *Data Bars* (p. E4–228).

- *Conditional formatting* formats only cells that meet specified criteria.
- *Highlight Cells Rules* use relational or comparison operators such as *Greater Than* or *Equals* to determine which cells are formatted.
- *Top/Bottom Rules* use ranking or averages to format cells.
- Use the *New Rule* dialog box to create a rule that uses a formula to determine which cells are formatted.
- *Data visualization* uses rules to format cells with *Icon Sets, Color Scales,* or *Data Bars*.
- Edit any conditional formatting rule with the *Manage Rules* command.
- Remove conditional formatting from a selected cell range or from the entire sheet with the *Clear Rules* command.

4.3 Sort data by one or more columns or by attribute (p. E4–235).

- *Sorting* is a process that arranges data in order, either *ascending* (A to Z) or *descending* (Z to A).
- Sort data by one or by multiple columns.
- Sort a single column using the *Sort A to Z* or *Sort Z to A* button in the *Sort & Filter* group on the *Data* tab.
- Sort multiple columns using the *Sort* dialog box. Click the *Sort* button on the *Data* tab.
- Perform a multiple column sort within the data by sorting in lowest to highest sort priority.
- Use the *Sort* dialog box to sort data by cell attribute including font color, cell fill color, or conditional formatting icon.
- Sort data in an Excel table using the *AutoFilter* arrows in the header row.

4.4 Filter data by using *AutoFilters* and by creating an *Advanced Filter* (p. E4–238).

- The *Filter* button [*Data* tab, *Sort & Filter* group] displays an *AutoFilter* arrow for each column heading in list-type data.
- Use an *AutoFilter* arrow to select records to be shown or hidden or to build a custom filter.
- A custom *AutoFilter* uses operators such as *Equals* or *Greater Than*, as well as AND and OR conditions.
- An *Advanced Filter* provides filter options such as using a formula in the filter definition.
- An *Advanced Filter* requires a criteria range in the same workbook and can display filtered results separate from the data.

4.5 Use subtotals, groups, and outlines for tabular data in a worksheet (p. E4–242).

- The *Subtotal* command inserts summary rows for sorted data using *SUM* or a statistical function.
- The *Subtotal* command formats the data as an *outline*, which groups records to be displayed or hidden.
- Outline buttons appear next to row and column headings and determine the level of detail shown in the data.
- An *Auto Outline* creates groups based on formulas that are located in a consistent pattern in a list.

- Define groups by sorting data, inserting blank rows, and using the *Group* button in the *Outline* group on the *Data* tab.

4.6 Import data into an Excel worksheet from a text file, a database file, and other sources (p. E4–248).

- **Import** text files into a worksheet to save time and increase accuracy.
- Common text file formats include .txt (text) and .csv (comma separated values).
- Data in a text file is **delimited** or **fixed width**.
- Text data are imported through a query and display in an Excel table.
- Copy data from a Word document into a worksheet.
- Import a table or a query into a worksheet from a **Microsoft Access database**.
- Many web sites offer data in Excel or text format for downloading into a worksheet.
- Data imported from a command in the *Get & Transform Data* group establishes a data connection so that the data can be refreshed.
- The **Flash Fill** command recognizes and copies typing actions from one or more cells and suggests data for the remaining rows in the same column.

4.7 Export Excel data as a text file and into a Word document (p. E4–254).

- Export data in a worksheet for use in another program or application.
- Export Excel data as a text file.
- Text file formats can be tab-, space-, or comma-delimited.
- Use the Windows or Office *Clipboard* to copy data from Excel into Word and other programs.

4.8 Build and format a *PivotTable* (p. E4–259).

- A **PivotTable** is a cross-tabulated summary report on its own worksheet.
- When a *PivotTable* is active, the *PivotTable Tools Analyze* and *Design* tabs are available.
- The *PivotTable Fields* pane displays on the right and is turned on and off from the *Show* group [*PivotTable Tools Analyze* tab].
- The *PivotTable Fields* pane includes a list of available fields and areas in the report where the fields can be positioned.
- Drag field names in the *PivotTable Fields* pane to reposition them and analyze data from a different perspective.
- Modify and format fields in a *PivotTable* using the *Field Settings* dialog box.
- Format *PivotTables* using the *PivotTable Tools Design* tab. Format selected cells using the *Home* tab.
- *PivotTable* layout options include subtotals and grand totals, repeated labels, and display formats.
- Refresh a *PivotTable* after editing the source data by clicking the *Refresh* button [*PivotTable Tools Analyze* tab, *Data* group].
- Click the *Fields, Items, & Sets* button [*PivotTable Tools Analyze* tab, *Calculations* group] to insert a calculated field in a *PivotTable*.
- A **PivotChart** is a chart based on a *PivotTable* and has similar features as the *PivotTable*.

Check for Understanding

The SIMbook for this text (within your SIMnet account) provides the following resources for concept review:

- Multiple-choice questions
- Short answer questions
- Matching exercises

Guided Project 4-1

For this project, you import a text file to complete the inventory worksheet for Wear-Ever Shoes. You use *Flash Fill* to enter product codes and sort the data by supplier and code. You use *AutoFilter* for several tasks, format data as an Excel table, prepare subtotals, build a *PivotTable,* and export data as a text file. [**Student Learning Outcomes 4.1, 4.2, 4.3, 4.4, 4.5, 4.6, 4.7, 4.8**]

Files Needed: ***WearEver-04.xlsx*** and ***WearEverText-04.txt*** *(Student data files are available in the* Library *of your SIMnet account.)*
Completed Project File Names: *[your initials] Excel 4-1.xlsx* and *[your initials] Excel 4-1Export.txt*

Skills Covered in This Project

- Import a text file.
- Sort data.
- Use *Flash Fill* to complete data.
- Use an *AutoFilter*.
- Set conditional formatting.
- Create an Excel table.
- Use the *Subtotal* command.
- Create and format a *PivotTable*.
- Export data as a tab-delimited file.

1. Open the ***WearEver-04*** workbook from your student data files and save it as [your initials] Excel 4-1.

2. Import a text file.
 a. Select cell **I3**. The text file includes headings that will display in row 4 after importing.
 b. Click the **From Text/CSV** button [*Data* tab, *Get & Transform Data* group].
 c. Find and select the ***WearEverText-04.txt*** file from your student data files in the *Import Data* window.
 d. Click **Import**.
 e. Click the **Delimiter** arrow in the *Navigator* window and choose **Tab** (Figure 4-75).
 f. Click the **Load** arrow and select **Load To**.
 g. Select **Existing worksheet**.
 h. Verify that cell **I3** displays as the location and click **OK**. The supplier name and phone number are imported and added to the list.

3. Select cells **I3:J40** and click the **Convert to Range** button [*Table Design* tab, *Tools* group] (Figure 4-76).

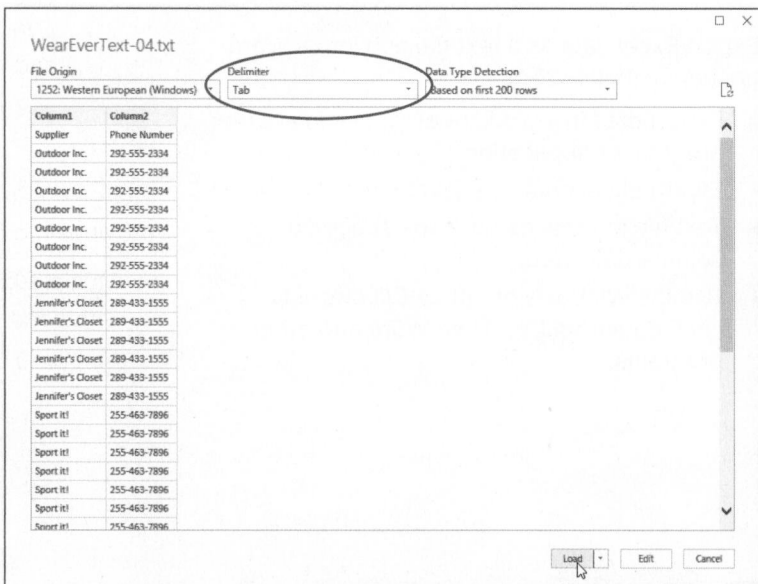

Figure 4-75 Delimiter character selected in the *Navigator* window

4. Click **OK** to remove the query definition, and close the *Queries & Connections* pane.

5. Use the **Format Painter** button to copy formatting from cell **H4** to cells **I4:J4**.

6. Select cells **I5:J40** and clear formats [*Home* tab, *Editing* group]. Format cells **I5:J40** with **Trebuchet MS** from the *Theme Fonts*.

7. Select cells **I3:J3** and clear all [*Home* tab, *Editing* group].

8. *AutoFit* columns **I:J**.

Figure 4-76 Data connection will be removed to create the table

9. Select cells **A1:J2** and click the **Launcher** in the *Alignment* group [*Home* tab]. From the *Horizontal* list, choose **Center Across Selection** and click **OK**.

10. Sort data in multiple columns.
 a. Select cell **A5** and click the **Sort** button [*Data* tab, *Sort & Filter* group].
 b. Select the **My data has headers** box if necessary.
 c. Click the **Sort by** arrow and choose **Supplier**.
 d. Verify that **Cell Values** is selected for *Sort On*.
 e. Choose **A to Z** for *Order*.
 f. Click **Add Level**.
 g. Click the **Then by** arrow and choose **Product**.
 h. Verify that **Cell Values** is selected for *Sort On* and that **A to Z** is selected for *Order*.
 i. Click **OK**. The data are in order by supplier name and then by product name.

11. Use *Flash Fill* to insert product codes.
 a. Insert a column between columns **B** and **C**.
 b. Type Code in cell **C4**.
 c. Type CWS in cell **C5** and press **Enter**.
 d. Type c in cell **C6** and press **Enter**. Regular *AutoComplete* completes the entries based on what is already in the column. The *Flash Fill* suggestion list does not appear because no recognizable pattern was identified.
 e. Click the **Fill** button [*Home* tab, *Editing* group] in cell **C7** and choose **Flash Fill**.
 f. *AutoFit* column **C**.

12. Apply conditional formatting.
 a. Select cells **F5:F40**, the quantity in stock.
 b. Click the **Conditional Formatting** button [*Home* tab, *Style* group].
 c. Click **Highlight Cells Rules** and select **Less Than**.
 d. Type 2 in the *Format cells that are LESS THAN* box.
 e. Click **OK** to accept the *Light Red Fill with Dark Red Text* format.

13. Use an *AutoFilter*.
 a. Select cell **A5** and click the **Filter** button [*Data* tab, *Sort & Filter* group].
 b. Click the *AutoFilter* arrow for the **Supplier** column.
 c. Deselect the **(Select All)** box to remove all the checkmarks.
 d. Select the **Jennifer's Closet** box.
 e. Click **OK**. The data are filtered to show only records from one supplier.

14. Copy the **Inventory** worksheet to the end and name the copy Women's. Set the tab color to **Gold, Accent 4** (eighth column).

15. Clear a filter and conditional formatting.
 a. Select the **Women's** sheet and click the *AutoFilter* arrow for the **Supplier** column.
 b. Select **Clear Filter from "Supplier"**.

c. Click the **Filter** button [*Data* tab, *Sort & Filter* group] to hide the *AutoFilter* arrows.

d. Click the **Conditional Formatting** button [*Home* tab, *Style* group].

e. Select **Clear Rules** and select **Clear Rules From Entire Sheet**.

16. Create an Excel table.
 a. Select cells **A4:K40** on the **Women's** sheet.
 b. Click the **Format as Table** button [*Home* tab, *Styles* group].
 c. Choose **Gold, Table Style Medium 5** in the *Table Styles* gallery.
 d. Confirm the range (A4:K40) in the *Format as Table* dialog box, that the *My table has headers* box is checked, and click **OK**.

17. Add a calculated column to a table.
 a. Insert a column at column **J**.
 b. Type Markup in cell **J4** and press **Enter**.
 c. Type = in cell **J5** and click cell **I5**.
 d. Type − for subtraction and click cell **H5** (Figure 4-77).
 e. Press **Enter** to copy the formula.

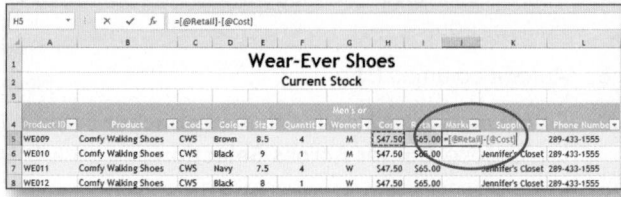

Figure 4-77 Add a calculated column to the table

18. Filter data in a table.
 a. Click the *AutoFilter* arrow for the **Men's or Women's** column.
 b. Deselect the **(Select All)** box to remove all the checkmarks.
 c. Select the **W** box and click **OK**.
 d. Press **Ctrl+Home**.

19. Copy the **Inventory** worksheet to the end and name the copy Subtotals. Set the tab color to **Black, Text 1** (second column).

20. Clear a filter and conditional formatting.
 a. Select the **Subtotals** sheet and clear the filter for the **Supplier**.
 b. Click the **Filter** button [*Data* tab, *Sort & Filter* group] to hide the *AutoFilter* arrows.
 c. Click the **Conditional Formatting** button [*Home* tab, *Style* group] and clear rules from the sheet.

Figure 4-78 *Subtotal* dialog box to count number of products by supplier

21. Use the *Subtotal* command.
 a. Select cell **J5** on the **Subtotals** sheet. The records are sorted by the "Supplier" column.
 b. Click the **Subtotal** button [*Data* tab, *Outline* group].
 c. Click the **At each change in** arrow and choose **Supplier**.
 d. Click the **Use function** arrow and choose **Count**.
 e. Check the **Supplier** box in the *Add subtotal to* area.
 f. Deselect any other selected fields in the *Add subtotal to* list (Figure 4-78).
 g. Click **OK**. A subtotal row displays at the bottom of each group and shows how many products are available from each supplier.
 h. Format the label in cell **I17** as **right-aligned**.
 i. **Right-align** the remaining subtotal labels in column **I** (Figure 4-79).

Figure 4-79 Subtotals inserted for each group

E4-274

22. Create a *PivotTable*.
 a. Click the **Inventory** sheet tab and select cell **A5**.
 b. Click the **PivotTable** button [*Insert* tab, *Tables* group].
 c. Verify that the *Table/Range* is **A4:K40** in the *Create PivotTable* dialog box and that the *New Worksheet* button is selected.

Figure 4-80 Blank *PivotTable* layout

 d. Click **OK**. A blank *PivotTable* layout displays on a new sheet (Figure 4-80).
 e. Name the sheet PivotTable.

23. Add fields in a *PivotTable*.
 a. Select the **Product** box in the *PivotTable Fields* pane to place it in the *Rows* area.
 b. Select the **Quantity** box to place it in the *Values* area.
 c. Drag the **Supplier** field name into the *Columns* area.

24. Format a *PivotTable*.
 a. Click the **More** button in the *PivotTable Styles* group [*PivotTable Tools Design* tab].
 b. Select **Light Orange, Pivot Style Medium 7**.
 c. Select the **Banded Rows** box [*PivotTable Tools Design* tab, *PivotTable Style Options* group].
 d. Select the **Banded Columns** box [*PivotTable Tools Design* tab, *PivotTable Style Options* group] (Figure 4-81).

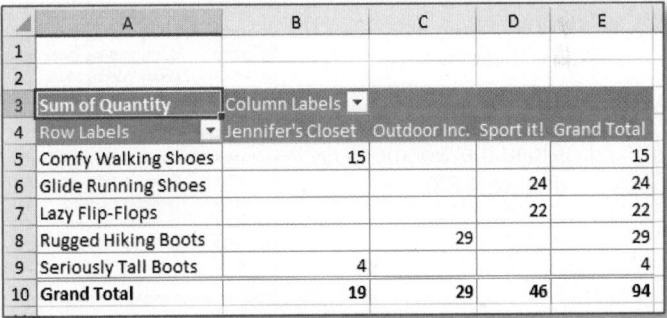

Figure 4-81 Formatted *PivotTable*

25. Copy the **Inventory** worksheet to the end and do not rename it.

26. Select the copied sheet, clear the filter from the **Supplier** column, and remove the *AutoFilter* arrows. Conditional formatting need not be cleared.

27. Export data as a tab-delimited file.
 a. Click cell **A1** in the copied sheet.
 b. Click the **File** tab and select **Export**.
 c. Select **Change File Type**.
 d. Select **Text (Tab delimited)** as the file type.
 e. Click **Save As**.
 f. Navigate to the save location for the exported data in the *Save as type* dialog box.
 g. Type [your initials]Excel 4-1Export as the file name.
 h. Click **Save**.
 i. Click **OK** in the message box to save only the current sheet (Figure 4-82).

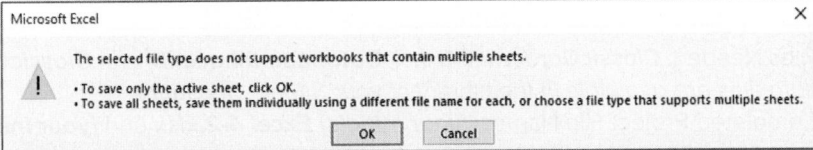

Figure 4-82 Only the current sheet is saved as a text file

j. Click **Yes** if a second message box notes that Excel features may be lost in the text file. The sheet is renamed, and the data are exported to a *.txt* file.

28. Save the workbook with the same file name.
 a. Click the **File** tab and choose **Save As**.
 b. Navigate to the folder for saved work.
 c. Select **Excel Workbook** as the *Save as type* in the *Save As* dialog box.
 d. Select *[your initials] Excel 4-1* or retype that file name.
 e. Click **Save** and click **Yes** to replace the .xlsx file that you saved at the beginning of this project.
 f. Close the workbook (Figure 4-83).

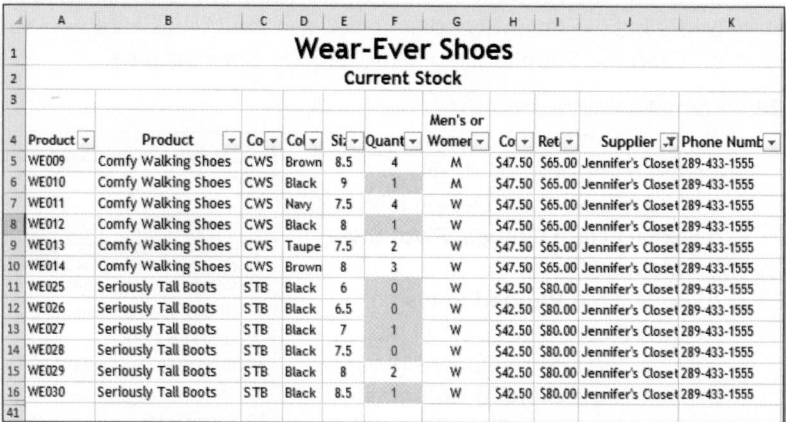

Figure 4-83 Excel 4-1 completed

Guided Project 4-2

Classic Gardens and Landscapes is building a workbook with data about revenue and promotion campaigns. You copy data from Word and import data from an Access database. You set conditional formatting, format an Excel table, sort and filter data, and build a *PivotTable* and *PivotChart*.
[Student Learning Outcomes 4.1, 4.2, 4.3, 4.4, 4.5, 4.6, 4.7, 4.8]

Files Needed: ***ClassicGardens-04.xlsx, Database-04.accdb,*** and ***ClassicGardensWord-04.docx*** *(Student data files are available in the* Library *of your SIMnet account.)*
Completed Project File Names: *[your initials]* **Excel 4-2.xlsx** and *[your initials]* **Excel 4-2Text.csv**

Skills Covered in This Project

- Copy data from Word.
- Use conditional formatting with an icon set.
- Prepare data for an *Auto Outline*.
- Import a table from a database file.
- Apply a table style and show a total row.
- Sort and filter data in a table.
- Build and format a *PivotTable*.
- Build a *PivotChart*.
- Filter data in a *PivotChart*.
- Export data as a comma-separated text file.

1. Open the ***ClassicGardens-04*** workbook from your student data files and save it as [your initials] Excel 4-2.

2. Select the **Quarterly** sheet; insert six columns between columns **G** and **H**.

3. Copy data from Word.
 a. Open the Word document ***ClassicGardensWord-04.docx*** from your student data files.
 b. Select all the data in Word and copy it.
 c. Select cell **H4** in the Excel workbook.
 d. Click the **Paste** button arrow [*Home* tab, *Clipboard* group] and choose **Match Destination Formatting**.
 e. Select cell **N5** and click the **AutoSum** button [*Home* tab, *Editing* group].
 f. Verify or select the range **B5:M5** and press **Enter**.
 g. Copy the formula to cells **N6:N9**.
 h. Select cells **H10:M10** and click the **AutoSum** button [*Home* tab, *Editing* group].

4. Apply conditional formatting.
 a. Select cells **N5:N9**.
 b. Click the **Quick Analysis** button.
 c. Verify that **Formatting** is selected.
 d. Choose **Icon Set** (Figure 4-84). The cells display a default icon to represent the upper, middle, or lower values of the range.

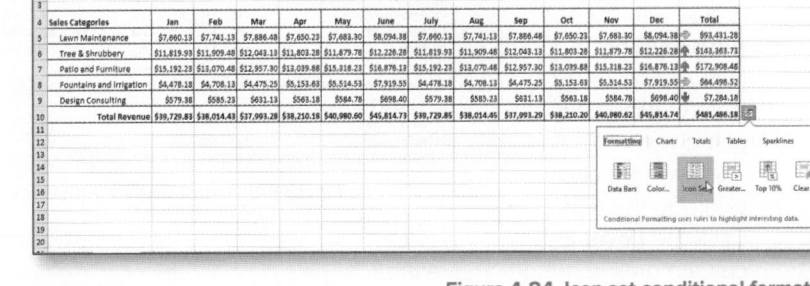

Figure 4-84 Icon set conditional formatting

5. *AutoFit* the columns and verify all data are visible.

6. Click the **AutoOutline** sheet tab.

7. Use *AutoSum* to calculate subtotals and totals.
 a. Select cells **E5:E18**, press **Ctrl** and select cells **I5:I18**, **M5:M18**, and **Q5:Q18** (Figure 4-85).
 b. Click the **AutoSum** button [*Home* tab, *Editing* group].

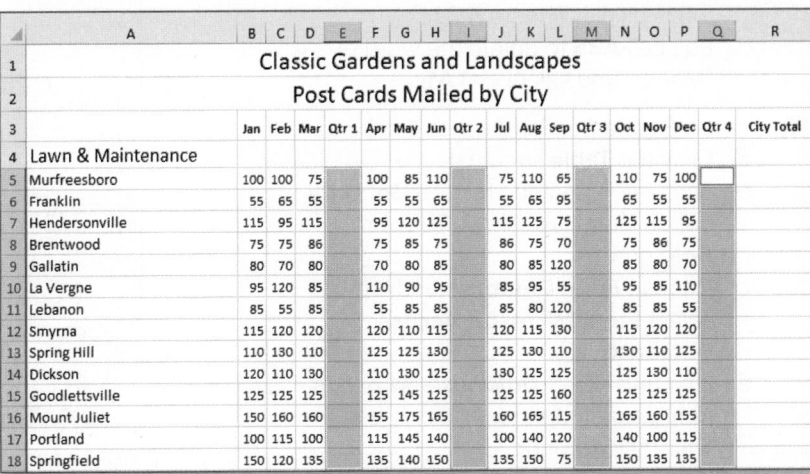

Figure 4-85 *SUM* function in a consistent pattern

c. Select cells **R5:R18** and click the **AutoSum** button [*Home* tab, *Editing* group]. Excel sums the *Qtr 1, Qtr 2, Qtr 3,* and *Qtr 4* columns (Q5, M5, I5, E5).

d. Select cells **B19:R19** and click the **AutoSum** button [*Home* tab, *Editing* group].

e. *AutoFit* columns to display all the data.

f. Select cells **E21:E25**, press **Ctrl** and select cells **I21:I25**, **M21:M25**, and **Q21:Q25**.

g. Click the **AutoSum** button [*Home* tab, *Editing* group].

h. Use *AutoSum* in cells **R21:R25** and verify that the *SUM* function refers to columns Q, M, I, and E.

i. Select cells **B26:R26** and click the **AutoSum** button [*Home* tab, *Editing* group].

j. Select cells **E28:E33**, **I28:I33**, **M28:M33**, **Q28:Q33** and use *AutoSum*.

k. Complete the *SUM* function for cells **R28:R33** and then for cells **B34:R34**.

l. *AutoFit* the columns.

8. Insert formulas to calculate monthly totals.

a. Type = in cell **B35** to start a formula.

b. Click cell **B19**, type +, click cell **B26**, type +, click cell **B34**, and press **Enter**. The formula is =**B19 + B26 + B34**.

c. Copy the formula in cell **B35** to cells **C35:R35**.

d. *AutoFit* columns to display all the data.

9. Create an *Auto Outline*.

a. Click cell **B5**.

b. Click the arrow for the **Group** button [*Data* tab, *Outline* group] and choose **Auto Outline** (Figure 4-86). The *Auto Outline* command uses column and row formulas to group the data.

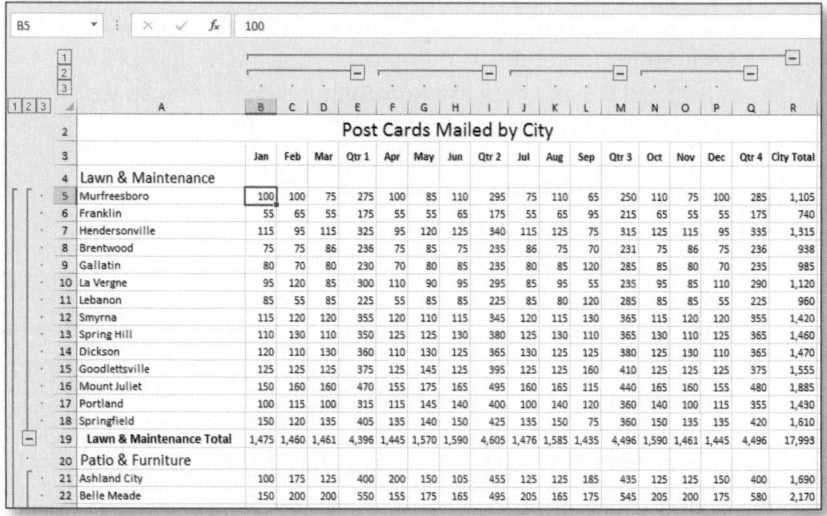

Figure 4-86 *Auto Outline* with three row levels and three column levels

c. Click the **Level 2** column outline button (above the column headings). Only the quarter totals display (Figure 4-87).

d. Edit cell **A35** to delete the word "Month" and select cell **A1**.

10. Import a table from an Access database.

a. Click the **Table** sheet tab.

b. Select cell **A4** and click the **Get Data** button [*Data* tab, *Get & Transform Data* group].

c. Choose **From Database** and then select **From Microsoft Access Database**.

d. Find and select *Database-04.accdb* from your student data files in the *Import Data* window.

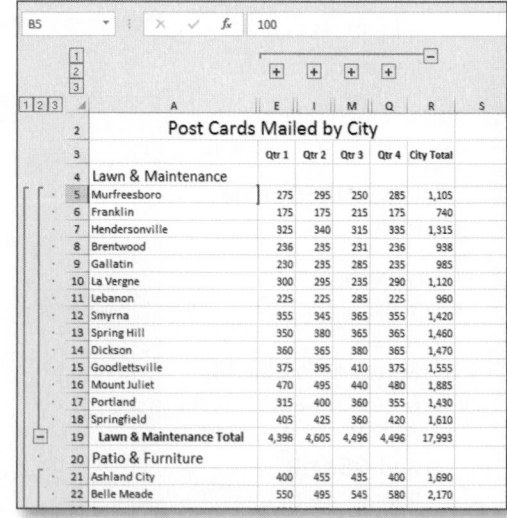

Figure 4-87 Outline collapsed at Level 2 column group

e. Click **Import**.
f. Click **tblMailings** in the *Navigator* dialog box (Figure 4-88).
g. Click the **Load** arrow and choose **Load To**.
h. Select **Existing worksheet**, verify that cell **A4** is the destination cell, and click **OK**.

11. Apply a table style and show a total row.
 a. Click cell **B5** in the table.
 b. Click the **More** button [*Table Tools Design* tab, *Table Styles* group].
 c. Choose **White, Table Style Medium 15**.
 d. Select the **Total Row** box [*Table Tools Design* tab, *Table Style Options* group].

Figure 4-88 *Navigator* dialog box for an Access database

 e. Click cell **C30** (January total) and choose **Sum**. Then copy the formula to cells **D30:M30**.

12. Sort and filter data in an Excel table.
 a. Click the *AutoFilter* arrow for **City**.
 b. Choose **Sort A to Z**.
 c. Click the *AutoFilter* arrow for **City**.
 d. Select **Text Filters** and **Equals**.
 e. Type c* in the first criteria box to select cities that begin with "C."
 f. Select the **Or** radio button.
 g. Select **equals** as the second operator.
 h. Type m* in the second criteria box to select cities that begin with "M" (Figure 4-89).
 i. Click **OK**.

Figure 4-89 *Custom AutoFilter* for cities that begin with "C" or "M"

13. Select cells **A1:N1**, merge and center the labels, and change the font size to **18 pt**. (Figure 4-90).

14. Repeat these steps for cells **A2:N2** (Figure 4-90).

15. Close the *Queries & Connections* pane and select the **Pivot Source** sheet tab.

16. Create a *PivotTable*.
 a. Select cell **A5**.
 b. Click the **Recommended PivotTables** button [*Insert* tab, *Tables* group].

	A	B	C	D	E	F	G	H	I	J	K	L	M	N
1					Classic Gardens and Landscapes									
2					Post Card Mailings by City									
3														
4	ID	City	Jan	Feb	Mar	Apr	May	Jun	Jul	Aug	Sep	Oct	Nov	Dec
9	18	Carthage	75	85	95	95	125	100	110	105	105	110	95	125
10	19	Centerville	150	100	85	100	85	150	85	150	100	85	85	85
11	20	Charlotte	150	175	205	175	215	135	205	175	255	135	205	205
12	21	Coopertown	150	225	200	235	200	145	195	250	200	145	200	235
13	22	Cross Plains	200	200	210	200	215	210	210	200	265	215	210	210
24	12	Mount Juliet	150	160	160	155	175	165	160	165	115	165	160	155
25	1	Murfreesboro	100	100	75	100	85	110	75	110	65	110	75	100
30	Total		975	1045	1030	1060	1100	1015	1040	1155	1105	965	1030	1115
31														

Figure 4-90 Imported data sorted and filtered

c. Verify that the **Sum of # of Responses by Department** thumbnail is selected and click **OK**.
d. Select the **City** and **# Mailed** boxes in the *Choose fields to add to report* area to add them to the report.
e. Drag the **Department** field from the *Rows* area to the *Filters* area in the *PivotTable Fields* pane.

17. Insert a calculated field in a *PivotTable*.
 a. Click the **Fields, Items, and Sets** button [*PivotTable Tools Analyze* tab, *Calculations* group] and select **Calculated Field**.
 b. Click the **Name** box and type Response Ratio.
 c. Click the **Formula** box and delete the zero and the space after the equals sign.
 d. Double-click **# Responses** in the *Fields* list and type / for division.
 e. Double-click **#Mailed** in the *Fields* list and click **OK** (Figure 4-91).

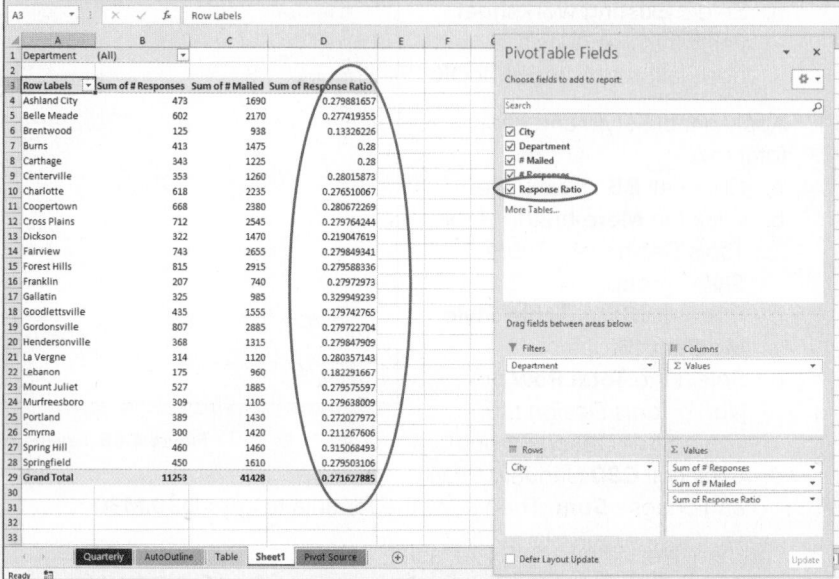

Figure 4-91 *PivotTable* with calculated field

18. Format a *PivotTable*.
 a. Right-click cell **B4** and select **Value Field Settings** from the context menu.
 b. Click **Number Format**.
 c. Choose **Number** as the *Category* and select zero decimal places.
 d. Select the **Use 1000 Separator (,)** box.
 e. Click **OK** to close each dialog box.
 f. Apply the same number format for "Sum of # Mailed" field.
 g. Select cell **D4** and format the field to use **Percentage** with 2 decimal places.
 h. Click the **More** button [*PivotTable Tools Design* tab, *PivotTable Styles* group].
 i. Select **Ice Blue, Pivot Style Medium 9** [*PivotTable Tools Design* tab, *PivotTable Styles* group].
 j. Select the **Banded Rows** box [*PivotTable Tools Design* tab, *PivotTable Styles Options* group].
 k. Select the **Banded Columns** box [*PivotTable Tools Design* tab, *PivotTable Styles Options* group] (Figure 4-92).

	A	B	C	D
1	Department	(All)		
2				
3	Row Labels	Sum of # Responses	Sum of # Mailed	Sum of Response Ratio
4	Ashland City	473	1,690	27.99%
5	Belle Meade	602	2,170	27.74%
6	Brentwood	125	938	13.33%
7	Burns	413	1,475	28.00%
8	Carthage	343	1,225	28.00%
9	Centerville	353	1,260	28.02%
10	Charlotte	618	2,235	27.65%
11	Coopertown	668	2,380	28.07%
12	Cross Plains	712	2,545	27.98%
13	Dickson	322	1,470	21.90%
14	Fairview	743	2,655	27.98%
15	Forest Hills	815	2,915	27.96%
16	Franklin	207	740	27.97%
17	Gallatin	325	985	32.99%
18	Goodlettsville	435	1,555	27.97%
19	Gordonsville	807	2,885	27.97%
20	Hendersonville	368	1,315	27.98%
21	La Vergne	314	1,120	28.04%
22	Lebanon	175	960	18.23%
23	Mount Juliet	527	1,885	27.96%
24	Murfreesboro	309	1,105	27.96%
25	Portland	389	1,430	27.20%
26	Smyrna	300	1,420	21.13%
27	Spring Hill	460	1,460	31.51%
28	Springfield	450	1,610	27.95%
29	Grand Total	11,253	41,428	27.16%

Figure 4-92 Formatted *PivotTable*

19. Create and format a *PivotChart*.
 a. Click the **PivotChart** button [*PivotTable Tools Analyze* tab, *Tools* group].
 b. Select **Bar** as the chart type and **Clustered Bar** as the subtype.
 c. Click **OK**.
 d. Position the chart object so that its top-left corner is at cell **F3**.
 e. Drag the bottom-right selection handle to reach cell **P24**.
 f. Click the **More** button [*PivotChart Tools Design* tab, *Chart Styles* group] and choose **Style 5**.
 g. Click the **Shape Outline** button [*PivotChart Tools Format* tab, *Shape Styles* group] and select **Blue, Accent 1** (fifth column).

20. Filter data in a *PivotChart*.
 a. Click the **Department** filter button in the chart.
 b. Select the **Select Multiple Items** box.
 c. Deselect the **(All)** box.
 d. Select the **Landscape Design** box and click **OK**.
 e. Select cell **A13** to deselect the *PivotTable* and *PivotChart* (Figure 4-93).
 f. Name the sheet PivotTable.

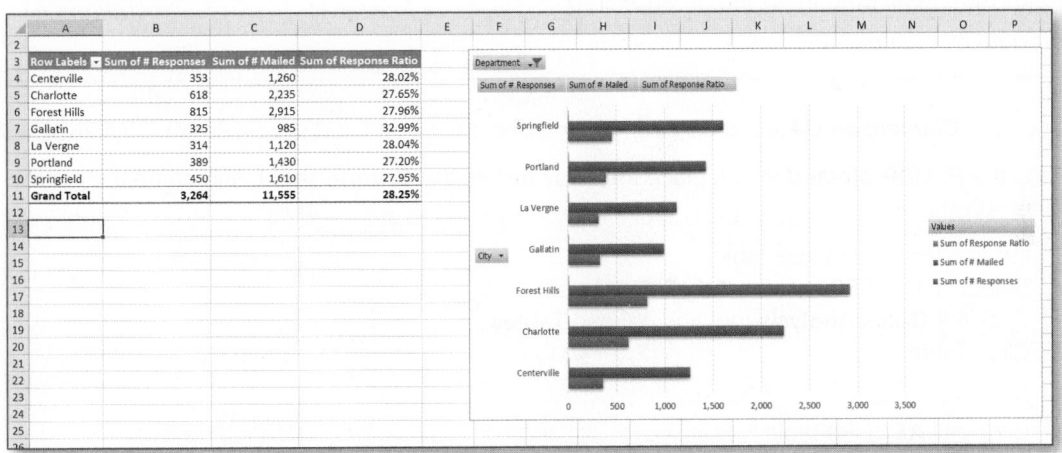

Figure 4-93 Filtered data in *PivotChart* and *PivotTable*

21. Export data as a comma-separated file.
 a. Click the **Quarterly** sheet tab.
 b. Click the **File** tab and select **Export**.
 c. Select **Change File Type**.
 d. Select **CSV (Comma delimited)** as the file type.
 e. Click **Save As**.
 f. Navigate to the save location for the exported data in the *Save as type* dialog box.
 g. Type [your initials]Excel 4-2Text as the file name.
 h. Click **Save**.
 i. Click **OK** in the message box to save the current sheet. The sheet is renamed, and the data are exported to a *.csv* file.
 j. Close the *Possible Data Loss* message bar if it opens.
 k. Rename the sheet as Quarterly.

22. Resave the workbook with the same file name.
 a. Click the **File** tab and choose **Save As**.
 b. Navigate to the folder for saved work.
 c. Select **Excel Workbook** as the *Save as type*.
 d. Select *[your initials] Excel 4-2* or retype the file name.
 e. Click **Save** and click **OK** to replace the file.

23. Save and close the workbook. Close Word.

Guided Project 4-3

Clemenson Imaging analyzes expense reports from field representatives as well as patient and image data. To complete the worksheets, you format data as a table and build an advanced filter. You import a comma-separated text file (.csv) and use the *Subtotal* command. Finally, you display data in a *PivotTable*. [Student Learning Outcomes 4.1, 4.2, 4.3, 4.4, 4.5, 4.6, 4.7, 4.8]

Files Needed: ***Clemenson-04.xlsx, ClemensonText-04.csv***, and ***ClemensonWord.docx*** *(Student data files are available in the* Library *of your SIMnet account.)*
Completed Project File Names: *[your initials] **Excel 4-3.xlsx*** and *[your initials] **Excel 4-3Word.docx***

Skills Covered in This Project

- Format data as an Excel table.
- Build an *Advanced Filter*.
- Apply conditional formatting to filtered results.
- Sort data by multiple columns.
- Import a comma-separated text file.
- Use the *Subtotal* command.
- Export data via the *Clipboard*.
- Create a *PivotTable*.

1. Open the ***Clemenson-04*** workbook from your student data files and save it as [your initials] Excel 4-3.

2. Copy the **Past&Projected** sheet, place the copy before the **Criteria** sheet, and name the copied sheet Adv Filter.

3. Create and format an Excel table.
 a. Select cells **A4:E60** on the **Adv Filter** sheet.
 b. Click the **Quick Analysis** tool and choose **Tables**.
 c. Click **Table**.

4. Apply a table style.
 a. Click cell **A5** in the table.
 b. Click the **More** button [*Table Tools Design* tab, *Table Styles* group].
 c. Select **White, Table Style Medium 15**.

5. Create an output range for an *Advanced Filter*.
 a. Select cells **A4:E4** and copy and paste them to cell **G4**.
 b. Type Extract Range in cell **G3** and set the font to **Cambria 16 pt**.
 c. Adjust column widths for columns **G:K** to show the labels.
 d. Adjust row **4** to a height of **33.75 (45 pixels)**.

6. Create an *Advanced Filter*.
 a. Click the **Criteria** sheet tab.
 b. Type >12/31/18 in cell **A3** to find records after 2018.
 c. Type mri in cell **B3**.
 d. Type >12/31/19 in cell **A4**, to find records after 2019.
 e. Type ct scan in cell **B4**. This criteria will find records dated 2019 or later for MRIs *and* records for CT scans dated 2020 or later (Figure 4-94).
 f. Click cell **A5** on the **Adv Filter** sheet.
 g. Click the **Advanced** button [*Data* tab, *Sort & Filter* group].
 h. Select the **Copy to another location** radio button.

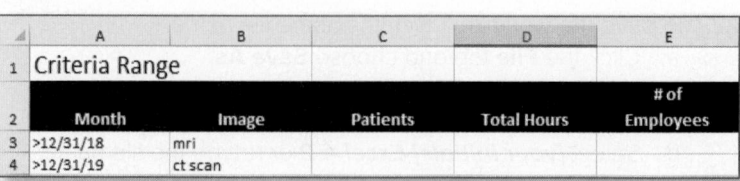

	A	B	C	D	E
1	Criteria Range				
2	Month	Image	Patients	Total Hours	# of Employees
3	>12/31/18	mri			
4	>12/31/19	ct scan			

Figure 4-94 Criteria for *Advanced Filter*

i. Verify that the **List range** is cells **A4:E60**. If the range is incorrect, click and drag to select the range including the header row.
j. Click the **Criteria range** box and select cells **A2:B4** on the **Criteria** sheet.
k. Click the **Copy to** box and select cells **G4:K4** on the **Adv Filter** sheet.
l. Click **OK** in the *Advanced Filter* dialog box.

7. Sort data in the output range.
 a. Select cell **G5** and click the **Sort** button [*Data* tab, *Sort & Filter* group].
 b. Click the **Sort by** arrow and choose **Image** for the first level.
 c. Verify that the **Sort On** selection is **Cell Values** and the **Order** is **A to Z**.
 d. Click **Add Level** and choose **Month** as the **Then by** selection.
 e. Verify or select **Cell Values** and **Oldest to Newest** for the second level.
 f. Click **OK**.

8. Apply conditional formatting and borders.
 a. Select the cells with values in column I.
 b. Click the **Conditional Formatting** button [*Home* tab, *Styles* group].
 c. Choose **Highlight Cells Rules** and **Greater Than**.
 d. Type 750 and choose **Green Fill with Dark Green Text**.
 e. Click **OK**.
 f. Select the extract range starting at cell **G5** and apply **All Borders** (Figure 4-95). (Your results may be different from Figure 4-95 depending on the current date.)
 g. Press **Ctrl+Home**.

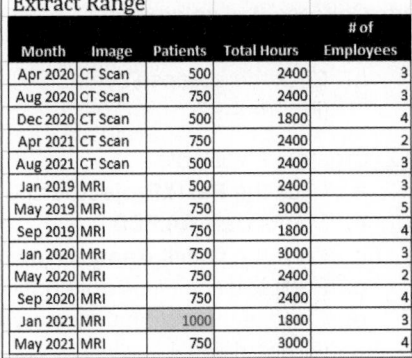

Extract Range

Month	Image	Patients	Total Hours	# of Employees
Apr 2020	CT Scan	500	2400	3
Aug 2020	CT Scan	750	2400	3
Dec 2020	CT Scan	500	1800	4
Apr 2021	CT Scan	750	2400	2
Aug 2021	CT Scan	500	2400	3
Jan 2019	MRI	500	2400	3
May 2019	MRI	750	3000	5
Sep 2019	MRI	750	1800	4
Jan 2020	MRI	750	3000	3
May 2020	MRI	750	2400	2
Sep 2020	MRI	750	2400	4
Jan 2021	MRI	1000	1800	3
May 2021	MRI	750	3000	4

Figure 4-95 *Advanced Filter* results

9. Import a comma-separated values text file.
 a. Click the **Expense Info** sheet tab.
 b. Select cell **A4**.
 c. Click the **From Text/CSV** button [*Data* tab, *Get & Transform Data* group].
 d. Find and select the ***ClemensonText-04.csv*** file from your student data files in the *Import Data* window.
 e. Click **Import**.
 f. Verify that **Comma** is selected as the **Delimiter** in the *Navigator* window.
 g. Click the **Load** arrow and select **Load To**. Select **Existing worksheet**.
 h. Verify that cell **A4** displays as the destination and that **Table** is how the data will be imported.
 i. Click **OK** to import the text data (Figure 4-96).
 j. Cut and paste (or drag and drop) the labels in row **3** to replace the labels in row **4**.
 k. Select cell **A5** and click the **Convert to Range** button [*Table Design* tab, *Tools* group]. Click **OK** to remove the query definition.
 l. Select cells **A4:D31** and clear the formats [*Home* tab, *Editing* group].
 m. Select cells **A4:D31**, if necessary, and change the font size to **11 pt**.
 n. Select the labels in row **4** and center align them.
 o. Format the dates in column **C** with the **Short Date** format.
 p. Select columns **A:D** and size each column to **12.14 (90 pixels)** wide. Deselect the columns.

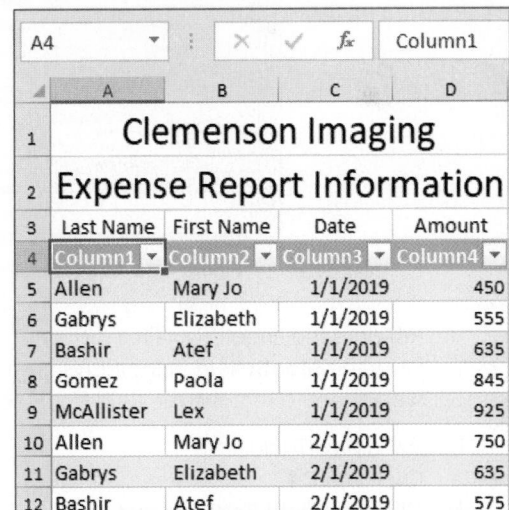

Figure 4-96 CSV file imported as a table

10. Use the *Subtotal* command.
 a. Close the *Queries & Connections* pane and click cell **A5**.
 b. Click the **Sort A to Z** button [*Data* tab, *Sort & Filter* group] to sort by last name.
 c. Click the **Subtotal** button [*Data* tab, *Outline* group].
 d. Verify or choose **Last Name** for the **At each change in** box.
 e. Click the **Use function** arrow and choose **Average**.
 f. Check the **Amount** box in the *Add subtotal to* area.
 g. Click **OK**.
 h. Format the values in column **D** as **Currency** with zero decimal places.

11. Collapse outline groups.
 a. Click the collapse symbol (−) for Allen in row **8**.
 b. Click the collapse symbol (−) for McAllister (Figure 4-97).

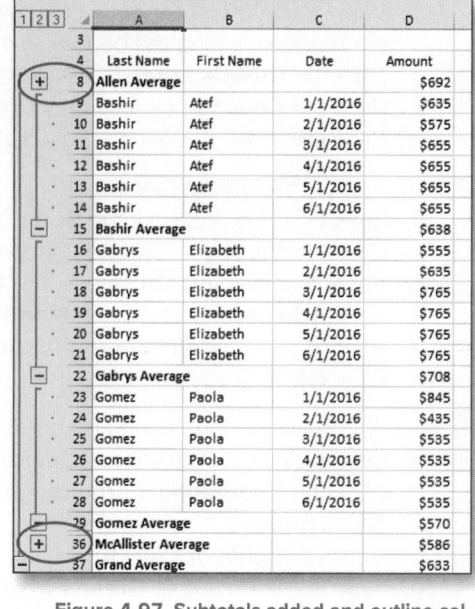

Figure 4-97 Subtotals added and outline collapsed for two groups

12. Create a *PivotTable*.
 a. Click the **Past&Projected** sheet tab.
 b. Select cells **A4:E60**.
 c. Click the **Quick Analysis** tool and choose **Tables**.
 d. Point to each *PivotTable* option to see the *Live Preview*.
 e. Choose the option that shows a sum of the employees, the total hours, and the patients by image (Figure 4-98).

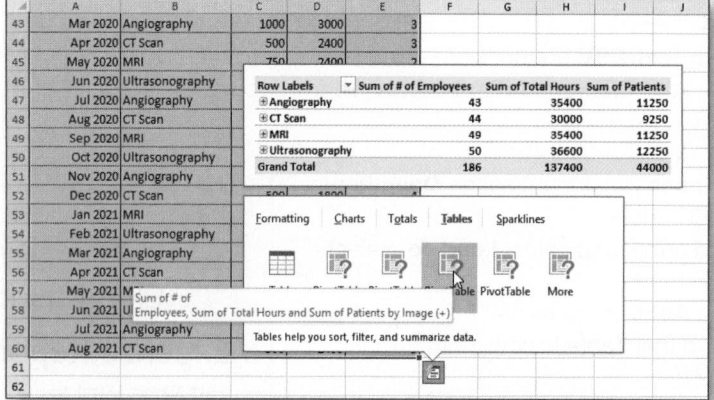

Figure 4-98 Suggested *PivotTable* choices from the *Quick Analysis* tool

 f. Rename the sheet PivotTable.
 g. Drag the **Month** field in the *Rows* area in the *PivotTable Fields* pane out of the pane and into the worksheet to remove the field from the *PivotTable*.

13. Format a *PivotTable*.
 a. Click cell **C4**.
 b. Click the **Field Settings** button [*PivotTable Tools Analyze* tab, *Active Field* group].
 c. Click **Number Format**.
 d. Choose **Number** as the *Category*.
 e. Select the **Use 1000 Separator (,)** box and set zero decimal places.
 f. Click **OK** to close each dialog box.
 g. Apply the same number format for the "Sum of Patients" field.

h. Click the **More** button [*PivotTable Tools Design* tab, *PivotTable Styles* group].

i. Select **Dark Gray, Pivot Style Dark 9** [*PivotTable Tools Design* tab, *PivotTable Styles* group].

j. Select the **Banded Rows** box [*PivotTable Tools Design* tab, *PivotTable Styles Options* group].

	A	B	C	D
1				
2				
3	Row Labels ▼	Sum of # of	Sum of Total Hours	Sum of Patients
4	Angiography	43	35,400	11,250
5	CT Scan	44	30,000	9,250
6	MRI	49	35,400	11,250
7	Ultrasonography	50	36,600	12,250
8	Grand Total	186	137,400	44,000

Figure 4-99 *PivotTable* with new settings

k. Select the **Banded Columns** box [*PivotTable Tools Design* tab, *PivotTable Styles Options* group] (Figure 4-99).

14. Create and format a *PivotChart*.
 a. Click the **PivotChart** button [*PivotTable Tools Analyze* tab, *Tools* group].
 b. Select **Bar** as the chart type and **Stacked Bar** as the subtype.
 c. Click **OK**.
 d. Position the chart object so that its top-left corner is at cell **A12**.
 e. Drag the bottom-right selection handle to reach cell **J30**.
 f. Click the **More** button [*PivotChart Tools Design* tab, *Chart Styles* group] and choose **Style 8**.
 g. Click the **Change Colors** button [*PivotChart Tools Design* tab, *Chart Styles* group].
 h. Select **Monochromatic Palette 1** in the *Monochromatic* group.
 i. Deselect the **# of Employees** box in the *PivotChart Fields* pane (Figure 4-100).
 j. Click cell **A1**.

Figure 4-100 *PivotChart* object

15. Export data using the *Clipboard*.
 a. Click the **Adv Filter** sheet tab.
 b. Starting at cell **G4**, select the cells in the *Extract Range* and click the **Copy** button [*Home* tab, *Clipboard* group].
 c. Open the **ClemensonWord-04** Word document from your student data files. Enable editing if prompted.

d. Press **Ctrl+End** to position the insertion point.

e. Click the arrow with the **Paste** button [*Home* tab, *Clipboard* group] and choose **Paste Special**.

f. Select **Microsoft Excel Worksheet Object** in the *Paste Special* dialog box.

g. Select the **Paste link** radio button in the *Paste Special* dialog box and click **OK**. (The Excel data in your document may be different from the figure.)

h. Click the **Center** button [*Home* tab, *Paragraph* group].

i. Save the Word document as *[your initials] Excel 4-3Word* in your usual folder (Figure 4-101).

j. Close Word.

16. Save and close the Excel workbook.

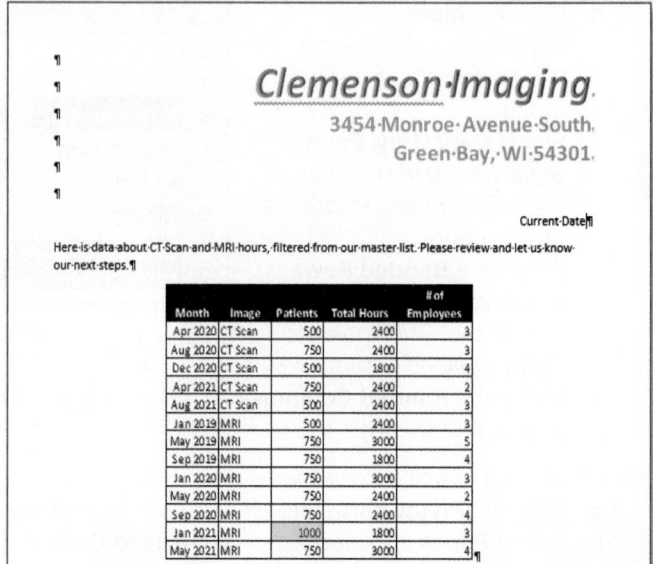

Figure 4-101 Word document with pasted Excel object

Independent Project 4-4

Eller Software Services has received contract revenue information in a text file. You import, sort, and filter the data. You also create a *PivotTable,* prepare a worksheet with subtotals, and format related data as an Excel table.

[Student Learning Outcomes 4.1, 4.3, 4.4, 4.5, 4.6, 4.8]

Files Needed: ***EllerSoftware-04.xlsx*** and ***EllerSoftwareText-04.txt*** *(Student data files are available in the Library of your SIMnet account.)*
Completed Project File Name: *[your initials] Excel 4-4.xlsx*

Skills Covered in This Project

- Import a text file.
- Use *AutoFilters.*
- Sort data by multiple columns.
- Create a *PivotTable.*

- Format fields in a *PivotTable.*
- Use the *Subtotal* command.
- Format data in an Excel table.
- Sort data in an Excel table.

1. Open the ***EllerSoftware-04*** workbook from your student data files and save it as [your initials] Excel 4-4.

2. Import the ***EllerSoftwareText-04.txt*** file from your student data files and load it to begin in cell **A4**. The text file is tab-delimited.

3. Format the values in column **H** as **Currency** with zero decimal places.

4. Click cell **G4** and use the *AutoFilter* arrow to sort by date oldest to newest.

5. Click cell **F4** and use the *AutoFilter* arrow to sort by product/service name in ascending order.

6. Filter the *Date* column to show only contracts for **September** using the **All Dates in the Period** option.

7. Edit the label in cell **A2** to display Contract Amounts for September.

8. Select cells **A1:H2** and press **Ctrl+1** to open the *Format Cells* dialog box. On the *Alignment* tab, choose **Center Across Selection**.

9. Change the font size for cells **A1:H2** to **20 pt**. (Figure 4-102) and close the *Queries & Connections* pane.

Figure 4-102 Imported data sorted and filtered

10. Copy the **Contracts** sheet to the end and name the copy Data.

11. Clear the date filter.

12. Select cell **A5** and click the **PivotTable** button [*Insert* tab, *Tables* group]. The range is identified as the *EllerSoftwareText* file.

13. Verify that **New Worksheet** is selected, deselect the **Add this data to the Data Model** button, and click **OK**.

14. Name the sheet PivotTable.

15. Show the **Product/Service** and **Contract** fields in the *PivotTable*.

16. Drag the **Contract** field from the *Choose fields to add to report* area below the **Sum of Contract** field in the *Values* area so that it appears twice in the report layout and the pane (Figure 4-103).

Figure 4-103 "Contract" field appears twice in the report

17. Select cell **C4** and click the **Field Settings** button [*PivotTable Tools Analyze* tab, *Active Field* group]. Type Average Contract as the *Custom Name*, choose **Average** as the calculation, and set the *Number Format* to **Currency** with zero decimal places.

18. Select cell **B4** and set its *Custom Name* to Total Contracts and the number format to **Currency** with zero decimal places.

19. Apply **Brown, Pivot Style Dark 3**.

20. Select the **Data** sheet tab and copy cells **A1:A2**. Paste them in cell **A1** on the **PivotTable** sheet.

21. Select **Align Left** for cells **A1:A2** and **16 pt**. as the font size. Edit the label in cell **A2** to display Contract Amounts, September through December (Figure 4-104).

22. Copy the **Data** sheet to the end and name the copy Subtotals.

23. Select cell **D5** and sort by **City** in **A to Z** order.

24. Select cell **A5** and convert the table to a range. Select cells **A5:H31** and apply **No Fill** [*Home* tab, *Font* group].

25. Use the *Subtotal* command to show a **SUM** for the contract amounts for each city.

26. Edit the label in cell **A2** to display Contract Amounts by City.

27. Format the sheet to **Landscape** orientation, center the page horizontally, and scale it to fit one page.

28. Click the **Billable Hours** sheet tab and select cell **A4**.

29. Click the **Format as Table** button [*Home* tab, *Styles* group], use **Orange, Table Style Medium 10**, and remove the data connections.

30. Type 5% Add On in cell **E4** and press **Enter**.

31. Build a formula in cell **E5** to multiply cell **D5** by **105%** and press **Enter** to copy the formula.

32. Select cells **A1:A2** and left align them. Then select cells **A1:E2**, click the **Launcher** for the *Alignment* group [*Home* tab], and select **Center Across Selection** from the *Horizontal* list.

33. Use the *AutoFilter* arrows to sort by date in oldest to newest order.

34. Save and close the workbook (Figure 4-105).

	A	B	C
1	Eller Software Services		
2	Contract Amounts, September through December		
3	Row Labels	Total Contracts	Average Contract
4	Accounting Software	$22,150	$3,692
5	ERP: Enterprise Resource Planning	$37,000	$12,333
6	POS: Point of Sale Software	$34,225	$5,704
7	Technical	$1,400	$1,400
8	Technical Support	$4,290	$858
9	Training	$7,300	$1,217
10	Grand Total	$106,365	$3,939
11			

Figure 4-104 Completed *PivotTable*

Eller Software Services
Billable Hours

Client Name	Product/Service	Date	Billable	5% Add On
Robert Gneiss	ERP: Enterprise Resource Planning	9/1/2019	6.00	6.3
Glenn Ladewig	Accounting Software	9/1/2019	5.00	5.25
Karen Talon	Accounting Software	9/1/2019	3.50	3.675
Charlie Lindberg	ERP: Enterprise Resource Planning	9/1/2019	4.00	4.2
Shelly Vicko	Accounting Software	9/15/2019	5.00	5.25
Arnold Robert	Accounting Software	9/15/2019	5.00	5.25
Karen Talon	Accounting Software	10/1/2019	5.50	5.775
Craig Brand	Technical Support	10/1/2019	8.00	8.4
Arthur Weston	Technical Support	10/1/2019	3.00	3.15
Richard Malinowski	Technical Support	10/1/2019	4.50	4.725
Elizabeth Jones	Technical Support	10/1/2019	3.50	3.675
Heather Guyan	Training	10/7/2019	3.25	3.4125
Terri Olander	POS: Point of Sale Software	10/15/2019	6.50	6.825
Paula Valentine	Training	10/15/2019	4.00	4.2
Paula Valentine	Training	10/15/2019	4.00	4.2
Mike Gunderson	Technical Support	10/28/2019	4.75	4.9875
Jeremie Midboe	POS: Point of Sale Software	11/1/2019	3.50	3.675
Susan Charlotte	ERP: Enterprise Resource Planning	11/1/2019	6.00	6.3
Wade Whitworth	Accounting Software	11/14/2019	5.00	5.25
Paula Valentine	Training	11/15/2019	4.00	4.2
Hilary Marschke	Training	11/15/2019	5.00	5.25
Christine Barton	POS: Point of Sale Software	11/15/2019	4.00	4.2
Hilary Marschke	Training	11/15/2019	5.00	5.25
Christine Barton	POS: Point of Sale Software	11/15/2019	2.00	2.1
Juan Garcia	Training	11/15/2019	4.00	4.2
Shelly Vicko	Accounting Software	11/16/2019	5.00	5.25
Thomas Larson	Training	12/5/2019	5.00	5.25
Michelle Cronin	POS: Point of Sale Software	12/15/2019	4.00	4.2
Michelle Cronin	POS: Point of Sale Software	12/15/2019	4.00	4.2
Amir Atef	Training	12/15/2019	4.00	4.2
Martin Green	Accounting Software	12/15/2019	5.00	5.25
Patricia Glunz	POS: Point of Sale Software	12/15/2019	3.25	3.4125
Mike Gunderson	Technical Support	12/18/2019	4.50	4.725
Richard Malinowski	Technical Support	1/5/2020	3.00	3.15
Robert Lawlor	Technical Support	1/8/2020	2.75	2.8875
Wade Whitworth	Accounting Software	2/2/2020	6.00	6.3
Heather Guyan	Training	2/3/2020	4.50	4.725
Robert Gneiss	ERP: Enterprise Resource Planning	2/5/2020	7.00	7.35
Susan Charlotte	ERP: Enterprise Resource Planning	3/5/2020	8.00	8.4
Martin Green	Accounting Software	3/7/2020	4.00	4.2
Hilary Marschke	Training	3/8/2020	5.00	5.25
Jerri Salzman	POS: Point of Sale Software	3/9/2020	4.50	4.725
Thomas Larson	Training	3/18/2020	4.00	4.2
Paula Valentine	Training	4/5/2020	4.00	4.2
Charlie Lindberg	ERP: Enterprise Resource Planning	4/5/2020	6.00	6.3
Arthur Weston	Technical Support	5/5/2020	6.00	6.3
Wade Whitworth	Accounting Software	5/17/2020	5.00	5.25

Eller Software Services
Contract Amounts by City

Client Name	Address	Phone Number	City	Zip	Product/Service	Date	Contract
Martin Green	127 Oak Street	218-555-2353	Bemidji	56601	Accounting Software	12/15/2019	$950
Mike Gundeson	304 Irvine Avenue	218-555-9021	Bemidji	56601	Technical Support	10/28/2019	$990
Heather Guyan	134 East Street	218-555-2313	Bemidji	56601	Training	10/7/2019	$1,500
Paula Valentine	127 Oak Street	218-555-2313	Bemidji	56601	Training	10/15/2019	$950
			Bemidji Total				**$4,390**
Jerri Salzman	800 Lake Avenue	218-555-8927	Brainerd	56401	POS: Point of Sale Software	9/15/2019	$7,000
Terri Olander	459 10th Avenue	218-555-8977	Brainerd	56401	POS: Point of Sale Software	10/15/2019	$6,525
Christine Barton	902 Clinton Street	218-555-8977	Brainerd	56401	POS: Point of Sale Software	11/15/2019	$5,500
Michelle Cronin	800 Lake Avenue	218-555-8977	Brainerd	56401	POS: Point of Sale Software	12/15/2019	$4,500
Patricia Glunz	902 Gunter Street	218-555-8900	Brainerd	56401	POS: Point of Sale Software	12/15/2019	$3,200
			Brainerd Total				**$26,725**
Glenn Ladewig	1600 Highway 2	218-555-4211	Cass Lake	56633	Accounting Software	9/1/2019	$4,500
Karen Talon	1600 Highway 2	218-555-4287	Cass Lake	56633	Accounting Software	9/1/2019	$4,000
Wade Whitworth	1822 Highway 2	218-555-4211	Cass Lake	56633	Accounting Software	9/2/2019	$5,000
Thomas Larson	1044 Highway 2	218-555-1234	Cass Lake	56633	Training	10/15/2019	$2,500
			Cass Lake Total				**$16,200**
Shelly Vicko	402 2nd Avenue SE	218-555-3456	Deer River	56636	Accounting Software	9/15/2019	$4,500
Arnold Robert	500 2nd Avenue SW	218-555-3456	Deer River	56636	Accounting Software	9/15/2019	$3,000
			Deer River Total				**$7,500**
Jeremie Midboe	Pilot Knob Road	651-555-2789	Eagan	55121	POS: Point of Sale Software	11/1/2019	$7,500
			Eagan Total				**$7,500**
Charlie Lindberg	345 Lyndale Avenue	612-555-2156	Minneapolis	55401	ERP: Enterprise Resource Planning	9/1/2019	$12,000
Robert Gneiss	245 Western Avenue	612-555-2356	Minneapolis	55401	ERP: Enterprise Resource Planning	9/1/2019	$10,000
Susan Charlotte	507 Lyndale Avenue	612-555-2177	Minneapolis	55401	ERP: Enterprise Resource Planning	11/1/2019	$15,000
Robert Lawlor	245 West 3rd Avenue	612-555-2376	Minneapolis	55401	Technical	9/1/2019	$1,400
			Minneapolis Total				**$38,400**
Craig Brand	554 2nd Street	320-555-4433	Saint Cloud	56301	Technical Support	10/1/2019	$1,050
Arthur Weston	554 3rd Street	320-555-4433	Saint Cloud	56301	Technical Support	10/1/2019	$750
Richard Malinowski	309 Fifth Street	320-555-4433	Saint Cloud	56301	Technical Support	10/1/2019	$750
Elizabeth Jones	450 Fifth Street	320-555-4422	Saint Cloud	56301	Technical Support	10/1/2019	$750
Hilary Marschke	245 West 3rd Avenue	320-555-5443	Saint Cloud	56301	Training	11/15/2019	$750
Juan Garcia	400 South Avenue	320-555-5448	Saint Cloud	56301	Training	11/15/2019	$800
Amir Atef	300 South Avenue	320-555-5443	Saint Cloud	56301	Training	12/15/2019	$800
			Saint Cloud Total				**$5,650**
			Grand Total				**$106,365**

Figure 4-105 Excel 4-4 completed

Independent Project 4-5

Boyd Air is monitoring flight arrival status, as well as capacities. Before formatting the data as an Excel table, you will export it as a text file for use in the reservation software. You will filter the data in the table, build a *PivotTable,* and create a *PivotChart.*
[Student Learning Outcomes 4.1, 4.2, 4.3, 4.4, 4.7, 4.8]

File Needed: **BoydAir-04.xlsx** *(Student data files are available in the* Library *of your SIMnet account.)*
Completed Project File Names: *[your initials]* **Excel 4-5.xlsx** and *[your initials]* **Excel 4-5Export.txt**

Skills Covered in This Project

- Export data as a text file.
- Format data as an Excel table.
- Use a number filter in a table.

- Set conditional formatting with an icon set.
- Filter data by cell icon.
- Create and format a *PivotTable.*
- Create and format a *PivotChart.*

1. Open the **BoydAir-04** workbook from your student data files and save it as [your initials] Excel 4-5.

2. Export the data to a tab-delimited text file named *[your initials]* **Excel 4-5Export** in your usual location for saving work. The sheet is renamed after the data are exported.

3. Rename the sheet tab Stats.

4. Use the *Save As* command to save and replace *[your initials] Excel 4-5* as an **Excel Workbook**.

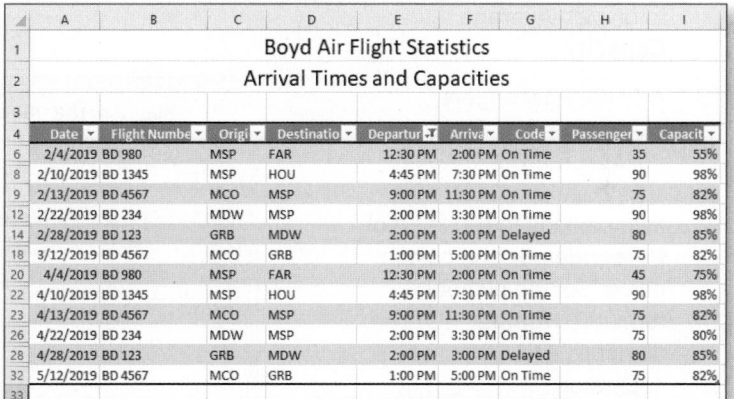

Figure 4-106 Filter results for *Departure Time* field

5. Select cell **A4** and format the data as an Excel table using **Green, Table Style Medium 21**.

6. Copy the **Stats** sheet to the end and name the copy PM Flights.

7. Select the **PM Flights** sheet, and use a *Greater Than* filter to display flights with a departure time after 12:00 PM (Figure 4-106).

8. Select the **Stats** worksheet, select cells **I5:I32**, and set conditional formatting to use **3 Flags** from the *Icon Sets*.

9. Build a two-level *Custom Sort* for the *Capacity* column to sort by icon. Show the green flag at the top, followed by the yellow flag. The red flag will default to the bottom (Figure 4-107).

Figure 4-107 Custom sort for the *3 Flags* icon set

10. Select the **Stats** worksheet, select cells **A4:I32**, and use the *Quick Analysis* tool to create a *PivotTable* to display average of capacity by origin (Figure 4-108).

11. Rename the sheet PivotTable&Chart.

12. Select cell **B3** in the *PivotTable* and use **Field Settings** to set a **Number Format** of **Percentage** with two decimal places. Edit the *Custom Name* to display **Average Capacity**.

13. Add the **Passengers** field to the *PivotTable Values* area with a sum calculation. Edit the field settings to display **# of Passengers** as the custom name. Set the number format to **Number** with zero decimals and a thousand's separator.

14. Use **White, Pivot Style Light 8** for the *PivotTable* and show banded rows and columns.

15. Add a **3-D Pie PivotChart** to the sheet and position the chart object to start in cell **E3**. Size the chart to reach cell **N22**.

16. Select the legend in the chart and change the font size to **11** from the *Home* tab.

17. Show **Data Labels** on the chart positioned at the **Inside End**. Select a data label and format all labels from the *Home* tab as **bold** and **10 pt**.

18. Select cell **A1** and save and close the workbook (Figure 4-109).

Figure 4-108 *PivotTable* suggestions from the *Quick Analysis* tool

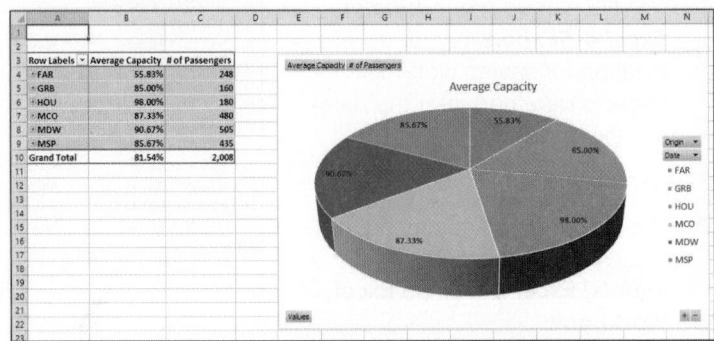

Figure 4-109 Excel 4-5 completed

Independent Project 4-6

Life's Animal Shelter has a list of suppliers in a worksheet to be copied to Word. You will also build an advanced filter to show suppliers for specific product categories and define groups based on supplier name. Your final task is to create an Excel table for sorting and filtering.
[Student Learning Outcomes 4.1, 4.3, 4.4, 4.5, 4.7]

File Needed: **LAShelter-04.xlsx** *(Student data files are available in the* Library *of your SIMnet account.)*
Completed Project File Names: *[your initials] Excel 4-6.xlsx* and *[your initials] Excel 4-6Word.docx*

Skills Covered in This Project

- Copy Excel data to Word.
- Create an advanced filter.
- Use *Flash Fill* to complete a column.

- Format data as a table.
- Filter data.
- Define groups in a worksheet.

1. Open the **LAShelter-04** workbook from your student data files and save it as [your initials] Excel 4-6.

2. Select the **LAS Suppliers** sheet, select cells **A4:D32**, and copy them to the Windows *Clipboard*.

3. Open Word and create a new document.

4. Paste the data into Word with the **Use Destination Styles** option (Figure 4-110).

5. Save the Word document as [your initials] Excel 4-6Word.docx.

6. Close the Word document and exit Word.

7. Press **Esc** to remove the moving border, and click the **Criteria** sheet tab.

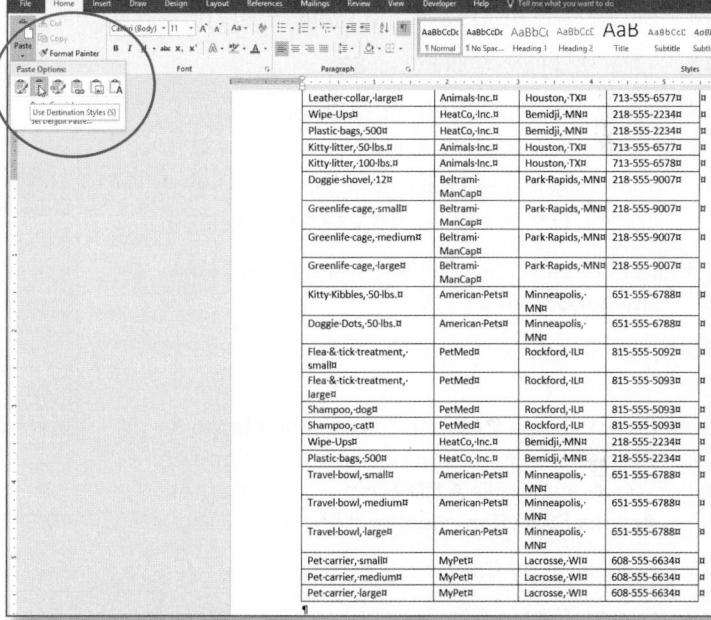

Figure 4-110 Word *Paste Options* for Excel data

8. Type *cage* in cell **A2** and type *carrier* in cell **A3**. This is *OR* criteria that will find products that include either the word "cage" or the word "carrier."

9. Select the **LAS Suppliers** sheet and format the labels in row **4** as **bold** and **centered** to distinguish the header row from other data.

10. Click cell **A5** on the **LAS Suppliers** sheet.

11. Build an advanced filter that uses the data on the **LAS Suppliers** sheet, the criteria range on the **Criteria** sheet, and cells **F6:G6** as the output range. In the *Advanced Filter* dialog box, select the **Unique records only** box (Figure 4-111).

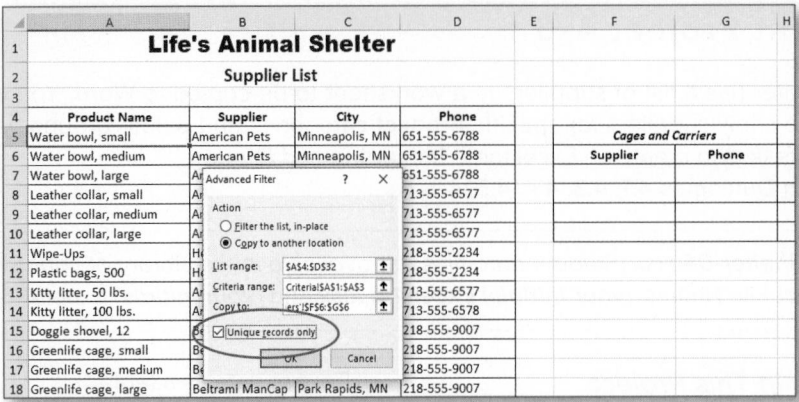

Figure 4-111 Advanced filter to select unique records

12. Replace the criteria on the **Criteria** sheet with *bowl* and *collar* to build a second advanced filter and show the filtered results where indicated on the **LAS Suppliers** sheet.

13. Select cells **A4:D32** on the **LAS Suppliers** sheet and copy them to cell **A4** on the **Table** sheet. Remove all borders.

14. Select cells **A5:D32** on the **Table** sheet and sort the data by product name in ascending order.

15. Type (651) 555-6788 in cell **E5**.

16. Type (2 in cell **E6** and press **Enter** when the *Flash Fill* suggestion appears.

17. Type Phone in cell **E4** and delete column **D**. Set column **D** to a width of **15.71 (115 pixels)**.

18. Format the data as a table using **Blue, Table Style Medium 2**.

19. Filter the data to show the suppliers located in Minnesota.

20. Select cells **A1:A2** and remove the **Merge & Center** command. Set both cells to **Align Left**. Then select cells **A1:D2** and use the **Center Across Selection** command (Figure 4-112).

21. Select the **By City** worksheet tab.

22. Sort by **City** in **A to Z** order.

23. Insert a row at row **5** and type Bemidji in cell **A5**. Left align the label.

24. Insert a row at row **10** and type Houston in cell **A10. Bold** the label.

25. Insert blank rows and type labels for the remaining cities.

26. Select the row headings for rows **6:9** and click the **Group** button [*Data* tab, *Outline* group]. Do not include the row with the city name in the group.

27. Repeat the command to group the rows for each city (Figure 4-113).

Figure 4-112 Completed table

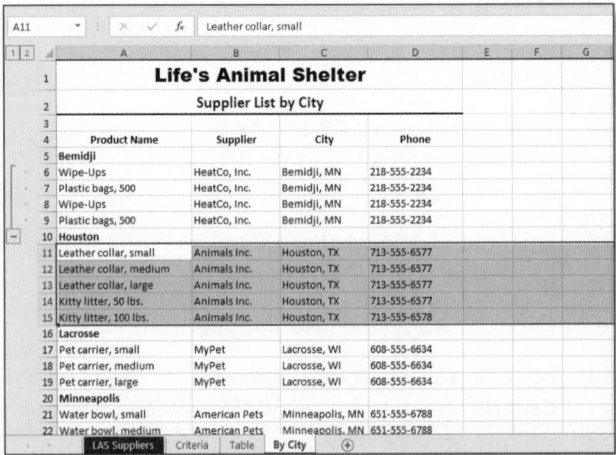

Figure 4-113 Data manually defined in groups

28. Select and delete column **C**.

29. Collapse the *Houston* and *Minneapolis* groups (Figure 4-114).

Figure 4-114 Excel 4-6 completed

30. Save and close the workbook.

Improve It Project 4-7

Placer Hills Real Estate wants its latest *PivotTable* to show sales by agent listing. In the source data, you highlight certain listings for insurance purposes. In a separate table, you create a calculation column to determine the number of market days.
[Student Learning Outcomes 4.1, 4.2, 4.8]

File Needed: ***PlacerHills-04.xlsx*** *(Student data files are available in the* Library *of your SIMnet account.)*
Completed Project File Name: ***[your initials] Excel 4-7.xlsx***

Skills Covered in This Project

- Pivot fields in a *PivotTable*.
- Format fields in a *PivotTable*.
- Add a field to a table.
- Set conditional formatting with a formula.

1. Open the ***PlacerHills-04*** workbook from your student data files and save it as [your initials] Excel 4-7.

2. Select the **Listings** sheet and use a conditional formatting formula for cells **A5:A26**. The formula is **=k5 = "frame"** to determine if the construction is frame. Set the format to use light blue fill from the second row, fourth column in the *Background Colors* (*Fill* tab in the *Format Cells* dialog box.).

3. Select the **PivotTable** sheet, deselect the **City** field in the *PivotTable Fields* pane, and drag the **Agent ID** field from the *Columns* area to the *Rows* area.

4. Drag the **Sale Price** field into the *Values* area so that it is shown twice in the *PivotTable*.

5. Format the first occurrence of the **Sale Price** field to show a sum with **Currency** format, zero decimals, and a custom name of Total Sales. Format the second occurrence to show an average with the same **Currency** format and the name Average Sale.

6. Apply **Light Gray, Pivot Style Light 15**.

7. Select cells **A3:C9** in the *PivotTable*. Click the **Border** button [*Home* tab, *Font* group] and apply **All Borders**. Select cell **A1**.

8. Select the **Table** sheet tab.

9. Type Days in cell **O4**. In cell **O5**, build an *IF* formula to display the number of days on the market. The *logical_test* determines if the sale date is greater than the list date. The *value_if_true* argument is the sale date minus the list date. For the *value_if_false* argument, press the **spacebar** once in the entry box in the *Function Arguments* dialog box; Excel displays the space within quotation marks " " in the completed formula. This inserts a space in the cell when no sale date is available. (If you type the formula, enclose a space in quotation marks for the *value_if_false* argument.)

10. Select cell **A4** on the **Table** sheet tab and click the **PivotTable** button [*Insert* tab, *Tables* group]. Verify that the highlighted cell range is *Table1* and that the *PivotTable* will be placed in a new worksheet. Deselect the **Add this data to the Data Model** box near the bottom of the dialog box. (If you select this box, you will not be able to create a calculated field in step 13.) Name the sheet PivotTable 2.

11. Place the **Listing ID** field in the *Rows* area and the **List Price** and **Sale Price** fields in the *Values* area. Format the values as **Currency** with no decimals.

12. Edit the labels in row 3 to Listing, List, Sale.

13. Insert a calculated field named Difference and build a formula that subtracts the sale price from the list price. Change the display label in the *PivotTable* for the calculated field to Variance and *AutoFit* the column.

14. Select all the cells in the *PivotTable* and apply **All Borders**.

15. Save and close the workbook (Figure 4-115).

Placer Hills Real Estate
Agent Listings

Listing ID	Listed	Agent ID	List Price	Address	City	Sq Ft	Beds	Baths	Garage	Construction	Year Built	Sale Date	Sale Price
10025	5/30/2019	160	$255,000	3420 Milburn Street	Rocklin	1900	4	3	3 Car Attached	Frame	2001	6/22/2019	$228,900
10027	6/4/2019	127	$335,000	2128 Wedgewood	Roseville	1184	3	2	1 Car Detached	Stone	1999	7/10/2019	$345,000
10033	6/9/2019	103	$334,500	4336 Newland Heights Drive	Rocklin	1840	2	2	2 Car Detached	Frame	1999	10/13/2019	$327,000
10042	6/22/2019	168	$385,000	131 Aeolia Drive	Auburn	1905	3	2	2 Car Detached	Brick	1965	9/15/2019	$385,000
10045	6/23/2019	168	$274,500	12355 Krista Lane	Auburn	2234	3	3	2 Car Attached	Brick	1984	8/17/2019	$260,000
10052	7/16/2019	103	$227,000	1096 Kinnerly Lane	Lincoln	1948	3	3	3 Car Attached	Brick	1995	10/1/2019	$238,000
10054	7/16/2019	168	$297,000	272 Lariat Loop	Lincoln	1571	2	1	2 Car Attached	Stone	2002	9/16/2019	$265,900
10069	7/24/2019	151	$239,600	1255 Copperdale	Auburn	1456	3	2	2 Car Detached	Frame	1995	8/30/2019	$237,000
10172	9/23/2019	160	$329,000	324 Center Point	Roseville	1480	2	2	3 Car Detached	Frame	1991	11/1/2019	$319,000
10177	10/5/2019	160	$326,500	411 Marion Street	Auburn	1950	3	2	2 Car Attached	Stone	2001	12/5/2019	$315,000
10180	10/8/2019	151	$425,999	17523 Oleander	Sacramento	2100	3	3	2 Car Attached	Brick	2000	12/15/2019	$415,000
10183	10/11/2019	168	$525,000	1044 Lake Street	Elk Grove	1755	2	2	1 Car Detached	Frame	2012	12/28/2019	$505,500
10186	10/14/2019	103	$345,000	15802 Centennial	Davis	1950	3	2	2 Car Detached	Stone	1998	1/4/2020	$340,000
10189	10/17/2019	127	$589,000	14313 Clearview	Sacramento	2200	3	3	3 Car Attached	Brick	2000		
10192	10/20/2019	103	$489,000	12222 South Ann Street	Elk Grove	2100	3	3	2 Car Detached	Frame	2000	1/24/2020	$425,000
10195	10/23/2019	168	$319,000	2330 West 120 Street	Davis	1700	2	2	1 Car Attached	Stone	1992	2/3/2020	$310,000
10198	10/26/2019	127	$439,000	7240 Westbrook Drive	Sacramento	1900	3	2	2 Car Attached	Brick	2001		
10201	10/29/2019	103	$505,000	419 Harlem Avenue	Elk Grove	2000	3	3	2 Car Attached	Brick	2002	2/23/2020	$500,000
10204	11/1/2019	151	$312,000	9023 Evergreen Lane	Davis	1850	3	2	2 Car Attached	Stone	2003		
10207	11/4/2019	151	$489,000	4230 Madison Street	Sacramento	1900	2	2	2 Car Attached	Brick	2005	3/15/2020	$475,000
10210	11/7/2019	160	$499,000	1330 Harrison Street	Elk Grove	2100	3	3	3 Car Attached	Frame	1990	3/25/2020	$465,000
10213	11/10/2019	160	$299,000	401 Lombard Avenue	Davis	1650	2	2	1 Car Attached	Frame	1995		

Placer Hills Real Estate
Sales by Agent Listing

Row Labels	Total Sales	Average Sale
103	$1,830,000	$366,000
127	$345,000	$345,000
151	$1,127,000	$375,667
160	$1,327,900	$331,975
168	$1,726,400	$345,280
Grand Total	$6,356,300	$353,128

	A	B	C	D
1				
2				
3	Listing	List	Sales	Variance
4	10025	$255,000	$228,900	$26,100
5	10027	$335,000	$345,000	-$10,000
6	10033	$334,500	$327,000	$7,500
7	10042	$385,000	$385,000	$0
8	10045	$274,500	$260,000	$14,500
9	10052	$227,000	$238,000	-$11,000
10	10054	$297,000	$265,900	$31,100
11	10069	$239,600	$237,000	$2,600
12	10172	$329,000	$319,000	$10,000
13	10177	$326,500	$315,000	$11,500
14	10180	$425,999	$415,000	$10,999
15	10183	$525,000	$505,500	$19,500
16	10186	$345,000	$340,000	$5,000
17	10189	$589,000		$589,000
18	10192	$489,000	$425,000	$64,000
19	10195	$319,000	$310,000	$9,000
20	10198	$439,000		$439,000
21	10201	$505,000	$500,000	$5,000
22	10204	$312,000		$312,000
23	10207	$489,000	$475,000	$14,000
24	10210	$499,000	$465,000	$34,000
25	10213	$299,000		$299,000
26	Grand Total	$8,239,099	$6,356,300	$1,882,799

Placer Hills Real Estate
Agent Listings

Listing ID	Listed	Agent ID	List Price	Address	City	Sq Ft	Beds	Baths	Garage	Construction	Year Built	Sale Date	Sale Price	Days
10025	5/30/2019	160	$255,000	3420 Milburn Street	Rocklin	1900		3	3 Car Attached	Frame	2001	6/22/2019	$228,900	23
10027	6/4/2019	127	$335,000	2128 Wedgewood	Roseville	1184	3	2	1 Car Detached	Stone	1999	7/10/2019	$345,000	36
10033	6/9/2019	103	$334,500	4336 Newland Heights Drive	Rocklin	1840	2	2	2 Car Attached	Frame	1999	10/13/2019	$327,000	126
10042	6/22/2019	168	$385,000	131 Aeolia Drive	Auburn	1905		2	2 Car Detached	Brick	1965	9/15/2019	$385,000	85
10045	6/23/2019	168	$274,500	12355 Krista Lane	Auburn	2234	3	3	2 Car Attached	Brick	1984	8/17/2019	$260,000	55
10052	7/16/2019	103	$227,000	1096 Kinnerly Lane	Lincoln	1948	3	3	3 Car Attached	Brick	1995	10/1/2019	$238,000	77
10054	7/16/2019	168	$297,000	272 Lariat Loop	Lincoln	1571	2	1	2 Car Attached	Stone	2002	9/16/2019	$265,900	62
10069	7/24/2019	151	$239,600	1255 Copperdale	Auburn	1456		2	2 Car Detached	Frame	1995	8/30/2019	$237,000	37
10172	9/23/2019	160	$329,000	324 Center Point	Roseville	1480	2	2	3 Car Detached	Frame	1991	11/1/2019	$319,000	39
10177	10/5/2019	160	$326,500	411 Marion Street	Auburn	1950	3	2	2 Car Attached	Stone	2001	12/5/2019	$315,000	61
10180	10/8/2019	151	$425,999	17523 Oleander	Sacramento	2100	3	2	2 Car Attached	Brick	2000	12/15/2019	$415,000	68
10183	10/11/2019	168	$525,000	1044 Lake Street	Elk Grove	1755	2	2	1 Car Detached	Frame	2012	12/28/2019	$505,500	78
10186	10/14/2019	103	$345,000	15802 Centennial	Davis	1950	3	2	2 Car Detached	Stone	1998	1/4/2020	$340,000	82
10189	10/17/2019	127	$589,000	14313 Clearview	Sacramento	2200	3	3	3 Car Attached	Brick	2000			
10192	10/20/2019	103	$489,000	12222 South Ann Street	Elk Grove	2100	3	3	2 Car Detached	Frame	2000	1/24/2020	$425,000	96
10195	10/23/2019	168	$319,000	2330 West 120 Street	Davis	1700	2	2	1 Car Attached	Stone	1992	2/3/2020	$310,000	103
10198	10/26/2019	127	$439,000	7240 Westbrook Drive	Sacramento	1900	3	2	2 Car Attached	Brick	2001			
10201	10/29/2019	103	$505,000	419 Harlem Avenue	Elk Grove	2000	3	3	2 Car Attached	Brick	2002	2/23/2020	$500,000	117
10204	11/1/2019	151	$312,000	9023 Evergreen Lane	Davis	1850	3	2	2 Car Attached	Stone	2003			
10207	11/4/2019	151	$489,000	4230 Madison Street	Sacramento	1900	2	2	2 Car Attached	Brick	2005	3/15/2020	$475,000	132
10210	11/7/2019	160	$499,000	1330 Harrison Street	Elk Grove	2100	3	3	3 Car Attached	Frame	1990	3/25/2020	$465,000	139
10213	11/10/2019	160	$299,000	401 Lombard Avenue	Davis	1650	2	2	1 Car Attached	Frame	1995			

Figure 4-115 Excel 4-7 completed

Challenge Project 4-8

For this project, you build a worksheet for a company that sells four varieties of socks in four eastern states. When the data are complete, format the data as an Excel table.
[Student Learning Outcomes 4.1, 4.2, 4.3]

File Needed: None
Completed Project File Name: *[your initials] Excel 4-8.xlsx*

Create a new workbook and save it as [your initials] Excel 4-8. Modify your workbook according to the following guidelines:

- Type the labels State, Month, Style, Pairs, and Price in cells **A4:E4**.
- Type Connecticut, Maine, New Hampshire, and Vermont in cells **A5:A8**.

- Type January in cell **B5**, and copy the month to cells **B6:B8**.
- Type the style name for one type of sock sold by the company in cell **C5**. Copy the name to cells **C6:C8**.
- Enter values for how many pairs were sold in each state in January in cells **D5:D8**. In column E, enter and copy a price for this sock style.
- Copy cells **A5:E8** and paste the range in cell **A9** to create a February group. Edit the month and the number of pairs sold.
- Copy cells **A5:E12** and paste the range in cell **A13** to create the data for another sock style. In this range, edit the style name, the number of pairs sold, and the price. The price is the same for all rows in this group.
- Copy and paste cells **A13:E20** to cell **A21** and then again to cell **A29** to complete two more ranges for two sock styles, so that you have January and February data for four sock styles for each state.
- Set conditional formatting to show one of the state names in a format different from the other states.
- Name the sheet Data and make a copy named Table. Clear the conditional formatting from the **Table** sheet.
- Select the **Table** sheet, and format the data as an Excel table with a light table style.
- Type Total in cell **F4** and create a formula to calculate the dollar amount of sales in the column. Show a total row for the table with results for the number of pairs and sales dollars.
- Add additional formatting to the table as needed.
- Use the *AutoFilter* arrows to sort by style and then by state.
- Enter a name for the company in cell **A1**. Enter a label in cell **A2** that describes the data.

Challenge Project 4-9

For this project, you explore the Bureau of Labor Statistics web site to download data for use in a worksheet. After you have arranged and formatted the data, you copy it to a Word document.
[Student Learning Outcomes 4.1, 4.2, 4.6, 4.7]

File Needed: None
Completed Project File Names: *[your initials] Excel 4-9.xlsx* and *[your initials] Excel 4-9Word.docx*

Create a new workbook and save it as [your initials] Excel 4-9. Modify your workbook according to the following guidelines:

- Go to www.bls.gov/data.
- Review the subject areas and choose one to explore. Find a topic and subtopic which provides an .xlsx file for download.
- Download or copy the data into your worksheet.
- Format the data as an Excel table (if it is not already formatted) or apply a different table style.
- Determine and apply conditional formatting for an aspect of the data.
- Determine and set a different sort order.
- Add a main title to your worksheet and set other format attributes to effectively display your information.
- Copy all or a logical portion of the data to a new Word document and save the Word document as [your initials] Excel 4-9Word.docx.

Challenge Project 4-10

For this project, you create a worksheet that lists names, birth dates, and hair color for 20 people. You format the list as a table for sorting and filtering. You convert the table to a range and use the *Subtotal* command.
[Student Learning Outcomes 4.1, 4.3, 4.4, 4.5]

File Needed: None
Completed Project File Name: *[your initials] Excel 4-10.xlsx*

Create a new workbook and save it as [your initials] Excel 4-10. Modify your workbook according to the following guidelines:

- Type your first name, your last name, your birthdate, and your hair color in a row using one column for each item.
- Type data for 19 more people, using fictitious or real data. Use birthdates that are the same year as yours, as well as four other years, so that your list has only five different years. Use at least three hair colors in your list, such as brown, blond, red.
- Format the data as a table and apply a table style.
- Sort the date by birthdate with the youngest people listed first. Then, filter the data to show only those records from the first year listed in the data.
- Make a copy of the sheet and convert the table to a normal range. Use the *Subtotal* command to count the number of persons with each hair color.

Source of screenshots Microsoft Office 365 (2019): Word, Excel, Access, Powerpoint.

Microsoft® Office

IN PRACTICE

access

©Chris Ryan/Getty Images

CHAPTER OVERVIEW

Microsoft Access (Access) is the leading PC-based database management system (DBMS) software in both the personal and business market. Access helps you organize and manage personal, business, and educational data in a structure known as a database. This software makes it easy for you to ensure your data are accurate, organized, and usable. This chapter covers the basics of working with a relational database and using the Access database management system.

STUDENT LEARNING OUTCOMES (SLOs)

After completing this chapter, you will be able to:

SLO 1.1 Explain data organization concepts, use the Access *Navigation Pane*, and identify objects (p. 3).

SLO 1.2 Create a database; set database properties; understand database object naming conventions and data types; create and manipulate database objects; and open, close, back up, and recover a database (p. 12).

SLO 1.3 Create a table in *Datasheet* view, edit the default primary key, add a new field, edit field and table properties, save a table, and enter records into a table (p. 21).

SLO 1.4 Import data records from Excel (p. 33).

SLO 1.5 Navigate table records in *Datasheet* view and customize a datasheet by modifying field order, row height, column width, field alignment, font style and size, row colors, and gridlines. Hide and unhide fields and add total rows (p. 35).

SLO 1.6 Search, sort, and filter records in a table (p. 46).

CASE STUDY

Throughout this book, you have the opportunity to put into practice the application features you are learning. Each chapter begins with a case study that introduces you to the Pause & Practice projects in the chapter. These Pause & Practice projects give you a chance to apply and practice key skills. Each chapter contains three to five Pause & Practice projects.

The first Pause & Practice is designed to orient you to using Access and enables you to explore the different parts of the Access interface and navigation mechanism. For this project, you open an existing database for the College of Sciences that tracks information about classes it offers. The remaining Pause & Practice projects are designed to help you learn how to build a database for Central Sierra Insurance. Central Sierra Insurance is a multi-office insurance company that handles all lines of commercial and personal insurance policies. Central Sierra regularly hires qualified personnel, and it needs to create an effective way to organize and manage the information

ACCESS

about its employees. Lanita McCartney has asked you to create a simple database containing information about its employees. This database is created as a blank database with one table. As you progress through the Pause & Practice projects, you incorporate many of the features you are learning in this chapter to construct and enhance this database.

Pause & Practice 1-1: Explore the tabs of the Access *Ribbon* and *Navigation Pane* in an existing database, and use *Datasheet* and *Design* views of a table.

Pause & Practice 1-2: Create a new blank database. Customize the table using *Datasheet*

View to edit the primary key, add new fields, save the table, reopen the table, edit field properties, and add employee records.

Pause & Practice 1-3: Import data into the table created in *Pause & Practice 1-2*. Modify the table and refine the datasheet layout by modifying the field order, row height, column width, and field alignment; selecting a display font and size; displaying gridlines; alternating row colors; hiding fields; and adding totals.

Pause & Practice 1-4: Use the employee table to search for data, sort the records on a single field and on multiple fields, and filter the records using single and multiple criteria.

SLO 1.1

Understanding Database Concepts

Organizations can generate a tremendous amount of data. Think about a few of the pieces of data captured by FedEx when you send a package or envelope: the sender's first and last name, sender's street address, sender's city, sender's state, sender's ZIP Code, recipient's first and last name, recipient's street address, recipient's city, recipient's state, recipient's ZIP Code, date sent, package weight, and type of service (for example, next-day air, ground service). Every day, FedEx delivers millions of packages and documents. This translates into millions of sender names, addresses, recipient names, addresses, and so forth, captured each day. To stay in business, FedEx must have an efficient and effective way to capture, process, and store these data to ensure that it delivers your package on time and to the right location.

Databases are used by many organizations to manage data. A ***database*** is an organized collection of integrated and related tables. A ***database management system (DBMS)*** is software that enables you to create a database; manage the data in the database by adding, deleting, and updating records; sort and retrieve data; and create queries and reports relating to that data. In this book, you learn about Microsoft Access, the leading PC-based DBMS software application.

Using a database management system, people can build applications to enable organizations to track orders and deliveries, manage retail sales and inventory, maintain employee payroll records, update patient data, and track student progress. Throughout this chapter, you learn more about these database concepts by using the Access DBMS to create a simple database.

Organize Data

Like the majority of the DBMSs available today, Access is a ***relational database***, which means that the data are organized into a collection of related tables. Each table stores data about one type, or grouping, of information represented in the system. For example, a database application used by a retail store contains a table with details about its customers, a table with details about the products it sells, and a table with details about the orders its customers have made for the various products. The different tables are related, or connected, to one another through common fields.

The first step in creating a database is to determine the best way to organize the required data. To do so, you need to understand the *hierarchy of data* used in relational databases. In Access, the hierarchy is organized from the smallest to the largest grouping of data. A *field* is a collection of characters that describes one aspect of a business object or activity—a single unit of data. A *record* is a collection of related data fields. A *table* is a collection of related records. Visually, you see the table containing rows and columns. Each row is the equivalent of a record. A row contains many different columns or fields. A *database* is a collection of related tables. An example of how this hierarchy works for a database that a university might use is shown in Table 1-1.

Table 1-1: Hierarchy of Data

Unit	Description	Examples
Field	A single unit of data	Date Enrolled, Student First Name, Student Last Name, Student ID
Record	A collection of related fields	All of the fields for one student stored together
Table	A collection of related records	A record for each of the students at the university stored together
Database	A collection of integrated and related tables	The collection of the student, faculty, and course tables for the entire university

How do you know how many tables you need or which fields belong in which tables? Often the database design plan is already completed for you, and you simply need to build the design. At this point, the simplest answer to the question about how many tables you need is this: Create a separate table for each major subject or grouping of information you will store in the database. Later, in *SLO 2.6: Understanding and Designing Relational Databases*, you will learn a more formal set of steps to create a well-designed database.

The Access Interface

The interface is how you interact with Access to create, modify, delete, and use different objects, or parts, of your database application. An open database should look similar to Figure 1-1. The *Ribbon* displays across the top of the window. Below the *Ribbon*, the window is divided into the *Navigation Pane* and the work area. The **Navigation Pane** lists each object in your database application. The work area uses a tabbed interface to display all objects that have been opened. In Figure 1-1, both the *Classes* table and the *InstructorInfo* form are open. The *Classes* table is active. Click a different tab to bring it to the top and make it the active object. The **Status** bar displays at the bottom and contains information about the current database or database object if one is open.

The *Ribbon* in Access contains five primary tabs: *File*, *Home*, *Create*, *External Data*, and *Database Tools*. Access also has several *contextual tabs* that become available to you when you are working on different tasks. The *Ribbon* provides the common Office functions, like copy, paste, and file management, but many of the *Ribbon* tabs are unique to Access. The *Ribbon* also contains the *Tell Me* help feature. You enter text in the *Tell Me* search box and Access displays command options that take you directly to the actions you want to perform.

 MORE INFO

Depending on configuration changes made to the Access program installed on your computer, you may see a sixth tab titled *Add-Ins*.

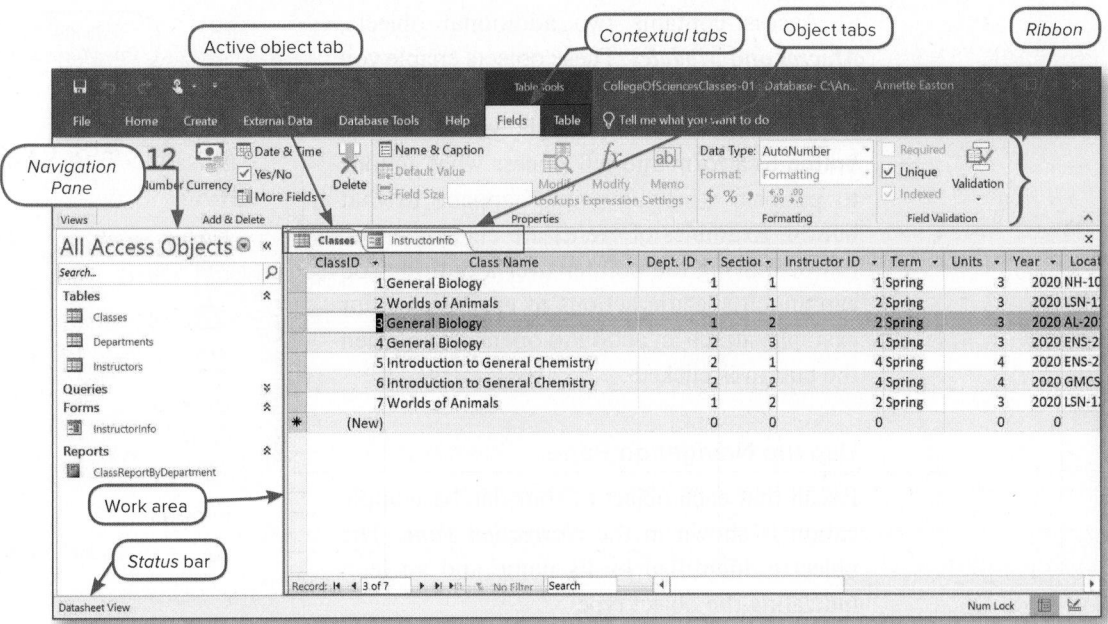

Figure 1-1 The Access Interface

Examine Access Objects

An Access database application typically contains many different components, such as tables and reports. In Access, these components are called *objects*. The major objects in Access are *tables*, *forms*, *reports*, and *queries*. At a minimum, your database must contain at least one table. These objects are described in Table 1-2.

Table 1-2: Major Access Objects

Object	Purpose	Additional Information	Navigation Pane Icon
Table	Stores data records	Once a table is created, you can begin entering data. Create a separate table for each type or grouping of information. When you view data in a table, it appears in a tabular format, very much like a spreadsheet.	
Form	Used to create an interface to view, add, update, and delete data in a table	Although you can do these tasks directly in a table, a form usually provides an easier way to interact with the data. Forms also enable you to view only one record at a time and to view fields from multiple tables at the same time.	
Query	Used to find data in your database	Queries enable you to specify criteria to locate specific records. Queries can also be used to perform actions such as updating or deleting records.	
Report	Used to view and print the data in your database	Reports enable you to create a formatted, and more professional, way to view and print the contents of your database.	

> **MORE INFO**
>
> Forms, queries, and reports provide different ways to interact with the data in your tables. As a result, they are related to the tables on which they are based.

Access contains two additional objects, **Macros** and **Modules**. These objects enable you to add functionality to the forms and reports in your database. For example, you can add a button to a form and tell Access what actions to perform when an event happens to that button. Examples of events are clicking a button or moving the pointer over a button. You can attach specific actions to each event. For example, attach an action to open a form when the button is clicked.

Use the Navigation Pane

Recall that each object in your database application is shown in the *Navigation Pane*. The object is identified by its name and an icon indicating the object type.

The top bar of the *Navigation Pane* contains the ***Shutter Bar Open/Close Button***, which

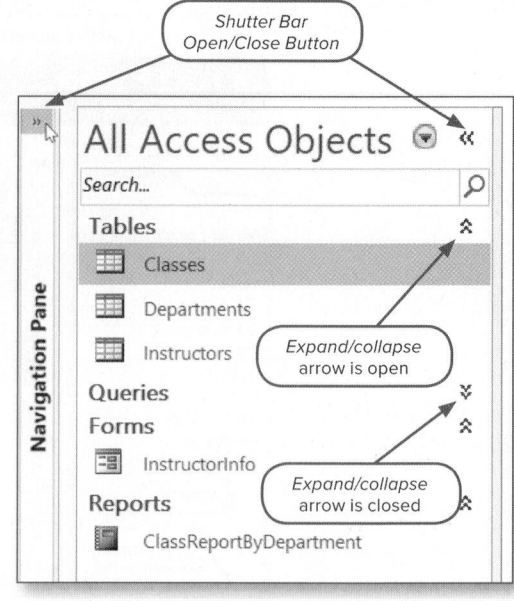

Figure 1-2 *Shutter Bar* of the *Navigation Pane*

opens and closes the pane. If the pane is closed, as shown on the left side of Figure 1-2, you will only see the phrase "Navigation Pane."

- Open the *Navigation Pane* by clicking the **Shutter Bar Open/Close Button**.
- The objects inside your database display, as shown on the right side of Figure 1-2.

> **ANOTHER WAY**
>
> **F11** opens and closes the *Navigation Pane*.

The *Navigation Pane* displays your objects in ***groups***, which you can expand and collapse. This is useful if you have many objects in your database and wish to narrow down those that are visible. Click the **expand/collapse** arrow to the right of the group name to change the current display. When a group is collapsed, like the *Queries* group in Figure 1-2, only the name of the group displays. The objects contained within that group do not display.

You can customize what displays in the *Navigation Pane* and the way objects are organized by using the ***Navigation menu*** (Figure 1-3).

The top half of the *Navigation* menu allows you to select a ***category***, the highest organizational level in the *Navigation Pane*. The standard categories are:

- **Custom**: Groups objects based on custom categories that you create
- **Object Type**: Groups objects on the basis of their type
- **Tables and Related Views**: Groups different objects according to the tables on which they are based
- **Created Date**: Groups objects on the basis of the week associated with the date they were created
- **Modified Date**: Groups objects on the basis of the week associated with the date they were last modified

The bottom half of the *Navigation* menu enables you to filter by a specific group within that category. Filtering enables you to limit

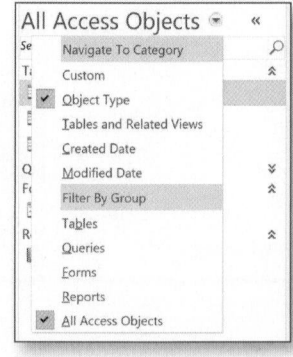

Figure 1-3 *Navigation* menu

the objects that display in the *Navigation Pane*. The choices in *Filter by Group* will change based on the selected category. The *Title* bar of the *Navigation Pane* shows the current filter selection.

The *Navigation Pane* in Figure 1-2 reflects the settings selected in Figure 1-3; it shows all objects grouped by the category of *Object Type* and the filter of *All Access Objects*. These are the default selections in the *Navigation* menu. Within a group, Access displays the objects in alphabetical order.

▶ **HOW TO:** Modify the Navigation Pane Category and Group Filter

1. Click the **Navigation Pane** arrow, shown in Figure 1-4, to open the *Navigation* menu.
2. Select the **desired category**.
 - The *Navigation* menu closes.
 - The *Navigation Pane* updates to display the objects based on your category selection.
3. Click the **Navigation Pane** arrow to open the *Navigation* menu.
4. Select the **desired filter selection**.
 - The *Navigation* menu closes.
 - The *Navigation Pane* updates to display the objects based on your filter selection.

Figure 1-4 Modify the *Navigation Pane*

You can adjust the width of the *Navigation Pane* as needed. Increase the width to see the complete text of longer object names. Decrease the width when you wish to have more space in the Access work area to display and edit objects.

▶ **HOW TO:** Modify the Navigation Pane Width

1. Place your pointer on the right border of the *Navigation Pane*. The resize pointer appears as a white two-pointed arrow (Figure 1-5).
2. Click, hold, and drag the resize pointer to increase or decrease the width of the *Navigation Pane*.
3. Release the resize pointer. The pane changes to the new width.

Figure 1-5 Resize the *Navigation Pane*

Use Datasheet and Design View of a Table

Because the *table* is the primary object of a database, it is useful to dig a little bit deeper into this object as you learn about the Access interface.

You can open tables directly from the *Navigation Pane*. Access provides two ways to open and view a table: *Datasheet* view and *Design* view.

- To open a table in ***Datasheet view***, double-click the table name in the *Navigation Pane*. Use *Datasheet* view to enter, modify, delete, or view the data records. You can also use *Datasheet* view to define or modify the structure of a table.
- To open a table in ***Design view***, right-click the table name in the *Navigation Pane* and select **Design View** from the context menu. *Design* view enables you to build or modify the basic

structure or functionality of an object. You see all the details, or properties, about the fields in your table in *Design* view.

Click to open the *View* menu

To switch between views of an open table, click the **View** button [*Home* tab, *Views* group] as shown in Figure 1-6 and select the desired view. The view option that is currently selected displays with a gray icon.

Figure 1-7 illustrates *Datasheet* view of a table. The name of the table displays in the tab at the top of the datasheet. Each row represents a record in the table and each column represents a field. The gray cell on the left of each row is the *record selector*. The record selector turns yellow when field(s) are selected on a particular row, indicating the active row. A rose-colored border surrounds the *active cell*. The active cell is the field where you enter or edit data. The last row in a table is the *append row*, identified with an asterisk in the record selector of that row. A new record is added to a table by entering the data in fields of the append row. The horizontal and vertical scroll sliders automatically display if the Access window is not wide enough or tall enough to display all of the rows and columns. Move the sliders to adjust what displays in the window. You may also see columns that display a series of # symbols. This occurs if the width of a column with numeric data is not large enough to display the entire contents.

Figure 1-6 *View* menu of a table

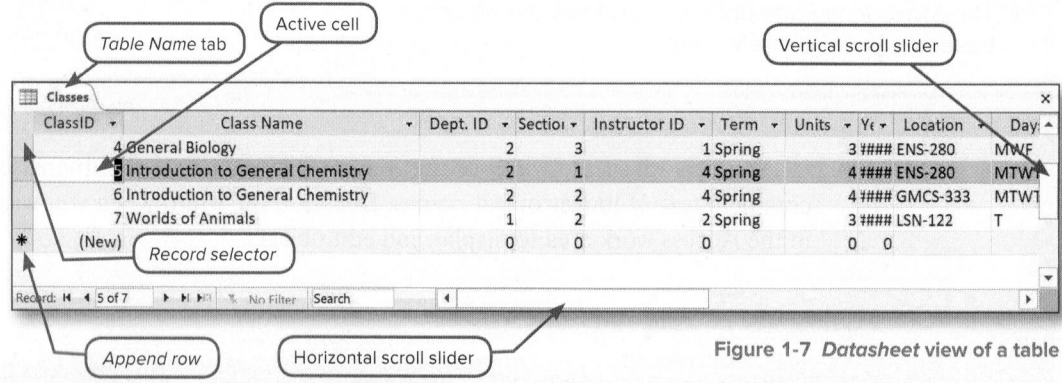

Figure 1-7 *Datasheet* view of a table

PAUSE & PRACTICE: ACCESS 1-1

For this project, you explore a database that tracks information about classes that are offered in the College of Sciences. This database contains three tables, one query, one form, and one report. You open the database, explore the Access *Ribbon*, explore the *Navigation Pane*, and work with *Datasheet* and *Design* views of a table.

File Needed: **CollegeOfSciencesClasses-01.accdb** *(Student data files are available in the Library of your SIMnet account.)*
Completed Project File Name: None

1. Open the database used by the College of Sciences.
 a. Double-click the **CollegeOfSciencesClasses-01** file in your student data files folder. This launches Access and opens the sample database application (Figure 1-8). The *Navigation Pane* opens and the *Home* tab is selected.

b. Click the **Enable Content** button in the *Security Warning* message bar if prompted.

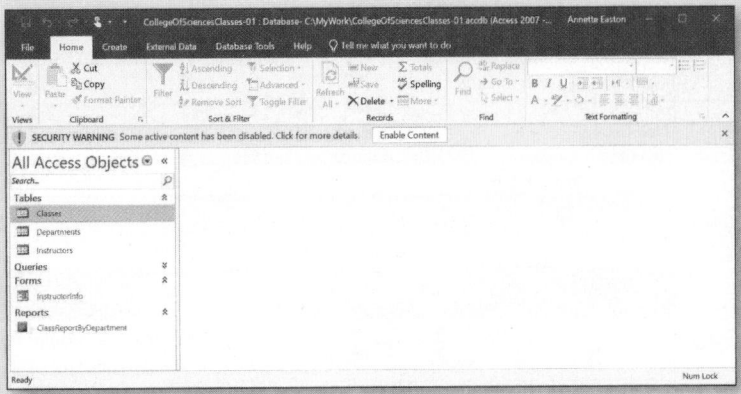

MORE INFO

Because viruses and worms may be transmitted in files, Microsoft warns you when you open a database file. If you trust the source of the file, enable the content so that you can use the database.

Figure 1-8 *CollegeOfSciencesClasses-01* database

2. Explore the Access *Ribbon*.
 a. Click the **File** tab to open the *Backstage* view (Figure 1-9). The *Backstage* view in Access provides file management capabilities to open, close, and save a database; create a new database; and print or publish a database.
 b. Click the arrow to return to the Access *Ribbon*.
 c. Click the **Home** tab. The *Home* tab (Figure 1-10) offers common Office functions, the ability to change the way you view an object, and searching and sorting functions. All icons are currently dimmed because no object is selected or open.

Click the arrow to return to the Access *Ribbon*

Figure 1-9 *Backstage* view

Figure 1-10 *Home* tab

d. Click the **Create** tab. The *Create* tab (Figure 1-11) contains tools to create all the objects you use in your database. The icons are grouped on the basis of the type of object you need to build.

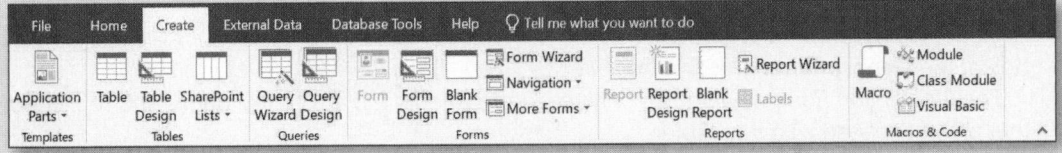

Figure 1-11 *Create* tab

e. Click the **External Data** tab. The *External Data* tab (Figure 1-12) provides functionality to link to other applications and data files. The icons are grouped based on the type of connectivity you need.

Figure 1-12 *External Data* tab

Figure 1-13 *Database Tools* tab

f. Click the **Database Tools** tab. The *Database Tools* tab (Figure 1-13) provides information about your database and additional functions to help you manage the database.

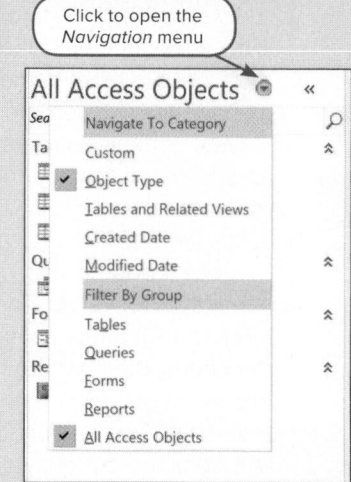

Figure 1-14 Explore the *Navigation Pane*

3. Explore the *Navigation Pane*.
 a. Click the **Navigation Pane** arrow to the right of *All Access Objects*. The *Navigation* menu displays on top of the *Navigation Pane* (Figure 1-14). This *Navigation Pane* displays objects by the *Object Type* category, and the filter is to show *All Access Objects*.
 b. Click anywhere outside the *Navigation* menu to close the menu.
 c. Click the **expand/collapse** arrow on the right edge of the *Tables* group (Figure 1-15). The *Tables* group collapses, leaving no table objects visible. The arrow changes to an expand arrow.
 d. Click the **expand/collapse** arrow in the *Tables* group to reopen the *Tables* group and display the three tables.
 e. Click the **Navigation Pane** arrow next to *All Access Objects*.
 f. Select the **Tables and Related Views** category.
 g. Click the **Navigation Pane** arrow again.
 h. Select **All Tables** in the *Filter By Group* area. The *Navigation Pane* updates and should look similar to Figure 1-16.
 This view shows each of the tables and all of the other objects that are associated with each table. For example, the report object named *ClassReportByDepartment* is associated with each of the three tables. However, the form object *InstructorInfo* is only associated with the *Instructors* table.
 i. Click the **Navigation Pane** arrow.
 j. Select the **Departments** group in the *Filter by Group*.
 The *Navigation Pane* now shows only the *Departments* table with the query and report objects that are associated with that table.
 k. Click the **Navigation Pane** arrow.
 l. Click the **Object Type** category. The *Navigation Pane* should have returned to show all of your objects by the *Object Type* category.

Figure 1-15 The *Tables* group

4. Explore *Datasheet* and *Design* views of a table.
 a. Double-click the **Classes** table to open the table in *Datasheet View*, as shown in Figure 1-17.

b. Press the **right arrow** key 10 times to navigate across the fields of the first record. You should stop at the *Time* field.

c. Press the **right arrow** key once more to navigate to the *Click to Add* column. *Datasheet View* allows you to add new fields into your table at the same time that you are looking at the data values.

d. Press the **right arrow** key once more to navigate to the *ClassID* of the second row.

e. Press the **down arrow** key five times to navigate down to *ClassID 7*, the last of the data records. If you were to navigate into the append row, identified by the asterisk in the record selector, you would be able to add a new class into the table by entering the data values.

Figure 1-16 *Tables and Related Views* category

Figure 1-17 *Datasheet View* of *Classes* table

f. Click the **record selector** of the first row. The entire row should be selected.

g. Click **View** [*Home* tab, *Views* group] to show the two possible table views (Figure 1-18) and then select **Design View**. Your screen should look similar to Figure 1-19. *Design* view shows you the details, or properties, of the different fields in your table.

h. Use the **scroll bar**, if necessary, to navigate down to see all the fields in the *Classes* table. Look for the last field, *Time*. You could add additional fields into the table by typing the name into the blank *Field Name* cell below *Time*.

i. Close the *Classes* table by clicking the **X** in the upper-right corner of the *Classes* table window.

j. Close the *CollegeOfSciencesClasses-01* database by clicking the **Close** button [*File* tab].

Figure 1-18 Two table views

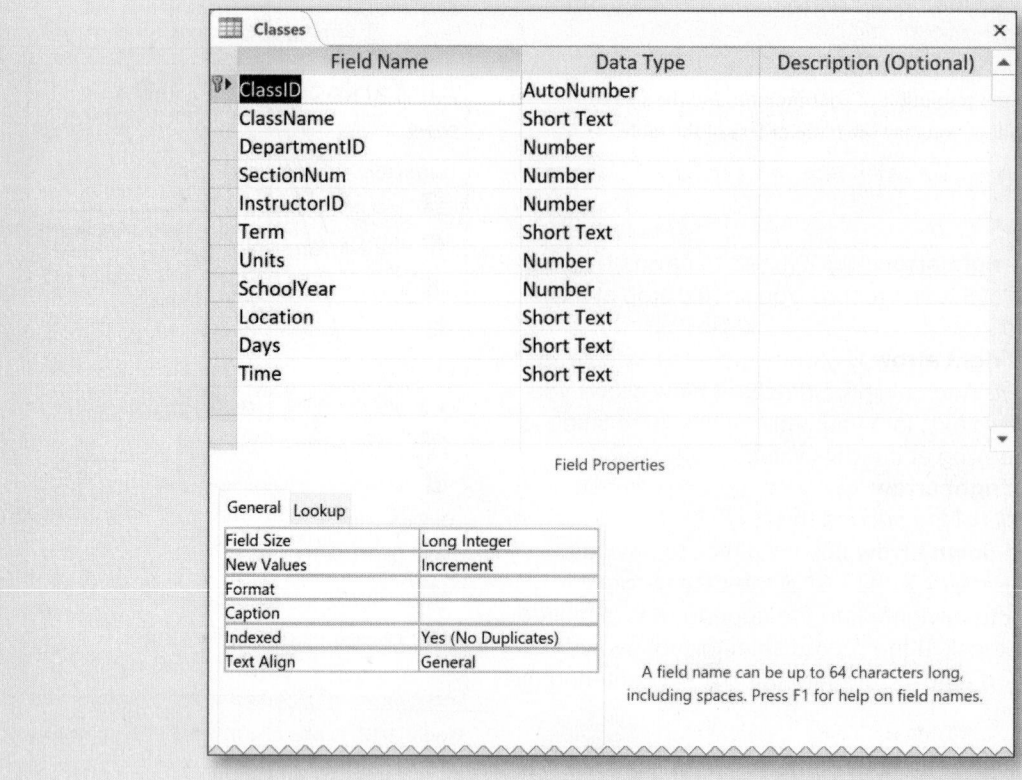

Figure 1-19 *Design* view of *Classes* table

Creating and Managing a Database

In Access, the database application file stores all of the separate objects that you create and use. The database file must be created before you can create and use any other objects. By default, the database file will be saved as a *.accdb* file. You can create a new database file by using a prebuilt template as a starting point or a blank database if you wish to start from scratch.

Templates

A *template* is a predesigned database that contains various pre-built objects. A template provides you with a complete, ready-to-use database application. After creating a database based on a template, use the new database directly or customize the database to better meet your needs. Templates are a great starting point if your needs are addressed in the template.

You can choose from several templates that are installed with Access. In addition, other templates are available at Office.com.

▶ **HOW TO: Create a New Database Using a Template**

1. Click the **File** tab to open the *Backstage* view if an Access database is already open.

 • If Access is closed, open Access. The *Start* page displays showing the *Recent* list on the left and thumbnails of sample templates on the right. In this case, skip to step 3.

2. Click the **New** button. The list of sample templates displays (Figure 1-20). The templates may display in a different order based on the most recently selected template.

3. Select the template you wish to use.

4. Type the file name for your database in the *File Name* box.

5. Click the **Browse for a location to put your database** button (Figure 1-21) to select the location on your computer or USB drive to save the database and click **OK**.

6. Click the **Create** button.

 • The new database opens.
 • A *Welcome* form may display based on the template selected. Click the **Get Started** button on the *Welcome* form.

7. Click the **Enable Content** button in the *Security Warning* message bar if prompted.

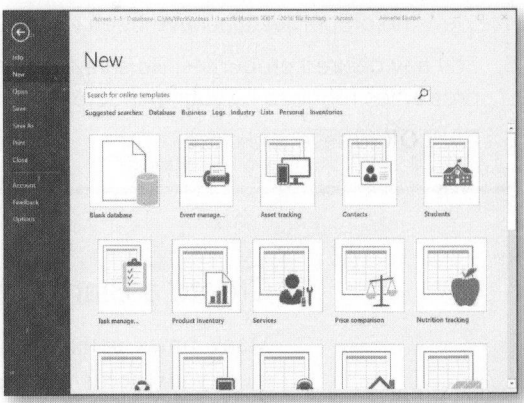

Figure 1-20 Create a new database from a template

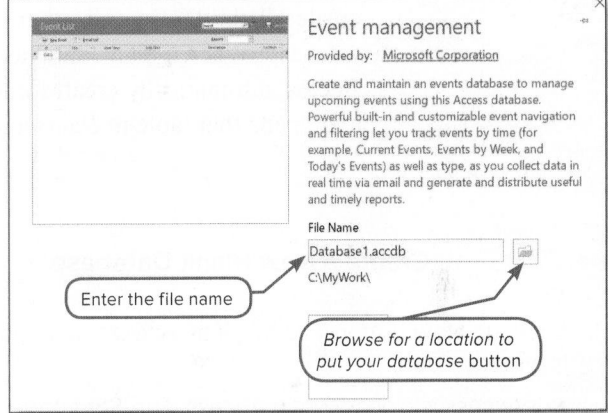

Figure 1-21 Select the file location and enter the file name

Database Properties

Every database contains details, or properties, about the database. The properties include information about the date the database was created and its author. View common file properties in the ***Database Properties*** dialog box available via the ***View and edit database properties*** link on the *Backstage* view. You can edit the properties on the *Summary* tab. However, you cannot edit properties on many of the other tabs. For example, the *Size* or *Modified Properties* on the *General* tab are automatically updated by the system.

▶ **HOW TO:** View and Edit Database Properties

1. Click the **File** tab to open the *Backstage* view and then click the **Info** button.

2. Click the **View and edit database properties** link (Figure 1-22) to open the *Database Properties* dialog box.

3. Click the **Summary** tab (Figure 1-23).

> **MORE INFO**
>
> Some properties may already be completed, depending on the settings selected when Office was installed on the computer.

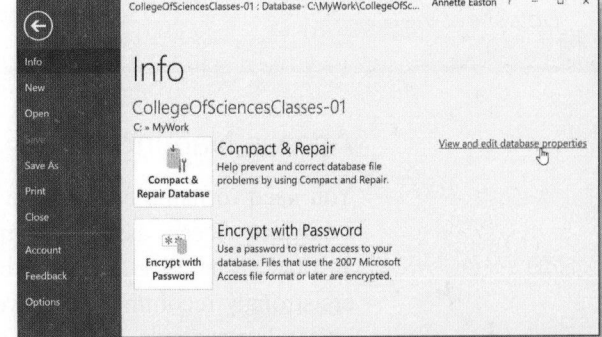

Figure 1-22 Open the database properties

4. View the properties that have been entered.

5. Edit any desired properties. Be sure to complete any properties required by your instructor.

6. Click **OK** to save and close.

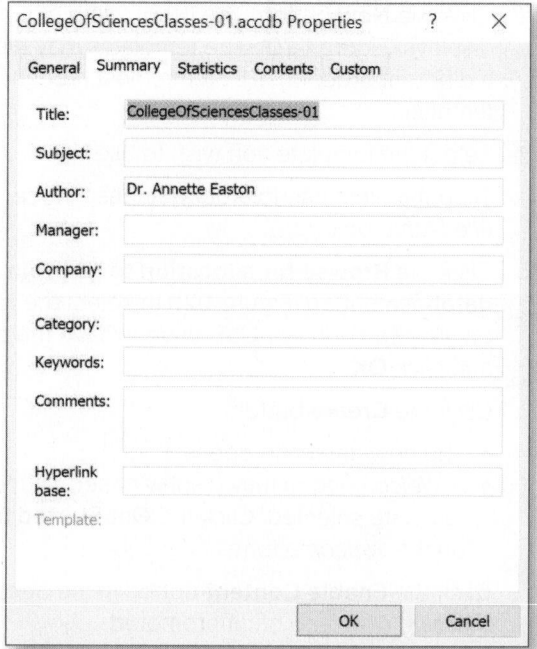

Figure 1-23 *Database Properties* dialog box

Create a Blank Database

Many times a template does not exist to meet your needs or it requires significant modifications to meet your requirements. In these cases, you can create a blank database. With the ***Blank database*** option, you create all the tables and other objects that you need. When a blank database is created, Access automatically creates one new table and opens that table in *Datasheet View*.

▶**HOW TO:** Create a New Blank Database

1. Click the **New** button [*File* tab] if an Access database is already open.

 • If Access is closed, open Access. The *Start* page displays where you can open a new blank database.

> **ANOTHER WAY**
>
> **Ctrl+N** opens the *Backstage* view with the *New* button selected.

2. Select **Blank database** (Figure 1-24).

3. Type the file name in the *File Name* box.

4. Click the **Browse for a location to put your database** button to select the location on your computer or USB drive to save the database and click **OK**.

5. Click the **Create** button. The database is created. A new table is automatically created and opens in *Datasheet View*.

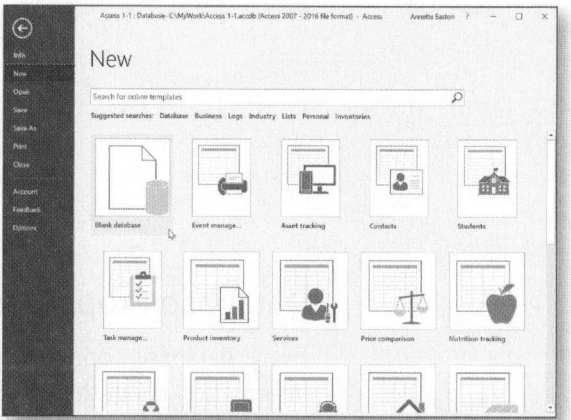

Figure 1-24 Create a new blank database

> **MORE INFO**
>
> Access automatically suggests a generic file name for your database, such as *Database1.accdb*. Be sure to change that name to a name that is more meaningful and related to the purpose of your database.

Access Naming Rules

You need to name each of the objects you create and use in Access. When you first create an object, Access assigns a generic name, such as *Table1* or *Form1*. The first time you save an object, the *Save As* dialog box prompts you to enter a different name. Database designers strongly recommend that you use a meaningful name that describes the contents of the object. For example, in the *CollegeOfSciencesClasses-01* database, the tables are named *Classes*, *Departments*, and *Instructors*. This makes it easy to understand the object's purpose. Each

object typically contains several fields. Form and report objects may also have other components such as buttons or labels. These components are called controls (see *SLO 4.2: Creating and Customizing a Form in Layout View*).

Your instructor or employer may have specific guidelines to follow when naming objects, fields, and controls. In addition to those guidelines, pay attention to the following Access naming rules:

- Names can have a maximum of 64 characters.
- The characters can be letters, numbers, and spaces. You can also use special characters except a period (.), exclamation point (!), square brackets ([]), and an accent grave (`).
- The name can't begin with a space.

Although spaces are allowed within a name, most database designers avoid using them due to possible naming conflicts with other applications. Instead, when creating a compound word name, it is a good idea to start each word with a capital letter (for example, *PhoneNumber* or *DepartmentName*). Sometimes database designers will also include a prefix in the object name such as, *tblAccounts* or *frmSales*. The most common prefixes are *tbl*, used for a table; *frm*, used for a form; *rpt*, used for a report; and *qry*, used for a query.

Data Types

Each field in your database must be assigned a specific ***data type***. The data type determines which properties can be manipulated and how that field can be used. Before you start to create and manipulate tables, it is important to learn about the types that are explained in Table 1-3.

Table 1-3: Access Data Types

Data Type	Description
Short Text	Used to store alphanumeric data (text, or combinations of text and numbers). Also used to store numbers that are not used in calculations, such as phone numbers. The maximum length is 255 characters.
Long Text	Used to store text longer than 255 characters or text containing rich-text formatting. The maximum length that displays is limited to the first 64,000 characters.
Number	Used to store numbers that are used in mathematical calculations. The number can be positive or negative. Seven field size choices are available for the number data type which determine the range of possible values and amount of storage space required.
Large Number	Used to store integer numbers ranging from −9,223,372,036,854,775,808 to 9,223,372,036,854,775,807. Compatible with the *BigInt* data type in SQL databases. Note: An Access database that uses the *Large Number* data type cannot be opened by a version of Access lower than Access 2016 version number 16.0.7812.
Date/Time	Used to store dates and times.
Currency	Used to store numbers representing currency values. This type does not allow rounding off during calculations. Accurate to 15 digits on the left side of the decimal point and four digits on the right side.
AutoNumber	Used to instruct Access to insert a unique number each time a new record is added. Choose sequential (increments by 1) or random numbers. The field value cannot be updated after the record is created. If a record is deleted, the *AutoNumber* value is not reused. Only one *AutoNumber* field, with a Field Size of *Long Integer,* is allowed in each table.
Yes/No	Used to store fields with two possible values, such as *Yes/No, True/False,* or *On/Off.* Displays as a check box. A *Yes/No* data type field contains −1 if it is checked, and 0 if it is unchecked.
OLE Object	Used to display OLE objects (spreadsheets, documents, pictures, sounds) that were created in other programs.
Hyperlink	Used to store a hyperlink to another file or web page.
Attachment	Used to attach pictures, images, and Office files.
Calculated	Used to store the results of a calculation. Typically, the equation references fields in the same table.
Lookup Wizard	Technically, this is not a data type. It is used to convert your field into a combo box that enables you to choose a value from another table or from a list of values.

Create and Save Database Objects

Databases typically contain many different objects. Each object is initially created using the *Create* tab. Once the object is created, you use one of the different views to define the object or to change the object.

▶ HOW TO: Create a New Object

1. Click the **Create** tab on the *Ribbon*.
2. Click the **object** button of the object you wish to create.
 - You may be prompted to save an open object before Access creates the new object.
 - The button choice determines the view that displays when the object opens. For example, selecting the **Table** button opens a table in *Datasheet View,* whereas selecting the **Table Design** button opens a table in *Design View*.
 - Wizard buttons, such as *Query Wizard,* launch a wizard that guides you through the steps to creating that object.

To keep a permanent copy of an object, you need to save it. When an object is created, Access automatically assigns it a name. The first time you save an object, you are prompted to change the default name in the *Save As* dialog box.

▶ HOW TO: Save an Object

1. Click the **Save** button [*File* tab]. The *Save As* dialog box opens if this is the first time you save the object.
2. Type the name you wish to use in the *Save As 'Object Name'* box. Instead of displaying the phrase "Object Name," Access displays the type of object you are saving. For example, Figure 1-25 is a *Save As* dialog box for a form.
3. Click **OK**.

Figure 1-25 *Save As* dialog box

Once an object has been saved, you must save it again to store any changes that have been made. In addition to clicking the **Save** button [*File* tab], you can also re-save the object by clicking the **Save** button on the *Quick Access* toolbar or by pressing **Ctrl+S**.

Sometimes you need to make a copy of an object. This may be done to have a backup of the original object or because another object has the same initial characteristics.

▶ HOW TO: Save a Copy of an Object

1. Select the desired object if not already selected or open.
2. Click the **Save As** button [*File* tab].
3. Click the **Save Object As** button in the *File Types* area and the **Save Object As** button in the *Database File Types* area (Figure 1-26).
4. Click the **Save As** button to open the *Save As* dialog box (Figure 1-27).
 - Access suggests the default object name of "Copy of" and the original object name.
 - Access selects the same object type as the original object.

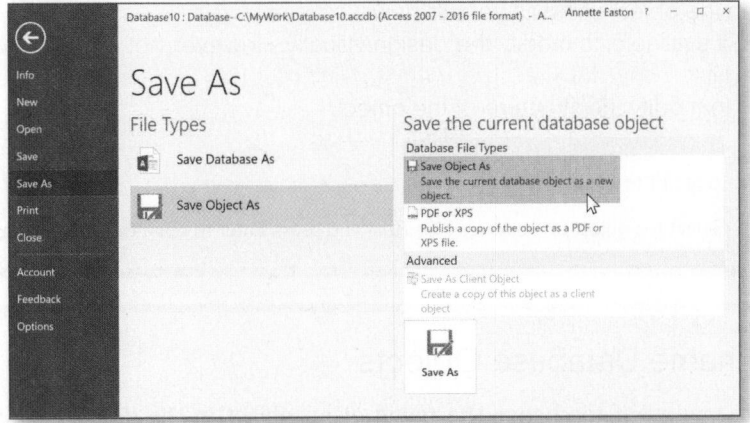

Figure 1-26 *Save Object As* button

5. Type the name you wish to use in the *Save 'Object name'* to box.

6. Select the type of object you wish to create.

 • Make a duplicate of the object by selecting the same object type.
 • Create a different type of object, based on the original objects settings, by selecting another object type.

7. Click **OK**.

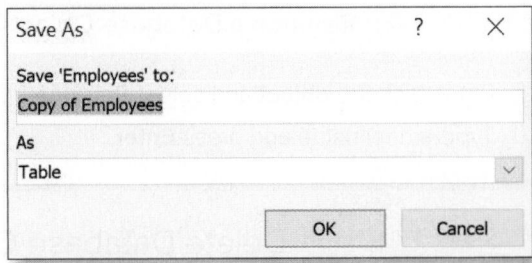

Figure 1-27 *Save As* dialog box

▶ ANOTHER WAY

Press the **F12** function key to open the *Save As* dialog box.

Use *Copy* and *Paste* to save a copy. Right-click the object in the *Navigation Pane* and select **Copy**. Then right-click in a blank area of the *Navigation Pane* and select **Paste** to open the *Paste 'Object name' As* dialog box.

Open Database Objects

You can open objects directly from the *Navigation Pane*. The selection you make when opening an object determines the view that displays. Each object type has a default view in which it opens when you double-click the object name in the *Navigation Pane*. This default view displays the contents of the object.

• *Datasheet* view is the default view for tables and queries.
• *Form* view is the default view for forms.
• *Report* view is the default view for reports.

▶HOW TO: Open a Datasheet Object

1. Click the **Shutter Bar Open/Close Button** or press **F11** if the *Navigation Pane* is closed.

2. Right-click the object name and select the desired view from the context menu (Figure 1-28). The object opens in the work area.

Figure 1-28 Select an open option on the context menu

- Select **Open** to open the object using its default view.
- Select **Layout View**, if available, to modify the design visually. However, not all design changes can be made in *Layout* view.
- Select **Design View** to modify the structure of the object.

ANOTHER WAY

Select the object in *the Navigation Pane* and press **Enter** to open the object using its default view.

Rename Database Objects

You may want to change the name of an object in the database. An object must be closed before it can be renamed.

> **HOW TO:** Rename a Database Object

1. Right-click the **object** and select **Rename** from the context menu.
2. Type a new name and press **Enter**.

Delete Database Objects

Occasionally, you have objects that you no longer need or want in the database. Be cautious when you delete objects because it is not possible to undo the action. An object must be closed before it can be deleted.

Delete an object by selecting it in the *Navigation Pane* and clicking the **Delete** button [*Home* tab, *Records* group]. Click **Yes** in the dialog box to confirm the deletion.

ANOTHER WAY

Right-click the object name in the *Navigation Pane* and select **Delete** from the context menu. Click **Yes** in the dialog box to confirm the deletion.

Close and Open a Database

When you are finished working on a database, you should close the database file. You won't actually save the database file before closing it. Instead, you are prompted to save each of the separate database objects as you work on them. Access also automatically saves many changes to your database file, such as records you add into a table.

> **HOW TO:** Close a Database

1. Click the **Close** button [*File* tab] to close a database.
 - The current database closes. Access remains open and you are positioned on the *Home* tab (Figure 1-29). Notice that the *Navigation Pane* does not display because a database is not open.

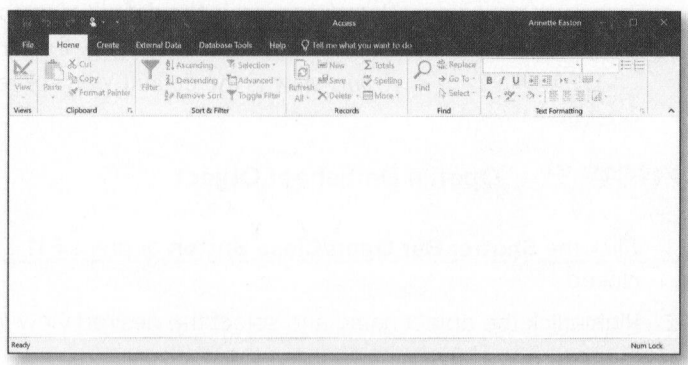

Figure 1-29 Access *Home* tab when a database is closed

A1-18

▶HOW TO: Open a Database

1. Click the **Open** button [*File* tab] to open an existing database.
2. Click the **Browse** button. The *Open* dialog box displays.
3. Select the database file and click the **Open** button.
 - You can also double-click the file name to open the database.

Back Up and Recover a Database

A backup copy of a database is necessary to completely restore your database. If you have several users of your database, you must be certain that all users have closed the database before you perform a backup procedure. Your organization's database administrator, in conjunction with the information systems manager, should determine a regular schedule for backups.

▶HOW TO: Back Up a Database

1. Click the **File** tab to open the *Backstage* view.
2. Click the **Save As** button. Your screen should look similar to Figure 1-30, with *Access Database* selected in the *Save Database As* area.

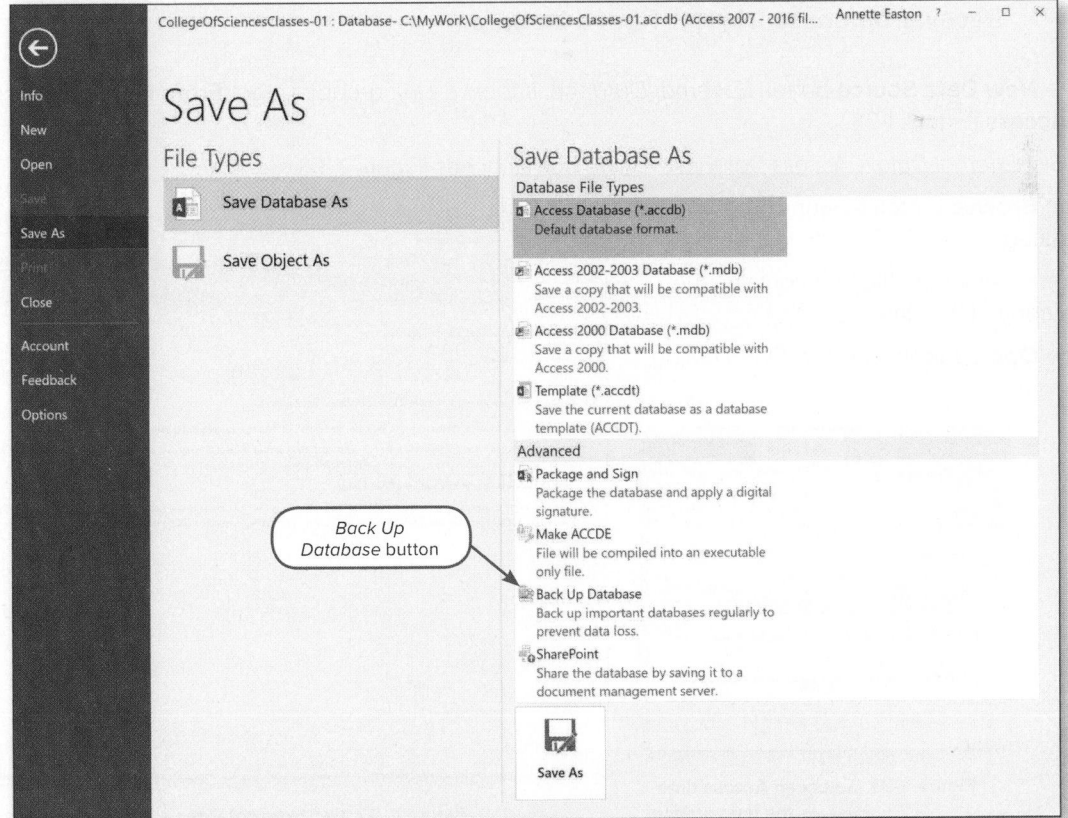

Figure 1-30 Back up a database

3. Select **Back Up Database** in the *Advanced* grouping of the *Save Database As* section.

4. Click the **Save As** button.

 - Select the desired location in which to store the backup database file.
 - Access suggests a filename, such as *CollegeOfSciencesClasses-01_2020-01-28,* which adds today's date to the end of the file name. This is a good practice, because you can quickly determine when a backup copy was created.
 - As desired, click the **File Name** box and change the default name.
 - Click the **Save** button.

The *Back Up Database* option creates a copy of your database, but the current database file remains open and you continue to work in that file.

> ### ANOTHER WAY
>
> Use the *Access Database* file type instead of *Back Up Database* and select the **Save As** button to create a copy of the database. In this case, the open database switches to the new copy you created.

If the original database file becomes damaged, use the backup file to recover the database. Copy the backup file to replace the original and then start working with this replacement file.

If the entire database is not damaged, you can choose to recover only the damaged database objects from the backup file. Open the original database file. Before starting the steps to recover the objects, you should delete the damaged object from the current database or rename the original object to reflect that it is an old or bad copy. For example, rename the *Classes* table to *Classes_Old* or *Classes_Damaged.*

▶HOW TO: Recover Database Objects from a Backup

1. Click the **New Data Source** button [*External Data* tab, *Import & Link* group], select **From Database**, and then select **Access** (Figure 1-31).

 - The *Get External Data – Access Database* dialog box launches (Figure 1-32).

2. Click the **Browse** button to launch the *File Open* dialog box.

3. Locate and select the file that contains the backup copy of the database.

4. Click the **Open** button. The *File Open* dialog box closes.

Figure 1-31 Select an Access database as the data source

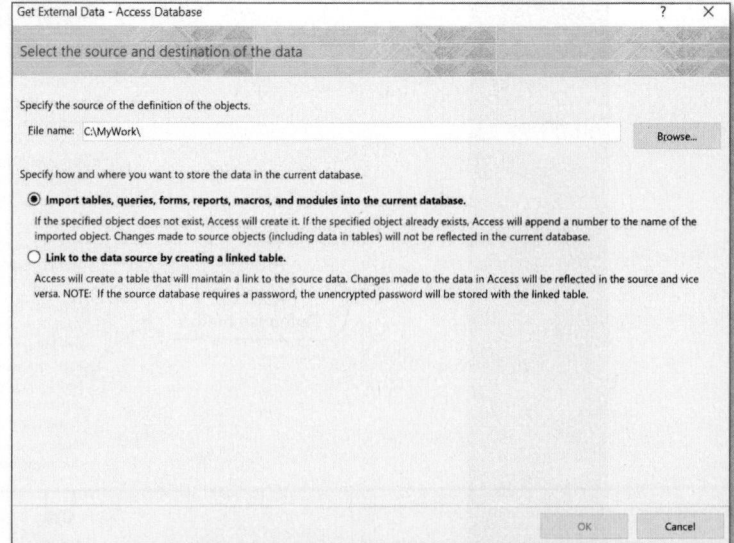

Figure 1-32 *Get External Data – Access Database* dialog box

5. Select the **Import tables, queries, forms, reports, macros, and modules into the current database** radio button.

6. Click **OK** to open the *Import Objects* dialog box (Figure 1-33).

7. Click the tab corresponding to the type of object you wish to import.

8. Select the objects you wish to import.
 - You can select multiple objects on a tab.
 - Click the **Select All** button to select all of the objects on the tab.

9. Repeat steps 7 and 8 to select objects from a different tab.

10. Click **OK**. The *Save Import Steps* screen displays.

11. Click the **Close** button.

12. Open the object to verify that the object was successfully recovered.

Figure 1-33 *Import Objects* dialog box

Creating and Using a Table in Datasheet View

Recall that when you create a new blank database, Access automatically creates one table for you. You can add tables using several different methods. In this section, you learn how to use *Datasheet* view to quickly create a table and enter data records. When using a database application, as you will learn later, *Datasheet* view is primarily used to enter, modify, delete, or view the data records.

No matter what method you use to create a table, you need to define the fields that are included within the table. You also need to describe the specific details, or *field properties*, of each of the fields. The basic field properties include the field name, data type, and size.

Create a New Table in Datasheet View

Databases typically contain multiple tables. You can add a new table to your database from the *Create* tab. Tables created using the *Table* button automatically open in *Datasheet* view.

▶ HOW TO: Create a New Table in Datasheet View

1. Click the **Create** tab on the *Ribbon*.

2. Click the **Table** button in the *Tables* group (Figure 1-34). A new table opens in *Datasheet* view.

 The *Ribbon* updates (Figure 1-35) because the *Table Tools* contextual tabs are now available, with the **Fields** tab selected.

Figure 1-34 *Table* button

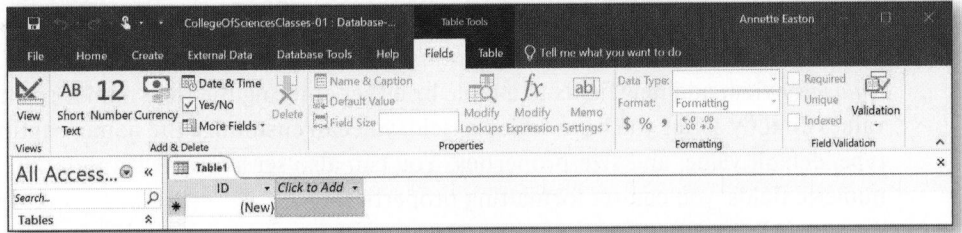

Figure 1-35 *Table Tools* contextual tabs

Edit the Default Primary Key

A ***primary key*** is a field that contains a unique value for each record. This is the way that one record can be distinguished from another. For example, the *InstructorID* field was designated as the primary key in the *Instructors* table in the *CollegeOfSciencesClasses-01* database, because each instructor has a unique ID number. When you enter values into a record, Access requires that you enter a value in any field designated as a primary key.

When a new table is created in *Datasheet* view, Access automatically includes one field, named *ID*, and designates it as the primary key. This field is assigned the *AutoNumber* data type to ensure that each record has a unique value.

> ### MORE INFO
>
> While not absolutely required, it is strongly recommended that each table has a field designated as the primary key.

In *Datasheet* view, you can change the following field properties of the *ID primary key* field: *Name*, *Caption*, *Description*, and *Data Type*.

▶HOW TO: Edit the Default Primary Key

1. Double-click the cell containing the **ID** *field name* (column header) in your table to select it (Figure 1-36).

2. Type the new name for your field and press the **down arrow** key. This action updates the change to the field name and keeps you in the same column.

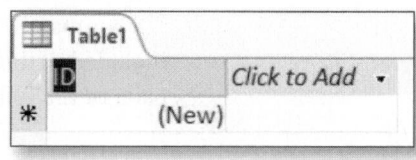

Figure 1-36 *Field name* column header

3. Change the default *Data Type* of *AutoNumber* as desired.

 • Click the **Data Type** [*Table Tools Fields* tab, *Formatting* group] drop-down arrow to display the list of data types (Figure 1-37).
 • Select the desired **Data Type** property.

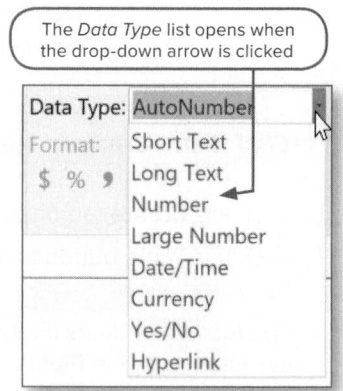

The *Data Type* list opens when the drop-down arrow is clicked

Figure 1-37 Field data types

Add New Fields

You must create a field for each of the different pieces of information you want to keep in your table. For example, *ClassID*, *ClassName*, and *DepartmentID* are three of the fields in the *Classes* table in the *CollegeOfSciencesClasses-01* database. In *Datasheet* view, add new fields to a table by either entering the field names or entering the data values directly. After you have added a field, you can customize the name, caption, description, type, default value, and size properties. You can also set a few field validation properties. On numeric fields, you can set formatting properties.

Add New Fields by Entering Field Names

You can add new fields into a table by entering the field name and selecting the data type.

▶HOW TO: Add New Fields by Entering Field Names

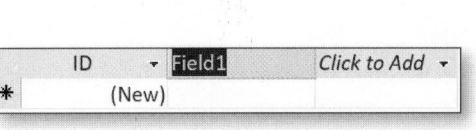

1. Click the **Click to Add** column header. The drop-down list of data types displays (Figure 1-38).

 - Technically, the *Rich Text* option is not a data type. Rather it assigns additional formatting selections to the *Long Text* data type.

2. Select the appropriate data type.

 - The new field is added and assigned a default field name, such as *Field1,* as shown in Figure 1-39.

3. Type the desired field name in the column header.

 - Recall that each field name is limited to 64 characters.
 - Each field in a table must have a unique name.

Figure 1-39 *Field name* column header

Figure 1-38 *Click to Add* data types

4. Press the **Enter** key. You move to the next column with the list of data types displayed.

5. Repeat steps 2 through 4 to add the additional fields into your table.

You can also add fields by selecting the data type first and then entering the field name. The more commonly used data types have buttons in

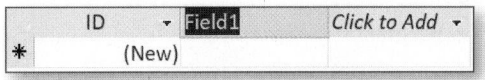

Figure 1-40 Data type buttons

the *Add & Delete* group on the *Table Tools Fields* tab (Figure 1-40). When adding fields using a data type button, the new field is inserted to the right of the currently selected field.

▶HOW TO: Add New Fields Using a Data Type Button

1. Click the appropriate data type button in the *Add & Delete* group on the *Table Tools Fields* tab.

 - The new field is added and assigned a default field name, such as *Field1*.

2. Type the field name in the column header.

3. Press the **Enter** key.

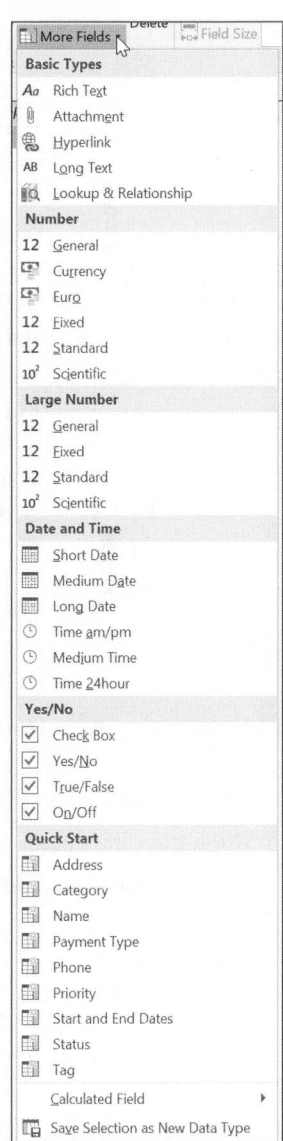

Use the ***More Fields*** [*Table Tools Fields* tab, *Add & Delete* group] drop-down list, shown in Figure 1-41, to select additional choices of the basic data type options when adding a new field.

Technically, not all of these choices are data types. Rather, they assign additional formatting selections to a data type. For example, within the *Date and Time* group, select format options for the ways to store the date or time. *Short Date* formats a date to display as 12/15/2020; *Medium Date* displays as 15-Dec-20.

Figure 1-41 *More Fields* drop-down list

The *Quick Start* group provides a set of fields that you can add by making just one choice. For example, selecting the *Phone* quick start data type adds four fields into your table: *Business Phone*, *Home Phone*, *Mobile Phone*, and *Fax Number*.

Most fields added using the *More Fields* button are inserted to the right of the currently selected field. However, fields added from the *Quick Start* group are inserted to the left of the currently selected field.

▶**HOW TO:** Add New Fields Using the More Fields Button

1. Click the **More Fields** button [*Table Tools Fields* tab, *Add & Delete* group] to display the drop-down list.
2. Select the appropriate data type.
3. Type the field name in the column header.
4. Press the **Enter** key.

Add New Fields by Entering Data

You can add new fields into a table by entering the data values in the append row. Recall that the append row is always the last row in the table and is identified with the asterisk icon in the record selector of that row.

Add a new field by clicking the first *Click to Add* cell on the append row.

A field on the append row with *(New)* displayed, as shown in Figure 1-42, indicates an *AutoNumber* data type. The data value for this field is automatically completed by Access. You can add a new field by entering data in the cell to the right of *(New)*.

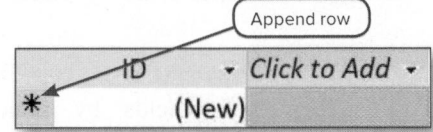

Figure 1-42 Append row with an *AutoNumber* field

If the *ID* field (the default, primary key) does not display *(New)* in the append row, the data type has been changed from an *AutoNumber* type (Figure 1-43). To add another field, first enter a value into the *ID* field and then add a new field by entering data in the *Click to Add* cell.

Figure 1-43 Append row without an *AutoNumber* field

▶**HOW TO:** Add New Fields by Entering Data

1. Click the **cell** in the first *Click to Add* column.
2. Type the data value into the cell.
3. Click the **Click to Add** column header (Figure 1-44) to add the field.
 - Access assigns a default field name, such as *Field1*, and selects that column.
 - *Click to Add* becomes the next column.
 - Access automatically assigns a data type for the field based on the contents that you enter. As desired, you can change the data type.
4. Repeat steps 1 through 3 to add all the additional fields into your table.

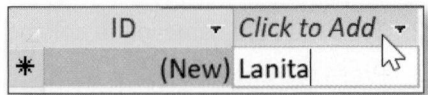

Figure 1-44 Add new field by entering data

▶ ANOTHER WAY

Press the **Tab** key or the **Enter** key to add the field and move to the next column.

Remember that you need to verify that Access assigned the correct data type to each field. You should also assign a descriptive field name. You can either edit these field properties after entering each field or after all the fields have been added.

When using the *Click to Add* option, the new field always adds to the right of the last field in your table. Occasionally, you may wish to add a field between existing fields.

▶HOW TO: Add New Fields between Existing Fields

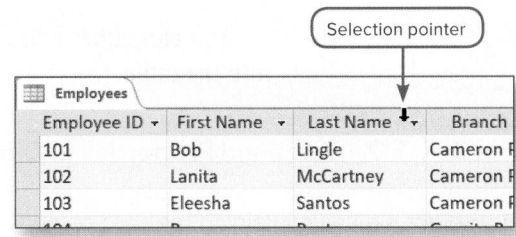

Selection pointer

1. Put your pointer on the field name of the column to the right of where you wish to insert a new field. The selection pointer appears as a black down arrow (Figure 1-45).

2. Click to select that column. The column is highlighted in blue.

3. Right-click to open the context menu.

4. Select **Insert Field** (Figure 1-46). The new field is inserted to the left of the selected field, as shown in Figure 1-47. It is assigned a default field name, such as *Field1*.

5. Double-click the field name to change the name.

Figure 1-45 Selection pointer

Figure 1-47 New field added with default field name

Delete Fields

You may need to delete a field from a table that was either created in error or is no longer needed in a table.

Figure 1-46 Select *Insert Field* on the context menu

▶HOW TO: Delete a Field

1. Place your pointer over the field name of the field you wish to delete. The selection pointer appears as a black down arrow.

2. Click to select that column.

3. Click the **Delete** button [*Table Tools Fields* tab, *Add & Delete* group] to delete the field. Access displays a message box asking you to confirm the deletion.

4. Click **Yes** to delete the field.

> **ANOTHER WAY**
>
> Right-click to open the context menu and select **Delete Field**.

> **MORE INFO**
>
> The *Undo* button cannot be used to undo deletions of table fields.

Edit Properties in Datasheet View

In *Datasheet* view, you can change a limited number of the field properties. Recall that the properties of each field describe the field's details or characteristics. The majority of the field properties are changed in *Design* view. The properties that you can set in *Datasheet* view include:

- *Name*: Each field in a table must be given a unique name.
- *Caption*: The caption is an alternative to the field name that displays in the datasheet. Captions often include spaces and multiple words.

- *Description*: The description describes the purpose or meaning of a field if the field name by itself does not clearly convey the purpose or intended content. It displays in the lower-left corner of the datasheet in the *Status* bar.
- *Data Type*: Select a data type that matches the characteristics of the stored data.
- *Field Size*: Enter the smallest, sufficient field size to ensure best performance. In *Datasheet* view, you can only modify this property for a field with a *Short Text* data type.

You can either edit the field properties as you add each field or after you add all the fields into the table.

▶ **HOW TO:** Edit Field Properties in Datasheet View

1. Select the cell containing the field name (column header) you wish to change.
2. Click the **Name & Caption** button [*Table Tools Fields* tab, *Properties* group].
 - The *Enter Field Properties* dialog box opens (Figure 1-48).
3. Type a new value in the *Name* property as desired.
4. Type a value in the *Caption* property as desired.
5. Type a value in the *Description* property as desired.
6. Click **OK** to close the dialog box.
7. Click the **Data Type option** drop-down arrow [*Table Tools Fields* tab, *Formatting* group].
8. Select the desired **Data Type** property.
9. Type a new value in the *Field Size* property [*Table Tools Fields* tab, *Properties* group] (Figure 1-49).

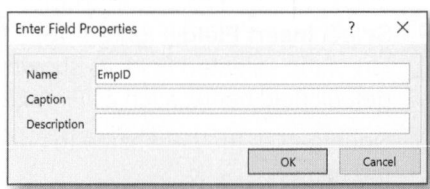

Figure 1-48 *Enter Field Properties* dialog box

Figure 1-49 *Field Size* property

Add a Table Description

In addition to the field and database properties you have learned about, database objects also have their own properties. One of the table properties you can set is *Description*. Use this property to provide a more informative summary of the table contents.

▶ **HOW TO:** Add a Table Description

1. Right-click the table name in the *Navigation Pane* and select **Table Properties** from the context menu. The *Table Properties* dialog box opens (Figure 1-50). Instead of displaying the word "Table," Access displays the table name.
2. Type a description in the *Description* property.
3. Click **OK**.

Figure 1-50 *Table Properties* dialog box

▶ MORE INFO

The table properties can be displayed in the *Navigation Pane*, although it generally is not necessary to do this. To display the table properties, right-click the *Title* bar of the *Navigation Pane*, select **View By**, and then select **Details**.

Save a Table

When you create a new table, Access automatically assigns a generic name to the table, such as *Table1*. The first time you save a table, you are prompted to change the default name in the *Save As* dialog box.

If you close *Table1* (the default table that comes with a new database) without saving it, Access deletes the table. This occurs even if you have entered data into the table.

▶HOW TO: Save a New Table

1. Click the **Save** button [*File* tab]. If this is the first time you are saving the table, the *Save As* dialog box displays.
2. Type the name you wish to use in the *Table Name* box.
3. Click **OK**.

> ▶ **ANOTHER WAY**
>
> Open the *Save As* dialog box by clicking the **Save** button on the *Quick Access* toolbar or by pressing **Ctrl+S**.

If you later make changes to a table, many of those changes will automatically be saved by Access. However, it is a good idea for you to re-save the table to ensure those changes are stored. Click the **Save** button [*File* tab], click the **Save** button on the *Quick Access* toolbar, press **Ctrl+S** or right-click the tab with the table name, and select **Save** from the context menu to save the changes. Because the table has been saved once, the *Save As* dialog box does not open again.

Close a Table

When you finish using a table, you should close the table. Routinely closing unneeded objects prevents you from making accidental changes to those objects.

To close a table, click the **X** (*Close* button) in the upper-right corner of the datasheet. You can also press **Ctrl+W** or **Ctrl+F4** to close a table, or right-click the tab with the table name and select **Close** from the context menu.

Open a Table

You can open an existing table in either *Datasheet* view or *Design* view. Once a table is open, you can easily switch views as desired.

▶HOW TO: Open a Table in Datasheet View

1. Click the **Shutter Bar Open/Close Button** or press **F11** if the *Navigation Pane* is closed.
2. Double-click the table name. The table opens in *Datasheet* view.

> ▶ **ANOTHER WAY**
>
> Select the table in the *Navigation Pane* and press **Enter**.
>
> Right-click the table in the *Navigation Pane* and select **Open** from the context menu.

HOW TO: Open a Table in Design View

1. Click the **Shutter Bar Open/Close** if the *Navigation Pane* is closed or press **F11**.
2. Select the table in the *Navigation Pane* and press **Ctrl+Enter**.

> **ANOTHER WAY**
>
> Right-click the table in the *Navigation Pane* and select **Design View** from the context menu.

Rename a Table

You may want to change the name of a table in the database, and it is easy to do this. However, you need to be aware of potential problems that may occur. Tables are the basis for many of the other database objects you create. For example, a report is created to provide a way to view and print the data in a table. The report depends on the table as its source of the data and is directly linked to the table. As a result, it is important to verify that objects that depend on a table still work correctly after a table is renamed.

HOW TO: Rename a Table

1. Close the table if it is open.
2. Right-click the table name in the *Navigation Pane* and select **Rename** from the context menu.
3. Type a new name and press **Enter**.

Add, Edit, and Delete Records

Datasheet view provides an easy way to add data values into your table, edit records already in the table, or delete records from a table.

Add the data by entering all the values for one record. After you finish entering the values for one record and navigate to the next record, Access automatically saves the record in the table.

> **MORE INFO**
>
> Your table must be saved at least once to initiate the automatic saving of data records.

If you realize you made an error in entering a value, you can make a correction several ways.

- If you have navigated out of a field, click the field and change the value.
- If you are still typing in the field, click the **Undo** button to undo the typing.

ANOTHER WAY

> Press **Esc** to undo a change to the current field. If more than one field has been changed on the current record, all changes will be undone.

- If you have moved to the next field, undo a change to the previous field by clicking the **Undo** button.
- To undo all the changes to an unsaved record, click the **Undo** button twice.

Once you navigate out of the current record, the *Undo* button won't remove changes.

One benefit of a database is that it automatically verifies the contents of what you enter, based on the different properties you have assigned. For example, you are required to enter a value into the primary key field. Additionally, each primary key field must have a unique value. If you enter a primary key value that is already used, Access displays an error message. Similarly, if you enter a value that violates the data type property, Access displays an error message.

▶HOW TO: Add Records in a Table

1. Click the first empty cell in the append row.

> **ANOTHER WAY**
>
> Click **New** [*Home* tab, *Records* group] to move automatically to the first empty cell in the append row.

2. Type the data value.
 - The append row asterisk changes to a pencil icon (Figure 1-51), indicating that you are editing a record that has not yet been saved.
 - A new append row is added.

3. Press the **Tab** key to move to the next field.

Figure 1-51 Pencil icon indicates editing an unsaved record

> **ANOTHER WAY**
>
> Press **Enter** to move to the next field.
>
> Press **Shift+Tab** to move to the preceding field.

4. Continue entering all remaining data values for the record, pressing **Tab** or **Enter** after each value.
 - After you press the **Tab** or **Enter** key of the last field, you advance to the first field of the next record.
 - If you enter a duplicate value for the primary key (Figure 1-52), Access displays an error message (Figure 1-53) when you navigate out of the record.
 - If you enter a value that does not match the data type, Access displays an error message when you navigate out of that field (Figure 1-54).

Employee ID ▾	First Name ▾	Last Name ▾
101	Bob	Lingle
🖉 101	Lanita	McCartney
*		

Figure 1-52 Duplicate primary key values

Figure 1-53 Duplicate values error message

Figure 1-54 Data type error message

You can edit an existing record in a table by clicking the cell of the field you wish to change. The append row asterisk changes to a pencil icon, indicating that you are editing a record. Make the necessary corrections in the field. When you navigate out of that field, Access automatically saves the changes.

Sometimes you need to delete a record from a table in your database.

▶ HOW TO: Delete a Record from a Table

1. Click the **record selector** cell of the record you wish to delete (Figure 1-55).
2. Click the **Delete** button [*Home* tab, *Records* group].
 - Access displays a message box warning you about the record deletion and informing you that it is not possible to undo a delete operation.
 - Click the **Yes** button if you want to confirm the delete operation.

Figure 1-55 Select the record before deleting

> ▶ **ANOTHER WAY**
>
> Right-click the selected record in the table and select **Delete Record** from the context menu.

PAUSE & PRACTICE: ACCESS 1-2

Businesses regularly use databases to organize and manage data in a useful and meaningful manner. For this project, you create a database to manage data about the employees of Central Sierra Insurance.

File Needed: None
Completed Project File Name: *[your initials] PP A1-2.accdb*

1. Create a new blank database.
 a. Open Access or click the **New** button [*File* tab] if an Access database is already open.
 b. Select **Blank database**.
 c. Name the database [your initials] PP A1-2 in the *File name* box.
 d. Browse to the location on your computer or storage device to save the database and click **OK**.
 e. Click **Create**. The database opens with a new table showing in *Datasheet* view (Figure 1-56).

Figure 1-56 *Datasheet* view of *Table 1* after a new database is created

2. Modify the default primary key.
 a. Double-click the **ID** field name (column header) in your table and type EmpID. Press the **down arrow** key to update the name and to stay in the same column.
 b. Click the **Name & Caption** button [*Table Tools Fields* tab, *Properties* group]. The *Enter Field Properties* dialog box opens (Figure 1-57).

Figure 1-57 *Enter Field Properties* dialog box

c. Type Employee ID in the *Caption* property.
d. Type Unique Employee Identification Number in the *Description* property.
e. Click **OK**.
f. Select **Short Text** in the *Data Type* option selection box [*Table Tools Fields* tab, *Formatting* group] (Figure 1-58).
g. Type 5 in the *Field Size* property [*Table Tools Fields* tab, *Properties* group].
h. Press the **Enter** key.

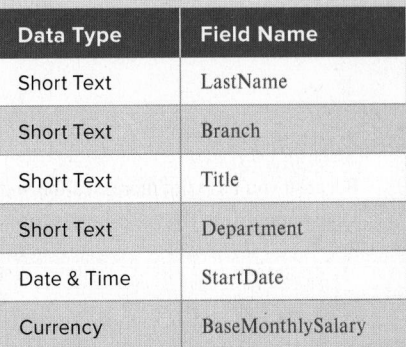

Figure 1-58 *Data Type* selection box

3. Add new fields into the table.
 a. Click the **Click to Add** column header.
 b. Select **Short Text** in the drop-down list of data types.
 c. Type FirstName to replace *Field1*.
 d. Press the **Enter** key to move to the next column.
 e. Continue entering the additional fields by selecting the data type and typing the field name for each field listed in Table 1-4. After you complete the *BaseMonthlySalary* field, don't select anything in the *Click to Add* column that displays.

Table 1-4

Data Type	Field Name
Short Text	LastName
Short Text	Branch
Short Text	Title
Short Text	Department
Date & Time	StartDate
Currency	BaseMonthlySalary

4. Save and close the table.
 a. Click the **Save** button or press **Ctrl+S** to save all of the modifications you have made to the table.
 b. Type Employees as the new table name.
 c. Click **OK**.
 d. Close the *Employees* table by clicking the **X** in the upper-right corner of the table (Figure 1-59).

Figure 1-59 Close the *Employees* table

5. Reopen the table in *Datasheet* view to edit the field properties.
 a. Double-click the **Employees** table to open it in *Datasheet* view.
 b. Click the **FirstName** field name.
 c. Click the **Name & Caption** button [*Table Tools Fields* tab, *Properties* group].
 d. Type First Name in the *Caption* property and press **Tab**.
 e. Type Employee's First Name in the *Description* property.
 f. Click **OK**.
 g. Type 25 in the *Field Size* property [*Table Tools Fields* tab, *Properties* group] and press **Enter**.
 h. Continue changing the remaining field properties in the table using the information in Table 1-5. Repeat steps 5b through 5g for each field.
 i. Click the **Save** button to save the changes to the table.

Table 1-5

Field Name	Caption	Description	Size
LastName	Last Name	Employee's Last Name	25
Branch		Branch Assigned To	30
Title		Current Job Title	40
Department		Department Assigned To	40
StartDate	Start Date	Date Employment Started	N/A
BaseMonthlySalary	Base Monthly Salary	Current Base Monthly Salary	N/A

6. Add the employee records into the *Employees* table.
 a. Click the first empty cell in the append row. Recall that the append row is always the last row in the table. It is identified with the asterisk icon in the record selector of that row.
 b. Type 101 in the *EmpID* field. Remember that if you entered a caption for a field, the caption displays as the column header in *Datasheet* view. The data entry instructions reference the actual field name. If a description was entered, it displays on the left side of the *Status* bar.
 c. Press the **Tab** key to move to the next field.
 d. Type Bob in the *FirstName* field. Press the **Tab** key to move to the next field.
 e. Type Lingle in the *LastName* field. Press the **Tab** key to move to the next field.
 f. Type Cameron Park in the *Branch* field. Press the **Tab** key to move to the next field.

> **MORE INFO**
>
> Because you have not increased the width of any fields, you may not be able to see the entire contents of all fields. Date and currency values that are too wide display with a series of pound sign symbols (######).

 g. Type Chief Executive Officer in the *Title* field. Press the **Tab** key to move to the next field.
 h. Type Administration in the *Department* field. Press the **Tab** key to move to the next field.
 i. Type 1/1/2017 in the *StartDate* field. Press the **Tab** key to move to the next field.
 j. Type 15000 in the *BaseMonthlySalary* field. Press the **Tab** key to move to the start of the next record.
 k. Continue entering the remaining records into the *Employees* table using the data values in Table 1-6. The values that you enter are not "wrapped" in the table cells when you enter them.

Table 1-6

Emp ID	FirstName	LastName	Branch	Title	Department	Start Date	Base Monthly Salary
102	Lanita	McCartney	Cameron Park	Chief Operating Officer	Administration	1/1/2017	12000
103	Eleesha	Santos	Cameron Park	Insurance Agent	Health and Benefits	2/10/2017	5580
104	Roy	Baxter	Granite Bay	Insurance Agent	Property and Casualty	2/11/2017	4500
115	Tami	Chan	Cameron Park	Administrative Assistant	Health and Benefits	5/8/2017	3100

7. Close the table by clicking the **X** in the upper-right corner. Because the data records are automatically saved when you enter them into the table, it is not necessary to save the table before closing.

8. Double-click the **Employees** table to reopen it in *Datasheet* view. Your completed table should look similar to Figure 1-60 and display all five records.

Figure 1-60 PP A1-2 completed

9. Close the table by clicking the **X** in the upper-right corner of the datasheet.

10. Close the database by clicking the **Close** button [*File* tab].

Importing Data Records from Excel

You have already learned how to add data records into a table using *Datasheet* view. Occasionally, companies may have their data stored in another file. In cases like these, you can import the data records into Access instead of having to enter all the data values.

In this section, you learn how to import data from an Excel file into a table that you have already created. You append (add) the new data to any existing data records already in the table. Prior to importing the file, you need to ensure that the Excel file is formatted correctly.

- The first row of the Excel file must contain the names of all of the fields in the Access table.
- The data fields don't need to be in the same order.
- All of the fields in the table do not need be in the Excel file as long as the *Required* property allows the field to be empty. With the exception of a primary key field, the default setting for other fields is to not require a value to be filled in. In *SLO 2.2: Setting Field Properties*, you will learn how to change the *Required* property.
- If the fields are not of the same data type (for example, the Access field data type is *Number* but the Excel file field contains *Text*), Access still imports the file but the contents of that field are left empty. In this case, the *Required* property must allow the field to be empty.

Close the Access table before starting the import. If the table is not closed, you are prompted to close it during the import process.

▶**HOW TO:** Import Data from Excel

1. Click the **New Data Source** button [*External Data* tab, *Import & Link* group], select **From File** and then select **Excel** (Figure 1-61).
 - The *Get External Data – Excel Spreadsheet* dialog box launches (Figure 1-62).
2. Click the **Browse** button to launch the *File Open* dialog box.
3. Locate and select the Excel file that contains the records you want to import.
4. Click the **Open** button. The *File Open* dialog box closes.
5. Select the **Append a copy of the records to the table** radio button.

Figure 1-61 *Excel* button

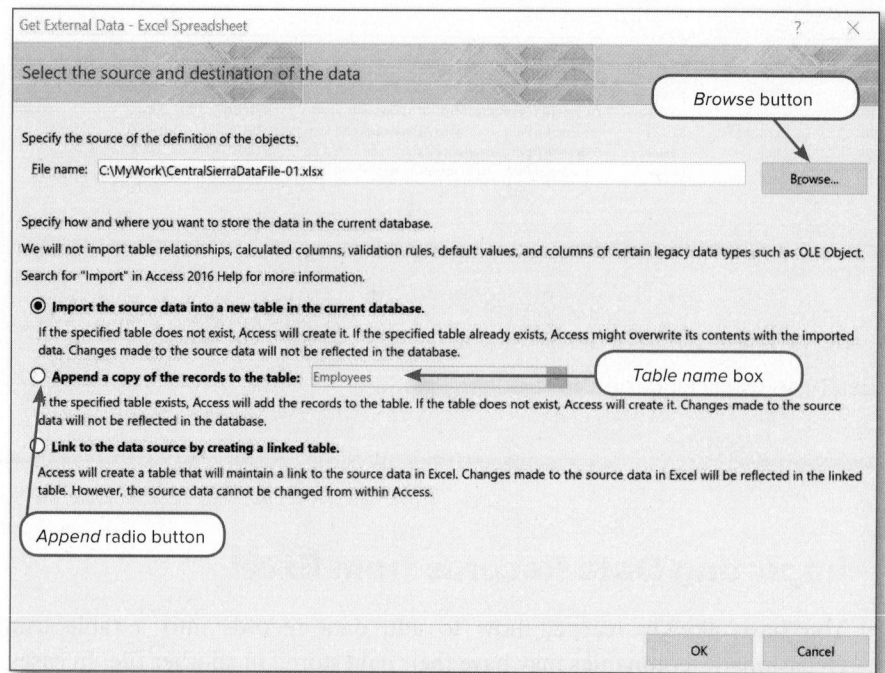

Figure 1-62 *Get External Data – Excel Spreadsheet* dialog box

6. Click the **drop-down arrow** in the *table name* box and select the desired table.

7. Click **OK** to launch the *Import Spreadsheet Wizard* (Figure 1-63). The data records should display in the *Wizard* window.

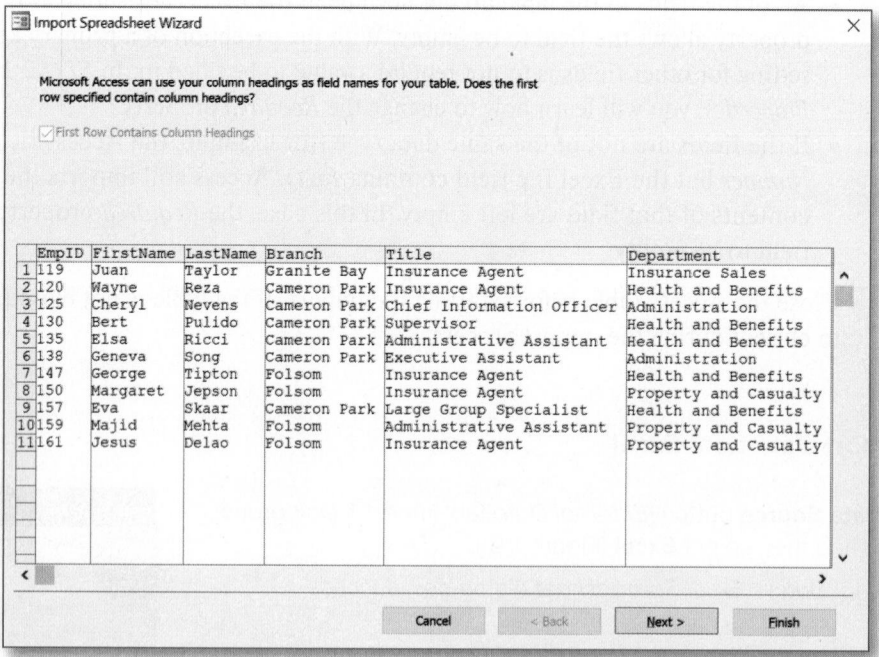

Figure 1-63 *Import Spreadsheet Wizard*

8. Click the **Next** button to advance to the next page of the *Wizard*.

• Access confirms the name of the table to append the records.

9. Click **Finish**.
 - The *Wizard* displays the *Save Import Steps* screen.
 - If you are frequently going to repeat an import process, you can save the steps to perform the action more quickly.
10. Click the **Close** button.
11. Open the table to verify that the records were successfully added into the table.

SLO 1.5

Exploring Datasheet View

As you have seen, you can use *Datasheet* view to add new fields into a table. However, the primary use of *Datasheet* view is to add, modify, delete, or view the data records. The *Navigation* buttons are used to move among the fields and records in *Datasheet* view. *Datasheet* view also provides many options to adjust the display of your data within a table. You can also choose to hide fields and to display totals in *Datasheet* view. This section reviews how to navigate among records, how to adjust *Datasheet* view display settings, how to hide fields, and how to add total rows.

Navigation Buttons

Access provides many different ways to navigate among the data records stored in your tables. For example, you can navigate using the keyboard arrow keys and the scroll bar.

Figure 1-64 *Navigation* bar

This works fine on tables that do not have too many records. However, in many cases, you may want to get to a specific record more quickly.

The *Navigation bar* provides additional methods to move among table records. It is located in the bottom-left corner of a table viewed in *Datasheet* view. The *Navigation* bar contains navigation buttons, a filter status message, and a *Search* box (Figure 1-64). Searching and filtering will be explained in *SLO 1.6: Using Search, Sort, and Filter Tools to Find Records in a Table*.

The *Navigation* buttons are located on the left side of the *Navigation* bar. The functionality of each button is explained in Table 1-7.

Table 1-7: Navigation Buttons in Access

Button	Description	
◄	Move to the first record of the table.	
◄	Move to the previous record of the table.	
4 of 16	The number of the current record, along with the total number of records. Type the number of the record where you wish to move.	
►	Move to the next record in the table.	
►		Move to the last record of the table.
►*	Create a new record.	

Refine the Datasheet Layout

You can adjust the default display settings in *Datasheet* view several ways. The settings change both the view of the table on the screen and the printed contents of a table.

Sometimes you may be given specific design guidelines based on company standards. Other times you need to use your judgment to evaluate the best way to have the data display. For example, the default column width or row height of a field may not be large enough to display the entire contents. You may wish to adjust the alignment, change the display font and size, or adjust the row colors and display gridlines. You can also hide and unhide table fields and add totals to the table.

If you make a change to the datasheet layout that you do not like, the *Undo* button cannot be used to reverse those changes. However, several options are available for making a correction:

- You can repeat the steps you followed to make the changes and select the previous settings.
- You can close the table without saving your changes. Keep in mind that if you close the table without saving changes, you lose all of the changes made since the last save.

Modify the Field Order

You may need to modify the order in which the fields display in a datasheet. You can move a single column, or move a group of adjacent columns.

▶**HOW TO: Modify the Field Order**

1. Place your pointer over the field name of the column you wish to move.
 - The selection pointer appears (Figure 1-65).
2. Click to select the column.
 - The selected column is highlighted in blue.
 - The pointer changes to the normal pointer.

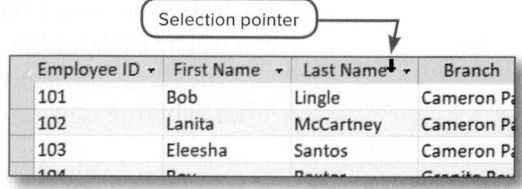

Figure 1-65 Selection pointer

▶ **MORE INFO**

Move a group of adjacent columns by selecting all of the desired columns. To select multiple columns, click to select the first column, and before you release the selected column, drag the selection pointer to the adjacent columns.

3. Click, hold, and drag the pointer to move the column to the new location.
 - A black, vertical line (Figure 1-66) moves with you to indicate the location where the column will be moved.
4. Release the pointer.
 - The column moves to the new location (Figure 1-67).

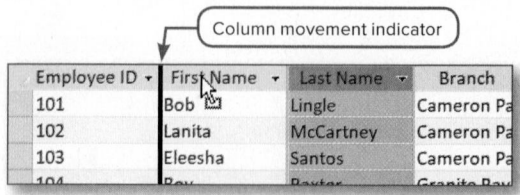

Figure 1-66 Column movement indicator

Press **Ctrl+Spacebar** to select the current column.

Press **Shift+Right Arrow** to increase the selection to include the adjacent column to the right.

Press **Shift+Left Arrow** to increase the selection to the adjacent column to the left.

Employee ID ▾	Last Name ▾	First Name ▾	Branch
101	Lingle	Bob	Cameron P...
102	McCartney	Lanita	Cameron P...
103	Santos	Eleesha	Cameron P...
104	Baxter	Roy	Granite B...

Figure 1-67 Moved column

Select a Display Font Face and Font Size

Access provides many of the standard text formatting options available in other Microsoft Office programs. These formatting options are found in the *Text Formatting* group on the *Home* tab as displayed in Figure 1-68.

The *font face* specifies the shape of the text. The *font size* specifies the size

Figure 1-68 *Text Formatting* group on the *Home* tab

of text, measured in *points* (pt.). A point is equal to 1/72 of an inch. *Font style* options include **bolding**, *italicizing*, and <u>underlining</u>.

> **MORE INFO**
>
> The default font face and size in Microsoft Access are Calibri and 11 pt. As desired, change the default font face and size.

The type of change you wish to apply determines the specific menu options you select.

- Change the font face by clicking the **Font** drop-down list in the *Text Formatting* group [*Home* tab] and selecting the desired font.
- Change the size of the font by clicking the **Font Size** drop-down list in the *Text Formatting* group [*Home* tab] and selecting the size.
- Change the style of the font by clicking the desired style button in the *Text Formatting* group [*Home* tab].

Changes to a font face, size, or style are applied to the entire datasheet. If you want only specific content to have a different format, select the **Rich Text** option available on the **More Fields** button [*Table Tools Fields* tab, *Add & Delete* group] when adding the field in *Datasheet* view. Rich text is a special text format applied to a *Long Text* data type that enables you to store formatted text.

Modify the Row Height

Adjust the *row height* to change the amount of space that displays between rows. When you change the row height in Access, all of the rows change to the new height.

▶HOW TO: Modify the Row Height

1. Place your pointer on the border of a record selector of a row in your table.

 - Because your changes affect all the rows, it does not matter which row you select.
 - The resize arrow appears (Figure 1-69).

2. Click, hold, and drag the resize arrow to increase or decrease the height of the rows.

 - A black, horizontal line moves to indicate the new height (Figure 1-70).

3. Release the resize arrow.

 - The rows change to the new height.
 - The content of columns that are narrower than needed automatically wraps within the cell (Figure 1-71).

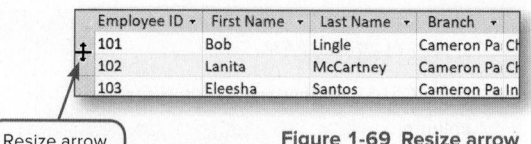

Figure 1-69 Resize arrow

Figure 1-70 Row height indicator

Figure 1-71 Changed row height

▶HOW TO: Modify the Row Height Using the Context Menu

1. Click the **record selector** of a row in your table.

 - The selected row is highlighted in blue.
 - Because your changes affect all the rows, it does not matter which row you select.

2. Place your pointer over the record selector and right-click to open the context menu (Figure 1-72).

3. Select **Row Height** to open the *Row Height* dialog box.

4. Type the desired height in the *Row Height* box.

5. Click **OK** to close the dialog box.

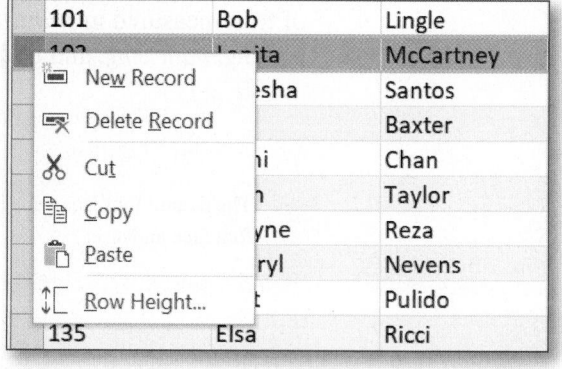

Figure 1-72 *Row* Context menu

Modify the Column Width

Adjust the *column width* to change the amount of text that displays. You can set each field to a desired width. You can also select a set of adjacent columns and set the same width to all of them in one operation.

▶HOW TO: Modify the Column Width of Selected Fields

1. Place your pointer on the right border of the field name of the column you wish to change. The resize arrow appears (Figure 1-73).

 - If you wish to change the width of adjacent columns, you must first select all of the columns. Click and hold to select the first column, then drag the selection pointer to the adjacent columns (Figure 1-74).

Figure 1-73 Resize arrow

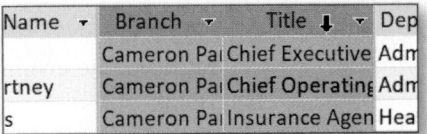
- Place your pointer over the border of the right-most field.

2. Click, hold, and drag the resize arrow to increase or decrease the width of the field(s).

 - A black, vertical line moves with you to indicate the new width.

3. Release the resize arrow.

 - The field column(s) changes to the new width.

Access can also automatically adjust the width of the column(s) to fit the widest entry. To have Access *AutoFit* the column(s) width to the widest entry, double-click instead of click and drag when the resize arrow appears. You can also use *AutoFit* to change all the datasheet columns by selecting the entire datasheet.

▶ HOW TO: Modify the Column Width of All Fields Using AutoFit

1. Click the **Select All** button (Figure 1-75), in the upper-left corner of the datasheet, to select the entire datasheet. All of the rows and columns are highlighted in blue.

2. Place your pointer on the right border of any of the field names.

3. Double-click the **resize arrow** (Figure 1-76).

 - All the fields automatically adjust to their widest entry or to the width of the field caption if that is larger than the contents.

Figure 1-75 *Select All* button

Figure 1-76 Adjust the column width of all fields

Modify the Field Alignment

The data type determines the default *field alignment*, or position relative to the edges, of each field.

- Left-aligned data types include *Short Text*, *Long Text*, and *Hyperlink*.
- Right-aligned data types include *Number*, *Large Number*, *Date/Time*, *Currency*, and *Calculated*.
- Center-aligned data types include *Yes/No* and *Attachment*. You are not able to change the alignment of fields with these *Yes/No* and *Attachment* data types.

Change the default alignment by selecting the field and then clicking the desired alignment button in the *Text Formatting* group [*Home* tab] (Figure 1-77). Alignment changes to a field are applied across all the database records, not just one cell. Figure 1-77 also illustrates several other buttons useful in formatting a datasheet.

Figure 1-77 *Text Formatting* group buttons

Display Gridlines

Gridlines help visually frame the rows and columns in a datasheet with a border. The default settings in Access display both vertical and horizontal gridlines in a gray color.

The gridline display options include:

- Both vertical and horizontal gridlines
- Only horizontal gridlines
- Only vertical gridlines
- No gridlines

To change the gridline settings, click the **Gridlines** button in the *Text Formatting* group [*Home* tab] to display the gallery of gridline options (Figure 1-78) and then select the desired setting.

Figure 1-78 Gridlines display options

> **MORE INFO**
>
> You can also change the default gridline settings in Microsoft Access.

Display Alternate Row Colors

Alternate row colors help you easily scan the records and fields in your datasheet. You can change the alternating colors that display or remove the colors altogether.

To change the alternate row color settings, click the **Alternate Row Color** button in the *Text Formatting* group [*Home* tab] (Figure 1-77) to display the gallery of color options. Select the desired color.

Use the Datasheet Formatting Dialog Box

If you are going to apply several changes to the datasheet layout, you may wish to use the ***Datasheet Formatting*** dialog box.

HOW TO: Make Multiple Formatting Changes with the Datasheet Formatting Dialog Box

1. Click the **Text Formatting launcher** [*Home* tab, *Text Formatting* group] to open the *Datasheet Formatting* dialog box (Figure 1-79).
2. Select the desired settings of the different options.
3. Click **OK** when finished.

The *Datasheet Formatting* dialog box enables you to change several other formatting options that are not available through the *Home* tab. These options include the **Cell Effect**, **Background Color**, and **Gridline Color**.

Figure 1-79 *Datasheet Formatting* dialog box

Hide and Unhide Table Fields

If a table has many fields, it may not be possible to see all of them at the same time. You can hide data to optimize your screen space. Access does not provide any visual indications that table columns have been hidden.

HOW TO: Hide a Table Field

1. Select the column to be hidden.
2. Click the **More** button [*Home* tab, *Records* group] and then select **Hide Fields**.

> **ANOTHER WAY**
>
> Right-click the field column heading and select **Hide Fields** from the context menu.

To hide multiple adjacent columns, select all the columns before selecting **Hide Fields** from either the *More* button or context menu. Remember that you click the first column heading, press and hold the **Shift** key, and then select the last column.

To redisplay hidden fields, you need to unhide the columns.

HOW TO: Unhide Table Fields

1. Click the **More** button [*Home* tab, *Records* group] and then select **Unhide Fields** to open the *Unhide Columns* dialog box (Figure 1-80). Checked fields display in the table, and unchecked fields are hidden.

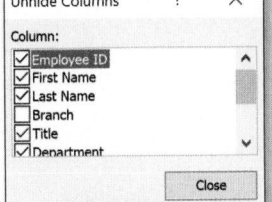

> **ANOTHER WAY**
>
> Right-click any field column heading and select **Unhide Fields** from the context menu.

Figure 1-80 *Unhide Columns* dialog box

2. Click all of the field check boxes that you wish to unhide.

3. Click **Close**.

Add Total Rows

At times you may wish to have Access calculate totals based on the data in a table. For example, you may wish to know the total salary amount for all Central Sierra employees. In chapter 3, you will learn how to use queries to summarize data, but you can also summarize data in a table with a *Total* row. After you add a *Total* row to the *Datasheet* view of the table, you then select the fields to calculate, as well as the type of calculation.

▶HOW TO: Add a Total Row

1. Click the **Totals** button [*Home* tab, *Records* group].
 - A *Total* row is added below the append row.
 - The *Totals* button on the *Ribbon* is gray to indicate that a *Total* row has been added.

2. Click the *Total* row cell of the field you wish to summarize, click the **drop-down arrow** in that cell, and select the desired function (Figure 1-81).
 - The available functions vary depending on the data type of the field.
 - The table updates and the calculated value displays in the *Total* row cell.
 - You can add totals to multiple fields in the table.
 - As records are added or deleted, the totals automatically recalculate.

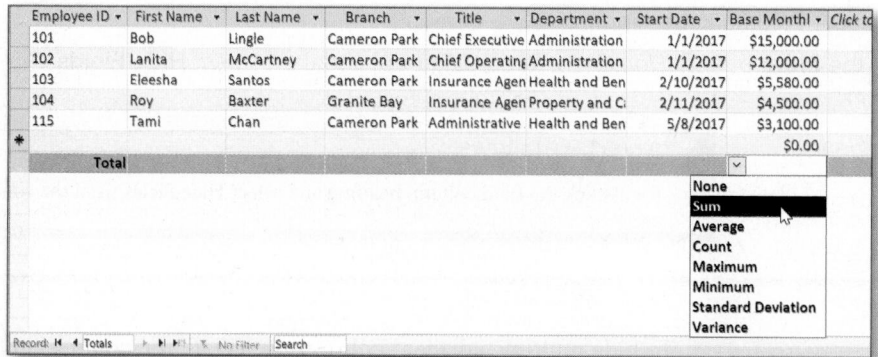

Figure 1-81 *Total* row in a table

To remove a *Total* row from a table, click the **Totals** button [*Home* tab, *Records* group].

Save Changes

If you make changes to the design settings of the datasheet layout, you must save the table for those changes to be permanent. Select one of the previously discussed options for saving the design changes to your table.

For this project, you import additional data into the *Employee* table. You also modify the field order, font size, row height, column width, and field alignment of your *Employee* table. Finally, you enhance the *Datasheet* view by modifying the gridline settings, alternating row colors, hiding a field, and adding totals.

Files Needed: *[your initials] PP A1-2.accdb* and *CentralSierraDataFile-01.xlsx* (*Student data files are available in the* Library *of your SIMnet account.*)
Completed Project File Name: *[your initials] PP A1-3.accdb*

1. Open the *[your initials] PP A1-2* database file that you created in *Pause & Practice 1-2*.

2. Save a new copy of your database.
 a. Select the **Save As** button [*File* tab]. The *Access Database* button should be selected in the *Save Database As* area.
 b. Click the **Save As** button.
 c. Select the desired location in which to store the copy of your database.
 d. Name the database [your initials] PP A1-3 in the *File name* box.
 e. Click the **Save** button.
 f. Click the **Enable Content** button in the *Security Warning* message bar if prompted.

3. Import data into the *Employees* table.
 a. Click the **New Data Source** button [*External Data* tab, *Import & Link* group], select **From File**, and then select **Excel** to launch the *Get External Data – Excel Spreadsheet* dialog box.
 b. Click the **Browse** button to launch the *File Open* dialog box.
 c. Locate and select the *CentralSierraDataFile-01* Excel file.
 d. Click the **Open** button. The *File Open* dialog box closes.
 e. Select the **Append a copy of the records to the table** radio button.
 f. Click the **drop-down arrow** in the *table name* box and select the **Employees** table if needed.
 g. Click **OK** to launch the *Import Spreadsheet Wizard*. The data records should display in the *Wizard* window as shown in Figure 1-82.

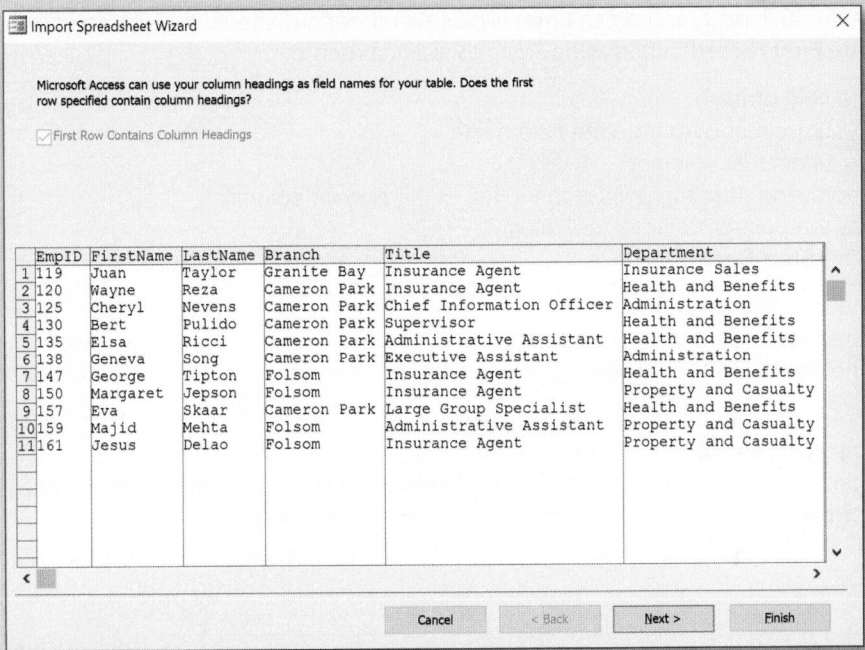

Figure 1-82 *Import Spreadsheet Wizard*

h. Click the **Next** button to advance to the next page of the *Import Spreadsheet Wizard*.
i. Verify that the *Import to Table* box contains the *Employees* table and click **Finish**.
j. Click the **Close** button. It is not necessary to save these import steps.

4. Open the **Employees** table in *Datasheet* view to verify that the 11 records imported correctly. The table should contain a total of 16 records and appear like that shown in Figure 1-83. Depending on the height and width of your Access window, you may see fewer rows and columns. Additionally, the horizontal and vertical scroll sliders may display if the window is not large enough to display all of the data.

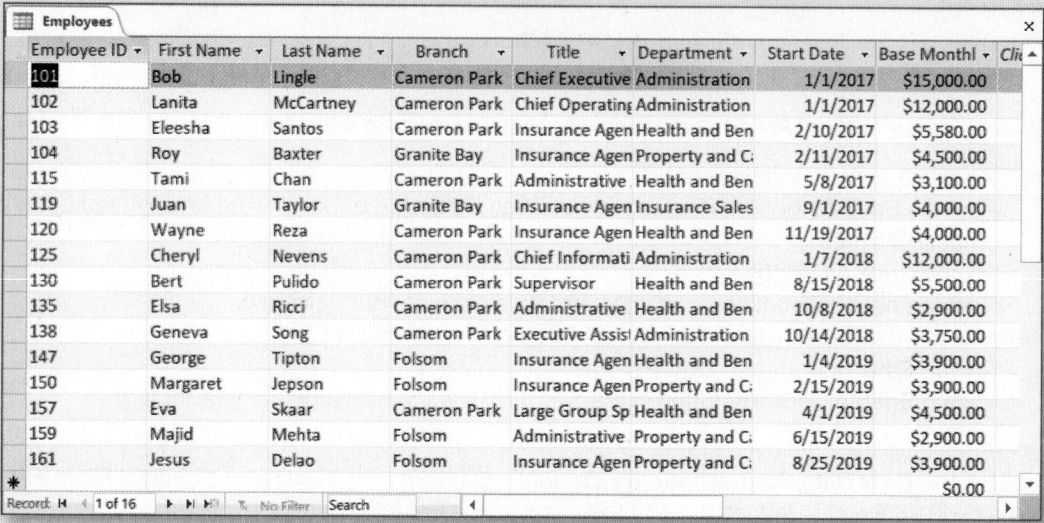

Employee ID	First Name	Last Name	Branch	Title	Department	Start Date	Base Monthl	Cli
101	Bob	Lingle	Cameron Park	Chief Executive	Administration	1/1/2017	$15,000.00	
102	Lanita	McCartney	Cameron Park	Chief Operating	Administration	1/1/2017	$12,000.00	
103	Eleesha	Santos	Cameron Park	Insurance Agen	Health and Ben	2/10/2017	$5,580.00	
104	Roy	Baxter	Granite Bay	Insurance Agen	Property and C	2/11/2017	$4,500.00	
115	Tami	Chan	Cameron Park	Administrative	Health and Ben	5/8/2017	$3,100.00	
119	Juan	Taylor	Granite Bay	Insurance Agen	Insurance Sales	9/1/2017	$4,000.00	
120	Wayne	Reza	Cameron Park	Insurance Agen	Health and Ben	11/19/2017	$4,000.00	
125	Cheryl	Nevens	Cameron Park	Chief Informati	Administration	1/7/2018	$12,000.00	
130	Bert	Pulido	Cameron Park	Supervisor	Health and Ben	8/15/2018	$5,500.00	
135	Elsa	Ricci	Cameron Park	Administrative	Health and Ben	10/8/2018	$2,900.00	
138	Geneva	Song	Cameron Park	Executive Assist	Administration	10/14/2018	$3,750.00	
147	George	Tipton	Folsom	Insurance Agen	Health and Ben	1/4/2019	$3,900.00	
150	Margaret	Jepson	Folsom	Insurance Agen	Property and C	2/15/2019	$3,900.00	
157	Eva	Skaar	Cameron Park	Large Group Sp	Health and Ben	4/1/2019	$4,500.00	
159	Majid	Mehta	Folsom	Administrative	Property and C	6/15/2019	$2,900.00	
161	Jesus	Delao	Folsom	Insurance Agen	Property and C	8/25/2019	$3,900.00	
							$0.00	

Record: ◄ ◄ 1 of 16 ► ►I ►I* ⊠ No Filter Search

Figure 1-83 *Datasheet* view of the *Employees* table

5. Use the *Navigation* buttons to move among records.
 a. Click the **Next record** button to navigate to the second record.
 b. Click the **Next record** button three more times to navigate to the fifth record.
 c. Click the **Last record** button to navigate to the last record.
 d. Click the **Current record** box. It changes from displaying 16 of 16 to simply displaying 16.
 e. Delete the 16, type 7, and press **Enter**. The seventh record should now be selected.
 f. Click the **First record** button to navigate to the first record.

6. Change the field order.
 a. Place your pointer over the **Title** field name.
 b. Click to select that column.
 c. Click, hold, and drag the pointer to the left of the *Branch* column.
 d. Release the pointer to move the column.
 e. Move the **Start Date** column to the right of the *Base Monthly Salary* column.

7. Change the font face and size.
 a. Click the **Font** drop-down list [*Home* tab, *Text Formatting* group] and select **Arial**.
 b. Click the **Font Size** drop-down list [*Home* tab, *Text Formatting* group] and select **12**.

8. Change the row height using the context menu.
 a. Click the **record selector** of a row in your table.
 b. Place the pointer over the record selector and right-click to open the context menu.
 c. Select **Row Height** to open the *Row Height* dialog box.
 d. Type 17 in the *Row Height* box.
 e. Click **OK**.

9. Change the width of the table columns.
 a. Click the **Select All** button in the upper-left corner of the datasheet.
 b. Place your pointer on the right border of any of the field names.

c. Double-click the **resize arrow** to *AutoFit* the columns. The column widths automatically adjust.

d. Click any cell to release the *Select All* setting.

e. Place your pointer over the *Base Monthly Salary* column, right-click the field name to open the context menu and select **Field Width** to open the *Column Width* dialog box.

f. Type 10 in the *Column Width* dialog box and click **OK**. The table should now look similar to Figure 1-84. The *Base Monthly Salary* column displays a series of # symbols in cells where the width is not wide enough to display the field content. Depending on the width of your Access window, the number of rows that display the # symbols may vary.

Employee ID ▾	First Name ▾	Last Name ▾	Title ▾	Branch ▾	Department ▾	Base M(▾	Start Date ▾	Click to A ▴
101	Bob	Lingle	Chief Executive Officer	Cameron Park	Administration	5,000.00	1/1/2017	
102	Lanita	McCartney	Chief Operating Officer	Cameron Park	Administration	######	1/1/2017	
103	Eleesha	Santos	Insurance Agent	Cameron Park	Health and Benefits	5,580.00	2/10/2017	
104	Roy	Baxter	Insurance Agent	Granite Bay	Property and Casualty	4,500.00	2/11/2017	
115	Tami	Chan	Administrative Assistant	Cameron Park	Health and Benefits	3,100.00	5/8/2017	
119	Juan	Taylor	Insurance Agent	Granite Bay	Insurance Sales	4,000.00	9/1/2017	
120	Wayne	Reza	Insurance Agent	Cameron Park	Health and Benefits	4,000.00	11/19/2017	
125	Cheryl	Nevens	Chief Information Officer	Cameron Park	Administration	######	1/7/2018	
130	Bert	Pulido	Supervisor	Cameron Park	Health and Benefits	5,500.00	8/15/2018	
135	Elsa	Ricci	Administrative Assistant	Cameron Park	Health and Benefits	2,900.00	10/8/2018	
138	Geneva	Song	Executive Assistant	Cameron Park	Administration	3,750.00	10/14/2018	
147	George	Tipton	Insurance Agent	Folsom	Health and Benefits	3,900.00	1/4/2019	
150	Margaret	Jensen	Insurance Agent	Folsom	Property and Casualty	3,900.00	2/15/2019	

Record: I◀ ◀ 1 of 16 ▶ ▶I ▶❑ ☒ No Filter Search

Vertical scroll slider

Horizontal scroll slider

Figure 1-84 Adjusted column widths of the *Employees* table

10. Increase the width of any columns that display a series of # symbols.

a. Move the horizontal scroll slider at the bottom of the datasheet to the right so that the *Base Monthly Salary* column moves to the middle of the window. This enables you to increase the width of this column more easily.

b. Place your pointer over the *Base Monthly Salary* column, right-click the field name to open the context menu and select **Field Width** to open the *Column Width* dialog box.

c. Type 23 in the *Column Width* dialog box and click **OK**. The column should now be wide enough to display the contents instead of the # symbols.

d. Repeat these steps for all columns that are too narrow.

11. Change the field alignment.

a. Move the horizontal scroll slider all the way to the left of the datasheet window if needed.

b. Select the **Employee ID** column.

c. Click the **Center** button [*Home* tab, *Text Formatting* group].

12. Hide a field.

a. Select the **Branch** column.

b. Click the **More** button [*Home* tab, *Records* group] and then select **Hide Fields**.

13. Add a total row.

a. Click the **Totals** button [*Home* tab, *Records* group].

b. Click the *Total* row cell of the *BaseMonthlySalary* field, click the **drop-down arrow** in that cell and select the **Sum** function.

14. Change the gridlines and alternate row colors using the *Datasheet Formatting* dialog box.

a. Click the **Text Formatting launcher** [*Home* tab, *Text Formatting* group].

b. Click the **Alternate Background Color** drop-down list in the *Datasheet Formatting* dialog box (Figure 1-85) and select **Blue-Gray, Text 2, Lighter 80%** (fourth column, second row in the *Theme Colors* category).

Figure 1-85 *Datasheet Formatting* dialog box

c. Uncheck the **Horizontal** check box in the *Gridlines Shown* area.
d. Click the **Gridline Color** drop-down list and Select **Blue-Gray, Text 2, Darker 25%** (fourth column, fifth row in the *Theme Colors* category).
e. Click **OK** to close the dialog box.
f. Click the *Employee ID* cell for **Employee 102** as shown in Figure 1-86. Depending on your window width, you may need to scroll to see all of the columns. The slightly darker blue color shown in the second row indicates that this is the current record.

15. Press **Ctrl+S** to save the table.

16. Click the **X** in the upper-right corner of the datasheet to close the table.

17. Close the database by clicking the **Close** button [*File* tab].

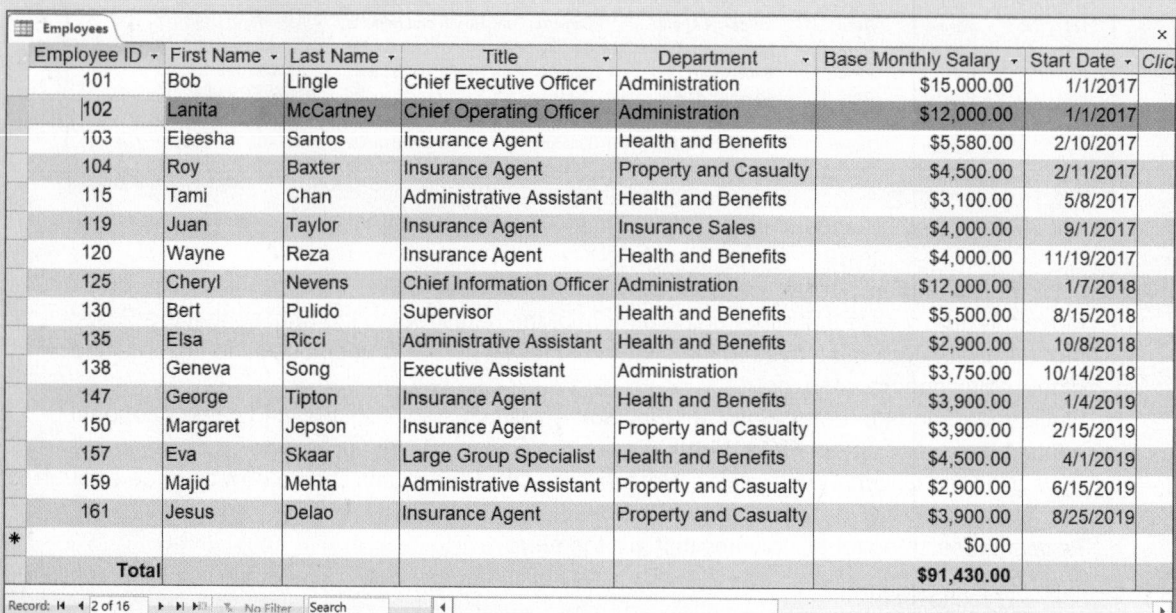

Employee ID	First Name	Last Name	Title	Department	Base Monthly Salary	Start Date	Clic
101	Bob	Lingle	Chief Executive Officer	Administration	$15,000.00	1/1/2017	
102	Lanita	McCartney	Chief Operating Officer	Administration	$12,000.00	1/1/2017	
103	Eleesha	Santos	Insurance Agent	Health and Benefits	$5,580.00	2/10/2017	
104	Roy	Baxter	Insurance Agent	Property and Casualty	$4,500.00	2/11/2017	
115	Tami	Chan	Administrative Assistant	Health and Benefits	$3,100.00	5/8/2017	
119	Juan	Taylor	Insurance Agent	Insurance Sales	$4,000.00	9/1/2017	
120	Wayne	Reza	Insurance Agent	Health and Benefits	$4,000.00	11/19/2017	
125	Cheryl	Nevens	Chief Information Officer	Administration	$12,000.00	1/7/2018	
130	Bert	Pulido	Supervisor	Health and Benefits	$5,500.00	8/15/2018	
135	Elsa	Ricci	Administrative Assistant	Health and Benefits	$2,900.00	10/8/2018	
138	Geneva	Song	Executive Assistant	Administration	$3,750.00	10/14/2018	
147	George	Tipton	Insurance Agent	Health and Benefits	$3,900.00	1/4/2019	
150	Margaret	Jepson	Insurance Agent	Property and Casualty	$3,900.00	2/15/2019	
157	Eva	Skaar	Large Group Specialist	Health and Benefits	$4,500.00	4/1/2019	
159	Majid	Mehta	Administrative Assistant	Property and Casualty	$2,900.00	6/15/2019	
161	Jesus	Delao	Insurance Agent	Property and Casualty	$3,900.00	8/25/2019	
*					$0.00		
Total					**$91,430.00**		

Record: ◄ ◄ 2 of 16 ► ►► ►▣ ⁞ No Filter Search

Figure 1-86 PP A1-3 completed

SLO 1.6

Using Search, Sort, and Filter Tools to Find Records in a Table

When the number of records in a database table increases, it is important to be able to quickly and easily organize and locate specific records. Access provides a number of ways to find data, change the order of how records display, and limit the records that display in the datasheet.

Search Data in a Table

The search functions enable you to find data by looking for specific values. The *Search* box on the *Navigation* bar is a quick and easy way to locate the first record containing a specific value. The *Find* button in the *Find* group [*Home* tab] provides a more powerful way to search for records.

▶HOW TO: Find Data in a Table Using the Search Box

1. Click the **Search** box in the *Navigation* bar.
2. Enter the search value you want to locate.
 - Access evaluates the criteria as you enter each character and moves to the first field that matches those criteria (Figure 1-87).

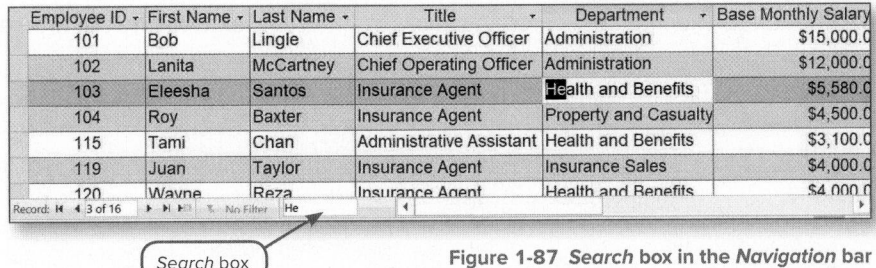

Employee ID ▾	First Name ▾	Last Name ▾	Title ▾	Department ▾	Base Monthly Salary
101	Bob	Lingle	Chief Executive Officer	Administration	$15,000.0
102	Lanita	McCartney	Chief Operating Officer	Administration	$12,000.0
103	Eleesha	Santos	Insurance Agent	Health and Benefits	$5,580.0
104	Roy	Baxter	Insurance Agent	Property and Casualty	$4,500.0
115	Tami	Chan	Administrative Assistant	Health and Benefits	$3,100.0
119	Juan	Taylor	Insurance Agent	Insurance Sales	$4,000.0
120	Wayne	Reza	Insurance Agent	Health and Benefits	$4,000.0

Record: H ◀ 3 of 16 ▶ H Hᐩ ▾ No Filter He

Search box

Figure 1-87 *Search box in the* Navigation *bar*

 - As you type more data into the *Search* box, Access continues to locate the first field that matches. The search is not case sensitive. A search for Health matches health, Health, and HEALTH.
 - If a match is not found, the field or record that was previously selected remains highlighted.

▶HOW TO: Find Data in a Table Using the Find Button

1. Click the **Find** button [*Home* tab, *Find* group] (Figure 1-88) to open the *Find and Replace* dialog box (Figure 1-89).
 - If you want to search only in a specific field, select that field before you click the *Find* button.

Figure 1-88 *Find button*

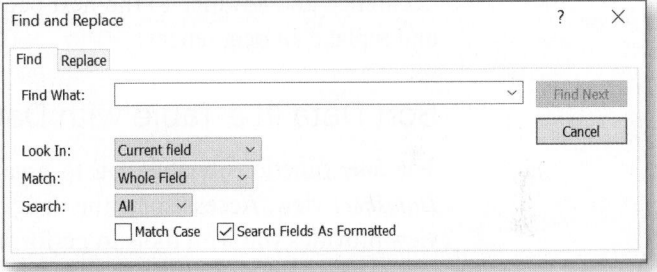

Figure 1-89 *Find and Replace dialog box*

▶ **ANOTHER WAY**

Select a column and then right-click to open the context menu. Select **Find** to open the *Find and Replace* dialog box.

Press **Ctrl+F** to open the *Find and Replace* dialog box.

▶ **MORE INFO**

The initial settings of your dialog box may be different. If you previously searched for a value and did not clear out that value, the previous search criteria displays in the *Find What* box.

2. Enter the search value you want to search in the *Find What* box.
3. Click the **Look In** drop-down list to select either **Current field** or **Current document**. If *Current field* is selected, the search only looks for a match in the current field.
4. Click the **Match** drop-down list to select the appropriate option.
 - **Any Part of Field**: The search value must be somewhere in the field. Use this option to find a value that contains the search value anywhere in the field.

- **Whole Field**: The search value must match the entire contents of a field. Use this option to find an exact match.
- **Start of Field**: The search value is at the beginning of the field. Use this option to find a value that starts with a certain character or number.

5. Click the **Search** drop-down list to select **All**, **Up**, or **Down**. Selecting *Up* or *Down* searches in that direction from the current record only.

6. Check the **Match Case** check box to perform a case-sensitive search and limit the results to the case of the search value.

7. Click the **Find Next** button to execute the search. Access searches the table to find the first record that meets the criteria.
 - If that is the desired record, click the **Cancel** button to close the *Find and Replace* dialog box or click the **Find Next** button to continue searching.
 - If the search value does not exist in the table, Access displays an information message box, indicating the record was not found.

ANOTHER WAY

If the *Find and Replace* dialog box is closed, press **Shift+F4** to find the next record that meets the criteria.

8. Click **Cancel** to close the *Find and Replace* dialog box.

As desired, you can change data using the *Replace* tab on the *Find and Replace* dialog box. Press **Ctrl+H** to open the *Find and Replace* dialog box with the *Replace* tab selected. Enter the search value in the *Find What* box. Enter the replacement value in the *Replace With* box. Click **Find Next** to find the first occurence of the data. Click the **Replace** button to replace just that occurence and advance to the next occurence. Or you can click the **Replace All** button to find and replace all occurences.

Sort Data in a Table with Datasheet View

The *Sort* functions enable you to organize your data. By default, when you open a table in *Datasheet* view, Access sorts the data records in ascending order by the first field. *Datasheet* view provides you with tools to perform a simple sort. You can sort the datasheet by one field, or a set of adjacent fields, in ascending or descending order.

- *Ascending order* is *lowest to highest* for a numeric field or *A to Z* for a text field.
- *Descending order* means *highest to lowest* for a numeric field or *Z to A* for a text field.

Sort Data on a Single Field

The simplest sort is to sort the datasheet on one field. You can either use the *Ascending* or *Descending* buttons in the *Sort & Filter* group [*Home* tab] or open the drop-down list for the desired column.

▶HOW TO: Sort Data in a Table on a Single Field Using the Sort & Filter Group

1. Click the **field name** to select the column you wish to sort.

ANOTHER WAY

Instead of selecting the column, just click any cell in the desired column.

2. Click either the **Ascending** or **Descending** button [*Home* tab, *Sort & Filter* group] (Figure 1-90).

- The datasheet updates to show the results of the sort. Figure 1-91 shows the employee records sorted in descending order by the *Department* field.
- The *field name* cell changes to display either an up or down sort indicator arrow to the right of the drop-down arrow to visually indicate that the

Figure 1-90 *Sort & Filter* group on the *Home* tab

Employee ID ▾	First Name ▾	Last Name ▾	Title ▾	Department ↓	Base Monthly Salary
159	Majid	Mehta	Administrative Assistant	Property and Casualty	$2,900.0
150	Margaret	Jepson	Insurance Agent	Property and Casualty	$3,900.0
104	Roy	Baxter	Insurance Agent	Property and Casualty	$4,500.0
161	Jesus	Delao	Insurance Agent	Property and Casualty	$3,900.0
119	Juan	Taylor	Insurance Agent	Insurance Sales	00.0
130	Bert	Pulido	Supervisor	Health and Benefits	$5,500.0
103	Eleesha	Santos	Insurance Agent	Health and Benefits	$5,580.0

Sort Indicator arrow

Figure 1-91 Employee records sorted on the *Department* field

datasheet has been sorted on this field. If you want the table records to remain in this sorted order, you must save the table.

HOW TO: Sort Data in a Table on a Single Field Using the Drop-Down List

1. Click the **drop-down arrow** to the right of the field name you wish to sort.

- The column turns blue, indicating it has been selected.
- The drop-down list opens (Figure 1-92).

2. Select either **Sort A to Z** or **Sort Z to A** on the drop-down list.

- The datasheet updates to show the results of the sort.
- If you are sorting a numeric field, the drop-down list options are *Sort Smallest to Largest* and *Sort Largest to Smallest*.

ANOTHER WAY

Right-click to open the context menu, then select the desired sort order.

Figure 1-92 *Sort* drop-down list

Sort Data on Multiple Fields

Sometimes sorting your datasheet on multiple fields makes it easier to organize the data records. In *Datasheet* view, you can sort on multiple adjacent fields using the same sort order.

- The left-most selected field is sorted first.
- If identical items appear in the first field, the second field is sorted.
- This process continues for all additional selected fields.

> ### MORE INFO
>
> If the fields that you wish to sort together are not adjacent, you first need to move them together. Refer back to the "Modify the Field Order" section in *SLO 1.5: Exploring Datasheet View* if necessary.

1. Click and hold the pointer over the *Field name* of the first column you want to sort. With the selection pointer still displayed, drag the pointer to the adjacent columns.
2. Release the pointer.

▶ **ANOTHER WAY**

Press **Ctrl+Spacebar** to select the first column you want to sort.

Press **Shift+Right Arrow** to increase the selection to include the adjacent column to the right or press **Shift+Left Arrow** to increase the selection to the adjacent column to the left.

3. Click either the **Ascending** or **Descending** button [*Home* tab, *Sort & Filter* group].

 - The datasheet updates to show the results of the sort. Figure 1-93 shows the employee records sorted in ascending order by the *Department* [Administration, Health and Benefits, Insurance Sales, and Property and Casualty] and the *Title* [Administrative Assistant, Chief Executive Officer, Chief Information Officer, Chief Operating Officer, Executive Assistant, etc.] fields.
 - In the example shown in Figure 1-93, column entries "tie" for the *Department,* so the *Title* field determines which record appears at the top of each *Department*.

First Name ▾	Last Name ▾	Department	Title
Bob	Lingle	Administration	Chief Executive Officer
Cheryl	Nevens	Administration	Chief Information Officer
Lanita	McCartney	Administration	Chief Operating Officer
Geneva	Song	Administration	Executive Assistant
Tami	Chan	Health and Benefits	Administrative Assistant
Elsa	Ricci	Health and Benefits	Administrative Assistant
Eleesha	Santos	Health and Benefits	Insurance Agent
Wayne	Reza	Health and Benefits	Insurance Agent
George	Tipton	Health and Benefits	Insurance Agent
Eva	Skaar	Health and Benefits	Large Group Specialist
Bert	Pulido	Health and Benefits	Supervisor
Juan	Taylor	Insurance Sales	Insurance Agent

Department sort indicator ⟶ *Title sort Indicator*

Figure 1-93 Employee records sorted on *Department* and *Title* fields

Remove Sorting Criteria

To return the records in your datasheet to their original order, remove the *Sort* criteria.

Click the **Remove Sort** button [*Home* tab, *Sort & Filter* group] to remove all *Sort* criteria.

▶ **MORE INFO**

If you open a table with a previously saved sort, clicking **Remove Sort** removes the sort.

Filter Data in a Table with Datasheet View

The ***Filter*** functions are helpful in limiting the number of records that display in your datasheet. Several different filter options are available.

Create a Filter by Selection

Filter by Selection enables you to display only the records that match the value in the fields you have selected.

▶HOW TO: Filter Data Using Filter by Selection

1. Click the cell that contains the value you wish to filter.
 - You can select only part of the cell contents as desired.
2. Click the **Selection** button in the *Sort & Filter* group on the *Home* tab (Figure 1-94).
 - The drop-down list shows the available filter options.
 - The available filter options depend on the data type of the field and what criterion is selected. If you only select part of a field, the beginning of the field, or the end of the field, the options differ.
3. Select the desired filter option.
 - The datasheet updates to show the results of the filter.
 - The filter status message changes, indicating the datasheet is filtered.
 - The *Field name* cell displays a *Filter* symbol to the right of the drop-down arrow, indicating this field has been filtered (Figure 1-95).
 - Once a filter has been applied, switch between viewing the complete dataset and the filtered results by clicking the *Toggle Filter* button [*Home* tab, *Sort & Filter* group], shown in the top image in Figure 1-96. When toggled off, the filter status message, shown in the bottom image of Figure 1-96, changes to *Unfiltered* to indicate that a filter exists but is toggled off.

Figure 1-94 *Selection* button in the *Sort & Filter* group

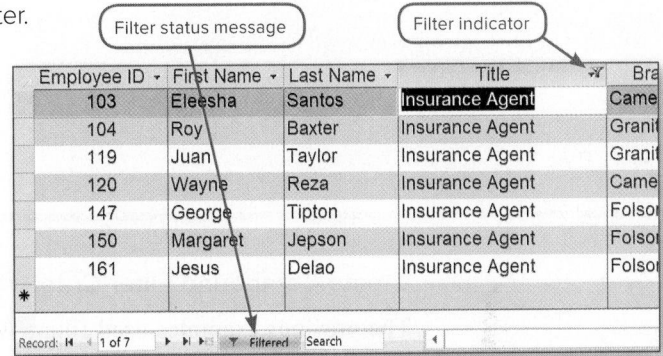

Figure 1-95 Filtered datasheet

> **ANOTHER WAY**
>
> After selecting the desired cell, right-click to open the context menu and then select the desired filter option.

Figure 1-96 *Toggle Filter* button and updated filter status message

Create a Text Filter, Number Filter, or Date Filter

A Text, *Number*, or *Date Filter* filters the records in your database by displaying the records that match the search criteria that you enter, instead of matching criteria you have selected from a cell. Although similar to using a *Filter by Selection*, these filters provide additional options.

▶HOW TO: Filter Data Using a Text, Number, or Date Filter

1. Click the **drop-down arrow** to the right of the field name you wish to filter.
2. Select **Text Filters** on the drop-down list (Figure 1-97).
 - The button name is context sensitive and determined by the type of field you are filtering.
 - The drop-down list displays the available filter options.
 - The filter options are also context sensitive and change based on the type of field.

3. Select the desired filter option on the drop-down list to open the *Custom Filter* dialog box (Figure 1-98). The content of this dialog box depends on the filter option selected.

4. Type the word or value you wish to filter.

5. Click **OK**.

 * The datasheet updates to show the results of the filter.
 * The filter status message changes, indicating the datasheet is filtered.
 * The *Field name* cell displays a *Filter* symbol to the right of the drop-down arrow that indicates this field has been filtered.

Figure 1-97 *Filter* drop-down list

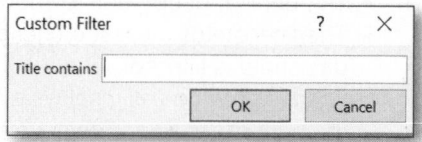

Figure 1-98 *Custom Filter* dialog box

Create Compound Filter Criteria

The previous examples used filters with one search value or criterion. You can create a more complex filter using compound criteria. **Compound criteria** combine more than one search value using the *AND* and *OR* logical operators.

* ***AND logical operator***: The filtered records must contain all of the criteria values.
* ***OR logical operator***: The filtered records must contain at least one of the criteria values.

Generally, searches using *OR* criteria return more results than searches using *AND* criteria. This is because the *AND* operator requires all the criteria to match while the *OR* operator requires only one of the criteria to match.

You can specify compound criteria on one field, or use compound criteria across several fields in your datasheet.

▶**HOW TO:** Filter Data Using "OR" Compound Criteria on One Field

1. Click the **drop-down arrow** to the right of the field name you wish to filter.

 * The drop-down list opens.
 * Initially, all the check boxes are selected.

2. Click the **(Select All)** check box to clear all the check boxes.

3. Click all of the check boxes on the drop-down list that contain the desired criteria (Figure 1-99).

> MORE INFO
>
> Selecting multiple criteria in the same field is an *OR* condition. The returned records contain the first value or the second value or the third value, and so on.

Figure 1-99 *Filter* drop-down list showing *OR* criteria

4. Click **OK**.
 - The datasheet updates to show the results of the filter.

▶**HOW TO:** Filter Data Using "AND" Compound Criteria on Multiple Fields

1. Click the **drop-down arrow** to the right of the first field name you wish to filter.
 - The drop-down list opens.
 - Initially, all the check boxes are selected.
2. Click the **(Select All)** check box to clear all the check boxes.
3. Click all of the check boxes on the drop-down list that contain the desired criteria.
4. Click **OK**.
 - The datasheet updates to show the results of the filter.
5. Click the **drop-down arrow** to the right of the second field name you wish to filter.
6. Click the **(Select All)** check box to remove that criterion.
7. Click all of the check boxes on the drop-down list that contain the desired criteria (Figure 1-100).
8. Click **OK**.
 - The datasheet updates to show the results of the additional filter.
 - Only the records that meet both of the criteria display.
9. Add a filter to additional columns by repeating the earlier steps.

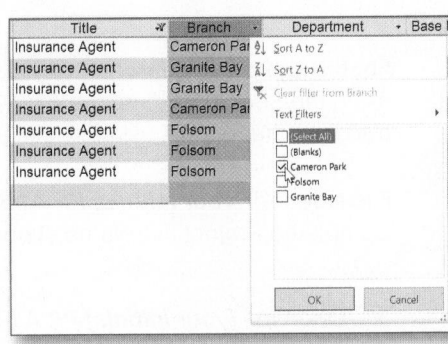

Figure 1-100 Using filters on multiple fields to create *AND* criteria

> ▶ **MORE INFO**
>
> Adding a filter to a second field is an *AND* condition. The returned records match the filter from both fields.

Remove Filter Criteria

To return the records in your datasheet to their original unfiltered state, you must remove the *Filter* criteria. You can remove a filter from just one field or you can remove all of the filters.

▶**HOW TO:** Remove Filter Criteria from a Single Field

1. Click the **drop-down arrow** to the right of the first field name where you wish to remove a filter.
 - The drop-down list opens.
2. Select **Clear filter from Field name** to remove the filter.
 - The phrase "Field name" will not display, but instead the actual field name that has been filtered displays.
 - The datasheet updates to show the results of this filter being removed.

> ▶ **ANOTHER WAY**
>
> Click a cell of the desired field. Right-click to open the context menu and then select the **Clear filter from** option.

1. Click the **Advanced** button [*Home* tab, *Sort & Filter* group] to open the drop-down list.
2. Select **Clear All Filters**.

PAUSE & PRACTICE: ACCESS 1-4

For this project, you first unhide fields and remove totals. You then search for data in the *Employees* table using the *Search* box and the *Find* button. Next, you sort the table using single and multiple fields. You also filter the records using single and multiple criteria.

File Needed: *[your initials] PP A1-3.accdb*
Completed Project File Name: *[your initials] PP A1-4.accdb*

1. Open the *[your initials] PP A1-3* database file you created in *Pause & Practice 1-3*.
2. Save a new copy of your database.
 a. Select the **Save As** button [*File* tab]. The *Access Database* button should be selected in the *Save Database As* area.
 b. Click the **Save As** button.
 c. Select the desired location in which to store the copy of your database.
 d. Name the database [your initials] PP A1-4 in the *File name* box.
 e. Click the **Save** button.
 f. Click the **Enable Content** button in the *Security Warning* message bar if prompted.
3. Open the **Employees** table in *Datasheet* view. The changes you made to the datasheet layout in *Pause & Practice 1-3* should be reflected (Figure 1-101).

Employee ID	First Name	Last Name	Title	Department	Base Monthly Salary	Start Date	Cli
101	Bob	Lingle	Chief Executive Officer	Administration	$15,000.00	1/1/2017	
102	Lanita	McCartney	Chief Operating Officer	Administration	$12,000.00	1/1/2017	
103	Eleesha	Santos	Insurance Agent	Health and Benefits	$5,580.00	2/10/2017	
104	Roy	Baxter	Insurance Agent	Property and Casualty	$4,500.00	2/11/2017	
115	Tami	Chan	Administrative Assistant	Health and Benefits	$3,100.00	5/8/2017	
119	Juan	Taylor	Insurance Agent	Insurance Sales	$4,000.00	9/1/2017	
120	Wayne	Reza	Insurance Agent	Health and Benefits	$4,000.00	11/19/2017	
125	Cheryl	Nevens	Chief Information Officer	Administration	$12,000.00	1/7/2018	
130	Bert	Pulido	Supervisor	Health and Benefits	$5,500.00	8/15/2018	
135	Elsa	Ricci	Administrative Assistant	Health and Benefits	$2,900.00	10/8/2018	
138	Geneva	Song	Executive Assistant	Administration	$3,750.00	10/14/2018	
147	George	Tipton	Insurance Agent	Health and Benefits	$3,900.00	1/4/2019	
150	Margaret	Jepson	Insurance Agent	Property and Casualty	$3,900.00	2/15/2019	
157	Eva	Skaar	Large Group Specialist	Health and Benefits	$4,500.00	4/1/2019	
159	Majid	Mehta	Administrative Assistant	Property and Casualty	$2,900.00	6/15/2019	
161	Jesus	Delao	Insurance Agent	Property and Casualty	$3,900.00	8/25/2019	
*					$0.00		
Total					**$91,430.00**		

Record: ◀ ◀ 1 of 16 ▶ ▶ ▶☐ No Filter Search ◀

Figure 1-101 PP A1-4 Starting *Datasheet* view

4. Unhide a field.
 a. Click the **More** button [*Home* tab, *Records* group] and then select **Unhide Fields** to open the *Unhide Columns* dialog box.
 b. Click the **Branch** field check box.
 c. Click **Close**.

5. Click the **Totals** button [*Home* tab, *Records* group] to remove the totals.

6. Click the **Save** button to save the changes to the table.

7. Use the *Search* box to find records.
 a. Type Health in the *Search* box in the *Navigation* bar. The *Department* field for **Employee 103** should be selected.
 b. Clear the *Search* box.
 c. Type Folsom in the *Search* box. The *Branch* field for **Employee 147** should be selected.
 d. Clear the *Search* box.
 e. Click the *Employee ID* cell for **Employee 101**.

8. Use the *Find* button to find records.
 a. Click the **Find** button [*Home* tab, *Find* group] to open the *Find and Replace* dialog box.
 b. Type Insurance in the *Find What* box.
 c. Click the **Look In** drop-down arrow and select **Current document** if it is not already displayed. This option searches for a match in all fields in the table.
 d. Click the **Match** drop-down arrow and select **Any Part of Field** if it is not already displayed. This option finds a match if the search value is somewhere in a field.
 e. Click the **Search** drop-down arrow and select **All** If it is not already displayed. Selecting this option searches through all the records.
 f. Uncheck the **Match Case** check box if it is checked.
 g. Select the **Find Next** button to execute the search. The search starts from the currently selected field. Access searches the table to find the first record that meets the criteria. The *Title* field for **Employee 103** should be selected. If you had not clicked out of the *Branch* field in step 7e, the *Title* field for Employee 150 would have been selected.
 h. Click the **Find Next** button again to find the next occurrence of *Insurance*. The *Title* field for **Employee 104** should be selected.
 i. Continue clicking the **Find Next** button until the *Department* field for **Employee 119** is selected.
 j. Click the **Cancel** button to close the *Find and Replace* dialog box.

9. Sort the datasheet on a single field using the drop-down list.
 a. Click the **drop-down arrow** to the right of the *Start Date* field.
 b. Select **Sort Newest to Oldest** on the drop-down list. Employee 161, the most recently hired employee, should be in the first row of the datasheet.
 c. Click the **Remove Sort** button [*Home* tab, *Sort & Filter* group] to remove the sort criteria.
 d. Click any cell to deselect the *Start Date* column.

10. Sort the datasheet on multiple fields using the *Sort & Filter* group.
 a. Click and hold the pointer over the *Branch* field name, the first column you wish to sort. With the selection pointer still displayed, drag the pointer to the *Department* field name.
 b. Release the pointer.
 c. Click the **Descending** button [*Home* tab, *Sort & Filter* group]. Employee 104, the employee from Granite Bay in the Property and Casualty department, should be in the first row of the datasheet.
 d. Click the **Remove Sort** button [*Home* tab, *Sort & Filter* group] to remove the sort criteria.
 e. Click any cell to deselect the columns.

11. Filter the datasheet using *Filter by Selection*.
 a. Click after the "t" in the phrase "**Insurance Agent**" in the *Title* cell for **Employee 103**.
 b. Click the **Selection** button [*Home* tab, *Sort & Filter* group].
 c. Select **Equals "Insurance Agent"** from the drop-down list. The datasheet should display only the seven employees who are insurance agents.

 d. Click the **drop-down arrow** to the right of the *Title* field name.

 e. Select **Clear filter from Title** to remove the filter. The datasheet updates to show all the records.

12. Filter the datasheet using a *Text Filter*.

 a. Click the **drop-down arrow** to the right of the *Title* field name.

 b. Select **Text Filters** on the drop-down list and select **Contains** from the drop-down list.

 c. Type Assistant in the *Title contains* box.

 d. Click **OK**. The datasheet should display only the four employees who have "Assistant" as part of their title.

 e. Click the **Toggle Filter** button [*Home* tab, *Sort & Filter* group] to switch back to viewing all the records.

 f. Click the **Toggle Filter** button again to switch back to the filtered records.

 g. Click the **drop-down arrow** to the right of the *Title* field name.

 h. Select the **Clear filter from Title** button to remove the filter. The datasheet updates to show all the records.

13. Filter the datasheet using compound criteria on multiple fields.

 a. Click the **drop-down arrow** to the right of the *Title* field name.

 b. Click the **(Select All)** check box to remove that criterion.

 c. Select the **Insurance Agent** check box on the drop-down list.

 d. Click **OK**. The datasheet should display only the seven employees who are insurance agents.

 e. Click the **drop-down arrow** to the right of the *Branch* field name.

 f. Click the **(Select All)** check box to remove that criterion.

 g. Click the **Cameron Park** check box on the drop-down list.

 h. Click **OK**. The datasheet should display only the two employees who are insurance agents at the Cameron Park branch.

 i. Click the **Advanced** button [*Home* tab, *Sort & Filter* group].

 j. Select the **Clear All Filters** button. The datasheet updates to show all the records.

14. Click the **X** in the upper-right corner of the datasheet to close the table.

15. Select the **No** button when asked to save changes to the design of the *Employees* table.

16. Close the database by clicking the **Close** button [*File* tab].

Chapter Summary

1.1 Explain data organization concepts, use the Access *Navigation Pane,* and identify objects (p. A1-3).

- The **hierarchy of data** helps organize the data into fields, records, tables, and a database.
- The major Access **objects** are **tables**, **forms**, **reports**, and **queries**.
- A database must contain at least one table.
- The **Navigation Pane** displays all of the objects in a database. You can open objects directly from the *Navigation Pane.*

1.2 Create a database; set database properties; understand database object naming conventions and data types; create and manipulate database objects; and open, close, back up, and recover a database (p. A1-12).

- Create a new database from a **template**, a ready-to-use database application that comes complete with objects already created.
- **Database properties** are details about the database including title, author, company, subject, date created, and date last modified.
- Create a **Blank database** when you want to build your database application from scratch.
- Assign a meaningful name to each database object. The name must adhere to the Access naming rules.
- Each field in a database must be assigned a specific **data type** that determines what properties can be manipulated and how that field can be used.
- In *Backstage* view, close, open, and create a backup copy of your database. Use the backup copy to recover a damaged database.

1.3 Create a table in *Datasheet* view, edit the default primary key, add a new field, edit field and table properties, save a table, and enter records into a table (p. A1-21).

- Use *Datasheet* view to enter, modify, delete, or view data records.
- Create and edit a new table using *Datasheet* view.
- Each table should have a **primary key**, a field that contains a unique value for each record.
- Add new fields in *Datasheet* view by entering data values or field names.

- The properties of each field describe the details or characteristics about the field. You can modify some of these properties in *Datasheet* view.
- Each table must be saved with a unique name. You can also add a description to the table properties.
- When entering records into a datasheet, Access verifies that the content of each field matches the data type. After a record is entered, it is automatically saved into the table.

1.4 Import data records from Excel (p. A1-33).

- You can import data records from an Excel file into an Access table with the *Append* option.
- The first row of the Excel file must contain the field names from the Access table. The format of the fields should match, otherwise not all the data values may be imported.

1.5 Navigate table records in a datasheet view and customize a datasheet by modifying field order, row height, column width, field alignment, font style and size, row colors, and gridlines. Hide and unhide fields and add total rows (p. A1-35).

- Use the **Navigation bar** to move among records in a table.
- Move the columns in a datasheet to change their order.
- Change the **font face**, **size**, and **style** in your datasheet. The changes are reflected in the entire datasheet.
- You can increase or decrease the **row height** in Access, but all of the rows change to the new height.
- Adjust each field to a unique **column width**. Numeric or date fields display a series of # symbols (####) if the column is not wide enough to display the entire contents.
- **Field alignment** dictates how content is aligned horizontally within a cell with respect to the edges. Align cells *left, center,* or *right.*
- **Gridlines** visually frame the rows and columns in a datasheet with a border.
- **Alternate row colors** help you easily scan the records and fields in your datasheet.
- Use the *Datasheet Formatting* dialog box if you are going to make several changes to the datasheet layout.

- Fields can be hidden in *Datasheet* view.
- Add a *Total* row to summarize data in a table.

1.6 Search, sort, and filter records in a table (p. A1-46).

- The **Search** box and the **Find** button enable you to find data with a specific value quickly.
- When you open a table in *Datasheet* view, the data records are sorted in ascending order by the first field.
- An **ascending order** sort is from lowest to highest; a **descending order** sort is from highest to lowest.
- In *Datasheet* view, if you sort on multiple fields, they all must be sorted in the same sort order.

- The **Filter** functions display only the set of records that meet specified criteria. The available filter options vary based on the data type of the field and what criterion is selected.

Check for Understanding

The SIMbook for this text (within your SIMnet account) provides the following resources for concept review:

- Multiple-choice questions
- Short answer questions
- Matching exercises

Guided Project 1-1

For this project, you create and use a new database based on the *Updated: Event management* template. As the vice president of events for the *Green Club* at your university, you are trying to find an efficient way to keep track of the events your club has planned this semester. After creating the database, use the *Navigation Pane* to explore the objects that exist in this database, edit field properties of the table, enter records, and modify the datasheet layout.
[Student Learning Outcomes 1.1, 1.2, 1.3, 1.5]

File Needed: None
Completed Project File Name: *[your initials] Access 1-1.accdb*

Skills Covered in This Project

- Create a database from a template.
- Use the *Navigation Pane*.
- Edit properties in *Datasheet* view.
- Save a table.
- Enter records.
- Change the datasheet layout.
- Explore Access objects.

1. Create a new database based on a template.
 a. Open Access or click the **New** button [*File* tab] if an Access database is already open.
 b. Select the **Event management** template (Figure 1-102). *Note: If you experience a problem downloading the template, close the dialog box and skip to step 2.*
 c. Enter [your initials] Access 1-1 in the *File Name* box.
 d. Click the **Browse for a location to put your database** button to change the location in which to save your database and click **OK**.
 e. Click the **Create** button. The database opens.
 f. Skip to step 3.

Figure 1-102 *Event Management* template available online

2. Open the ***EventManagement-01*** database from your student data files.
 a. Select the **Save As** button [*File tab*]. The **Access Database** button should be selected in the *Save Database As* area.
 b. Click the **Save As** button.
 c. Select **Yes** in the message box to have Access close the open objects.
 d. Enter [your initials] Access 1-1 the *File Name* box.
 e. Select the location in which to save your database.
 f. Click the **Save** button. The database opens.

3. Complete step 3 if the *Welcome* form displays (Figure 1-103). This form displays based on the selections made on your computer.
 a. Click the **Play** button to view a video about using the *Events Database*.
 b. Uncheck the **Show Welcome when this database is opened** check box.
 c. Click the **Get Started** button.

4. Click the **Enable Content** button in the *Security Warning* message bar (Figure 1-104). If the *Welcome* form displays again, click **Get Started**.

Figure 1-103 *Welcome* form

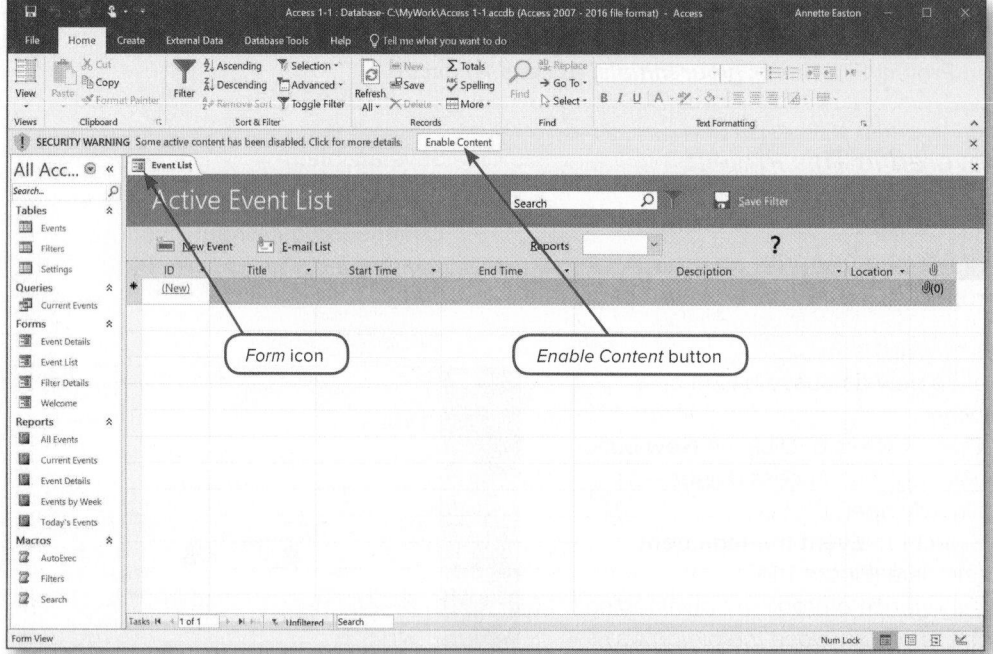

Figure 1-104 *Event Database* beginning navigation

The events database system is now ready to explore. This database contains many database objects that you have not yet used, like forms and reports. Often, the objects in a template will contain more advanced database features. In the events database, when the database opens, an *Event List* form opens automatically. You know it is a form because the *Form* icon displays on the object tab, along with the name of the form. This form was designed to display data using a datasheet layout. You can also use this form to enter data into the database. You can now explore the database table in this template to see if it meets your needs.

5. Use the *Navigation Pane* to view the database objects.
 a. Click the **Navigation Pane** arrow next to the *All Access Objects* category to open the *Navigation* menu, shown on the right side of Figure 1-105. Note that the *Navigation Pane* is set to display all objects grouped by object type.
 b. Click the arrow to close the *Navigation* menu without making any selections.
 c. Notice that the *Events* template comes with 16 pre-built objects:
 • 3 tables
 • 1 query
 • 4 forms
 • 5 reports
 • 3 macros

The *Event List* form is linked to the *Events* table. When no records are in the table, nothing displays in the form.

d. Close the **Event List** form by clicking the **X** in the right corner.

6. View the *Events* table in *Datasheet* view and edit field properties.

a. Double-click the **Events** table to open it in *Datasheet* view. No records have been entered into the database table (Figure 1-106).

b. Double-click the cell containing the **ID** field name (column header).

c. Type Event ID for the field name and press the **down arrow** key.

d. Click the **Title** field name.

Figure 1-105 View the *Navigation Pane* display

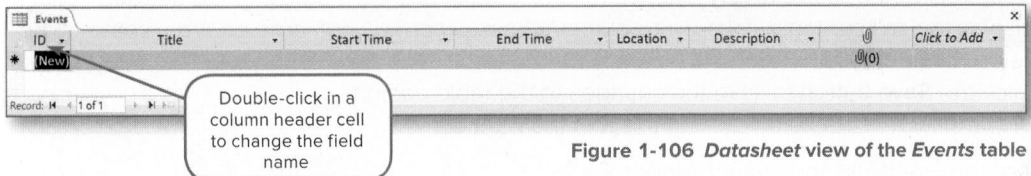

Figure 1-106 *Datasheet* view of the *Events* table

e. Click the **Table Tools Fields** tab. Remember that this contextual tab only displays when you are editing a table.

f. Click the **Name & Caption** button [*Table Tools Fields* tab, *Properties* group].

g. Type Event Title in the *Caption* property and click **OK**.

h. Type 100 in the *Field Size* property [*Table Tools Fields* tab, *Properties* group] and press **Enter**.

i. Click the **Start Time** field name. In the *Formatting* group [*Table Tools Fields* tab], notice that the *Data Type* property is set to *Date/Time* and the *Format* property is set to *General Date*.

j. Click the **Save** button to save the changes to the table design. With the changes to the field properties saved, the table is ready for you to begin to enter data records.

7. Enter a data record into the *Events* table to test the table structure.

a. Click the **Event Title** cell in the append row.

b. Type Member Welcome and Kickoff Meeting. The pencil icon displays, indicating that this record has not yet been saved.

c. Press the **Tab** key to move to the *Start Time* field and type 7:00 PM.

d. Press the **Tab** key to move to the *End Time* field. The message box in Figure 1-107 opens. If a message box opens after leaving a field, it indicates that the data entered does not match what was expected for that field.

e. Click **OK** to return to the *Start Time* field. It appears that this template has a discrepancy in the *Start Time* field. You need to fix this discrepancy before the Green Club can use the database. Because we need to explore this field further, delete the text you entered and leave that field blank for now.

Figure 1-107 Error message box

f. Press the **Tab** key to move to the *End Time* field. Because you did not enter a value for the *Start Time,* leave the *End Time* field blank for now.

g. Press the **Tab** key to move to the *Location* field and type Recreation Center Room 202.

h. Press the **Tab** key to move to the *Description* field and type Member Meeting.

i. Press the **Tab** key to move to the *Attachment* field.
j. Press the **Tab** key because you do not have an attachment to enter. The pencil icon no longer displays because the record has been saved.

8. Change the layout of the *Events* table.
 a. Click to select the **Location** column.
 b. Click, hold, and drag the pointer to move the *Location* column to the left of the *Start Time*.
 c. Change the *Font Face* to **Times New Roman** [*Home* tab, *Text Formatting* group].
 d. Change the *Font Size* to **12** [*Home* tab, *Text Formatting* group].
 e. Click the **Select All** button in the upper-left corner of the datasheet.
 f. Place your pointer on the right border of any of the *Field* names (Figure 1-108).

Figure 1-108 Adjust column widths in the table

 g. Double-click the **resize arrow**. The width of all the fields should adjust to the needed width to display the cell contents. If the width of the Access window is not large enough, some of the fields will be smaller.
 h. Click the **Save** button to save the changes to the table design.
 i. Close the *Events* table by clicking the **X** in the right corner.

9. Explore the *Event List* and *Event Details* forms.
 a. Double-click the **Event List** form in the *Forms* group of the *Navigation Pane*. The *Event List* form opens (Figure 1-109). The *Member Welcome* record you entered into the *Events* table displays. Recall that a form object provides a more user-friendly interface to view, add, update, and delete data in a table. It can also include additional features beyond those available in a table. For example, the *Event List* form, part of the template, has been customized to include a menu with direct links to additional forms and reports in the database.

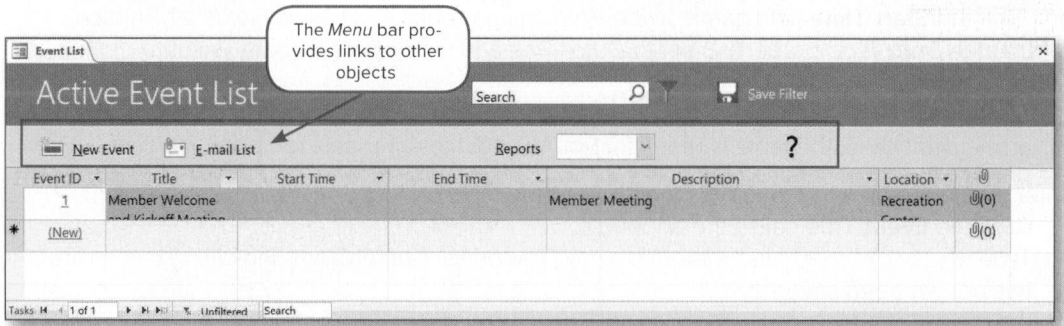

Figure 1-109 *Event List* form

 b. Click the **New Event** button in the *Menu* bar of the *Event List* form to open the *Event Details* form (Figure 1-110). This form provides an easy interface to enter a new record into the database. Do not enter any additional data records because the properties of the time fields are not quite right at this point.
 c. Click the **Close** button to close the *Event Details* form.

10. Explore the other database objects.
 a. Look at the objects displayed in the *Navigation Pane*. You should still see the same objects shown earlier in Figure 1-105.
 b. Look at the *Tables* group. You see the *Events* table, the *Filters* table, and the *Settings* table. You also want your database to store information about the members of the Green Club. As a result,

you realize that this database template is not right for you yet. You recognize that you will need to learn more about how to modify existing databases to create additional tables or how to build your own database from scratch.

11. Close the *Event List* form by clicking the **X** in the right corner.

12. Close the database by clicking the **X** in the right corner of the application window.

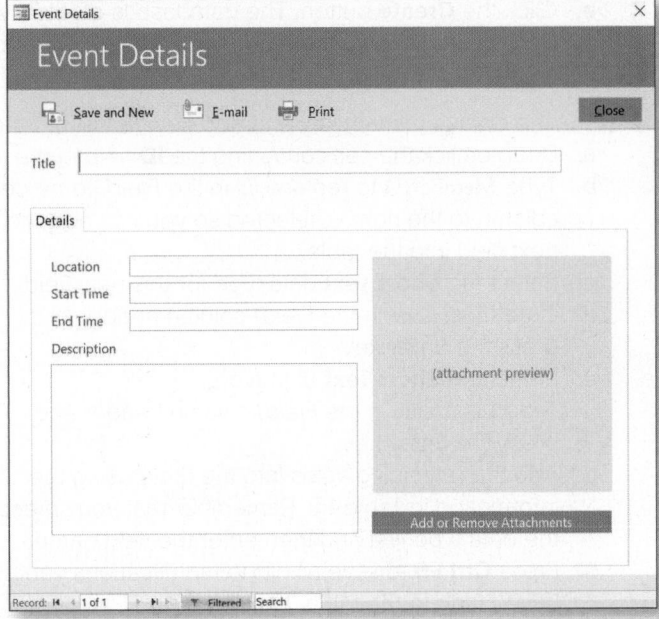

Figure 1-110 *Event Details* form

Guided Project 1-2

American River Cycling Club is a local cycling club. For this project, you create a database, containing one table, to store information about club members. After creating the database, add fields into the table, edit field properties, enter records, modify the datasheet layout, hide table fields, import data and sort and filter the data in the table.
[Student Learning Outcomes 1.2, 1.3, 1.4, 1.5, 1.6]

File Needed: ***MembersDataFile-01.xlsx*** (Student data files are available in the Library of your SIMnet account.)
Completed Project File Name: ***[your initials] Access 1-2.accdb***

Skills Covered in This Project

- Create a blank database.
- Edit the default primary key.
- Add a new field into a table.
- Edit properties in *Datasheet* view.
- Save a table.
- Enter records.

- Change the datasheet layout.
- Hide table fields.
- Import records.
- Sort data in a table.
- Filter data in a table.

1. Create a new blank database.
 a. Open Access or click the **New** button [*File* tab] if an Access database is already open.
 b. Select **Blank database**.
 c. Enter [your initials] Access 1-2 in the *File Name* box.
 d. Click the **Browse** button to change the location in which to save your database and click **OK**.

e. Click the **Create** button. The database is created. A new table is created and opens in *Datasheet* view. If a table does not display, click the **Table** button [*Create* tab, *Tables* group] to create a new table.

2. Edit the default primary key and add new fields into the table.
 a. Double-click the cell containing the **ID** field name (column header).
 b. Type MemberID to replace *ID* in the *Field name* cell and press the **Enter** key. The *Click to Add* column to the right is selected so you can add the next field into the table.
 c. Select the **Short Text** data type for this new field.
 d. Type FirstName in the *Field1* column header and press the **Enter** key.
 e. Select the **Short Text** data type.
 f. Type LastName in the *Field1* column header and press the **Enter** key.
 g. Add the remaining fields into the table using the information in Table 1-8. Remember that you select the data type first and then enter the field name.
 h. Press **Ctrl+S** to save all of the modifications you have made to the table.
 i. Type Members as the new table name.
 j. Click **OK**.

Table 1-8

Data Type	Field Name
Short Text	Address
Short Text	City
Short Text	State
Short Text	ZIPCode
Hyperlink	EmailAddress
Short Text	CellPhoneNumber

3. Edit the field properties of the *Members* table.
 a. Click the **MemberID** field name.
 b. Click the **Name & Caption** button [*Table Tools Fields* tab, *Properties* group].
 c. Type Member ID in the *Caption* property. Because the field names in this table provide a clear description of the content, it is not necessary to enter anything into the *Description* property.
 d. Click **OK**.
 e. Select the **FirstName** field name.
 f. Click the **Name & Caption** button [*Table Tools Fields* tab, *Properties* group].
 g. Type First Name in the *Caption* property.
 h. Click **OK**.
 i. Type 20 in the **Field Size** property [*Table Tools Fields* tab, *Properties* group].
 j. Change the remaining field properties in the table using the information in Table 1-9.
 k. Click the **Save** button to save the changes to the table. With the changes to the field properties saved, the table is ready for you to begin to enter data records. Remember that even though you have changed the caption that displays as the column header in *Datasheet* view, the field names have not changed.

Table 1-9

Field Name	Caption	Size
LastName	Last Name	25
Address		45
City		25
State		2
ZIPCode	ZIP	5
EmailAddress	Email	N/A
CellPhoneNumber	Cell Phone	12

4. Enter the member records into the *Members* table.
 a. Click the **FirstName** cell in the append row.
 b. Type Geneva. The pencil icon displays, indicating that this record has not yet been saved.
 c. Press the **Tab** key to move to the next field.
 d. Type Lingle in the *LastName* field. Press the **Tab** key to move to the next field.
 e. Type 1850 Stoneridge Court in the *Address* field. Press the **Tab** key.
 f. Type Cameron Park in the *City* field. Press the **Tab** key.
 g. Type CA in the *State* field. Press the **Tab** key.

h. Type 95682 in the *ZIPCode* field. Press the **Tab** key.
i. Type glingle@gmail.com in the *EmailAddress* field. Press the **Tab** key.
j. Type 780-886-6625 in the *CellPhoneNumber* field. Press the **Tab** key. The pencil icon no longer displays. You move to the *MemberID* field in the append row.
k. Tab to the next field. Enter the information from Table 1-10 into the *Members* table. Remember that after you tab out of the *CellPhoneNumber* field you move to the *MemberID* field. Because *MemberID* is an *AutoNumber* field, do not enter a value and simply tab to the next field.

Table 1-10

FirstName	LastName	Address	City	State	ZIPCode	EmailAddress	Cell PhoneNumber
Cheryl	Wilson	7105 High Street	Folsom	CA	95630	cwilson@mcc.com	916-451-8325
Ryan	Thomas	2227 Alexandra Drive	Auburn	CA	95602	rthomas@gmail.com	916-753-5586
Roy	Baxter	705 First Street	Rocklin	CA	95677	roy@centralsierra.com	780-886-2471

5. Change the layout of the *Members* table.
 a. Click to select the **ZIP** column.
 b. Right-click to open the context menu.
 c. Select **Field Width**.
 d. Type 7 in the **Column Width** cell.
 e. Click **OK** to close the dialog box.
 f. Click the **Center Alignment** button [*Home* tab, *Text Formatting* group].
 g. Click to select the **State** column.
 h. Place your pointer on the right border of the **State** field name.
 i. Double-click the **resize arrow** to adjust the *Column Width* using *AutoFit*.
 j. Click the **Center Alignment** button.
 k. Click the **Alternate Row Color** drop-down list [*Home* tab, *Text Formatting* group] and select **Blue-Gray, Text 2, Lighter 80%** (fourth column, second row in the *Theme Colors* category).
 l. Press **Ctrl+S** to save the changes to the layout.
 m. Close the *Members* table by clicking the **X** in the right corner.

6. Import data from Excel into the *Members* table.
 a. Click the **New Data Source** button [*External Data* tab, *Import & Link* group], select **From File** and then select **Excel** to launch the *Get External Data – Excel Spreadsheet* dialog box.
 b. Click the **Browse** button to launch the *File Open* dialog box.
 c. Locate and select the ***MembersDataFile-01*** Excel file.
 d. Click the **Open** button. The *File Open* dialog box closes.
 e. Select the **Append a copy of the records to the table** radio button.
 f. Click the **drop-down arrow** in the *table name* box and select the **Members** table if needed.
 g. Click **OK** to launch the *Import Spreadsheet Wizard*. The data records should display in the *Import Spreadsheet Wizard* window.
 h. Click the **Next** button to advance to the next page of the *Import Spreadsheet Wizard*.
 i. Verify that the *Import to Table* box contains the *Members* table.
 j. Click **Finish**.
 k. Click the **Close** button.

7. Open the *Members* table in *Datasheet* view. Your table should contain the 14 records shown in Figure 1-111.

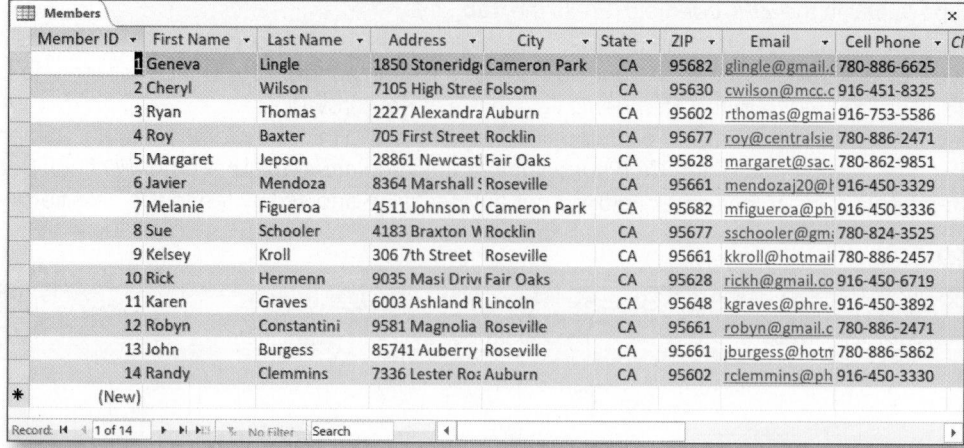

Figure 1-111 *Members* table after import

8. Hide the *State* field.
 a. Select the **State** column.
 b. Click the **More** button [*Home* tab, *Records* group] and then select **Hide Fields**.
 c. Press **Ctrl+S** to save the changes to the table.

9. Sort the *Members* table.
 a. Click the **drop-down arrow** to the right of the **City** field name.
 b. Select **Sort A to Z** on the drop-down list. The records display in ascending order by the *City* field.
 c. Click the **Remove Sort** button [*Home* tab, *Sort & Filter* group] to remove the sort criteria.
 d. Click to select the **ZIP** column.
 e. Click, hold, and drag the pointer to move the **ZIP** column to the left of the *Last Name* column.
 f. Click anywhere to deselect the *ZIP* column.
 g. Click and hold the pointer over the **ZIP** column. With the selection pointer still displayed, drag the pointer to the *Last Name* column. Release the pointer.
 h. Click the **Ascending** button [*Home* tab, *Sort & Filter* group]. The records display in ascending order by the *ZIP* column. In cases of the same *ZIP* Code, the records are sorted in ascending order by the last name. Your table should look similar to Figure 1-112.

 Sort indicator arrow

Member ID ▾	First Name ▾	ZIP ◂	Last Name ◂	Address ▾
14	Randy	95602	Clemmins	7336 Lester Roa
3	Ryan	95602	Thomas	2227 Alexandra
10	Rick	95628	Hermenn	9035 Masi Drive
5	Margaret	95628	Jepson	28861 Newcast
2	Cheryl	95630	Wilson	7105 High Stree
11	Karen	95648	Graves	6003 Ashland R

 i. Click the **Remove Sort** button [*Home* tab, *Sort & Filter* group] to remove the sort criteria.

 Figure 1-112 Records sorted on *ZIP* and *Last Name*

 j. Click anywhere to deselect the columns.
 k. Move the **ZIP** column to the right of the *City* column.

10. Filter the *Members* table using *Filter by Selection*.
 a. Select **916** in the *Cell Phone* cell for *Member ID 2*.
 b. Click the **Selection** button [*Home* tab, *Sort & Filter* group].
 c. Select **Begins with "916"** from the drop-down list (Figure 1-113).
 The datasheet should display only the seven members who have a cell phone area code of 916.
 d. Click the **drop-down arrow** to the right of the *Cell Phone* field name.
 e. Select **Clear filter from Cell Phone** to remove the filter.

11. Filter the datasheet using a *Text Filter*.
 a. Click the **drop-down arrow** to the right of the *Email* field name.

b. Select **Text Filters** on the drop-down list and select **Contains** from the second drop-down list (Figure 1-114). Notice in Figure 1-114 that the second drop-down list displays to the left. The exact position varies based on the width of your screen and location of the Access window.

Figure 1-113 *Filter by Selection*

c. Type gmail in the *Email contains* box.

d. Click **OK**. The datasheet should display only the five members who have *gmail* as part of their email addresses.

e. Click the **Toggle Filter** button [*Home* tab, *Sort & Filter* group] to switch back to viewing all the records.

f. Click the **Toggle Filter** button again to switch back to the filtered records.

g. Click the **drop-down arrow** to the right of the *Email* field name.

h. Select **Clear filter from Email** to remove the filter.

12. Close the *Members* table by clicking the **X** in the right corner. Select the **No** button in the dialog box. Do *not* save any of the changes made to the table.

Figure 1-114 *Text Filter*

13. Review the completed *Members* table.
 a. Double-click the **Members** table to view the table. The table should look similar to Figure 1-115. Note that the sorting and filtering changes were not saved.
 b. Close the table by clicking the **X** in the right corner.

Figure 1-115 Completed *Members* table

14. Add database properties using the *Database Properties* dialog box.
 a. Click the **File** tab to open the *Backstage* view. The **Info** button should be selected.
 b. Click the **View and edit database properties** link to open the *Database Properties* dialog box.
 c. Type American River Members in the *Title* area.
 d. Type Taylor Mathos in the *Author* area.
 e. Type ARCC in the *Company* area.
 f. Click **OK** to save the changes.

15. Close the database by clicking the **X** in the right corner of the application window.

Guided Project 1-3

San Diego Sailing Club is a local sailing club with a fleet of sailboats that members can rent. For this project, you create a database, containing one table, to store information about rental sailboats. After creating the database, you add fields to the table, edit field properties, enter records, import data, modify the datasheet layout, add a total row, and filter the data in the table.
[Student Learning Outcomes 1.2, 1.3, 1.4, 1.5, 1.6]

File Needed: ***SailboatDataFile-01.xlsx*** *(Student data files are available in the* Library *of your SIMnet account.)*
Completed Project File Name: *[your initials] **Access 1-3.accdb***

Skills Covered in This Project

- Create a blank database.
- Edit the default primary key.
- Add a new field into a table.
- Edit properties in *Datasheet* view.

- Save a table.
- Enter records.
- Change the datasheet layout.
- Add a total row.
- Import records.
- Filter data in a table.

1. Create a new blank database.
 a. Open Access or click the **New** button [*File* tab] if an Access database is already open.
 b. Select **Blank database**.
 c. Enter [your initials] Access 1-3 in the *File Name* box.
 d. Click the **Browse** button to change the location in which to save your database and click **OK**.
 e. Click the **Create** button. The database is created. A new table is created and opens in *Datasheet* view.

2. Edit the default primary key and add new fields into the table.
 a. Double-click the cell containing the **ID** field name (column header).
 b. Type BoatID in the *Field name*.
 c. Press the **down arrow** key to update the field name and stay in the same column.
 d. Select the **Short Text** data type [*Table Tools Fields* tab, *Formatting* group] from the drop-down list. Because the boats already have an ID number assigned to them, do not use the *AutoNumber* data type in Access.
 e. Click the **Click to Add** column header.
 f. Select the **Short Text** data type.
 g. Type BoatType in the *Field name* column header and press the **Enter** key.
 h. Select the **Short Text** data type.
 i. Type Length in the *Field name* column header and press the **Enter** key.

j. Enter the remaining fields into the table using the information in Table 1-11. Remember that you select the data type first and then enter the field name. After you enter the last field name, *ModelYear,* press the **down arrow** key to move to the first column of the append row.

k. Press **Ctrl+S** to save all of the modifications you have made to the table.

l. Type SailboatFleet as the new table name.

m. Click **OK**.

3. Edit the field properties of the *SailboatFleet* table.
 a. Click the **BoatID** field name.
 b. Select the **Name & Caption** button [*Table Tools Fields* tab, *Properties* group].
 c. Type Boat ID in the *Caption* property. Because all of the field names in this table provide a clear description of their content, it is not necessary to enter any additional information in the *Description* property.
 d. Click **OK**.
 e. Type 4 in the *Field Size* property [*Table Tools Fields* tab, *Properties* group].
 f. Select the **BoatType** field name.
 g. Click the **Name & Caption** button [*Table Tools Fields* tab, *Properties* group].
 h. Type Boat Type in the *Caption* property.
 i. Click **OK**.
 j. Type 25 in the *Field Size* property [*Table Tools Fields* tab, *Properties* group].
 k. Change the remaining field properties using the information in Table 1-12.
 l. Click the **Save** button to save the changes to the table. With the changes to the field properties saved, the table is ready for you to begin to enter data records.

Table 1-11

Data Type	Field Name
Number	Seats
Number	Sleeps
Currency	FourHourRentalRate
Currency	FullDayRentalRate
Yes/No	GalleyWithStove
Short Text	ModelYear

Table 1-12

Field Name	Caption	Size
Length		8
Seats		N/A
Sleeps		N/A
FourHourRentalRate	4 Hr Rate	N/A
FullDayRentalRate	Full Day Rate	N/A
GalleyWithStove	Galley w/ Stove	N/A
ModelYear	Model Year	4

4. Enter the data records into the *SailboatFleet* table.
 a. Click the **BoatID** field cell in the append row.
 b. Type 1150. The pencil icon displays, indicating that this record has not yet been saved.
 c. Press the **Tab** key to move to the next field.
 d. Type Capri 22 Mk II in the *BoatType* field. Press the **Tab** key to move to the next field.
 e. Type 24'8" in the *Length* field. Press the **Tab** key to move to the next field.
 f. Type 6 in the *Seats* field. Press the **Tab** key to move to the next field.
 g. Type 4 in the *Sleeps* field. Press the **Tab** key to move to the next field.
 h. Type 65 in the *FourHourRate* field. Press the **Tab** key to move to the next field.
 i. Type 89 in the *FullDayRate* field. Press the **Tab** key to move to the next field.
 j. Leave the check box blank in the *GalleyWithStove* field. Press the **Tab** key to move to the next field.
 k. Type 2007 in the *ModelYear* field. Press the **Tab** key to move to the next record. The pencil icon no longer displays.
 l. Continue entering the remaining records into the table using the information in Table 1-13. Click the **GalleyWithStove** field check box to indicate a "Y" value.
 m. Press **Ctrl+S** to save the table.
 n. Close the *SailboatFleet* table by clicking the **X** in the right corner.

Table 1-13

BoatID	BoatType	Length	Seats	Sleeps	4 Hr Rate	Full Day Rate	GalleyWith Stove	Model Year
1010	Catalina 270	28'4"	8	6	139	179	Y	2004
1146	Hunter 33	33'6"	10	6	299	349	Y	2006
1015	Catalina 270	28'4"	8	6	139	179	Y	2005
1185	Hunter 36	35'6"	10	6	349	389	Y	2012

5. Import data from Excel into the *SailboatFleet* table.
 a. Click the **New Data Source** button [*External Data* tab, *Import & Link* group], select **From File** and then select **Excel** to launch the *Get External Data – Excel Spreadsheet* dialog box.
 b. Click the **Browse** button to launch the *File Open* dialog box.
 c. Locate and select the ***SailboatDataFile-01*** Excel file.
 d. Click the **Open** button. The *File Open* dialog box closes.
 e. Select the **Append a copy of the records to the table** radio button.
 f. Click the **drop-down arrow** in the *Table Name* box and select the **SailboatFleet** table if needed.
 g. Click **OK** to launch the *Import Spreadsheet Wizard*. The data records should display in the *Wizard* window.
 h. Click the **Next** button to advance to the next page of the *Import Spreadsheet Wizard*.
 i. Verify that the *Import to Table* box contains the *SailboatFleet* table.
 j. Click **Finish**.
 k. Click the **Close** button.

6. Open the *SailboatFleet* table in *Datasheet* view. Your table should have the 20 records as shown in Figure 1-116.

Boat ID	Boat Type	Length	Seats	Sleeps	4 Hr Rate	Full Day Rate	Galley w/ Sto	Model Year
1010	Catalina 270	28'4"	8	6	$139.00	$179.00	✓	2004
1015	Catalina 270	28'4"	8	6	$139.00	$179.00	✓	2005
1146	Hunter 33	33'6"	10	6	$299.00	$349.00	✓	2006
1150	Capri 22 Mk II	24'8"	6	4	$65.00	$89.00	☐	2007
1152	Capri 22 Mk II	24'8"	6	4	$65.00	$89.00	☐	2007
1164	Capri 22 Mk II	24'8"	6	4	$65.00	$89.00	☐	2010
1168	Hunter 33	33'6"	10	6	$299.00	$349.00	✓	2010
1175	Beneteau 40	39'10"	12	6	$489.00	$529.00	✓	2011
1180	Beneteau 373	36'11"	10	6	$369.00	$409.00	✓	2012
1185	Hunter 36	35'6"	10	6	$349.00	$389.00	✓	2012
1190	Beneteau 373	36'11"	10	6	$369.00	$409.00	✓	2012
1200	Beneteau 373	36'11"	10	6	$369.00	$409.00	✓	2013
1205	Beneteau 40	39'10"	12	6	$489.00	$529.00	✓	2014
1225	Hunter 36	35'6"	10	6	$349.00	$389.00	✓	2014
1254	Hunter 36	35'6"	10	6	$349.00	$389.00	✓	2015
1310	Beneteau 373	36'11"	10	6	$369.00	$409.00	✓	2016
1342	Hunter 33	33'6"	10	6	$299.00	$349.00	✓	2017
1401	Capri 22 Mk II	24'8"	6	4	$65.00	$89.00	☐	2018
1410	Beneteau 40	39'10"	12	6	$489.00	$529.00	✓	2018
1419	Hunter 33	33'6"	10	6	$299.00	$349.00	✓	2018
*			0	0	$0.00	$0.00	☐	

Record: I◀ ◀ 1 of 20 ▶ ▶I ▶❋ ⏫ No Filter Search

Figure 1-116 *SailboatFleet* table records after import

7. Change the layout of the *Sailboat Fleet* table.
 a. Change the *Font Face* to **Times New Roman** [*Home* tab, *Text Formatting* group].
 b. Change the *Font Size* to **12** [*Home* tab, *Text Formatting* group].
 c. Click to select the **Length** column.

d. Press **Shift+Right Arrow** twice to select the *Seats* and *Sleeps* columns.
e. Place your pointer on the right border of the *Sleeps* field.
f. Double-click to adjust the *Column Width* using *AutoFit*.
g. Select the **BoatType** field.
h. Place your pointer on the right border of the *Boat-Type* field. The pointer changes to the resize arrow.
i. Click, hold, and drag the pointer to the right to increase the width of the *BoatType* field so that you can see the entire data value in the *BoatType* column.
j. Select the **Boat ID** field.
k. Click the **Center Alignment** button [*Home* tab, *Text Formatting* group].
l. Select the **Length** field.
m. Click the **Center Alignment** button.
n. Click anywhere to deselect the column.
o. Open the *Datasheet Formatting* dialog box (Figure 1-117) by clicking the **Text Formatting launcher** in the bottom-right corner of the *Text Formatting* group [*Home* tab].

Figure 1-117 *Datasheet Formatting* dialog box

p. Click the **Alternate Background Color** drop-down list in the *Datasheet Formatting* dialog box and select **Green, Accent 6, Lighter 80%** (tenth column, second row in the *Theme Colors* category).
q. Click the **Gridline Color** drop-down list and select **Green, Accent 6, Darker 25%** (tenth column, fifth row in the *Theme Colors* category).
r. Click **OK** to close the dialog box.

8. Add a total row.
 a. Click the **Totals** button [*Home* tab, *Records* group].
 b. Click the *Total* row cell of the *FourHourRentalRate* field, click the **drop-down arrow** in that cell and select the **Average** function.
 c. Click the *Total* row cell of the *FullDayRentalRate* field, click the **drop-down arrow** in that cell and select the **Average** function.
 d. Press **Ctrl+S** to save the changes to the layout. The updated layout should look similar to Figure 1-118.

Boat ID ▾	Boat Type ▾	Length ▾	Seats ▾	Sleeps ▾	4 Hr Rate ▾	Full Day Ra ▾	Galley w/ St ▾	Model Year ▾
1010	Catalina 270	28'4"	8	6	$139.00	$179.00	✓	2004
1015	Catalina 270	28'4"	8	6	$139.00	$179.00	✓	2005
1146	Hunter 33	33'6"	10	6	$299.00	$349.00	✓	2006
1150	Capri 22 Mk II	24'8"	6	4	$65.00	$89.00		2007
1152	Capri 22 Mk II	24'8"	6	4	$65.00	$89.00		2007
1164	Capri 22 Mk II	24'8"	6	4	$65.00	$89.00		2010
1168	Hunter 33	33'6"	10	6	$299.00	$349.00	✓	2010
1175	Beneteau 40	39'10"	12	6	$489.00	$529.00	✓	2011
1180	Beneteau 373	36'11"	10	6	$369.00	$409.00	✓	2012
1185	Hunter 36	35'6"	10	6	$349.00	$389.00	✓	2012
1190	Beneteau 373	36'11"	10	6	$369.00	$409.00	✓	2012
1200	Beneteau 373	36'11"	10	6	$369.00	$409.00	✓	2013
1205	Beneteau 40	39'10"	12	6	$489.00	$529.00	✓	2014
1225	Hunter 36	35'6"	10	6	$349.00	$389.00	✓	2014
1254	Hunter 36	35'6"	10	6	$349.00	$389.00	✓	2015
1310	Beneteau 373	36'11"	10	6	$369.00	$409.00	✓	2016
1342	Hunter 33	33'6"	10	6	$299.00	$349.00	✓	2017
1401	Capri 22 Mk II	24'8"	6	4	$65.00	$89.00		2018
1410	Beneteau 40	39'10"	12	6	$489.00	$529.00	✓	2018
1419	Hunter 33	33'6"	10	6	$299.00	$349.00	✓	2018
*			0	0	$0.00	$0.00		
Total					$286.20 ▾	$325.00		

Figure 1-118 Formatted datasheet layout

9. Filter the *SailboatFleet* table using compound criteria and sort the filtered results.
 a. Click the **drop-down arrow** to the right of the *Seats* field name.
 b. Select **Number Filters** on the drop-down list and select **Greater Than** from the second drop-down list (Figure 1-119).
 c. Type 8 in the *Seats is greater than or equal to* box.
 d. Click **OK**. The datasheet should display only the 16 boats that can seat at least eight people.
 e. Click the **drop-down arrow** to the right of the *4 Hr Rate* field name.
 f. Select the **Number Filters** on the drop-down list and select **Less Than** from the second drop-down list.
 g. Type 350 in the *4 Hr Rate is less than or equal to* box.
 h. Click **OK**. The datasheet should display only the nine boats that can seat at least eight people and have a four-hour rate of less than or equal to $350.
 i. Click to select the **Length** column.
 j. Click the **Ascending** button [*Home* tab, *Sort & Filter* group] to sort the filtered results by the *Length* field. In Figure 1-120, notice the filter symbols next to the field names of the *Seats* and *4 Hr Rate* fields and the *Sort symbol* next to the *Length* field name. Also notice that the averages updated on the *Total* row to reflect the values for this selected group of records.

Figure 1-119 *Number Filters*

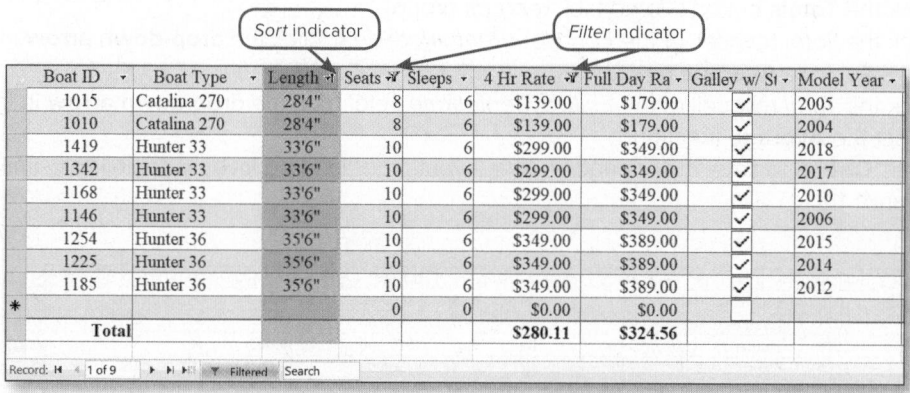

Figure 1-120 **Filtered and sorted records**

 k. Click the **Toggle Filter** button [*Home* tab, *Sort & Filter* group] to switch back to the unfiltered records. Notice that the records remain sorted.
 l. Click the **Remove Sort** button [*Home* tab, *Sort & Filter* group] to remove the sort criteria.
 m. Click the **Advanced** button [*Home* tab, *Sort & Filter* group] and select the **Clear All Filters** button. The datasheet should update to show all the records.

10. Close the *SailboatFleet* table by clicking the **X** in the right corner.

11. Click the **No** button in the dialog box. You do not need to save any of the changes as a result of sorting or filtering the table.

12. Close the *San Diego Sailing* database by clicking the **X** in the right corner of the application window.

Independent Project 1-4

Courtyard Medical Plaza (CMP) is a full-service medical office complex. For this project, you create a database, containing one table, to store information about the physicians who work at CMP. After creating the database, you add fields into the table, edit field properties, enter records, import data, modify the datasheet layout, and sort and filter the data in the table.
[Student Learning Outcomes 1.2, 1.3, 1.4, 1.5, 1.6]

File Needed: *PhysiciansDataFile-01.xlsx (Student data files are available in the Library of your SIMnet account.)*
Completed Project File Name: *[your initials] Access 1-4.accdb*

Skills Covered in This Project

- Create a blank database.
- Edit the default primary key.
- Add a new field into a table.
- Edit properties in *Datasheet* view.
- Save a table.
- Enter records.
- Import records.
- Change the datasheet layout.
- Sort data in a table.
- Filter data in a table.

1. Create a new blank database.
 a. Name the database [your initials] Access 1-4.
 b. Change the location where you save the database if needed.

2. Edit the default primary key and add new fields into the table.
 a. Change the **ID** field name to DoctorID. Keep this field as an *AutoNumber* data type.
 b. Enter the remaining fields into the table using the information in Table 1-14. After you enter the last field name, *MoveInDate,* press the **down arrow** key to move to the first column of the append row.
 c. Save the table as Physicians.

3. Edit the field properties of the *Physicians* table using the information in Table 1-15.

4. Save the table after updating the properties.

5. Enter the data records shown in Table 1-16 into the *Physicians* table. Remember that the *DoctorID* field is automatically entered by Access.

Table 1-14

Data Type	Field Name
Short Text	LastName
Short Text	FirstName
Short Text	OfficeNumber
Short Text	PrimarySpecialty
Date & Time	MoveInDate

Table 1-15

Field Name	Caption	Size
DoctorID	Doctor ID	N/A
LastName	Last Name	25
FirstName	First Name	20
OfficeNumber	Office	3
PrimarySpecialty	Specialty	30
MoveInDate	Tenant Since	N/A

Table 1-16

Last Name	First Name	Office Number	Specialty	Move-In Date
Beyer	Robert	101	Cardiovascular Disease	2/15/2015
Scher	Elizabeth	115	Pediatrics	4/1/2017
Ostrander	Emy	101	Cardiovascular Disease	11/8/2017
Foster	Margaret	200	Pediatrics	7/1/2008

6. Save and close the *Physicians* table.

7. Import the remaining data records from Excel into the *Physicians* table.
 a. Launch the *Get External Data – Excel Spreadsheet* dialog box.
 b. Locate and select the **PhysiciansDataFile-01** Excel file.
 c. Append the records to the *Physicians* table.
 d. Launch the *Import Spreadsheet Wizard*.
 e. Finish the *Import Spreadsheet Wizard*. Close the *Wizard* after the records have imported.

8. Open the *Physicians* table in *Datasheet* view. Your table should contain 16 records.

9. Change the layout of the *Physicians* table.
 a. Change the *Font Size* to **12**.
 b. Use *AutoFit* to increase the column width of the *Specialty* field.
 c. Use *AutoFit* to increase the column width of the *Tenant Since* field.
 d. **Center-align** the *Doctor ID, Office,* and *Tenant Since* fields.
 e. Change the *Alternate Row Color* to **Blue**, **Accent 1**, **Lighter 60%** (fifth column, third row in the *Theme Colors* category).
 f. Save the changes to the layout.

10. Sort the *Physicians* table in ascending order by the *Specialty* field.

11. Remove the sort criteria.

12. Filter the *Physicians* table to find the doctors who moved in on or after 1/1/2013 and who have a specialty in Pediatrics. The table should look similar to Figure 1-121.

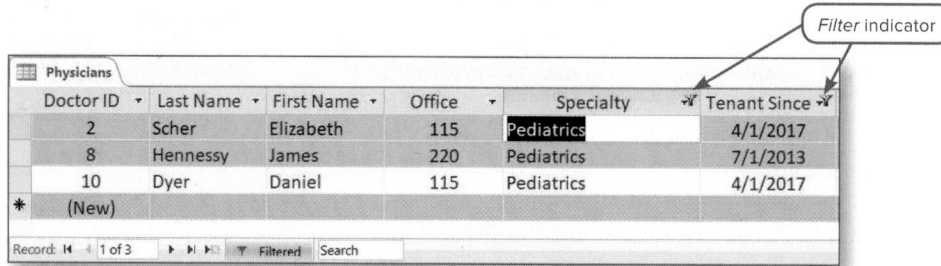

Figure 1-121 Records filtered on *Specialty* and *Tenant Since*

13. Clear all the filters. The datasheet updates to show all the records.

14. Close the *Physicians* table.

15. Do not save any of the changes as a result of sorting or filtering the table.

16. Add the following database properties.
 a. *Title*: Courtyard Medical Plaza Physicians
 b. *Author*: Caroline Rios
 c. *Company*: CMP
 d. Click **OK** to save the changes.

17. Close the database.

Independent Project 1-5

Life's Animal Shelter (LAS) is an animal adoption agency that strives to keep its expenses down and donations up and is mainly run by volunteers. LAS does not turn any animal away, and its goal is to find homes for all animals within six months of their arrival. Julie Freed, one of the volunteers, has begun building a database for LAS. For this project, you work with her database, which currently has one table that contains information about the pets currently at LAS. Add one field into the table, edit field properties, enter data into records, modify the datasheet layout, and sort and filter the data in the table. [Student Learning Outcomes 1.1, 1.2, 1.3, 1.5, 1.6]

File Needed: *LifesAnimalShelter-01.accdb (Student data files are available in the Library of your SiMnet account.)*
Completed Project File Name: *[your initials] Access 1-5.accdb*

Skills Covered in This Project

- Open an existing database.
- Use the *Navigation Pane*.
- Edit field properties in *Datasheet* view.
- Add a new field into a table.
- Save a table.
- Enter records.
- Change the datasheet layout.
- Sort data in a table.
- Filter data in a table.

1. Open the **LifesAnimalShelter-01** database from your student data files.

2. Save a new copy of your database.
 a. Select the **Save As** button [*File tab*]. The **Access Database** button should be selected in the *Save Database As* area.
 b. Click the **Save As** button.
 c. Select the desired location in which to store the copy of your database.
 d. Type [your initials] Access 1-5 in the *File name* box.
 e. Click the **Save** button.

3. Enable content in the security warning.

4. Open the *Navigation Pane*.

5. Open the *Pets* table in *Datasheet* view.

6. Edit the field properties of the *Pets* table using the information in Table 1-17. For several of the fields you see a *Some data may be lost* warning message display when you change the field size. The sizes provided are large enough based on the data entered, so no data will be lost. Click the **Yes** button to make the change.

Table 1-17

Field Name	Caption	Size
ID	Pet ID	N/A
PetName	Pet Name	15
Type		10
Breed		40
Age		8
Gender		1
Details	Why I'd make a great companion	N/A

7. Save the table after updating the properties.

8. Add a new field, to the left of the *Details* field. Remember that the field name is still *Details* even though the caption is changed to *Why I'd make a great companion*.
 a. Select the **Details** column.
 b. Right-click to open the context menu.
 c. Select **Insert Field**.

9. Edit the field properties using the following information:
 a. *Field Name*: Color
 b. *Data Type*: **Short Text**
 c. *Size*: 25

10. Save the table after updating the properties of this new field.

11. Enter the data values shown in Table 1-18 into the *Color* field.

Table 1-18

Pet ID	Pet Name	Color
1	Abby	Black
2	Alec	Tan
3	Allie	Brown
4	Barnaby	White
5	Lilith	Black/White
6	Martin	Brown Tabby/White
7	Sasha	Tan/White
8	Tate	Black/White
9	Elsa	White/Brown
10	Hubert	White/Brown
11	Bessie	Black/White
12	Connie	Tortoise Shell
13	Topaz	Brown Tabby
14	Lady	Black Brindle/White
15	Ashley	White/Brown
16	Peanut Butter	Tan/White

12. Change the layout of the *Pets* table.
 a. Use *AutoFit* to decrease the column width of the *Pet ID, Type, Age,* and *Gender* fields.
 b. **Center-align** the *Pet ID* and *Gender* fields.
 c. Change the *Alternate Row Color* to **Light Gray, Background 2, Darker 10%** (third column, second row in the *Theme Colors* category).
 d. Set the *Column Width* of the *Details* field to 65.
 e. Set the *Row Height* of the table to 110.
 f. Save the changes to the layout.

13. Filter the *Pets* table to find the **Dogs** and **Cats** with **Brown** as part of their coloring. The resulting table should look similar to Figure 1-122. Your records may display in a different order.

14. Sort the filtered results in ascending order by the *Gender* field.

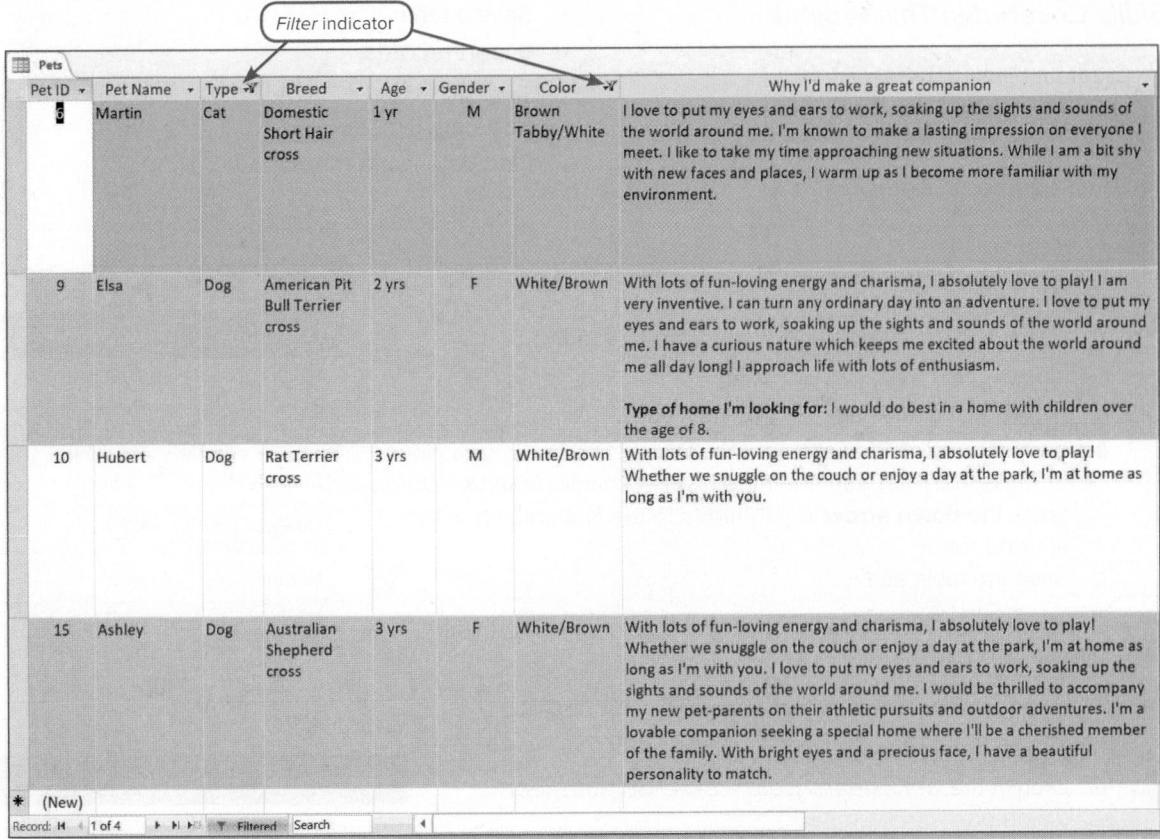

Figure 1-122 Records filtered on *Type* and *Color*

15. Remove the sort criteria. Clear all the filters. The datasheet will update to show all the records.

16. Close the *Pets* table.

17. Do not save any of the changes as a result of sorting or filtering the table.

18. Add the following database properties.
 a. *Company*: LAS
 b. *Author*: Student Name
 c. *Comments*: Pets table updated on [enter today's date]
 d. Click **OK** to save the changes.

19. Close the database.

Independent Project 1-6

Boyd Air is a national airline company. For this project, you will create a database, containing one table, to store information about the airplanes in Boyd Air's fleet. After creating the database, add fields into the table, edit field properties, import data, modify the datasheet layout, and find data using the *Search* box.
[Student Learning Outcomes 1.2, 1.3, 1.4, 1.5, 1.6]

File Needed: ***AirplaneDataFile-01.xlsx*** *(Student data files are available in the* Library *of your SIMnet account.)*
Completed Project File Name: *[your initials] **Access 1-6.accdb***

Skills Covered in This Project

- Create a blank database.
- Edit the default primary key.
- Add new fields into a table.
- Edit properties in *Datasheet* view.
- Save a table.
- Import records.
- Change the datasheet layout.
- Sort data in a table.
- Find data using the *Search* box.

1. Create a new blank database.
 a. Name the database [your initials] Access 1-6.
 b. Change the location to save your database if needed.

2. Add new fields into the table.
 a. Do not make any changes to the *ID* field.
 b. Enter the remaining fields into the table using the information in Table 1-19. After you enter the last field name, *InServiceDate*, press the **down arrow** key to move to the first column of the append row.
 c. Save the table as Fleet.

3. Edit the field properties of the *Fleet* table using the information in Table 1-20.

4. Save and close the table after updating the properties.

5. Import data from Excel into the *Fleet* table.
 a. Launch the *Get External Data – Excel Spreadsheet* dialog box.
 b. Locate and select the **AirplaneDataFile-01** Excel file.
 c. Append the records to the *Fleet* table.
 d. Launch the *Import Spreadsheet Wizard*.
 e. Finish the *Import Spreadsheet Wizard*. Close the *Wizard* after the records have imported.

6. Open the *Fleet* table in *Datasheet* view. Your table should contain 17 records.

7. Change the layout of the *Fleet* table.
 a. Change the *Font Size* to **12**.
 b. Select the entire datasheet and use *AutoFit* to adjust all the fields to their correct size.
 c. **Center-align** the *Aircraft ID, First Class,* and *Coach* fields.
 d. Remove the gridlines.
 e. Save the changes to the layout.

8. Sort the *Fleet* table in descending (newest to oldest) order according to the *In-Service* field. The table should look similar to Figure 1-123.

9. Remove the sort criteria.

10. Use the *Search box* to find Dash8.

11. Delete the value from the *Search* box.

12. Close the *Fleet* table.

13. Do not save any of the changes as a result of sorting the table.

Table 1-19

Data Type	Field Name
Short Text	PlaneModel
Short Text	Manufacturer
Short Text	Length
Number	FirstClassSeats
Number	CoachSeats
Date & Time	InServiceDate

Table 1-20

Field Name	Caption	Size
ID	Aircraft ID	N/A
PlaneModel	Model	25
Manufacturer		20
Length		7
FirstClassSeats	First Class	N/A
CoachSeats	Coach	N/A
InServiceDate	In-Service	N/A

Figure 1-123 Records sorted on *In-Service* field

14. Add the following database properties.
 a. *Title*: Boyd Air Fleet Data
 b. *Author*: Marcus Sampson
 c. *Company*: Boyd Air
 d. Click **OK** to save the changes.

15. Close the database.

Improve It Project 1-7

Placer Hills Real Estate (PHRE) is a real estate company with regional offices throughout central California. Kelsey Kroll, one of the managers, began building a database. The database has one table that contains information about the real estate properties currently listed for sale. You add one field into the table, edit field properties, enter data into records, modify the datasheet layout, and sort and filter the data in the table.
[Student Learning Outcomes 1.1, 1.2, 1.3, 1.5, 1.6]

File Needed: *PlacerHills-01.accdb (Student data files are available in the* Library *of your SIMnet account.)*
Completed Project File Name: *[your initials] Access 1-7.accdb*

Skills Covered in This Project

- Open a database.
- Use the *Navigation Pane*.
- Edit the default primary key.
- Add a new field into a table.

- Edit properties in *Datasheet* view.
- Save a table.
- Enter records.
- Change the datasheet layout.
- Sort data in a table.
- Filter data in a table.

1. Open the **PlacerHills-01** database from your student data files.

2. Save a new copy of your database.
 a. Select the **Save As** button [*File tab*]. The **Access Database** button should be selected in the *Save Database As* area.
 b. Click the **Save As** button.
 c. Select the desired location in which to store the copy of your database.
 d. Type [your initials] Access 1-7 in the *File name* box.
 e. Click the **Save** button.

3. Enable content in the security warning.

4. Open the *Navigation Pane*.

5. Open the *Listings* table in *Datasheet* view.

6. Edit the field properties of the *Listings* table using the information in Table 1-21. For several of the fields, you see a *Some data may be lost* warning message when you change the field size. Because the new field sizes are sufficient for the existing data, click the **Yes** button to continue.

7. Save the table after updating the properties.

8. Add a new field, to the left of the *Agent* field.

9. Edit the field properties using the following information:
 a. *Field Name*: Construction
 b. *Data Type*: Short Text
 c. *Size*: 5

10. Save the table after updating the properties.

11. Enter the data values shown in Table 1-22 into the new *Construction* field.

12. Change the layout of the *Listings* table.
 a. Change the *Font Size* to **12**.
 b. Select the entire datasheet and use *AutoFit* to adjust all the fields to their correct size. Remember that if the width of the Access window was not wide enough, some of the columns may still be too small. You can adjust the width of those columns individually.
 c. **Center-align** the *SqFt*, *Beds*, *Baths*, *Built*, and *Construction* fields.
 d. Change the *Gridline Color* to **Green 5** (seventh column, sixth row in the *Standard Colors* category).
 e. Set the *Row Height* of the table to 16.
 f. Save the changes to the layout.

13. Add the following database properties and save the changes:
 a. *Company*: PHRE
 b. *Comments*: Listings table updated [enter today's date]
 c. Click **OK** to save the changes.

Table 1-21

Field Name	Caption	Size
ListingID		N/A
DateListed	Date Listed	N/A
ListPrice	List Price	N/A
Address		35
City		20
SqFt		N/A
Beds		N/A
Baths		N/A
Garage		18
YearBuilt	Built	N/A
ListingAgent	Agent	25

Table 1-22

ListingID	Construction
10022	Frame
10023	Stone
10024	Brick
10027	Stone
10030	Stone
10031	Brick
10040	Frame
10042	Brick
10043	Stone
10044	Brick
10045	Brick
10046	Brick
10048	Frame
10052	Brick
10053	Frame
10054	Stone

14. Sort the *Listings* table in descending order by the *List Price* field. *ListingID 10024* should be at the top of the datasheet and *ListingID 10053* should be at the bottom of the datasheet.

15. Remove the sort criteria.

16. Filter the *Listings* table to find the listings of homes that are at least 2000 square feet, have 3 or 4 bathrooms, and are brick construction.

17. Sort the filtered results in ascending order by the *List Price* field. Your datasheet should look similar to Figure 1-124.

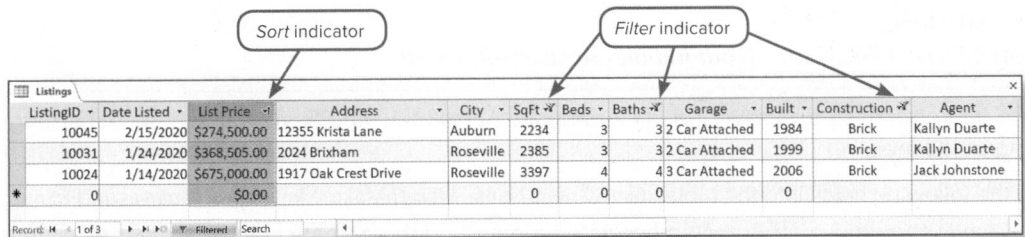

Figure 1-124 Records sorted on *List Price*

18. Remove the sort criteria.

19. Clear all the filters. The datasheet updates to show all the records.

20. Close the *Listings* table. Do not save any of the changes as a result of sorting or filtering the table.

21. Close the database.

Challenge Project 1-8

Create a database for an organization to which you belong. Add the necessary fields into the table. Be sure to edit the field properties as needed. Enter several rows of data into the table. Ensure that the datasheet layout is easy to read.
[Student Learning Outcomes 1.2, 1.3, 1.5, 1.6]

File Needed: None
Completed Project File Name: *[your initials] Access 1-8.accdb*

Create a new database and save it as [your initials] Access 1-8. Modify your database according to the following guidelines:

- Enter at least five fields into the table.
- Save the table.
- Edit the field properties to match the needs of the database.
- Enter several records into the table.
- Change the layout as desired to create a professional-looking layout.
- Sort the records by one of the fields.

Challenge Project 1-9

Create a database for a small bakery. The database should contain one table to store information about the different items sold by the bakery. Be sure to include a table field to store the item category. Examples of the content for the item categories might include cupcakes, cakes, pies, cookies, and candy. Create the table by adding fields and modifying properties. Enter data into the table. Ensure that the datasheet layout is easy to read.
[Student Learning Outcomes 1.2, 1.3, 1.5, 1.6]

File Needed: None
Completed Project File Name: *[your initials] Access 1-9.accdb*

Create a new database and save it as [your initials] Access 1-9. Modify your database according to the following guidelines:

- Add the following fields into the table: ItemID, ItemName, CostToMake, Mark-UpPercentage, and ItemCategory.
- The *ItemID* should use an *AutoNumber* data type and be the primary key. Select appropriate data types for the other fields.
- Save the table.
- Edit the field properties to match the needs of the database.
- Enter several records into the table.
- Change the layout as desired to create a professional-looking layout.
- Find a record where the category is *Cupcakes*, using the *Search* box.
- Use the *Filter by Selection* to find all the records for which the category is *Cupcakes*.

Challenge Project 1-10

Create a database for a travel agency. The database should contain one table to store information about upcoming cruises. Create the table by adding fields and modifying properties. Enter data into the table. Ensure that the datasheet layout is easy to read.
[Student Learning Outcomes 1.2, 1.3, 1.5, 1.6]

File Needed: None
Completed Project File Name: *[your initials] Access 1-10.accdb*

Create a new database and save it as [your initials] Access 1-10. Modify your database according to the following guidelines:

- Add the following fields to the table: TripID, TripName, NumberOfDays, DepartureCity, DestinationCity, DepartureDate, and CostPerPerson.
- The *TripID* should use an *AutoNumber* data type and be the primary key. Select appropriate data types for the other fields.
- Save the table as Trips.
- Edit the field properties, like *Field Size,* to match the needs of the database.
- Enter several records into the table for trips of various lengths. Search the web if you need help finding examples of data to enter.
- Change the layout as desired to create a professional-looking layout.
- Create a filter using compound criteria to locate all cruises that leave from a select city and have the same trip length.

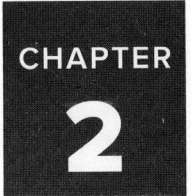

CHAPTER 2

Using Design View, Data Validation, and Relationships

CHAPTER OVERVIEW

In chapter 1, you learned to use *Datasheet* view to create and view tables. Many database designers prefer to create tables in *Design* view because it is easier to change the various field and table properties. Additionally, several database properties can only be changed using *Design* view. This chapter covers the basics of creating a table in *Design* view, using data validation rules to ensure your data is valid, and creating relationships among different tables in a database.

STUDENT LEARNING OUTCOMES (SLOs)

After completing this chapter, you will be able to:

SLO 2.1 Create a table in *Design* view; add new fields; define a primary key; delete fields; save, close, rename, and open a table; and switch between *Datasheet* and *Design* views (p. A2-84).

SLO 2.2 Set field properties including *Field Size, Format, Caption, Default Value, Required,* and *New Values* (p. A2-88).

SLO 2.3 Explain data integrity and data validation concepts and options (p. A2-95).

SLO 2.4 Create field and record validation rules, test rules, create validation text, create lookup fields, and define an input mask (p. A2-97).

SLO 2.5 Change field properties after records are added into a table (p. A2-111).

SLO 2.6 Explain relational database principles, understand the steps that must be taken to design a database, create relationships between tables, implement referential integrity, and delete and edit relationships (p. A2-117).

SLO 2.7 Preview and print the contents of a table (p. A2-127).

SLO 2.8 Manage a database using the *Compact & Repair Database* utility (p. A2-129).

CASE STUDY

Mary's Rentals is a privately owned equipment rental company. For the Pause & Practice projects in this chapter, you develop a database that contains information about the company's products. As you progress through the chapter, you incorporate many of the skills you are learning to construct and enhance this database.

Pause & Practice 2-1: Create a new blank database. Customize the table using *Design*

view to store equipment information. Add new fields, define the primary key, edit field properties, and save the table.

Pause & Practice 2-2: Refine your equipment table design by adding a field validation rule and a table validation rule, adding validation text, testing the validation rules, creating a lookup field, and defining an input mask.

A2-83

Pause & Practice 2-3: Add a second table to store the service history of the equipment. Define a relationship between the equipment and service history tables. Print the contents of the equipment table. Use the *Compact & Repair Database* utility to manage the database.

SLO 2.1

Creating a Table in Design View

Design view is used to create a table from scratch. When creating the table, you define the fields that are included in the table and set their properties. You can also make changes to the fields in an existing table using *Design* view. This section teaches you to create a table in *Design* view, add new fields, define a primary key, delete fields, and save a table.

Create a New Table in Design View

To add a new table into a database, use the *Create* tab. Tables created using the **Table Design** button automatically open in *Design* view.

▶HOW TO: Create a New Table in Design View

1. Click the **Create** tab on the *Ribbon*.
2. Click the **Table Design** button in the *Tables* group (Figure 2-1).

 Figure 2-1 *Table Design* button on the *Create* tab

 - A new table opens in *Design* view (Figure 2-2).
 - The table is assigned a generic name such as *Table1*.
 - The *Design* tab, a *Table Tools* contextual tab, is now available and selected.
 - The new table does not contain any fields.
 - The *Design* view window is divided into two areas. The top half displays the *Field Name*, *Data Type*, and *Description* for all fields in the table. The lower half displays the detailed field properties of the selected field.

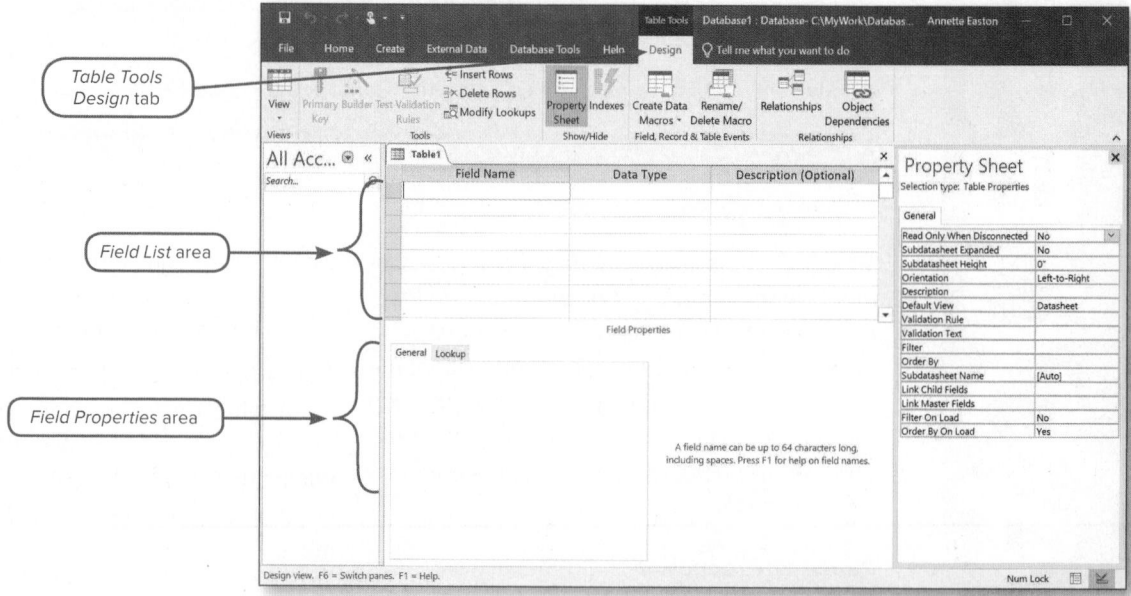

Figure 2-2 New table in *Design* view

- Depending on the settings the last time Access was used, the *Property Sheet* for the table may display to the right of the table.
- This sheet contains properties that apply to the entire table, not just a specific field.
- Because you don't need to modify table properties now, click the **Property Sheet** button [*Table Tools Design* tab, *Show/Hide* group] to close the *Property Sheet* if it is open.

The *Table Tools Design* tab contains buttons to perform a variety of tasks. The more commonly used buttons (*Primary Key, Insert Rows* and *Delete Rows*) are located in the *Tools* group (Figure 2-3) and explained in the following sections.

Figure 2-3 *Table Tools Design* tab, *Tools* group

Add New Fields

Add new fields into a table by entering a field name in the first blank row in the field list. When you add a new field, you must enter values for the *Field Name* and *Data Type* properties. Enter values for other available properties as desired.

1. Click the **Field Name** property box in the first blank row in the field list.
2. Type the desired name in the property box (Figure 2-4).
 - Each field must have a unique name.
 - As needed, review the *Access Naming Rules* section in *SLO 1.2: Creating and Managing a Database* to ensure that you create a valid field name.
 - Use the naming conventions required by your instructor or employer.

Figure 2-4 *Field Name* property box

3. Press **Enter** to add the field.
 - You move to the *Data Type* property with the *Short Text Data Type* selected.
 - The *Field Properties* of this field now display in the lower half of the *Design* view window.

> **ANOTHER WAY**
>
> Press **Tab** to add the field and move to the *Data Type* column.

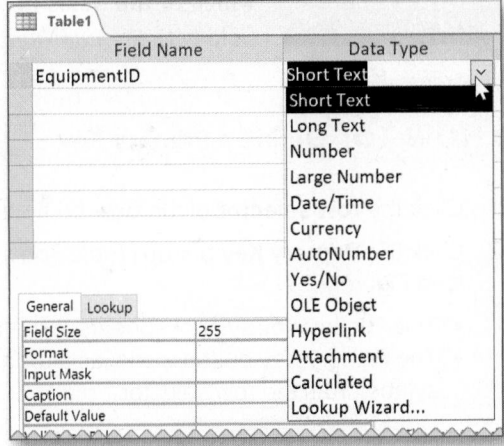

4. Click the **drop-down arrow** in the *Data Type* property box (Figure 2-5).
 - The list of data types displays.
5. Select the appropriate **Data Type**.

Figure 2-5 *Data Type* options in *Design* view

6. Press **Enter** to move to the *Description* property box. Recall from chapter 1 that the contents of the *Description* property displays in the lower left of the *Status* bar when the table is viewed in *Datasheet* view.

7. Type a value in the **Description** property box as desired (Figure 2-6).

8. Press **Enter** to move to the *Field Name* property box of the next row.

9. Repeat steps 2–8 to add the additional fields into your table.

Description (Optional)
Unique ID assigned to each piece of equipment

Figure 2-6 Enter the field's description in the *Description* property

Sometimes, you may need to add a new field between existing fields in a table. To add this new field, you must first insert a new row. After the row has been inserted, follow the steps above to add the new field.

▶**HOW TO: Insert a Blank Row to Add a New Field between Existing Fields**

1. Click the **row selector** of the row where the new field should be added. In *Design* view, the gray box to the left of a field name is called the ***row selector***.

2. Click the **Insert Rows** button [*Table Tools Design* tab, *Tools* group] (see Figure 2-3).
 - A new blank row is entered above the selected row (Figure 2-7).
 - Follow the steps in *How To: Add a New Field* to enter the details about the new field.

ANOTHER WAY

Right-click the **row selector** to open the context menu and then select **Insert Rows**.

Field Name	Data Type
EquipmentID	Short Text
ProductName	Short Text
DailyRentalRate	Currency

Row selector box

Figure 2-7 New row inserted into table

Define a Primary Key

Recall that a ***primary key*** is a field that contains a unique value for each record. When a table is created in *Design* view, a primary key field is not automatically assigned. You must determine which of the fields in your table uniquely identifies each record. If needed, add an additional field with an *AutoNumber Data Type* to serve as the primary key.

▶**HOW TO: Define a Primary Key**

1. Click the **row selector** of the desired field.

2. Click the **Primary Key** button [*Table Tools Design* tab, *Tools* group] (see Figure 2-3).
 - The *Primary Key* symbol appears in the row selector box (Figure 2-8).
 - The *Primary Key* button works as a toggle. Pressing it again will remove the symbol from the row selector.

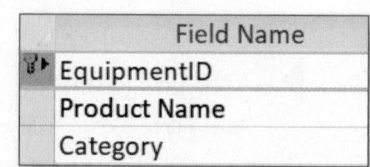

Field Name
EquipmentID
Product Name
Category

Figure 2-8 *Primary Key* symbol

ANOTHER WAY

Right-click the **row selector** of the desired field to open the context menu and then select **Primary Key**.

Delete Fields in a Table

The steps to delete a field in a table are straightforward. However, before you delete a field, it is important to realize that this may impact other parts of your database. If you have queries, forms, and reports that contain this field, you must also modify those objects to remove this field.

▶ **HOW TO:** Delete a Field in a Table

1. Click the **row selector** of the field to delete.
2. Click the **Delete Rows** button [*Table Tools Design* tab, *Tools* group] (see Figure 2-3). If the table contains data, Access displays an information message (Figure 2-9) asking you to confirm the deletion of the field and data in the table.

Figure 2-9 Delete field confirmation message

▶ **ANOTHER WAY**
Right-click the **row selector** of the desired field to open the context menu and then select **Delete Rows**.

Save, Close, Rename, and Open a Table

The save, close, and open operations on a table work the same whether you are in *Datasheet* or *Design* view.

- Save a new table by clicking the **File** tab and then clicking the **Save** button. The *Save As* dialog box opens if this is the first time you save the table. Type a new name for the table to replace the generic name assigned by Access.

▶ **ANOTHER WAY**
Recall from chapter 1 that you can also use **Ctrl+S**, the **Save** icon on the *Quick Access* toolbar, or the **F12** function key to open the *Save As* dialog box.

- Close a table by clicking the **X** in the upper-right corner of the table. If you close a new table without saving it, Access deletes the table.
- Rename a table by right-clicking the table name in the *Navigation Pane* and selecting **Rename** from the context menu. Remember that a table must be closed before you can rename it.
- Open a table in *Design* view by selecting the table name in the *Navigation Pane* and pressing **Ctrl+Enter**. You can also right-click the table name in the *Navigation Pane* and select **Design View** from the context menu.

Property Update Options Smart Tag

After the table has been named and saved for the first time, the **Property Update Options** smart tag becomes available. The smart tag displays after you tab out of the *Description* property box and you have entered or modified text in the *Description* property. Hover over the smart tag and click the arrow to display the list of options (Figure 2-10).

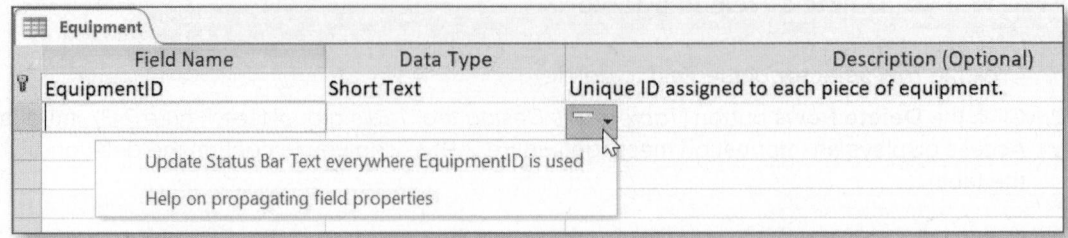

Figure 2-10 *Property Update Options* button

As desired, select the **Update Status Bar Text** option. This choice is most appropriate if you have created many different objects in your database and later change the *Description* property of a field. Selecting this option updates the description in all objects containing controls linked to this field. For example, you may have a text box control on a form object that is linked to the table field. When a field property can be passed to a control, it is called an ***inheritable property***. Not all field properties are able to be inherited. As a result, the *Property Update Options* smart tag only displays when the value of an inheritable property, such as the description, has been changed.

Switch between Datasheet and Design Views

Recall that ***Datasheet view*** is used to enter records into a table. When creating, and later using, a table, you may find that you need to switch between looking at the data records and looking at the properties of the different fields. When a table is open, Access provides three ways to easily switch between different table views.

Figure 2-11 *View* button

- Click the **View** button [*Home* tab, *Views* group] and then select the desired view option (Figure 2-11).
- Click the icon on the *View* button [*Home* tab, *Views* group] to directly switch to the alternate view (Figure 2-12). The icon that displays in the *View* button is the opposite of the current view. For example, because Figure 2-12 shows the datasheet icon, this means that the current view of the table is *Design* view.
- Click the desired view icon from the right side of the *Status* bar (Figure 2-13), located at the bottom of the Access window. The icon that has a gray background is the current view of the table.

Figure 2-12 *View* button icon

SLO 2.2

Setting Field Properties

Field properties describe the specific details of each field. When you add a field into the table, you enter values for the field name, data type, and description properties. You can set many additional

Design View icon

Figure 2-13 Table *View* icons in the *Status* bar

Datasheet View icon

field properties depending on the needs of your database. The available properties vary based on the data type of the field. Field properties are grouped into *General* and *Lookup* properties, and are displayed on their respective tabs in the *Field Properties* area in the lower half of the *Design* view window. This section introduces the more common *General* tab field properties of *Field Size*, *Format*, *Caption*, *Default Value*, and *Required*. Additionally, the *New Values* property of an *AutoNumber* field is described.

In order for the changes you make on any of the properties to be permanent, you must save the table. You can either save the table after each change or after all of your changes have been made.

Be sure to click the **row selector** of the correct field in the table before setting any of the properties discussed in this section.

Set the Field Size

The *Field Size* property determines the maximum number of characters allowed in a *Short Text* field or the range of possible values in a *Number* or *AutoNumber* field.

- A *Short Text* field can have a size from 0 to 255.
- A *Number* field can have seven possible field sizes that are explained in Table 2-1.

Table 2-1: Number Data Type Field Sizes

Unit	Description
Byte	Stores numbers from 0 to 255. Does not use decimal places.
Integer	Stores numbers from −32,768 to 32,767. Does not use decimal places.
Long Integer	Stores numbers from −2,147,483,648 to 2,147,483,647. Does not use decimal places. This is the default field size for a number data type.
Single	Stores numbers from -3.4×1038 to 3.4×1038 with a precision of 7 significant digits.
Double	Stores numbers from -1.797×1038 to 1.797×1038 with a precision of 15 significant digits.
Replication ID	Stores a globally unique identifier (GUID) randomly generated by Access.
Decimal	Stores numbers from −1028 to 1028 with a precision of 28 significant digits.

- An *AutoNumber* field can use either the *Long Integer* or *Replication ID* field size.

The other data types do not have a *Field Size* property because their size is controlled by the database. The *Field Size* property, if available, is the first property on the *General* tab.

▶**HOW TO:** **Set the Field Size Property**

1. Click the **Field Size** property box for a *Short Text* field, and type the desired field size (Figure 2-14).

 - The default size of a *Short Text* field is 255.

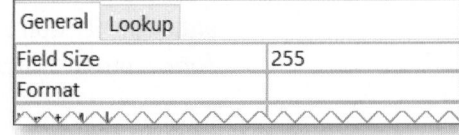

Figure 2-14 *Field Size* property

> ▶ MORE INFO
>
> Use the smallest field size that allows for the required processing or storage.

2. Click the **drop-down arrow** in the *Field Size* property for a *Number* or *AutoNumber* field, and select the desired number field size (Figure 2-15).

- The default selection for a *Number* field is *Long Integer*.
- The drop-down list of an *AutoNumber* field only contains *Long Integer* and *Replication ID*.

General	Lookup	
Field Size	Integer	⌄
Format	Byte	
Decimal Places	Integer	
Input Mask	Long Integer	
Caption	Single	
Default Value	Double	
Validation Rule	Replication ID	
Validation Text	Decimal	
Required	Yes	

Figure 2-15 Field sizes for a *Number* data type

The Format Property

The *Format* property controls the way a field displays in a table; it doesn't change what is actually stored. The choices available vary by the data type selected. Data types like *Number*, *Currency*, *Date/Time*, and *Yes/No* have predefined formats from which you can select. For *Short Text* and *Long Text* data types, you can create a custom format.

To enter a value in the *Format* property box, either select the predefined format or enter the desired formatting characters to create a custom format.

Number and Currency Field Formats

Click the **drop-down arrow** in the *Format* property box of a *Number* or *Currency* field to display the list of predefined formats (Figure 2-16).

If you don't select a format, Access uses the *General Number* format for a number field, although it won't display in the *Format* property box. A *Currency* field defaults to the *Currency* format.

General	Lookup		
Field Size	Long Integer		
Format			⌄
Decimal Places		General Number	3456.789
Input Mask		Currency	$3,456.79
Caption		Euro	€3,456.79
Default Value		Fixed	3456.79
Validation Rule		Standard	3,456.79
Validation Text		Percent	123.00%
Required		Scientific	3.46E+03
Indexed	No		
Text Align	General		

Figure 2-16 Predefined formats for *Number* and *Currency* data types

Date/Time Field Formats

Click the **drop-down arrow** in the *Format* property box of a *Date/Time* field to display the list of predefined formats (Figure 2-17). You can choose formats that display only the date, only the time, or both.

If you don't select a format, Access uses the *General Date* format, although it won't display in the *Format* property box.

General	Lookup		
Format			⌄
Input Mask		General Date	11/12/2015 5:34:23 PM
Caption		Long Date	Thursday, November 12, 2015
Default Value		Medium Date	12-Nov-15
Validation Rule		Short Date	11/12/2015
Validation Text		Long Time	5:34:23 PM
Required		Medium Time	5:34 PM
Indexed		Short Time	17:34
IME Mode	No Control		
IME Sentence Mode	None		

Figure 2-17 Predefined field formats for the *Date/Time* data type

Yes/No Field Formats

Click the **drop-down arrow** in the *Format* property of a *Yes/No* field to display the list of predefined formats shown in Figure 2-18.

If you don't select a format, Access uses the *Yes/No* format.

General	Lookup		
Format		Yes/No	⌄
Caption		True/False	True
Default Value		Yes/No	Yes
Validation Rule		On/Off	On
Validation Text			
Indexed	No		
Text Align	General		

Figure 2-18 Predefined field formats for the *Yes/No* data type

Short Text and Long Text Field Formats

Short Text and *Long Text* fields do not have any predefined formats. You can use formatting symbols to create a custom format and change the way the data display. More than one symbol may be used if multiple formatting effects are needed. Four common formatting symbols are described in Table 2-2.

Table 2-2: Short Text and Long Text Field Formatting Symbols

Character	Description
<	The less than symbol (<) displays characters in lowercase. For example, if **FL** or **Fl** is entered into a field with a format of <, the entry displays as **fl**. This must be the first of the formatting symbols if multiple symbols are used.
>	The greater than symbol (>) displays characters in uppercase. For example, if **fl** or **Fl** is entered into a field with a format of >, the entry displays as **FL**. This must be the first of the formatting symbols if multiple symbols are used.
@	Enter one at symbol (@) for each character in the size of the field. If the field content contains fewer characters than the field size, the content displays with leading spaces. For example, if **ABC** is entered into a field of size 5 with a format of @@@@@, this entry displays as **space, space, ABC**.
[color]	Applies a color to this field only. The color must be enclosed in brackets. The possible colors are black, blue, cyan, green, magenta, red, yellow, or white. This formatting symbol only works when applied in conjunction with one of the other formatting symbols. For example, a format of >[blue] displays that field's contents in uppercase with a blue color.

Recall that *Short Text* and *Long Text* data types default to display left-justified. In chapter 1, you learned to change the alignment of a field in *Datasheet* view. The at symbol (@) does not change the alignment, but when leading spaces are included for field contents that are less than the field size, the displayed contents do not appear to be left-justified.

The Caption Property

The *Caption* property contains the text that displays in the column header to identify a field in *Datasheet* views of tables, forms, queries, and reports. Captions often include spaces and multiple words as compared to the field name. Access displays the field name as the caption if you do not enter a caption value.

To enter a value for the *Caption* property, click the **Caption** property box and type the desired value.

Set the Default Value

You can use the *Default Value* property to automatically insert a specified value into a new record in a table. For example, Access can enter today's date into an *OrderDate* field. Or, if most of a company's customers live in California, a default value of **CA** can be entered for a *State* field. Using a default value doesn't prevent the user from changing that value if needed (for example, when a customer is from Nevada (NV) instead of California (CA)). The default value is only inserted into the field at the time a new record is created. It does not automatically update later if field values are modified.

To enter a value in the *Default Value* property, click the **Default Value** property box and type the desired value.

The Required Property

You can specify whether a user must enter a value into a field or whether the user can skip the field and leave it blank. If a field must have a value, you should set the *Required* property to *Yes*. The default value for the *Required* property is *No*.

To set the *Required* property, click the **Required** property box and select **Yes**.

When building tables, you may wish to set the required property last. This enables you to more easily test different features in the table without being forced to enter a value for every field. This is especially helpful when you are adding different types of validation rules into the table. This skill is covered in the next section.

The New Values Property

As you learned in chapter 1, an *AutoNumber Data Type* is often used as a primary key field because it guarantees a unique value. The value of an *AutoNumber* field is set automatically when you create a new record. When creating this type of field, you can choose whether the values are set to be sequential (increment by 1) or random. This is controlled in the *New Values* property box (Figure 2-19), located on the *General* tab. The default value for the *New Values* property is *Increment*, which produces sequential numbers that increase by 1.

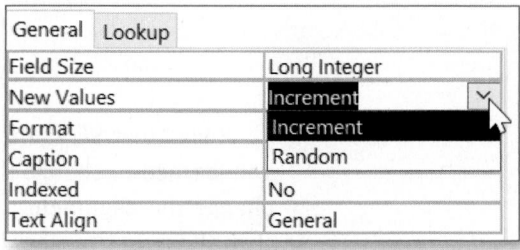

To set the *New Values* property to random numbers, click the **New Values** property box and select **Random**.

Figure 2-19 *New Values* property options

It is important to note that when a new record is created, the first value assigned is to the *AutoNumber* field. If you ultimately do not save that record, or the record is later deleted, the *AutoNumber* value is still considered used. A subsequent record will be assigned the next available value in sequence or an unused random number. Additionally, once you have set an *AutoNumber* field to use random values and have saved that table, you cannot change back to use incremental values.

Pause & Practice: Access 2-1

For this Pause & Practice, you create a new database for Ryan Thomas, operations director for Mary's Rentals. You use *Design* view to create a table to store information about the rental equipment. In addition, you modify the field properties to enhance the functionality of this table.

File Needed: ***EquipmentDataFile-02.xlsx*** *(Student data files are available in the Library of your SIMnet account.)*
Completed Project File Name: *[your initials] **PP A2-1.accdb***

➡

1. Create a new blank database.
 a. Open Access or click the **New** button [*File* tab] if an Access database is already open.
 b. Click **Blank database**.
 c. Type [your initials] PP A2-1 in the *File Name* box.
 d. Click the **Browse** button to change the location in which to save the database and click **OK**.
 e. Click the **Create** button. The database opens with a new table showing in *Datasheet* view.

2. Switch to *Design* view and save the table.
 a. Click the **View** button [*Table Tools Fields* tab, *Views* group] and select the **Design View** option. You are prompted to save the table.
 b. Type Equipment as the new table name.
 c. Click **OK**. The table displays in *Design* view with the default primary key selected.

3. Modify the default primary key.
 a. Click the **ID** *Field Name* property box in your table and type EquipmentID. Press **Tab** to move to the *Data Type* property.
 b. Click the **drop-down arrow** in the *Data Type* property box.
 c. Select the **Short Text** data type. Press **Tab** to move to the *Description* property.
 d. Type Unique ID assigned to each piece of equipment in the *Description* property box. Press **Tab** to move to the next row (Figure 2-20).

> **MORE INFO**
>
> The default *AutoNumber* data type was not appropriate for the *EquipmentID* field because Mary's Rentals already has assigned ID numbers to their equipment. Choose a *Short Text* data type for fields not used in arithmetic operations, even if the field contains numbers.

4. Add new fields into the table.
 a. Type ProductName in the *Field Name* property box of the second row. Press **Tab** to move to the *Data Type* property.

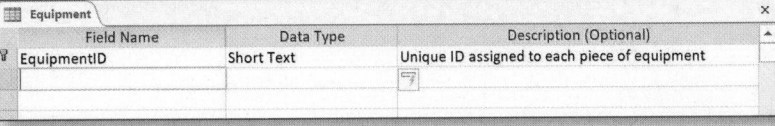

Figure 2-20 Add fields into the *Equipment* table

 b. Select the **Short Text** *Data Type*. Press **Tab** to move to the *Description* property.
 c. Do not enter a description; instead, press **Tab** to move to the next row.
 d. Continue adding the remaining fields into the *Equipment* table using the information in Table 2-3.

Table 2-3

Field Name	Data Type	Description
Category	**Short Text**	Type of equipment
DailyRentalRate	**Currency**	
WeeklyRentalRate	**Currency**	Must be greater than the DailyRentalRate
MonthlyRentalRate	**Currency**	Must be greater than the WeeklyRentalRate
DatePurchased	**Date/Time**	Date we purchased the equipment; not necessarily the date the equipment was made
Comments	**Long Text**	Additional information about the equipment

5. Save all of the modifications to the *Equipment* table.

6. Set the field properties in the *Equipment* table.
 a. Click the **row selector** of the *EquipmentID* field.
 b. Type 5 in the *Field Size* property box in the *Field Properties* area.
 c. Click the **Required** property box and select **Yes** if necessary.
 d. Click the **row selector** of the *ProductName* field.
 e. Continue changing the remaining field properties in the *Equipment* table using the information in Table 2-4.

Table 2-4

Field Name	Field Size	Format
ProductName	45	>[Blue]
Category	30	
DatePurchased		Medium Date

The *Required* property will be set for several of the other fields in *Pause & Practice 2-2* after you have added data validation features into the table design.

7. Save the table. Your completed table design should be similar to Figure 2-21.

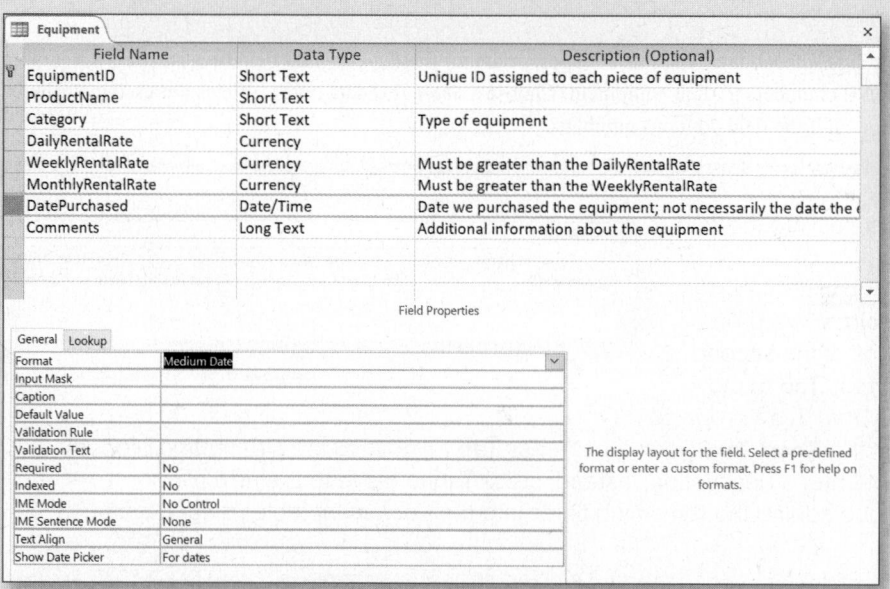

Figure 2-21 *Design* view of the completed *Equipment* table

8. Close the table.

9. Import data records from Excel into the *Equipment* table.
 a. Launch the *Get External Data – Excel Spreadsheet* dialog box.
 b. Locate and select the **EquipmentDataFile-02** Excel file.
 c. Append the records to the *Equipment* table.
 d. Launch the *Import Spreadsheet Wizard*. Note that the file only contains values for the *EquipmentID*, *ProductName*, and *Comments* fields. You will adjust the properties of the other fields in *Pause & Practice 2-2* before adding the additional data values.
 e. Finish the *Import Spreadsheet Wizard*. Close the *Wizard* after the records have imported.

10. Open the *Equipment* table in *Datasheet* view. The table should contain 10 records. Access automatically displays a value of $0.00 in currency data type fields that do not have any data.

The *ProductName* values display in uppercase blue text as a result of entering >[Blue] in the *Format* property in step 6e.

11. Modify the row height of the table. Recall from chapter 1 that you can change the row height through the context menu.
 a. Select any row in the table.
 b. Right-click to open the context menu and select **Row Height**.
 c. Enter 58 in the *Row Height* box and click **OK**.

12. Modify the field width of the *ProductName* and *Comments* columns. Recall from chapter 1 that you can change the column width through the context menu.
 a. Select the *ProductName* column.
 b. Right-click to open the context menu and select **Field Width**.
 c. Enter 23 in the *Column Width* box and click **OK**.
 d. Repeat steps a–c to change the *Comments* field to a column width of 26.

13. Improve the formatting display of the *Comments* field. You can force a line break in a text field to have text appear on a second line. Press the **Ctrl+Enter** keys at the point where you want the line break to occur.
 a. For EquipmentID 09863, position and click the pointer before the B in "Bucket" and then press **Ctrl+Enter**. "Bucket" now starts on a second line.
 b. For EquipmentID 10015, position and click the pointer before the W in "Weight" and then press **Ctrl+Enter**.
 c. For EquipmentID 10103, position and click the pointer before the 6 in "67"L," and then press **Ctrl+Enter**. The completed table will be similar to Figure 2-22.

EquipmentIC ▾	ProductName ▾	Category ▾	DailyRentalR ▾	WeeklyRenta ▾	MonthlyRent ▾	DatePurchas ▾	Comments ▾
09863	BACKHOE COMPACT ALLMAND DIESEL		$0.00	$0.00	$0.00		Lift Capacity: 2100 lbs Bucket Size: 16" only
10015	GENERATOR PORTABLE MAKITA 1000W		$0.00	$0.00	$0.00		Size: 19-1/2"L x 11-3/4"W x 17-1/2"H Weight: 55 lbs
10047	SKIP LOADER 4X4		$0.00	$0.00	$0.00		Subject to Environmental Fee
10103	GENERATOR TOWABLE POWERPRO 25KW		$0.00	$0.00	$0.00		Overall L x W x H: 67"L x 28"W x 3"H
10129	LEVEL SITE LASER		$0.00	$0.00	$0.00		

Figure 2-22 PP A2-1 completed

14. Save and close the table.

15. Close the database.

SLO 2.3

Understanding Data Integrity and Data Validation

The usefulness of your database depends on the quality of the data being stored. It is critical that all data entered into a table is verified to make sure that it is accurate.

The process of verifying the accuracy, or integrity, of the data is known as *data validation*. Data validation uses the data integrity rules that have been defined in the field and table properties. *Data integrity rules* ensure that the data in a database is accurate and consistent. The more common data integrity rules are described in Table 2-5.

Table 2-5: Data Integrity Rules

Rule Focus	Description
Data format	Ensures that a value entered into a field matches the data type established for that field; meets any size constraints; and meets any required formatting, such as beginning with a number or letter, or matching a month/day/year format
Range	Ensures that a value entered into a field falls within the range of acceptable values that have been established
Consistency	Ensures that a value entered into a field is consistent with a value in another field
Completeness	Ensures that a field contains a value if it is required

Data integrity rules are included as part of the ***metadata***, the descriptions about what the different data fields represent and their formats. In Access, metadata is entered into the different field properties. An example of the metadata for the *Order Details* table in *Northwind Traders*, a sample database available in the Access online templates, is shown in Figure 2-23.

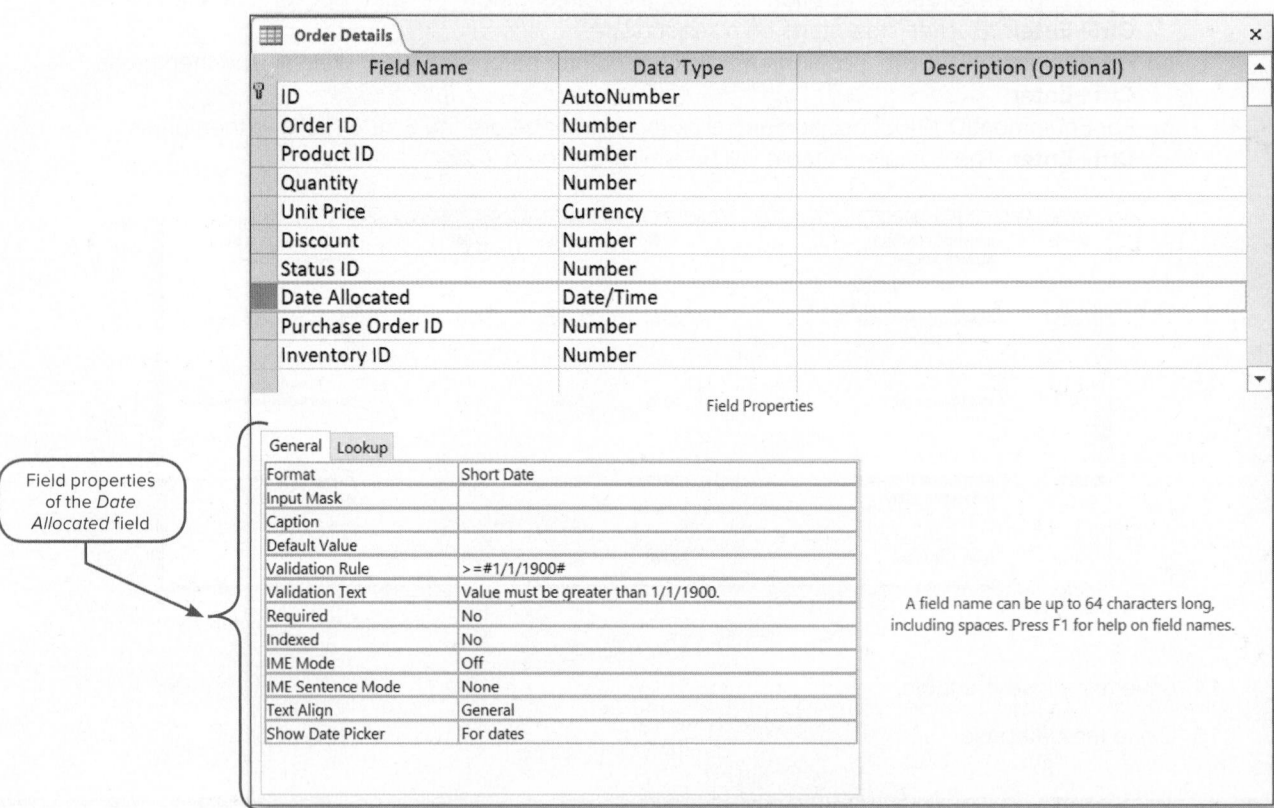

Figure 2-23 Metadata of the *Order Details* table in *Northwind Traders*

One of the key advantages to a database is that the DBMS automatically uses the metadata for the data integrity rules to perform data validation. Based on the metadata shown for the *Date Allocated* field, the database performs data validation using the following data integrity rules:

- The field must have *Date/Time* data and must follow the *Short Date* format (the *Data Type* and *Format* properties).
- The date must be greater than or equal to 1/1/1900 (the *Validation Rule* property).
- The user may leave this field blank (the *Required* property).

Integrating Data Validation in Tables

You learned how to set the *Data Type* and *Required* properties in *SLO 2.2: Setting Field Properties*. Those properties are used to implement data format and completeness data integrity rules. The material that follows describes additional properties used to implement data format, consistency, and range data integrity rules. In Access, these can be created using field and record validation rules. This section explains how to create validation rules in *Design* view, although they can also be entered in *Datasheet* view. Additionally, you learn how to use lookup fields to ensure range integrity and how to use an input mask to help users enter data in the correct format. Remember to save your table after you make changes to any of these properties.

Field Validation Rules

Field validation rules are used to create range and data format integrity rules that limit entries to a certain range of values or to make sure entries match a specified format. You enter the specific rule into the ***Validation Rule*** property of a field. Access checks field validation rules when a user navigates out of the field. If the data violates the rule, Access requires the user to fix the problem before he or she can leave the field.

Validation rules cannot be used on fields with data types of *Attachment*, *AutoNumber*, *OLE Object*, and the *ReplicationID Field Size* choice of a *Number* field.

> **MORE INFO**
>
> If you want your rule to compare two or more fields, you must use a record validation rule.

In Access, the rules are called ***expressions***. They are written using the common operators shown in Table 2-6.

Table 2-6: Operators Used in Access Expressions

Arithmetic	Comparison	Logical
−	<	And
+	<=	Or
*	>	Not
/	>=	Xor
^	=	
	<>	
	Between	
	In	
	Like	

The content of your expression depends on the data type of the field, along with the specific restriction you are trying to implement. Validation rules ignore the case of the text when making an evaluation. Examples of entries for validation rules, along with an explanation of their effects, are shown in Table 2-7.

Table 2-7: Using and Understanding Field Validation Rules

Validation Rule Example	Explanation of Effect
<5	Value entered must be less than 5.
<>0	Value entered must not equal 0.
>=#1/1/2020#	Value entered must be greater than or equal to 1/1/2020. *Tip*: Dates must be surrounded by the **#** sign.
"M" OR "F"	Value entered must be the letter M or the letter F. *Tip*: Text values must be surrounded by double quotation marks.
>=#1/1/2020# AND <#1/1/2021#	Value entered must be a date from 2020.
"A" OR > "M"	Value entered must be the letter A or a letter that comes after M in the alphabet.
IN ("CA", "NV", "AZ")	Value entered must be either CA, NV, or AZ.
Not Null	The field must be filled in. While this can be enforced with the required property, using this validation rule enables you to include a custom validation message like "The Equipment ID field cannot be empty." *Tip*: **Null** means no value in the field.

The *Yes/No* data type defaults to display data using a check box. A check indicates *Yes*, while an unchecked box indicates *No*. Internally, Access stores *Yes* as a −1 and *No* as 0. Expressions written to check the contents of a *Yes/No* data type should compare the contents to either a −1 or a 0.

Use the *Like* comparison operator to find a value that is similar to (or like) another value. When using *Like*, you typically incorporate one of the *wildcard characters* available in Access. Examples of three of the wildcard characters and their effects are shown in Table 2-8.

Table 2-8: Using Wildcard Characters in Validation Rules

Wildcard Character	Matches	Example	Explanation of Example
?	Any single character (numbers are also considered characters)	Like "C????"	Values entered must be 5 characters long and begin with the letter C. *Tip*: Even if the field size is larger than 5, this rule requires that exactly 5 characters are entered.
*	Any number of characters	Like "MA*"	Values entered must begin with MA, but can be any length up to the maximum field size.
#	Any single numeric digit	Like "##"	Values entered must contain two numeric digits.

When using wildcards, the criteria of your expression must be enclosed in quotation marks. You can combine multiple wildcards to achieve the desired criteria.

▶ HOW TO: Create a Field Validation Rule

1. Click the **row selector** of the desired field.
2. Click the **Validation Rule** property box (Figure 2-24). The *Build* button displays at the right of the property box.

3. Type the text of the desired rule.

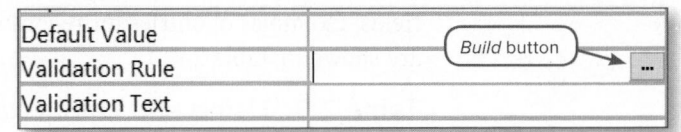

Default Value	
Validation Rule	Build button ...
Validation Text	

Figure 2-24 *Validation Rule property box*

You can also use the *Expression Builder* to enter your validation rules. The **Expression Builder** is a dialog box that provides access to built-in functions, constants, and operators. It also provides a larger window in which to type your expression. This can be useful when you have a long expression.

▶ **HOW TO:** Create a Field Validation Rule Using the Expression Builder

1. Click the **row selector** of the desired field.
2. Click the **Validation Rule** property box (see Figure 2-24) and click the **Build** button. The *Expression Builder* dialog box opens.

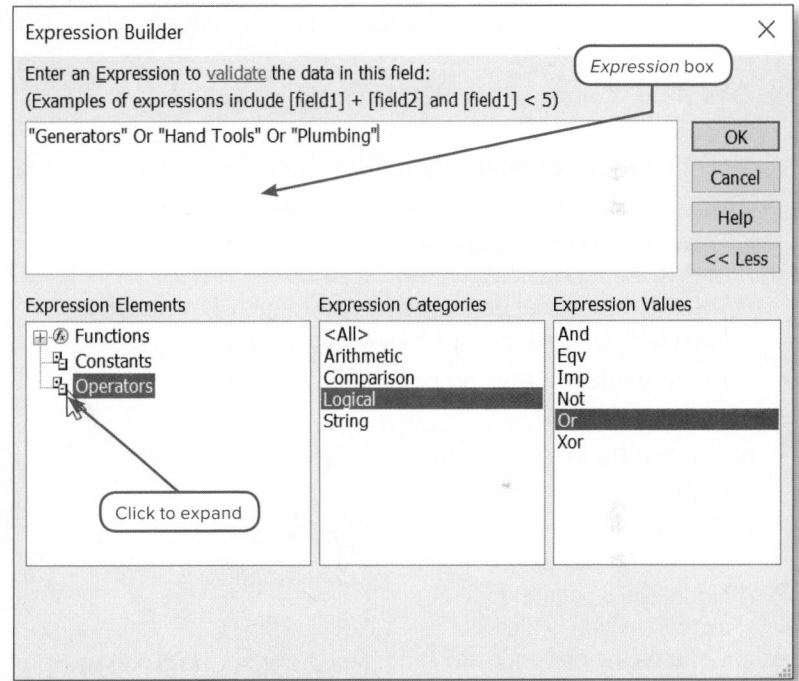

▶ **ANOTHER WAY**

Open the *Expression Builder* dialog box by pressing **Ctrl+F2** or clicking the **Builder** button [*Table Tools Design* tab, *Tools* group].

3. Type the text of the desired rule in the *Expression* box (Figure 2-25).
 - You can click to expand the items in the **Expression Elements** area to display the available choices.
 - Instead of typing, double-click choices in the **Expression Categories** and **Expression Values** areas to add them to the *Expression* box.

Figure 2-25 *Expression Builder dialog box*

Record Validation Rules

Record validation rules are used to create consistency data integrity rules that compare fields in the same table. You can also use them to create range and data format integrity rules that limit entries to a certain range of values or to a specified format. You enter the specific rule into the *Validation Rule* property of the table, located on the table's *Property Sheet*. The rule is checked when a user attempts to navigate out of the record. If the data the user has entered in the record violates the rule, Access requires the user to fix the problem before he or she can leave the record.

Expressions written for a record validation rule can use the same operators and wildcard characters used in field level validation rules. However, they typically are written to compare

fields. Examples of entries for record validation rules, along with an explanation of the effects, are shown in Table 2-9.

Table 2-9: Using and Understanding Record Validation Rules

Record Validation Rule Example	Explanation of Effect
([Field1] is Null) XOR ([Field2] is Null)	You must enter a value into either *Field1* or *Field2*, but not into both fields. *Tip*: The *XOR* logical operator prevents both fields from having a value; both fields would be allowed to have a value if *OR* were used instead.
[Field1] <> [Field2]	You may not enter the same value into both *Field1* and *Field2*.
([Field1] > [Field2]) AND ([Field2] > 10)	*Field1* must be greater than *Field2*, and *Field2* must have a value greater than 10. *Tip*: When using the *AND* operator, all parts of the condition must be true.

Substitute the actual field names in your table for the placeholders of *Field1*, *Field2*, etc. Be sure to include your field name inside square brackets, as shown in the examples.

▶ **HOW TO:** Create a Record Validation Rule

1. Click the **Property Sheet** button [*Table Tools Design* tab, *Show/Hide* group] (Figure 2-26).
 - The *Property Sheet* for the table opens (Figure 2-27).
 - This sheet contains properties that apply to the entire table, not just a specific field.
 - The *Property Sheet* button works as a toggle. If the sheet is open and you click the button, the sheet closes.
2. Click the **Valdation Rule** property box.
3. Type the text of the desired rule directly in the property box or click the **Build** button to open the *Expression Builder* dialog box.
 - The example valida-tion rule shown in Figure 2-28 uses the *Date()* function, which captures the current date from the computer. This example rule requires that the value in the *DatePurchased* field is greater than or equal to the current date.

Property Sheet

Selection type: Table Properties

General

Read Only When Disconnected	No
Subdatasheet Expanded	No
Subdatasheet Height	0"
Orientation	Left-to-Right
Description	
Default View	Datasheet
Validation Rule	
Validation Text	
Filter	
Order By	
Subdatasheet Name	[Auto]
Link Child Fields	
Link Master Fields	
Filter On Load	No
Order By On Load	Yes

Figure 2-26 *Property Sheet* button

| Validation Rule | [DatePurchased] >= Date() |

Figure 2-28 Example record validation rule

Figure 2-27 *Property Sheet* of a table

▶ MORE INFO

Adjust the width of the *Property Sheet* by dragging the resize pointer on the left border of the *Property Sheet*.

Test Validation Rules

When using validation rules, it is important that you test the rules. Two different considerations are available for testing.

- Test to ensure the rule is written correctly.

 These tests ensure that the logic is valid, and the rule works as you intended. If several fields have validation rules, it is easiest to test each rule as you write it. This helps you focus on a specific rule instead of trying to test all of them at the same time.

 To test a validation rule, you must create *test data*, a set of data created to test an application. The test data should include a sample of every valid condition, as well as samples of as many invalid conditions as possible. Table 2-10 illustrates several examples about creating test data.

Table 2-10: Test Data Examples for Validation Rules

Validation Rule	Examples of Test Data	Result of Test
"M" OR "F"	M	Valid (test of M condition); should be accepted.
	F	Valid (test of F condition); should be accepted.
	X	Invalid; error message should display.
=#1/1/2020# AND <#1/1/2021#	12/15/2019	Invalid (below the range); error message should display.
	7/7/2020	Valid; should be accepted.
	2/13/2021	Invalid (above the range); error message should display.
([Field1] is Null) XOR ([Field2] is Null)	Field1 null and Field2 null	Invalid (both can't be null); error message should display.
	Field1 = 5 and Field2 = 7	Invalid (both can't have a value); error message should display.
	Field1 null and Field2 = 7	Valid (only Field2 has a value); should be accepted.
	Field1 = 5 and Field2 null	Valid (only Field1 has a value); should be accepted.

- Test to ensure that any data already in the table is verified against the new rules.

 Test existing data by clicking the **Test Validation Rules** button [*Table Tools Design* tab, *Tools* group] (Figure 2-29).

 Access displays a message box explaining the test and alerting you to the fact that this operation could take a long time depending on the number of records of data in your table.

 If you click **Yes** to proceed, Access displays an error message (Figure 2-30) if any data are found to violate validation rules. Select whether to continue testing other rule violations.

 If you continue testing, Access displays an error message (Figure 2-31) indicating which rule is violated.

 You must return to *Datasheet* view, locate any records that have invalid data, and then make the necessary corrections.

Figure 2-29 *Test Validation Rules* button

Figure 2-30 Validation rule violation error message

Figure 2-31 Message box for data validation errors

Create Validation Text

When the data entered violate a validation rule, Access automatically displays a message box alerting the user to the problem. The message box text includes the condition entered into the validation rule. Unfortunately, the message, as shown in Figure 2-32, is often not very clear to a typical user of your database.

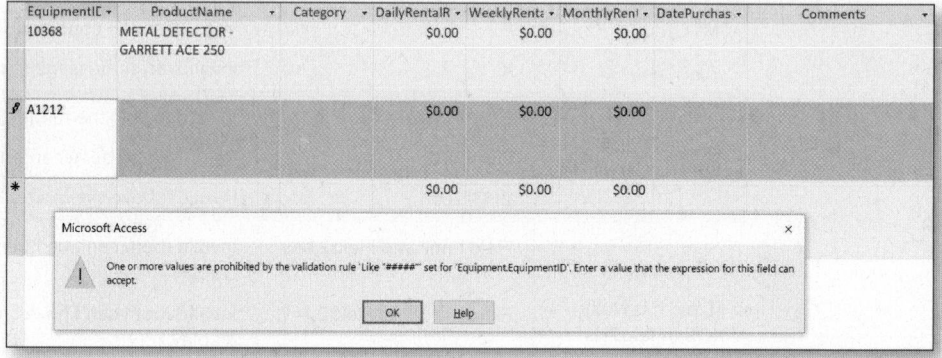

Figure 2-32 Default message when entering data that violate a validation rule

You can use the *Validation Text* property to enter a custom message that displays instead of the default message. Be clear and concise in your message. Include the reason the entry is invalid and suggest how to correct the problem. For example, "The EquipmentID must contain 5 numbers" is a better error message than "Invalid entry in EquipmentID field" or "Please enter a valid EquipmentID."

For a field validation rule, place the custom message in the *Validation Text* property of that field. For a record validation rule, place the custom message in the *Validation Text* property of the table.

▶ HOW TO: Create Validation Text

1. Click the **row selector** of the desired field or open the *Property Sheet* for the table by clicking the **Property Sheet** button [*Table Tools Design* tab, *Show/Hide* group].
2. Click the **Validation Text** property box.
3. Type the text of the desired message. An example message is shown in the *Validation Text* property box in Figure 2-33.

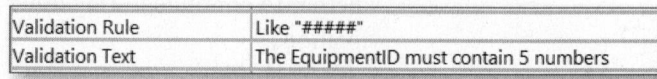

Validation Rule	Like "#####"
Validation Text	The EquipmentID must contain 5 numbers

Figure 2-33 Example validation text

Because the *Validation Text* property box is not very wide, you can also enter the message in the *Zoom* window. The *Zoom* window (Figure 2-34) enables you to see the entire message that you are entering, which might not be visible in the smaller property box.

Open the *Zoom* window by right-clicking the **Validation Text** property box and selecting the **Zoom** button or by pressing **Shift+F2**.

As desired, click the **Font** button to change the default font used in the *Zoom* window. However, this does not affect the font that displays in the message box.

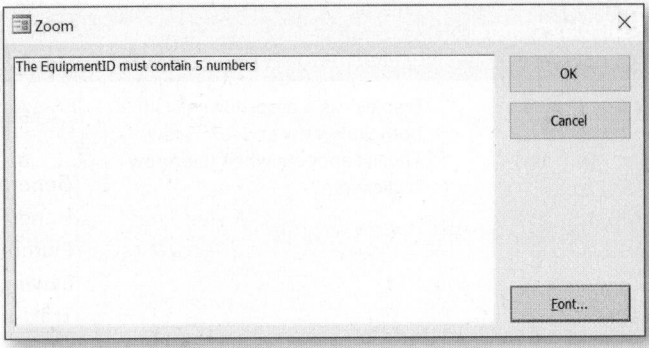

Figure 2-34 Create a custom validation text message in the *Zoom* window

Create a Lookup Field

Lookup fields display a list of data values from which the user can choose. Lookup fields are another way to implement *range* integrity rules and are an alternative to validation rules because they also limit what can be entered into a field. They are very helpful when the actual choices are lengthy or prone to typing mistakes. Lookup fields can be used on any field that is defined as a data type of *Number*, *Short Text*, or *Yes/No*, but are most commonly used on *Number* and *Short Text* fields.

The list of values in a lookup field can either be directly entered into the properties of the field or automatically filled in from values in another table or query. In this section, you learn to create a lookup field by entering the list of values.

One of the choices you make when creating a lookup field is to determine the way that the list displays. This choice is made in the field's **Display Control** property on the *Lookup* tab. *Text* and *Number* fields have three options for the *Display Control* property. The appearance and behavior of the control depends on whether you are viewing the data in *Datasheet* view of a table or whether you are viewing it in a form. Because you select the type of control when creating the lookup field, it is important to understand the differences now. The *Display Control* property of a field is initially set based on the field's data type. *Text Box* is the default choice for the *Display Control* property of *Short Text* and *Number* fields. The three options available to a lookup field are explained in Table 2-11, which includes samples of how the control displays in a table or form. To create a lookup field, you would change the *Display Control* property from *Text Box* to one of the other two options.

Table 2-11: Understanding Display Control Options

Display Control Choice	Explanation	Table Sample	Form Sample
Text Box	Displays the contents of a field and also enables the user to type a value into that field. This is the default choice.	Category ▾	Category
List Box	*Table* view: Displays as a drop-down list. The list appears when the arrow is clicked. *Form* view: Displays as a box showing all possible choices.	Category ▾ ⌄ Generators Hand Tools Plumbing Sawing, Cutting Tractors	Category: Generators Hand Tools Plumbing Sawing, Cutting & Grinding Tractors

Continued

Display Control Choice	Explanation	Table Sample	Form Sample
Combo Box	Displays as a drop-down list in both table view and form view. The list appears when the arrow is clicked.	Category ▾ Generators Hand Tools Plumbing Sawing, Cutting Tractors	Category Generators Hand Tools Plumbing

Notice that a *List Box* and *Combo Box* display the same way in *Datasheet* view of a table but are different when displayed on a form. Because the *List Box* control takes up more space on a form, and users don't always find it intuitive to understand and don't know to make a selection, you may want to opt to use the *Combo Box* display control choice.

Once the *Display Control* property is set to either *List Box* or *Combo Box*, additional properties become available on the *Lookup* tab. Several of the more commonly used properties are described in Table 2-12.

Table 2-12: Common Lookup Field Properties

Property	Explanation	Setting Contents
Row Source Type	Designates whether the values for the different list choices come from a table, query, or list.	*Table/Query*: Values will come from a table or query that you specify. *Value List*: Values will come from a list of choices you enter. *Field List*: Values will come from a list of field names from a table.
Row Source	Contains the name of the table or query, or the actual list of values.	If the *Row Source Type* is **Table/Query** or **Field List**, enter the name of the table or query. If the *Row Source Type* is **Value List**, enter the choices.
List Rows	Contains the number of rows to display in the list. The default number is 16. A scroll bar automatically appears when you enter more choices than rows. Available only if the *Display Control* is a *Combo Box*.	Enter the number of rows to display.
Limit to List	Designates whether a user can enter a value into the field that is not on the list. The default choice is *No*. Available only if the *Display Control* is a *Combo Box*.	*Yes*: Restricts the user to picking an entry from the list. *No*: Enables users to pick from the list or enter a new value.
Allow Value List Edits	Designates whether the list of items can be edited. The default choice is *No*.	*Yes*: Enables the user to add to, change, and delete the values in the list. *No*: Restricts the user from editing the list.

In Table 2-11, the form sample *Combo Box* image illustrates changes made in both the *List Rows* and *Allow Value List Edits* properties. The *List Rows* property has been changed to three. Because the list has five items, the scroll bar appears. The *Allow Value List Edits* property

Figure 2-35 *Edit List Items* button

Figure 2-36 *Edit List Items* dialog box

has been changed to *Yes*. The **Edit List Items** button appears below the list when the user tabs into that field. When you hover over the button, it turns gray (Figure 2-35). Click the button to open the *Edit List Items* dialog box (Figure 2-36).

▶ **ANOTHER WAY**

Press **Ctrl+E** to open the *Edit List Items* dialog box, or right-click the **lookup field** to open the context menu and then select the **Edit List Items** button.

The *Edit List Items* dialog box enables the user to add new items to the list, change existing items, or delete items from the list. Be cautious about giving this type of control to your users.

Because the *Combo Box* is the more common display control, we will concentrate on creating and using this type of lookup field.

HOW TO: Create a Combo Box Lookup Field by Typing a List of Values

1. Click the **row selector** of the desired field.
2. Select the **Lookup** tab in the *Field Properties* area in the lower half of the *Design view* window (Figure 2-37).

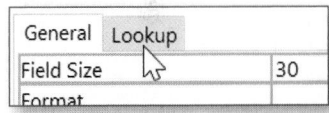

Figure 2-37 Select the *Lookup* tab

3. Click the **Display Control** property box and select **Combo Box**.
 - After you select the *Combo Box* display control, additional properties will become available on the *Lookup* tab, as shown in Figure 2-38.
4. Click the **Row Source Type** property box, click the **drop-down arrow** and select **Value List**.
 - This choice indicates that you will enter the list of possible choices.
5. Type the list of choices into the **Row Source** property box.
 - Separate each choice with a semicolon (**;**).
 - If the choice contains a comma (**,**) as punctuation, the choice must be surrounded by quotation marks (**" "**).
6. Edit the **List Rows** property, as desired, to set the number of rows that display.

General	Lookup	
Display Control	Combo Box	∨
Row Source Type	Table/Query	
Row Source		
Bound Column	1	
Column Count	1	
Column Heads	No	
Column Widths		
List Rows	16	
List Width	Auto	
Limit To List	No	
Allow Multiple Values	No	
Allow Value List Edits	No	
List Items Edit Form		
Show Only Row Source Values	No	

Figure 2-38 Additional properties on the *Lookup* tab

7. Edit the **Limit To List** property as desired.
 - Select **Yes** if you want to restrict the user to picking a choice only from the list.
8. Edit the **Allow Value List Edits** property as desired.
 - Select **Yes** if you want to enable the user to change the values in the list while entering or viewing data.

▶HOW TO: Create a Combo Box Lookup Field Using the Lookup Wizard

1. Click the **row selector** of the desired field.
2. Click the property box for the **Data Type** property and click the **drop-down arrow** to display the list of data types.
3. Select **Lookup Wizard** (Figure 2-39). The *Lookup Wizard* dialog box opens.
4. Select the radio button for **I will type in the values that I want.** (See Figure 2-40.)

Figure 2-39 *Lookup Wizard* option in the *Data Type* property list

Figure 2-40 First step of the *Lookup Wizard*

5. Click the **Next** button.
 - The next step of the *Lookup Wizard* displays.
 - Initially no items display in the list.
6. Click the **first cell** in the *Col1* column.
7. Type the first value in the list.
8. Press the **down arrow** key to move to the next row.
9. Continue typing all values in the list (Figure 2-41).
10. Click the **Next** button when done entering all items on the list.
 - The final step of the *Lookup Wizard* displays (Figure 2-42).
 - The label defaults to the original field name you entered.
11. Change the field name as desired.
12. Click the **Limit To List** check box as desired. Checking this box sets the *Limit to List* property to **Yes**.
13. Click the **Finish** button when done. As desired, you can edit the *List Rows* and *Allow Value List Edits* properties on the *Lookup* tab.

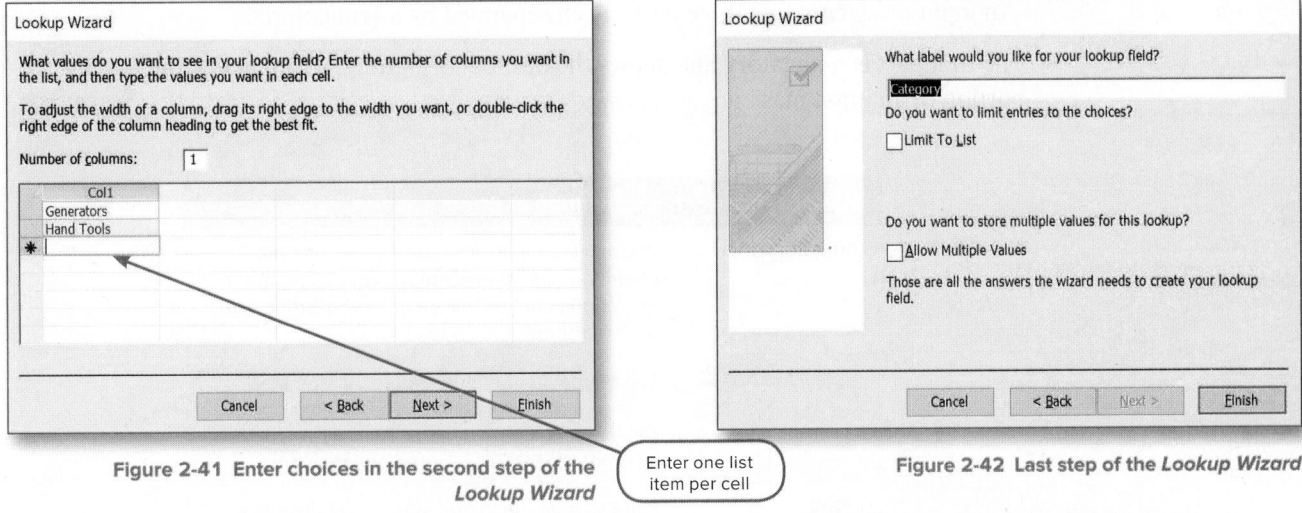

Figure 2-41 Enter choices in the second step of the *Lookup Wizard*

Enter one list item per cell

Figure 2-42 Last step of the *Lookup Wizard*

Define an Input Mask

An ***input mask*** forces a user to enter data using a specific format. For example, you can require a user to enter a phone number with an area code in the (123) 123-4567 format. Input masks help enforce *data format* data integrity rules.

An input mask can only be used on fields with data types of *Short Text*, *Number* (excluding the *ReplicationID* field size), *Large Number*, *Currency*, or *Date/Time*. You can type the mask directly into the *Input Mask* property box, or you can select the *Build* button to launch the **Input Mask Wizard**. However, the *Input Mask Wizard* only works on *Short Text* or *Date* fields.

Before you learn how to create an input mask, it is important to learn fundamental rules about the parts of a mask and the characters a mask can contain. An input mask uses a variety of characters that control how and what kind of data is acceptable. Common special characters are explained in Table 2-13.

Table 2-13: Input Mask Special Characters

Character	Explanation of Effect
0	User must enter a number (0 to 9).
9	User can enter a number (0 to 9), but it is not required.
#	User can enter a number (0 to 9), space, or plus or minus sign, but it is not required. If not filled in, Access enters a blank space.
L	User must enter a letter (A to Z, upper- or lowercase).
?	User can enter a letter (A to Z, upper- or lowercase), but it is not required.
A	User must enter a letter or a number.
a	User can enter a letter or a number, but it is not required.
&	User must enter any character or a space.
C	User can enter any character or a space, but it is not required.
!	In a text field, when fewer characters are entered than specified in the mask, the blank spaces are placed on the left side of the field instead of the default right side of the field. This is not the same as right-justifying the field.
""	Characters entered inside the quotation marks display as written.
\	Characters following the backslash display as written.

An input mask contains three parts, each separated by a semicolon.

- The first part is mandatory and shows the desired formatting. Examples of the mandatory portion of an input mask are as follows.

Mask Example	Explanation of Effect
(000) 000-0000	You must enter an area code along with the phone number (**0** indicates a required number). The phone number will be entered starting with the area code.
(999) AAA-AAAA	The phone number does not require an area code (**9** indicates optional). The number portion can be numbers or digits. This mask would allow an entry of 555-STAR for the phone number.
!9999	You can enter up to four numbers (**9** indicates optional). The exclamation point (**!**) indicates that if fewer than four numbers are entered, the data display right-justified with the blank spaces to the left. For example, if 12 is entered, it would display as " 12" instead of "12 ". because 12 only contains two numbers, the two empty spaces display before the 12.
"WN "9999	The data must start with WN, a blank space, and be followed with up to 4 numbers. because the exclamation point (**!**) is not used, the numbers will be left-justified because the blank spaces will be to the right.

When you enter the mask characters, Access may add additional special characters to ensure the mask displays as desired. For example, if you enter (000) 000-0000 as the mask, Access converts it to \(000") "000\-0000. Access inserted the backslash (\) in front of the open parenthesis ((), to indicate that this character displays as written. Access also inserted quotation marks ("") around the close parenthesis ()) and space. Finally, another backslash (\) was inserted in front of the dash (—) to indicate that this character displays as written.

- The second part of the input mask is optional and indicates whether the mask characters, such as parentheses, dashes, etc., are stored with the data. Not storing the characters saves space; this can be significant in large databases. If you do store the characters, make sure the field size is large enough to store the data value and the characters. The two possible symbols are **0** and **1**. A **0** tells Access to store the characters; a **1** or blank tells Access not to store the characters.
- The third part of the mask is also optional and specifies what symbol displays in the mask as the user enters the data. The default symbol is the underscore (_). You can select a different symbol as desired. If this part of the mask is left blank, Access behaves as if the underscore (_) was selected.

Based on the mask characters entered, Access may add additional special characters to ensure the mask displays as desired. Three examples of input masks follow. Recall that a semicolon (;) separates the different parts of the mask. The parts of each mask are identified, along with displaying a sample of how the mask would appear (Figures 2-43 through 2-45).

Example 1

User entered: (000) 000-0000;0

Access adjusted: \(000") "000\-0000;0;

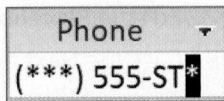

Datasheet view sample:

Figure 2-43 Example 1
Input Mask display

Part 1	Part 2	Part 3
\(000") "000\-0000	0	Empty
The backslash (\) in front of the open parenthesis ((), the quotation marks ("") around the close parenthesis ()) and space, and the backslash (\) in front of the dash (−), indicates that these characters display as written.	The mask characters are stored along with the data. This format requires a field size of 14 to store the phone number digits and the mask characters, including the blank space between the area code and the number.	The default underscore (_) displays as the placeholder character.

Example 2

User entered: (999) AAA-AAAA;;*

Access adjusted: \(999") "AAA\-AAAA;;*

Datasheet view sample:

Figure 2-44 Example 2
Input Mask display

Part 1	Part 2	Part 3
\(999") "AAA\-AAAA	Empty	*
The backslash (\) in front of the open parenthesis ((), the quotation marks ("") around the close parenthesis ()) and space, and the backslash (\) in front of the (−), indicates that these characters display as written.	The mask characters are not stored along with the data. This format requires a field size of ten to store the phone number.	An asterisk (*) displays as the placeholder character.

Example 3

User entered: WN 9999;1

Access adjusted: "WN "9999;1;_

Datasheet view sample:

Figure 2-45 Example 3
Input Mask display

Part 1	Part 2	Part 3
"WN "9999	1	_
The database designer wanted WN and a space to appear at the beginning, along with up to four additional numbers.	The mask characters are not stored with the data. This format requires a field size of four to store the flight number.	The underscore (_) displays as the placeholder character.

1. Click the **row selector** of the desired field.

2. Click the **Input Mask** property box.

3. Click the **Build** button to launch the *Input Mask Wizard* dialog box (Figure 2-46).

ANOTHER WAY

Type the rule directly into the property box.

Figure 2-46 *Input Mask Wizard*, step 1

4. Select the pre-formatted mask you wish to use or an option that you can modify.

5. Click the **Next** button to move to the next step of the *Input Mask Wizard* (Figure 2-47).

6. Edit the **Input Mask** as desired.

7. Edit the **Placeholder character** as desired.

8. Click the **Next** button to move to the next step of the *Input Mask Wizard* (Figure 2-48).

Figure 2-47 *Input Mask Wizard*, step 2

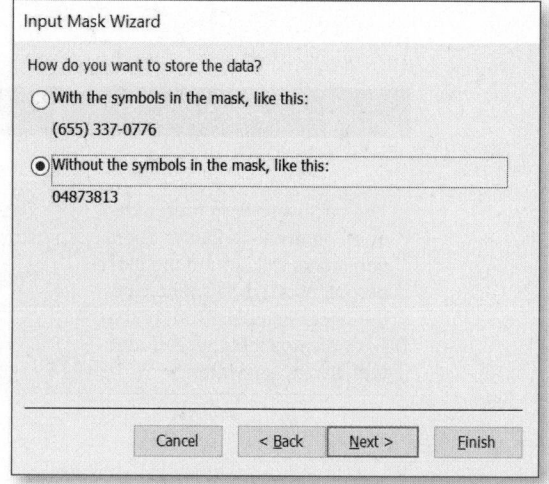

Figure 2-48 *Input Mask Wizard*, step 3

9. Select the appropriate radio button based on whether you are storing the symbols with the data. Be sure that the field width is large enough to also store the symbol because it takes space as well.

10. Click the **Finish** button.

11. Make any needed adjustments to the input mask directly in the property box.

MORE INFO

The input mask displays only when a user clicks into that field. Based on the characters used, sometimes a mask may not display until the user begins to enter data.

Changing Field Properties after Records Are Added into a Table

In chapter 1, you learned to use *Datasheet* view to add records into a table. Ideally, you will have decided on the final structure of all your tables before you begin to enter data, but there may be times you need to make a change to the field properties on a table that already contains data.

Making the change is straightforward. Open the table in *Design* view and follow the steps previously described for the specific property. However, you cannot change the *Data Type* property of a field to the *AutoNumber* type if any data has been added into the table. Additionally, once you have set an *AutoNumber* field to use random values, you can't change back to use incremental values. If a change is permitted, you must use caution when making changes to the table design after records are added.

You just learned that the field properties are used to specify the data integrity rules. Keep in mind that changes to several of the properties may result in unintended consequences. When you save the changes, Access displays a message box warning you about the potential problems. Examples of different problem situations and the resulting warnings include the following.

- If you reduce the *Field Size*, Access warns you that data may be lost (Figure 2-49). If you click *Yes* to continue, Access truncates the contents of any data values that are larger than the new field size. Be certain that the field is large enough that you don't lose any data because you can't undo this change.

Figure 2-49 *Field Size* change warning message

- If you change the *Required* property to *Yes*, Access warns you that data integrity rules have changed (Figure 2-50). If you click *Yes* to test the data with the new rules, Access validates the existing data. This could take a long time depending on the number of records in the table.

Figure 2-50 Data integrity rule change warning message

- If any records violate the new rule, another message box displays, similar to Figure 2-51.
 You must decide whether to keep the new rule. This message only appears once to let you know that data have violated the rule, not once for each record that violates the rule. If you proceed with the change, you must open the table and individually correct each violation of this new rule.

Figure 2-51 Validation error warning message

- If you change any of the validation rules, you should test the changes as described earlier in this chapter by clicking the *Test Validation Rules* button [*Table Tools Design* tab, *Tools* group]. Again, you must individually correct each violation of a new rule.

PAUSE & PRACTICE: ACCESS 2-2

For this Pause & Practice, you add features to enhance the data integrity in the *Equipment* table. You add field and record level validation rules and validation text, use the *Lookup Wizard* to create a combo box, and add an input mask. You also test the validation rules. Finally, you add data into the *Equipment* table.

File Needed: *[your initials] PP A2-1.accdb*
Completed Project File Name: *[your initials] PP A2-2.accdb*

1. Open the *[your initials] PP A2-1* database file created in *Pause & Practice 2-1*.

2. Save a new copy of your database as [your initials] PP A2-2.

3. Enable content in the security warning.

4. Open the *Equipment* table in *Design* view.

5. Add a field validation rule and validation text.
 a. Click the **row selector** of the *EquipmentID* field.
 b. Click the **Validation Rule** property box.
 c. Type Like "#####" in the *Validation Rule* property box.
 d. Click the **Validation Text** property box.
 e. Type The Equipment ID must contain 5 numbers in the *Validation Text* property box. The completed properties should match those shown in Figure 2-52.

| General | Lookup | |
|---|---|
| Field Size | 5 |
| Format | |
| Input Mask | |
| Caption | |
| Default Value | |
| Validation Rule | Like "#####" |
| Validation Text | The Equipment ID must contain 5 numbers |
| Required | Yes |
| Allow Zero Length | Yes |
| Indexed | Yes (No Duplicates) |
| Unicode Compression | No |
| IME Mode | No Control |
| IME Sentence Mode | None |
| Text Align | General |

Figure 2-52 Completed properties of the *EquipmentID* field

6. Test the field validation rule.
 a. Switch to *Datasheet* view to test the rule. If prompted, save the changes to your table. You may also be prompted with a box that states that the data integrity rules have changed and asked whether you want to test the existing data. Click **No**.
 b. Click the **EquipmentID** cell in the append row.
 c. Type A1212 in the *EquipmentID* field. This value is incorrect because it contains letters. Press **Tab** or **Enter** to move to the next field. A message box should display the validation text message you entered in step 5 (Figure 2-53).

<p style="text-align:center">Figure 2-53 Error message displays validation text from a field validation rule</p>

 d. Click **OK** to acknowledge the error.
 e. Delete the contents and type 123 in the *EquipmentID* field. Press **Tab** to move to the next field. This value is incorrect because it contains only three numbers. The message box should display the validation text message.
 f. Click **OK** to acknowledge the error.
 g. Type 12345 in the *EquipmentID* field. Press **Tab** to move to the next field. This value is correct and you should be moved to the *ProductName* field.
 h. Click the **record selector** for *EquipmentID 12345*. Remember that, in *Datasheet* view, the record selector is the gray cell on the left of each row.
 i. Click the **Delete** button [*Home* tab, *Records* group] to delete this test record. A message box displays. Click **Yes** to confirm the deletion.
 j. Switch back to *Design* view of the table.

7. Add a record validation rule.
 a. Display the *Property Sheet* for the *Equipment* table if necessary by clicking the **Property Sheet** button [*Table Tools Design* tab, *Show/Hide* group].
 b. Click the **Validation Rule** property box.
 c. Click the **Build** button to open the *Expression Builder* dialog box.
 d. Enter [WeeklyRentalRate]>[DailyRentalRate] And [MonthlyRentalRate]>[WeeklyRentalRate] in the *Expression Builder*. Instead of typing the field names, you can double-click them in the *Expression Categories* area and add them to the *Expression* box.
 e. Click **OK** to close the *Expression Builder*.
 f. Right-click the **Validation Text** property box and select the **Zoom** button.
 g. Type The Weekly Rate must be greater than the Daily Rate and the Monthly Rate must be greater than the Weekly Rate. in the *Zoom* window. Click **OK**.
 h. Close the *Property Sheet* window.

8. Test the record validation rule.
 a. Switch to *Datasheet* view to test the rule. If prompted, save the changes to your table. You may also be prompted that the data integrity rules have changed and asked whether you want to test the existing data. Click **No**.

b. For *EquipmentID 09863*, select the **$0.00** in the *DailyRentalRate* field and then type 160 to replace that value. Select the **$0.00** in the *WeeklyRentalRate* field, type 160, and select the **$0.00** in the *MonthlyRentalRate* field and type 160.

c. Press the **down arrow** key to leave the current record. This causes the record level rule to execute. The message box should display the validation text message (Figure 2-54) because the *WeeklyRentalRate* is not greater than the *DailyRentalRate* and the *MonthlyRentalRate* is not greater than the *WeeklyRentalRate*. This test is checking if the *And Compound Condition* is working correctly.

Figure 2-54 Error message displays validation text from a record validation rule violation

d. Click **OK** to acknowledge the error.

e. Delete the contents in the *MonthlyRentalRate* field and type 640.

f. Press the **down arrow** key to exit the current record. The message box should display the validation text message because the *WeeklyRentalRate* is not greater than the *DailyRentalRate*, the first half of the compound condition.

g. Click **OK** to acknowledge the error.

h. Delete the contents in the *WeeklyRentalRate* field and type 640.

i. Press the **down arrow** key to exit the current record. The message box should display the validation text message because the *MonthlyRentalRate* is not greater than the *WeeklyRentalRate*, the second half of the compound condition.

j. Click **OK** to acknowledge the error.

k. Delete the contents in the *MonthlyRentalRate* field, and type 1920.

l. Press the **down arrow** key to leave the current record. The record changes should be successfully saved.

m. Switch back to *Design* view of the table.

9. Modify the *Category* field to use a *Combo Box*.

a. Click the **row selector** of the *Category* field.

b. Click the **Data Type** property box, click the **arrow**, and select **Lookup Wizard**. The *Lookup Wizard* dialog box opens.

c. Select the **I will type in the values that I want** radio button.

d. Click the **Next** button.

e. Leave 1 in the *Number of columns* box and click the **first cell** in the *Col1* column.

f. Type Generators.

g. Press the **down arrow** key to move to the next row.

h. Enter the values from Table 2-14.

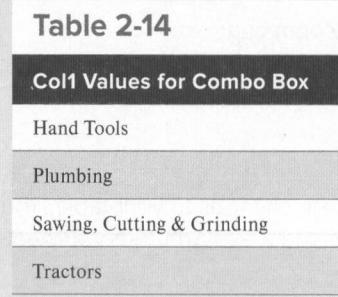

Table 2-14

Col1 Values for Combo Box
Hand Tools
Plumbing
Sawing, Cutting & Grinding
Tractors

i. Click the **Next** button when done entering all the items.
j. Click the **Limit To List** check box.
k. Click the **Finish** button.
l. Save your changes to the table.

10. Add an input mask to the *DatePurchased* field.
 a. Click the **row selector** of the *DatePurchased* field.
 b. Click the **Input Mask** property box.
 c. Click the **Build** button or press **Ctrl+F2**. The *Input Mask Wizard* dialog box opens.
 d. Select the **Medium Date** *Input Mask* (Figure 2-55).
 e. Click the **Next** button. The next screen of the *Input Mask Wizard* displays the characters used in the mask along with the *Placeholder* character (Figure 2-56). Recall from Table 2-2 that the **>** symbol causes text to display in uppercase while the **<** symbol causes text to display in lowercase. The effect of those symbols in the middle part of this input mask is to display a three-character month. The first character is uppercase and the last two are lowercase, such as Sep or Oct.

Figure 2-55 *Medium Date Input Mask* option Figure 2-56 *Medium Date Input Mask* characters

f. Click the **Next** button to accept the input mask without making any changes and to accept the suggested *Placeholder character*.
g. Click the **Finish** button.

11. Set the **Required** property to **Yes** for the *DatePurchased* field. Continue setting the **Required** property to **Yes** for the following fields: *ProductName, Category, DailyRentalRate, WeeklyRentalRate,* and *MonthlyRentalRate*.

12. Save the changes to the *Equipment* table. If prompted to test existing data against the new rules, click **No**.

13. Switch to *Datasheet* view and enter the data from Table 2-15 into the *Equipment* table. Remember that the *EquipmentID* value has already been entered. The values for the *ProductName* column, located between the *EquipmentID* and *Category* fields, have also been entered. Those data values are not repeated in Table 2-15. Additionally, you already entered the rental rate values for the first record when you were testing the validation rules.

 Because you created an input mask for the *DatePurchased* field, those data values have been provided using the mask format to ease data entry.

Table 2-15

Equipment ID	Category	Daily Rental Rate	Weekly Rental Rate	Monthly Rental Rate	Date Purchased
09863	Tractors	160	640	1920	10-Oct-17
10015	Generators	30	120	360	16-Dec-17
10047	Tractors	225	900	2700	09-Feb-18
10103	Generators	120	360	1080	20-Jul-18
10129	Hand Tools	60	240	720	02-Aug-18
10235	Hand Tools	10	30	60	01-Feb-19
10236	Plumbing	35	140	420	01-Feb-19
10237	Plumbing	200	800	2400	01-Feb-19
10283	Sawing, Cutting & Grinding	120	480	1440	15-Mar-19
10368	Hand Tools	15	45	135	11-Nov-19

14. Save the table. The *Datasheet* view should look similar to Figure 2-57.

Figure 2-57 PP A2-2 completed

15. Close the table.

16. Close the database.

Understanding and Designing Relational Databases

As you learned earlier, a database is a collection of integrated and related tables. So far, we have concentrated on learning the steps to build and use a table in Access. Because most databases have more than one table, the next step is to learn how to create a collection of integrated and related tables.

Relational Principles

Recall that Access is a relational database management system. The data in a *relational database* is organized into a collection of related tables. Each table stores data about one part of the system.

Consider, for example, the Mary's Rentals database. In addition to the *Equipment* table you have been building, Mary's Rentals needs separate tables to store details about employees, customers, customer orders, information about which equipment has been rented in each order, and the service history for the equipment.

The different tables are related, or connected, to each other through common fields. You can create these relationships and view them in the **Relationships window**. Figure 2-58 illustrates how the different tables in Mary's Rentals are connected. The lines connecting the different tables show which fields are connected to each other.

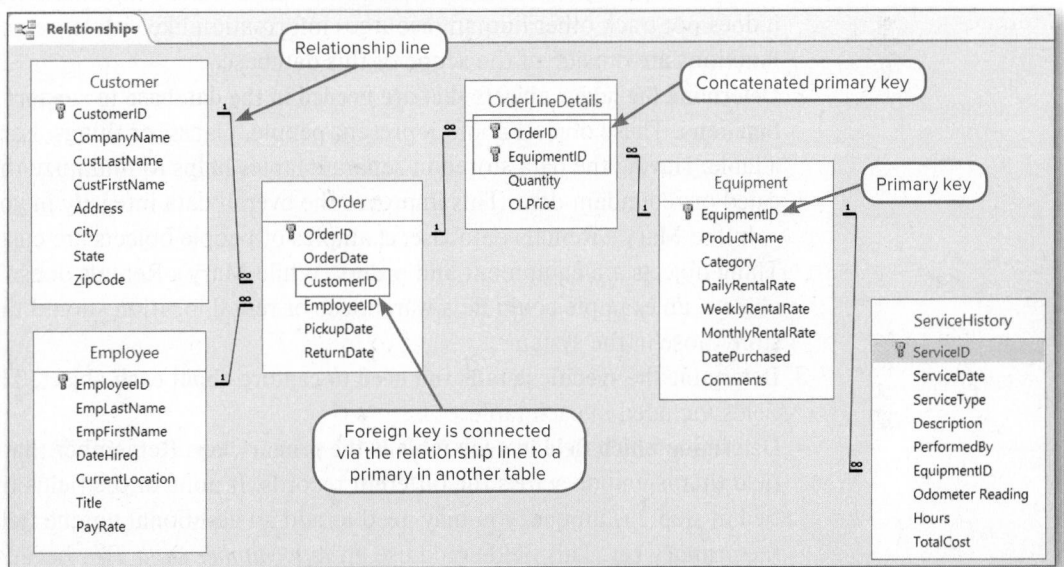

Figure 2-58 *Relationships* window for Mary's Rentals database

To be considered relational, a database must meet certain specifications. Many of the specifications are familiar to you because of the work you have already done in building tables. We use Mary's Rentals to illustrate these specifications.

- The data in the database must be stored in tables.
- The rows of the table must represent records. In the *Equipment* table, for example, each record contains the data about one particular piece of equipment.
- The columns of the table must represent fields. A field contains one specific piece of data about a record. In the *Equipment* table, *EquipmentID* and *ProductName* are the first two fields (see Figure 2-58).
- Each row must have a unique identifier or primary key. The primary key enables the DBMS to locate a specific record in the database. The primary key can either be one field in the

table or a combination of several fields. If a primary key is made up of more than one field, as in the *OrderLineDetails* in Figure 2-58, it is called a ***concatenated key*** or ***composite key***.

- Each table must have a relationship with at least one other table. In order to have a relationship, the two tables must have a field in common with each other. This common field is created by adding the primary key field from one table into the related table. In the related table, this added field is known as a ***foreign key***. After the foreign key is added into a table, you create a relationship between the two tables by linking the foreign key to the primary key. The foreign key enables you to establish the relationship with another table.

The Steps to Design a Relational Database

For a database to be of value to an organization, it must be well-designed. It is important to spend time early in the database development process analyzing the needs of the business so you can create a database that meets the needs of the business. The following seven steps will help you create a well-designed database:

1. **Determine the purpose of the database and the scope of the functions that will be performed.**

 For example, the purpose of the Mary's Rentals database is to manage inventory and customer orders. The functions that must be performed include all tasks needed to record customers and their orders, from the initial taking of an order all the way to checking a rental return back in to the location.

 While the Mary's Rentals database does contain basic information about the employees, it does not track other human resources information like sick leave or vacation time. Those functions are outside of the scope of this database.

2. **Determine the major objects that are needed in the database to support its purpose and functions.** These objects could represent people, places, or things. Each object is built as a table. Having the data stored in separate tables helps to minimize the amount of duplicated or redundant data. This improves the overall data integrity in your database.

 In the Mary's Rentals database, examples of people objects are customers or employees. Thing objects are equipment and orders. While Mary's Rentals doesn't have any place objects, an example could be a warehouse or rental location should the company choose to store those in the system.

3. **Determine the specific details you need to capture about each object.** These details are the fields included in each table.

4. **Determine which field in each table is the primary key.** Remember that the primary key is a field that is unique across the different records. If none of the fields that you have identified in step 3 is unique, you may need to add an additional unique field that can serve as the primary key. This field could use an *AutoNumber Data Type* because it guarantees a unique value. Sometimes, you might need to combine more than one field together to create a concatenated primary key.

5. **Determine the data type and size of each field.** Each field must be defined as containing only a specific type of data such as numbers, text, or dates. Additionally, you should decide how big each field could be.

 For example, you might allow 40 characters for a street address field, while a ZIP code field should be limited to nine numbers.

6. **Determine any additional restrictions on what kinds of data can be stored in the fields.** You may wish to further limit the data that can be entered to increase data integrity.

 For example, you may determine that certain fields must be filled in, while others are optional, or other fields may be limited to a select list of choices.

7. **Determine how the different tables are related to each other.** This step requires that you look at your different tables and see how they are related to each other. In this way, you can create a foreign key in different tables.

One relationship in Figure 2-58 is between the *Customer* and *Order* tables. In this case, the *CustomerID* was placed into the *Order* table as the foreign key so that the company would know which customer was associated with a particular order. You learn how to perform this step in the next section.

Three Types of Relationships

Three different types of relationships may exist between tables in a database: one-to-one, one-to-many, and many-to-many. When designing your database, it is critical that you understand how your tables are related to each other and that you select the correct relationship type. One type of relationship is not better than another; a relationship is simply a reflection of the reality of how the tables are associated. The one-to-many type relationship is the most common.

> ▶ MORE INFO
>
> When describing relationships, the following shorthand notation is often used:
>
> 1:1 (one-to-one)
>
> 1:M (one-to-many)
>
> M:N (many-to-many)

Additionally, when describing table relationships, you sometimes will refer to a table based on the side of the relationship to which it belongs. For example, in a 1:M relationship, one table may be called the "1" table, while the other table may be called the "M" table. In a many-to-many relationship (M:N), the letter N is commonly used in the shorthand notation to differentiate the second side of the relationship.

One-to-One Relationship

In a ***one-to-one relationship***, one row of data in *Table A* may be associated with only one row of data in *Table B*. For example, a business may have a table containing information about employees. Because the employees frequently travel internationally, they also have another table to store information about employee passports. Each employee has only one passport and a passport belongs to only one employee.

Figure 2-59 shows the visual representation of a one-to-one relationship in Access.

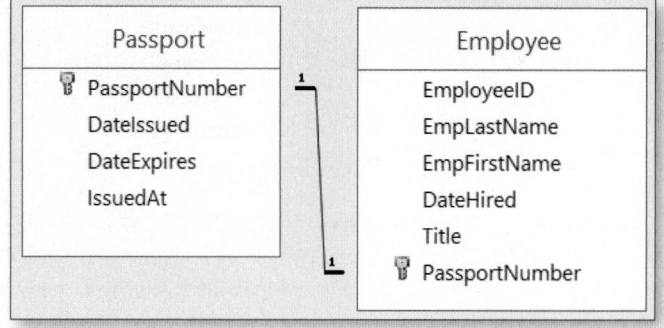

Figure 2-59 One-to-one relationship

One-to-Many Relationship

In a ***one-to-many relationship***, one row of data in *Table A* may be associated with many rows of data in *Table B*. In Mary's Rentals, a one-to-many relationship exists between the *Customer* and *Order* tables. A customer can have many orders, but a particular order is associated with only one customer.

In Access, the "many" side of a relationship is indicated with the *infinity symbol*. Figure 2-60 shows the visual representation of a 1:M relationship.

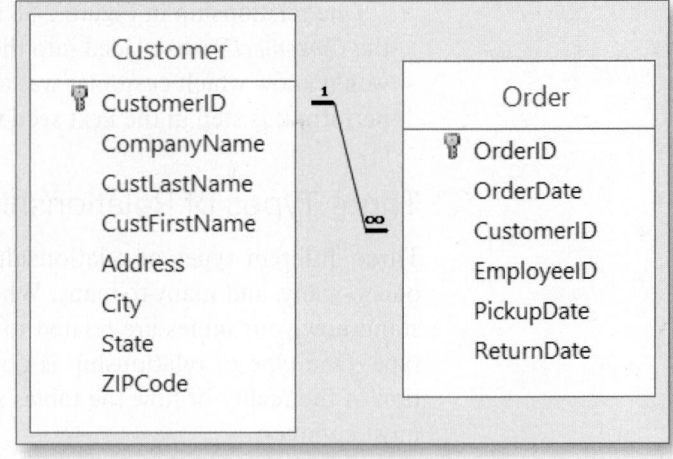

Figure 2-60 One-to-many relationship

Many-to-Many Relationship

In a *many-to-many relationship*, many rows of data in *Table A* may be associated with many rows of data in *Table B*. In Mary's Rentals, a many-to-many relationship exists between the *Order* and *Equipment* tables. An order can be for many different pieces of equipment, and a particular piece of equipment can be on many different orders (obviously not at exactly the same time).

A relational database does not directly support M:N relationships. They require the creation of a third table, *Table C*. This third table is a *junction* or *intersection table* that matches up the records across the two tables. With the creation of the junction table, the M:N relationship converts into two 1:M relationships. This results in a 1:M relationship between *Table A* and *Table C*, and another 1:M relationship between *Table B* and *Table C*.

Figure 2-61 shows the visual representation of a M:N relationship. The *OrderLineDetails* table is the junction table in this example. A junction table contains the primary key fields from each of the "1" tables. In this case, *OrderLineDetails* contains the primary key field of *OrderID* from the *Order* table and the primary key field of *EquipmentID* from the *Equipment* table. The combination of *OrderID* and *EquipmentID* creates a concatenated primary key in the junction table.

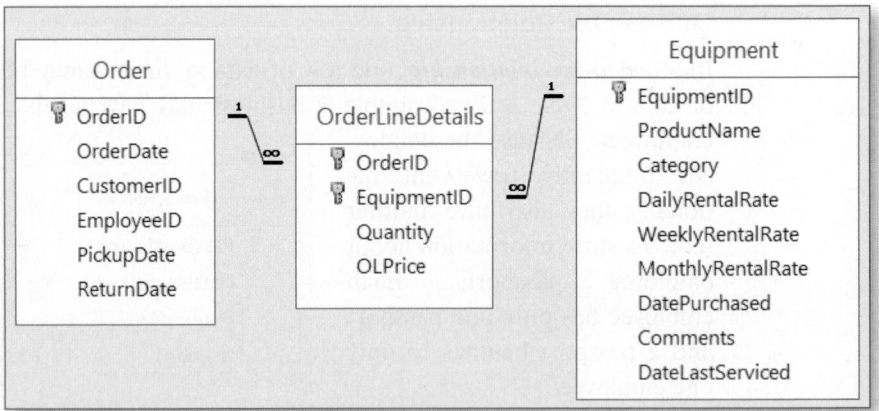

Figure 2-61 A many-to-many relationship is converted into two one-to-many relationships

Understand a Foreign Key

Recall that a foreign key is the field in common between two tables. When designing your tables, it is important to know how to create a foreign key. In the seventh step of designing a database, you determine how the tables are related to each other and determine what the foreign key is. By the time you get to step 7, you already have each of the tables in your database defined.

For example, in *Independent Project 1-5*, you built a database containing a pet table for Life's Animal Shelter. The shelter also needs a table to store information about owners who adopt the pets. Working through step 6 of designing a database would result in the *Owners* and *Pets* tables shown in Figure 2-62. At this point, a common field does not exist.

Step 7 requires you to identify what type of relationship exists between the *Owners* and

Figure 2-62 *Owners* and *Pets* tables without a field in common

Pets tables. An owner could adopt many pets, but a pet belongs to only one owner. This is a 1:M relationship.

- For a 1:M relationship, you create the foreign key by taking the primary key field from the *1* table and adding it as an extra field into the *M* table. This added field is known as the foreign key.

In the Life's Animal Shelter example, you take the *OwnerID* from the *Owners* table and add it in as a foreign key into the *Pets* table (Figure 2-63). Although not required, many database designers prefer to start the foreign key field name with the letters *FK*.

- For a 1:1 relationship, you create the foreign key by taking the primary key from either table and adding it into the other table. You must set

Figure 2-63 Add the foreign key into the "M" table in a relationship

the **Indexed** property of the foreign key field to *Yes (No Duplicates)* for Access to recognize a 1:1 relationship.

- If you determine that you have a M:N relationship, you first need to create the junction table and convert the M:N relationship into two 1:M relationships. The junction table contains the primary key fields from each of the *1* tables, along with any other fields that describe that junction.

Remember that the foreign key field is always the primary key of another table. Sometimes, it is the primary key in both. (An example of this is shown and explained later in Figure 2-67.)

The actual addition of the foreign key into the related table is done in *Design* view of the table. When adding the foreign key field, set the field properties to be the same *Data Type* and *Field Size* as the primary key in the *1* table. If the primary key or foreign key field is an *AutoNumber Data Type*, then the other field should be made a *Long Integer Data Type*. The foreign key field name can be anything. Often, it will either be the exact same name as the primary key or the name of the primary key preceded by *FK*.

Adding the foreign key into the table does not establish the relationship. This is done as a separate step, described in the next section. The addition of the foreign key enables you to relate the tables.

Create Relationships between Tables

You can add relationships after you have added the foreign keys into the tables. Relationships should be set before any data are added into the tables that contain the foreign keys. While the process of creating the relationship is very straightforward, you need to make several decisions about how Access enforces the relationship.

Define a Relationship Using the Relationships Window

You can create a relationship directly in the *Relationships* window.

Figure 2-64 *Show Table* dialog box

▶**HOW TO: Define a Relationship Using the Relationships Window**

1. Click the **Relationships** button [*Database Tools* tab, *Relationships* group].

 - If this is the first time you are establishing relationships for your database, the *Show Table* dialog box appears (Figure 2-64).
 - Click the **Show Table** button [*Relationship Tools Design* tab, *Relationships* group] if the *Show Table* dialog box does not display or if you need to re-open the dialog box.

2. Select the **first table** to add.

3. Click the **Add** button.

4. Continue adding the remaining tables.

5. Click the **Close** button when all tables have been added.

 - The tables appear in the *Relationships* window.
 - Sometimes, the size of the table object is not large enough to display the entire field name of all of the table fields. This is the case for the *Equipment* table shown in Figure 2-65.
 - If you want, adjust the size of the table objects to see more fields. Point to a border of the table until the pointer changes to the resize pointer. Drag the pointer to increase or decrease the table.

6. Click, hold, and drag the **primary key** field from the *1* table on top of the **foreign key** field in the related table (see Figure 2-65).

 - The pointer displays a small plus sign box when it is dragged onto the related table.
 - The related table is either a *1* table or an *M* table, depending on the type of relationship.

Figure 2-65 Drag the primary key to the foreign key to create a relationship

A2-122

7. Release the pointer when you are positioned on top of the **foreign key** field in the related table. The *Edit Relationships* dialog box opens (Figure 2-66).

8. Verify that the field names displayed are correct. If necessary, you can use the drop-down arrows to make any corrections.

9. Check the **Enforce Referential Integrity** box.
 - The check boxes for *Cascade Update Related Fields* and *Cascade Delete Related Records* become available.
 - As desired, check those boxes.

10. Click **Create**.
 - The *Relationships* window updates with the relationship line added (Figure 2-67). The *1* and infinity symbols display indicating that referential integrity is enforced and that there is a one-to-many relationship between the two tables.
 - As you can see in Figure 2-67, the *EquipmentID* field is the primary key of the *Equipment* table and is part of a concatenated primary key in the *OrderLineDetails* table. It also is a foreign key in the *OrderLineDetails* table because it links back to the primary key in the *Equipment* table.

11. Save the changes made to the relationships.

12. Click **Close** [*Relationship Tools Design* tab, *Relationships* group] if you are finished with all changes to the relationships.

Figure 2-66 *Edit Relationships* dialog box

Figure 2-67 Completed relationships window

> **ANOTHER WAY**
>
> You can also create a relationship using the *Lookup Wizard*. Select the **foreign key** field, select the **Lookup wizard** data type and select the option **I want the lookup field to get the values from another table or query**.

Once a relationship has been created, when you view the *1* table in *Datasheet* view you can see the related records. A plus sign appears to the left of the first column, indicating that this table is related to another table.

- View related records by clicking the **plus sign**. The plus sign changes to a minus sign. Figure 2-68 shows the related records for *EquipmentID 10015*.
- You can enter additional records into the related table directly from this view.
- Click the **minus sign** to hide the related records.

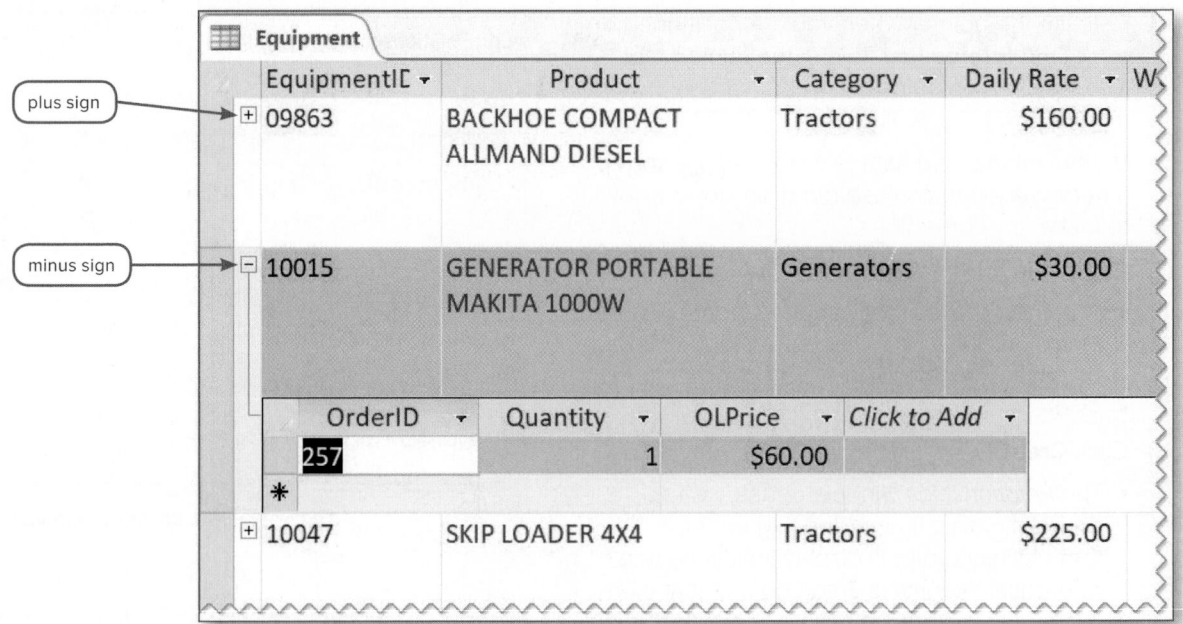

Figure 2-68 Click the plus sign to show related records in *Datasheet* view

Enforce Referential Integrity

When creating a relationship, you must decide if you want to enforce referential integrity. *Referential integrity* ensures that records in associated tables have consistent data. For example, if you enter a row of data in the *OrderLineDetails* table, when you enter a value in the *EquipmentID* field it should match an *EquipmentID* value that already exists in the *Equipment* table. This ensures consistency and integrity of the database.

If you create a relationship and do not enforce referential integrity, you can have records in the associated table that do not match a record in the *1* table.

For example, if a doctor's office does not require a patient to declare a primary physician, the *PhysicianID* field on a *Patient* table may be left blank. While this is possible, in the majority of cases you will want to enforce referential integrity.

Enforce referential integrity by selecting the **Enforce Referential Integrity** check box in the *Edit Relationships* dialog box.

In addition to requiring that the foreign key value of a record in the associated table matches a primary key value in the *1* table, when referential integrity has been enforced Access prohibits two other actions.

- First, Access does not allow you to delete a record from the *1* table if that record has related records in an associated table. For example, at a school you may have a table with student information and another table containing information about student parking tickets. If referential integrity is enforced, Access does not allow you to delete a student record from the *Student* table if that student has any rows of data in the *ParkingTicket* table. This ensures that all parking tickets remain linked to the student who got the ticket. This restriction means that a student can't exit the school system without first paying all their parking tickets.
- Second, Access does not allow you to change the value of the primary key field in the *1* table if that record has related records in an associated table. Assuming that *StudentID* is the primary key in the *Student* table, the student is not allowed to change the value of their *StudentID* if they have any parking ticket records in the *ParkingTicket* table.

You may determine that valid reasons exist to override these constraints. If referential integrity has been enforced, the *Cascade Update Related Fields* and *Cascade Delete Related Records* options become available.

Cascade Updates

Sometimes, it is desirable to allow the primary key value of the *1* table to be changed. For example, if a *StudentID* value has been stolen, the student must be assigned a new ID. In cases like this, you want to be able to change the value of the primary key and have Access find all related records and change the value in the foreign key to match the new primary key value.

To allow the primary key value to be changed and have Access cascade updates in the related table, select the **Cascade Update Related Fields** check box in the *Edit Relationships* dialog box. You can do this only if you have selected the *Enforce Referential Integrity* option in the *Edit Relationships* dialog box.

Cascade Deletes

There may be situations when you want to delete a record from the *1* table and have Access automatically delete all the related records in the associated table. For example, if a record is deleted from the *Order* table because an order is canceled, all of the records in the *OrderLineDetails* table (the specific products this customer had ordered) should be deleted as well. In cases like this, you want to be able to make this deletion and have Access delete all the related records.

To allow a record in the *1* table to be deleted and have Access delete all associated records in the related table, select the **Cascade Delete Related Records** check box in the *Edit Relationships* dialog box. You can do this only if you have selected the *Enforce Referential Integrity* option.

Save a Relationship

If you have made any changes to the relationships, you need to save those changes.

Click the **Save** button on the *Quick Access* toolbar to save any changes made to the relationships.

Delete a Relationship between Tables

If a relationship has been created in error, or you need to make changes to the fields involved in the relationship, or you no longer need to have a particular relationship, you can delete it. You must close all of the tables involved in the relationship, as well as any objects that are based on those tables before you can delete a relationship.

▶ **HOW TO:** Delete a Relationship between Tables

1. Click the **Relationships** button [*Database Tools* tab, *Relationships* group].
 - The *Relationships* window appears.
2. Select the **relationship line** you wish to delete (Figure 2-69).
 - The middle part of the line thickens once it has been selected.
3. Right-click the **relationship line** to open the context menu.

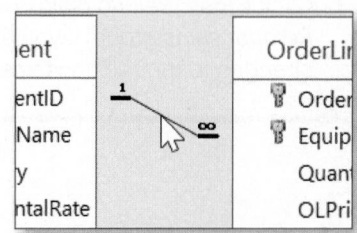

Figure 2-69 Select the relationship line

4. Click **Delete** (Figure 2-70).

 - A confirmation message appears asking you to confirm the deletion. Click **Yes** to confirm the deletion.

5. Click the **Save** button to save your changes.

6. Click **Close** [*Relationship Tools Design* tab, *Relationships* group] if you are finished with all deletions to the relationships.

Figure 2-70 *Delete* option in the context menu

Edit a Relationship between Tables

Occasionally, you need to make changes to an existing relationship between tables.

> ▶**HOW TO:** Edit a Relationship between Tables

1. Click the **Relationships** button [*Database Tools* tab, *Relationships* group].

 - The *Relationships* window appears.

2. Select the **relationship line** you wish to edit.

3. Click **Edit Relationships** [*Relationship Tools Design* tab, *Tools* group] (Figure 2-71). The *Edit Relationships* dialog box opens (Figure 2-72).

Figure 2-71 *Edit Relationships* button

> ▶ **ANOTHER WAY**
> Right-click the **relationship line** to open the context menu and then select **Edit Relationship**.

4. Change the referential integrity options or selected fields.

5. Click **OK**.

6. Save the changes made to the relationships.

7. Click **Close** [*Relationship Tools Design* tab, *Relationships* group] if you are finished with all changes to the relationships.

Figure 2-72 *Edit Relationships* dialog box

SLO 2.7

Printing the Contents of a Table

Occasionally, you may wish to print a simple list of all records in a table. You can do this with the *Print* button on the *Backstage* view. Three options are available after selecting the *Print* button:

- *Quick Print*: Sends the contents of the current object immediately to the printer.
- *Print*: Enables you to select different print options before sending the contents to the printer.
- *Print Preview*: Enables you to preview the way the table records will print before actually sending them to the printer.

Preview the Data Records

Previewing the way that your table records will print is a good idea. This enables you to check that the formatting is appropriate and to make changes to any settings before printing.

▶ **HOW TO:** Preview the Data Records before Printing

1. Select the **table** you want to print from the *Navigation Pane*. The table can be closed or it can be open in *Datasheet* view when you print records.
2. Click the **Print** button [*File* tab] to display the printing options.
3. Click the **Print Preview** button.
 - The *Print Preview* tab opens and shows a preview of how the table will print (Figure 2-73).
 - The default print settings include the table name and current date at the top of the report and the page number at the bottom of the report. Access calls these three items *Headings*.
4. Review the *Navigation* bar to determine if additional pages will print. In Figure 2-73, the darkened *Next Page* button indicates additional pages.

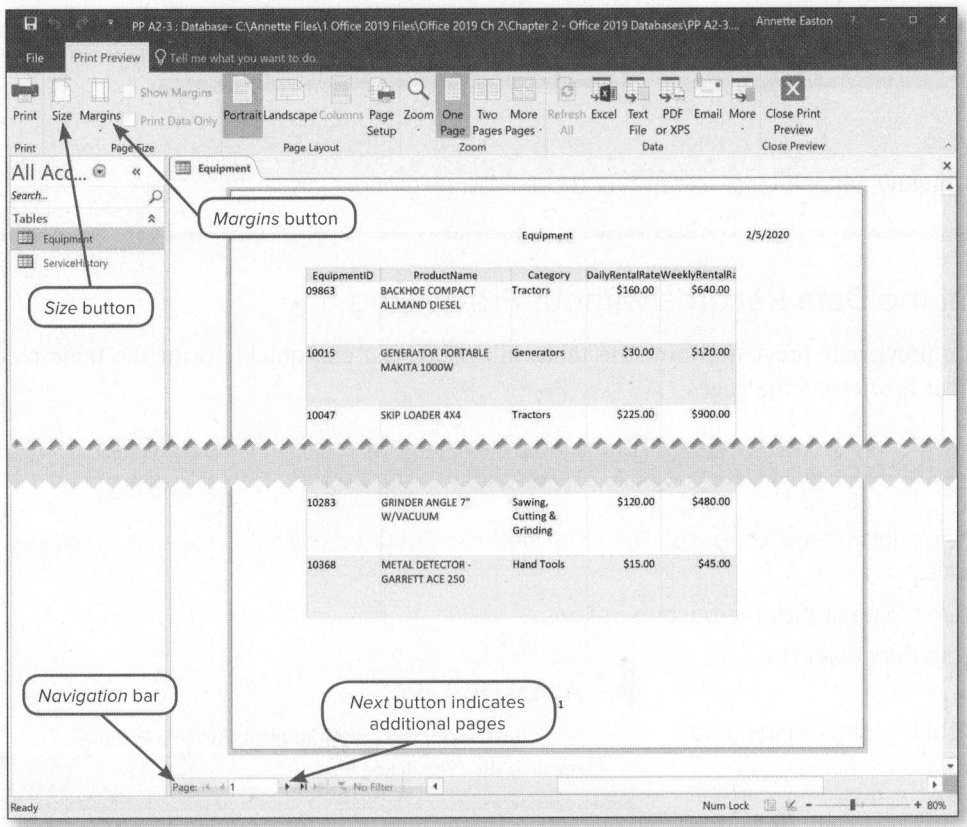

Figure 2-73 *Print Preview* of table records

5. Adjust the page orientation by clicking the **Portrait** or **Landscape** buttons [*Print Preview* tab, *Page Layout* group].

6. Click the **Page Setup** button [*Print Preview* tab, *Page Layout* group] or press **S** to open the *Page Setup* dialog box (Figure 2-74).

7. Adjust the margins on the *Print Options* tab.

8. Adjust the paper size on *Page* tab. You can also adjust the page orientation on the *Page* tab.

> **ANOTHER WAY**
>
> Set the paper size, and margins by clicking the **Size** or **Margins** buttons [*Print Preview* tab, *Page Size* group].

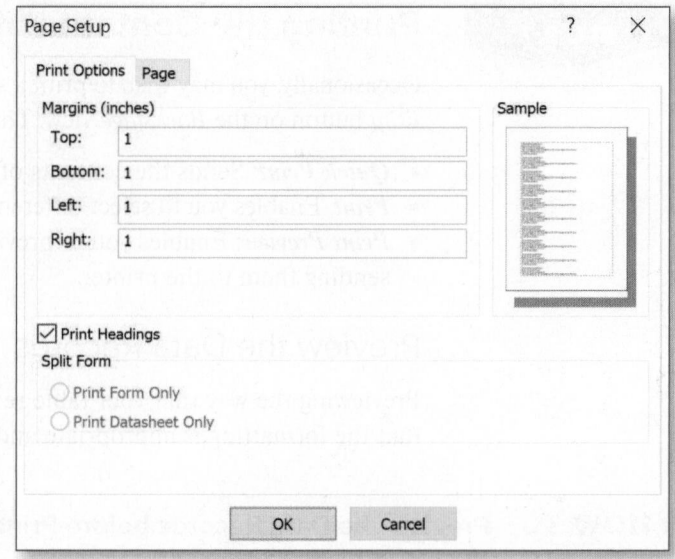

Figure 2-74 *Page Setup* dialog box

9. Remove the *Headings* from the printout by deselecting the **Print Headings** check box on the *Print Options* tab of the *Page Setup* dialog box.

10. Click **OK** to close the *Page Setup* dialog box.

11. Click the **Print** button [*Print Preview* tab, *Print* group] when ready to print.

 - The *Print* dialog box displays.
 - In the *Print* dialog box, you can change the number of copies, page range, and printer as desired.

> **ANOTHER WAY**
>
> Press **P** or **Ctrl+P** to open the *Print* dialog box from *Print Preview* view.

12. Click **OK** to print the table.

13. Click the **Close Print Preview** button [*Print Preview* tab, *Close Preview* group].

Print the Data Records without Previewing

If you previously previewed how the table will print, you can quickly print the table records without previewing the pages.

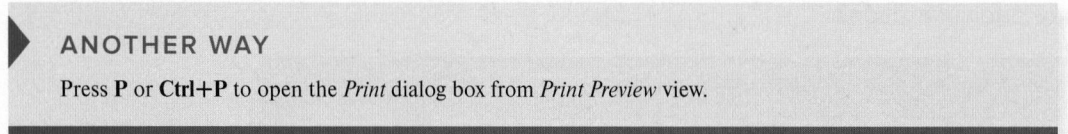

HOW TO: Print Table Records

1. Select the **table** you want to print from the *Navigation Pane*. The table can be closed or it can be open in *Datasheet* view when you print records.

2. Click the **Print** button [*File* tab] to display the printing options.

3. Click the **Print** button. The *Print* dialog box displays.

4. Change the number of copies, page range, and printer as desired.

> **ANOTHER WAY**
>
> Click the **Quick Print** button to print the table without opening the *Print* dialog box.

5. Click **OK**.

Queries and *Reports* provide advanced options to create more attractive and formatted printouts of table data. You can also use them to print only a subset of the table data. These objects are covered in chapters 3 and 4.

Using the Compact & Repair Database Utility

Over time, as you use your database, the database file becomes larger. Much of this is due to additional records being added into the tables. However, part of the increased size is due to certain ways that Access operates. In order to accomplish certain functions, Access creates temporary objects. These objects are not always automatically deleted when the function has been performed. Additionally, when you delete database objects, that space is not always released.

As the database file grows, it takes longer to perform tasks such as adding and deleting records, querying tables, and printing reports. With really large databases, this can result in a significant decrease in processing speed.

Another concern is that a database file may become corrupted. In Access, this is most likely to occur if the database is shared over a network and numerous users make frequent edits to *Long Text* fields. A corrupted database doesn't typically result in lost data; rather, certain forms or pieces of the code may be lost or become unusable.

You can use the ***Compact & Repair Database*** utility to reduce the chances of corruption and to reclaim unused space from temporary and deleted objects. Before running this process, be sure to create a backup copy of your database. Additionally, if this is a multi-user database, no one can be using the database at the time the compact and repair is performed.

▶ HOW TO: Compact and Repair a Database

1. Click the **File** tab. The *Info* button should be selected.

2. Click the **Compact & Repair Database** button (Figure 2-75).

Figure 2-75 *Compact & Repair Database* button

- If Access is not able to repair everything in a corrupted database, it creates a table named *MSysCompactErrors*. This table opens automatically and contains information about the objects that could not be repaired.

ANOTHER WAY

Click the **Compact and Repair Database** button [*Database Tools* tab, *Tools* group] to compact and repair the database.

PAUSE & PRACTICE: ACCESS 2-3

In this Pause & Practice, you add a second table to store the service history of the equipment. Next, you define a relationship between the *Equipment* and *Service History* tables. You also print the contents of the *Equipment* table and manage the database using the *Compact & Repair Database* utility.

Files Needed: *[your initials] PP A2-2.accdb* and ***ServiceHistoryDataFile-02.xlsx*** *(Student data files are available in the* Library *of your SIMnet account.)*
Completed Project File Name: *[your initials] PP A2-3.accdb* and *[your initials] PP A2-3_YYYY-MM-DD.accdb*

1. Open the *[your initials] PP A2-2* database file created in *Pause & Practice 2-2*.

2. Save a new copy of your database as [your initials] PP A2-3.

3. Enable content in the security warning.

4. Click the **Table Design** button [*Create* tab, *Tables* group] to open a new table in *Design* view.

5. Add new fields into the table.
 a. Type ServiceID in the *Field Name* property box of the first row. Press **Tab** to move to the *Data Type* property.
 b. Select the **Short Text** *Data Type*. Press **Tab** to move to the *Description* property.
 c. Type Unique ID number for the service request.
 d. Click the **Primary Key** button [*Table Tools Design* tab, *Tools* group].
 e. Press **Tab** to move to the next row.
 f. Continue adding the remaining fields into the new table using the information in Table 2-16.

Table 2-16

Field Name	Data Type	Description
ServiceDate	**Date/Time**	Date service was completed
ServiceType	**Short Text**	Indicates whether service was maintenance, repair, or inspection
Description	**Short Text**	General description of the nature of the service performed
PerformedBy	**Short Text**	Employee ID number of the repair person
FKEquipmentID	**Short Text**	Must match an EquipmentID value in the Equipment table – (this is the foreign key)
OdometerReading	**Number**	Odometer reading at time of repair (for vehicles only)
Hours	**Number**	Total number of hours the equipment has been in use
TotalCost	**Currency**	Cost of the service (parts and labor)

6. Save the table as ServiceHistory.

7. Set the field properties in the *ServiceHistory* table.
 a. Click the **row selector** of the *ServiceID* field.
 b. Type 6 in the *Field Size* property box in the *Field Properties* area.
 c. Set the *Required* property to **Yes** if necessary.
 d. Click the **row selector** of the *ServiceDate* field.
 e. Continue changing the remaining field properties in the *ServiceHistory* table using the information in Table 2-17.
 f. Save the table.

Table 2-17

Field Name	Field Size	Format	Required
ServiceDate		General Date	Yes
ServiceType	15		Yes
Description	255		Yes
PerformedBy	3		Yes
FKEquipmentID	5		Yes
TotalCost		Currency	Yes

8. Modify the *ServiceType* field to use a *Combo Box*.
 a. Click to select the **ServiceType** field.
 b. Click the property box for the **Data Type** property, click the **arrow**, and select **Lookup Wizard**. The *Lookup Wizard* dialog box opens.
 c. Select the radio button for **I will type in the values that I want**.
 d. Click the **Next** button.
 e. Click the **first cell** in the *Col1* column.
 f. Type Maintenance.
 g. Press the **down arrow** key to move to the next row.
 h. Type Repair. Press the **down arrow** key to move to the next row.
 i. Type Inspection.
 j. Click the **Next** button.
 k. Click the **Limit To List** check box.
 l. Click the **Finish** button.

9. Save and close the table.

10. Create a relationship between the *Equipment* and *ServiceHistory* tables.
 a. Click the **Relationships** button [*Database Tools* tab, *Relationships* group]. If this is the first time you have established relationships for your database, the *Show Table* dialog box appears.
 b. Click the **Show Table** button [*Relationship Tools Design* tab, *Relationships* group] if the *Show Table* dialog box does not display.
 c. Select the **Equipment** table and click the **Add** button.
 d. Select the **ServiceHistory** table and click the **Add** button.
 e. Click the **Close** button. The tables display in the *Relationships* window.
 f. Adjust the size of the table objects to see all of the fields.
 g. Drag the **EquipmentID** from the *Equipment* table on top of the **FKEquipmentID** in the *ServiceHistory* table. The pointer displays a small plus sign box when it is dragged onto the related table (Figure 2-76).

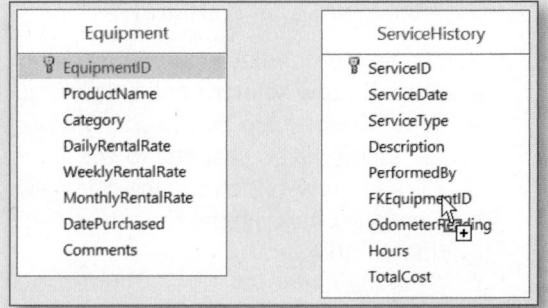

Figure 2-76 Create the relationship between the *Equipment* and *ServiceHistory* tables

h. Release the pointer when you are positioned on top of the *FKEquipmentID* field. The *Edit Relationships* dialog box opens.

i. Verify that the field names displayed are correct. If necessary, click the **drop-down arrows** to make any corrections.

j. Check the **Enforce Referential Integrity** check box.

k. Check the **Cascade Update Related Fields** check box.

l. Check the **Cascade Delete Related Records** check box. The completed *Edit Relationships* dialog box should be similar to Figure 2-77.

Figure 2-77 Select referential integrity options in the *Edit Relationships* dialog box

m. Click **Create**. The *Relationships* window updates with the relationship line added (Figure 2-78). The 1 and infinity symbols display indicating that referential integrity is enforced and that there is a one-to-many relationship between the two tables.

n. Save the changes made to the relationships.

o. Click **Close** [*Relationship Tools Design* tab, *Relationships* group].

11. Import data into the *ServiceHistory* table.
 a. Launch the *Get External Data – Excel Spreadsheet* dialog box.
 b. Locate and select the ***ServiceHistoryDataFile-02*** Excel file.
 c. Append the records to the *ServiceHistory* table.
 d. Launch the *Import Spreadsheet Wizard*.
 e. Finish the *Import Spreadsheet Wizard*. Close the *Wizard* after the records have imported.

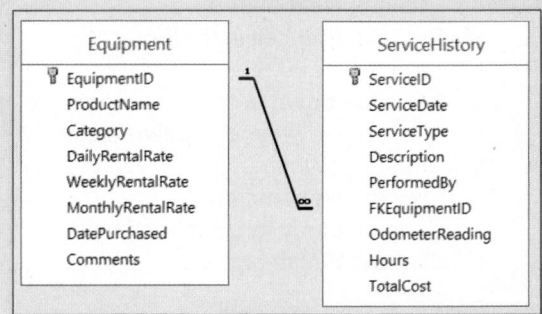

Figure 2-78 Completed relationship between the tables

12. Open the *Equipment* table in *Datasheet* view.
 a. Click the **plus sign** for *EquipmentID 09863* to display the related records. You should see the four entries in the *ServiceHistory* table for this piece of equipment (Figure 2-79).
 b. Click the **minus sign** to hide the related records.
 c. Close the table.

EquipmentID	ProductName	Category	DailyRentalR	WeeklyRentz	Monthly
⊟ 09863	BACKHOE COMPACT ALLMAND DIESEL	Tractors	$160.00	$640.00	$1,9

ServiceID	ServiceDate	ServiceType	Description	PerformedB	OdometerRe
A13428	1/15/2020	Maintenance	6-month servic	151	1789
A13719	10/15/2019	Maintenance	6-month servic	151	3772
B29876	9/14/2019	Repair	Replaced dama	132	3216
C00217	3/1/2020	Inspection	Required annu;	177	5308
*					0

| ⊞ 10015 | GENERATOR PORTABLE MAKITA 1000W | Generators | $30.00 | $120.00 | $3 |

Figure 2-79 Display related records for *EquipmentID* 09863

13. Prepare to print the *Equipment* table.
 a. Verify that the *Equipment* table is selected in the *Navigation Pane* and then click the **Print** button [*File* tab] to display the printing options.
 b. Click the **Print Preview** button to open the *Print Preview* tab and view a preview of how the table will print.
 c. Click the **Landscape** button [*Print Preview* tab, *Page Layout* group] to change the page orientation.
 d. Click the **Margins** button [*Print Preview* tab, *Page Size* group] and select the **Normal** button as shown in Figure 2-80. The report preview should appear as shown in Figure 2-81. Depending on the default font or printer settings, the *Comments* field may appear on a separate page and you may see a different number of records on the page.

Figure 2-80 *Margins* options in *Print Preview*

Equipment								2/5/2020
EquipmentID	ProductName	Category	DailyRentalRate	WeeklyRentalR	MonthlyRentalR	DatePurchased	Comments	
09863	BACKHOE COMPACT ALLMAND DIESEL	Tractors	$160.00	$640.00	$1,920.00	10-Oct-17	Lift Capacity: 2100 lbs Bucket Size: 16" only	
10015	GENERATOR PORTABLE MAKITA 1000W	Generators	$30.00	$120.00	$360.00	16-Dec-17	Size: 19-1/2"L x 11-3/4"W x 17-1/2"H Weight: 55 lbs	
10047	SKIP LOADER 4X4	Tractors	$225.00	$900.00	$2,700.00	09-Feb-18	Subject to Environmental Fee	
10103	GENERATOR TOWABLE POWERPRO 25KW	Generators	$120.00	$360.00	$1,080.00	20-Jul-18	Overall L x W x H: 67"L x 28"W x 3"H	
10129	LEVEL SITE LASER	Hand Tools	$60.00	$240.00	$720.00	02-Aug-18		
10235	WHEELBARROW	Hand Tools	$10.00	$30.00	$60.00	01-Feb-19		
10236	SNAKE DRAIN 1/2" ELECTRIC	Plumbing	$35.00	$140.00	$420.00	01-Feb-19	General Brand - Easy Rooter Jr	
10237	PIPELINE INSPECTION CAMERA - 85'	Plumbing	$200.00	$800.00	$2,400.00	01-Feb-19	85' Cable	

Page 1

Figure 2-81 *Print Preview* of *Equipment* table records

14. Click the **Close Print Preview** button [*Print Preview* tab, *Close Preview* group].

15. Compact and repair the database.
 a. Click the **Save As** button [*File* tab].
 b. Ensure that *Save Database As* is selected in *File Types*.
 c. Select **Back Up Database** in the *Advanced* grouping of the *Save Database As* area.
 d. Click the **Save As** button.
 e. Accept the default name in the *File name* box and click the **Save** button.
 f. Click the **File** tab. The *Info* button should be selected.
 g. Click the **Compact & Repair Database** button.

16. Close the database.

Chapter Summary

2.1 Create a table in *Design* view; add new fields; define a primary key; delete fields; save, close, rename, and open a table; and switch between *Datasheet* and *Design* views (p. A2-84).

- **Design view** provides the most flexibility when you are creating tables and setting field properties.
- Add new fields in *Design* view by entering the field name and selecting the data type.
- Use the *Property Update Options* smart tag to have Access update the value of an *inheritable property* in all of the controls that are based on that field.
- Each table should have a **primary key**, a field that contains a unique value for each record.
- Add a new field between existing fields by inserting a row, and delete a field by deleting a row.
- Save any changes to the table design for them to be permanent.

2.2 Set field properties including *Field Size*, *Format*, *Caption*, *Default Value*, *Required*, and *New Values* (p. A2-88).

- The field properties in *Design* view are grouped into *General* and *Lookup* properties.
- The **Field Size** property sets the maximum number of characters allowed or the maximum value of a number.
- Use the **Format** property to control the appearance of the data in a table.
- Choose from predefined formats for *Number*, *Currency*, *Date/Time*, and *Yes/No* data types.
- Create custom formats for *Short Text* and *Long Text* data types.
- Customize the **Caption** property to change the contents that appear as a column header.
- The contents of the **Default Value** property are automatically entered into a field when a new record is added to a table.
- Require a user to enter a value for a field by setting the **Required** property.
- Use the **New Values** property to select sequential and random values of an *AutoNumber* field.

2.3 Explain data integrity and data validation concepts and options (p. A2-95).

- **Data validation** is the process of verifying the accuracy, or integrity, of the data.

- Create **data integrity rules** to ensure that the data are accurate and consistent.
- *Data format*, *range*, *consistency*, and *completeness* are the most common types of data integrity rules.
- **Metadata** are the descriptions about what the different data fields represent and their formats.

2.4 Create field and record validation rules, test rules, create validation text, create lookup fields, and define an input mask (p. A2-97).

- **Field validation rules** create *range* and *data format* integrity rules by limiting what can be entered into a field.
- *Consistency* integrity rules compare fields in the same table. These **record validation rules** are entered into the validation rule property for the table.
- It is a good idea to create several cases of **test data** and use it to test the validation rules to ensure the rule works as desired.
- Enter custom error messages into the **Validation Text** property. This message displays when data are entered that violate a validation rule.
- **Lookup fields** display a list of predefined choices from which the user can select.
- Apply an **input mask** to a field to require the user to enter the data in a predefined format.

2.5 Change field properties after records are added into a table (p. A2-111).

- If you change field properties after data have been added into the tables, Access warns you that the change could result in lost data or inconsistent data.
- Pay attention to the warning messages because it may be impossible to undo the changes and recover any lost data.

2.6 Explain relational database principles, understand the steps that must be taken to design a database, create relationships between tables, implement referential integrity, and delete and edit relationships (p. A2-117).

- A **relational database** contains data that are organized into a collection of related tables. To be considered relational, a database must meet a set of specifications.

- It is important to follow the steps to designing a relational database to ensure that your set of tables and relationships are correct.
- Relationships are the connections among different tables. Relationships can be classified as *one-to-one*, *one-to-many*, and *many-to-many*.
- A *foreign key* is a field in common across tables and is the mechanism that enables tables to be related.
- Once the foreign key has been added into a table, the relationships can be established through the *Relationships window*.
- Referential integrity ensures that records in related tables are consistent.
- Depending on the needs of the business, you can decide whether to use the *Cascade Update Related Fields* and *Cascade Delete Related Records* options.

2.7 Preview and print the contents of a table (p. A2-127).

- Use the *Backstage* view to print the contents of a table.
- *Print Preview* enables you to see how the records appear before printing. Use the *Print* *Preview* tab to change paper size, margins, and page orientation.

2.8 Manage a database using the *Compact & Repair Database* utility (p. A2-129).

- Over time, the size of your database increases due to added data, as well as temporary and deleted objects.
- In larger databases, functions such as adding and deleting records, querying tables, and running reports take longer.
- The *Compact & Repair Database* utility reclaims unused space and repairs databases that have become corrupted.

Check for Understanding

The SIMbook for this text (within your SIMnet account) provides the following resources for concept review:

- Multiple-choice questions
- Short answer questions
- Matching exercises

Guided Project 2-1

Central Sierra Insurance wants to expand the database you created in *Pause & Practice 1-4*. To ensure consistency, the starting file is provided for you. For this project, you use *Design* view to create a second table, edit field properties, and integrate data integrity rules. You also create a relationship between the two tables and enforce referential integrity constraints. Finally, you view how the table records will print using *Print Preview*.
[Student Learning Outcomes 2.1, 2.2, 2.3, 2.4, 2.5, 2.6, 2.7]

File Needed: *CentralSierra-02.accdb (Student data files are available in the* Library *of your SIMnet account.)*
Completed Project File Name: *[your initials] Access 2-1.accdb*

Skills Covered in This Project

- Create a table using *Design* view.
- Add fields into a table.
- Edit field properties in *Design* view.
- Define an input mask.
- Use the *Lookup Wizard* to create a drop-down list.

- Save a table.
- Enter records.
- Verify the existence of a foreign key.
- Create a 1:M relationship between tables.
- Enforce referential integrity.
- View a table in *Datasheet* view and expand related records.
- Preview table results for printing.

1. Open the **CentralSierra-02** database file.

2. Save a new copy of your database as [your initials] Access 2-1.

3. Enable content in the security warning.

4. Click the **Table Design** button [*Create* tab, *Tables* group] to open a new table in *Design* view.

5. Add new fields into the table and set field properties.
 a. Type Branch in the *Field Name* property box of the first row. Press **Tab** to move to the *Data Type* property.
 b. Select the **Short Text** *Data Type*. Press **Tab** to move to the *Description* property.
 c. Type Unique branch name.
 d. Click the **Primary Key** button [*Table Tools Design* tab, *Tools* group].
 e. Press **Tab** to move to the next row.
 f. Add the remaining fields into the table using the information in Table 2-18.

Table 2-18

Field Name	Data Type	Description
Address	**Short text**	Street address of the branch
City	**Short text**	Branch city
State	**Short text**	Branch state
ZIP	**Short text**	Branch ZIP Code
Phone	**Short text**	Branch main phone number
DateOpened	**Date/Time**	Date the branch first opened

g. Save the table as Branches. It is a good idea to periodically save a table when you are creating it so you don't lose your work.
h. Click the **row selector** to select the *Branch* field.
i. Type 30 in the *Field Size* property box in the *Field Properties* area.
j. Set the *Required* property to **Yes** if necessary.
k. Click the **row selector** to select the *Address* field.
l. Change the remaining field properties in the *Branches* table using the information in Table 2-19.

Table 2-19

Field Name	Field Size	Format	Default Value	Required
Address	40			Yes
City	20			Yes
State	2		CA	Yes
ZIP	9			Yes
Phone	10			Yes
DateOpened		Medium Date		Yes

m. Save the table.

6. Create an input mask for the *ZIP* field.
 a. Click to select the **ZIP** field.
 b. Click the property box for the *Input Mask* property.
 c. Click the **Build** button to launch the *Input Mask Wizard*.
 d. Select the **Zip Code** *Input Mask*.
 e. Click the **Next** button.
 f. Click the **Next** button without making any changes to the *Input Mask* or *Placeholder character*.
 g. Select the **Without the symbols in the mask, like this** radio button if necessary.
 h. Click the **Finish** button.
 i. Save the table.

7. Create an input mask for the *Phone* field.
 a. Click to select the **Phone** field.
 b. Click the property box for the *Input Mask* property.
 c. Click the **Build** button to launch the *Input Mask Wizard*.
 d. Select the **Phone Number** *Input Mask*.
 e. Click the **Next** button.
 f. Click the **Next** button without making any changes to the *Input Mask* or *Placeholder character*.
 g. Select the **Without the symbols in the mask, like this** radio button if necessary.
 h. Click the **Finish** button.
 i. Save the table.

8. Enter records into the *Branches* table.
 a. Change to *Datasheet* view of the table.
 b. Enter the records in Table 2-20 into the *Branches* table. The *DateOpened* values will display in the *Medium Date* format, DD-Mon-YY, after you enter them.

Table 2-20

Branch	Address	City	State	ZIP	Phone	DateOpened
Cameron Park	3360 Coach Lane	Cameron Park	CA	95682-8454	530-672-3232	1/1/2017
Folsom	75 Natoma Street, #B1	Folsom	CA	95630-2640	916-458-5555	1/1/2019
Granite Bay	6132 Del Oro Road	Granite Bay	CA	95746-9007	916-791-8787	2/1/2017

c. Save and close the table.

9. Modify the *Department* field in the *Employees* table to use a *Combo Box*.
 a. Open the *Employees* table in *Design* view.
 b. Click to select the **Department** field.
 c. Click the property box for the **Data Type** property, click the **arrow**, and select **Lookup Wizard**. The *Lookup Wizard* dialog box opens.
 d. Select the **I will type in the values that I want** radio button.
 e. Click the **Next** button.
 f. Click the **first cell** in the *Col1* column.
 g. Type Administration.
 h. Press the **down arrow** key to move to the next row.
 i. Type Health and Benefits. Press the **down arrow** key to move to the next row.
 j. Type Insurance Sales. Press the **down arrow** key to move to the next row.
 k. Type Property and Casualty.
 l. Click the **Next** button.
 m. Click the **Limit To List** check box.
 n. Click the **Finish** button.
 o. Save the table. If prompted to test the existing data against the new rules, click **Yes**.

10. Verify the existence of a foreign key and create a one-to-many relationship between the *Branches* and *Employees* tables. The *Branch* field is the field in common across the two tables. It is the primary key in the *Branches* table.
 a. Open both tables in *Design* view and verify that the *Branch* field has the same *Data Type* and *Field Size* in both tables.
 b. Edit the *Description* property of the *Branch* field in the *Employees* table to read Branch Assigned To – Must match a branch in the Branches table.
 c. Save and close any tables that you may have opened.
 d. Click the **Relationships** button [*Database Tools* tab, *Relationships* group].
 e. Select the **Branches** table in the *Show Table* dialog box and click the **Add** button.
 f. Select the **Employees** table and click the **Add** button.
 g. Click the **Close** button.
 h. Adjust the size of the table objects to see all of the fields if needed.
 i. Drag the **Branch** field from the *Branches* table on top of the **Branch** field in the *Employees* table. Release the pointer. The *Edit Relationships* dialog box opens.
 j. Verify that the field names displayed are correct. If necessary, use the drop-down arrows to make any corrections.
 k. Click the **Enforce Referential Integrity** check box.
 l. Click the **Cascade Update Related Fields** check box.
 m. Leave the *Cascade Delete Related Records* check box not selected. The company does not want to delete employees just because they may close a branch. This enables them to reassign employees.
 n. Click **Create**. The *Relationships* window updates with the relationship line added. The *1* and infinity symbols display indicating that referential integrity is enforced and that there is a one-to-many relationship between the two tables.
 o. Save the changes made to the relationships.
 p. Click **Close** [*Relationship Tools Design* tab, *Relationships* group].

11. Open the *Employees* table in *Datasheet* view and enter the record in Table 2-21 into the table to test the new drop-down list.

 Table 2-21

Emp ID	FirstName	LastName	Branch	Title	Department	Start Date	Base Monthly Salary
200	Timothy	Hansen	Cameron Park	Insurance Agent	Health and Benefits	9/15/2019	3900

12. Save and close the table.

13. Open the *Branches* table in *Datasheet* view.
 a. Adjust the width of the fields so that the entire field contents shows for each field.
 b. Click the **plus sign** to the left of the *Branch* field for the *Cameron Park* branch. You should see the 11 employees assigned to Cameron Park.
 c. Click the **minus sign** to close the related records.

14. Preview the data records in the *Branches* table before printing.
 a. Click the **Print** button [*File* tab] to display the printing options.
 b. Click the **Print Preview** button. The *Print Preview* tab opens and shows a preview of how the table will print.
 c. Click the **Landscape** button [*Print Preview* tab, *Page Layout* group] to change the page orientation. The report preview should appear similar to that in Figure 2-82.

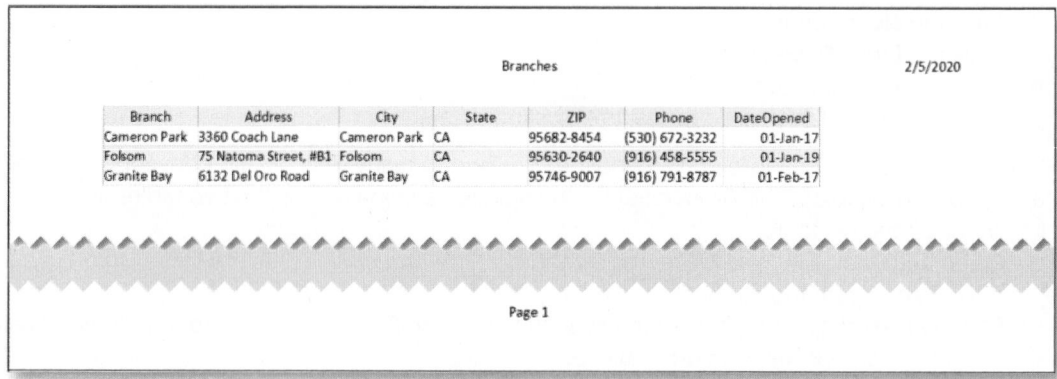

Figure 2-82 *Print Preview* of *Branches* table records

 d. Click the **Close Print Preview** button.

15. Save and close the *Branches* table.

16. Close the database.

Guided Project 2-2

San Diego Sailing Club wants to expand the database created in *Guided Project 1-3*. To ensure consistency, the starting file is provided for you. For this project, you use *Design* view to create a second table, edit field properties, and integrate data integrity rules. You also create a relationship between the two tables, enforce referential integrity constraints, and preview records for printing. Finally, you create a backup, and compact and repair the database.
[Student Learning Outcomes 2.1, 2.2, 2.3, 2.4, 2.5, 2.6, 2.7, 2.8]

File Needed: *SanDiegoSailing-02.accdb* (Student data files are available in the Library of your SIMnet account.)
Completed Project File Name: *[your initials] Access 2-2.accdb* and
[your initials] Access 2-2_YYYY-MM-DD.accdb

Skills Covered in This Project

- Create a table using *Design* view.
- Add fields into a table.
- Edit field properties in *Design* view.
- Create a validation rule and validation text.
- Save a table.
- Create a 1:M relationship between tables.
- Enforce referential integrity.
- Preview a table for printing.
- Compact and repair a database.

1. Open the **SanDiegoSailing-02** database file.

2. Save a new copy of your database as [your initials] Access 2-2.

3. Enable content in the security warning.

4. Click the **Table Design** button [*Create* tab, *Tables* group] to open a new table in *Design* view.

5. Add new fields into the table and set field properties.
 a. Type RentalID in the *Field Name* property box of the first row. Press **Tab** to move to the *Data Type* property.
 b. Select the **Short Text** *Data Type*. Press **Tab** to move to the *Description* property.
 c. Type Unique ID assigned to each rental.
 d. Click the **Primary Key** button [*Table Tools Design* tab, *Tools* group].
 e. Press **Tab** to move to the next row.
 f. Add the remaining fields into the table using the information in Table 2-22.

 ### Table 2-22

Field Name	Data Type	Description
FKBoatID	**Short Text**	Must match a BoatID in the SailboatFleet table
RentalDate	**Date/Time**	Date of rental
FourHourRental?	**Yes/No**	Yes is a 4-hour rental; No is a daily rental
MemberID	**Short Text**	ID number of member renting the boat

 g. Save the table as SDRentals.
 h. Click the **row selector** of the *RentalID* field.
 i. Type 5 in the *Field Size* property box in the *Field Properties* area.
 j. Type Rental ID in the *Caption* property box.
 k. Change the remaining field properties in the *SDRentals* table using the information in Table 2-23.

 ### Table 2-23

Field Name	Field Size	Format	Caption
FKBoatID	4		Boat ID
RentalDate		**Short Date**	Rental Date
FourHourRental?		**Yes/No**	Four Hour Rental?
MemberID	4		Member Number

6. Save the table.

7. Create a field validation rule and validation text for the *RentalDate* field.
 a. Click to select the **RentalDate** field.
 b. Click the **Validation Rule** property box.
 c. Type >=#1/1/2020#.

d. Click the **Validation Text** property box.

e. Type The Rental Date must be greater than or equal to 1/1/2020.

f. Save the table and switch to *Datasheet* view.

g. Type 1 in the *RentalID* field. **Tab** to the *RentalDate* field and type 7/5/2019.

h. Press **Tab**. The message box should display the contents of your *Validation Text* property. Click **OK**. Type 7/5/2020 in the *RentalDate* field.

i. Press **Tab**. You should successfully move to the *FourHourRental?* field.

j. Click the **record selector** box to select this data record and click **Delete** [*Home* tab, *Records* group] because you no longer need this sample data. Remember that in *Datasheet* view, the record selector is the gray cell on the left of each row.

k. Click **Yes** to confirm deletion of this record.

l. Close the *SDRentals* table.

8. Create a one-to-many relationship between the *SailboatFleet* table and the *SDRentals* table.

a. Click the **Relationships** button [*Database Tools* tab, *Relationships* group].

b. Select the **SailboatFleet** table in the *Show Table* dialog box and click the **Add** button.

c. Select the **SDRentals** table and click the **Add** button.

d. Click the **Close** button.

e. Adjust the size of the table objects to see all of the fields if needed.

f. Drag the **BoatID** field from the *SailboatFleet* table on top of the **FKBoatID** field in the *SDRentals* table as shown in Figure 2-83. The *Edit Relationships* dialog box opens.

g. Verify that the field names displayed are correct. If necessary, click the **drop-down arrows** to make any corrections.

h. Click the **Enforce Referential Integrity** check box.

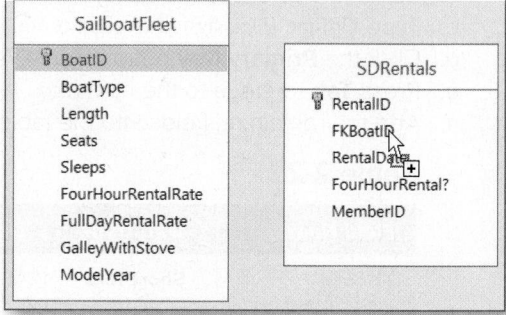

Figure 2-83 Drag the *BoatID* to the FKBoatID to create a relationship

i. Click the **Cascade Update Related Fields** check box.

j. Leave the *Cascade Delete Related Records* check box not selected. The club does not want to delete rental records just because it may take a boat out of service. This enables the club to keep a record of the rental.

k. Click **Create**. The *Relationships* window updates with the relationship line added. The *1* and infinity symbols display indicating that referential integrity is enforced and that there is a one-to-many relationship between the two tables.

l. Save the changes made to the relationships.

m. Click **Close** [*Relationship Tools Design* tab, *Relationships* group].

9. Enter records into the *SDRentals* table.

a. Open the *SDRentals* table in *Datasheet* view.

b. Enter the records in Table 2-24 into the *SDRentals* table.

Table 2-24

Rental ID	Boat ID	Rental Date	Four Hour Rental?	Member Number
08032	1152	1/15/2020	Yes	1122
08033	1146	1/15/2020		1386
08040	1010	2/2/2020	Yes	1122
08045	1010	2/9/2020		1386
08046	1152	2/9/2020	Yes	1427
08050	1152	2/15/2020	Yes	1122

c. Save the table.

10. Edit field properties in the *SDRentals* table.
 a. Click the **Design View** icon (Figure 2-84) in the *Status* bar to switch to *Design* view.
 b. Change the *Required* property for all fields except *FourHourRental?* to **Yes**.
 c. Save the changes to your table. Access displays a message box warning you that data integrity rules have changed. Click **Yes** to test your data against the new rules.
 d. Close the *SDRentals* table.

Figure 2-84 *Design View* icon in the *Status* bar

11. View the related data in the *SailboatFleet* table.
 a. Open the *SailboatFleet* table in *Datasheet* view.
 b. Click the **plus sign** to the left of the *BoatID* field *for BoatID 1010*. You should see two rentals for this boat.
 c. Close the *SailboatFleet* table.

12. Preview the data records in the *SailboatFleet* table for printing.
 a. Select the **SailboatFleet** table in the *Navigation Pane*.
 b. Click the **Print** button [*File* tab] to display the printing options.
 c. Click the **Print Preview** button. The *Print Preview* tab opens and shows a preview of how the table will print.
 d. Click the **Landscape** button [*Print Preview* tab, *Page Layout* group] to change the page orientation.
 e. Click the **Close Print Preview** button.

13. Back up the database and use *Compact & Repair Database* to reclaim unused space.
 a. Click the **Save As** button [*File* tab].
 b. Ensure that *Save Database As* is selected in the *File Types*.
 c. Select **Back Up Database** in the *Advanced* grouping of the *Save Database As* area.
 d. Click the **Save As** button.
 e. Accept the default name in the *File name* box and click the **Save** button.
 f. Click the **File** tab. The *Info* button should be selected.
 g. Click the **Compact & Repair Database** button.

14. Close the database.

Guided Project 2-3

American River Cycling Club wants to expand the database created in *Guided Project 1-2*. To ensure consistency, the starting file is provided for you. The *Members* table has been modified to unhide the *State* field. For this project, you use *Design* view to create a second table, edit field properties, and integrate data integrity rules. You also create a relationship between the two tables and enforce referential integrity constraints. Finally, you import data and view the related table records.
[**Student Learning Outcomes 2.1, 2.2, 2.3, 2.4, 2.5, 2.6**]

Files Needed: ***AmericanRiver-02.accdb*** and ***RaceResultsDataFile-02.xlsx*** (*Student data files are available in the* Library *of your SIMnet account.*)
Completed Project File Name: ***[your initials] Access 2-3.accdb***

Skills Covered in This Project

- Create a table using *Design* view.
- Add fields into a table.
- Edit field properties in *Design* view.
- Use the *Lookup Wizard* to create a drop-down list.
- Save a table.
- Create a 1:M relationship between tables.
- Enforce referential integrity.
- View a table in *Datasheet* view and expand related records.

1. Open the **AmericanRiver-02** database file.

2. Save a new copy of your database as [your initials] Access 2-3.

3. Enable content in the security warning.

4. Click the **Table Design** button [*Create* tab, *Tables* group] to open a new table in *Design* view.

5. Add new fields into the table and set field properties.
 a. Type RaceID in the *Field Name* property box of the first row. Press **Tab** to move to the *Data Type* property.
 b. Select the **Short Text** *Data Type*. Press **Tab** to move to the *Description* property.
 c. Type Unique race ID number.
 d. Press **Tab** to move to the next row.
 e. Type FKMemberID in the *Field Name* property box. Press **Tab** to move to the *Data Type* property.
 f. Select the **Number** *Data Type*. Press **Tab** to move to the *Description* property.
 g. Type Must match a MemberID in the Members table.
 h. Click the **row selector** to select the *RaceID* field. Press and hold the **Shift** key. Click the **row selector** to select the *FKMemberID* field.
 i. Click the **Primary Key** button [*Table Tools Design* tab, *Tools* group]. The *Primary Key* symbol should appear on both the *RaceID* and *FKMemberID* fields, indicating a concatenated primary key, as shown in Figure 2-85.

	Field Name	Data Type	Description (Optional)
🔑▶	RaceID	Short Text	Unique race ID number
🔑	FKMemberID	Number	Must match a MemberID in the Members table

Figure 2-85 *RaceID* and *FKMemberID* make a concatenated primary key

 j. Click the **Field Name** property box of the cell below *FKMemberID*.
 k. Add the remaining fields into the table using the information in Table 2-25.

Table 2-25

Field Name	Data Type	Description
Place	**Number**	Place finished in the race
Time	**Date/Time**	Total time
Division	**Short Text**	Division in which the member participated
AgeGroup	**Short Text**	Age group in which the member participated

 l. Save the table as RaceResults.
 m. Click the **row selector** of the *RaceID* field.
 n. Type 3 in the *Field Size* property box in the *Field Properties* area.

o. Change the remaining field properties in the *RaceResults* table using the information in Table 2-26.

Table 2-26

Field Name	Field Size	Format	Caption
FKMemberID			Member ID
Place	Integer		
Time		Short Time	
Division	1		
AgeGroup	13		

6. Save the table.

7. Modify the *Division* field to use a *Combo Box*.
 a. Click to select the *Division* field.
 b. Click the property box for the *Data Type* property, click the **arrow**, and select **Lookup Wizard**.
 c. Select the **I will type in the values that I want** radio button.
 d. Click the **Next** button.
 e. Click the **first cell** in the *Col1* column and type M.
 f. Press the **down arrow** key to move to the next row.
 g. Type F.
 h. Click **Next**.
 i. Click the **Limit To List** check box.
 j. Click **Finish**.
 k. Save and close the table.

8. Create a one-to-many relationship between the *Members* table and the *RaceResults* table.
 a. Click the **Relationships** button [*Database Tools* tab, *Relationships* group].
 b. Select the **Members** table in the *Show Table* dialog box and click the **Add** button.
 c. Select the **RaceResults** table and click the **Add** button.
 d. Click the **Close** button.
 e. Adjust the size of the table objects to see all of the fields if needed.
 f. Drag the **MemberID** field from the *Members* table on top of the **FKMemberID** field in the *RaceResults* table, as shown in Figure 2-86. The *Edit Relationships* dialog box opens.
 g. Verify that the field names displayed are correct. Use the drop-down arrows to make any corrections.
 h. Click the **Enforce Referential Integrity** check box.
 i. Click the **Cascade Update Related Fields** check box.
 j. Leave the *Cascade Delete Related Records* check box not selected. The club does not want to delete race records just because a member may leave the club. This enables the club to keep a record of the race.
 k. Click **Create**. The *Relationships* window updates with the relationship line added. The *1* and infinity symbols display indicating that referential integrity is enforced.

Figure 2-86 Drag the *MemberID* to the *FKMemberID* to create a relationship

l. Save the changes made to the relationships.

m. Click **Close** [*Relationship Tools Design* tab, *Relationships* group].

9. Import data from Excel into the *RaceResults* table.

 a. Launch the *Get External Data – Excel Spreadsheet* dialog box.

 b. Locate and select the **RaceResultsDataFile-02** Excel file.

 c. Append the records to the **RaceResults** table.

 d. Launch the *Import Spreadsheet Wizard*.

 e. Finish the *Import Spreadsheet Wizard*. Close the *Wizard* after the records have imported.

10. Open the *RaceResults* table in *Datasheet* view. Your table should contain the 24 records shown in Figure 2-87.

RaceID	Member ID	Place	Time	Division	AgeGroup
1	1	2	2:15	F	>=20 and <30
1	2	3	2:20	F	>=30 and <40
1	4	3	2:16	M	>=30 and <40
1	5	1	2:12	M	>=30 and <40
1	8	4	2:22	F	>=30 and <40
1	11	5	2:23	F	>=30 and <40
2	1	1	0:47	F	>=20 and <30
2	8	2	0:51	F	>=30 and <40
2	11	3	0:52	F	>=30 and <40
3	1	3	1:07	F	>=20 and <30
3	2	1	1:06	F	>=30 and <40
3	5	2	1:07	M	>=30 and <40
3	6	4	1:08	M	>=30 and <40
3	7	6	1:10	F	>=20 and <30
3	8	7	1:11	F	>=30 and <40
3	10	5	1:09	M	>=20 and <30
4	1	3	0:43	F	>=20 and <30
4	7	2	0:42	F	>=20 and <30
4	10	1	0:40	M	>=20 and <30
5	1	1	2:10	F	>=20 and <30
5	3	5	2:20	M	>=30 and <40
5	8	2	2:11	F	>=30 and <40
5	9	4	2:16	F	<20
5	12	3	2:14	F	<20
*	0	0			

Record: ◄ ◄ 1 of 24 ► ►I ►► No Filter Search

Figure 2-87 *RaceResults* table records after import

11. Edit field properties in the *RaceResults* table.

 a. Click the **Design View** icon in the *Status* bar to switch to *Design* view.

 b. Change the *Required* property for all fields to **Yes**.

 c. Save the changes to your table. Access displays a message box warning you that data integrity rules have changed. Click **Yes** to test your data against the new rules.

 d. Close the *RaceResults* table.

12. View the related data records in the *Members* table.

 a. Open the *Members* table in *Datasheet* view.

 b. Click the **plus sign** to the left of the *MemberID* field for *Geneva Lingle*, *MemberID* 1. You should see the five races in which Geneva has participated.

c. Click the **plus sign** to the left of the *MemberID* field for the *Ryan Thomas, MemberID* 3. You should see the one race in which Ryan has participated. Your screen should look similar to Figure 2-88.

Figure 2-88 *Members* table with related *RaceResults* table records

d. Close the *Members* table.

13. Close the database.

Independent Project 2-4

Courtyard Medical Plaza wants to expand the database created in *Independent Project 1-4*. To ensure consistency, the starting file is provided for you. For this project, you use *Design* view to create a second table, edit field properties, integrate data integrity rules, and enter data. You also create a relationship between the two tables, enforce referential integrity constraints, and import data. Finally, you preview how the records will print.

[Student Learning Outcomes 2.1, 2.2, 2.3, 2.4, 2.5, 2.6, 2.7]

Files Needed: *CourtyardMedicalPlaza-02.accdb* and *RentInvoicesDataFile-02.xlsx* (Student data files are available in the Library of your SIMnet account.)
Completed Project File Name: *[your initials] Access 2-4.accdb*

Skills Covered in This Project

- Create a table using *Design* view.
- Add fields into a table.
- Edit field properties in *Design* view.
- Create and test a record validation rule.
- Save a table.
- Enter records.
- Create a 1:M relationship between tables.
- Enforce referential integrity.
- View a table in *Datasheet* view and expand related records.
- Preview table results for printing.

1. Open the **CourtyardMedicalPlaza-02** database file.

2. Save a new copy of your database as [your initials] Access 2-4.

3. Enable content in the security warning.

4. Create a new table using *Table Design*.
 a. Add the fields in Table 2-27 into the table and set the field properties.

 ### Table 2-27

Field Name	Data Type	Description
InvoiceID	**Number**	Unique invoice number
InvoiceDate	**Date/Time**	Date invoice created
DueDate	**Date/Time**	Date bill is due
AmountDue	**Currency**	Total rent amount due
FKDoctorID	**Number**	Must match a DoctorID in the Physicians table
Description	**Short Text**	Brief summary of charges

 b. Set *InvoiceID* as the primary key.
 c. Save the table as RentInvoices.
 d. Change the field properties in the *RentInvoices* table using the information in Table 2-28.

 ### Table 2-28

Field Name	Field Size	Format	Caption
InvoiceID	**Integer**		
InvoiceDate		**Medium Date**	Invoice Date
DueDate		**Medium Date**	Due Date
AmountDue			Amount Due
FKDoctorID			Doctor ID
Description	40		

5. Save the table.

6. Create and test a record validation rule in the *RentInvoices* table.
 a. Open the *Property Sheet* for the *RentInvoices* table.
 b. Type [DueDate]>=([InvoiceDate]+10) in the *Validation Rule* property for the table.
 c. Type The Due Date must be at least 10 days after the Invoice Date. as *Validation Text*.
 d. Close the *Property Sheet* window.
 e. Switch to *Datasheet* view to test the rule. If prompted, save the changes to your table.

f. Type 1 in the *InvoiceID* field. Press **Tab** to move to the *InvoiceDate* field.

g. Type 1/1/2020. Press **Tab** to move to the *DueDate* field.

h. Type 1/5/2020.

i. Press the **down arrow** key to leave the current record. The message box should display the validation text message (Figure 2-89) because the *DueDate* is not at least 10 days after the *InvoiceDate*.

j. Click **OK** to acknowledge the error.

k. Delete the contents in the *DueDate* field and type 1/11/2020.

l. Verify that the record adds successfully.

m. Delete this record because you no longer need this sample data.

n. Close the *RentInvoices* table.

Figure 2-89 Error message displays valida-
tion text from a record validation rule violation

7. Create a one-to-many relationship between the *Physicians* table and the *RentInvoices* table.

a. Open the *Relationships* window and add the two tables.

b. Adjust the size of the table objects to see all of the fields if needed.

c. Drag the **DoctorID** field from the *Physicians* table on top of the **FKDoctorID** field in the *RentInvoices* table as shown in Figure 2-90.

d. Make the correct choices to *Enforce Referential Integrity* and *Cascade Update Related Fields*.

e. Leave the *Cascade Delete Related Records* check box not selected. Courtyard Medical Plaza does not want to delete invoice records just because a doctor may move out of the office complex. This enables Courtyard Medical Plaza to keep all rental records.

f. Create the relationship.

g. Save the changes and close the *Relationships* window.

Figure 2-90 Drag the *DoctorID* to the
FKDoctorID to create a relationship

8. Import data from Excel into the *RentInvoices* table.

a. Launch the *Get External Data – Excel Spreadsheet* dialog box.

b. Locate and select the **RentInvoicesDataFile-02.xlsx** Excel file.

c. Append the records to the *RentInvoices* table.

d. Launch the *Import Spreadsheet Wizard*.

e. Finish the *Import Spreadsheet Wizard*. Close the *Wizard* after the records have imported.

9. Open the *RentInvoices* table in *Datasheet* view. Your table should contain 27 records.

a. Use *AutoFit* to adjust the field width of all the columns.

b. Save the changes to your table.

10. Edit field properties in the *RentInvoices* table.

a. Use *Design* view to change the *Required* property for all fields to **Yes**.

b. Save the changes to your table. Access displays a message box warning you that data integrity rules have changed. Test your data against the new rules.

c. Close the *RentInvoices* table.

11. Open the *Physicians* table in *Datasheet* view.

a. Click the **plus sign** to the left of the *DoctorID* field for *Robert Beyer, DoctorID 1*. You should see the three invoices sent to Dr. Beyer.

b. Click the **plus sign** to the left of the *DoctorID* field for the *Emy Ostrander, DoctorID 3*. Notice that Dr. Ostrander does not have any invoices. Based on the way Courtyard Medical processes billing, they only send the bill to the one doctor listed on the lease. Your screen should be similar to Figure 2-91.

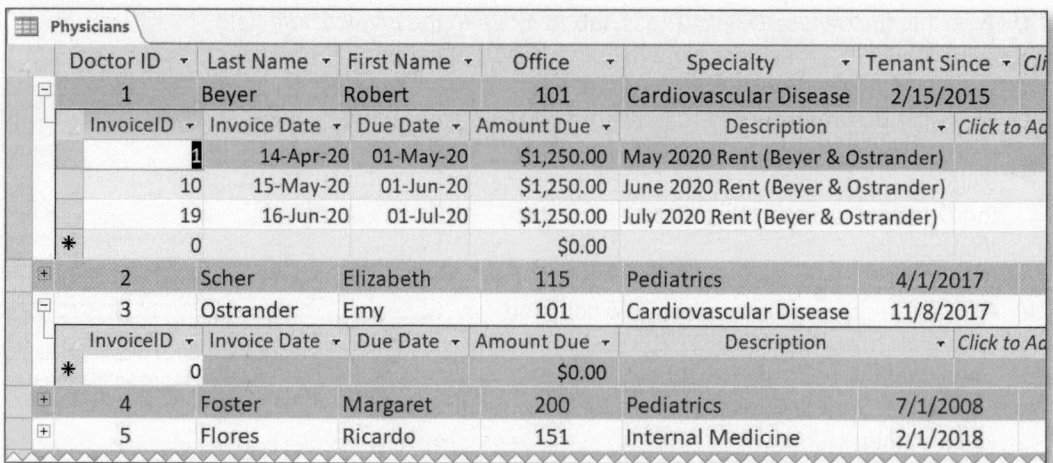

Figure 2-91 *Physicians* table with related *RentInvoices* table records

 c. Close the *Physicians* table.

12. Preview the data records in the *RentInvoices* table for printing.
 a. Select the **RentInvoices** table in the *Navigation Pane*.
 b. Use *Print Preview* to show a preview of how the table will print.
 c. Close the *Print Preview*.

13. Close the database.

Independent Project 2-5

Life's Animal Shelter wants to expand the database created in the *Independent Project 1-5*. To ensure consistency, the starting file is provided for you. In this project, you use *Design* view to create a second table, edit field properties, integrate data integrity rules, and enter data. You also create a relationship between the two tables and enforce referential integrity constraints. Finally, you add data using the relationship between tables.
[Student Learning Outcomes 2.1, 2.2, 2.3, 2.4, 2.6]

File Needed: ***LifesAnimalShelter-02.accdb*** *(Student data files are available in the* Library *of your SIMnet account.)*
Completed Project File Name: *[your initials]* ***Access 2-5.accdb***

Skills Covered in This Project

- Create a table using *Design* view.
- Add fields into a table.
- Edit field properties in *Design* view.
- Create an input mask.
- Create a validation rule and validation text.

- Save a table.
- Enter records.
- Create a foreign key.
- Create a 1:M relationship between tables.
- Enforce referential integrity.
- View a table in *Datasheet* view and expand related records.

1. Open the *LifesAnimalShelter-02* database file.

2. Save a new copy of your database as [your initials] Access 2-5.

3. Enable content in the security warning.

4. Create a new table using *Table Design*.
 a. Add the fields in Table 2-29 into the table and set field properties.

 Table 2-29

Field Name	Data Type	Description	Field Size
OwnerID	**Short Text**	Unique owner ID	4
OwnerLastName	**Short Text**	Last name	20
OwnerFirstName	**Short Text**	First name	20
Address	**Short Text**	Street address	40
City	**Short Text**		20
State	**Short Text**		2
ZIP	**Short Text**	ZIP Code	5
Phone	**Short Text**	Contact phone number	10

 b. Set *OwnerID* as the primary key.
 c. Select the **State** field and type TX in the *Default Value*.
 d. Save the table as Owners.

5. Create an input mask for the *Phone* field.
 a. Select the **Phone** field.
 b. Use the **Phone Number** *Input Mask*.
 c. Don't make any changes to the mask or placeholder character and select the **Without the symbols in the mask, like this** radio button.
 d. Finish the *Input Mask Wizard*.
 e. Save the table.

6. Create and test a field validation rule.
 a. Select the **OwnerID** field.
 b. Type Like "####" in the *Validation Rule*.
 c. Type You must enter a 4-digit Owner ID as *Validation Text*.
 d. Save the table and switch to *Datasheet* view.
 e. Test the rule by typing 11 in the first row of the *OwnerID* column.
 f. Move to the *OwnerLastName* field. The message box should display the validation text message (Figure 2-92) because the *OwnerID* is not four digits long.
 g. Click **OK** to acknowledge the error.
 h. Delete the contents and type 1111 into the *OwnerID* field.
 i. Verify that you successfully moved to the *OwnerLastName* field because 1111 meets the validation rule criteria.
 j. Delete this test data record.

Figure 2-92 Field validation rule error message

7. Enter the records in Table 2-30 into the *Owners* table. Life's Animal Shelter doesn't have any data about the owners stored electronically so you are unable to import any data. Because the *State* field has a default value of TX, you can simply accept that value and tab to the next field.

Table 2-30

Owner ID	OwnerLast Name	OwnerFirst Name	Address	City	State	ZIP	Phone
0100	Smith	Albert	11 Lakewood Drive	Abilene	TX	79601	325-614-9333
0101	Weston	Mark	2601 Nonesuch Road	Abilene	TX	79606	325-555-1112
0102	Rivera	Angela	2548 Laney Road	Denton	TX	76208	940-321-8020
0103	Moyer	Silvia	6867 Anglebluff Circle	Dallas	TX	75248	972-380-6188
0104	Wills	Mason	2421 Klondike Drive	Dallas	TX	75228	214-224-5555

8. Save and close the table.

9. Determine the foreign key field. Currently, a field is not common across the *Owners* and *Pets* tables. A one-to-many relationship exists between the two tables because an owner could adopt many pets, but each pet is only adopted by one owner. The foreign key comes by taking the primary key field from the *1* table and adding it in as an additional field in the *M* table.
 a. Open the *Pets* table in *Design* view.
 b. Add the foreign key field below the *Details* field using the information in Table 2-31.

Table 2-31

Field Name	Data Type	Description	Field Size
FKOwnerID	**Short Text**	Must match an OwnerID in the Owners table	4

 c. Save and close the *Pets* table.

10. Create a one-to-many relationship between the *Owners* and *Pets* tables.
 a. Open the *Relationships* window and add the two tables.
 b. Enlarge the table objects, if needed, to see all of the fields.
 c. Drag the **OwnerID** field from the *Owners* table on top of the **FKOwnerID** field in the *Pets* table. Release the pointer. The *Edit Relationships* dialog box displays.
 d. Select the choices to **Enforce Referential Integrity** and **Cascade Update Related Fields**.
 e. Leave the *Cascade Delete Related Records* check box not selected. The shelter does not want to delete pet records when it deletes information about an owner.
 f. Create the relationship.
 g. Save the changes and close the *Relationships* window.

11. Enter the following data into the specified records in the *Pets* table to reflect which pets have been adopted:
 a. Open the *Pets* table in *Datasheet* view.
 b. Type 0100 in the *FKOwnerID* field for *PetID 1*.
 c. Type 0103 in the *FKOwnerID* field for *PetID 3*.
 d. Type 0100 in the *FKOwnerID* field for *PetID 12*.
 e. Type 0104 in the *FKOwnerID* field for *PetID 14*.
 f. Close the *Pets* table.

12. View the related data records in the *Owners* table.
 a. Open the *Owners* table in *Datasheet* view.
 b. Click the **plus sign** to the left of the *OwnerID* field for *Albert Smith*, *OwnerID 0100*. You should see the two pets adopted by Albert.
 c. Close the *Owners* table.

13. Close the database.

Independent Project 2-6

The New York Department of Motor Vehicles tracks information about drivers, including accidents in which they have been involved. The starting database file is provided for you. For this project, you use *Design* view to edit a table and integrate data integrity rules. You also create a relationship between the two tables and enforce referential integrity constraints. Finally, you view how the table records will print using *Print Preview*.
[Student Learning Outcomes 2.1, 2.2, 2.3, 2.4, 2.5 2.6, 2.7]

File Needed: ***NewYorkDMV-02.accdb*** *(Student data files are available in the* Library *of your SIMnet account.)*
Completed Project File Name: *[your initials]* ***Access 2-6.accdb***

Skills Covered in This Project

- Edit a table using *Design* view.
- Edit field properties in *Design* view.
- Create a lookup field.
- Save a table.

- Enforce referential integrity.
- View a table in *Datasheet* view and expand related records.
- Preview table results for printing.

1. Open the ***NewYorkDMV-02*** database file.

2. Save a new copy of your database as [your initials] Access 2-6.

3. Enable the contents in the security warning.

4. Edit field properties of the *Tickets* table in *Design* view.
 a. Select a **Short Date** *Format* for the *TicketDate* field.
 b. Create a *Lookup Field* for the *PrimaryFactor* field with the following choices and limit the choices to those on the list: Alcohol, Backing Unsafely, Driver Distraction, Driver Inexperience, Failure to Yield R.O.W., Passing/Lane Violations, Traffic Control Disregarded, Turning Improperly, Unsafe Speed.
 c. Change all fields to be *Required*.
 d. Save the changes to the table. If prompted to test existing data against the new rules, click **Yes**.
 e. Close the table.

5. Edit field properties of the *Drivers* table in *Design* view.
 a. Open the *Drivers* table in *Design* view.
 b. Change all fields to be *Required*.
 c. Create a lookup field on the *Gender* field with the choices of M and F. Select **Yes** in the *Limit To List* property.
 d. Assign a *Default Value* of NY to the *State* field.

e. Save the changes to the table. If prompted to test existing data against the new rules, click **Yes**.

f. Close the table.

6. Review table relationships.

a. Open the *Relationships* window. Notice the relationship line does not have any symbols on the end points. This indicates that referential integrity has not been enforced (Figure 2-93).

b. Close the *Relationships* window.

c. Open the *Tickets* table in *Datasheet* view to see the impact of not enforcing referential integrity.

d. Enter the test data record in Table 2-32 into the *Tickets* table. Be sure to press **Enter** or **Tab** after you have entered the officer badge number so that the record is added into the table.

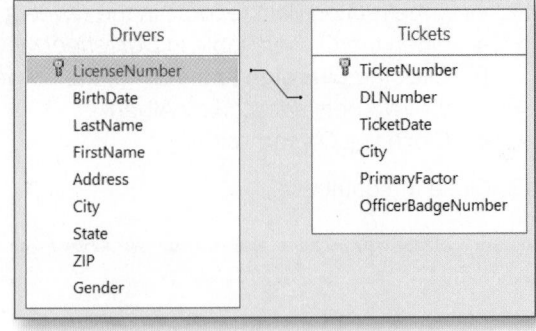

Figure 2-93 Referential Integrity is not enforced

Table 2-32

Ticket Number	DL Number	Ticket Date	City	Primary Factor	Officer Badge Number
1234567890	99999999	7/1/2020	New York	Unsafe Speed	123456789

e. Open up the *Drivers* table in *Datasheet* view. Keep the *Tickets* table open. Notice that no data record exists for a driver with the *LicenseNumber* of *99999999*. When referential integrity is not enforced, Access permits you to enter data records that don't need to have a corresponding record in the related table.

f. Click to expand the **plus sign** for *LicenseNumber 10000501 (Diego Acosta)*. You should see the two tickets Diego received. Notice that the relationship exists even if referential integrity is not enforced.

g. Close the *Drivers* table.

h. Delete the test data record from the *Tickets* table.

i. Save and close the *Tickets* table.

7. Edit referential integrity constraints.

a. Open the *Relationships* window.

b. Select the **relationship line** and click **Edit Relationships**.

c. Select the choices to **Enforce Referential Integrity** and **Cascade Update Related Fields**.

d. Leave the *Cascade Delete Related Records* check box not selected. You do not want to delete ticket records if you delete information about a driver.

e. Click **OK** to save the changes to the relationship.

f. Save the changes and close the *Relationships* window.

8. Test the referential integrity constraints.

a. Open the *Tickets* table in *Datasheet* view.

b. Enter the test data record in Table 2-33 into the *Tickets* table.

Table 2-33

Ticket Number	DL Number	Ticket Date	City	Primary Factor	Officer Badge Number
1234567890	99999999	7/1/2020	New York	Unsafe Speed	123456789

c. Click **OK** when Access displays a message box (Figure 2-94) indicating that you cannot add this ticket record because it requires a related record in the *Drivers* table.

Microsoft Access ✕

⚠ You cannot add or change a record because a related record is required in table 'Drivers'.

OK Help

Figure 2-94 Error message when referential integrity is violated

d. Press **Esc** to delete the record contents.

9. Enter the valid records in Table 2-34 into the *Tickets* table.

Table 2-34

Ticket Number	DL Number	Ticket Date	City	Primary Factor	Officer Badge Number
4235895082	12394163	2/21/2020	Utica	Unsafe Speed	A00045729
4235895110	39992387	2/28/2020	Utica	Unsafe Speed	A00045729

10. Save and close the table.

11. Preview the data records in the *Drivers* table for printing.
 a. Select the **Drivers** table in the *Navigation Pane*.
 b. Use *Print Preview* to show a preview of how the table will print.
 c. Change the page to a **Landscape** orientation. A darkened *Next Page* button in the *Navigation* bar indicates additional pages.
 d. Use the **Navigation** buttons to move to the second page if necessary.
 e. Close the *Print Preview*.

12. Close the database.

Improve It Project 2-7

Placer Hills Real Estate expanded the database created in *Improve It Project 1-7*. To ensure consistency, the starting file is provided for you. For this project, you use *Design* view to edit properties in a table and integrate data integrity rules. You edit data records, create a relationship between the two tables, and enforce referential integrity constraints. Finally, you view how the table records will print using *Print Preview*.
[Student Learning Outcomes 2.1, 2.2, 2.3, 2.4, 2.6, 2.7]

File Needed: ***PlacerHills-02.accdb*** *(Student data files are available in the* Library *of your SIMnet account.)*
Completed Project File Name: ***[your initials] Access 2-7.accdb***

Skills Covered in This Project

- Edit a table using *Design* view.
- Edit field properties in *Design* view.
- Create an input mask.
- Save a table.

- Create a foreign key.
- Create a 1:M relationship between tables.
- Enforce referential integrity.
- View a table in *Datasheet* view and expand related records.
- Preview table results for printing.

1. Open the **PlacerHills-02** database file.

2. Save a new copy of your database as [your initials] Access 2-7.

3. Enable the contents in the security warning.

4. Open the *Agents* table in *Datasheet* view (Figure 2-95).

EmployeeNu ▾	LastName ▾	FirstName ▾	DateHired ▾	Phone ▾
103	Bidou	Simon	Saturday, May 9, 2015	5306487689
127	Weatherby	Kelly	Tuesday, November 10, 2015	9169873756
133	Burgess	John	Friday, June 23, 2017	5302784699
151	Chung	Rick	Tuesday, October 9, 2018	9168236940
160	Johnstone	Jack	Friday, January 18, 2019	9165551679
160	Duarte	Kallyn	Friday, February 15, 2019	9167441614
169	Montoya	Gerardo	Thursday, March 21, 2019	9165345991

Figure 2-95 *Datasheet* view of the *Agents* table

 a. Look at the *DateHired* and *Phone* fields. The manager of the real estate office wants those to be formatted differently.
 b. Notice that both Jack Johnstone and Kallyn Duarte have the same value in the *EmployeeNum* field. If the employee number is supposed to be unique, something must not be set correctly with the primary key in this table.
 c. Change Kallyn Duarte's *EmployeeNum* to be 168, the correct value.

5. Change to *Design* view to make needed corrections to the *Agents* table.
 a. Notice that the table does not have a primary key. Although Access recommends that you assign a primary key in a table, Access lets you create a table without one.
 b. Set the *EmployeeNum* as the primary key.
 c. Set the *Format* property of the *DateHired* field to use *Short Date*.
 d. Create an input mask for the *Phone* field. Select the **Phone Number** *Input Mask*. Don't make any changes to the mask or placeholder character and select the **Without the symbols in the mask, like this** radio button. Complete the *Input Mask Wizard*.
 e. Change all fields to be *Required*.
 f. Save the table.
 g. Switch to *Datasheet* view to ensure that the formatting shows as desired.
 h. Adjust the field width of the *DateHired* field to 13. Remember that you can select the column, right-click to open the context menu and then select **Field Width** to change the width to a specific size.
 i. Adjust the field width of the Phone field to 16.
 j. Save and close the *Agents* table.

6. Open the *Listings* table in *Datasheet* view to help determine the type of relationship and the foreign key field. A one-to-many relationship exists between the *Agents* and *Listings* tables because an agent can list many different properties, but a property is listed by only one agent. The foreign key comes by taking the primary key field from the *1* table and adding it in as an additional field in the *M* table. In this case, the *EmployeeNum* should also be added into the *Listings* table.

Notice that the *Listings* table has a field that stores the agent's name. However, it doesn't have the foreign key. To minimize redundant data, you will change the *Agent* field so that it will now store the agent's employee number instead of the agent's name. This requires changing the data values as well as field properties.

7. Edit the data values in the *Agent* field in the *Listings* table.
 a. Click the **arrow** to the right of the *Agent Field Name* and select **Sort A to Z**. Because the employee name values begin with the first name, the sort isn't alphabetical by last name. However, the sort makes it easier to change the data values because all the property listings by the same agent are grouped together.
 b. Type 169 in the *Agent* field for *Gerardo Montoya*.
 c. Change each of the six records for *Jack Johnstone* to have the value of 160 for the *Agent* field. After entering the first value, you can use copy and paste to enter the remaining values.
 d. Continue changing the remaining records using the information in Table 2-35.

Table 2-35

Number of Records to Change	Agent Name	New Value for Agent Field
3	John Burgess	133
5	Kallyn Duarte	168
9	Kelly Weatherby	127
4	Rick Chung	151
4	Simon Bidou	103

 e. Remove the sort from the *Agent* field.
 f. Save the table.

8. Switch to *Design* view in the *Listings* table to edit the properties of the foreign key.
 a. Select the **ListingAgent** field.
 b. Change the field name to ListingAgentNumber. In this database, Placer Hills prefers that the foreign key have a unique name instead of choosing to use *FKEmployeeNum* as the name of the field.
 c. Change the *Description* to read Must match an EmployeeNum in the Agents table.
 d. Change the field size to 3.
 e. Save and close the table. Access warns you that the field size has been changed and that you may lose data. Your values meet this new size. Click **Yes**.

9. Create a one-to-many relationship between the *Agents* table and the *Listings* table.
 a. Open the *Relationships* window and add the two tables.
 b. Enlarge the table objects, if needed, to see all of the fields.
 c. Drag the **EmployeeNum** field from the *Agents* table on top of the **ListingAgentNumber** field in the *Listings* table as shown in Figure 2-96.
 d. Select the correct choices to **Enforce Referential Integrity** and **Cascade Update Related Fields**.

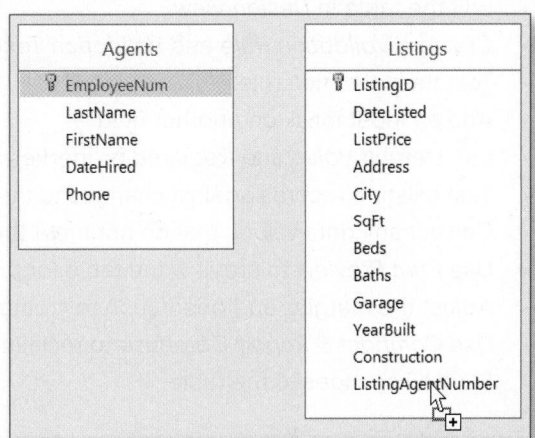

Figure 2-96 Drag the *EmployeeNum* to the *ListingAgentNumber* to create a relationship

 e. Leave the *Cascade Delete Related Records* check box not selected. You do not want to delete property listing records just because an agent may leave the company. This enables you to keep a record of the listings.

 f. Create the relationship.

 g. Save the changes and close the *Relationships* window.

10. Open the *Agents* table in *Datasheet* view.

 a. Click to expand the records for Kelly Weatherby. There should be nine properties listed.

 b. Close the *Agents* table.

11. Preview the data records in the *Listings* table for printing.

 a. Select the **Listings** table in the *Navigation Pane*.

 b. Use *Print Preview* to show a preview of how the table will print.

 c. Change the page to **Landscape** orientation.

 d. Close the *Print Preview*.

12. Close the database.

Challenge Project 2-8

Modify the database you created in *Challenge Project 1-8*. Use *Design* view to edit field properties. Change any data that violates these properties, preview the table for printing, and compact and repair the database.

[Student Learning Outcomes 2.2, 2.3, 2.4, 2.5, 2.7, 2.8]

File Needed: *[your initials] Access 1-8.accdb*
Completed Project File Name: *[your initials] Access 2-8.accdb*

Open the database *[your initials] Access 1-8* and save a copy of it as [your initials] Access 2-8.

Modify your database according to the following instructions:

- Edit the table in *Design* view.
- Create a *Validation Rule* and *Validation Text* for at least one of the fields in your table.
- Test the validation rule.
- Add an input mask on another field.
- Edit *Default Value* and *Required* properties for the fields as appropriate.
- Test existing records against changes to the properties.
- Correct any data values that do not meet the new data integrity rules.
- Use *Print Preview* to preview the table for printing.
- Adjust the margins and orientation to create an easy-to-read printout. Print the table as desired.
- Use *Compact & Repair Database* to reclaim any unused space.
- Save all changes to the table.

Challenge Project 2-9

Blue Lake Sports is a nationally recognized sporting goods company. It has a growing internship program at its corporate office to offer experience to college students. You have been asked to create a database to store information about the internship program. Create two tables, create a relationship between the tables, and add data into the database.
[Student Learning Outcomes 2.1, 2.2, 2.3, 2.4, 2.6]

File Needed: None
Completed Project File Name: *[your initials] Access 2-9.accdb*

Open a new database and save it as [your initials] Access 2-9.

Modify your database according to the following instructions:

- Create a table using *Design* view to store information about the interns.
- Add a field named InternID. Use a *Short Text* data type and designate it as the primary key.
- Add the following fields: LastName, FirstName, Phone, University, Major, and InternshipStartDate.
- Select appropriate data types and field sizes for the fields.
- Use the *Lookup Wizard* to create a drop-down list for *University* and add at least three choices to the list.
- Save the table as Intern.
- Enter several records into the table.
- Create a second table using *Design* view to store information about the different departments in which an intern can work.
- Add a field named DepartmentName. Use a *Short Text* data type and designate it as the primary key.
- Add the following fields: DeptMgrLastName, DeptMgrFirstName, OfficeNumber, and Division.
- Select appropriate data types and field sizes for the fields.
- Use the *Lookup Wizard* to create a drop-down list for *Division* and add the choices of Golf, Water Sports, and Children.
- Save the table as Department.
- Enter several rows of data. Use the following values for the *DepartmentName*: Sales-Golf, Accounting-Golf, HR-Golf, Sales-Water Sports, Accounting-Water Sports, HR-Water Sports, Sales-Children, Accounting-Children, HR-Children.
- An intern can only be assigned to one department, but a department may have several interns. Add the correct foreign key into the *Intern* table. Don't make that field required yet.
- Create the one-to-many relationship. Enforce referential integrity and cascade updates and deletes. Save the changes to the relationship.
- Edit the data records in the *Intern* table to add values into the foreign key field. Edit the *Intern* table to make the foreign key field required.
- Save all changes to the table.
- Open the *Department* table in *Datasheet* view. Expand the plus sign for several departments to see the associated interns assigned to this department.

Challenge Project 2-10

Modify the database you created in *Challenge Project 1-10* for a travel agency. Your database contains a table about upcoming cruises. Use *Design* view to create a new table to store information about the different ships on which passengers can cruise. Create a relationship between the tables, and add data into the new table.

[**Student Learning Outcomes 2.1, 2.2, 2.3, 2.4, 2.6**]

File Needed: *[your initials] **Access 1-10.accdb***
Completed Project File Name: *[your initials] **Access 2-10.accdb***

Open the database *[your initials] **Access 1-10*** and save a copy of it as [your initials] Access 2-10.

Modify your database according to the following instructions:

- Create a table using *Design* view to store information about the ships.
- Add a field named ShipID. Use a *Short Text* data type and designate it as the primary key.
- Add the following fields: ShipName, CruiseLineName, DateLaunched, NumberOfPassengers, and CountryOfRegistry.
- Select appropriate data types and field sizes for the fields.
- Use the *Lookup Wizard* to create a drop-down list for the *CruiseLineName* and add at least three choices to the list.
- Save the table as Ships.
- Enter several records into the table for various ships. Search the web if you need help finding examples of data to enter.
- Edit the *Trips* table you created in *Challenge Project 1-10*. Add the foreign key field of ShipID. It must have the same data type and field size you assigned in the *Ships* table.
- Create a one-to-many relationship between the two tables, because a ship can be used for many different cruises, but a specific cruise is only on one ship. Enforce referential integrity and cascade updates and deletes. Save the changes to the relationship.
- Edit the data records in the *Trips* table to add values into the *ShipID* field.
- Save all changes to the table.
- Open the *Ships* table in *Datasheet* view. Expand the plus sign for several ships to see the associated trips the ships are taking.

Source of screenshots Microsoft Office 365 (2019): Word, Excel, Access, Powerpoint.

Creating and Using Queries

CHAPTER OVERVIEW

Queries provide a powerful way to find and analyze data in databases. In chapter 1, you learned to use the *Search*, *Sort*, and *Filter* tools to find data. These are good tools, but over time, as the number of records stored in your databases increases, those tools become less helpful. Learning to create and use queries helps you to quickly and easily access your data and manage your databases. This chapter covers the basics of creating a query, adding criteria to a query, using different query options, integrating calculated fields, and creating summary queries.

STUDENT LEARNING OUTCOMES (SLOs)

After completing this chapter, you will be able to:

SLO 3.1 Understand queries and use the *Simple Query Wizard* to create and run a query (p. A3-162).

SLO 3.2 Create a query in *Design* view, add fields, and save and run a query (p. A3-163).

SLO 3.3 Add criterion into a query, use comparison operators, and create criteria with wildcards (p. A3-169).

SLO 3.4 Integrate sorting and limiting fields and records that display (p. A3-175).

SLO 3.5 Use the *AND* and *OR* operators to include multiple criteria in a query (p. A3-178).

SLO 3.6 Create and use a parameter query (p. A3-184).

SLO 3.7 Build a query that uses a calculated field (p. A3-189).

SLO 3.8 Create and use a summary query using aggregate functions (p. A3-194).

CASE STUDY

For the Pause & Practice projects in this chapter, you develop queries for Placer Hills Real Estate. As you progress through the Pause & Practice projects, you use the features you learn in this chapter to find and analyze data in a database with queries.

Pause & Practice 3-1: Create, run, and add criterion to a query in *Design* view. Edit and save a copy of a query.

Pause & Practice 3-2: Create queries using sorting and multiple criteria.

Pause & Practice 3-3: Create queries using a parameter and calculated fields.

Pause & Practice 3-4: Create a summary query that uses aggregate functions.

Understanding Queries and Using the Simple Query Wizard

A *query* finds data in your database by enabling you to ask a question. For example, in a music database you can create a simple query that shows all the albums that you own. Queries may include a criterion to search for only specific records. For example, in a university database, create a query to "show only the students who are taking a course in the biology department." You can also create a query that includes multiple criteria to further narrow your search. For example, a query in the Central Sierra Insurance database might use three criteria to find all of the employees who work as insurance agents in the Cameron Park branch who were hired after January 1, 2019.

You can create a query in *Design* view or with the **Query Wizard**. In this section, you use the **Simple Query Wizard** option.

When you build a query, you must tell Access where to find the data. The data source for a query can be a table or another query. The *Simple Query Wizard* enables you to select the specific table(s) and queries, as well as the specific fields to include in the query. After you create a query, run it to see the results. If you need to change the query once it has been created, you can edit it using *Design* view.

▶**HOW TO: Create a Query Using the Simple Query Wizard**

1. Click the **Create** tab on the *Ribbon*.
2. Click the **Query Wizard** button in the *Queries* group (Figure 3-1) to launch the *Query Wizard*.
3. Select **Simple Query Wizard** in the *New Query* dialog box (Figure 3-2).
4. Click **OK**.
 - The *Simple Query Wizard* launches (Figure 3-3).
 - The values displayed in the *Tables/Queries* box and the *Available Fields* window vary depending on the contents of your database.

Figure 3-1 *Query Wizard* button

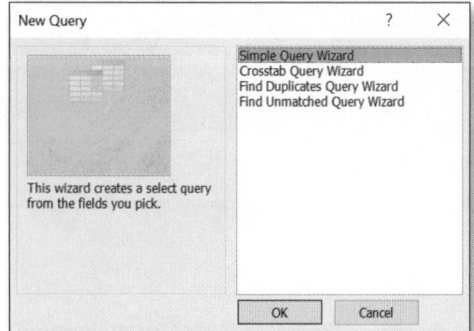

Figure 3-2 Select the query type in the *New Query* dialog box

Figure 3-3 *Simple Query Wizard*

5. Click the **Tables/Queries** drop-down arrow and select the *Table* or *Query* name.
6. Select a field to include in the query from those displayed in the *Available Fields* window.
7. Click the **Move Single Field** button.
 - The field moves into the *Selected Fields* window (Figure 3-4).
 - The *Remove Single Field* and *Remove All Fields* buttons become active.

Figure 3-4 Use the *Move Fields* buttons to select the fields to display in a query

8. Continue moving all required fields, changing the selected *Table* or *Query* if needed.

> ▶ **ANOTHER WAY**
>
> Use the **Move All Fields** button (see Figure 3-4) to select all of the fields in the query.

9. Click the **Next** button when you have finished adding fields. The last page of the *Simple Query Wizard* displays (Figure 3-5).

 - The *Title* box displays a default *Query Title*. The title will also be used as the *Query Name*. The default name combines the *Table Name* with the word *Query*.
 - Because you may have several queries that use the same table as the data source, be sure to create a name that describes the function of the query.
 - If you have selected fields from related tables, the *Simple Query Wizard* may display another page to make a choice between a *Detail* or *Summary* query. Select the desired radio button and click **Next**. If shown, this page displays prior to the last page in Figure 3-5 where you name the query.

10. Change the title as desired.

11. Click **Finish** to run the query. Access automatically saves and executes the query.

 - The results display in *Datasheet* view (Figure 3-6).
 - The *Query Name* displays in the *Queries* group on the *Navigation Pane*.

12. Close the query when done.

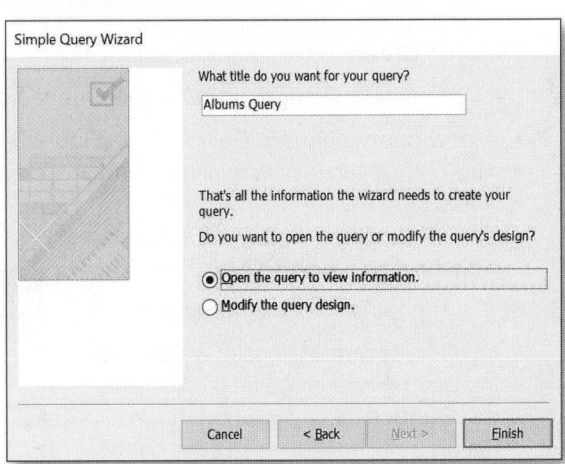

Figure 3-5 *Simple Query Wizard*, last page

> ▶ **MORE INFO**
>
> If you want to further edit the query, instead of running the query, select the **Modify the query design** radio button prior to clicking the *Finish* button. The query is saved and opens in *Design* view.

Album Name	Artist	Genre	ReleaseDate
1989	Taylor Swift	Pop	27-Oct-14
Seeds from the Underground	Kenny Garrett	Jazz	10-Apr-12
Thriller	Michael Jackson	Pop	30-Nov-82
Own the Night	Lady Antebellum	Country	13-Sep-11
Need You Now	Lady Antebellum	Country	26-Jan-10
19	Adele	Pop	10-Jun-08
Mylo Xyloto	Coldplay	Alternative	25-Oct-11
Greatest Hits (Volume One)	Queen	Rock	26-Oct-81
Melodrama	Lorde	Pop	16-Jun-17
The Thrill of It All	Sam Smith	Pop	03-Nov-17
Heart Break	Lady Antebellum	Country	09-Jun-17
Red Pill Blues	Maroon 5	Pop/Rock	03-Nov-17

Record: 1 of 50 No Filter Search

Figure 3-6 Query results display in *Datasheet* view

SLO 3.2

Creating, Running, and Editing a Query in Design View

While the *Simple Query Wizard* is useful when you want to see information quickly in your database, it doesn't enable you to take advantage of all the options available when creating a query. As a result, the most common way to create queries is with *Query Design*. In *Query Design*, you not only can specify the table(s) or queries to include, along with the fields from those objects, but you can also specify options to further restrict which records display, as well as how the results display. When you create and edit a query with *Query Design*, the *Design* tab, a *Query Tools contextual tab*, is available on the *Ribbon*.

Create a Query Based on a Single Table

Create a new query from the *Create* tab. Queries you create using the *Query Design* button automatically open in *Design* view.

> ▶ **HOW TO:** Create a New Query in Design View Using a Single Table

1. Click the **Create** tab on the *Ribbon*.
2. Click the **Query Design** button in the *Queries* group (Figure 3-7).
 - A new query opens in *Design* view (Figure 3-8).
 - The *Design* tab is now available and selected.
 - The *Query Design* window opens.
 - The *Show Table* dialog box displays with the *Tables* tab selected.

Figure 3-7 *Query Design* button

3. Select the table to use in the query.
 - If your new query is based on an existing query instead of a table, first click the **Queries** tab in the *Show Table* dialog box and then select the query.
 - If you accidentally close the *Show Table* dialog box and need to reopen it, click the **Show Table** button [*Query Tools Design* tab, *Query Setup* group].
4. Click **Add** to add the table into the *Query Design* window.

> **ANOTHER WAY**
>
> Double-click a table name in the *Show Table* dialog box to add it into the *Query Design* window.

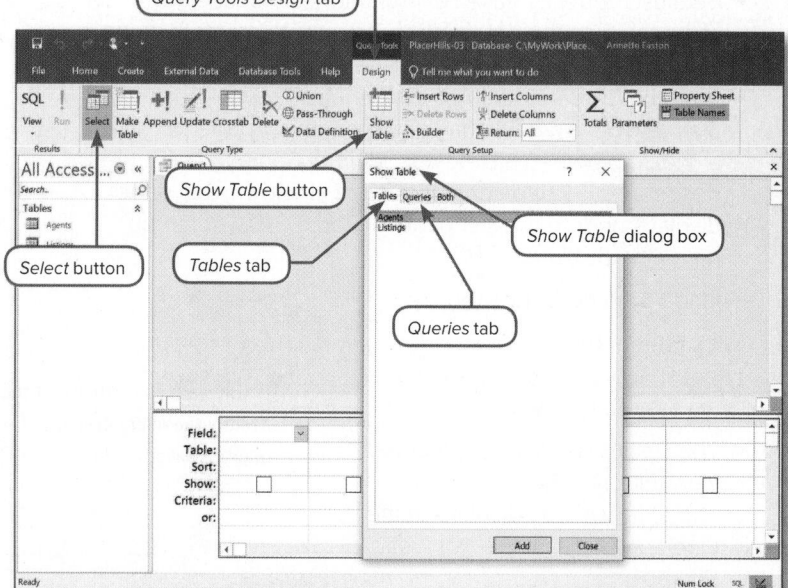

Figure 3-8 Create a new query in *Design* view

5. Click the **Close** button to close the *Show Table* dialog box.
 - The *Query Design* window (Figure 3-9) is divided into two sections. The top half shows the table you added into the query. The bottom half shows the query design grid. The **query design grid** contains the fields which have been included in the query, along with details about criteria and how the query results display. You learn to add fields in the next *How To*.
 - Increase the size of the table object in the window to display all of the fields as desired. Point to a border of the table until the pointer changes to the resize pointer. Drag the pointer to increase or decrease the table.
 - The **divider bar** separates the two sections. You can adjust the size of either section by moving the divider bar up or down.

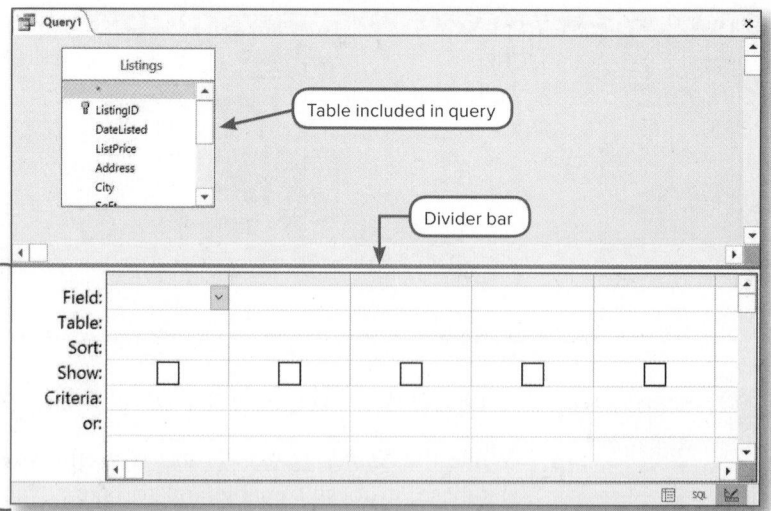

Figure 3-9 *Query Design* window

Notice that the *Select* button is highlighted in the *Query Type* group [*Query Tools Design* tab] shown in Figure 3-8. This indicates that the query is a select query. You can use **select queries** to locate, or select, data in the database. They are the most common type of query. In future chapters, you will learn about other query types that are action-based.

Add Fields into a Query

After you create a query, you need to add the fields into the query design grid. You can add as many fields as needed into the query. The query results display the fields in the order you place them into the query design grid.

Access provides three different ways to add fields into a query.

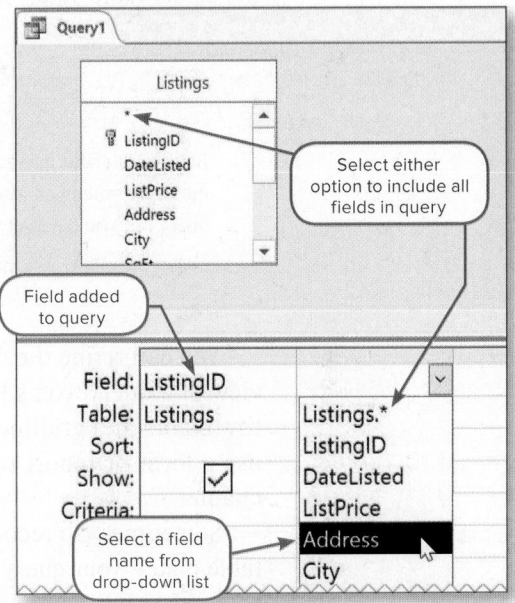

- Click, hold, and drag a **field name** from a *Table* displayed in the top part of the *Query Design* window to the first empty cell in the *Field* row of the query design grid. The *Field* and *Table* row cells in the query design grid update to display the contents (Figure 3-10).
- Double-click a **field name** from a *Table* in the top part of the *Query Design* window. The field is added to the first empty cell in the *Field* row of the query design grid.
- Click the **first empty cell** in the *Field* row of the query design grid. Click the **drop-down arrow** to display the list of field names. Select the desired field name (Figure 3-10).

To include all of the fields from a table in the query, either double-click the asterisk (*) symbol from the *Table* in the top part of the *Query Design* window or select the **TableName.*** choice from the drop-down list of fields displayed in the query design grid. Both options add TableName.* to the first empty cell in the *Field* row of the query design grid. Remember that the text "TableName" does not actually display; instead, the name of your table displays.

Figure 3-10 Add fields into a query

> ### MORE INFO
>
> If you want to apply criteria to individual fields, you must add each field separately instead of using the asterisk (*) symbol.

Run a Query

To see the results of a query, you need to execute, or run, the query. Running a newly written query ensures that you have created your query correctly. It is an important part of the database design and testing process.

- Click the **Run** button [*Query Tools Design* tab, *Results* group] to execute, or run, a query (Figure 3-11).

Figure 3-11 *Run* button

The results of the query display in *Datasheet* view (Figure 3-12). If the query results in more records than can display in the window, scroll bars automatically display.

Datasheet view of a query operates like *Datasheet* view of a table. This means you can change, add, and delete records in this view. Making changes to the data shown in *Datasheet* view of a query changes the actual table data.

ListingID	Address	City	List Price	SqFt	Beds	Baths	Garage
10022	525 Riverdale	Lincoln	$337,600.00	2755	3	2	2 Car Detached
10023	615 Silver Hill Court	Lincoln	$339,600.00	1600	3	2	2 Car Attached
10024	1917 Oak Crest Drive	Roseville	$675,000.00	3397	4	4	3 Car Attached
10025	3420 Milburn Street	Rocklin	$216,600.00	1900	4	3	3 Car Attached
10027	2128 Wedgewood	Roseville	$130,000.00	1184	3	2	1 Car Detached
10029	3998 Rawhide Road	Rocklin	$1,295,000.00	6685	7	6	4 Car Attached
10030	1720 Grey Owl Circle	Roseville	$389,900.00	2182	3	2	3 Car Attached
10031	2024 Brixham	Roseville	$368,505.00	2385	3	2	2 Car Attached
10032	4018 Legend Drive	Rocklin	$829,000.00	3821	4	4	3 Car Attached
10033	4336 Newland Heights Drive	Rocklin	$334,500.00	1840	2	2	2 Car Attached
10034	3535 Camino Cielo	Lincoln	$965,000.00	5159	5	5	4 Car Attached
10040	3935 Cedar Mist Lane	Auburn	$299,999.00	1056	3	2	2 Car Detached
10042	131 Aeolia Drive	Auburn	$385,000.00	1905	3	2	2 Car Detached
10043	1575 Oak Ridge Way	Auburn	$357,000.00	2266	3	3	3 Car Attached

Figure 3-12 Query results display in *Datasheet* view

> **MORE INFO**
>
> Be careful about using the *Datasheet* view results of a query to add data. You will encounter error messages when you attempt to add data in *Datasheet* view if you have not included all the fields in a query but you have set data integrity properties to require all fields.

You can refine the datasheet layout using the skills you learned in chapter 1. In *Datasheet* view of a query, you can change the font type, font size, font color, column width, alternate row colors and gridlines. To further customize the appearance of the query results, you can use a form or report to display the query results. These objects are introduced in the next chapter.

Sometimes, no records show when you run a query. This may be because no records in the table match your query criteria. However, if you expect results to display but none are shown when you run the query, you need to explore the potential causes. Check that the criterion value entered into the query matches the way the values are entered into the table. Additionally, verify that the query design is correct. You may have accidentally included the wrong field in the query and, as a result, no values match the criteria entered. Finally, the data may have been entered wrong when they were added to the table.

Switch between Datasheet and Design Views

When creating, and later using, a query, you may find that you need to switch between looking at the query results and looking at the query design. When a query is open, Access provides three ways to easily switch between different query views.

- Click the **View** button [*Home* tab, *Views* group] and then select the desired view option. Selecting *Datasheet View* executes the query, just like pressing the *Run* button. In addition to *Datasheet* and *Design* views, you will see an *SQL View* button. SQL is introduced in a later chapter.
- Click the **icon** on the *View* button [*Home* tab, *Views* group] to directly switch to the alternate view. The icon that displays in the *View* button is the opposite of the current view. For example, if the datasheet icon shows, this means that the current view of the query is *Design* view.
- Click the desired view **icon** from the right side of the *Status* bar, located at the bottom of the Access window. The icon that has a gray background is the current view of the table.

Save and Close a Query

When you create a query, Access automatically assigns a generic name to the query, such as *Query1*. The first time you save the query, the *Save As* dialog box displays and you are prompted to change the default name.

Because you may have several queries based off the same table, change the generic name to a name that describes the function of the query.

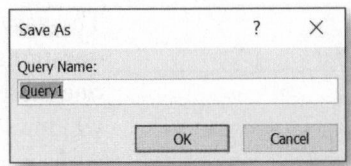
Figure 3-13 *Save As* dialog box for a query

- Save a new query by clicking the **Save** button [*File* tab]. Type a new name for the query in the *Query Name* box (Figure 3-13) and click **OK**.

> **ANOTHER WAY**
>
> To open the *Save As* dialog box, use **Ctrl+S**, the **Save** button on the *Quick Access* toolbar, or the **F12** function key.

Once a query has been saved, it displays in the *Queries* group of the *Navigation Pane* (Figure 3-14).

- Close a query by clicking the **X** in the upper-right corner of the query. If you close a new query without saving it, Access deletes the query. You can close the query from either *Design* view or *Datasheet* view.

Open a Saved Query

Open a saved query in *Design* view by right-clicking the query name in the *Navigation Pane* and selecting **Design View** from the context menu (Figure 3-15).

If you double-click a query name in the *Navigation Pane*, the query executes and the results show in *Datasheet* view.

Figure 3-14 Saved queries display in the *Navigation Pane*

Rename a Query

You may want to change the name of a query in the database, and it is easy to do this. The query should be closed before you rename it.

Figure 3-15 Use the context menu to open a query in *Design View*

> **HOW TO:** Rename a Query

1. Right-click the **query name** in the *Navigation Pane* and select **Rename** from the context menu.
2. Type a new name and press **Enter**.

Create a Query Based on Multiple Tables

The vast majority of databases contain multiple, related tables. As a result, many of the questions that you want to ask about the data require that you get data from more than one table. When building a query, you can add more than one table into the *Query Design* window. Be sure to include only tables that are related to each other, or you may end up with more records than anticipated, and records may be displayed in a way that doesn't make sense.

▶ **HOW TO:** Create a New Query in Design View Using Multiple Tables

1. Click the **Create** tab on the *Ribbon*.
2. Click the **Query Design** button in the *Queries* group to open the *Show Table* dialog box.
3. Select the **first table** you want to use in the query.
4. Click **Add** to add the table into the **Query Design** window.
5. Select the **second table** you want to use in the query.
6. Click **Add** to add the table into the **Query Design** window.
 - The *Query Design* window updates to show both tables (Figure 3-16).
 - A relationship line displays showing the relationship.
7. Continue adding all required tables.

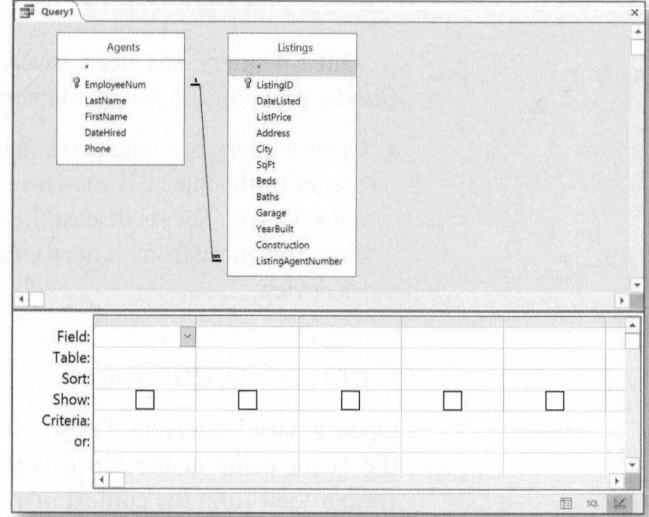

> ▶ **ANOTHER WAY**
>
> Select the first table name. Press and hold the **Shift** or **Ctrl** key. Select any additional table names. Click **Add** to add all the tables into the *Query Design* window.

Figure 3-16 *Query Design* window displays all the tables used in a query

8. Click the **Close** button to close the *Show Table* dialog box.
 - You can now add fields and run and save the query following the steps you have learned.

Edit Fields in Query Design

When building a query, you may need to insert a field between two fields that already are placed in the query design grid. Alternatively, you may need to delete a field from the query design grid if you determine it is no longer needed. The *Query Setup* group [*Query Tools Design* tab] contains the ***Insert Columns*** or ***Delete Columns*** buttons to add or delete a field (Figure 3-17).

Figure 3-17 *Insert Columns* and *Delete Columns* buttons

1. Locate the query design grid. Put your pointer in the small cell above the field name to the right of where you wish to insert a new field (Figure 3-18) and click the **Selection** pointer to select that column. The column is highlighted in black.

2. Click the **Insert Columns** button [*Query Tools Design* tab, *Query Setup* group]. The new column displays and becomes the selected column (Figure 3-19).

3. Add a field into that column by clicking the **Field** row cell of the new column, clicking the **drop-down arrow**, and selecting the desired field name.

Figure 3-18 Select a column in the query design grid

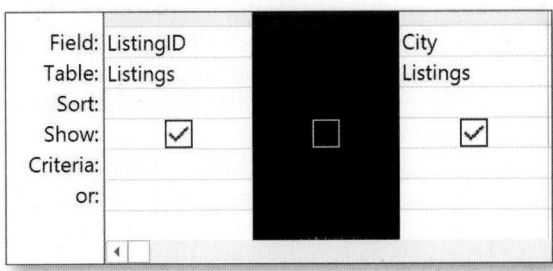

Figure 3-19 A new column inserted between existing fields

1. Select the **column** in the query design grid of the field that you wish to delete.

2. Click the **Delete Columns** button [*Query Tools Design* tab, *Query Setup* group] to delete the selected field.

SLO 3.3

Adding a Criterion to a Query

You can add a criterion into a query to search for records that meet a specific value. The type of criterion you enter, along with the way you enter the criterion, depends on the data type of the field. Use *expressions* to write the criterion. In chapter 2, you learned to create expressions when you created a validation rule. The expressions that you write for criterion work the same way. Enter the criterion expression directly in the criteria cell or in the *Expression Builder*.

When you enter the specific criterion value, be sure to format the value correctly based on the data type of the field.

- Criterion for *Number, Large Number, Currency,* and *AutoNumber* data types include the actual number value not surrounded by any special symbols.
- Criterion for *Short Text* and *Long Text* data types are enclosed within quotation marks. Access ignores the case of the text in the criterion when making an evaluation.
- Criterion for *Date/Time* data types are enclosed within pound (#) symbols.
- Criterion for *Yes/No* data types use either *Yes* or *No.* Use *Yes* to find records where the check box is selected and use *No* to find records where the check box is not selected.

Single Criterion

In the simplest criterion expression, you only enter the criteria value. Access evaluates this criterion as an "equal to" comparison. In other words, it will find all data that are "equal to" the criterion.

▶ HOW TO: Add a Criterion into the Query

1. Click the **Criteria** row cell of the desired field.
2. Type the criterion expression you want to enter.

 - The criterion shown in Figure 3-20 creates a query that finds all property listings in the *City* of "Roseville".
 - As desired, you can include the equals sign in the expression. In this example, you could enter either ="Roseville" or "Roseville" because they both evaluate the same way.
 - If your criterion expression is longer than the column width, increase the width of the column. Position the pointer at the border of a column, in the small cell above the field name. The pointer turns into the resize arrow. Click and drag the **resize arrow** to resize the column.
 - You can also enter the criteria into the *Expression Builder*. Open the *Expression Builder* dialog box by right-clicking the **Criteria** row cell and selecting **Build** from the context menu (Figure 3-21) or by pressing **Ctrl+F2**.

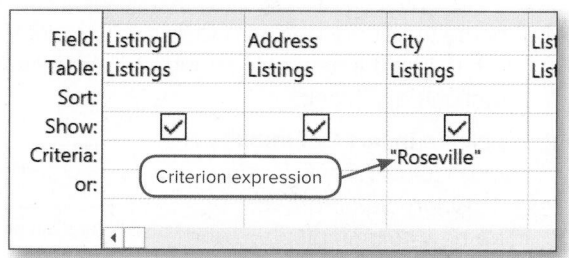

Figure 3-20 Enter a criterion into a query

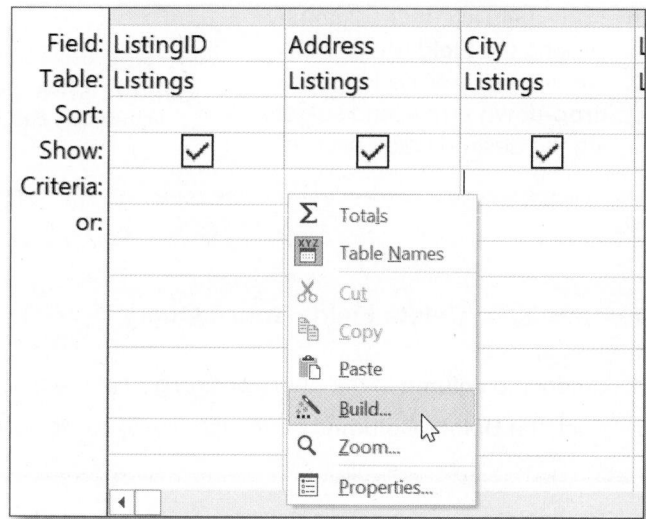

Figure 3-21 Select the *Build* button to open the *Expression Builder*

When entering an expression, the ***IntelliSense*** tool may suggest a list of possible values. Figure 3-22 shows an example of an *IntelliSense* list. A description of the selected item also displays. The list automatically appears if the text you enter into an expression matches the text in a function or object name. The list updates as you type additional text. Select an item from the list, press **Esc** to hide the list, or simply continue typing your value.

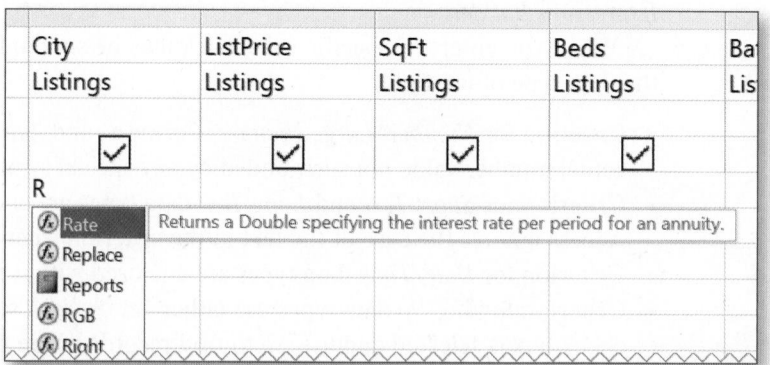

Figure 3-22 The *IntelliSense* tool suggests possible functions based on the value you have entered

After adding a criterion to a query, remember to test the query to make sure you wrote the criterion expression correctly. Test the query by running it and then comparing the results to your expected results.

If no records in the database match the query criterion, the datasheet still displays but no records appear. If this occurs and you expect that records in the table should display as a result of the query, verify that the query criterion was entered correctly or that data values were entered correctly when the record was added into the table.

Comparison Operators

When you want to search for values beyond an "equal to" comparison, you need to include a comparison operator in the expression. A *comparison operator* is used to compare two values in an expression. Usually, the comparison operator appears at the beginning of the expression, although that depends on the exact structure of the expression.

The operators are summarized in Table 3-1.

Table 3-1: Comparison Operators

Operator	Explanation	Example
<	Less than	<5
<=	Less than or equal to	<=100
>	Greater than	>#1/1/2014#
>=	Greater than or equal to	>="B24"
=	Equal to	="CA"
<>	Not equal to	<>0
Between	Between these two values	Between 10 and 20
In	Contained in this list of values	In(1, 5, 10)
Like	Similar to this value	Like "C??"

A criterion can also have the value of *Is Null* or *Is Not Null*. Use *Is Null* to find records where the value is not entered for a specific field. Use *Is Not Null* to find records where the field contains a value.

Sometimes, *Date/Time* fields use a function as the criteria value. *Functions* are pre-built procedures that perform a specific task. A common function used with *Date/Time* fields is *Date()*, which returns the current date from your computer. Two criterion examples using the *Date()* function in a *ShippingDate* field are explained below.

- *<=Date()*: Finds records that have a *ShippingDate* value that is on or before today's date.
- *Between Date() and Date()+7*: Finds records that have a *ShippingDate* value that is one of the next 7 days. In this example, the criterion includes an arithmetic formula as part of the comparison.

Use Wildcards in Criteria

You can use the *Like* comparison operator in a criterion to find records containing data that is similar to, or like, the criterion value. When using *like*, you typically incorporate one of the *wildcard characters* available in Access. When you use a wildcard, the criterion of your expression must be enclosed in quotation marks, even when you use *Number*, *Large Number*, *Currency*, and *AutoNumber* data types.

Examples of wildcard characters and their effects in a query criterion are illustrated in the following material.

The ? Wildcard Character

Use the ? wildcard character to match any single character in a specific position. Remember that numbers are also considered characters. Review the following example:

Field (Type and Size)	Example Criterion	Explanation of Example
PhoneNumber (Text, Size 10) [The input mask symbols are not stored with the data.]	Like "9?????????"	Finds records where the phone number contains 10 characters and starts with a 9.

If you use the criterion above to search the sample data shown in Figure 3-23, only the highlighted record values are returned by the query. The second record, phone number 987-3116, does start with a 9, but it is not 10 characters long.

If you wrote the criterion as *Like "9???????"*, which would require a value of exactly 8 characters, no records would be returned because none of the phone numbers in Figure 3-23 contains only 8 characters.

Figure 3-23
Sample phone data

The * Wildcard Character

Use the * wildcard character to match any number of characters, as shown in the following example:

Field (Type and Size)	Example Criterion	Explanation of Example
SongTitle (Text, Size 70)	Like "love *"	Finds records where the song title starts with the word love. Note the blank space after the letter "e" and before the asterisk.

Due to the blank space between the word "love" and the asterisk, this query finds only the complete word of "love" and not songs where the title contains the letters of the word "love" within a word, such as "beloved" or "lover". This criterion would find "Love for All Seasons". However, it will not find songs with the title of "Leave Love Alone" or "Make You Feel My Love" because in these titles "love" is not the first word.

If you change the criterion to *Like "* love"*, the only songs found would be those that end with the word "love". For example, it would find "Make You Feel My Love".

If you change the criterion to *Like "* love *"*, the only songs found would be those that contain the word "love" somewhere in the middle ("love" cannot be the first or last word). This query would find "Leave Love Alone".

If you are interested in finding songs that contain the letters of the word "love", you can remove the spaces. For example, the query *Like "*Love*"*, would find song titles that contain the letters of the word "love" anywhere in the title. This would find "Love for All Seasons", "Leave Love Alone", "Make You Feel My Love" and it would also find "She Will Be Loved" and "Lovers in a Dangerous Time".

> **MORE INFO**
>
> You must pay attention to the proper placement of the * wildcard, along with any characters and spaces, to ensure that the query returns the correct results.

Review another example below used on a currency field:

Field (Type and Size)	Example Criterion	Explanation of Example
Sales Price (Currency, Size N/A)	Like "*.99"	Finds records where the sales price ends with .99.

This criterion finds records where the price is .99, 2.99, or 345.99. It will not find records where the price is 1.09 or 3.995.

You can combine multiple wildcards together. For example, using the criterion of *Like "*1?"* combines the * and ? wildcards. Using this criterion on the *PhoneNumber* field in Figure 3-23 would return the phone numbers of () 987-3116 and (916) 744-1614. This criterion returns records with a phone number of any length, as long as a "1" is the second to last digit.

The # Wildcard Character

Use the # wildcard character to match any single numeric digit. Review the following example:

Field (Type and Size)	Example Criterion	Explanation of Example
SqFt (Number, Size Long Integer)	Like "2###"	Finds records where the square footage starts with a 2 and contains 4 digits.

This criterion finds houses that are in the 2,000 to 2,999 square foot range. It does not find a house with 255 square feet or with 20,000 square feet because those don't meet the 4-digit specification. Remember that the comma (,) in 2,000, as an example, only displays as part of the formatting and is not stored as a character in the actual table.

A second example of # wildcard character is shown below:

Field (Type and Size)	Example Criterion	Explanation of Example
Sales Price (Currency, Size N/A)	Like "###.99"	Finds records where the sales price contains three digits to the left of the decimal point and ends with .99.

This criterion finds records where the price is 100.99 or 345.99. It will not find records where the price is .99, 2.99 or 1043.99.

PAUSE & PRACTICE: ACCESS 3-1

For this Pause & Practice, you use *Design* view to create three queries for the Placer Hills Real Estate Company.

File Needed: **PlacerHills-03.accdb** *(Student data files are available in the* Library *of your SIMnet account.)*
Completed Project File Name: **[your initials] PP A3-1.accdb**

1. Open the **PlacerHills-03** database file.

2. Save a new copy of your database as [your initials] PP A3-1.

3. Enable content in the database.

4. Create a new query in *Design* view.
 a. Click the **Query Design** button [*Create* tab, *Queries* group] to open the *Show Table* dialog box.
 b. Select the **Agents** table if needed, and click the **Add** button.
 c. Select the **Listings** table and click the **Add** button.
 d. Click the **Close** button in the *Show Table* dialog box.
 e. Increase the size of the table objects to display all of the fields.
 f. Double-click the **ListingID** field from the *Listings* table in the *Query Design* window. The field is added to the first empty column in the query design grid.
 g. Double-click the **Address** field to add it into the query design grid.
 h. Continue adding the following fields into the query design grid: **City**, **ListPrice**, **SqFt**, **Beds**, **Baths**, **Garage**, **FirstName**, **LastName** and **Phone**. Note that the last three fields come from the *Agents* table. The completed query should look similar to Figure 3-24.

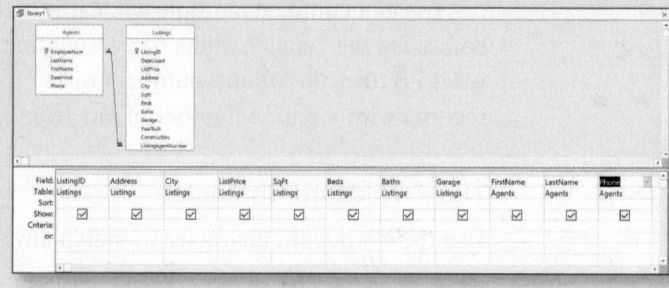

Figure 3-24 Completed query design

5. Click the **Run** button [*Query Tools Design* tab, *Results* group] to run the query. The query should open in *Datasheet* view and display 57 records.

6. Click the **View** button [*Home* tab, *Views* group] and select the **Design View** option to switch back to *Design* view.

7. Save the query.
 a. Click the **Save** button [*File* tab].
 b. Type ShowAllListings in the *Query Name* box.
 c. Click **OK**. The query name displays in the *Navigation Pane* in the *Queries* group.

8. Add a criterion to the query to find all listings in Roseville.
 a. Type Roseville in the **Criteria** row cell of the *City* field. When you enter criterion into a *Short Text* or *Long Text* field, you can either enter quotation marks around the criterion, or if you omit the quotation marks, Access automatically enters them for you.
 b. Tab out of that field. Notice that Access automatically puts quotation marks around the text criteria (Figure 3-25).

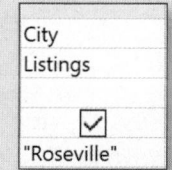

Figure 3-25 Query criterion

9. Click the **Run** button [*Query Tools Design* tab, *Results* group] to run the query. The query should open in *Datasheet* view and display the 11 listings located in Roseville (Figure 3-26).

ListingID	Address	City	List Price	SqFt	Beds	Baths	Garage	FirstName	LastName	Phone
10024	1917 Oak Crest Drive	Roseville	$675,000.00	3397	4	4	3 Car Attached	Jack	Johnstone	(916) 555-1679
10027	2128 Wedgewood	Roseville	$130,000.00	1184	3	2	1 Car Detached	Kelly	Weatherby	(916) 987-3756
10030	1720 Grey Owl Circle	Roseville	$389,900.00	2182	3	2	3 Car Attached	Simon	Bidou	(530) 648-7689
10031	2024 Brixham	Roseville	$368,505.00	2385	3	3	2 Car Attached	Kallyn	Duarte	(916) 744-1614
10049	1773 Melanzane Drive	Roseville	$599,900.00	4390	4	5	3 Car Attached	Kelly	Weatherby	(916) 987-3756
10055	954 Court Street	Roseville	$429,900.00	2580	3	3	2 Car Attached	Kelly	Weatherby	(916) 987-3756
10060	1110 Kimberly Court	Roseville	$399,900.00	3765	4	4	3 Car Detached	Kelly	Weatherby	(916) 987-3756
10080	1089 Marseille Lane	Roseville	$274,000.00	1645	2	2	2 Car Attached	Simon	Bidou	(530) 648-7689
10081	1520 Arrowwood Lane	Roseville	$340,000.00	2370	4	3	3 Car Attached	Jack	Johnstone	(916) 555-1679
10110	227 Balsam Creek	Roseville	$559,600.00	1976	4	2	1 Car Detached	John	Burgess	(530) 278-4699
10117	1924 Wildwood Way	Roseville	$279,000.00	1676	3	3	2 Car Attached	Rick	Chung	(916) 823-6940

Record: 1 of 11 No Filter Search

Figure 3-26 Query results for listings in Roseville

10. Save a copy of this query.
 a. Click the **Save As** button [*File* tab].
 b. Select the **Save Object As** button in the *File Types* area and then click the **Save As** button. Access suggests the new query name of *Copy of ShowAllListings*.
 c. Type ListingsInRoseville in the *Save 'ShowAllListings' to* box.
 d. Click **OK**. The two queries now display in the *Navigation Pane* in the *Queries* group.
 e. Close the query.

11. Right-click the **ShowAllListings** query name in the *Navigation Pane* and select **Design View** from the context menu to open the query.

12. Type Like "*Attached" in the *Criteria* row cell of the *Garage* field. This criterion will find all listings that have an attached garage, no matter how many cars.

13. Run the query. Your results should display 37 listings that have an attached garage.

14. Save a copy of the query using the name ListingsWithAttachedGarage.

15. Close the query.

16. Close the database.

Controlling the Display of Query Results

Access provides a variety of options to help control the way query results display. For example, you may wish to have the results display in a sorted order. Or you may need to include a field in a query to apply a criterion, but you don't want that field to display in the results. At other times, a query may show duplicate records and you want to show only records that contain unique values. This section describes ways to control the display of query results.

Unique Values Property

A well-designed database is structured to minimize redundant data. As a result, most queries display unique records in the results. However, sometimes, the structure of a particular query causes duplicated records to display.

For example, a music database may have two tables: one that stores information about each album owned and another that stores information about the songs that are on each album. The *Query* window showing those tables is displayed in Figure 3-27. As you know, it is possible for a song to appear on multiple albums. For example, "Billie Jean" appears on two of Michael Jackson's albums, *Thriller* and *Number Ones*.

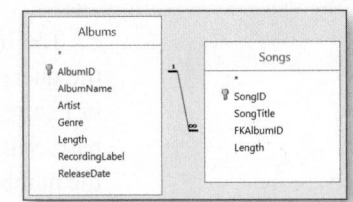

Figure 3-27 *Query* window shows the relationship between the *Albums* and *Songs* tables

If you write a query to find the names of all the songs in the database, you would see that song name appear once for each album that includes this song. In the query results, this would appear as duplicated data. You can use the ***Unique Values*** property to direct Access to only display records that don't include duplicated values. Don't confuse the *Unique Values* property with the ***Unique Records*** property. *Unique Records* checks all the fields in a table (not just those included in the query).

▶HOW TO: Display Unique Values in Query Results

Figure 3-28 *Show/Hide* group buttons

1. Open the query in *Design* view.
2. Click anywhere in the top half of the *Query Design* window to deselect any fields that are selected.
3. Click the **Property Sheet** button [*Query Tools Design* tab, *Show/Hide* group] (Figure 3-28).
 - The *Property Sheet* for the query opens (Figure 3-29).
 - In the *Show/Hide* group, the *Table Names* button is highlighted when the query design grid displays the *Table* row below the *Field* row. The *Table Names* button works as a toggle. Clicking it when it is highlighted removes the *Table* row from the query design grid.
 - Verify that the *Selection type* in the *Property Sheet* displays *Query Properties*. If the *Selection type* displays *Field Properties*, you still had a field selected before opening the *Property Sheet* and you must repeat step 2.
4. Click the **Unique Values** property box and select **Yes**.
5. Close the *Property Sheet*.

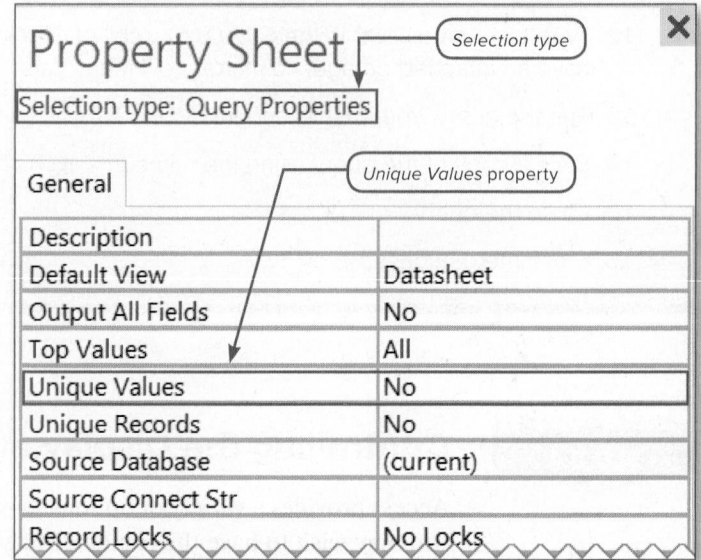

Figure 3-29 *Property Sheet* of a query

▶ **ANOTHER WAY**

Press the **F4** key, or the **Alt+Enter** keys, to open or close the *Property Sheet*.

The usefulness of the *Unique Values* property depends on the query structure. For example, if you run the query shown in Figure 3-30, you see one record for every song in the database. Setting the *Unique Values* property to *Yes* does not reduce the number of records displayed, because including the field of *AlbumName* creates unique records in the results (assuming the same *SongTitle* is not included on an album twice).

The query shown in Figure 3-31 does not include the *AlbumName* field. Setting the *Unique Values* property to *Yes* on this query results in fewer records being displayed. With this query, "Billie Jean" only appears one time in the query results.

Field:	AlbumName	SongTitle	Artist
Table:	Albums	Songs	Albums
Sort:			
Show:	☑	☑	☑
Criteria:			
or:			

Figure 3-30 *Unique Values* property has no impact when fields create unique records

Field:	SongTitle	Artist
Table:	Songs	Albums
Sort:		
Show:	☑	☑
Criteria:		
or:		

Figure 3-31 Not including the *AlbumName* field results in unique values

Show Option for Query Fields

Most of the time, you want all of the fields placed into the query design grid to display in the query results. Occasionally,

you don't want a field to display because it would show unnecessary or duplicated values. The query shown in Figure 3-32 displays all the songs that are on albums by "The Beatles".

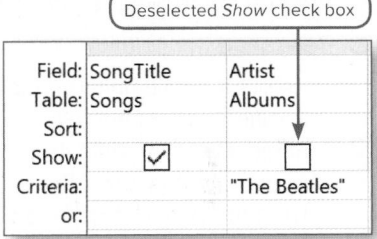

Figure 3-32 *Show* row check box for fields

This query produces a datasheet like that shown in Figure 3-33. The *Artist* field is needed in the query because you included a criterion on that field to limit the records displayed to songs by "The Beatles". But displaying the *Artist* is not really necessary here, because you know that all of these songs are by "The Beatles".

- To hide a query field in the query results, deselect the **Show** row check box in the query design grid of your query (Figure 3-34).

Song Title	Artist
Come Together	The Beatles
Something	The Beatles
Maxwell's Silver Hammer	The Beatles
Oh! Darling	The Beatles
Octopus's Garden	The Beatles
I Want You (She's So Heavy)	The Beatles
Here Comes the Sun	The Beatles
Because	The Beatles
You Never Give Me Your Money	The Beatles

Figure 3-33 Query results

In order to determine if a query is working correctly, first run the query with all fields displayed so you can verify the accuracy of the query. Only after you are confident with the query design should you deselect the *Show* row check box of the appropriate fields.

Apply Sorting

Access can display the results of a query in sorted order. You can sort on one or more fields.

- To sort the results of a query, click the **Sort** row cell of the desired field.
- Click the **drop-down arrow** and select **Ascending** or **Descending** (Figure 3-35).

Deselected *Show* check box

Field:	SongTitle	Artist
Table:	Songs	Albums
Sort:		
Show:	☑	☐
Criteria:		"The Beatles"
or:		

Figure 3-34 Deselect the *Show* row check box

> **MORE INFO**
>
> To remove sorting from a field, click the **Sort** row cell, click the **drop-down arrow**, and select **(not sorted)**.

Field:	ListingID	Address	City
Table:	Listings	Listings	Listings
Sort:			
Show:	☑	☑	Ascending
Criteria:			Descending
or:			(not sorted)

Figure 3-35 *Sort* option of a query

Access sorts data based on the order of the columns. If you are sorting on multiple fields, you need to decide the sorting order of the fields. For example, in a table containing a list of all properties for sale, a client may want the query results sorted by the *City*, *Construction*, and *SqFt* fields. Many possible combinations of sorted results are available in this instance. The two sort examples shown here use an *Ascending* sort order on each field.

Figure 3-36 shows results sorted first by *City*, next by *Construction*, and last by *SqFt*. The highlighted cells emphasize the impact of the sorting. Because *City* is the first sort field and alphabetically Auburn is the first city in the database, this results in all properties in Auburn appearing first. Within the "Auburn"

ListingID	Address	City	Construction	SqFt
10042	131 Aeolia Drive	Auburn	Brick	1905
10045	12355 Krista Lane	Auburn	Brick	2234
10040	3935 Cedar Mist Lane	Auburn	Frame	1056
10069	1255 Copperdale	Auburn	Frame	1456
10177	9030 Upper Valley Road	Auburn	Frame	2635
10144	863 Holly Hill Drive	Auburn	Frame	2876
10043	1575 Oak Ridge Way	Auburn	Stone	2266
10150	423 Welterwood	Lincoln	Brick	1482
10046	1735 Andover Lane	Lincoln	Brick	1552
10052	1096 Kinnerly Lane	Lincoln	Brick	1948
10074	1827 Delouch Drive	Lincoln	Brick	2575
10072	406 E Street	Lincoln	Frame	1100
10062	2811 Cardinal Drive	Lincoln	Frame	2061
10116	611 Ledgestone Court	Lincoln	Frame	2353

Figure 3-36 Records sorted by the *City*, *Construction* and *SqFt* fields

properties, homes made of brick appear first. Finally, within the "Auburn" and "Brick" properties, the property with the smallest square footage appears at the top of the list.

Figure 3-37 is sorted differently. In this example, the query is sorted first by *Construction*, next by *City*, and last by *SqFt*. In these results all properties with brick construction appear first. Within the "Brick" properties, those in Auburn appear first. Finally, within the "Brick" and "Auburn" properties, the smallest square footage appears at the top of the list.

ListingID	Address	Construction	City	SqFt
10042	131 Aeolia Drive	Brick	Auburn	1905
10045	12355 Krista Lane	Brick	Auburn	2234
10150	423 Welterwood	Brick	Lincoln	1482
10046	1735 Andover Lane	Brick	Lincoln	1552
10052	1096 Kinnerly Lane	Brick	Lincoln	1948
10074	1827 Delouch Drive	Brick	Lincoln	2575
10073	736 Oakdale	Brick	Newcastle	766
10166	1852 Wedgewood	Brick	Newcastle	2234
10031	2024 Brixham	Brick	Roseville	2385
10024	1917 Oak Crest Drive	Brick	Roseville	3397
10044	446 Manzanita Way	Brick	Weimer	1885
10040	3935 Cedar Mist Lane	Frame	Auburn	1056
10069	1255 Copperdale	Frame	Auburn	1456
10177	9030 Upper Valley Road	Frame	Auburn	2635
10144	863 Holly Hill Drive	Frame	Auburn	2876
10072	406 E Street	Frame	Lincoln	1100

Figure 3-37 Records sorted by the *Construction*, *City* and *SqFt* fields

▶ HOW TO: Sort a Query Using Multiple Fields

1. Add the fields into the query design grid from left to right based on the desired sort order.

2. Rearrange the column order by moving a column if the fields are already placed in the query design grid.

 - Select the column to be moved. The column turns black.
 - Position the pointer in the small cell above the field name. Click and hold the pointer. A black vertical line appears to the left of the selected column (Figure 3-38).
 - Drag the pointer to the new location. The line moves with you to indicate the location where the column will be moved.
 - Release the pointer to complete the move.

3. Click the **Sort** row cell, click the **drop-down arrow**, and select **Ascending** or **Descending** for each of the sort fields.

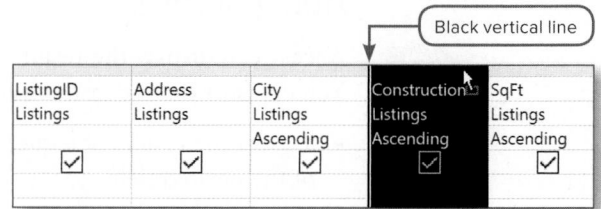

Figure 3-38 The black vertical line indicates the new location of the column

> ▶ MORE INFO
>
> When writing queries, you may need to combine sorting and show options. For example, you may wish to have the first sort field display in a different position in the query results. In this case, you would include the field twice. The first would be included to the left of the query to designate the *Sort* selection and to deselect the *Show* box. The same field would be added a second time in the desired position to show the value.

SLO 3.5

Defining Multiple Criteria in a Query

The previous examples created queries that used at most one condition or criterion. Many times, the questions that you want to ask about the data are more complex and require the use of compound criteria. *Compound criteria* combine more than one criterion using the *AND* or *OR* logical operators and enable you to ask questions using multiple conditions.

The AND Operator

The *AND* logical operator requires that a record meet all of the individual conditions specified in order to be included in the results. Use an *AND* condition in one field or across multiple fields.

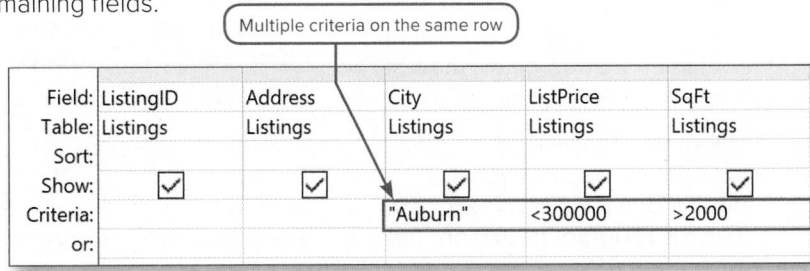

▶HOW TO: Use AND Compound Criteria in Multiple Fields

1. Click the **Criteria** row cell of the first field.
2. Type the text of the desired criterion expression.
3. Click the **Criteria** row cell of the second field.
4. Type the text of the second desired criterion expression.
5. Continue entering the criterion in the remaining fields.

- The query shown in Figure 3-39 finds the properties in Auburn that have a list price of less than $300,000 and have more than 2,000 square feet.
- Values entered in cells on the same *Criteria* row of the query design grid create an *AND* condition.

Multiple criteria on the same row

Field:	ListingID	Address	City	ListPrice	SqFt
Table:	Listings	Listings	Listings	Listings	Listings
Sort:					
Show:	☑	☑	☑	☑	☑
Criteria:			"Auburn"	<300000	>2000
or:					

Figure 3-39 Query criteria entered on the same row creates an *AND* condition

Occasionally, you need to use the *AND* operator in a single field. In these cases, the *AND* operator is typically combined with another comparison operator such as *Between*, > or <. Remember that all criterion included together on a row are treated as *AND* conditions.

▶HOW TO: Use AND Compound Criteria in a Single Field

1. Click the **Criteria** row cell of the field.
2. Type the text of the desired condition, including the word "AND" between each part of the condition.

- The query shown in Figure 3-40 finds listings with a square footage that is greater than or equal to 2,000 square feet and less than or equal to 3,000 square feet.
- This condition could also be written using the *Between* operator. The condition in Figure 3-41 uses *Between* and returns the same results as the condition shown in Figure 3-40, which uses the >= and <= operators.

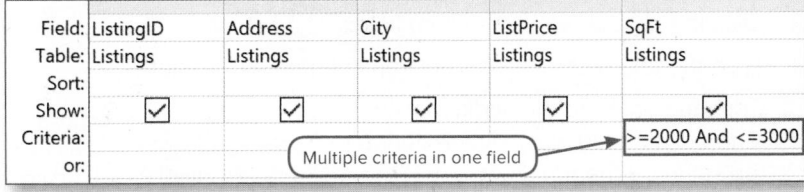

Field:	ListingID	Address	City	ListPrice	SqFt
Table:	Listings	Listings	Listings	Listings	Listings
Sort:					
Show:	☑	☑	☑	☑	☑
Criteria:					
or:			Multiple criteria in one field		>=2000 And <=3000

Figure 3-40 Use the word "AND" between compound criteria in the same field

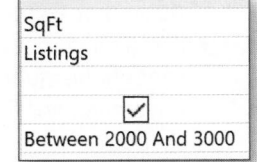

SqFt
Listings
☑
Between 2000 And 3000

Figure 3-41 *Between* operator

> ▶ MORE INFO
>
> The case used to write "AND" has no impact on the query. "AND" or "And" or "and" all evaluate the same.

The OR Operator

The *OR* logical operator requires a record to meet at least one of the individual conditions specified in order to be included in the results. With the *OR* operator you can specify multiple criterion in one field, or you can use compound criteria across several fields.

▶HOW TO: Use OR Compound Criteria in Multiple Fields

1. Click the **Criteria** row cell of the first field.

2. Type the text of the desired criterion expression.

3. Click the **or** row cell of the second field.

4. Type the text of the second desired criterion expression.

5. Continue entering criterion on the remaining fields, each time entering the value on the row below the last row you entered a value.

 - The query shown in Figure 3-42 finds the properties that are in Auburn or have a list price of less than $300,000 or have more than 2,000 square feet.

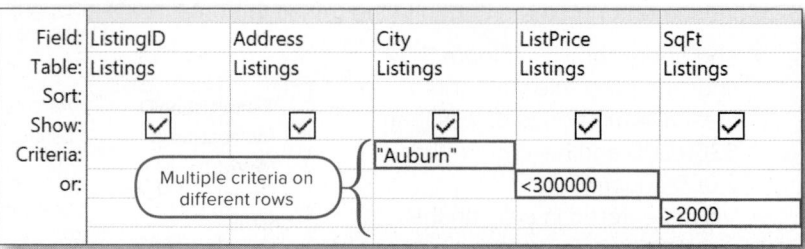

Field:	ListingID	Address	City	ListPrice	SqFt
Table:	Listings	Listings	Listings	Listings	Listings
Sort:					
Show:	☑	☑	☑	☑	☑
Criteria:			"Auburn"		
or:	Multiple criteria on different rows			<300000	
					>2000

Figure 3-42 Query criteria entered on different rows creates an *OR* condition

Entering multiple criteria in the same field is an *OR* condition. The returned records match the first value *or* the second value *or* the third value, and so on.

▶HOW TO: Use OR Compound Criteria in a Single Field

1. Click the **Criteria** row cell of the first field.

2. Type the text of the desired criterion expression.

3. Click the **or** row cell of the same field.

4. Type the text of the second desired criterion expression.

5. Continue entering the additional criterion in the field, each time entering the value on the next row.

 - The query shown in Figure 3-43 finds the properties that are in Auburn or Roseville.
 - If you save, close, and then reopen this query, Access will have changed the criteria to read "Auburn" Or "Roseville" in the one cell on the *Criteria* row instead

Field:	ListingID	Address	City	ListPrice	SqFt
Table:	Listings	Listings	Listings	Listings	Listings
Sort:					
Show:	☑	☑	☑	☑	☑
Criteria:			"Auburn"		
or:			"Roseville"		

Figure 3-43 Place compound criteria in separate rows of the same field to create an *OR* condition

of in two cells, as shown in Figure 3-43. If the query only has this type of criteria, you can type the *OR* criteria directly in one cell or on separate rows.

Combine the AND and OR Operators

You can create a query that combines both the *AND* and *OR* operators. These types of conditions can be logically complex. Keep in mind that all criterion included on a row are treated as *AND* conditions, while criterion entered on separate rows are treated as *OR* conditions.

Compare the queries in Figures 3-44 and 3-45. The query in Figure 3-44 returns all properties in Auburn that have a list price less than $300,000 and have more than 2,000 square feet or any property in Roseville, no matter the list price or square footage. The *ListPrice* and *SqFt*

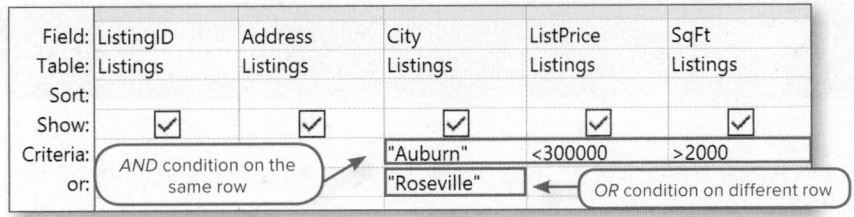

Figure 3-44 The *ListPrice* and *SqFt* criteria only apply to the city of Auburn

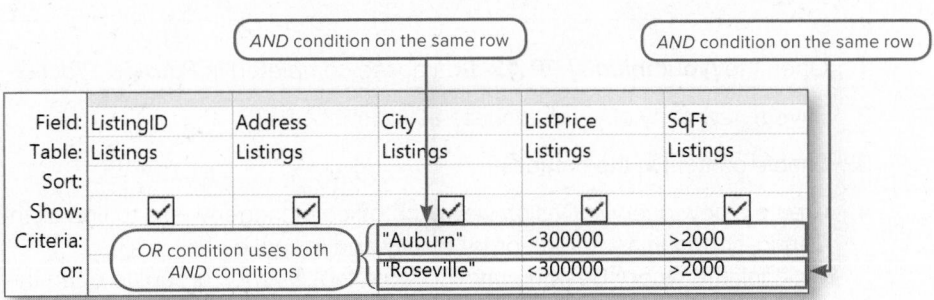

Figure 3-45 The *ListPrice* and *SqFt* criteria apply to both cities

criteria are only applied to the city of Auburn, because they are only included on the row with the *City* criterion for Auburn.

The query in Figure 3-45 returns all properties in Auburn that have a list price less than $300,000 and have more than 2,000 square feet, or all properties in Roseville that have a list price less than $300,000 and have more than 2,000 square feet. If you want to have the *ListPrice* and *SqFt* criteria apply to both cities, you need to repeat the criteria on both rows.

Finally, consider the query in Figure 3-46. This query returns all properties in Auburn that have a list price less than $300,000, or all properties in Roseville no matter their list prices or square footages, or all properties in Lincoln with square footage between 2,000 and 3,000 square feet.

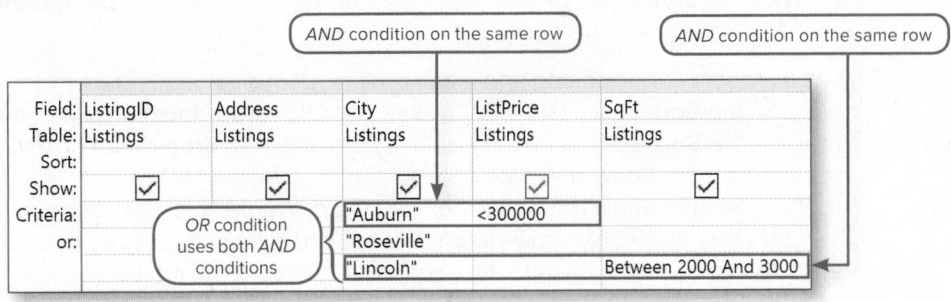

Figure 3-46 The *ListPrice* criteria apply to Auburn and the *SqFt* criteria apply to Lincoln

As these examples illustrate, compound conditions can become very complex. Spend the time to understand what you need the query to do before you attempt to build the query in Access. Now that you have learned about compound criteria, you can write more complex criteria. For example, in a music database you can now write a query to find songs where the word "I" is at the beginning, end, or in the middle of the title. Using the compound criteria of *Like "I *" Or Like "* I *" Or Like "* I"* would find songs that begin, contain, or end with the word "I".

For this Pause & Practice, you use *Design* view to create two additional queries for Placer Hills Real Estate.

File Needed: *[your initials] PP A3-1.accdb*
Completed Project File Name: *[your initials] PP A3-2.accdb*

1. Open the *[your initials] PP A3-1* database completed in *Pause & Practice 3-1*.

2. Save a new copy of your database as [your initials] PP A3-2.

3. Enable content in the database.

4. Create a new query in *Design* view. The office manager wants to find all the listings by agent Rick Chung, sorted in ascending order by city and list price.
 a. Click the **Query Design** button [*Create* tab, *Queries* group] to open the *Show Table* dialog box.
 b. Select the **Agents** table. Press and hold the **Shift** key and select the **Listings** table. Click the **Add** button.
 c. Click the **Close** button in the *Show Table* dialog box.
 d. Increase the size of the table objects to display all of the fields.
 e. Double-click the **FirstName** field from the *Agents* table in the *Query Design* window. The field is added to the first empty column in the query design grid.
 f. Double-click the **LastName** field to add it into the query design grid.
 g. Continue adding the following fields into the query design grid: **ListingID**, **SqFt**, **Address**, **City**, and **ListPrice**.

5. Click the **Save** button and save the query as ListingsByRickChung.

6. Add criteria to the query.
 a. Type Rick in the *Criteria* row cell of the *FirstName* field.
 b. Type Chung in the *Criteria* row cell of the *LastName* field.
 c. Click the **Run** button [*Query Tools Design* tab, *Results* group] to execute the query. The query should open in *Datasheet* view and display nine records.
 d. Click the **View** button [*Home* tab, *Views* group] and select the **Design View** option to switch back to *Design* view of the query.

7. Edit the query to add sorting and modify show options.
 a. Click the **Sort** row cell for the *City* field, click the **drop-down arrow**, and select **Ascending**.
 b. Click the **Sort** row cell for the *ListPrice* field, click the **drop-down arrow**, and select **Ascending**.
 c. Deselect the **Show** row check box for the *FirstName* field.
 d. Deselect the **Show** row check box for the *LastName* field. Because you tested the query in step 6, you know that it only shows Rick's listings, and it is not necessary to display that information.
 e. Save the changes made to the query. The query should look similar to Figure 3-47.

Field:	FirstName	LastName	ListingID	SqFt	Address	City	ListPrice
Table:	Agents	Agents	Listings	Listings	Listings	Listings	Listings
Sort:						Ascending	Ascending
Show:	☐	☐	☑	☑	☑	☑	☑
Criteria:	"Rick"	"Chung"					
or:							

Figure 3-47 *Design* view of the query criteria

f. Click the **Run** button [*Query Tools Design* tab, *Results* group] to execute the query. The query should open in *Datasheet* view and look similar to Figure 3-48.

g. Close the query.

8. Create a new query in *Design* view to help an agent locate the potential properties that meet the requirements of her client.

a. Click the **Query Design** button [*Create* tab, *Queries* group] to open the *Show Table* dialog box.

b. Select the **Listings** table and click the **Add** button.

c. Click the **Close** button in the *Show Table* dialog box.

d. Increase the size of the table object to display all of the fields.

e. Double-click the **ListingID** field to add it into the query design grid.

f. Continue adding the following fields into the query design grid: **Address**, **City**, **ListPrice**, **SqFt**, **Beds**, **Baths**, and **Garage**.

9. Save the query as ListingsForBrandonBuchanon.

10. Add criteria to the query. A client, Brandon Buchanon, is looking for homes in Rocklin or Roseville. The properties must have at least three bedrooms and at least two bathrooms and at least 1,800 square feet. Properties must have a garage, but it doesn't matter if it is attached or detached. In general, the list prices shouldn't exceed $550,000. However, if the house is in Rocklin, Brandon is willing to spend up to $600,000.

a. Type Rocklin in the *Criteria* row cell of the *City* field.

b. Type <=600000 in the *Criteria* row cell of the *ListPrice* field.

c. Type >=1800 in the *Criteria* row cell of the *SqFt* field, >=3 in the *Criteria* row cell of the *Beds* field, >=2 in the *Criteria* row cell of the *Baths* field, and Like "??Car*" in the *Criteria* row cell of the *Garage* field. Note that because the criterion for the *Garage* field requires two characters before "Car" it will exclude Carport from the results.

d. Type Roseville in the *or* row cell of the *City* field.

e. Type <=550000 in the *or* row cell of the *ListPrice* field.

f. Type >=1800 in the *or* row cell of the *SqFt* field, >=3 in the *or* row cell of the *Beds* field, >=2 in the *or* row cell of the *Baths* field, and Like "??Car*" in the *or* row cell of the *Garage* field. The completed criteria in the query design grid should match Figure 3-49.

Figure 3-48 *Datasheet* view of the *ListingsByRickChung* query results

Field:	Address	City	ListPrice	SqFt	Beds	Baths	Garage
Table:	Listings	Listings	Listings	Listings	Listings	Listings	Listings
Sort:							
Show:	☑	☑	☑	☑	☑	☑	☑
Criteria:		"Rocklin"	<=600000	>=1800	>=3	>=2	Like "??Car*"
or:		"Roseville"	<=550000	>=1800	>=3	>=2	Like "??Car*"

Figure 3-49 Completed query criteria in the query design grid

11. Add sorting to the query.

a. Select **Ascending** in the **Sort** row cell for the *City* field.

b. Select **Descending** in the **Sort** row cell of the *ListPrice* field.

12. Save the changes to the query and click the **Run** button [*Query Tools Design* tab, *Results* group] to execute the query. The query should open in *Datasheet* view and display the 11 records shown in Figure 3-50.

13. Close the query.

14. Close the database.

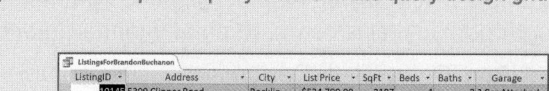

Figure 3-50 *Datasheet* view of the *ListingsFor BrandonBuchanon* query results

Creating and Using a Simple Parameter Query

SLO 3.6

The query examples covered so far in this chapter use criteria that have been entered into, or hardcoded into, the query. In *SLO 3.3: Adding a Criterion to a Query*, you saw a query that displayed all the property listings in Roseville—those that have a *City* listed as "Roseville". The criteria property box for that query had the value of "Roseville". What if you wanted to locate all the properties in Lincoln or all the properties in Auburn? You could create a separate query for each situation and enter the specific criteria value into each query. But this would not be very efficient.

It is more efficient to create a parameter query. A ***parameter query*** asks you to enter the specific criteria value when you run the query. This enables you to write one query but use it for many different values of the criteria. Figure 3-51 is an example of the *Enter Parameter Value* dialog box for the *City* field. When you see this box, enter the specific value, such as "Roseville" or "Lincoln", click **OK**, and the desired results are shown.

Figure 3-51 *Enter Parameter Value* dialog box

If you enter a value that is not located in the database, the query returns an empty datasheet.

To create a parameter query, you follow the same steps you learned to create a query with criteria. However, instead of entering a specific value for the criteria, you need to format the criteria expression so that Access prompts you for a ***parameter value***.

Create a Parameter

Parameters must follow a few simple rules.

- Your parameter is the specific phrase that you want to display in the dialog box, for example "Enter the City". Be sure to enter a phrase that gives clear instructions about the kind of information to enter into the dialog box, along with any formatting instructions.
- Enter your parameter into the *Criteria* row cell for the desired field.
- Enclose the parameter within square brackets.
- You can include a comparison operator, like < or >=, before the parameter.

▶ **HOW TO: Create a Parameter**

1. Select *Design* view of the query, and click the **Criteria** row cell of the desired field.

2. Type the parameter. An example parameter value is shown in Figure 3-52. You can use the *Expression Builder* to enter the parameter. This may be helpful when the parameter contains a longer phrase that is harder to enter into the *Criteria* row cell.

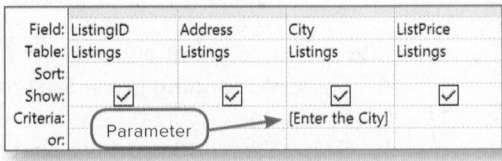

Figure 3-52 Sample parameter in the *Criteria* cell

3. Click **Run** [*Query Tools Design* tab, *Results* group] to execute the query. The *Enter Parameter Value* dialog box displays. Either press **Cancel** or enter a value and click **OK**.

> ▶ MORE INFO
>
> The actual phrase entered inside the square brackets has no impact on how the parameter and the query function. *[Enter the City]*, *[]*, and *[City?]* all collect the same information, but the first option is more user-friendly when it appears in the dialog box.

You can include more than one parameter in the same field if you need to enter multiple values. For example, a client at the Placer Hills Real Estate Company is looking for properties between 1,800 and 2,500 square feet. You already learned how to use the *Between* operator to write a compound criteria expression. To create a more flexible query, you can incorporate multiple parameters with the *Between* operator.

▶ HOW TO: Use Multiple Parameters in a Field

1. Select *Design* view of the query and click the **Criteria** row cell of the desired field.
2. Right-click and select **Zoom**, or press **Shift+F2**, to open the *Zoom* box.
3. Type the criteria expression including the parameters. An example expression using two parameters is shown in Figure 3-53.

ANOTHER WAY

The *Zoom* box is an alternative to the *Expression Builder*. It provides a larger area in which to enter an expression, but it does not show any of the *Expression Elements* displayed in the lower portion of the *Expression Builder*.

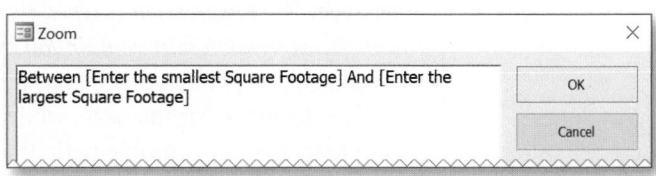

Figure 3-53 Example expression that contains two parameters in a field

4. Click **OK**.
5. Click **Run** [*Query Tools Design* tab, *Results* group] to execute the query. The first *Enter Parameter Value* dialog box displays (Figure 3-54).
6. Enter the value and click **OK**. The second *Enter Parameter Value* dialog box displays (Figure 3-55).

Figure 3-54 First *Enter Parameter Value* dialog box

Figure 3-55 Second *Enter Parameter Value* dialog box

7. Enter the value and click **OK**. After all the *Enter Parameter Value* dialog boxes have displayed, the query runs.

You can use parameters in more than one field in a query. For example, a realtor may want to locate the properties listed for sale in a specific city that have a list price less than a maximum dollar value. The realtor wants the query to prompt the user to specify the city and the maximum list price each time it runs. Figure 3-56 shows the query design grid for that query. When the query executes, the *Enter Parameter Value* dialog boxes display in the order that the fields are listed in the query. In this example, the *City* parameter displays before the *ListPrice* parameter. This example also includes the **<=** comparison operator with the *ListPrice* parameter.

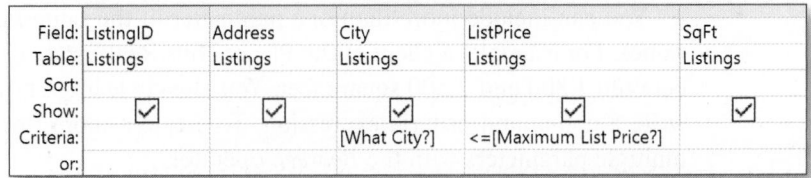

Field:	ListingID	Address	City	ListPrice	SqFt
Table:	Listings	Listings	Listings	Listings	Listings
Sort:					
Show:	☑	☑	☑	☑	☑
Criteria:			[What City?]	<=[Maximum List Price?]	
or:					

Figure 3-56 Query design grid with multiple parameters

The Parameter Data Type

The *Enter Parameter Value* dialog box accepts any type of input entered by the user. However, the data type of the field determines what is valid in terms of performing the actual comparison. Consider what happens when a letter is entered into the *Enter Parameter Value* dialog box of a field with a number data type. When Access executes the query, if the value entered into the dialog box doesn't match the data type of the field, by default Access displays the following message: *"The expression is typed incorrectly, or it is too complex to be evaluated. For example, a numeric expression may contain too many complicated elements. Try simplifying the expression by assigning parts of the expression to variables."*

The default error message, while absolutely correct in terms of content, may be confusing for a user. Also, it is problematic that even if you create multiple *Enter Parameter Value* dialog boxes, the message only shows once when the query is executed. The user doesn't know if he or she made only one mistake or several.

To make dialog boxes easier to understand, Access enables you to specify the data type that a parameter can accept. If you have specified a data type, and the user enters a value that doesn't match the data type, a more helpful error message displays (Figure 3-57).

Figure 3-57 Error message when the data type has been specified

If you specify the data type, Access also checks the data type when you click **OK** on the *Enter Parameter Value* dialog box. If the data type is not correct, after displaying the message box, Access returns you back to the *Enter Parameter Value* dialog box to re-enter an acceptable value.

▶ **HOW TO:** Specify the Parameter Data Type

1. Click the **Parameters** button [*Query Tools Design* tab, *Show/Hide* group] (Figure 3-58).

 - The *Query Parameters* dialog box opens.
 - Recall that the *Table Names* button is highlighted when the query design grid displays the *Table* row.

2. Click the first cell in the *Parameter* column.

3. Type the name of your parameter.

 - Make sure that you enter the text exactly as it appears in the *Criteria* property box.
 - The square brackets around the text are optional.

Figure 3-58 *Parameters* button

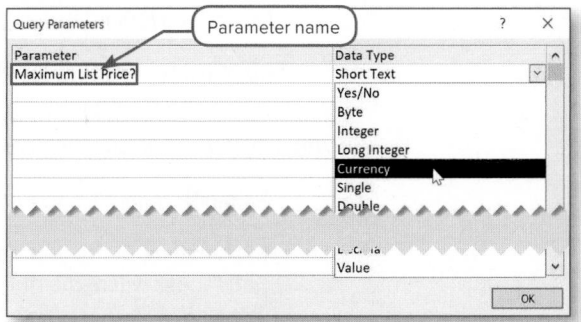

Figure 3-59 Assign a data type to a parameter

4. Click the **Data Type** cell, click the **drop-down arrow**, and select the correct data type (Figure 3-59).
5. Enter additional parameters in the dialog box if needed.
6. Click **OK** when you are finished.

Use Wildcards in a Parameter Query

You can use the *Like* comparison operator and wildcards in a parameter when writing the query criteria. Remember, the *Like* comparison operator helps you find records containing data that are similar to, or *like*, the criterion value. Recall that the * symbol represents any number of characters, the **?** represents any single character, and the **#** represents any single number.

Access provides three common ways to structure a criteria expression with a parameter that uses wildcards. You can include a wildcard character at the end, a wildcard character at the beginning, or a wildcard character at the beginning and the end. The following examples, using our music database scenario, illustrate each of these methods. These examples also introduce the **& *concatenation operator*** which combines, or concatenates, two text values into one.

- *Like [Enter Prompt Text Inside the Brackets] & " *"*

This parameter includes the * wildcard character at the end. It finds records where the data in the field begin with the value entered into the parameter. To limit the results to finding a complete word, the criteria include a space before the asterisk. This treats the parameter value entered as a separate word, not just letters.

Example: *Like [Enter the first word of the song] & " *"*

> **Explanation**: If the user enters "love" into the *Enter Parameter Value* dialog box, this query finds songs where the title starts with the word "love". For example, this query finds "Love for All Seasons" and "Love This Pain". However, it does not find the songs with the title of "Leave Love Alone", "Make You Feel My Love", or "Lovesong".

Compare the difference in the next example that removes the space before the asterisk.

Example: *Like [Enter the first word of the song] & "*"*

> **Explanation**: If the user enters "love" into the *Enter Parameter Value* dialog box, this query finds songs where the title starts with the first four letters "love". It still finds all the songs that begin with the word "love" but will now also find "Lovesong".

- *Like "* " & [Enter Prompt Text Inside the Brackets]*

This parameter includes the * wildcard character at the beginning. It finds records where the data in the field end with the value entered into the parameter. To limit the results to finding a complete word, the criteria include a space after the asterisk.

> **Example**: *Like "* " & [Enter the last word of the song]*
>
> **Explanation**: If the user enters "love" into the *Enter Parameter Value* dialog box, this query finds songs where the title ends in the word "love". For example, the query finds "Make You Feel My Love". It does not find "Love for All Seasons", "Leave Love Alone", or "50 Ways to Leave Your Lover".

- *Like "* " & [Enter Prompt Text Inside the Brackets] & " *"*

This parameter includes the * wildcard character at the beginning and at the end. It finds records where the data in the field contain the value entered into the parameter in the middle of the field. In this example, a space displays after the first asterisk, and a space displays before the second asterisk, which limits the results to finding the complete word.

> **Example**: *Like "* " & [Enter the song word] & " *"*
>
> **Explanation**: If the user enters "love" into the *Enter Parameter Value* dialog box, this query finds songs with titles that contain the word "love" in the middle. For example, the query finds "Leave Love Alone". It would not find "Love for All Seasons", "Make You Feel My Love", or "50 Ways to Leave Your Lover". The phrase inside the parameter was changed just to clarify the prompt. Recall that the phrase content has no impact on the query results.

The next example removes the spaces before and after the asterisks.

> **Example**: *Like "*" & [Enter the song word] & "*"*
>
> **Explanation**: If the user enters "love" into the *Enter Parameter Value* dialog box, this query finds songs with titles that contain the letters "love". This creates a very flexible query, because the user can enter only part of the parameter value. In this case, all the songs listed in the other examples would be located.

It is important to remember that the entry the user types in the *Enter Parameter Value* dialog box affects how the query functions. For example, with the criterion of *Like "*" & [Enter the song word] & "*"*, if you type "love" (with a space after the "e"), Access returns a different set of records than if the user types "love" or "love" (with two spaces).

This last example illustrates a powerful option for a database user. In addition to being able to enter all, or only part, of the parameter value to see the selected records, the user could leave the *Enter Parameter Value* dialog box blank to display all records.

For this reason, the parameter text for this option is often changed so the user knows this flexibility. For example, in the parameter above, the parameter text could read *[Enter the song word, or Leave blank to select all songs]*.

If you don't need the complete flexibility to enter part of the parameter value or to leave it blank, you could simplify the parameter by including the asterisk portion only at the beginning or at the end. Both of the following examples return all records if the *Enter Parameter Value* dialog box is left blank.

- *Like "*" & [Enter the song word, or Leave blank to select all songs]*
- *Like [Enter the song word, or Leave blank to select all songs] & "*"*

However, as you learned above, these two examples return different records depending on the parameter value entered.

You will most likely use the *Zoom* box (Figure 3-60) or *Expression Builder* to enter a parameter query that contains wildcards due to the length of the expression.

Zoom
Like [Enter the first word of the song] & " *"

Figure 3-60 The *Zoom* box provides a large area to enter a parameter

Adding Calculated Fields to a Query

SLO 3.7

A *calculated field* is a field that gets its value from a calculation instead of a value that is entered into the field. The calculation, or formula, can reference other fields in the database. For example, if a database that stores sales transactions contains the fields of *UnitPrice* and *Quantity*, the *Total Cost* of an item purchased is calculated by multiplying the *UnitPrice* by the *Quantity*.

Unlike a regular table field, a calculated field is not stored in the database. Why not simply store the *TotalCost* field in the database instead of having the database calculate it? To help avoid redundant data and ensure integrity in your database, most database designers recommend that you don't store fields in your database if the field can be calculated using data from other fields.

When writing a formula for a calculated field, use the traditional mathematical operators shown in Table 3-2. Remember that Access evaluates formulas using the standard order of operations. When more than one operator appears in an equation, Access evaluates the equation from left to right, performing calculations based on their precedence level.

Table 3-2: Order of Operations Characters and Precedence Level

Character	Operator	Order of Operation
()	Parentheses	First
^	Exponent	Second
*	Multiplication	Third
/	Division	Third
−	Subtraction	Fourth
+	Addition	Fourth

Enter a Formula in a Calculated Field

A formula for a query field has two parts that are separated by a colon (:). The first part is the name you assign to the calculated field. The second part is the formula, or what Access refers to as an expression. A generic example of a formula is written as *FieldName:Expression*. The expression can reference other fields and can include other **constants**, hardcoded values entered into a formula. The expressions must obey the following rules:

- Any fields included in the expression must be enclosed within square brackets.
- Any fields that are needed in the expression must be in tables included in the query.

For example, when you apply these rules to the *Total Cost* example described earlier, the formula for a calculated field that determines the *Total Cost* of an item is written as *TotalCost:[UnitPrice]*[Quantity]*.

▶HOW TO: Add a Calculated Field to a Query

1. Right-click the **first empty cell** in the *Field* row of the query design grid and select either **Zoom** to open the *Zoom* box or **Build** to open the *Expression Builder*.

2. Enter the formula following the rules described on the previous page.

 - Figure 3-61 is an example of a formula that calculates the potential commission on the sale of a home.
 - Notice the formula contains the name assigned to the field, a colon, and the expression.

3. Click **OK** in the *Zoom* box or *Expression Builder* when you are finished entering the formula.

Figure 3-61 Enter the formula for a calculated field

You can adjust the *Format* properties to change how the calculated field displays.

▶HOW TO: Format a Calculated Field in a Query

1. Click to select the **calculated field** in the query design grid.

2. Press **F4** to open the *Property Sheet* for that field.

3. Click the **Format** property box, click the **drop-down arrow**, and select the desired format option (Figure 3-62).

4. Click the **Decimal Places** property box and select the desired number of decimal places.

 - This property does not display for date and time formats.
 - If the *Decimal Places* property box does not display in the *Property Sheet* after selecting a numeric format option, you may need to first run the query and then return to *Design* view to enter a value.

5. Press **F4** to close the *Property Sheet*.

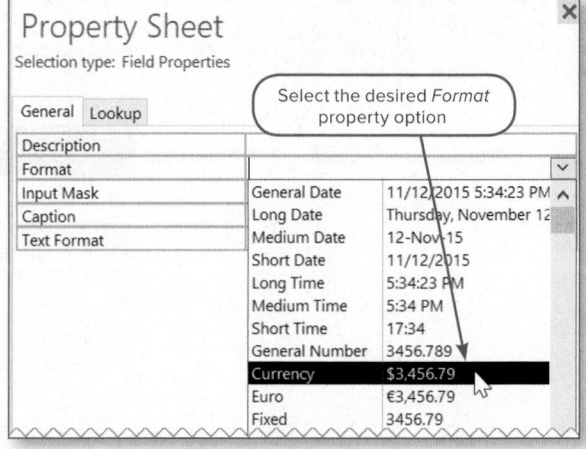

Figure 3-62 Format options

Remember to run your query to verify that your calculated field works as planned.

Troubleshoot Calculated Fields

You may encounter three common problems with a calculated field.

- An *Enter Parameter Value* dialog box displays when you run the query.

 If you are not expecting an *Enter Parameter Value* dialog box to display, pay attention to the contents of the parameter phrase. In Figure 3-63, the dialog box is asking the user to enter a value for "List Price".

Figure 3-63 *Enter Parameter Value* dialog box for the *List Price* field

In *Design* view, review the formula that you have entered into the calculated field. Notice in Figure 3-64 that the field name enclosed in the square brackets is *List Price*. Recall that the field in the database was actually named *ListPrice* (no space between *List* and *Price*).

If this occurs, edit the expression so that it includes valid field names.

Figure 3-64 Review the field name entered into the parameter

- A field is missing a name.

Each field must have a name. If you forget to include a field name when you enter the formula, Access assigns the field a generic field name such as *Expr1* by default. This default field name displays in both the query design grid (Figure 3-65) and the *Datasheet* view of the results (Figure 3-66). If this happens, edit the expression and change the field to an appropriate name.

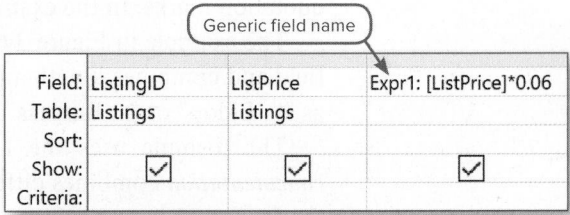

Figure 3-65 A generic field name like *Expr1* is assigned by Access if you do not name the field

- The formula does not provide the correct answer.

In cases like this, you need to review the structure of the formula. Make sure that you have used the correct fields and have written the formula correctly according to the order of operations.

ListingID ▾	List Price ▾	Expr1 ▾
10022	$337,600.00	$20,256.00
10023	$339,600.00	$20,376.00
10024	$675,000.00	$40,500.00

Figure 3-66 The *Expr1* field name in *Datasheet* view

Functions in a Calculated Field

Access provides a variety of ***functions***, predefined formulas to perform a specific task. Recall in *SLO 3.3: Adding a Criterion to a Query*, you used the *Date()* function as part of the query criteria. Functions can also be used in a formula. Access groups the functions by the type of task they perform. Table 3-3 highlights a few of the functions available in Access.

Table 3-3: Examples of Access Functions

Function	Category	Explanation
Max	SQL Aggregate	Finds the largest value
Round	Math	Rounds the value
UCase	Text	Converts the value to uppercase
Left	Text	Finds a specific number of characters from the left of the field
IIf	Program Flow	Performs a comparison and does one of two alternatives
Year	Date/Time	Returns the year portion of a date field

A function is typically included as part of a formula. This means that when you use a function, you need to follow the general rules about how to write a formula.

Some of the functions listed in this table are described in various chapters of the book but not all of the Access functions are introduced. If you are writing a complex formula, be sure to utilize the ***Access Help System*** to see if a function might make your task easier. In this section, to help you learn how to use a function in a calculated field, the *Left* function is introduced.

The *Left* function uses the format of *Left(string, length)*. Functions typically have different parameters, or arguments, that you must include with the function. The *Left* function has two parameters: **string** and **length**. The function analyzes the content of the string parameter and extracts a certain number of characters, as indicated in the length parameter, from the left of the string parameter. For example, *Left("California",2)* returns the value of "*Ca*", while *Left("California",5)* returns the value of "*Calif*".

Both the string and length parameters are required, and each can be either a field or a constant. You must enclose fields in square brackets, while text constants are enclosed in quotation marks. In the example, *Left([State],2)*, the *State* field is used as the string parameter.

The example in Figure 3-67 shows a formula that finds the first character of the *FirstName* field and combines it with a period, a space, and the *LastName*. This formula displays a name as "S. Bidou" or "J. Burgess".

The formula uses the *Left* function with the & concatenation operator. Recall that **concatenation** combines different parts of an equation together. You used the & operator with the *Like* special operator to combine different parts of an expression together in *SLO 3.6: Creating and Using a Simple Parameter Query*. Often, concatenation is used to combine different fields together. For example, use it to combine a first and last name, or to combine the city, state, and ZIP Code into one field.

▶ **HOW TO:** Use the Left Function in a Calculated Field

1. Add the fields from the database tables into the query grid.
2. Click the **first empty cell** in the *Field* row of the query design grid.
3. Right-click and select either **Zoom** to open the *Zoom* box or **Build** to open the *Expression Builder*.
4. Enter the formula, including the appropriate function.
 • The example in Figure 3-67 uses the *Left* function.
5. Click **OK** in the *Zoom* box or *Expression Builder* when finished entering the formula.

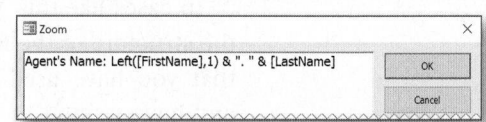

Figure 3-67 Example of a formula that uses the *Left* function

Remember to run your query to verify that your calculated field works. The most challenging part of working with a calculated field is not the actual process of entering the formula into a field. Rather, it is the process of determining what the formula must do, structuring the formula correctly, verifying the results, and fine-tuning the display formatting.

PAUSE & PRACTICE: ACCESS 3-3

For this Pause & Practice, you use *Design* view to create a query for Placer Hills Real Estate that uses calculated fields. Then, you save a copy of that query and modify it to include a parameter.

File Needed: *[your initials] PP A3-2.accdb*
Completed Project File Name: *[your initials] PP A3-3.accdb*

1. Open the *[your initials] PP A3-2* database completed in *Pause & Practice 3-2*.
2. Save a new copy of your database as [your initials] PP A3-3.

3. Enable content in the database.

4. Create a new query in *Design* view. The office manager wants to calculate the potential commission on the listed properties. The query should display the agent's name, listing ID, list price, and potential commission for each property. The agent's name should be formatted as the first initial, a period, a space, and the last name (for example, *J. Johnstone*). To help understand the logic behind queries, you build this query in stages.
 a. Click the **Query Design** button [*Create* tab, *Queries* group] to open the *Show Table* dialog box.
 b. Select the **Agents** table if needed, and click the **Add** button.
 c. Select the **Listings** table and click the **Add** button.
 d. Click the **Close** button in the *Show Table* dialog box.
 e. Increase the size of the table objects to display all of the fields.
 f. Right-click the **first empty cell** in the *Field* row of the query design grid and select **Build** to open the *Expression Builder*.
 g. Type Agent's Name:Left([FirstName], 1) & ". " & [LastName] in the *Expression Builder* box.
 h. Click **OK**.
 i. Drag the **ListingID** field into the second cell in the *Field* row of the query design grid.
 j. Drag the **ListPrice** field into the third cell in the *Field* row of the query design grid. Your completed query design grid should look similar to Figure 3-68.

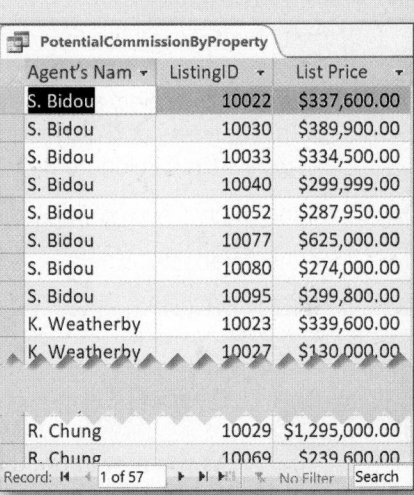

Field:	Agent's Name: I	ListingID	ListPrice
Table:		Listings	Listings
Sort:			
Show:	☑	☑	☑
Criteria:			
or:			

Figure 3-68 Query design grid

5. Click the **Save** button and save the query as PotentialCommissionByProperty.

6. Click the **Run** button [*Query Tools Design* tab, *Results* group] to execute the query. The query should open in *Datasheet* view and display all 57 records (Figure 3-69).

7. Adjust the width of the *Agent's Name* field.
 a. Right-click the **Agent's Name** cell to open the context menu and select **Field Width**.
 b. Click the **Best Fit** button.

PotentialCommissionByProperty

Agent's Nam ▼	ListingID ▼	List Price ▼
S. Bidou	10022	$337,600.00
S. Bidou	10030	$389,900.00
S. Bidou	10033	$334,500.00
S. Bidou	10040	$299,999.00
S. Bidou	10052	$287,950.00
S. Bidou	10077	$625,000.00
S. Bidou	10080	$274,000.00
S. Bidou	10095	$299,800.00
K. Weatherby	10023	$339,600.00
K. Weatherby	10027	$130,000.00
R. Chung	10029	$1,295,000.00
R. Chung	10069	$239,600.00

Record: ◄ ◄ 1 of 57 ► ►► ►◄ No Filter Search

Figure 3-69 Query results

8. Edit the query to add a field to calculate the potential commission and format that field.
 a. Click the **View** button [*Home* tab, *Views* group] and select the **Design View** option to switch back to *Design* view of the query.
 b. Right-click the **Field** cell of the fourth column and select **Zoom**.
 c. Type Potential Commission:[ListPrice]*.06 in the *Zoom* box.
 d. Click **OK**.
 e. Click to select the **Potential Commission** field if needed. Verify that the **Show** check box is selected.
 f. Press **F4** to open the *Property Sheet*. If the *Show* check box was not selected, the *Property Sheet* displays the query properties instead of the field properties.
 g. Click the **Format** property box, click the **drop-down arrow**, and select **Currency**.
 h. Press **F4** to close the *Property Sheet*.

9. Save and test the query.
 a. Click the **Save** button to save the changes to the query.
 b. Click the **Run** button [*Query Tools Design* tab, *Results* group] to execute the query. The query should open in *Datasheet* view. All 57 records display. Each record now also shows the new *Potential Commission* field (Figure 3-70).

10. Add a parameter to find properties by agent. Because the *Agents* table stores the data as first and last name, you need to add those fields to the query.
 a. Click the **View** button [*Home* tab, *Views* group] and select the **Design View** option to switch back to *Design* view.
 b. Double-click the **FirstName** field to add it into the query design grid.
 c. Double-click the **LastName** field to add it into the query design grid.
 d. Type [Enter the Agent's First Name] in the *Criteria* row cell for the *FirstName* field.
 e. Type [Enter the Agent's Last Name] in the *Criteria* row cell for the *LastName* field.
 f. Deselect the **Show** row check box for the *FirstName* field.
 g. Deselect the **Show** row check box for the *LastName* field.

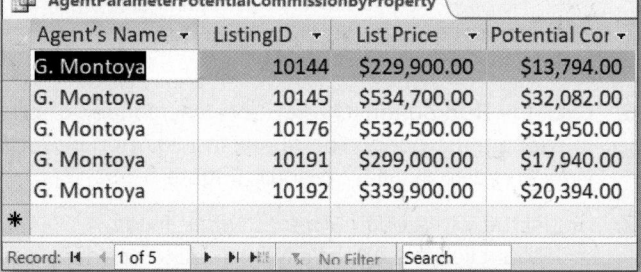

Agent's Name ▾	ListingID ▾	List Price ▾	Potential Cor ▾
S. Bidou	10022	$337,600.00	$20,256.00
S. Bidou	10030	$389,900.00	$23,394.00
S. Bidou	10033	$334,500.00	$20,070.00
S. Bidou	10040	$299,999.00	$17,999.94
S. Bidou	10052	$287,950.00	$17,277.00

Figure 3-70 Updated query results

11. Save a copy of the query.
 a. Click the **Save As** button [*File* tab].
 b. Select the **Save Object As** button and then click the **Save As** button.
 c. Replace the suggested name with AgentParameterPotentialCommissionByProperty and click **OK**.

12. Click the **Run** button [*Query Tools Design* tab, *Results* group].
 a. Enter Gerardo in the *Enter the Agent's First Name* box of the *Enter Parameter Value* dialog box.
 b. Click **OK**.
 c. Enter Montoya in the *Enter the Agent's Last Name* box of the *Enter Parameter Value* dialog box.
 d. Click **OK**. The query should open in *Datasheet* view and display the five records shown in Figure 3-71.

13. Close the query.

14. Close the database.

AgentParameterPotentialCommissionByProperty

Agent's Name ▾	ListingID ▾	List Price ▾	Potential Cor ▾
G. Montoya	10144	$229,900.00	$13,794.00
G. Montoya	10145	$534,700.00	$32,082.00
G. Montoya	10176	$532,500.00	$31,950.00
G. Montoya	10191	$299,000.00	$17,940.00
G. Montoya	10192	$339,900.00	$20,394.00

Record: ◄ ◄ 1 of 5 ► ►I ►► ⅞ No Filter Search

Figure 3-71 Parameter query results

SLO 3.8

Creating and Using a Summary Query

As you now know, queries help locate data in a database by asking a question. Up to this point, the queries you have worked with have all been structured to find sets of records. But, sometimes, the question that you want answered involves getting summarized results. For example, you may want to know the total number of Pop/Rock albums that you own, or the average listing price of properties for sale, or the total number of dogs available for adoption. A *summary query* analyzes a set of records and displays summarized results. Recall that you learned how to add a *Total* row to a table in *SLO 1.5: Exploring Datasheet View*. By including the totals in a summary query and not directly in the table, you can add criteria to narrow the summarized results.

Aggregate Functions

A summary query works by using an aggregate function. *Aggregate functions* perform calculations on a group of records. The most common aggregate functions are explained in Table 3-4. When used in a summary query, the function calculates an answer based only on the records that match the query's criteria.

Table 3-4: Common Aggregate Functions

Function	Explanation	Supported Data Types
Avg	Finds the average value of the field	*AutoNumber, Currency, Date/Time, Large Number, Number*
Count	Counts the number of records that have a value in the field	All data types
Max	Finds the maximum value of the field	*AutoNumber, Currency, Date/Time, Large Number, Number, Text*
Min	Finds the minimum value of the field	*AutoNumber, Currency, Date/Time, Large Number, Number, Text*
Sum	Finds the total value of the field	*AutoNumber, Currency, Date/Time, Large Number, Number*

> **MORE INFO**
>
> If the *Max* or *Min* function is used on a field with a **Short Text** data type, "A" is the smallest value and "Z" is the largest value.

Build a Summary Query

The basic building blocks of a summary query are the same as they are for the select queries you have already built. A summary query uses a **Total** row that is added into the query design grid of the query.

When you add a *Total* row to a query, each field in the query has the value in the *Total* row initially set to *Group By* (Figure 3-72). In most cases, you will change the *Group By* value to an appropriate aggregate function for at least one of the fields. If you don't change at least one of the fields, the query results show one record for each row of data. Generally, this is not your desired result in creating a summary query.

Figure 3-72 The *Total* row contains *Group By* or an aggregate function

Figure 3-73 shows the result of the query in Figure 3-72, with the *Total* row for all three fields set to *Group By*. The only difference between this query and one that doesn't include the *Total* row is that the results in this query are grouped by *City* and *Construction*.

If you change the query to use the *Avg* function in the *ListPrice* field, the query displays the results shown in Figure 3-74. Notice that the *Field Name* also changes to indicate the nature of the aggregate function. In this case, it changes to *AvgOfListPrice*.

This revised query answers the question "What is the average list price of homes, grouped by city and within each city by construction type?" Or, in other words, "By city and construction type, show the average price of the homes that are listed." Scanning through the results, you see that the highest average list price ($683,510) is for stone homes in Rocklin. The results also show that in Weimar, brick homes had the lowest average list price of $209,000.

City	Construction	List Price
Auburn	Brick	$274,500.00
Auburn	Brick	$385,000.00
Auburn	Frame	$229,900.00
Auburn	Frame	$239,600.00
Auburn	Frame	$299,999.00
Auburn	Frame	$329,900.00
Auburn	Stone	$357,000.00
Lincoln	Brick	$131,000.00
Lincoln	Brick	$287,950.00
Lincoln	Brick	$299,900.00
Lincoln	Brick	$329,900.00
Rocklin	Frame	$292,900.00
Rocklin	Frame	$299,800.00

Record: ◄ ◄ 1 of 57 ► ►► ⧉ No Filter Search

Figure 3-73 Query results when all fields use *Group By* in the *Total* row

City	Construction	AvgOfListPrice
Auburn	Brick	$329,750.00
Auburn	Frame	$274,849.75
Auburn	Stone	$357,000.00
Lincoln	Brick	$262,187.50
Lincoln	Frame	$448,657.14
Lincoln	Stone	$318,300.00
Newcastle	Brick	$459,800.00
Newcastle	Frame	$264,375.00
Newcastle	Stone	$489,000.00
Rocklin	Frame	$430,446.15
Rocklin	Stone	$683,510.00
Roseville	Brick	$521,752.50
Roseville	Frame	$387,116.67
Roseville	Stone	$359,833.33
Weimar	Stone	$307,600.00
Weimer	Brick	$209,000.00
Weimer	Frame	$227,450.00

Record: ◄ ◄ 1 of 17 ► ►► ⧉ No Filter Search

Figure 3-74 Query results with the *Avg* aggregate function

To be most effective, a summary query should include only the fields that you want to group by and the fields that you want to aggregate. For example, if you wish to find the average list price for each city, you must remove the *Construction* field from the query.

▶ **HOW TO:** Create a Summary Query

1. Click the **Query Design** button [*Create* tab, *Queries* group].
2. Select the first table to use in the query from the *Show Table* dialog box.
3. Click the **Add** button to add the table into the *Query Design* window.
4. Continue adding all required tables.
5. Click the **Close** button to close the *Show Table* dialog box.
6. Add the desired fields into the query design grid.
7. Click the **Totals** button [*Query Tools Design* tab, *Show/Hide* group] (Figure 3-75).
 - The *Total* row is added into the query design grid below the *Table* row.
 - The *Total* row value for each field in the query design grid is set to *Group By*.

> **MORE INFO**
>
> You cannot use the *Group By* choice in fields that have *Long Text*, *OLE Object*, and *Hyperlink* data types.

Figure 3-75 *Totals* button

Once you have created the summary query, you need to select the appropriate aggregate functions.

▶ HOW TO: Use an Aggregate Function in a Summary Query

1. Click the **Total** row cell of the desired field.
2. Click the **drop-down arrow** and select the desired aggregate function (Figure 3-76).
 - The query in Figure 3-76 answers the question "How many homes are listed for sale in each city, grouped by construction type?"
3. Repeat steps 1 and 2 for any additional fields that will be aggregated.

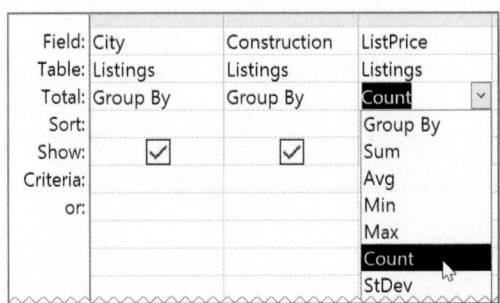

Figure 3-76 Select the aggregate function from the drop-down list

Occasionally, you may want to create a summary query where you want to see multiple calculations on the same field. For example, you may want to find the best and worst place finish that each member had in a race. Or for our real estate database, you might want to see the average, maximum, and minimum list price for all properties.

▶ HOW TO: Use Multiple Aggregate Functions on a Field

1. Click the **Total** row cell of the desired field.
2. Click the **drop-down arrow** and select the desired aggregate function.
3. Add the field into another column in the query design grid.
4. Click the **drop-down arrow** and select the desired aggregate function.
5. Continue adding the same field and selecting the aggregate function for as many calculations as you want to include.
 - Figure 3-77 shows an example of a query that aggregates the average, maximum, and minimum on the *ListPrice* field.
 - A sample of the query results is shown in Figure 3-78.

Figure 3-77 Include a field multiple times to use more than one aggregate function on the same field

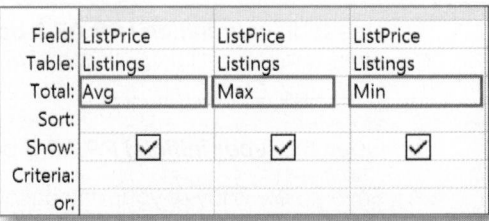

AvgOfListPrice ▾	MaxOfListPrice ▾	MinOfListPrice ▾
$382,245.16	$1,295,000.00	$104,900.00

Figure 3-78 Query results with multiple aggregate functions

A summary query can also include criteria to limit the results. For example, you may want to find the lowest-priced three-bedroom home in a specific city, or the average price of homes listed between two dates. When you use a summary query, the way that you include criteria changes a little. You need to select the *Where* option from the drop-down list of aggregate functions, in addition to adding the specific criteria.

▶ HOW TO: Use Criteria in a Summary Query

1. Click the **Total** row cell of the field that will have the criteria.
2. Click the **drop-down arrow** and select **Where**.
 - The *Show* row check box is deselected.
 - To include the criteria field in the query results, you must add that field into another column in the query design grid, leave *Group By* as the selection in the *Total* row, and click the **Show** row check box of that field.

3. Click the **Criteria** row cell of the field and enter the criteria.
 - Figure 3-79 shows an example of the query design grid that calculates and displays the average *ListPrice* for properties listed after *3/1/2020*.
 - The query results do not include the *DateListed* field because the *Show* row check box is deselected and the field was not added into another column in the query design grid.

Figure 3-79 Select the *Where* option in the *Total* row when using critieria in a summary query

In order to get the results you desire, you need to spend time planning the structure of a summary query before you build it. You must decide which fields to include in the query, which aggregate functions to use, and any additional criteria needed to limit the results.

PAUSE & PRACTICE: ACCESS 3-4

For this Pause & Practice, you create a summary query for the Placer Hills Real Estate Company.

File Needed: *[your initials] PP A3-3.accdb*
Completed Project File Name: *[your initials] PP A3-4.accdb*

1. Open the *[your initials] PP A3-3* database file completed in *Pause & Practice 3-3*.

2. Save a new copy of your database as [your initials] PP A3-4.

3. Enable content in the database.

4. Create a new summary query in *Design* view. The Placer Hills Real Estate Company wants to know the total number of properties each agent has listed and the average list price of those properties. It wants to display the agent's first and last name, as well as the two summary fields. To help you understand the logic behind queries, you build this query in stages.
 a. Click the **Query Design** button [*Create* tab, *Queries* group] to open the *Show Table* dialog box.
 b. Select the **Agents** table, press and hold the **Shift** key, select the **Listings** table, and click the **Add** button.
 c. Click the **Close** button in the *Show Table* dialog box.
 d. Increase the size of the table objects to display all of the fields.
 e. Click the **drop-down arrow** in the first *Field* row cell of the query design grid and select **Agents.FirstName**.
 f. Click the **second cell** in the *Field* row, click the **drop-down arrow**, and select **Agents.LastName**.
 g. Click the **third cell** in the *Field* row, click the **drop-down arrow**, and select **Listings.ListPrice**.
 h. Click the **fourth cell** in the *Field* row, click the **drop-down arrow**, and select **Listings.ListPrice**. (Yes, you add this field twice!)
 i. Click the **Totals** button [*Query Tools Design* tab, *Show/Hide* group] to add the *Total* row to the query.

5. Add the aggregate functions into the query.
 a. Click the **Total** row cell of the first *ListPrice* field.
 b. Click the **drop-down arrow** and select **Count**.

c. Click the **Total** row cell of the second
 ListPrice field.
d. Click the **drop-down arrow** and select **Avg**.
 The completed query design grid should
 look similar to Figure 3-80.

6. Click the **Save** button and save the query as
 ListingCountAndAvgListPriceByAgent.

Figure 3-80 Aggregate functions added to query

7. Click the **Run** button [*Query Tools Design* tab, *Results* group] to execute the query. The query should
 open in *Datasheet* view and display 7 records.

8. Adjust the column width of the *CountOfListPrice* and *AvgOfListPrice* fields to display the entire col-
 umn name.
 a. Select the **CountOfListPrice** column, right-click to open the context menu, and select
 Field Width.
 b. Click **Best Fit**.
 c. Select the **AvgOfListPrice** column,
 right-click to open the context
 menu, and select **Field Width**.
 d. Click **Best Fit**. The *Datasheet* view
 should be similar to Figure 3-81.

9. Click the **Save** button to save the
 changes.

10. Close the query.

11. Close the database.

ListingCountAndAvgListPriceByAgent			
FirstName ▾	LastName ▾	CountOfListPrice ▾	AvgOfListPrice ▾
Gerardo	Montoya	5	$387,200.00
Jack	Johnstone	9	$406,513.33
John	Burgess	5	$381,800.00
Kallyn	Duarte	8	$408,188.13
Kelly	Weatherby	13	$355,007.69
Rick	Chung	9	$395,000.00
Simon	Bidou	8	$356,093.63

Record: ◄ ◄ 1 of 7 ► ►│ ►▸ ⛉ No Filter Search

Figure 3-81 Query results for summary query

Chapter Summary

3.1 Understand queries and use the *Simple Query Wizard* to create and run a query (p. A3-162).

- Use **queries** to find data in your database.
- Build queries from tables, other queries, or both.
- Use the **Simple Query Wizard** to quickly build a query by specifying the tables or queries to use and then selecting the desired fields from those objects.
- Edit a query created with the *Simple Query Wizard* in *Design* view.

3.2 Create a query in *Design* view, add fields, and save and run a query (p. A3-163).

- The **Query Design** button opens *Design* view to build queries.
- *Design* view provides the most flexibility when creating queries.
- Add tables or queries into the *Query Design* window by selecting them from the *Show Table* dialog box.
- Add fields into the **query design grid** if you want them to appear in the query.
- Run a query to execute the query and have the query locate records in the database.
- Query results display in *Datasheet* view.
- Save each query with a unique name.

3.3 Add criterion into a query, use comparison operators, and create criteria with wildcards (p. A3-169).

- Add criterion into a query to search for specific records.
- Enter a criterion **expression** into the *Criteria* row of the query design grid. Type the expression directly into a *Criteria* row cell, or enter it using the **Expression Builder**.
- Expressions can include the standard **comparison operators**.
- Combine the **Like** comparison operator with the *?*, ***, and *#* **wildcard characters** for greater flexibility in the criterion value.

3.4 Integrate sorting and limiting fields and records that display (p. A3-175).

- Set the **Unique Values** property to have Access evaluate the fields in the query and avoid including duplicated values.
- The **Unique Records** property checks all the fields in a table, not just those included in the query.

- Deselecting the *Show* row check box prevents a field from displaying in the query results.
- Sort query results in ascending or descending order in one or more fields.
- If sorting on multiple fields, the fields must be placed into the query design grid in order of sort priority.

3.5 Use the *AND* and *OR* operators to include multiple criteria in a query (p. A3-178).

- **Compound criteria** combine more than one criterion using the **AND** and **OR** operators; this enables you to create a more complex query.
- Criteria written in different fields but on the same criteria row are evaluated as an *AND* comparison.
- Criteria written on different criteria rows are evaluated as an *OR* comparison.
- Combine *AND* and *OR* operators in one query.

3.6 Create and use a parameter query (p. A3-184).

- A **parameter query** asks the user to enter a specific criteria value at the time the query is run.
- When a parameter query is included, the *Enter Parameter Value* dialog box displays before the query executes.
- The **parameter** is the text phrase you enter into the *Criteria* row cell of the field. You must enclose the parameter in square brackets.
- A query can include multiple parameters, on one or more fields.
- If you specify the data type of the parameter, Access displays a more user-friendly message if a user makes an error when entering the parameter value.
- Combine the *Like* comparison operator with wildcard characters for increased flexibility in a parameter.

3.7 Build a query that uses a calculated field (p. A3-189).

- **Calculated fields** get their value from a calculation instead of being stored in a table.
- Use a calculated field instead of a table field if the database can calculate the field's value using data stored in other fields.
- Add a calculated field into the query design grid of a query.
- The formula expression for a calculated field is in the format *FieldName:Expression*.

- Formulas use the standard mathematical operators and order of operations.
- Access provides a variety of **functions**, which are predefined formulas that perform a specific task.
- Include a function as part of an expression in a calculated field.

3.8 Create and use a summary query using aggregate functions (p. A3-194).

- A **summary query** analyzes a set of records and then displays summarized results.
- Add a *Total* row into a query to turn it into a summary query.
- Summary queries use **aggregate functions**, functions that perform calculations on a group of records.

- Common aggregate functions include *Avg*, *Count*, *Max*, *Min*, and *Sum*.
- Summary queries can summarize several different fields or perform different calculations on the same field.

Check for Understanding

The SIMbook for this text (within your SIMnet account) provides the following resources for concept review:

- Multiple-choice questions
- Short answer questions
- Matching exercises

Guided Project 3-1

You have built a database to store information about a friend's music collection. You want to write three queries to help answer questions about the songs in the database. To ensure consistency, the starting file is provided for you. Use *the Simple Query Wizard* to create a query, use *Design* view to edit the query, and add criteria. After saving and testing the query, save a copy of the query to add a parameter. Finally, create a third query that includes summary query capabilities.
[**Student Learning Outcomes 3.1, 3.2, 3.3, 3.4, 3.5, 3.6, 3.8**]

File Needed: ***MusicDatabase-03.accdb*** *(Student data files are available in the* Library *of your SIMnet account.)*
Completed Project File Name: *[your initials] Access 3-1.accdb*

Skills Covered in This Project

- Create a query using the *Simple Query Wizard*.
- Edit a query in *Design* view.
- Add compound criteria to a query.
- Execute a query.
- Save a query.
- Add a parameter to a query.
- Sort query results.
- Edit a query to add an aggregate function.

1. Open the ***MusicDatabase-03.accdb*** database file.

2. Save a new copy of your database as [your initials] Access 3-1.

3. Enable content in the database.

4. Open the *Albums* table in *Datasheet* view to view the contents. You should see 50 different records.

5. Click the **plus sign** to the left of *AlbumID 1*, to see the 13 songs that are on Taylor Swift's *1989* album.

6. Close the table.

7. Create a new query using the *Simple Query Wizard*.
 a. Click the **Query Wizard** button [*Create* tab, *Queries* group] to launch the *Query Wizard*.
 b. Select **Simple Query Wizard** in the *New Query* dialog box.
 c. Click **OK** to launch the *Simple Query Wizard* (Figure 3-82).
 d. Select **AlbumName** in the *Available Fields* window.
 e. Click the **Move Single Field** button to move the field into the *Selected Fields* window.
 f. Select **Artist** in the *Available Fields* window.
 g. Click the **Move Single Field** button.
 h. Continue moving over the **Genre** and **ReleaseDate** fields.
 i. Click the **Tables/Queries** drop-down arrow and select the **Songs** table.

Figure 3-82 *Simple Query Wizard*

j. Select **SongTitle** in the *Available Fields* window.
k. Click the **Move Single Field** button. The completed *Selected Fields* window should match Figure 3-83.
l. Click the **Next** button. The second page of the *Simple Query Wizard* displays. Because of the relationship between the two tables, Access asks you whether you want a detail or summary query.
m. Leave the radio button selected for **Detail** and click the **Next** button.
n. Change the title in the *Title* box to SongsOnAlbums.
o. Click **Finish** to save and run the query. The query results should match those shown in Figure 3-84, displaying 634 total records.

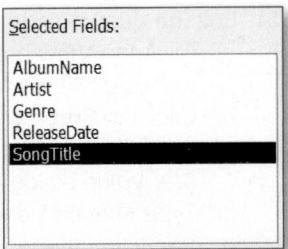

Figure 3-83 Completed *Selected Fields* window

Album Name	Artist	Genre	ReleaseDate	Song Title
1989	Taylor Swift	Pop	27-Oct-14	Welcome to New York
1989	Taylor Swift	Pop	27-Oct-14	Blank Space
1989	Taylor Swift	Pop	27-Oct-14	Style
1989	Taylor Swift	Pop	27-Oct-14	Out of the Woods
1989	Taylor Swift	Pop	27-Oct-14	All You Had to Do Was Stay
1989	Taylor Swift	Pop	27-Oct-14	Shake It Off
When We Were Young	Lady Antebellum	Country	3-Sep-11	Friday Night
Own the Night	Lady Antebellum	Country	13-Sep-11	When You Were Mine
Own the Night	Lady Antebellum	Country	13-Sep-11	Cold As Stone

Record: 1 of 634 No Filter Search

Figure 3-84 Query results of *SongsOnAlbums* query

8. Edit the query in *Design* view to add criteria to find songs on pop albums released after 1/1/2017.
 a. Click the **View** button [*Home* tab, *Views* group] and select the **Design View** option to switch back to *Design* view of the query.
 b. Type Pop in the *Criteria* row cell of the *Genre* field.
 c. Tab out of that field. Notice that Access automatically puts quotation marks around the text criteria.
 d. Click the **Run** button [*Query Tools Design* tab, *Results* group] to run the query. The query should open in *Datasheet* view and display the 191 songs that were on pop albums.
 e. Switch back to *Design* view and type >=#1/1/2017# in the *Criteria* row cell of the *ReleaseDate* field.
 f. Click the **Run** button [*Query Tools Design* tab, *Results* group]. The query should display 36 songs from Taylor Swift's *Reputation*, Lorde's *Melodrama*, and Sam Smith's *The Thrill of It All* albums.

9. Save a copy of the query.
 a. Click the **Save As** button [*File* Tab].
 b. Select the **Save Object As** button and then click the **Save As** button.
 c. Replace the suggested object name in the *Save 'SongsOnAlbums' to* box with SongsOnPopAlbumsAfterJan2017.
 d. Click **OK**.
 e. Close the query.

10. Edit the *SongsOnAlbums* query in *Design* view to add a parameter for the *Artist* field.
 a. Locate the *Queries* group of the *Navigation Pane*, and select the **SongsOnAlbums** query. Right-click to open the context menu and select the **Design View** option to open the query in *Design* view.
 b. Type [Show songs by which Artist?] in the *Criteria* row cell of the *Artist* field.
 c. Click the **Run** button [*Query Tools Design* tab, *Results* group] to run the query. The *Enter Parameter Value* dialog box displays.
 d. Type Maroon 5 and click **OK** (Figure 3-85). The query should open in *Datasheet* view and display the 67 songs on albums released by Maroon 5.

Figure 3-85 *Enter Parameter Value* dialog box

11. Edit the query to add sorting.
 a. Click the **View** button [*Home* tab, *Views* group] and select the **Design View** option to switch back to *Design* view of the query.
 b. Click the **Sort** row cell of the *ReleaseDate* field, click the **drop-down arrow**, and select **Descending**.
 c. Click the **Run** button [*Query Tools Design* tab, *Results* group] to run the query. The *Enter Parameter Value* dialog box displays.
 d. Type Maroon 5 and click **OK**.
 e. Verify that the results display in descending order on the *ReleaseDate* field.

12. Save a copy of the query.
 a. Click the **Save As** button [*File* Tab].
 b. Select the **Save Object As** button and then click the **Save As** button.
 c. Replace the suggested object name in the *Save 'SongsOnAlbums' to* box with SongCountArtistParameter.

13. Edit the query to add a *Total* row.
 a. Click the **View** button [*Home* tab, *Views* group] and select the **Design View** option to switch back to *Design* view of the query.
 b. Click the **Totals** button [*Query Tools Design* tab, *Show/Hide* group].
 c. Click the **Total** row cell for the *SongTitle* field.
 d. Click the **drop-down arrow** and select **Count**.

14. Click the **Save** button to save the query.

15. Test the query.
 a. Click the **Run** button [*Query Tools Design* tab, *Results* group] to run the query. The *Enter Parameter Value* dialog box displays.
 b. Type Maroon 5 and click **OK**. The query should open in *Datasheet* view and display the *CountOfSongTitle* on the five albums by Maroon 5.
 c. Extend the width of the *ReleaseDate* and *CountofSongTitle* columns so that your datasheet is similar to Figure 3-86.
 d. Save the changes to query.

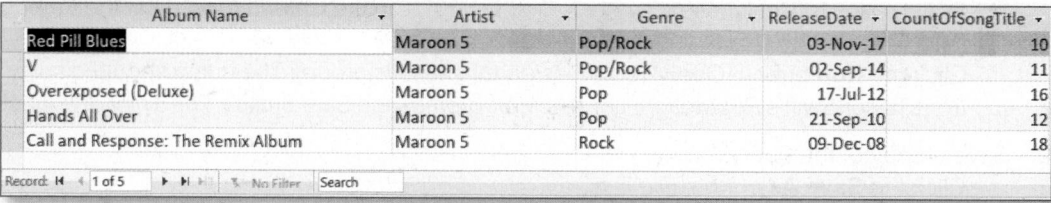

Figure 3-86 Query results with *Count* aggregate function

16. Close the query.

17. Close the database.

Guided Project 3-2

San Diego Sailing Club wants to create three queries. To ensure consistency, the starting file is provided for you. Use *Design* view to create, edit, add aggregate functions, and add criteria to a query to find the total dollar value of the rentals for each boat in its fleet. After saving and testing the query, create a second query that uses aggregate functions and a parameter. Finally, create a query to find which boat types have been rented.
[Student Learning Outcomes 3.2, 3.3, 3.4, 3.5, 3.6, 3.8]

File Needed: **SanDiegoSailing-03.accdb** *(Student data files are available in the* Library *of your SIMnet account.)*
Completed Project File Name: *[your initials] Access 3-2.accdb*

Skills Covered in This Project

- Create a query using *Design* view.
- Add fields to a query.
- Add criteria to a query.
- Execute a query.

- Save and test a query.
- Save a copy of a query.
- Add a parameter.
- Use aggregate functions.
- Use the *Unique Values* property.

1. Open the **SanDiegoSailing-03.accdb** database file.

2. Save a new copy of your database as [your initials] Access 3-2.

3. Enable content in the database.

4. Create a new summary query in *Design* view. The Sailing Club wants to find out the total dollar value of the full day rentals, by boat, from the boats that have been rented. If a boat has been rented, a record displays in the *SDRentals* table.
 a. Click the **Query Design** button [*Create* tab, *Queries* group] to open the *Show Table* dialog box.
 b. Select the **SailboatFleet** table and click the **Add** button.
 c. Select the **SDRentals** table and click the **Add** button.
 d. Click the **Close** button in the *Show Table* dialog box.
 e. Increase the size of the table objects to display all of the fields.
 f. Click the **drop-down arrow** in the first *Field* row cell of the query design grid and select **SDRentals.FKBoatID**.
 g. Click the **second cell** in the *Field* row, click the **drop-down arrow**, and select **SailboatFleet.BoatType**.
 h. Click the **third cell** in the *Field* row, click the **drop-down arrow**, and select **SailboatFleet.FullDayRentalRate**.
 i. Click the **fourth cell** in the *Field* row, click the **drop-down arrow**, and select **SDRentals.FourHourRental?**.
 j. Click the **Totals** button [*Query Tools Design* tab, *Show/Hide* group].
 k. Click the **Run** button [*Query Tools Design* tab, *Results* group] to execute the query. The query should open in *Datasheet* view and display 16 records (Figure 3-87). This query only shows boats that have been rented. At most, a *Boat ID* appears in two rows; one row if the *Four Hour Rental?* box is checked and another row if the *Four Hour Rental?* box is not checked.

Boat ID	Boat Type	Full Day Rate	Four Hour Re
1010	Catalina 270	$179.00	✓
1010	Catalina 270	$179.00	
1015	Catalina 270	$179.00	✓
1015	Catalina 270	$179.00	
1146	Hunter 33	$349.00	
1150	Capri 22 Mk II	$89.00	✓
1152	Capri 22 Mk II	$89.00	✓
1152	Capri 22 Mk II	$89.00	
1164	Capri 22 Mk II	$89.00	✓
1168	Hunter 33	$349.00	
1185	Hunter 36	$389.00	
1225	Hunter 36	$389.00	✓
1225	Hunter 36	$389.00	
1310	Beneteau 373	$409.00	
1401	Capri 22 Mk II	$89.00	✓
1419	Hunter 33	$349.00	✓

Record: ◄ ◄ 1 of 16 ► ►► ►► No Filter Search

Figure 3-87 Sailboat query results

5. Edit the query to add aggregate functions. Because you are looking only for rentals that were for a full day, use the "No" value on the *FourHourRental?* field.
 a. Click the **View** button [*Home* tab, *Views* group] and select the **Design View** option to switch back to *Design* view of the query.
 b. Click the **Total** row cell for the *FullDayRentalRate* field.
 c. Click the **drop-down arrow** and select **Sum**.
 d. Click the **Total** row cell for the *FourHourRental?* field.
 e. Click the **drop-down arrow** and select **Where**. This causes the *Show* row check box for the *FourHourRental?* field to be deselected.
 f. Click the **Criteria** row cell for the *FourHourRental?* field and enter No. The *IntelliSense* feature in Access may suggest the value of "Now" while you are typing. Press the **Esc** key to hide the list and then tab out of the field. The query window should look similar to Figure 3-88.

Field:	FKBoatID	BoatType	FullDayRentalRa	FourHourRental
Table:	SDRentals	SailboatFleet	SailboatFleet	SDRentals
Total:	Group By	Group By	Sum	Where
Sort:				
Show:	☑	☑	☑	☐
Criteria:				No
or:				

Figure 3-88 Query design grid for the summary query with criteria

g. Click the **Run** button. The query should open in *Datasheet* view and display eight records (Figure 3-89). The *Boat ID* now displays only once because the criteria limits the results only to the full day rentals.

Boat ID ▾	Boat Type ▾	SumOfFullDa ▾
1010	Catalina 270	$895.00
1015	Catalina 270	$179.00
1146	Hunter 33	$698.00
1152	Capri 22 Mk II	$178.00
1168	Hunter 33	$349.00
1185	Hunter 36	$389.00
1225	Hunter 36	$1,556.00
1310	Beneteau 373	$409.00

Record: I◄ ◄ 1 of 8 ► ►I ►❋ ☜ No Filter Search

Figure 3-89 Results from completed *SummaryOfFullDayRentalsByBoat* query

6. Click the **Save** button and save the query as FullDayRentalsByBoatSummary.

7. Verify that that query works correctly.
 a. Open the *SDRentals* table in *Datasheet* view.
 b. Click the **drop-down arrow** in the *Boat ID* field name cell and select the **Sort A to Z** option.
 c. Click the **drop-down arrow** in the *Four Hour Rental?* field name cell and select the **Sort Cleared to Selected** option. You can see that *Boat ID 1010* has five full day rentals. From Figure 3-87 you know that the full day rate for that boat is $179.00 and 5 × $179 = $895.00. This matches the results of your query.
 d. Click the **Remove Sort** button [*Home* tab, *Sort & Filter* group].
 e. Close the *SDRentals* table. If prompted, do not save the changes to the table.

8. Save a copy of the query.
 a. Click the **Save As** button [*File* Tab].
 b. Select the **Save Object As** button and then click the **Save As** button.
 c. Replace the suggested name with FullDayRentalsByBoatSummaryWithParameter. This second query will enable the Sailing Club to enter the date range for the summary query and also will count the number of rentals.

9. Edit the query to add additional fields and an aggregate function and parameters.
 a. Click the **Design View** icon in the *Status* bar.
 b. Drag the **FullDayRentalRate** field from the *SailboatFleet* table to the fifth column in the query design grid. (Yes, this field is in the query twice!)
 c. Click the **Total** row cell for this field, click the **drop-down arrow**, and select **Count**.
 d. Drag the **RentalDate** field from the *SDRentals* table to the sixth column in the query design grid.
 e. Click the **Total** row cell for this field, click the **drop-down arrow**, and select **Where**. This causes the *Show* row check box for the *RentalDate* field to be deselected.
 f. Click the **Criteria** row cell of the *RentalDate* field.
 g. Right-click and select **Zoom**.
 h. Type Between [Enter the Start Date] And [Enter the End Date] in the *Zoom* box to add the two parameters.
 i. Click **OK**. The query window should look similar to Figure 3-90.
 j. Click the **Save** button and save the changes to the query.

10. Test the query.
 a. Click the **Run** button.
 b. Enter 2/1/2020 in the *Enter the Start Date* box of the *Enter Parameter Value* dialog box.

Field:	FKBoatID	BoatType	FullDayRentalRate	FourHourRental?	FullDayRentalRate	RentalDate
Table:	SDRentals	SailboatFleet	SailboatFleet	SDRentals	SailboatFleet	SDRentals
Total:	Group By	Group By	Sum	Where	Count	Where
Sort:						
Show:	☑	☑	☑	☐	☑	☐
Criteria:				No		Between [Enter
or:						

Figure 3-90 Query window with aggregate functions and a parameter

c. Click **OK**.
d. Enter 2/28/2020 in the *Enter the End Date* box of the *Enter Parameter Value* dialog box.
e. Click **OK**. The query should open in *Datasheet* view and display the records shown in Figure 3-91.

Boat ID ▾	Boat Type ▾	SumOfFullDa ▾	CountOfFull ▾
1010	Catalina 270	$716.00	4
1015	Catalina 270	$179.00	1
1152	Capri 22 Mk II	$89.00	1
1185	Hunter 36	$389.00	1

Record: ◄ ◄ 1 of 4 ► ►I ►▣ No Filter Search

Figure 3-91 Query results with *Sum* and
Count aggregate functions and parameter

f. Click the **Save** button to save the changes made to the query.
g. Close the query.

11. Review the *FullDayRentalsByBoatSummaryWithParameter* query.
 a. Reopen the query in *Design* view. Notice that Access has reordered the position of the fields. The two fields (*FullDayRentalRate* and *RentalDate*) that use the *Where* option on the *Total* row have been moved to the right side of the query design grid. This does not affect the way the query runs.
 b. Close the query.

12. Create a new query in *Design* view. The Sailing Club wants to find out what boat types have been rented so it can decide whether to adjust pricing or marketing of its boat types. If a boat has been rented, a record of that rental exists in the *SDRentals* table.
 a. Click the **Query Design** button [*Create* tab, *Queries* group] to open the *Show Table* dialog box.
 b. Select the **SDRentals** table if needed, press and hold the **Shift** key, select the **SailboatFleet** table, and click the **Add** button.
 c. Click the **Close** button in the *Show Table* dialog box.
 d. Click the **drop-down arrow** in the first *Field* row cell in the query design grid and select **SDRentals.FKBoatID**.
 e. Click the **Sort** row, click the **drop-down arrow**, and select **Ascending**.
 f. Click the **second cell** in the *Field* row, click the **drop-down arrow**, and select **SailboatFleet.BoatType**.
 g. Click the **Run** button [*Query Tools Design* tab, *Results* group] to execute the query. The query should open in *Datasheet* view and display 28 records (Figure 3-92). Notice that in a number of instances the same *Boat ID* displays multiple times, once for each time that boat was rented.

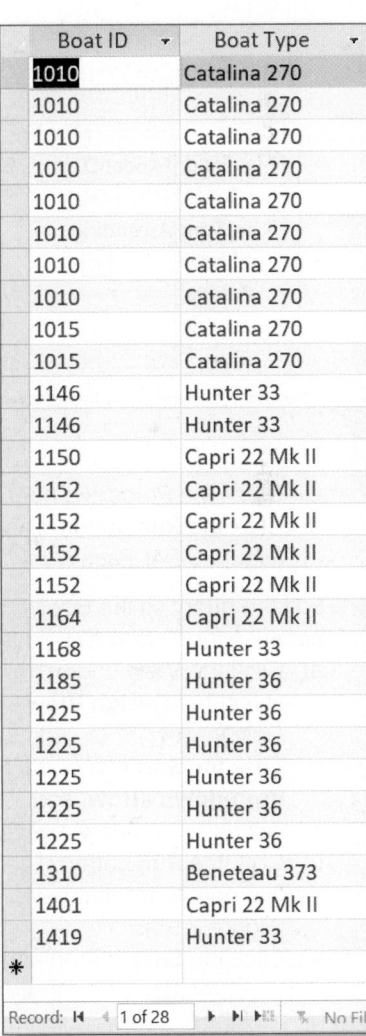

Boat ID ▾	Boat Type ▾
1010	Catalina 270
1010	Catalina 270
1010	Catalina 270
1010	Catalina 270
1010	Catalina 270
1010	Catalina 270
1010	Catalina 270
1010	Catalina 270
1015	Catalina 270
1015	Catalina 270
1146	Hunter 33
1146	Hunter 33
1150	Capri 22 Mk II
1152	Capri 22 Mk II
1152	Capri 22 Mk II
1152	Capri 22 Mk II
1152	Capri 22 Mk II
1164	Capri 22 Mk II
1168	Hunter 33
1185	Hunter 36
1225	Hunter 36
1225	Hunter 36
1225	Hunter 36
1225	Hunter 36
1225	Hunter 36
1310	Beneteau 373
1401	Capri 22 Mk II
1419	Hunter 33
*	

Record: ◄ ◄ 1 of 28 ► ►I ►▣ No Filt

Figure 3-92 *BoatID* query results

13. Edit the query to display *Unique Values*.
 a. Click the **Design View** icon in the *Status* bar to switch back to *Design* view of the query.
 b. Click the **Property Sheet** button [*Query Tools Design* tab, *Show/Hide* group] to open the *Property Sheet*.
 c. Click anywhere in the *Query Window* so that the *Selection type* in the *Property Sheet* displays *Query Properties*.
 d. Click the **Unique Values** property box and select **Yes**. The query window should look similar to Figure 3-93.

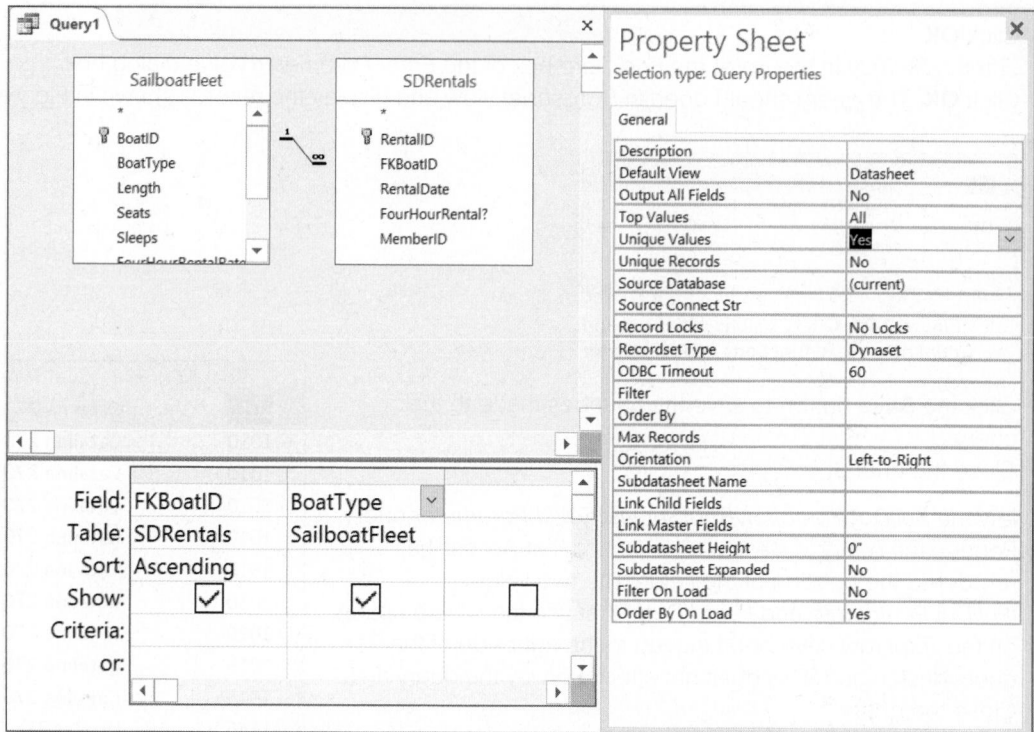

Figure 3-93 Set the *Unique Values* property in the *Property Sheet* of the query

 e. Close the *Property Sheet*.
 f. Click the **Run** button. The query should open in *Datasheet* view and display 12 records (Figure 3-94). Each *Boat ID* now displays only once, but the *Boat Types* are still repeated.

14. Edit the query so the *Boat Type* displays only once. The *Boat Type* is displaying more than once because the *FKBoatID* field is different for each boat.
 a. Click the **View** button [*Home* tab, *Views* group] and select the **Design View** option to switch back to *Design* view.
 b. Click the **Sort** row of the **FKBoatID** field, click the **drop-down arrow**, and select **(not sorted)**.
 c. Deselect the **Show** row check box for the **FKBoatID** field.
 d. Click the **Run** button. The query should display the five boat types that have been rented at least once (Figure 3-95).
 e. Click the **Save** button and save the query as BoatTypesRented.
 f. Close the query.

15. Close the database.

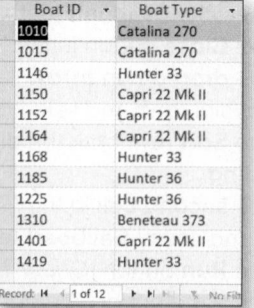

Figure 3-94 Query results with repeated *BoatType* values

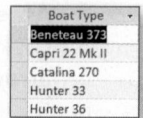

Figure 3-95 Unique records for *BoatType*

Guided Project 3-3

The American River Cycling Club wants to run three queries on its database. The first query finds which members have participated in races and where they placed in each race. The second query is based on the first one, which you enhance to include a parameter so the club can search only for a particular place finish. Finally, the third query displays division and age group information about the members. To ensure consistency, the starting file is provided for you. Use *Design* view and the *Simple Query Wizard* to create and edit the queries, add criteria, calculated fields, and a parameter. Save and test the queries to ensure they work correctly.

[Student Learning Outcomes 3.1, 3.2, 3.6, 3.7, 3.8]

File Needed: ***AmericanRiver-03.accdb*** *(Student data files are available in the* Library *of your SIMnet account.)*
Completed Project File Name: *[your initials]* ***Access 3-3.accdb***

Skills Covered in This Project

- Create a query using the *Simple Query Wizard.*
- Create a query using *Design* view.
- Add fields to a query.
- Execute a query.
- Save and test a query.
- Add calculated fields to a query.
- Add a parameter to a query.
- Use *Group By* in a summary query.

1. Open the ***AmericanRiver-03.accdb*** database file.

2. Save a new copy of your database as [your initials] Access 3-3.

3. Enable content in the database.

4. Create a new query in *Design* view to find which members have participated in races and what place they got in each race.
 a. Click the **Query Design** button [*Create* tab, *Queries* group] to open the *Show Table* dialog box.
 b. Select the **Members** table and click the **Add** button.
 c. Select the **RaceResults** table and click the **Add** button.
 d. Click the **Close** button in the *Show Table* dialog box.
 e. Increase the size of the table objects to display all of the fields.
 f. Click the **first cell** in the *Field* row of the query design grid.
 g. Press **Ctrl + F2** to open the *Expression Builder.*
 h. Type MemberName:Left([First Name],1) & ". " & [LastName] into the window.
 i. Click **OK**.
 j. Double-click the **RaceID** field from the *RaceResults* table to add it into the query design grid.
 k. Double-click the **Place** field from the *RaceResults* table to add it into the query design grid. Your completed query design grid should look similar to Figure 3-96.

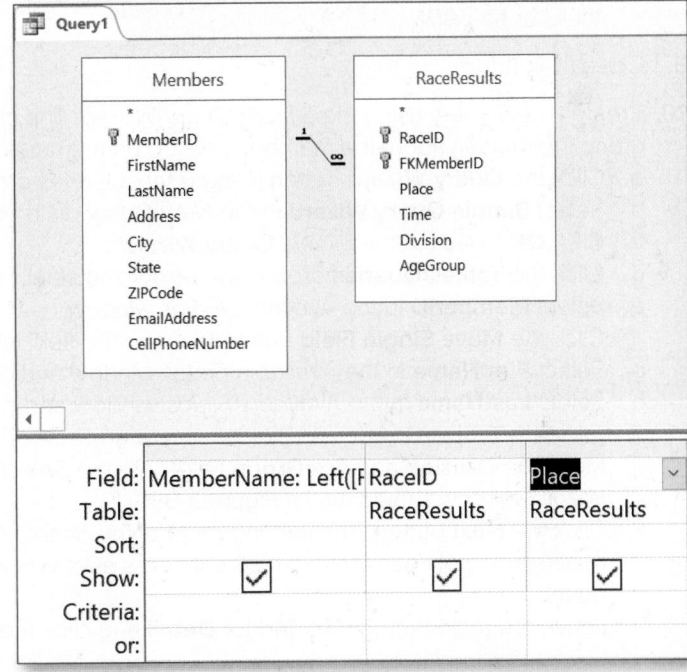

Figure 3-96 Query design grid

5. Click the **Save** button and save the query as MemberRaceResults.

6. Click the **Datasheet View** icon in the *Status* bar to run the query. The query should open in *Datasheet* view and display 36 records. A sample of the results is shown in Figure 3-97.

7. Save a copy of the query.
 a. Click the **Save As** button [*File* Tab].
 b. Select the **Save Object As** button and then click the **Save As** button.
 c. Replace the suggested name with MemberRaceResultsPlaceParameter.

8. Edit the *MemberRaceResultsPlaceParameter* query to add a parameter.
 a. Click the **View** button [*Home* tab, *Views* group] and select the **Design View** option to switch back to *Design* view of the query.
 b. Type [Show members who finished in what place? (Enter a number)] in the **Criteria** row of the *Place* field. You can use the *Zoom* box or *Expression Builder* to enter the parameter.
 c. Click the **Save** button to save the query.
 d. Click the **Run** button to test the query. The *Enter Parameter Value* dialog box displays.
 e. Enter 1 and click the **OK** button. The query results should display the five records shown in Figure 3-98.
 f. Switch back to *Design* view and then run the query again.
 g. Click the **OK** button in the *Enter Parameter Value* dialog box without entering a value. The query results should display with no records showing because no records match the place value "null," or no value.

Figure 3-97 Query results

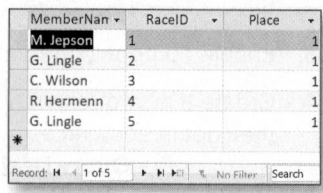

Figure 3-98 Query results

9. Close the query.

10. Create a new query using the *Simple Query Wizard*. The club wants to display division and age group information about the members, based on the races in which they competed.
 a. Click the **Query Wizard** button [*Create* tab, *Queries* group] to launch the *Query Wizard*.
 b. Select **Simple Query Wizard** in the *New Query* dialog box.
 c. Click **OK** to launch the *Simple Query Wizard*.
 d. Click the **Tables/Queries** drop-down arrow and select the **Members** table.
 e. Select **MemberID** in the *Available Fields* window.
 f. Click the **Move Single Field** button to move the field into the *Selected Fields* window.
 g. Select **FirstName** in the *Available Fields* window and click the **Move Single Field** button.
 h. Select **LastName** in the *Available Fields* window and click the **Move Single Field** button.
 i. Click the **Tables/Queries** drop-down arrow and select the **RaceResults** table.
 j. Move the **Division** and **AgeGroup** fields into the *Selected Fields* window. The completed *Query Wizard* window should match Figure 3-99.
 k. Click the **Next** button. The second page of the *Simple Query Wizard* displays. Because of the relationship between the two tables, Access asks you whether you want a detail or summary query.
 l. Leave the radio button selected for **Detail** and click the **Next** button.

m. Change the title in the *Title* box to MemberDivisionAndAgeGroup.
n. Click **Finish** to save and run the query. The query results display 36 total records, one for each of the records in the *RaceResults* table.

11. Edit the query in *Design* view to add a *Total* row. This enables you to group the records to remove the duplicate records.
 a. Click the **Design View** icon in the *Status* bar to switch back to *Design* view of the query.
 b. Click the **Totals** button [*Query Tools Design* tab, *Show/Hide* group]. *Group By* displays in the *Total* row for each field.
 c. Click the **Save** button to save the query.

12. Click the **Run** button. The query should open in *Datasheet* view and display 17 records (Figure 3-100). Notice that two records still display for Marco Guzman, indicating that he has run races in two age groups. He must have had a birthday that caused him to change age groups.

13. Close the query.

14. Close the database.

Figure 3-99 Completed *Simple Query Wizard*

Figure 3-100 Query results of *Member DivisionAndAgeGroup* query

Independent Project 3-4

You are creating a parameter query for the music database you have worked with in previous projects. To ensure consistency, the starting file is provided for you. Use *Design* view to create the query. Edit the query to add criteria. After saving and testing the query, edit the query to add a parameter.
[Student Learning Outcomes 3.2, 3.3, 3.4, 3.5, 3.6]

File Needed: ***MusicDatabase-03.accdb*** *(Student data files are available in the* Library *of your SIMnet account.)*
Completed Project File Name: *[your initials]* ***Access 3-4.accdb***

Skills Covered in This Project

- Create a query in *Design* view.
- Edit a query in *Design* view.
- Add compound criteria to a query.
- Execute a query.
- Save a query.
- Sort query results.
- Add a parameter to a query.

1. Open the **MusicDatabase-03.accdb** database file.

2. Save a new copy of your database as [your initials] Access 3-4.

3. Enable content in the database.

4. Open the *Songs* table in *Datasheet* view to verify that the table contains 634 songs.

5. Close the table.

6. Create a new query in *Design* view. The query finds songs with lengths that are within a certain range.
 a. Add both tables into the *Query Design* window.
 b. Increase the size of the table objects to display all of the fields.
 c. Add the following fields into the query in the order listed: **AlbumName**, **Artist**, **SongTitle**, and **Length** (from the *Songs* table).

7. Save the query as 3to4MinuteSongs-Artist-or-AlbumChoice.

8. Enter the following criteria in the *Length* field: Between #0:03:00# and #0:04:00#. Due to the way Access stores times, Access changes this criteria to read: *Between #12:03:00 AM# And #12:04:00 AM#*.

9. Save the changes and run the query. The datasheet should display 338 songs.

10. Change to *Design* view to edit the query and add a parameter. The parameter should enable the user to enter either the *Album Name* or the *Artist Name* to find songs.
 a. Type [Enter the Album Name] as the criteria for the *AlbumName* field.
 b. Click the *Or* row, and type [Enter the Artist Name] as the criteria for the *Artist* field.
 c. Copy the criteria in the *Length* field and paste it into the *Or* row cell of the *Length* field. You need the *Length* criteria to be in both the *Criteria* row and the *Or* row.

11. Sort the results to display in ascending order by song length.

12. Save the changes to the query. The completed query design grid should be similar to Figure 3-101.

Field:	AlbumName	Artist	SongTitle	Length
Table:	Albums	Albums	Songs	Songs
Sort:				Ascending
Show:	☑	☑	☑	☑
Criteria:	[Enter the Album Name]			Between #12:03:00 AM# And #12:04:00 AM#
or:		[Enter the Artist Name]		Between #12:03:00 AM# And #12:04:00 AM#

Figure 3-101 Query design grid of query showing multiple parameters and compound criteria

13. Run the query to verify that it works.
 a. Type Need You Now in the *Enter the Album Name Enter Parameter Value* dialog box, and click **OK**.
 b. Don't enter anything in the *Enter the Artist Name Enter Parameter Value* dialog box, and click **OK**. The datasheet should show the four (out of 11) songs from this album that meet the criteria (Figure 3-102). You can verify the song count on this album by looking in the *Songs* table for *AlbumID 5*.

Album Name	Artist	Song Title	Length
Need You Now	Lady Antebellum	Love This Pain	3:03
Need You Now	Lady Antebellum	Perfect Day	3:21
Need You Now	Lady Antebellum	Something 'Bout a Woman	3:41
Need You Now	Lady Antebellum	American Honey	3:44

Record: H ◄ 1 of 4 ► H ►◻ ◻ No Filter Search

Figure 3-102 Query results for *Need You Now* songs between 3 and 4 minutes long

14. Switch back to *Design* view and then run the query again.
 a. Don't enter anything in the *Enter the Album Name Enter Parameter Value* dialog box, and click **OK**.
 b. Type Lady Antebellum in the *Enter the Artist Name Enter Parameter Value* dialog box, and click **OK**. The datasheet should show the 47 (out of 71) songs from this artist that meet the criteria (Figure 3-103). You can verify the song count for this artist by looking in the *Albums* table for *Lady Antebellum* and expanding the **plus sign**.

Album Name	Artist	Song Title	Length
Heart Break	Lady Antebellum	You Look Good	3:01
Golden	Lady Antebellum	Better Off Now (That You're Gone)	3:03
Need You Now	Lady Antebellum	Love This Pain	3:03
Heart Break	Lady Antebellum	This City	3:04
747	Lady Antebellum	Freestyle	3:04
747	Lady Antebellum	Sounded Good at the Time	3:06
Heart Break	Lady Antebellum	Heart Break	3:07
On This Winter's Night	Lady Antebellum	Christmas (Baby Please Come Home)	3:09
Heart Break	Lady Antebellum	Think About You	3:09
On This Winter's Night	Lady Antebellum	Silent Night (Lord of My Life)	3:11
Golden	Lady Antebellum	Can't Stand the Rain	3:11
Heart Break	Lady Antebellum	Good Time to Be Alive	3:11
Golden	Lady Antebellum	Downtown	3:16
Golden	Lady Antebellum	All for Love	3:16
Heart Break	Lady Antebellum	Army	3:17
Own the Night	Lady Antebellum	We Owned the Night	3:17
747	Lady Antebellum	Bartender	3:18
On This Winter's Night	Lady Antebellum	This Christmas	3:19
On This Winter's Night	Lady Antebellum	I'll Be Home for Christmas	3:20
747	Lady Antebellum	She Is	3:21

Record: 1 of 47 No Filter Search

Figure 3-103 Query results for *Lady Antebellum* songs between 3 and 4 minutes long

15. Close the query.

16. Close the database.

Independent Project 3-5

The State of New York Department of Motor Vehicles wants to create three queries. The first query provides summary data on the number of tickets by city and violation. The second query summarizes the total tickets by violation. The third query provides summary data for the total fines assessed against each driver who has had a ticket. To ensure consistency, the starting file is provided for you. Use *Design* view to create the summary queries. Edit the queries to add fields, aggregate functions, and sorting. Finally, save and run the queries.
[Student Learning Outcomes 3.2, 3.4, 3.8]

File Needed: **NewYorkDMV-03.accdb** (Student data files are available in the Library of your SIMnet account.)

Completed Project File Name: **[your initials] Access 3-5.accdb**

Skills Covered in This Project

- Create a summary query in *Design* view.
- Edit a query in *Design* view.
- Add fields to a query.
- Execute a query.
- Save a query.
- Sort query results.
- Add aggregate functions.

1. Open the **NewYorkDMV-03.accdb** database file.

2. Save a new copy of your database as [your initials] Access 3-5.

3. Enable content in the database.

4. Create a new summary query in *Design* view. The query counts the number of tickets issued by city and violation.
 a. Add the *Tickets* table into the *Query Design* window.
 b. Increase the size of the table object to display all of the fields.
 c. Add the following fields into the query: **City**, **PrimaryFactor**, and **TicketNumber**.
 d. Add the *Total* row to the query.
 e. **Group By** the *City* and *PrimaryFactor* fields and **Count** the *TicketNumber* field.

5. Save the query as TicketCountByCityAndFactor.

6. Run the query. The datasheet should display 22 records.

7. Adjust the field column widths using **AutoFit** or **Best Fit**. The datasheet should be similar to Figure 3-104.

8. Save the changes to the query.

9. Save a copy of the query as TicketCountByFactor.

10. Edit the *TicketCountByFactor* query in *Design* view. The query should show the total tickets issued for each violation factor, sorted in descending order by count.
 a. Delete the *City* field.
 b. Sort the *TicketNumber* field in descending order.

11. Save and run the query. The datasheet should match Figure 3-105.

12. Close the query.

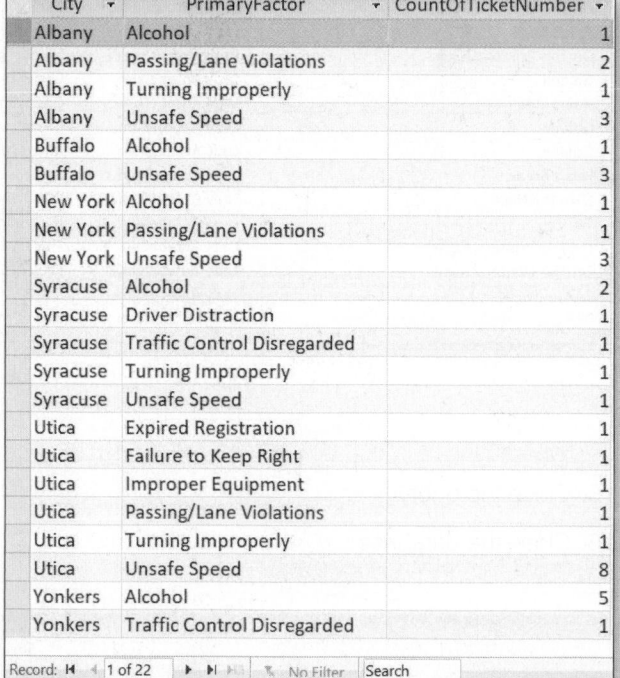

Figure 3-104 Summary query results counting tickets by city and factor

Figure 3-105 Summary query results counting tickets by factor

13. Create a new summary query in *Design* view. The query provides summary data on the total fines assessed against each driver.
 a. Add both tables into the *Query Design* window.
 b. Increase the size of the table objects to display all of the fields.
 c. Add the following fields into the query: **LicenseNumber**, **FirstName**, **LastName**, **Fine**, and **TicketNumber**.
 d. Add the **Total** row to the query.
 e. **Group By** the *LicenseNumber*, *FirstName*, and *LastName* fields, **Sum** the *Fine* field and **Count** the *TicketNumber* field.
 f. Sort the *Fine* field in descending order.

14. Save the query as TicketsByDriver.

15. Run the query. The datasheet should display 24 drivers who have received tickets, sorted in descending order by the total dollar amount of their fines (Figure 3-106).

16. Close the query.

17. Close the database.

LicenseNumb ▾	FirstName ▾	LastName ▾	SumOfFine ▾	CountOfTick ▾
15500786	Brian	Shin	$1,040.00	4
12348692	Michael	Finch	$845.00	3
10004387	Miranda	Jones	$800.00	2
15503625	Corey	Norman	$800.00	2
39989780	Kevin	Nguyen	$625.00	4
12389049	Bonnie	Hirshman	$530.00	2
12344537	Austin	Davis	$520.00	2
12348279	Sharon	Altier	$495.00	3
39998181	Ellie	Nassiri	$400.00	1
10000501	Diego	Acosta	$345.00	3
39992366	Mark	Watson	$180.00	1
12346123	Claudia	Schooler	$150.00	1
15502325	Ron	Stokes	$130.00	1
10003086	Mark	Williams	$120.00	1
12345838	Eric	Wilson	$120.00	1
18957217	Jessica	Healy	$105.00	2
12394163	Jake	Harvey	$90.00	1
18955806	Nancy	Smith	$90.00	1
15500914	Michelle	Taylor	$90.00	1
12388795	Caroline	Doiron	$90.00	1
10004372	Caterina	Malek	$90.00	1
12345678	Emily	Garcia	$60.00	1
10001786	Sandra	Johnson	$60.00	1
39992387	Kiana	Caton	$45.00	1

Record: ◄ ◄ 1 of 24 ► ►I ►□ 🏷 No Filter Search

Figure 3-106 Summary query results of tickets by driver

Independent Project 3-6

Courtyard Medical Plaza wants to create a query to provide details about its tenants and their rental payment history. The starting database file is provided for you. Use *Design* view to create the query. Edit the query to add calculated fields. After saving and testing the query, edit the query to add a parameter. [**Student Learning Outcomes 3.2, 3.3, 3.4, 3.5, 3.6, 3.7**]

File Needed: ***CourtyardMedicalPlaza-03.accdb*** (*Student data files are available in the* Library *of your* SIMnet *account.*)
Completed Project File Name: *[your initials] **Access 3-6.accdb***

Skills Covered in This Project

- Create a query in *Design* view.
- Edit a query in *Design* view.
- Add compound criteria to a query.
- Execute a query.
- Save a query.
- Add calculated fields to a query.
- Sort query results.
- Add a parameter to a query.

1. Open the ***CourtyardMedicalPlaza-03.accdb*** database file.

2. Save a new copy of your database as [your initials] Access 3-6.

3. Enable content in the database.

4. Create a new query in *Design* view. The query should display the rental invoice history.
 a. Add both tables into the *Query Design* window.
 b. Increase the size of the table objects to display all of the fields.
 c. Add the following fields into the query: **LastName**, **InvoiceID**, **DueDate**, **DateReceived**, **AmountDue**, and **Discount**.
 d. Run the query to make sure it works. The datasheet should display 54 records.

5. Save the query as InvoiceHistory.

6. Change to *Design* view to edit the query to add calculated fields.
 a. Insert a column to the left of *InvoiceID*.
 b. Add a calculated field in the inserted column to concatenate the *FirstName* and *LastName* fields using the following formula: Doctor: [FirstName] & " " & [LastName].
 c. Don't show the *LastName* field. In the next step you will use that for query criteria.
 d. Insert a column to the left of *Discount*.
 e. Add a calculated field in the inserted column to determine the number of days early the rent was paid using the following formula: DaysPaidEarly: [DueDate]-[DateReceived].
 f. Enter a calculated field to the right of the *Discount* field to determine the net amount of rent due with the following formula: NetRent: [AmountDue]-[Discount].

7. Save your changes and run the query. The datasheet should look similar to Figure 3-107 and display a total of 54 records.

Doctor	InvoiceID	Due Date	DateReceived	Amount Due	DaysPaidEarly	Discount	NetRent
Robert Beyer	1	01-May-20	4/30/2020	$1,250.00	1		
Robert Beyer	10	01-Jun-20	5/29/2020	$1,250.00	3	$25.00	$1,225.00
Robert Beyer	19	01-Jul-20	6/30/2020	$1,250.00	1		
Robert Beyer	28	01-Aug-20	8/1/2020	$1,250.00	0		
Robert Beyer	37	01-Sep-20	9/1/2020	$1,250.00	0		
Robert Beyer	46	01-Oct-20	9/30/2020	$1,250.00	1		
Elizabeth Scher	2	01-May-20	5/1/2020	$1,100.00	0		
Elizabeth Scher	11	01-Jun-20	6/1/2020	$1,100.00	0		

Figure 3-107 Query results showing concatenated and calculated fields

8. Edit the query to add parameters to search either by last name or by a date range.
 a. Type [Enter the last name or leave blank to select all doctors] as the criteria for the *LastName* field.
 b. Click the *Or* row, and type Between [Enter the Starting Date] And [Enter the Ending Date] as the criteria for the *DueDate* field.

9. Sort the results in ascending order by *LastName* and *DueDate*.

10. Save the query.

11. Run the query.
 a. Type Flores in the *Enter the last name Enter Parameter Value* dialog box and click **OK**.
 b. Don't enter anything in the *Enter the Starting Date Enter Parameter Value* dialog box; click **OK**.
 c. Don't enter anything in the *Enter the Ending Date Enter Parameter Value* dialog box; click **OK**. The datasheet should show the six payments received from Dr. Flores (Figure 3-108). Dr. Flores paid his rent early three months this year.

Doctor	InvoiceID	Due Date	DateReceived	Amount Due	DaysPaidEarly	Discount	NetRent
Ricardo Flores	4	01-May-20	4/29/2020	$1,350.00	2	$13.50	$1,336.50
Ricardo Flores	13	01-Jun-20	5/28/2020	$1,350.00	4	$27.00	$1,323.00
Ricardo Flores	22	01-Jul-20	6/29/2020	$1,350.00	2	$13.50	$1,336.50
Ricardo Flores	31	01-Aug-20	8/1/2020	$1,350.00	0		
Ricardo Flores	40	01-Sep-20	9/1/2020	$1,350.00	0		
Ricardo Flores	49	01-Oct-20	10/1/2020	$1,350.00	0		

Record: I◄ ◄ 1 of 6 ► ►I ►▣ 🔍 No Filter | Search

Figure 3-108 Query results when name parameter is completed

12. Switch back to *Design* view and then run the query again.
 a. Don't enter anything in the *Enter the last name Enter Parameter Value* dialog box; click **OK**.
 b. Type 9/1/2020 in the *Enter the Starting Date Enter Parameter Value* dialog box and click **OK**.
 c. Type 10/1/2020 in the *Enter the Ending Date Enter Parameter Value* dialog box and click **OK**. The datasheet should show the 18 invoices with a due date between 9/1/2020 and 10/1/2020 (Figure 3-109).

Doctor	InvoiceID	Due Date	DateReceived	Amount Due	DaysPaidEar	Discount	NetRent
Robert Beyer	37	01-Sep-20	9/1/2020	$1,250.00	0		
Robert Beyer	46	01-Oct-20	9/30/2020	$1,250.00	1		
Juan Camacho	41	01-Sep-20	8/27/2020	$1,100.00	5	$22.00	$1,078.00
Juan Camacho	50	01-Oct-20	10/1/2020	$1,100.00	0		
Ricardo Flores	40	01-Sep-20	9/1/2020	$1,350.00	0		
Ricardo Flores	49	01-Oct-20	10/1/2020	$1,350.00	0		
Margaret Foste	39	01-Sep-20	8/29/2020	$1,350.00	3	$27.00	$1,323.00
Margaret Foste	48	01-Oct-20	9/29/2020	$1,350.00	2	$13.50	$1,336.50
James Henness	42	01-Sep-20	9/1/2020	$1,600.00	0		
James Henness	51	01-Oct-20	10/1/2020	$1,600.00	0		
Steven Norman	45	01-Sep-20	8/30/2020	$1,600.00	2	$16.00	$1,584.00
Steven Norman	54	01-Oct-20	10/1/2020	$1,600.00	0		
Rick Plice	43	01-Sep-20	9/1/2020	$1,400.00	0		
Rick Plice	52	01-Oct-20	10/1/2020	$1,400.00	0		
Elizabeth Scher	38	01-Sep-20	9/1/2020	$1,100.00	0		
Elizabeth Scher	47	01-Oct-20	10/1/2020	$1,100.00	0		
Robyn Singh	44	01-Sep-20	9/1/2020	$1,650.00	0		
Robyn Singh	53	01-Oct-20	9/28/2020	$1,650.00	3	$33.00	$1,617.00

Record: H ◀ 1 of 18 ▶ H ▶ No Filter Search

Figure 3-109 Query results when date parameters are completed

13. Close the query.

14. Reopen the query in *Design* view. Notice that Access has moved the *LastName* field to the right side of the query design grid and also entered a copy of the *DueDate* field with the *Show* row check box deselected. This is due to the way Access processes the query (Figure 3-110).

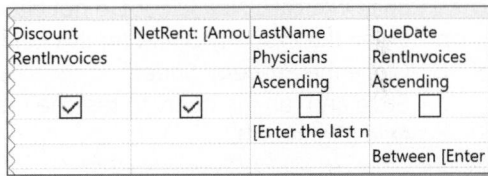

Figure 3-110 Updated query design grid

15. Close the query.

16. Close the database.

Improve It Project 3-7

Central Sierra needs help with their database. One of the administrative assistants has created two queries to provide information about the employees. Unfortunately, the queries are not working correctly. For this project, determine why the queries don't work and make the necessary corrections. The starting file is provided for you. Use *Design* view to edit the queries. Use calculated fields, compound criteria, and parameters, and save the queries and test that they work correctly.
[Student Learning Outcomes 3.2, 3.3, 3.4, 3.5, 3.6, 3.7, 3.8]

File Needed: **CentralSierra-03.accdb** (Student data files are available in the Library of your SIMnet account.)
Completed Project File Name: **[your initials] Access 3-7.accdb**

Skills Covered in This Project

- Edit a query in *Design* view.
- Add compound criteria to a query.
- Execute a query.
- Save a query.
- Add calculated fields to a query.
- Add a parameter to a query.

1. Open the **CentralSierra-03.accdb** database file.

2. Save a new copy of your database as [your initials] Access 3-7.

3. Enable the contents in the security warning.

4. Run the *NewSalaryCostSummary* query. The results display in *Datasheet* view (Figure 3-111). The query is supposed to summarize results by department and, within the department by title, the total salary cost and the total cost of potentially giving a 3% raise to all employees. Several errors need to be repaired.

First Name	Last Name	Title	Department	SumOfBas	Expr1
Albert	Quiroga	Large Group Specialist	Health and Benefits	$4,500.00	4635
Bert	Pulido	Supervisor	Health and Benefits	$5,500.00	5665
Bob	Lingle	Chief Executive Officer	Administration	$15,000.00	15450
Charlene	Althouse	Large Group Specialist	Property and Casualty	$4,700.00	4841
Cheryl	Nevens	Chief Information Officer	Administration	$12,000.00	12360
Chris	Robles	Insurance Agent	Health and Benefits	$3,900.00	4017
Eleesha	Santos	Insurance Agent	Health and Benefits	$5,580.00	5747.4
Timothy	Hansen	Insurance Agent	Health and Benefits	$3,900.00	4017
Todd	DeRenzis	Administrative Assistant	Insurance Sales	$2,800.00	2884
Wayne	Reza	Insurance Agent	Health and Benefits	$4,000.00	4120

Record: 1 of 29 No Filter Search

Figure 3-111 *NewSalaryCostSummary* query results

5. Edit the query in *Design* view to remove the unneeded columns that cause the summary query to display too many records.
 a. Delete the *FirstName* column.
 b. Delete the *LastName* column.
 c. Save and run the query to test the results. The datasheet should now show only 14 records.

6. Edit the query in *Design* view to repair the calculated field name and formatting.
 a. Open the *Zoom* box for the *Expr1* field to change the default *Expr1* name to SumOfPotentialNewSalary. Do not change the existing formula.
 b. Open the *Property Sheet* for this field and change the *Format* property to **Currency**.
 c. Close the *Property Sheet*.
 d. Save and run the query to test the results. The datasheet should show the improved calculated field (Figure 3-112).

Title	Department	SumOfBas	SumOfPot
Administrative Assistant	Administration	$3,000.00	$3,090.00
Administrative Assistant	Health and Benefits	$6,000.00	$6,180.00
Administrative Assistant	Insurance Sales	$5,400.00	$5,562.00
Administrative Assistant	Property and Casualty	$2,900.00	$2,987.00
Chief Executive Officer	Administration	$15,000.00	$15,450.00

Figure 3-112 Query results with improvements to calculated field and removal of name fields

7. Edit the query in *Design* view to fix the grouping order. The results are supposed to display the records grouped by the department, and then within each department by the job titles.
 a. Move the *Department* field to the left of the *Title* field.
 b. Save and run the query to test the results. The datasheet should show the records with the correct grouping (Figure 3-113).

Department	Title	SumOfBas	SumOfPot
Administration	Administrative Assistant	$3,000.00	$3,090.00
Administration	Chief Executive Officer	$15,000.00	$15,450.00
Administration	Chief Information Officer	$12,000.00	$12,360.00
Administration	Chief Operating Officer	$12,000.00	$12,360.00
Administration	Executive Assistant	$3,750.00	$3,862.50
Health and Benefits	Administrative Assistant	$6,000.00	$6,180.00

Figure 3-113 Query results with improved grouping

8. Edit the query in *Design* view to enhance the functionality and improve the appearance. In addition to calculating the sum of both the *Base Salary* and the *Potential New Salary* fields, management would like to see the average of both of those fields, as well as the total number of employees in each area.
 a. Insert a new column to the left of the *BaseMonthlySalary* column.
 b. Click the **drop-down arrow** in the *Field* row of this new column and select **EmpID**. Set this field to use the **Count** aggregate function.
 c. Add the **BaseMonthlySalary** field into the first empty cell in the *Field* row. *BaseMonthlySalary* will be in the query design grid twice. Set this field to use the **Avg** aggregate function.
 d. Type the following formula into the first empty cell in the *Field* row: AvgOfPotentialNewSalary: Avg([BaseMonthlySalary]*1.03).
 e. Set the *Total* row cell for this field to **Expression**.
 f. Format this field to use **Currency**.
 g. Save and run the query to test the results. Adjust the column widths as necessary to improve the appearance. The datasheet should now be similar to that shown in Figure 3-114.

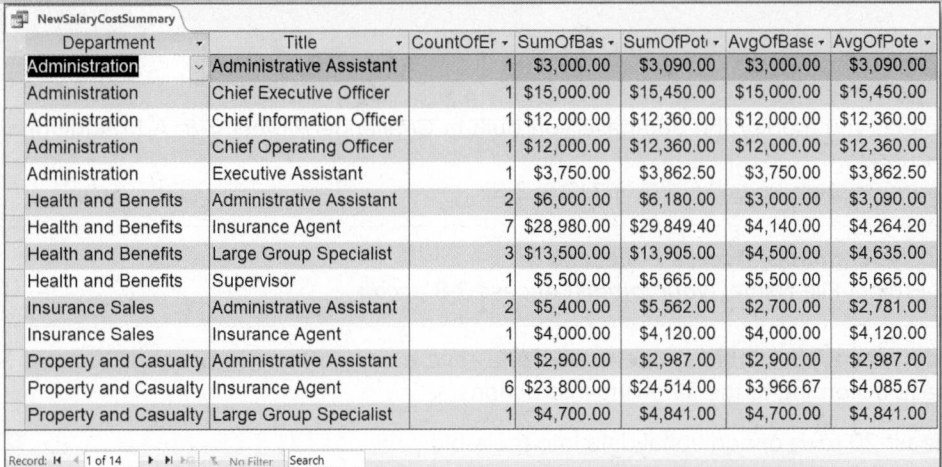

Department	Title	CountOfEr	SumOfBas	SumOfPot	AvgOfBase	AvgOfPote
Administration	Administrative Assistant	1	$3,000.00	$3,090.00	$3,000.00	$3,090.00
Administration	Chief Executive Officer	1	$15,000.00	$15,450.00	$15,000.00	$15,450.00
Administration	Chief Information Officer	1	$12,000.00	$12,360.00	$12,000.00	$12,360.00
Administration	Chief Operating Officer	1	$12,000.00	$12,360.00	$12,000.00	$12,360.00
Administration	Executive Assistant	1	$3,750.00	$3,862.50	$3,750.00	$3,862.50
Health and Benefits	Administrative Assistant	2	$6,000.00	$6,180.00	$3,000.00	$3,090.00
Health and Benefits	Insurance Agent	7	$28,980.00	$29,849.40	$4,140.00	$4,264.20
Health and Benefits	Large Group Specialist	3	$13,500.00	$13,905.00	$4,500.00	$4,635.00
Health and Benefits	Supervisor	1	$5,500.00	$5,665.00	$5,500.00	$5,665.00
Insurance Sales	Administrative Assistant	2	$5,400.00	$5,562.00	$2,700.00	$2,781.00
Insurance Sales	Insurance Agent	1	$4,000.00	$4,120.00	$4,000.00	$4,120.00
Property and Casualty	Administrative Assistant	1	$2,900.00	$2,987.00	$2,900.00	$2,987.00
Property and Casualty	Insurance Agent	6	$23,800.00	$24,514.00	$3,966.67	$4,085.67
Property and Casualty	Large Group Specialist	1	$4,700.00	$4,841.00	$4,700.00	$4,841.00

Record: I◄ ◄ 1 of 14 ► ►I ►⊞ ℅ No Filter Search

Figure 3-114 Completed *NewSalaryCostSummary* query results

9. Save any changes and close the query.

10. Run the *InsuranceAgentsBranchParameter* query. Enter Folsom in the *Enter Parameter Value* dialog box. The results display in datasheet view (Figure 3-115). The query is supposed to list the insurance agents in a particular branch or show all the insurance agents if the branch prompt is left blank. You have identified several errors that need to be fixed, including that all the insurance agents displayed even though you entered a branch.

11. Edit the query to fix the parameter problem.
 a. Open the query in *Design* view. Notice that the branch parameter is actually on the *Department* field and not the *Branch* field.
 b. Change that column to contain the *Branch* field.
 c. Run the query again and enter Folsom. The results now display the branch, but you still have employees from all the branches.
 d. Switch to *Design* view to review the criteria. The *Branch* parameter is on the "or" row. It needs to be on the same row as "Insurance Agent".
 e. Move the parameter to the criteria row to fix that problem.
 f. Open the *Zoom* window to review the *Branch* parameter. It isn't designed correctly, because it won't allow the field to be left blank and show all the insurance agents.
 g. Edit the parameter as follows: Like [Enter the branch or leave blank to select all branches] & "*".
 h. Save and run the query. Type Folsom. Only the four agents at the Folsom branch should display.
 i. Change back to *Design* view and then run the query again and leave the dialog box empty. All 14 agents should display.

Employee	Title	Department
EleeshaSant	Insurance Agent	Health and Benefits
RoyBaxter	Insurance Agent	Property and Casualty
JuanTaylor	Insurance Agent	Insurance Sales
WayneReza	Insurance Agent	Health and Benefits
LazaroNeto	Insurance Agent	Health and Benefits
TheresaNguy	Insurance Agent	Property and Casualty
GeorgeTiptor	Insurance Agent	Health and Benefits
MargaretJeps	Insurance Agent	Property and Casualty
ShoukatAli	Insurance Agent	Health and Benefits
ChrisRobles	Insurance Agent	Health and Benefits
JesusDelao	Insurance Agent	Property and Casualty
LaryAdamser	Insurance Agent	Property and Casualty
MayelaRome	Insurance Agent	Property and Casualty
TimothyHans	Insurance Agent	Health and Benefits
*		

Record: I◄ ◄ 1 of 14 ► ►I ►⊞ ℅ No Filter Search

Figure 3-115 *InsuranceAgentsBranchParameter* query results are not correct

12. Edit the query to fix the *Employee* field. Notice that there isn't a space between the names.
 a. Edit the formula in the *Employee* field as follows: Employee: [FirstName] & " " & [LastName].
 b. Run the query. Enter Granite Bay. The results should show only the five insurance agents at the Granite Bay branch.
 c. Use **AutoFit** to adjust the width of all the columns. The datasheet should now be similar to that shown in Figure 3-116.

13. Save and close the query.

14. Close the database.

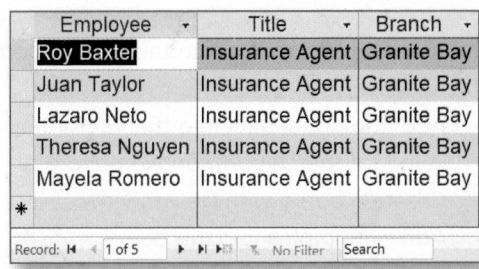

Employee	Title	Branch
Roy Baxter	Insurance Agent	Granite Bay
Juan Taylor	Insurance Agent	Granite Bay
Lazaro Neto	Insurance Agent	Granite Bay
Theresa Nguyen	Insurance Agent	Granite Bay
Mayela Romero	Insurance Agent	Granite Bay
*		

Record: I◄ ◄ 1 of 5 ► ►I ►⊞ ℅ No Filter Search

Figure 3-116 Completed *InsuranceAgentsBranch-Parameter* query

Challenge Project 3-8

For this project, you modify the database you built in *Challenge Project 2-8*. Add additional data and create two queries.
[Student Learning Outcomes 3.1, 3.2, 3.3, 3.4, 3.5]

File Needed: *[your initials] Access 2-8.accdb*
Completed Project File Name: *[your initials] Access 3-8.accdb*

Open the database *[your initials] Access 2-8* and save a copy of it as [your initials] Access 3-8. Modify your database according to the following instructions:

- Add at least 20 rows of additional data into the table.
- Create a query with the *Simple Query Wizard*.
- Add at least three of the fields into the query.
- Edit the query in *Design* view and add a criterion to one of the fields.
- Apply sorting to one of the fields.
- Save and run the query.
- Create a second query in *Design* view.
- Add all of the fields into a query.
- Add compound criteria to the query using an *OR* condition on one of the fields combined with an *AND* condition on at least one other field.
- Save and run the query.
- Adjust the width of the columns in the query so that they are sized appropriately.
- Save any changes that you made.

Challenge Project 3-9

Modify the database you created in *Challenge Project 2-9* for Blue Lake Sports. Your database contains a table with information about the different departments at Blue Lake Sports and a related table with information about Interns who are working at Blue Lake. Add additional data and create one query.
[Student Learning Outcomes 3.2, 3.3, 3.6, 3.7]

File Needed: *[your initials] Access 2-9.accdb*
Completed Project File Name: *[your initials] Access 3-9.accdb*

Open the database *[your initials] Access 2-9* and save a copy of it as [your initials] Access 3-9. Modify your database according to the following instructions:

- Add additional data into the *Department* table so that you have at least 10 different departments if necessary.
- Add additional data into the *Intern* table so that there are at least 30 interns. When entering the value for the *DepartmentName* foreign key, don't assign all of the interns to the same department.
- Create a query with *Design* view.
- Add both tables into the query.
- Add the *DepartmentName* and *Division* fields (from the *Department* table).
- Add a calculated field to concatenate the intern's *FirstName* and *LastName* fields.

- Save and run the query.
- Edit the query to add a parameter. The parameter should enable the user to enter the division he or she wishes to query. Write this parameter using wildcards so that if the user leaves the *Enter Parameter Value* dialog box empty, the query returns all the records. You may want to review the "Use Wildcards in a Parameter Query" section in *SLO 3.6: Creating and Using a Simple Parameter Query* for help with this task.
- Save and run the query.
- Verify that the query works correctly when the user enters a specific division and that it returns all the records if the dialog box is left blank.
- Adjust the width of the columns in the query so that they are sized appropriately.
- Save any changes that you made.

Challenge Project 3-10

Modify the database you created in *Challenge Project 2-10* for a travel agency. Your database contains a table with information about the different ships and a related table with information about upcoming cruises. Add additional data and create two queries.
[Student Learning Outcomes 3.2, 3.3, 3.4, 3.5, 3.7, 3.8]

File Needed: *[your initials] Access 2-10.accdb*
Completed Project File Name: *[your initials] Access 3-10.accdb*

Open the database *[your initials] Access 2-10* and save a copy of it as [your initials] Access 3-10. Modify your database according to the following instructions:

- Add at least 10 rows of additional data into the *Trips* table. When entering the value for the *ShipID* foreign key, don't assign all of the trips to the same ship.
- Create a query with *Design* view.
- Add both tables into the query.
- Add the *ShipName*, *CruiseLineName*, and *NumberOfPassengers* fields (from the *Ships* table) and the *TripName* and *CostPerPerson* fields (from the *Trips* table).
- Add a field to calculate the potential revenue for each trip. The *PotentialRevenue* is the *CostPerPerson* times the *NumberofPassengers*.
- Sort the results in ascending order by the potential revenue.
- Save and run the query.
- Adjust the width of the columns in the query so that they are sized appropriately.
- Save any changes that you made.
- Create a *Summary* query in *Design* view to count how many trips each Cruise Line has scheduled.
- Add both tables into the query.
- Add the *TripID* field and the *CruiseLineName* field into the query.
- Add the *Total* row.
- Count by the *TripID* field.
- Save and run the query.
- Adjust the width of the columns in the query so that they are sized appropriately.
- Save any changes that you made.

Source of screenshots Microsoft Office 365 (2019): Word, Excel, Access, Powerpoint.

Creating and Using Forms and Reports

CHAPTER OVERVIEW

Forms and reports enhance the usability of your Access database. Forms provide a user-friendly interface to view, add, update, and delete data in a database. Reports offer a professional way to view and print data, making it easier for your user to understand information in your database. This chapter introduces the Access tools that enable you to create and customize forms and reports.

STUDENT LEARNING OUTCOMES (SLOs)

After completing this chapter, you will be able to:

SLO 4.1 Create a simple form using quick create options, and save, modify, and delete a form (p. A4-223).

SLO 4.2 Create a blank form, understand controls and control layouts, customize a form in *Layout* view, adjust control positions, add a title, date, or logo to a form, and create a form from a template (p. A4-231).

SLO 4.3 Restrict a form to data entry, limit user edits and deletions on a form, add command buttons, and test a form (p. A4-241).

SLO 4.4 Create a simple report with the *Report Wizard*, and save, modify, and delete a report (p. A4-248).

SLO 4.5 Create a blank report, understand controls and control layouts, customize a report in *Layout* view, adjust control positions, and add a title, logo, date, and page numbers to a report (p. A4-256).

SLO 4.6 Enhance a report by adding grouping, sorting, and totals to a report in *Layout* view (p. A4-265).

SLO 4.7 Integrate conditional formatting into a report (p. A4-269).

SLO 4.8 Preview, modify print settings, print a report, and format and print a report with multiple columns (p. A4-271).

ACCESS

CASE STUDY

For the Pause & Practice projects in this chapter, you develop forms and reports for the Placer Hills Real Estate and Central Sierra Insurance databases. As you progress through the Pause & Practice projects in this chapter, you incorporate many of the features you learn in this chapter to build forms and reports used to display, add, edit, and delete data in a database.

Pause & Practice 4-1: Create and view forms using the *Form Wizard*, the *Form* button, and *Split Form*.

Pause & Practice 4-2: Create a form using the *Blank Form* button. Modify the form to restrict it to data entry, add buttons, and test the form.

Pause & Practice 4-3: Create and view a report using the *Report Wizard*. Create a report using the *Blank Report* button. Modify the report to improve its layout.

Pause & Practice 4-4: Create and preview a report with grouping and conditional formatting.

Creating and Working with a Simple Form

A *form* is an object you use to create an interface to easily view, add, update, and delete data in a database. Most forms in a database are directly connected to a table or query, the source of the data. Access calls these *bound forms* because they link to the data source. *Unbound forms*, forms that don't have a connection to a data source, can be used to help operate the database. For example, a database may have an unbound form that contains no data but has buttons that perform different actions in the database like printing reports or opening forms. In this chapter, you learn how to create forms that are bound to a table.

Forms provide flexible access to data in a database. You can create a form with fields from one or more tables or queries. The form may also contain only a subset of the fields from the table. You also can choose to display only one record at a time or multiple records. This flexibility helps you create forms that look attractive and are more user-friendly than *Datasheet* view of a table. Ideally, a well-designed form makes it easier for users to work with the database and prevents mistakes in adding, updating, or deleting data.

Access offers three view choices for most forms. Use *Form view* to enter and view data. *Design view* enables you to change the form. *Layout view* enables you to alter the design of a form and see the effects of the changes in real time. However, not all design changes can be made in *Layout* view. Forms created with a *Datasheet* layout also have a *Datasheet view* option.

Access provides several different ways to create a form. These options are available in the *Forms* group [*Create* tab] (Figure 4-1). Some of the options are quick, while others take a little more effort but provide greater flexibility and enable you to create more specialized types of forms. In this section, you are introduced to three quick ways to build a form: the *Form Wizard*, the *Form* button, and the *Split Form* options.

Figure 4-1 Form creation options

The Form Wizard

The *Form Wizard* steps you through the process of quickly creating a form. When you build a bound form, you must tell Access where to find the data. Use the *Form Wizard* to select the specific table(s) and queries along with the specific fields to include in the form. You can also select the layout for the form. After you create the form, you use *Form* view to enter and view data in your database. If you need to change the form once it has been created, edit it using *Layout* view or *Design* view.

When you use the *Form Wizard* to create a form based on one table, you can select from four different layout options. Note that Figures 4-2 through 4-5 show *Form* view for each of the sample forms.

- *Columnar.* The form displays the fields in one column (Figure 4-2). The field names display to the left

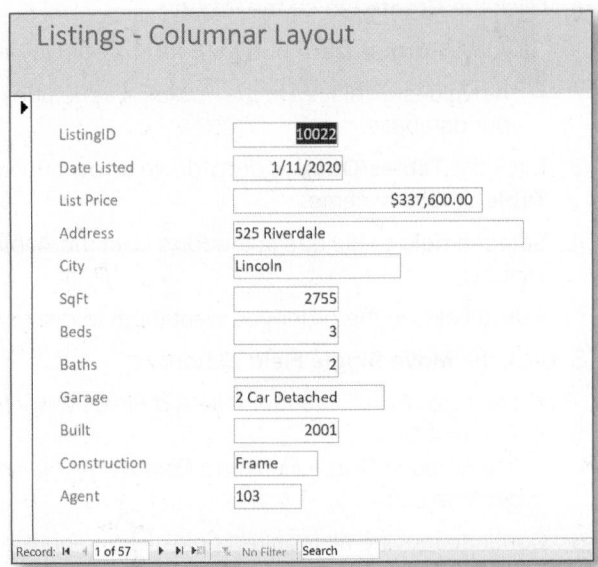

Figure 4-2 Columnar form layout

of the field, and the name of the form displays in a header section at the top of the form. A columnar layout shows only one record at a time. You use the *Navigation* buttons to move from one record to another.

- **Tabular**. The form displays the fields in a table (row and column) format (Figure 4-3). The header section at the top of the form displays the name of the form and the field names as column heads.

- **Datasheet**: The form displays in the Access *Datasheet* layout (Figure 4-4). The field names are the column heads.

- **Justified**: The form displays the fields in a horizontal, justified layout (Figure 4-5). The field names are above each field. The form name displays in a header section. Only one record displays at a time.

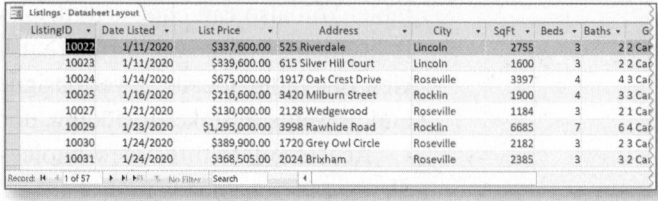

Figure 4-3 Tabular form layout

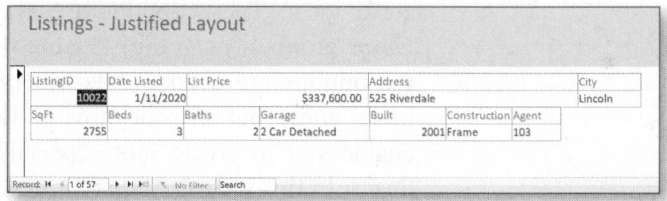

Figure 4-4 Datasheet form layout

Figure 4-5 Justified form layout

▶ **HOW TO: Create a Form Using the Form Wizard**

1. Click the **Create** tab on the *Ribbon*.
2. Click the **Form Wizard** button [*Forms* group] to launch the *Form Wizard*.
 - The values displayed in the *Tables/Queries* box and the *Available Fields* window are based on the contents of your database.
3. Click the **Tables/Queries** drop-down arrow and select the **Table** or **Query** name.
4. Select a **field** to include in the form from the *Available Fields* window.
 - Add fields in the order you want them to display in the form.
5. Click the **Move Single Field** button.
 - The field moves into the *Selected Fields* window (Figure 4-6).
 - The *Remove Single Field* and *Remove All Fields* buttons become active.
6. Continue moving all required fields, changing the selected *Table* or *Query* if needed.

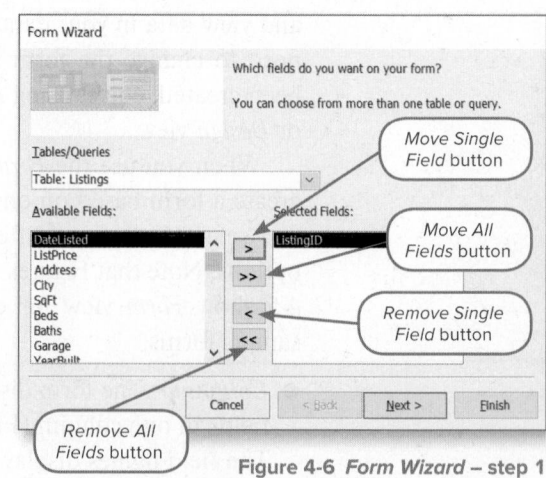

Figure 4-6 *Form Wizard* – step 1

7. Click the **Next** button when you are finished adding all fields. The second page of the *Form Wizard* displays (Figure 4-7).

8. Select the radio button of the form layout that you want.

9. Click the **Next** button. The last page of the *Form Wizard* displays (Figure 4-8).

10. Change the form **Title** as desired. The suggested title is the name of the table or query used to create the form. The title will also be used as the *Form Name*.

11. Click **Finish** to open the form to view the data.

 - Access automatically saves the form.
 - The form shows in *Form* view (Figure 4-9).
 - Most of the fields appear in text boxes.

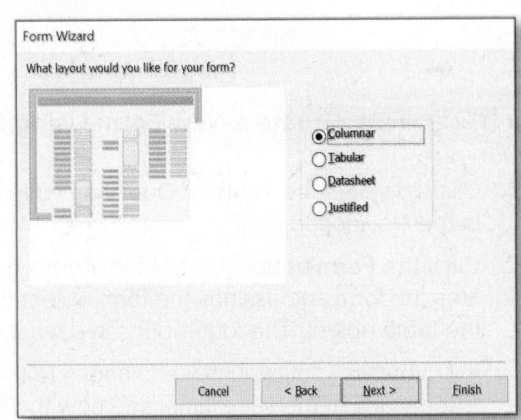

Figure 4-7 Select the form layout

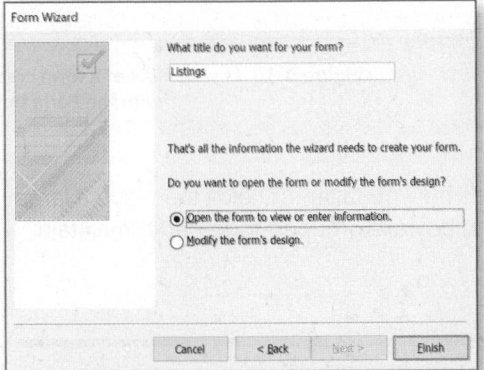

Figure 4-8 Enter the form title in the last step of the *Form Wizard*

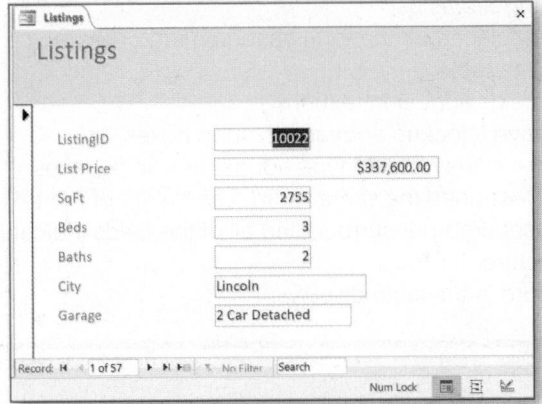

Figure 4-9 *Form* view of the completed form

 - Fields that have a lookup appear in combo boxes.
 - Fields that are a *Yes/No* data type appear as check boxes.
 - The size of a field depends on the data type and the field size.
 - The first record in the table displays.
 - The form name displays in the *Forms* group in the *Navigation Pane*.

12. Close the form.

The Form Button

The *Form* button is the quickest way to create a form. However, it does not give you any options during the initial creation process. After you have created the form, you can edit the form in *Layout* view or *Design* view.

▶**HOW TO:** Create a New Form Using the Form Button

1. Click to select the **Table** or **Query** on which to base the form in the *Navigation Pane*.

2. Click the **Form** button [*Create* tab, *Forms* group]. Access creates the form and assigns the form object the same name as the table object. The form opens in *Layout* view (Figure 4-10).

 - *Layout* view lets you make changes to the design of the form, and at the same time, see how the form looks with data displaying.
 - The orange selector border around a text box is an indicator that you are in *Layout* view. The *Layout View* icon is also selected in the *Status* bar.
 - The fields are placed on the form based on the order they are listed in the table.
 - Most of the fields appear in text boxes.
 - Fields that have a lookup appear in combo boxes.
 - Fields that are a *Yes/No* data type appear as check boxes.
 - All fields are assigned the same width. The height of the text boxes may be taller for fields that have a large size. The dashed border surrounding all of the fields indicates that they are grouped together to maintain uniform structure.
 - The first record in the table displays.

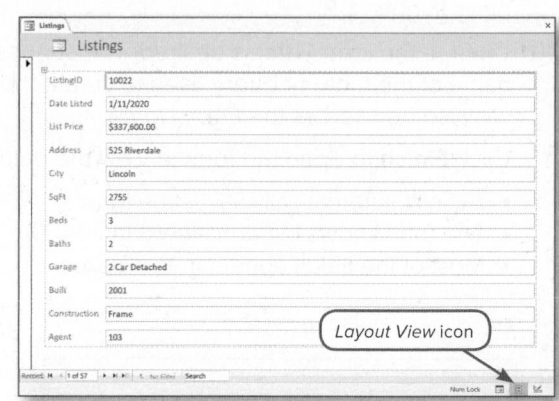

Figure 4-10 *Layout* view of a form created with the *Form* button

When a new form is created, the initial layout of the fields depends on the number of fields in the table and the size of the Access window when the form is created. A layout like the one shown in Figure 4-11 results if you have a smaller Access window before you click the *Form* button.

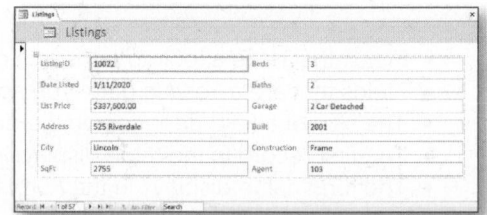

Figure 4-11 A smaller Access window results in a different field layout

The Split Form

A ***split form*** enables you to view data in two different ways at the same time. The top section of the form displays one record in a columnar mode, while the bottom section displays a *Datasheet* view. The two sections are synchronized so that when you navigate to a record, the selected record displays in the top section and is also highlighted in the lower section. This type of form enables you to see many records at once in the *Datasheet* view while giving you access to edit a single record. After you create a split form, use *Layout* view or *Design* view to edit it.

▶ HOW TO: Create a Split Form Using a Single Table

1. Click to select the table on which to base the form in the *Navigation Pane*.

2. Click the **More Forms** button [*Create* tab, *Forms* group] and select **Split Form** (Figure 4-12).

 - The form opens in *Layout* view (Figure 4-13).

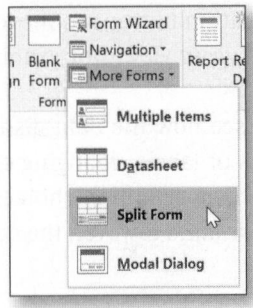

Figure 4-12 *More Forms button options*

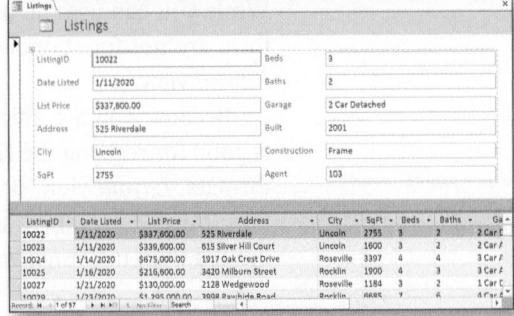

Figure 4-13 Split form in *Layout* view

View or Modify a Form

As you know, Access provides three different view options for most forms. Depending on how you created the form, it may initially display in any of the view options. When you double-click a form name in the *Navigation Pane*, it opens in *Form* view. Recall that you use *Form* view to enter and view data. After you create a form using one of the three quick methods just described, you may want to make modifications to the form. You can modify a form using either *Design* view or *Layout* view.

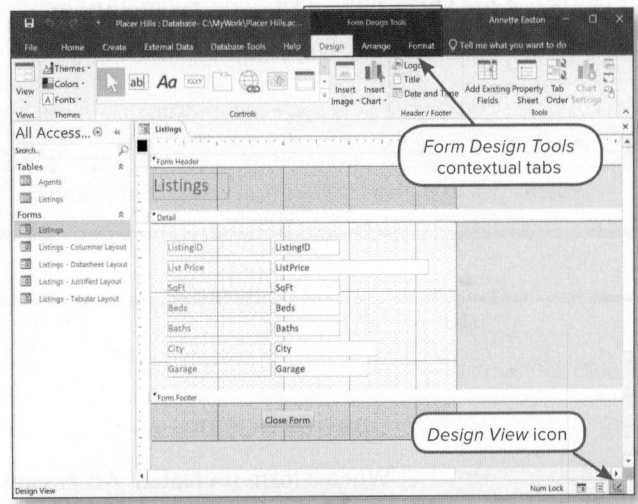

Figure 4-14 *Design* view of a form

Design view shows you the completed structure of the form (Figure 4-14) so you can modify any aspect of a form. *Design* view has a distinctive look, but you can also tell you are in *Design* view from the *Status* bar at the bottom of the Access window. You can modify the header, detail, and footer sections of the form. *Design* view is good for adding labels and images into a form, editing text boxes, resizing the form sections, and changing form properties. In *Design* view, the different editing choices are organized into three *Form Design Tools* contextual tabs: *Design*, *Arrange*, and *Format*.

Layout view enables you to make changes to the design of a form while seeing how the form looks with data displaying. The *Layout* view of the form in Figure 4-14 is shown in Figure 4-15. *Layout* view looks very similar to *Form* view, but you can tell what view you are in from the *Status* bar at the bottom of the Access window.

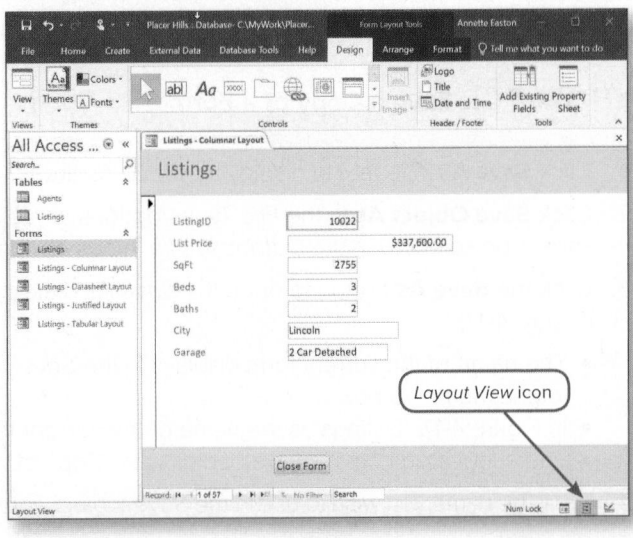

Figure 4-15 *Layout* view of a form

While you can use the navigation buttons to move among different records, other parts of the form are not functional in *Layout* view. For example, the *Close Form* button does not work in *Layout* view.

Because you are able to see how the data display while modifying the design, *Layout* view is good for resizing the fields or labels, changing colors or text alignment, or applying different formats. *Layout* view also provides editing choices on the three *Form Layout Tools* contextual tabs: *Design*, *Arrange*, and *Format*. However, the editing options located on those tabs are more limited than in *Design* view.

▶ **HOW TO: Switch Form Views to View or Modify a Form**

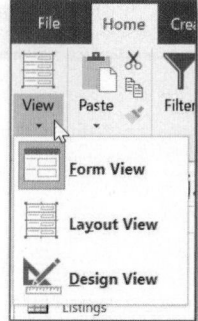

1. Click the **View** button [*Home* tab] (Figure 4-16).
2. Select **Form View**, **Layout View**, or **Design View**.
3. View the results or make any desired modifications.

▶ **ANOTHER WAY**

Select a view icon from the lower-right corner of the *Status* bar.

Figure 4-16 View options for a form

Save a Form

When a form is created, Access automatically assigns it a name. When you create a form using the *Form Wizard*, Access automatically saves the form during the creation process. If you created a form with the *Form* or *Split Form* buttons, or if you have made any modifications to the design of the form created with the wizard, you need to save those changes. Save changes to a form by pressing **Ctrl+S** or the **Save** icon on the *Quick Access* toolbar. The first time you save an object, you are prompted to change the default name in the *Save As* dialog box.

After a form has been created and saved, you may need to make a copy of that form. This may be done to have a backup of the original form or because another form will have the same initial characteristics.

▶ **HOW TO: Save a Copy of a Form**

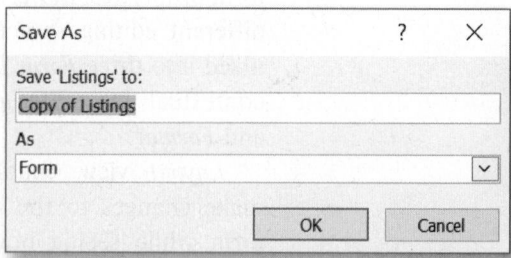

1. Click **Save As** [*File* tab] to display the *Save As* area.
2. Click **Save Object As** in the *File Types* options. *Save Object As* should be selected in the *Database File Types* options.
3. Click the **Save As** button to open the *Save As* dialog box (Figure 4-17).
 - The name of the current form displays in the *Save 'object name' to* box.
 - In Figure 4-17, "Listings" is the name of the current form.
 - The suggested name always begins with "Copy of."
4. Type the name you wish to use in the *Save 'object name' to* box.
5. Click **OK**.

Figure 4-17 Save As dialog box

▶ **ANOTHER WAY**

Press **F12** to open the *Save As* dialog box.

Once a form has been saved, it displays in the *Forms* group of the *Navigation Pane*. As you add more objects into your database, the number of objects displayed in the *Navigation Pane* increases (Figure 4-18). This is one of the reasons why it is important to use object names that effectively and immediately convey the meaning or purpose of the object. For example, in Figure 4-18, you don't know whether the *Listings* form and *Listings* report contain all the fields and information from the *Listings* table or whether differences exist, as you can see from the query names.

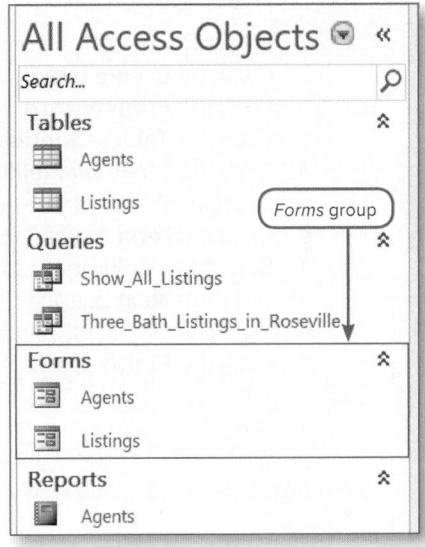

Figure 4-18 *Forms group on the Navigation Pane*

Open a Saved Form

If you double-click a form name in the *Navigation Pane*, the form opens in *Form* view. If the form was created using a *Datasheet* layout, it opens in *Datasheet* view.

Open a saved form in *Layout* view or *Design* view by right-clicking the form name in the *Navigation Pane* and selecting **Layout View** or **Design View** from the context menu (Figure 4-19).

Delete a Form

Occasionally, you have forms that you no longer need or want in the database.

Delete a form by selecting the form name in the *Navigation Pane* and clicking the **Delete** button [*Home* tab, *Records* group].

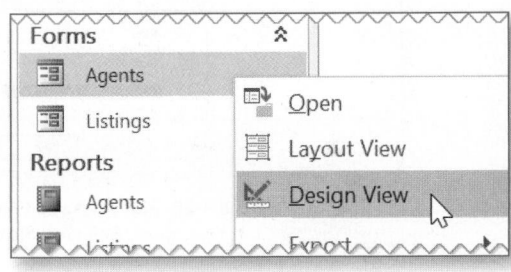

Figure 4-19 Context menu of a form

> **ANOTHER WAY**
>
> Right-click the form name in the *Navigation Pane* and select **Delete** from the context menu.

PAUSE & PRACTICE: ACCESS 4-1

For this Pause & Practice, you create three versions of a form using three quick creation methods. You create a form using the *Form Wizard*, the *Form* button, and the *Split Form* button.

File Needed: **PlacerHills-04.accdb** (Student data files are available in the Library of your SIMnet account.)
Completed Project File Name: **[your initials] PP A4-1.accdb**

1. Open the **PlacerHills-04** database from your student data files.

2. Save a new copy of the database as [your initials] PP A4-1.

3. Enable content in the database.

4. Create a form using the *Form Wizard*.
 a. Click the **Create** tab on the *Ribbon*.
 b. Click the **Form Wizard** button in the *Forms* group to launch the *Form Wizard*.
 c. Click the **Tables/Queries** drop-down arrow and select the **Listings** table.
 d. Click the **Move All Fields** button to move all of the fields from the *Available Fields* window to the *Selected Fields* window (Figure 4-20).
 e. Click the **Next** button to move to the second page of the *Form Wizard*.
 f. Select the **Columnar** radio button if necessary.
 g. Click the **Next** button to move to the last page of the *Form Wizard*.
 h. Type Listings - Form Wizard in the *Title* box.
 i. Click the **Finish** button. The form opens in *Form* view (Figure 4-21).

Figure 4-20 Move desired fields into the *Selected Fields* window

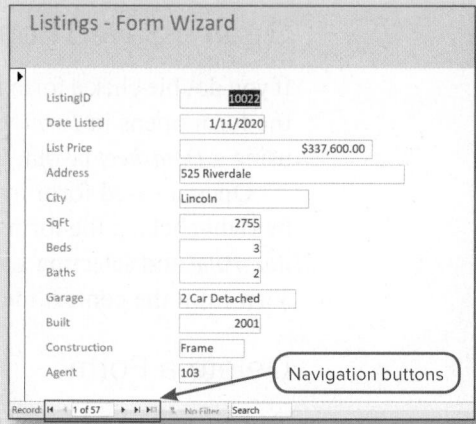

Figure 4-21 *Listings* form created using the *Form Wizard*

 j. Use the navigation buttons to move among records.
 k. Close the form.

5. Create a form using the *Form* button.
 a. Click to select the **Listings** table in the *Navigation Pane*.
 b. Click the **Form** button [*Create* tab, *Forms* group] to create the form.
 c. Click to select the **Listings** label in the *Header* section (Figure 4-22). The layout of your fields may be different depending on the size of the Access window when you created the form.
 d. Click inside the label to open the edit mode.
 e. Edit the label to read Listings – Form Button.
 f. Save the form. Enter Listings – Form Button as the *Form Name* and click **OK**.
 g. Switch to *Form* view by clicking the **View** button [*Form Layout Tools Design* tab, *Views* group] and selecting **Form View**.
 h. Use the navigation buttons to move among records.
 i. Close the form.

6. Create a form using the *Split Form* button.
 a. Click to select the **Listings** table in the *Navigation Pane*.

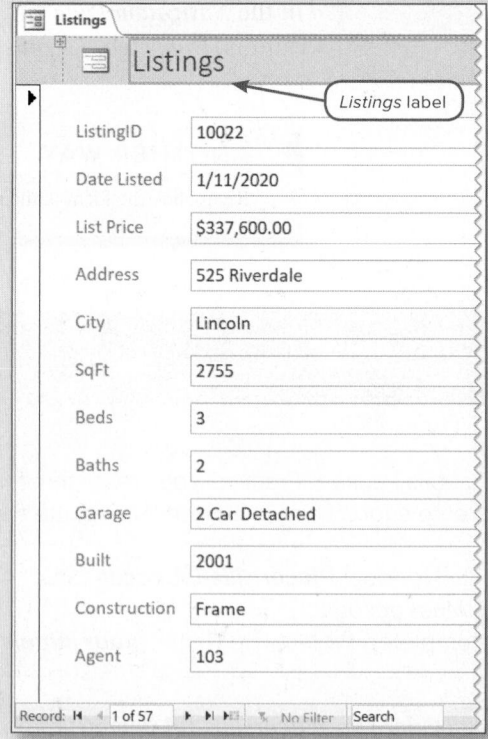

Figure 4-22 *Listings* form created using the *Form* button

b. Click the **More Forms** button [*Create tab, Forms* group] and select **Split Form** to create the form shown in Figure 4-23.

c. Click to select the **Listings** label in the *Header* section.

d. Click inside the label to open the edit mode.

e. Edit the label to read Listings – Split Form.

f. Save the form. Enter Listings – Split Form as the *Form Name* and click **OK**.

g. Switch to *Form* view by clicking the **View** button [*Form Layout Tools Design* tab, *Views* group] and selecting **Form View**.

h. Use the navigation buttons to move among records. Notice that, as you change records, the selected record displays in the top section and is also highlighted in the *Datasheet* view in the lower section.

i. Close the form.

7. Close the database.

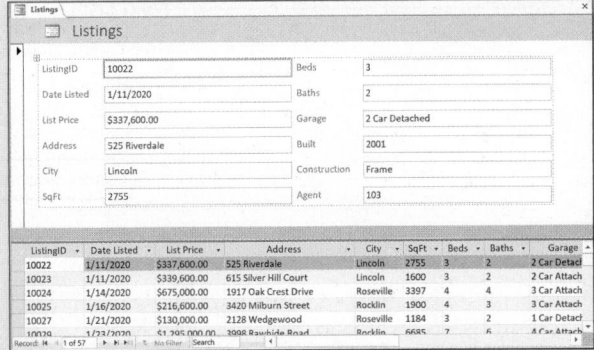

Figure 4-23 *Listings* form created using *Split Form*

Creating and Customizing a Form in Layout View

As you have learned, *Layout* view provides an easy way to modify a form while seeing how the form looks with data displaying. The functions of the form do not work in *Layout* view. However, you can use the navigation buttons to move among different records. In this section, you first learn how to create a blank form. After that, you explore the layout of a form and learn how to make modifications using *Layout* view. Finally, you learn to create a form from a template.

Create a Form Using the Blank Form Button

Sometimes, it is easier to start with a completely blank form and add the fields, labels, or buttons that you need directly onto the form.

▶HOW TO: Create a Blank Form

1. Click the **Blank Form** button [*Create* tab, *Forms* group].
 - A new blank form opens in *Layout* view (Figure 4-24).
 - The *Field List* pane displays. The *Field List* contains the list of the tables in your database.
2. Click the **Show all tables** link to display the database tables.
3. Click the **plus sign** to the left of a table name to see the fields in the table (Figure 4-25).
4. Click the **minus sign** to the left of a table name to collapse the list of fields in the table.

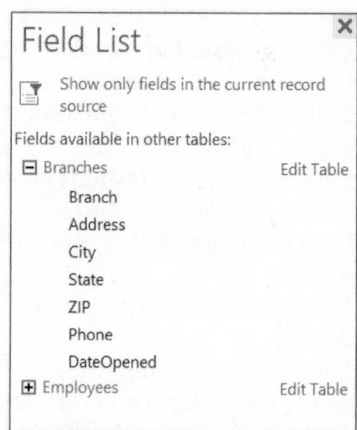

Figure 4-24 Blank form in *Layout* view Figure 4-25 Expanded *Field List*

After you create the blank form, you are ready to start adding items onto the form. Remember to save the form and any changes you make to it.

Form Controls

In Access, the fields, labels, buttons, and so forth are all known as *controls*. You can add controls to a form in either *Layout* view or *Design* view.

The controls are located in the *Controls* group of the *Form Layout Tools Design* tab. The controls available in *Layout* view are shown in Figure 4-26.

Figure 4-26 *Controls* group for a form

Controls can be bound, unbound or calculated. *Bound* controls are linked to a data source. For example, a text box that gets its value from a field in a table is a bound control. *Unbound* controls are not linked to a data source. For example, a label on a form that contains a form title is an unbound control. Finally, *calculated* controls contain an expression. For example, a text box that gets its value from an expression is a calculated control. The most common controls and their usage are described in Table 4-1.

Table 4-1: Common Form Controls

Control	Explanation
Text Box	Used to display data on a form or to accept data from a user when entering a value.
Label	Displays the content contained in its caption property. Does not accept any input from the user. You can edit the wording in a label on the form.
Button	Used to add a command button that performs an action such as *Close Form*, *Open Form*, *Delete Record*, etc.
Combo Box	Displays or accepts data in a drop-down list. Used for lookup fields.
Check Box	Used to display or accept data for a field with a *Yes/No* data type.

As you read this book, you will learn more about these controls and how they are used in a database.

Form Control Layouts

Control layouts provide a structure that helps to align the different controls on your form. This gives your form a more uniform appearance. Forms are not required to include a control layout, although some of the form creation methods place all fields in a control layout by default. The two primary control layout options are tabular and stacked:

- *Tabular.* The layout organizes data in rows and columns. Labels identifying the different fields are above the data values in a header section. Figure 4-27 shows a tabular layout in *Layout* view. The tabular layout starts with each field having a fairly large column width. This can make it difficult to see all the fields on the screen at one time.

Figure 4-27 **Tabular control layout**

- *Stacked*: The layout organizes data vertically. The labels are to the left of the data control. The fields all have the same width. Figure 4-28 shows a stacked layout in *Layout* view.

Figure 4-28 **Stacked control layout**

The small icon in the upper-left corner of a layout is the *layout selector*. It displays when a control inside the layout has been selected.

Add Fields to a Control Layout

When a new blank form is created, no controls appear on the form. You can add any desired table fields to the form in *Layout* view. When you add a table field to a form, Access automatically determines the type of control to add based on the value in the *Display Control* property of the field. Recall that the *Display Control* property is initially set based on the field's data type. Most data types use *Text Box* to display the data, but *Yes/No* data types use a *Check Box*. If you created a lookup field, the *Display Control* property would be either *List Box* or *Combo Box*. When a table field is added to a form, Access adds a control for that field and also adds an attached label control. The label control displays the field name or the caption, if one has been entered for the field.

▶ **HOW TO: Add Fields into the Control Layout of a Blank Form**

1. Open the form in *Layout* view.
2. Click the **Add Existing Fields** button [*Form Layout Tools Design* tab, *Tools* group] if the *Field List* is not open (Figure 4-29).

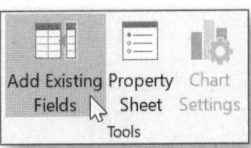

Figure 4-29 *Add Existing Fields* button

> ▶ **ANOTHER WAY**
>
> Press **Alt+F8** to show or hide the *Field List*.

3. Click the **Show all tables** link if the database tables do not show.
4. Click the **plus sign** next to the desired table name to display the fields.

5. Double-click the desired **field name**.

- The field is added into a stacked layout (Figure 4-30). A label control, associated with the field name, is also added to the form.
- The most recently added field is highlighted with an orange border.
- The next field added to the form appears below the orange-bordered field.

6. Continue adding the remaining fields.

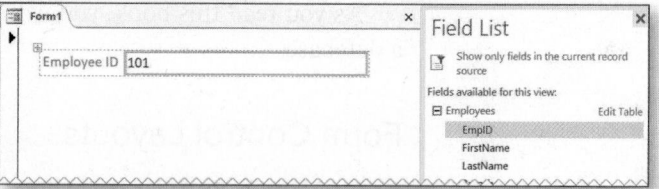

Figure 4-30 Add fields into a stacked layout of a blank form

> **ANOTHER WAY**
>
> Click, hold, and drag a **field** from the *Field List* into the form window to add it into the control layout.

▶ HOW TO: Add Fields between Existing Fields in a Control Layout

1. Open the form in *Layout* view.
2. Click the **Add Existing Fields** button [*Form Layout Tools Design* tab, *Tools* group] or press **Alt+F8** if the *Field List* is not open.
3. Click the **plus sign** next to the desired table name to display the fields.
4. Select the desired **field name** to add to the form. The field is highlighted in rose.
5. Click, hold, and drag the **field** to the desired location in the control layout. A rose-colored line indicates the position of the new field (Figure 4-31).

- The rose-colored line appears both vertically and horizontally as you move to the new location.
- If the line is positioned horizontally, the existing rows move down to accommodate the inserted field.
- If the line is positioned vertically, the existing fields move to the right to accommodate the inserted field.

6. Release the pointer to add the field and its label.

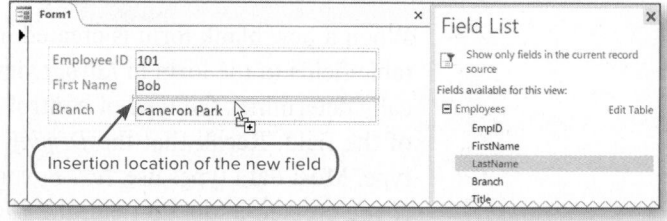

Figure 4-31 Drag a field to the desired location

Delete Fields from a Control Layout

As you saw in *SLO 4.1: Creating and Working with a Simple Form*, if you use the *Form* button to create a form, all table fields are automatically added to the control layout of the form. However, you may not want to keep all of the fields on the form. Although they are added together, the text box and the label are two separate controls associated with a field. If you select and delete the text box, the label is automatically deleted. However, if you only select and delete the label, the text box control remains on the form. Additionally, deleting a label or text box control does not automatically delete the row or column that contains the control from the control layout.

▶**HOW TO:** Delete a Field from a Control Layout

1. Open the form in *Layout* view.

2. Select the **text box control** of the field to delete.

3. Right-click to open the context menu.

4. Select the desired delete option (Figure 4-32). The choices work differ-
 ently depending on the control layout.

 • In a stacked layout, select **Delete** to delete both the text box and label,
 but you keep the empty row in the control layout.
 • In a stacked layout, select **Delete Row** to delete the text box, label, and row containing the controls.
 • In a tabular layout, select **Delete** to delete the text box, but the label and column are not deleted.
 • In a tabular layout, select **Delete Column** to delete the text box, label, and column containing the controls.

Figure 4-32 Context menu to delete a field

If necessary, you can delete the entire control layout. After selecting a control in the form, click the **layout selector** to select the entire layout and then press **Delete**.

Customize a Form in Layout View

Use *Layout* view to modify a form and to see the effects of the modifications in real time. In this section, you learn how to change control layouts, adjust control widths and heights, and add and delete rows and columns in a control layout.

These options are available through the buttons in the *Table* and *Rows & Columns* groups on the *Form Layout Tools Arrange* tab (Figure 4-33).

Figure 4-33 Customize a form layout using options in the *Table* and *Rows & Columns* groups

Change Control Layouts

When you create a form using one of the quick create options, the form starts with either a stacked or tabular layout. As you add and delete fields on the form, you may wish to change its layout.

▶**HOW TO:** Change Control Layouts

1. Open the form in *Layout* view.

2. Select one of the fields in the control layout. The orange border surrounds the selected field.

3. Click the **Select Layout** button [*Form Layout Tools Arrange* tab, *Rows & Columns* group]. The orange border sur-
 rounds all of the controls in the layout.

> **ANOTHER WAY**
> Click the **layout selector** to select all of the controls.

4. Select either the **Stacked** or **Tabular** button [*Form Layout Tools Arrange* tab, *Table* group]. The form updates to
 show the new layout.

Adjust Control Widths and Heights

Often, the initial width of the form fields is much larger than needed. Keep in mind that in a stacked layout, all of the fields have the same width. That means that when you change the width you need to ensure that the column is wide enough to fit the largest field.

▶ HOW TO: Change Field Column Widths

1. Open the form in *Layout* view.
2. Select the **text box control** of the desired field in the control layout. The orange border surrounds the selected field.
3. Place your pointer over the right edge of the text box until it changes to the resize arrow.
4. Click, hold, and drag the **resize arrow** to increase or decrease the width of the text box.
 - The field(s) update to show the new width.
 - In a stacked layout, all fields change together to maintain the same width (Figure 4-34).
 - In a tabular layout, you can set the width of each field individually (Figure 4-35).

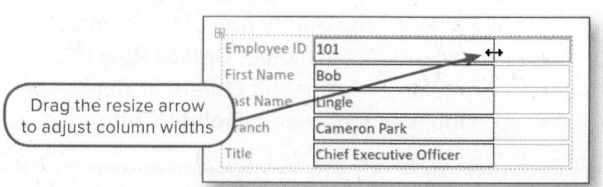

Figure 4-34 Adjust the width of all fields in a stacked layout

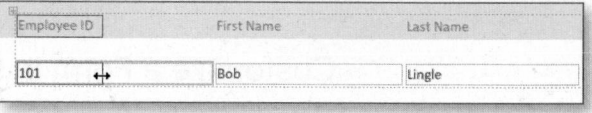

Figure 4-35 Adjust the width of a single field in a tabular layout

Change the height of a field using a very similar process. After you select the control, place your pointer over the lower edge of the control. Click, hold, and drag the **resize arrow** up or down to adjust the height. If you have a stacked layout, you can set the height of each field individually. However, in a tabular layout, all fields change together to maintain the same the height.

These same instructions can be used to change the width or height of many other controls, like labels and command buttons.

You can also change the width or height of a control on the *Format* tab of the *Property Sheet*. This enables you to enter a precise value.

▶ HOW TO: Change Control Width or Height Using the Property Sheet

1. Open the form in *Layout* view.
2. Select one of the controls in the control layout. The orange border surrounds the selected field.
3. Press **F4** or click the **Property Sheet** button [*Form Layout Tools Design* tab, *Tools* group].
4. Enter the value in the *Width* or *Height* property box on the *Format* tab (Figure 4-36).
 - You must press **Enter** or **Tab** after entering the value so that Access recognizes a changed value.
 - The form updates to show the modified control.

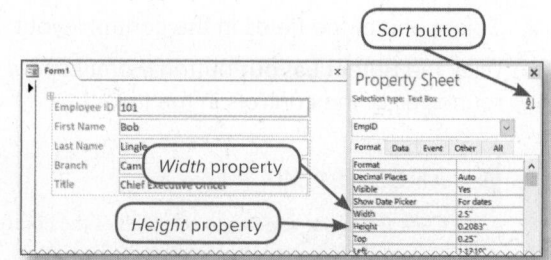

Figure 4-36 Adjust the width and height in the *Property Sheet*

Add and Delete Rows and Columns in a Control Layout

Often, you want to make minor modifications to the control layout. For example, you may want to create a second column in a stacked layout, or you may want to delete a row if you removed fields from the control layout.

▶ HOW TO: Add a Column to a Control Layout

1. Open the form in *Layout* view.
2. Select a control in the column adjacent to the place where you want to add a new column.
3. Click the **Select Column** button [*Form Layout Tools Arrange* tab, *Rows & Columns* group].
4. Click the **Insert Left** or **Insert Right** button [*Form Layout Tools Arrange* tab, *Rows & Columns* group].
 - The new column is added to the control layout (Figure 4-37).
 - A light gray, dotted border surrounds each cell in the added column.

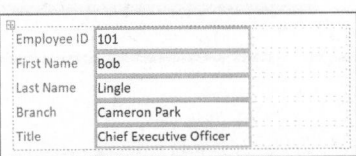

Figure 4-37 A dotted border surrounds each cell in the added column

▶ HOW TO: Add a Row to a Control Layout

1. Open the form in *Layout* view.
2. Select a control in the row adjacent to the place where you want to add a new row.
3. Click the **Select Row** button [*Form Layout Tools Arrange* tab, *Rows & Columns* group].
4. Click the **Insert Above** or **Insert Below** button [*Form Layout Tools Arrange* tab, *Rows & Columns* group].
 - The new row is added to the control layout (Figure 4-38).
 - A light gray, dotted border surrounds each cell in the added row.

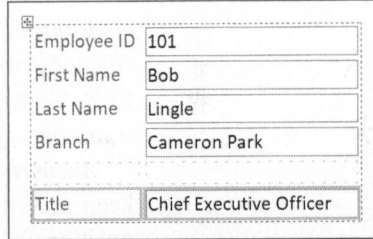

Figure 4-38 A dotted border surrounds each cell in the added row

▶ HOW TO: Delete a Row or Column from a Control Layout

1. Open the form in *Layout* view.
2. Select a control in the row or column you wish to delete.
3. Click the **Select Row** or **Select Column** button [*Form Layout Tools Arrange* tab, *Rows & Columns* group].
4. Right-click to open the context menu.
5. Select **Delete Row** or **Delete Column**.

Move a Control within a Layout

After you make a modification to the control layout, you may want to move a control from one part of the layout to another.

▶ **HOW TO:** Move a Control within a Layout

1. Open the form in *Layout* view.
2. Select the **control** that you wish to move. The orange border surrounds that control and the pointer changes to the move arrow.
3. Click the control, hold, and drag the **control** to the new location. A rose color highlights the destination cell (Figure 4-39).

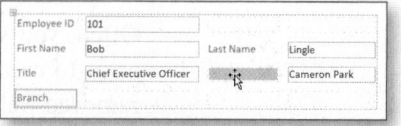

Figure 4-39 Drag a control to a new location in the form layout

> **ANOTHER WAY**
> Select multiple controls by pressing and holding **Shift** when you select controls.

Adjust Control Positioning on a Form

Depending on the design of your form, you may wish to make changes to the way controls are positioned on the form. Use the *Position* group [*Form Layout Tools Arrange* tab] to make these changes to the controls. The effects are visible when the form is viewed in *Form* or *Layout* view.

Control Margins set how much margin space surrounds the text inside a control. It is measured from the upper-left corner of the control to the position of the text inside the control. The margin options are *None*, *Narrow*, *Medium*, and *Wide*. Each option places slightly more space in the margin.

Control Padding sets how much space is between the controls. The padding options are *None*, *Narrow*, *Medium*, and *Wide*. Each option places slightly more space between the controls. Compare the space between the text boxes in Figures 4-38 and 4-39. Figure 4-38 illustrates narrow padding, while Figure 4-39 illustrates medium padding.

Anchoring is used to keep a control in a certain position on the form, even as the form is resized. If controls are placed inside a control layout, the entire layout is anchored, not individual controls. The *Anchoring* options are shown in Figure 4-40.

Figure 4-40 Select an *Anchoring* option

Figure 4-41 shows an example of controls anchored in a variety of locations. As the form is increased or decreased in size, the controls stay in their relative location. If controls are not anchored, as the form is decreased in size you may need to use the scroll bars to see all of the controls. Figure 4-41 also illustrates two *Control Margin* settings. The *LastName* field is set to *Narrow*, while the *FirstName* field is set to *Medium*. Notice that the lower part of "Bob" is cut off in the text box. Be sure that the height and width of the control is large enough so that the text can fully display.

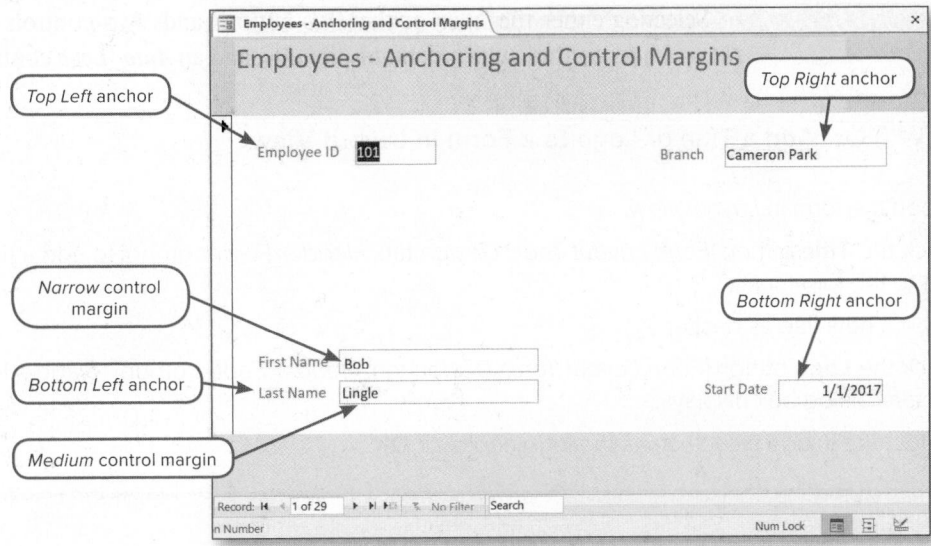

Figure 4-41 *Anchoring* and *Control Margin* examples

▶ HOW TO: Adjust Control Positioning on a Form

1. Open the form in *Layout* view.
2. Select the desired control or control layout.
3. Click the **Form Layout Tools Arrange** tab.
4. Click the **Control Margins**, **Control Padding**, or **Anchoring** button.
5. Select the desired option.

Add a Title, Date, or Logo to a Form

It is good design practice to title each form. This helps identify the form for the user. You can also display the current date and add a logo to forms. These controls are added to a form from the *Header/Footer* group [*Form Layout Tools Design* tab] (Figure 4-42). If the form does not already contain a **header section**, adding any of these items automatically adds a header section to the form.

Figure 4-42 *Header/ Footer* group options

▶ HOW TO: Add a Date to a Form in Layout View

1. Open the form in *Layout* view.
2. Click the **Date and Time** button [*Form Layout Tools Design* tab, *Header/ Footer* group] to add the *Auto_Date* and/or *Auto_Time* controls into the header section of the form. The *Date and Time* dialog box displays (Figure 4-43).
3. Select the check boxes and radio buttons corresponding to your choices.
4. Click **OK**.

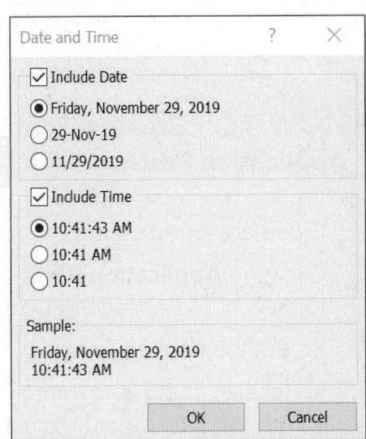

Figure 4-43 *Date and Time* dialog box

Selecting either the *Logo* or the *Title* buttons adds two controls into the header section: an ***Auto_Header*** control, which contains the title, and an ***Auto_Logo*** control, which contains the logo.

▶ **HOW TO:** Add a Title or Logo to a Form in Layout View

1. Open the form in *Layout* view.
2. Click the **Title** button [*Form Layout Tools Design* tab, *Header/Footer* group] to add a title to the form. The title is set to the form name.
3. Type a new title as desired.
4. Click the **Logo** button [*Form Layout Tools Design* tab, *Header/Footer* group] to add a logo to the form. The *Insert Picture* dialog box displays.
5. Select the image file to use as the logo and click **OK**.

Figure 4-44 shows a form with a date and time, a title, and a logo. The background of the *Auto_Date* control has been set to a different color. With the *Auto_Header* control selected, notice that the

Figure 4-44 Controls in the header section

width of the control overlaps onto the *Auto_Date* control. If necessary, you may need to adjust the width or location of these controls.

Create a Form from a Template with Application Parts

Another option to creating a form is to use a pre-built form template. In *SLO 1.2: Creating and Managing a Database*, you learned that Access has a variety of templates that you can use to create a complete database. Access also has a set of ***Application Parts***, pre-built parts of a database that can be added into an existing database. These parts include ten pre-built forms from which you can choose. The *Application Parts* gallery displays the pre-built form options. If you place your pointer over a form in the gallery, a *ScreenTip* displays information about the basic layout of that form (Figure 4-45).

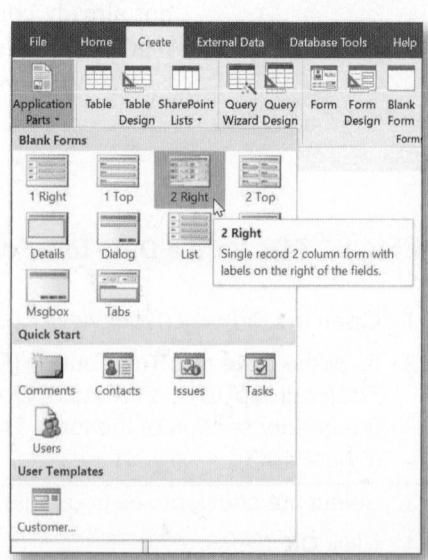

▶ **HOW TO:** Create a Form from a Template with Application Parts

1. Close any open objects.
2. Click the **Application Parts** button [*Create* tab, *Templates* group] to display the *Application Parts* gallery.
3. Select the desired form.
 - Access creates the form and assigns it a default name.
 - The form does not automatically open but displays in the *Navigation Pane*.

Figure 4-45 *Application Parts* gallery

Although Access categorizes these as *Blank Forms* in the gallery, they do contain various controls and formatting layouts. For example, they typically have an existing control layout and placeholder labels. However, a form that is created from *Application Parts* is not yet directly linked to a table in the database, just like a form created with the *Blank Form* button. After creating it, you must customize the form to link it to specific fields in a database table(s) and to modify or add controls on the form.

You can use the the skills you have learned in this section to make these modifications in *Layout* view. However, you will notice a difference when adding fields into an *Application Parts* form compared to a form created with the *Blank Form* button, because the placeholder labels already exist.

▶ **HOW TO:** Add Fields to a Form Created with Application Parts

1. Open the form in *Layout* view.
2. Click the **Add Existing Fields** button [*Form Layout Tools Design* tab, *Tools* group] if the *Field List* is not open.
3. Click the **plus sign** next to the desired table name to display the fields.
4. Click to select the desired field name.
5. Press and hold the **Ctrl** key and drag the field to the placeholder control on the form. Release the **Ctrl** key.
 - The field is added into the layout and highlighted with an orange border (Figure 4-46).
 - Edit the caption in the label as desired.
6. Continue adding additional fields as desired.

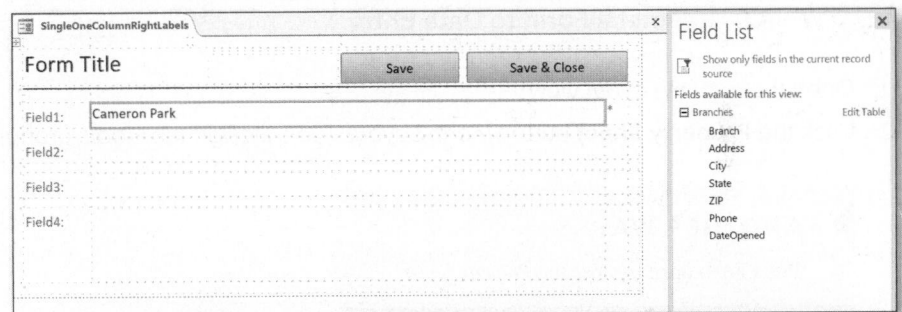

Figure 4-46 Add a field to an *Application Parts* form

Facilitating Data Input with a Form

Forms enable you to view, change, or delete data already in a database or to add new data into a database. Sometimes, you use a form for all these purposes, but at other times you may want to create a single-purpose form. When using a form for data entry, it is important to design it to help minimize potential data entry mistakes, as well as to make the data entry efficient. Use the *Property Sheet* of the form to select the desired settings to limit actions available in a form (Figure 4-47).

The following form properties, located on the *Data* tab, control actions available in a form:

- *Data Entry*: Determines whether a form is restricted to data entry. The default setting is *No*.

Figure 4-47 Properties to limit actions available in a form

- ***Allow Additions***: Determines whether a user can use the form to add data into the database. The default setting is *Yes*.
- ***Allow Deletions***: Determines whether a user can use the form to delete a record from the database. The default setting is *Yes*.
- ***Allow Edits***: Determines whether a user can use the form to change values in a record in the database. The default setting is *Yes*.

Recall that you can press the **Sort** button in the *Property Sheet* to sort the properties in ascending order (see Figure 4-36 if needed). This can be helpful to find a specific property more quickly.

Restrict a Form to Data Entry

Restrict a form to only allow data entry when you don't want users to have access to all the data records that exist in the database. This enables you to limit some activities to authorized users. Additionally, this feature can prevent users from accidentally changing or deleting existing records in the table.

▶HOW TO: Restrict a Form to Data Entry

1. Open the form in *Layout* view.
2. Click the **Property Sheet** button [*Form Layout Tools Design* tab, *Tools* group].

ANOTHER WAY
Press **F4** to open or close the *Property Sheet*.

3. Click the **drop-down arrow** in the *Selection* box of the *Property Sheet* and select **Form**.
4. Click to select the **Data** tab of the *Property Sheet* if necessary.
5. Select **Yes** in the *Data Entry* property box to restrict the form to data entry.
6. Select **Yes** in the *Allow Additions* property box.

A form that has been restricted to data entry does not show any existing records when viewed. This means that a user cannot delete or edit records. As a result, the settings in the *Allow Deletions* and *Allow Edits* property boxes don't have an impact.

Limit Edits and Deletions on a Form

Sometimes, you want users to be able to view existing records in a database but not to be able to edit or delete them. You can establish these limits through the *Property Sheet*.

▶HOW TO: Limit Edits and Deletions on a Form

1. Open the form in *Layout* view.
2. Click the **Property Sheet** button [*Form Layout Tools Design* tab, *Tools* group] to open the *Property Sheet*.
3. Click the **drop-down arrow** in the *Selection* box of the *Property Sheet* and select **Form**.

4. Select **No** in the *Data Entry* property box. The additional property selections you make in step 5 determine how users can access and change the data currently in the database.

5. Set the desired form properties.
 * Select **Yes** or **No** in the *Allow Additions* property box. If set to *Yes*, this will override the *Data Entry* property and enable records to be added into the database.
 * Select **Yes** or **No** in the *Allow Deletions* property box.
 * Select **Yes** or **No** in the *Allow Edits* property box.

Add a Command Button

A ***command button*** is a type of control that can perform a number of different actions. For example, command buttons can be set to print the current form, close the current form, navigate to the next record, or open another form. Buttons make a form more user-friendly.

The quickest way to add a command button to a form is to use the *Command Button Wizard*. The ***Command Button Wizard*** creates a button and attaches all of the necessary functionality to the button. The functionality is contained in a *Macro* and is attached to the ***On Click*** property of the button. Recall that a ***Macro*** is a database object that enables you to write and attach code to different objects and controls in your database.

The *Command Button Wizard* groups the available functionality into six different categories. Those categories and the available actions are shown in Table 4-2.

Table 4-2: Groupings of Categories and Actions in the Command Button Wizard

Category	Actions
Record Navigation	*Find Next* *Find Record* *Go To First Record* *Go To Last Record* *Go To Next Record* *Go To Previous Record*
Record Operations	*Add New Record* *Delete Record* *Duplicate Record* *Print Record* *Save Record* *Undo Record*
Form Operations	*Apply Form Filter* *Close Form* *Open Form* *Print a Form* *Print Current Form* *Refresh Form Data*
Report Operations	*Mail Report* *Open Report* *Preview Report* *Print Report* *Send Report to File*
Application	*Quit Application*
Miscellaneous	*Auto Dialer* *Print Table* *Run Macro* *Run Query*

The *Command Button Wizard* does not launch unless you first turn on the *Control Wizards* tool. The *Control Wizards* tool directs Access to launch an available wizard when adding controls to an object.

The *Control Wizards* tool uses an on/off setting. If the icon is gray-colored, the *Control Wizards* are on; if the icon is white, the *Control Wizards* are off.

▶HOW TO: Add a Command Button Using the Command Button Wizard

1. Open the form in *Layout* view.
2. Click the **Form Layout Tools Design** tab.
3. Click the **More** arrow at the far right of the *Controls* group (Figure 4-48) to expand the *Controls* group. If the *Use Control Wizards* button does not have a gray-colored background, select the **Use Control Wizards** button to turn on the wizard (Figure 4-49).

Figure 4-48 *Controls* group

Figure 4-49 *Use Control Wizards* button

4. Click **Button** in the *Controls* group. Move the pointer to the desired location in the control layout and click a **cell** (Figure 4-50) to launch the *Command Button Wizard* (Figure 4-51).

 - If the *Command Button Wizard* does not launch, *Control Wizards* is not turned on.
 - Delete the button that was placed on the form.
 - Repeat step 3 to turn the *Control Wizards* on.
 - Repeat step 4 to add a button.

Figure 4-50 Position the button control onto the form

Figure 4-51 *Command Button Wizard*, page 1

5. Select a **Category** and **Action** for the button.
6. Click **Next** to move to the second page of the *Command Button Wizard*.
7. Choose whether you want the button to display words or an image (Figure 4-52).
8. Click **Next** to move to the last page of the wizard.
9. Enter a name for the button as desired and click **Finish**.

 - The button name is important if you are going to modify the macro code attached to the button.
 - You may want the name to reference the form name and button action. For example, *EmployeeForm-CloseButton*.
 - The button displays in the form (Figure 4-53).

A4-244

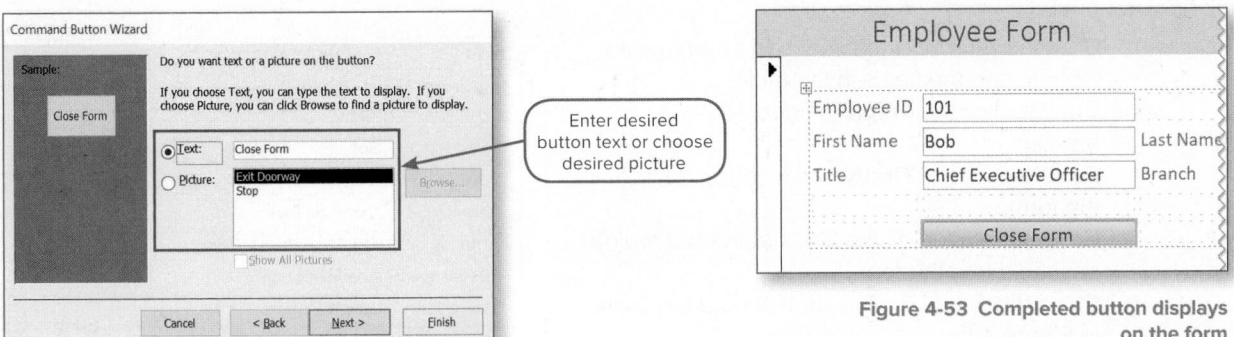

Figure 4-52 *Command Button Wizard, page 2*

Figure 4-53 **Completed button displays on the form**

Test a Form

After you have built your form, it is important to switch to *Form* view and test the functionality of the form. You may have forgotten to add or delete a field on the form or you may want to change the text in a label to make it more user-friendly. You may also realize that you selected the wrong action to assign to a button.

Switch to *Form* view by clicking the **Views** button [*Form Layout Tools Design* tab] and selecting **Form View**. If you are in *Design* view, you can also press **F5** to switch to *Form* view.

Test the functionality of the form by performing the following tasks:

- Navigate through several records, ensuring that the width of the fields is appropriate.
- Review the overall layout to ensure that the structure is easy-to-use and intuitive for the user.
- Test all buttons to ensure they behave as expected.
- Make any needed corrections and re-test as appropriate.

PAUSE & PRACTICE: ACCESS 4-2

For this Pause & Practice, you build a form using the *Blank Form* button for the Central Sierra Insurance database. You modify the form to restrict it to data entry, add buttons, and test the form. This database contains an existing query and report that are used later in the chapter.

File Needed: ***CentralSierra-04.accdb*** *(Student data files are available in the* Library *of your SIMnet account.)*
Completed Project File Name: ***[your initials] PP A4-2.accdb***

1. Open the ***CentralSierra-04*** database from your student data files.

2. Save the database as [your initials] PP A4-2.

3. Enable content in the database.

4. Create a new form using the *Blank Form* button.
 a. Click the **Blank Form** button [*Create* tab, *Forms* group]. A new blank form opens in *Layout* view.
 b. Cick the **Show all tables** link in the *Field List* pane.

c. Click the **plus sign** to expand the *Employees* table to see the fields in the table.
d. Double-click the **EmpID** field to add it to the form.
e. Double-click the **FirstName** field to add it to the form.
f. Continue adding all the fields from the *Employees* table into the form.
g. Close the *Field List*. The form should be similar to Figure 4-54.

5. Modify the control layout.
a. Click one of the fields on the form. An orange border surrounds it.
b. Click the **Select Layout** button [*Form Layout Tools Arrange* tab, *Rows & Columns* group] or click the **layout selector**. All the cells in the layout are bordered in orange.
c. Place your pointer over any field. Click, hold, and drag the **control layout** down about ¼" and to the right about ¼" (Figure 4-55), and then release the pointer.
d. Select the **Base Monthly Salary** label.
e. Place your pointer over the right edge of the label until it becomes the resize arrow.
f. Click, hold, and drag the **resize arrow** to increase the width of the label to make the entire caption visible.
g. Navigate to record number 10. This record contains the employee with the longest title.
h. Click the **Title** text box. Remember that the text box control displays the actual data. In this form, the text boxes are located to the right of the label.
i. Decrease the width of the text box to remove the excess space.

6. Add a new column and new rows to the control layout.
a. Select the **Base Monthly Salary** text box.
b. Click the **Select Row** button [*Form Layout Tools Arrange* tab, *Rows & Columns* group].
c. Click the **Insert Below** button [*Form Layout Tools Arrange* tab, *Rows & Columns* group] to add a blank row.
d. Click the **Insert Below** button again to add a second blank row.
e. Select the **Base Monthly Salary** text box.
f. Click the **Select Column** button [*Form Layout Tools Arrange* tab, *Rows & Columns* group].
g. Click the **Insert Right** button [*Form Layout Tools Arrange* tab, *Rows & Columns* group] to add a blank column.

7. Adjust the height and width of the new column and rows.
a. Select a **cell** in the new column.
b. Place your pointer over the right edge of the cell until it becomes the resize arrow.
c. Click, hold, and drag the **resize arrow** to increase the width of the cell. Make the width approximately the same as the first column.
d. Select a **cell** in the bottom blank row.
e. Press **F4** to open the *Property Sheet*.
f. Click the **Format** tab if necessary.
g. Type .4" in the *Height* property box and press **Enter**.

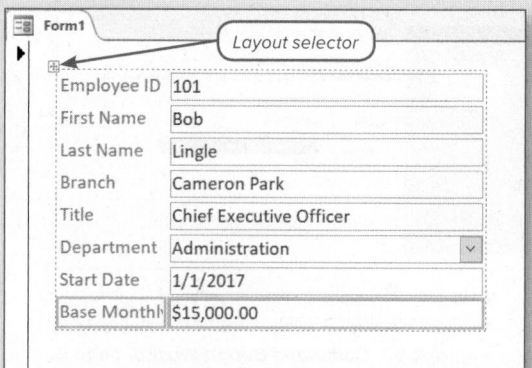

Figure 4-54 Employee form after adding all fields

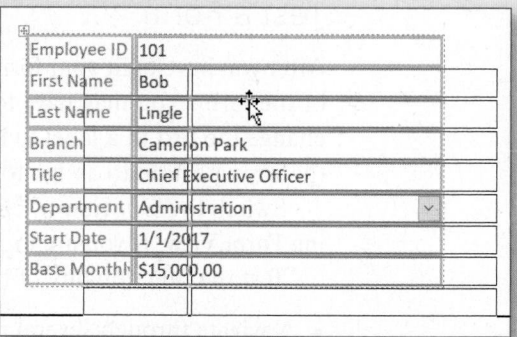

Figure 4-55 Drag the control layout to a new location

h. Press **F4** to close the *Property Sheet*. The completed form should look similar to Figure 4-56.

8. Add command buttons to the form.
 a. Click the **Form Layout Tools Design** tab.
 b. Click the **More** arrow on the far right of the *Controls* group and select the **Use Control Wizards** button if it does not already have a gray-colored border indicating it is selected.
 c. Click **Button** in the *Controls* group. Click the left-most **cell** in the bottom row to launch the *Command Button Wizard*. If the *Command Button Wizard* does not launch, *Control Wizards* is not turned on. Delete the button that was added to the form and go back to step 8b.
 d. Select the **Record Operations** *Category* and the **Save Record** *Action* of the button.
 e. Click **Next** to move to the second page of the *Command Button Wizard*.
 f. Select the **Text** radio button and change the wording to read Save Employee Record.
 g. Click **Next** to move to the last page of the wizard.
 h. Enter AddEmpForm-SaveButton as the name for the button and click **Finish**. The button displays in the form (Figure 4-57). The text in the button wraps depending on the width of the column.
 i. Add a second button to the form. Place the button in the middle cell of the last row.
 j. Select the **Record Operations** *Category* and the **Add New Record** *Action* of the button.
 k. Click **Next** to move to the second page of the *Command Button Wizard*.
 l. Select the **Text** radio button and change the wording to read Add New Employee.
 m. Click **Next** to move to the last page of the wizard.
 n. Enter AddEmpForm-AddButton as the name for the button and click **Finish**.
 o. Add a third button to the form. Place the button in the right-most cell of the last row.
 p. Select the **Form Operations** *Category* and the **Close Form** *Action* of the button.
 q. Click **Next** to move to the second page of the wizard.
 r. Select the **Text** radio button and accept the existing wording of "Close Form."
 s. Click **Next** to move to the last page of the wizard.
 t. Enter AddEmpForm-CloseButton as the name for the button and click **Finish**.

9. Add a title to the form.
 a. Click the **Title** button [*Form Layout Tools Design* tab, *Header/Footer* group].
 b. Change the wording to read Add New Employee and press **Enter**. The form should look similar to Figure 4-58.

10. Restrict the form to data entry.
 a. Press **F4** to open the *Property Sheet*.
 b. Click the **drop-down arrow** in the *Selection* box of the *Property Sheet* and select **Form**.
 c. Click to select the **Data** tab if necessary.
 d. Select **Yes** in the *Data Entry* property box.
 e. Select **Yes** in the *Allow Additions* property box if necessary.
 f. Close the *Property Sheet*.

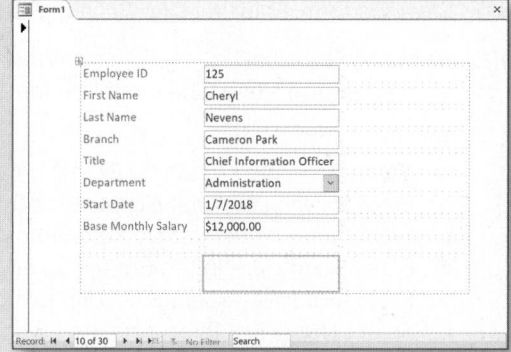

Figure 4-56 Employee form after adding and modifying rows and columns

Figure 4-57 Button added to form

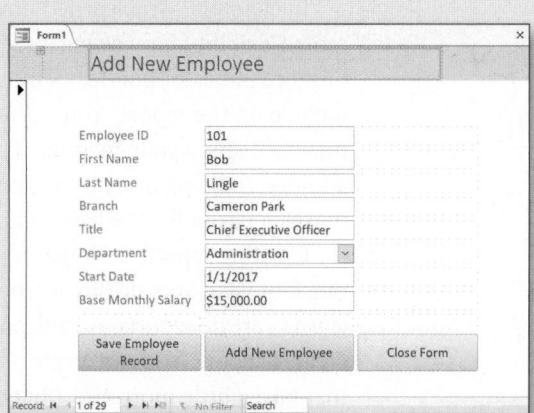

Figure 4-58 Completed form after adding a title and three buttons

11. Save the form. Enter AddNewEmployee as the *Form Name*.

12. Switch to *Form* view by clicking the **View** button [*Form Layout Tools Design* tab, *Views* group] and selecting **Form View**. The complete form displays.

13. Test the form.
 a. Enter 165 in the *Employee ID* text box.
 b. Enter Susan in the *First Name* text box.
 c. Enter Stone in the *Last Name* text box.
 d. Enter Granite Bay in the *Branch* text box.
 e. Enter Insurance Agent in the *Title* text box.
 f. Select Health and Benefits in the *Department* combo box.
 g. Enter 9/2/2019 in the *Start Date* text box.
 h. Enter 3800 in the *Base Monthly Salary* text box. The completed form should match the data shown in Figure 4-59.
 i. Click the **Save Employee Record** button.
 j. Click the **Add New Employee** button. A blank record should display in the form. In the *Navigation* bar, you can navigate back to the record you just entered, but you cannot view any other records in the table because the form is restricted to data entry.
 k. Click the **Close Form** button.

Employee ID	165
First Name	Susan
Last Name	Stone
Branch	Granite Bay
Title	Insurance Agent
Department	Health and Benefits
Start Date	9/2/2019
Base Monthly Salary	$3,800.00

Figure 4-59 Employee record values to enter in form

14. Double-click the **Employees** table to open it in *Datasheet* view.

15. Scroll down to find the new record for employee 165 that you added into the database.

16. Close the table.

17. Close the database.

Creating and Working with a Simple Report

A **report** is an object you can use to create an organized and professional output of the data in a database. Unlike forms, reports do *not* enable you to modify the underlying data. The reports in your database are directly connected to a table or query, the source of the data.

In chapter 2, you learned how to print the data records in a table. Reports provide a great deal more flexibility for viewing and printing the data in a database. A report can have fields from one or more tables or queries. Similar to a form, you select which fields from the tables or queries to include on the report. You also select grouping and summarizing options when you are choosing how to display your records. This flexibility helps you create reports that look professional, in addition to being more user-friendly than *Datasheet* view of a table. Ideally, a well-designed report makes it easier for the user to understand the information contained in the database.

Creating reports is similar to creating forms. You can apply much of what you already learned about creating forms as you learn to create reports. Access provides several different ways to create a report. You can create a report quickly or create reports that take a little more effort but provide a great deal more flexibility when it comes to report design and specialization. In this section, you are introduced to two ways to build a report: the *Report Wizard* and the *Blank Report* options. These options are available in the *Reports* group [*Create* tab] (Figure 4-60).

Figure 4-60 Report creation options

The Report Wizard

The **Report Wizard** steps you through the process of quickly creating a report. While you will probably need to fine-tune the initial report design, it provides a good starting point. The *Report Wizard* asks you which tables and queries you want to base the report on and which specific fields you want to include in the report. Additionally, you must determine if you want to group the data by any fields, sort on any fields, and choose the layout and orientation of the report. Your layout choices change based on whether you group the data or not.

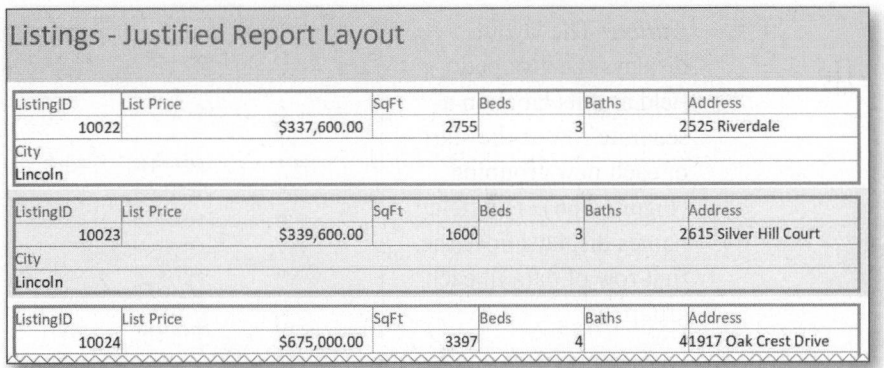

Listings - Columnar Report Layout	
ListingID	10022
List Price	$337,600.00
SqFt	2755
Beds	3
Baths	2
Address	525 Riverdale
City	Lincoln
ListingID	10023
List Price	$339,600.00
SqFt	1600

Figure 4-61 Columnar report layout

The three layout choices for reports without grouping are columnar, tabular, and justified:

- *Columnar.* The layout displays the fields in one column (Figure 4-61). The field labels appear to the left of the data.
- *Tabular.* The layout displays the fields in a table (row and column) format. The field names display above the data (Figure 4-62).

Listings - Tabular Report Layout

ListingID	List Price	SqFt	Beds	Baths	Address	City
10022	$337,600.00	2755	3	2	525 Riverdale	Lincoln
10023	$339,600.00	1600	3	2	615 Silver Hill Court	Lincoln
10024	$675,000.00	3397	4	4	1917 Oak Crest Drive	Roseville
10025	$216,600.00	1900	4	3	3420 Milburn Street	Rocklin
10027	$130,000.00	1184	3	2	2128 Wedgewood	Roseville

Figure 4-62 Tabular report layout

- *Justified*: The layout displays the fields in a horizontal, justified layout (Figure 4-63). The field names display above each field.

Listings - Justified Report Layout

ListingID	List Price		SqFt	Beds	Baths	Address
10022		$337,600.00	2755	3		2525 Riverdale
City						
Lincoln						
ListingID	List Price		SqFt	Beds	Baths	Address
10023		$339,600.00	1600	3		2615 Silver Hill Court
City						
Lincoln						
ListingID	List Price		SqFt	Beds	Baths	Address
10024		$675,000.00	3397	4		41917 Oak Crest Drive

Figure 4-63 Justified report layout

Grouping is useful when you want to organize and summarize the data in your report. For example, you could group all properties from the same city together or you could group all

the songs from a particular artist together. The three layout choices for a grouped report are stepped, block, and outline:

- ***Stepped***: The layout displays the fields in a table layout (Figure 4-64). The field names display in a row above the data. If the report is longer than one page, the field names appear at the top of each page. The grouped field displays in the left-most column. The data value appears in its own row at the start of each new grouping.

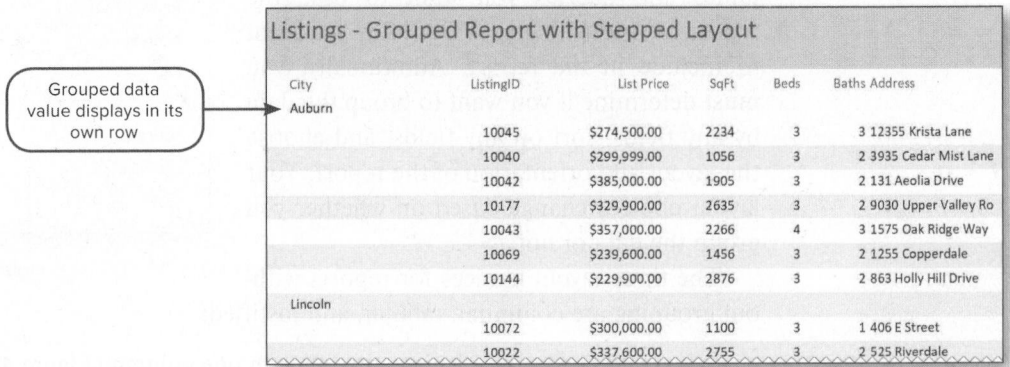

Figure 4-64 Stepped layout in a grouped report

- ***Block***: The layout is very similar to a stepped layout; it has a table layout and field names at the top. The major difference is that the grouped field appears in the same row as the first record for that grouping (Figure 4-65). If the report is longer than one page, the field names appear at the top of each page. Additionally, the data rows are grouped a little more tightly together, meaning that more data can appear on each page.

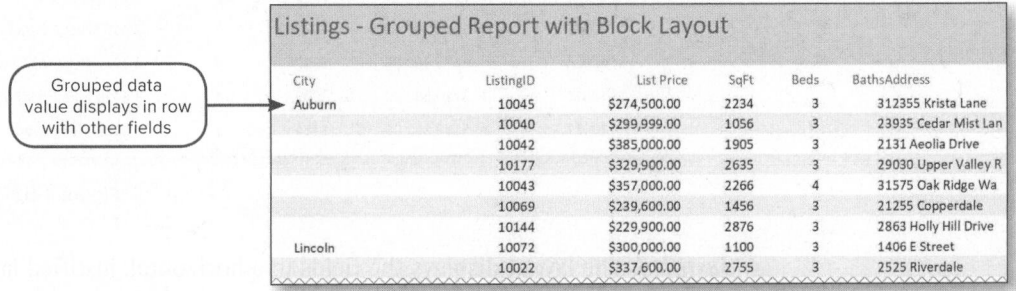

Figure 4-65 Block layout in a grouped report

- ***Outline***: The layout displays the grouped field and its label on a separate row at the start of each new grouping (Figure 4-66). The field names display above the first row of data in each grouping.

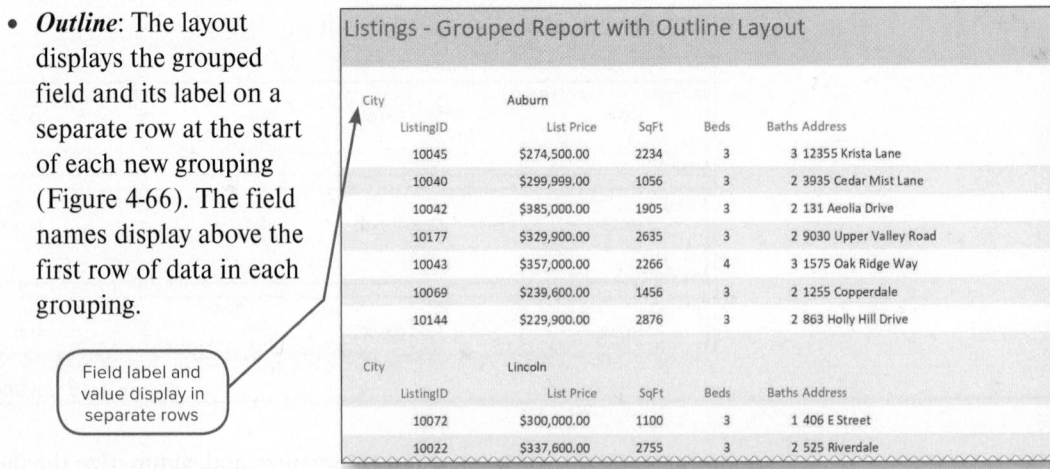

Figure 4-66 Outline layout in a grouped report

With grouped reports, you also have the option to have Access automatically calculate various summary values across the different groups. You can decide to display only the summary values (Figure 4-67) or to display both the detail records and summary values for each group (Figure 4-68).

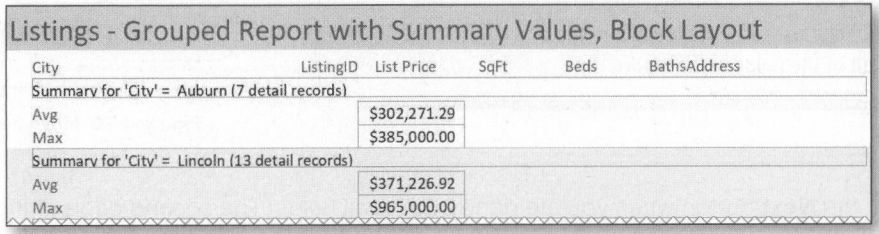

Figure 4-67 Grouped report with summary values only

Figure 4-68 Grouped report with detail and summary values

After you have created a report using the *Report Wizard*, you can preview the report or open it in *Design* view to modify the layout. If you need to make changes to the report later, you can edit it using *Layout* view or *Design* view.

▶ HOW TO: Create a Report Using the Report Wizard

1. Click the **Create** tab on the *Ribbon*.
2. Click the **Report Wizard** button [*Reports* group] to launch the *Report Wizard* (Figure 4-69).
 - The values displayed in the *Tables/Queries* box and the *Available Fields* window change based on the contents of your database.
3. Click the **Tables/Queries** drop-down arrow and select the *Table* or *Query* name.
4. Select a **field** to include in the *Report* from those displayed in the *Available Fields* window.
 - Add fields in the order you want them to display in the report.
5. Click the **Move Single Field** button.
 - The field moves into the *Selected Fields* window.
 - The *Remove Single Field* and *Remove All Fields* buttons become active.

Figure 4-69 *Report Wizard*, step 1

6. Continue moving all required fields (Figure 4-70), changing the selected *Table* or *Query* if needed.

> **ANOTHER WAY**
>
> Click the **Move All Fields** button to quickly include all of the fields in the report.

Figure 4-70 Move fields into the *Selected Fields* window

7. Click the **Next** button when you are done adding all fields. The second page of the *Report Wizard* displays (Figure 4-71).

8. Select any fields you want to use to group the data.

 • When you select fields on which to group, Access moves those fields to the left-most columns of the report.

9. Click the **Next** button. The next page of the *Report Wizard* displays (Figure 4-72).

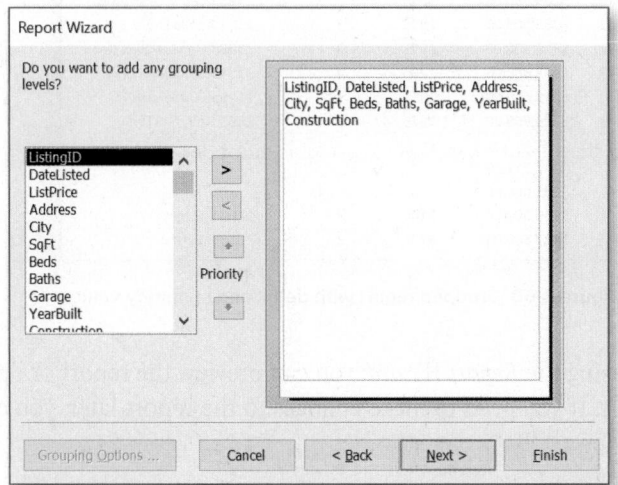

Figure 4-71 Select grouping levels

Figure 4-72 Select sorting and summary options

10. Select any fields you want to use to sort the report and select either **Ascending** or **Descending** sort order.

 • The *Summary Options* button only displays if you added grouping levels in step 8.

 • Click the **Summary Options** button to open the *Summary Options* dialog box, select the fields to calculate and choose the desired functions. You can choose from the *Sum*, *Avg*, *Min*, and *Max* functions. You can also choose whether to display only summary values or both detail and summary values.

11. Click the **Next** button. The next page of the *Report Wizard* displays (Figure 4-73).

12. Select the desired layout and orientation. If you added grouping levels, the layout choices change to *Stepped*, *Block*, and *Outline*.

Figure 4-73 Select layout and orientation options

13. Deselect the check box that fits all fields on one page as desired. If this box is selected, some fields may not be wide enough to display their full contents.

14. Click the **Next** button. The last page of the *Report Wizard* displays (Figure 4-74).

15. Change the title.

16. Select the radio button to either **Preview the report** or to **Modify the report's design**.

17. Click **Finish**.

- Access saves the report using the name provided in the title.
- The report shows in either *Print Preview* view or *Design* view depending on the selection made in step 16.
- Most of the fields appear in text boxes.
- Fields that have a lookup appear in a combo box.
- Fields that are a *Yes/No* data type appear as a check box.
- The size of a field depends on the data type and the field size.
- The report name displays in the *Reports* group on the *Navigation Pane*.

18. Close the report.

- If the report was opened in *Print Preview* view, when you close *Print Preview* you are in *Design* view. You need to close that when you are done with the report.

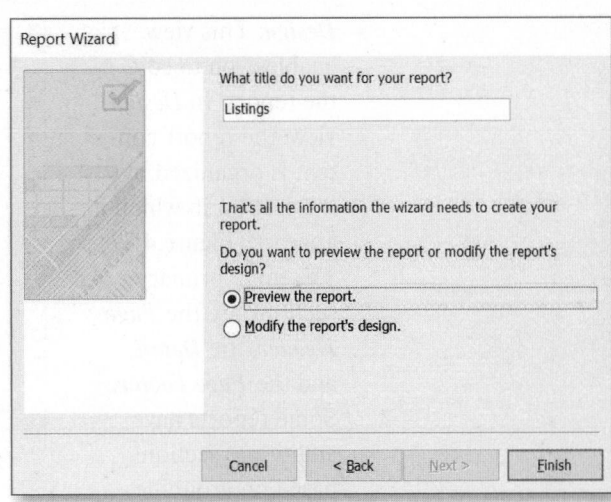

Figure 4-74 Enter the title in the last step of the *Report Wizard*

View or Modify a Report

Access provides four different view options for a report:

- **Report**: This view is used to execute the report and see the results (Figure 4-75). When you double-click a report in the *Navigation Pane*, it opens in *Report* view. In *Report* view, you see all the data contained in the report. However, you do not see it separated into separate pages. Use the scroll bars to see parts of the report not visible on the screen.

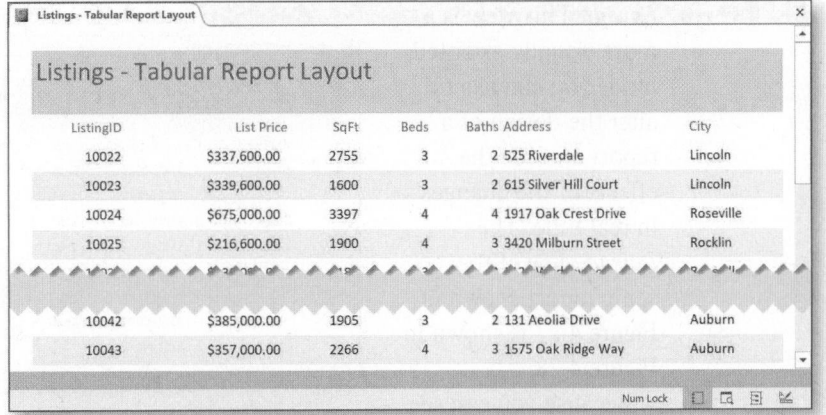

Figure 4-75 *Report* view of a report

- **Print Preview**: This view (Figure 4-76) lets you see how the report will look in print. In *SLO 4.8: Printing a Report*, you will learn to use the *Print Preview* tab to make modifications to the print settings, such as margins, page orientation, page size, and so forth.

- **Design**: This view
 enables you to edit
 the report. In *Design*
 view, the report con-
 tent is organized by
 the section in which it
 appears (Figure 4-77).
 The three primary
 sections are the **Page
 Header**, the **Detail**,
 and the **Page Footer**.
 Some reports have
 additional sections
 based on grouping
 levels that have been added.

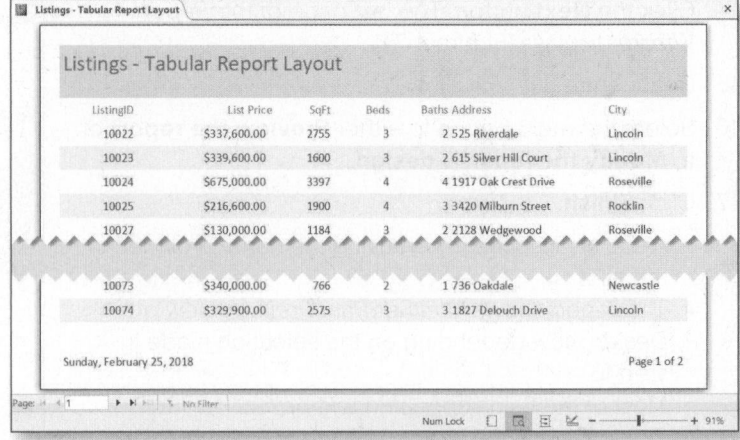

Figure 4-76 *Print Preview* view of a report

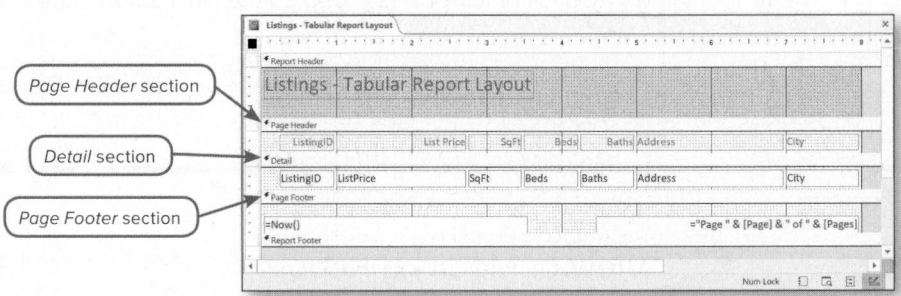

Figure 4-77 *Design* view of a report

Design view is good for adding labels and images into a report, editing text boxes, resiz-
ing the report sections, and changing some report properties. When you are working in
Design view, Access organizes your editing choices into four **Report Design Tools** contex-
tual tabs: **Design**, **Arrange**, **Format**, and **Page Setup**.

- **Layout**: This view is a
 more visually oriented
 mode you can use to
 alter the design of a
 report and see the
 effects of the changes
 in real time. The
 Layout view of the
 same report shown in
 Figure 4-77 is shown in
 Figure 4-78.

 Because you can see
 how the data display at

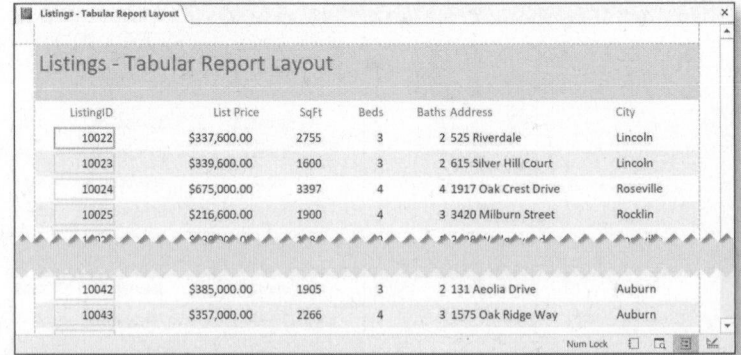

Figure 4-78 *Layout* view of a report

the same time you are able to modify the design, *Layout* view is good for resizing fields or
labels, changing colors or text alignment, or applying different formats. Like *Design* view,
Layout view organizes your editing choices into the same four *Report Design Tools* con-
textual tabs: *Design*, *Arrange*, *Format*, and *Page Setup*. However, not all design options are
available while in *Layout* view.

A4-254

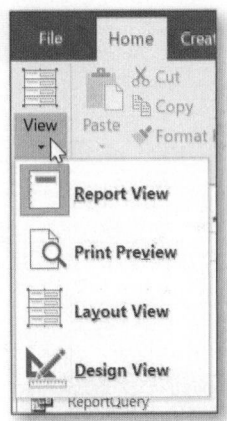

▶ HOW TO: Switch Report Views to View or Modify a Report

1. Click the **View** button [*Home* tab].
2. Select **Report View**, **Print Preview**, **Layout View**, or **Design View** (Figure 4-79).
3. View the results or make any modifications.

> ▶ **ANOTHER WAY**
> Select a view icon from the lower-right corner of the *Status* bar.

Figure 4-79 *View options for a report*

Save a Report

When a report is created, Access automatically assigns it a default name. When you create a report using the *Report Wizard*, Access automatically saves the report during the creation process. If you created a report using any of the other report options, or if you have made any modifications to the design of the report created with the wizard, you need to save those changes. Save changes to a report by pressing **Ctrl+S** or clicking the **Save** icon on the *Quick Access* toolbar. The first time you save a report, you are prompted to change the default name in the *Save As* dialog box.

After a report has been created and saved, you may need to make a copy of that report. This may be done to have a backup of the original report or because another report will have the same initial characteristics.

▶ HOW TO: Save a Copy of a Report

1. Click **Save As** [*File* tab] to display the *Save As* area.
2. Click **Save Object As** in the *File Types* options. *Save Object As* should be selected in the *Database File Types* options.
3. Click the **Save As** button to open the *Save As* dialog box (Figure 4-80).
 - The name of the current report displays in the *Save 'object name' to* box.
 - In Figure 4-80, *Listings – Tabular Report Layout* is the name of the current report.
 - The suggested name always begins with "Copy of."
4. Type the name you wish to use in the *Save 'object name' to* box.
5. Click **OK**.

Figure 4-80 *Save As dialog box*

> ▶ **ANOTHER WAY**
> Press **F12** to open the *Save As* dialog box.

Once a report has been saved, it displays in the *Reports* group of the *Navigation Pane*.

Open a Saved Report

If you double-click a report name in the *Navigation Pane*, the report opens in *Report* view.

Open a saved report in *Print Preview* view, *Design* view, or *Layout* view by right-clicking the report name in the *Navigation Pane* and selecting **Print Preview**, **Design View**, or **Layout View** from the context menu.

Delete a Report

Occasionally, you have reports that no longer are needed in the database.

Delete a report by selecting the report name in the *Navigation Pane* and clicking the **Delete** button [*Home* tab, *Records* group].

> ▶ **ANOTHER WAY**
>
> Right-click the report name in the *Navigation Pane* and select **Delete** from the context menu.

Creating and Customizing a Report in Layout View

In *Layout* view, you can modify a report and see how the report looks with data displaying. In this section, you first learn how to create a blank report and then you explore the layout of a report and modify the report in *Layout* view.

The Blank Report Button

Sometimes, it is easier to start with a completely blank report and then add the fields, labels, or other controls.

▶ **HOW TO:** Create a Blank Report

1. Click the **Blank Report** button [*Create* tab, *Reports* group].
 - A new blank report opens in *Layout* view (Figure 4-81).
 - The *Field List* pane displays.
2. Click the **Show all tables** link to display the database tables.
3. Click the **plus sign** to the left of a table name to see the fields in the table.
4. Click the **minus sign** to the left of a table name to collapse the list of fields in the table.

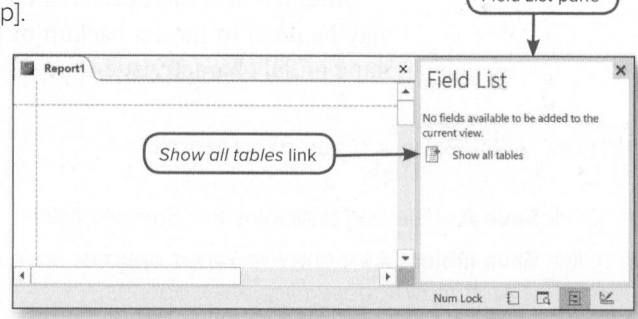

Figure 4-81 Blank report in *Layout* view

After you create the blank report, you are ready to add items to the report. Remember to save the report and any changes you make to it.

Report Controls

Recall that the fields, labels, buttons, and so forth are all known as *controls*. In a report, you add controls in either *Layout* view or *Design* view. The controls are accessed in the *Controls* group of the *Report Layout Tools Design* tab. The report controls available in *Layout* view are shown in Figure 4-82.

Figure 4-82 *Controls* group for a report

Like controls on forms, controls on reports are either *bound* to a data value, *unbound* and not linked to a data source, or *calculated* and their value comes from an expression. As you work through the book, you are introduced to a variety of report controls.

Report Control Layouts

Like forms, ***control layouts*** provide a structure to align the controls on your report. The two primary layout options are tabular and stacked:

- ***Tabular***: This layout organizes data in rows and columns. Labels identifying the different fields are above the data values (Figure 4-83).
- ***Stacked***: This layout organizes data vertically. The labels are to the left of the data control (Figure 4-84).

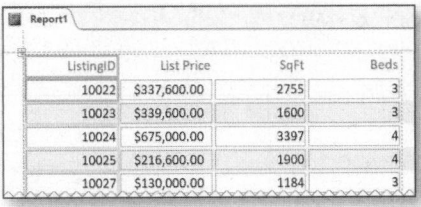

Figure 4-83 Tabular control layout in a report

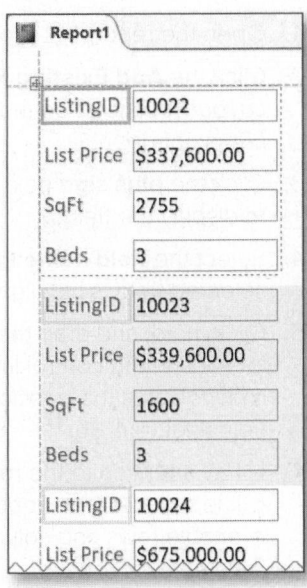

Figure 4-84 Stacked control layout in a report

Add and Delete Fields in a Control Layout

A new blank report initially has no controls. You can add table fields to the report in *Layout* view.

▶HOW TO: Add Fields into the Control Layout of a Blank Report

1. Open the report in *Layout* view.
2. Click the **Add Existing Fields** button [*Report Layout Tools Design* tab, *Tools* group] if the *Field List* is not open.

> ▶ **ANOTHER WAY**
> Press **Alt+F8** to show or hide the *Field List*.

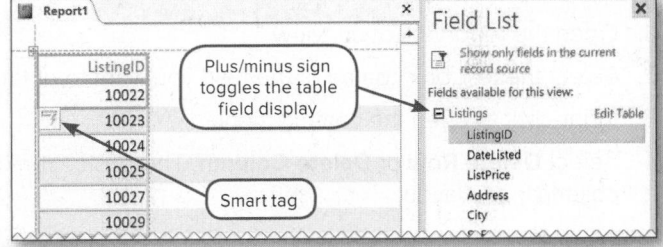

Figure 4-85 Add fields into a report

3. Click the **Show all tables** link if the database tables do not show.
4. Click the **plus sign** next to the table name to display the fields.
5. Double-click the **field name** to add the field into the report.
 - The field is added into a tabular layout (Figure 4-85).
 - Click the **smart tag icon** to change to a stacked layout.
 - The most recently added field is highlighted with an orange border.
6. Continue adding the remaining fields.

> ▶ **ANOTHER WAY**
> Click, hold, and drag a **field** from the *Field List* into the report window to add it into the control layout.

▶HOW TO: Add Fields between Existing Fields in a Control Layout

1. Open the report in *Layout* view.
2. Click the **Add Existing Fields** button [*Report Layout Tools Design* tab, *Tools* group] if the *Field List* is not open.
3. Click the **plus sign** next to the desired table name to display the fields.
4. Select the **field name** to add to the report. The selected field is highlighted in rose.
5. Click, hold, and drag the **field** to the desired location in the control layout. A rose-colored line indicates the position of the new field (Figure 4-86).

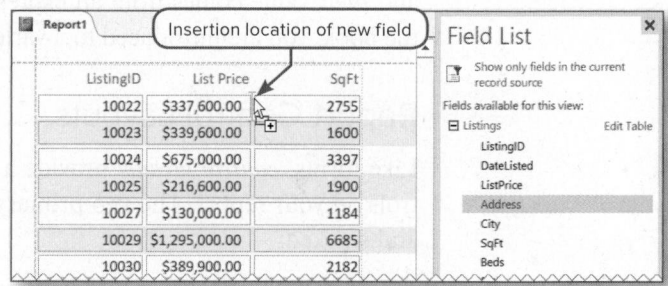

Figure 4-86 Add fields between existing fields in a control layout

- Pay attention to the rose-colored line's placement. Reports enable rows and columns to be combined.
- Figure 4-87 shows the new field being added into a row of a tabular layout.
- Figure 4-88 shows the resulting report. This could create a confusing report organization.

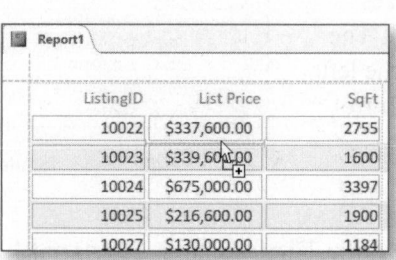

Figure 4-87 Insert a new field as a row in a tabular layout

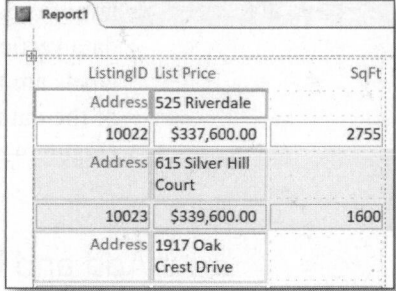

Figure 4-88 Report after new field added

As you improve the layout of a report, you may need to delete a field from the report.

▶HOW TO: Delete a Field from a Control Layout

1. Open the report in *Layout* view.
2. Select the text box control of the field you want to delete.
3. Right-click to open the context menu.
4. Select **Delete Row** or **Delete Column**. The choice removes the field, the associated label, as well as the row or column in the layout.

Customize a Report in Layout View

You can make a number of modifications to a report in *Layout* view. In this section, you learn how to change control layouts, adjust column widths, and add and delete rows and columns in a control layout.

These options are available through the buttons in the *Table* and *Rows & Columns* groups on the *Report Layout Tools Arrange* tab (Figure 4-89).

Figure 4-89 Customize a report layout using options in the *Table* and *Rows & Columns* groups

Change Control Layouts

When you create a report, the report starts with either a stacked or tabular layout. As you add and delete fields on the report, you may wish to change its layout.

▶ HOW TO: Change Control Layouts

1. Open the report in *Layout* view.
2. Select one of the fields in the control layout. The orange border surrounds that field.
3. Click the **Select Layout** button [*Report Layout Tools Arrange* tab, *Rows & Columns* group] or click the **layout selector**. The orange border surrounds all of the controls in the layout.
4. Select either the **Stacked** or **Tabular** button [*Report Layout Tools Arrange* tab, *Table* group]. The report updates with the new layout.

Adjust Column Widths

Sometimes, the initial width of the report fields needs to be adjusted. Keep in mind that in a stacked layout, all of the fields have the same width. As a result, when changing the width, you need to ensure that the column is wide enough to fit the largest field. In a tabular layout, you can set the width of each field individually.

▶ HOW TO: Change Field Column Widths Using the Property Sheet

1. Open the report in *Layout* view.
2. Select the text box control of the field in the control layout. The orange border surrounds that field.
3. Press **F4** or click the **Property Sheet** button [*Report Layout Tools Design* tab, *Tools* group].
4. Click the **Format** tab if necessary.
5. Type the new value in the *Width* property (Figure 4-90) and press **Enter**. Remember that a series of **#** symbols indicates that the column is not wide enough to display the contents.

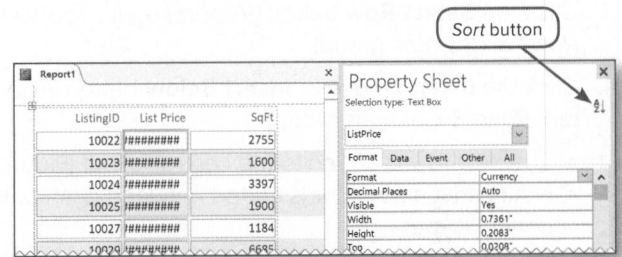

Figure 4-90 Adjust the width of a report field

> **MORE INFO**
>
> Sometimes, it can be difficult to locate the desired property in the *Property Sheet*. Click the **Sort** button (Figure 4-90) in the *Property Sheet* to sort the properties in ascending order.

> **ANOTHER WAY**
>
> You can also change the width of a text box control by using the resize arrow. Select the control. Place your pointer on the right edge of the control. Click, hold, and drag the **resize arrow** to increase or decrease the width of the control.

Add and Delete Rows and Columns in a Control Layout

Often, you want to make minor modifications to the control layout. For example, you may want to create a second column in a stacked layout, or you may want to delete a row if you removed fields from the control layout. You can make these modifications using buttons in the *Rows & Columns* group of the *Report Layout Tools Arrange* tab.

▶ HOW TO: Add a Column to a Control Layout

1. Open the report in *Layout* view.
2. Select a control in the column adjacent to where you want to add a new column.
3. Click the **Select Column** button [*Report Layout Tools Arrange* tab, *Rows & Columns* group].
4. Click the **Insert Left** or **Insert Right** button [*Report Layout Tools Arrange* tab, *Rows & Columns* group].
 - The new column is added to the control layout (Figure 4-91).
 - A light gray, dotted border surrounds the cells in the added column.

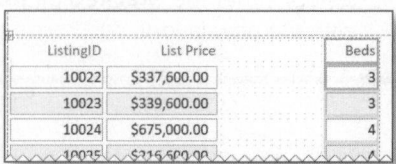

Figure 4-91 A dotted border surrounds each cell in the added column

▶ HOW TO: Add a Row to a Control Layout

1. Open the report in *Layout* view.
2. Select a control in the row adjacent to where you want to add a new row.
3. Click the **Select Row** button [*Report Layout Tools Arrange* tab, *Rows & Columns* group].
4. Click the **Insert Above** or **Insert Below** button [*Report Layout Tools Arrange* tab, *Rows & Columns* group].
 - The new row is added to the control layout (Figure 4-92).
 - Notice that a new row is added between each of the existing rows in the control layout.
 - A light gray, dotted border surrounds the cells in the new rows.

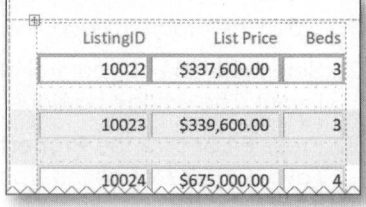

Figure 4-92 A dotted border surrounds each cell in the added row

▶ HOW TO: Delete a Row or Column from a Control Layout

1. Open the report in *Layout* view.
2. Select a control in the row or column you wish to delete.
3. Click the **Select Row** or **Select Column** button [*Report Layout Tools Arrange* tab, *Rows & Columns* group].
4. Right-click to open the context menu.
5. Select **Delete Row** or **Delete Column**.

Move a Control within a Layout

As you modify the control layout, you may need to move a control from one part of the layout to another.

▶HOW TO: Move a Control within a Layout

1. Open the report in *Layout* view.

2. Select the control that you wish to move.

 - The orange border surrounds that control.
 - To move the entire row or column including labels, click the **Select Row** or **Select Column** button [*Report Layout Tools Arrange* tab, *Rows & Columns* group].

3. Click the control, hold, and drag the **control** to the new location. A rose-colored line highlights the new location (Figure 4-93).

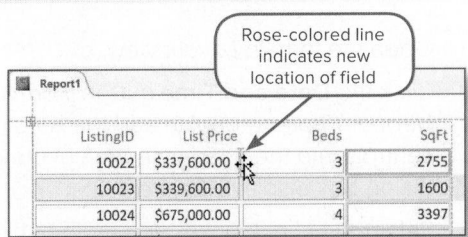

Figure 4-93 Drag a control to the new location

> ▶ **ANOTHER WAY**
>
> Select multiple controls by pressing and holding **Shift** and selecting multiple controls. You can then move them together.

Adjust Control Positioning on a Report

As with a form, you may wish to make changes to the way controls are positioned on a report. These changes can be made to a report from the *Position* group [*Report Layout Tools Arrange* tab].

Control Margins set how much margin space surrounds the text inside a control. It is measured from the upper-left corner of the control to the position of the text inside the control. The margin options are *None*, *Narrow*, *Medium*, and *Wide*. Each option places slightly more space in the margin.

Control Padding sets how much space is between the controls. The padding options are *None*, *Narrow*, *Medium*, and *Wide*. Each option places slightly more space between the controls.

▶HOW TO: Adjust Control Positioning on a Form

1. Open the report in *Layout* view.
2. Select the desired control or control layout.
3. Click the **Report Layout Tools Arrange** tab.
4. Click the **Control Margins** or **Control Padding** button.
5. Select the desired option.

Add a Title, Logo, Date, or Page Numbers to a Report

It is good database design to title each report. This enables the user to quickly understand the purpose of the report. You also may want to have a logo, the current date, and page numbers displayed in a report. These controls can be added to a report from the *Header/Footer* group [*Report Layout Tools Design* tab] (Figure 4-94). If the report does not already contain a header section, adding a title, logo, or the date and time automatically adds a header section to the report.

Figure 4-94 *Header/Footer* group options

▶HOW TO: Add a Date to a Report in Layout View

1. Open the form in *Layout* view.
2. Click the **Date and Time** button [*Form Layout Tools Design* tab, *Header/Footer* group] to add the *Auto_Date* and/or *Auto_Time* controls into the header section of the report. The *Date and Time* dialog box displays (Figure 4-95).
3. Select the check boxes and radio buttons corresponding to your choices.
4. Click **OK**.

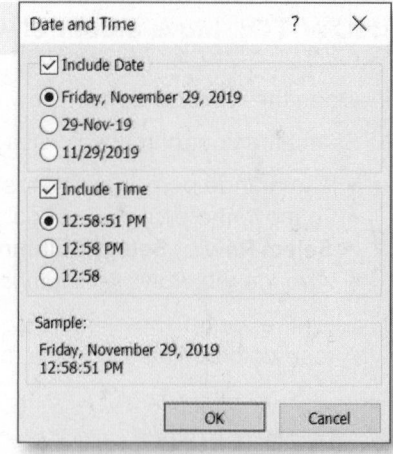

Figure 4-95 *Date and Time* dialog box

Selecting either the *Logo* or the *Title* button adds two controls into the header section, an *Auto_Header* control which contains the title and an *Auto_Logo* control which contains a logo.

▶HOW TO: Add a Title or Logo to a Report in Layout View

1. Open the report in *Layout* view.
2. Click the **Title** button [*Report Layout Tools Design* tab, *Header/Footer* group] to add a title into the header section of the report. The title is set to the report name.
3. Type a new title as desired.
4. Click the **Logo** button [*Report Layout Tools Design* tab, *Header/Footer* group] to add a logo to the report. The *Insert Picture* dialog box displays.
5. Select the image file to use as the logo and click **OK**.

When adding page numbers, you make several choices regarding the format and placement. Keep in mind that while a page number will display when the report is viewed in *Report* or *Layout* view, the value displayed is one. Only *Print Preview* view actually shows the separate report pages with the correct page number displayed.

▶HOW TO: Add Page Numbers to a Report in Layout View

1. Open the report in *Layout* view.
2. Click the **Page Numbers** button [*Report Layout Tools Design* tab, *Header/Footer* group] to open the *Page Numbers* dialog box (Figure 4-96).
3. Select the radio buttons corresponding to the appropriate *Format* and *Position* of the page numbers. If the *Bottom of Page* position is selected, a footer section is added to the report as needed.
4. Select the alignment of the page numbers.
5. Deselect the check box to **Show Number on First Page** as desired.

Figure 4-96 *Page Numbers* dialog box

6. Click **OK**. The page numbers appear in either the header or footer section (Figure 4-97).

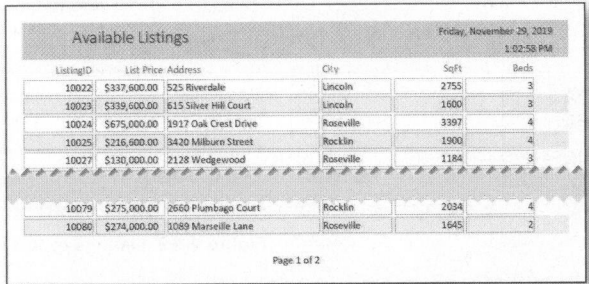

Figure 4-97 *Print Preview* of a report with controls in the
header and footer sections

PAUSE & PRACTICE: ACCESS 4-3

For this Pause & Practice, you create two reports for the Placer Hills Real Estate database. Create one report using the *Report Wizard* and a second report using the *Blank Report* button.

File Needed: *[your initials] PP A4-1.accdb*
Completed Project File Name: *[your initials] PP A4-3.accdb*

1. Open the *[your initials] PP A4-1* database file that you created in *Pause & Practice 4-1*.

2. Save a new copy of your database as [your initials] PP A4-3.

3. Enable content in the database.

4. Create a report using the *Report Wizard*.
 a. Click the **Report Wizard** button [*Create* tab, *Reports* group] to launch the *Report Wizard*.
 b. Click the **Tables/Queries** drop-down arrow and select the **Listings** table.
 c. Click the **Move All Fields** button.
 d. Select the **ListingAgentNumber** field in the *Selected Fields* window and click the **Remove Single Field** button.
 e. Remove the *Construction*, *YearBuilt*, *Garage*, and *DateListed* fields. The *Report Wizard* should look similar to Figure 4-98.
 f. Click the **Next** button to move to the second page of the *Report Wizard*.
 g. Do not group the data. Click the **Next** button to move to the third page of the *Report Wizard*.
 h. Sort the *ListPrice* field in ascending order.
 i. Click the **Next** button to move to the fourth page of the *Report Wizard*.
 j. Select a **Tabular** layout and **Portrait** orientation if necessary.
 k. Click the **Next** button to move to the last page of the *Report Wizard*.
 l. Type Listings-Report Wizard in the *Title* box.

Figure 4-98 Select report fields

m. Click the **Finish** button. The report opens in *Print Preview* view (Figure 4-99). Notice that the *ListPrice* field moved to the left-most column because you are sorting on that field.

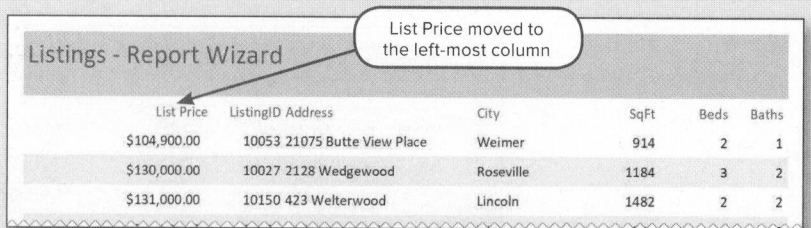

Figure 4-99 Listings report created using the *Report Wizard*

n. Use the navigation buttons to move among pages.
o. Click the **Close Print Preview** button.
p. Close the report.

5. Create a report using the *Blank Report* button.
 a. Click the **Blank Report** button [*Create* tab, *Reports* group] to open a new, blank report in *Layout* view.
 b. Click the **Show all tables** link in the *Field List* pane if necessary.
 c. Click the **plus sign** to expand the *Listings* table if necessary.
 d. Double-click the **ListingID** field to add it to the report.
 e. Double-click the **ListPrice** field to add it to the report
 f. Add the **SqFt**, **Beds**, **Baths**, **Address**, **City**, and **Garage** fields to the report. The report should look similar to Figure 4-100.

Figure 4-100 Add fields into a tabular layout of a blank report

 g. Close the *Field List*.

6. Save the report. Enter Listings – Blank Report Button as the *Report Name*.

7. Add a title and page numbers to the report.
 a. Click the **Report Layout Tools Design** tab if necessary.
 b. Click the **Title** button [*Header/Footer* group]. Accept the default wording of the title.
 c. Click the **Page Numbers** button [*Header/Footer* group].
 d. Select the **Page N of M** radio button in the *Format* group.
 e. Select the **Bottom of Page [Footer]** radio button in the *Position* group.
 f. Select **Left** in the *Alignment* drop-down list.
 g. Click **OK**.

8. Adjust the width of the report columns.
 a. Select a text box in the *ListingID* column.
 b. Click the **Property Sheet** button [*Report Layout Tools Design* tab, *Tools* group].
 c. Click the **Format** tab if necessary.
 d. Type .62" in the *Width* property box and press **Enter**. Don't worry if Access adjusts the actual value to a slightly different number, such as .6201".
 e. Select a text box in the *SqFt* column, type .5" in the *Width* property box and press **Enter**.
 f. Select a text box in the *Beds* column. Press and hold the **Shift** key and select a text box in the *Baths* column, type .5" in the *Width* property box, and press **Enter**. Both columns adjust to the new width.
 g. Select a text box in the *Address* column, type 2" in the *Width* property box, and press **Enter**.
 h. Select a text box in the *ListPrice* column, type 1.1" in the *Width* property box, and press **Enter**.
 i. Press **F4** to close the *Property Sheet*.

9. Save the report.

10. Preview the report by selecting the **View** button [*Report Layout Tools Design* tab, *Views* group] and selecting **Print Preview**. The report should look similar to Figure 4-101.

11. Click the **Close Print Preview** button.

12. Close the report.

13. Close the database.

Listings - Blank Report Button							
ListingID	List Price	SqFt	Beds	Baths	Address	City	Garage
10022	$337,600.00	2755	3	2	525 Riverdale	Lincoln	2 Car Detached
10023	$339,600.00	1600	3	2	615 Silver Hill Court	Lincoln	2 Car Attached
10024	$675,000.00	3397	4	4	1917 Oak Crest Drive	Roseville	3 Car Attached
10079	$275,000.00	2034	4	3	2660 Plumbago Court	Rocklin	2 Car Attached
10080	$274,000.00	1645	2	2	1089 Marseille Lane	Roseville	2 Car Attached
10081	$340,000.00	2370	4	3	1520 Arrowwood Lane	Roseville	3 Car Attached

Page 1 of 2

Figure 4-101 Completed listings report created using the *Blank Report* option

Adding Grouping, Sorting, and Totals

As you learned in the *Report Wizard* section, you can choose to sort records in a report on different fields, to add grouping to a report, or to add totals to a report. Add a **group** to a report when you want to organize and summarize your data. For example, you could group all employees from the same branch together in an insurance agency database, or you could group all the songs from a particular artist together in a music database. When you create a grouping, Access can automatically calculate various summary values across the different groups. You can also combine sorting with grouping. Finally, totals can also be added to a report independent of grouping or sorting being used. The features are located on the *Report Layout Tools Design* tab.

Figure 4-102 *Grouping & Totals group options*

You add grouping and sorting to a report using the *Group & Sort* button [*Report Layout Tools Design* tab, *Grouping & Totals* group] (Figure 4-102). Add totals using the *Totals* button [*Report Layout Tools Design* tab, *Grouping & Totals* group].

Sorting

Data sorting is a very useful Access reports feature. Sorting makes it easier to read and understand reports because it places all like data together. Access enables you to sort on multiple fields, with each field having its own sort order.

▶**HOW TO:** Add a Sort to a Report

1. Open the report in *Layout* view.

2. Click the **Group & Sort** button [*Report Layout Tools Design* tab, *Grouping & Totals* group] to open the *Group, Sort, and Total* pane at the bottom of the report.

3. Click **Add a sort** in the *Group, Sort, and Total* pane.

4. Select the field you want to sort by from the field list (Figure 4-103).

 • The report updates to display the data sorted in ascending order by the selected field.

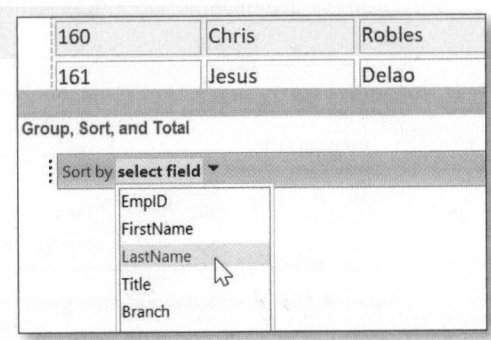

Figure 4-103 Select a sort field

- The *Group, Sort, and Total* pane updates to show how the report is being sorted (Figure 4-104).
- The default sort order is *with A on top* for text fields, *oldest to newest* for date fields, and *smallest to largest* for number fields.

5. Change the sort order by clicking the arrow to the right of the default sort order and selecting the new sort order. The default sort order in Figure 4-104 is *with A on top*.

Figure 4-104 Updated *Group, Sort, and Total* pane

6. Close the *Group, Sort, and Total* pane by clicking the **X** in the upper-right corner of the *Group, Sort, and Total* pane. Be careful not to click the *Delete* symbol inside the pane or you remove the sort.

Add a Group to a Report

When you add a group in *Layout* view, a new section is added using a stepped layout. You can group on more than one field.

▶ HOW TO: Add a Group to a Report

1. Open the report in *Layout* view.
2. Click the **Group & Sort** button [*Report Layout Tools Design* tab, *Grouping & Totals* group] to open the *Group, Sort, and Total* pane at the bottom of the report.
3. Click **Add a group** in the *Group, Sort, and Total* pane.
4. Select the field you want to group on from the field list (Figure 4-105).
 - The selected field moves to the left-most column (Figure 4-106).
 - The report changes to a stepped layout.
 - The *Group, Sort, and Total* pane updates to show how the report is being grouped (Figure 4-107).
5. Change the sort order of the grouping by clicking the arrow to the right of the default sort order and selecting the new sort order. The default sort order of the grouping in Figure 4-106 is *with A on top*.

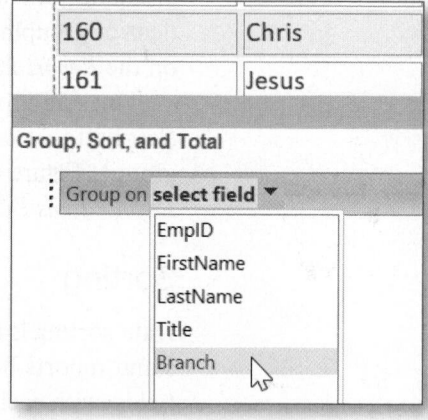

Figure 4-105 Select a group field

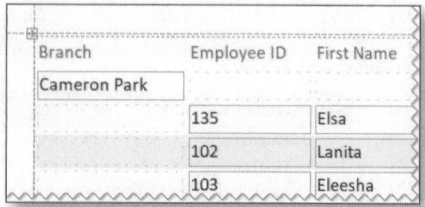

Figure 4-106 Updated report after grouping added

Figure 4-107 Updated *Group, Sort, and Total* pane

6. Close the *Group, Sort, and Total* pane by clicking the **X** in the upper-right corner of the *Group, Sort, and Total* pane. Be careful not to click the *Delete* symbol inside the pane or you remove the group.

Group and Sort Options

You can modify the report design after adding a sort or group section. You can also change the location or format of the grouping field in the control layout.

Other modifications are available. Click **More** in the *Group, Sort, and Total* pane to display the options shown in Figure 4-108 and explained in Table 4-3. Click **Less** to close the expanded list of options.

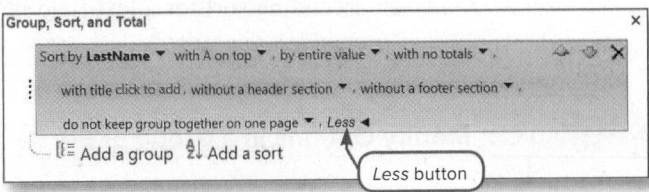

Figure 4-108 Expanded options in *Group, Sort, and Total* pane

Table 4-3: Options in the Group, Sort, and Total Pane

Category	Options	Explanation
Sorting	Ascending	The grouping field is sorted in ascending order.
	Descending	The grouping field is sorted in descending order.
Grouping	By entire value	The grouping is based on the entire value in the selected field.
	By partial value	The grouping is based on only part of the field. For example, in a text field, the grouping could be "by first character," which would group together all values that start with the same letter. In a date field, the grouping could be by year or month.
	Custom	The grouping is based on a specific number of characters that you provide.
Totals	Select the field and type of calculation	You choose which field in the report should be calculated, along with the calculation. Choices include *Sum, Average, Count, Maximum,* and *Minimum.*
	Show grand totals	Calculates overall totals for all records.
	Show group totals as percent of grand total	Displays the group totals as a percent of the grand total.
	Show in header or footer section	Determines which section displays the totals.
Title		Changes the wording in the label of the grouping field.
Header section	With a header section / without a header section	Determines whether to include a header section in the report.

Continued

Category	Options	Explanation
Footer section	With a footer section/ without a footer section	Determines whether to include a footer section in the report.
Keep group together	Do not keep group together on one page	Enables a group to be split across multiple pages if it can't all fit in the space remaining on a page.
	Keep whole group together on one page	Starts a group on the following page if it can't all fit in the space remaining on a page.
	Keep header and first record together on one page	Prevents a header from printing on the bottom of a page unless at least one record of the group can also be printed with the header.

The wording for some of the options depends on the data type of the field. For example, an ascending sort for a text field is "*with A on top*," while an ascending sort for a date field is "*from oldest to newest*."

▶HOW TO: Modify Options in a Group or Sort

1. Open the report in *Layout* view.
2. Click the **Group & Sort** button [*Report Layout Tools Design* tab, *Grouping & Totals* group] if the *Group, Sort, and Total* pane is not open.
3. Click **More** in the *Group, Sort, and Total* pane.
4. Select the **arrow** of the desired option and select the new option choice (Figure 4-109).
 - The report updates to reflect the new option.
 - The expanded list of options closes.

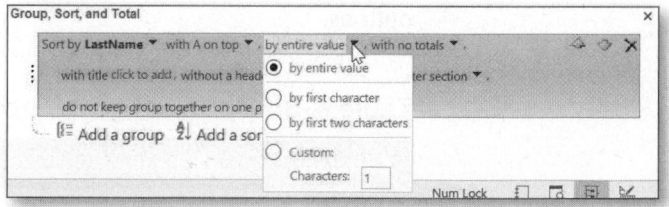

Figure 4-109 Expanded grouping options in *Group, Sort, and Total* pane

> ### MORE INFO
> Add additional options by selecting **More** again.

5. Click **Less** to close the expanded list of options if you decide not to make any modifications.
6. Close the *Group, Sort, and Total* pane by clicking the **X** in the upper-right corner of the *Group, Sort, and Total* pane.

Add Totals to a Report

You can add totals to a report to allow performance of overall calculations based on your data. Calculation options include *Sum*, *Average*, *Count Records*, *Count Values*, *Max*, *Min*, *Standard Deviation*, and *Variance*. The options available for non-numeric fields are limited to *Count Records* and *Count Values*.

▶HOW TO: Add Totals to a Report

1. Open the report in *Layout* view.
2. Select a text box in the field you want to total.

3. Click the **Totals** button [*Report Layout Tools Design* tab, *Grouping & Totals* group].

4. Select the desired calculation (Figure 4-110).
 - The report updates with the total added to the bottom of the report.

5. Repeat steps 2–4 to add additional total calculations to the report.

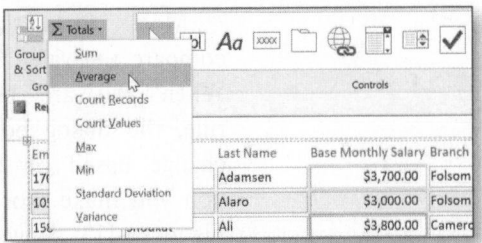

Figure 4-110 *Totals* button options

In a report with grouping or sorting, add totals by selecting the **with no totals** choice in the *Group, Sort, and Total* pane and then select the desired total options (Figure 4-111).

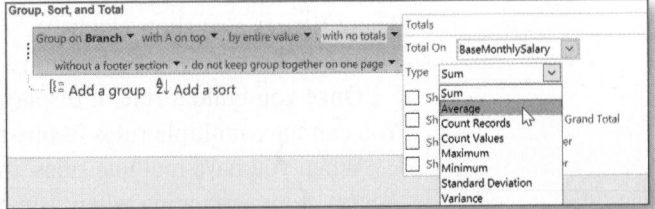

Figure 4-111 Total options in *Group, Sort, and Total* pane

SLO 4.7

Using Conditional Formatting in a Report

Conditional formatting enables you to format only values that meet a certain condition. This helps you focus the user's attention to certain records in a report.

Conditional Formatting Rules

The formatting rules are defined in the *New Formatting Rule* dialog box (Figure 4-112). When building a rule, you must select the *rule type*, conditions, and the desired formatting.

The most common rule type is *Check values in the current record or use an expression*. Use the *Compare to other records* rule type to create data bars, which enable you to compare values across data records.

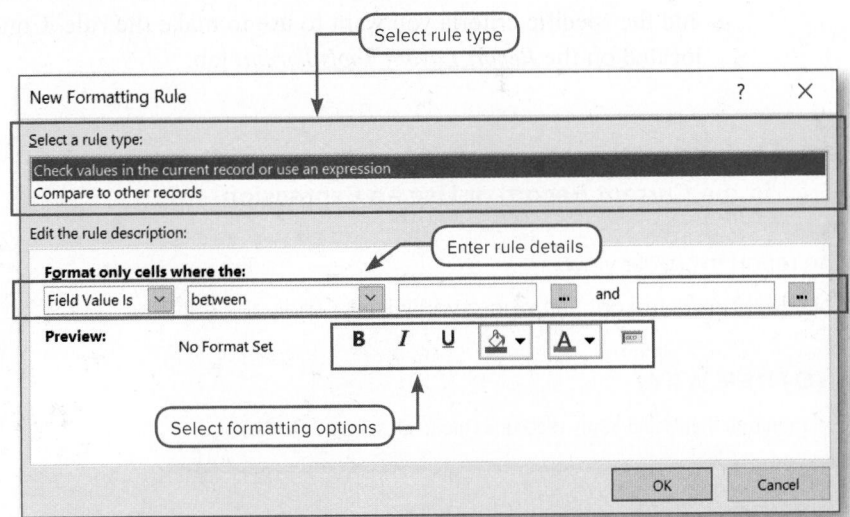

Figure 4-112 *New Formatting Rule* dialog box

Most formatting rules compare the value in a field. When you are building a rule, the dialog box options change based on the selection you make. For example, Figure 4-113 shows a place where you enter only one data value based on the selection of the *less than* comparison. Compare this to Figure 4-114, where you enter two data values for a *between* comparison. These figures also show examples of different formatting options.

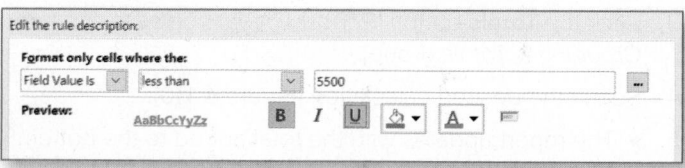

Figure 4-113 Example rule with *less than* comparison and one data value

Figure 4-114 Example rule with *between* comparison and two data values

Once you build a rule, it displays in the *Conditional Formatting Rules Manager* dialog box. You can have multiple rules in one report and even multiple rules for the same field.

When you have multiple rules, the order in which they are listed is very important, because Access stops evaluating when a match is found. For example, the rule in Figure 4-115 shows *BaseMonthlySalary* values that are less than 5,000 in blue instead of the desired brown color. That is because a value less than 5,000 is also less than 10,000. The evaluation stops after the condition in the first rule is met. To correct this situation, select the *Value < 10000* rule and click the **Move Down** arrow to make it the second rule instead of the first. As appropriate, you can also click the **Move Up** arrow to change the position of a rule.

Figure 4-115 *Conditional Formatting Rules Manager* dialog box with multiple rules

Add Conditional Formatting to a Report

To add conditional formatting, you need to determine which fields will have formatting applied and the specific criteria you want to use to make the rule. Conditional formatting features are located on the *Report Layout Tools Format* tab.

HOW TO: Add Conditional Formatting to a Report to Check Values in the Current Record or Use an Expression

1. Open the report in *Layout* view.
2. Select any text box in the column where you wish to apply the criteria.

Figure 4-116 *Conditional Formatting button*

> **ANOTHER WAY**
> Select multiple fields and apply the same rule to all selected fields.

3. Click the **Conditional Formatting** button [*Report Layout Tools Format* tab, *Control Formatting* group] (Figure 4-116) to open the *Conditional Formatting Rules Manager* dialog box (Figure 4-117).

- The selected field displays in the *Show formatting rules for* box.
- If more than one field is selected, *Multiple* displays in the box.

4. Change the field to format in the *Show formatting rules for* box if necessary.

5. Click the **New Rule** button to open the *New Formatting Rule* dialog box.

6. Select **Check values in the current record or use an expression** in the *Select a rule type* box.

7. Click the appropriate **arrows** to select the desired comparison.

8. Type the comparison values into the boxes.

9. Select formatting options as desired.

10. Click **OK**. The completed rule displays in the *Conditional Formatting Rules Manager* dialog box (Figure 4-118).

11. Add another rule to either the same field or a different field as desired.

12. Click **Apply** to have Access evaluate the data in the report and apply the formatting to the values that meet the criteria.

13. Click **OK** when you are finished building all rules.

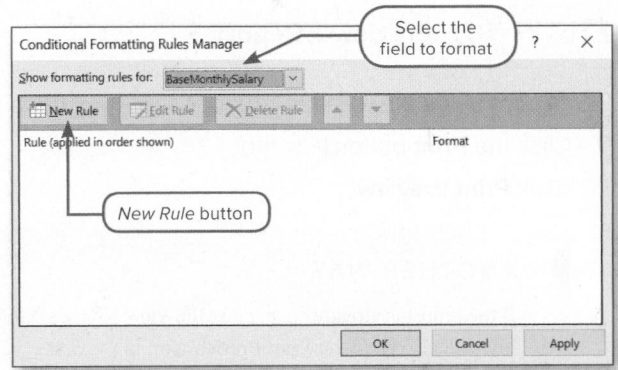

Figure 4-117 *Conditional Formatting Rules Manager* dialog box

Figure 4-118 Completed rule

Manage Conditional Formatting Rules

You can also edit or delete existing rules from the *Conditional Formatting Rules Manager* dialog box. The *Conditional Formatting Rules Manager* only displays rules for one field at a time. If you created rules for multiple fields, you must select the desired field first in the *Show formatting rules for* box to view the rules for that specific field.

To edit an existing rule, select the rule in the *Conditional Formatting Rules Manager* dialog box and click the **Edit Rule** button. The *Edit Formatting Rule dialog* box opens. This dialog box is similar to the *New Formatting Rule* dialog box, and you set options the same way.

To delete an existing rule, select the rule in the *Conditional Formatting Rules Manager* dialog box and click the **Delete Rule** button. Because you are not prompted to confirm the deletion, use caution to avoid an accidental deletion.

SLO 4.8

Printing a Report

Reports can be viewed on screen, but most reports are designed to be printed. To ensure that your report prints as desired, take the time to review it in *Print Preview* view.

Preview a Report

Recall that *Print Preview* enables you to see how your report appears on a printed page. The options on the *Print Preview* tab let you adjust the size and margins of the page, change the orientation, and change the zoom level as needed.

▶HOW TO: Preview a Report

1. Click to select the desired report in the *Navigation Pane*.
2. Click the **Print** button [*File* tab].
3. Click **Print Preview**.

> ▶ **ANOTHER WAY**
>
> If the report is already open, click the **View** button [*Home* tab, *Views* group] and select **Print Preview**.
> You can also click the **Print Preview** icon in the *Status* bar.

4. Make any desired adjustments to the report (Figure 4-119).

Figure 4-119 Adjust printing options while viewing a report in *Print Preview*

5. Click the **Print** button [*Print Preview* tab, *Print* group] to open the *Print* dialog box if you are ready to print. Choose desired options and click **OK** to print the report.
6. Click the **Close Print Preview** button.

Print a Report without Print Preview

If you already know that your report is designed correctly, you can print the report without previewing it first.

▶ HOW TO: Print a Report without Using Print Preview

1. Click to select the desired report in the *Navigation Pane*.
2. Click the **Print** button [*File* tab].
3. Choose the desired print option.
 - Click **Quick Print** to print the report on the default printer without making any changes.
 - Click **Print** to open the *Print* dialog box and customize printing options. Select a printer, desired printing options, and click **OK** to print.

Format and Print a Report with Multiple Columns

Occasionally, the fields in a report may not take up the full width of a report. For example, if you were printing a list of employees and their office phone numbers, or the song titles on different music albums, the fields would not span the entire width of the page. In these cases, you can choose to print the report using multiple columns. You do not make any special property settings or changes when designing the report. Instead, you choose the columns option when printing.

▶ HOW TO: Print a Report with Multiple Columns

1. Click to select the desired report in the *Navigation Pane*.
2. Click the **Print** button [*File* tab].
3. Click **Print Preview**.

> ▶ **ANOTHER WAY**
>
> If the report is already open, click the **View** button [*Home* tab, *Views* group] and select **Print Preview**.

4. Click the **Columns** button [*Print Preview* tab, *Page Layout* group]. The *Page Setup* dialog box opens with the *Columns* tab selected (Figure 4-120).
5. Enter the number of columns to print.
6. Enter the width of the columns.
7. Select the desired *Column Layout* option.
8. Edit any other column settings.
9. Click **OK**. The report preview updates (Figure 4-121). Review the updated report to ensure that you made the correct selections in the dialog box.
10. Save the report.
11. Click **Print** to open the *Print* dialog box and customize printing options. Select a printer, desired printing options, and click **OK** to print.

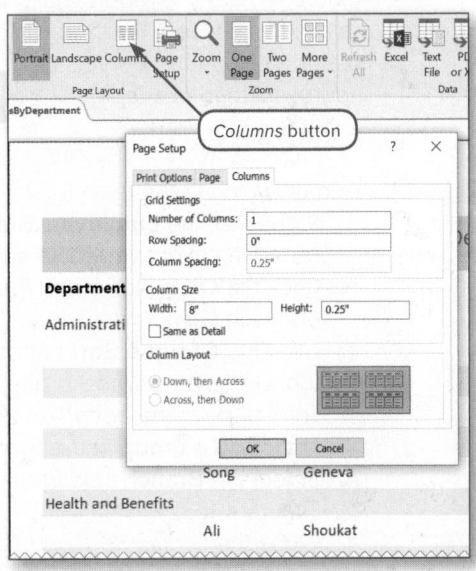

Figure 4-120 *Columns* tab of the *Page Setup* dialog box

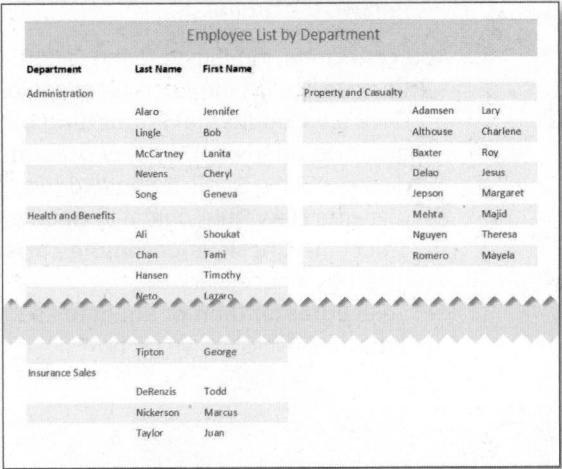

Figure 4-121 Multiple column report preview

For this Pause & Practice, you edit a report based on a parameter query. You modify the report to add grouping and conditional formatting. Finally, you preview the report.

File Needed: *[your initials] PP A4-2.accdb*
Completed Project File Name: *[your initials] PP A4-4.accdb*

1. Open the *[your initials] PP A4-2* database file that you created in *Pause & Practice 4-2*.

2. Save a new copy of your database as [your initials] PP A4-4.

3. Enable content in the database.

4. Double-click the **EmployeesBranchParameter** query.

5. Leave the value blank in the *Enter Parameter Value* dialog box, and click **OK**. The query executes and displays the results shown in Figure 4-122. The report you edit in this Pause & Practice was created using this query as the data source instead of a table.

Employee	Title	Branch	Base Monthly Salary
Bob Lingle	Chief Executive Officer	Cameron Park	$15,000.00
Lanita McCartney	Chief Operating Officer	Cameron Park	$12,000.00
Eleesha Santos	Insurance Agent	Cameron Park	$5,580.00
Roy Baxter	Insurance Agent	Granite Bay	$4,500.00
Jennifer Alaro	Administrative Assistant	Folsom	$3,000.00

Figure 4-122 *EmployeeBranchParameter* query results

6. Close the query.

7. Add grouping to the report.
 a. Right-click the **EmployeesBranchParameterReport** report and select **Layout View** to open the report in *Layout* view. The query executes.
 b. Click the **OK** button in the *Enter Parameter Value* dialog box without entering a value. The report opens in *Layout* view.
 c. Click the **Group & Sort** button [*Report Layout Tools Design* tab, *Grouping & Totals* group] to open the *Group, Sort, and Total* pane at the bottom of the report.
 d. Click **Add a group** in the *Group, Sort, and Total* pane.
 e. Select the **Branch** field from the *Group on select field* list (Figure 4-123).
 f. Close the *Group, Sort, and Total* pane by clicking the **X** in the upper-right corner of the *Group, Sort, and Total* pane. Be careful not to click the *Delete* symbol inside the pane or you remove the group.

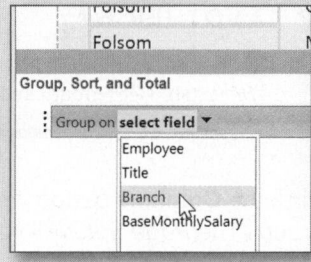

Figure 4-123 Group on the *Branch* field

8. Add conditional formatting to the report.
 a. Click any cell in the *Base Monthly Salary* column.
 b. Click the **Conditional Formatting** button [*Report Layout Tools Format* tab, *Control Formatting* group] to open the *Conditional Formatting Rules Manager* dialog box. *BaseMonthlySalary* displays in the *Show formatting rules for* box.
 c. Click the **New Rule** button to open the *New Formatting Rule* dialog box.
 d. Select the **Check values in the current record or use an expression** rule type in the *Select a rule type* box if necessary.
 e. Select **greater than or equal to** as the comparison.
 f. Type 10000 into the value box.

g. Select **Bold** and a **red** font. The *New Formatting Rule* dialog box should be similar to Figure 4-124.

h. Click **OK**. The completed rule displays in the *Conditional Formatting Rules Manager* dialog box (Figure 4-125).

i. Click **Apply**.

j. Click **OK**.

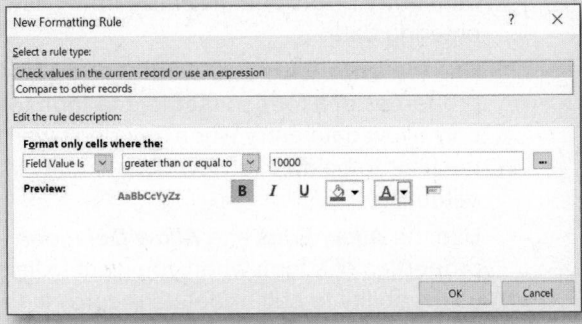

Figure 4-124 *New Formatting Rule* dialog box for *BaseMonthlySalary* field

Figure 4-125 Completed rule for *BaseMonthlySalary* field

9. Save and close the report.

10. Preview the way the report will print.

a. Right-click the **EmployeesBranchParameterReport** report and select **Print Preview**. The query executes.

b. Click **OK** in the *Enter Parameter Value* dialog box without entering a value.

c. Click the **Zoom** button arrow and select **Fit to Window**.

d. Click the **Margins** button arrow and select **Normal**. If a message displays that the section width is greater than the page width, click **OK** to acknowledge the message. Your report should look similar to Figure 4-126.

e. Close the *Print Preview* of the report.

11. Close the database.

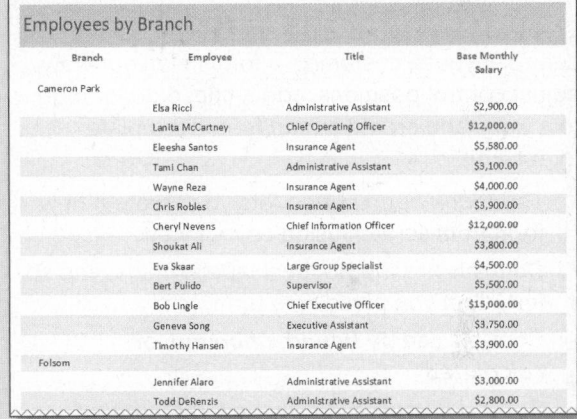

Figure 4-126 Completed report with grouping and conditional formatting

Chapter Summary

4.1 Create a simple form using quick create options, and save, modify, and delete a form (p. A4-223).

- *Forms* enable you to view, add, update, and delete data in a database.
- Build forms from tables, queries, or both.
- *Bound forms* are linked to the data source; *unbound forms* don't have a connection to a direct link to a data source.
- The *Form Wizard* lets you quickly build a form by specifying the tables or queries to use, selecting the desired fields and the desired layout of the form.
- Use the *Form* button to create a form in one click.
- A *split form* lets you view data in two ways on the same form by combining both a columnar display and a datasheet display.
- Edit a form in *Design view* or *Layout view* and modify any aspect of the form's design.

4.2 Create a blank form, understand controls and control layouts, customize a form in *Layout* view, adjust control positions, add a title, date, or logo to a form, and create a form from a template (p. A4-231).

- The *Blank Form* button lets you create a new form from scratch using *Layout* view.
- *Controls* are the buttons, labels, fields, and so forth that you place on a form.
- Controls can be *bound*, *unbound*, or *calculated*.
- *Control layouts* provide the structure that aligns the controls on a form.
- The two primary control layouts are *tabular* and *stacked*.
- Save each form with a unique name.
- Change the *Control Margins*, *Control Padding*, or *Anchoring* properties of a control to modify its position on a form.
- Titles, dates, and logos can be added to a form.
- Create a form from a template with application parts, and then modify it to meet your needs.

4.3 Restrict a form to data entry, limit user edits and deletions on a form, add command buttons, and test a form (p. A4-241).

- When designing a form for data entry, choose design options that help minimize potential data entry errors and maximize efficiency for entering data.
- Use the *Data Entry* and *Allow Additions* properties of a form to restrict the form to only allow data entry when you don't want the user to be able to view data already in the database.
- Use the *Allow Edits* and *Allow Deletions* properties of a form when you want to limit the user's ability to edit or delete records in the database.
- Add *command buttons* to a form to automate user tasks.
- Use the *Command Button Wizard* to easily add buttons to a form.
- After you build a form, test it to ensure that it functions as desired.

4.4 Create a simple report with the *Report Wizard*, and save, modify, and delete a report (p. A4-248).

- Use *reports* to create an organized and professional output of the data in a database.
- Build reports from tables, queries, or both.
- The *Report Wizard* lets you quickly build a report by specifying the tables or queries to use, selecting the desired fields, selecting any grouping or sorting options, and specifying the layout of the report.
- *Report* view executes a report and displays the results.
- *Print Preview* view shows how a report will look in print while also enabling you to make modifications to the print settings.
- Modify reports in *Design* view or *Layout* view.

4.5 Create a blank report, understand controls and control layouts, customize a report in *Layout* view, adjust control positions, and add a title, logo, date, and page numbers to a report (p. A4-256).

- The *Blank Report* button lets you create a new report from scratch using *Layout* view.
- Control layouts provide the structure that aligns the controls on a report.
- The two primary control layouts are tabular and stacked.

- The fields, labels, and so forth that you place on a report are controls. Controls can be bound, unbound, or calculated.
- Change the **Control Margins** or **Control Padding** properties of a control to modify its position on a report.
- It is good design practice to include titles, logos, dates, and page numbers on a report.
- Save each report with a unique name.

4.6 Enhance a report by adding grouping, sorting, and totals to a report in *Layout* view (p. A4-265).

- Sorting the records in a report makes it easier to read and understand the data contained in the report.
- Sort a report in ascending or descending order on one or more fields.
- Add a **group** to a report to organize and summarize the data.
- A report can contain multiple groups.
- Within a grouping level, you can choose to include header or footer sections, integrate sorting, and include summary totals.
- Totals enable you to perform overall calculations based on the data in the report.
- Calculation options include *Sum*, *Average*, *Count Records*, *Count Values*, *Max*, *Min*, *Standard Deviation*, and *Variance*.

4.7 Integrate conditional formatting into a report (p. A4-269).

- **Conditional formatting** enables you to format only values that meet a specified condition.

- A report can contain multiple formatting rules.
- When using multiple rules, the order of specifying the rules is important because Access stops evaluating once it finds a rule that matches the data.
- You can add, modify, and delete rules from the *Conditional Formatting Rules Manager* dialog box.

4.8 Preview, modify print settings, print a report, and format and print a report with multiple columns (p. A4-271).

- To ensure that your report prints as desired, review it in *Print Preview* view.
- Adjust the print settings related to page size, margins, and page orientation using the *Print Preview* mode.
- Print a report directly from the *Backstage* view without using *Print Preview*.
- Format and print a report using multiple columns to make better use of the spacing on a page.

Check for Understanding

The SIMbook for this text (within your SIMnet account) provides the following resources for concept review:

- Multiple-choice questions
- Short answer questions
- Matching exercises

Guided Project 4-1

In this project, you enhance the functionality of the database you built for your friend's music collection by building a form to display information about the albums and a report to show all of the songs on each album. To ensure consistency, the starting file is provided for you. Use the *Form Wizard* to create a form and *Layout* view to edit the form. Create a report using the *Report Wizard*, edit the report in *Layout* view, add totals to the report, and view the report using *Print Preview*.
[Student Learning Outcomes 4.1, 4.2, 4.4, 4.5, 4.6, 4.8]

File Needed: **MusicDatabase-04.accdb** *(Student data files are available in the Library of your SIMnet account.)*
Completed Project File Name: *[your initials] Access 4-1.accdb*

Skills Covered in This Project

- Create a form using the *Form Wizard*.
- Edit a form in *Layout* view.
- Add the current date to a form.

- Create a report using the *Report Wizard*.
- Edit a report in *Layout* view.
- Add totals to a report.
- View a report using *Print Preview*.

1. Open the **MusicDatabase-04.accdb** database file.

2. Save the database as [your initials] Access 4-1.

3. Enable content in the database.

4. Create a form using the *Form Wizard*.
 a. Click the **Form Wizard** button [*Create* tab, *Forms* group] to launch the *Form Wizard*.
 b. Click the **Tables/Queries** drop-down arrow and select the **Albums** table if necessary.
 c. Click the **Move All Fields** button to move all of the fields from the *Available Fields* window to the *Selected Fields* window.
 d. Click the **Next** button to move to the second page of the *Form Wizard*.
 e. Select the **Columnar** radio button if necessary.
 f. Click the **Next** button to move to the last page of the *Form Wizard*.
 g. Type MusicAlbums in the *Title* box.
 h. Click **Finish**. The form opens in *Form* view.
 i. Use the navigation buttons to move to record album 29. This album has the longest album name.

5. Edit the form column widths in *Layout* view.
 a. Click the **View** button [*Home* tab, *Views* group] and select **Layout View**.
 b. Close the *Field List* if it is open.
 c. Select the **AlbumName** text box.
 d. Click the **Property Sheet** button [*Form Layout Tools Design* tab, *Tools* group].
 e. Click the **Format** tab if necessary.
 f. Type 3.2" in the *Width* property box and press **Enter**.
 g. Select the **Artist** text box, type 3.2" in the *Width* property box and press **Enter**.
 h. Select the **Genre** text box. Press and hold the **Shift** key and select the **Length** text box, type 1.5" in the *Width* property box and press **Enter**.

 i. Select the **RecordingLabel** text box, type 3.2" in the *Width* property box and press **Enter**.
 j. Press **F4** to close the *Property Sheet*.
6. Edit the form header section.
 a. Click to select the **MusicAlbums** label in the header section.
 b. Click inside the label to open the edit mode.
 c. Insert a space between "Music" and "Albums".
 d. Click the header section outside the *Music Albums* label.
 e. Click the **Date and Time** button [*Form Layout Tools Design* Tab, *Header/Footer* group].
 f. Select the radio button to display the date using the **mm/dd/yyyy** format.
 g. Deselect the check box to **Include Time**.
 h. Click **OK**.
 i. Click the **Form View** icon in the *Status* bar. The completed form should look similar to Figure 4-127. Depending on the width of the Access window, your date field may be further to the right in your form header.

7. Save the form.

8. Close the form.

9. Create a report using the *Report Wizard*.
 a. Click the **Report Wizard** button [*Create* tab, *Reports* group] to launch the *Report Wizard*.
 b. Click the **Tables/Queries** drop-down arrow in the box and select the **SongsOnAlbums** query. This report is based on a query instead of a table.
 c. Select the **AlbumName** field.
 d. Click the **Move Single Field** button.

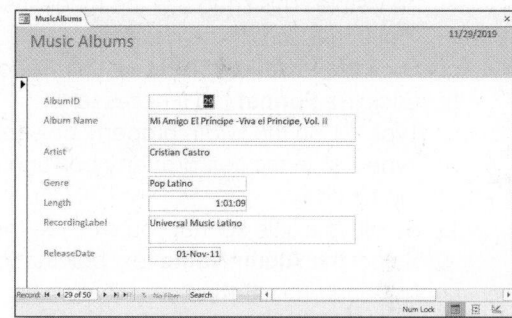

Figure 4-127 Completed *MusicAlbums* form

 e. Continue adding the **Artist** and **SongTitle** fields. Remember that you can click the **Remove Single Field** button if you accidentally add a field that is not needed.
 f. Click the **Next** button to move to the next page of the *Report Wizard*.
 g. Choose to view the data **by Albums**. The *Report Wizard* should look similar to Figure 4-128. Click **Next**.

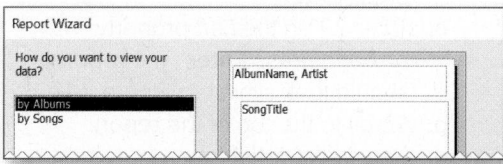

Figure 4-128 Select to view the data *by Albums* in the *Report Wizard*

 h. Do not group the data. Click the **Next** button to move to the next page of the *Report Wizard*.
 i. Do not sort the data. Click the **Next** button to move to the next page of the *Report Wizard*.
 j. Select a **Stepped** layout and **Portrait** orientation if necessary.
 k. Click the **Next** button to move to the last page of the *Report Wizard*.
 l. Type SongsOnAlbums in the *Title* box.
 m. Click the **Finish** button. The report opens in *Print Preview* view (Figure 4-129).
 n. Click the **Next Page** navigation button three times to move to the fourth page of the report. You should see the *Blunderbuss* album.
 o. Click the **Last Page** navigation button. You should be on page 19 of the report. Don't worry if your report contains 20 pages. This could be caused by different default settings in Access.
 p. Click the **Close Print Preview** button. The report displays in *Design* view.

Figure 4-129 *SongsOnAlbums* report

10. Edit the report header section.
 a. Close the *Field List* pane, if it is open.
 b. Click to select the **SongsOnAlbums** label in the header section.
 c. Click inside the label to open the edit mode.
 d. Insert a space between "Songs" and "On" and "Albums".
 e. Click the header section outside the *Songs On Albums* label.

11. Edit the report column widths using *Layout* view.
 a. Switch the report to *Layout* view.
 b. Click the **Find** button [*Home* tab, *Find* group]. The *Find* dialog box displays.
 c. Type Orbit in the *Find What* box.
 d. Click the **Match** drop-down arrow and select **Any Part of Field**.
 e. Click **Find Next**. The "The Chieftains in Orbit (with NASA Astronaut Cady Coleman)" song from the *Voice of Ages* album by *The Chieftains* should be selected, although the entire title may not be visible. This song has the longest song title.
 f. Close the *Find* dialog box.
 g. Click the **Property Sheet** button [*Report Layout Tools Design* tab, *Tools* group].
 h. Click the **Format** tab if necessary.
 i. Type 4.1" in the *Width* property box and press **Enter**.
 j. Type 3.8" in the *Left* property box and press **Enter**. The *Left* property indicates the left position of the text box.
 k. Scroll up a little so that you can see the album name, *Voice of Ages*, for this song if necessary.
 l. Select the **AlbumName** text box that contains "Voice of Ages," type 1.6" in the *Width* property box and press **Enter**.
 m. Type .5" in the *Height* property box and press **Enter**.
 n. Select the **Artist** text box that contains "The Chieftains," type 2.5" in the *Width* property box and press **Enter**.
 o. Type 1.9" in the *Left* property box and press **Enter**. The report should look similar to Figure 4-130.
 p. Scroll to the top of the report.
 q. Select the **Artist** label, type 1.5" in the *Width* property box and press **Enter**.

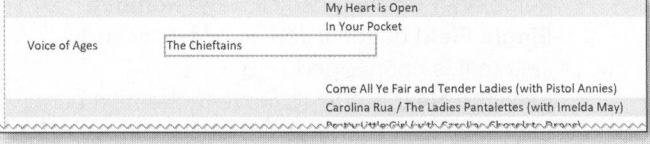

Figure 4-130 Report fields after adjusting size and location

 r. Type 1.9" in the *Left* property box and press **Enter**.
 s. Select the **Song Title** label, type 1.5" in the *Width* property box, and press **Enter**.
 t. Type 3.8" in the *Left* property box and press **Enter**.
 u. Close the *Property Sheet*.

12. Add totals to the report to count the number of songs on each album.
 a. Click the **Report Layout Tools Design** tab.
 b. Select a text box in the *SongTitle* column.
 c. Click the **Totals** button in the *Grouping & Totals* group.
 d. Select **Count Records**. The report updates to display the count below the last song on each album. A grand total displays at the end of the report.

13. Save the report.

14. Switch to *Print Preview* view. The completed report should look similar to Figure 4-131.

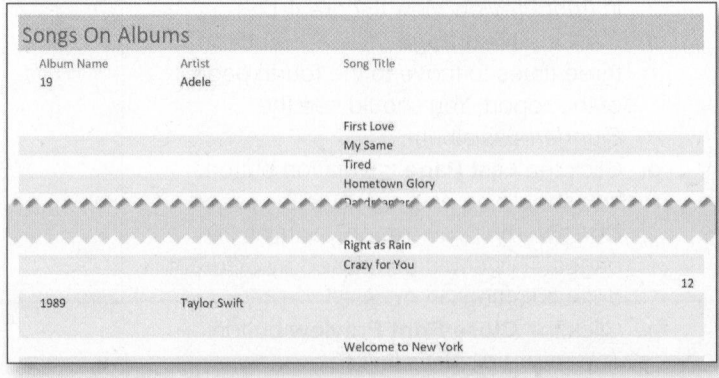

Figure 4-131 Completed report

15. Close the *Print Preview* of the report.

16. Close the report.

17. Close the database.

Guided Project 4-2

San Diego Sailing Club wants to add forms and a report to their database. To ensure consistency, the starting file is provided for you. Use the *Blank Form* button to create the form and *Layout* view to modify the form, save a copy of the form, edit form properties, and add command buttons. Create a report using the *Report Wizard* and use *Layout* view to modify the report.
[Student Learning Outcomes 4.1, 4.2, 4.3, 4.4, 4.5]

File Needed: ***SanDiegoSailing-04.accdb*** *(Student data files are available in the* Library *of your SIMnet account.)*
Completed Project File Name: ***[your initials] Access 4-2.accdb***

Skills Covered in This Project

- Create a form using the *Blank Form* button.
- Edit a form in *Layout* view.
- Save a copy of the form.

- Add a title to a form.
- Add buttons to a form.
- Set form properties.
- Create a report using the *Report Wizard*.
- Edit a report in *Layout* view.

1. Open the ***SanDiegoSailing-04*** database from your student data files.

2. Save the database as [your initials] Access 4-2.

3. Enable content in the database.

4. Create a new form using the *Blank Form* button.
 a. Click the **Blank Form** button [*Create* tab, *Forms* group]. A new blank form opens in *Layout* view.
 b. Click the **Show all tables** link in the *Field List* pane.
 c. Click the **plus sign** to expand the *SailboatFleet* table to see the fields in the table.
 d. Double-click the **BoatID** field to add it to the form.
 e. Double-click the **BoatType** field to add it to the form.
 f. Continue adding all the fields from the *SailboatFleet* table to the form. The form should look similar to Figure 4-132.
 g. Close the *Field List*.

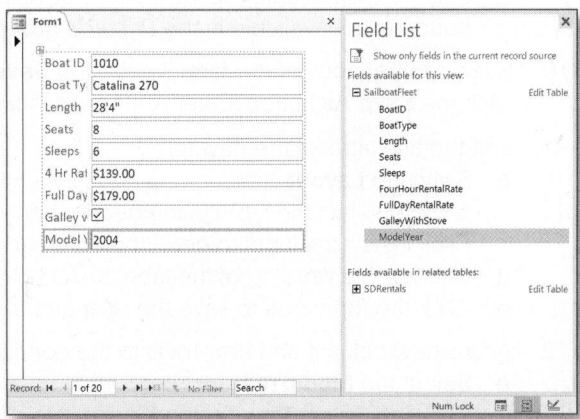

Figure 4-132 Add fields from the *SailboatFleet* table onto the form

5. Modify the control layout.
 a. Click one of the fields on the form. An orange border surrounds it.
 b. Click the **Select Layout** button [*Form Layout Tools Arrange* tab, *Rows & Columns* group] or click the **layout selector**. All the cells in the layout are bordered in orange.
 c. Place your pointer over any field. Click, hold, and drag the **control layout** down about 1" and to the right about 1", and then release the pointer (Figure 4-133).
 d. Select the **Galley w/ Stove** label.
 e. Click the **Property Sheet** button [*Form Layout Tools Design* tab, *Tools* group].
 f. Click the **Format** tab if necessary.
 g. Type 1.1" in the *Width* property box and press **Enter**.
 h. Navigate to record number 4.
 i. Select the **BoatType** text box, type 1.3" in the *Width* property box, and press **Enter**.

6. Add a title control to the form.
 a. Click the **Title** button [*Form Layout Tools Design* tab, *Header/Footer* group].
 b. Change the wording of the label in the header section to View Sailboat Fleet Data.
 c. Click the form area to save the changes to the label. The form should look similar to Figure 4-134.

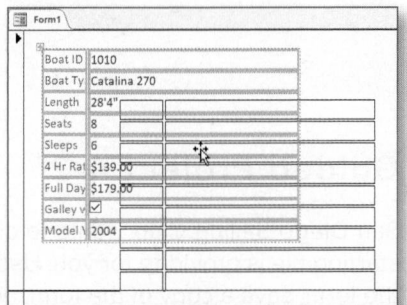

Figure 4-133 Move the control layout

7. Modify the form to limit user edits and deletions.
 a. Click the **drop-down arrow** in the *Selection* box of the *Property Sheet* and select **Form**.
 b. Click the **Data** tab.
 c. Select **No** in the *Data Entry* property box if necessary.
 d. Select **No** in the *Allow Additions* property box.
 e. Select **No** in the *Allow Deletions* property box.
 f. Select **No** in the *Allow Edits* property box.
 g. Close the *Property Sheet*.

8. Save the form. Enter ViewSailboatFleet as the *Form Name*.

9. Test the form.
 a. Switch to **Form** view.
 b. Try to change the value in the *BoatID* text box. You should not be able to edit the value. Notice that the *New (blank) record* icon is not visible in the *Navigation* bar and that the *Delete Record* button is not available in the *Records* group [*Home* tab].

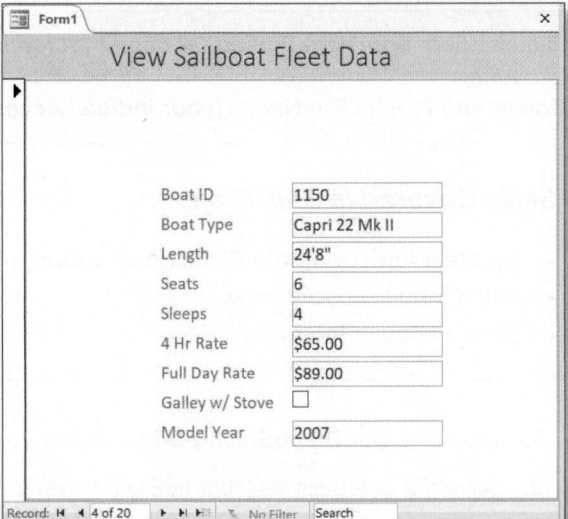

Figure 4-134 Updated form

10. Save another copy of the form by clicking **Save As** [*File* tab] and then selecting **Save Object As** and click the **Save As** button. Enter AddNewSailboat as the *Form Name*.

11. Edit the title label of the new form.
 a. Switch to **Layout** view.
 b. Click to select the label in the header section.
 c. Click inside the label to open the edit mode.
 d. Change the wording of the label to Add New Sailboat.
 e. Click the form area to save the changes to the label.

12. Add a new column and new rows to the control layout of the form.
 a. Select the **ModelYear** text box.
 b. Click the **Select Row** button [*Form Layout Tools Arrange* tab, *Rows & Columns* group].

c. Click the **Insert Below** button [*Form Layout Tools Arrange* tab, *Rows & Columns* group] to add a blank row.

d. Click the **Insert Below** button again to add a second blank row.

e. Select the **Model Year** text box.

f. Click the **Select Column** button [*Form Layout Tools Arrange* tab, *Rows & Columns* group].

g. Click the **Insert Right** button [*Form Layout Tools Arrange* tab, *Rows & Columns* group] to add a blank column.

13. Adjust the height and width of the new rows and column.

a. Select a **cell** in the new column.

b. Click the **Property Sheet** button [*Form Layout Tools Design* tab, *Tools* group].

c. Click the **Format** tab if necessary.

d. Type 1.1" in the *Width* property box and press **Enter**.

e. Select a **cell** in the bottom blank row.

f. Type .45" in the *Height* property box and press **Enter**. The revised control layout on the form should look like Figure 4-135.

g. Close the *Property Sheet*.

Figure 4-135 Modified control layout

14. Add command buttons to the form.

a. Click the **Form Layout Tools Design** tab if necessary.

b. Click the **More** arrow at the far right of the *Controls* group and select the **Use Control Wizards** button if it does not already have a gray-colored border indicating it is selected.

c. Click **Button** in the *Controls* group. Move the pointer to the left-most cell in the bottom row of the control layout and click. The *Command Button Wizard* launches.

d. Select the **Record Operations** *Category* and the **Save Record** *Action* of the button.

e. Click **Next** to move to the second page of the *Command Button Wizard*.

f. Select the **Text** radio button and change the wording to read Save Sailboat Record.

g. Click **Next** to move to the last page of the *Wizard*.

h. Accept the default button name because you will not modify the button code and click **Finish**. The button displays in the form.

i. Add a second button to the form. Place the button in the middle cell of the last row.

j. Select the **Record Operations** *Category* and the **Add New Record** *Action* of the button. Click **Next**.

k. Select the **Text** radio button and change the wording to read Add New Sailboat. Click **Next**.

l. Accept the default button name because you will not modify the button code and click **Finish**.

m. Add a third button onto the form. Place the button in the right-most cell of the last row.

n. Select the **Form Operations** *Category* and the **Close Form** *Action* of the button. Click **Next**.

o. Select the **Text** radio button and use the existing "Close Form" wording. Click **Next**.

p. Accept the default button name because you will not modify the button code and click **Finish**. The form should look similar to Figure 4-136.

q. Save the form.

Figure 4-136 Modified *AddNewSailboat* form

15. Restrict the form to data entry.
 a. Click the **Property Sheet** button [*Form Layout Tools Design* tab, *Tools* group] to open the *Property Sheet*.
 b. Click the **drop-down arrow** in the *Selection* box of the *Property Sheet* and select **Form**.
 c. Click to select the **Data** tab if necessary.
 d. Select **Yes** in the *Data Entry* property box.
 e. Select **Yes** in the *Allow Additions* property box.
 f. Close the *Property Sheet*.
 g. Save the form.

16. Switch to *Form* view by clicking the **View** button [*Form Layout Tools Design* tab, *Views* group] and selecting **Form View**. The complete form displays.

17. Test the form.
 a. Enter 1425 in the *Boat ID* text box.
 b. Enter Catalina 270 in the *Boat Type* text box.
 c. Enter 28'4" in the *Length* text box.
 d. Enter 8 in the *Seats* text box.
 e. Enter 6 in the *Sleeps* text box.
 f. Enter 139 in the *4 Hr Rate* text box.
 g. Enter 179 in the *Full Day Rate* text box.
 h. Select the **Galley w/ Stove** check box.
 i. Enter 2018 in the *Model Year* text box. The completed form should match the data shown in Figure 4-137.
 j. Click the **Save Sailboat Record** button.
 k. Click the **Add New Sailboat** button. A blank record should display in the form.
 l. Click the **Close Form** button.

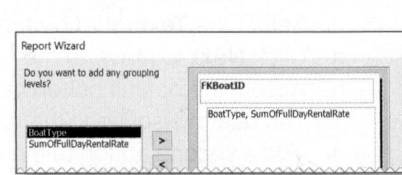

Figure 4-137 Sample data

18. Create a report using the *Report Wizard*.
 a. Click the **Report Wizard** button [*Create* tab, *Reports* group] to launch the *Report Wizard*.
 b. Click the **Tables/Queries** drop-down arrow and select the **FullDayRentalsByBoatSummary** query.
 c. Click the **Move All Fields** button and click **Next**. The next page of the *Report Wizard* displays the grouping as shown in Figure 4-138.
 d. Click the **Next** button to move to the next page of the *Report Wizard*.
 e. Do not sort the data. Click the **Next** button to move to the next page of the *Report Wizard*.
 f. Select a **Block** layout and **Portrait** orientation. Click **Next**.
 g. Click the **Finish** button without making any changes to the suggested title. The report opens in *Print Preview* view (Figure 4-139).
 h. Click the **Close Print Preview** button. The report displays in *Design* view.

Figure 4-138 Suggested data grouping

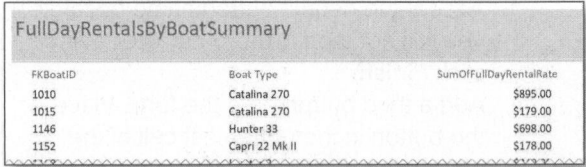

Figure 4-139 *Print Preview* view of report

19. Edit the report labels using *Layout* view.
 a. Switch the report to **Layout** view.
 b. Click to select the **FullDayRentalsByBoatSummary** label in the header section.
 c. Click inside the label to open the edit mode.
 d. Insert a space between each of the words and add Report as the last word.
 e. Click the header section outside the label.

f. Edit the labels of the column headers. Change *FKBoatID* to Boat ID and *SumOfFullDayRentalRate* to Total Income from Full Day Rentals.

g. Save the report.

h. Switch to **Report** view. The report should look similar to Figure 4-140.

i. Close the report.

20. Close the database.

Full Day Rentals By Boat Summary Report		
Boat ID	Boat Type	Total Income from Full Day Rentals
1010	Catalina 270	$895.00
1015	Catalina 270	$179.00
1146	Hunter 33	$698.00
1152	Capri 22 Mk II	$178.00
1168	Hunter 33	$349.00
1185	Hunter 36	$389.00
1225	Hunter 36	$1,556.00
1310	Beneteau 373	$409.00

Friday, November 29, 2019 Page 1 of 1

Figure 4-140 Completed report in *Report* view

Guided Project 4-3

Life's Animal Shelter wants to add a report and form to its database. To ensure consistency, the starting file is provided for you. You edit a report that was created based on a query. In *Layout* view, add a title, grouping, and totals. Next, add conditional formatting to the report, preview the results, and adjust print settings. Finally, you create a split form and adjust control positions on the form.
[Student Learning Outcomes 4.1, 4.5, 4.6, 4.7, 4.8]

File Needed: ***LifesAnimalShelter-04.accdb*** (Student data files are available in the Library of your SIMnet account.)
Completed Project File Name: ***[your initials] Access 4-3.accdb***

Skills Covered in This Project

- Modify a report in *Layout* view.
- Add grouping and sorting to a report.
- Add conditional formatting to a report.
- Add totals to a report.
- Preview a report.
- Create a split form.
- Adjust control positions.

1. Open the ***LifesAnimalShelter-04*** database from your student data files.

2. Save the database as [your initials] Access 4-3.

3. Enable content in the database.

4. Right-click the **PetsWithoutMatchingOwner** report and select **Layout View** to open the report in *Layout* view.

5. Change the report to a **landscape** orientation.
 a. Click the **Report Layout Tools Page Setup** tab.
 b. Click the **Landscape** button [*Page Layout* group].

6. Adjust the width of the report columns
 a. Select a text box in the *Why I'd make a great companion* column.
 b. Press and hold **Shift** and click to select the **Why I'd make a great companion** label.
 c. Press **F4** to open the *Property Sheet* and click the **Format** tab if necessary.
 d. Enter 3.2" in the *Width* property. You must press **Enter** or **Tab** after entering the value so that Access recognizes a changed value.
 e. Enter 7" in the *Left* property.

f. Select a text box in the *Color* column. Press and hold **Shift** and click to select the **Color** label.

g. Enter 1.5" in the *Width* property.

h. Enter 5.3" in the *Left* property.

i. Set the *Width* property of the *Gender* column and label to .6" and set the *Left* property to 4.6".

j. Set the *Width* property of the *Age* column and label to .5" and set the *Left* property to 4".

k. Set the *Width* property of the *Breed* column and label to 1.3" and set the *Left* property to 2.5".

l. Click a text box in the *Breed* column to select only the text box and to deselect the *Breed* label.

m. Enter .5" in the *Height* property.

n. Set the *Width* property of the *Type* column and label to .7" and set the *Left* property to 1.7".

o. Set the *Width* property of the *Pet Name* column and label to .8" and set the *Left* property to .8". The report should look similar to Figure 4-141.

p. Save the report.

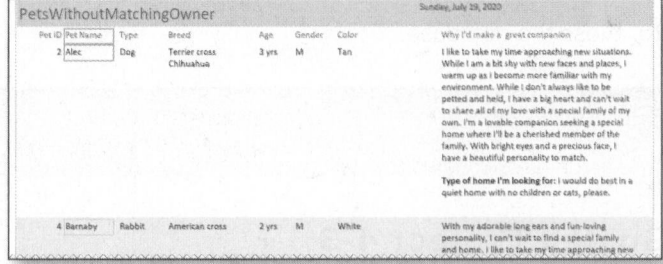

Figure 4-141 *PetsWithoutMatchingOwner* report

7. Edit the header and footer sections.

a. Click the text box containing the *Date*.

b. Enter 7.4" in the *Left* property.

c. Click to select the title label and then click the label again to open the edit mode.

d. Change the label to **Pets Available for Adoption**.

e. Click outside the label to save the changes.

f. Scroll down to the bottom of the report and select the **page number** text box.

g. Enter 9" in the *Left* property.

h. Press **F4** to close the *Property Sheet*.

8. Add grouping and sorting to the report.

a. Click the **Group & Sort** button [*Report Layout Tools Design* tab, *Grouping & Totals* group] to open the *Group, Sort, and Total* pane at the bottom of the report.

b. Click **Add a group** in the *Group, Sort, and Total* pane.

c. Select the **Type** field from the *Group on select field* list.

d. Click **More** in the *Group, Sort, and Total* pane.

e. Select the **do not keep group together on one page** arrow and then select **keep header and first record together on one page** (Figure 4-142).

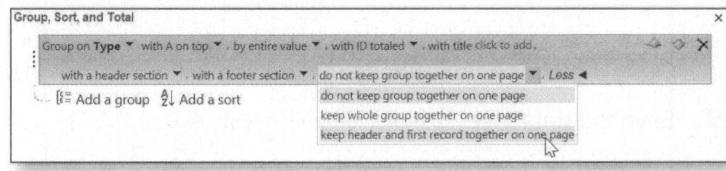

f. Click **Add a sort** in the *Group, Sort, and Total* pane.

Figure 4-142 *Keep header and first record together on one page* option

g. Select the **ID** field from the *Sort by select field* list.

h. Close the *Group, Sort, and Total* pane by clicking the **X** in the upper-right corner of the *Group, Sort, and Total* pane. Be careful not to click the *Delete* symbol inside the pane or you remove the group.

i. Scroll to the top of the report. The first record should be for "Martin," *Pet ID* number 6. Because the grouping uses a stepped layout, the word "Cat" appears in the *Type* column on the line above Martin.

9. Add conditional formatting to the report.

a. Click any cell in the *Gender* column.

b. Click the **Conditional Formatting** button [*Report Layout Tools Format* tab, *Control Formatting* group] to open the *Conditional Formatting Rules Manager* dialog box. *Gender* displays in the *Show formatting rules for* box.

c. Click the **New Rule** button to open the *New Formatting Rule* dialog box.

d. Select the **Check values in the current record or use an expression** rule type in the *Select a rule type* box if necessary.

e. Select **equal to** as the comparison.

f. Type M into the value box.

g. Select **bold** and choose the **Dark Blue** font color from the *Standard Colors*.

h. Click **OK**. The completed rule displays in the *Conditional Formatting Rules Manager* dialog box (Figure 4-143).

i. Click **Apply**.

j. Click **OK**.

k. Save the report.

Figure 4-143 Conditional formatting rule

10. Add totals to the report to count how many of each type of pet is available.

a. Select a text box in the **Pet ID** column.

b. Click the **Totals** button [*Report Layout Tools Design* tab, *Grouping & Totals* group].

c. Select **Count Records**. The report updates to show the total at the end of each group and a grand total at the end of the report.

d. Save the report.

11. Preview the report.

a. Select the **View** button [*Report Layout Tools Design* tab, *Views* group] and select **Print Preview**. The report should look similar to Figure 4-144.

b. Click the **One Page** button [*Print Preview* tab, *Zoom* group] if necessary.

c. Use the navigation arrows to move among pages.

d. Click the **Close Print Preview** button.

12. Close the report.

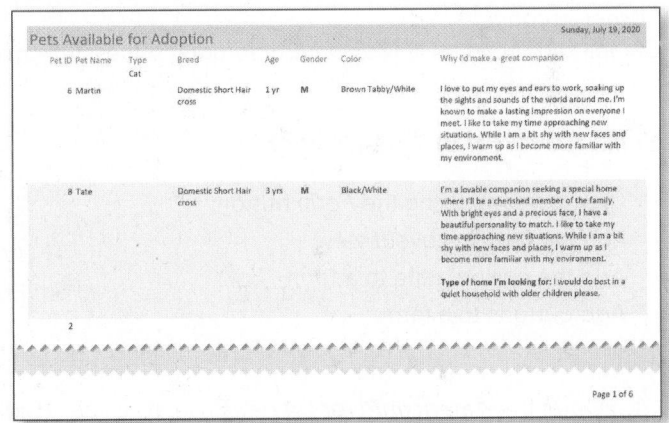

Figure 4-144 *Print Preview* of completed report

13. Create a split form and adjust control positions on the form.

a. Click to select the **Owners** table in the *Navigation Pane*.

b. Click the **More Forms** button [*Create* tab, *Forms* group] and select **Split Form** to create a new form. Depending on the width of the Access window, your form may display the fields in two columns in the top half of the form.

c. Click the **Form Layout Tools Arrange** tab.

d. Click the **Select Layout** button.

e. Click the **Control Padding** button.

f. Select **Medium**.

g. Click inside the form to deselect the control layout. The completed form should look similar to Figure 4-145.

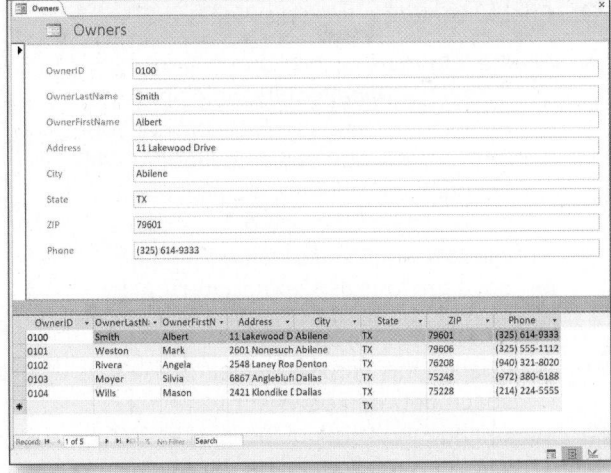

Figure 4-145 Completed split form

A4-287

h. Save the form. Accept the suggested form name by clicking **OK**.
i. Switch to *Form* view by clicking the **Form View** icon in the *Status* bar.
j. Use the navigation buttons to move among records.
k. Close the form.

14. Close the database.

Independent Project 4-4

American River Cycling wants to add a report and form to their database. To ensure consistency, the starting file is provided for you. Create a form with the *Form* button. Edit the form in *Layout* view and add a button. Create a report using the *Blank Report* option. In *Layout* view, modify the layout and add a title and grouping. Preview the results.
[Student Learning Outcomes 4.1, 4.2, 4.3, 4.5, 4.6, 4.8]

File Needed: ***AmericanRiver-04.accdb*** (Student data files are available in the Library of your SIMnet account.)
Completed Project File Name: ***[your initials] Access 4-4.accdb***

Skills Covered in This Project

- Create a form using the *Form* button.
- Edit the form in *Layout* view.
- Add the current date to a form.
- Add buttons to a form.
- Set form properties.
- Create a blank report.
- Edit the report in *Layout* view.
- Add grouping to a report.
- Preview a report.

1. Open the ***AmericanRiver-04*** database from your student data files.

2. Save the database as [your initials] Access 4-4.

3. Enable content in the database.

4. Create a form using the *Form* button.
 a. Select the **RaceResults** table and create a new form using the *Form* button. Your form should look similar to Figure 4-146, although the layout may be different depending on the size of the Access window when you created the form.
 b. Save the form as ViewRaceResults.

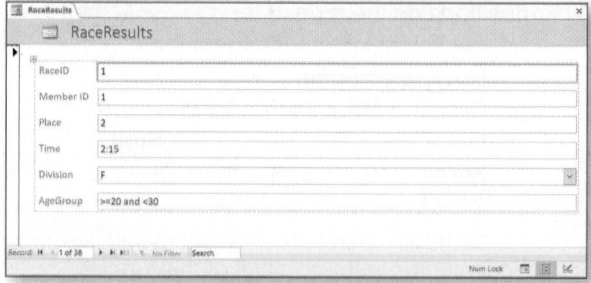

Figure 4-146 *RaceResults* form created with *Form* button

5. Edit the form in *Layout* view.
 a. Change the wording of the *RaceResults* label to read Member Race Results. Be careful to enter a space between each word.
 b. Change the *Width* of the label to 2.4".
 c. Change the *Width* of the *RaceID* text box to be 1". Remember that all the fields in this column change to the new width.

d. Add two rows below the *AgeGroup* field.
e. Change the *Height* of the bottom row to .4".
f. Move the control layout down about ½" and to the right about 1" as shown in Figure 4-147.
g. Add the date to the form. Choose the *DD-Mon-YY* format. If necessary, deselect the **Include Time** check box so that only the date is added.
h. Select the **Auto_Date** control in the header and change the width of the *Auto_Date* control to 1".
i. Change the *Left* property of the *Auto_Date* control to 4.75". The form should be similar to Figure 4-147, although you have not yet added the button.

Figure 4-147 Completed *ViewRaceResults* form

6. Add a button to the form.
 a. Add a command button into the right-most cell in the second added row. The button should close the form [*Form Operations* category].
 b. Choose the **Text** radio button and use the suggested wording.
 c. Save the button as ViewFormCloseButton.

7. Edit the form properties to limit user edits and deletions.
 a. Set the *Data Entry*, *Allow Additions*, *Allow Deletions*, and *Allow Edits* properties to **No** in the *Property Sheet* of the form.
 b. Close the *Property Sheet*.
 c. Save the form.

8. Switch to *Form* view. The complete form should look similar to Figure 4-147.
 a. Use the navigation buttons to move among records.
 b. Close the form.

9. Create a report using the *Blank Report* button.
 a. Add all the fields from the *Members* table. The report should look similar to Figure 4-148.

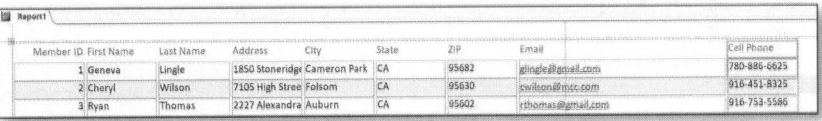

Figure 4-148 Add fields into a blank report

10. Add grouping into the report.
 a. Group the report on the *City* field.
 b. Save the report as ClubMembers.

11. Modify the layout of the report.
 a. Select the **Report Layout Tools Page Setup** tab.
 b. Click **Margins** [*Page Size* group] and select **Normal**.
 c. Change the page layout to **Landscape**. Notice the light gray, vertical, dashed line to the left of the cell phone field. This indicates that the cell phone column does not fit on the same page as the other fields.
 d. Change the *Width* of the *Member ID* column to .8".
 e. Change the *Width* of the *Address* column to 1.7".
 f. Change the *Width* of the *State* and *ZIP* columns to .5".

g. Change the *Width* of the *Email* column to 2".

h. Close the *Property Sheet*.

i. Add a title to the report and enter **List of Club Members** as the title text.

j. Add page numbers to the bottom of the report. Use the **Page N of M** format and **Center** the alignment.

12. Save the changes made to the report.

13. View the report in *Print Preview*.
 a. Adjust the zoom to **One Page**. The report should look similar to Figure 4-149.
 b. Close *Print Preview*.

List of Club Members

City	Member ID	First Name	Last Name	Address	State	ZIP	Email	Cell Phone
Auburn								
	3	Ryan	Thomas	2227 Alexandra Drive	CA	95602	rthomas@gmail.com	916-753-5586
	14	Randy	Clemmins	7336 Lester Road	CA	95602	rclemmins@phre.com	916-450-3330
	18	Dean	Teague	2112 Stonebrook Court	CA	95602	teague.dean@sac.rr.com	916-599-2222
Cameron Park								
	7	Melanie	Figueroa	4511 Johnson Court	CA	95682	mfigueroa@phre.com	916-450-3336
	1	Geneva	Lingle	1850 Stoneridge Court	CA	95682	glingle@gmail.com	780-886-6625
Fair Oaks								
	10	Rick	Hermenn	9035 Masi Drive	CA	95628	rickh@gmail.com	916-450-6719
	5	Margaret	Jepson	28861 Newcastle Road	CA	95628	margaret@sac.rr.com	780-862-9851
Folsom								
	2	Cheryl	Wilson	7105 High Street	CA	95630	cwilson@mcc.com	916-451-8325
Lincoln								
	11	Karen	Graves	6003 Ashland Road	CA	95648	kgraves@phre.com	916-450-3892
Rocklin								
	4	Roy	Baxter	705 First Street	CA	95677	roy@centralsierra.com	780-886-2471
	8	Sue	Schooler	4183 Braxton Way	CA	95677	sschooler@gmail.com	780-824-3525
Roseville								
	12	Robyn	Constantini	9581 Magnolia Way	CA	95661	robyn@gmail.com	780-886-2471
	6	Javier	Mendoza	8364 Marshall Street	CA	95661	mendozaj20@hotmail.com	916-450-3329
	13	John	Burgess	85741 Auberry Road	CA	95661	jburgess@hotmail.com	780-886-5862
	15	Amber	Harrison	488 Yale Drive	CA	95661	aharrison24@gmail.com	780-824-1111
	16	Mark	Pohlman	7377 Acorn Glen Loop	CA	95661	mpohlman@hotmail.com	916-541-5339

Page 1 of 2

Figure 4-149 *Print Preview* of completed report

14. Close the report.

15. Close the database.

Independent Project 4-5

The State of New York Department of Motor Vehicles wants to add a form and a report to its database so users can more easily view the information about drivers. To ensure consistency, the starting file is provided for you. Create a split form and edit the form in *Layout* view. Next, create a report using the *Blank Report* option. In *Layout* view, modify the layout, add a title, grouping, sorting, and totals. Preview the results.
[Student Learning Outcomes 4.1, 4.2, 4.3, 4.5, 4.6, 4.8]

File Needed: **NewYorkDMV-04.accdb** *(Student data files are available in the Library of your SIMnet account.)*
Completed Project File Name: ***[your initials] Access 4-5.accdb***

Skills Covered in This Project

- Create a form using the *Form* button.
- Edit a form in *Layout* view.
- Add the current date to a form.
- Move fields within the control layout.
- Test the functionality of a form.
- Create a blank report.
- Edit a report in *Layout* view.
- Add grouping and sorting to a report.
- Add totals to a report.
- Preview a report.

1. Open the **NewYorkDMV-04** database from your student data files.

2. Save the database as [your initials] Access 4-5.

3. Enable content in the database.

4. Create a split form. Recall that when creating a split form, the width of the Access window affects whether the fields are placed in one or two columns. Before creating the form, you adjust the size of the Access window to ensure that the initial layout of the form includes two columns.
 a. Click the **Restore Down** button if necessary so that the Access window is not maximized.
 b. Click the **Create** tab. If needed, reduce the width of the Access window so that there is minimal extra space to the right of the icons displayed on the *Ribbon*.
 c. Select the **Drivers** table in the *Navigation Pane* and create a split form. Your form should look similar to Figure 4-150. If your form does not have two columns, close the form without saving. Adjust the height and width of the Access window to make it a bit smaller and then create the form again.

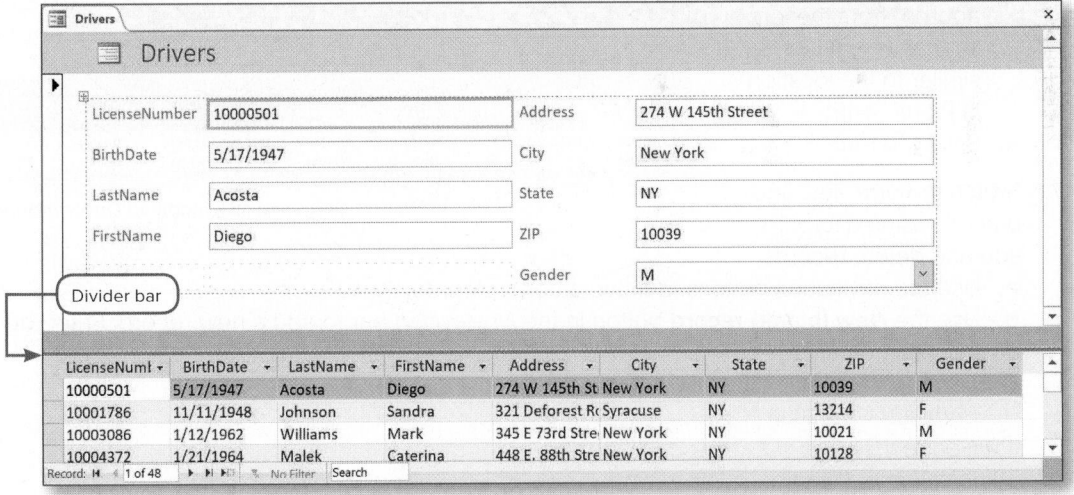

Figure 4-150 Split form based on *Drivers* table

 d. Save the form as DriverInformation.

5. Edit the form in *Layout* view.
 a. In the *Datasheet* portion of the form, use the resize arrow to decrease the column width of the *State*, *ZIP*, and *Gender* fields and to increase the width of the *Address* field. You can't use the *Property Sheet* to set the width of columns in the *Datasheet* portion of the form.

b. In the single record portion of the form, change the label for *LicenseNumber* to License# and insert spaces between the words in the labels for *BirthDate*, *LastName*, and *FirstName*.

c. Add the date and time to the form header. Choose the radio buttons for the long date and time formats.

d. Enter 5.5" in the *Left* property for the *Date* and the *Time* controls.

6. Move controls within the layout to customize the layout.

a. Add two rows below the *Gender* field so you have some room to move the different fields. If necessary, you can drag the divider bar down to increase the available space in the single record portion of the form.

b. Add one row above the *License#* field.

c. Move the *License#* label to the cell in the top row.

d. Move the *License#* text box to the cell below the label.

e. Continue moving the labels and text boxes so that your fields are placed similar to those in Figure 4-151. You may need to move some labels and text boxes to a temporary location in the layout during this process. Don't worry that the row heights and column widths may not yet match Figure 4-151.

f. Delete any unused rows and columns in the layout.

g. Select a **cell** in the left column and change the *Width* to 1.8".

h. Change the *Width* of the middle column to 1.8".

i. Change the *Width* of the right column to 1".

j. Change the *Height* of the rows that contain labels to .2".

k. Change the *Height* of the rows that contain text boxes to .25".

l. Move the control layout from the far left to about 1" from the left, so that its location is similar to the location in Figure 4-151.

m. Save the form.

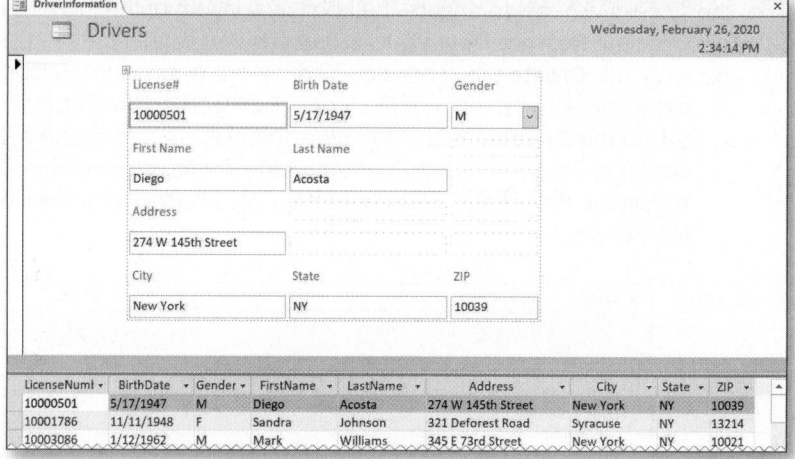

Figure 4-151 Modified *DriverInformation* form

7. Switch to *Form* view and practice using a form to add and delete records.

a. Use the navigation buttons to move among records.

b. Use the **New (blank) record** button in the *Navigation* bar to add a new record. Enter the following data values:

LicenseNum#: 39998200
BirthDate: 3/3/2000
Gender: F
FirstName: Patricia
LastName: Lozada
Address: 12846 Sandy Point Drive
City: Utica
State: NY
ZIP: 13502

c. Navigate to the first record.

d. Navigate back to the last record. This should be the record you added.
e. Navigate to the sixth record. This should be Steve Miller's record.
f. Delete the record by clicking the **Delete** button arrow [*Home* tab, *Records* group] and then selecting **Delete Record**. Click **Yes** in the dialog box to confirm the deletion.
g. Close the form when done.

8. Create a report using the *Blank Report* button. Add all the fields from the *Tickets* table into the report.

9. Modify the layout of the report.
 a. Modify the *TicketNumber*, *DLNumber*, *TicketDate*, and *PrimaryFactor* column labels by inserting a space between "Ticket" and "Number", "DL" and "Number", "Ticket" and "Date", and "Primary" and "Factor".
 b. Change the *OfficerBadgeNumber* column label to **Officer#**. The updated labels should match those in Figure 4-152.
 c. Change the *Width* of the *DL Number*, *Ticket Date*, and *Officer#* columns to .85".

Ticket Number	DL Number	Ticket Date	City	Primary Factor	Officer#	Fine
4235879527	12348279	11/4/2019	Buffalo	Unsafe Speed	A00032567	$360.00
4235879530	12346123	11/7/2019	New York	Passing/Lane Violations	A00061444	$150.00

Figure 4-152 Adjusted column width of report fields

 d. Change the *Width* of the *Primary Factor* column to 2".
 e. Change the *Width* of the *Fine* column to .75".
 f. Add a title to the report header and enter **Ticket Report by City** as the title text.
 g. Add page numbers. Use the **Bottom of Page [Footer]** position, **Page N of M** format, and **Center** the alignment.
 h. Save the report as **TicketsByCity**.

10. Add grouping and sorting to the report.
 a. Group the report on the *City* field.
 b. Sort the report on the *Ticket Date* field in *from oldest to newest* order.
 c. Save the report.

11. Add totals to the report.
 a. Calculate the average dollar value of the *Fine* field. The average appears at the end of each group and an overall average appears at the end of the report.
 b. Scroll to the bottom of the report. Change the *Height* of the *Fine Average* text box for both the group and the overall average to .25".
 c. Apply the **bold** format, on the *Report Layout Tools Format* tab, to the *Fine Average* text box for both the group and the overall average.
 d. Save the report.

12. View the report in *Print Preview*.
 a. Adjust the zoom to **One Page**.
 b. Navigate to the second page of the report. Notice that the Utica group of tickets is spread across two pages. Don't worry if the Syracuse group of tickets is spread across two pages instead of the Utica group. This could be caused by different default settings in Access.
 c. Close *Print Preview*.

13. Choose **keep whole group together on one page** for the *Group on City* in the *Group, Sort, and Total* pane.

14. Save the report.

15. Preview the report again.
 a. Adjust the zoom to **One Page**. The report should look similar to Figure 4-153.
 b. Navigate to the second page. Notice that the Utica tickets are all on the second page. If the Syracuse group was spread across two pages in step 12b, then the Syracuse group will now be on the second page.
 c. Close *Print Preview*.

16. Close the report.

17. Close the database.

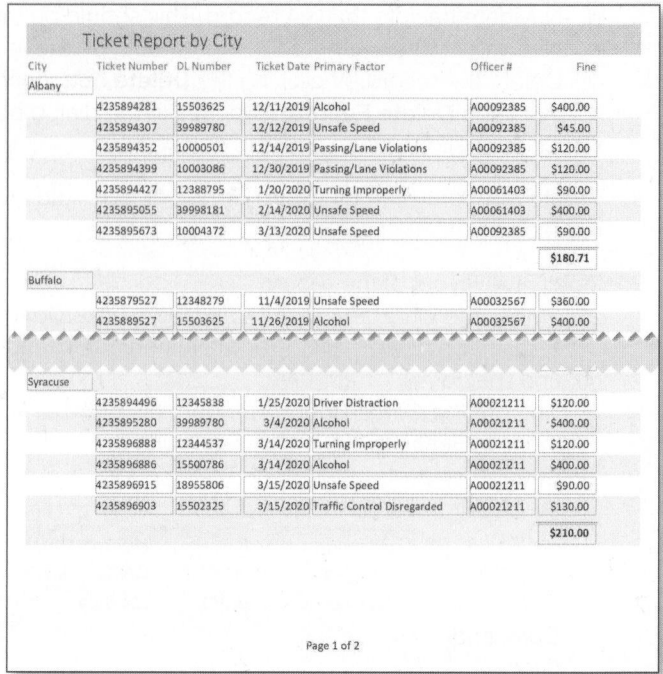

Figure 4-153 Completed *TicketsByCity* report

Independent Project 4-6

Courtyard Medical Plaza wants to add a form and a report to its database. To ensure consistency, the starting file is provided for you. Create a blank form and modify the form in *Layout* view. Edit properties to restrict the form to data entry and add buttons. Next, create a report using the *Report Wizard*. In *Layout* view, modify the layout, add sorting, and add conditional formatting. Finally, preview the results. [Student Learning Outcomes 4.2, 4.3, 4.4, 4.5, 4.6, 4.7, 4.8]

File Needed: **CourtyardMedicalPlaza-04.accdb** (*Student data files are available in the* Library *of your SIMnet account.*)
Completed Project File Name: **[your initials] Access 4-6.accdb**

Skills Covered in This Project

- Create a form using the *Form* button.
- Edit a form in *Layout* view.
- Add the current date to a form.
- Move fields within the control layout.
- Restrict a form to data entry.
- Create a report using the *Report Wizard*.
- Edit a report in *Layout* view.
- Add grouping and sorting to a report.
- Add totals to a report.
- Add conditional formatting to a report.
- Preview a report.

1. Open the **CourtyardMedicalPlaza-04** database from your student data files.

2. Save the database as [your initials] Access 4-6.

3. Enable content in the database.

4. Create a form using the *Blank Form* button.
 a. Add all the fields from the *Physician* table in the following order: **DoctorID**, **FirstName**, **LastName**, **PrimarySpecialty**, **OfficeNumber**, and **MoveInDate**.
 b. Close the *Field List*.
 c. Save the form as AddNewPhysician.

5. Edit the form in *Layout* view, add a new column and new rows to the control layout, and modify their size.
 a. Add two rows below the *Tenant Since* row.
 b. Add one column to the right of the existing columns.
 c. Adjust the *Width* of each column to 1.6".
 d. Adjust the *Height* of the last row to .4".

6. Add command buttons, a title, and the date to the form.
 a. Add a button into the bottom row of the left-most column to save a record [*Record Operations Category*].
 b. Change the wording to Save Physician Record.
 c. Name the button AddPhysicianFormSaveButton.
 d. Add a second button into the bottom row of the middle column to add a new record [*Record Operations Category*].
 e. Change the wording to Add New Physician.
 f. Name the button AddPhysicianFormAddButton.
 g. Add a third button into the bottom row of the right-most column to close the form [*Form Operations Category*].
 h. Use the existing wording for the button.
 i. Name the button AddPhysicianFormCloseButton.
 j. Add a title to the form header. Edit the title to include spaces between the words.
 k. Add the date to the form. Use the *DD-Mon-YY* format. If necessary, deselect the **Include Time** check box so that only the date is added.
 l. Enter 1.1" in the *Width* property and 4" in the *Left* property for the *Auto_Date* control.
 m. Save the changes to the form. The revised form should look similar to Figure 4-154.

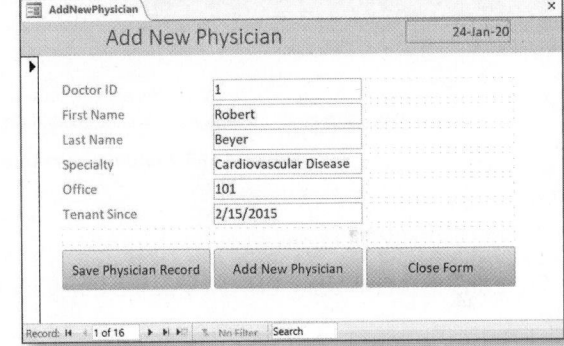

Figure 4-154 *AddNewPhysician* form

7. Restrict the form to data entry.
 a. Open the *Property Sheet* for the form if necessary and select the **Data** tab.
 b. Click the **drop-down arrow** in the *Selection* box of the *Property Sheet* and select **Form**.
 c. Select **Yes** in the *Data Entry* property box.
 d. Select **Yes** in the *Allow Additions* property box if necessary. Recall that when both the *Data Entry* and *Allow Additions* properties are set to *yes*, the values in the *Allow Deletions* and *Allow Edits* properties do not have an impact
 e. Save the form.
 f. Close the form.

8. Create a report using the *Report Wizard*.
 a. Launch the *Report Wizard*.
 b. Add all the fields from the *RentInvoices* table in the following order: **InvoiceID**, **FKDoctorID**, **InvoiceDate**, **Description**, **DueDate**, **DateReceived**, **AmountDue**, and **Discount**.
 c. Accept the suggested grouping by *FKDoctorID* on the second page of the *Report Wizard*.

d. Add summary options on the third page of the *Report Wizard*. In the *Summary Options* dialog box, select the **Sum** of the *AmountDue* field and select the **Detail and Summary** radio button for the *Show* option if necessary (Figure 4-155).

e. Choose a **Stepped** layout and **Landscape** orientation and deselect the *Adjust the field width so all fields fit on a page* check box.

f. Click the **Finish** button without making any changes to the suggested title. The preview of the report should look similar to Figure 4-156. Don't worry if not all fields are visible, or if some of your fields overlap or display the # symbols indicating that the column width is too narrow. You resize the columns in step 9. The wording for the summary line was automatically added using the totals created by the *Report Wizard*.

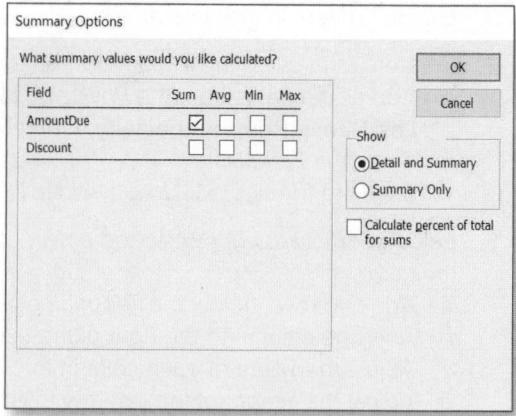

Figure 4-155 *Summary Options* dialog box

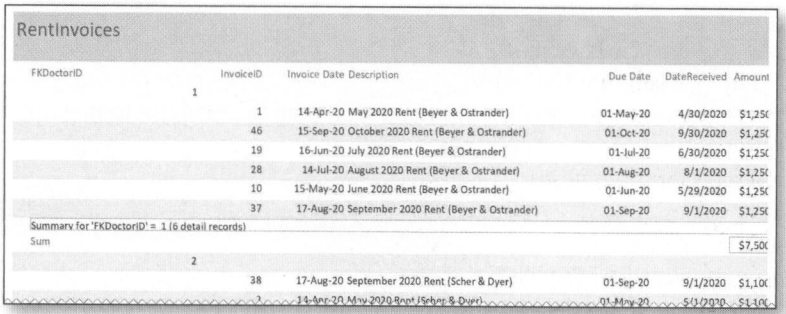

Figure 4-156 *RentInvoices* report created using the *Report Wizard*

g. Close *Print Preview*.

9. Edit the report using *Layout* view so that your report matches Figure 4-157.

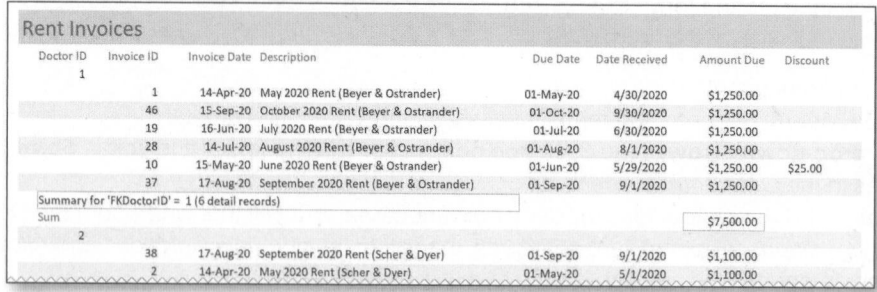

Figure 4-157 *RentInvoices* report after editing the layout

a. Switch to *Layout* view and open the *Property Sheet* if necessary.

b. Select both the *FKDoctorID* label and text box and change the *Width* to .6".

c. Change the *Width* of the *InvoiceID* label and text box to .75" and change the *Left* property to 1".

d. Change the *Width* of the *Invoice Date* label and text box to 1" and change the *Left* property to 1.9".

e. Change the *Width* of the *Description* label and text box to 2.8" and change the *Left* property to 3".

f. Change the *Width* of the *Due Date* label and text box to 1" and change the *Left* property to 6".

g. Change the *Width* of the *DateReceived* label and text box to 1" and change the *Left* property to 7.1".

h. Change the *Width* of the *Amount Due* label and text box to 1" and change the *Left* property to 8.3". Don't worry that you still don't see the entire value. It will be corrected when you change the next column.

i. Change the Width of the *Discount* label and text box to .7" and change the *Left* property to 9.4".

j. Edit the title label and the *InvoiceID* and *DateReceived* field labels by inserting a space between "Rent" and "Invoices", "Invoice" and "ID", and "Date" and "Received".

k. Remove the "FK" from the *FKDoctorID* label and insert a space between "Doctor" and "ID". The updated labels should match Figure 4-157.

l. Change the *Width* of the text box that displays the sum of the *Amount Due* for each doctor to 1" and change the *Left* property to 8.3".

m. Click to select a *Summary for 'FKDoctorID'* text box and change the *Width* to 6" and the *Height* to .2".

n. Scroll to the bottom of the report. Change the *Width* of the text box that displays the grand total of the *Amount Due* to 1" and change the *Left* property to 8.3".

o. Scroll to the lower-right corner of the report to find the text box with the page number. Click to select the page number and change the *Width* to 1" and change the *Left* property to 9.4".

p. Save the report.

q. Switch to *Report* view. Scroll to the top of the report if necessary. The report should look similar to Figure 4-157.

r. Switch back to *Layout* view.

10. Add an *oldest to newest* sort on the *InvoiceDate* field in the *Group, Sort, and Total* pane.

11. Add conditional formatting to the report so that any *Discount* values that *are greater than or equal to $20* display in a **bold**, **green** font. Don't include the **$** symbol when entering the criteria. Choose the **Green 5** font from the *Standard Colors* (seventh column, sixth row).

12. Save your changes.

13. View the report in *Print Preview*.
 a. Click **One Page** [*Print Preview* tab, *Zoom* group]. The report should look similar to Figure 4-158.
 b. Close *Print Preview*.

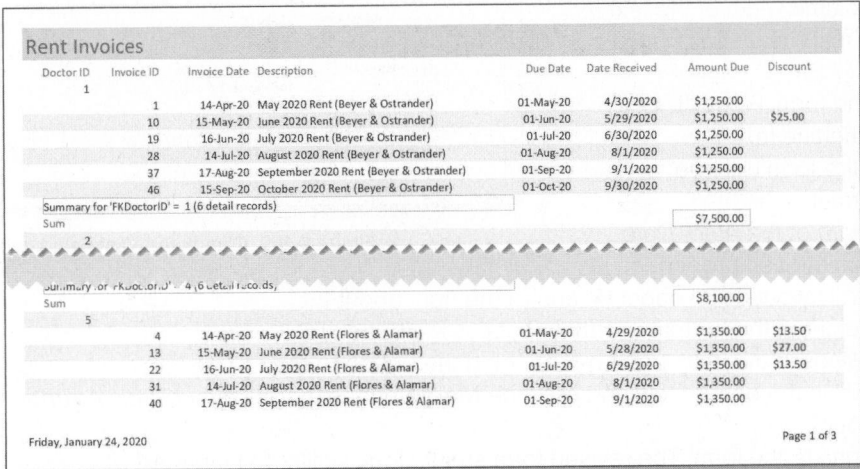

Figure 4-158 Completed *RentInvoices* report

14. Close the report.

15. Close the database.

Improve It Project 4-7

Mary's Rentals wants to improve its database. To ensure consistency, the starting file is provided for you. You improve the functionality of a form by editing controls on the form, modifying the layout, and limiting edits and deletions. Improve the usability of a report by modifying the layout and adding grouping and sorting. Finally, preview how the report will print.
[Student Learning Outcomes 4.2, 4.3, 4.5, 4.6, 4.8]

File Needed: ***MarysRentals-04.accdb*** *(Student data files are available in the Library of your SIMnet account.)*
Completed Project File Name: *[your initials]* **Access 4-7.accdb**

Skills Covered in This Project

- Edit a form in *Layout* view.
- Add a title and date to a form.
- Move fields within the control layout.
- Set properties to limit user edits and deletions.

- Test the functionality of a form.
- Edit a report in *Layout* view.
- Add grouping and sorting to a report.
- Preview a report.

1. Open the ***MarysRentals-04*** database from your student data files.

2. Save the database as [your initials] Access 4-7.

3. Enable content in the database.

4. Edit the *ViewEquipment* form in *Layout* view so that your form matches Figure 4-159.
 a. Increase the column width of the labels to 1.5" so that the entire caption displays.
 b. Edit the label contents to insert blank spaces between the words. For example, change *EquipmentID* to *Equipment ID*.
 c. Increase the column width of the text boxes to 3" so that the entire contents displays.
 d. Add a title to the form. Enter View Equipment as the title text.
 e. Add a date to the form with the *DD-Mon-YY* format.
 f. Change the *Width* of the *Auto_Date* control to 1" and the *Left* property to 5".
 g. Move the control layout down about ¼" and to the right about ½".
 h. Increase the height of the bottom row that contains the button to .3".
 i. Fix the misspellings in the button text by changing the button to read Close Form.
 j. Select both cells in the bottom row and click the **Merge** button [*Form Layout Tools Arrange* tab, *Merge/Split* group].
 k. Save the changes to the form. The revised form should look similar to Figure 4-159.

5. Edit the form properties to restrict user additions, edits, and deletions.

6. Test the form.
 a. Save the form.
 b. Switch to *Form* view and navigate through the records.

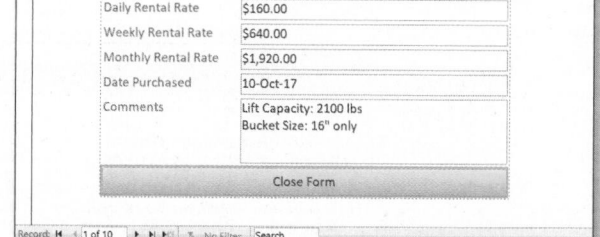

Figure 4-159 Completed *ViewEquipment* form

c. Try to change the value of one of the fields. That action should be restricted.
 d. Close the form.

7. Add grouping and sorting into the *ServiceHistory* report.
 a. Open the report in *Layout* view.
 b. Group the report on the *FKEquipmentID* field.
 c. Change to the option to **keep header and first record together on one page**.
 d. Sort the report on the *ServiceDate* field in *oldest to newest* order.

8. Edit the report in *Layout* view.
 a. Remove the *FK* from the *FKEquipmentID* label and insert a space between "Equipment" and "ID".
 b. Edit the captions in the labels, including the title, to insert spaces between the words.
 c. Select **Center** alignment on the *Report Layout Tools Format* tab for the *Service Date* label and text box and the *Hours* label and text box.
 d. Change the *Total Cost* label to be **right aligned**.
 e. Save the report.

9. View the report in *Print Preview*.
 a. Adjust the zoom to **One Page**. The report should look similar to Figure 4-160.
 b. Close *Print Preview*.

10. Close the report.

11. Close the database.

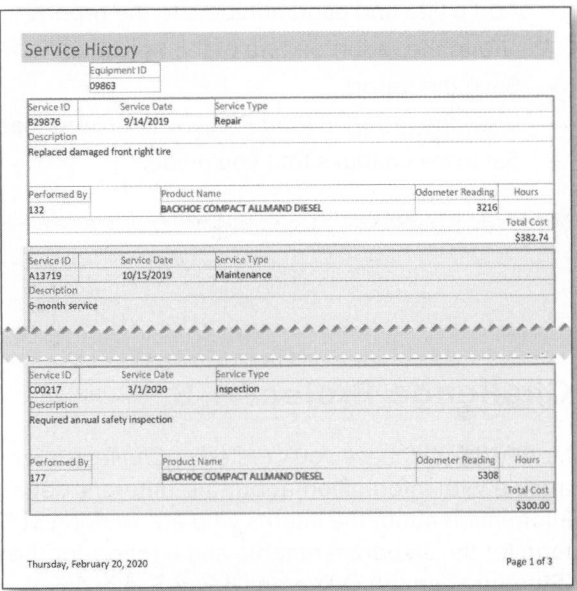

Figure 4-160 Completed *ServiceHistory* report

Challenge Project 4-8

For this project, you modify the database you built in *Challenge Project 3-8*, by creating one form and two reports.
[Student Learning Outcomes 4.1, 4.2, 4.3, 4.4, 4.5, 4.6, 4.8]

File Needed: *[your initials] Access 3-8.accdb*
Completed Project File Name: *[your initials] Access 4-8.accdb*

Open the database *[your initials] Access 3-8* and save a copy of it as [your initials] Access 4-8.

Modify your database according to the following instructions:

* Create a form for your table using the *Form Wizard*.
* Add all the fields to the form.
* In *Layout* view, adjust the column widths as necessary so they are sized appropriately.
* Change the form properties to restrict the form to limit user edits and deletions.

- Add one button to the form to close the form.
- Save the form and view it in *Form* view to ensure it works as desired.
- Create a report using the *Report Wizard* to show all the fields from one of your queries.
- Adjust the column widths as necessary so they are sized appropriately.
- Save the report and view it in *Print Preview* to ensure that it will print as desired.
- Create a second report using the *Blank Report* option.
- Add all the fields from the table into the report.
- Edit the layout as needed to adjust the column widths and page orientation.
- Add a title and page numbers to the report.
- Group the report on one of the fields.
- Save the report.
- View the report in *Print Preview* to ensure that it will print as desired.
- Save any changes that you made.

Challenge Project 4-9

Modify the database you created in *Challenge Project 3-9* for Blue Lake Sports. Your database contains a table with information about the different departments at Blue Lake Sports and a related table with information about the interns who are working at Blue Lake, along with the query you created. Create a form for the *Department* table and a report for the *Intern* table.
[Student Learning Outcomes 4.2, 4.3, 4.5, 4.6, 4.7, 4.8]

File Needed: *[your initials] Access 3-9.accdb*
Completed Project File Name: *[your initials] Access 4-9.accdb*

Open the database *[your initials] Access 3-9* and save a copy of it as [your initials] Access 4-9.

Modify your database according to the following instructions:

- Create a form for the *Department* table using the *Blank Form* button.
- Add all the fields to the form.
- Adjust the column widths as necessary so they are sized appropriately.
- Add a title to the form.
- Add a button to the form to close the form.
- Save the form and view it in *Form* view to ensure it works as desired.
- Create a report using the *Blank Report* tool to show all the fields in the *Intern* table.
- Adjust the column widths as necessary so they are sized appropriately.
- Group the report on the *FKDepartmentName* field.
- Sort the records by intern *LastName*.
- Add totals to count the total number of interns in each department.
- Add conditional formatting to the *University* field. Make the font a different color for each of the university values contained in the database. You need to add several rules for the *University* field (one for each value).

- Edit the title of the report to indicate the contents.
- Save the report.
- View the report in *Print Preview* and adjust the orientation and margins as necessary.
- Save any changes that you made.

Challenge Project 4-10

Modify the database you created in *Challenge Project 3-10* for a travel agency. Your database contains a table with information about the different ships and a related table with information about upcoming cruises, along with the queries you added. Add a form to allow new ships to be added into the database. Add a report to display trip information, grouped by number of days. Modify both the form and report to improve the overall functionality.
[Student Learning Outcomes 4.2, 4.3, 4.4, 4.5, 4.6, 4.8]

File Needed: *[your initials] Access 3-10.accdb*
Completed Project File Name: *[your initials] Access 4-10.accdb*

Open the database *[your initials] Access 3-10* and save a copy of it as [your initials] Access 4-10.

Modify your database according to the following instructions:

- Create a form for the *Ships* table using the *Blank Form* button.
- Add all the fields to the form.
- Adjust the column widths as necessary so they are sized appropriately.
- Add a title to the form.
- Change the form properties to restrict the form to data entry.
- Add three buttons to the form: Save a Record, Add New Record, and Close the Form.
- Save the form and view it in *Form* view to ensure it works as desired.
- Create a report using the *Report Wizard* to show all the fields in the *Trips* table.
- Group the report on the *NumberOfDays* field.
- Sort the records by cost per person.
- Add totals to calculate the average cost per person.
- Adjust the column widths as necessary so they are sized appropriately.
- Edit the title of the report to indicate the contents.
- Save the report.
- View the report in *Print Preview* and adjust the orientation and margins as necessary.
- Save any changes that you made.

Microsoft® Office

IN PRACTICE

powerpoint

©Chris Ryan/Getty Images

Creating and Editing Presentations

CHAPTER OVERVIEW

Microsoft PowerPoint is the leading presentation software. Whether you need to create a quick display or a very polished presentation with dazzling graphics, creative animation effects, and video, PowerPoint has all the tools you need. You can use PowerPoint for slide shows with computer projection equipment in meeting rooms, for self-running presentations viewed by individuals, or for presentations shown on the web. This chapter covers the basics of starting and editing a PowerPoint presentation.

STUDENT LEARNING OUTCOMES (SLOs)

After completing this chapter, you will be able to:

SLO 1.1 Create, open, and save a presentation (p. P1-3).

SLO 1.2 Work with slides, layouts, placeholders, and text (p. P1-13).

SLO 1.3 Navigate between slides and organize content by reproducing and rearranging slides (p. P1-25).

SLO 1.4 Change theme colors and fonts (p. P1-32).

SLO 1.5 Insert headers and footers to add identifying information (p. P1-35).

SLO 1.6 Insert, resize, and align a picture from a file (p. P1-40).

SLO 1.7 Apply and modify transition effects to add visual interest (p. P1-43).

SLO 1.8 Preview a presentation and print slides, handouts, and outlines (p. P1-45).

SLO 1.9 Apply presentation properties (p. P1-48).

CASE STUDY

Each chapter in this book begins with a case study that introduces you to the Pause & Practice projects in the chapter. These Pause & Practice projects give you a chance to apply and practice key skills. Each chapter contains three to five Pause & Practice projects.

Hamilton Civic Center (HCC) is a nonprofit community fitness center that partners with the local hospital for educational events. Doctors and nurses provide classes on a variety of health and wellness issues for adults. HCC also works with local schools to support their academic programs and sponsors events for children.

In this chapter, you develop a presentation about training for an upcoming marathon that is being promoted to HCC members.

Pause & Practice 1-1: Create a presentation and develop text content.

Pause & Practice 1-2: Apply a presentation theme, change theme colors and fonts, and edit content.

Pause & Practice 1-3: Add interest with pictures, apply transitions, and print supplements.

Creating, Opening, and Saving Presentations

PowerPoint provides several ways to start, view, and save a presentation. Always save your presentation if you will need to access it again. If you close the presentation before saving it, your content is lost.

PowerPoint Start and Open Pages

When you launch PowerPoint, the *Start* page opens with several options for starting a new presentation or opening an existing presentation.

If you prefer to work on text content only, click the **Blank Presentation** thumbnail to go directly to your first slide to begin developing content. You can select a *Theme* with a background design and then add your content. When you click a theme, a dialog box opens where you can choose from four or more *Variants* showing different color and font combinations. Variants may have different graphics, too. You can also search for themes by topic or search word.

If you choose *Open Other Presentation*, you will go to PowerPoint's *Open Page* on *Backstage* view where you can access files saved in different locations. *Backstage* view is used to control many aspects of your presentation. While you are working, click the *File* tab to access *Backstage* view.

▶ HOW TO: Use the PowerPoint Start Page

1. Launch PowerPoint and the *Start* page displays (Figure 1-1).

2. Open a saved presentation in the *Recent* list on the left by clicking the file name.

3. Start a new blank presentation.
 - Click the **Blank Presentation** thumbnail to go directly to your first slide.
 - Press **Esc** to close the *Start* page and go directly to your first slide.

4. Start a new presentation with a theme.
 - Double-click a **Theme** to open the presentation with the theme default *Variant* colors.
 - Click a **Theme** to open a dialog box (Figure 1-2) that shows *Variants* with different color combinations. Select a *Variant* on the right and click **Create**.

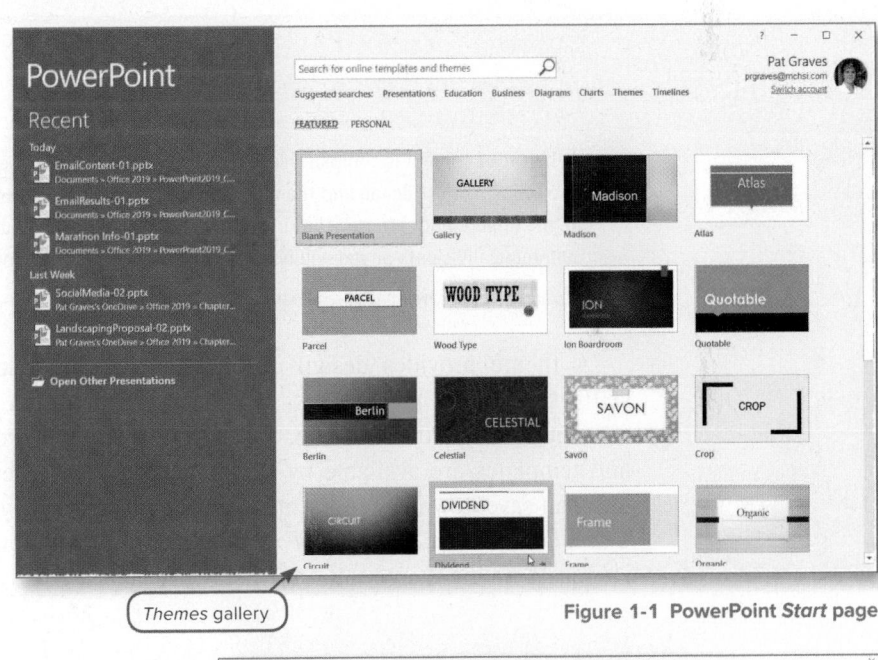

Figure 1-1 PowerPoint *Start* page

Figure 1-2 Theme *Variants*

5. Open a saved presentation by clicking the **Open Other Presentations** link on the left.
 - The *Open* page appears where you can select the file location (Figure 1-3).
 - To pin a file that you frequently open, click the pin icon on the right of the file name so it is then listed in the *Pinned* area at the top.
 - Click **OneDrive – Personal** or **This PC** to see the folders and files in these locations. Click the presentation name to open it.
 - Click **Browse** to locate files using the *Open* dialog box (Figure 1-4). Double-click the file name to open the presentation and close the dialog box.

Figure 1-3 *Backstage* view

Figure 1-4 *Open* dialog box

> **MORE INFO**
>
> When your content is complete, save your presentation (discussed on pages P1-9 – P1-11) and then close it by clicking the **File** tab and then clicking **Close**. To close PowerPoint, click the **Close** button (an **X**) in the upper-right corner of the title bar. If you click the **Close** button before saving, the presentation automatically closes or you will be prompted to save your presentation if any changes have been made.

A theme provides design consistency through background graphics, colors, and font settings. A *template* contains the characteristics of a theme and usually provides sample content you can edit or delete. When you start a new PowerPoint presentation, many themes and templates are available by searching online, or they can be downloaded at Office.com. You can save downloaded themes and templates so they are available for future use. *SLO 1.4: Changing Theme Colors and Fonts* provides information about searching within PowerPoint and customizing theme settings.

> **MORE INFO**
>
> For instructions to set up a Microsoft account, refer to *SLO Intro.1: Using Windows 10* in *Intro Chapter 1: Windows 10, Office 365/2019, and File Management*. Your computer must be connected to the internet to access *OneDrive* files or download themes and templates.

▶ HOW TO: Create a New Presentation from Online Templates and Themes

1. Launch PowerPoint to display the *Start* page.
 - If PowerPoint is open, click the **File** tab on the left to open the *Backstage* view and click **New**.

2. Use one of these methods to search for templates and themes:

 - In the search box, type a search word, such as modern, and click the **Start searching** button (Figure 1-5).
 - Click one of the *Suggested searches* for general topics.

3. The *Category* list on the right provides links for common documents using PowerPoint and other Office applications (Figure 1-6).

4. Click a thumbnail to open a dialog box with a description (Figure 1-7).

5. Click **Create** and the presentation opens.

 - The presentation may contain sample content that you need to delete before adding your content.

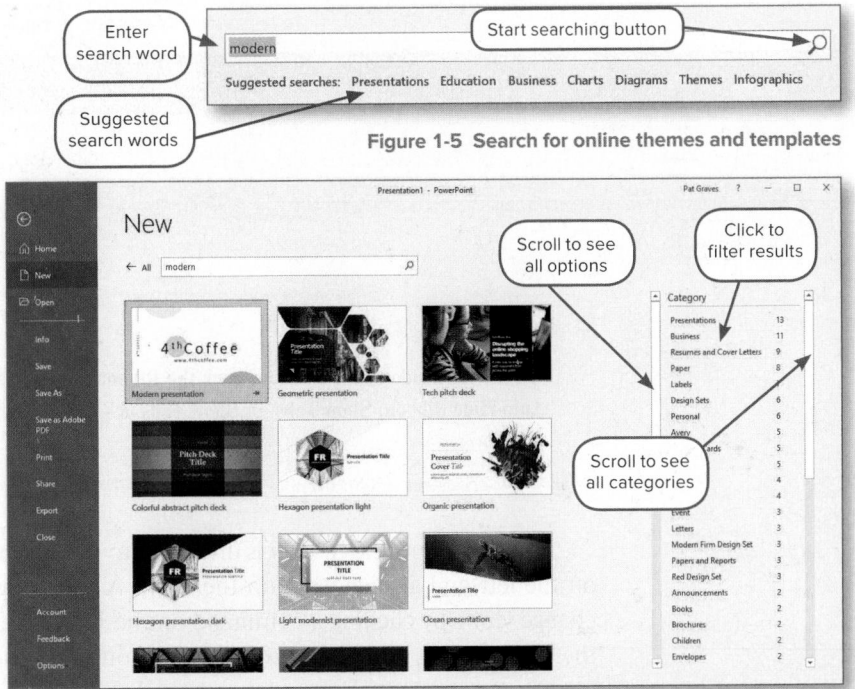

Figure 1-5 Search for online themes and templates

Figure 1-6 Search results for online themes and templates

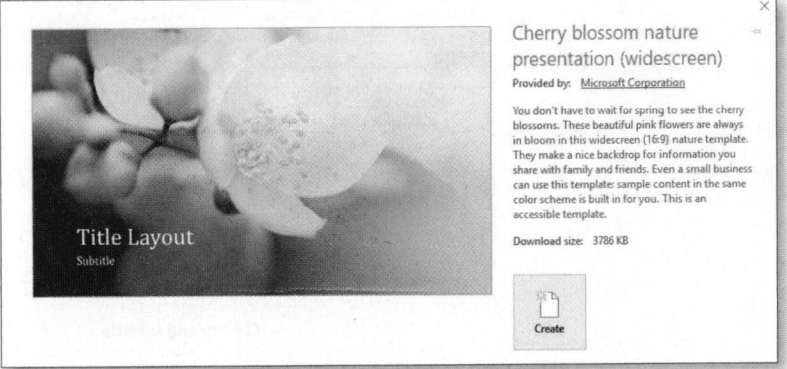

Figure 1-7 Template with description and sample content

> **ANOTHER WAY**
>
> In *Normal* view, press **Ctrl+O** to access the *Open* page on *Backstage* view. Press **Ctrl+F12** (or **Fn+Ctrl+F12** if necessary for your computer) to access the *Open* dialog box.

Views

PowerPoint provides different views to help you create slides, organize them, and display them in a slide show. When you start a new presentation, it opens in *Normal* view. The *Ribbon* displays across the top of the window and has named tabs with commands organized in groups (Figure 1-8). Additional tabs, such as the *Drawing Tools Format* tab, open depending on your current activity. Several tabs contain commands similar to those in Word, whereas other tabs display features that are unique to PowerPoint.

Figure 1-8 PowerPoint *Ribbon* with *Home* tab displayed

> **MORE INFO**
>
> On the right side of the title bar, click the **Ribbon Display Options** button to select from three options: **Auto-Hide Ribbon, Show Tabs**, or **Show Tabs or Commands**. The last option is used for figures in this book.

The area below the *Ribbon* is divided into panes where you work on slides: a *Thumbnail* pane on the left and a *Slide* pane on the right. A *Notes* pane may display below the slide. You can change views by clicking a command on the *View* tab [*Presentation Views* group] (Figure 1-9) or the *View* buttons on the *Status* bar at the bottom of the window.

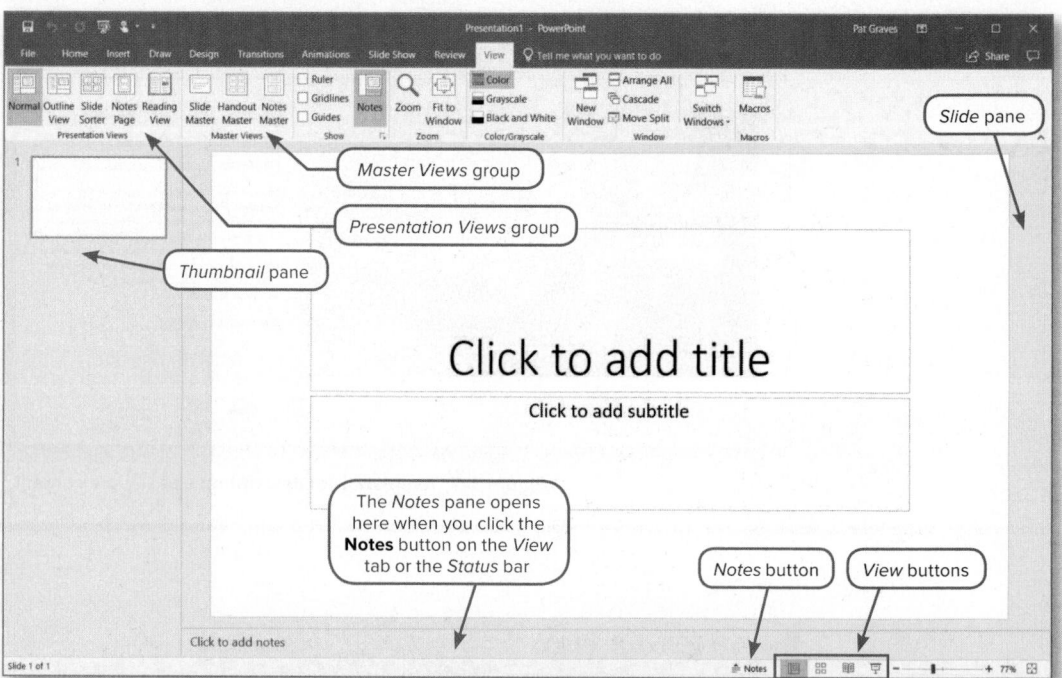

Figure 1-9 *Normal* view with *View* tab and *Notes* pane displayed

The *View* tab displays five *Presentation Views* that include the following:

- *Normal View*. The default view where you enter content and move between slides as you develop them. Click the **Notes** button to open a *Notes* pane below the slide to add speaker notes for individual slides.
- *Outline View*. The left pane displays slide titles and bulleted text instead of slide thumbnails.
- *Slide Sorter View*. Slides appear as thumbnails, so it is easy to reorganize slides and apply transition effects to control how the slides advance.
- *Notes Page View*. Each slide appears at the top of a page with space below the slide where you type speaker notes.

- *Reading View:* The slide show displays at full-screen or another window size controlled by the viewer. Navigation controls are in the *Status* bar at the bottom of the window.

The *Master Views* group includes the following: **Slide Master, Handout Master,** and **Notes Master.** These views are used to change formatting that affects the whole presentation.

The *View* buttons located on the *Status* bar provide easy access to different PowerPoint views regardless of which *Ribbon* tab is currently open (Figure 1-10).

Figure 1-10 *View buttons*

Two additional views are very important for the delivery of your presentation:

- *Slide Show View:* Slides appear one at a time at full-screen size for audience viewing.
- *Presenter View:* Speaker notes and other features display that are helpful for delivering a presentation. For more on this feature, see "Presenter View" in *SLO 3.5: Controlling Display Options.*

While developing your presentation, test it in *Slide Show* view so you can see the content in the way your audience will see it, and rehearse your presentation before using it.

HOW TO: Start Slide Show View

1. Begin your slide show with the current slide using one of these methods.
 - Click the **Slide Show** button [*Status* bar].
 - Click the **From Current Slide** button [*Slide Show* tab, *Start Slide Show* group] (Figure 1-11).

Figure 1-11 *Slide Show* tab

2. Begin your slide show with the first slide regardless of which slide is the current slide.
 - Press **F5** or click the **From Beginning** button [*Slide Show* tab, *Start Slide Show* group].
3. Move through the slides by clicking the screen or pressing one of several keys on the keyboard: **Spacebar, Enter, Page Down, Down Arrow,** or **N**.

When you point to a pane border in *Normal* view, your pointer changes to a *resize arrow* (two arrows). Then you can click and drag the border to adjust pane sizes to better focus on one aspect of your presentation. For example, thumbnails become larger when you increase the size of the thumbnail pane, and you have more room to write speaker notes if you increase the size of the notes pane. In each case, the slide becomes a little smaller.

▶HOW TO: Adjust Pane Sizes in Normal View

1. Point to the pane border separating the *Thumbnail* pane and the *Slide* pane.

2. Click the **resize pointer** (Figure 1-12) and drag the pane border to the right or left to increase or decrease thumbnail size.

3. Click the **Notes** button [*View* tab, *Show* group or *Status* bar] if the *Notes* pane is not open.

4. Point to the pane border separating the *Slide* pane and the *Notes* pane.

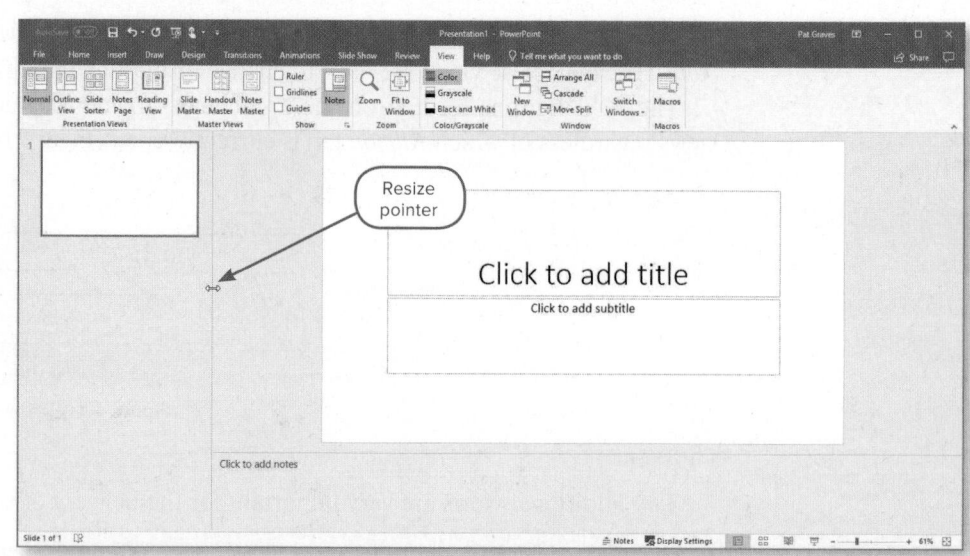

Figure 1-12 *Thumbnail* pane and *Notes* pane sizes are increased

5. Click the **resize pointer** and drag the *Notes* pane border up or down to increase or decrease the *Notes* pane size.

6. Click the **resize pointer** and drag the *Notes* pane border down to the bottom of the window or click the **Notes** button on the *Status* bar to remove this pane.

Click the **Zoom** button [*View* tab, *Zoom* group] to open the *Zoom* dialog box and then increase or decrease the current slide size in *Normal* view.

▶HOW TO: Use the Zoom Dialog Box

1. Click the **Zoom** button [*View* tab, *Zoom* group].
 - The *Zoom* dialog box opens with the current size percentage displayed.

2. Select a preset zoom percentage such as 200% (Figure 1-13) or enter a percentage number, such as 150%.

3. Click **OK**. The slide size increases and you see only a portion of the slide so you can work with more detail in that area.
 - Select lower zoom percentages to see a smaller slide.

4. Click the **Fit to Window** button [*View* tab, *Zoom* group] to return to the default setting so the entire slide displays.
 - You can also click the **Zoom** button, select **Fit**, and click **OK** to return to the default setting.

Figure 1-13 *Zoom* dialog box

Zoom controls on the right side of the *Status* bar are always available regardless of which tab is open. The current slide size percentage is shown; at 100%, the slider is in the center. Click the **Zoom Out** button or the **Zoom In** button to move in 10% increments.

▶HOW TO: Use the Zoom Controls

Figure 1-14 *Zoom* controls

1. Click the **Zoom Out** button several times to decrease the view to 50% (Figure 1-14).
2. Drag the **Zoom** slider to the center.
3. Click the **Zoom In** button several times to increase the view to 150%.
4. Click the line on the left or right of the **Zoom** slider to increase or decrease the percentage.
5. Click the **Fit slide to current window** button to return to the default setting.
6. Click the percentage to open the *Zoom* dialog box. Select a percentage and click **OK** to close the dialog box.

Save and Close a Presentation

PowerPoint assigns each new presentation a generic name such as *Presentation1* that appears in the title bar. You should change this name to a more meaningful name and select a location to save your file. When you save files to *OneDrive*, the *AutoSave* feature is automatically turned on and your file will be updated as you make changes without the need for you to save again. The *AutoSave* feature displays on the *Quick Access* toolbar.

▶HOW TO: Save a Presentation for the First Time

1. Click the **File** tab to open the *Backstage* view.
2. Click **Save** or **Save As** to display the *Save As* page (Figure 1-15).
 - Once a file is saved, click **Save As** to create a second copy of the presentation in another location.
 - You can modify the second copy while saving the first copy as the original file.
3. Select the location (*Backstage* view, *Save As* page) where you want to save your presentation: *Recent, OneDrive, This PC,* or *Add a Place* to create a new location.

Figure 1-15 *Save As* page on the *Backstage* view

 - If the file is saved in *OneDrive, AutoSave* is turned on and *Save As* is not available.
 - If you need to change the presentation without affecting your original file, select **Save a Copy** and give the second version a different name.
4. When saving to *OneDrive* or *This PC* (*Backstage* view, *Save As* page), select an appropriate folder and name the file.
 - If you select the wrong folder, click the blue **up arrow** (see Figure 1-15) to move up one level and select again.
 - Type a file name in the box that appears at the top and click the **Save** button.
 - The file is saved as a PowerPoint Presentation file type with the .pptx extension.
 - Click the **More Options** link to open the *Save As* dialog box.

5. Click the **Browse** button (*Backstage* view, *Save As* page) to open the *Save As* dialog box (Figure 1-16).
 - Browse to the appropriate folder to save the file.
 - Double-click to open the folder.
 - Create a new folder if necessary. Click the **New folder** button, name the folder, and click **Open**.
 - Type the presentation name in the *File name* area and click the **Save** button.

Figure 1-16 *Save As* dialog box

When saving for the first time, you can also click the **Save** button on the *Quick Access* toolbar, or press **Ctrl+S**, to open the *Save As* page on the *Backstage* view. As you revise your presentation, simply click the **Save** button on the *Quick Access* toolbar to resave it with the same name in the same location.

If you want to create a second version of that file, click the **File** tab and then click **Save As** to open the *Save As* dialog box. You can then resave it with a different name in the same or different location. If your file is on *OneDrive*, changes are automatically saved; therefore, click **Save a Copy** and resave the file with a different name. The original presentation is not affected by any changes made to the second presentation.

> **ANOTHER WAY**
> Press **F12** (or **Fn+F12** if necessary for your computer) to open the *Save As* dialog box.

You can save PowerPoint presentations in a variety of formats. By default, PowerPoint presentations are saved with the .pptx file extension. To change the type of presentation format, select the format of your choice from the *Save as type* area in the *Save As* dialog box (Figure 1-17).

The most common save formats used for PowerPoint are listed in Table 1-1.

When you finish a presentation, save your final version and then close the presentation by clicking the **File** tab and then clicking **Close** or clicking the **Close** button [X] in the upper-right corner of the title bar.

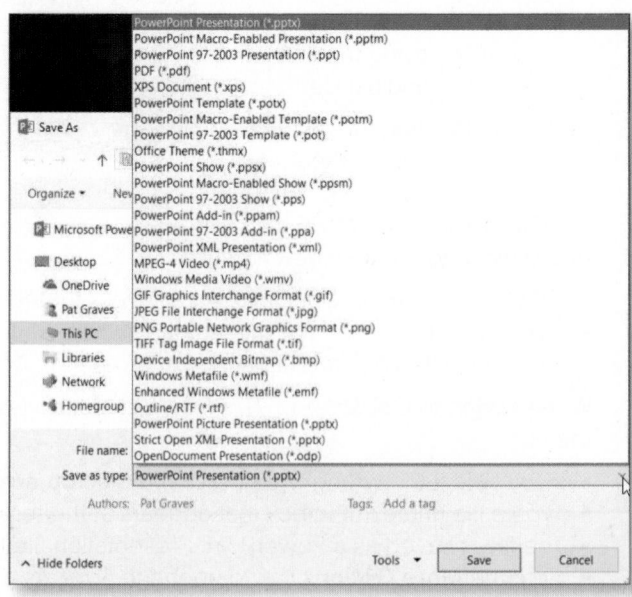

Figure 1-17 *Save As* file types

Table 1-1: Save Formats

Type of Presentation	File Extension	Uses of This Format
PowerPoint Presentation	.pptx	PowerPoint presentation compatible with 2007–2019 and 365 software versions that use an XML-enabled file format. This is the default file format.
PowerPoint 97-2003 Presentation	.ppt	PowerPoint presentation compatible with 1997–2003 software versions. Newer software features are not supported.
PDF (Portable Document Format)	.pdf	Similar to pictures of slides, with each slide shown as a separate page. The file size may be smaller than the original presentation, so this format often works well for presentations shared electronically.
PowerPoint Template	.potx	PowerPoint template that can be used to format presentations.
Windows Media Video or Mpeg-P4 Video	.wmv or .mp4	PowerPoint presentation saved as a video that will play on many media players. Four resolution sizes are available and all create large file sizes.
Outline/RTF	.rtf	A presentation text-only outline with a small file size for easy sharing.
PowerPoint Picture Presentation	.pptx	PowerPoint presentation that converts each slide into an image. It helps to reduce file size or create images for inclusion in other documents.
Open Document Presentation	.odp	PowerPoint presentation that can be opened in applications that use the *Open Document Presentation* format, such as Google.Docs or Open Office.org.

> **MORE INFO**
>
> Other file formats are used to save individual slides or images on slides. These graphic file formats include .jpg, .png, .tif, .bmp, .wmf, or .emf. These formats are explained on page P1-41.

Share and Export Options

While working on a presentation in *Normal* view, you can share it with others. If you have saved the file on your local computer, click the **Share** button in the upper-right corner of your PowerPoint window. The *Share* dialog box opens prompting you to upload your file (Figure 1-18).

When the file is on *OneDrive*, click the **Share** button to open the *Share* pane. In this pane, enter addresses to invite people, control sharing options, and send an attachment or create a sharing link to send.

Figure 1-18 *Share* button and dialog box

> **ANOTHER WAY**
>
> Click **File** to open the *Backstage* view and then click **Share** to open the *Share* pane.

▶HOW TO: Share a Presentation

1. Save your file on *OneDrive*.

2. Click the **Share** button in the upper-right corner of your PowerPoint window to open the *Share* pane (Figure 1-19).

3. Type an email address or enter an address from your address book to invite people to share the file.

4. Choose **Can edit** or **Can view** to control permission (Figure 1-20).

5. Type a brief note.

6. Click **Share** to send.

Or

7. Click **Send as attachment** at the bottom of the *Share* pane.

8. Choose **Send a copy** or **Send a PDF**. Your email program opens so you can send the file.

Or

9. Click **Get a sharing link** at the bottom of the *Share* pane.

10. Click either **Create an edit link** or **Create a view-only link** to control permission. The address to your file on *OneDrive* appears (Figure 1-21).

11. Click **Copy** and then paste the link in a message or document where you want it available to the recipient.

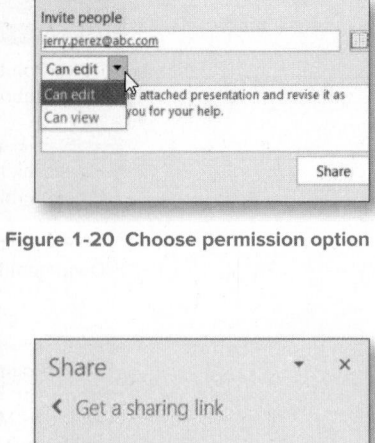

Figure 1-20 Choose permission option

Figure 1-19 *Share* pane

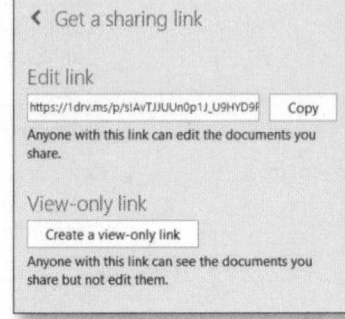

Figure 1-21 Get a sharing link

PowerPoint enables you to *export* your presentation by saving it in different file formats. Click the **File** tab and choose **Export** to access the following options (Figure 1-22):

- *Create PDF/XPS Document*: Converts your presentation to preserve formatting and reduce file size for easier distribution

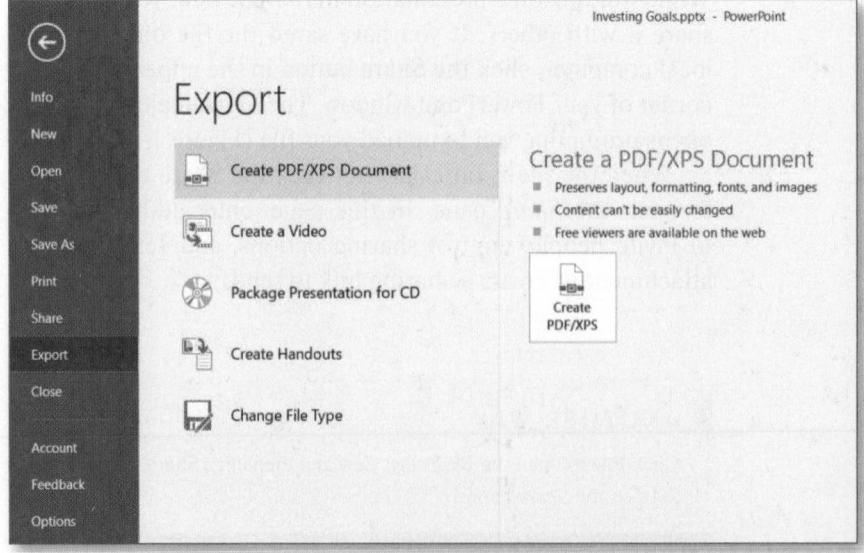

Figure 1-22 *Export* options

- *Create a Video*: Saves your presentation as a video
- *Package Presentation for CD*: Saves your presentation and all linked or embedded files
- *Create Handouts*: Transfers slides and notes to a Word document that you can re-format
- *Change File Type*: Saves your presentation or individual slides in different file formats

Working with Slides, Layouts, Placeholders, and Text

In *Normal* view, use placeholders to enter slide text and other objects. **Placeholders** are rectangular boxes that, by default, have no fill color or border. You may emphasize a placeholder by adding color or resize a placeholder to fit content. The available placeholders and their positions are controlled by the slide *layout*.

When you start a new presentation, the first slide has a *Title Slide* layout with two place-holders: a presentation title and a subtitle. You can add text directly into these placeholders or you can type slide text in *Outline* view. The font, font size, and alignment are preset, but you can change them as you develop your presentation. Keep in mind that text should be brief, straight to the point, and easy to read.

Add Slides and Choose Layouts

Click the **New Slide** button (top half) on the *Home* tab to add a slide. After a title slide, PowerPoint automatically inserts a **Title and Content** layout. This layout is used for develop-ing most slides; it has a placeholder for the slide title and a placeholder for bulleted text or content such as pictures, tables, or charts. From that point forward, each time you click the top of the **New Slide** button, you add a new slide with the same layout as the previous one (unless you use the *Title Slide* layout again). If you click the **New Slide** drop-down arrow (bottom half), you see a gallery of layouts, such as the ones shown in Figure 1-23, for a blank presentation using the *Office Theme*.

Layouts provide a starting point for your slide designs. You can change layouts or customize each slide for the content you are developing. The available layouts vary based on the current theme. The most common layouts are described in Table 1-2.

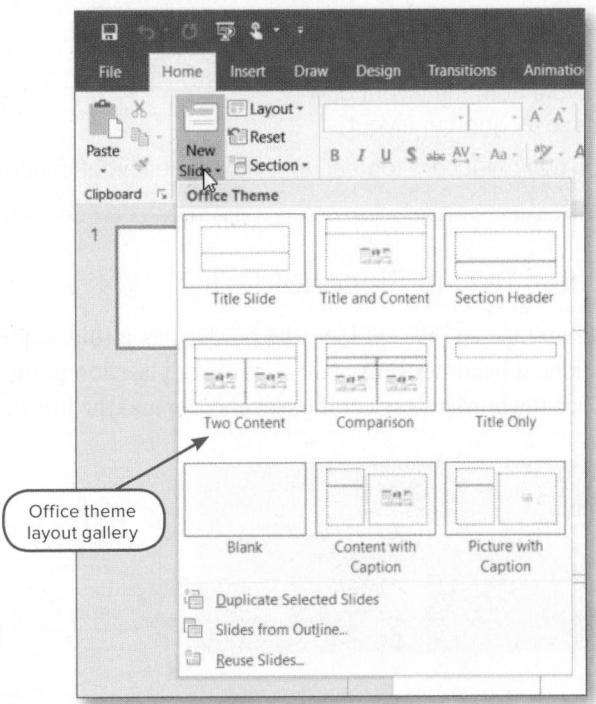

Figure 1-23 Slide layouts

Table 1-2: Slide Layouts

Layout Name	Layout Description
Title Slide	A layout used for a presentation's opening slide. It contains a title and a subtitle placeholder.
Title and Content	A layout used for the body of a presentation. It contains a slide title placeholder and a larger placeholder for different kinds of content.
Section Header	This layout is similar to a *Title Slide* layout and usually has a slightly different appearance. It can divide a lengthy presentation or introduce different topics or speakers.
Two Content	This layout has a slide title placeholder and two smaller content placeholders to display either two brief lists or a list and a graphic object, such as a picture or chart.
Comparison	A layout similar to the *Two Content* layout (slide title placeholder and two content placeholders). It works better for comparing two lists because a heading area is above each content placeholder.
Title Only	A layout with only one placeholder for the title (usually at the top) of the slide.
Blank	This layout has no placeholders.
Content with Caption	A layout similar to the *Two Content* layout (slide title placeholder and two content placeholders). One placeholder is designated for content, such as a table or chart, while the other placeholder is meant for descriptive text.
Picture with Caption	This layout has a large placeholder for a picture and another placeholder for descriptive text.

▶ HOW TO: Choose and Change Slide Layouts

1. Choose a layout for a new slide using one of these methods:
 - Click the **New Slide** button [*Home* tab, *Slides* group] to insert a slide with the default layout.
 - Click the **New Slide** drop-down arrow [*Home* tab, *Slides* group] and select a layout from the layout gallery. The current theme name will appear at the top.
2. Change the layout of a selected slide by following these steps:
 - Click the **Layout** button [*Home* tab, *Slides* group].
 - Select a different layout from the layout gallery.
 - Repeat this process to try another layout.
3. Click the **Undo** button [*Quick Access* toolbar] to remove the layout change.

Enter Text in Placeholders

On an inactive placeholder, the border has a thin, dotted line. When you click inside the placeholder, it becomes active with a blinking insertion point where you type or edit text (Figure 1-24). Click the border to select the placeholder and the line becomes solid (Figure 1-25). *Sizing handles*

Figure 1-24 Placeholders for text Figure 1-25 Selected placeholder to move or resize

are small white circles that appear on the corners and sides when you type text or select the border. Also, a **_rotation handle_** that is a circular arrow appears at the top.

By default, PowerPoint automatically fits text in a placeholder. Therefore, keep your wording concise so text does not become too small. Depending on the font that is used, title text for individual slides is usually 36–44 points. Title text for a *Title Slide* layout is usually 54–72 points.

> ### MORE INFO
>
> A point is a unit of measurement in typography used to represent the height of text characters and the space between lines. The number of points in one inch is 72. The default widescreen slide size is 13.33″ × 7.5″ (*Width* × *Height*).

In body placeholders, a bullet (a small symbol such as a circle or square) automatically appears when you type text and press **Enter**. Bullets help mark the beginning of a line, so people recognize separate items. Subpoints are indented below a bulleted item. Be sure your list is brief, usually no more than six items, and the text size is 20–28 points. Larger font sizes are very important if you are presenting in a large room so your audience can read slide text from a distance. However, if you are preparing a presentation to be viewed on a computer or online, you can use smaller font sizes.

Bulleted lists are appropriate when items require no particular order. If you need to show items in order, use a numbered list instead.

HOW TO: Work with Lists

1. Add a slide with a *Title and Content* layout and type the slide title.
2. Enter bulleted text on the slide.
 - Click after the first bullet in the body placeholder and type text.
 - Press **Enter** to type another bulleted item using the same list level.
 - Press **Tab** or click the **Increase List Level** button [*Home* tab, *Paragraph* group] (Figure 1-26) to indent a bulleted item to the right (Figure 1-27) to create a subpoint.

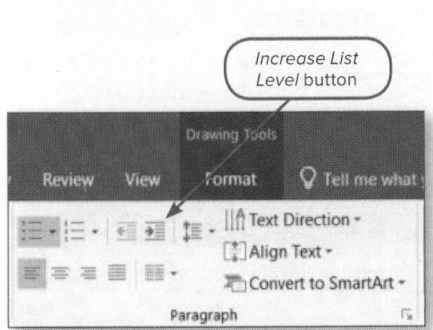

Figure 1-26 Paragraph group on the *Home* tab

Figure 1-27 Bulleted list slide

3. Enter bulleted text in *Outline* view.
 - Click the **Outline View** button [*View* tab, *Presentation Views* group] and the *Outline* pane opens on the left.
 - All text appears in the *Outline* pane and on the slide.
 - Use the *Outline* pane when you need to enter several text slides.

4. Decrease the list level by moving a bulleted item to the left.
 - Place your insertion point at the beginning of the text and press **Shift+Tab** or click the **Decrease List Level** button [*Home* tab, *Paragraph* group] (Figure 1-28).

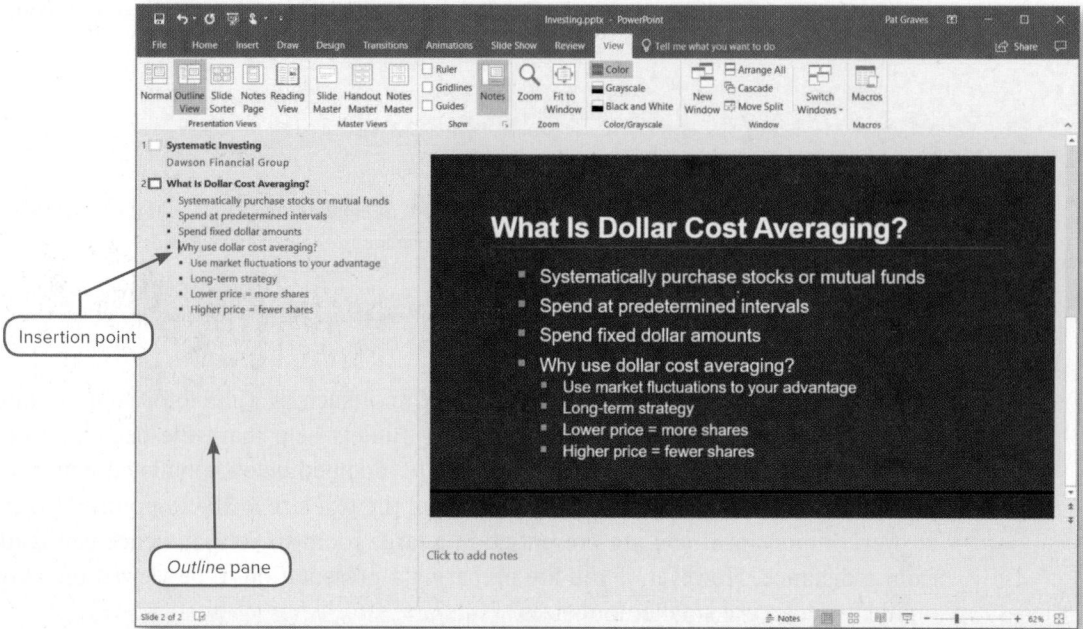

Figure 1-28 Slide in *Outline* view with bulleted text before list level changes

- In the *Outline* pane, a first-level bulleted item will change to a slide title.
- Change text capitalization as needed for a title (Figure 1-29).

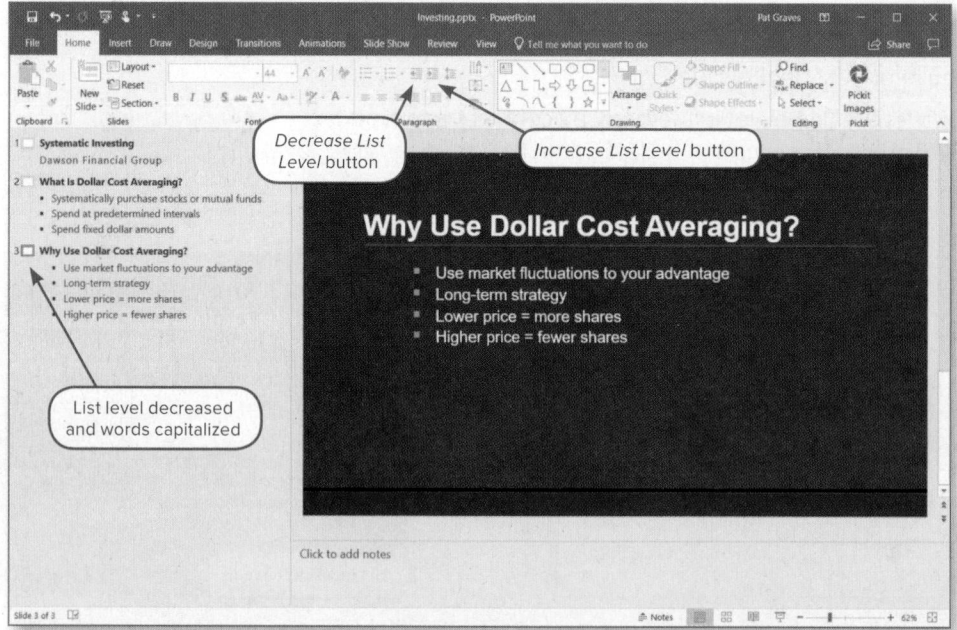

Figure 1-29 New slide created by decreasing the list level

5. Convert a bulleted list to a numbered list by selecting the text to be changed and then clicking the **Numbering** button [*Home* tab, *Paragraph* group].

Align, Move, and Resize Placeholders

Horizontal alignment and *vertical alignment* control how text is positioned within placeholders. A small margin automatically appears in placeholders so the text within them does not touch the border.

▶ HOW TO: Align Text and Placeholders

1. Select placeholder text and align it within a placeholder using these options:
 - *Horizontal*: Choose **Align Left**, **Center**, **Align Right**, or **Justify** (aligns text on both the left and right) [*Home* tab, *Paragraph* group]. *Justify* is rarely used on slides because it can cause irregular spacing between words.
 - *Vertical*: Click **Align Text** [*Home* tab, *Paragraph* group] and then choose **Top**, **Middle**, or **Bottom** (Figure 1-30).

2. Select a placeholder and align it to the slide using these options:
 - Click the **Arrange** button [*Home* tab, *Drawing* group] and then choose **Align** (Figure 1.31) or click the **Align** button [*Drawing Tools Format* tab, *Arrange* group] (Figure 1-32).
 - When one placeholder is selected, **Align to Slide** is automatically selected.
 - *Horizontal*: Choose **Align Left**, **Align Center**, or **Align Right**.
 - *Vertical*: Choose **Align Top**, **Align Middle**, or **Align Bottom**.

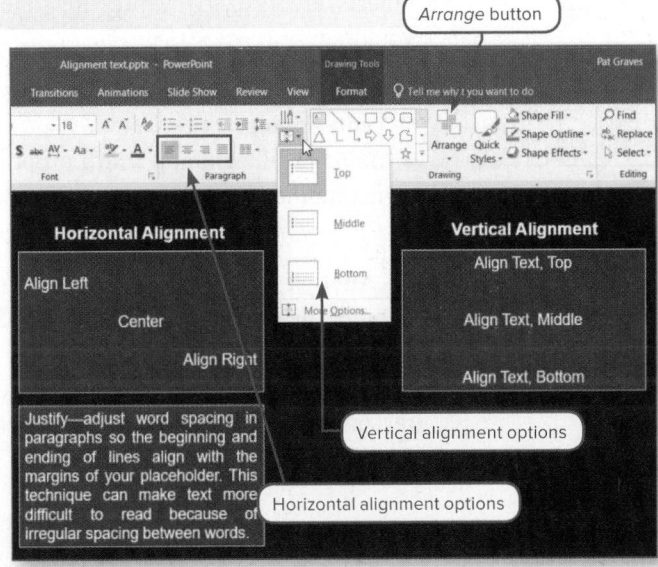

Figure 1-30 *Align Text* within placeholders

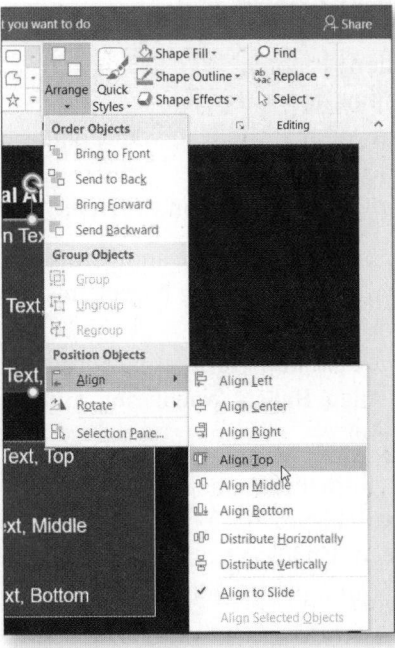

Figure 1-31 *Align* options on the *Home* tab

Figure 1-32 *Align* options on the *Drawing Tools Format* tab

Move a placeholder by pointing to its border so your pointer changes to a *move arrow* (with four points) (Figure 1-33). Click to select the placeholder and drag it to a new position without changing its shape.

Figure 1-33 Move and resize pointers

To increase or decrease placeholder size, point to a corner or side *sizing handle* until your pointer changes to a resize pointer (with two points) (see Figure 1-33). As you drag to resize, your pointer changes to a *crosshair* and the placeholder color is faded (Figure 1-34). When you release the pointer, the circle handles appear again and color is restored. Drag a corner sizing handle (with a diagonal resize pointer) to change both the horizontal and vertical dimensions at the same time.

Figure 1-34 Resize a placeholder

You can control the way placeholders and other objects are resized by pressing one of three keys as you drag:

- *Ctrl*: The placeholder size changes from a fixed center point.
- *Shift*: The height and width proportions are maintained as the size changes.
- *Ctrl+Shift*: The placeholder resizes from the center and remains in proportion.

Another way to precisely resize a placeholder and other objects is to enter the exact dimensions in the *Size* group on the *Drawing Tools Format* tab (Figure 1-35).

If you don't like a change that you made moving, aligning, and resizing placeholders, click the **Reset** button in the *Slides* group on the *Home* tab.

Figure 1-35 *Size* group

Edit Text

Notice that your pointer changes when you are working with text. When you see a blinking insertion point, PowerPoint is waiting for you to type text. When you point to text, your pointer changes to a text selection tool so you can click and drag to select text.

Figure 1-36 *Clipboard, Slides, Font,* and *Paragraph* groups on the *Home* tab

Commands for editing text are on the *Home* tab in three groups (Figure 1-36):

- *Clipboard group*: **Cut, Copy, Paste,** and **Format Painter**
- *Font group*: Character formatting commands such as **Bold, Italic, Underline, Change Case, Font,** and **Font Size**
- *Paragraph group*: Paragraph formatting commands such as **Align, Bullets, Numbering,** and **Increase List Level**

Also, many text formatting options are available on the mini toolbar (Figure 1-37), which appears when text is selected. Undo or redo actions using commands on the *Quick Access* toolbar.

Figure 1-37 Mini toolbar

▶ HOW TO: Delete Text

1. Press **Delete** to remove text to the right of the insertion point.
2. Press **Backspace** to remove text to the left of the insertion point.
3. Select text and press **Delete** to remove several words at one time.

Click outside a text placeholder to deselect it. Handles no longer appear.

Change Text Case

Text *case* refers to how text is capitalized. In several themes, text appears in a placeholder in uppercase (all capital) letters. Be careful when using uppercase letters, because they may not be as easy to read as text with initial caps (the first letter only is capitalized). People can generally read lowercase text faster than uppercase text. Also, uppercase words in email are thought to represent shouting, and this negative connotation might carry over to your presentation if you overuse capital letters. Use uppercase letters when you really want to emphasize selected words or brief phrases.

▶ HOW TO: Change Case

1. Select the text to be changed.
2. Click the **Change Case** button [*Home* tab, *Font* group].
3. Choose from the options **Sentence case**, **lowercase**, **UPPERCASE**, **Capitalize Each Word**, or **tOGGLE cASE** (Figure 1-38).
 - *Toggle Case* changes text from uppercase to lowercase or lowercase to uppercase.

Figure 1-38 *Change Case* options

Change List Bullet Symbols

You can change the bullet symbol in a placeholder if it seems inappropriate or if its color blends too much with the slide background.

▶ HOW TO: Change Bullet Symbols

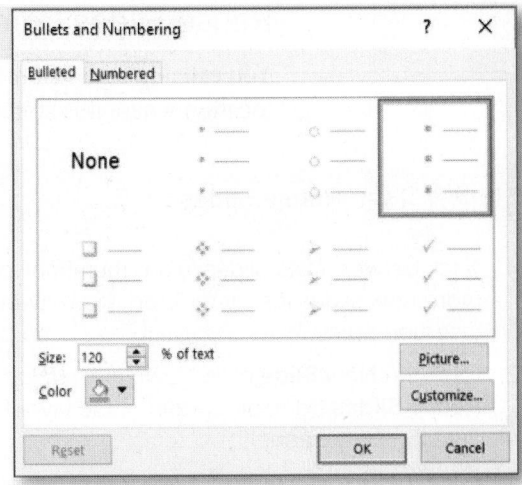

1. Select the text or placeholder where you want to change the bullet.
 - Select text in the placeholder to change the bullet for one or more bulleted items.
 - Select the bulleted placeholder to change all bullets in the placeholder.
2. Click the **Bullets** drop-down arrow [*Home* tab, *Paragraph* group] and then select **Bullets and Numbering** to open the *Bullets and Numbering* dialog box (Figure 1-39).

Figure 1-39 *Bullets and Numbering* dialog box

3. Select one of the pre-defined bullets.

 - Enter a different number in the *Size* box to increase or decrease the bullet size.
 - Click the **Color** button to select a different bullet color.

4. Click the **Customize** button to open the *Symbol* dialog box (Figure 1-40), where many symbols display in several fonts.

 - Select a symbol and a *Character code* appears. This is a unique number that your computer uses to identify the symbol.
 - Click **OK** to add that symbol to the *Bullets and Numbering* dialog box.
 - Select the bullet and click **OK** to change the bullets on selected text.

Figure 1-40 *Symbol* dialog box

The three *Wingdings* fonts have most of the available character bullets from the *Symbols* dialog box. You can also select picture bullets that are more decorative from the *Bullets and Numbering* dialog box.

The Format Painter

To copy formatting from text, shapes, or pictures and apply these settings to another selection, use the *Format Painter*. You can apply the changes on the same slide or on different slides.

▶HOW TO: Use the Format Painter

1. Select the text or other object with the format that you want to copy.
2. Click the **Format Painter** button [*Home* tab, *Clipboard* group] (see Figure 1-36). Your pointer changes to a paintbrush.
3. Move the paintbrush over the text or other object you want to change and click to apply the formatting.
4. Apply the change to multiple selections by first double-clicking the **Format Painter** button.
5. Press **Esc** to stop formatting or click the **Format Painter** button again.

Reuse Slides from Another Presentation

You can add slides from another presentation without opening it as long as you can access the location where it is stored.

▶HOW TO: Reuse Slides

1. Click between two slides in the thumbnail pane where you want one or more new slides inserted. A red line between the slides indicates your insertion point.
2. Click the **New Slide** drop-down arrow [*Home* tab, *Slides* group] and select **Reuse Slides** from the bottom of the layout gallery. The *Reuse Slides* pane automatically opens.
3. Click the **Browse** button in the *Reuse Slides* pane (Figure 1-41) to open the *Browse* dialog box.

Figure 1-41 *Reuse Slides* pane

4. Find the location where your presentation with the slides you need is saved and select the file name.

5. Click **Open**. The slides in this second presentation appear in the *Reuse Slides* pane with text showing their titles (Figure 1-42).

6. Click the slides you want to insert in your current presentation.

 • By default, the reused slides will appear with the formatting of your current presentation.

 • If you want the inserted slides to retain their design from the original presentation, select the **Keep source formatting** checkbox at the bottom of the *Reuse Slides* pane before inserting them.

7. Click the **Close** button at the top of the *Reuse Slides* pane.

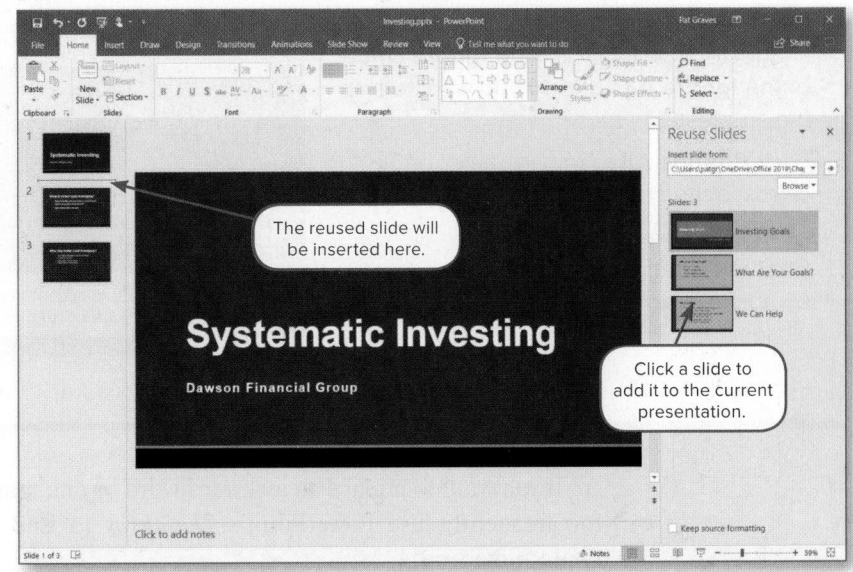

Figure 1-42 Reuse slides

> MORE INFO
>
> When task panes open, they are docked on the right side of the PowerPoint window. If you have a wide computer screen and you are using PowerPoint in a window size that does not fill the screen, you can drag a pane away from the window so your slide size becomes larger. Double-click the pane to dock it on the right of the window again.

Check Spelling and Word Usage

PowerPoint's *AutoCorrect* feature repairs many simple errors, such as changing "teh" to "the" or "recieve" to "receive," as you enter text on your slides. You can customize *AutoCorrect* options to include words that you frequently misspell or abbreviate when the word should be spelled.

PowerPoint automatically adds a red, wavy line below words it does not recognize. Use the *Spelling* feature to correct errors at any time during a presentation but always when you are making your final adjustments. You still need to carefully read the content to find any words that may have been missed, such as names or words that might not be in the spelling dictionary. If your audience sees mistakes when viewing your slide show, your credibility is undermined.

▶ **HOW TO: Check Spelling**

1. Click the **Spelling** button [*Review* tab, *Proofing* group] (Figure 1-43). The *Spelling* pane opens on the right (Figure 1-44).

2. Consider each word that is identified and whether or not the suggested spelling is correct.

3. Click the **Audio** button on the *Spelling* pane to hear the word pronounced.

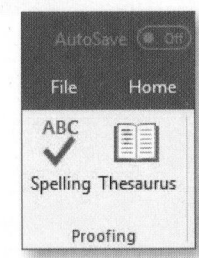

Figure 1-43 *Spelling* button on the *Review* tab

4. Click the **Change** button to insert a suggested spelling; click the **Ignore Once** or the **Ignore All** button if you want to skip the suggestion.

5. Click **Change All** to replace all incorrect words in the presentation with the correct spelling

6. Click **OK** when the spell check is complete. The *Spelling* pane automatically closes.

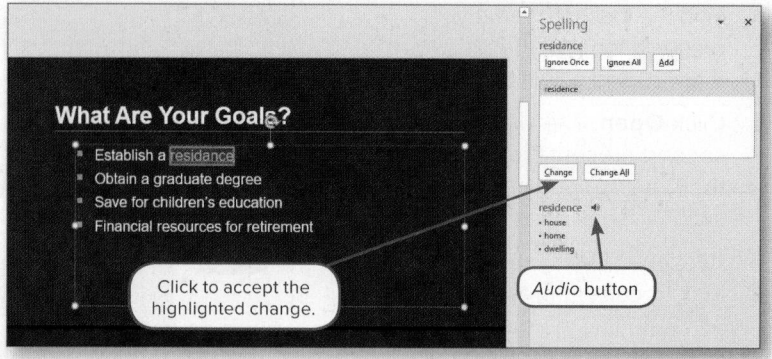

Figure 1-44 *Spelling* pane

If you want to replace an awkward word or one that is used too frequently, use PowerPoint's **Thesaurus** to find a more appropriate word.

▶**HOW TO:** Use the Thesaurus

1. Click the word you want to change.

2. Click the **Thesaurus** button [*Review* tab, *Proofing* group]. The *Thesaurus* pane opens, and the selected word appears in the search box (Figure 1-45). Words with similar meanings appear below it.

3. Click a word in this list to see more options; click the **Back arrow** to return to the original list.

4. Click the **Down arrow** to the right of a word in this list or **right-click** the word and choose **Insert**. The selected word on your slide is replaced with the new word.

5. Click the **Close** button at the top of the *Thesaurus* pane.

Use PowerPoint Designer with Listed Information

The *PowerPoint Designer* feature provides a quick way to select attractive layouts. When you use *Designer* for the first time, a message appears asking if you want to try *Design Ideas* because you are using *Office intelligent services* (Figure 1-46). Click **Turn on**.

Office 2019 Note: *PowerPoint Designer* is not available in Office 2019.

The *Design Ideas* pane automatically opens when various graphic objects and sometimes when text is entered in a bulleted list. If this pane does not open automatically, click the **Design Ideas** button [*Design* tab, *Designer* group]. Suggested slides display as thumbnails in the *Design Ideas* pane.

For slides with text in a bulleted list, *Designer* shows layouts with different background designs, and most provide a **SmartArt** graphic to display your information in a more visual way. Write your list so *Designer* makes relevant suggestions. Be very concise and phrase listed items in the same way beginning with verbs or nouns. Use bulleted lists or numbered lists.

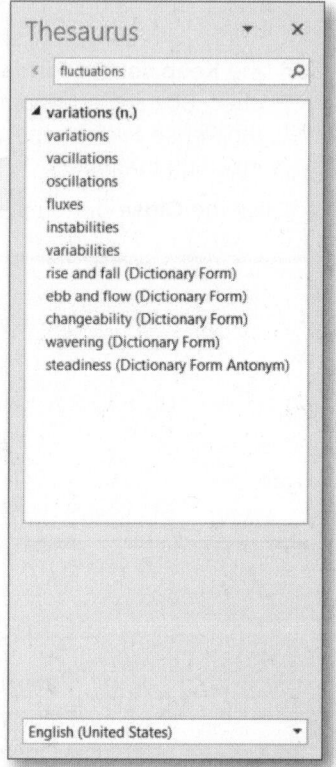

Figure 1-45 *Thesaurus* word choices

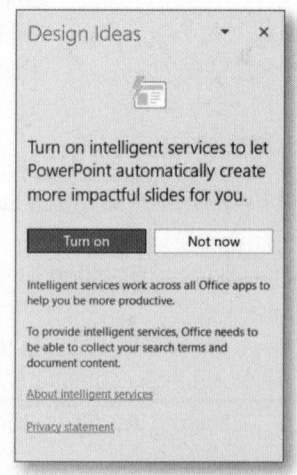

Figure 1-46 *Design Ideas* permission request

Designer can recognize content for a timeline or a list of procedural steps/statements that begin with a verb. You must decide which of the layouts displayed is appropriate for your content. You will use *PowerPoint Designer* with pictures and other objects later in this chapter.

▶ HOW TO: Use the Design Ideas Pane for Listed Information

1. Start a new presentation or open an existing presentation that uses one of PowerPoint's themes.

2. Click the **New Slide** drop-down arrow [*Home* tab, *Slides* group] and select the **Title and Content** layout.

3. Type the title in the title placeholder.

4. Type the bulleted text.

 - The *Design Ideas* pane opens with thumbnails of different layouts (Figure 1-47).
 - If the *Design Ideas* pane does not automatically open, click the **Design Ideas** button [*Design* tab, *Designer* group] to open the pane.
 - **Office 2019 Note**: *PowerPoint Designer* is not available in Office 2019.

5. Scroll down to see all suggested layouts.

6. Click a thumbnail to apply it to your current slide (Figure 1-48).

 - If you want to try another layout, simply click a different thumbnail.

7. Leave the *Design Ideas* pane open and it will continue to generate design ideas as you develop other slides.

8. Close the *Design Ideas* pane by clicking the **X** at the top of the pane.

9. Reopen the *Design Ideas* pane at any time while you are developing a presentation.

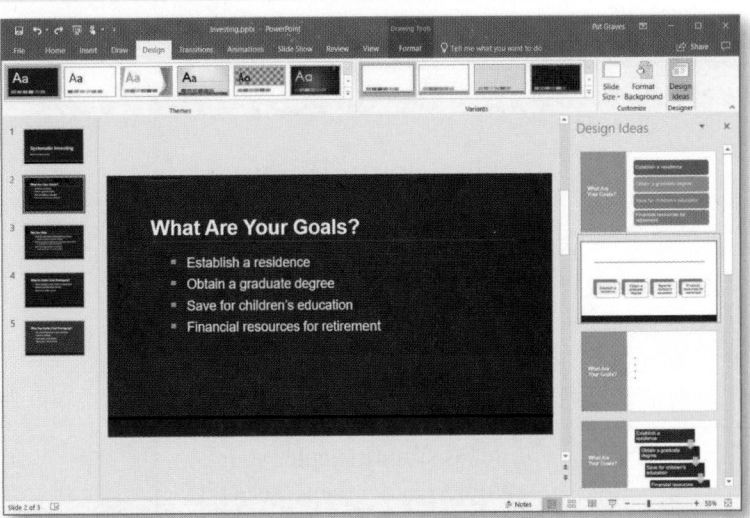

Figure 1-47 *Design Ideas* pane with suggested layouts

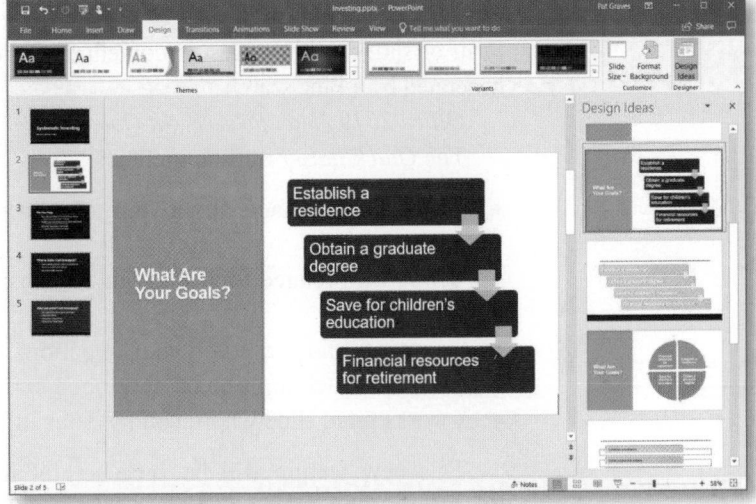

Figure 1-48 *Design Ideas* pane with changed layout

Office intelligent services can be enabled on the *PowerPoint Options* dialog box also. You might check this setting when you complete a routine Office update.

▶ HOW TO: Enable Office Intelligent Services

1. Click the **File** tab to open the *Backstage* view.

2. Select **Account**.

3. Examine the *Office Updates* text to confirm your software is current.

4. Click **Update Options** if your software is not current (Figure 1-49) and then select **Update Now**.

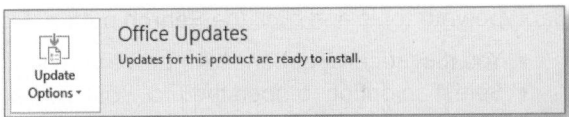

Figure 1-49 *Update Options*

5. Click the **File** tab again and click **Options** to open the *PowerPoint Options* dialog box (Figure 1-50).

6. Select the *General* tab and check **Enable Services** under the *Office intelligent services* heading.

7. Click **OK**.

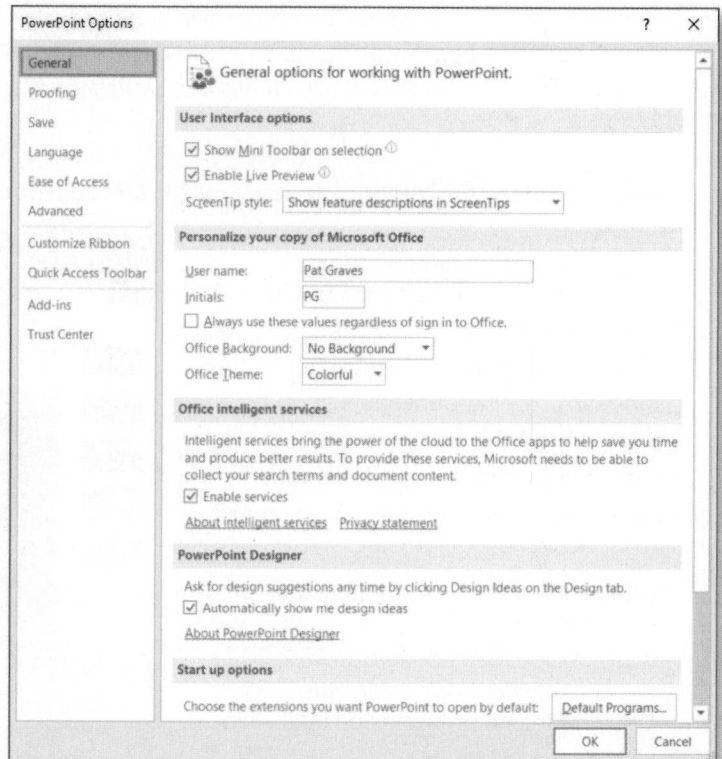

Figure 1-50 *PowerPoint Options* dialog box

Use PowerPoint QuickStarter to Research Content

PowerPoint QuickStarter can help you develop your presentation with both research and design ideas. You first enter your topic and then select starter slides to begin your research. *QuickStarter* then provides an outline (in the form of slides) with suggested content and links to suitable articles and related images that are generated by a Bing search.

Office 2019 Note: PowerPoint QuickStarter is not available in Office 2019.

The *QuickStarter* outline includes:

- A slide with key facts about your topic from online sources that appear on the slide and in the *Notes* pane.
- A slide with related topics for you to consider in your research.
- A title slide.
- A contents slide based on your selections.
- A slide for each topic to be developed and suggestions in the *Notes* pane.
- A works cited slide where you list your information sources.

This new feature will be very helpful to you after you gain more experience in using PowerPoint and designing slide content. *Office intelligent services* must be enabled to use the *QuickStarter*. Select this option on the *PowerPoint Options* dialog box.

▶**HOW TO:** Enter a Topic and Select Slides

1. Click the **File** tab to open the *Backstage* view and select **New**.

2. Click the **QuickStarter** theme to open a search dialog box.

3. Type your topic and click the **Search** button (Figure 1-51).

 - You may receive options to improve your search results.
 - Select an option to open the *Pick your starter slides* dialog box.

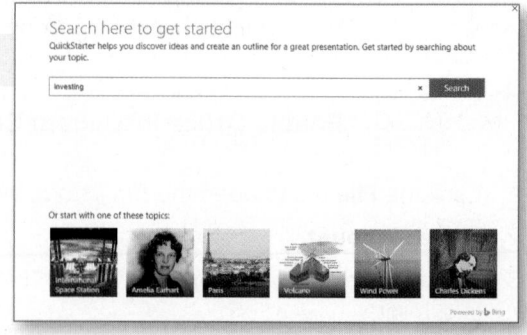

Figure 1-51 Start Searching

4. Select your starter slides that will help you develop your content (Figure 1-52).

5. Click the **Next** button to open the *Pick a Look* dialog box.

6. Select a design theme and click the **Create** button (Figure 1-53).

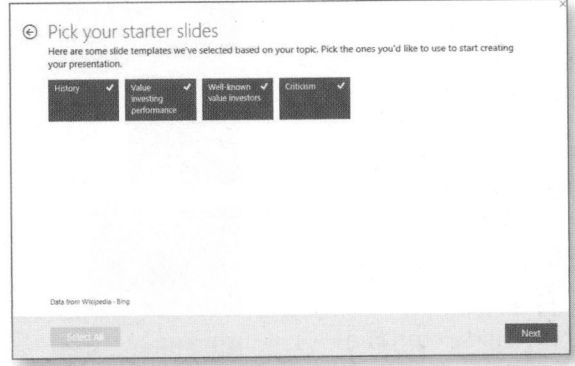

Figure 1-52 Select starter slides

Figure 1-53 Pick a look

- Your slides appear with suggested content (Figure 1-54).
- The first two slides have helpful research information.
- Slide 3 is the title slide.

7. Edit the slides as you begin inserting your content (Figure 1-55).

8. Save and close the presentation.

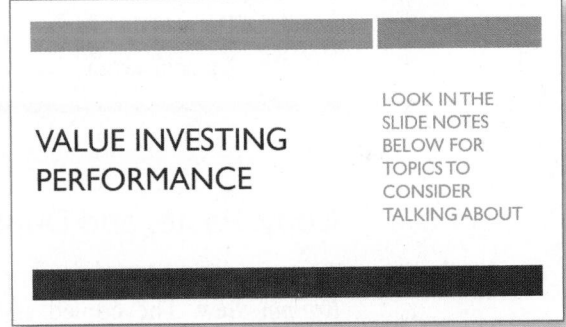

Figure 1-55 Suggested content

Figure 1-54 QuickStarter slide layouts

Navigating between Slides and Organizing Content

When developing a presentation, you might need to move between slides as ideas occur to you or when you have new information to add. You can rearrange slides at any time. However, always carefully examine your sequence when all slides are complete. The final order must be logical to you and to your audience.

Navigate between Slides

In *Normal* view, you can move between slides by clicking the **Next Slide** and **Previous Slide** buttons, clicking scroll arrows, or dragging the scroll box to the right of the window. You can also click thumbnails or use keyboard shortcuts.

▶HOW TO: Navigate between Slides

1. Use one of these methods to move between slides using the scroll bar and buttons on the right:
 - Click the **Next Slide** button or the **down arrow** on the scroll bar to go to the next slide.
 - Click the **Previous Slide** button or **up arrow** on the scroll bar to go to the previous slide.
 - Click above or below the scroll box to move between slides one at a time.
 - Drag the scroll box up or down to move to a specific slide, using the slide indicator (Figure 1-56).

2. Use one of these methods to move between slides using the *Thumbnail* pane:
 - Click a slide thumbnail to make that slide active.
 - Click between slide thumbnails to select a position for a new slide. A red line indicates your insertion point.

Figure 1-56 Navigate between slides

▶ **ANOTHER WAY**

Home	First slide
End	Last slide
Page Down or **down arrow**	Next slide
Page Up or **up arrow**	Previous slide

Copy, Paste, and Duplicate Slides

To reuse a slide's content or format, copy the thumbnail in *Normal* view. The copied slide is stored in your computer's temporary storage area called the *Clipboard*. The original slide remains in its position. Paste the copied slide where you need it and edit the text as necessary.

▶HOW TO: Copy and Paste Slides

1. Select the thumbnail of the slide to be copied.
2. Copy the slide using one of these methods:
 - Press **Ctrl+C**.
 - Click the **Copy** button [*Home* tab, *Clipboard* group].
3. Move the insertion point to the place between slides where you want the copied slide to appear.
 - A red line indicates your insertion point.
4. Paste the slide using one of these methods:
 - Press **Ctrl+V**.
 - Click the **Paste** button [*Home* tab, *Clipboard* group] (Figure 1-57).

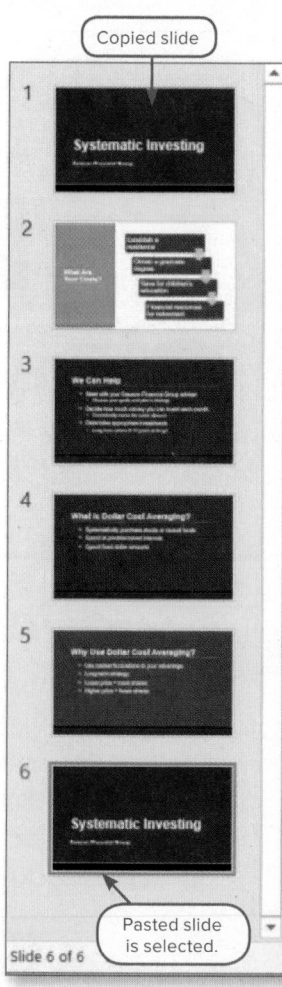

Figure 1-57 Copy and paste a selected slide

5. Use the context menu to copy and paste slides.
 - Right-click a slide thumbnail to be copied and select **Copy**.
 - Move your insertion point to the place where you want to paste the copied slide.
 - Right-click and select **Paste**.
6. Edit the text on the new slide as needed.

Duplicating also creates a second copy of a slide. You can drag the second slide to a different position.

▶ **HOW TO:** Duplicate Slides

1. Select the thumbnail of the slide to be duplicated.
2. Press **Ctrl+D** to duplicate the slide.
 - The second slide appears immediately after the original slide and the new slide is selected.
 - You can also right-click a slide thumbnail and select **Duplicate Slide** from the context menu.
 - When you use the *Duplicate Slide* command, a copy of the slide is not placed on the *Clipboard*.

▶ **ANOTHER WAY**

Ctrl+X	Cut
Ctrl+C	Copy
Ctrl+V	Paste
Ctrl+Z	Undo
Ctrl+Y	Redo
Ctrl+D	Duplicate

Select Multiple Slides

If you need to make the same changes to more than one slide, select multiple slide thumbnails.

▶ **HOW TO:** Select Multiple Slides

1. Select multiple adjacent slides (in order) by selecting the first slide and then pressing **Shift** while you click the last slide (Figure 1-58).
2. Select multiple nonadjacent slides (not in order) by selecting the first slide and then pressing **Ctrl** while you click each of the slides you need to select (Figure 1-59).

Figure 1-58 Adjacent slides selected

Figure 1-59 Nonadjacent slides selected

Rearrange Slide Order

You can rearrange slides at any time while developing a presentation. In the *Thumbnail* pane, drag slide thumbnails up or down. On the *Outline* view, drag the slide icons. You can also cut slides and paste them into different positions. However, when your presentation has more slides than can be seen in the *Thumbnail* pane, it is best to rearrange slides using *Slide Sorter* view (Figure 1-60).

The *Slide Sorter* view enables you to see your presentation as a whole. The thumbnails are arranged from left to right in rows. By default, they are shown at a 100% size. Click buttons on the *Status* bar to change this percentage. The **Zoom In** button will increase the slide thumbnail size if you need to see the slide content better; the **Zoom Out** button will decrease the slide thumbnail size and you see more slides at one time.

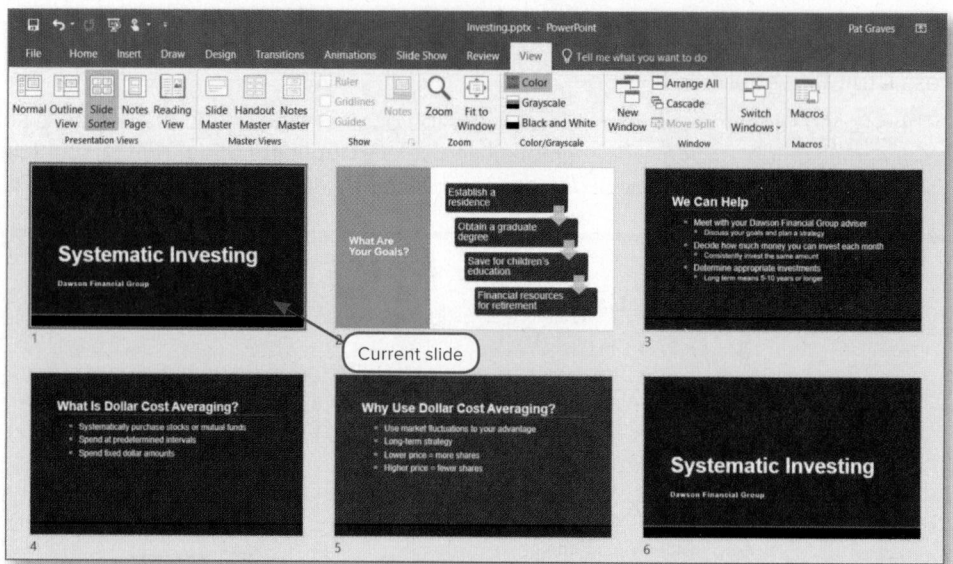

Figure 1-60 *Slide Sorter* view

▶ **HOW TO:** Rearrange Slides in Slide Sorter View

1. Click the **Slide Sorter** button on the *Status* bar.
2. Click the **Zoom In** or **Zoom Out** buttons to adjust the size of the thumbnails.
3. Click and drag the slide thumbnails into their new positions (Figure 1-61).

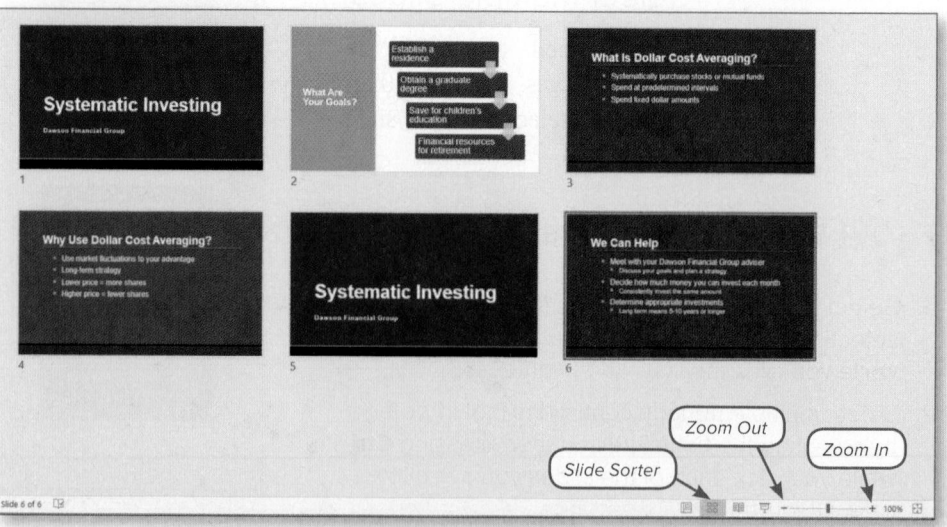

Figure 1-61 Slides rearranged

Delete Slides

Remove slides by deleting slide thumbnails in *Normal* view and *Slide Sorter* view or by deleting the slide icon in *Outline* view. You can also click the **Cut** button on the *Home* tab in the *Clipboard* group. This method is helpful because if you change your mind about the deletion, you can paste the deleted slides back into the presentation from the *Clipboard*.

▶ HOW TO: Delete Slides

1. Right-click the slide thumbnail (or the *Slide* icon in *Outline* view). Click **Delete Slide** from the context menu.

Or

2. Select the slide thumbnail (or the *Slide* icon in *Outline* view). Press **Delete** or click **Cut** [*Home* tab, *Clipboard* group].

PAUSE & PRACTICE: POWERPOINT 1-1

For this project, you develop the text for a presentation about upcoming marathon events at the Hamilton Civic Center. This presentation promotes event preparation for participants. You start with a blank presentation, add slides, reuse slides from another presentation, and change formatting.

File Needed: *Marathon Info-01.pptx* (Student data files are available in the Library *of your SIMnet account.*)
Completed Project File Name: ***[your initials] PP P1-1.pptx***

1. Open PowerPoint and click **Blank Presentation** to start a new presentation.
 a. Press **Ctrl+N** if PowerPoint is already open, or click the **File** tab, click **New**, and then click **Blank Presentation**.

2. Name and save the presentation.
 a. Press **F12** to open the *Save As* dialog box.
 b. Browse to the location where you want to save your files and double-click to open the appropriate folder (Figure 1-62).
 • If necessary, click the **New Folder** button, type a name for the new folder, and then double-click to open it.
 c. Type [your initials] PP P1-1 in the *File name* area.

Figure 1-62 *Save As* dialog box

 d. Verify that the *Save as type* area displays "PowerPoint Presentation."

 e. Click **Save**. The *Save As* dialog box closes.

3. Display slide 1. Type the following text in the placeholders:

 Title: Take the Right Steps

 Subtitle: Train for a Marathon

4. Click the **New Slide** button [*Home* tab, *Slides* group] twice to add two new slides.

 • The slide thumbnails appear blank, but the slides have the *Title and Content* layout with two placeholders.

5. Type the following text on slides 2 and 3:

 Slide 2 Title: What Is Your Goal?

 Bulleted items: • Run the second half faster

 • Beat a time you've run before

 • Or

 • Finish the marathon

 Slide 3 Title: Start Early to Be Ready

 Bulleted items: • Begin 5-16 weeks in advance

 • Get a physical checkup

 • Prepare gear for running

 • Join a training group

 • Enjoy camaraderie

 • Be accountable

 • Run 3-4 times a week

6. Change a slide layout and adjust text.

 a. Display slide 3. Click the **Layout** button [*Home* tab, *Slides* group] and select the **Two Content** layout.

 b. Select the last four bulleted items on the left placeholder and press **Ctrl+X** to cut them.

 c. Click the right placeholder and press **Ctrl+V** to paste them.

 d. Delete any extra bullets by placing your insertion point on that line and pressing **Backspace**.

 e. Select the middle two bulleted items on the right placeholder and press **Tab** or click the **Increase List Level** button [*Home* tab, *Paragraph* group] to format them as indented subpoints under the first-level item (Figure 1-63).

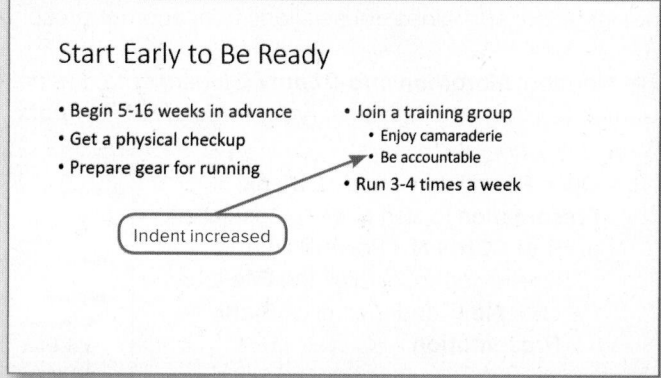

Figure 1-63 *Two Content* layout

7. Insert three slides from another presentation.

 a. Display slide 3. Click the **New Slide** drop-down arrow and select **Reuse Slides**.

 b. On the *Reuse Slides* pane, click the **Browse** button to open the *Browse* dialog box. Locate your student data files.

 c. Select the presentation ***MarathonInfo-01*** and click **Open**.

 • This presentation has spelling errors that you will fix later.

 d. Click three slides (Figure 1-64) to insert them:

 Practice Runs

 Eat Energy Foods

 Get Running Apparel

 e. Close the *Reuse Slides* pane.

8. Rearrange slides.
 a. Click the thumbnails and drag them up or down so the six slides are in this order:
 1 Take the Right Steps
 2 What is Your Goal?
 3 Start Early to Be Ready
 4 Get Running Apparel
 5 Eat Energy Foods
 6 Practice Runs

9. Insert and duplicate a new slide.
 a. Display slide 6. Click the **New Slide** drop-down arrow and select the **Title Only** layout.
 b. Type Look It UP! in the title placeholder on slide 7 (Figure 1-65).
 c. Select the title text and change the *Font Size* to **72 pt**.
 d. Select this slide thumbnail and press **Ctrl+D** to duplicate it to create slide 8.

10. Edit and duplicate a slide.
 a. Display slide 8. Replace the title with the text Mark It DOWN!
 b. Select this slide thumbnail and press **Ctrl+D** to duplicate it to create slide 9.

11. Display slide 9. Change the title text to See You THERE!

12. Display slide 1. Click the **Spelling** button [*Review* tab, *Proofing* group] and correct each of the spelling errors ("performance," "soreness," "banana," and "yogurt").

13. Close the *Design Ideas* pane if it opens.

14. Save and close the presentation (Figure 1-66). You will continue to work on this presentation for *Pause & Practice 1-2* and *Pause & Practice 1-3*.

Figure 1-64 Reuse slides

Figure 1-65 Placeholder text resized

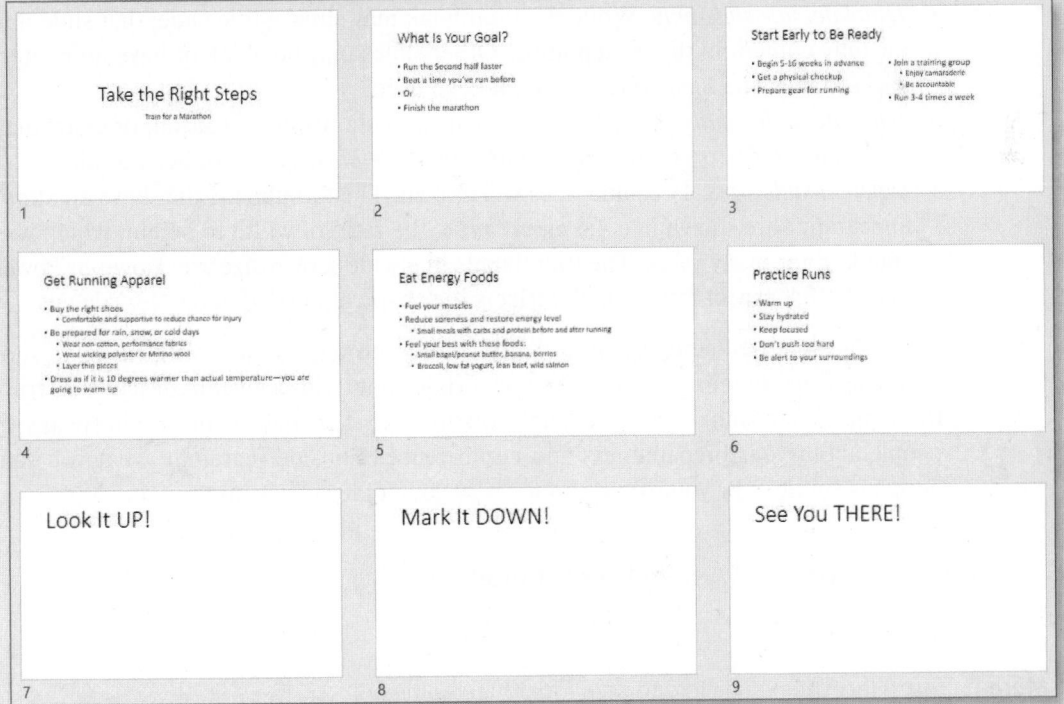

Figure 1-66 PP P1-1 completed

Changing Theme Colors and Fonts

In PowerPoint, you can quickly change theme colors and fonts using the *Design* tab. If you want to make additional theme changes, use the *Slide Master* tab. The **Slide Master** stores information about slide backgrounds, layouts, colors, and fonts for each theme. In this section, you change theme colors and fonts using both tabs so you learn which method is the most efficient.

When you start a new presentation and search online for templates and themes, you may find backgrounds with artwork or pictures that match your topic perfectly. The file names you see below each thumbnail do not distinguish between themes and templates. Many of the presentations that appear in a search will have the PowerPoint default file extension (.pptx). Those saved as template files will have a different file extension (.potx). Depending on how your software is set up, you may not see these file extensions when you open files.

> ## MORE INFO
>
> To display file extensions, open your *File Explorer* window. Click the **View** tab and select **File name extensions**.

You can search through general categories or enter a specific search word to get more targeted results. Themes and templates are provided by Microsoft and other companies.

Your searches will provide results that include the following:

- *Theme*: A slide show with background graphics and text treatments but no content. Different layouts control where slide objects are positioned. You can control design elements with the *Slide Master* to create custom designs.
- *Template*: A slide show with the characteristics of a theme but also with sample content on several slides. Edit the content or remove individual slides that you do not need for your presentation. Control design elements with the *Slide Master* to create custom designs.
- *Template, title slide only*: While the thumbnail may show a title slide, that slide might be the only content in the presentation. Other slides may be blank or have no related graphic background. The *Slide Master* has not been used.
- *Template, individual slide only*: Thumbnails may show only a diagram or chart that can be revised for a new presentation. Usually, the *Slide Master* has not been used.
- *Different slide sizes*: Two slide sizes will appear. The thumbnails that have an almost square appearance are shown in a 4:3 **aspect ratio**, the ratio of width to height, which was the standard for many years. The thumbnails in a wide-screen size are shown in PowerPoint's default 16:9 aspect ratio, which reflects the shape of current computer screens.

People who frequently see presentations become very familiar with the slide show designs that appear in common software. Seeing a slide show with a custom design that truly matches the topic is refreshing. Caring enough to match your theme to your topic speaks volumes to people about your preparedness and competence. Consider carefully what you select so the design is suitable for your topic and for how your slide show is used.

▶ **HOW TO:** Apply a Theme to an Existing Presentation

1. Click the **Design** tab.
2. Click the **More** button in the *Themes* gallery to see additional themes.
3. Point to a thumbnail to see a live preview of the theme on the current slide (Figure 1-67).
4. Click the thumbnail to apply the theme.

Figure 1-67 *Design* tab and *Themes* gallery

▶ **ANOTHER WAY**

To apply two themes in one presentation, apply your first theme to all slides, and then select the slides that should be different. Right-click another theme and select **Apply to Selected Slides**. Be careful when using this option so that your content does not seem disjointed.

Change Theme Colors

When changing theme colors, select colors that are appropriate for your topic. Also consider where you will present. Because of room lighting, colors for a slide show projected on a large screen are not as clear or vibrant as what you see on a computer screen directly in front of you. These differences can influence your color choices. Be sure your text is easy to read with a high contrast between the text and background colors (dark on light or light on dark).

Every presentation, even a blank one, begins with a set of colors that have been chosen to work well together. With each built-in theme, PowerPoint provides *Variants* on the *Design* tab that show different theme colors and may have different graphics. Many more theme colors are available.

▶ **HOW TO: Change Theme Colors Using the Design Tab**

1. Click the **Design** tab.
2. Click the **More** button [*Variants* group].
3. Select **Colors** and a drop-down list appears showing theme colors (Figure 1-68).
4. Point to a set of theme colors to see a live preview of those colors on your current slide.
 - A *Blank Presentation* theme uses *Office* theme colors. Slides will show a live preview only if the background color has changed.
5. Click the colors or a theme name to apply it to all slides.

Figure 1-68 *Design* tab and *Theme Colors*

In each set of theme colors, the first two colors represent the background and text colors; the remaining six show accent colors. Once you select theme colors, you can apply a light or dark variation of background and text colors. Click the **More** button [*Design* tab, *Variants* group] and select **Background Styles**. Point to a color in the gallery to see a live preview; click a color to apply it.

Not all themes you find online permit color changes in the same way. It depends on how the background design was created. For more on customizing theme colors, see *SLO 3.1: Creating Custom Theme and Background Colors*.

Change Theme Fonts

Select your fonts carefully. Some fonts can seem very traditional and serious; others appear more playful and flamboyant. Use fonts that are appropriate for your presentation topic.

Consider how legible the font is with the background color you are using. Letters can appear very thin and are not easy to read unless you apply bold. Also consider issues related to where you present. The lighting and room size affect how readable the text is on a large screen, and you must use large font sizes. If you are designing a presentation to show to a single person on your notebook or tablet computer, you can use smaller font sizes.

Every presentation, even one with a blank background, begins with a pair of *Theme Fonts*. The heading font is used for slide titles and the body font is used for all other text. Occasionally, the same font is used for both. You can view or change *Theme Fonts* from the *Design* tab or from the *Slide Master* tab.

> ▶ **HOW TO: Change Theme Fonts Using the Design Tab**
>
> 1. Click the **Design** tab.
> 2. Click the **More** button [*Variants* group].
> 3. Select **Fonts** and a drop-down list appears showing theme fonts.
> 4. Point to a pair of theme fonts to see a live preview of those fonts applied to the current slide (Figure 1-69).
> 5. Click a theme font pair to apply it to all slides.

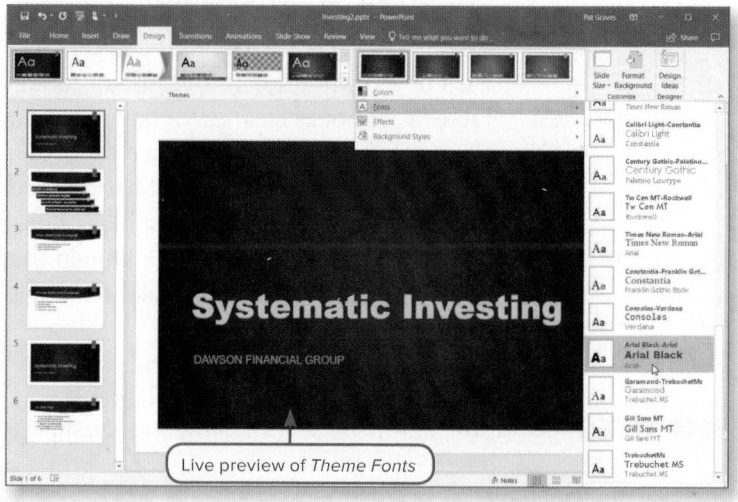

Figure 1-69 *Design* tab and *Theme Fonts*

Use the Slide Master to Change Theme Colors and Fonts

The *Slide Master* tab shows commands for changing the background, and they all work the same as using the *Design* tab. However, the *Slide Master* enables you to change other design elements. For example, you could customize the background by adding a company logo to all slides in a presentation. Each *Slide Master* has a variety of layouts, shown in the pane on the left, that control positioning of different types of content. If you are adding graphics or changing only specific layout colors, then select only the layout you want to change. Changes made on the first layout at the top of this pane generally apply to all other layouts.

▶ HOW TO: Change Theme Colors and Fonts Using the Slide Master

1. Click the **View** tab.

2. Click the **Slide Master** button [*Master Views* group] (Figure 1-70) to open the *Slide Master* tab.

3. Scroll up to select the first layout, the *Slide Master* layout, at the top of the *Thumbnails* pane so your changes will affect all layouts.

4. Click the **Colors** button [*Background* group] and a drop-down list appears with theme colors.

5. Point to a set of theme colors to see a live preview of those colors on your current *Slide Master* layout.

6. Click the colors or a theme color name to apply it to all *Slide Master* layouts.

7. Click the **Background Styles** button [*Slide Master* tab, *Background* group] to change the background to a light or dark variation (Figure 1-71).

 - You can apply different *Background Styles* to various *Slide Master* layouts.

8. Click the **Fonts** button [*Slide Master* tab, *Background* group] and a drop-down list appears showing theme fonts.

9. Point to a pair of theme fonts to see a live preview of those fonts applied to the current layout.

10. Click a theme font pair to apply it to all layouts.

11. Click the **Close Master View** button [*Slide Master* tab, *Close* group].

Figure 1-70 *Slide Master* button on the *View* tab

Figure 1-71 *Background Styles*

 SLO 1.5

Inserting Headers and Footers

If you want to include identifying information on all slides of a presentation, use the *Header & Footer* command on the *Insert* tab (Figure 1-72). **Footers** have placeholders for the date and time, slide number, and footer text. These placeholders often appear across the bottom of the slide, but they may appear in different places depending on the theme. You can choose to show footers on all slides or only on selected slides.

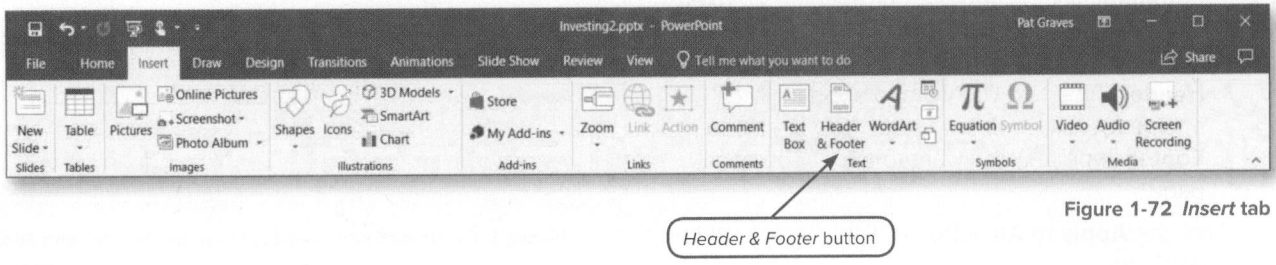

Figure 1-72 *Insert* tab

Header & Footer button

Create a Slide Footer

When you enter information using the *Header and Footer* dialog box, placeholders appear on the slides. You can move these placeholders if you wish.

▶HOW TO: Create a Slide Footer

1. Click the **Insert** tab.

2. Click the **Header & Footer** button [*Text* group]. The *Header and Footer* dialog box displays.

 - The **Slide** tab is automatically open (Figure 1-73).

3. Click the check boxes to select the following as needed:

 - **Date and time**: Choose between **Update automatically** to show the current date or **Fixed** to enter a specific date.
 - **Slide number**: Each slide is numbered.
 - **Footer**: Type text you want to appear on each slide.

4. Check the box for **Don't show on title slide** if you do not want footer information to appear on any slide created with the *Title Slide* layout.

5. Apply your choices by clicking one of these buttons:

 - **Apply**: the settings are applied to the current slide only.
 - **Apply to All**: the settings are applied to all slides.

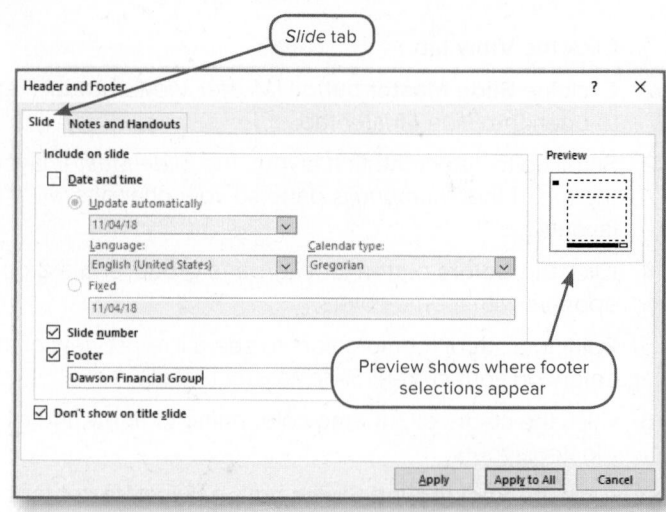

Figure 1-73 *Slide* tab in the *Header and Footer* dialog box

Create a Notes and Handouts Header

Because notes and handouts are usually printed documents, they can include *header* information that appears at the top of each page. Control all settings for notes and handouts in the same way you control slide footers.

▶HOW TO: Create a Notes and Handouts Header

1. Click the **Insert** tab.

2. Click the **Header & Footer** button [*Text* group]. The *Header and Footer* dialog box displays.

3. Click the **Notes and Handouts** tab (Figure 1-74).

4. Click the check boxes to select the following as needed:

 - **Date and time**: Choose between **Update automatically** to show the current date or **Fixed** to enter a specific date.
 - **Page number**: Each page is numbered.
 - **Header**: Type text you want to appear on each page.
 - **Footer**: Type text you want to appear on each page.

5. Click the **Apply to All** button to apply your settings to all pages.

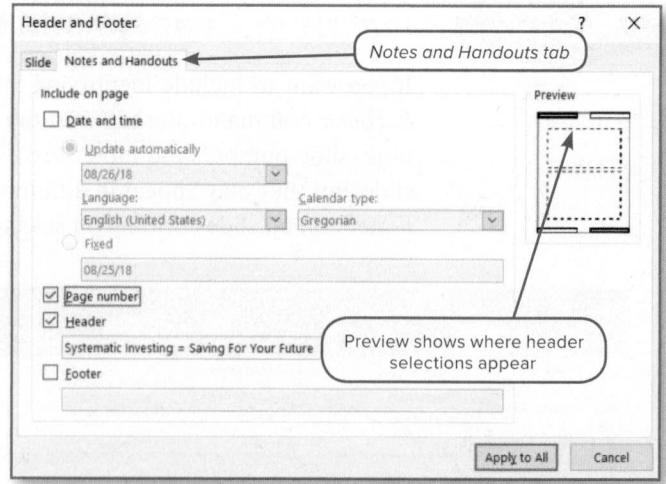

Figure 1-74 *Notes and Handouts* tab in the *Header and Footer* dialog box

If you leave items blank in the *Header and Footer* dialog box, empty placeholders show on your slide but no information appears in *Slide Show* view.

For this project, you continue working on the presentation about training for a marathon. You add a theme and then change theme colors and fonts to revise two individual slides. Finally, you add a footer to your slides and add page numbering to the notes and handout pages.

File Needed: *[your initials] PP P1-1.pptx*
Completed Project File Name: *[your initials] PP P1-2.pptx*

1. Open the presentation you completed in *Pause & Practice 1-1*.
 a. Click the **File** tab to open the *Backstage* view and click **Open** on the left.
 b. Click **Browse** to open the *Open* dialog box.
 c. Locate the folder where your files are saved.
 d. Select the *[your initials] PP P1-1* presentation and click **Open**.

2. Rename and save the presentation.
 a. Click the **File** tab to open the *Backstage* view and select **Save As** on the left.
 b. Click **Browse** to open the *Save As* dialog box.
 c. Locate the folder where you want to save this file.
 d. Change the file name to [your initials] PP P1-2.
 e. Click **Save** to save the presentation and close the *Save As* dialog box.

3. Apply a theme.
 a. Click the **Design** tab.
 b. Click the **More** button [*Themes* group] to open the *Themes* gallery (Figure 1-75).
 c. Click the **Facet** theme so it is applied to all slides.

Figure 1-75 *Themes* gallery

4. Change theme colors and the background style.
 a. Click the **More** button [*Design* tab, *Variants* group] and select **Colors**.
 b. Scroll down the list and select the **Aspect** theme.
 c. Click the **More** button again and select **Background Styles**.
 d. Select **Style 4**, which applies a solid black background (Figure 1-76).

5. Change theme fonts.
 a. Click the **More** button [*Design* tab, *Variants* group] and select **Fonts**.
 b. Scroll down the list and click the **TrebuchetMS** font pair (Figure 1-77).

Figure 1-76 *Background Styles*

6. Modify and move the title.
 a. Display slide 1. Select the title placeholder and apply these font changes: **60 pt.**, **Bold** [*Home* tab, *Font* group], and **Align Left** [*Home* tab, *Paragraph* group].
 b. Click the **Arrange** button [*Home* tab, *Drawing* group], select **Align**, and then select **Align Top**.
 c. Select the word **Right**. Click the **Change Case** button [*Home* tab, *Font* group] and select **UPPERCASE**.
 d. Resize the placeholder by dragging the right horizontal sizing handle so the text fits on one line.

7. Modify and move the subtitle.
 a. Select the subtitle placeholder on slide 1 and apply these font changes: **36 pt.**, **Bold** [*Home* tab, *Font* group], and **Align Left** [*Home* tab, *Paragraph* group].
 b. Point to the subtitle placeholder border so your pointer changes to a four-pointed arrow.
 c. Click and drag to move this placeholder below the title.
 d. Select both the title and subtitle placeholders.
 e. Click the **Arrange** button [*Home* tab, *Drawing* group], select **Align**, and then select **Align Left**.

8. Change the bullet.
 a. Display slide 2. Select the bulleted text and click the **Bullets** drop-down arrow [*Home* tab, *Font* group].
 b. Select **Bullets and Numbering**.
 c. Change the *Size* to **100%** of text.
 d. Click the **Color** button (Figure 1-78) and select **Red, Accent 2**.
 e. Click the **Customize** button to open the *Symbol* dialog box.
 f. Change the *Font* to **Wingdings** (Figure 1-79). Select the **Black Square** (Character code 110).
 g. Click **OK** to insert the symbol and close the *Symbol* dialog box.
 h. Click **OK** again to close the *Bullets and Numbering* dialog box.
 i. Click to position your insertion point before the word "**Or**" on the third bulleted item.
 j. Press **Backspace** to remove the bullet from this item only.
 k. Apply **Bold** to the word "Or."
 l. Deselect the bulleted text placeholder.

Figure 1-77 Change *Theme Fonts*

Figure 1-78 Change bullet size and color

Figure 1-79 *Symbol* dialog box

Figure 1-80 *Header and Footer* dialog box with changes

9. Add a slide footer.
 a. Click the **Header & Footer** button [*Insert* tab, *Text* group] on slide 2.
 b. Select **Slide number** and **Footer** on the *Slide* tab (Figure 1-80).
 c. Type Take the Right Steps, Train for a Marathon in the *Footer* text box.
 d. Select **Don't show on title slide**.
 e. Click the **Apply** button. The dialog box closes and the footer appears only on this slide.
 f. Press **Shift** and click the footer and the page number placeholders to select them both. Increase the *Font Size* to **18 pt**. [*Home* tab, *Font* group].

10. Save and close the presentation (Figure 1-81).

Figure 1-81 PP P1-2 completed

Working with a Picture from a File

An old adage says "A picture is worth a thousand words." That saying is still true today, because pictures, or photographs, bring a sense of realism to a presentation. Pictures are commonly referred to as images and can include drawings that are saved in a digital format because PowerPoint supports different graphic file types.

Select pictures appropriate for your topic. Include pictures from web sites only if you have the permission of the image owner to avoid copyright infringement. For academic purposes, you may include images if you reference their sources as you would any other research citation.

Insert a Picture and Select a Design Ideas Layout

To insert a picture, click the *Pictures* button in the *Images* group on the *Insert* tab. Be aware that pictures can increase the file size of your presentation dramatically.

If you are using Microsoft's Intelligent Services, *Alt Text* (Alternative Text) that describes the picture briefly appears at the bottom of the picture. If that text is not accurate, click the **Alt Text** button to open the *Alt Text* pane and type a description. You will learn more about *Alt Text* in *SLO 2.3: Working with Pictures*.

Office 2019 Note: The *Alt Text* does not automatically display at the bottom of the picture when using Office 2019. Use the *Alt Text* pane to check description wording and revise it as needed.

▶**HOW TO:** Insert a Picture

1. Click the **Insert** tab.
2. Click the **Pictures** button (*Images* group).
3. Select the drive and folder where your picture is saved.
4. Select the file you want to insert (Figure 1-82).
5. Click **Insert**.
 - The *Design Ideas* pane automatically opens on the right showing different ways to feature the picture you just inserted.
 - *Office 2019 Note*: *PowerPoint Designer* is not available in Office 2019.
 - *Alt Text* (Alternative Text) that describes the picture briefly appears at the bottom of the picture.
 - *Office 2019 Note*: No text will display at the bottom of the picture when using Office 2019.
6. Click one of the *Design Ideas* thumbnails (Figure 1-83) to apply that layout to your slide.
 - If you want to try another layout, click the **Undo** button on the *Quick Access* toolbar and then click another thumbnail to apply that layout.
 - Close the *Design Ideas* pane by clicking the **X** at the top of the pane.

Figure 1-82 *Insert Picture* dialog box

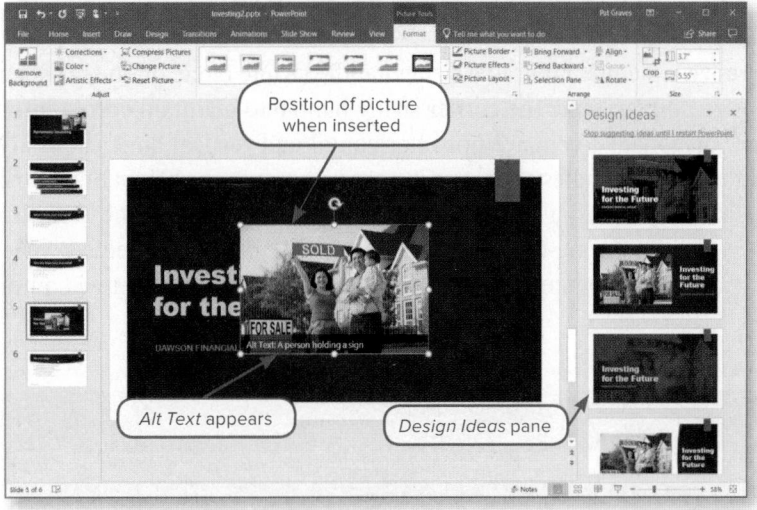

Figure 1-83 *Design Ideas* pane with picture layouts

> ## ANOTHER WAY
>
> Once you have located your picture file, insert the picture by double-clicking the file name.

The graphic file formats used by PowerPoint for pictures and illustrations are listed in Table 1-3.

Table 1-3: Graphic File Formats

Picture File Type	Extension	Uses of This Format
JPEG (Joint Photographic Experts Group)	.jpg	Used for photographs and complex graphics. Handles gradual color blending well. Produces a smaller file size than most other formats. Transparency is not supported.
PNG (Portable Network Graphics)	.png	Used for photographs and complex graphics. Supports transparency so areas removed from the image appear blank on the slide.
GIF (Graphics Interchange Format)	.gif	Suited for line art and simple drawings because it is limited to 256 colors. Used for simple animated graphics. Does not handle gradual color blending well. Supports transparency.
Windows Metafile and Enhanced Windows Metafile	.wmf and .emf	Used for simple 16-bit or 32-bit graphics.
Device Independent Bitmap	.bmp	Images usually display well in their original size, but if you increase size, they will be distorted.
TIFF (Tagged Image File Format)	.tiff	Designed for print publications. Produces high-quality images with large file sizes. Supports transparency.
SVG (Scalable Vector Graphics)	.svg	Used for the simple, one-color images called *Icons*. You can customize icons with no loss to image quality.

Resize a Picture

To resize a picture, point to a sizing handle (white circle on the border). Your pointer changes to a resize pointer. Drag the corner sizing handle to maintain correct proportions. Corner handles move diagonally to change both horizontal and vertical dimensions at the same time. Dragging the top or side handles can cause distortion because the height or width is changed independently.

Precisely resize a picture by entering dimensions in the *Size* group on the *Picture Tools Format* tab (Figure 1-84) that appears when a picture is selected. When you change the *Height* or *Width* measurement [*Size* group], the other measurement will automatically adjust.

Reset Picture button Enter sizes

Figure 1-84 *Picture Tools Format* tab

You can resize a picture to make it smaller and still retain its clarity, but pictures may become blurred or distorted if their size is increased. If you change the size incorrectly, restore the picture's original dimensions by clicking the **Reset Picture** drop-down arrow [*Picture Tools Format* tab, *Adjust* group] and selecting **Reset Picture & Size**. Depending on the picture's resolution, you may need to resize it again to fit your slide.

Align a Picture

As you place pictures and other graphic objects on slides, consider how they are aligned rather than positioning them randomly. Align selected pictures and other objects with each other or with the slide by clicking **Align Selected Objects** or **Align to Slide** (see "Align, Move, and Resize Placeholders" in *SLO 1.2: Working with Slides, Layouts, Placeholders, and Text*.) Click the **Align** button [*Picture Tools Format* tab, *Arrange* group] and select the alignment from the drop-down list (Figure 1-85):

- *Horizontal alignment*: **Align Left**, **Align Center**, or **Align Right**
- *Vertical alignment*: **Align Top**, **Align Middle**, or **Align Bottom**

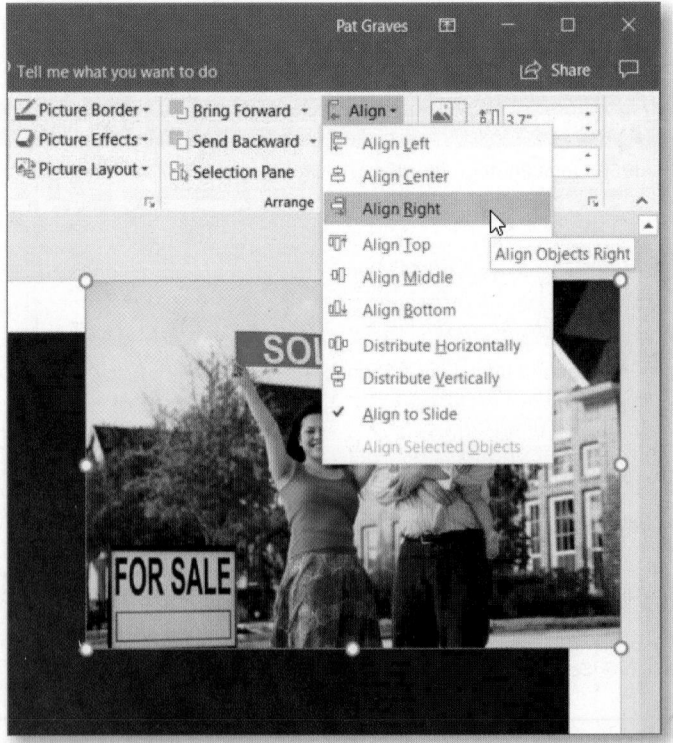

Figure 1-85 *Align Top* and *Align Right*

The picture shown in Figure 1-85 displays the following alignment: **Align to Slide**, **Align Right**, and **Align Top**.

Applying and Modifying Transitions

A *transition* is the visual effect of movement when one slide changes to the next slide. PowerPoint provides these effects on the *Transitions* tab (Figure 1-86) in the *Transition to This Slide* group.

Figure 1-86 *Transitions* tab

Each slide can have only one transition. You can set transitions for one slide at a time in *Normal* view or apply the same transition to all slides. If you want to use different transitions, select thumbnails in *Normal* view or *Slide Sorter* view and click a transition to apply it to those slides. Once a transition has been applied, an icon symbolizing movement appears with the slide thumbnail.

In the *Timing* group, select the **Advance Slide** option 1) **On Mouse Click** (the default) which enables the speaker to control timing or 2) **After** when the number of seconds is specified to automate the transitions. *On Mouse Click* also works if you are using a stylus to click. If you are using a tablet computer, you can swipe to change slides.

You can add sound to a transition such as an audio recording or music that would play in the background as slides change. *Duration*, shown in seconds, controls how fast the slides change. *Duration* seconds vary based on the selected transition effect. Movement might be barely visible if the duration is fast; a slower duration of five or more seconds will cause the movement to be much more noticeable. Enter a different number to change the duration and experiment to see what works best for your content.

▶ **HOW TO: Apply Transitions**

1. Select the slide thumbnail where you want a transition to appear.
2. Click the **Transitions** tab.
3. Click the **More** button [*Transition to This Slide* group] to see additional transitions (Figure 1-87) organized by the following categories:
 - *Subtle*
 - *Exciting*
 - *Dynamic Content*
4. Apply one transition to all slides in the presentation.
 - Select a transition effect.
 - Select **On Mouse Click** [*Timing* group] if it is not already selected.
 - Click the **Apply to All** button [*Timing* group].

Figure 1-87 *Transitions* gallery

5. Apply a different transition to selected slides.
 - Click the **Slide Sorter** button on the *Status* bar.
 - Press **Ctrl** as you click to select one or more slides to apply a different transition.
 - Click a different transition effect to apply it to the selected slides. The movement displays on the selected slides.
 - Select **On Mouse Click** [*Timing* group] if it is not already selected (Figure 1-88).

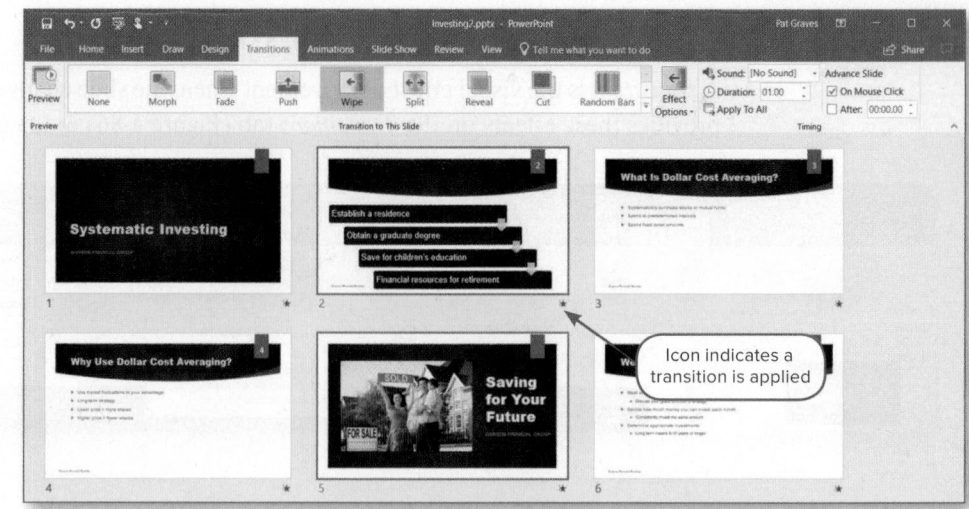

Figure 1-88 Change transitions on selected slides in *Slide Sorter* view

6. Preview slides in different views to test the movement.
 - *Slide Sorter* view: Click the **Slide Sorter** button on the *Status* bar. Select a slide thumbnail and click **Preview** [*Transitions* tab, *Preview* group]. Repeat for other slides.
 - *Normal* view: Click the **Normal View** button on the *Status* bar. Select a slide and click **Preview**. Click the **Next Slide** button to advance from slide to slide.
 - *Slide Show* view: Click the **Slide Show** button [*Status* bar] and press **N** to advance from slide to slide starting from the current slide.
 - *Slide Show* view: Click the **From Beginning** button [*Slide Show* tab, *Start Slide Show* group] to view the slide show from the first slide. Click to advance from slide to slide.

Although it is possible to apply different transitions on every slide in a presentation, it is neither practical nor advisable. People are very accustomed to PowerPoint use today and know that slides are going to change. Random movements using many different transitions do not entertain an audience and may be distracting or even annoying. Control movement skillfully to reinforce your message. For example, you could apply a "quiet" transition for most of your presentation (similar to turning pages in a book or an e-reader) and then apply a more "energetic" transition to key slides to grab attention or signal the beginning of a new topic. Use the *Slide Sorter* view to see more slides at once and decide which slides might benefit from a different movement.

One of the transitions, *Morph*, works differently than other transitions because you can change individual objects on the slide instead of the entire slide. One object must be the same on each slide and then slide objects will appear to animate as one slide changes to the second slide. You can develop two slides—one is your final slide, then create a duplicate slide that goes before it. On the duplicate slide, you apply changes such as moving or recoloring objects. Then when the slides change, the *Morph* transition creates a blending effect as objects on the slide change into the final slide.

Select Effect Options

Effect Options control the direction of transition movement. Each transition can have only one effect option, but most transitions provide two or more options from which to choose. Apply these options as you apply your transitions or later when you are editing your presentation.

▶**HOW TO:** Select Effect Options

1. Select a slide with a transition.

2. Click the **Effect Options** button [*Transition* tab, *Transition to This Slide* group] to see a drop-down list showing directional movements (Figure 1-89).

3. Select an effect option to apply it.

4. Apply the effect option to multiple transitions if appropriate:

 • Click **Apply To All** [*Transition* tab, *Timing* group] if this movement is appropriate for all slides.
 • If different transitions have been applied, select the slide thumbnails in *Slide Sorter* view with the same transition and then apply the appropriate effect option.

5. Preview the slides in *Slide Show* view to test all transitions and effect options.

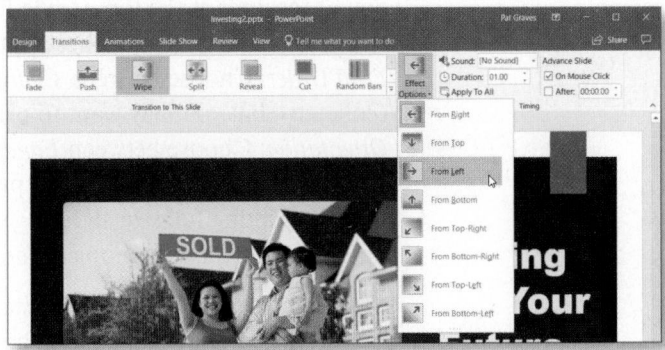

Figure 1-89 Transition *Effect Options*

<div style="background:#6b6b6b">SLO 1.8</div>

Exploring Print Options

You may want to proofread your presentation content on paper or review the slides with a colleague. You may need audience handouts or your own printed materials to use while you are presenting. PowerPoint provides convenient ways to preview and print presentation slides, handouts, notes pages, or outlines.

Preview a Presentation

Before printing, check your slides to ensure everything looks as you intended. The *Backstage* view [*File* tab, *Print* button] displays each slide or handout page in your presentation as it will look when printed. Use the navigation controls at the bottom of the window to go through the slides or pages one at a time. You can also use the scroll bar on the right. Adjust slide or page size using the *Zoom* controls on the lower right.

The look of your slides in *Backstage* view is influenced by the selected printer. The preview image shows in color if you are printing with a color printer or in *grayscale* (shades of black) if you are printing with a printer that prints only black. In a work setting, you may have a small desktop printer for printing rough draft copies with black print and a network printer for printing more expensive, high-quality color pages. If you design slides in color and plan to print slides or handouts in grayscale, preview your slides in grayscale to confirm that all text is readable. You may need to adjust a few colors to get good results.

In *Backstage* view, select a printer from the available list of local and network printers. *Settings* are shown as buttons with the current setting displayed. Click the list arrow on each button for a list of options:

• *Which Slides to Print*: Choose *Print All Slides*, *Print Selection*, *Print Current Slide*, or *Custom Range* using slide numbers entered in the *Slides* box such as slides 1–3 (a range of one through three) or slides 1–3, 5, 8 (a range followed by individual slides).
• *What to Print*: Choose *Full Page Slides*, *Notes Pages*, *Outline*, or *Handouts*. You can print handouts with one, two, three, four, six, or nine slides on a page with the sequence of slides arranged horizontally or vertically. You can also specify *Frame Slides*, *Scale to Fit Paper* (increases slide size), or *High Quality*.

- *Print Side*: Choose between *Print One Sided* or *Print on Both Sides*. You can choose to *Flip pages on long edge* or *Flip pages on short edge* to control how pages will turn if they are bound together at the top or side like a book. However, not all printers can print on both sides, so you may not see these options.
- *Print Order*: Choose between *Collated* and *Uncollated*. Usually slides print in order (collated), but you may want to print multiple copies page by page (uncollated).
- *Orientation*: Choose between *Landscape* and *Portrait*. By default, slides print in landscape orientation; notes and handouts print in portrait orientation. This option is not available if you are printing full-size slides.
- *Color Range*: Choose among *Color*, *Grayscale*, or *Pure Black and White*.

Below the print *Settings* in *Backstage* view, you can click the *Edit Header & Footer* link to open the *Header and Footer* dialog box and then enter or revise information.

Print a Slide

The default print settings print each slide on letter-size paper. Adjust print settings as needed to print the current or selected slides.

▶HOW TO: Print a Slide in Grayscale

1. Click the **File** tab.
2. Click **Print** on the left.
3. Select an appropriate printer.
4. Locate the *Settings* area. Click the list arrow for each box and choose options from the drop-down list, such as the following:
 - *Which Slides to Print*: **Print Current Slide**
 - *What to Print*: **Full Page Slides**
 - *Print Order*: **Collated**
 - *Color Range*: **Grayscale** (Figure 1-90)
5. Click the *Edit Header & Footer* link to open the *Header and Footer* dialog box to enter or revise information.
6. Enter the number of copies if you need more than one.
7. Click the **Print** button at the top.

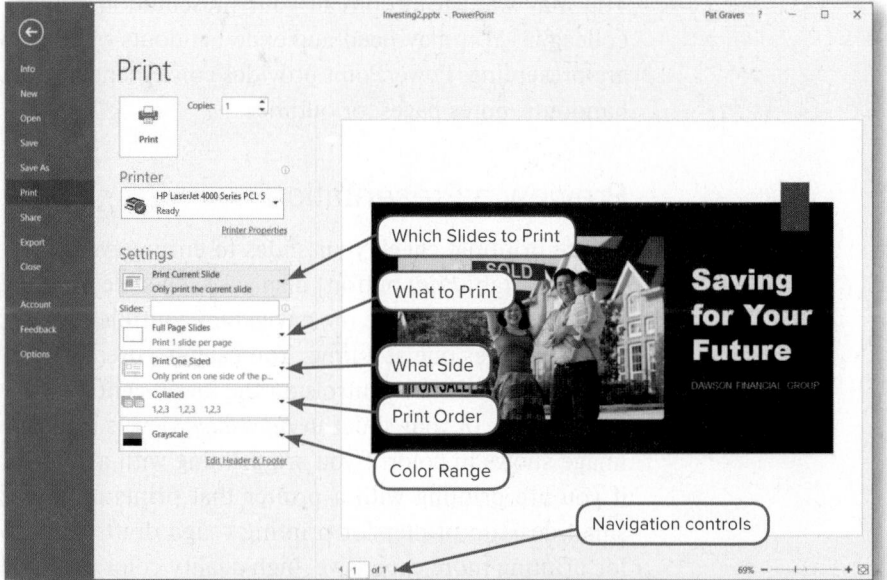

Figure 1-90 Print settings for a full-size slide

Print a Handout

Handouts print one to nine slides on a page. Use these pages as audience handouts or for your own reference during a presentation. Select **Scale to Fit Paper** to increase slide size. Select **Frame Slides** to show a slide border, which is helpful when printing slides with a white background on white paper. Depending on the number of slides, changing the *Page Orientation* from **Portrait** to **Landscape** may increase slide size.

When preparing handouts for an audience, consider which slides are important for the audience to have. You can specify which slides to include and reduce the number of pages required for printing.

HOW TO: Print a Handout for Selected Slides in Color

1. Click the **File** tab.
2. Click **Print** on the left.
3. Select a color printer.
4. Locate the *Settings* area. Click the list arrow for each box and choose options from the drop-down list, such as the following:

 - *Which Slides to Print*: Type the specific slides needed (1, 3–4, 6) in the *Slides* box to print a *Custom Range*.
 - *What to Print*: **6 Slides Horizontal**
 - *Print Order*: **Collated**
 - *Orientation*: **Portrait Orientation**
 - *Color Range*: **Color** (Figure 1-91)

5. Click the *Edit Header & Footer* link to open the *Header and Footer* dialog box to enter or revise information.
6. Type the number of copies if you need more than one.
7. Click the **Print** button at the top.

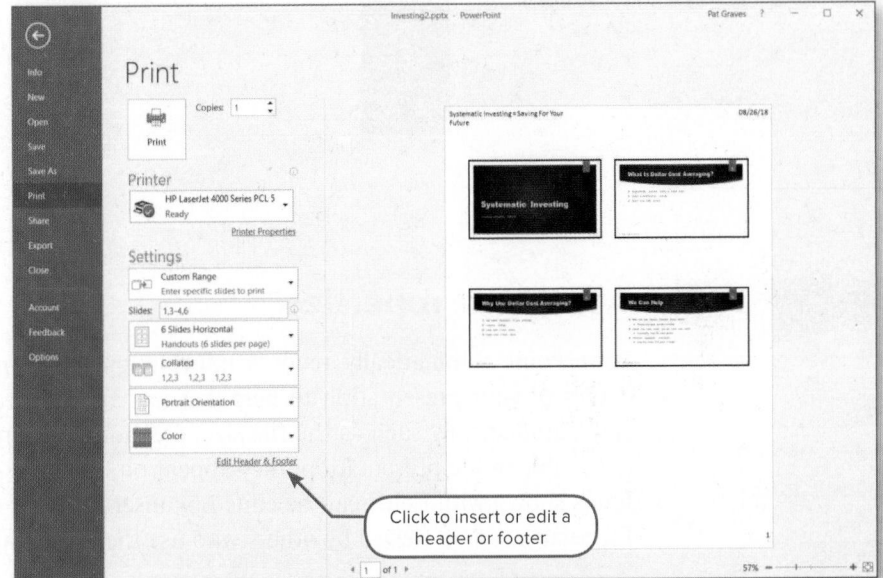

Figure 1-91 Print settings for a handout

Print an Outline

If a presentation consists of mostly slides with titles and bulleted lists, printing an outline is a very concise way to display the content. Only the text is shown.

HOW TO: Print an Outline in Pure Black and White

1. Click the **File** tab.
2. Click the **Print** button on the left.
3. Select an appropriate printer.
4. Locate the *Settings* area. Click the list arrow and choose options from the drop-down list, such as the following:

 - *Which Slides to Print*: **Print All Slides**
 - *What to Print*: **Outline**
 - *What Side*: **Print One Sided** (this option will not be available if your printer cannot duplex print).
 - *Print Order*: **Collated**

- Orientation: **Portrait Orientation**
- Color Range: **Pure Black and White** (Figure 1-92)

5. Click the *Edit Header & Footer* link to open the *Header and Footer* dialog box to enter or revise information.

6. Enter the number of copies if you need more than one.

7. Click the **Print** button at the top.

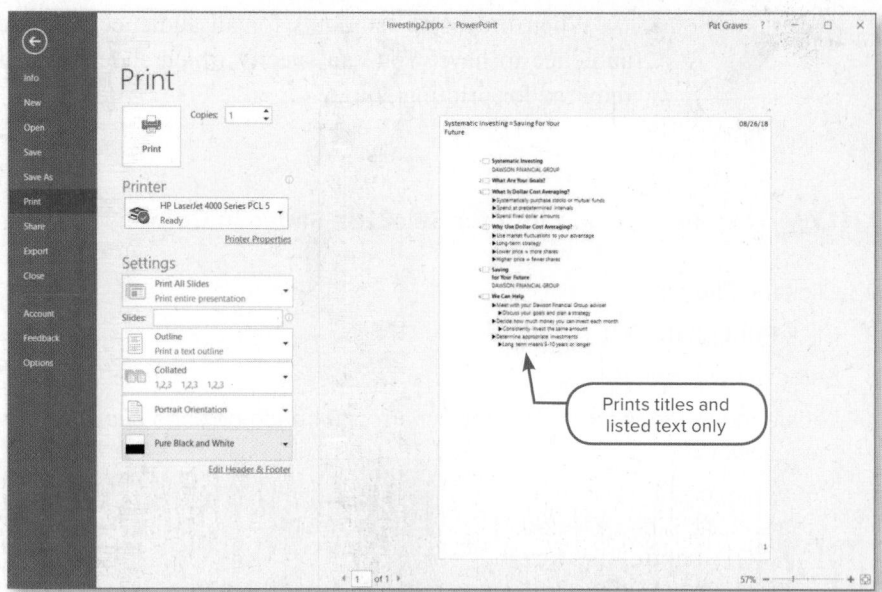

Figure 1-92 Print settings for an outline

SLO 1.9

Applying Properties

PowerPoint automatically records information called *properties*, or *metadata*, that identify details of your presentation to help you manage and track files. Some information is generated automatically such as the file size, creation date, and number of slides. These details are not visible in the presentation; they appear on the *Backstage* view or the *Properties* dialog box. Items shown with fields can be edited by inserting your own content such as title and author. Properties can be viewed by others who use the presentation.

▶ **HOW TO:** Add Properties Using Backstage View

1. Click the **File** tab to display the *Backstage* view.

2. Click **Info** if it is not already selected.

3. Point to the properties listed on the right. The property field names are followed by the information for the current presentation.

 - Properties that are automatically generated cannot be changed.
 - When you point to a property text box, a red border displays (Figure 1-93). Click the box to edit or add content.

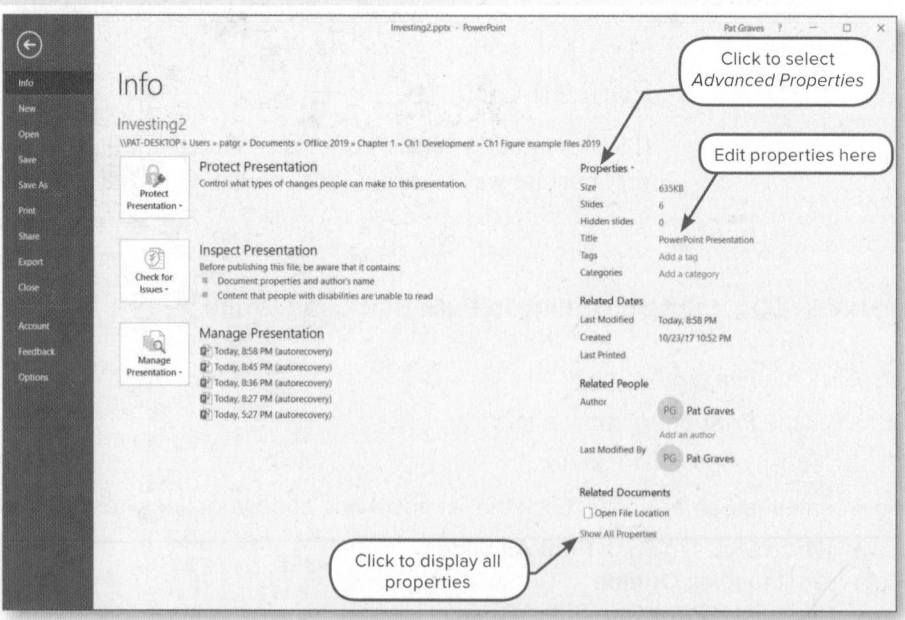

Figure 1-93 Document properties on the *Backstage* view

4. Click **Show All Properties** to access additional information.

5. Click a text box and type information to edit the document property.

6. Click the **Back arrow** in the upper-left corner of the *Backstage* view to return to your presentation.

To open the *Properties* dialog box, click the **File** tab to display the *Backstage* view and then click **Info**. Click the **Properties** button and select **Advanced Properties**. Properties are organized in the following five tabs: *General*, *Summary*, *Statistics*, *Contents*, and *Custom* (Figure 1-94). You can edit properties on the *Summary* tab.

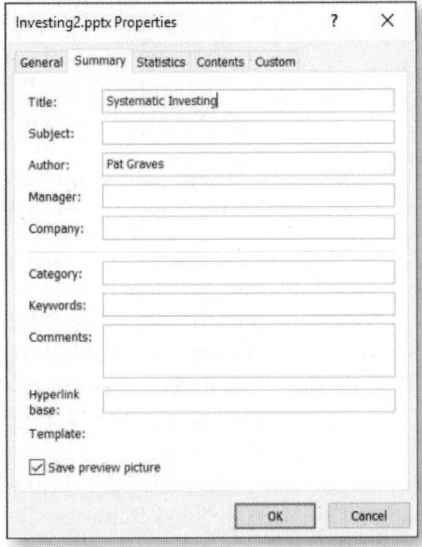

Figure 1-94 *Properties* dialog box

PAUSE & PRACTICE: POWERPOINT 1-3

For this final Pause & Practice project, you finish the presentation about training for a marathon. You insert, resize, and align several pictures, apply transitions, change the presentation properties, and print a handout.

Files Needed: *[your initials] PP P1-2.pptx, PP P1-2_2019.pptx, RunnersGroup-01.jpg, RunnerWoman-01.jpg*, and *MarathonSchedule-01.jpg* (Student data files are available in the Library of your SIMnet account.)
Completed Project File Name: *[your initials] PP P1-3.pptx*

1. Open the presentation you completed in *Pause & Practice 1-2*.
 a. Click the **File** tab to open the *Backstage* view and click **Open** on the left.
 b. Click **Browse** to open the *Open* dialog box.
 c. Locate the folder where your files are saved.
 d. Select the *[your initials] PP P1-2* presentation and click **Open**. If you are using Office 2019, open **PP P1-2_2019** and skip step 3 because it uses the *Design Ideas* pane.

2. Rename and save the presentation.
 a. Click the **File** tab to open the *Backstage* view and select **Save As** on the left.
 b. Click **Browse** to open the **Save As** dialog box.
 c. Locate the folder where you want to save this file.
 d. Change the file name to [your initials] PP P1-3.
 e. Click **Save** to save the presentation and close the *Save As* dialog box.

3. Insert, resize, and align a picture on the slide.
 a. Display slide 1. Click the **Insert** tab, and then click the **Pictures** button [*Images* group].
 b. Locate your student data files.

c. Select **RunnersGroup-01** and click **Insert** (or double-click the file name) to insert the picture.
 - The *Design Ideas* pane automatically opens.
 - Scroll down to review all the suggested layouts.
d. Click a thumbnail with a layout similar to Figure 1-95.
 - Because the picture is already blurred to reflect the speed of running, it looks fine if the picture is stretched.

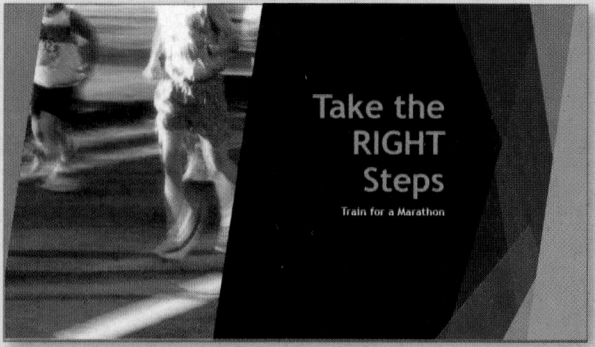
Figure 1-95 Picture of runners inserted with *Design Ideas* layout

4. Insert and align a picture.
a. Display slide 6. Click the **Insert** tab and click the **Pictures** button.
b. Locate your student data files.
c. Select **RunnerWoman-01** and click **Insert** (or double-click the file name) to insert the picture.
 - No resizing is required for this picture.
d. Select the picture and click the **Align** button [*Picture Tools Format* tab, *Arrange* group] and select **Align Right** (Figure 1-96).
 - The *Design Ideas* pane automatically closes when alignment is applied.

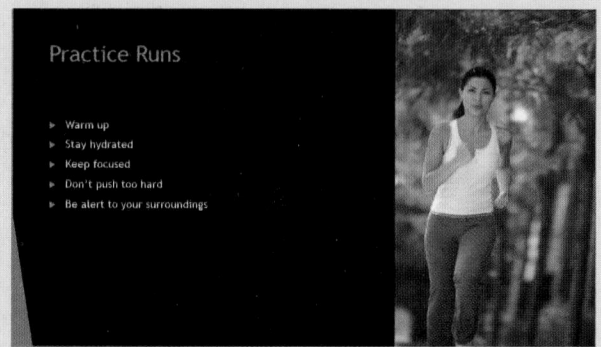
Figure 1-96 Picture aligned

5. Add a new slide and insert a picture of a table.
a. Display slide 6 if necessary. Click the **New Slide** drop-down arrow [*Home* tab, *Slides* group].
b. Select the **Title Only** layout.
c. Type the title Upcoming Marathons.
d. Click the **Insert** tab, and then click the **Pictures** button [*Images* group].
e. Locate your student data files.
f. Select **MarathonSchedule-01** and click **Insert** (or double-click the file name) to insert the picture.
 - Close the *Design Ideas* pane if it opens.
g. Click the **Alt Text** button [*Picture Tools Format* tab, *Accessibility* group] to open the *Alt Text* pane.
 - Delete text that may automatically appear.
h. Type the description Marathon Schedule.
i. Increase the picture *Width* to **8.5"** (*Picture Tools Format* tab, *Size* group).
j. Move the table so it is approximately centered in the black area (Figure 1-97).

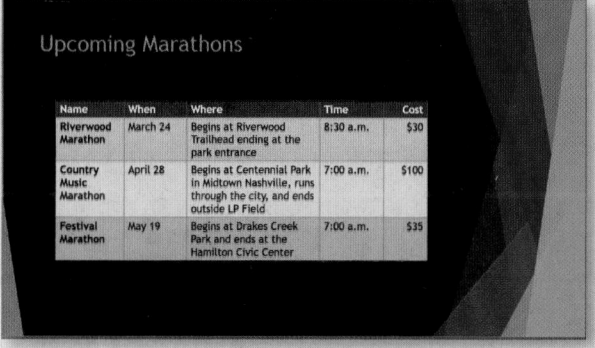
Figure 1-97 Picture of a table inserted and positioned

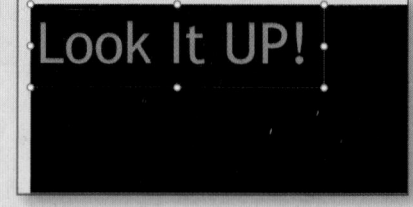
Figure 1-98 Title placeholder aligned top and left

6. Adjust placeholder size and alignment.
a. Display slide 8. Select the title placeholder and resize it horizontally on the right side so the text fits in the placeholder without extra horizontal space or word wrapping.
b. Click the **Align** button [*Drawing Tools Format* tab, *Arrange* group] and select **Align Left**. Repeat to select **Align Top** (Figure 1-98).
c. Display slide 9. Repeat steps 6a and 6b using **Align Center** and **Align Bottom**.

 d. Display slide 10. Repeat steps 6a and 6b using **Align Right** and **Align Middle**.
 e. Change the *Font Color* for the word "THERE!" on slide 10 to **Tan**, **Text 2** (row 1/column 4) [*Home* tab, *Font* group].

7. Apply one transition to all slides.
 a. Click the **Slide Sorter** button [*Status* bar].
 b. Click the **Transitions** tab.
 c. Select slide 1 and click the **Wipe** transition (*Subtle* group) from the gallery.
 d. Click **Effect Options** [*Transition* tab, *Transition to This Slide* group].
 e. Select **From Left** (Figure 1-99).

Figure 1-99 Transition *Effect Options*

 f. Click **Apply To All** [*Transition* tab, *Timing* group].

8. Select each of the following slides and apply different transitions (listed first) and effect options to emphasize the content.
 Slide 2: **Zoom** (*Exciting* group), **Out**
 Slide 7: **Doors** (*Exciting* group), **Horizontal**
 Slide 8: **Pan** (*Dynamic* group), **From Bottom**
 Slide 9: **Pan** (*Dynamic* group), **From Top**
 Slide 10: **Pan** (*Dynamic* group), **From Left**

9. Test transition movements.
 a. Select *Slide Sorter* view, and press **Ctrl+A** to select all slides.
 b. Click **Preview** [*Transitions* tab] to see the movements.
 c. Select the first slide and click the **Slide Show** button [*Status* bar].
 d. Click to advance each slide so you can see the movements in *Slide Show* view. At the end, click or press **Esc** to exit *Slide Show* view.

10. Change presentation properties.
 a. Click the **File** tab to open the *Backstage* view.
 b. Click **Info** on the left if it is not already selected. The properties display on the right.
 c. Click the *Title* field and type Train for a Marathon.
 d. Click the **Properties** button, then select **Advanced Properties** to open the *Properties* dialog box (Figure 1-100).

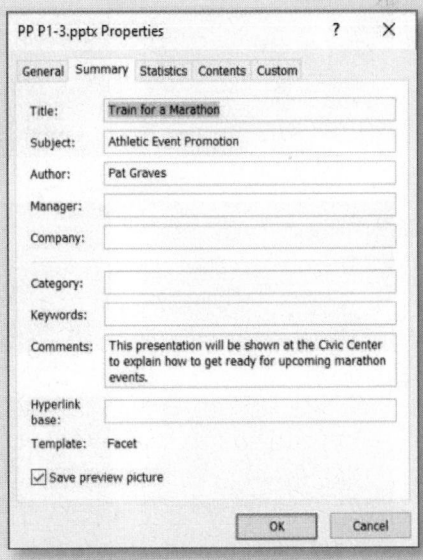

Figure 1-100 *Properties* dialog box

e. Click the **Summary** tab and type the following information in the respective fields:
 Title: Train for a Marathon *(already entered)*
 Subject: Athletic Event Promotion
 Author: Your Name *(unless it already appears)*
 Comments: This presentation will be shown at the Civic Center to explain how to get ready for upcoming marathon events.
f. Click **OK** to close the *Properties* dialog box and return to *Backstage* view.

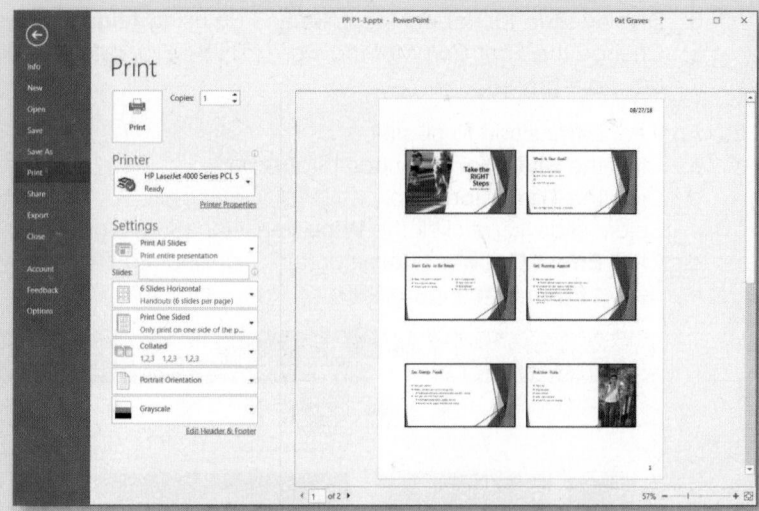

Figure 1-101 *Print* settings for a handout

11. Print slides as a handout. If your computer is not connected to a printer, skip step e.
 a. Click the **Print** button on the left.
 b. Select the appropriate printer.
 c. Change the following *Settings* by clicking the list arrow for each option (repeat as necessary for more than one change) (Figure 1-101):
 Which Slides to Print: **Print All Slides**
 What to Print: **Handouts, 6 Slides Horizontal, Frame Slides, Scale to Fit Paper**
 Print Order: **Collated**
 Orientation: **Portrait Orientation**
 Color Range: **Grayscale** (or **Color** if you prefer)
 d. Preview the handout by clicking the navigation buttons to see both pages.
 e. Click the **Print** button at the top of the *Backstage* view if you are connected to a printer.
 • Skip this step if you are not connected to a printer.
 f. Click the **Back arrow** to close *Backstage* view.

12. Press **Ctrl+S** to save the presentation (or click **Save** on the *File* tab or the *Quick Access* toolbar). Close the presentation (Figure 1-102).

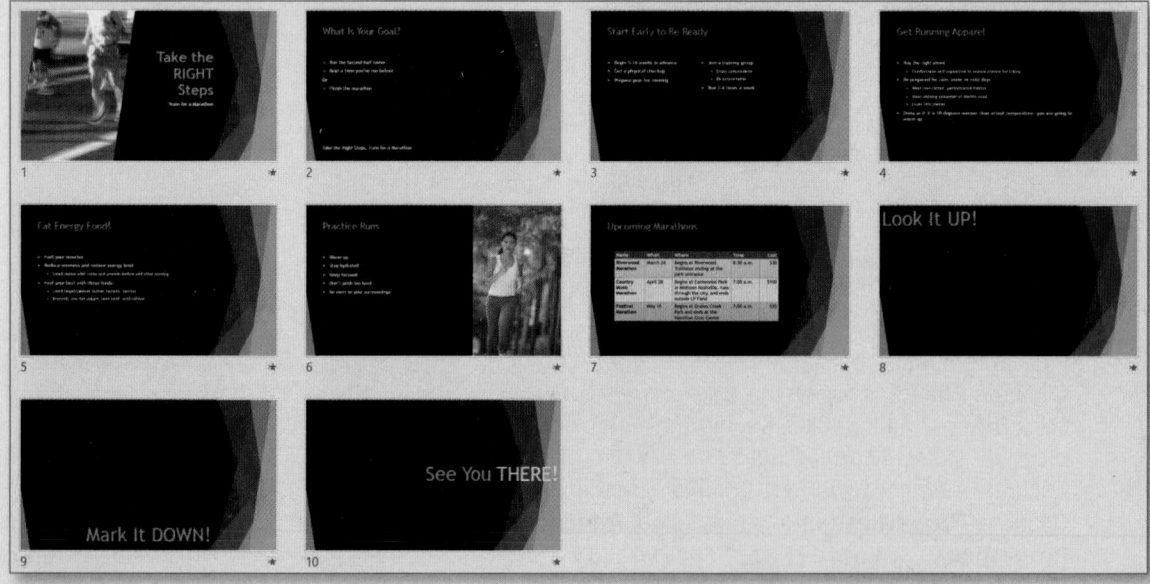

Figure 1-102 PP P1-3 completed

Chapter Summary

1.1 Create, open, and save a presentation (p. P1-3).

- Start developing presentation content with a blank presentation, a **Theme**, an existing presentation, or a **Template**.
- PowerPoint views enable you to look at your content in different ways.
- Use the **Zoom** feature to adjust the size of the current slide.
- The standard file format for presentation files has an extension of .pptx.
- *Backstage* view provides a variety of save and send options. For example, save a presentation as a PDF file or email a presentation file as an attachment.
- Additional themes and templates are available by searching online through PowerPoint or downloading them at Office.com.

1.2 Work with slides, layouts, placeholders, and text (p. P1-13).

- Use **placeholders** for presentation text and objects such as pictures, tables, and charts. Resize, reposition, and align text placeholders on slides.
- The *New Slide* button displays a gallery of slide layouts with placeholders arranged for different content.
- Change fonts using commands on the *Home* tab or the mini toolbar.
- *Change Case* changes the way words are capitalized.
- Format bulleted lists by changing the bullet symbol, size, and color.
- Use the **Format Painter** to copy formatting from one object and apply it to another object.
- The *Reuse Slides* feature enables you to insert slides from another presentation.
- Although potential spelling errors are automatically marked, use the *Spelling* dialog box to check for errors.
- Use the **Thesaurus** to find synonyms for words in your presentation.
- The **Design Ideas** pane provides a variety of slide layouts for listed text. This feature is not available in Office 2019.
- **PowerPoint QuickStarter** provides research and design ideas to start a presentation. This feature is not available in Office 2019.

1.3 Navigate between slides and organize content by reproducing and rearranging slides (p. P1-25).

- Move selected slides using a variety of methods to rearrange their sequence.
- Copy, paste, duplicate, and delete slides using the *Slides* pane or *Slide Sorter* view.

1.4 Change theme colors and fonts (p. P1-32).

- Presentation themes provide a cohesive look through the consistent use of background designs, colors, and font treatments.
- Consider the topic and tone of your presentation when choosing theme colors and fonts.

1.5 Insert headers and footers to add identifying information (p. P1-35).

- Both headers and footers are used for notes pages and handouts. They are applied to all pages or to individual pages.
- Footers usually appear at the bottom of slides but can appear in other locations. They are applied to all slides, all slides except the title slide, or to individual slides.

1.6 Insert, resize, and align a picture from a file (p. P1-40).

- PowerPoint supports different graphic file types; insert almost any digital image into slide shows.
- Use **sizing handles** or enter exact dimensions to increase or decrease a picture's size.
- Avoid distortion when resizing pictures by maintaining accurate height and width ratios.
- Align pictures with one another or with the slide.
- The **Design Ideas** pane provides a variety of slide layouts for inserted pictures. This feature is not available in Office 2019.

1.7 Apply and modify transition effects to add visual interest (p. P1-43).

- A **transition** is the visual effect that appears when one slide changes into another slide.
- The **Effect Options** command enables you to control the direction of transition movement.
- Apply transitions to one slide, multiple slides, or to all slides in a presentation.

1.8 Preview a presentation and print slides, handouts, and outlines (p. P1-45).

- Use *Backstage* view to examine each slide in your presentation before printing.
- The printer you select influences how slides appear in *Backstage* view.
- **Grayscale** shows shades of black.
- **Print Settings** control which slides to print, what to print, and the print order, orientation, and color range.

1.9 Apply presentation properties (p. P1-48).

- **Properties** are automatically recorded in your presentation file.
- Add properties such as subject, keywords, or category to help manage and track files.
- Edit properties in *Backstage* view under *Info* or by opening the *Properties* dialog box.

Check for Understanding

The SIMbook for this text (within your SIMnet account) provides the following resources for concept review.

- Multiple-choice questions
- Matching exercises
- Short answer questions

Guided Project 1-1

Jason Andrews is a sales associate for Classic Gardens and Landscaping (CGL) and frequently talks to customers when they visit the CGL showroom. For this project, you prepare a presentation he can use when introducing customers to CGL services.
[Student Learning Outcomes 1.1, 1.2, 1.3, 1.4, 1.5, 1.6]

Files Needed: *GardenView-01.jpg*, *CGLLogo-01.png*, and *PowerPoint 1-1_2019.pptx* (Student data files are available in the Library of your SIMnet account.)
Completed Project File Name: *[your initials] PowerPoint 1-1.pptx*

Skills Covered in This Project

- Create a new presentation using a theme.
- Change theme colors and background style.
- Change theme fonts.
- Add slides.
- Use *PowerPoint Designer* to apply slide layouts.
- Change font size.
- Rearrange slides.
- Use the *Format Painter*.
- Insert a footer.
- Check spelling.
- Adjust placeholder position.
- Insert, align, and resize a picture.
- Save a presentation.

1. Create a new presentation using a theme. If you are using Office 2019, open **PowerPoint 1-1_2019** and skip steps 1a and 1b, step 3, and step 12 as you complete this project.
 a. Click the **File** tab, and then click **New**.
 b. Double-click the **Ion** theme (Figure 1-103).

2. Save the presentation as [your initials] PowerPoint 1-1.

3. Change the theme colors.
 Office 2019 Note: Skip this step.
 a. Click the **Design** tab.
 b. Click the **More** button [*Variants* group] to select each of the following options:
 Colors: Scroll down the list and select the **Paper** theme.
 Background Styles: Select **Style 3** from the gallery (third option/first row) (Figure 1-104).
 Fonts: Select the **Candara** font group.

4. Type the following text in the placeholders on slide 1. Press **Ctrl+Enter** to move between placeholders.
 Title: Creating Beautiful Outdoor Spaces
 Subtitle: Jason Andrews, Sales Associate

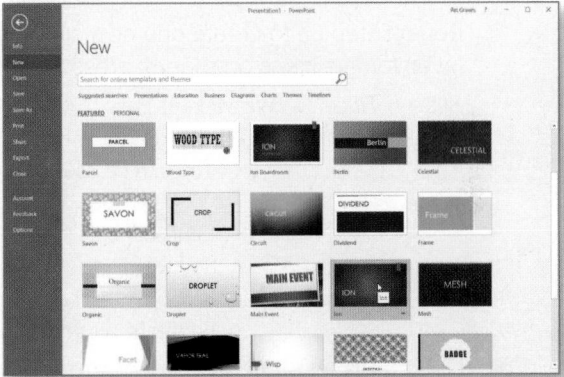

Figure 1-103 *Ion* theme selected

Figure 1-104 *Background Styles*

5. Format the title and subtitle.
 a. Apply **Bold** and **Shadow** [*Home* tab, *Font* group] to both the title and subtitle.
 b. Change the title *Font Size* to **66 pt**. and resize the title placeholder to remove extra space at the top.
 c. Change the subtitle *Font Size* to **28 pt**.

6. Add slides.
 a. Click the **New Slide** button [*Home* tab, *Slides* group] to add a slide that automatically has the **Title and Content** layout. Type the following text for slide 2:

Title:	Our Services
Bulleted items:	• Garden center
	• Tree nursery
	• Gift shop
	• Delivery and installation
	• Patios and irrigation systems

 b. Repeat step 6a to create two new slides with the following text.

Slide 3 Title:	Available Products
Bulleted items:	• Shrubs, perennials, annuals
	• Soils and mulches
	• Garden décor including fountains
	• Shade trees and evergreen screening trees
	• Flowering or ornamental trees
	• Trees and plants for Christmas
Slide 4 Title:	Why Sustainable Design?
Bulleted items:	• Energy efficiency increased
	• Water efficiency increased
	• Dependency on chemicals decreased
	• Vigor assured through native and hardy plants

 c. Repeat step 6a to create one new slide with the following text. Press **Tab** to indent (increase list level) for five items on slide 5; press **Shift+Tab** to decrease the list level.

Slide 5 Title:	We Make It Easy
Bulleted items:	• We can do the entire project or we can assist
	• You can do as much, or as little, as you like
	• We will provide:
	• Landscape design planning or just advice
	• Soil testing
	• Low-cost delivery
	• Fountain set up

 d. Click the **New Slide** drop-down arrow [*Home* tab, *Slides* group] and click the **Title Slide** layout. Type this text in the placeholders:

Title:	Call for a Consultation
Subtitle:	615-792-8833

7. Move the slide 5 thumbnail before slide 4.

8. Apply **Bold** and use the *Format Painter*.
 a. Display slide 2, select the title text placeholder, and apply **Bold** [*Home* tab, *Font* group].
 b. Double-click the **Format Painter** button [*Home* tab, *Clipboard* group] so you can apply this change more than one time.
 c. Press **Page Down** and click the title text placeholder on slide 3.
 d. Repeat for slides 4 and 5.
 e. Click the **Format Painter** button or press **Esc** to stop applying formatting.

9. Create a footer with the company name in the footer text.
 a. Click the **Header & Footer** button [*Insert* tab, *Text* group] to open the *Header and Footer* dialog box.
 b. Check the following options on the *Slide* tab: **Date and time** with **Update automatically, Slide number**, and **Footer** (Figure 1-105).
 c. Type Classic Gardens and Landscapes in the *Footer* text box.
 d. Select **Don't show on title slide**.
 e. Click the **Apply to All** button.

Figure 1-105 *Header and Footer* dialog box

10. Click the **Spelling** button [*Review* tab, *Proofing* group] and correct any spelling errors you find.

11. Change case.
 a. Display slide 1 and select the subtitle.
 b. Click the **Change Case** button [*Home* tab, *Font* group] and select **Capitalize Each Word**.

12. Apply a *Design Ideas* layout to make the title slide more distinctive. **Office 2019 Note**: The *Design Ideas* pane will not open when using Office 2019, so skip this step.
 a. Display slide 1 and click the **Insert** tab.
 b. Click the **Pictures** button to open the *Insert Picture* dialog box.
 c. Locate your student data files and select *GardenView-01*.
 d. Click **Insert** and the *Design Ideas* pane opens (Figure 1-106).
 e. Click the layout similar to Figure 1-107 to apply it. Text sizes will automatically adjust for this new layout.

13. Click the **Pictures** button, locate your student data files, select *CGL Logo-01*. Click **Insert**.
 a. Close the *Design Ideas* pane if it opens.
 b. Resize the logo *Width* to **5"** [*Picture Tools Format* tab, *Size* group] and the *Height* will automatically adjust.
 c. Drag the logo to the bottom right of the slide.

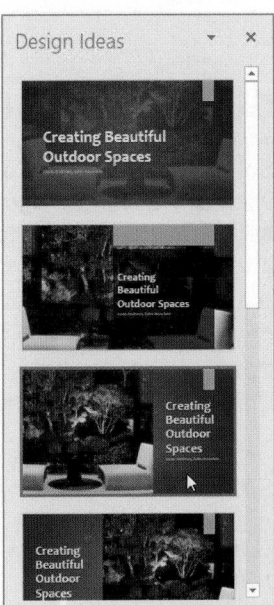

Figure 1-106 *Design Ideas* pane

14. Edit text on the last slide.
 a. Select slide 6.
 b. Increase the *Font Size* for the subtitle phone number to **48 pt.** and apply **Bold**.
 c. Move the subtitle phone number down to fit evenly between the title and the bottom of the slide.

Figure 1-107 Title slide completed

15. Save and close the presentation (Figure 1-108).

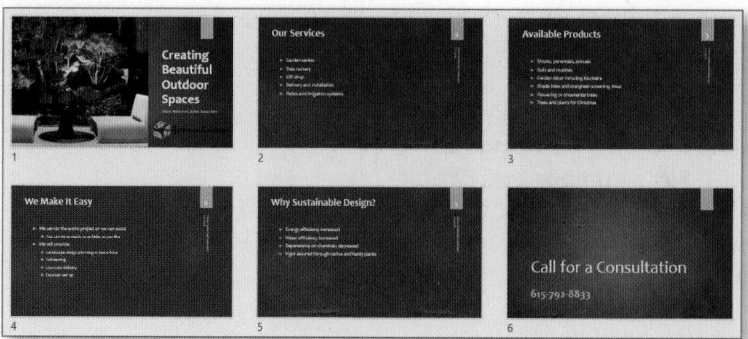

Figure 1-108 PowerPoint 1-1 completed

Guided Project 1-2

Solution Seekers, Inc., a management consulting firm, is preparing a series of brief presentations to be used in a training program for new hires. For this project, you develop a presentation about how to get better results when writing email messages.
[Student Learning Outcomes 1.1, 1.2, 1.3, 1.6, 1.7, 1.8, 1.9]

Files Needed: **E-mailResults-01.pptx**, **E-mailContent-01.pptx**, **AtSymbol-01.jpg**, and **PowerPoint 1-2_2019.pptx** (Student data files are available in the Library of your SIMnet account.)
Completed Project File Name: **[your initials] PowerPoint 1-2.pptx**

Skills Covered in This Project

- Open a presentation.
- Change bullets.
- Reuse slides from another presentation.
- Rearrange slides.
- Check spelling.
- Insert a picture.
- Use *PowerPoint Designer* to apply slide layouts.
- Apply transitions.
- Preview a presentation.
- Change presentation properties.
- Print a handout.
- Save a presentation.

1. Open and resave a presentation.
 a. Click the **File** tab, select **Open**, and click **Browse**.
 b. Locate your student data files and double-click **E-mailResults-01** to open the presentation. If you are using Office 2019, open **PowerPoint 1-2_2019** and skip step 7 as you complete this project.
 - *Note*: If the presentation opens in *Protected View*, click the **Enable Editing** button in the *Message* bar at the top of the presentation so you can modify it.
 c. Press **F12** (or **Fn+F12** if necessary for your computer) to open the *Save As* dialog box and save this presentation as [your initials] PowerPoint 1-2 in the appropriate location.

2. Change the bullets for additional emphasis.
 a. Display slide 2. Select the bulleted text.
 b. Click the **Bullets** drop-down arrow [*Home* tab, *Paragraph* group].

c. Select **Bullets and Numbering** to open the *Bullets and Numbering* dialog box.

d. Change the *Size* to **80%** of text.

e. Click the **Color** button and select **Orange, Accent 6** (last color/first row) (Figure 1-109).

f. Click the **Customize** button to open the *Symbol* dialog box.

g. Scroll down the *Font* list and select **Wingdings 3** (Figure 1-110).

h. Select the **Black Right-Pointing Pointer** (Character code 117).

i. Click **OK** to close the *Symbol* dialog box. Click **OK** again to close the *Bullets and Numbering* dialog box.

3. Reuse slides from another presentation to follow slide 2, the current slide.

a. Click the **New Slide** drop-down arrow and select **Reuse Slides**.

b. Click **Browse** on the *Reuse Slides* pane to open the *Browse* dialog box. Locate your student data files.

c. Select the presentation *E-mailContent-01* and click **Open**.

 • This presentation has spelling errors that you will correct later.

d. Click all three slides on the *Reuse Slides* pane to insert them (Figure 1-111).

e. Close the *Reuse Slides* pane.

4. Use the *Thumbnail* pane to rearrange the six slides in this order:

 1 Getting Results with E-mail
 2 Ask These Questions
 3 Why?
 4 Write a Meaningful Subject Line
 5 Organize It!
 6 Keep It Short

5. Select slide 1. Click the **Spelling** button [*Review* tab, *Proofing* group].

a. Correct all spelling errors: "receive," "Careless," "organized," "capture," "response," and "separate."

b. Click **OK** when the spell check is complete.

c. Close the *Design Ideas* pane if it opens.

6. Use *Format Painter* to change list bullets.

a. Display slide 2 and select the body placeholder with the bulleted text.

b. Double-click the **Format Painter** button [*Home* tab, *Clipboard* group] so you can apply what you have copied more than one time.

c. Press **Page Down** and click the list on slide 3 to apply the change for the first-level bullets.

Figure 1-109 Change bullet color

Figure 1-110 Change bullet symbol

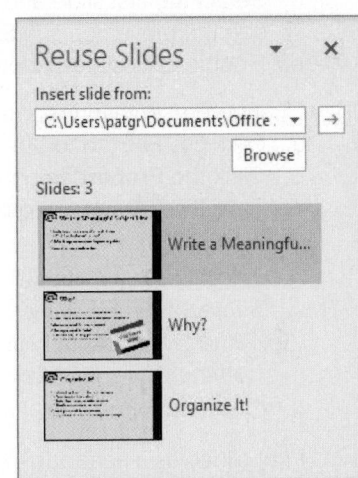

Figure 1-111 *Reuse Slides* pane

d. Repeat for slides 4 and 5.
e. Press **Esc** to end formatting or click the **Format Painter** button again.
 - Changing bullets for all slides could also be accomplished using the *Slide Master*.

7. Insert a picture and apply a *Design Ideas* layout.
 Office 2019 Note: The *Design Ideas* pane will not open when using Office 2019, so skip this step.
 a. Select slide 6 and delete the picture on the right.
 b. Click the **Insert** tab, and then click the **Pictures** button.
 c. Locate your student data files.
 d. Select *At-Symbol-01* and click **Insert**. The *Design Ideas* pane opens.
 e. Click the thumbnail similar to the layout in Figure 1-112.
 f. Close the *Design Ideas* pane.

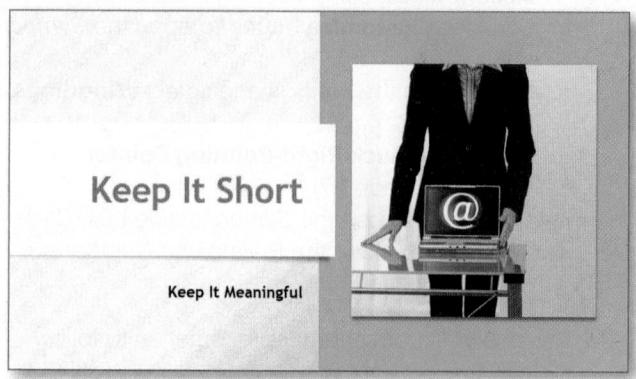

Figure 1-112 Ending slide with *Design Ideas* layout

8. Select the picture on slide 6 and click the **Alt Text** button [*Picture Tools Format* tab, *Accessibility* group] to open the *Alt Text* pane.
 - Delete text that may automatically appear.
 a. Type the description A person showing notebook features.
 b. Close the *Alt Text* pane.
 c. Select the title text, "Keep It Short." Click the **Font Color** button [*Home* tab, *Font* group] and select **Orange, Accent 6** (last color/first row).

9. Apply one transition and effect option to all slides.
 a. Click the **Transitions** tab.
 b. Click the **Switch** transition from the gallery (*Exciting* group).
 c. Click **Effect Options** [*Transition to This Slide* group] and select **Left**.
 d. Click **Apply To All** [*Timing* group].

10. Preview the presentation in both *Slide Sorter* and *Slide Show* views.
 a. Click the **Slide Sorter** button [*Status* bar].
 b. Click the **Zoom Out** button (*Status* bar), if necessary, to see all slide thumbnails.
 c. Press **Ctrl+A** to select all slides. Click **Preview** [*Transitions* tab] to examine the movements in *Slide Sorter* view.
 d. Select the first slide and click the **Slide Show** button [*Status* bar]. Advance through the slides to see the movements in *Slide Show* view.
 e. Double-click slide 1 to open the slide in *Normal* view.

11. Change presentation properties.
 a. Click the **File** tab to open *Backstage* view and display the **Info** area.
 b. Click the **Properties** button and select **Advanced Properties**.
 c. Type the following information in the respective fields on the **Summary** tab. The title may appear automatically.

Title:	Getting Results with E-mail
Subject:	Writing
Author:	Your Name (unless it already appears)
Comments:	This presentation is for the new hire seminar.

 d. Click **OK** to close the *Properties* dialog box.

12. Print slides as a handout.
 a. Click the **Print** button on the left of the *Backstage* view.
 b. Select the appropriate printer.

 c. Change the following *Settings* by clicking the button list arrow for each option:

Which Slides to Print:	**Print All Slides**
What to Print:	**Handouts, 6 Slides Horizontal, Frame Slides, Scale to Fit Paper**
Print Order:	**Collated**
Orientation:	**Portrait**
Color Range:	**Grayscale** (or **Color** if you prefer)

 d. Click the **Print** button at the top of the *Backstage* view.
- Skip this step if you are not connected to a printer.

13. Save and close the presentation (Figure 1-113).

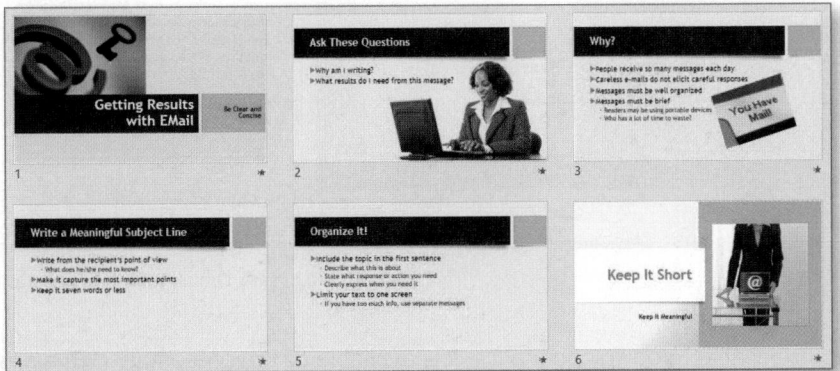

Figure 1-113 PowerPoint 1-2 completed

Guided Project 1-3

At Placer Hills Real Estate, realtors are always thinking of ways to help sellers make their homes more marketable and help buyers find the right home. For this project, you prepare a presentation for realtors to use when they speak with individual clients to explain how sellers can provide an added-value benefit by offering a home warranty.
[Student Learning Outcomes 1.1, 1.2, 1.5, 1.6, 1.7, 1.9]

Files Needed: ***PHRELogo-01.png*** and ***BuyerIncentive-01.pptx*** *(Student data files are available in the Library of your SIMnet account.)*
Completed Project File Name: ***[your initials] PowerPoint 1-3.pptx***

Skills Covered in This Project

- Create a new presentation using an online template.
- Change font size.
- Adjust picture position.
- Insert a picture.

- Reuse slides from another presentation.
- Check spelling.
- Insert a footer.
- Apply transitions.
- Change presentation properties.
- Save a presentation.

1. Create a new presentation using an online template.
 a. Click the **File** tab, and then click **New**.
 b. Type the word sales in the search box and click the **Start Searching** button or press **Enter**.
 c. Select the **Business product overview presentation** to open a description (Figure 1-114). Click **Create** to download the presentation.

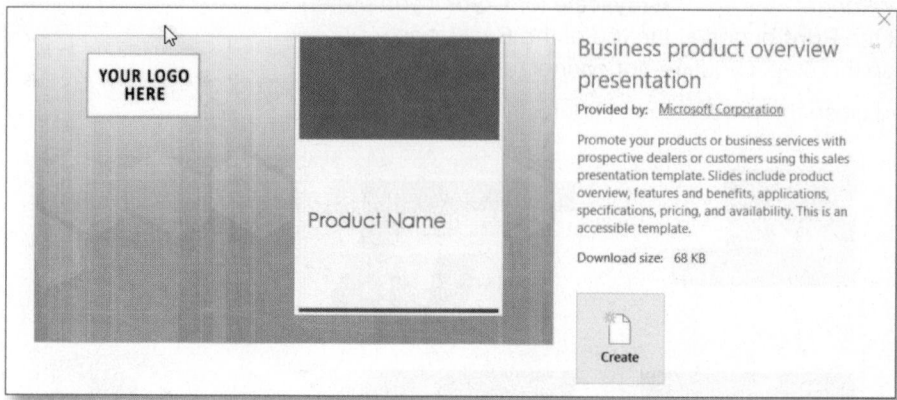

Figure 1-114 Online template description

 • If you are unable to download the file, it is available as the presentation ***BusinessProduct Overview-01*** in your student data files.
 d. Select slide 1 in the *Thumbnail* pane and then press **Ctrl+A** to select all slides.
 e. Press **Delete** to remove all slides so you can use only the template.
2. Click the **New Slide** button [*Home* tab, *Slides* group] to insert a slide with the *Title Slide* layout.
3. Select the "Insert product photo here" placeholder and press **Delete**.
4. Type the following text in the placeholders:

 Title: Compete with New Homes

 Subtitle: Angie O'Connor, Sales Associate
5. Save the presentation as [your initials] PowerPoint 1-3 in the appropriate location.
6. Increase the title *Font Size* to **48 pt**. and apply **Bold** [*Home* tab, *Font* group].
7. Reduce the size of the subtitle placeholder to fit the text and move it to the bottom of the slide below the white rectangle.
8. Insert the PHRE company logo.
 a. Click the **Pictures** button [*Insert* tab, *Images* group] and locate your student data files.
 b. Select ***PHRELogo-01*** and click **Insert** (or double-click the file name) to insert the logo.
 c. Position this logo in the lower right of the white rectangle (Figure 1-115).
9. Click the **Alt Text** button [*Picture Tools Format* tab, *Accessibility* group] to open the *Alt Text* pane.

 a. Delete text that may automatically appear.
 b. Type the description The Placer Hills Real Estate logo.
 c. Close the *Alt Text* pane.
10. Reuse slides from another presentation.
 a. Click the **New Slide** drop-down arrow and select **Reuse Slides**.
 b. Click **Browse** on the *Reuse Slides* pane to open the *Browse* dialog box. Locate your student data files.

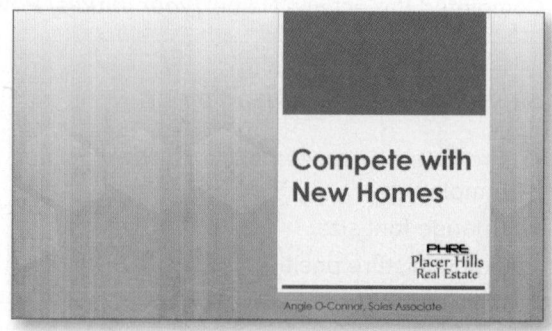

Figure 1-115 Title slide completed

c. Select the presentation ***BuyerIncentive-01*** and click **Open**.
d. Click slides **2–6** (starting with the "Seller Needs" slide) on the *Reuse Slides* pane to insert them (Figure 1-116).
e. Close the *Reuse Slides* pane.

11. Click the **Spelling** button [*Review* tab, *Proofing* group] and correct the following spelling errors: "Competitive", "maintained", "replacement", and "deductible". Click **OK**.

12. Display slide 6. Resize the picture using the center sizing handles on all four sides to stretch the picture to cover the white rectangle.

13. Click the **Alt Text** button [*Picture Tools Format* tab, *Accessibility* group] to open the *Alt Text* pane.
 a. Delete text that may automatically appear.
 b. Type the description A picture of a home with a sold sign in the yard.
 c. Close the *Alt Text* pane.

14. Add a footer.
 a. Click the **Header & Footer** button [*Insert* tab, *Text* group].
 b. On the *Slide* tab, select **Slide number** and **Footer**.
 c. In the *Footer* text box, type Placer Hills Real Estate.
 d. Select **Don't show on title slide**.
 e. Click the **Apply to All** button.
 f. The footer appears in small text on the lower right.
 g. Delete the page number that is at the top of the picture on slide 6.

15. Apply one transition to all slides.
 a. Select slide 1. Click the **More** button [*Transitions* tab, *Transition to This Slide* group] to open the gallery. Click the **Box** effect (*Exciting* group).
 b. Click **Effect Options** [*Transitions* tab, *Transition to This Slide* group]. Select **From Bottom** (Figure 1-117).
 c. Click **Apply To All** [*Transitions* tab, *Timing* group].
 d. Click the **Slide Show** button [*Status* bar] and advance through the slides to see the movements in *Slide Show* view.

16. Change presentation properties.
 a. Click the **File** tab, then click **Info**.
 b. Click the **Properties** button and select **Advanced Properties** to open the *Properties* dialog box.
 c. Type the following information as needed in the respective fields on the *Summary* tab:

 Title: Compete with New Homes
 Subject: Sales Strategies
 Author: Angie O'Connor
 Comments: Seller can offer a home warranty to encourage buyer purchase.

 d. Click **OK** to close the *Properties* dialog box.

17. Save and close the presentation (Figure 1-118).

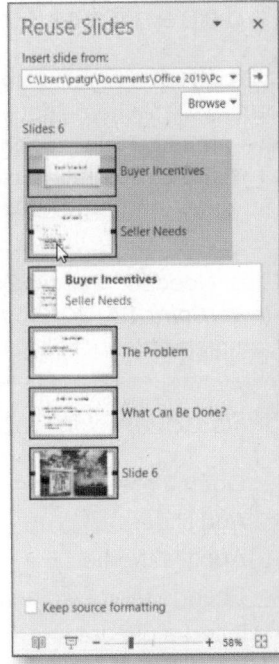

Figure 1-116 *Reuse Slides* pane

Figure 1-117 *Transition Effect Options*

Figure 1-118 **PowerPoint 1-3 completed**

Independent Project 1-4

Wilson Home Entertainment Systems (WHES) assists customers with everything from a single television purchase to a home network installation to the design and construction of an elaborate home theater. For this project, you work on a presentation that sales representatives can use to describe the capabilities of WHES to potential customers.
[Student Learning Outcomes 1.1, 1.2, 1.4, 1.6, 1.7, 1.9]

Files Needed: **SpecialEnvironment-01.pptx**, **WHESLogo-01.png**, **Family-01.jpg**, **Theater1-01.jpg**, and **PowerPoint 1-4_2019.pptx** *(Student data files are available in the* Library *of your SIMnet account.)*
Completed Project File Name: **[your initials] PowerPoint 1-4.pptx**

Skills Covered in This Project

- Open a presentation.
- Add slides.
- Apply a theme.
- Change theme colors.
- Insert a picture.

- Adjust placeholders.
- Apply a *Design Ideas* layout.
- Check spelling.
- Apply transitions.
- Change presentation properties.
- Save a presentation.

1. Open the presentation **SpecialEnvironment-01**. If you are using Office 2019, open **PowerPoint 1-4_2019** and skip steps 3 and 8 as you complete this project.
 - *Note*: If the presentation opens in *Protected View*, click the **Enable Editing** button in the *Message* bar at the top of the presentation so you can modify it.

Figure 1-119 Change variant

2. Save the presentation as [your initials] PowerPoint 1-4.
3. Apply a theme and change theme colors.

 Office 2019 Note: Skip this step.
 a. Select the **Integral** theme and the third **Variant** (Figure 1-119).
 b. Select **Colors** and the **Orange Red** theme colors.

4. Insert a new slide after slide 2 with the *Title and Content* layout. Type the following text for slide 3:

Slide 3 title:	Sales
Bulleted items:	• Authorized dealer for the highest-quality home theater technology in the industry
	• Televisions
	• Projectors
	• Blu-Ray Players
	• Cables

5. Insert, adjust, and align pictures.
 a. Display slide 1 and delete the popcorn picture.
 b. Delete the subtitle placeholder.
 c. Insert **Family-01** and **WHESLogo-01** from your student data files. The pictures may overlap, but you will move them in the next steps.
 d. Close the *Design Ideas* pane if it opens.
 e. Increase the family picture size (*Height* **5"** and *Width* **7.52"**) and align it on the top right (Figure 1-120).
 f. Position the logo on the white area so it covers the small vertical line below the picture.

6. Change the presentation title.
 a. Move the title placeholder up to the red area on the left.
 b. Change the *Font Color* to **White, Background 1** (first color/first row) and increase the *Font Size* to **66 pt**.

c. Apply **Bold** and **Shadow**.
d. Resize the title placeholder so it word wraps as shown.

7. Click the **Spelling** button and correct the following spelling errors: "cabling", "television", and "calibration".

8. Insert a picture and apply a *Design Ideas* layout.

 Office 2019 Note: The *Design Ideas* pane will not open when using Office 2019, so skip this step.

 a. Display slide 2.
 b. Insert **Theater1-01** from your student data files and the *Design Ideas* pane opens.
 c. Click a layout with a picture background (Figure 1-121).
 d. Close the *Design Ideas* pane.
 e. Select the body text placeholder and change the *Font Size* to **36 pt**.

9. Display slide 6. Increase the picture size (*Width* **11"** and *Height* automatically adjusts) and center it horizontally in the space below the text.

10. Apply one transition to all slides.
 a. Select the **Cube** transition.
 b. Apply the **From Bottom** effect option.
 c. Click **Apply To All**.

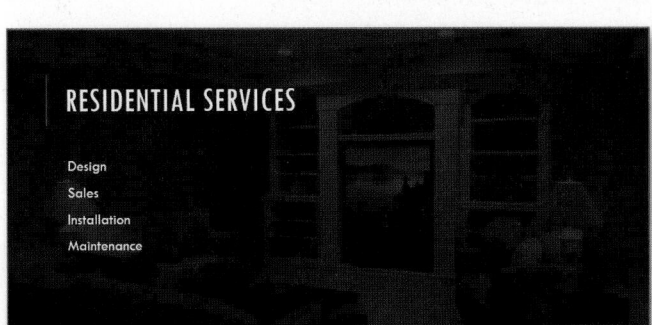

Figure 1-120 Title slide completed

Figure 1-121 *Design Ideas* layout applied

11. Open the *Properties* dialog box and insert the following presentation properties as needed on the *Summary* tab:

 Title: Create Your Special Environment
 Subject: Residential Services
 Author: Liam Martin

12. Close the *Properties* dialog box.

13. Save and close the presentation (Figure 1-122).

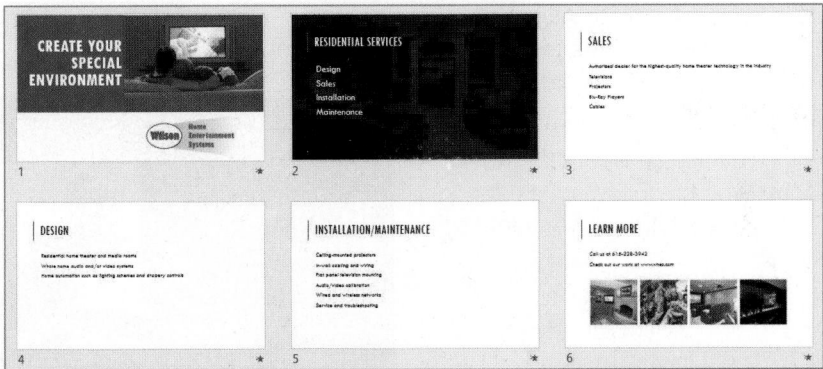

Figure 1-122 PowerPoint 1-4 completed

Independent Project 1-5

The advising offices in the Sierra Pacific Community College (SPCC) District work to assist students throughout the completion of their academic programs. Because SPCC has a large population of students who are retraining themselves for different types of employment, job-related information is especially important. For this project, you prepare a presentation about writing resumes.
[Student Learning Outcomes 1.1, 1.2, 1.3, 1.4, 1.7, 1.8]

Files Needed: ***ResumeUpdates-01*** and ***ResumeContent-01.pptx*** *(Student data files are available in the Library of your SIMnet account.)*
Completed Project File Name: ***[your initials] PowerPoint 1-5.pptx***

Skills Covered in This Project

- Open a presentation.
- Change theme background style and fonts.
- Change case.
- Adjust sizing and alignment.
- Add slides.
- Reuse slides from another presentation.
- Check spelling.
- Apply transitions.
- Print a handout.
- Save a presentation.

1. Open the **ResumeUpdates-01** presentation from your student data files.
 - *Note*: If the presentation opens in *Protected View*, click the **Enable Editing** button in the *Message* bar at the top of the presentation so you can modify it.

2. Save the presentation as [your initials] PowerPoint 1-5.

3. Change theme style and font.
 a. Select the *Design* tab and click the button in the *Variants* group.
 b. Select **Background Styles** and choose **Style 4** (last option/first row) (Figure 1-123).
 c. Repeat step 4a, select **Fonts**, and choose **Georgia**.

4. Adjust placeholder sizing and text.
 a. Display slide 1 and select the title placeholder. Change text alignment to **Align Left**.
 b. Resize the title placeholder so the text word wraps on two lines.
 c. Select the subtitle placeholder and change text alignment to **Align Left** (Figure 1-124).

5. Insert two new slides after slide 2 with the *Title and Content* layout. Type the following text for slides 3 and 4. Indent the subpoints on slide 3 (the last three items).

 Slide 3 title: Accomplishments, Not Duties
 Bulleted items: • Include only the most impressive details about your career

Figure 1-123 *Background Styles*

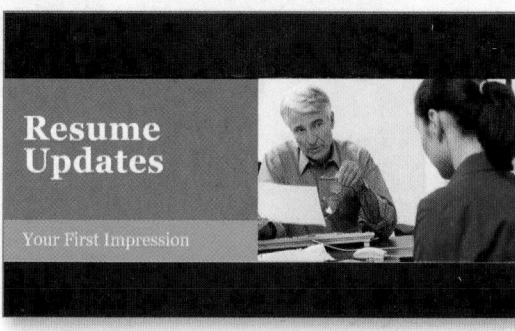

Figure 1-124 **Title slide completed**

- Quantify your day-to-day tasks
 - How many times?
 - What was the result?
 - How much money was saved?

Slide 4 title: Proofread
Bulleted items:
- Employers take spelling and grammar errors as signs of carelessness
- Ask a trusted friend or colleague to look at your resume

6. Reuse slides from another presentation.
 a. Move your insertion point after slide 3.
 b. Open the *Reuse Slides* pane and browse to find **ResumeContent-01** from your student data files.
 c. Insert all three slides and close the *Reuse Slides* pane.

7. Display slide 8, the last slide. Adjust placeholders and insert text.
 a. Select the title placeholder and change text alignment to **Align Left**. Type Success!.
 b. Resize the title placeholder to fit the text.
 c. Delete the subtitle placeholder.

8. Click the **Spelling** button [*Review* tab, *Proofing* group] and correct the following spelling errors: "redundant," "achievements," and any other errors you find.

9. Apply the **Reveal** transition with the **Through Black from Right** effect option to all slides.

10. Print slides as an outline (Figure 1-125).

11. Save and close the presentation (Figure 1-126).

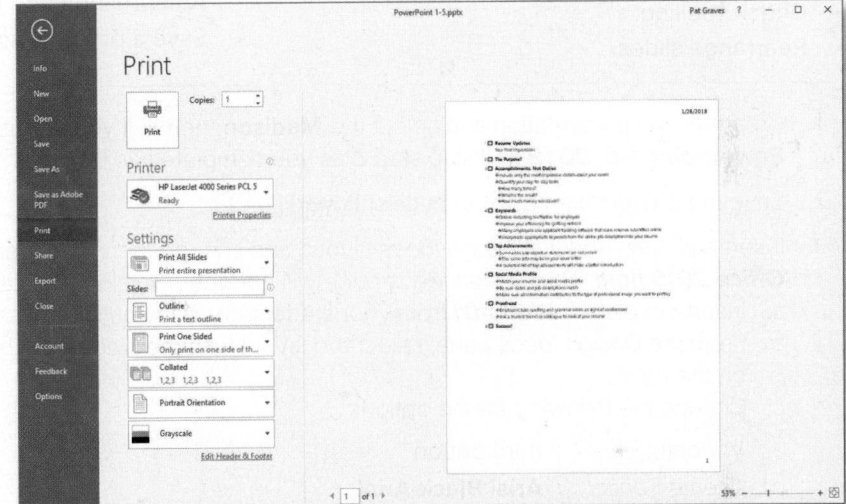

Figure 1-125 Print settings for an outline

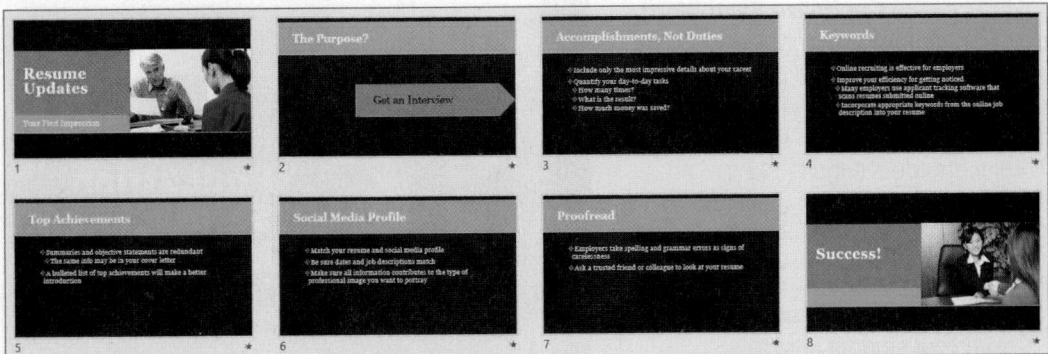

Figure 1-126 PowerPoint 1-5 completed

Independent Project 1-6

At the Hamilton Civic Center, workshops are offered to the community to address fitness, health, and wellness issues. For this project, you develop a presentation for an upcoming series about helping families become more active.

[Student Learning Outcomes 1.1, 1.2, 1.3, 1.4, 1.5, 1.6, 1.7, 1.9]

Files Needed: **PedestrianSafety-01.pptx, Walk1-01.jpg, Walk2-01.jpg**, and **PowerPoint 1-6_2019.pptx** *(Student data files are available in the* Library *of your SIMnet account.)*
Completed Project File Name: **[your initials] PowerPoint 1-6.pptx**

Skills Covered in This Project

- Create a new presentation using a theme.
- Change theme colors and fonts.
- Change case.
- Reuse slides from another presentation.
- Check spelling.
- Rearrange slides.

- Insert a picture.
- Apply *Design Ideas* layouts.
- Adjust placeholders.
- Insert a footer.
- Apply transitions.
- Add presentation properties.
- Save a presentation.

1. Create a new presentation and select the **Madison** theme. If you are using Office 2019, open **PowerPoint 1-6_2019** and skip step 3 as you complete this project.

2. Save the presentation as [your initials] PowerPoint 1-6.

3. Insert a picture, apply a *Design Ideas* layout, and change theme options
 Office 2019 note: The *Design Ideas* pane will not open, so skip this step.
 a. Insert the picture **Walk1-01** from your student data files on slide 1.
 b. From the *Design Ideas* pane, select the layout with the picture on the left and a larger text area on the right.
 c. Change the following theme options:

Variant:	third option
Theme Fonts:	**Arial Black-Arial**

4. Display slide 1 and type the following text:

Title:	Pedestrian Safety Matters
Subtitle:	Keeping that new year's resolution to be more active

5. Adjust text.
 a. Select the subtitle text and change the case to **Capitalize Each Word**.
 b. Change subtitle *Font Size* to **24 pt.,** click **Align Left**, and move the placeholder up.
 c. Align the left side of both placeholders (Figure 1-127).

6. Reuse slides from another presentation.
 a. Open the *Reuse Slides* pane and browse to find **PedestrianSafety-01** from your student data files.
 b. Insert all five slides and close the *Reuse Slides* pane.

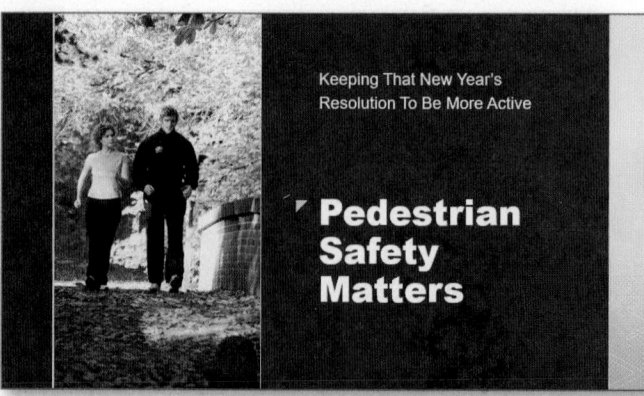

Figure 1-127 Title slide completed

7. Display slide 2. Put your insertion point in front of the word "Guard" and press **Enter** to show this text as the last item in the list.

8. Display slide 1. Click the **Spelling** button [*Review* tab, *Proofing* group] and correct the following spelling errors: "pedestrians," "aggressive," "Remember," "traffic," "Regardless," and "cloudy."

9. Adjust slide order as follows:
 1. Pedestrian Safety Matters (title slide)
 2. Take a Walk
 3. Respect Your Surroundings
 4. Wear the Right Outfits
 5. Increase Your Visibility
 6. Use Caution

10. Add a footer with the text Pedestrian Safety Matters. Apply it to all slides except the title slide.

11. Insert and position a picture.
 a. Display slide 6. From your student data files, insert the picture *Walk2-01*.
 b. Close the *Design Ideas* pane if it opens.
 c. Move the picture to the upper-left corner of the slide (see Figure 1-128).

12. Apply the **Push** transition with the **From Right** effect option to all slides.

13. Preview the transitions in *Slide Show* view.

14. Open the *Properties* dialog box and insert the following presentation properties as needed on the *Summary* tab:

 Title: Pedestrian Safety Matters
 Subject: Active Lifestyle
 Author: Anna Lorenzo

15. Close the *Properties* dialog box.

16. Save and close the presentation (Figure 1-128).

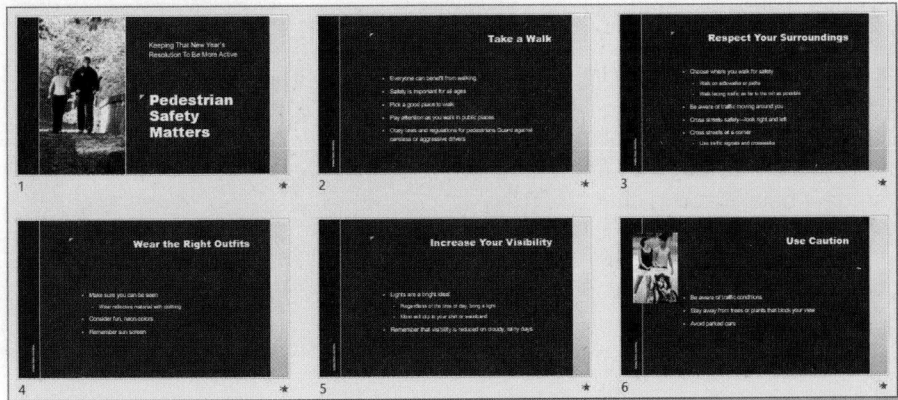

Figure 1-128 PowerPoint 1-6 completed

Improve It Project 1-7

For this project, you revise a presentation for Margaret Jepson, insurance agent at Central Sierra Insurance. You adjust theme colors and fonts, and add information to the slide show, including a picture. [Student Learning Outcomes 1.1, 1.2, 1.3, 1.4, 1.5, 1.6, 1.7, 1.8, 1.9]

Files Needed: ***TotaledCar-01.pptx***, ***Travel-01.jpg***, and ***CSILogo-01.png*** *(Student data files are available in the* Library *of your SIMnet account.)*
Completed Project File Name: *[your initials] **PowerPoint 1-7.pptx***

Skills Covered in This Project

- Open a presentation.
- Change theme colors.
- Check spelling.
- Insert a picture.

- Adjust placeholders.
- Insert a footer.
- Apply transitions.
- Change presentation properties.
- Print a handout.
- Save a presentation.

1. Open the presentation ***TotaledCar-01*** from your student data files.
 - *Note*: If the presentation opens in *Protected View*, click the **Enable Editing** button in the *Message* bar at the top of the presentation so you can modify it.

2. Save the presentation as [your initials] PowerPoint 1-7.

3. Change the following theme options:

Theme Colors:	**Blue Green**
Background Style:	**Style 3**
Theme Font:	**Trebuchet MS**

4. Format text and insert a picture logo.
 a. Display slide 1 and change the title *Font Size* to **66 pt**.
 b. Resize the title placeholder to fit the text on two lines.
 c. Delete the subtitle placeholder.
 d. Insert the picture ***CSILogo-01*** from your student data files and change the *Width* to **5"**.
 e. Position the logo on the shape across the bottom of the slide (Figure 1-129).
 f. Close the *Design Ideas* pane if it opens.

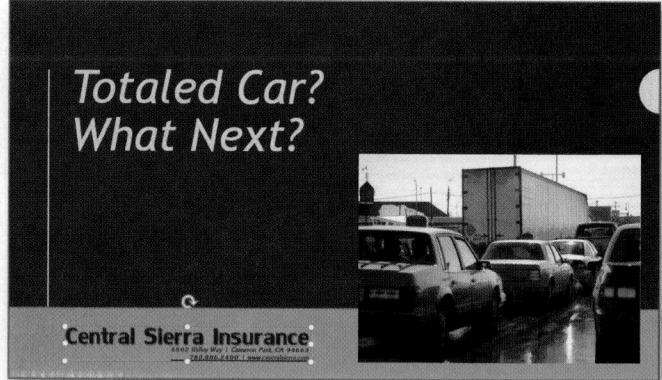

Figure 1-129 Title slide completed

5. Change a layout and insert a picture.
 a. Display slide 5. Change the slide layout to **Section Header**.
 b. Type the following text on two lines in the placeholder near the top of the slide.
 - The text is right-aligned and this placeholder right aligns with the title placeholder below.

 780-886-2400
 Margaret Jepson

c. Insert the picture **Travel-01** and change the *Width* to **7"**.
　　d. Position the picture on the left (Figure 1-130).
　　e. Close the *Design Ideas* pane if it opens.

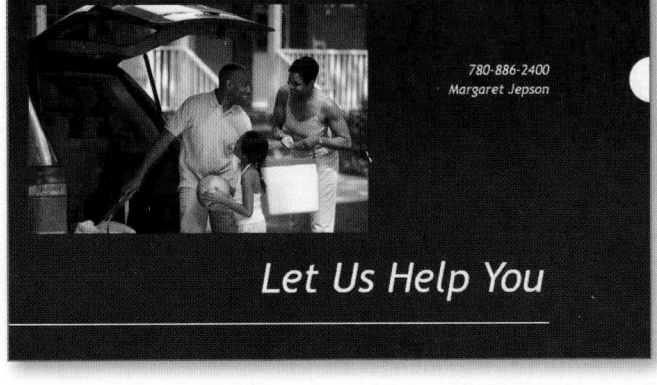

6. Add footer text and slide numbering to all slides except the title slide.

　　Slide footer text: The Totaled Car

7. Add header text and page numbering to the handout.

　　Handout header text: Central Sierra Insurance

Figure 1-130　Slide 5 completed

8. Apply and preview transitions.
　　a. Select the **Clock** transition (*Exciting* group) with the **Counterclockwise** effect option.
　　b. Apply this transition to all slides.
　　c. Preview the transitions.

9. Open the *Properties* dialog box and insert the following presentation properties as needed on the *Summary* tab.

　　Title:　　　　Totaled Car? What Next?
　　Subject:　　Accident Insurance
　　Author:　　Margaret Jepson

10. Print a handout with the following options: **6 Slides Horizontal, Frame Slides**, and **Scale to Fit Paper**.

11. Save and close the presentation (Figure 1-131).

Figure 1-131　PowerPoint 1-7 completed

Challenge Project 1-8

For this project, tell the story of your favorite vacation. Create six slides that introduce the topic and describe your main points with bulleted lists. Insert photographs to illustrate locations and resize them to fit with related text by using layouts available in the *Design Ideas* pane.
[Student Learning Outcomes 1.1, 1.2, 1.4, 1.5, 1.6, 1.7, 1.9]

File Needed: None
Completed Project File Name: *[your initials] PowerPoint 1-8.pptx*

Create a new presentation and save it as [your initials] PowerPoint 1-8. Modify your presentation according to the following guidelines:

- Apply an online theme with an appropriate background for your topic. Delete the slides that appear.
- Develop your content on six slides using one or more of the following slide layouts: *Title Slide*, *Title and Content*, *Section Header*, and *Title Only*.
- Insert three or more pictures and add appropriate *Alt Text* to each picture.
- Add a footer.
- Apply transitions.
- Check spelling and include presentation properties.

Challenge Project 1-9

Think about different jobs for which you are qualified. On the internet, research four different jobs and identify several characteristics and requirements for each job. Many online resources provide job-related information, such as www.careerbuilder.com or the *Occupational Outlook Handbook* at www.bls.gov/ooh.
[Student Learning Outcomes 1.1, 1.2, 1.3, 1.4, 1.5, 1.6, 1.7, 1.8, 1.9]

File Needed: None
Completed Project File Name: *[your initials] PowerPoint 1-9.pptx*

Create a new presentation and save it as [your initials] PowerPoint 1-9. Modify your presentation according to the following guidelines:

- Select an appropriate theme and use the *Design* tab to change colors and fonts as needed for your topic.
- Create a distinctive title slide.
- Write bulleted lists describing the characteristics and requirements of each different job with no more than six lines of bulleted text on each slide.
- Apply transitions.
- Check spelling and include presentation properties.
- Print handouts with six slides on a page.

Challenge Project 1-10

For this project, develop a presentation about how a speaker can manage nervous tendencies when presenting in front of an audience. Include information from your own experiences and refer to online resources, such as www.presentationmagazine.com.
[Student Learning Outcomes 1.1, 1.2, 1.3, 1.4, 1.5, 1.6, 1.7, 1.8, 1.9]

File Needed: None
Completed Project File Name: *[your initials] PowerPoint 1-10.pptx*

Create a new presentation and save it as [your initials] PowerPoint 1-10. Modify your presentation according to the following guidelines:

- Select an appropriate theme and use the *Design* tab to change colors and fonts as needed for your topic.
- Create a distinctive title slide.
- Write bulleted lists describing typical causes of nervousness and suggest ways to control nervousness when presenting.
- Insert pictures to illustrate concepts and add appropriate *Alt Text* to each picture.
- Apply transitions.
- Check spelling and include presentation properties.
- Print an outline of the presentation.

Illustrating with Pictures and Information Graphics

CHAPTER OVERVIEW

Today we are surrounded by information graphics. We see them in television programming, web sites, and published material of all kinds. We interpret signage that helps us get from place to place and readily recognize many iconic images that help us with everyday tasks. These graphics communicate visually and can be more effective than long passages of text.

PowerPoint enables you to create information graphics—to visually display your content so your audience will quickly grasp what you are presenting. You can choose from many options, such as shapes or icons, pictures to illustrate, diagrams to show processes, and charts to show data relationships. You can achieve professional results with your slide design, the colors you apply, and the effects you choose.

STUDENT LEARNING OUTCOMES (SLOs)

After completing this chapter, you will be able to:

SLO 2.1 Work with shapes, styles, effects, and colors (p. P2-75).

SLO 2.2 Work with icons and 3D models (p. P2-87).

SLO 2.3 Search for pictures and illustrations, modify picture appearance, and compress picture file size (p. P2-93).

SLO 2.4 Use tables to organize information in a grid format of columns and rows (p. P2-103).

SLO 2.5 Format a table by applying styles, colors, and effects (p. P2-108).

SLO 2.6 Show processes and relationships with *SmartArt* graphics (p. P2-113).

SLO 2.7 Format a *SmartArt* graphic by applying styles, colors, and effects (p. P2-116).

SLO 2.8 Create charts that show relationships between data values and emphasize data in different ways based on the chart type and chart elements (p. P2-121).

SLO 2.9 Format a chart by applying preset styles or customizing individual chart elements (p. P2-126).

CASE STUDY

Classic Gardens and Landscapes (CGL) is a landscape design company that creates beautiful and low-maintenance landscapes for outdoor living spaces. Frank and Sandra Hunter recently bought a new home from a builder. It has minimal landscaping, so they contacted Gerod Sunderland, a landscape designer for CGL, to discuss improvements.

Gerod visited the property and designed plans with several options for trees, shrubs, and plants. You have been asked to prepare a

POWERPOINT

presentation illustrating his key points for his meeting with the Hunters.

Pause & Practice 2-1: Add visual interest with picture enhancements and creative text designs.

Pause & Practice 2-2: Prepare a table.

Pause & Practice 2-3: Create an organization chart and convert text to a *SmartArt* graphic.

Pause & Practice 2-4: Create column and pie charts with an enhanced appearance.

Working with Shapes, Styles, Effects, and Colors

You learned in chapter 1 that PowerPoint provides options in the form of galleries, drop-down lists, and dialog boxes. These features are convenient and enable you to make selections quickly. PowerPoint's *Ribbon* is dynamic, so how the tabs display commands can vary because the software adapts to the screen size on the device you are using. Even with a large screen, you may use PowerPoint in a different window size rather than expanding it to fill your whole screen.

If a portion of the gallery is open on the *Ribbon*, click the gallery's **More** button to open the complete gallery. If the gallery is represented by a button, then click the button to open the complete gallery. This difference is illustrated in Figure 2-1.

Figure 2-1 *Shapes* button on the *Insert* tab and the *Shapes* gallery on the *Home* tab

Shapes and Text Boxes

Shapes can emphasize key points. For example, insert an arrow to point to an object, or add a line to connect two related objects. You can draw a variety of shapes using drawing tools from PowerPoint's **Shapes** gallery (Figure 2-2). Because this gallery is frequently used, it is on the *Home*, *Insert*, and the *Drawing Tools Format* tabs. Shapes are grouped in the following categories:

- *Recently Used Shapes*
- *Lines*
- *Rectangles*
- *Basic Shapes*
- *Block Arrows*
- *Equation Shapes*
- *Flowchart*
- *Stars and Banners*
- *Callouts*
- *Action Buttons*

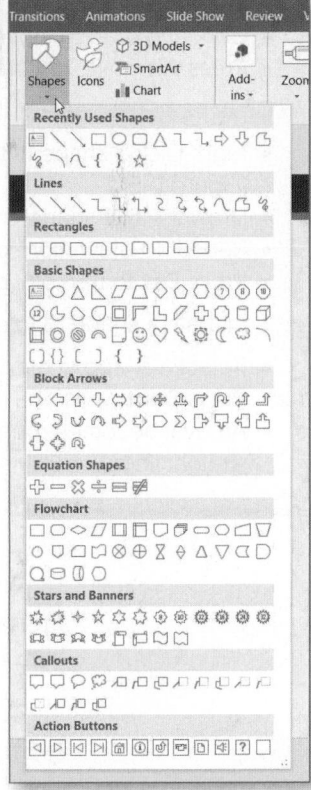

Figure 2-2 Complete *Shapes* gallery

To insert a shape, select the shape you want from the *Shapes* gallery and use the following features to draw and adjust your shape:

- *Crosshair*: A large plus sign used to draw the shape.
- *Sizing handles*: White circles on the corners and sides of the shapes used to change shape size.
- *Rotation handle*: A circular arrow on the top of the shape to angle shapes.
- *Adjustment handle*: Yellow circles used to change curves or points.

▶ **HOW TO:** Draw One or More Shapes

1. Click the **Insert** tab.
2. Click the **Shapes** button [*Illustrations* group] to display the *Shapes* gallery.
3. Select a shape in the *Shapes* gallery and your pointer becomes a crosshair (Figure 2-3).
4. Click and drag the crosshair on your slide to draw the shape in the approximate size you need (Figure 2-4).
 - The shape appears with sizing handles and a rotation handle.
 - The shape may have adjustment handles that you drag to change areas within it such as the tip of an arrow or star.
5. Resize a shape.
 - Click a sizing handle on your shape and your pointer changes from a resize pointer to a crosshair.
 - Drag the crosshair to change the size.
6. Move a shape.
 - Point in a shape on your slide and your pointer changes to a move pointer (four-tipped arrow).
 - Click and drag to move the shape.
 - Press **Alt** while you drag for smooth movement.
7. Draw more than one of the same shape.
 - Right-click a shape in the *Shapes* gallery and click **Lock Drawing Mode** (Figure 2-5).
 - Draw the first shape on your slide.
 - Repeat to draw more of the same shape.
 - Press **Esc** to turn off *Lock Drawing Mode*.
8. Constrain a shape to keep horizontal and vertical dimensions the same.
 - Select a shape in the *Shapes* gallery.
 - Press **Shift** while you drag the crosshair on your slide.
 - An oval becomes round, a rectangle becomes square, and lines become straight lines.

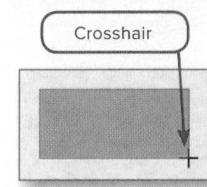

Figure 2-3 Crosshair drawing a shape

Figure 2-4 Shape with handles

Figure 2-5 *Lock Drawing Mode*

When you select a shape on your slide, the *Drawing Tools Format* tab becomes available. On this tab the *Shapes* gallery displays on the left in the *Insert Shapes* group. Use the ***Edit Shape*** button to access the gallery to select a different shape.

▶ MORE INFO

Press **Ctrl+D** to duplicate a selected shape.

▶ HOW TO: Change a Shape

1. Select the shape to be changed.
2. Click the **Edit Shape** drop-down arrow [*Drawing Tools Format* tab, *Insert Shapes* group] (Figure 2-6).
3. Select **Change Shape** and click a different shape from the *Shapes* gallery.
4. Click a blank area on the slide to deselect the shape.
5. Click **Undo** [*Quick Access* toolbar] to return to your original shape.

Figure 2-6 *Change Shape*

Add text to shapes and format the text as you do with text in a placeholder.

By using a ***text box***, you can add text anywhere on a slide without using placeholders. For example, you can add notations to identify slide objects or insert brief phrases you want to emphasize. Text boxes can be sized and moved around like any other shape.

The text in shapes or in text boxes does not appear in *Outline* view.

▶ HOW TO: Draw a Text Box

1. Click the **Insert** tab.
2. Click the **Text Box** button [*Text* group] and your pointer changes to an insertion point. Create a text box using one of the following methods:
 - Click the slide background to place your insertion point where you want the text to appear. Begin typing and the text box expands as you enter text because it has no defined width. The *Home* tab displays.
 - Click and drag to change the pointer to a crosshair and draw a text box (Figure 2-7) in the approximate width you need. The *Home* tab displays. The text box height adjusts as you type text.
3. Resize if necessary, by dragging sizing handles or entering *Height* and *Width* sizes [*Drawing Tools Format* tab, *Size* group] (Figure 2-8).
4. Click and drag the text box to move it to an appropriate position on the slide.

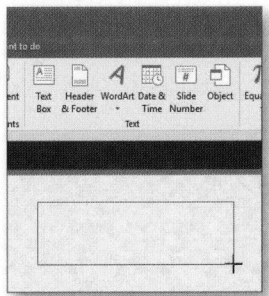

Figure 2-7 Draw a text box

Figure 2-8 Size measurements

If you are using a touch screen, the *Draw* tab is automatically available. When you select a pen from this tab, inking mode is turned on so you can draw shapes, drawings, or formulas. You can even replay a drawing to show how it was created. Drawing is possible with a mouse or your finger, but a digital pen is more precise and feels more natural for drawing and writing.

If you want to use these features and the *Draw* tab is not displayed on your computer, click the **File** tab and select **Options** to open the *PowerPoint Options* dialog box. Select **Customize Ribbon** and then check **Draw** on the right list to add that tab. Click **OK**. The *Draw* tab appears on the ribbon between the *Insert* and *Design* tabs.

Office 2019 Note: The *Draw* tab does not have *Ink to Text*, *Ink to Shape*, or *Ink Replay*.

Style Galleries and Effect Options

Style galleries provide collections of preset effects for shapes, pictures, or other objects. You can customize all effects using the related button such as **Shape Effects**, **Picture Effects**, or **Text Effects** to access drop-down galleries. You can choose from *Shadow, Reflection, Glow, Soft Edges, Bevel, 3D Rotation,* or *Transform* described in Table 2-1. You can also apply one or more effects without first using styles from a gallery.

Table 2-1: Effect Options

Effect	Options
Shadow	**Shadow** effects appear in three groupings. An **Outer** shadow shows behind an object from different directions. An **Inner** shadow makes part of the object looked raised. A **Perspective** shadow shows below so the object appears to float.
Reflection	A **Reflection** shows a mirror image below an object, like a reflection on a shiny surface or on water. You can control how close the reflection is to the object.
Glow	**Glow** provides a colored area around an object that fades into the background color on your slide. Glow colors by default are based on the current theme colors, but other colors are available. The size of the *Glow* is measured in points.
Soft Edges	Shapes and other objects have either straight edges or well-defined curves. **Soft Edges** creates a feathered edge that gradually blends into the background color. The size of the blending area is measured in points from the edge of the object inward. The larger the point size, the less you see of the object.
Bevel	**Bevel** effects add light and dark areas to create a dimensional appearance. Objects or text can look raised or inset.
3D Rotation	**3D Rotation** effects include **Parallel**, **Perspective**, and **Oblique** options that create an illusion of depth by rotating an object from front to back.
Transform	**Transform** is a *Text Effect* used to change the shape of words. It is not available for shapes or pictures.

Outline Weight and Style

All shapes have a fill and outline color. Emphasize a shape outline by making it wider with a contrasting color; deemphasize a shape outline by making it thinner. You can show no outline or match its color to the shape to make the outline disappear.

Many of the options for shape outlines also apply to lines (straight or curved) that you draw.

Select a shape or line and click the **Shape Outline** drop-down arrow [*Drawing Tools Format* tab, *Shape Styles* group]. Click one of the following options in the drop-down list to choose from additional variations (Figure 2-9):

- *Weight*: Displays line thickness measured in points
- *Dashes*: Displays lines made with various combinations of dots and dashes (Figure 2-10)
- *Arrows*: Displays arrowheads or other shapes for both ends of a line

Figure 2-10 *Shape Outline Dashes*

Figure 2-9 *Shape Outline Weight*

At the bottom of each drop-down list, select **More Lines** to open the *Format Shape* pane (Figure 2-11) where you can customize the following *Line* options:

Figure 2-11 *Format Shape pane*

- *Color*: Provides color choices
- *Transparency*: Adjusts transparency percentages so more or less of the background color shows through the selected object
- *Width*: Controls the thickness of lines measured in points
- *Compound type*: Provides outlines with two or more lines in different thicknesses
- *Dash type*: Displays lines made with various combinations of dots and dashes
- *Cap type*: Controls the look (*Square*, *Round*, or *Flat*) of the ends of lines; it is usually applied to single lines or arrows
- *Join type*: Controls the look (*Round*, *Bevel*, *Miter*) for the connection point where two lines meet (for example, at the corner of a rectangle or square)
- *Begin and End Arrow type*: Controls the shape for both ends of an arrow
- *Begin and End Arrow size*: Controls the size of the shape at both ends of an arrow

The *Format Shape* pane is a convenient place to change many options. Figure 2-11 shows the *Shape Options* selected at the top of the pane with the *Fill & Line* tab displayed. *Line* options for a *Solid line* are selected. Different options appear if you choose a *Gradient* line. Above the *Line* option, you can select the *Fill* option to change shape colors. Click the arrow in front of these options to expand or collapse each list.

Additional tabs under *Shape Options* include *Effects* and *Size & Properties* with related options on each tab. Click the icons at the top of the pane to select these tabs.

> ## ANOTHER WAY
>
> Right-click a shape and then select **Format Shape** from the context menu to open the *Format Shape* pane.

Solid and Gradient Colors

Theme colors are named in the *Theme Colors* gallery indicating their use as a background or accent color for the presentation design theme being used. However, all colors can be used for various objects in your presentation.

Theme colors applied on shapes and text will automatically change if you select a different presentation design theme with different theme colors. When *Standard* colors (or custom colors you create) are used, they remain in effect even if theme colors change.

This section explains how colors are arranged in PowerPoint and describes different ways to "mix" custom colors or match specific colors. The same techniques for choosing colors apply to fill and outline colors. Color selection is important to create slides that are easy to read with colors appropriate for your topic. For example, you may want to create a certain mood for your presentation, match company colors, or match the colors of a product you are promoting.

▶ HOW TO: Change Solid Colors and Apply Theme Styles or Theme Presets

1. Apply a *Theme Color* to a selected shape by clicking the **Shape Fill** drop-down arrow [*Drawing Tools Format* tab, *Shape Styles* group] to open the ***Themes Colors*** gallery (*Figure 2-12*).

 - Colors are arranged in a grid of columns and rows.
 - The first four colors on the top row represent background and text colors.
 - The remaining six colors on the top row represent accent colors.
 - Colors in columns below the top row show lighter and darker variations of the top-row colors.
 - Below the *Theme Colors* is a single row of *Standard Colors* arranged in the order of a rainbow.

2. Point to a color and a *ScreenTip* shows its name. Click to apply the color.

3. Apply a ***Theme Style*** or ***Preset Style*** to a selected shape by clicking the **More** button on the *Shape Styles* gallery [*Drawing Tools Format* tab, *Shape Styles* group] (Figure 2-13).

4. Point to a theme style and a *ScreenTip* shows its name. Click to apply the style.

Figure 2-12 *Theme Colors* gallery

Figure 2-13 *Theme Styles* and *Presets* for shapes

Gradient colors blend two or more colors together. Using the *Format Shape* pane, you can select from preset colors or customize your own gradient color by changing the colors and how they blend.

▶ HOW TO: Change Gradient Colors Using the Format Shape Pane

1. Select a shape and click the **Shape Fill** drop-down arrow [*Drawing Tools Format* tab, *Shape Styles* group].

2. Select **Gradient** to choose from a gallery of light and dark variations of the current fill color that blend the colors in different directions (Figure 2-14).

3. Click **More Gradients** at the bottom of the gallery to open the *Format Shape* pane to customize the colors.

4. Select **Gradient fill** and apply *Fill* options from the following:

 - *Preset gradients*: Theme color variations (Figure 2-15)
 - *Type*: *Linear*, *Radial*, *Rectangular*, or *Path*
 - *Direction*: Options change based on the selected *Type*.
 - *Angle*: The percentage changes with each *Type* and *Direction*.
 - *Gradient stops*: Shapes on the gradient bar that you move to control where colors change (Figure 2-16).

Figure 2-14 Gradient color variations for the selected color

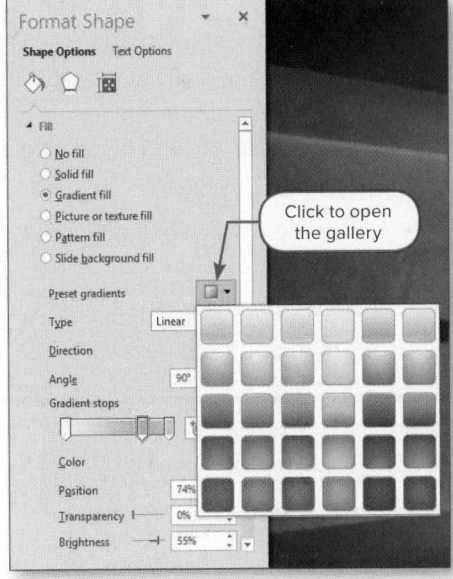

Figure 2-15 Preset gradients based on theme colors

5. Select a *Gradient stop* and change its settings to control color blending:
 - *Delete a stop*: Click the **Remove gradient stop** button or drag the stop down to remove it from the gradient bar.
 - *Add a stop*: Click the **Add gradient stop** button or click the gradient bar where you want the stop to appear.
 - *Color*: Select the stop and then change the color.
 - *Position*: Enter a different percentage or drag the stop on the gradient bar to change its position.
 - *Transparency*: Click the arrows to change the percentage. When *Transparency* is 0%, the color is opaque (solid). As the percentage increases, the color becomes increasingly transparent and more of the slide background color shows through.
 - *Brightness*: Click the arrows to change the percentage. As the percentage decreases from 100%, the color softens.

Figure 2-16 Gradient stops

6. Check **Rotate with shape** to maintain the color settings when a shape or text is rotated so it angles on the slide.

7. Select **No line** or **Solid line** under *Line* options to control if an outline shows around a shape or text.

8. Click the **X** at the top of the pane to close the *Format Shape* pane.

Custom Colors

The *Colors* dialog box provides many solid color options on the *Standard* tab and options to mix a unique color on the *Custom* tab. Colors that you select or mix are not affected by any changes made to theme colors.

▶HOW TO: Use the Standard Tab to Select a Color

1. Select a shape and click the **Shape Fill** drop-down arrow [*Home* tab, *Drawing* group or *Drawing Tools Format* tab, *Shape Styles* group].

2. Click **More Fill Colors** to open the *Colors* dialog box.
 - Select the *Standard* tab (Figure 2-17).
 - Colors are arranged in a honeycomb shape with colors blending from white to black below.

3. Click a color to apply it.
 - Notice the *New* color that appears on the right above the *Current* color.

4. Adjust the *Transparency* as needed.

5. Click **OK** to apply the new color.

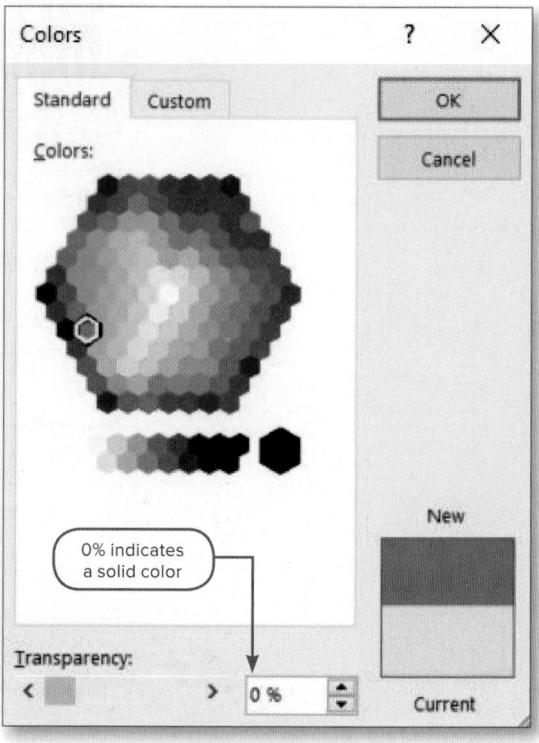

Figure 2-17 *Standard* tab in *Colors* dialog box

When you need more precision to select a color, use the *Custom* tab on the *Colors* dialog box. Colors are arranged like a rainbow, and you drag a crosshair to select a different color. Drag up or down to change the color intensity and then move a slider to adjust how light or dark the color appears. The **RGB Color model** is typically used for computer displays and colors are formed by blending values of the three numbers for *Red*, *Green*, and *Blue*. Highly saturated colors at the top have higher number values (255 maximum). Use these numbers to match color values in different shapes or objects such as a business or college logo.

▶HOW TO: Use the Custom Tab to Mix a Color

1. Select a shape and click the **Shape Fill** drop-down arrow [*Home* tab, *Drawing* group or *Drawing Tools Format* tab, *Shape Styles* group].

2. Click **More Fill Colors** to open the *Colors* dialog box.

3. Click the *Custom* tab (Figure 2-18) and a crosshair is positioned for the *Current* color.
 - Drag the crosshair horizontally to select a different color. Notice the new color that appears on the right above the *Current* color.
 - When the crosshair is at the top, colors are highly **saturated** (intense and vibrant).
 - As you move the crosshair down, colors become less saturated (duller and less intense).

Figure 2-18 *Custom* tab in *Colors* dialog box

4. Drag the slider on the right to adjust the **luminosity** (lightness or brightness).
 - Drag up to add white and increase the luminosity.
 - Drag down to add black and decrease the luminosity.
5. Adjust the *Transparency* as needed.
6. Click **OK** to apply the new color.

Color Matching with the Eyedropper

To match the exact color in PowerPoint, use the *Eyedropper* tool. The *Eyedropper* is a pointer that looks like a pen. You can match the fill or outline color of a selected shape on your slide by clicking the tip of the *Eyedropper* on a color within a picture or other object on the same slide.

▶ HOW TO: Use the Eyedropper

1. Insert a shape that you want to color on a slide.
2. Insert a picture or other object that will be your color source on the same slide.
3. Select the shape.
4. Click the **Shape Fill** drop-down arrow [*Home* tab, *Drawing* group or *Drawing Tools Format* tab, *Shape Styles* group] and select **Eyedropper**.
5. Move your pointer (now an eyedropper) around in the picture and a live preview of each color appears. Pause to see a *ScreenTip* showing the *RGB* (Red Green Blue) values (Figure 2-19).
6. Click to select a color and it is applied to your selected shape.

Or

7. Press **Esc** to cancel the *Eyedropper* without selecting a color.

Figure 2-19 *Eyedropper* live preview and *RGB* colors

To match a color anywhere on your computer screen, left-click and hold as you drag the eyedropper to other areas of the screen outside the PowerPoint window.

Picture, Texture, or Pattern Fills

You can fill shapes with more than colors. The following options are available by clicking the **Shape Fill** drop-down arrow [*Drawing Tools Format* tab, *Shape Styles* group] or from the *Format Shape* pane.

- *Picture fill*: Fills the shape with a picture from a file or from an online search
- *Texture fill*: Applies an image such as woven fabric or wood
- *Pattern fill*: Applies a mixture of two colors in various dotted or crosshatch designs

▶ HOW TO: Apply Picture, Texture, or Pattern Fills

1. Select a shape and click the **Shape Fill** drop-down arrow [*Home* tab, *Drawing* group or *Drawing Tools Format* tab, *Shape Styles* group].
2. Select **Picture** from the drop-down list to open the *Insert Pictures* dialog box. Browse or search for a picture.

3. Select the picture and click **Insert**. The picture fills the shape.

Or

4. Select **Texture** from the drop-down list to open the gallery (Figure 2-20). Click a texture to fill the shape or click **More Textures** to open the *Format Shape* pane.

 • Select **Picture or texture fill** and then click the **File** button or the **Online** button to search for textures that are saved as a picture.

Or

5. Select a shape and right-click. Select **Format Shape** from the callout menu to open the *Format Shape* pane.

 • Click **Fill**, if necessary, to display *Fill* options.
 • Select **Pattern fill** (Figure 2-21).
 • Click a pattern to fill the shape.
 • Change *Foreground* and *Background* colors as needed.
 • Click other patterns to see how different these colors look in different patterns.

6. Close the *Format Shape* pane.

Figure 2-20 *Texture* fills

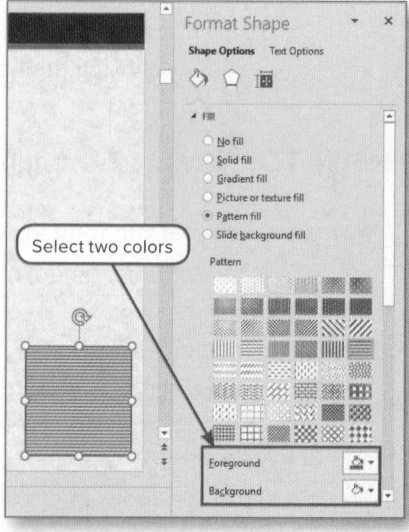

Figure 2-21 *Pattern* fills on the *Format Shape* pane

Use the *Format Background* pane to insert textures and patterns for a slide background. Inserting online pictures is covered in *SLO 2.3: Working with Pictures*.

WordArt Styles and Text Effects

Text effects can be functional or decorative. For example, slide titles may be easier to read with a shadow to improve contrast with the slide background color. Or, you can use interesting fill and outline treatments or even change the shape of text to provide a bold focal point on a slide. One way is to start by inserting *WordArt*.

▶**HOW TO:** Apply WordArt Styles

1. Click the **WordArt** button [*Insert* tab, *Text* group] to open the *WordArt Styles* gallery (Figure 2-22).

 • *WordArt* styles are preset text effects showing a variety of solid, gradient, and pattern fill colors.
 • Point to a style and a *ScreenTip* shows its name.

2. Click to select a style.

 • A text box displays on your slide with sample text that you edit to create a *WordArt* object (Figure 2-23).

Figure 2-22 *WordArt Styles* gallery

3. Use the *Font* group [*Home* tab] to apply the following character formatting:

- Select a different font or attribute such as **Bold** or **Italic**.
- Change the *Font Size* by entering a point size or using the **Increase Font Size** and **Decrease Font Size** buttons.
- Click the **Character Spacing** button to control the distance between letters by expanding or condensing the spacing.

Figure 2-23 *WordArt* as it first appears

> **MORE INFO**
>
> When using text in a large size, *Tight* character spacing conserves space yet keeps the text easy to read.

You can also start with text in a placeholder or text box and then apply text effects. With either method, you use commands in the *WordArt Styles* group [*Drawing Tools Format* tab] (Figure 2-24) to customize your text. These commands—*Text Fill, Text Outline, and Text Effects*—are similar to the *Shape* commands.

Figure 2-24 *WordArt Styles* group

▶ HOW TO: Apply Text Effects

1. Select a *WordArt* object or text in a placeholder or text box.
2. Click the **More** button [*Drawing Tools Format* tab, *WordArt Styles* group] to open the *WordArt Styles* gallery.

 - Point to a style to see a live preview applied to your text (Figure 2-25).
 - Click a style to apply it.

3. Use the *WordArt Styles* group [*Drawing Tools Format* tab] to change colors and add special effects:

 - Click the **Text Fill** drop-down arrow to select **Theme** or other color options.
 - Click the **Text Outline** drop-down arrow to select **Theme** or other color options, as well as line *Weight* and *Style*.
 - Click the **Text Effects** button and select from *Shadow, Reflection, Glow, Bevel, 3D Rotation,* or *Transform* effects and then choose the option you prefer.

Or

4. Select a *WordArt* object or text box and right-click to open the context menu. Click **Format Shape** to open the *Format Shape* pane.

 - Select **Shape Options** to change *Fill* or *Line* options.
 - Select **Text Options** to change *Text Fill* or *Text Outline* options.

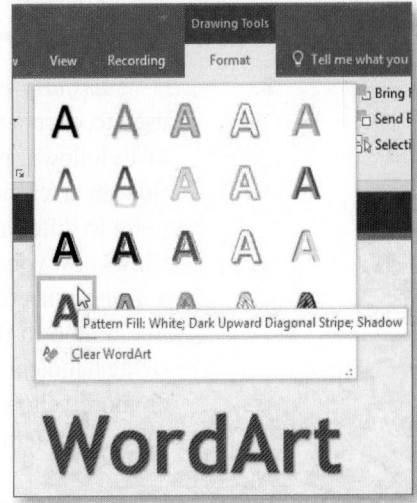

Figure 2-25 *WordArt* object with a style applied

Changing the text outline color and increasing line weight emphasizes the outline just as it does on shapes. Different line styles can create interesting effects. Using pictures or patterns as fill colors can add a creative touch when text displays in a large size. A variety of different colors and effects are shown in Figure 2-26.

Figure 2-26 *Text Fill*, *Text Outline*, and *Text Effects* samples

Transform effects are unique to text and are used to warp a word or phrase to different shapes or to follow a path. For example, text can angle, flow in a circle, and arc up or down. As you point to different *Transform* effects, a live preview shows how your text will look in that shape. Once a *Transform* effect has been applied, text size is not limited to the font size because you can drag sizing handles. *Transform* effects also provide one or more yellow adjustment handles that control the slant of letters or the curve of text.

▶ **HOW TO:** Apply a Transform Effect

1. Select a *WordArt* object (or any text).
2. Click the **Text Effects** button [*Format* tab, *WordArt Styles* group].
3. Select **Transform** from the drop-down list (Figure 2-27) to open the *Transform* gallery.
 - Point to an effect to see a live preview applied to your text.

Figure 2-27 *Transform Fade Up* effect applied

4. Click an effect to apply it.

5. Adjust your text as needed using sizing and adjustment handles.

Working with Icons and 3D Models

Icons are images (*Scalable Vector Graphics* or SVG files) that you can resize, rotate, or color with no loss of image quality. *3D Models* are three-dimensional images that you can rotate 360 degrees, tilt up and down, pan, or zoom.

Insert and Format Icons

The *Insert Icons* dialog box displays icons as single-color images grouped in categories. After you insert an icon, you can change its color or apply graphic styles. Because icons are two-dimensional, you can change their size by adjusting *Height* and *Width*. Because icons are simple images, you can use them for more of an abstract effect rather than using a picture that provides a realistic image.

▶ **HOW TO:** Insert Icons

1. Click the **Icons** button [*Insert* tab, *Illustrations* group] (Figure 2-28) to open the *Insert Icons* dialog box.

 • The icons are all solid-black images.

2. Scroll down to see more icons or click a category name in the *Navigation* pane on the left to quickly jump to that category.

3. Select one or more icons (Figure 2-29).

 • A red square and a check mark appear with each selected icon.

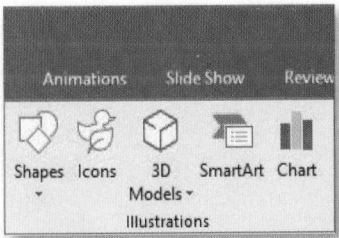

Figure 2-28 *Icons* button in the *Illustrations* group

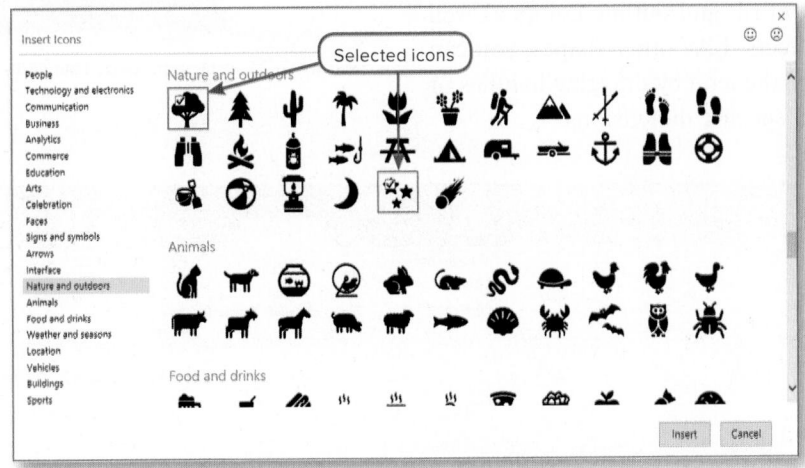

Figure 2-29 *Insert Icons* dialog box

4. Click the **Insert** button.

 • The icon appears in a small size in the center of your slide.
 • Move and resize the icon as needed.

The *Design Ideas* pane may open automatically when you insert an icon. If it does not, click the **Design Ideas** button [*Designer* group, *Graphics Tools Format* tab]. Click a *Design Ideas* layout to apply it.

Office 2019 Note: The *Design Ideas* pane is not available in Office 2019.

In Figure 2-30, an icon was inserted on the title slide of a blank presentation and layouts display in the *Design Ideas* pane.

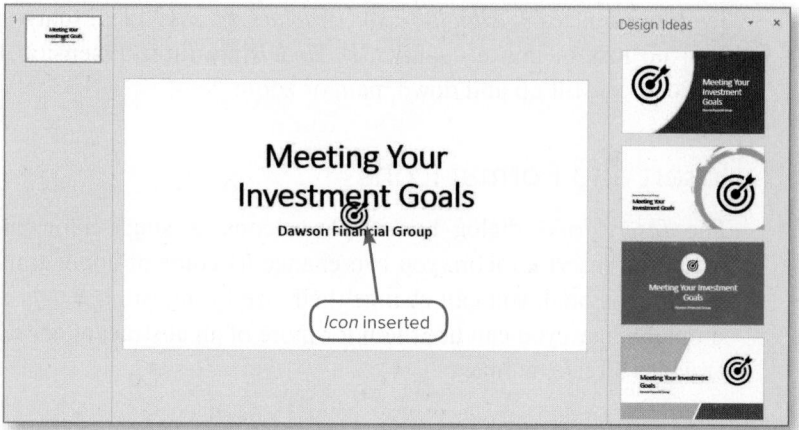

Figure 2-30 The *Design Ideas* pane with layouts for an icon inserted on a blank presentation title slide

If you selected more than one icon to insert, they will be stacked together. Click each one and move it to a different position, or select a layout such as Figure 2-31 from the *Design Ideas* pane.

With an icon selected, the *Graphics Tools Format* tab (Figure 2-32) appears with commands similar to the *Drawing Tools Format* tab to control fill and outline colors as well as effects. Like other shapes, you can resize the icon by dragging handles or enter specific dimensions.

Figure 2-31 A *Design Ideas* title slide layout with four icons

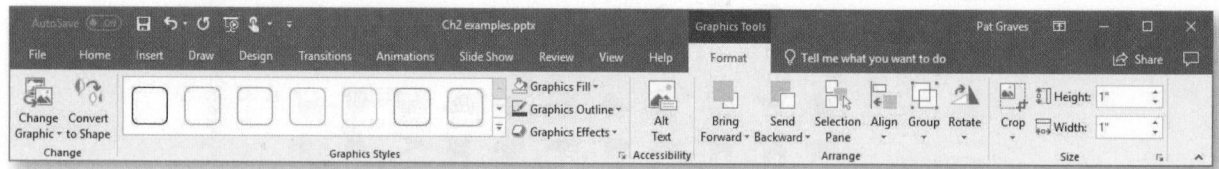

Figure 2-32 *Graphics Tools Format* tab

▶ **HOW TO:** Apply Icon Colors, Styles, and Effects

1. Select an icon on your slide and drag sizing handles to resize.
 - You can also enter *Height* and *Width* sizes on the *Graphics Tools Format* tab [*Size* group].
2. Click the **Graphics Fill** drop-down arrow [*Graphics Tools Format* tab, *Graphic Styles* group].
 - Point to a color to see a live preview applied to your icon.

- A *ScreenTip* shows the color name.
- Click to select a color and the icon displays as a solid color with no outline.

3. Click the **Graphics Outline** drop-down arrow and select a contrasting color so the outline displays (Figure 2-33).

 - Click the **Graphics Outline** drop-down arrow again to change line *Weight* or *Dashes*.

4. Click the **More** button [*Graphics Tools Format* tab, *Graphic Styles* group] to display style *Presets* (Figure 2-34) appearing in accent colors.

 - *First row*: White fill, accent color outlines
 - *Second row*: Accent color fills, no outline
 - *Third row*: Accent color fills, black outline
 - *Fourth row*: Transparent fill, accent color outlines

5. Point to a style to see a live preview applied to your icon.

 - A *ScreenTip* shows the style name.

6. Click the **Graphics Effects** button [*Graphics Tools Format* tab, *Graphic Styles* group], select an effect, and click an option from the gallery.

 - If you try an effect you don't like, click **Undo**.

7. Click the **Change Graphic** button [*Graphic Tools Format* tab, *Change* group] to replace your icon with a different image.

 - Select from available sources: **From a File**, **From Online Sources**, or **From Icons**.

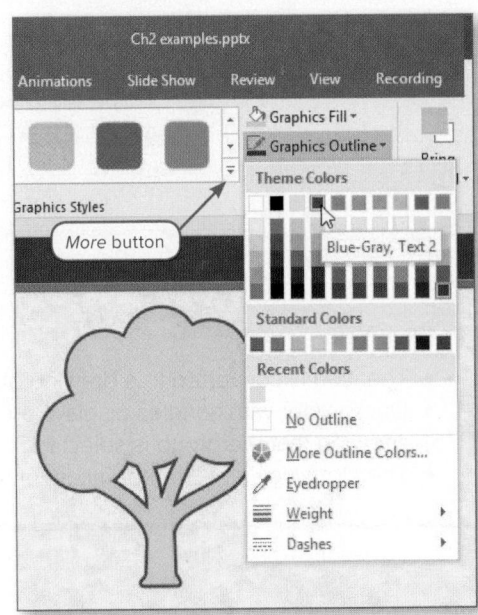

Figure 2-33 *Graphics Outline* color applied

Figure 2-34 *Graphics Styles* gallery and *Icon* style

Because icons have a solid color, the *Graphics Tools Format* tab provides only solid fill and outline colors for the entire image. Click the **Convert to Shape** button to change the icon into a Microsoft Office drawing object. After an icon is converted, it cannot be resaved as an icon.

> **HOW TO: Convert an Icon to a Shape**

1. Select an icon on your slide and resize as needed.

 - Notice that the icon has one border with handles.

2. Click the **Convert to Shape** button [*Graphics Tools* tab, *Change* group].

 - A message box appears asking you to confirm that you want to convert the selected object to a Microsoft Office drawing object (Figure 2-35).

Figure 2-35 Convert icon to a drawing object message

3. Click **Yes**.

- The icon is converted to a drawing object that consists of shapes in a group.
- One border with handles displays around the entire icon (Figure 2-36) showing that the group is selected.
- The *Drawing Tools Format* tab is now available.

After an icon is converted into a drawing object, you can select individual shapes within a group. Use the *Drawing Tools Format* tab to change the colors, sizes, or position of shapes within the group.

Figure 2-36 An *Icon* is converted to a shape and a single border with handles displays

▶ **HOW TO:** Modify an Icon as a Drawing Object

1. Insert an icon and click the **Convert to Shape** button [*Graphics Tools* tab, *Change* group] to change the icon to a drawing object.

- One border with handles displays around the entire icon.
- Multiple shapes are combined in a group to create the icon.

2. Click each shape in the icon to see its border and handles (Figure 2-37).

- Press **Ctrl+Click** to select more than one shape within the group.
- You can move or delete shapes within the group.

3. Select individual shapes and recolor or apply styles (Figure 2-38).

4. Click the group border to move the icon to a different position.

Figure 2-37 The shapes within the group are selected

Figure 2-38 Each shape within the group is recolored and repositioned

The title slide examples in Figure 2-39 show how these simple graphics can be used in different ways as drawing objects. In *Example 1* on the left, the flower basket was ungrouped and the various shapes recolored with a shadow and bevel effect applied. In *Example 2* on the right, the bridge was created by removing part of an icon and duplicating the remaining shapes that are placed over a gray rectangle. The bridge has a reflection effect over a picture of water at the bottom of the slide.

Figure 2-39 Title slides with icons converted to drawing objects and used in different ways

> **MORE INFO**
>
> Separate an icon's shapes to use them in different ways on your slide. Select the group, click the **Group** button [*Drawing Tools Format* tab, *Arrange* group], and select **Ungroup**. Then you can work with the individual shapes independently.

Insert and Adjust 3D Models

Icons and other shapes are two-dimensional graphics (2D) because they are measured in *Height* and *Width*. A three-dimensional graphic (3D) also has the dimension of *Depth*. In upcoming projects, you will show depth when you apply shadow and perspective effects to pictures and other objects.

3D Models are more complex computer graphics with the three-dimensional shape of an object that can be seen from any angle by tilting or rotating the object. 3D models are used for computer-generated imagery (CGI) in gaming and animated films, and for computer-aided design in manufacturing, architectural design, and 3D printing.

Microsoft provides an online collection of 3D models. When you insert one of these 3D models on your slide, you can use a control on the image to rotate or tilt. On the *3D Model Tools Format* tab, select **Pan & Zoom** to show a close up or distant view of your image or adjust the area of the image that is displayed. You cannot edit 3D models in PowerPoint. If you want to create 3D models, try Microsoft's *Paint 3D* application. You can search for additional 3D models on the web.

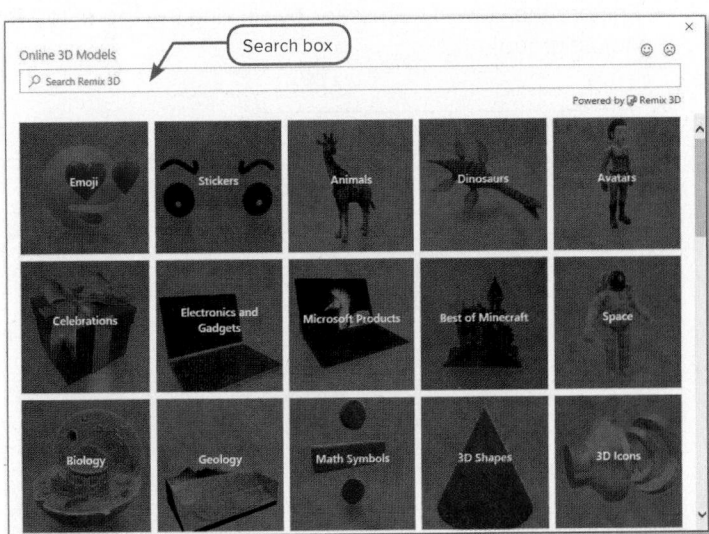

Figure 2-40 *Online 3D Models* dialog box

> **HOW TO:** Insert and Adjust a 3D Model

1. Select the slide where you will insert the *3D Model*.
2. Click the **3D Models** button [*Insert* tab, *Illustrations* group] to open the *Online 3D Models* dialog box (Figure 2-40).
 - You can also click the **3D Models** drop-down arrow to select **From a File** or **From Online Sources**.

3. Locate a *3D Model* using one of these methods:
 - Click one of the thumbnails to open a category of *3D Models*.
 - Enter a search word and press **Enter** to see available *3D Models*.
4. Click a *3D Model* thumbnail to insert it on your slide.
5. Select the *3D Model* and adjust its size as appropriate by using the resize handles or entering *Height* and *Width* measurements [*3D Model Tools Format* tab, *Size* group] (Figure 2-41).

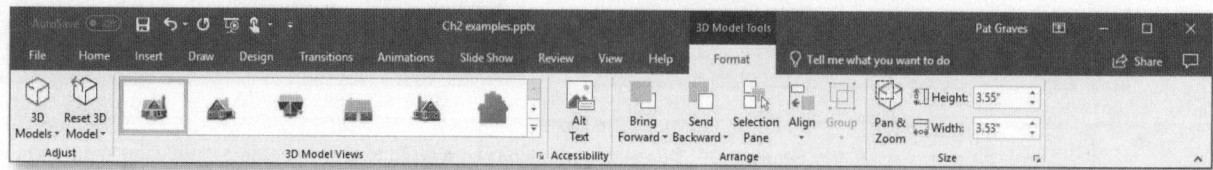

Figure 2-41 *3D Model Tools Format* tab

6. Change the view of the selected *3D Model* using one of these methods:
 - Click the **More** button [*3D Model Tools Format* tab, *3D Model Views* group] to open the gallery of rotation views (Figure 2-42) and select a different view option.
 - Click and drag the **3D control** that appears at the center of the *3D Model* (Figure 2-43) to tilt the image or rotate it in any direction.
 - Use the rotation handle at the top of the *3D Model* shape to rotate in a clockwise or counterclockwise movement.

7. Click the **Pan & Zoom** button [*3D Model Tools Format* tab, *3D Model Views* group] and a *Zoom* button (magnifying glass) appears on the right (Figure 2-44).

Figure 2-42 *3D Model Views* gallery

8. Zoom out to show a distance view of the *3D Model.*
 - Click the **Zoom** button and drag down as the *3D Model* becomes smaller to appear more distant (see Figure 2-44).
 - Restore the view, if necessary, by clicking the top of the **Reset 3D Model** button [*3D Model Tools Format* tab, *Adjust* group].

Figure 2-43 *Tilt* and *Rotate* a *3D Model*

Figure 2-44 Zoom out to show a *3D Model* distance view

9. Zoom in to show a close-up portion of the *3D Model*.

 • Click the **Zoom** button and drag up to zoom in and the *3D Model* appears closer (Figure 2-45).

10. *Pan* to control how your *3D Model* fits within its frame.

 • Display a different area by clicking and dragging the *3D Model* within its frame.
 • Use the **Zoom** button to increase or decrease the area displayed within the frame.
 • Restore the view if necessary.

11. Position the *3D Model* as needed on your slide.

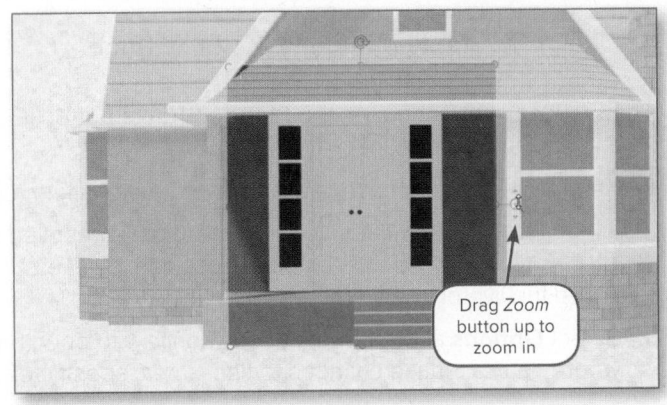

Figure 2-45 Zoom in to show a *3D Model* close up view

SLO 2.3

Working with Pictures

In chapter 1, you inserted pictures from files, changed their size, and aligned them on the slide. In this section, you adjust pictures to enhance their appearance. You will also use PowerPoint's search capabilities to find images that illustrate presentation concepts and consider various licensing requirements for the use of images available online.

Apply Picture Styles and Effects

When you select a picture on a slide, the *Picture Tools Format* tab becomes available. *Styles* provide a preset gallery of options such as framing pictures or adding a reflection.

▶ HOW TO: Apply a Picture Style

1. Insert a picture on your slide.
2. Select the picture and click the **Picture Tools Format** tab.
3. Click the **More** button on the gallery [*Picture Styles* group] to see the preset effects (Figure 2-46).

 • Point to a style to see a live preview applied to your picture.
 • A *ScreenTip* shows the style name.

4. Click a style to apply it to your picture.
5. Change to a different style by selecting a new style from the gallery.

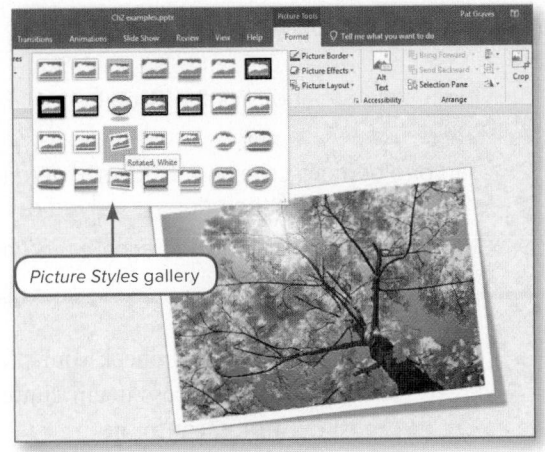

Figure 2-46 Picture style applied

Picture Effects are similar to *Shape Effects*. Each different effect has many options you can adjust. For presentations with pictures on multiple slides, it is usually best to apply similar styles or effects for consistency. If you make pictures look different, be sure you have a reason so the changes do not appear random.

▶HOW TO: Apply or Modify Picture Effects

1. Select a picture and click the **Picture Effects** button [*Picture Tools Format* tab, *Picture Styles* group].
2. Select an effect in the drop-down list to see a gallery (Figure 2-47) of options.
 - Point to an effect option to see a live preview applied to your picture.
 - Move your picture to a temporary position, if necessary, so you can better see the live preview.
3. Select **Options** at the bottom of each gallery to open the *Format Picture* pane where you can make changes to fine-tune a specific effect.
 - Right-click a picture and select **Format Picture** from the context menu to open the *Format Picture* pane.
4. Remove a picture style by selecting the picture and clicking the **Reset Picture** button [*Picture Tools Format* tab, *Adjust* group].

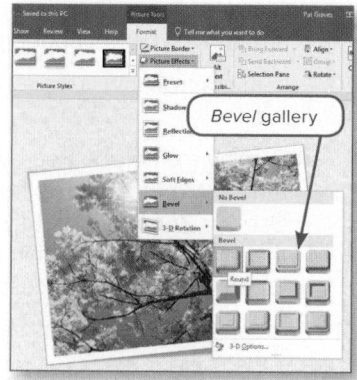

Figure 2-47 *Picture Effects*

Crop a Picture

You can *crop* (trim) unwanted areas of a selected picture by dragging black *cropping handles* on the corners and sides of the picture that appear when you click the **Crop** button. When you point to these handles, your pointer changes to a black shape that resembles the cropping handle. Be careful when dragging so you move a cropping handle and not a sizing handle.

Figure 2-48 Cropped area of a picture

▶HOW TO: Crop a Picture

1. Select a picture and click the **Crop** button [*Picture Tools Format* tab, *Size* group].
2. Drag one or more cropping handles toward the center of the picture; the area to be removed from the edges is grayed out (Figure 2-48).
3. Click the **Crop** button again to accept this change.

Always check your pictures and crop them as needed to be sure they have a strong focal point. Excess detail clutters a picture and does not help your viewers quickly grasp what you want them to see.

> **MORE INFO**
>
> The *Design Ideas* pane can provide slide layouts for multiple pictures. Once a layout is applied, then apply picture styles and effects.

Change Picture Colors

Pictures are made up of many colors to achieve the realism that digital photographs portray. PowerPoint's *Color* feature enables you to vary picture colors. For example, you might want a picture to look old or to look faded so text over the picture is easy to read.

▶ HOW TO: Change Picture Colors

1. Select a picture you want to change.

2. Click the **Color** button [*Picture Tools Format* tab, *Adjust* group] to open a gallery of color options (Figure 2-49).

 - The current option within each group is highlighted.

3. Select one or more options from the following groups to customize your picture colors:

 - **Color Saturation**: Colors are more muted as you move from the center to the left as saturation becomes lower; colors are more intense as you move from the center to the right as saturation increases.
 - **Color Tone**: Colors on the left have cool tones and lower temperature values; colors on the right have warm tones and higher values.
 - **Recolor**: Options on the first row include *Grayscale*, *Sepia*, *Washout*, and percentages of *Black and White*. The second and third rows display dark and light monotone variations of accent colors.

4. Click **Picture Color Options** at the bottom of the gallery to open the *Format Picture* pane with the *Picture Color* options displayed to further adjust a picture.

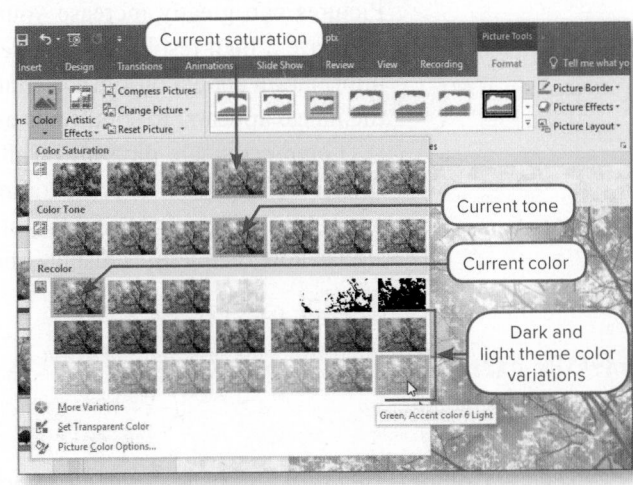

Figure 2-49 *Color* gallery

Set a Transparent Color

An image with a white background works well on a slide with a white background (or on a typical Word document) because you see just the image. However, a white background can detract from an image if you place it on a slide background with a contrasting color.

Use the *Set Transparent Color* feature to remove a single-color background. Because this feature removes only one color, it does not work well for pictures that have a lot of detail and many colors.

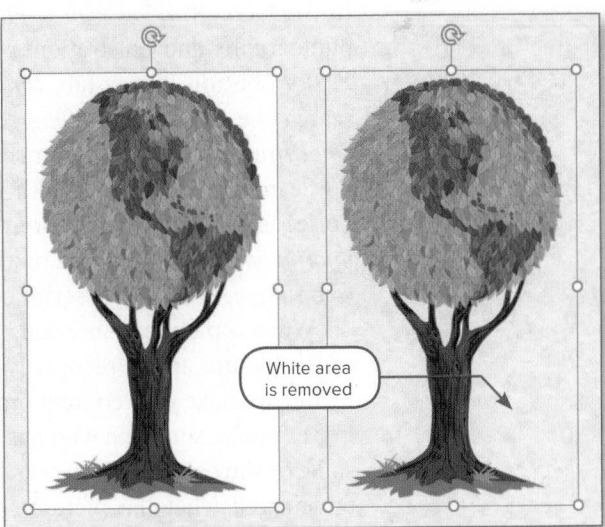

▶ HOW TO: Set a Transparent Color

1. Select a picture.

2. Click the **Color** button [*Picture Tools Format* tab, *Adjust* group].

3. Click **Set Transparent Color** and your pointer changes to a pen tool.

4. Point to the area of the picture you want to remove and click.

 - All of the area with that color value disappears, revealing what is behind the picture (Figure 2-50).

Figure 2-50 *Set Transparent Color* applied

Compress Pictures

Pictures can greatly increase your presentation file size, especially when pictures are large and have a high resolution. A *pixel* is an abbreviated term for *picture element*, a single unit of information about color in a digital image. The more pixels used in an image, the more realistic the image appears. Resolution is expressed in *pixels per inch (ppi)*.

Compress single pictures or all pictures at one time to reduce the picture resolution and, therefore, reduce your presentation's file size. Choose an option for the image quality you need. Also delete cropped areas of pictures to remove unused information. Compression only affects how the pictures display and not the original picture files.

▶ HOW TO: Compress Picture File Size

Figure 2-51 *Compress Pictures* dialog box

1. Select a picture.
2. Click the **Compress Picture** button [*Picture Tools Format* tab, *Adjust* group] to open the *Compress Pictures* dialog box (Figure 2-51).
3. Deselect **Apply only to this picture** if you want the compression to apply to all pictures in the presentation.
4. Select **Delete cropped areas of pictures** if you have cropped pictures.
5. Select the appropriate *Resolution*.
 - Options include *High fidelity*, *HD (330 ppi)*, *Print (220 ppi)*, *web (150 ppi)*, *E-mail* (96 ppi), or the *default resolution*.
 - Options will be grayed out if they are not available for your selected picture.
6. Click **OK** to close the dialog box.

Insert Online Pictures and Illustrations

In *SLO 1.6: Working with a Picture from a File*, you learned how to insert pictures (digital photographs and illustrations) saved on your computer or other locations. Click the *Online Pictures* button [*Insert* tab, *Images* group] to open the *Online Pictures* dialog box where you search the web using a *Bing* search box, access pictures organized by topics, or search on *OneDrive*. You can filter your search in several ways.

Search results appear with thumbnail pictures that have a *Creative Commons* license, so no fee is required for use. Sources may require that credit is given. Each picture has a *More information and actions* box on the lower right. When you click this box, the picture's pixel size, web source, and brief description appears.

When a picture is inserted, *Alternative Text* (called **Alt Text**) appears briefly at the bottom of the picture and is recorded in the *Alt Text* pane. This text provides information about the picture to make your content more accessible to individuals with special needs or impairments. For example, someone who has a vision problem might use software that reads screen content so he or she can hear the words that cannot be seen. A picture's *Alt Text* would help that person understand what the picture shows even though it could not be seen. Therefore, accurate descriptions are important.

Office 2019 Note: *Alt Text* is not automatically provided in Office 2019. Click the **Alt Text** button to add *Alt Text*.

Text that is automatically provided, however, may not be as descriptive as needed. To edit *Alt Text*, select the picture, click the **Alt Text** button [*Picture Tools Format* tab, *Accessibility* group] or **right-click** and select **Edit Alt Text**. The *Alt Text* pane opens showing the current information for this picture. Revise the existing text as needed. You can provide *Alt Text* for other objects in your presentations, also. A text box below the picture provides licensing information and is grouped with the picture.

▶HOW TO: Search for and Insert a Picture or Illustration

1. Click the **Online Pictures** button [*Insert* tab, *Images* group] (Figure 2-52) to open the *Online Pictures* dialog box.

 - A *Bing* search box displays.
 - Thumbnail pictures of general topics are arranged in alphabetical order.

2. Type one or more keywords In the *Bing* search box (Figure 2-53).

3. Press **Enter** to activate the search.

 - Thumbnails of pictures matching your keyword appear (Figure 2-54).
 - Check **Creative Commons only** on the upper left to restrict your results.
 - Click the **Filter** icon to select criteria to restrict your results.

4. Click to select a picture and a checkmark appears on the picture.

 - Press **Ctrl** while you click to select more than one picture.
 - Click the picture's *More information and actions* button (black with three dots) and click the web address to view the picture in a larger size on its source page.
 - Close the web browser and return to your presentation.

5. Click the **Insert** button. The picture downloads and the *Online Pictures* dialog box closes.

 - An *Alt Text* statement briefly appears at the bottom of the picture.
 - A caption below the picture provides a link to the picture's source and to Creative Commons information. The picture and caption are grouped.
 - Click the slide background to deselect the picture and caption.

6. Select the picture only (not the caption) and click the **Alt Text** button [*Picture Tools Format* tab, *Accessibility* group].

 - The *Alt Text* pane opens with the current information for this picture.

7. Edit the *Alt Text* as needed and then close the *Alt Text* pane.

Figure 2-52 *Online Pictures* button

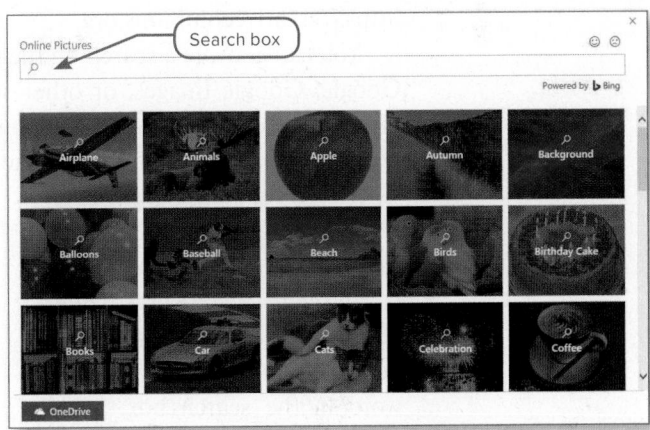

Figure 2-53 *Online Pictures* dialog box

Figure 2-54 Pictures from search

The source that appears in a caption may not be the original source of an image. It is best to reference the original source of an image if possible. You decide if you prefer to leave the notation here, edit it in some way, or include the information on a source slide at the end of your presentation.

Creative Commons Licensing

A Creative Commons (CC) license enables the free distribution of copyrighted work when the creator wants to give people the right to copy, use, or remix by building upon the work. This right is usually for non-commercial purposes. The creator can make requirements for attribution so the creator is credited for the work. You can read more about these requirements at https://creativecommons.org.

You can activate a search on the Creative Commons site for images, music, and video using Google, Google Images, or other search engines to locate work listed with the CC license. However, the results cannot be guaranteed because no registration is required to use a CC license. You still need to contact the creator (copyright holder) directly or contact the web site where you found the content.

Another way to find images that you can save for future use is through Microsoft's *Bing* search engine at www.bing.com. Select an **Images** search, type a word in the search box, press **Enter**, and the results display. If filter options are not displayed, click **Filter** in the upper-right corner to display them. Click the **License** button (Figure 2-55) to filter your results to one of the following criteria:

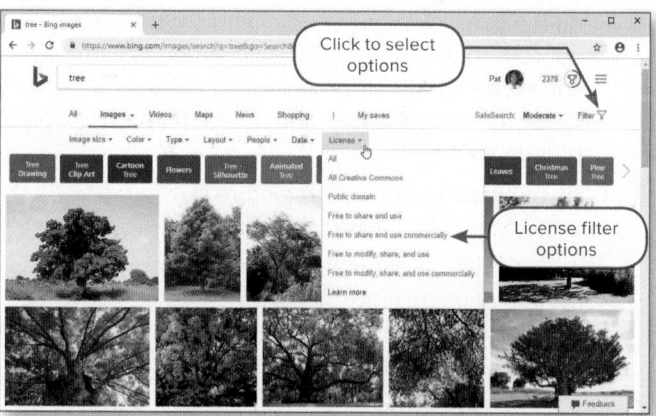

Figure 2-55 Image search at *Bing.com*

- *All*
- *All Creative Commons*
- *Public domain*
- *Free to share and use*
- *Free to share and use commercially*
- *Free to modify, share, and use*
- *Free to modify, share, and use commercially*

Bing does not verify CC licensing; you still need to go to the image's web site to determine the actual licensing being used.

When Gerod Sunderland shares his landscaping proposal with homeowners, he provides detailed printed information and uses a presentation to illustrate concepts. For this project, you add pictures and other objects to his presentation and apply a variety of styles and colors to enhance the content.

File Needed: **LandscapingProposal-02.pptx** (Student data files are available in the Library of your SIMnet account.)
Completed Project File Name: **[your initials] PP P2-1.pptx**

1. Open the presentation **LandscapingProposal-02** from your student data files.

2. Save the presentation as [your initials] PP P2-1.

3. Add a rectangle.
 a. Display slide 1 and click the **Shapes** button [*Insert* tab, *Illustrations* group].
 b. Select the **Rectangle** shape.
 c. Click and drag to draw a rectangle across the top of the slide.

Figure 2-56 Change *Shape Fill* color

 d. Change the rectangle *Height* to **.4"** and *Width* to **13.33"** [*Drawing Tools Format* tab, *Size* group].
 e. Click the **Shape Fill** drop-down arrow [*Drawing Tools Format* tab, *Shape Styles* group] and select **Green, Accent 6** (last color/first row) (Figure 2-56).
 f. Click the **Shape Outline** drop-down arrow [*Drawing Tools Format* tab, *Shape Styles* group] and select **No Outline**.
 g. Position the rectangle below the orange line.

4. Add text effects.
 a. Select the title on slide 1 and click the **Text Effects** button [*Drawing Tools Format* tab, *WordArt Styles* group].
 b. Select **Bevel** and then **Round** (Figure 2-57).
 c. Click the **Text Effects** button again, select **Shadow**, and then select **Offset: Bottom Right** (first option/*Outer* group).

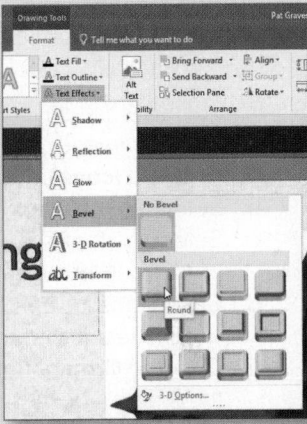

Figure 2-57 Apply *Text Effects*

5. Apply color transparency to a picture.
 a. Select the leaf picture on slide 1.
 b. Click the **Color** button [*Picture Tools Format* tab, *Adjust* group].
 c. Select **Set Transparent Color** and the pointer changes to a pen tool.
 d. Click the white area around the leaf so it becomes transparent (Figure 2-58).

6. Apply effects and use the *Format Painter*.
 a. Display slide 2 and select the left heading placeholder above the list.

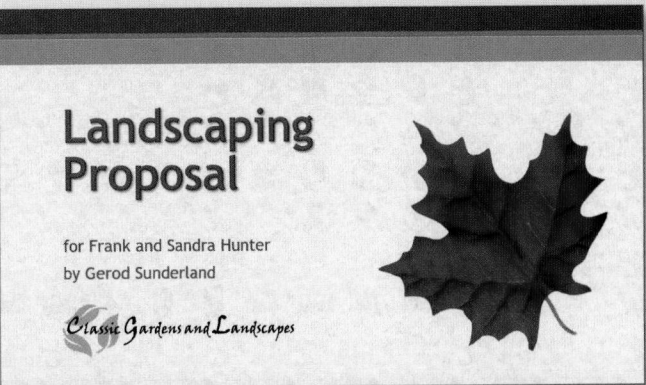

Figure 2-58 Slide 1 completed

b. Click the **Shape Fill** drop-down arrow [*Drawing Tools Format* tab, *Shape Styles* group] and select **Texture**.

c. Click the **Papyrus** option (first row).

d. Apply **Bold** [*Home* tab, *Font* group].

e. With the placeholder still selected, click the **Format Painter** button [*Home* tab, *Clipboard* group].

f. Click the list heading placeholder on the right to apply the copied format.

g. Press **Esc** to turn off the *Format Painter*.

7. Add a frame shape.

a. Display slide 3. Resize the bulleted text placeholder on the bottom and the right so the placeholder border fits the text.

b. Click the **Shapes** button [*Insert* tab, *Illustrations* group] and select the **Frame** shape (*Basic Shapes* group).

c. Click and drag to draw a frame below the list.

d. Adjust the frame size (*Height* **1"** and *Width* **3.3"**) [*Drawing Tools Format* tab, *Size* group]. Keep the frame selected for the next step.

e. Type Allow three days.

f. Change the *Font Size* to **24 pt**.

8. Change to a different shape and color.

a. Select the frame shape on slide 3. Click the **Edit Shape** button [*Drawing Tools Format* tab, *Insert Shapes* group] and select **Change Shape**.

b. Click the **Rectangle: Beveled** shape (*Basic Shapes* group).

c. Change the *Shape Fill* [*Drawing Tools Format* tab, *Shape Styles* group] to **Gold, Accent 4** (eighth color/first row) (Figure 2-59).

Figure 2-59 *Rectangle: Beveled* shape positioned below list

9. Insert and format an icon on slide 3 to create a decorative background image.

a. Click the **Icons** button [*Insert* tab, *Illustrations* group] to open the *Insert Icons* dialog box.

b. Select **Weather and seasons** in the navigation area on the left.

c. Select the **leaf** (Figure 2-60) and click **Insert**.

 • A small icon displays, and the *Graphics Tools Format* tab opens.

d. Change the *Height* to **7"** [*Graphics Tools Format* tab, *Size* group] and the *Width* automatically adjusts.

 • The leaf may cover other objects, but you will position it later.

e. Click the **Crop** button [*Graphics Tools Format* tab, *Size* group] and crop all four sides to better fit the shape (Figure 2-61). Click **Crop**.

Figure 2-60 *Insert Icons* dialog box

Figure 2-61 Cropped icon

f. Change the *Height* of the cropped image to **6"**.

g. Click the **Align** button [*Graphics Tools Format* tab, *Arrange* group] and choose **Align Left**. Repeat to choose **Align Bottom**.

h. Click the **Graphics Fill** drop-down arrow [*Graphics Tools Format* tab, *Graphics Styles* button] and choose **Green, Accent 6, Lighter 60%** (last color/third row).

i. Click the **Send Backward** drop-down arrow [*Graphics Tools Format* tab, *Arrange* group] and click **Send to Back**.

10. Search for and insert an online picture on slide 3.

 a. Click the **Online Pictures** button [*Insert* tab, *Images* group] to open the *Online Pictures* dialog box.

 b. Type the words new plant in soil in the *Bing* search box.

 c. Click **Search** (or press **Enter**) to activate the search. Results will be similar to Figure 2-62.

 d. Locate a picture of a plant in soil.

 e. Click the picture's *More information and actions* box to see the picture's size information and its web address. Make a note of this web address for step 11.

 f. Select the picture and then click **Insert**.

 • The picture is inserted and grouped with a text box below that contains links to source information.

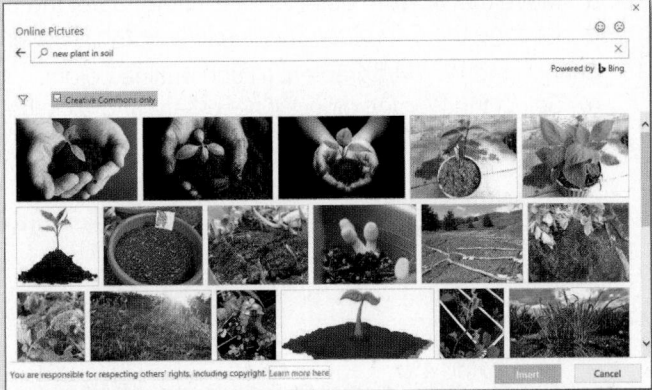

Figure 2-62 *Online Pictures* search results

11. Delete the text box below the picture because you have already documented source information.

12. Resize, crop, and add text.

 a. Select the picture on slide 3 and change its size as needed to fit in the blank area on the right of the slide.

 b. Click the **Crop** button [*Picture Tools Format* tab, *Size* group] and crop a little space from all four edges to focus more on the plant.

 c. Click the **Crop** button again to accept the crop.

 d. Click the **More** button [*Picture Tools Format* tab, *Picture Styles* group] and select the **Rotated, White** picture style.

 e. Insert a text box [*Insert* tab, *Text* group] and type the picture's source information.

 f. Position the text box below the picture (see Figure 2-63).

 g. Select the bulleted list placeholder and move it down to fit over the green leaf. If necessary, move the *Bevel* shape.

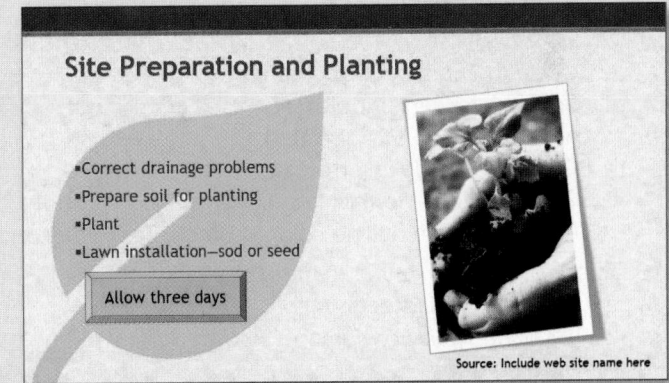

Figure 2-63 Slide 3 completed

13. Compress a picture to reduce presentation file size.

 a. Select the picture on slide 3 and click **Compress Pictures** [*Picture Tools Format* tab, *Adjust* group].

 b. Deselect **Apply only to this picture**.

 c. Select **Use default resolution** for the *Target output*.

 d. Click **OK**.

14. Add *WordArt* text.
 a. Display slide 8 and click the **WordArt** button [*Insert* tab, *Text* group].

 b. Select the **Gradient Fill: Gold, Accent color 4; Outline: Gold, Accent color 4** (third option/second row) from the *Style* gallery.

Figure 2-64 *WordArt with gradient fill applied*

 c. Type Thank you for your business! in the *WordArt* text box.
 d. Move the *WordArt* object so it is at the top of the picture (Figure 2-64).
 e. Change the *Character Spacing* [*Home* tab, *Font* group] to **Tight**.

15. Change the *WordArt* gradient fill and outline colors.
 a. Select the *WordArt* object, if necessary, and click the **Text Fill** drop-down arrow [*Drawing Tools Format* tab, *WordArt Styles* group].
 • Select **Gradient** and click **More Gradients** to open the *Format Shape* pane.
 • All gradient options appear in the pane.
 b. Select the second gradient stop (at Position **4%**).
 • Click the **Remove gradient stop** button.
 c. Select the left gradient stop (at Position **0%**) (Figure 2-65).
 • Click the **Color** button and select **Green, Accent 6, Lighter 40%** (last color/fourth row).
 d. Select the right gradient stop.
 • Click the **Color** button and select **Green, Accent 6, Darker 50%** (last color/bottom row).
 e. Close the *Format Shape* pane.
 f. Select the *WordArt* object, if necessary, and click the **Text Outline** drop-down arrow [*Drawing Tools Format* tab, *WordArt Styles* group].
 • Change the outline color to **Black, Text 1** (second color/first row).

Figure 2-65 *Format Shape pane*

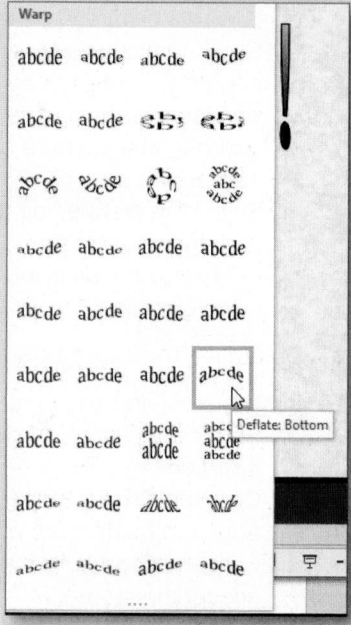

Figure 2-66 *WordArt Transform gallery*

16. Apply a *Transform* effect to the *WordArt*.
 a. Click the **Text Effects** button [*Drawing Tools Format* tab, *WordArt Styles* group].
 b. Select **Transform** from the drop-down list. Click the **Deflate Bottom** effect from the *Transform* gallery (Figure 2-66).
 c. Resize the *WordArt* (*Height* **2"** and *Width* **10"**).
 d. Click **Align** [*Drawing Tools Format* tab, *Arrange* group] and click **Align Center** so the *WordArt* fits across the top of the picture (Figure 2-67).

Figure 2-67 *Deflate Bottom Transform* effect applied and adjusted

17. Save and close your presentation (Figure 2-68).

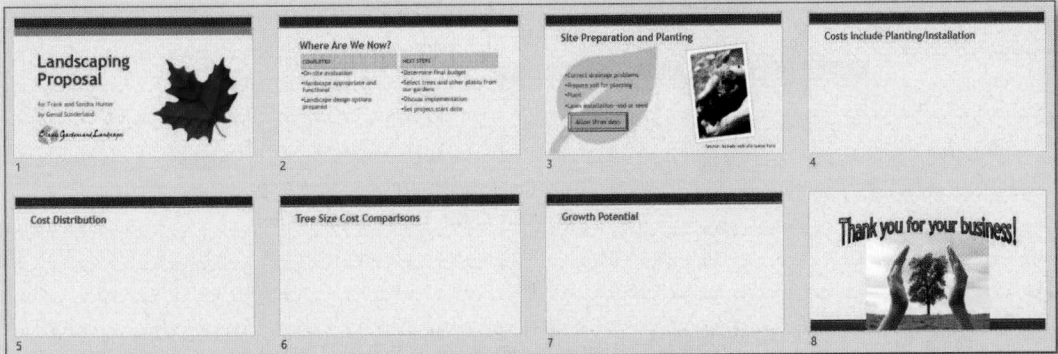

Figure 2-68 PP P2-1 completed

Creating a Table

Tables show data in an organized and easy-to-read format because information is arranged in *columns* (vertical) and *rows* (horizontal). The intersection of a column and a row is a *cell*. *Border* lines and *shading* show the table structure. Working with PowerPoint tables is much like working with tables in Word. Create a table from a content placeholder when you create a new slide or by using options on the *Insert* tab.

Once you create a table, you can change its size as well as column width and row height. Use table formatting to emphasize the content and help your audience interpret the data. If you plan to project your slides on a large screen, be sure your table information is concise so that you can use a minimum font size of 20 points. If a table requires a lot of detailed information, then prepare the table as a full-page handout with body text at an 11- to 12-point size. You could prepare a PowerPoint slide to reference the handout as you explain the table, or perhaps show only a portion of the table on a slide.

Insert and Draw Methods

You can create the columns and rows of a table in different ways. Click the **Table** button [*Insert* tab, *Tables* group] to visually select columns and rows by dragging over them. The table dimensions (such as *3x4 Table* meaning three columns by four rows) are shown at the top of the drop-down list. By default, columns and rows appear on the slide with even sizing, but you can adjust column width and row height as you add information.

▶ **HOW TO: Insert a Table and Select Columns and Rows**

1. Display the slide where you want the table.
2. Click the **Insert** tab.
3. Click the **Table** button [*Tables* group] to open the drop-down list.
4. Drag across and down to select the number of columns and rows you need (Figure 2-69).

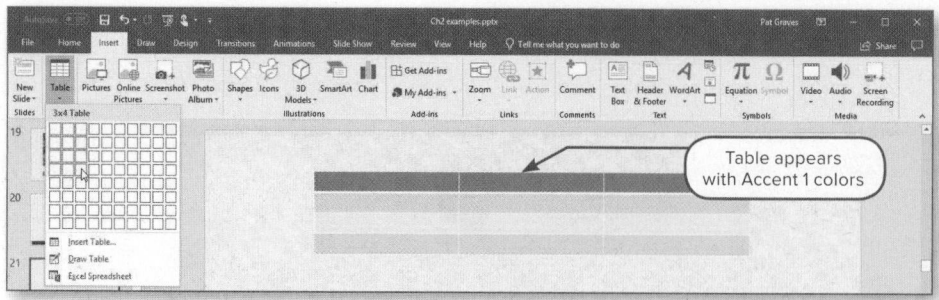

Figure 2-69 Table cells selected

5. Release the pointer to insert the table.

Use the **Insert Table** command [*Insert* tab, *Tables* group] to create a table by entering a specific number of columns and rows.

▶ **HOW TO:** Insert a Table and Enter the Number of Columns and Rows

1. Display the slide where you want to insert the table.
2. Click the **Insert** tab.
3. Click the **Table** button [*Tables* group] to open the drop-down list.
4. Click **Insert Table** and the *Insert Table* dialog box opens (Figure 2-70).
5. Specify the number of columns and rows.
6. Click **OK** to close the *Insert Table* dialog box and insert the table.

Figure 2-70 *Insert Table* dialog box

On a new slide with the *Title and Content* layout, click the **Insert Table** icon in the content placeholder to open the *Insert Table* dialog box. Enter the number of columns and rows to create the table. Because of the placeholder size, the table width will be slightly wider than when you click the **Table** button on the *Insert* tab to create a table.

The final way to create a table is by drawing the table area and dividing it into columns and rows. This method works well when space is limited on the slide because of other content.

▶ **HOW TO:** Draw a Table

1. Display the slide where you want the table.
2. Click the **Insert** tab.
3. Click the **Table** button [*Tables* group] to open the drop-down list.
4. Click **Draw Table** and your pointer changes to a pen.
5. Drag the pen to draw the outside border of the table in the size you want.
6. Click the **Draw Table** button [*Table Tools Design* tab, *Draw Borders* group] to activate the pen again.

7. Drag the pen inside the table to insert horizontal and vertical lines that divide the table into rows and columns (Figure 2-71).

- Start dragging near but not touching the outside border.
- The lines will expand on both ends to reach the borders.

8. Press **Esc** to turn off the pen tool.

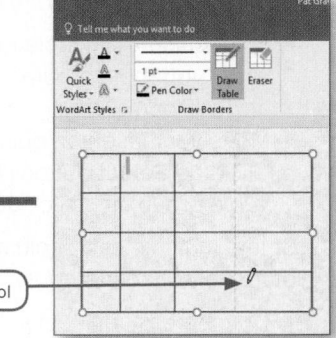

Figure 2-71 *Draw Table*

Regardless of the method you use to create a table, the *Table Tools Design* tab (Figure 2-72) and *Table Tools Layout* tab (Figure 2-73) are available when the table is active.

Figure 2-72 *Table Tools Design tab*

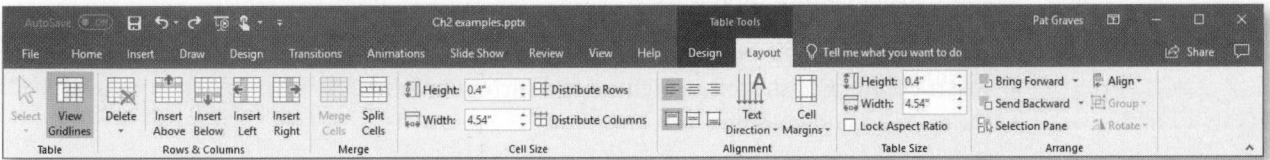

Figure 2-73 *Table Tools Layout tab*

Move and Select

Your insertion point indicates where you are within a table. To move from cell to cell, use one of the following methods:

- Press **Tab** to move to the next cell on the right (or the first cell in the next row).
- Press **Shift+Tab** to move to the previous cell on the left.
- Press arrow keys to move in different directions from the current cell.
- Click a cell to move the insertion point to that cell.

Where you point within a table influences whether you select individual cells, columns, rows, or the entire table. Your pointer changes to a selection pointer (a black arrow that points in different directions based on what you are selecting).

▶ **HOW TO: Select Cells, Columns, Rows, and the Table**

1. Select a cell by pointing inside the left border and clicking when your pointer turns into a black arrow that angles (Figure 2-74).

2. Select a column by using one of the following methods:

 - Point above the column's top border and click when your pointer turns into a downward-pointing black arrow (Figure 2-75).
 - Move your insertion point to any cell in the column. Click the **Select** button [*Table Tools Layout* tab, *Table* group] and click **Select Column**.

Figure 2-74 *Select table cell*

3. Select a row by using one of the following methods:
 - Point outside the table to the left of a row and click when your pointer turns into a right-pointing black arrow (Figure 2-76).
 - Move your insertion point to any cell in the row. Click the **Select** button [*Table Tools Layout* tab, *Table* group] and click **Select Row**.

Figure 2-75 Select table column

4. Select multiple cells, columns, or rows by using one of the following methods:
 - Drag across adjacent cells.
 - Press **Shift** as you click additional adjacent cells.
5. Select an entire table by using one of the following methods:

Figure 2-76 Select table row

 - Drag across all cells in the table.
 - Move your insertion point to any cell in the table. Click the **Select** button [*Table Tools Layout* tab, *Table* group] and click **Select Table**.

Insert and Delete Rows and Columns

After you begin entering table content, you may need to add rows or columns. You can change a table's structure in several ways:

- Insert rows above or below the current row.
- Insert columns to the left or right of the current column.
- Delete rows and columns.

▶ **HOW TO:** Insert and Delete Rows and Columns

1. Click a table cell next to where you want to add a row or column.
2. Click the **Insert Above** or **Insert Below** buttons [*Table Tools Layout* tab, *Rows & Columns* group] to add a row.
3. Click the **Insert Left** or **Insert Right** buttons [*Table Tools Layout* tab, *Rows & Columns* group] to add a column.
4. Click a table cell where you want to delete a row or column.
5. Click the **Delete** button and select **Delete Rows** or **Delete Columns** [*Rows & Columns* group] (Figure 2-77).

Figure 2-77 *Delete* button with options

▶ **ANOTHER WAY**

Right-click a row or column and insert or delete a row or column by selecting the appropriate option from the mini toolbar or context menu.

Merge and Split Cells

Use the *Merge Cells* command to combine two or more cells in a row or column. For example, you can merge all the cells in the top row of a table so a title will span all columns. Use the *Split Cells* command to divide any single cell into two or more cells.

▶HOW TO: Merge and Split Cells

1. Select the cells to be merged.
2. Click the **Merge Cells** button [*Table Tools Layout* tab, *Merge* group] to combine those cells into one cell.
3. Select the cell (or cells) to be split.
4. Click the **Split Cells** button [*Table Tools Layout* tab, *Merge* group] to open the *Split Cells* dialog box and enter the number of columns and rows that you need.
5. Click **OK** to close the dialog box.

> ▶ **ANOTHER WAY**
>
> Click the **Eraser** button [*Table Tools Design* tab, *Draw Borders* group]. Use the eraser pointer to click a border within the table to remove it and merge cells. Press **Esc** to turn off the *Eraser*.

Adjust Sizing

You often need to resize tables to display information appropriately. Column widths will vary based on content, but row height should usually be consistent. When even spacing is desired, click the *Distribute Rows* button or the *Distribute Columns* button to allocate row or column space evenly within the size of the table.

▶HOW TO: Resize a Table, Cells, Columns, and Rows

1. Resize a table using one of these methods.
 - Enter sizes in the *Height* and *Width* boxes [*Table Tools Layout* tab, *Table Size* group].
 - Click and drag table sizing handles as you would to resize a shape.
2. Resize a cell, column, or row using one of these methods.
 - Point to a cell, column, or row border. When your pointer changes to a splitter (Figure 2-78), click and drag to increase or decrease the size of the cell, column, or row.
 - Select the cell, column, or row to change; then enter the size you want in the *Height* and *Width* boxes [*Table Tools Layout* tab, *Cell Size* group].

Figure 2-78 Change column width

3. Resize a column to fit the text within it. Point to a column border and double-click when your pointer changes to a splitter.
4. Distribute column width evenly. Select the columns to be changed and click the **Distribute Columns** button [*Table Tools Layout* tab, *Cell Size* group].
5. Distribute row height evenly. Select the rows to be changed and click the **Distribute Rows** buttons [*Table Tools Layout* tab, *Cell Size* group.

> ▶ **MORE INFO**
>
> To maintain column width proportions, press **Shift** as you drag table sizing handles or select **Lock Aspect Ratio** [*Table Tools Layout* tab, *Table Size* group] before entering *Height* or *Width* sizes.

Formatting a Table

Format text in a table the same way you format any other text such as changing fonts and text effects. You can also change cell margins and text direction. While shading and borders may appear decorative, these effects can make a table easier to interpret. For example, shading individual rows helps the reader focus on one line of text; shading on a column draws attention to text in that vertical space. PowerPoint provides many preset styles using color combinations derived from theme colors. Customize effects to create a unique design.

PowerPoint's *Designer* feature will suggest different slide layouts for tables. Click the **Design Ideas** button [*Design* pane, *Designer* group] to open the *Design Ideas* pane with several slide background designs or different table styles. It is usually best to apply one of these layouts before customizing your table. If you customize the table first, not all of the layout options presented in the *Design Ideas* pane will retain those changes.

Office 2019 Note: PowerPoint's *Designer* feature is not available in Office 2019, so the *Design Ideas* pane will not open.

Table Style Options and Effects

On the *Table Tools Design* tab, the ***Table Styles*** gallery provides options for a table's design. The first style on each row of options displays in black and white, while the other six styles are in theme accent colors. Table styles are arranged in the following categories:

- *Best Match for Document*
- *Light*
- *Medium*
- *Dark*

Each table style is influenced by the features checked for ***Table Style Options*** [*Table Tools Design* tab]. Fill colors that emphasize table cells vary depending on which of the following options you select:

- ***Header Row*** or ***Total Row***: The first or last row has a darker color and has bold text in a contrasting color.
- ***First Column*** or ***Last Column***: The first or last column has a darker color and has bold text in a contrasting color.
- ***Banded Rows*** or ***Banded Columns***: The rows or columns have alternating colors. *Banded Rows* improves reading across the table. *Banded Columns* emphasizes the separate columns.

▶ **HOW TO:** Apply a Table Style and Options

1. Click anywhere in the table you want to format.
2. Click the **More** button [*Table Tools Design* tab, *Table Styles* group] to see the complete gallery (Figure 2-79). The current style is highlighted.
3. Point to a style to see a live preview. *ScreenTips* identify each style name.
4. Click a style to apply it.

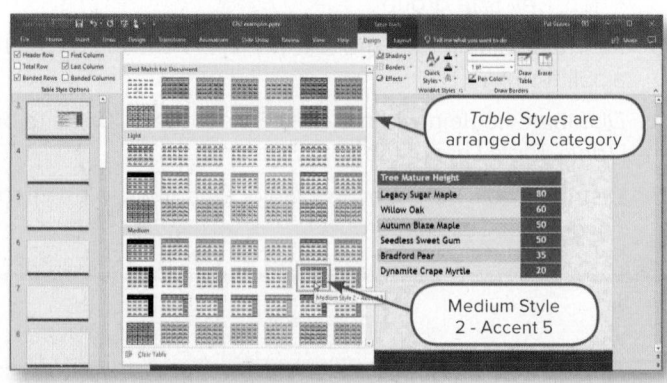

Figure 2-79 *Table Styles*

5. Adjust *Table Style Options* as needed.
 - Check **Header Row** and **Banded Rows** [*Table Tools Design* tab, *Table Style Options* group].
 - Deselect **Banded Rows** and select **Banded Columns** [*Table Tools Design* tab, *Table Style Options* group].

If you want to remove table formatting, click the **More** button [*Table Tools Design* tab, *Table Styles* group] and click **Clear Table**. To emphasize the table or cells within the table, such as a heading row, apply effects to selected areas.

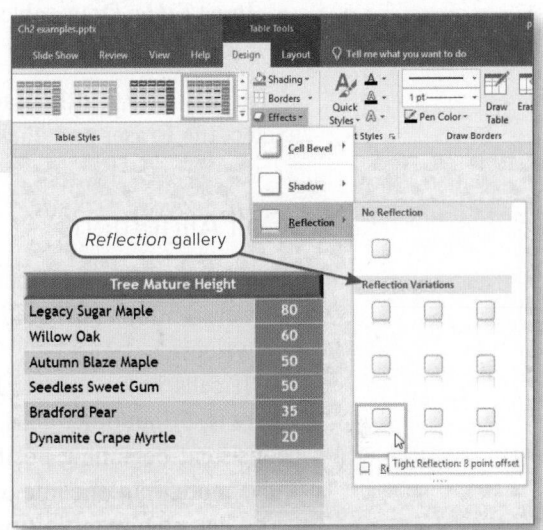

▶ HOW TO: Apply Table Effects

1. Select the table, or the cells, to format.
2. Click the **Effects** button [*Table Tools Design* tab, *Table Styles* group (Figure 2-80).
3. Select one of the following effects:
 - **Cell Bevel**
 - **Shadow**
 - **Reflection**
4. Point to an option to see a live preview. *ScreenTips* identify each option name.
5. Click an option to apply it.

Figure 2-80 *Reflection Effects*

Shading and Border Colors

After you apply a built-in table style, you can change colors to emphasize your content or better match other aspects of your presentation. Select the cells you want to change and click the **Shading** drop-down arrow [*Table Tools Design* tab, *Table Styles* group] to select a different color (Figure 2-81). The icon for *Shading* is the same as the icon for *Shape Fill*.

Border lines separate cells and outline the edge of the table, but not all table styles show border lines. To add lines, use the **Borders** button [*Table Tools Design* tab, *Table Styles* group] and each available option shows where the border line will be applied when that option is selected (Figure 2-82).

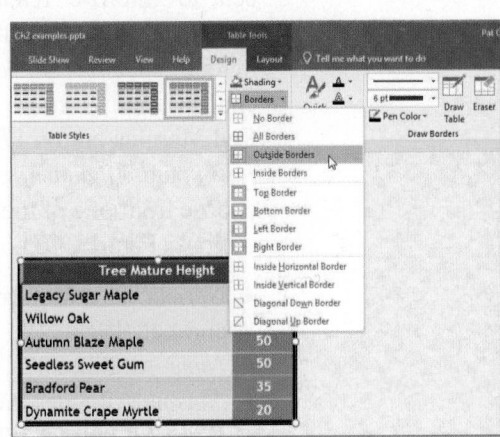

Figure 2-82 *Pen Weight* changed and *Outside Borders* applied

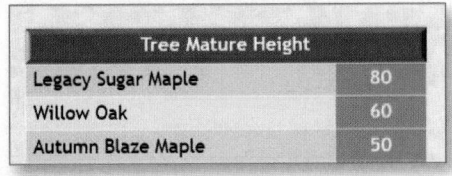

Figure 2-81 Shading emphasizes content

Click the **Pen Weight** button [*Table Tools Design* tab, *Draw Borders* group] to change line thickness before you apply a border line. Then select the appropriate area before you apply a border line. Remove borders from selected cells by clicking the **Borders** button and selecting **No Border**.

Also, you can apply, change, and remove borders using the *Pen* tools [*Table Tools Design* tab, *Draw Borders* group]:

- *Pen Color*: Change line color.
- *Pen Style*: Choose a different line style.
- *Pen Weight*: Change line thickness.
- *Draw Table*: Draw table area, as well as column and row border lines.
- *Eraser*: Remove border lines.

It may take a little practice to use the pen to change table lines and not start a new table. Select the **Eraser** and click each border line you need to remove.

Cell Alignment

Within cells, text is aligned on the left by default, which is appropriate for words and phrases. However, numbers should usually be right-aligned so your audience can more easily interpret the values.

If cells have a single line of text, center the text vertically in the cells. If cells contain more text than other cells, top alignment generally works best because reading is easier with a consistent beginning position. Bottom alignment works well for column headings when they have more than one line of text.

Click alignment buttons [*Table Tools Layout* tab, *Alignment* group] to control horizontal and vertical alignment within cells:

- *Horizontal alignment*: **Align Left**, **Center**, **Align Right**
- *Vertical alignment*: **Align Top**, **Center Vertically**, **Align Bottom**

Cell Margins and Text Direction

Add space between the border lines of a cell and the text in the cell to improve readability of the table. The default internal margin spacing is *Normal*. To change the spacing, click the **Cell Margins** button [*Table Tools Layout* tab, *Alignment* group] and choose from one of the following options (Figure 2-83):

- *Normal*: Top/Bottom **.05"** and Left/Right **.1"**
- *None*: All Sides **0"**
- *Narrow*: All Sides **0.05"**
- *Wide*: All Sides **0.15"**

Click **Custom Margins** to open the *Cell Text Layout* dialog box to enter other measurements.

Figure 2-83 *Cell Margins* options

Text is, by default, arranged horizontally in each cell. Be careful when changing text direction because your text may not be as easy to read. Click the **Text Direction** button [*Table Tools Layout* tab, *Alignment* group] and choose one of the following four options (Figure 2-84):

- *Horizontal*
- *Rotate all text 90°*
- *Rotate all text 270°*
- *Stacked*

Figure 2-84 *Text Direction* options

PAUSE & PRACTICE: POWERPOINT 2-2

For this project, you create a table of costs, insert a row of data, and format the table to blend with other colors used in the landscaping presentation. You also add a text box to show an alternative cost.

File Needed: *[your initials] PP P2-1.pptx* (Student data files are available in the Library of your SIMnet account.)
Completed Project File Name: *[your initials] PP P2-2.pptx*

1. Open the presentation *[your initials] PP P2-1* and save it as [your initials] PP P2-2.

2. Create a table.
 a. Display slide 4 and click the **Insert Table** icon on the content placeholder to open the *Insert Table* dialog box.
 b. Enter 4 columns and 5 rows. Click **OK** to close the dialog box and create the table.
 c. Type the text in Table 2-2 beginning with the column headings.
 d. Click and drag across the table to select all cells. Change the *Font Size* to **20 pt**. [*Home* tab, *Font* group] (Figure 2-85).

3. Adjust table sizing and alignment.
 a. Adjust column width by pointing to each border separating the columns and double-clicking when your pointer changes to a splitter.
 - For the right side of the "Totals" column, deselect the table and then point just inside the right border so your pointer will change to a splitter and then double-click.

Table 2-2

Item	Quantity	Cost Each	Totals
Trees—shade	3	500	1,500
Trees—ornamental	3	150	450
Perennials	30	12	360
Hydroseeding sq. ft.	8,000	.10	800

Costs Include Planting/Installation

Item	Quantity	Cost Each	Totals
Trees—shade	3	500	1,500
Trees—ornamental	3	150	450
Perennials	30	12	360
Hydroseeding sq. ft.	8,000	.10	800

Figure 2-85 Table as it first appears with *Font Size* change

b. Point above the "**Quantity**" column and click when your pointer turns into a black arrow. Drag across the "**Cost Each**" and "**Totals**" columns to select all three cells in those columns. Click the **Align Right** button [*Table Tools Layout* tab, *Alignment* group].

4. Insert rows and add text.
 a. Click the "**Perennials**" cell and click the **Insert Above** button [*Table Tools Layout* tab, *Rows & Columns* group].
 b. Add the following text to the newly inserted row:

 Shrubs 10 40 400

 c. Click the "**Hydroseeding**" cell and click the **Insert Below** button [*Table Tools Layout* tab, *Rows & Columns* group].
 d. Select the last three cells on the new row and click the **Merge Cells** button [*Table Tools Layout* tab, *Merge* group].
 e. Add the following text:

 Total 3,510

5. Select table styles, options, and shading.
 a. Click the **More** button [*Table Tools Design* tab, *Table Styles* group] and select the **Medium Style 3, Accent 6** style.
 b. Check **Header Row**, **Total Row**, and **Banded Rows** [*Table Tools Design* tab, *Table Style Options* group] if they are not already checked.
 c. Select a row with gray shading. Click the **Shading** drop-down arrow [*Table Tools Design* tab, *Table Styles* group] and select **Green, Accent 6, Lighter 80%** (last color/second row). Repeat for the remaining two gray rows.
 d. Select the last row. Click the **Shading** drop-down arrow and select **Green, Accent 6, Lighter 60%** (last color/third row).
 e. Select the first row. Click the **Effects** button [*Table Tools Design* tab, *Table Styles* group], click **Cell Bevel**, and select **Slant** (Figure 2-86).

Item	Quantity	Cost Each	Totals
Trees—shade	3	500	1,500
Trees—ornamental	3	150	450
Shrubs	10	40	400
Perennials	30	12	360
Hydroseeding sq. ft.	8,000	.10	800
Total			3,510

Figure 2-86 Style, row shading, and *Bevel* effect applied

6. Add borders and a shadow effect.
 a. Select the table.
 b. Click the **Pen Color** button [*Table Tools Design* tab, *Draw Borders* group] and select **Green, Accent 6, Darker 50%** (last color/bottom row).
 c. Click the **Pen Weight** button [*Table Tools Design* tab, *Draw Borders* group] and select **6 pt**.
 d. Click the **Borders** drop-down arrow [*Table Tools Design* tab, *Table Styles* group] and select **Outside Borders**.
 e. Select the table and click the **Effects** button [*Table Tools Design* tab, *Table Styles* group]. Click **Shadow** and select **Offset: Bottom Right** in the *Outer* group.

7. Center the table on the slide.
 a. Click the **Align** button [*Table Tools Layout* tab, *Arrange* group] and select **Align Center**.
 b. Click **Align** again and select **Align Middle**.

8. Insert a text box.
 a. Click the **Text Box** button [*Insert* tab, *Text* group] and click the slide area below the table to start a text box. Type the following text:

 Sod cost for 8,000 sq. ft. @ .60 = $4,800

b. Change the *Font Size* to **20 pt**. [*Home* tab, *Font* group].
c. Click the **Shape Fill** drop-down arrow [*Home* tab, *Drawing* group] and select **Green, Accent 6, Lighter 60%** (last color/third row).
d. Resize the text box as necessary so the text fits on one line. Move it to the lower right of the slide (Figure 2-87).

9. Save and close your presentation (Figure 2-88).

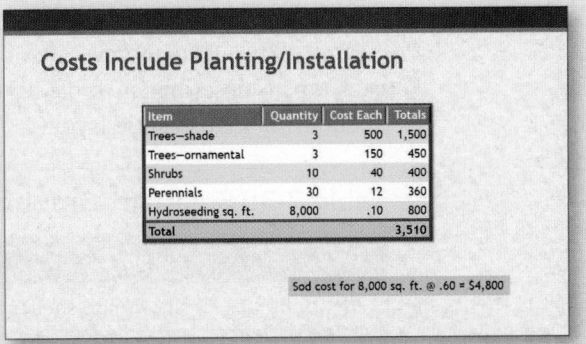

Figure 2-87 Slide 4 table completed

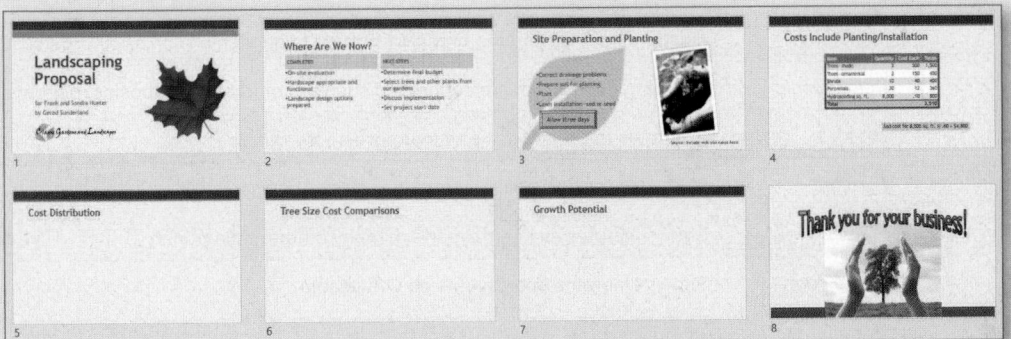

Figure 2-88 PP P2-2 completed

SLO 2.6

Creating a SmartArt Graphic

To clearly illustrate concepts such as processes, cycles, or relationships, create a diagram using *SmartArt graphics* to help your audience see connections or sequences. This is a very important communication strategy; the shapes of the diagram are concisely labeled for each concept and the shapes are connected in various ways. For example, you can show subtopics radiating from a central topic or sequential steps in a workflow.

The *SmartArt Tools Design* tab (Figure 2-89) provides options for the overall layout and styles of the *SmartArt* graphics. You can add shapes and rearrange the order of shapes.

The *SmartArt Tools Format* tab (Figure 2-90) provides options to customize shape and text styles, fill colors, outline colors, and effects.

Figure 2-89 *SmartArt Tools Design* tab

Figure 2-90 *SmartArt Tools Format* tab

SmartArt Layouts

SmartArt layouts (diagrams) are organized by type in the *Choose a SmartArt Graphic* dialog box; each type is described in Table 2-3. When you select a layout, PowerPoint provides information about using that specific layout.

Table 2-3: SmartArt Graphic Layout Types and Purposes

Type	Purpose
List	Shows non-sequential or grouped information
Process	Displays sequential steps in a process or workflow
Cycle	Displays a continuing sequence or concepts related to a central idea
Hierarchy	Illustrates a decision tree or top-to-bottom relationship such as an organizational chart
Relationship	Shows concepts that are connected such as contrasting, opposing, or converging
Matrix	Illustrates the relationship of four parts to the whole
Pyramid	Illustrates proportional or interconnected relationships
Picture	Shows pictures as integral parts of many different diagrams
Office.com	Shows diagrams from layouts on Office.com

▶ HOW TO: Create a SmartArt Graphic

1. Use one of these methods to open the *Choose a SmartArt Graphic* dialog box:
 - Create a new slide and click the **Insert a SmartArt Graphic** icon on the content placeholder.
 - Display the slide where you want to insert the *SmartArt* graphic and click the **SmartArt** button [*Insert* tab, *Illustrations* group].
2. Select a type from the list on the left (Figure 2-91).
3. Click a layout in the gallery to select it.
4. Click **OK** to close the dialog box.
 - The *SmartArt* graphic appears on the slide with sample text.

Figure 2-91 *Choose a SmartArt Graphic* dialog box

When you insert a *SmartArt* graphic using the *SmartArt* button on the *Insert* tab, the initial size of the *SmartArt* frame may be different than if you inserted the *SmartArt* graphic using the content placeholder on a new slide with a *Title and Content* layout. You may need to resize the frame for your content to fit appropriately on your slide.

If the layout you choose has picture placeholders on the shapes, such as the *Continuous Picture List* layout shown in Figure 2-92, click

Figure 2-92 *SmartArt Continuous Picture List* layout

each picture icon to open the *Insert Pictures* dialog box. Locate the picture you want to use and click **Insert**. The picture is sized automatically and shaped to fit the current picture placeholder.

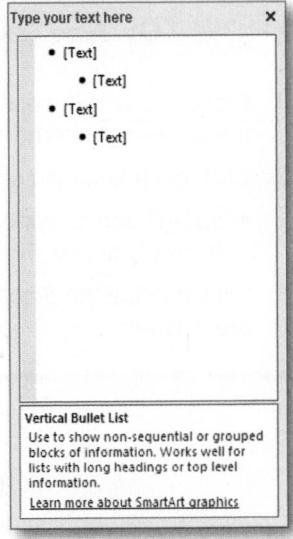

Add Text

Click the **Text Pane** button [*SmartArt Tools Design* tab, *Create Graphic* group] to open a pane beside your layout (Figure 2-93). As you type in the pane, *SmartArt* text appears as a bulleted list and in the *SmartArt* shapes on the slide. Text becomes smaller in the shapes as you enter more text, so it is important to use only a few words. You can resize or move the *Text pane*.

List layouts often work well if you have two levels of bulleted text: Level 1 (the first line) and Level 2 (text indented to a sublevel). The two levels of text are arranged differently based on the selected *SmartArt* layout.

Figure 2-93 *SmartArt Text* pane

▶HOW TO: Type SmartArt Text Using the Text Pane

1. Open the *Text* pane, if necessary, by using one of the following methods:
 - Click the **Text Pane** button [*SmartArt Tools Design* tab, *Create Graphic* group].
 - Click the smaller **Text Pane** button on the left side of the *SmartArt* frame.
2. Type text after the first bullet to add Level 1 text.
3. Press **Enter** to add a new item in the *Text* pane.
 - Another shape appears in your *SmartArt* layout, and shape sizes automatically adjust.
4. Press **Tab** in the *Text* pane to indent for Level 2 text (Figure 2-94).
 - Notice in this example that Level 1 text is in a shape and Level 2 text is in a bulleted list below the shape.
5. Press **Shift+Tab** in the *Text* pane to go from Level 2 text to Level 1 text.
6. Use arrow keys to move through the listed items.
7. Remove a shape by deleting the related bulleted text in the *Text* pane.
8. Close the *Text* pane.
 - Click outside the *SmartArt* layout and the *Text pane* automatically closes.
 - If you want to keep the current *SmartArt* layout active, click the *Text* pane's **Close** button or the **Text Pane** button [*SmartArt Tools Design* tab, *Create Graphic* group] to close the pane.

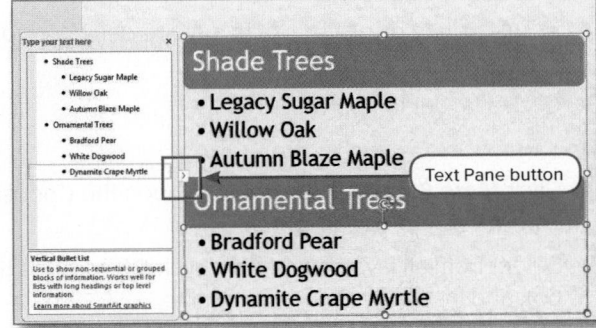

Figure 2-94 *SmartArt Text* pane with *SmartArt* layout

Another way to add text is to type directly into each *SmartArt* shape. Text resizes as you type, so be concise to avoid text becoming too small for easy reading. Pressing **Tab** does not move your insertion point between shapes. You can paste copied text, but you cannot drag text into a *SmartArt* shape.

►HOW TO: Type Text in SmartArt Shapes

1. Close the *Text Pane*, if open, by clicking the **Close** button in the upper-right corner of the pane.

2. Click each *SmartArt* shape to select it and type your text.
 - Sizing handles appear on the individual shape as you type or edit your text (Figure 2-95).

3. Click outside the *SmartArt* frame, or press **Esc**, when you are finished.

Figure 2-95 Add text in the *SmartArt Continuous Picture List* layout

If you already have bulleted text on your slide, you can quickly change that text to a *SmartArt* graphic. The gallery layouts that first appear are designed for listed information, but you can access all the other layouts, too.

►HOW TO: Convert Text to a SmartArt Graphic

1. Select the bulleted text placeholder or click anywhere in the placeholder that you want to convert to a *SmartArt* graphic.

2. Click the **Convert to SmartArt Graphic** button [*Home* tab, *Paragraph* group] (Figure 2-96).
 - The gallery displays layouts that are designed to show listed information.

3. Click a layout to apply it.

Or

4. Click **More SmartArt Graphics** to open the *Choose a SmartArt Graphic* dialog box.

5. Select from all layouts and then click **OK** to close the dialog box and insert the *SmartArt* graphic.

Figure 2-96 *Convert to SmartArt* graphic

SLO 2.7

Formatting a SmartArt Graphic

When you create a *SmartArt* graphic, it appears using the first accent color in the current color theme. Before customizing colors and effects, try PowerPoint's *Designer* feature. Click the **Design Ideas** button [*Design* pane, *Designer* group] to open the *Design Ideas* pane with slide layouts showing different background designs and different SmartArt layouts positioned in different ways. If you customize the *SmartArt* first, the colors and effects are not retained.

Office 2019 Note: PowerPoint's *Designer* feature is not available in Office 2019, so the *Design Ideas* pane will not open.

Once you are satisfied with the slide layout, use options on the *SmartArt Tools Design* tab to select styles, change colors, rearrange shape order, add shapes, or change layouts.

SmartArt Styles

The **SmartArt Styles** gallery provides different effects for emphasizing the diagram shapes. In the **3D** group, the styles have a dimensional effect. When choosing these styles, be sure that your diagram is not distorted or difficult to interpret.

▶ HOW TO: Apply SmartArt Styles

1. Select the *SmartArt* graphic.
2. Click the **SmartArt Tools Design** tab.
3. Click the **More** button [*SmartArt Styles* group] to open the *SmartArt Styles* gallery (Figure 2-97).
4. Point to a style to see a live preview.
 - The style name displays as a *ScreenTip*.
5. Click a style to apply it.

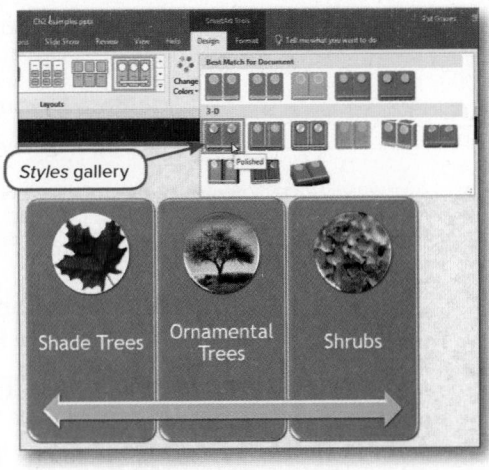

Figure 2-97 *SmartArt* graphic styles

Change Colors

The ***Change Colors*** gallery provides a quick way to change all the colors in a *SmartArt* graphic at the same time. Color options are arranged in groups. The *Primary Theme Colors* group shows variations of text and background colors, the *Colorful* group shows options with four different theme colors, and the remaining six groups each show variations of *Accent* color.

Change individual shape colors within a *SmartArt* graphic as you would any other shape.

HOW TO: Change SmartArt Colors

1. Select the *SmartArt* graphic.
2. Click the **Change Colors** button [*SmartArt Tools Design* tab, *SmartArt Styles* group] and select a gallery option to change colors for the entire diagram (Figure 2-98).

Or

3. Change the color of a selected shape within a diagram by clicking the **Shape Fill** drop-down arrow or the **Shape Outline** drop-down arrow [*SmartArt Tools Format* tab, *Shape Styles* group] and choosing an appropriate color.

Figure 2-98 *SmartArt* graphic *Change Colors* options

Change Layouts

You may find that the *SmartArt* graphic layout you have chosen is not appropriate for the process or relationship you are trying to show, or you might need a layout that displays two levels of information.

▶ HOW TO: Change Layouts

1. Select the *SmartArt* graphic.
2. Click the **SmartArt Tools Design** tab and click the **More** button [*Layouts* group] to open the *Layouts* gallery (Figure 2-99).
3. Point to a layout to see a live preview of that layout.

Figure 2-99 *SmartArt* graphic layouts

4. Click a layout to apply it.

Or

5. Click **More Layouts** to open the *Choose a SmartArt Graphic* dialog box.

6. Select from all layouts and then click **OK** to close the dialog box and apply the new layout.

Add Shapes

The *Add Shape* button on the *SmartArt Tools Design* tab inserts shapes in relation to the selected shape. Options vary based on the *SmartArt* layout you are using and include the following:

- *Add Shape After*: The new shape is at the same level and follows the selected shape.
- *Add Shape Before*: The new shape is at the same level and before the selected shape.
- *Add Shape Above*: The new shape is one level above the selected shape and all shapes below the new shape are demoted.
- *Add Shape Below*: The new shape is one level below the selected shape.
- *Add Assistant*: The new shape is below the selected shape and above other shapes. This option is only available for organization charts.

▶HOW TO: Add Shapes

1. Select the shape closest to where you want to add a shape.
2. Click the **SmartArt Tools Design** tab.
3. Click the **Add Shape** drop-down arrow [*Create Graphic* group] (Figure 2-100) and select the position where you want to add the new shape.

Figure 2-100 *Add Shape* options

To change the flow of a diagram, click the **Right to Left** button [*SmartArt Tools Design* tab, *Create Graphic* group].

PAUSE & PRACTICE: POWERPOINT 2-3

For this project, you create an organization chart showing the CGL employees who will be managing various aspects of the landscaping for Frank and Sandra Hunter. You also convert one of the existing lists to a *SmartArt* graphic and rearrange slide objects for an interesting appearance. The *SmartArt* styles applied blend with other colors in the presentation.

File Needed: **[your initials] PP P2-2.pptx** *(Student data files are available in the* Library *of your SIMnet account.)*
Completed Project File Name: **[your initials] PP P2-3.pptx**

1. Open the presentation **[your initials] PP P2-2** and save it as [your initials] PP P2-3.

2. Create a new slide and insert a *SmartArt* graphic.
 a. Display slide 1. Click the **New Slide** drop-down arrow and select the **Title and Content** layout.
 b. Type the slide title Your CGL Team.
 c. Click the **Insert a SmartArt Graphic** icon on the content placeholder to open the *Choose a SmartArt Graphic* dialog box.
 d. Select the *Hierarchy* type from the list on the left.

e. Click the **Organization Chart** layout and click **OK** to close the dialog box and insert the *SmartArt* graphic.

3. Insert text.
 a. Select each *SmartArt* shape and type the names and job titles in Table 2-4 starting with the top shape.
 b. Press **Enter** after each name within a shape. Let the job titles word wrap as needed (Figure 2-101).

4. Change the organization chart using the *SmartArt Tools Design* tab.
 a. Change the flow by clicking the **Right to Left** button [*Create Graphic* group].
 b. Click the **More** button [*SmartArt Styles* group] and select the **Inset** effect (Figure 2-102).

Table 2-4

Top shape	Gerod Sunderland Landscape Designer
Assistant shape	Marie Foster Master Gardener
Bottom row, first shape	Allen Cooper Construction Manager
Bottom row, second shape	Bill Granger Horticulturist
Bottom row, third shape	Jason Andrews Sales Associate

Figure 2-101 Slide 2 organization chart

Figure 2-102 *SmartArt* graphic styles

c. Click the **Change Colors** button [*SmartArt Styles* group] and scroll down to select **Gradient Loop - Accent 6** (fourth color/last row) (Figure 2-103).

5. Change bulleted text to a *SmartArt* graphic.
 a. Display slide 4.
 b. Select the bulleted text placeholder, click the **Convert to SmartArt** button [*Home* tab, *Paragraph* group], and select the **Vertical Bullet List** (first option).
 • The *SmartArt* list fills the size of the bulleted text placeholder (Figure 2-104).

Figure 2-104 *SmartArt* graphic shapes as they originally appear

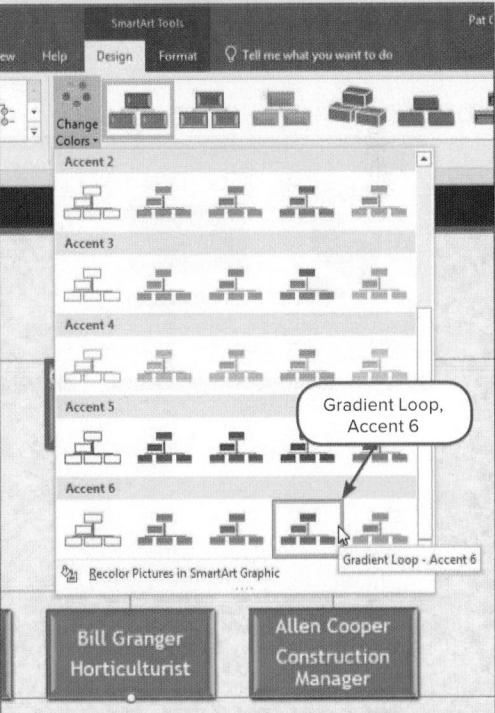

Figure 2-103 New colors applied

6. Change the *SmartArt* graphic and adjust other objects for a better slide design.
 a. Select the *SmartArt* frame (not individual shapes) and resize it (*Height* **3"** and *Width* **5"**) [*SmartArt Tools Format* tab, *Size* group].
 b. Change the style to **Inset** [*SmartArt Tools Design* tab, *SmartArt Styles* group].
 c. Click the **Change Colors** button [*SmartArt Tools Design* tab, *SmartArt Styles* group] and select **Gradient Range - Accent 6** (third option/*Accent 6* group).
 d. Click the **Font Color** button [*Home* tab, *Font* group] and change the color to **Black, Text 1** (second color/ first row).
 e. Rearrange slide objects (Figure 2-105)
 • Position the picture over the leaf.
 • Move the source notation below the picture.
 • Move the *SmartArt* and beveled shape to the right.
 • Click **Arrange**, select **Align**, and select **Align Right**.

Figure 2-105 Slide 4 completed

7. Save and close your presentation (Figure 2-106).

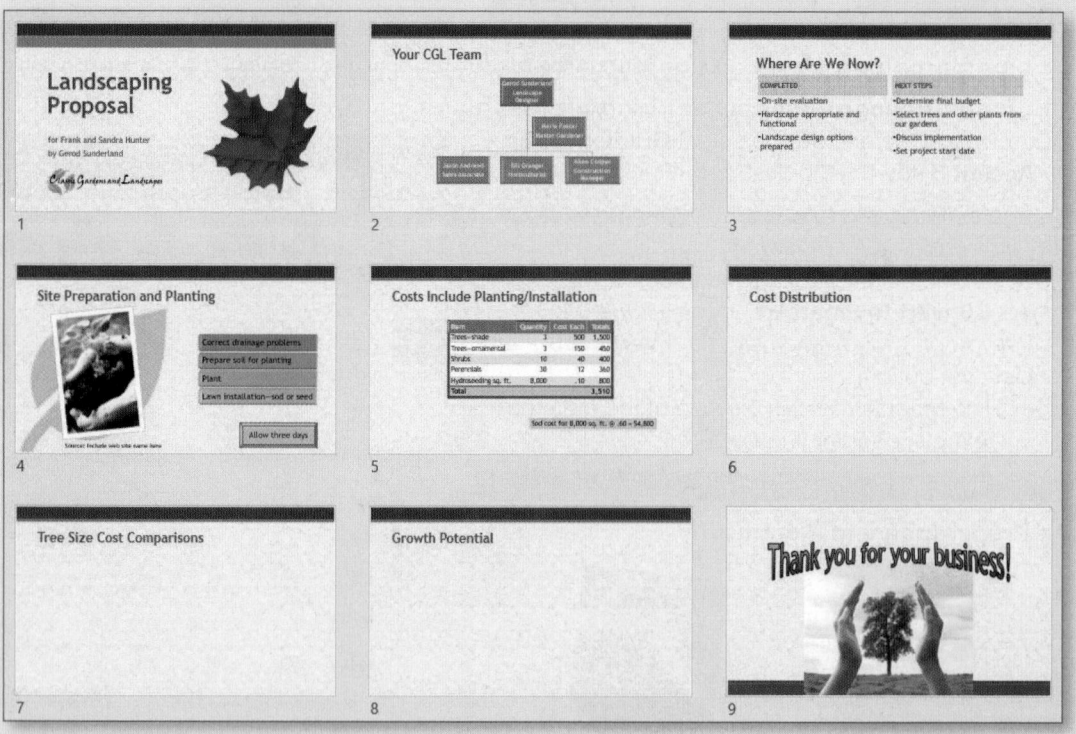

Figure 2-106 PP P2-3 completed

Creating a Chart

Charts help viewers interpret and compare data. If you have large amounts of data, create your chart in Excel and copy it to a PowerPoint slide. However, for most situations, PowerPoint's *Chart* feature will provide all the options you need.

To insert a chart in PowerPoint 2019, click the **Insert Chart** icon on a new slide content placeholder or click the **Insert** tab and click the **Chart** button [*Illustrations* group] to add a chart to an existing slide. You can choose a chart type to control how data are represented, such as with columns, bars, lines, or pie slices. Chart types and their purposes are described in Table 2-5.

Table 2-5: Chart Types and Purposes

Type	Purpose
Column	Shows a comparison of values or data changes over time. Categories are shown on the horizontal axis and values are shown on the vertical axis. Columns may be clustered to show a range of values or groupings. Columns in a category may be stacked to emphasize the total category value rather than the subsections that make up the category.
Line	Shows data changes over time; works well to show trends with multiple data series plotted at even intervals. Categories are shown on the horizontal axis, and values are shown on the vertical axis. Markers can indicate individual values.
Pie	Shows the values in a data series in proportional sizes that create the whole pie. Values cannot be negative or zero values. Percentages or actual values can be displayed near or on pie slices. This category also includes *Doughnut* charts that show parts of a whole but can contain more than one data series as rings.
Bar	Similar to column charts except bars are horizontal; works well for comparison of values. Categories are shown on the vertical axis, and values are shown on the horizontal axis.
Area	Shows changes in data over time; emphasizes the total values across a trend.
X Y (Scatter)	Shows the relationships between data using values on both the X and Y axes to plot data points; works well to emphasize where data sets have similar values. This category also includes *Bubble* charts.
Map	Shows categories across geographical regions and compares values.
Stock	Shows fluctuation of stock prices with high, low, and close values displayed over time.
Surface	Shows the differences between two sets of data. Instead of values, color bands represent the same range of values, as in a topographic map showing land elevations.
Radar	Shows the combined values of several data series with values relative to a center point.
Treemap	Displays categories by color arranged in a structure that helps to compare proportions within a hierarchy.
Sunburst	Displays data in a circular pattern of rings that create a hierarchy with the highest level in the center. With multiple categories, this chart shows how the outer rings relate to the inner rings.
Histogram	Shows the distribution of data grouped by frequencies. Can include a cumulative total.
Box & Whisker	Shows multiple data sets organized by quartiles (ranked data divided into four equal groups) and shown as proportional boxes. Variability is shown as lines above or below the boxes. Outliers are plotted as individual points.
Waterfall	Shows how an initial value is affected by the addition of positive and negative values with columns that reflect a running total.
Funnel	Shows values, usually decreasing gradually, for the stages in a process.
Combo	Combines two charts, such as a column chart with a line chart displayed over it.

> **MORE INFO**
>
> Search for more chart information using one of these methods. Click the **Tell me** box on the *Ribbon* after the last tab, type chart types, and choose **Get Help**. Or click the **Help** tab, click **Help**, type chart types, and click **Search**. Available information appears in the *Help* pane with links to descriptions with examples and instructions.

The *Chart Tools Design* tab (Figure 2-107) and the *Chart Tools Format* tab (Figure 2-108) are available when a chart is active.

Figure 2-107 *Chart Tools Design* tab

Figure 2-108 *Chart Tools Format* tab

When you insert a chart in PowerPoint, a ***worksheet*** opens with sample data in rows and columns. A group of data values from each column is a ***data series***; a group of data values from each row is a ***category***. Edit the worksheet sample data by entering your own information, or copy and paste data from Excel, Word, or Access.

Because the worksheet and PowerPoint chart are linked, the changes you make to the worksheet are automatically reflected in the chart.

▶ HOW TO: Insert a Chart

1. Click the **Insert** tab, then click the **Chart** button [*Illustrations* group].

 - You can also click the **Insert Chart** icon on a new slide content placeholder.
 - In the *Insert Chart* dialog box (Figure 2-109), chart types are listed on the left and a variety of chart layouts for each type appear on the right.
 - A *ScreenTip* identifies chart names.

2. Click a layout to select a chart.

Figure 2-109 *Insert Chart* dialog box

3. Click **OK** to close the dialog box and insert the chart.

 - A worksheet automatically opens showing sample data that you edit (Figure 2-110).

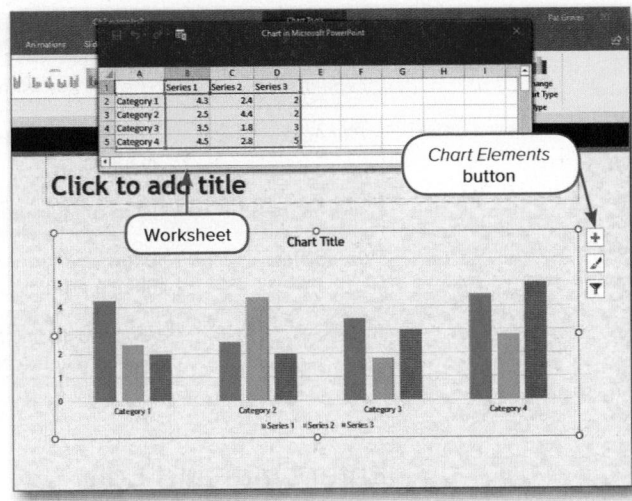

Figure 2-110 Worksheet linked to a chart

> **MORE INFO**
>
> The size of a chart frame will vary based on whether you insert a chart on an existing slide or you create a chart when adding a new slide using the *Title and Content* layout. Resize the chart frames as needed.

The chart frame displays *chart elements*, the objects that make up the chart. Chart elements vary based on the type of chart used. You can see which chart elements are shown by clicking the **Chart Elements** button, the top button (with a green plus sign) on the right of the chart frame. You can add or remove elements by changing selections from the list. Other chart elements appear in the drop-down list box in the *Current Selection* group on the *Chart Tools Format* tab and in the *Format* pane when you are working on the chart. Chart elements are defined in Table 2-6.

Table 2-6: Chart Elements and Definitions

Element	Definition
Y-Axis (Vertical)	Also called the *Value Axis*; displayed vertically with numbers usually arranged on the left of a chart
X-Axis (Horizontal)	Also called the *Category Axis*; displayed horizontally with word or number labels across the bottom of the chart
Axis Titles	Both the Y-Axis and the X-Axis can include titles to name values or categories
Chart Area	The background area where the entire chart displays in a frame
Chart Title	A chart may include a title
Data Labels	Used to identify a data series or its individual points; may include values
Data Markers	The graphical representation of values shown as columns, bars, slices, or data points
Data Table	The data that creates the chart displays in table format below the chart
Error Bars	Used to show margins of error or standard deviation amounts
Floor	Area at the bottom of a 3D chart to create an illusion of depth
Gridlines	Lines that appear behind a chart to help the viewer judge values

Continued

Element	Definition
Legend	The key that identifies each data series by color
Plot Area	The rectangle between the vertical and horizontal axes that appears behind the data markers
Tick Marks	Lines of measurement on an axis that help to interpret values on each axis
Trendline	Shows averages on 2D charts that are not stacked and can extend beyond actual data to predict future values
Walls	Areas, including *Back Walls* and *Side Walls*, of a 3D chart behind the data markers that help to create an illusion of depth

Enter Data and Edit

After you replace the worksheet sample data with your data, you can close the worksheet. As you work on the chart in PowerPoint, you can open the worksheet again if you need to make changes.

▶ **HOW TO: Edit Data in the Worksheet**

1. Select the chart you want to modify.
2. Click the top of the **Edit Data** button [*Chart Tools Design* tab, *Data* group] to display the worksheet (Figure 2-111) so you can make changes in PowerPoint.

 - If you need to modify the data in Excel, click the **Edit Data** drop-down arrow and choose **Edit Data in Excel** to open Excel and display the worksheet.
 - If your worksheet is open and you decide to use Excel, click the **Edit Data in Microsoft Excel** button in the worksheet title bar.
 - You can click and drag the Excel window to a different location or resize it if needed.

3. Replace cell contents (Figure 2-112) by clicking the **cell** and typing your data.

Figure 2-111 *Edit Data* button

4. Move around the worksheet by clicking your pointer in a cell or using keyboard shortcuts as follows:

 - Press **Enter** to move the insertion point down one row.
 - Press **Shift+Enter** to move the insertion point up one row.
 - Press **Tab** to move the insertion point to the next cell on the right.
 - Press **Shift+Tab** to move to the next cell on the left.
 - Press arrow keys to move in any direction.

5. Click the worksheet **Close** button to return to the PowerPoint chart.

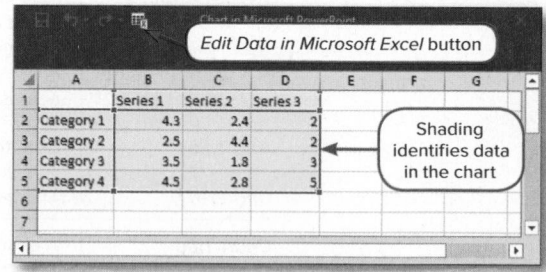

Figure 2-112 Default worksheet data

> MORE INFO
>
> Remove the sample data on the worksheet by clicking the **Select All** button (above the row 1 heading and to the left of the column A heading) and then pressing **Delete**.

Adjust worksheet columns if necessary to show all data. Columns not wide enough to display text will truncate the text so part of it will not display until you make the column wider. If a cell displays number signs (###) rather than the values you entered, make the column wider to display cell contents.

- Change column width by pointing to the top of the column and dragging the splitter or double-click the line between columns to auto fit the contents.
- Be sure the shading of the selected rows and columns (see Figure 2-112) correctly identifies the category, series, and data cells. Drag a corner sizing handle to adjust.
- Columns in a worksheet with blank cells must be deleted so the related chart displays without a blank space.
- You can add new columns or rows in the worksheet or edit the worksheet in Excel.

HOW TO: Modify the Worksheet

1. Select the chart you want to modify.
2. Click the top of the **Edit Data** button [*Chart Tools Design* tab, *Data* group].
3. Adjust column width. Position your pointer on the vertical line to the right of the column heading (Figure 2-113), then use one of these methods:
 - Drag to the correct width.
 - Double-click and the column automatically adjusts to fit the widest data in that column.
 - Right-click to open the context menu and select **Column Width**, then type the width number in the *Column Width* dialog box. Click **OK** to close the dialog box.

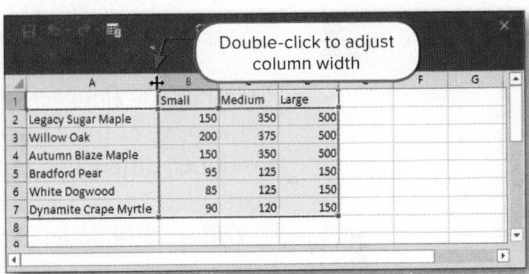

Figure 2-113 Adjust column width

4. Add or delete columns and rows.
 - Right-click to open the context menu and select **Insert**. Choose **Table Columns to the Left** or **Table Rows Above**.
 - Right-click to open the context menu and select **Delete**. Choose **Table Columns** or **Table Rows**.
5. Use Excel to modify data.
 - Click the **Edit Data** drop-down arrow [*Chart Tools Design* tab, *Data* group] and choose **Edit Data in Excel**. The Excel window displays.
 - Click a cell where you need to add a cell, row, or column. Click the **Insert** drop-down arrow [*Home* tab, *Cells* group] and select the option you need.
 - Adjust column width and edit titles and data values as needed.
 - Close Excel to return to the chart on your slide.

In PowerPoint, switch the data series by clicking the **Switch Row/Column** button [*Chart Tools Design* tab, *Data* group]. In a column chart, for example, data displayed on the X-axis (bottom) and Y-axis (left) will be reversed.

Change Chart Type

Click the **Change Chart Type** button [*Chart Tools Design* tab, *Type* group] to open the *Change Chart Type* gallery where you can choose from the many different layouts. For example, Figure 2-114 shows data in a line chart and Figure 2-115 shows the same data in a clustered column chart.

Figure 2-114 Line chart

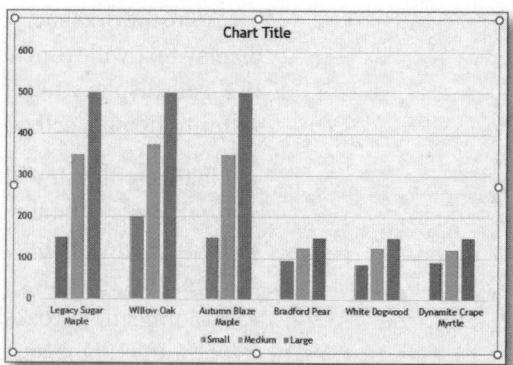
Figure 2-115 Clustered column chart

SLO 2.9

Formatting a Chart

PowerPoint's *Designer* feature will suggest different slide layouts for charts. The layouts that appear in the *Design Ideas* pane show several slide background designs with the chart positioned differently. It is usually best to apply one of these layouts before you customize your chart.

Office 2019 Note: PowerPoint's *Designer* feature is not available in Office 2019, so the *Design Ideas* pane will not open.

This section focuses on ways to modify a chart by applying preset styles or customizing individual chart elements.

Chart Styles and Colors

The **Chart Styles** gallery [*Chart Tools Design* tab] provides preset effects for chart elements including the chart background. Click the *More* button to see styles arranged by number. Click a style to apply it (Figure 2-116).

Figure 2-116 *Chart Styles* gallery

> **MORE INFO**
>
> If your PowerPoint window is narrow, you may need to click the **Quick Styles** button [*Chart Tools Design* tab] to open the *Chart Styles* gallery.

Click the *Change Colors* button [*Chart Tools Design* tab] to select **Colorful** or **Monochromatic** (shades of one color based on theme colors) combinations (Figure 2-117). The colors you choose then show in all the available chart styles. Be careful when selecting colors so the chart shapes (columns, bars, lines, or pie slices) are easy to distinguish for value comparisons. The colors also need to coordinate with your overall presentation (Figure 2-118).

Figure 2-117 *Chart Colors* gallery

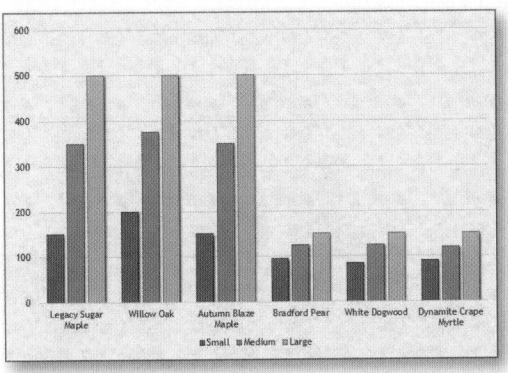

Figure 2-118 Chart style applied and colors changed

If possible, avoid arranging red and green colors together. People who have difficulty recognizing colors are more likely to have problems with red and green colors because they can look beige or gray.

> ### ANOTHER WAY
> Access *Chart Styles* and *Chart Colors* using the *Chart Styles* button (with a paintbrush icon) to the right of each chart.

Format Chart Elements

You can select chart elements (objects) and apply formatting in several ways. When a chart element is selected, the related options for that element display when the *Format* pane opens.

▶ HOW TO: Format a Chart Element

1. Select a chart element and click the **Chart Tools Format** tab.
 - Change shapes by clicking the **Shape Fill**, **Shape Outline**, or **Shape Effects** drop-down arrows [*Shape Styles* group].
 - Change text by clicking the **Text Fill**, **Text Outline**, or **Text Effects** drop-down arrows [*WordArt Styles* group].
 - Choose appropriate colors and effects.
2. Open the *Format* pane using one of these methods:
 - Double-click a shape or text element.
 - Right-click a shape or text element and choose **Format** from the context menu.
3. Click the **Chart Elements** button beside the chart to open a list.
 - Select an element (Figure 2-119).
 - Click the triangle beside each element to select from different options.
 - Click **More Options** to open the *Format* pane.

4. Click the **Chart Elements** drop-down arrow [*Chart Tools Format* tab, *Current Selection* group].
 - Select an element from the list.
 - Click **Format Selection** [*Chart Tools Format* tab, *Current Selection* group] to open the *Format* pane.

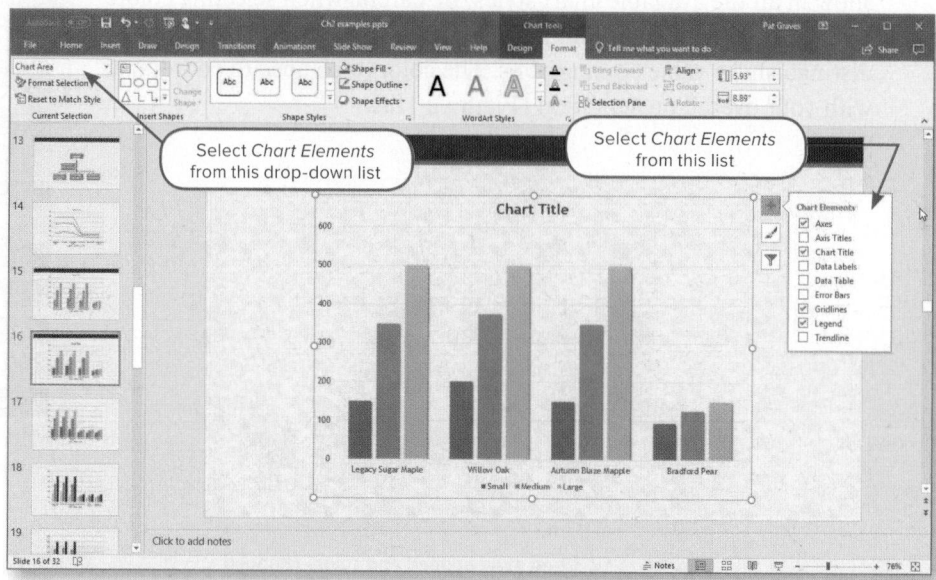

Figure 2-119 Choose options using the *Chart Elements* button

To change the chart area size, point to any sizing handle (the white circles on the chart frame) and resize by dragging. You can resize chart elements but be careful not to distort size relationships.

You can fill a *chart area* or a *plot area* with a picture to create an interesting background (Figure 2-120) related to your topic. Be careful that text is easy to read on the picture and simplify the chart as much as possible. Columns or bars can be filled with simple images that each fill a column or can be stacked (Figure 2-121). Be careful when using pictures to avoid a cluttered chart so it communicates a general relationship of data values that is easy to understand.

Vary colors to feature certain chart elements or to make text easy to read. In the *Clustered Column* chart shown in

Figure 2-120 Column chart *plot area* with a picture fill and *data series* with a picture fill

Figure 2-121 Bar chart *plot area* with a solid fill and *data series* with a stacked picture fill

Figure 2-122, the *chart area* has a solid fill. The *plot area* has a yellow gradient fill with the darkest color at the bottom which helps to emphasize the height of the columns. In the *3D Column Chart* shown in Figure 2-123, the column heights (especially for the shorter columns) are not as easy to compare as they are in Figure 2-122.

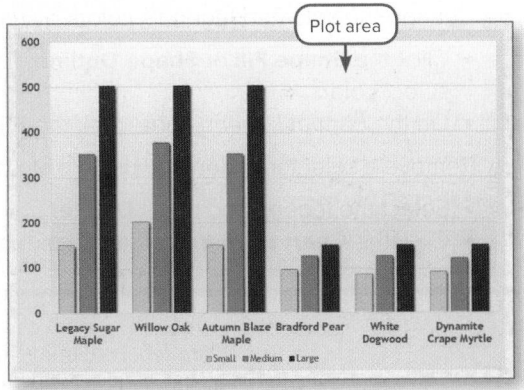

Figure 2-122 Chart *plot area* with gradient fill

Legend and Data Labels

The *legend* is usually displayed on the right, but you can move it to other positions, display it horizontally above or below the plot area, or delete it. The legend can blend with the chart's plot color or can be displayed using different fill and border colors to emphasize it more. However, the colors used to identify each data series must always be easy to interpret and compare. If you have only one data series, no legend is needed.

On the *Format Legend* pane, both **Legend Options** and **Text Options** display three different tabs to control settings.

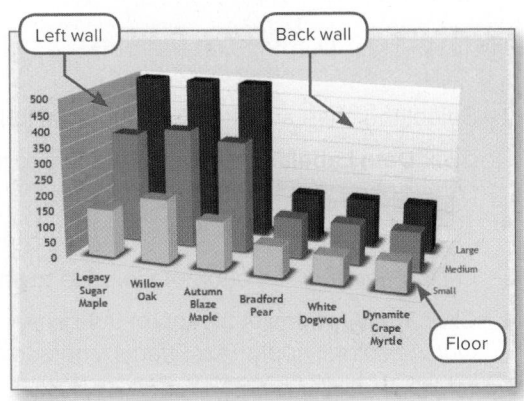

Figure 2-123 *3D Column* chart

▶ **HOW TO:** Change Legend Position and Colors

1. Select the legend and drag it to another position within the chart area.
2. Click the **Chart Elements** button beside the chart, click the legend triangle, and then select a position.
3. Open the *Format Legend* pane (Figure 2-124) with **Legend Options** displayed so you can change the legend position. Use one of these methods:
 - Double-click the legend.
 - Right-click the legend and choose **Format Legend**.
 - Click the **Chart Elements** button beside the chart, click the legend triangle, and then click **More Options**.
 - Click the **Chart Tools Format** tab, select **Legend** in the *Chart Elements* drop-down list box, and click **Format Selection**.
4. On the *Format Legend* pane under **Legend Options**, choose a legend position: **Top**, **Bottom**, **Left**, **Right**, or **Top Right**.
 - Select **Show the legend without overlapping the chart** to prevent the legend from appearing over other chart elements (Figure 2-125).

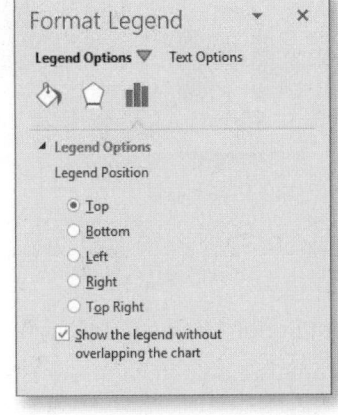

Figure 2-124 *Format Legend* pane

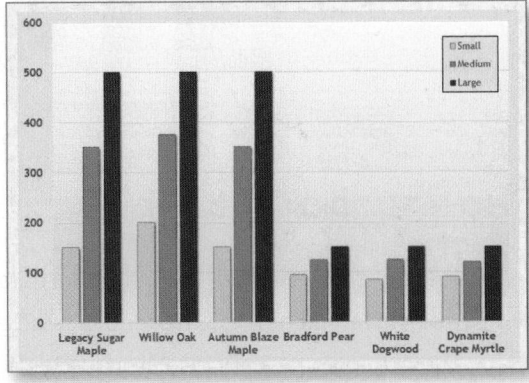

Figure 2-125 Legend moved and recolored

5. Change the selected legend's colors by using one of the following methods:
 - Click the **Shape Fill** or **Shape Outline** drop-down arrows [*Chart Tools Format* tab, *Shape Styles* group] and select colors.
 - On the *Format Legend* pane, click the **Fill & Line** tab and then select *Fill* and *Border* colors.
6. Remove a selected legend by using one of the following methods:
 - Select the legend and press **Delete**.
 - Click the **Chart Elements** button beside the chart and deselect the **Legend**.

Data labels display values for each data series. These labels appear in different places based on the chart style. Use the *Format Data Labels* pane to customize labels. Both **Label Options** and **Text Options** display multiple tabs to control settings.

▶ HOW TO: Display Data Labels

1. Select the chart and then click the **Chart Element** button beside the chart to open the list of *Chart Elements*.
2. Click **Data Labels** and click the triangle to select a position or click **More Options** to open the *Format Data Labels* pane with **Label Options** at the top of the pane selected.
 - Control the display and position of the value on the **Label Options** tab.
3. Click other tabs at the top of the pane to change *Fill & Line*, *Effects*, and *Size & Properties* options.
4. Click **Text Options** at the top of the pane, and then select tabs at the top of the pane to control *Text Fill & Outline* colors, apply *Text Effects*, and add a *Text Box* options.

Using data labels above or inside columns enables the viewer to see the exact data value as well as the size relationships that the columns represent. However, the columns must be wide enough to display the numbers without overlapping. If the columns are too narrow (Figure 2-126), using a data table is more effective. In a data table, the legend is automatically included, so it was removed from the plot area in Figure 2-127.

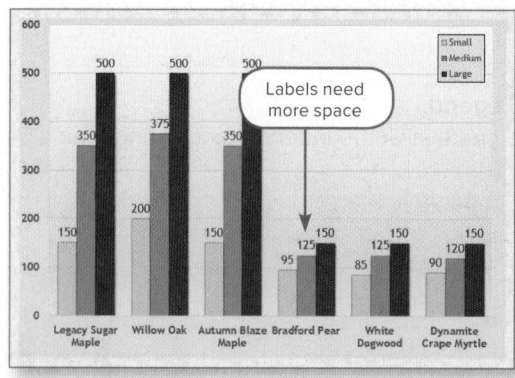

Figure 2-126 Data labels Figure 2-127 Data table

▶ HOW TO: Display a Data Table

1. Select the chart and then click the **Chart Element** button beside the chart to open the list of *Chart Elements*.
2. Deselect **Data Labels** and **Legend** if these elements are selected.
 - They will automatically display in the table.
3. Click **Data Table** and the table appears below the chart.

4. Point to any number in the data table, right-click to open the context menu, and select **Format Data Table** to open the *Format Data Table* pane.
5. Select **Table Options** and choose tabs at the top of the pane to make changes.
 - Select the *Fill & Line* tab (paint bucket) or the *Effects* tab (pentagon) to make color and effect changes.
 - Select *Table Options* (chart) to control table borders and the legend key (the color that identifies each data series).
6. Select **Text Options** and choose tabs at the top of the pane to make changes.
 - Select *Text Fill & Outline* or *Text Effects* to make color and effect changes.
 - Select *Textbox* to add text.

A pie chart has one data series. Each slice represents a value and the size of the slice illustrates its relationship to the whole. The number of slices is best limited to six or seven slices; too many slices make a pie chart difficult to interpret.

Unlike a column or line chart, a pie chart does not have axes or axes titles. Data labels are often used instead of a legend because they are easier to interpret. Format data labels to display on the slices or outside the slices (Figure 2-128).

Figure 2-128 **Pie chart data label positions**

Be sure to select an option that makes it easy for the viewer to match the number with the related slice. Usually, the label font size must be increased. The *Format Data Labels* pane has many options for you to explore (Figure 2-129).

Figure 2-129 *Format Data Labels* pane

Explode a Pie Slice

You can *explode* (separate) pie chart slices by dragging the pie slices away from the center. How-ever, when all slices are separated, no single slice is emphasized. For better results, design a pie chart as you want it to look and then drag one slice away from the pie to emphasize that slice. Consider, also, how your colors are applied so the most noticeable or brightest color is used for the slice that you want to emphasize (Figure 2-130).

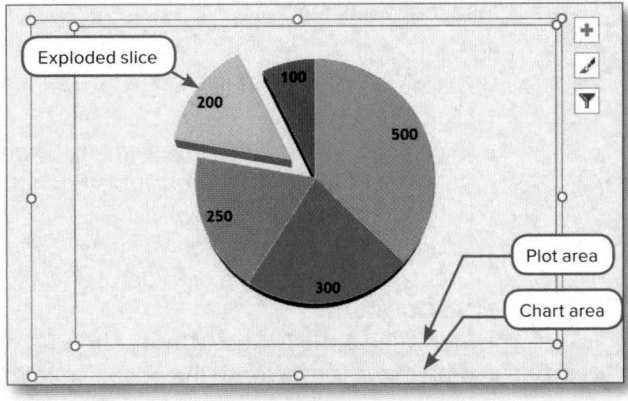

Figure 2-130 *3D Pie* chart with an exploded slice

►HOW TO: Explode a Pie Slice

1. Select the chart (*Chart Area*) and click the pie object (*Plot Area*).
2. Click again to select just one pie slice.
 - Check the handles to be sure you have selected the correct slice and not a label on the slice.
 - Confirm your selection [*Chart Tools Format* tab, *Current Selection* group].
3. Click and drag slightly away from the center of the pie so the slice is emphasized.

As you drag a pie slice away from the center, the entire pie becomes smaller. You can enlarge the pie by resizing the plot area. Removing the legend creates more space for the pie, too.

PAUSE & PRACTICE: POWERPOINT 2-4

For this project, you create a pie and two clustered column charts showing the cost distribution for CGL landscaping, cost comparisons for tree sizes, and the height of mature trees being considered for the new landscape.

Files needed: ***[your initials] PP P2-3.pptx*** and ***Trees-02.jpg*** *(Student data files are available in the Library of your SIMnet account.)*
Completed Project File Name: ***[your initials] PP 2-4.pptx***

1. Open the presentation file ***[your initials] PP P2-3*** and save it as [your initials] PP P2-4.

2. Create a 3D pie chart.
 a. Select slide 6, "**Cost Distribution**."
 b. Click the **Insert Chart** icon on the content placeholder.
 c. Select the **Pie** chart type, and then select the **3D Pie** layout. Click **OK**.
 d. Replace the worksheet sample data with the data in Table 2-7 beginning with the column heading. Point to the top of the worksheet column and then click and drag the splitter to resize columns as needed.

3. Resize the worksheet window, if necessary, so you can proof all entries.
 - To make corrections, double-click a cell, position your insertion point, and then edit the cell contents.
 - Be sure all chart data is selected (Figure 2-131).

4. Close the worksheet.

5. Format the 3D pie chart.
 a. Delete the **Cost** chart title in the chart area because it duplicates the slide title.
 b. Click **Style 3** [*Chart Tools Design* tab, *Chart Styles* group].
 c. Verify that **Chart Area** [*Chart Tools Format* tab, *Chart Elements* group] is selected in the drop-down list.
 d. Click the **Shape Fill** drop-down arrow [*Chart Tools Format* tab, *Shape Styles* group] and select **No Fill**.
 e. Click the **Shape Outline** drop-down arrow [*Chart Tools Format* tab, *Shape Styles* group] and select **No Outline**.
 f. Select the **Series "Cost" Data Labels** [*Chart Tools Format* tab, *Chart Elements* group] in the drop-down list. Increase the *Font Size* to **20 pt**. [*Home* tab, *Font* group].

Table 2-7

	Cost
Trees--Shade	1,500
Trees--Ornamental	450
Shrubs	400
Perennials	360
Hydroseeding sq. ft	800

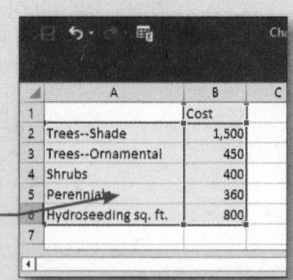

Shading defines chart area data

Figure 2-131 Worksheet linked to a chart

g. Click the **Legend** and increase the *Font Size* to **20 pt**. [*Home* tab, *Font* group].
h. Click and drag the legend to the upper-right corner of the **Chart Area**.
i. Select the **Plot Area** [*Chart Tools Format* tab, *Current Selection* group] from the drop-down list.
j. Drag the corner sizing handles to increase the plot area height so it matches the chart area height.
 - The pie chart increases in size. (Figure 2-132).
k. Select the single slice for "**Trees— Ornamental**" and explode that slice by dragging it down slightly.

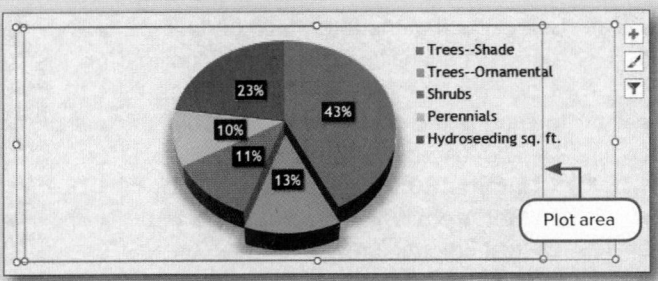

Figure 2-132 Slice exploded and legend repositioned

6. Create a clustered column chart.
 a. Select slide 7, "**Tree Size Cost Comparisons**." Click the **Insert Chart** icon on the content placeholder.
 b. Click the **Clustered Column** layout and click **OK**.
 c. Replace the worksheet data with the data in Table 2-8 beginning with the column headings.
 d. Close the worksheet. If you need to check the data, click the **Edit Data** button [*Chart Tools Design* tab, *Data* group].
 e. Delete the chart title in the chart area.
 f. Change the chart style to **Style 8** [*Chart Tools Design* tab, *Chart Styles* group] which has a dark fill for the chart area.

Table 2-8

	Small	Medium	Large
Legacy Sugar Maple	150	350	500
Willow Oak	200	375	500
Autumn Blaze Maple	150	350	500
Bradford Pear	95	125	150
White Dogwood	85	115	150
Dynamite Crape Myrtle	90	120	150

7. Add chart elements.
 a. Click the **Chart Elements** button on the right side of the chart to display the list of elements (Figure 2-133).
 b. Select the following elements: **Axes**, **Axis Titles**, **Data Table**, **Gridlines**, and **Legend** if they are not already selected.
 - The **Data Table** automatically appears below the columns.

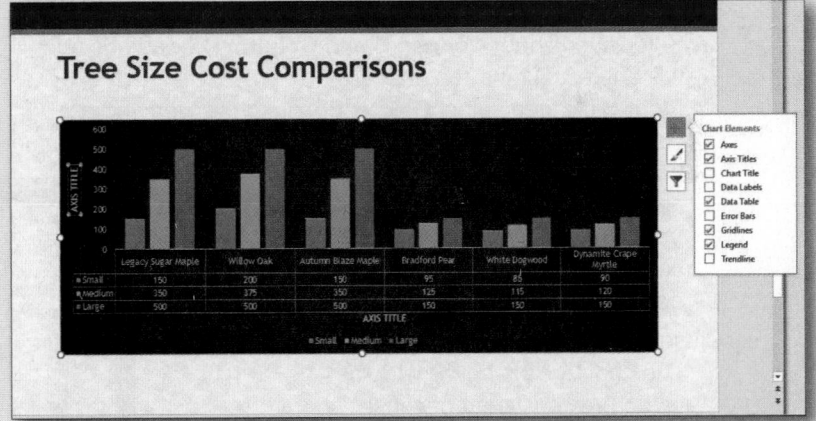

Figure 2-133 *Clustered Column* chart with *Style 8* applied and chart elements listed on the right

8. Adjust chart formatting by selecting the following elements in the chart area. If necessary, confirm that you have the correct element selected [*Chart Tools Format* tab, *Current Selection* group].
 a. Select the *Vertical (Value) Axis Title* (rotated text on the Y-axis) and edit the text by typing Tree Cost.
 b. Select the *Horizontal (Category) Axis Title* (X-axis) below the data table and press **Delete**.
 c. Select the **Legend** below the data table and press **Delete**.
 d. Drag the chart area center sizing handle down to increase the height. Adjust the chart area size (*Height* **5"** and *Width* **11.5"**) [*Chart Tools Format* tab, *Size* group].

e. Move the chart area up slightly so the blank space above and below the chart is even.

f. Select each of the following chart elements and click **Shape Fill** [*Chart Tools Format* tab, *Shape Styles* group] to change the colors (Figure 2-134):

- *Chart Area*: **Gold, Accent 4, Lighter 60%** (eighth color/third row)
- *Plot Area*: **White, Background 1** (first color/first row)
- *"Large" Series*: **Green, Accent 6, Darker 50%** (last color/last row)
- *"Medium" Series*: **Green, Accent 6** (last color/first row)
- *"Small" Series*: **Green, Accent 6, Lighter 60%** (last color/third row)

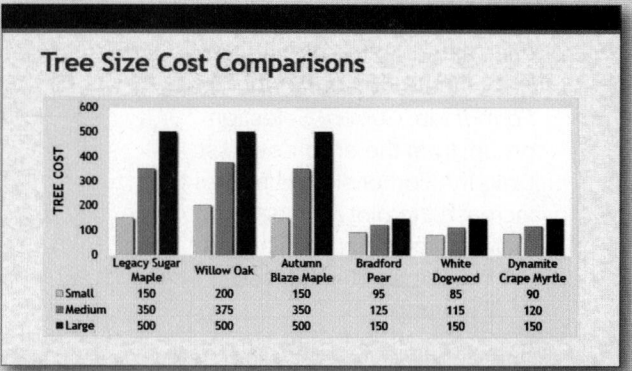

Figure 2-134 Completed chart

g. Select each of the following text elements. Change the *Font Color* [*Home* tab, *Font* group] to **Black, Text 1** (second color/first row) and change the *Font Size*:

- *Data Table*: **18 pt**.
- *Vertical (Value) Axis*: **18 pt**.
- *Vertical (Value) Axis title*: **20 pt**.

9. Create another clustered column chart.

a. Select slide 8, **"Growth Potential."** Click **Chart** [*Insert* tab, *Illustrations* group] because this slide does not have a content placeholder.

b. Click the **Clustered Column** layout and click **OK** to close the dialog box.

c. Replace the worksheet data with the data in Table 2-9 beginning with the column headings.

d. Delete the extra columns in the worksheet.

- Select worksheet **Column C** and **Column D** headings and the entire columns are selected.
- Right-click, then select **Delete**. Because the worksheet columns C and D are now empty, the remaining chart columns (for *Height*, one data series) have expanded to fill the chart area on the slide (Figure 2-135).
- Verify that data is correctly selected and adjust worksheet borders if necessary.

e. Close the worksheet.

- The chart area is not as wide as in the previous chart because you inserted the chart directly on the slide rather than inserting it through a content placeholder that had different proportions.

Table 2-9

	Height
Legacy Sugar Maple	80
Willow Oak	60
Autumn Blaze Maple	50
Bradford Pear	35
White Dogwood	20
Dynamite Crape Myrtle	20

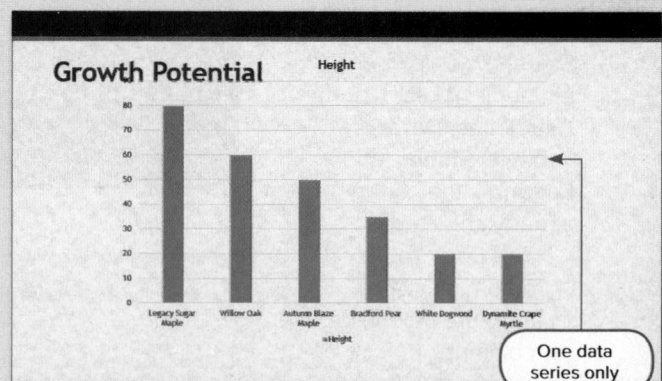

Figure 2-135 *Column* chart as it first appears

10. Format the chart.

a. Delete the chart title and the legend.

b. Resize the chart area (*Height* **5.5"** and *Width* **10"**) [*Chart Tools Format* tab, *Size* group].

c. Position the chart evenly on the slide below the slide title.

d. Click the **More** button [*Chart Tools Design* tab, *Chart Styles* group] and change the chart style to **Style 14** (the last style).

e. Select the columns and change the *Shape Fill* to **Green, Accent 6** (last color/first row).

f. Select the **Vertical (Value) Axis**. Change *Font Color* to **Black, Text 1** (second color/first row), the *Font Size* to **20 pt.**, and apply **Bold**.

g. Select the **Horizontal (Category) Axis**. Change *Font Color* to **Black, Text 1** (second color/first row), the *Font Size* to **18 pt.**, and apply **Bold**.

11. Select the *Chart Area* and apply a picture fill.

a. Select **Chart Area** [*Chart Tools Format* tab, *Current Selection* group] from the drop-down list.

b. Click **Format Selection** to open the *Format Chart Area* pane.

c. Click **Fill** and select **Picture or texture fill**.

d. Click the **File** button and browse to your student data files. Select **Trees-02** and click **Insert**.

e. Change the *Transparency* percentage to **60%** (by dragging the slider or typing the percentage) to soften the picture's colors because it is behind the columns and text (Figure 2-136).

f. Close the *Format Chart Area* pane.

Figure 2-136 Chart resized, colors changed, and a picture fill

12. Apply a transition.

a. Click the **Wipe** [*Transitions* tab, *Transition to This Slide* group].

b. Click **Effect Options** and select **From Left** [*Transitions* tab, *Transition to This Slide* group].

c. Click **Apply to All** [*Transitions* tab, *Timing* group].

13. Save and close your presentation (Figure 2-137).

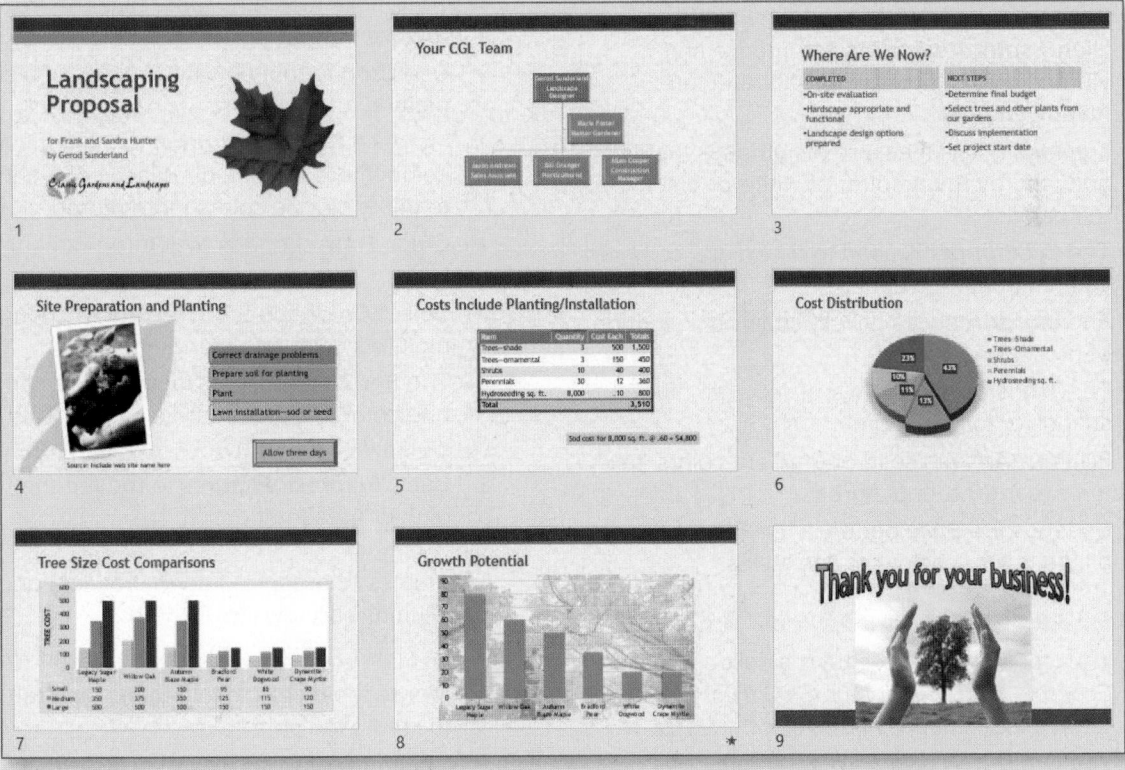

Figure 2-137 PP P2-4 completed

Chapter Summary

2.1 Work with shapes, styles, effects, and colors (p. P2-75).

- Change shape size by entering exact height and width sizes or by dragging sizing handles.
- Use **Lock Drawing Mode** to draw the same shape multiple times.
- Use **text boxes** to position text anywhere on a slide.
- PowerPoint's various **style** galleries provide collections of preset effects for shapes, pictures, or other objects.
- Line **Weight** is the line thickness measured in points.
- **Dashes** show lines with a combination of dots and dashes.
- When you apply **Theme Colors** to shapes, the colors change when a different theme is applied.
- **Standard Colors** do not change when a different theme is applied.
- Computer screens use the **RGB model** that displays colors by blending values for *red*, *green*, and *blue*.
- Highly **saturated** colors are intense and vibrant; colors that are not saturated are muddy and dull.
- **Luminosity** is a measure of lightness that is adjusted by the amount of white or black in the color.
- The **Eyedropper** is used to match any color on your computer screen.
- The **WordArt** styles gallery shows a collection of preset text effects.
- The **Transform** effect warps text into different shapes or follows a path.
- Fill **WordArt** with solid or gradient colors, textures, patterns, or pictures.
- Use the **Line Style** option in the **Format Shape** dialog box to customize line styles.

2.2 Work with icons and 3D models (p. P2-87)

- The **Icons** dialog box shows a collection of *Scalable Vector Graphics (SVG files)* that are ready-made images in one color.
- The **Graphics Tools Format** tab provides options to customize icons similar to the

Drawing Tools Format tab options for customizing shapes.

- The **Convert to Shape** feature changes an *Icon* to a drawing object that may consist of several shapes that can be formatted separately.
- **3D Models** are computer graphics with the three-dimensional shape of an object that can be seen from any angle by tilting or rotating the object.
- The **Zoom** enables you to change to a distant or close-up view of a **3D Model**.

2.3 Search for pictures and illustrations, modify picture appearance, and compress picture file size (p. P2-93).

- Use the **Online Pictures** dialog box to search for online pictures and illustrations.
- **Alt Text** is alternative text that identifies a picture or graphic object; used with screen readers to accommodate individuals with visual impairments.
- The **Picture Styles** gallery shows a collection of preset picture effects.
- To remove a picture style, click the **Reset Picture** button.
- Use **Crop** to trim unwanted areas of a selected picture.
- Increase **Color Saturation** to make picture colors more vibrant; decrease color saturation to make picture colors more muted.
- **Color Tone** changes a picture's cool or warm tones.
- Select **Color** and then **Recolor** to change a picture's color to a monotone color.
- The **Set Transparent Color** feature can make one color in a picture transparent. This feature works well to remove white backgrounds.
- Use **Compress Pictures** to reduce the file size of your presentation.

2.4 Use tables to organize information in a grid format of columns and rows (p. P2-103).

- Insert and delete table **columns** and **rows**.
- **Merge** table cells to join them; **split** table cells to create multiple cells.
- Column width usually varies based on content; row height is usually a consistent size.

2.5 Format a table by applying styles, colors, and effects (p. P2-108).

- Apply **WordArt Styles** to table text.
- **Table Styles** provide options for a table's design using theme accent colors.
- **Table Style Options** control how columns and rows are emphasized to feature areas of the table.
- Use border lines to separate cells and shading to emphasize cells.
- Horizontal cell alignment options include *Align Left*, *Center*, or *Align Right*; vertical cell alignment options include *Align Top*, *Center Vertically*, or *Align Bottom*.

2.6 Show processes and relationships with *SmartArt* graphics (p. P2-113).

- Use **SmartArt graphics** to create diagrams that illustrate concepts such as processes, cycles, or relationships.
- **SmartArt layouts** are organized by categories.
- Each layout includes information about how you can use it or the meaning it conveys.
- Type text directly in each **SmartArt** shape or type text in the **Text Pane**.
- Change bulleted text to a **SmartArt** graphic by clicking the **Convert to SmartArt Graphic** button.

2.7 Format a *SmartArt* graphic by applying styles, colors, and effects (p. P2-116).

- **SmartArt Styles** provide a gallery of **Effect Options**.
- The **Change Colors** button provides a gallery of color options arranged in categories.

- The **Add Shape** button inserts shapes in relation to the selected shape.
- Format or individually resize shapes within a **SmartArt** graphic.

2.8 Create charts that show relationships between data values and emphasize data in different ways based on the chart type and chart elements (p. P2-121).

- Charts in PowerPoint are linked to worksheets. Changes made to the data will automatically appear in the chart.
- Charts created in Excel can be edited in PowerPoint when they are linked.
- A group of data values is a **data series**.
- **Chart Layouts** are arranged in categories including *Column*, *Line*, *Pie*, *Bar*, and *Area*.
- The **Chart Area** displays the entire chart including all **chart elements**.
- The **Plot Area** provides a background for **Data Markers**, the columns, bars, slices, or shapes that represent data.

2.9 Format a chart by applying preset styles or customizing individual chart elements (p. P2-126).

- **Chart Styles** provide a gallery of preset effects for chart elements.
- The **Legend** is a key that identifies each data series by color.
- The **Change Colors** button provides a gallery of colorful or monochromatic colors for chart elements.
- Customize chart elements individually to enhance their appearance.
- To emphasize a pie slice, **explode** it by separating the slice from the rest of the pie chart.

Check for Understanding

The SIMbook for this text (within your SIMnet account) provides the following resources for concept review.

- Multiple-choice questions
- Matching exercises
- Short answer questions

Guided Project 2-1

Guest satisfaction has always been important to the success of Paradise Lakes Resort (PLR) in Minnesota. The general manager plans to use feedback from social media to identify problems and to guide improvements at the resort. In this project, you illustrate a presentation the general manager will use to explain these concepts to employees at PLR.
[Student Learning Outcomes 2.1, 2.2, 2.3, 2.6, 2.7]

File Needed: ***SocialMedia-02.pptx*** *(Student data files are available in the* Library *of your SIMnet account.)*
Completed Project File Name: ***[your initials] PowerPoint 2-1.pptx***

Skills Covered in This Project

- Apply a picture style.
- Adjust size dimensions.
- Apply text effects.

- Insert a text box.
- Create a *SmartArt* graphic.
- Apply a *SmartArt* style and effects.
- Insert an icon and apply a style.

1. Open the presentation ***SocialMedia-02***. This design theme shows slide titles at the bottom of all slides except the title slide.

2. Save the presentation as [your initials] PowerPoint 2-1.

3. Resize a picture and apply a style.
 a. Select the lake picture on slide 1.
 b. Change the picture *Width* to **6"** [*Picture Tools Format* tab, *Size* group]. The *Height* automatically adjusts.
 c. Apply the **Metal Oval** picture style [*Picture Tools Format* tab, *Picture Styles* group].
 d. Position the picture on the left (Figure 2-138).

4. Adjust the title text to complement the wood decking shown in the picture.
 a. Select the title text "Improving Guest Satisfaction" on slide 1 and increase the *Font Size* to **60 pt**.
 b. Adjust the title placeholder to fit the text (see Figure 2-138). Keep the title text selected.
 c. Click the **Text Fill** drop-down arrow [*Drawing Tools Format* tab, *WordArt Styles* group], select **Texture**, and select **Medium Wood** (last option/bottom row).
 d. Click the **Text Effects** button, select **Shadow**, and select **Shadow Options**. The *Format Shape* pane opens. Change the following settings:
 Transparency: **20**%
 Blur: **5 pt**.
 Angle: **50°**
 Distance: **5 pt**.
 e. Close the *Format Shape* pane.

5. Insert a new slide with a *Title and Content* layout after slide 1.

Figure 2-138 Title slide

6. Add text and a shape.
 a. Display slide 2 and type the slide title Why Social Media? In this theme, the title placeholder is at the bottom of the slide.
 b. Type the following bulleted text:

 Revenue
 Market Share
 Guest Satisfaction
 Guest Loyalty

 c. Resize the bulleted list placeholder to fit the text and move the text to the right (Figure 2-139).
 d. Click the **Shapes** button [*Insert* tab, *Illustrations* group] to open the gallery. Select the **Arrow: Up** shape (*Block Arrow* group).
 e. Draw an arrow (*Height* **3.5"** and *Width* **2.5"**). Position the arrow to the left of the text. Keep the arrow selected for the next step.
 f. Click the **More** button [*Drawing Tools Format* tab, *Shape Styles* group] and apply the **Intense Effect - Orange, Accent 1** (second option/sixth row).

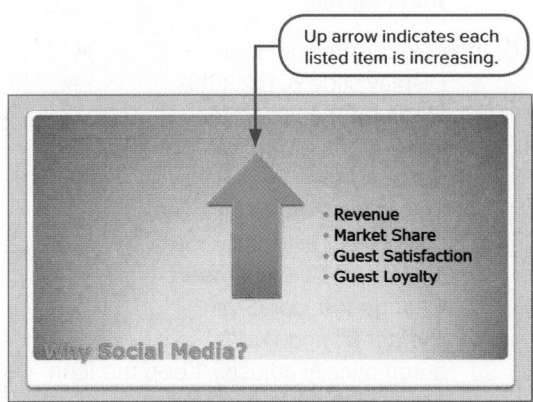

Figure 2-139 Slide 3 with a shape

7. Insert a new slide with a *Blank* layout after slide 4.

8. Create a *SmartArt* graphic and insert an additional shape on slide 5.
 a. Click the **Insert** tab.
 b. Click the **SmartArt** button and select the **Cycle** type.
 c. Select the **Continuous Cycle** layout and click **OK**.
 d. Add the following text to each shape starting with the top shape and continuing in a clockwise direction around the circle:

 More Rentals
 Rentals
 Social Media Comments
 Improvements
 Better Social Media Comments

 e. Select the "**Better Social Media Comments**" shape, click the **Add Shape** drop-down arrow [*SmartArt Tools Design* tab, *Create Graphic* group] and select **Add Shape After**.
 f. Type Higher Ratings in the new shape.
 g. Click the **SmartArt** frame so the entire layout is selected and then click the **Intense Effect** style [*SmartArt Tools Design* tab, *SmartArt Styles* group].
 h. Select all shapes with text by pressing **Ctrl** while you click each one. Change the *Font Size* to **20 pt**. and apply **Bold** [*Home* tab, *Font* group]. Keep all shapes selected.
 i. Resize the shapes horizontally (*Width* **2.75"**) so the word "Improvements" fits on one line (Figure 2-140).

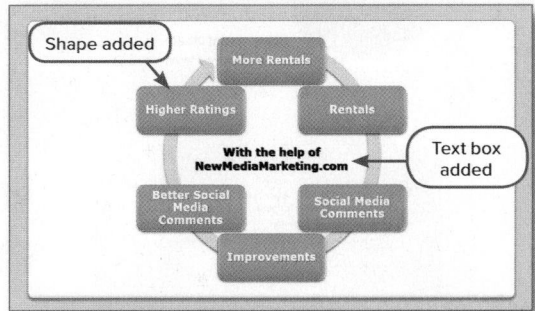

Figure 2-140 Slide 5 with *SmartArt* graphic and effects added

9. Insert a text box.
 a. Click the **Text Box** button [*Insert* tab, *Text* group] and click inside the cycle layout.
 b. Type With the help of NewMediaMarketing.com and resize the text box so that the text wraps on two lines (see Figure 2-140).

c. Change the *Font Size* to **20 pt**. and apply **Bold** [*Home* tab, *Font* group]. Click **Center** [*Home* tab, *Paragraph* group].

d. Adjust the text box size, if necessary.

e. Click **Arrange**, select **Align**, and select **Align Center** [*Home* tab, *Drawing* group]. Repeat to select **Align Middle**.

10. Insert and format an icon.

a. Display slide 6. Click the **Icons** button [*Insert* tab, *Illustrations* group] to open the gallery.

b. Select the **People** type and then select the family icon (Figure 2-141). Click **Insert**.

Figure 2-141 *Icon* selected in the *People* group

c. Change the icon *Size* (*Height* **5"** and *Width* automatically adjusts). Keep the icon selected for the next step.

d. Click the **More** button [*Graphics Tools Format* tab, *Graphics Styles* group] and apply the **Colored Fill - Accent 1, No Outline** (second option/second row).

e. Click the **Graphics Effects** button, select **Preset**, and click **Preset 2** (second option/first row).

f. Position the icon on the lower right (Figure 2-142).

Figure 2-142 Slide 6 with an icon and a style added

11. Apply a transition.

a. Click the **Reveal** transition effect [*Transitions* tab, *Transition to This Slide* group].

b. Click **Apply To All** [*Transitions* tab, *Timing* group].

12. Save and close the presentation (Figure 2-143).

Figure 2-143 PowerPoint 2-1 completed

Guided Project 2-2

For this project, you prepare a presentation with key points essential to maintain a healthy lifestyle and show examples of weight loss calorie requirements for men and women at different ages. The doctors at Courtyard Medical Plaza will use this presentation to encourage clients to be more active.
[Student Learning Outcomes 2.1, 2.2, 2.3, 2.4, 2.5, 2.6, 2.7]

File Needed: **StayingActive-02.pptx** (Student data files are available in the Library of your SIMnet account.)
Completed Project File Name: **[your initials] PowerPoint 2-2.pptx**

Skills Covered in This Project

- Apply text effects.
- Insert and format an icon.
- Create a *SmartArt* graphic.
- Apply a *SmartArt* style and effects.

- Insert an online picture.
- Crop a picture.
- Apply a picture style.
- Adjust size dimensions.
- Insert a text box.
- Insert and format a table.

1. Open the presentation **StayingActive-02**.

2. Save the presentation as [your initials] PowerPoint 2-2.

3. Format the presentation title.
 a. Select the title placeholder on slide 1.
 b. Click the **Text Effects** button [*Drawing Tools Format* tab, *WordArt Styles* group], click **Transform**, and select **Square** (first style/*Warp* group).
 - The text fills the title placeholder.
 c. Click the **Bring Forward** drop-down arrow [*Drawing Tools Format* tab, *Arrange* group], and select **Bring to Front**.
 - The green triangle on the left is behind the text.
 d. Click the **Text Fill** drop-down arrow [*Drawing Tools Format* tab, *WordArt Styles* group], select **Texture**, and click **More Textures** at the bottom of the gallery to open the *Format Shape* pane.
 e. Select **Pattern fill** and then choose the **Large checker board** pattern (fourth option/last row).
 f. Change the *Foreground Color* to **Aqua, Accent 1, Lighter 40%** (fifth color/fourth row).
 g. Change the *Background Color* to **White, Text 1** (second color/first row).
 h. Click **Text Fill** on the *Format Shape* pane to close those options.
 i. Click **Text Outline** on the *Format Shape* pane to open *Outline* options.
 j. Select **Solid line** and change the color to **Black, Background 1** (first color/first row).
 k. Click the **Text Effects** icon at the top of the pane. Select **Glow**.
 l. Change the *Color* to **Green, Accent 2, Lighter 60%** (sixth option/ third row) and the *Transparency* to **20%**. Verify the *Size* is **10 pt**. (Figure 2-144).
 m. Close the *Format Shape* pane.

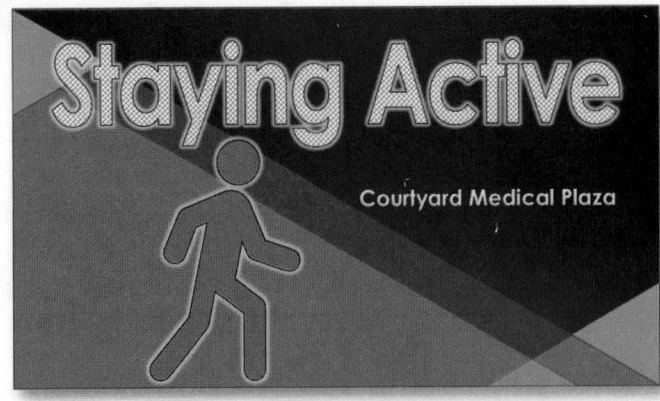

Figure 2-144 Title slide with text and graphics effects

4. Insert and format an icon on slide 1.

Figure 2-145 *Icon* selected in the *People* group

 a. Click the **Icons** button [*Insert* tab, *Illustrations* group] to open the gallery.
 b. Select the **People** type and then select the person walking icon (Figure 2-145). Click **Insert**.
 c. Change the icon size (*Height* **5.3"** and *Width* automatically adjusts). Keep the icon selected.
 d. Click the **Graphics Fill** drop-down arrow [*Graphics Tools Format* tab, *Graphics Styles* group] and select **Aqua, Accent 1** (fifth option/first row).
 e. Click the **Graphics Outline** drop-down arrow [*Graphics Tools Format* tab, *Graphics Styles* group] and select **Black, Background 1** (first option/first row).
 f. Click the **Graphics Effects** button [*Graphics Tools Format* tab, *Graphics Styles* group], select **Glow**, and click **Glow Options** to open the *Format Graphic* pane.
 g. Change the *Color* to **Green, Accent 2, Lighter 60%** (sixth option/third row) and the *Transparency* to **20%**. Verify the *Size* is **10 pt**.
 h. Position the icon on the left (see Figure 2-144).

5. Insert a *SmartArt* graphic, apply a style, and change colors using the *SmartArt Tools Design* tab.
 a. Display slide 2 and click the **SmartArt** icon on the content placeholder to open the *Choose a SmartArt Graphic* dialog box.
 b. Select the **Hierarchy** type and the **Horizontal Hierarchy** layout (last option/third row).
 c. Click **OK** to close the dialog box and insert the SmartArt graphic.
 d. Delete the three shapes on the right.
 e. Click the **Text Pane** button, if necessary, on the left of the *SmartArt* frame.
 f. Type Keep Moving after the first bullet.
 g. Type the following items after the indented bullets:

 Moderate Intensity Activity
 Count Steps (Press **Enter** to add another bullet.)
 Combine Aerobic and Strengthening

Figure 2-146 *SmartArt* graphic with style and colors changed

 h. Click the *Text Pane* **Close** button.
 i. Verify that the *SmartArt* frame is selected. Click the **Subtle Effect** *SmartArt* style [*SmartArt Tools Design* tab, *SmartArt Styles* group].
 j. Click the **Change Colors** button [*SmartArt Tools Design* tab, *SmartArt Styles* group] and select **Colorful Range - Accent Colors 4 to 5** (fourth option/*Colorful* section) (Figure 2-146).

6. Search for a picture and apply a picture style.
 a. Display slide 3. Click the **Online Pictures** button [*Insert* tab, *Images* group] to open the *Online Pictures* dialog box.
 b. Type the search word gardening and press **Enter**.
 • The *Search Results* dialog box opens.
 c. Select an appropriate picture (*Creative Commons only*) and click **Insert**.
 • Close the *Design Ideas* pane if it opens.
 • Delete the caption below the picture.
 d. Select the picture and click the **Rotated, White** picture style [*Picture Tools Format* tab, *Picture Styles* group].
 e. Resize the picture as needed so it fits on the right of the slide below the title.

7. Crop a picture and apply a picture style.
 a. Display slide 5 and select the picture.
 - Close the *Design Ideas* pane if it opens.
 b. Click the **Crop** button [*Picture Tools Format* tab, *Size* group] and crop the picture to focus only on the family. Click **Crop** again to accept your change.
 c. Select the **Rotated White** picture style [*Picture Tools Format* tab, *Picture Styles* group] to match the other picture.
 d. Move the picture to the right of the slide below the title.

8. Insert a new slide after slide 6 with a *Title and Content* layout.

9. Add text.
 a. Display slide 7. Type the title text Calorie Examples.
 b. Click the **Text Box** button [*Insert* tab, *Text* group], click below the title, and type Gaining 5 pounds a year.
 c. Apply **Bold** and change the *Font Size* to **20 pt**. [*Home* tab, *Font* group].
 d. Resize the text box as needed.
 e. Select the text box and the slide title. Click the **Arrange** button [*Home* tab, *Drawing* group], select **Align**, and select **Align Right**.

10. Insert a table, add text, and modify formatting.
 a. Click the **Table** icon on the content placeholder on slide 7.
 b. Enter **6** columns and **5** rows on the *Insert Table* dialog box. Click **OK** to close the dialog box.
 c. Type the text in Table 2-10 beginning with the column headings.

Table 2-10

Age	Height	Weight	Maintain	Fat Loss	Extreme Fat Loss
20	5 ft 10 in	200	2,647	2,118	1,600
25	5 ft 10 in	225	2,769	2,215	1,800
30	6 ft 2 in	240	2,916	2,333	1,920
35	6 ft 2 in	265	3,038	2,430	2,120

 d. Select all cells and change the *Font Size* to **20 pt**. [*Home* tab, *Font* group].
 e. Change to **Center** alignment [*Home* tab, *Paragraph* group].
 f. Adjust column width by double-clicking the border line between columns.
 - Deselect the table, if necessary, so your pointer changes to a splitter to adjust the right border of the last column so the text fits on one line.
 - When you stop dragging, the table is selected again. Verify that it is selected.
 g. Change the *Pen Color* to **Black, Background 1** (first color/first row).
 - Verify the *Pen Weight* is **1 pt**. [*Table Tools Design* tab, *Draw Borders* group].
 h. Click the **Borders** button, and select **All Borders** [*Table Tools Design* tab, *Table Styles* group].
 i. Select the second and third rows. Click the **Shading** drop-down arrow [*Table Tools Design* tab, *Table Styles* group] and select **Aqua, Accent 1, Lighter 80%** (fifth color/second row).
 j. Select the fourth and fifth rows. Click the **Shading** drop-down arrow [*Table Tools Design* tab, *Table Styles* group] and select **Aqua, Accent 1, Lighter 60%** (fifth color/third row) Figure 2-147.

Shading reflects the same person at two ages

Age	Height	Weight	Maintain	Fat Loss	Extreme Fat Loss
20	5 ft 10 in	200	2,647	2,118	1,600
25	5 ft 10 in	225	2,769	2,215	1,800
30	6 ft 2 in	240	2,916	2,333	1,920
35	6 ft 2 in	265	3,038	2,430	2,120

Figure 2-147 Table with formatting changes

k. Move the table up slightly.
l. Click the **Align** button [*Table Tools Layout* tab, *Arrange* group] and select **Align Center**.

11. Duplicate the table and edit the text in the second table.
 a. Select the table on slide 7 and press **Ctrl+D** to duplicate it.
 b. Position the second table centered near the bottom of the slide.
 c. Edit the content to match the text in Table 2-11:

Table 2-11

Age	Height	Weight	Maintain	Fat Loss	Extreme Fat Loss
20	5 ft 7 in	150	2,041	1,633	1,225
25	5 ft 7 in	175	2,163	1,730	1,400
30	5 ft 9 in	180	2,204	1,763	1,440
35	5 ft 9 in	205	2,325	1,860	1,640

12. Insert and format a shape to identify table contents on slide 7.
 a. Click the **Shapes** button [*Insert* tab, *Illustrations* group] and select the **Oval**. Draw an oval shape and adjust its *Size* (*Height* **0.9"** and *Width* **2"**) [*Drawing Tools Format* tab, *Size* group].
 b. Click the **Shape Fill** drop-down arrow [*Drawing Tools Format* tab, *Shape Styles* group] and select **Gold, Accent 5, Lighter 40%** (ninth color/fourth row).
 c. Click the **Shape Outline** drop-down arrow [*Drawing Tools Format* tab, *Shape Styles* group] and select **Green, Accent 2** (sixth color/first row). Repeat to change the *Weight* to **3 pt**.
 d. Type the word Female. Change the *Font Color* to **Black, Background 1** (first color/first row) and apply **Bold**.
 e. Click the **Edit Shape** button [*Drawing Tools Format* tab, *Insert Shapes* group] and select **Change Shape**.
 f. Select **Explosion: 8 Points** in the *Stars and Banners* group.
 g. Position this shape at the left corner of the bottom table (Figure 2-148).

13. Duplicate and edit a shape.
 a. Select the "**Female**" shape and press **Ctrl+D** to duplicate it.
 b. Position the second shape at the left corner of the top table.
 c. Change the text to Male.

14. Format the table.
 a. Display slide 8 and select the table. If necessary, change the *Pen Color* to **Black, Background 1** and the *Pen Weight* to **1 pt**. [*Table Tools Design* tab, *Draw Borders* group].
 b. Click **Borders** [*Table Tools Design* tab, *Table Styles* group] and select **All Borders**.
 c. Change the *Font Size* for all text to **20 pt**. [*Home* tab, *Font* group].
 d. Select all cells and click the **Center Vertically** button [*Table Tools Layout* tab, *Alignment* group].
 e. Change the *Table Size* (*Height* **4.5"** and *Width* **9"**) [*Table Tools Layout* tab, *Table Size* group].
 f. Click the **Align** button [*Table Tools Layout* tab, *Arrange* group] and select **Align Center**.

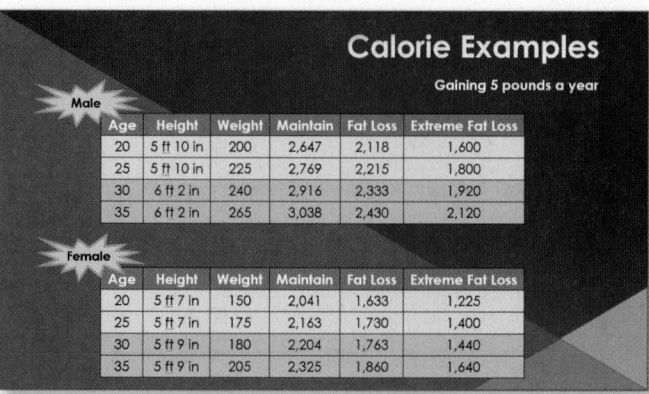

Figure 2-148 Slide 7 tables completed

15. Apply a transition.
 a. Click the **Cube** transition effect [*Transitions* tab, *Transition to This Slide* group].
 b. Click **Apply To All** [*Transitions* tab, *Timing* group].

16. Save and close the presentation (Figure 2-149).

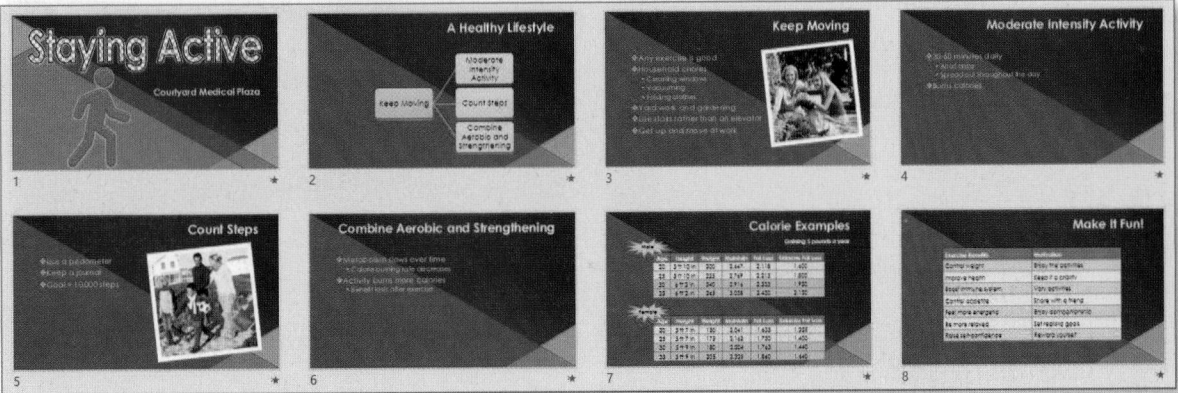

Figure 2-149 PowerPoint 2-2 completed

Guided Project 2-3

Solution Seekers, Inc., has been asked to develop a presentation for a meeting of personnel managers about how information technology is evolving. You will discuss skills needed, salaries, and job satisfaction and illustrate these concepts with *SmartArt* and charts.
[**Student Learning Outcomes 2.1, 2.5, 2.6, 2.7, 2.8**]

File Needed: ***InfoTech-02.pptx*** *(Student data files are available in the* Library *of your SIMnet account.)*
Completed Project File Name: ***[your initials] PowerPoint 2-3.pptx***

Skills Covered in This Project

- Apply text effects.
- Convert text to a *SmartArt* graphic.
- Apply a *SmartArt* style and effects.
- Create a pie chart.
- Format a table.
- Create a column chart.
- Apply chart styles.
- Format chart elements.
- Apply a picture style.
- Insert and align text boxes.

1. Open the presentation ***InfoTech-02***.

2. Save the presentation as [your initials] PowerPoint 2-3.

3. Apply text effects on slide 2.
 a. Resize the title placeholder (*Height* **3"** and *Width* **7.5"**) [*Drawing Tools Format* tab, *Size* group].
 - The text should fit on two lines.
 b. Select the title placeholder and click the **Text Effects** button [*Drawing Tools Format* tab, *WordArt Styles* group].
 c. Select **Transform** and click **Cascade Up** (third option/last row).

d. Click the **Text Fill** drop-down arrow [*Drawing Tools Format* tab, *WordArt Styles* group] and select **Teal, Accent 1, Darker 25%** (fifth color/fifth row).

e. Click the **Text Outline** drop-down arrow [*Drawing Tools Format* tab, *WordArt Styles* group] and select **Black, Background 2** (third color/first row).

f. Position the title on the left (Figure 2-150).

g. Delete the subtitle placeholder.

Figure 2-150 Slide 2 text effects applied

4. Convert bulleted text to a *SmartArt* graphic and modify the style and colors.

 a. Display slide 3. Select the bulleted text and click the **Convert to SmartArt** button [*Home* tab, *Paragraph* group].

 b. Select **More SmartArt Graphics** to open the *Choose a SmartArt Graphic* dialog box.

 c. Select the **Process** type and the **Increasing Arrows Process** layout (second option/third row).

 d. Click **OK** to close the dialog box.

 e. Apply the **Cartoon** style from the *3D* group [*SmartArt Tools Design* tab, *SmartArt Styles* group].

 f. Select the three white shapes and click the **Shape Fill** drop-down arrow [*SmartArt Tools Format* tab, *Shape Styles* group].

 g. Select **Tan, Text 2, Lighter 60%** (fourth color/third row) to soften the color.

 h. Select the three arrows and click the **Text Fill** drop-down arrow [*SmartArt Tools Format* tab, *WordArt Styles* group].

 i. Select **Black, Background 2** (third color/first row) (Figure 2-151).

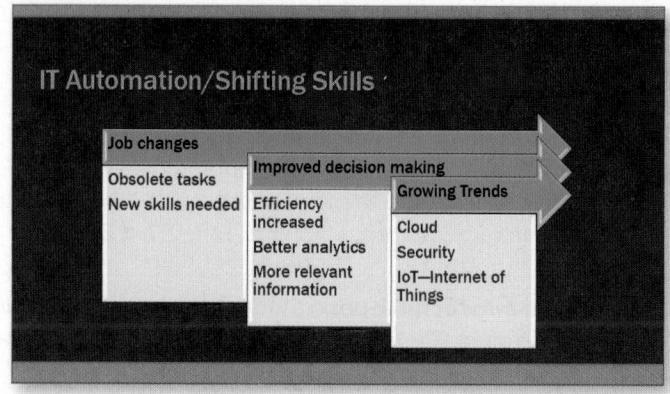

Figure 2-151 Slide 3 *SmartArt* graphic with color and style changes

5. Modify table formatting.

 a. Display slide 4 and select the two-column table on the left.

 b. Verify that **Header Row** and **Banded Rows** [*Table Tools Design* tab, *Table Style Options* group] are selected.

 c. Click the **More** button [*Table Tools Design* tab, *Table Style Options* group] to open the *Style* gallery.

 d. Apply the **Medium Style 2, Accent 1** style (second color/seventh row) [*Table Tools Design* tab, *Table Styles* group].

 e. Select the first row, click the **Text Fill** drop-down arrow and select **Black, Background 2** (third color/first row).

 f. Repeat steps 5 b–e for the single-column table on the right.

6. Insert a new slide after slide 4 with a *Title and Content* layout.

7. Create a bar chart.

 a. Select slide 5 and type the slide title Starting Salaries, Selected Jobs.

 b. Click the **Insert Chart** button on the content placeholder.

 c. Select the **Clustered Bar** chart and click **OK** to open the worksheet.

 d. Select **Columns C** and **D** on the worksheet, right-click, and select **Delete**.

 • By removing the blank column, the chart displays correctly with no blank space.

e. Replace the worksheet data for columns A and B with the data in Table 2-12.

f. Close the worksheet.

8. Modify a bar chart.
 a. Delete the "**Series 1**" *Chart Title* and *Legend*.
 b. Click the chart frame to select the **Chart Area**.
 c. Change the **Shape Fill** color to **Teal, Accent 1, Darker 50%** (fifth color/last row).
 d. Change the **Chart Area** *Width* to **12"**.
 e. Click the **Align** button [*Chart Tools Format* tab, *Arrange* group] and select **Align Center**.
 f. Select the **Vertical (Category) Axis** and change the *Font Size* to **18 pt**.
 g. Select the **Horizontal (Value) Axis** and change the *Font Size* to **18 pt**. (Figure 2-152).

9. Insert a new slide after slide 5 with a *Title and Content* layout.

10. Create a pie chart.
 a. Display slide 6 and type the slide title Employee Job Satisfaction.
 b. Click the **Insert Chart** icon in the content placeholder.
 c. Click the **Pie** chart type. Then select the **3D Pie**. Click **OK** to close the dialog box and open the worksheet.
 d. Replace the worksheet data with the data in Table 2-13 beginning with the column headings.
 e. Close the worksheet.

11. Modify a pie chart.
 a. Drag the chart title, "**Satisfaction %**," to the top left of the chart area. Increase the *Font Size* to **24 pt**. [*Home* tab, *Font* group].
 b. Click the **Chart Elements** button on the right side of the slide. Select the **Legend**, click the **right arrow** to see position options, and then select **Right**.
 c. Increase the legend *Font Size* to **20 pt**. [*Home* tab, *Font* group].
 d. Drag the legend to the bottom right of the chart area.
 e. Click the **Chart Elements** button again. Select **Data Labels**, click the **right arrow** to see position options, and then select **Inside End**.
 f. Click the **Chart Elements** list box arrow [*Chart Tools Format* tab, *Current Selection* group] and select **Series "Satisfaction %" Data Labels**.
 g. Increase the *Font Size* to **24 pt**. and apply **Bold** [*Home* tab, *Font* group] (Figure 2-153).

Table 2-12

Security Analyst	73,000
Project Manager	71,000
Applications Developer	68,500
Network Specialist	63,000
Computer Support Specialist	45,500
Help Desk Analyst	43,000

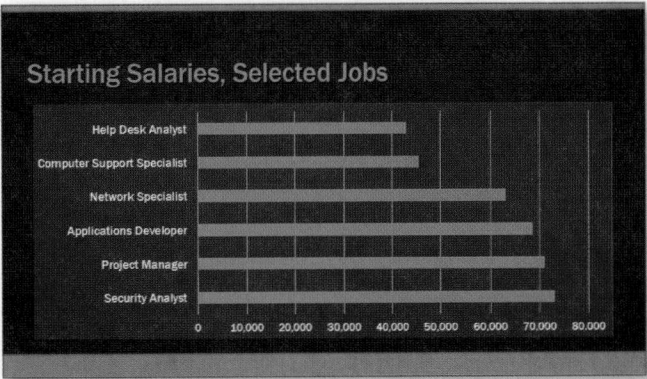

Figure 2-152 Slide 5 *Clustered Bar* chart completed

Table 2-13

	Satisfaction %
Very Satisfied	15
Somewhat Satisfied	37
Undecided	18
Somewhat Unsatisfied	22
Very Dissatisfied	8

Figure 2-153 Slide 3 *Pie* chart completed

12. Apply transitions.
 a. Click the **Blinds** transition effect [*Transitions* tab, *Transition to This Slide* group].
 b. Click **Apply To All** [*Transitions* tab, *Timing* group].
 c. Apply the **Zoom** transition to slide 6.

13. Save and close the presentation (Figure 2-154).

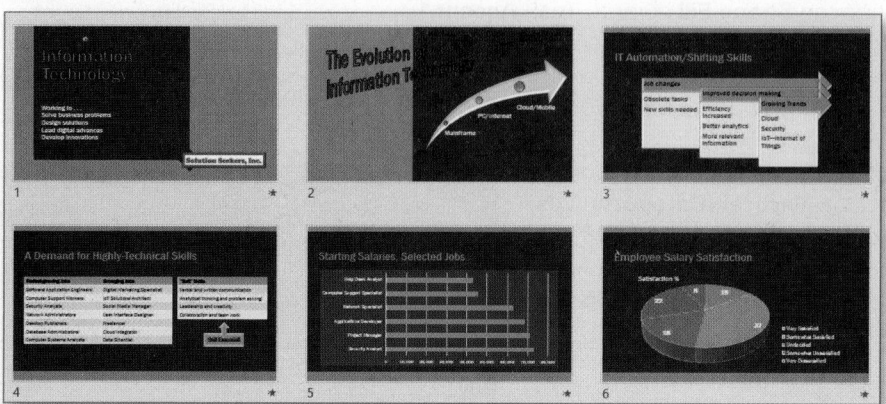

Figure 2-154 PowerPoint 2-3 completed

Independent Project 2-4

At Pool & Spa Oasis, sales associates must educate new spa owners about keeping spa water safe with proper maintenance. For this project, you prepare a presentation that emphasizes the routine to follow, explains pH level numbers, and lists available products that are typically used to balance water.
[Student Learning Outcomes 2.1, 2.3, 2.4, 2.5, 2.6, 2.7]

File Needed: ***Balancing-02.pptx*** (*Student data files are available in the Library of your SIMnet account.*)
Completed Project File Name: ***[your initials] PowerPoint 2-4.pptx***

Skills Covered in This Project

- Insert *WordArt* and apply effects.
- Adjust size dimensions.
- Insert an online picture.
- Apply a picture style.
- Create a *SmartArt* graphic.
- Apply a *SmartArt* style and effects.
- Insert and format a table.
- Insert a text box.
- Change solid and gradient colors.

1. Open the presentation ***Balancing-02***.

2. Save the presentation as [your initials] PowerPoint 2-4.

3. Change the title text arrangement.
 a. Display slide 1. Delete the title text "**Balancing Act**," but leave the word "**The**" as shown.
 b. Insert *WordArt* using the **Fill: White; Outline: Blue, Accent color 1; Glow: Blue, Accent color 1** (fourth option/second row) style.
 c. Type Balancing Act.
 d. Apply a **Shadow**, **Offset Right** *Text Effect*.

e. Click the **Character Spacing** button [*Home* tab, *Font* group] and choose **Tight**.

f. Apply the *Transform* text effect of **Cascade Up**.

g. Increase the *WordArt* size (*Height* **3"** and *Width* **9"**) and position it as shown in Figure 2-155.

4. Insert a picture and adjust text spacing.

a. Display slide 2.
 - The bulleted list placeholder on slide 2 has a gradient *Fill Color* so it cannot be resized without distorting the slide.

b. Place your insertion point in front of the word "correct" on the first indented line in the bulleted list.
 - Press **Shift+Enter** to insert a line break. The remaining text moves to the next line without starting a new paragraph.

c. Repeat to split the next line twice: before "microorganisms" and "Bromine."

d. Search for an online picture using the words hot tub and insert a picture similar to the one shown in Figure 2-156.
 - Close the *Design Ideas* pane if it opens.
 - Click the **Alt Text** button to open the *Alt Text* pane.
 - Delete the suggested text and type Picture of a hot tub.
 - Close the *Alt Text* pane.

e. Resize the picture to fit on the right side of the slide.
 - If a source notation is provided, resize it as needed and position it below the picture.

f. Apply the **Bevel Rectangle** picture style (last option/third row).

g. Position the picture on the lower right.

5. Insert a *SmartArt* graphic, add text, and change formatting.

a. Display slide 4. Insert a *SmartArt* graphic from the *Process* category with the **Continuous Block Process** layout (first option/third row).

b. Type Test Water, Add Necessary Products, and Enjoy! in the three shapes.

c. Resize the *SmartArt* graphic (*Height* **5"** and *Width* **9.5"**).

d. Apply the **Polished** *SmartArt* style (first **3D** option).

e. Select the **arrow** and apply a **Gradient** *Shape Fill*. Select **More Gradient** to open the *Format Shape* pane.

f. Select a *Preset gradient* of **Light Gradient - Accent 2** (second option/first row). The *Type* is **Linear** and change the *Direction* to **Linear Left** (last option/first row).

g. Modify the gradient stops:
 - *First stop*: Color **Light Blue, Background 2** (third color/first row); Position **0%**
 - *Second stop*: Color **Turquoise, Accent 2, Lighter 80%** (sixth option/second row); Position **40%**; Brightness **80%**
 - *Third stop*: Remove
 - *Fourth stop*: Color **Turquoise, Accent 2, Lighter 40%** (sixth option/fourth row); Position **100%**; Brightness **40%**

h. Close the *Format Shape* pane.

i. Apply **Bold** to all *SmartArt* text.

j. Position the *SmartArt* graphic evenly in the vertical space below the title. Choose **Align Center** for horizontal placement (Figure 2-157).

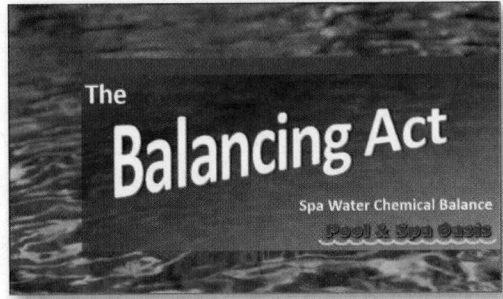

Figure 2-155 Slide 1 with *WordArt*

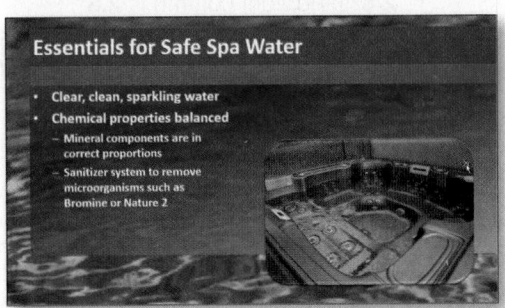

Figure 2-156 Slide 2 with inserted picture and picture style

Figure 2-157 Slide 4 *SmartArt* graphic with style and color changes

6. Insert a table, add text, and change formatting.
 a. Display slide 5. Insert a table with **3** columns and **4** rows.
 b. Verify that **Header Row** and **Banded Rows** are selected.
 c. Type the text in Table 2-14 beginning with the column headings.
 d. Change the *Font Size* to **20 pt**. for all table text.
 e. Apply the **Themed Style 1, Accent 1** table style (second style/first row).
 f. Select each column and adjust the *Cell Width* as follows: left column is **1.5"**, middle column is **2.8"**, and right column is **2.8"**.
 g. Change the alignment on the middle column to **Center**.
 h. Select the table and choose **Align Middle** and **Align Center** so the table is centered on the slide.

Table 2-14

Level	Numbers	Results
High	8.0	Alkaline, Scale
Good	7.2 – 7.6	Ideal pH Range
Low	6.0	Acidic, Corrosion

7. Insert a text box.
 a. Insert a text box below the table on slide 5. Type Drain and replace spa water every 60-90 days.
 b. Change the *Font Size* to **20 pt**.
 c. Change the *Shape Fill* to **Turquoise, Accent 2, Lighter 80%** (sixth option/second row).
 d. Resize the text box, if necessary, so the text fits on one line. Position it below the table aligned with the right of the table.

8. Copy and format a table.
 a. Select the table on slide 5 and copy it.
 b. Display slide 6 and paste the table.
 c. Delete the middle column.
 d. Select the table and change the *Table Width* to **9"**.
 e. Delete the table text and add three rows.
 f. Type the text in Table 2-15 beginning with the column headings.

Table 2-15

Products	Purpose
Sanitizer	Type needed depends on sanitizer system
Test Strips	Measure chemical levels
Shock Treatment	Breaks down organic or unfiltered material
Total Alkalinity	Increases or decreases to balance pH levels
Calcium Increaser	Balances dissolved calcium
Stain and Scale Prevention	Removes metallic impurities

 f. Adjust the column width as needed to avoid word wrapping within cells.
 g. Choose **Align Middle** and **Align Center** so the table is centered on the slide.

9. Apply the **Ripple** transition with the **From Top-Left** effect option to all slides.

10. Save and close the presentation (Figure 2-158).

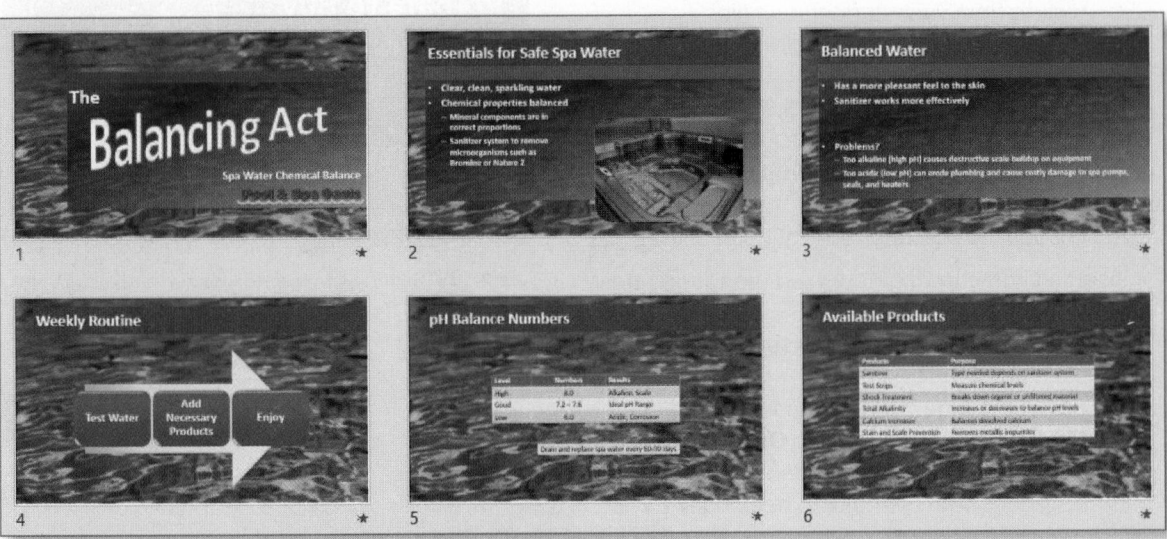

Figure 2-158 PowerPoint 2-4 completed

Independent Project 2-5

Prospective home buyers need to understand mortgage requirements and how to prepare to apply for a mortgage. Angie O'Connor at Placer Hills Real Estate wants to use a presentation on her notebook computer to help guide her discussions about these concepts with clients. For this project, you develop the presentation.
[Student Learning Outcomes 2.1, 2.3, 2.4, 2.5, 2.6, 2.7, 2.8, 2.9]

Files Needed: *PreparetoBuy-02.pptx* and *PlacerHillsSold-02.jpg* (Student data files are available in the Library of your SIMnet account.)
Completed Project File Name: *[your initials] PowerPoint 2-5.pptx*

Skills Covered in This Project

- Insert a picture.
- Crop a picture.
- Apply a picture style.
- Adjust size dimensions.
- Insert a chart and edit data.
- Apply chart styles.
- Format chart elements.
- Insert and format a table.
- Insert text boxes.
- Insert an icon.
- Convert text to a *SmartArt* graphic.
- Apply a *SmartArt* style and effects.

1. Open the presentation *PreparetoBuy-02*.

2. Save the presentation as [your initials] PowerPoint 2-5.

3. Insert and modify a picture.
 a. On slide 1, insert the **PlacerHillsSold-02** picture from your student data files.
 b. Crop the picture on the left and right (Figure 2-159).
 c. Resize the picture (*Height* **5.5"** and the *Width* automatically adjusts).
 d. Apply the **Rounded Diagonal Corner, White** picture style.
 e. Position the picture on the right side of the slide.

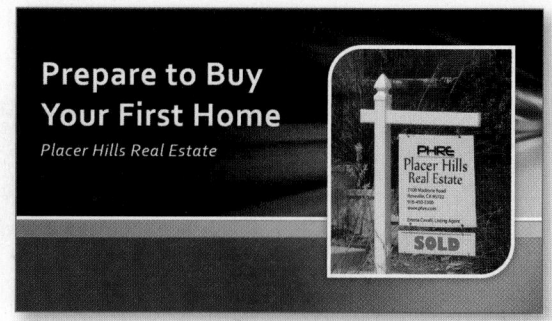

Figure 2-159 Slide 1 with inserted picture and picture style

4. Insert a chart showing how fixed mortgage rates have changed over time.
 a. Display slide 4. Click the **Insert Chart** button on the content placeholder.
 b. Select the **Line** chart type and then select the **Line with Markers** chart layout. Click **OK**.
 c. Replace the worksheet data with the data in Table 2-16 beginning with the column headings.

5. Adjust the worksheet.
 a. Be sure the selection area includes row 10 to avoid error messages.
 b. Delete worksheet **Column D** so the corresponding chart area on the slide is correct with no blank space (Figure 2-160).
 c. Close the worksheet.

6. Examine the line chart as it first appears (Figure 2-161).
 a. The line chart is accurate, but the data series lines are too thin and the data markers too small.
 b. The following changes (steps 6–12) improve the readability of the chart.

Table 2-16

	Rate	Points
1978	9.64	1.3
1983	13.24	2.1
1988	10.34	2.1
1993	7.31	1.6
1998	6.94	1.1
2003	5.83	0.6
2008	6.03	0.6
2013	3.98	0.7
2018	4.03	0.5

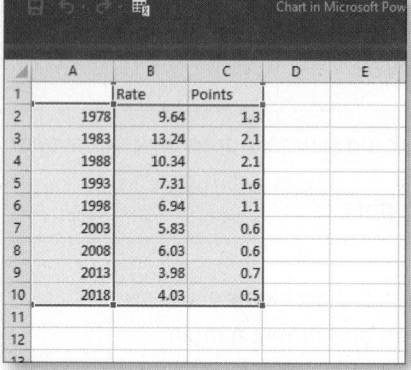

Figure 2-160 Worksheet linked to a chart

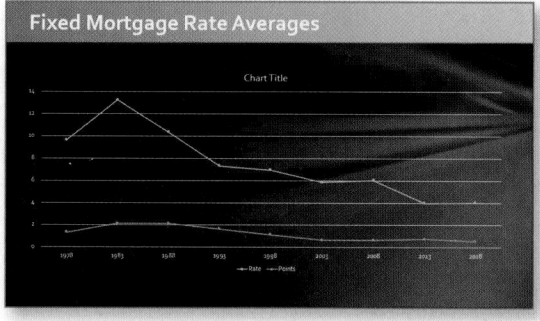

Figure 2-161 Line chart as it first appears

7. Delete the chart title.

8. Select the **Chart Area** and change the *Shape Fill* to **Brown, Background 2** (third color/first row).

9. Format the line and markers on the "Rate" series.
 a. Select the "Rate" line and right-click. Select **Format Data Series** to open the *Format Data Series* pane (Figure 2-162).
 b. Click the **Fill & Line** icon at the top of the pane.

Figure 2-162 Format Data Series pane

c. Click **Line** options and change the *Width* to **3 pt**.

d. Click **Marker** options at the top of the pane and select the following:
 - *Marker Options*: **Built-in**, *Type*: **Square**, and *Size*: **15** (Figure 2-163)
 - *Fill*: **Solid fill**, *Color*: **Orange, Accent 2** (sixth color/first row)

10. Format the line and markers on the "Points" series.

 a. Select the "Points" line. Click **Line** options and select the following:
 - *Line*: **Solid line**; *Color*: **Orange, Accent 4** (eighth color/first row)
 - *Width*: **3 pt**.

 b. Select **Marker** options and select the following:
 - *Marker Options*: **Built-in**; *Type*: **Diamond**; *Size*: **20**
 - *Marker Fill*: **Solid fill**; *Color*: **Red, Accent 5** (ninth color/first row)

11. Close the *Format Data Series* pane.

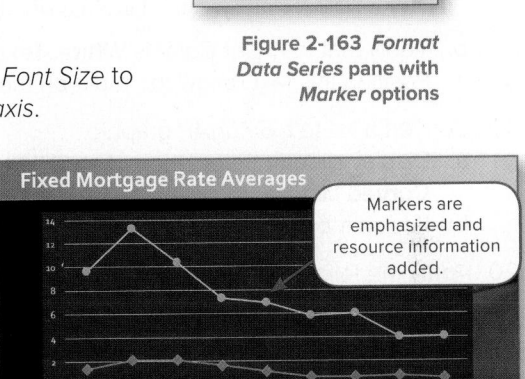

Figure 2-163 *Format Data Series* pane with *Marker* options

12. Select the *Horizontal (Category) axis* and increase the *Font Size* to **18 pt**. and apply **Bold**. Repeat for the *Vertical (Value) axis*.

13. Select the **Chart Area**, change the *Width* to **11"**, and select **Align Center**.

14. Move the chart up slightly to make room for a source notation at the bottom of the slide.

 a. Insert a text box and type the following on two lines with the web address on the second line:

 Information based on Freddie Mac survey data
 http://www.freddiemac.com/pmms/pmms30.html

 b. Position the text box below the chart on the right (Figure 2-164).

Figure 2-164 Slide 4 *Line* chart completed

15. Insert and format a table:

 a. Display slide 5 and insert a table with **5** columns and **3** rows.

 b. Type the text in Table 2-17 beginning with the column headings.

Table 2-17

Loan $200,000	Rate	Number of Payments	Monthly Payments Principle + Interest	Total Paid
15 Year Fixed	3.64	180	$1,444	$259,920
30 Year Fixed	4.31	360	$991	$356,760

c. Select all text and change the *Font Size* to **24 pt**. Adjust column width as needed.

d. Select columns **2–5** and change to **Center** alignment.

e. Select the first row and apply **Align Bottom** and change the *Shading* to **Gold, Accent 1, Darker 50%** (fifth color/bottom row) (Figure 2-165).

f. Choose **Align Middle** and **Align Center** so the table is centered on the slide.

Loan $200,000	Rate	Number of Payments	Monthly Payments Principle + Interest	Total Paid
15 Year Fixed	3.64	180	$1,444	$259,920
30 Year Fixed	4.31	360	$991	$356,760

Figure 2-165 Slide 5 table completed

16. Insert a text box.
 a. Type Home Price $250,000–Down Payment $50,000 (20%).
 b. Change the *Font Size* to **32 pt**. and apply **Bold**.
 c. Align the text box in the horizontal center above the table.

17. Click the **Icons** button and select the **Buildings** group.
 a. Select and insert the first **house** icon (fourth icon/first row).
 b. Change the *Graphics Fill* to **Red, Accent 5, Darker 25%** (ninth color/fifth row).
 c. Change the *Height* and *Width* to **1.5"**.
 d. Position the house icon on the left beside the "Home Price" text box.

18. Insert another text box.
 a. Type the following text on three lines:

 Loan cost only—add taxes and insurance costs.
 Lender rates are influenced by credit scores.
 Plan for a 20% down payment to avoid cost of points.

 b. Verify that the *Font Color* is **White, Text 1**.
 c. Position this text below the table on the right.

19. Convert a list to a *SmartArt* graphic.
 a. Display slide 6. Select the bulleted text and convert it to a *SmartArt* graphic with the **Vertical Curved List** layout.
 b. Resize the *SmartArt* frame on the right so it fits the longest line of text.

20. Apply the following changes to the *SmartArt* graphic:
 a. Change the colors to **Colorful Range - Accent Colors 2 to 3** (second option/*Colorful* group).
 b. Apply the **Moderate Effect** *SmartArt* style.
 c. Select all of the white circles and apply three changes:
 • *Shape Fill*: **Red, Accent 5, Darker 25%** (ninth color/fifth row)
 • *Shape Outline*: **Black, Background 1** (first color/first row)
 • *Bevel*: **Slant**

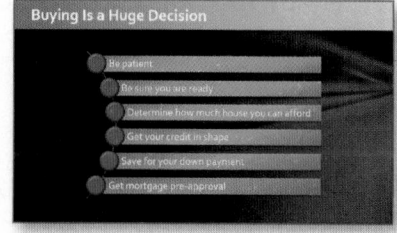

 d. Position the *SmartArt* graphic evenly in the vertical space below the title. Choose **Align Center** for horizontal placement (Figure 2-166).

21. Apply the **Shape** transition with the **Out** effect option to all slides.

22. Save and close the presentation (Figure 2-167).

Figure 2-166 Slide 6 *SmartArt* graphic with style and effects changed

Figure 2-167 PowerPoint 2-5 completed

Independent Project 2-6

Kathy Sung, Director of Services at Life's Animal Shelter (LAS), will speak to a luncheon group of businesspeople. For this project, you develop the presentation she will use to explain the needs of LAS and describe ways people can contribute through donations or by volunteering their time. [Student Learning Outcomes 2.1, 2.2, 2.3, 2.4, 2.5, 2.6, 2.7]

Files Needed: *YouCanHelp-02.pptx*, *CountryStroll-02.jpg*, *DayCare-02.jpg*, *Food-02.jpg*, *Groom-02.jpg*, and *RoyalTreatment-02.jpg* (*Student data files are available in the Library of your SIMnet account.*)
Completed Project File Name: *[your initials] PowerPoint 2-6.pptx*

Skills Covered in This Project

- Apply text effects.
- Apply a picture style.
- Set transparent color.
- Recolor a picture.
- Adjust size dimensions.

- Insert a text box.
- Insert and format a table.
- Insert icons.
- Convert text to a *SmartArt* graphic.
- Create a *SmartArt* graphic with pictures.
- Apply a *SmartArt* style and effects.

1. Open the presentation *YouCanHelp-02*.

2. Save the presentation as [your initials] PowerPoint 2-6.

3. Display slide 1 and adjust the title.
 a. Change the *Text Fill* color to **Dark Red, Accent 1, Darker 25%** (fifth color/fifth row).
 b. Apply the *Text Effect* of **Bevel** and choose **Angle** (first option/second row).
 c. Change the *Font Size* to **80 pt**.
 d. Resize the placeholder on the right so one word is on each line.

4. Resize a picture and remove a background color.
 a. Select the dog picture on slide 1.
 b. Increase the picture size (*Height* **6"** and *Width* automatically adjusts).
 c. Use *Set Transparent Color* to remove the white area in the picture.
 d. Position the dog picture on the left (Figure 2-168).

Figure 2-168 Slide 1 with picture added, white background removed

5. Apply a picture style.
 a. Display slide 2 and increase the picture size (*Width* **8"** and *Height* automatically adjusts).
 b. Apply the **Moderate Frame, Black** picture style.
 c. Choose **Align Center** and position the picture near the top of the slide.

6. Insert a text box and apply formatting.
 a. Insert a text box below the picture and type the following text:
 Our operating funds come through donations and pet adoption fees.
 b. Change the *Font Color* to **White, Background 1** (first color/first row).
 c. Change the *Font Size* to **20 pt**.
 d. Change the *Shape Fill* to **Black, Text 1** (second color/first row).
 e. Change the *Shape Outline* to **White, Background 1** and the *Weight* to **3 pt**.

f. Resize the text box so the text wraps on two lines (Figure 2-169).

g. Choose **Align Center** and position the text box below the picture.

7. Copy and paste a slide.
 a. Select the slide 2 thumbnail and press **Ctrl+C**.
 b. Move your insertion point after slide 3 and press **Ctrl+V**.

8. Format the new slide 4.
 a. Replace the text in the text box below the picture with the words We Need Your Help!
 b. Resize the text box to fit the text and center it horizontally under the picture.
 c. Select the picture and change the *Color* to **Orange, Accent color 2 Dark** (third option/ second *Recolor* row) (Figure 2-170).

9. Convert a list to a *SmartArt* graphic.
 a. Display slide 5 and convert the list to a **Vertical Bullet List** *SmartArt* graphic.
 b. Increase the *SmartArt* frame *Height* to **4.7"** so the text size increases.
 c. Reduce the *Width* to **9"**.
 d. Apply the **Cartoon** *SmartArt Style* (third *3D* option).
 e. Choose **Align Middle** and **Align Center** (Figure 2-171).

10. Insert a new slide after slide 5 with a *Title and Content* layout.
 a. Type the title Items We Need on slide 6.
 b. Insert a table with **3** columns and **5** rows.
 c. Type the text in Table 2-18 beginning with the column headings.

Figure 2-169 Slide 2 with picture and text box inserted

Figure 2-170 Slide 4 with picture recolored

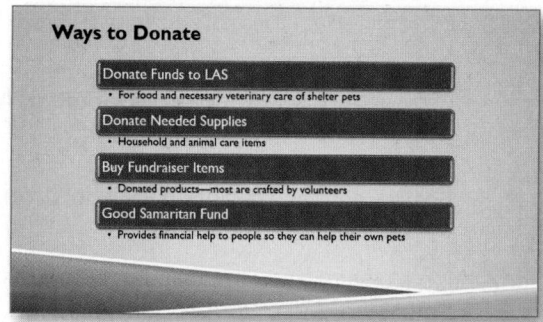

Figure 2-171 Slide 5 *SmartArt* graphic converted from bulleted text

Table 2-18

Cleaning	Paper Products and Bedding	Dog and Cat Play
Bleach	Paper Towels	Dog and Cat Treats
Pine Sol	Paper Plates	Chewies
Mop Heads	Plastic Containers with Lids	Collars
Towels	Blankets	Leashes

d. Increase the *Font Size* to **20 pt**.
e. Adjust column width so each column fits the longest line of text (Figure 2-172).
f. Center the table on the slide.

Cleaning	Paper Products and Bedding	Dog and Cat Play
Bleach	Paper Towels	Dog and Cat Treats
Pine Sol	Paper Plates	Chewies
Mop Heads	Plastic Containers with Lids	Collars
Towels	Blankets	Leashes

Figure 2-172 Slide 6 table completed

11. Insert and format two icons on slide 6.
 a. Click the **Icons** button to open the *Insert Icons* dialog box.
 b. Select the *Animals* group, choose both the **cat** and **dog** icons, and click **Insert**.
 c. Change the cat *Height* to **2"** and the *Width* automatically adjusts.
 d. Position the cat above the table (Figure 2-173).
 e. Change the dog *Height* to **3.5"** and the *Width* automatically adjusts.
 f. Position the dog below the table on the right.

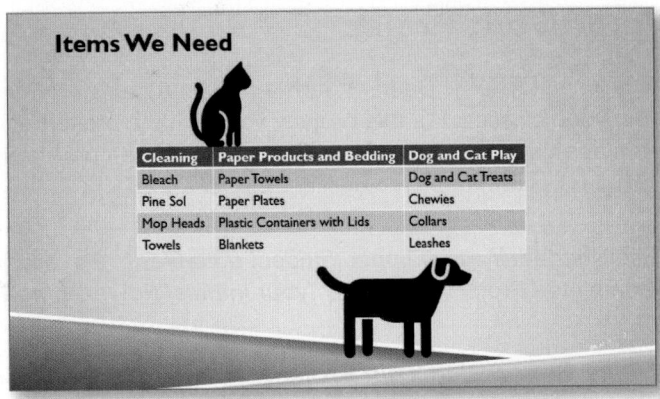

Figure 2-173 Icons inserted

12. Convert a list to a *SmartArt* graphic.
 a. Display slide 7 and convert the list to a **Picture Lineup** *SmartArt* graphic in the *Picture* group (first option/seventh row on the *Choose a SmartArt Graphic* dialog box).
 • Each picture placeholder is automatically sized.
 b. Insert five pictures (going from left to right) by following these steps:
 • Click the **Picture** icon on a shape to open the *Insert Pictures* dialog box.
 • Click **From a File**.
 • Browse to locate your student data files.
 • Select the related picture and click **Insert** (Figure 2-174):

 1 *DayCare-02*
 2 *CountryStroll-02*
 3 *RoyalTreatment-02*
 4 *Food-02*
 5 *Groom-02*

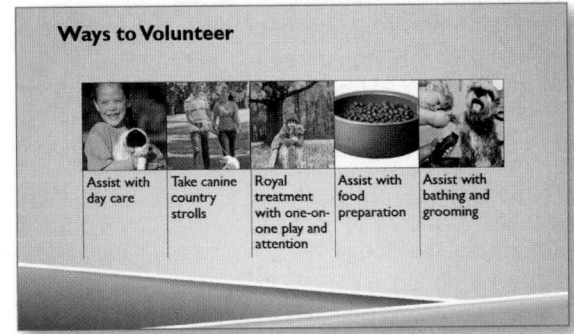

Figure 2-174 Slide 6 *SmartArt* graphic picture layout

13. Apply the **Gallery** transition to all slides.

14. Save and close the presentation (Figure 2-175).

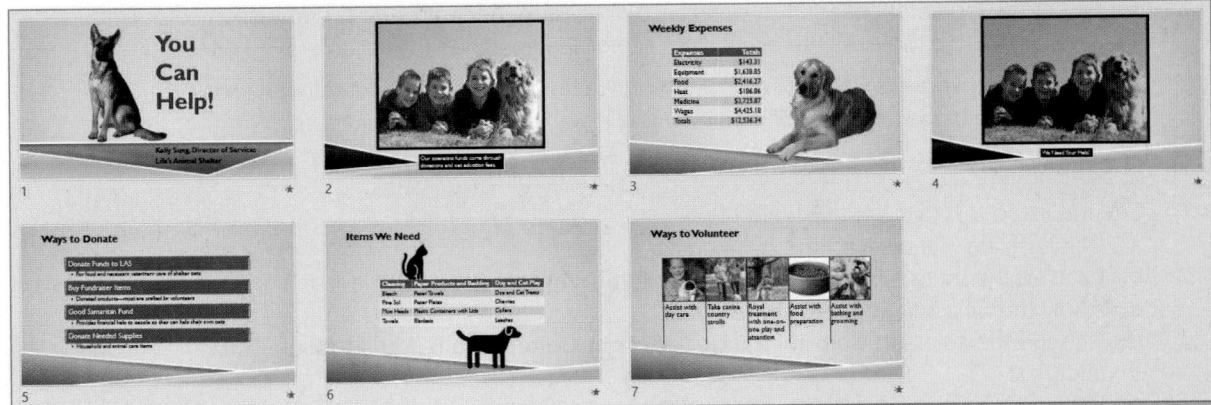

Figure 2-175 PowerPoint 2-6 completed

Improve It Project 2-7

The Hamilton Civic Center needs a presentation to explain benefits of yoga and encourage members to join yoga classes. For this project, you revise a presentation to add pictures, create a *SmartArt* graphic, and apply various styles and effects for a contemporary appearance.
[Student Learning Outcomes 2.1, 2.3, 2.4, 2.5, 2.6, 2.7]

File Needed: **Yoga-02.pptx** *(Student data files are available in the Library of your SIMnet account.)*
Completed Project File Name: *[your initials] **PowerPoint 2-7.pptx***

Skills Covered in This Project

- Apply text effects.
- Insert an online picture.
- Apply a picture style.
- Reposition slide objects.
- Convert text to a *SmartArt* graphic.
- Apply a *SmartArt* style and effects.
- Format a table.
- Compress pictures.

1. Open the presentation **Yoga-02** that has a *Standard* size (4:3 aspect ratio). The slide size is 10" × 7.5" compared to the slide size of 13.33" × 7.5" for the default *Widescreen* size (16:9 aspect ratio).

2. Save the presentation as [your initials] PowerPoint 2-7.

3. Format the title slide for a more dynamic appearance.
 a. Search online and insert a yoga picture (see Figure 2-176).
 b. Resize the picture as needed.
 c. Apply a **Bevel Rectangle** picture style.
 d. Select the title placeholder and apply the *Text Effect* **Transform** with the **Wave: Down** option (first option/fifth row in *Warp* group).

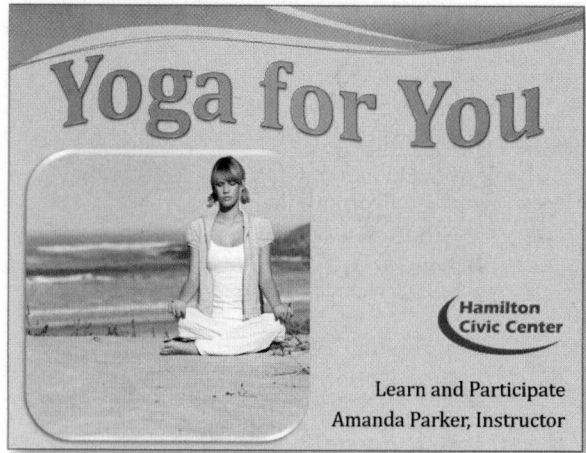

Figure 2-176 Title slide completed

4. Recolor the logo picture.
 a. Select the logo and change the picture *Color* to **Blue, Accent color 5 Light** (sixth color/fifth row).
 - This change replaces the black with a color that matches theme colors.
 b. Use *Set Transparent Color* to remove the white so your background color shows.
 c. Change the logo *Width* to **2.5"** and the *Height* will automatically adjust.

5. Arrange title slide objects as shown in Figure 2-176.

6. Change listed text to a *SmartArt* graphic.
 a. Display slide 3 and select the bulleted list.
 b. Convert the list to a *SmartArt* graphic using the **Vertical Block List** layout.
 c. Apply the *SmartArt* **White Outline** style.
 d. Change the colors to **Colorful Range – Accent Colors 4 to 5** (fourth option/*Colorful* section) (Figure 2-177).
 e. Position the *SmartArt* graphic evenly in the vertical space below the title. Choose **Align Center** for horizontal placement

7. Insert, position, and compress pictures.
 a. Display slide 4. Search online and insert an appropriate yoga picture.
 b. Resize the picture if needed and position it on the right.
 c. Apply a **Bevel Rectangle** picture style.
 d. Resize the bulleted text placeholder as needed to fit with the picture.
 e. Display slide 5. Repeat steps 7a–d.
 f. Select the picture and click **Compress Pictures**. Use default resolution, delete cropped areas of pictures, and apply compression to all pictures.

8. Modify the table.
 a. Display slide 6. Select the table text and increase the *Font Size* to **20 pt**.
 b. Apply the **Medium Style 2 – Accent 4** table style (fifth option/second row in *Medium* group).
 c. Select the title row and apply the *Cell Bevel* **Riblet** effect (second option/third row).
 d. Increase the table *Height* to **2.5"**.
 e. Center the text vertically in all cells.
 f. Add a **1 pt**. border to all cells using the **Blue, Accent 4, Darker 50%** pen color (eighth color/bottom row) (Figure 2-178).
 g. Choose **Align Middle** and **Align Center** so the table is centered on the slide.

9. Apply the **Dissolve** transition to all slides.

10. Save and close your presentation (Figure 2-179).

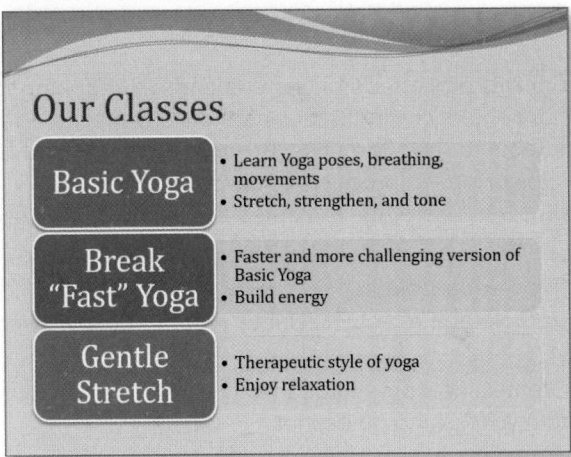

Figure 2-177 *SmartArt* graphic *Vertical Block List* layout

Classes	Days	Hours
Basic Yoga	Mon/Wed	4:15 – 5:15 p.m.
Break "Fast" Yoga	Tues/Thurs	7:00 – 8:10 a.m.
Gentle Stretch	Fri	10:00 – 11:30 a.m.

Figure 2-178 Slide 6 table

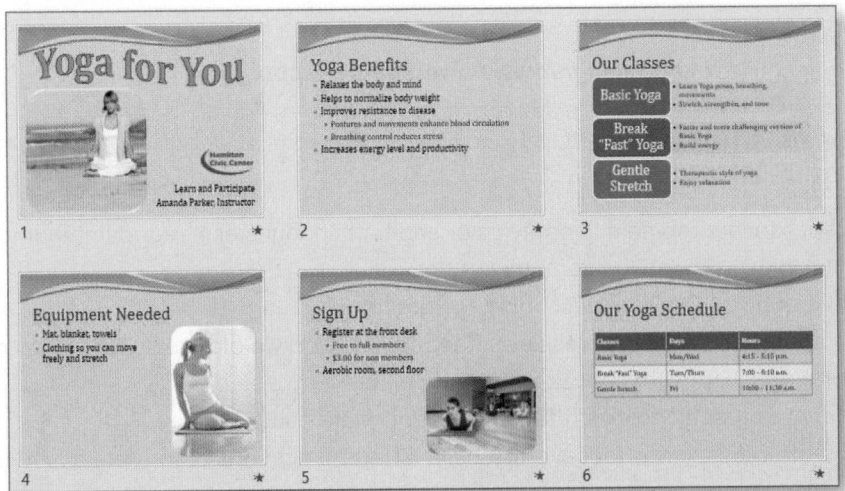

Figure 2-179 PowerPoint 2-7 completed

Challenge Project 2-8

For this project, do online comparison shopping for items you would be likely to buy, such as clothing, household products, or automotive supplies. Prepare slides describing the products and apply text effects to the slide titles. Prepare a chart that shows costs either for the same product at several web sites or similar products at the same site.
[Student Learning Outcomes 2.1, 2.2, 2.3, 2.4, 2.5, 2.6, 2.7, 2.8, 2.9]

File Needed: None
Completed Project File Name: *[your initials] PowerPoint 2-8.pptx*

Create a new presentation and save it as [your initials] PowerPoint 2-8. Modify your presentation according to the following guidelines:

- Select an appropriate theme and apply color and font changes as needed for your topic.
- Prepare a title slide and product description slides.
- Search online for a related image and insert it on the title slide.
- Add one or more shapes to emphasize a slide object.
- Insert an *Icon* and format it as a subtle, background image.
- Insert a *SmartArt* graphic to illustrate a process or relationship.
- Create a table summarizing findings.
- Create two charts to compare specific items.

Challenge Project 2-9

Using data from the United States Department of Labor published online by the Bureau of Labor Statistics (http://www.bls.gov), prepare a presentation explaining current trends in the labor force. For example, you could show unemployment rate comparisons from different regions or wage estimates for various occupations in different states.
Student Learning Outcomes 2.1, 2.3, 2.4, 2.5, 2.6, 2.7, 2.8, 2.9]

File Needed: None
Completed Project File Name: *[your initials] PowerPoint 2-9.pptx*

Create a new presentation and save it as [your initials] PowerPoint 2-9. Modify your presentation according to the following guidelines:

- Select an appropriate theme and apply color and font changes as needed for your topic.
- Create a title slide using a *Transform* text effect.
- Include several bulleted slides describing current trends.
- Search for appropriate pictures, resize as needed, and apply a picture style to each one.
- Add one or more shapes to emphasize a slide object.
- Insert a *SmartArt* graphic to illustrate a process or relationship.
- Prepare a table with salaries for several jobs in different locations or for data changing over time.
- Prepare a chart comparing employment statistics from your state or region.

Challenge Project 2-10

Create a presentation using information from one of your favorite coffee or soft drink manufacturers. For example, you can find facts at web sites such as www.thecoca-colacompany.com or www.pepsico.com to prepare a presentation comparing different products. You could show the diversity of the product line or list promotional products with pricing. From financial information provided on the sites, you could feature total revenue, total profits, or other interesting performance data in your presentation.
[Student Learning Outcomes 2.1, 2.2, 2.3, 2.4, 2.5, 2.6, 2.7, 2.8, 2.9]

File Needed: None
Completed Project File Name: *[your initials] PowerPoint 2-10.pptx*

Create a new presentation and save it as [your initials] PowerPoint 2-10. Modify your presentation according to the following guidelines:

- Select an appropriate theme and apply color and font changes as needed for your topic.
- Create a distinctive title slide using *WordArt* combined with an *Icon* or *3D Model* to create interest.
- Search online for appropriate pictures and insert three or more.
- Adjust picture sizes and apply picture styles.
- Prepare slides listing key factors contributing to the company's growth.
- Feature selected financial information in a table.
- Prepare a *SmartArt* graphic illustrating a specific process or relationship from historical or operational information.
- Create a chart showing comparisons for data such as net revenue, operating profit, or growth over time.

Preparing for Delivery and Using a Slide Presentation

POWERPOINT

CHAPTER OVERVIEW

This chapter shows you how to create new theme colors customized for your topic, apply animation so selected slide objects appear just at the right time in your presentation, and link to a video from a web site. You also explore PowerPoint's rehearsal features to help you perfect your delivery timing and techniques, project your presentation more effectively, and prepare a presentation to be self-running. Finally, you learn how to save a presentation on a CD or a folder.

STUDENT LEARNING OUTCOMES (SLOs)

After completing this chapter, you will be able to:

SLO 3.1 Create custom theme colors and background fills (p. P3-163).

SLO 3.2 Apply animation to add interest and reinforce content (p. P3-172).

SLO 3.3 Link to an online video (p. P3-175).

SLO 3.4 Use rehearsal techniques to prepare for presentation delivery (p. P3-182).

SLO 3.5 Control display options for different screen sizes (p. P3-185).

SLO 3.6 Present effectively and professionally using projection equipment (p. P3-191).

SLO 3.7 Use annotation pens to highlight information and save presentation markings (p. P3-195).

SLO 3.8 Prepare a self-running presentation that loops (p. P3-198).

SLO 3.9 Use the *Package Presentation for CD* feature to prepare a slide show for display on other computers (p. P3-200).

CASE STUDY

Specialists at Solution Seekers, Inc., frequently present to both large and small groups as they work with clients to improve business performance. Davon Washington is creating a series of seminars for new hires to help them be more productive and professional. For this project, you work with Davon to finish the presentation he has developed for a seminar on presentation planning.

Pause & Practice 3-1: Create custom theme and background colors. Add interest with animation and video.

Pause & Practice 3-2: Rehearse a presentation and prepare for a widescreen display.

Pause & Practice 3-3: Practice slide show delivery features.

Pause & Practice 3-4: Prepare a self-running presentation and package a presentation to a folder.

Creating Custom Theme and Background Colors

Themes create a unified appearance for your presentation. When you use themes effectively, the information you present on a topic is seen by your viewers as one "package" and not a collection of random slides. You may need to match specific colors in a company logo or a school's college colors, so in this section you will prepare custom theme colors that create a unique palette and help you work more efficiently. Then, you will explore different ways to apply pattern, gradient, and picture fills and consider issues to keep in mind when applying these fills to slide backgrounds.

Custom Theme Colors

As you worked with shapes, colors, and styles in previous chapters, you saw how theme colors are arranged across the top of the *Theme Colors* gallery. Recall that various percentages of each color appear below the top row colors (Figure 3-1). This section takes a closer look at how PowerPoint automatically applies theme colors to various graphics.

Four sample slides are shown in Figure 3-2 with the *Facet* theme and *Blue* theme colors. The white background is the *Background 1* color with decorative shapes in *Accent 1* and *Accent 2* colors.

- **Slide 1**: The photograph has a border of *Text 2* color.
- **Slide 2**: The first color samples show the two sets of *Background* and *Text* colors. The second color samples show *Accent colors 1–6*.
- **Slide 3**: The bullets and the *SmartArt* shapes are shown in the *Accent 1* color.
- **Slide 4**: The table has *Accent 2* color variations. The chart shows all six *Accent* colors. They appear based on the order data are entered in the worksheet.

Figure 3-1 *Theme Colors* gallery

Accent colors (Figure 3-3) appear from left to right in both the *Shape Styles* gallery and the *Table Styles* gallery (Figures 3-4 and 3-5). Other galleries show options in a similar way.

Creating custom theme colors can boost your productivity because the colors you choose are available to you in the galleries as you develop your slide show. When you save custom theme colors, the colors are also available to use again in another presentation. Keep the following guidelines in mind when you create custom theme colors:

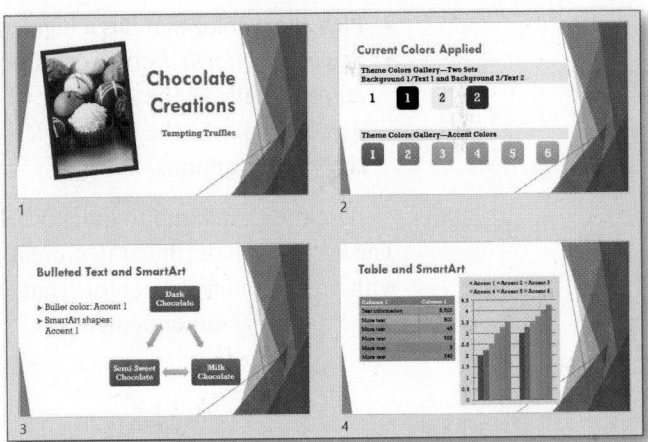

Figure 3-2 Sample slides showing graphics with *Blue* theme colors

Figure 3-3 *Blue* theme accent colors

- Select your background color first and then select other colors that work well on the background.

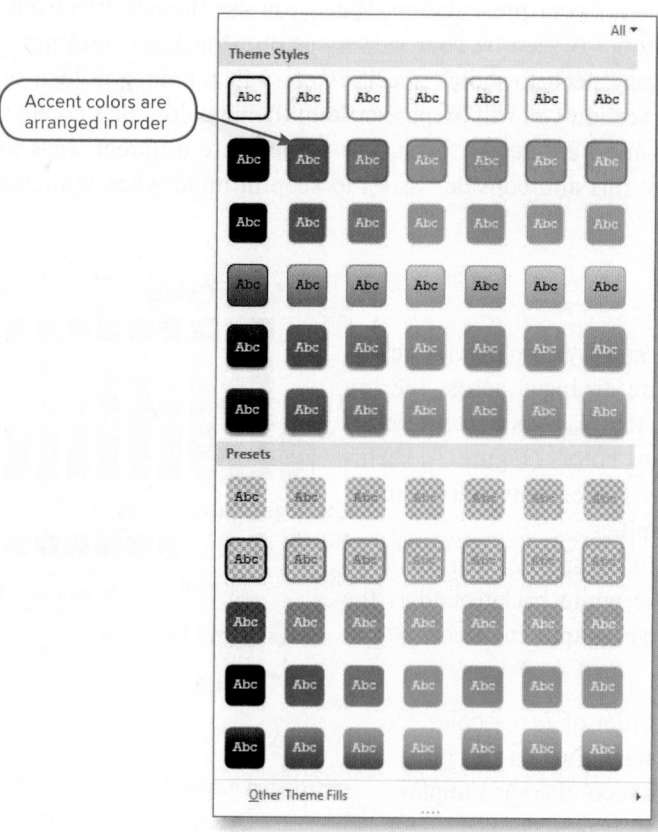

Accent colors are arranged in order

Figure 3-4 *Shape Styles* gallery

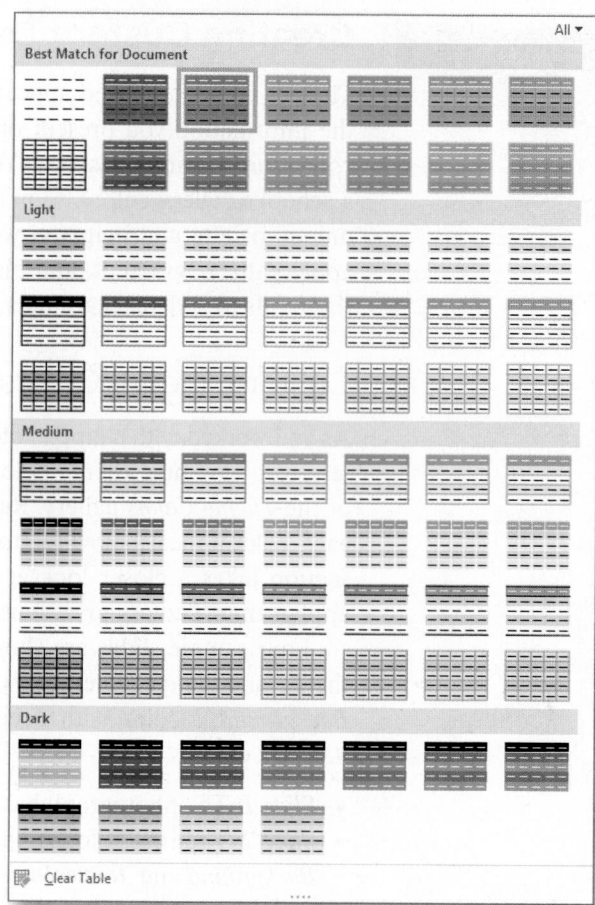

Figure 3-5 *Table Styles* gallery

- Pick a text color that has a high contrast with your background color so words are easy to read.
- Select the *Accent 1* color carefully because it will appear automatically as the fill color when you draw shapes. The *Accent 1* color is the first choice, also, in galleries that show color options.

Use the *Design* tab to quickly select built-in theme colors. The next example illustrates creating custom theme colors with brown and yellow colors that are more appropriate for a presentation about chocolate.

Current theme colors

▶ HOW TO: Create New Theme Colors

1. Start a new presentation using a design theme or open an existing presentation.
2. Click the **More** button [*Design* tab, *Variants* group].
3. Select **Colors** to open the list of built-in theme colors. The current color theme is selected (Figure 3-6).
4. Select **Customize Colors** to open the *Create New Theme Colors* dialog box (Figure 3-7).

Figure 3-6 *Theme Colors* gallery

Figure 3-7 *Create New Theme Colors* dialog box showing *Blue* theme colors

Figure 3-8 *Create New Theme Colors* dialog box showing custom colors

5. Change individual colors as needed to create your custom theme (Figure 3-8).

- Click a **Color** button to open the *Themes Colors* gallery.
- Select a different theme color or click **More Colors** to open the *Colors* dialog box.
- Click the **Standard** or **Custom** tab, choose a color, and click **OK**.
- Repeat for each of the colors you want to change.
- For this example, the *Text/Background – Dark 1* and *Light 1* colors do not require a change.

6. Name the new custom theme.

7. Click the **Save** button.

- The new custom theme is automatically applied.
- The name will appear in the *Custom* section of your list of available theme colors so you can use it again.

The same sample slides are shown in Figure 3-9 with the new colors. Controlling color this way is more efficient than using an existing theme and having to select a custom color each time you create various illustrations. If any slide text, such as a slide title, retains the original colors, click the **Reset** button [*Home* tab, *Slides* group] to update the colors.

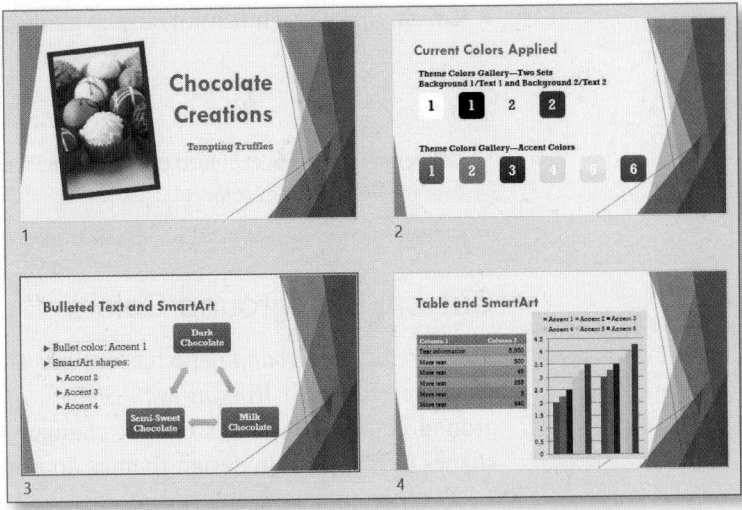

Figure 3-9 *Chocolate* theme colors applied to sample slides

Colors influence the tone or mood of your presentation. Consider the following title slides designed to illustrate this concept using the same *Facet* theme with different colors for contrasting tones. The picture on each slide provided color ideas and the font was changed to better reflect the tone (Figure 3-10).

- *Slides 1-2*: Varied and vibrant or similar with subtle differences
- *Slides 3-4*: Soothing and tranquil or lively and energetic
- *Slides 5-6*: Youthful or mature
- *Slides 7-8*: Historic or high-tech

When you think about colors for your topic, consider your audience and be respectful of cultural differences. People tend to assign meaning to colors based

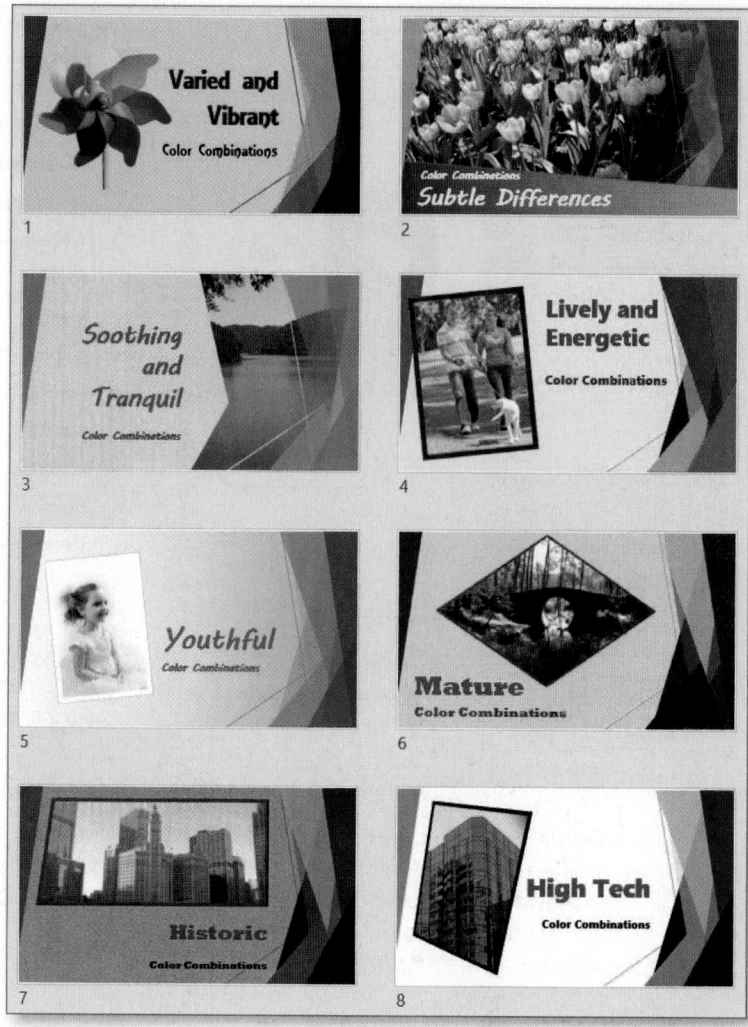

Figure 3-10 The *Facet* theme title slide with different color combinations

on their cultural background and life experiences. A few examples of colors that have symbolic meaning include the following:

- *White*: Purity and cleanliness in the American culture, death in some cultures
- *Red*: Health (red blood) in the medical field, loss (negative values) in the financial field
- *Green*: Sickness (infection) in the medical field, wealth (money) in the financial field

> **MORE INFO**
>
> To examine this concept further, look online for information about color meaning, color symbolism, or the psychology of color.

Custom Background Colors

The *Format Background* pane has options similar to those you have used on the *Format Shape* pane (see *SLO 2.1: Working with Shapes, Styles, Effects, and Colors*). When you change background colors, text colors do not change. Also, the position of placeholders or the graphic shapes that appear on design themes do not change.

When you choose colors and creative effects for backgrounds, remember that your color choices will fill the entire slide area behind everything else you design on a slide. These changes

are visible throughout the presentation if you apply them to all slides, so you should examine your changes at full screen size to be sure you are satisfied with the results.

You need to consider how your background affects text, too. If a theme or template has graphic shapes included in its design, then a solid color background fill is a good choice. Select a color that has a strong contrast from the color used for text (light on dark or dark on light).

Format a Background with Pattern and Gradient Fills

Two colors (the *Foreground* and the *Background*) create pattern fills. Two similar colors create a subtle pattern; two contrasting colors create a more obvious pattern. Notice the difference in two title slides prepared using the *Wisp* theme and a *Dark Horizontal* background pattern fill (Figure 3-11).

- *Slide 1 (Left)*: The text is difficult to read on a background with pattern colors that have a strong contrast.
- *Slide 2 (Right)*: The text is easier to read on a background with pattern colors that are similar.

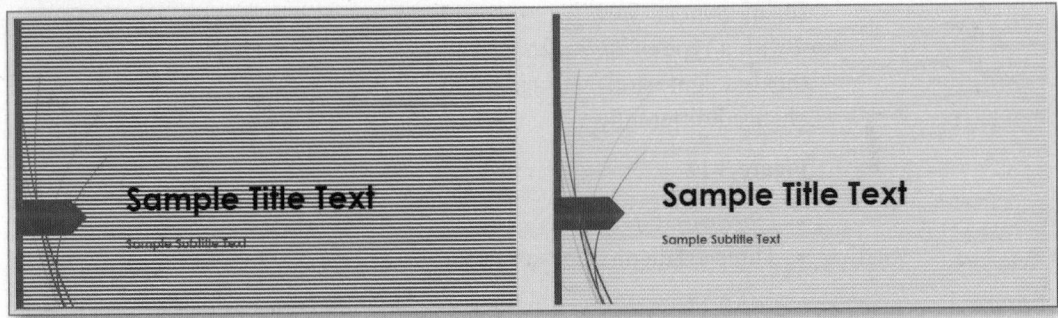

Figure 3-11 *Wisp* theme title slide with the same background pattern in different colors

▶ HOW TO: Add a Background Pattern Fill

1. Point to and right-click the slide background to open the context menu.
2. Click **Format Background** to open the *Format Background* pane.
3. Select the **Pattern fill** option.
4. Choose an appropriate *Foreground Color* and *Background Color*.
5. Choose one of the patterns. By default, this change is applied to the current slide only.
6. Click **Apply to All** to apply this change to the entire presentation.

Or

7. Click **Reset Background** if you want to restore the background's original design.
8. Close the *Format Background* pane.

> ### ▶ ANOTHER WAY
>
> Open the *Format Background* pane by clicking the **Format Background** button [*Design* tab, *Customize* group]. When using *Slide Master* view, click the **Background Styles** button [*Slide Master* tab, *Background* group], and then click **Format Background**.

Preset gradient colors are based on theme colors. You first choose the *Type* of gradient that controls how the colors blend, and then you choose the *Direction* of color change. Based on these choices, gradient stops appear on the color bar. You can select different colors for each gradient stop. Move, delete, or add gradient stops to modify how the colors blend. The color change is more gradual with more distance between the stops. Compare the title slides of the *Wisp* design theme shown in Figures 3-12 and 3-13. These two slides started with the same preset gradient fill of *Bottom Spotlight - Accent 4* with a type of *Linear*; however, the gradient stop settings were changed differently.

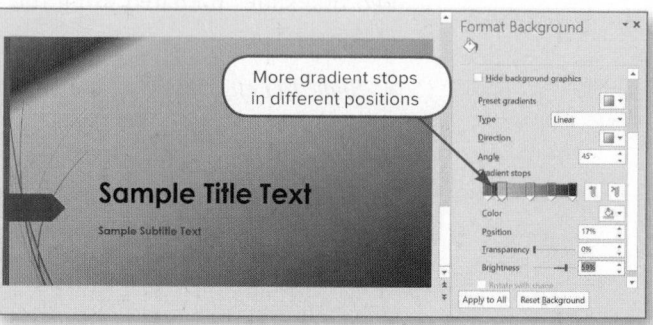

Figure 3-12 *Wisp* theme title slide with a custom background gradient fill

Figure 3-13 *Wisp* theme title slide with a custom background gradient fill showing different gradient stops

Figure 3-12

- *Linear Up* direction.
- Three gradient stops are used.

Figure 3-13

- *Linear Diagonal - Top Left to Bottom Right* direction.
- The three gradient stops on the left of the color bar are close together for a defined color change; three more stops on the right are spread apart for a more gradual color change.

▶ **HOW TO:** Add a Background Gradient Fill

1. Point to the slide background that you want to change and right-click to open the context menu.
2. Click **Format Background** to open the *Format Background* pane.
3. Select the **Gradient fill** option. By default, changes are applied to the current slide only.
4. Click the **Preset gradients** button and select a color such as **Light Gradient – Accent 2** (second option/first row) or **Top Spotlight – Accent 4** (fourth option/second row) from the gallery of options.
 - Each gallery shows all accent colors for the same gradient style.
5. Click the **Type** drop-down arrow and choose one of the options: **Linear**, **Radial**, **Rectangular**, **Path**, or **Shade from title**.
6. Click the **Direction** button and choose a direction for color blending if one is available.
 - The *Angle* degree is available only for the *Linear* type, and it automatically adjusts based on the direction you choose.
 - Type a different number in the *Angle* box or click the arrows to change the number in 10-degree increments.
7. Add or remove gradient stops.
 - Click the **Add gradient stop** button to add gradient stops.
 - Click the **Remove gradient stop** button or drag the gradient stop down to remove it from the color bar.

8. Change colors by selecting a gradient stop and clicking the **Color** button. Choose a different color.
9. Change color blending by selecting the gradient stop and dragging it to a different position on the color bar.
 - Drag the stops to rearrange them if you want to change the order.
 - Change percentages for each stop position to precisely adjust the positions.
10. Adjust *Brightness* and *Transparency* as needed.
11. Click the **Reset Background** button, if necessary, to restore the settings before you made changes.
 - Click the **Undo** button {*Quick Access* toolbar] to reapply the settings.
12. Click the **Apply to All** button to apply your finished background to every slide in your presentation.
13. Close the *Format Background* pane.

ANOTHER WAY

Access various *Background Styles* [*Design* tab, *Variants* group or *Slide Master* tab, *Background* group] that show light and dark color combinations based on theme colors.

Format a Background with Picture and Texture Fills

Pictures help you tell your story, communicate without words, and convey emotions that are difficult to express in words. Pictures can provide a dramatic background for your presentation. However, text over pictures may be difficult to read because pictures are comprised of many colors. Textures can use many colors, too, or show a lot of detail. Pictures in a small size can be used as textures to fill a slide with many small pictures. The examples in this section show you several ways to combine background pictures and text.

▶HOW TO: Add a Background Picture Fill

1. Point to and right-click the slide background to open the context menu.
2. Click **Format Background** to open the *Format Background* pane.
3. Select the **Picture or texture fill** option.
 - By default, changes are applied to the current slide only.
4. Click one of three buttons to select and insert a picture:
 - **File**: Opens the *Insert Picture* dialog box so you can search for and insert a picture from your collection.
 - **Clipboard**: Inserts a picture previously copied to the *Clipboard*. By default, the last picture copied is inserted. Open the *Clipboard* pane [*Home* tab, *Clipboard* group] to select a different picture from the ones you copied.
 - **Online**: Opens the *Online Pictures* dialog box so you can search for and insert a picture from online sources.
5. Use one of the following methods to soften the picture colors so text and other objects on the slide are easy to see:
 - Increase the *Transparency* percentage on the *Format Background* pane. This setting mutes the colors, but the original colors are still evident.
 - Click the **Picture** tab at the top of the *Format Background* pane, and then click **Picture Color**. Click the **Presets** button to choose from different saturation levels or click the **Recolor** button to choose from dark and light accent colors for a monochromatic effect.
 - If you decide not to change the picture's colors, click the **Reset** button to restore the picture to its original state.
6. Use a picture multiple times in a small size to fill the background.
 - Click the **Fill Option** on the *Format Background* pane and select **Tile picture as texture**.
 - Reposition the repeating pictures in the slide area by adjusting the **Offset** percentages (*Offset X* moves left and *Offset Y* moves down).
 - Adjust the size of the repeating pictures in the slide area by adjusting the **Scale** percentages (*Scale X* changes width and *Scale Y* changes height).

7. Click the **Reset Background** button, if necessary, to restore the settings before you made changes.
 - Click the **Undo** button {*Quick Access* toolbar] to reapply the settings.
8. Click the **Apply to All** button to apply your finished background to every slide in your presentation.
9. Close the *Format Background* pane.

> **MORE INFO**
>
> Change a slide background at any time while you are working on a presentation.

The following figures show options using the *Format Background* pane to soften background pictures or use placeholder fill colors so that text on pictures or textures is easy to read. A single flower that is almost a square image (Figure 3-14) is used differently in Figures 3-15 through 3-17. The first slide in each figure illustrates a problem, while the second and third slides show possible solutions. Figure 3-18 illustrates several options for using textures as a background.

Notice the following characteristics for the three slides shown in Figure 3-15:

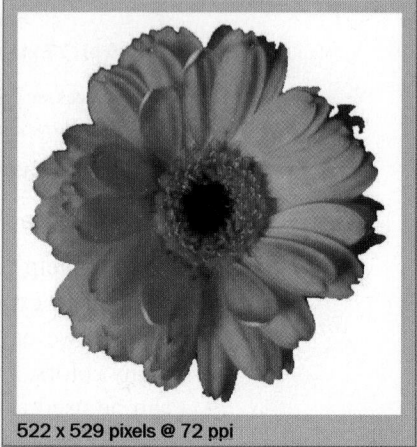

522 x 529 pixels @ 72 ppi

Figure 3-14 A flower picture used in background examples

- *Slide 1 (left)*: This picture is almost square (522 × 529 pixels). When it is stretched to fill the width of a widescreen display (*Height* 7.5" and *Width* 13.33"), part of the flower is cut off at the top and bottom. This is not necessarily a problem, just what happens if you use a square picture. The title text, however, is not easy to read over the dark colors of the flower. Text should be legible no matter what background designs you use.
- *Slide 2 (center)*: The title placeholder is the same width as the slide. A dark red fill is applied and the white text has a shadow so now the text is easy to read.
- *Slide 3 (right)*: The title placeholder treatment is the same as slide 2. The picture was recolored using the preset *Black and White: 25%* color. This creates a more abstract image.

Figure 3-15 A large square picture used as a background fill with color changes

Notice the following characteristics for the three slides shown in Figure 3-16:

- *Slide 4 (left)*: The large flower does not fill the slide when inserted in its original size, so now the complete flower appears. The *Tile picture as texture* option was selected with *Alignment* changed to *Center*. *Tiling* causes the picture to be repeated to fill the slide area so parts of the flower are shown around the center flower. Like slide 1 in Figure 3-15, the text is difficult to read.

- *Slide 5 (center)*: The title placeholder resembles slide 2 in Figure 3-15, but this time the fill color transparency is 30%. More of the flower shows, yet the text is still easy to read.
- *Slide 6 (right)*: The picture was recolored with preset *Gray - 25%, Background color 2 Light*. Black text is used with no shadow to avoid making the text appear blurred.

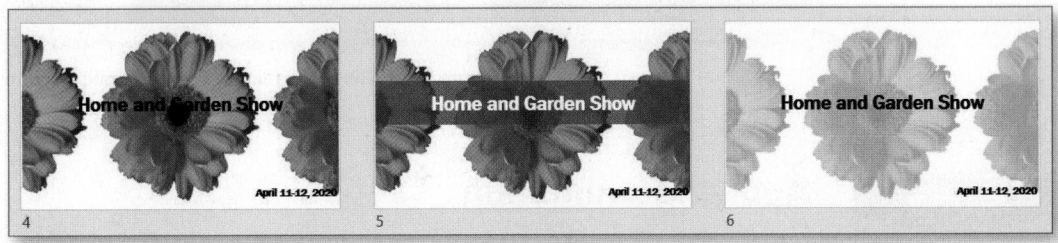

Figure 3-16 A large square picture used as a tiled background fill with color changes

If you tile a picture or texture that is small, many images fill the screen for an effect like tile on a wall. If these images are too large, then adjust the *Tiling Options* and reduce the *Scale* percentage to display each image in a smaller size. *Offset* points control how much the tiled images are indented from the left (*Offset X*) and top (*Offset Y*).

Notice the following characteristics for the three slides shown in Figure 3-17:

- *Slide 7 (left)*: The *Tile picture as texture* option was selected so many of these small flower images (200 × 203 pixels) fill the screen. *Alignment* was changed to *Top left*, and then *Offset* and *Scale* were adjusted. Like slide 4 in Figure 3-16, the text is difficult to read.
- *Slide 8 (center)*: The flower picture was recolored with preset *Grayscale*. The title placeholder colors were changed to a black fill with red text and the size was increased, too, for greater emphasis.
- *Slide 9 (right)*: The repeating picture for this slide is a small rectangle (40 × 77 pixels) with a bevel effect so it looks like a real tile. The title text is left aligned and the placeholder is filled with a gold color. A rectangle was added on the right so the date would be easy to read and to help create an asymmetrical focal point with the single large flower. This flower has a transparent background rather than white as in the previous examples.

Figure 3-17 Small pictures tiled for a background fill with color changes

Textures available on the *Format Background* pane are small images, so it is generally best to tile them because the effect is more pleasing. When stretched to fill a slide, the textures may be too bold or blurred. Notice the following characteristics for the slides shown in Figure 3-18:

- *Slide 10 (left)*: The *Paper bag* texture was applied and its bold appearance dominates the slide.
- *Slide 11 (center)*: The same texture was tiled so multiple small images repeat and no other change was made.
- *Slide 12 (right)*: The same texture was tiled and the *Mirror type* changed to *Both*. This creates a pattern with horizontal and vertical mirror images.

Figure 3-18 The same texture used as a background fill with different settings

SLO 3.2

Applying Animation

Animation is the movement of objects on a slide. Animation creates a more dynamic presentation and can help your audience focus on concepts.

Observe creative animation techniques by noticing how objects and text move in movies or in television commercials. As you decide what effects to use, select movements that enhance your content and support your message. Animation can be overdone when it is not used skillfully. Use animation sparingly because too much can be distracting.

When planning movement, also consider the transitions (the movement between slides). When a presentation is supporting a speaker, you want to keep the transitions calmer and apply animation effects to draw attention to information on selected slides only.

Add Entrance, Exit, and Emphasis Effects

Animation effects are arranged in categories that are shown in different colors on the gallery (Figure 3-19):

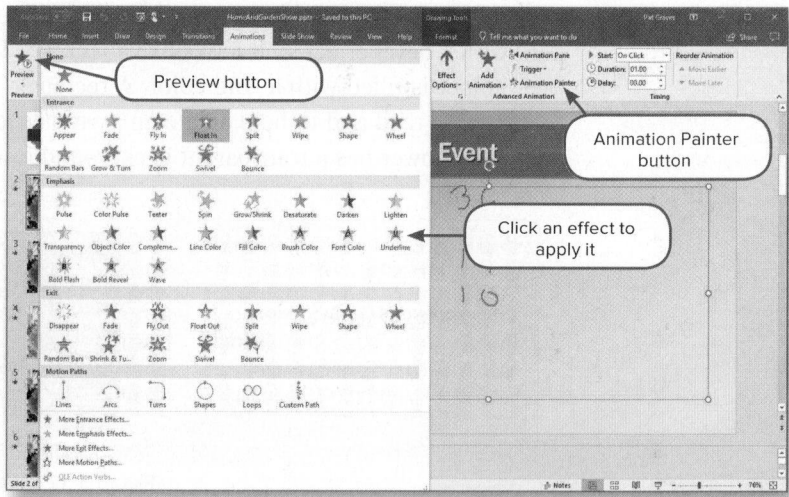

- *Entrance*: A movement that occurs when an object appears on the slide (green)
- *Emphasis*: A movement or color change that calls attention to an object that remains on the slide (yellow)
- *Exit*: A movement that occurs when an object leaves the slide (red)

Figure 3-19 *Animations* gallery

- *Motion Path*: Predefined movements or one a user draws to make an animated object move in a specific direction

Note that some effects are for text only. When animating objects, those effects are gray in the gallery and are not available.

Select an animated object and click the **Animation Painter** button [*Animations* tab, *Advanced Animation* group] to copy those settings. Click a second object to apply the same animation settings to that object.

▶HOW TO: Apply an Animation Effect

1. Select the text or object to animate.
2. Click the **Animations** tab.
3. Open the *Animations* gallery using one of these methods:
 - Click the **More** button on the gallery [*Animation* group].
 - Click the **Add Animation** button [*Advanced Animation* group].
4. Click an effect to apply it.
 - A number appears on the slide beside the text or object to show that it is animated.
5. Click the **Preview** button to test the animation.
6. Repeat to animate additional objects as desired.
 - Each animated object is numbered in sequence to show animation order.
7. Apply the same animation to another object.
 - Select an animated object and click the ***Animation Painter*** button.
 - Click another object to apply the animation.
8. Remove an animation by clicking the animation number and pressing **Delete** on your keyboard.

> ▶ MORE INFO
>
> Animation numbers display only when the *Animations* tab is open.

Effect Options, Timing, and Duration

Each different animation has ***Effect Options*** that control the direction of movement.

▶HOW TO: Change Effect Options

1. Select the animated object.
2. Click the **Effect Options** button [*Animations* tab, *Animation* group].
3. Select an appropriate **Direction** and **Sequence** if available.

For the *Float In* effect shown in Figure 3-20, two directions are available. Other effects have many different options. You select only one direction for each animation.

The sequence shown in this figure is *By Paragraph* because the animated object is a list. Animation numbers display before each bulleted item so they appear individually. If you choose *As One Object*, only one animation number displays and the complete list appears at the same time. If you choose *All at Once*, the same animation number displays for each text item and the complete list appears at the same time.

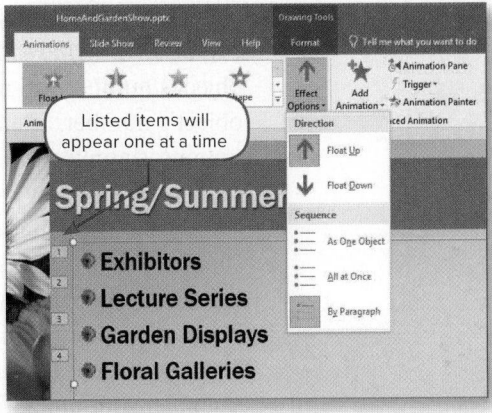

Figure 3-20 Animation and effect options applied

Remember that viewers cannot read text until it stops moving, so be careful when applying animation to text. If you will spend significant time discussing each item in a list, adding each item as you start talking about it is helpful. However, animating a list has no value if your statements are brief or if you discuss the complete list in general terms.

Adjust animation *Timing* using the following commands on the *Animations* tab in the *Timing* group:

- *Start*: When the *On Click* option is selected, the speaker controls when animation begins by clicking at an appropriate time. The *With Previous* or *After Previous* options cause the animation to occur automatically.
- *Duration*: By default, the time to complete each animation ranges from .50 to 2.00 seconds depending on the movement. Increasing the duration seconds extends the time an object is moving so the movement appears slower.
- *Delay*: The default setting is no delay, but enter seconds to start the animation after a specified time.
- *Reorder Animation*: When multiple objects are animated, click **Move Earlier** or **Move Later** to adjust the sequence of animation.

▶ HOW TO: Adjust Animation Timing and Duration

1. Select the animated object.
2. Click the **Start** drop-down arrow [*Animations* tab, *Timing* group] and select from **On Click**, **With Previous**, or **After Previous** (Figure 3-21).
3. Increase or decrease *Duration* by changing the seconds.
4. Enter seconds or click the *Delay* arrows to specify the time (in seconds) before the animation starts.
5. Click the **Preview** button [*Preview* group] to test the animation.
6. Reorder animation if necessary using the **Move Earlier** and **Move Later** buttons.

Figure 3-21 *Animations* tab, *Timing* group

When you animate several objects, check the animation numbers to be sure the sequencing is appropriate (Figure 3-22). Each number represents the click on which the animation occurs. If a single object's *Start* is **With Previous** or **After Previous**, then the object's number will match the previous object's number. If either of these *Start* options is applied to all objects, then the number will display as "0".

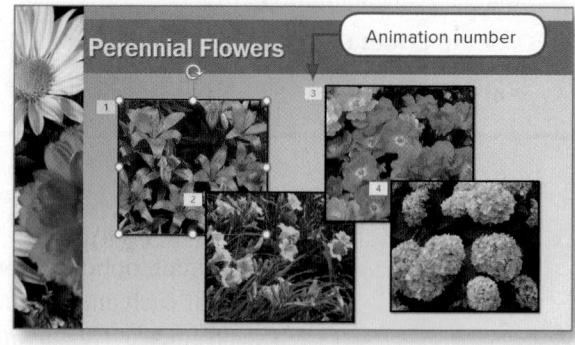

Figure 3-22 Numbers indicate animation order

If your presentation is designed to support you as a speaker, coordinate the animation timing with your speaking. This technique usually works best in small segments only because precise timing is almost impossible to predict when you are presenting in real time to an audience. If you are designing a self-running presentation for a trade show exhibit, for example, your animation can be much more dramatic and extensive because the slide show is not dependent on a speaker's pace.

Linking to an Online Video

Many videos are available online, but not all of them can be played within PowerPoint. When you search for a video using the *Insert Video* dialog box, the videos found from YouTube are most likely to play within PowerPoint as long as you have internet access. You click **Insert** to put the video on your slide, but the actual video is not saved in your presentation. An image of the video appears and the necessary information to link to it is saved in your presentation.

When you search for videos, you may find a compelling interview or demonstration that will enliven your presentation, but be sure the video relates to your topic and adds value.

▶ HOW TO: Link a Presentation to an Online Video

1. Select the PowerPoint slide where you want to show the video.
 - Be sure your computer has internet access.
2. Click the **Insert** tab.
3. Click the **Video** button [*Media* group] and select **Online Video** (Figure 3-23) to open the *Insert Video* dialog box (Figure 3-24).
4. Type a word in the *YouTube* search box and click the **Search** button.
5. Available videos appear showing thumbnails.
 - When you point to each one, a *ScreenTip* identifies its name.
 - Source information appears in the lower-left corner of the dialog box (Figure 3-25).

Figure 3-23 *Video* button on the *Insert* tab

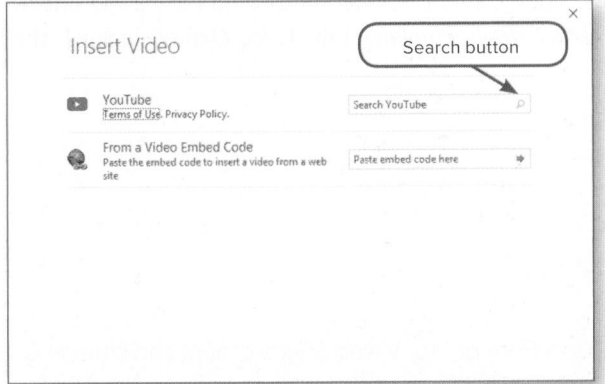

Figure 3-24 *Insert Video* dialog box showing search options

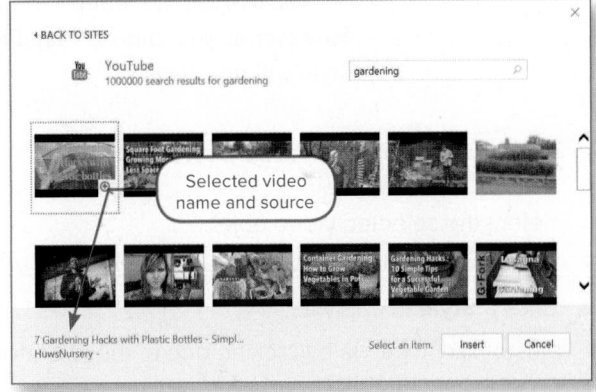

Figure 3-25 *Insert Video* dialog box showing search results

6. Click **Insert** and the video appears on your slide.
7. Add the appropriate source information as needed below the video.

▶ MORE INFO

A linked video will not play in a presentation that you send by email or one that you prepare on your computer and later view on your phone through Office Online. The link that creates a path to the file is broken.

Format an Online Video

When you change the size of an online video on your slide, be sure to maintain the correct aspect ratio. Drag the video object to reposition it on the slide just as you would a picture or shape. Styles can enhance the video's appearance.

▶ HOW TO: Resize an Online Video

1. Select the video object on your slide.
2. Change the video size by dragging handles or entering specific *Height* and *Width* measurements [*Video Tools Format* tab, *Size* group].

Or

3. Change the video size and maintain dimensions using the *Format Video* pane.

 - Right-click the video object and select **Format Video** or click the **Size** launcher [*Video Tools Format* tab, *Size* group] to open the *Format Video* pane (Figure 3-26).
 - Click the **Size & Properties** tab at the top of the pane.
 - Change *Height* and *Width* measurements or change the *Scale Height* and *Scale Width* percentages.
 - Check **Lock aspect ratio** and **Relative to original picture size** to maintain the video's aspect ratio as you resize.
 - Check **Best scale for slide show** to select a different resolution.
 - Close the *Format Video* pane.
4. Reposition the video object as needed.

Figure 3-26 *Format Video* pane

Video Styles are similar to picture styles. They frame the video and some have a 3D effect. However, if you choose **Play Full Screen** [*Video Tools Playback* tab, *Video Options* group], the style will not display.

▶ HOW TO: Apply a Video Style

1. Select the selected video object.
2. Click the **More** button [*Video Tools Format* tab, *Video Styles* group].
3. Click a **Style** to apply it.
4. Customize the style by clicking one of these buttons [*Video Tools Format* tab, *Video Styles* group] and selecting an appropriate option:

 - **Video Shape**: Display the video in any shape from the *Shapes* gallery. However, the video reverts to its default rectangular shape as it plays.
 - **Video Border**: Change the color or outline weight.
 - **Video Effects**: Apply an effect. *Shadow*, *Glow*, or *Reflection* seem to work best.

Play the Online Video

To play an online video in PowerPoint, the computer used to display your presentation must have internet access. The clarity you see in playback depends on the resolution of the original video and how it was compressed for online distribution. Resolution is expressed in pixel width and height. With more pixels, the image quality is better.

As with all computer technology, video capabilities continue to improve and many videos can be played at full-screen size from their online source. However, video sharing sites often

provide video in the standard definition size (640 × 480 pixels) or even smaller. Be careful when increasing the size of a video object on your slide to avoid reducing image quality. Test how the video plays before you use it in your presentation.

▶ HOW TO: Play an Online Video

1. Play the video in *Normal* view.
 - Click the **Play** button [*Video Tools Playback* tab, *Preview* group] or double-click the video to activate it.
 - Click the **Play** button at the center of the video to play it.
 - A timeline will appear below the video with playback controls to play, pause, mute, and access other options (Figure 3-27).

2. Play the video in *Slide Show* view.
 - Select the slide with the video and click the **Slide Show** button [*Status* bar] to start your slide show on the current slide.
 - Click the **Play** button in the middle of the video.
 - Click the **Play Full Screen** button on the video timeline to expand the video to fill your computer's screen. Not all videos enable this feature.
 - Press **Esc** twice to stop the slide show and return to *Normal* view.

Figure 3-27 Video playing in *Normal* view

3. Set the video to play at full screen size in *Slide Show* view.
 - Select **Play Full Screen** [*Video Tools Playback* tab, *Video Options* group]. This option will be grayed out if the video cannot be played at full screen size.

4. Set the video to start automatically and test it in *Slide Show* view.
 - Click the **Start** list box [*Video Tools Playback* tab, *Video Options* group] and select **Automatically**. For some videos, this may be the only option and it causes the video to be activated on the slide in *Slide Show* view.
 - Click the **Slide Show** tab and the **From Beginning** button [*Start Slide Show* group].
 - Advance to the slide with the video to test that it begins playing automatically. If it does not, click the **Play** button in the middle of the video.

5. Move your pointer so it does not appear on the video while it is playing.

6. Notice the clarity of the video as you play it. If you resized the video and the quality is degraded, click the **Reset Design** drop-down arrow [*Video Tools Format* tab, *Adjust* group] and click **Reset Design & Size** to restore the video to its original dimension.

7. Advance to the next slide when the video playback ends.

> **MORE INFO**
>
> If you find an online video that you want to use in PowerPoint, you may be able to link to it without searching for it in PowerPoint. Copy the video's embed codes (the host web address, name of the video, and playback size information) that are included with a video in a sharing section on the host page. Then, open the *Insert Video* dialog box and paste the embed codes. Information to link to the video is saved in your presentation, so internet access is required to play the video.

Obtain Permission

Linking to a video for classroom purposes falls under the guidelines of *fair use* for education and crediting the source may be sufficient. However, business use is different. Just like television programming or movies in a theater, videos are copyrighted by the creator. You need permission before you link to, display, or distribute video that is copyrighted. Obtaining permission is time consuming and can be expensive. If the creator does not give you permission, you must find another video and start the process again.

▶HOW TO: Obtain Permission to Use an Online Video

1. Go to the web site where the video is posted and identify the user name of the creator.
2. Click a link to go to more profile information, or in some cases, another web site.
3. Look for terms of use and find contact information.
4. Send an email message explaining the following:
 - How you want to use the video
 - What portion of the video you will use
 - When you will use the video
 - How you will show credits on the slide where the video is displayed
 - Your contact information for the creator's response

With the dynamic nature of the web, a video you find may be available for only a limited time. You may need to request a high-resolution copy of the video and the creator may charge you for this service.

▶ MORE INFO

The *Copyright Act of 1976* is the primary basis of copyright law in the United States. It specifies fair use that permits limited use for such purposes as research, teaching, and scholarship. The *Digital Millennium Copyright Act of 1998* addresses issues of online copyright infringement.

PAUSE & PRACTICE: POWERPOINT 3-1

Davon Washington has almost finished the slide show for his seminar on presentation planning. For this project, you create custom theme colors that better match the Solution Seekers, Inc., logo, modify a background style, animate several slide objects, and link to a video on a web site.

File Needed: **PresentationPlanning-03.pptx** (Student data files are available in the Library of your SIMnet account.)
Completed Project File Name: **[your initials] PP P3-1.pptx**

1. Open the presentation **PresentationPlanning-03**.
2. Save the presentation as [your initials] PP P3-1.

3. Create new theme colors.
 a. Click the **More** button [*Design* tab, *Variants* group].
 b. Click **Colors** and select **Customize Colors** to open the *Create New Theme Colors* dialog box (Figure 3-28).
 c. Click the *Text/Background - Light2* **Color** button and select **More Colors** to open the *Colors* dialog box.
 d. Click the **Custom** tab and enter the numbers for *Red*, *Green*, and *Blue* for this color from Table 3-1.
 e. Repeat steps 3 c - d for *Accent 1*, *Accent 2*, and *Accent 3* colors.
 f. Name the new custom theme Planning (Figure 3-29).

Table 3-1

	Text/Background – Light2	Accent 1	Accent 2	Accent 3
Red	234	3	102	181
Green	214	110	0	139
Blue	184	131	51	128

Figure 3-28 Original theme colors

 g. Click the **Save** button.
 • The new custom theme is saved in the *Custom* section of your list of available theme colors.

4. Apply a gradient fill as shown in Figure 3-30.
 a. Display slide 1.
 b. Point to the slide background and right-click. Select **Format Background** to open the *Format Background* pane.
 c. Select the **Gradient fill** option.
 d. Click the **Type** drop-down arrow and choose **Linear** if it is not selected.
 e. Click the **Direction** button and choose **Linear Diagonal – Top Right to Bottom Left** (third option/first row).
 • The *Angle* percentage automatically adjusts to 135°.
 f. Click the **Add gradient stop** button, if necessary, so you have four gradient stops.
 • The number of stops that first appear on the color bar is influenced by the gradient settings that were last used.
 g. Click each gradient stop from left to right (Figure 3-31) and adjust the *Color, Position, Brightness,* and *Transparency* values as needed to match values in Table 3-2.

Figure 3-29 *Planning* theme colors

Figure 3-30 Title slide with background gradient fill

Table 3-2

Gradient Stops	Stop 1	Stop 2	Stop 3	Stop 4
Color	Dark Teal, Accent 1 (fifth column/ first row)	Dark Teal, Accent 1, Lighter 60% (fifth column/ third row)	Tan, Text 2 (fourth column/ first row)	Tan, Text 2, Darker 50% (fourth column/ fourth row)
Position	0%	30%	70%	100%
Transparency	0%	50%	0%	0%
Brightness	0%	0%	0%	−50%

Figure 3-31 Gradient stops adjusted

5. Create a *Picture fill* background.
 a. Display slide 2 and select **Picture or texture fill** on the *Format Background* pane.
 b. Click the **File** button to open the *Insert Picture* dialog box.
 c. Locate your student data files, select **Presenter-03**, and click **Insert**.
 d. Click the **Picture** tab at the top of the *Format Background* pane and then click **Picture Color**.
 e. Click the **Recolor** button and choose **Tan, Background color 2 Light** (first option/third row) (Figure 3-32).
 f. Close the *Format Background* pane.

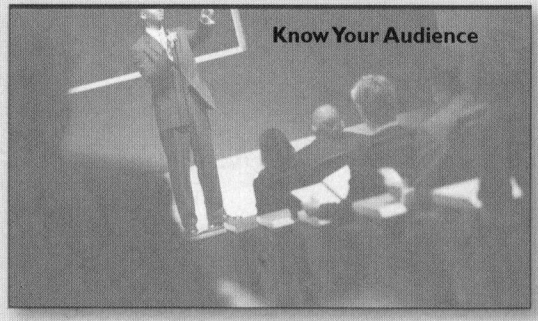

Figure 3-32 Background picture fill recolored

6. Apply a transition.
 a. Click the **Transitions** tab and apply the **Wipe** transition.
 b. Click the **Effect Options** button and select **From Left**.
 c. Click **Apply to All** [*Timing* group].

7. Apply animation on five slides.
 a. Display slide 4. Click the **Animations** tab.
 b. Select the two objects to be animated, the Down Arrow and "Possible body sequences" text box, that are listed on the first row of Table 3-3. Since two objects on slide 4 are animated, press **Ctrl** while you click both objects to select them.
 c. Click the **More** button on the *Animation* gallery [*Animation* group] or click the **Add Animation** button [*Advanced Animation* group] if the gallery is not open.
 d. Select the **Wipe** *Entrance* effect.
 e. Click the **Effect Options** button [*Animations* group] and select the **From Top** *Direction*.
 f. Change settings [*Timing* group] as needed for the following: *Start* is **On Click**, *Duration* is **02.00**, and *Delay* is **None**. Some of the settings will appear by default.
 g. Click the **Preview** button [*Preview* group] or **Slide Show** button [*Status* bar] to test the animation.
 h. Repeat steps 7b-g for the remaining four animations listed in Table 3-3.

8. Insert a new blank slide after slide 14.

9. Insert an online video, adjust its size, and add source information.
 a. Display slide 15. Click the **Video** button [*Insert* tab, *Media* group] and select **Online Video** to open the *Insert Video* dialog box.
 b. Type the words presentation skills in the *YouTube Search* box and click **Search**.

Table 3-3

Slide	Object	Animation Effect	Effect Options	Start	Duration	Delay
4	Down arrow and "Possible body sequences" text box	*Wipe* (Entrance)	*From Top*	*On Click*	*02.00*	None
5	"First impression" text	*Wave* (Emphasis)	*By Paragraph*	*After Previous*	*00.50*	None
7	Quoted text	*Bounce* (Entrance)	*As One Object*	*After Previous*	*02.00*	01:00
8	Road picture	*Grow & Turn* (Entrance)	*None*	*With Previous*	*02.00*	01:00
14	Heart	*Spin* (Emphasis)	*Clockwise, Two Spins*	*With Previous*	*02.00*	None

 c. Select an appropriate video from the search results and click **Insert**.

 d. Increase the size so the width is approximately **7"** wide.

 e. Apply the **Drop Shadow Rectangle** *Video Style* [*Video Tools* Format tab, *Video Styles* group] in the *Subtle* category.

 f. Click the **Align** button [*Video Tools Format* tab, *Arrange* group] and select **Align Center**. Repeat to select **Align Middle**.

 g. Click the **Play** button [*Video Tools Playback* tab, *Preview* group] to activate the video.

 h. Click the **Play** button on the video to test it.

 i. Add a text box below the video with source information.

10. Review your presentation in *Slide Show* view to text all transitions, animations, and video.

11. Save and close the presentation (Figure 3-33).

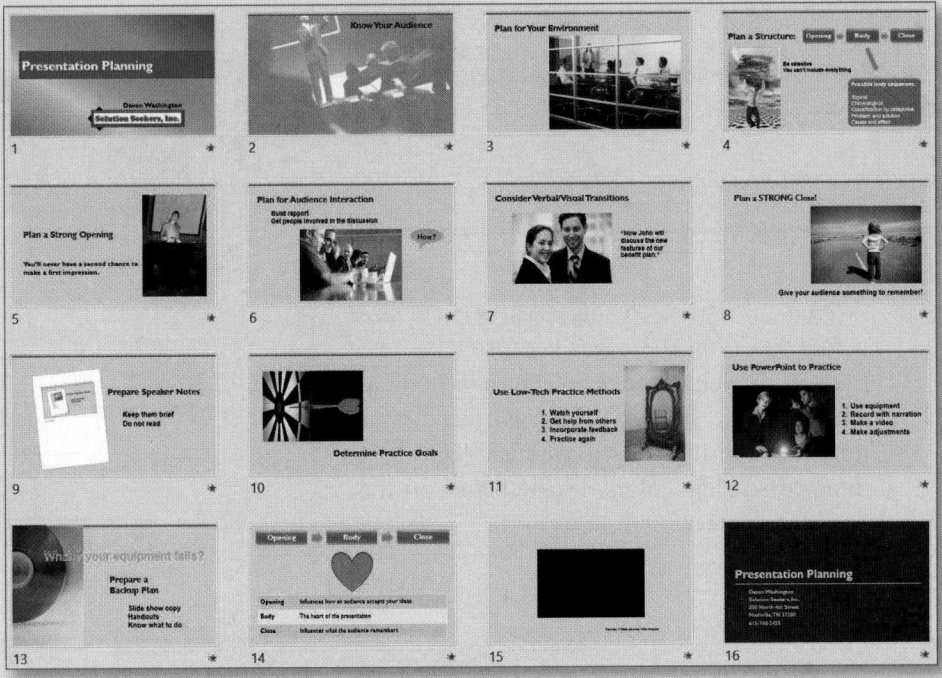

Figure 3-33 PP P3-1 completed

SLO 3.4

Using Rehearsal Techniques

Everyone, no matter how experienced, can benefit from rehearsing a presentation. Practicing your delivery ensures that each slide's information supports what you are saying. Practice builds confidence, too.

Speaker Notes

Speaker notes help you remember what you need to say in your presentation, but they should not be written as a script that you would read to your audience. Write notes as personal reminders, such as items to emphasize or terminology to define. For example, you could include statistics you want to mention, a quote you want to say but not show on a slide, a list of upcoming events, or additional resources for your

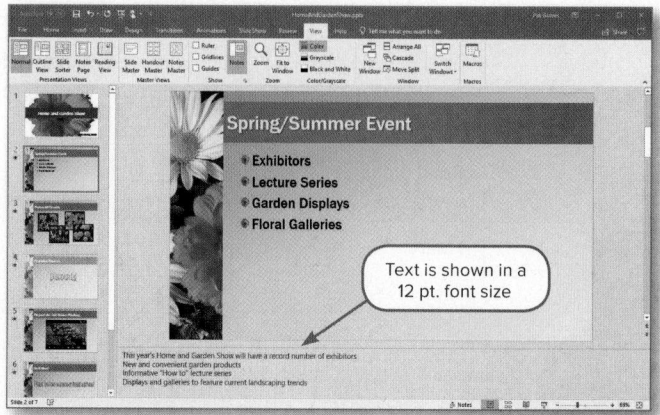

Figure 3-34 Increased *Notes* pane size

audience. As you decide what to include, plan for smooth and logical transitions between topics. Even if you don't use the speaker notes you prepare, having them available while you present can be comforting and help to reduce nervousness.

In *SLO 1.1: Creating, Opening, and Saving Presentations*, you learned how to adjust pane sizes and increase the *Notes* pane in *Normal* view to make writing notes easier (Figure 3-34). The *Notes Page* view, however, provides much more space to type text.

> ▶ **HOW TO: Use Notes Page View**
>
> 1. Click the **Notes Page** button [*View* tab, *Presentation Views* group] to show the slide at the top of a page with a large text box below.
> 2. Type your notes in the text box (Figure 3-35).

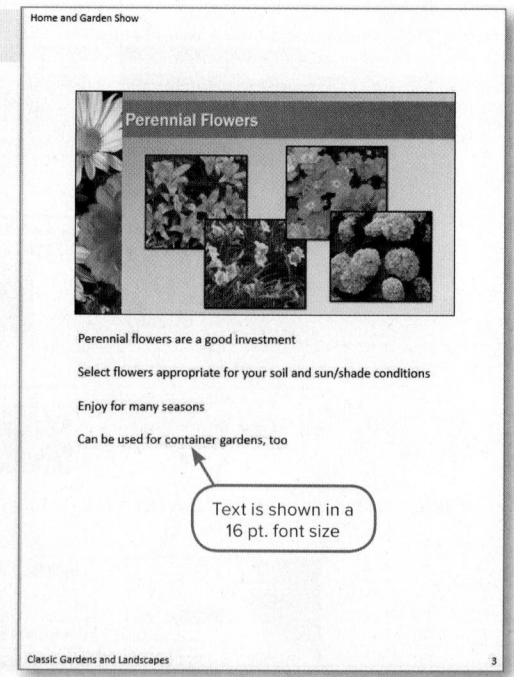

You may want to increase the font size before you print the pages because large text is easier for you to see on a lectern or podium while you are speaking. You will need your notes to be visible even if overhead lighting is dimmed so slide colors display better on the projection screen.

> ▶ **ANOTHER WAY**
>
> Printed handouts with a few handwritten reminders can work well for speaker notes.

Figure 3-35 *Notes Page* view with slide and text

▶HOW TO: Print Notes Pages

1. Click the **File** tab and click **Print**.
2. Choose **Notes Pages** for *Print Layout*, and check **Scale to Fit Paper** to make the slide images larger (Figure 3-36).
3. Omit the **Frame Slide** option for *Notes Pages*. A single-line border around the entire page is unnecessary.
4. Click the **Print** button.

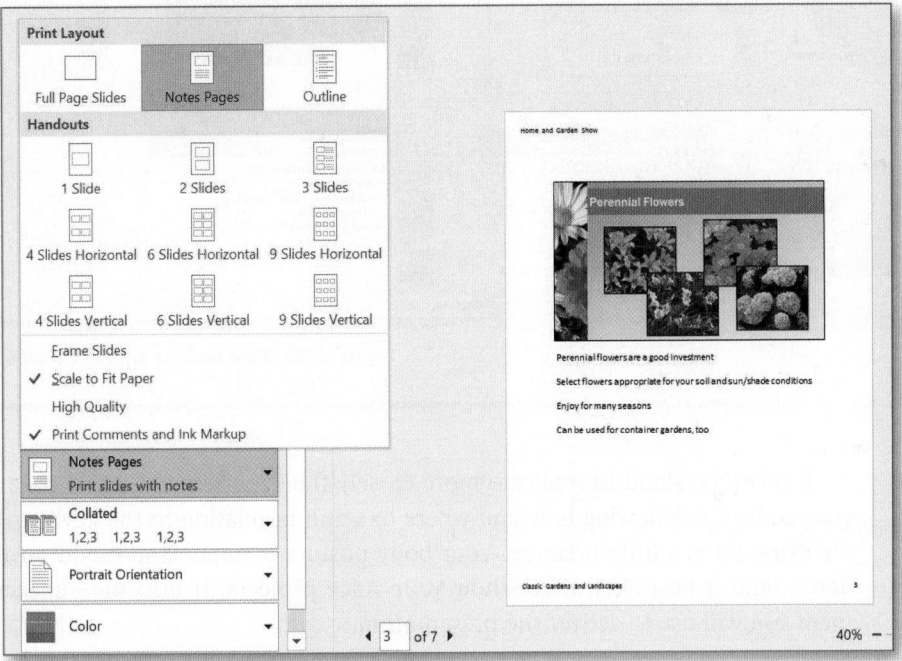

Figure 3-36 Print settings for *Notes Pages*

Rehearse Timings

PowerPoint's ***Rehearse Timings*** feature makes it easy to judge the pace of your presentation. Go through your presentation and practice what you will say while each slide displays. Use printed notes pages while you are practicing. The time you spend on each slide is recorded as you move through your presentation. The times appear below each slide in *Slide Sorter* view.

▶HOW TO: Rehearse Timings

1. Click the **Rehearse Timings** button [*Slide Show* tab, *Set Up* group] and your slide show starts.
 - A *Recording* dialog box appears in the upper-left corner (Figure 3-37). It shows the time each slide displays and the total elapsed time.
2. Click the **Next Slide** button (or press the **spacebar**) to advance.
3. Click the **Pause** or **Repeat** buttons as needed.
4. Click **Yes** when asked at the end of your presentation if you want to save your timings.

Figure 3-37 The Current slide time and total elapsed time

5. Click the **Slide Sorter** button [*Status bar*] to see the timings, in seconds, displayed below each slide (Figure 3-38).

- The seconds shown in this example are brief because they were recorded when testing the presentation. The times may be much longer in an actual presentation.

Figure 3-38 Slide timings appear below each slide thumbnail.

If possible, stand to replicate more closely the experience you will have when speaking to your audience. Knowing how and where to stand in relation to the keyboard and monitor you are using takes a little practice. Your body posture is important. Good posture reflects confidence, and it positively affects how your voice projects. If possible, rehearse with the equipment you will use to deliver the presentation.

Set Timings Manually

You can enter all timings manually, but it is quicker to rehearse your presentation, save the timings, and adjust the time as needed for individual slides. It takes practice to effectively cover your content in the time you have available to speak. Save the timings to automate the presentation if it is self-running. However, if you are presenting to an audience, do not use the timings so you control when the slides advance. Many variables will affect your delivery and you must be able to adjust what you say as you react to audience feedback.

▶HOW TO: Modify Timings

1. Click the **Normal View** button [*View* tab, *Presentation Views* group], if necessary.

2. Click the **Transitions** tab and be sure the **After** option is selected [*Transitions* tab, *Timing* group] and second numbers are showing (Figure 3-39).

3. Change the number of seconds for each slide, as needed, to increase or decrease the amount of time the slide displays.

4. Deselect the **On Mouse Click** option if you want the slides to advance automatically.

5. Present your slide show without using the saved timings by deselecting the **Use Timings** option [*Slide Show* tab, *Set Up* group].

Figure 3-39 *Transitions* tab, *Timings* group

6. Remove timings by clicking the **Record Slide Show** button [*Slide Show* tab, *Set Up* group], select **Clear**, and then select **Clear Timing on Current Slide** or **Clear Timings on All Slides** (Figure 3-40).

Figure 3-40 *Clear Timings* options

Prepare for Mishaps

Be sure you have backup copies of your presentation in case you experience equipment failure, and you need to switch to a different computer. In a worst-case situation, where both your computer and projector have malfunctioned, you can present using your handouts to support what you say. All experienced presenters encounter such problems at some time during their careers.

SLO 3.5

Controlling Display Options

As you learned in chapter 1, online themes and templates are available in different sizes called *Standard* and *Widescreen*. The default size for PowerPoint 365 and 2019 is *Widescreen*; the default size before PowerPoint 2013 was *Standard*. Therefore, you may encounter files that require updating to fit your current screen size, or you may need to adjust the size of your presentation to fit an older projection screen in a room where you will deliver your presentation.

Adjust Slide Size

Today widescreen computers (like television screens) use a 16:9 or 16:10 aspect ratio (the ratio of width to height) which is ideally suited to display high-definition video signals. A slide show designed in the 16:9 aspect ratio fills the screen to take advantage of this wide horizontal space. A slide show designed in the 4:3 aspect ratio (more square) and displayed on a widescreen will be positioned in the center of the screen with black areas on both sides.

Both of these slide sizes are available on the *Design* tab in the *Customize* group, and you change from one to the other by clicking the **Slide Size** button [*Customize* group] and choosing **Standard (4:3)** or **Widescreen (16:9)**. In the *Slide Size* dialog box, the *Standard (4:3)* size shows as *On-screen Show (4:3)* and numbers are not shown after *Widescreen*. Two other *On-screen Show* sizes are available, and you can create a custom size if necessary. These sizes are listed in Table 3-4 and illustrated as blue and green thumbnails in Figure 3-41.

Table 3-4: Slide Sizes

Aspect Ratios	Width in Inches	Height in Inches
Standard 4:3 or On-screen Show 4:3	10	7.5
On-screen Show 16:9	10	5.625
On-screen Show 16:10	10	6.25
Widescreen (default is 16:9)	13.333	7.5

Figure 3-41 Slide sizes illustrated

The two wide sizes available in the *Slide Size* dialog box (illustrated in Figure 3-41 on the right) look smaller because their width is 10″, the same as the *Standard 4:3* width. On your computer screen, they will look almost the same as the *Widescreen* size, but ruler measurements and object sizes will be different due to the difference in width and height.

Changing between slide show sizes is a simple process, but adjusting text and graphics to fit appropriately with different aspect ratios is time consuming. Both *Standard 4:3* and *Widescreen 16:9* sizes available on the *Design* tab have the same vertical measurement, so the slide width changes. If you change from 4:3 to 16:9 or 16:10 from the *Slide Size* dialog box, the vertical size is reduced, which compresses the slide vertically.

Be aware of these height and width differences when changing slide sizes. If you think you may need to change back to your original size, save the original presentation as a separate file before you begin making changes for the new size. By doing this, you avoid all the resizing changes that would be necessary to return to the original size.

▶ HOW TO: Change the Slide Size

1. Click the **Design** tab.
2. Click the **Slide Size** button [*Customize* group], and then click either **Standard (4:3)** or **Widescreen (16:9)** to select a different size.
 - A dialog box opens showing how your slide content will be affected.
3. Select either **Maximize** or **Ensure Fit** for the best scaling option.
4. Click **Custom Slide Size** to open the *Slide Size* dialog box. Sizes for printing and four sizes for on-screen viewing are available (Figure 3-42). Choose from the following:
 - *On-screen Show (4:3)*: 10″ × 7.5″ (Standard)
 - *On-screen Show (16:9)*: 10″ × 5.625″
 - *On-screen Show (16:10)*: 10″ × 6.25″
 - *Widescreen*: 13.333″ × 7.5″ (default 16:9)
5. Click **OK**. If necessary, select either **Maximize** or **Ensure Fit**.

Figure 3-42 *Slide Size* dialog box

Presenter View

Presenter View enables you to display your presentation on the screens of two or more monitors. For example, you could use a tablet or laptop and a large screen television. Or in a presentation room with built-in equipment, you might use a desktop computer with a ceiling-mounted projector and a large screen. The computer you are using must support the use of multiple monitors.

Setting up your monitors depends on your equipment. For example, if you are using a tablet or laptop, you can choose an option in PowerPoint to automatically extend your display to another monitor. By connecting a wireless display adapter into a television HDMI port, you can extend to that device. Specific instructions will vary depending on your equipment.

▶HOW TO: Modify PowerPoint Display Settings to Extend a Tablet or Laptop

1. Click the **File** tab and select **Options** to open the **PowerPoint Options** dialog box.
2. Select **Advanced**.
3. Select **Automatically extend display when presenting on a laptop or tablet** in the *Display* category.
4. Click **OK**.

If you have two monitors connected to one computer, you need to modify your computer's display settings to extend to the second monitor. This is a *Microsoft Windows* function. In addition to using the second monitor for display purposes, it is very convenient to use while you are working. Your pointer moves across both screens so you have a lot more workspace. Desktop computers usually have more than one video port so you can easily connect a second monitor with the appropriate cables.

▶HOW TO: Modify Windows Display Settings for Two Monitors

1. Connect a second monitor to your computer.
2. Click the *Windows* **Start** button and select **Settings** to open the Windows *Settings* dialog box.
3. Click **System** and then select **Display**. Two monitors will appear (Figure 3-43).
4. Click **Identify** and numbers appear on each monitor.
 - The *Orientation* should automatically be set for **Landscape**.
5. Click the **Multiple displays** list box arrow and select **Extend these displays**.
6. Select **Monitor 1** and choose **Make this my main display**.
 - Usually *Monitor 1* is on the left.
 - Drag the monitor shapes to control their positions.
 - Select each monitor shape and change the *Resolution* if necessary.
7. Click **Apply**.
8. Select **Advanced display settings** to make additional changes such as color calibration for both monitors.
9. Close the *Settings* dialog box.

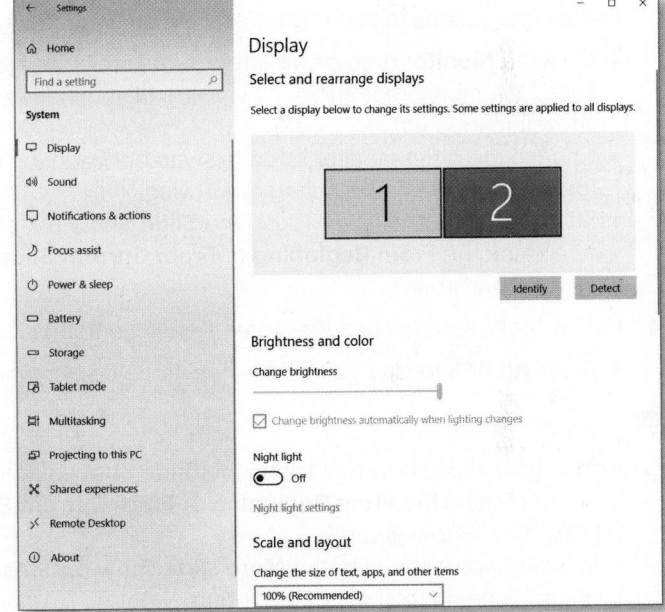

Figure 3-43 Customize *Display* settings using Windows 10

PowerPoint can automatically detect when two monitors are connected and will recognize one monitor as your primary monitor for *Presenter View*. The primary monitor shows your view of the presentation and includes the displayed slide, the navigation tools, the next slide, and an area for notes. The second monitor (or projector) displays the full-size slide show for your audience.

Using *Presenter View* is helpful because while you are speaking you can do the following:

- View the current slide and see the next slide in your presentation.
- Use convenient navigation tools.
- Have speaker notes available on the monitor for easy reading instead of needing printed notes.
- View thumbnails for all slides in the presentation and click thumbnails to display slides out of sequence.
- Zoom in to sections of a slide.
- Use pen tools without the audience seeing how you select pen options.
- Make the screen that's visible to your audience black yet still have speaker notes available to you.

To practice your presentation, it is possible to use *Presenter View* with only one monitor.

▶ HOW TO: Use Presenter View

1. Click the **Slide Show** tab.
2. Select **Use Presenter View** [*Monitors* group].
3. Follow these steps to use *Presenter View* on two monitors:
 - Click the **Monitor** drop-down arrow [*Monitors* group] to select the monitor for audience viewing of your full-size slide show (Figure 3-44).
 - Choose the other monitor listed to swap between the monitors used for *Presenter View* and audience viewing.
 - Start your slide show by clicking the **Slide Show** button [*Status* bar] or clicking the **From Beginning** or **From Current Slide** buttons [*Start Slide Show* group].
4. Follow these steps to use *Presenter View* on one monitor:
 - Press **Alt+F5** to start your slide show from the beginning.

 Or

 - Start your slide show by clicking the **Slide Show** button on the *Status* bar or clicking the **From Beginning** or **From Current Slide** buttons [*Start Slide Show* group].
 - In *Slide Show* view, click the **More slide show options** button on the control area on the bottom left (Figure 3-45).
 - Select **Show Presenter View**.
5. Review features of *Presenter View* (Figure 3-46).
 - The current slide displays on the left. The current notes appear on the lower right; the next slide appears in the upper-right.
 - Click buttons at the bottom of the notes pane to increase or decrease text size.
 - Notice the slide show time displayed above the slide. Click **Pause the timer** to stop the seconds from increasing, but this change does not affect automatic transitions. Click **Resume the timer** to continue the time.
 - Click **Restart the timer** to set the time back to **0:00:00**.

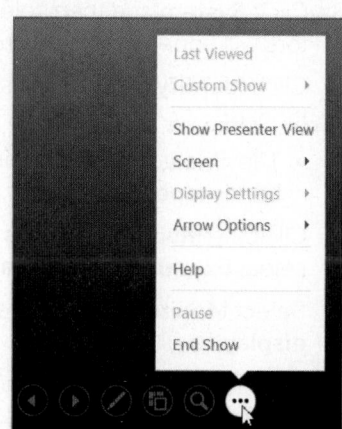

Figure 3-44 *Use Presenter View* option on the *Slide Show* tab

Figure 3-45 Control area in *Slide Show* view and *More slide show options* selected

Figure 3-46 *Presenter View* window

- Options above the slide include **Show Taskbar** so you can easily switch to other applications, **Display Settings** to swap monitors or duplicate a slide show, or **End Slide Show**.
- Click the **Advance to next animation or slide** button in the navigation area below the slide to move forward through your slides or click the **Return to the previous animation or slide** button to move back.

Figure 3-47 Control area in *Presenter View* and *More slide show options* selected

6. Review the control area options in *Presenter View* (Figure 3-47).
 - Click the **Pen and laser pointer tools** button to select options for marking on your slide.
 - Click the **See all slides** button to show slide thumbnails. Click a thumbnail to jump to a different slide out of sequence.
 - Click the **Zoom into the slide** button, drag the selection area over an object or text you want to magnify to show detail, and then click. The zoomed section of the screen displays for your audience. Click the same button again (now **Zoom out**) to return to normal screen size.
 - Click the **Black or unblack** button to make your second monitor appear blank and temporarily hide your current slide.
 - Click **More slide show options** to choose other options such as **Hide Presenter View** so PowerPoint displays on your primary monitor.
 - Press **Esc** or click **End Slide Show** to exit the slide show.

PAUSE & PRACTICE: POWERPOINT 3-2

For this project, you add speaker notes, print notes pages, and rehearse a presentation. You will use *Presenter View* to display your slide show.

File Needed: *[your initials] PP P3-1.pptx*
Completed Project File Name: *[your initials] PP P3-2.pptx*

1. Open the *[your initials] PP P3-1* presentation completed in *Pause & Practice 3-1*.
 - A *Security Warning* may appear because an online video was inserted in this presentation. Click **Enable Content**.

2. Save the presentation as [your initials] PP P3-2.

3. Create a visual transition between topics.
 a. Insert a new slide with the *Section Header* layout after slides 3, 9, and 15.
 b. Delete the subtitle placeholder on each new *Section Header* slide and type the title text as follows:
 - Slide 4 title: Presentation Structure (Figure 3-48)
 - Slide 10 title: Presentation Practice
 - Slide 16 title: Summary

Presentation Structure

Figure 3-48 *Section Header* slide layout

4. Prepare speaker notes for two slides that do not have notes.
 a. Display slide 11, "Prepare Speaker Notes," and click the **Notes Page** button [*View* tab, *Presentation Views* group].

b. Click the **Zoom In** button several times to increase the percentage to **120%** so you can easily see the text you will add.

c. Click inside the notes section below the slide.

d. Click the **Bullets** button [*Home* tab, *Paragraph* group] and type the following text. Add a blank line space between first-level bulleted text for easy reading (Figure 3-49):

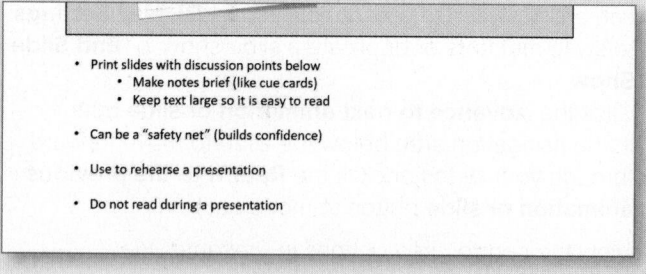

Figure 3-49 *Notes Page* view with text

- Print slide with discussion points below
 - Make notes brief (like cue cards)
 - Keep text large so it is easy to read
- Can be a "safety net" (builds confidence)
- Use to rehearse a presentation
- Do not read during a presentation

e. Click the **Next Slide** button [*Scroll* bar] or press **Page Down** to display the *Notes Page* for slide 12.

f. Click the **Bullets** button [*Home* tab, *Paragraph* group] and type the following text. Add a blank line space between first-level bulleted text.

- Experience is the best teacher
- Identify strengths and develop them
- Identify weaknesses and work to overcome them
- Reduce tendency to be nervous

g. Click the **Normal** button [*View* tab, *Presentation Views* group].

5. Print notes pages for slides 11 and 12.
 a. Click the **File** tab and click **Print**.
 b. Select the appropriate printer and make sure that you are printing just one copy.
 c. Type 11-12 for *Slides* to print a *Custom Range*.
 d. Click **Full Page Slides** button for *Print Layout* options. Choose **Notes Pages** and select **Scale to Fit Paper** (Figure 3-50).
 e. Click the **Print** button.

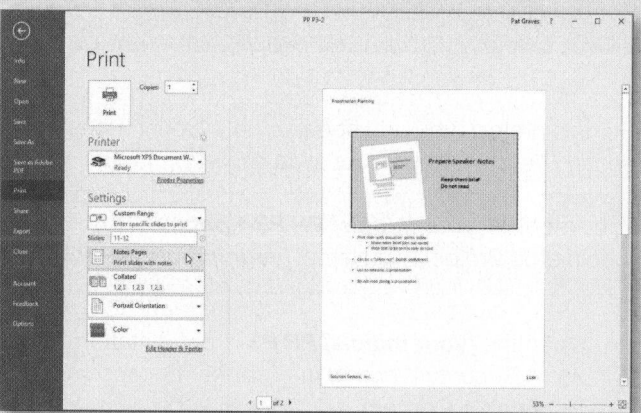

Figure 3-50 Print settings for *Notes Pages*

6. Rehearse your presentation and save timings.
 a. Click the **Slide Show** tab.
 b. Click the **Rehearse Timings** button [*Set Up* group] to begin your presentation in *Slide Show* view.
 - The *Recording* dialog box opens and timing begins.
 c. Click the **Next Slide** button to advance each slide after approximately 3–5 seconds (for the purpose of practicing this feature).
 d. Click **Yes** at the end of your presentation to save your timings.
 e. Click the **Slide Sorter** button [*Status* bar] to see the timings displayed below each slide.

7. Change how slides advance and modify presentation timings.
 a. Click the **Transitions** tab.
 b. Deselect **On Mouse Click** [*Transitions* tab, *Timing* group].
 c. Change the *After* timing to **3** seconds (shown as **00:03.00** in the *Timing* group and **00:03** below the slide in *Slide Show* view).
 d. Click the **Apply To All** button.

e. Change the *After* timing on the *Section Header* slides (slides 4, 10, and 16) to **1** second (shown as **00:01.00** in the *Timing* group and **00:01** below the slide in *Slide Show* view) (Figure 3-51).

Figure 3-51 PP P3-2 completed

8. Review your presentation using *Presenter View*.
 a. Click the **Slide Show** tab.
 b. Click **Use Presenter View** [*Monitors* group].
 c. Review your slides using one of these methods.
 • If you have two monitors, click the **From Beginning** button [*Start Slide Show* group].
 • If you have one monitor, start your slide show. Click the **More slide show options** button on the control area at the bottom left and select **Show Presenter View**.

9. Save and close the presentation.

Presenting Using Projection Equipment

When you look at the front of a presentation room from where people are seated, the ideal location for a speaker is to the left of the projection screen. People are conditioned to read from left to right, so it is natural for the audience to first look at the speaker and then at the projection screen. Many situations are less than ideal, however, so be flexible when you cannot control the speaker area. Keep the following guidelines in mind:

• Become familiar with your equipment so you won't feel awkward using it.
• Be sure the computer or other device you are using has an adequate battery charge (if you are using a wireless system to project your slide show).
• If possible, load your slide show before the audience enters the room so you are not seen scrambling around with preliminary preparations. Arrive early and test your presentation to be sure all content works correctly.
• Allow time to relax before your presentation starts. Almost everyone feels nervous before a presentation begins. This reaction is normal and just shows you are respectful of the situation. Harness your nervous energy in a positive way.

- Have your title slide displayed as people enter the room.
- If possible, greet people to make them feel welcome. Let people know that you are glad to have the opportunity to share with them.

Position Equipment

Using a computer while you speak can create challenges. With a desktop or notebook computer, you must see the computer screen when facing the audience and access the computer to advance slides. Controlling your slide show using a tablet computer or even a smartphone makes it easy to advance slides using a touch screen, but these devices must work with your projector or a television if you are using a wireless display adapter.

In presentation rooms, you may need to place your computer on a table. A podium (or lectern) may be available to hold your computer or printed notes pages. Be careful, however, that the podium does not create a barrier between you and the audience. Move away from it when you can.

Even if your computer has a wireless internet connection and is running on battery power, you may need to manage power cords for other equipment. Connections may not be convenient. Be sure to keep cables and cords away from the area where you and audience members walk, or tape cords to the floor for safety.

Navigate in a Slide Show

You have practiced advancing through a slide show by pressing the spacebar or clicking a slide. The following list shows other methods to advance, to go to specific slides, or to end a slide show.

During a slide show, buttons are on the lower left of each slide (Figure 3-52) when you point to that area.

Figure 3-52 Control area in *Slide Show* view

- *Previous* or *Next*: Move between slides.
- *Pen and laser pointer tools*: Shows the menu for pen options.
- *See all slides*: Displays slide thumbnails; click a thumbnail to jump to that slide. Click the **Back** button to return to your previous slide.
- *Zoom into the slide*: Provides a selection area you can drag over your slide to magnify a section of the screen to show detail. Drag the magnified area to show other portions of the screen in the large size. Right-click or press **Esc** to return to the current slide.
- *More slide show options*: Shows the menu for presentation options. For example, you can make the screen go black, change to *Presenter View*, or end a slide show.

Control Slide Display

The audience needs to focus on you, the speaker. Slides support your message, but you may not want a slide displayed all the time. Also, going from a blank screen to your next slide can seem dramatic.

Blank Slides

If you know in advance that you need to discuss a topic unrelated to your slides, then plan ahead and place one or more slides with a black background in specific places in your slide show. This way, the screen is blank and your audience can focus on what you are saying.

During a presentation, blank the screen by pressing **B** on your keyboard to display an empty black screen or **W** to display an empty white screen. Be careful about using white, however, because an all-white screen can create glare that will be unpleasant for your audience. Also, in the *Control* area in *Slide Show* view, click the **More slide show options** button, select **Screen**, and choose **Black Screen** or **White Screen** to blank your screen. Repeat these steps and choose **Unblack Screen** or **Unwhite Screen** to return to the slide. The same options are available when you right-click and use the context menu, too.

Hide and Reveal Slides

Hiding a slide is helpful when you have information that is not essential to your presentation, but you want to have that slide available if you need it, depending on time and audience interest. For example, you could hide slides containing information such as:

- References
- Additional pictures
- Additional details about a topic
- Optional charts, diagrams, or tables

Select one or more slides and click the **Hide Slide** button [*Slide Show* tab, *Set Up* group] (Figure 3-53). In *Normal* and *Slide Sorter* views, the slide thumbnail for a hidden slide appears grayed out with a diagonal line through the slide number.

During a slide show, display a hidden slide by typing the slide number and pressing **Enter**.

Figure 3-53 *Hide Slide* button and hidden slide 12

> ### MORE INFO
>
> Print hidden slides by clicking the **File** tab, then select **Print**. Click the **Print All Slides** option and select **Print Hidden Slides**.

Use Keyboard Shortcuts

Keyboard shortcuts are convenient if you have easy access to your keyboard while speaking. A complete list of Microsoft Office shortcuts is in *Appendix A*.

Table 3-5: Slide Show Navigation Shortcuts

Press	Action
N, spacebar, right arrow, down arrow, **Enter**, or **Page Down**	Advance to the next slide.
P, Backspace, left arrow, up arrow, or **Page Up**	Go to the previous slide.
Slide number, then **Enter**	Go to a particular slide.
Ctrl+S	Open *All slides* dialog box, select slide, and click **Go To**.
B or period	Blanks the screen to black.
W or comma	Blanks the screen to white.
S	Stop or restart an automatic show.
Plus sign	Zoom in.
Minus sign	Zoom out.
H or slide number, then **Enter**	Go to a hidden slide.

The presentation context menu is available during a slide show by right-clicking when you point anywhere on a slide (Figure 3-54).

Remote Control and Laser Pointer

A *remote control* enables you to move away from your computer as you are presenting to interact more naturally with your audience. You don't need to stay close to your computer to advance slides. Remote control devices come in many styles, from small clickers to clickers that resemble pens with USB storage. When presenting, be sure you have extra batteries available for the remote control.

Click through slides with a digital pen if it supports Bluetooth, and it is paired with your computer. With the appropriate wireless app installed, you can use a smartphone to remote-control your computer.

Remote controls may have a built-in laser pointer, or you can purchase a separate pointing device. A laser pointer shows a small dot (usually red) on the slide where you point. PowerPoint's *laser pointer* feature resembles this dot. To use this feature, press **Ctrl** and your left mouse button while you point on the screen and your pointer changes to a dot that can be red, green, or blue.

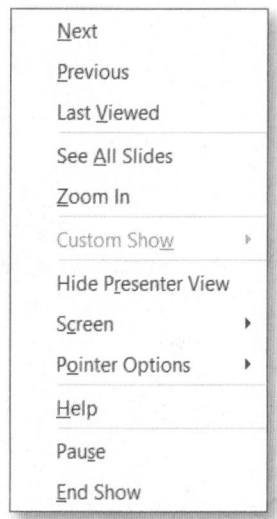

Figure 3-54 Presentation context menu

Figure 3-55 Change laser pointer color in the *Set Up Show* dialog box

▶ HOW TO: Change Laser Pointer Color

1. Click the *Set Up Slide Show* button [*Slide Show* tab, *Set Up* group] to open the *Set Up Show* dialog box (Figure 3-55).
2. Click the **Laser pointer color** list box arrow and select **red**, **green**, or **blue**.
3. Click **OK**.

A dot on the screen directs audience attention to a particular location. Be sure you show the dot long enough for your audience to find it and keep the dot steady. Do not bounce it around on the screen with random movements because this distracts viewers.

SLO 3.7 Using Annotation Pens

Call attention to information by writing or drawing on slides during a presentation. These markings are called *ink annotations*. While controlling the pointer to write with a hand-held mouse is a little awkward, using your finger, a stylus, or a digital pen to draw on a tablet is more natural. You can record audience feedback and make simple drawings on slides. When you reach the end of your presentation, you can save ink annotations. All markings, even if you draw a rectangle, are saved as lines and not as shapes.

To write or draw on a slide, use the *Pen*. To add a color overlay on text, use the *Highlighter* just as you would mark text to highlight information on paper. When you change *Ink Color*, be sure the color you select contrasts with the slide background so it is easy to see.

▶ HOW TO: Use the Pen and Highlighter

1. Start a slide show and go to the slide you want to annotate.
2. Select the *Pen* or *Highlighter* using one of the following methods:
 - Click the **Pen** button in the control area on the lower left (Figure 3-56) to open the context menu. Select an option.
 - Right-click anywhere on the slide to open the context menu and select **Pointer Options**. Select an option.
3. Begin writing or drawing on one or more slides.
4. Remove markings. Right-click, select **Pointer Options** from the context menu, and select **Eraser**. With the **Eraser** (Figure 3-57), click markings to delete each continuous pen stroke.
5. Change ink color. Right-click, select **Pointer Options** from the context menu, and select the **Ink Color** option. Select a different color (Figure 3-58).

Figure 3-56 Pen and laser pointer tools

Figure 3-57 Ink annotations and the *Eraser* tool

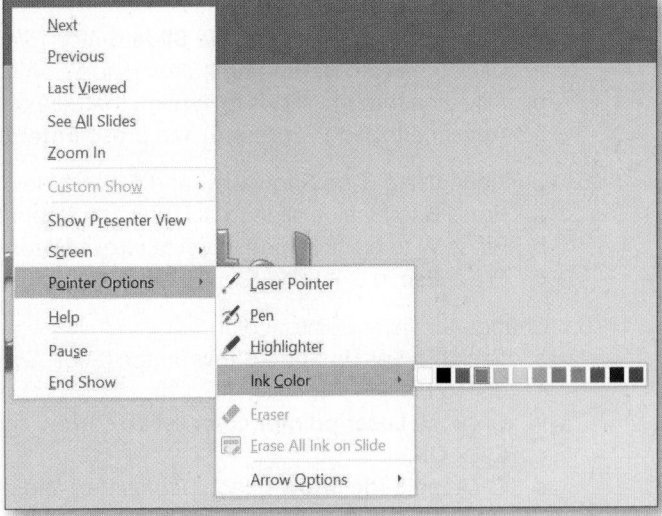

Figure 3-58 Change *Ink Color* for the *Pen* or *Highlighter*

6. Click **Keep** at the end of a presentation to save ink annotations. The markings are saved as lines that you can edit.

Pen tools are available in *Presenter View*, also, and options can be controlled with keyboard shortcuts.

Table 3-6: Ink Markup Shortcuts

Press	Action
Ctrl+P	Changes the pointer to a pen
Ctrl+A	Changes the pointer to an arrow
Ctrl+E	Changes the pointer to an eraser
Ctrl+M	Shows or hides ink markup
E	Erases markings on the screen

PAUSE & PRACTICE: POWERPOINT 3-3

For this project, you use PowerPoint features to present more effectively. You hide and reveal slides, blank slides, practice with the laser pointer, change pen colors, use the pen and highlighter, and save annotations.

File Needed: *[your initials] PP P3-2.pptx*
Completed Project File Name: *[your initials] PP P3-3.pptx*

1. Open the *[your initials] PP P3-2* presentation completed in *Pause & Practice 3-2*.
 - A *Security Warning* may appear because an online video was inserted in this presentation. Click **Enable Content**.

2. Save the presentation as [your initials] PP P3-3.

3. Click the **Transitions** tab and remove slide timings.
 a. Select **On Mouse Click** and deselect **After** [*Timing* group].
 b. Click **Apply To All** [*Timing* group].

4. Select slide 4 and click the **Hide Slide** button [*Slide Show* tab, *Set Up* group].
 a. Click the **From Beginning** button [*Slide Show* tab, *Start Slide Show* group] to start a slide show.
 b. Advance through slides to confirm that you automatically go from slide 3 to slide 5.
 c. Advance to slide 6, press **4**, and press **Enter** to show the hidden slide.

5. Continue using *Slide Show* view and blank slides.
 a. Press **B** to blank a slide to black. Press **B** to return to the slide.
 b. Press **W** to blank a slide to white. Press **W** to return to the slide.
 c. Press **Esc** to exit *Slide Show* view.

6. Change the laser pointer color.
 a. Click the **Set Up Slide Show** button [*Slide Show* tab, *Set Up* group] to open the *Set Up Show* dialog box.
 b. Click the **Laser pointer color** list box arrow and select **Blue**.
 c. Click **OK**.
 d. Click the **Slide Show** button [*Status* bar] and practice using the laser pointer in *Slide Show* view. Press **Ctrl** and the left mouse button as you move the pointer on your slide.

7. Use the pen and highlighter.
 a. Go to slide 7 in *Slide Show* view.
 b. Right-click to open the context menu, select **Pointer Options**, and then repeat for each of the following actions:
 - Select **Ink Color** and select the color **Blue**.
 - Select the **Pen**. Draw a circle around the shape with the word "How" (Figure 3-59).
 - Select the **Highlighter**.
 - Select **Ink Color** and select the color **Light Blue**.
 - Draw a line twice to highlight the word "involved."

Plan for Audience Interaction

Build rapport
Get people involved in the discussion

How?

Figure 3-59 Pen color changed

 c. Type **13** and press **Enter** to go to slide 13. Use the **Highlighter** to highlight the words "Get help" and "feedback."
 d. Type **17** and press **Enter** to go to slide 17. Use the **Highlighter** to highlight the words "how an audience," "accepts," "heart," "what an audience," and "remembers."
 e. Right-click to open the context menu, select **Pointer Options**, and then select **Eraser**. Click to remove the highlights from the words "how an audience" and "what an audience."
 f. Right-click again, select **Pointer Options**, and select **Eraser** to stop erasing and return to the pointer.
 g. Advance to the end of the presentation. When a message appears asking if you want to save your annotations, click **Keep**.

8. Save and close your presentation (Figure 3-60).

Figure 3-60 PP P3-3 completed

Preparing a Self-Running Presentation

A self-running slide show, also referred to as a *kiosk presentation*, runs continuously without someone being present to advance the slides. This type of presentation works well for trade shows or open house events where people walk up to a computer screen and watch the slide show. For example, self-running presentations can be used for marketing products to customers or to educate patients in medical office waiting rooms. You can record narration to accompany the slides or create a slide show to *loop* so it cycles continuously from beginning to end and automatically repeats.

Record a Slide Show with Narration

To record voice narration for your presentation, your computer must have a microphone, sound card, and speakers. With a camera, you can record yourself speaking. Like rehearsal, this feature helps you practice what you will say during a presentation and evaluates your vocal qualities. Prepare carefully what you will say as each slide displays. Use notes pages or other resources as references.

While narrating, PowerPoint records your use of the pen, highlighter, or eraser. You can stop your recording and listen to it. If you are not satisfied, then re-record over the first version. The audio and ink annotations are removed when you begin a new recording.

▶ HOW TO: Record Narration

1. Click the **Slide Show** tab.
2. Open the *Recording* window using one of these methods:
 - Click the top of the **Record Slide Show** button [*Set Up* group] to start recording on the current slide.
 - Click the **Record Slide Show** drop-down arrow [*Set Up* group] and then select **Record from Current Slide** or **Record from Beginning** (Figure 3-61).
3. Notice that the *Recording* window (Figure 3-62) is similar to *Presenter View*.
 - The current slide displays in the main pane.
4. Review the features of the *Recording* window:
 - *Record*: Click (or press **R**) to begin recording after a 3-second countdown.
 - *Stop*: Click (or press **Alt+S**) to stop recording.
 - *Replay*: Click to playback your recording.
 - *Notes*: Click to display notes at the top of the screen while you are speaking. You can increase or decrease the font size.
 - *Clear*: Select an option to remove existing recordings from the current slide or from all slides.

Figure 3-61 *Record Slide Show* options

Click to start recording

Figure 3-62 *Recording* window

- *Settings*: Select your microphone or camera.
- *Navigation*: Click the left button to go to the previous slide; click the right button to go to the next slide.
- *Timing*: Shows elapsed seconds as you move through your slides.
- *Inking tools*: Select the *Eraser*, *Pen*, or *Highlighter* and then click to select a color.
- *On/Off controls*: Click to control your microphone and camera.

5. Click the **Record** button.

- After the 3-second countdown, recording begins.

6. Speak clearly into your microphone as each slide displays.

- Narration and slide timings are automatically saved for each slide.
- Click the **Stop** button and then click **Replay** to review the recorded audio before advancing to the next slide.
- Replace a recording by clicking the **Record** button again.
- At the end of the slide show, click to exit.

7. Review your presentation in *Slide Show* view and listen to your narration.

8. Save your presentation.

> **ANOTHER WAY**
>
> The **Record Slide Show** button is also available on the *Recording* tab, and it has the same options.
> Use *PowerPoint Options* to add the *Recording* tab to your *Ribbon*.

The audio (and video if a camera is used) is embedded on each slide and, therefore, synchronized with timings for how long each slide displays in the presentation. You will see a small picture in the lower-right corner on recorded slides; audio is represented by a speaker icon and a web camera will show a still image from the web cam.

Review your presentation in *Slide Show* view. Press **Esc** if you need to end the slide show before reaching the last slide. Edit your recordings if necessary. For example, you can re-record individual slides within the presentation or change sequencing. You may notice unnecessary audio at the end of a recording. When that happens, reduce the **After** seconds [*Transitions* tab, *Timing* group] to "trim" seconds so the recording is automatically interrupted as you transition to the next slide. Remove a single narration by deleting the slide audio or web cam icon or clear timing and narration on all slides.

Once your presentation is complete, save your narrated slide show to a CD, a flash drive, or share it online as a presentation or even a video.

▶**HOW TO: Clear Timings or Narration**

1. Click the **Slide Show** tab.

2. Click the **Record Slide Show** drop-down arrow [*Set Up* group] and then select **Clear**.

3. Select from these options:

> *Clear Timing on Current Slide*
> *Clear Timing on All Slides*
> *Clear Narration on Current Slide*
> *Clear Narration on All Slides*

To display a narrated slide show without narration or timings, deselect **Play Narrations** and **Use Timings** [*Slide Show* tab, *Set Up* group]. You can also make this change when you set up a show. Click the **Set Up Show** button [*Slide Show* tab, *Set Up* group], and select **Show without narration** under *Show Options* and **Manually** under *Advance Slides*.

Set Up a Kiosk Presentation with Looping

Depending on how you plan to use a kiosk presentation, it may need different design guidelines than a slide show that is projected by a presenter. While other presentations provide minimal text because slides support the speaker's message, a kiosk presentation may contain more information because it is a stand-alone product. If your kiosk presentation is displayed in a public place with distractions, use splashy graphics to grab attention. On the other hand, if your kiosk presentation is for educational purposes in a quiet setting such as a doctor's office, the slides might be designed more like pages in a book with smaller text and more detailed information.

▶HOW TO: Set Up a Kiosk Presentation

1. Click the **Slide Show** tab.
2. Click the **Set Up Slide Show** button [*Set Up* group] to open the *Set Up Show* dialog box.
3. Choose the following settings:
 - *Show type*: **Browsed at a kiosk (full screen)** (Figure 3-63).
 - *Show options*: **Loop continuously until 'Esc'** is automatically selected and grayed out because you chose a kiosk.
 - *Show slides*: **All** or enter the first and last slide numbers you want to display.
 - *Advance slides*: **Use timings, if present** is automatically selected for a kiosk.
 - *Slide show monitor*: If you are using more than one monitor, select the appropriate monitor for the slide show.
 - *Resolution*: **Use Current Resolution** or the highest resolution possible for your equipment.
 - **Use Presenter View** is not available for a kiosk presentation.
4. Click **OK**.
5. Save the presentation with these changes.

Figure 3-63 *Set Up Show* dialog box

Packaging a Presentation for CD or Folder

The *Package Presentation for CD* feature enables you to easily transport one or more presentations for use on another computer. You can copy your presentation file and any linked files to a blank CD (CD-R, recordable or CD-RW, rewritable) or to a folder on your computer, network location, or removable drive.

▶HOW TO: Save a Presentation to a CD or Folder

1. Insert a CD in your CD/DVD drive if you are saving to that location.
2. Click the **File** tab and select **Export**.
3. Select **Package Presentation for CD**.

4. Click the **Package for CD** button to open the *Package for CD* dialog box.

5. Type a name for the CD (Figure 3-64).

6. Click the **Options** button to open the *Options* dialog box (Figure 3-65) and choose from the following options:

 - *Linked Files*: Preserves links and copies any external files such as audio or video files.
 - *Embedded TrueType fonts*: Assures that the fonts used in your presentation are available on the play-back computer.
 - *Password*: Enhances security for opening or modifying a presentation.
 - *Inspect*: Checks for inappropriate or private information.

7. Click **OK**.

8. Save the presentation using one of the following methods:

 - Click the **Copy to CD** button and click **Yes** to verify that you want to include linked files.
 - Click the **Copy to Folder** button to open the *Copy to Folder* dialog box (Figure 3-66). The CD name you entered will appear. Browse for the location to save the presentation. Select the option to **Open folder when complete** if you want to see all the files that are copied. Click **OK**.

9. Click **No** when the packaging process is complete to indicate that you don't need to make another copy. Click **Close**.

10. Test the presentation by loading it from the folder or from the CD.

Figure 3-64 *Package for CD* dialog box

Figure 3-65 *Options* dialog box

Figure 3-66 *Copy to Folder* dialog box

> **MORE INFO**
>
> If file size requirements exceed the storage capacity of a CD, save your presentation to a folder on your computer or flash drive. You could also convert your slide show to a video and then use DVD burning software to save the files to a DVD. PowerPoint does not support direct burning to DVDs.

PAUSE & PRACTICE: POWERPOINT 3-4

This project consists of two parts. In Part A, you record a presentation with audio if you have a microphone connected to your computer. In Part B, you prepare a kiosk presentation, set it to loop so it is self-running, and then use the *Package Presentation for CD* feature to save it to a folder.

File Needed: *[your initials] PP P3-2.pptx*
Completed Project File Name: *[your initials] PP P3-4a. pptx* and *[your initials] PP P3-4b.pptx*

Part A (A Microphone is Required to Record Narration)

1. Open the *[your initials] PP P3-2* presentation completed in *Pause & Practice 3-2*.

 • A *Security Warning* may appear because an online video was inserted in this presentation. Click **Enable Content**.

2. Save the presentation as [your initials] PP P3-4a and change to *Slide Sorter* view.

3. Keep five slides for this project and remove other slides.

 • Delete slide 4, "Presentation Structure."
 • Keep slide 1 "Presentation Planning" through slide 5 "Plan a Strong Opening."
 • Delete slide 6 "Plan for Audience Interaction" through slide 18 "Presentation Planning."

4. Select any slide and remove slide timings by selecting **On Mouse Click** [*Transition* tab, *Timings* group], change the **After** seconds to **00:00.00**, and deselect **After**. Click **Apply To All**.

5. Click the **Notes Page** button [*View* tab, *Presentation Views* group] and add notes to two slides.

 a. Display the *Notes Page* for slide 2. Add four items after the first line of text and add bullets [*Home* tab, *Paragraph* group] (Figure 3-67):

 > This knowledge will guide many decisions.
 > • What is their background?
 > • What is their educational level?
 > • How familiar are they with your topic?
 > • Are they likely to be accepting of your ideas or resistant?
 >
 > Keep the presentation focused on your objectives.

 Figure 3-67 Slide 2 speaker notes

 • What is their background?
 • What is their educational level?
 • How familiar are they with your topic?
 • Are they likely to be accepting of your ideas or resistant?

 b. Display the *Notes Page* for slide 3. Add two more bulleted items at the end of the bulleted text:

 • Overall cleanliness and organization of the room
 • Temperature level for comfort

 c. Print the notes pages for slides 2 and 3 to use as a reference when recording the slide show.

6. Click the **Normal** button [*Status* bar] to return to *Normal* view.

7. Click the **Record Slide Show** drop-down arrow [*Slide Show* tab, *Set Up* group] and select **Start Recording from Beginning**. The *Recording* window opens (Figure 3-68).

 a. Refer to your printed notes or click the **Notes** button at the top of the *Recording* window to see the notes you prepared to help you explain the concepts of each slide.

 b. Click the **Record** button.

 c. Speak clearly into your microphone as you go through the

Figure 3-68 *Recording* window

 slide show. If you don't have a microphone, go through the slide show to practice. Your timings will be saved and sound icons will appear even if no sound was recorded.

8. Review the presentation and listen to the narration.

9. Save and close the presentation.

Part B

1. Open the presentation *[your initials] PP P3-2* again.
 - A *Security Warning* may appear because an online video was inserted in this presentation. Click **Enable Content**.

2. Save the presentation as [your initials] PP P3-4b.

3. Apply timing so slides change rapidly.

 Figure 3-69 *Timing* group on the *Transitions* tab

 a. Confirm that **On Mouse Click** [*Transitions* tab, *Timing* group] is not selected.
 b. Change *Duration* to **01.00** and *After* to **00:02:00**.
 c. Click **Apply to All** (Figure 3-69).

4. Click the **Set Up Slide Show** button [*Slide Show* tab, *Set Up* group] to open the *Set Up Show* dialog box.
 a. Select the following settings (Figure 3-70):
 - *Show type*: **Browsed at a kiosk (full screen)**.
 - *Show options*: **Loop continuously until 'Esc'** is automatically checked for a kiosk.
 - *Show slides*: **All**.
 - *Advance slides*: **Use timings, if present** is automatically checked for a kiosk.
 - *Slide show monitor*: Select the appropriate monitor.
 - **Use Presenter View** is not available because you selected a kiosk presentation.
 b. Click **OK**.

 Figure 3-70 *Set Up Show* dialog box

5. Use the *Package Presentation for CD* feature to save a presentation to a folder.
 a. Click the **File** tab and select **Export**.
 b. Click **Package Presentation for CD** and click the **Package for CD** button to open the *Package for CD* dialog box.
 c. Type Planning for the name of the CD.

6. Click the **Options** button to open the *Options* dialog box and select the following:
 a. Choose **Linked Files** to preserve links and copy any external files such as audio or video files.
 b. Choose **Embedded TrueType fonts** to assure that the fonts you use in your presentation are available on the playback computer.
 c. Click **OK** and the dialog box closes.

7. Click the **Copy to Folder** button to open the *Copy to Folder* dialog box. The name you typed for the CD automatically appears.
 a. Click **Browse** to open the *Choose Location* dialog box and find the place where you want to save the presentation. Click **Select**.
 b. Select the option to **Open folder when complete**.
 c. Click **OK** and the dialog box closes.
 d. Click **Yes** if you receive a message about including linked files.
 - A *File Explorer* window opens showing the files in the open *Planning* folder (Figure 3-71).

 Figure 3-71 *File Explorer* window with *Package Presentation for CD* files

8. Move the *File Explorer* window so you can close the *Package for CD* dialog box.

9. Save and close your *[your initials] PP P3-4b* presentation.

10. Test the presentation saved to your *Planning* folder by opening it from the folder. Double-click the *[your initials] PP P3-4b* file name.

11. Close the presentation and folder.

Chapter Summary

3.1 Create custom theme colors and background fills (p. P3-163).

- Design themes create a unified appearance for your presentation.
- The *Accent 1* theme color is the color that appears, by default, each time you draw a shape.
- Create custom theme colors by selecting different colors for background, text, and accent colors. Select the background color first and then select other colors that work well on that background.
- Modify backgrounds using the **Format Background** dialog box to apply a custom pattern, gradient, or picture fill.
- Carefully control how text is placed over background pictures and other fills so text is easy to read.

3.2 Apply animation to add interest and reinforce content (p. P3-172).

- **Animation** adds movement to slide objects and text.
- Animation is applied through **Entrance**, **Exit**, and **Emphasis** effects.
- If more than one animation is used, each animation is numbered in sequence.
- **Effect Options** control the direction and sequence of movement.
- Animation **Start** options include *On Click*, *With Previous*, or *After Previous*.
- **Duration** is the time that it takes to complete an animation.

3.3 Link to an online video (p. P3-175).

- Search for an online video using the *Insert Video* dialog box.
- You need internet access, and a video must currently be available online if you want to link to it during a PowerPoint presentation.
- Some videos cannot be played effectively at full screen size because the resolution is too low.
- Format a video by applying a style.
- Playback controls appear at the bottom of the video.

3.4 Use rehearsal techniques to prepare for presentation delivery (p. P3-182).

- Type **speaker notes** using the *Notes* pane or *Notes Page* view.
- Print speaker notes for reference during a presentation.
- Use **Rehearse Timings** to practice and judge the pace of your presentation.
- Adjust timings to increase or decrease the number of seconds a slide displays.
- Prepare backup copies of your presentation and your notes.

3.5 Control display options for different screen sizes (p. P3-185).

- The dimensions of your slides vary based on the aspect ratio (the ratio of width to height) you use.
- PowerPoint's default slide size has a **Widescreen** aspect ratio of (16:9).
- **Presenter View** displays the current slide, next slide, notes, and navigation controls on one monitor, while the slide show displays on a second monitor or projection screen.
- Use *Presenter View* with one monitor or multiple monitors/devices.

3.6 Present effectively and professionally using projection equipment (p. P3-191).

- Use the slide show toolbar, context menu, or keyboard shortcuts to navigate to different slides in a presentation.
- To blank a slide to black, press **B**; to blank a slide to white, press **W**. Press the same letter to return to your slide.
- When you hide a slide, it is still in the presentation but will not display during a slide show unless you go to that specific slide by typing its number and pressing **Enter**.
- Use a **remote control** to advance slides so you can move away from your computer.
- Use PowerPoint's **laser pointer** to temporarily display a dot on the slide during a slide show.

3.7 Use annotation pens to highlight information and save presentation markings (p. P3-195).

- Use the **Pen** or **Highlighter** to mark or draw on a slide during a slide show.
- Use the **Eraser** to remove markings during a slide show.
- These markings, called **ink annotations**, can be saved at the end of the presentation.

3.8 Prepare a self-running presentation that loops (p. P3-198).

- If your computer has a microphone, sound card, and speakers, you can record a slide show with narration.
- A self-running presentation, a *kiosk presentation*, is set to automatically *loop* so it runs continuously.
- Use the *Set Up Show* dialog box to choose options for a kiosk presentation.

3.9 Use the *Package Presentation for CD* feature to prepare a slide show for display on other computers (p. P3-200).

- The *Package Presentation for CD* feature saves linked files to a CD or other location.
- To ensure that the fonts you used to create your presentation are available on the computer you will use to display your presentation, select *Embedded TrueType Fonts*.

Check for Understanding

The SIMbook for this text (within your SIMnet account) provides the following resources for concept review:

- Multiple-choice questions
- Matching exercises
- Short answer questions

Guided Project 3-1

One of the community colleges in the Sierra Pacific Community College District has finished construction of a new building for their business program. A dedication ceremony and open house is planned. For this project, you finalize the presentation for this special program.
[Student Learning Outcomes 3.1, 3.2, 3.4, 3.6]

Files Needed: **Dedication-03.pptx** and **Building-03.jpg** *(Student data files are available in the* Library *of your SIMnet account.)*
Completed Project File Names: *[your initials]* **PowerPoint 3-1.pptx**

Skills Covered in This Project

- Apply a background picture fill.
- Apply animation and effect options.
- Create and print notes pages.

- Rehearse a presentation and save timings.
- Use *Presenter View*.
- Use slide show navigation tools, keyboard shortcuts, and insert blank slides.

1. Open the **Dedication-03** presentation from your student data files.

2. Save the presentation as [your initials] PowerPoint 3-1.

3. Display slide 1. Apply a background picture fill with a softened effect to all slides.
 a. Point to the slide background and right-click to open the context menu. Click **Format Background** to open the *Format Background* pane.
 b. Select the **Picture or texture fill** option.
 c. Click the **File** button to open the *Insert Picture* dialog box.
 d. Locate your student data files, select the **Building-03** picture, and click the **Insert** button.
 e. Click the **Picture** button at the top of the pane and then click **Picture Color**. Click the **Recolor** button and select **Blue, Accent color 2 Dark** (third color/second row) (Figure 3-72).

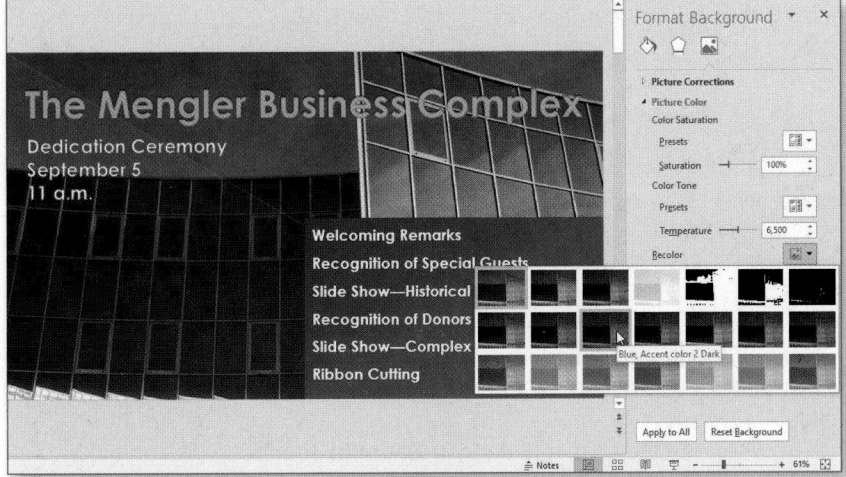

Figure 3-72 Picture background with *Recolor* options

 f. Click **Apply to All** so this picture is used as the background for all slides.

4. Restore the background picture to its original color on two slides.
 a. Display slide 1. On the *Format Background* pane under *Picture Color*, click the **Reset** button.
 b. Display slide 2 and click the **Reset** button again.

5. Prepare a black slide so the speaker can talk for a few moments with no slide displayed.
 a. Display slide 6. On the *Format Background* pane, click **Fill** at the top of the pane if it is not selected. Select the **Solid fill** option.
 b. Click the **Color** button and select **Black, Background 1** (first color/first row).
 c. Close the *Format Background* pane.

6. Apply a transition to all slides.
 a. Click the **Transitions** tab and apply the **Shape** transition.
 b. Click the **Effect Options** button [*Transition to This Slide* group] and select **Diamond**.
 c. Click **Apply to All** [*Timing* group] (Figure 3-73).

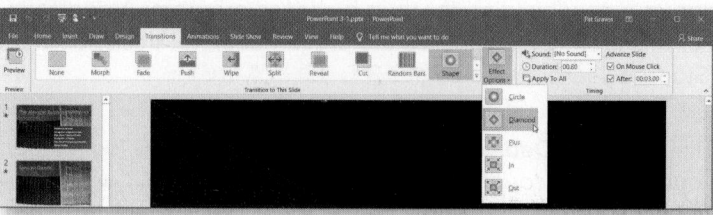

Figure 3-73 *Transition Effect Options*

7. Apply animation on five slides.
 a. Display slide 1. Click the **Animations** tab.
 b. Select the object to be animated, the text box for the agenda on the right, that is listed on the first row of Table 3-7.
 c. Click the **More** button on the *Animation* gallery [*Animation* group] or click the **Add Animation** button [*Advanced Animation* group] if the gallery is not open.
 d. Click the **Wipe** Entrance effect.
 e. Click the **Effects Options** button [*Animation* group] and select the **From Bottom** *Direction* and **By Paragraph** *Sequence*.
 f. Change settings [*Timing* group] as needed for the following: *Start* is **On Click** and *Duration* is **00.50**. Some of the settings will appear by default.
 g. Click the **Preview** button [*Preview* group] or **Slide Show** button [*Status* bar] to test the animation.
 h. Repeat steps b-g for the remaining four animations listed in Table 3-7.

Table 3-7

Slide	Object	Animation Effect	Effect Options	Start	Duration
1	Text box for the agenda on the right	*Wipe* (Entrance)	*From Bottom, By Paragraph*	*On Click*	*00.50*
3	Picture	*Shape* (Entrance)	*Diamond, Out*	*After Previous*	*02:00*
7	Text box about space design	*Zoom* (Entrance)	*Object Center, As One Object*	*On Click*	*00:50*
7	Text box about wireless access	*Zoom* (Entrance)	*Object Center, As One Object*	*On Click*	*00:50*
8	Text box with donor names	*Wipe* (Entrance)	*From Bottom, All At Once*	*After Previous*	*01:00*

8. Use *Slide Show* view to practice use of navigation tools, keyboard shortcuts, and blanking slides.
 a. Display slide 1 and click the **Slide Show** button [*Status* bar].
 b. Click the **Next** button in the control area to advance slides.
 c. Click the **See all slides** button in the control area to see slide thumbnails; click a thumbnail to jump to slide 4.
 d. Right-click anywhere on the slide and choose **Zoom In**. Right-click to zoom out to regular slide size.
 e. Press **N** to advance through animation or go to the next slide; press **P** to go to the previous animation or slide.
 f. Press **5** and press **Enter** to go to slide 5.
 g. Press **B** to blank a slide; press **B** to view the slide again.
 h. Press **Esc** to exit *Slide Show* view.

9. Prepare speaker notes on two slides.
 a. Select slide 1. Click the **Notes Page** button [*View* tab, *Presentation Views* group].

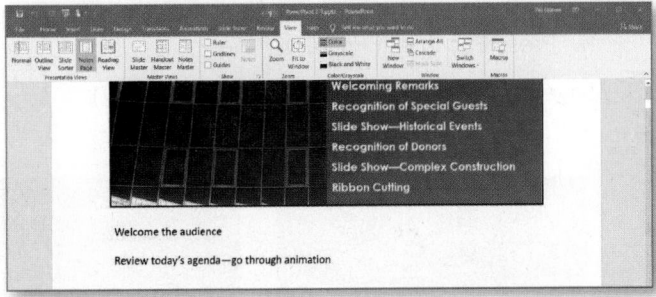

 b. Click the **Zoom** button on the *Notes Page* and increase the *Percent* to **150%** so you can more easily see the text. Click **OK**.
 c. Add the following text with a blank line between each item (Figure 3-74):

Figure 3-74 *Notes Page* view showing speaker notes

 Slide 1: Welcome the audience
 　　　　Review today's agenda—go through animation

 Slide 5: Fostered business innovation and involvement
 　　　　Developed the Business Development Institute
 　　　　Expanded internship opportunities

 d. Click the **Normal** button [*View* tab, *Presentation Views* group] to return to *Normal* view.

10. Print notes pages for slides 4 and 5.
 a. Click the **File** tab and click **Print**.
 b. Select the appropriate printer and verify that you are printing just one copy.
 c. Choose the following settings:
 • *Slides*: 4-5 to print a *Custom Range*.
 • *Print Layout*: **Notes Pages** and **Scale to Fit Paper** (Figure 3-75).
 d. Click the **Print** button.

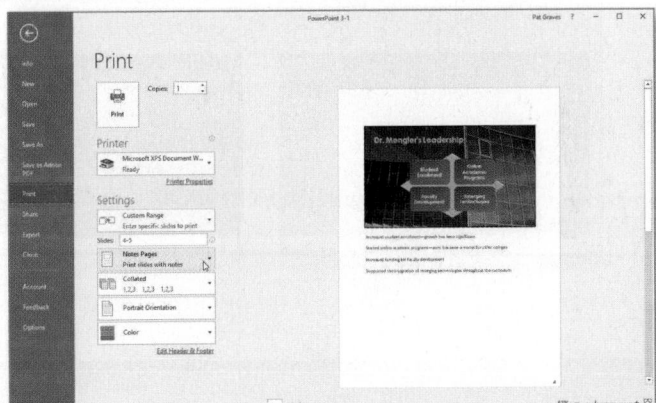

Figure 3-75 Print view of *Notes Page*

11. Rehearse and save timings.
 a. Click the **Rehearse Timings** button [*Slide Show* tab, *Set Up* group] to open the *Recording* dialog box and start timing.
 b. Click the **Next Slide** button to advance each slide and animation effect after approximately 3–5 seconds.
 c. Click **Yes** at the end of your presentation to save your timings. The timings display below each slide in *Slide Sorter* view.

12. Use *Presenter View* to review your presentation.
 a. Click the **Slide Show** tab.
 b. Deselect **Use Timings** [*Set Up* group].
 c. Click **Use Presenter View** [*Monitors* group].
 d. Click the **From Beginning** button [*Start Slide Show* group].
 • If you have one monitor, right-click and select **Show Presenter View**.
 e. Click the **Advance to next slide** button to review your slides.
 f. Click the **Zoom into the slide** button to magnify a section of the slide. Click **Zoom Out** (the same button) to return to the normal slide size (Figure 3-76).

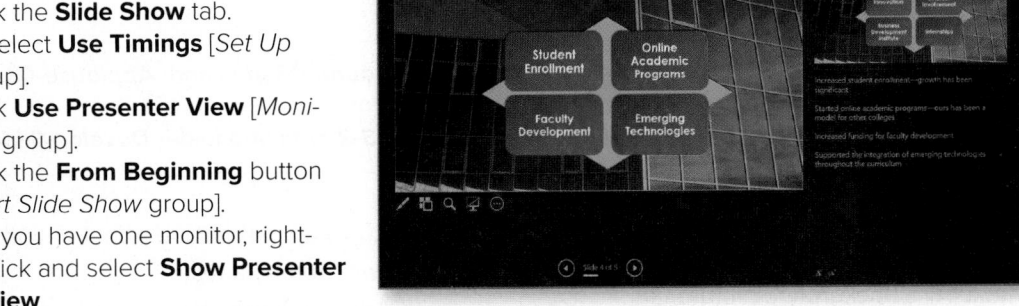

Figure 3-76 *Presenter View*

g. Click the **See all slides** button to view thumbnails of all slides. Click to display different slides.

h. Press **Esc** to exit *Presenter View*.

13. Save and close the presentation (Figure 3-77).

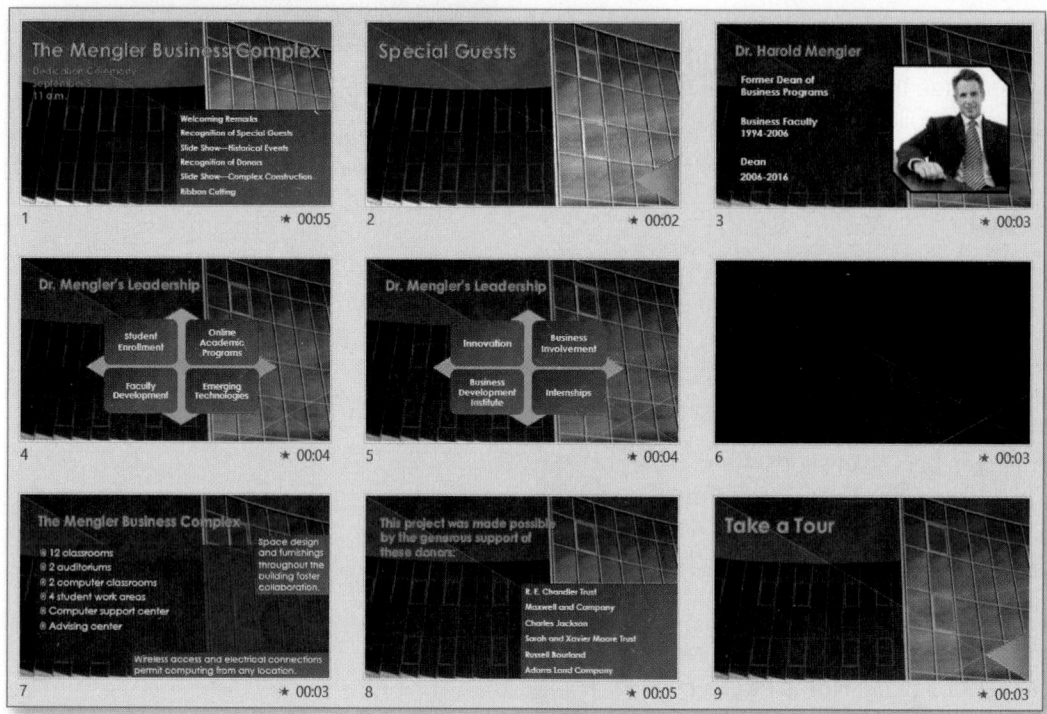

Figure 3-77 PowerPoint 3-1 completed

Guided Project 3-2

For the second training session for new hires on presenting effectively, Davon Washington, management consultant at Solution Seekers, Inc., is preparing guidelines for designing slides and developing content in a visual way. For this project, you finish the presentation that Davon has prepared and save it on a CD so participants can refer to it after the session.
[Student Learning Outcomes 3.1, 3.2, 3.4, 3.7, 3.9]

Files Needed: ***SlideShowDevelopment-03.pptx***, ***Background-03.jpg***, and ***Applause-03.jpg*** *(Student data files are available in the Library of your SIMnet account.)*
Completed Project File Names: ***[your initials] PowerPoint 3-2.pptx*** and folder ***Develop Slides***

Skills Covered in This Project

- Apply a background picture fill.
- Create custom theme colors.
- Apply animation and effect options.
- Print notes pages.
- Add ink annotations.
- Use the *Package Presentation for CD* feature.

1. Open the **SlideShowDevelopment-03** presentation from your student data files.

2. Save the presentation as [your initials] PowerPoint 3-2.

3. Apply a background picture fill to all slides.
 a. Point to the background and right-click. Select **Format Background** to open the *Format Background* pane.
 b. Select the **Picture or texture fill** option.
 c. Click the **File** button to open the *Insert Picture* dialog box.
 d. Locate your student data files, select **Background-03**, and click **Insert** (Figure 3-78).
 e. Click **Apply to All** so this picture is the background for all slides.

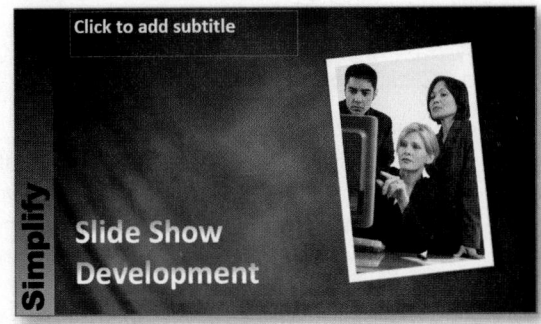

Figure 3-78 Title slide with new background picture fill

4. Display slide 12. Repeat step 3 to apply a different background picture, **Applause-03**, for this slide only.
 a. Change the *Offset left* to **−9%** and the *Offset top* to **−5%** for better picture positioning on the slide. (*Offset right* is 0% and *Offset bottom* is −9%.)
 b. Close the *Format Background* pane.

5. Prepare a new custom color theme to blend with the background picture.
 a. Click the **More** button [*Design* tab, *Variants* group].
 b. Click **Colors** and click **Customize Colors** to open the *Create New Theme Colors* dialog box.
 c. Change five accent colors using the numbers in Table 3-8.
 • For each change, click the color button and select **More Colors** to open the *Colors* dialog box.
 • Click the **Custom** tab and enter the numbers for *Red*, *Green*, and *Blue*.

Figure 3-79 New *Theme Colors*

Table 3-8

	Accent 1	Accent 2	Accent 3	Accent 4	Accent 5
Red	255	157	255	38	95
Green	247	175	217	203	30
Blue	220	210	82	236	60

 d. Name the new custom theme Development (Figure 3-79).
 e. Click the **Save** button.

6. Select the following slides and adjust text and object colors:
 a. *Slide 7*: Select the *SmartArt* graphic. Click the **Change Colors** button [*SmartArt Tools Design* tab, *SmartArt Styles* group] and select the **Colored Fill – Accent 5** style (second option/*Accent 5* category) (Figure 3-80).
 b. *Slide 12*: Select the text box. Click the **Shape Fill** drop-down arrow [*Home* tab, *Drawing* group] and select **Plum, Accent 5** (ninth color/first row).

Figure 3-80 *SmartArt* recolored

7. Apply a transition to all slides.
 a. Click the **Transitions** tab and apply the **Reveal** transition.
 b. Click the **Effect Options** button [*Transition to this Slide* group] and select **Smoothly from Right**.
 c. Change the *Duration* to **02:00** [*Timing* group].
 d. Click **Apply to All**.

8. Apply animation on four slides.
 a. Display slide 2. Click the **Animations** tab.
 b. Select the object to be animated, the Ducks, that is listed on the first row of Table 3-9.
 c. Click the **More** button on the *Animation* gallery [*Animation* group] or click the **Add Animation** button [*Advanced Animation* group] if the gallery is not open.
 d. Click the **Fly In** *Entrance* effect.
 e. Click the **Effects Options** button [*Animation* group] and select the **From Top** *Direction*.
 f. Change settings [*Timing* group] as needed for the following: *Start* is **On Click**, *Duration* is **02.00**, and *Delay* is **None**. Some of the settings will appear by default.
 g. Click the **Preview** button [*Preview* group] or **Slide Show** button [*Status* bar] to test the animation.
 h. Repeat steps b-g for the remaining animations (slides 2, 4, 5, and 6) listed in Table 3-9.

Table 3-9

Slide	Object	Animation Effect	Effect Options	Start	Duration
2	Ducks	*Fly In* (Entrance)	*From Left*	*On Click*	02.00
2	Slide Show Development text box	*Bounce* (Entrance)	None	*After Previous*	02.00
4 and 5	Grouped text box and up arrow	*Float In* (Entrance)	*Float Up*	*After Previous*	01.00
4 and 5	Grouped text box and down arrow	*Float In* (Entrance)	*Float Down*	*After Previous*	01.00
6	Color wheel	*Spin* (Emphasis)	*Clockwise, Two Spins*	*After Previous*	03.00

9. Display slide 1. Click the **Notes Page** button [*View* tab, *Presentation Views* group]. Advance through all slides and read the speaker notes to review tips for slide design.

10. Print notes pages for slides 7 and 11.
 a. Click the **File** tab and click **Print**.
 b. Select the appropriate printer and verify that you are printing just one copy.
 c. Choose the following settings:
 - *Slides*: 7, 11 for a *Custom Range*.
 - *Print Layout*: **Notes Pages** and **Scale to Fit Paper** (Figure 3-81).
 d. Click the **Print** button.

11. Add ink annotations on slides 4, 5, and 7.
 a. Display slide 4. Click the **Slide Show** button [*Status* bar] to start your slide show on this slide.
 b. Right-click to open the context menu, select **Pointer Options** and **Highlighter**. Highlight the word "**organization**" in the text box on the lower right.
 c. Display slide 5, repeat step 11b and highlight the words "**creative thinking**" in the text box.
 d. Display slide 7, right-click to open the context menu. Select **Pointer Options** and **Pen**. Circle the words "**Reduce words**" and "**keep the meaning**."
 e. Advance to the end of the presentation and click **Keep** to save your ink annotations.

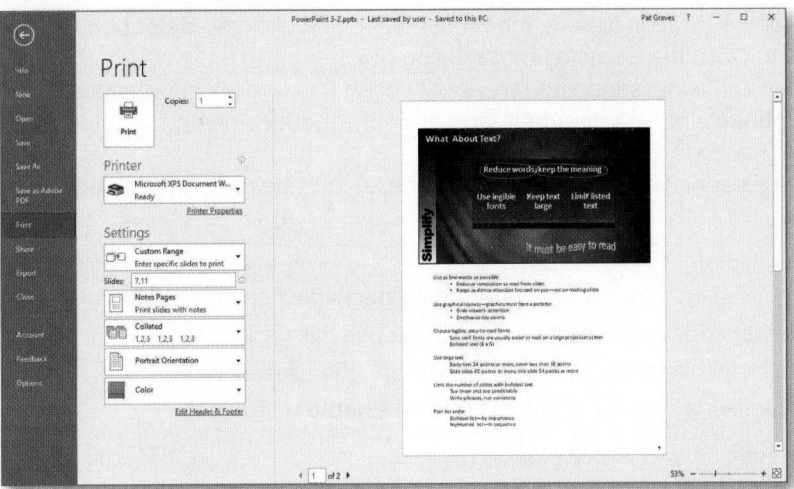

Figure 3-81 Print *Notes Pages*

12. Save the presentation (Figure 3-82).

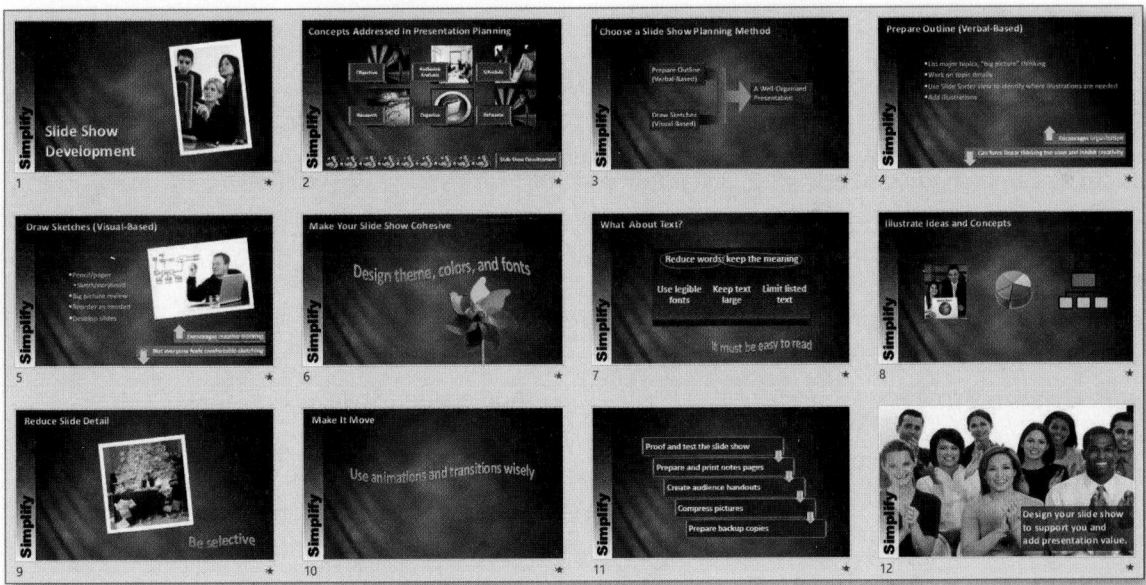

Figure 3-82 PowerPoint 3-2 completed

13. Use the *Package Presentation for CD* feature to save the presentation to a folder.
 a. Click the **File** tab and select **Export**.
 b. Click **Package Presentation for CD** and click the **Package for CD** button to open the *Package for CD* dialog box.
 c. Type Develop Slides to name the CD.
 d. Click the **Options** button to open the *Options* dialog box and select **Linked Files** and **Embedded TrueType fonts** (Figure 3-83).
 e. Click **OK**.
 f. Click the **Copy to Folder** button to open the *Copy to Folder* dialog box.
 • The folder name appears and is the same name you typed for the CD.
 • Deselect the **Open folder when complete** option.

Figure 3-83 *Package for CD* and *Options* dialog boxes

g. Browse for the location to save the presentation and click the **Select** button.
h. Click **OK** to close the *Copy to Folder* dialog box.
i. Click **Yes** when a message appears about comments and ink annotations.
j. Click **Continue** when another message appears about comments and ink annotations.
k. Close the *Package for CD* dialog box.
l. Close the presentation without saving because you saved it in step 12 and in the folder created in step 13.

14. Test the presentation.
 a. Open the *Develop Slides* folder where you "packaged" the presentation.
 - Notice that additional files have been saved in this folder.
 b. Double-click the file name in the folder to open the presentation.
 - If you receive a security warning, click the **Enable** button.

15. Test the presentation and then close it.

Guided Project 3-3

At an upcoming meeting of the American River Cycling Club, Eric Salinas will deliver a presentation about the importance of knowing your target heart rate and exercising with your heart rate at an appropriate target level. For this project, you finalize the presentation.
[Student Learning Outcomes 3.1, 3.3, 3.4, 3.8]

Files Needed: *HeartRateARCC-03.pptx* and *RiderAir.jpg* (*Student data files are available in the Library of your SIMnet account.*)
Completed Project File Name: *[your initials] PowerPoint 3-3.pptx*

Skills Covered in This Project

- Create custom theme colors.
- Apply a background picture fill.
- Link to a video on a web site.
- Add a video style.
- Use *Presenter View*.
- Create and print notes pages.
- Record a presentation with narration.

1. Open the **HeartRateARCC-03** presentation from your student data files.

2. Save the presentation as [your initials] PowerPoint 3-3.

3. Prepare a new custom color theme to blend with the heart picture on slide 3.
 a. Click the **More** button [*Design* tab, *Variants* group].
 b. Select **Colors** and click **Customize Colors** to open the *Create New Theme Colors* dialog box.
 c. Click the **Color** button for each change and select **More Colors** to open the *Colors* dialog box.
 d. Click the **Custom** tab and enter the *Red*, *Green*, and *Blue* numbers for the four colors in Table 3-10.

Table 3-10

	Text/Background – Dark 2	Accent 1	Accent 2	Accent 3
Red	24	36	204	227
Green	66	99	0	108
Blue	77	116	0	9

e. Name the new custom theme **ARCC** (Figure 3-84).
f. Click the **Save** button and the new colors will automatically be applied to all slides.

4. Format the title slide by adding a background picture fill.
 a. Display slide 1. Point to the background, right-click, and select **Format Background** to open the *Format Background* pane.
 b. Select the **Picture or texture fill** option.
 c. Click the **File** button to open the *Insert Picture* dialog box.
 d. Locate your student data files, select *RiderAir-03*, and click **Insert**.
 e. Click **Picture** at the top of the pane and select **Picture Color**.
 f. Click the **Recolor** button and select **Black and White**: **25%** (fifth option/first row) (Figure 3-85).
 g. Close the *Format Background* pane.

Figure 3-84 New ARCC color theme

5. Increase the subtitle *Font Size* on slide 1 to **36 pt**. and resize the placeholder so one word fits on each line.

6. Find and insert an online video.
 a. Display slide 5 and click the **Insert** tab.
 b. Click the **Video** button [*Media* group] and select **Online Video** to open the *Insert Video* dialog box.
 c. Type the words Col de la Madone in the *YouTube* search box and click the **Search** button.
 d. Select an appropriate video. Click **Insert**.
 e. Position the video to the left of the picture and resize it (*Width* **5.5"**) if necessary.
 f. Apply the **Metal Frame** video style [*Video Tools Format* tab, *Video Styles* group] (*Intense* group).
 g. Below the video, add the appropriate source information in a text box.
 h. Play the video in *Slide Show* view by clicking the **Start** button in the middle of the video.
 i. Press **Esc** to return to *Normal* view.

Figure 3-85 Title slide completed

7. Apply a transition.
 a. Choose the **Cube** transition [*Transitions* tab, *Transition to This Slide* group] with the **From Right** effect options.
 b. Click **Apply To All**.

8. Use *Presenter View* to review your presentation.
 a. Click the **Slide Show** tab.
 b. Click **Use Presenter View** [*Monitors* group].
 c. Click the **From Beginning** button [*Start Slide Show* group] to start your presentation.
 • If you have one monitor, right-click and select **Show Presenter View**.
 d. Click the **Advance to the next slide** button to advance slides as you review them.
 e. Click the **Make the text larger** button at the bottom of the *Notes* pane to increase the text size for notes on all slides. Scroll to read the text on slide 3 (Figure 3-86).
 f. Press **Esc** to end the slide show.

Figure 3-86 *Presenter View*

9. Print notes pages for slides 3 and 4.
 a. Click the **File** tab. Click **Print**.
 b. Select the appropriate printer and verify that you are printing just one copy.
 c. Choose the following settings:
 - *Slides*: 3-4 for a *Custom Range*.
 - *Print Layout*: **Notes Pages** and **Scale to Fit Paper**.
 d. Click the **Print** button.

10. Record a slide show with narration.
 a. Click the **Record Slide Show** drop-down arrow [*Slide Show* tab, *Set Up* group] and select **Record from Beginning** to open the *Record* window.
 b. Click the **Record** button (Figure 3-87).
 c. Speak clearly into your microphone as each slide displays.
 d. Click the **Advance to the Next Slide** button to advance each slide.

Figure 3-87 *Record* button

11. Save and close your presentation (Figure 3-88).

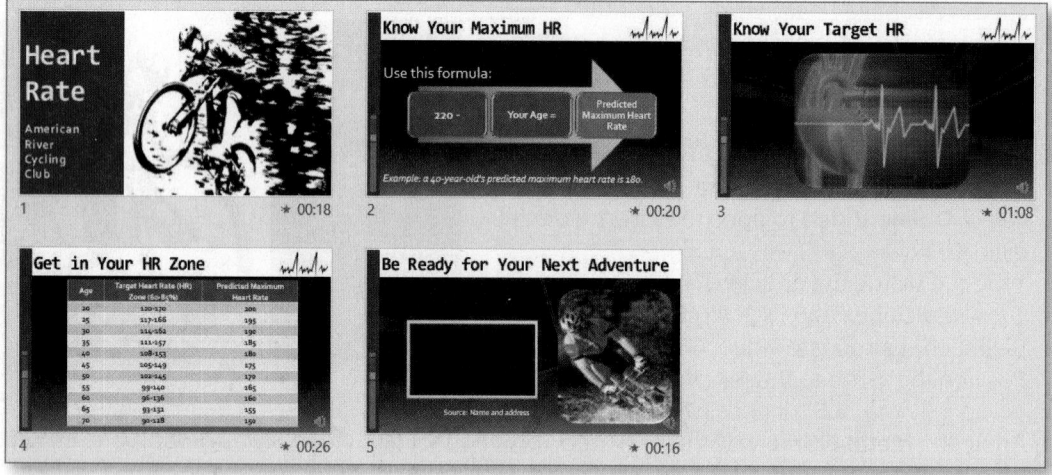

Figure 3-88 PowerPoint 3-3 completed

Independent Project 3-4

The sales representatives at Wilson Home Entertainment Systems review acceptable viewing distances when talking with clients who are in the early stages of planning a home theater or media room. They discuss options for televisions or projection systems for the spaces being planned. For this project, you complete a presentation to prepare clients for an in-home consultation.
[Student Learning Outcomes 3.1, 3.2, 3.4, 3.5, 3.7, 3.8]

Files Needed: ***ScreenSizes-03.pptx***, ***TVCabinet-03.jpg***, ***TVWallMount-03.jpg***, and ***Projector-03.jpg*** *(Student data files are available in the Library of your SIMnet account.)*
Completed Project File Name: ***[your initials] PowerPoint 3-4.pptx***

Skills Covered in This Project

- Change slide size.
- Apply a background picture fill.
- Apply animation and effect options.
- Rehearse a presentation and save timings.
- Use slide show navigation tools, keyboard shortcuts, and blank slides.
- Hide and reveal slides.
- Use the laser pointer feature.
- Use annotation pens.
- Prepare a kiosk presentation.

1. Open the **ScreenSizes-03** presentation (in the **Standard (4:3)** format) from your student data files.

2. Change slide size.
 a. Notice how the logo on slide 1 and the titles at the bottom of slides 5–7 are aligned on the bottom right.
 - The *Standard (4:3)* slide *Width* is 10" and *Height* is 7.5".
 b. Click the **Slide Size** button [*Design* tab, *Customize* group] and click **Widescreen (16:9)** (Figure 3-89).
 - The slide *Width* changes from 10" to 13.33" but the *Height* remains the same.
 - The logo and slide titles are not aligned because of the size change.

Figure 3-89 *Slide Size*

3. Save the presentation in the widescreen size as [your initials] PowerPoint 3-4.

4. Apply a picture fill background on three slides.
 a. Open the *Format Background* pane.
 b. Choose **Picture or texture fill** and insert the following pictures from your student data files:
 Slide 5: **TVCabinet-03**
 Slide 6: **TVWallMount-03**
 Slide 7: **Projector-03**
 c. Close the *Format Background* pane.

5. Right-align objects at the bottom of the following slides to better fit the widescreen size.
 Slides 5, 6, and 7: text boxes (Figure 3-90)
 Slides 1 and 8: WHES logo

6. Apply a transition.
 a. Choose the **Vortex** transition with the **From Bottom** effect option (Figure 3-91).
 b. Change the *Duration* to **3.00**.
 c. Apply these settings to all slides.

Figure 3-90 Background picture fill

Figure 3-91 *Vortex* transition effect options

7. Apply animation on four slides using the settings to match Table 3-11. After you complete the animation on slide 5, use the **Animation Painter** to copy these settings and apply them to the text boxes on slides 6 and 7.

Table 3-11

Slide	Object	Animation Effect	Effect Options	Start	Duration
2	Question mark	*Spin* (Emphasis)	*Counterclockwise, Two Spins*	*After Previous*	*02.00*
5, 6, 7	Text box	*Fly In* (Entrance)	*From Top-Left, As One Object*	*After Previous*	*00.50*

8. Rehearse the presentation and save timings.

9. Modify the timings to advance each slide after 5 seconds.

10. Hide slide 4.

11. Use the *Set Up Show* dialog box to change *Advance Slides* to **Manually**. Click **OK**.

12. Practice the following slide show features in *Slide Show* view:
 a. Use the control area buttons to move to the next slide.
 b. Press **B** to blank a slide. Press **B** to display the slide again.
 c. Right-click to open the context menu, select **Pointer Options**, and change the *Laser Pointer* color.
 d. Go to the hidden slide 4.
 e. Point to slide objects (*Height*, *Lighting*, and *Viewing Angle*) with the laser pointer.
 f. Use keyboard shortcuts. Press **2** and press **Enter** to go to slide 2.

13. Use *Presenter View* and practice making annotations on the presenter slide.
 a. Select the **Presenter View** button on the *Slide Show* tab.
 b. Start the slide show from the beginning.
 c. Click the **Pen** tool and change the *Ink Color* to **Red**.
 d. Go to slide 3 and circle the "**60-65**" and "**100**" television and screen sizes.
 e. Go to hidden slide 4. Circle the following phrases in the bulleted items: "**level with the middle**," "**reduce color clarity**," and "**visibility at all seats**."
 f. Keep annotations.

14. Prepare a kiosk presentation with looping.
 a. Select **Use Timings** on the *Slide Show* tab.
 b. Click the **Set Up Slide Show** button to open the *Set Up Show* dialog box.
 c. For *Show Slides*, select **All**.
 d. For *Advance Slides*, select **Use timings, if present** is automatically selected.
 e. Select **Browsed at a kiosk (full screen)** (Figure 3-92).
 f. Select the appropriate monitor.
 g. Click **OK**.

Figure 3-92 *Set Up Show* dialog box

15. Save and close the presentation (Figure 3-93).

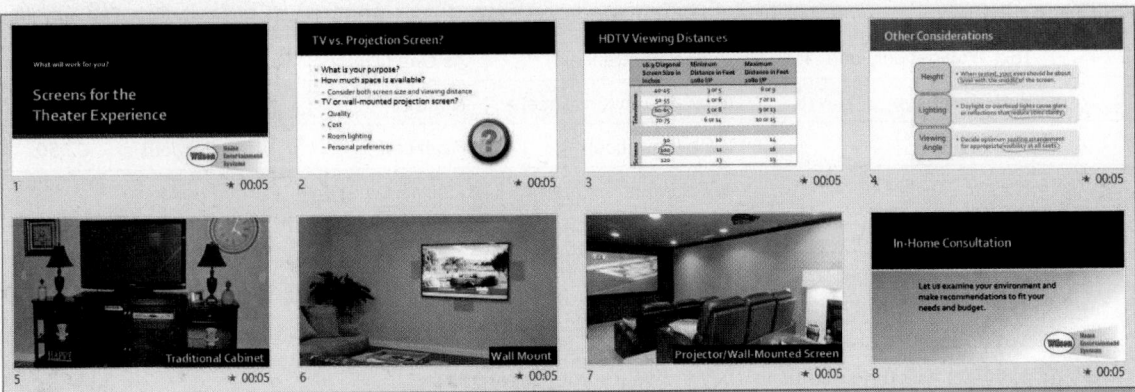

Figure 3-93 PowerPoint 3-4 completed

Independent Project 3-5

For the third training session for new hires on presenting effectively, Davon Washington, management consultant at Solution Seekers, Inc., is preparing guidelines for delivering a presentation with projection equipment. For this project, you finish the presentation that Davon has prepared.
[Student Learning Outcomes 3.2, 3.4, 3.7, 3.8]

File Needed: **PresentationDelivery-03.pptx** (Student data files are available in the Library of your SIMnet account.)
Completed Project File Name: **[your initials] PowerPoint 3-5.pptx**

Skills Covered in This Project

- Apply a background picture fill.
- Apply animation and effect options.
- Create and print notes pages.

- Hide and reveal slides.
- Rehearse a presentation and save timings.
- Use *Presenter View*.
- Use ink annotation pens.

1. Open the **PresentationDelivery-03** presentation from your student data files.

2. Save the presentation as [your initials] PowerPoint 3-5.

3. Apply the **Fade** transition with the **Smoothly** effect option. Change the *Duration* to **01.00**. Click **Apply To All**.

4. Apply animation on five slides and change effect options, start, and duration settings as listed in Table 3-12. Some of these settings will appear by default.

5. Prepare speaker notes on two slides. In the notes for slide 9, apply bullets and indent the bulleted text (Figure 3-94).

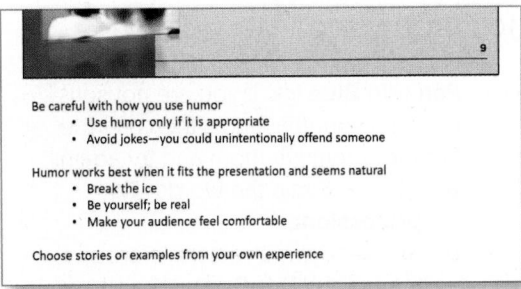

Figure 3-94 Speaker notes with bullets and indents

Table 3-12

Slide	Object	Animation Effect	Effect Options	Start	Duration
2	Text "You get only one . . . "	*Bounce* (Entrance)	*As One Object*	*After Previous*	02.00
5	Butterfly image	*Grow & Turn* (Entrance)	None	*After Previous*	02.00
7	Graphic	*Wipe* (Entrance)	*From Left*	*After Previous*	02.50
11	Text "Make it memorable"	*Bounce* (Entrance)	*As One Object*	*After Previous*	02.00
12	Success shape	*Grow/Shrink* (Emphasis)	*Both, Larger*	*After Previous*	02.50

Slide 2:
- Never underestimate the importance of a first impression
- If possible, welcome people as they arrive for your presentation

Slide 9:
- Be careful with how you use humor
 - Use humor only if it is appropriate
 - Avoid jokes—you could unintentionally offend someone
- Humor works best when it fits the presentation and seems natural
 - Break the ice
 - Be yourself; be real
 - Make your audience feel comfortable
- Choose stories or examples from your own experience

6. Print notes pages for slides 5, 6, and 7.

7. Hide slide 8.

8. Review the presentation to check transitions and animations.
 a. Select the *Transitions* tab and deselect **On Mouse Click**.
 b. Change *After* to **00:03:00** seconds.
 c. Click **Apply To All**.
 d. Start your slide show from the beginning and review all slide movements.

9. Use *Presenter View* to review your presentation.
 a. Deselect **Use Timings** [*Slide Show* tab, *Set Up* group] so you can advance through the slides at your own pace.
 b. Select **Use Presenter View**.
 c. Begin the presentation. If you have one monitor, right-click and select **Show Presenter View**.
 d. Navigate through slides using the **Advance to the next animation or slide** and **Return to the previous animation or slide** buttons.
 e. Click the **See all slides** button and click thumbnails to move to different slides.

10. Use *Presenter View* to add annotations on the following slides using the **Pen** with **Blue** ink. If you are not satisfied with your markings, then use the **Eraser** to remove them and try again.
 a. *Slide 2*: Circle the words "**Be professional**."
 b. *Slide 4*: Draw a rectangle around the words "**Eye Contact**" and "**Smile**" (Figure 3-95).

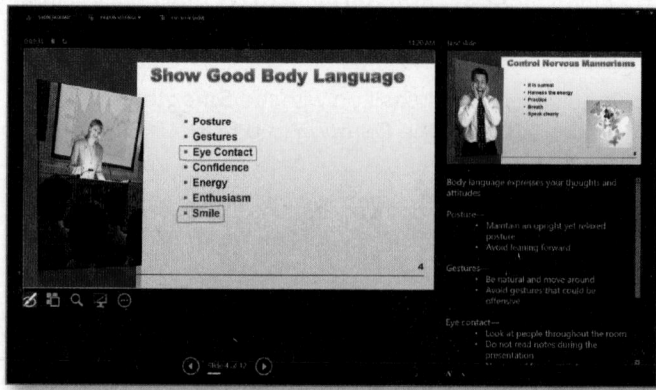

Figure 3-95 *Presenter View* showing ink annotations

c. *Slide 7*: Circle the words "**Avoid monotone**."
d. *Slide 10*: Circle "**End on time**."
e. Click **Keep** at the end of the presentation to save annotations.

11. Save and close your presentation (Figure 3-96).

Figure 3-96 PowerPoint 3-5 completed

Independent Project 3-6

At the Hamilton Civic Center (HCC), classes are offered for a variety of fitness activities. For this project, you complete a presentation to promote the water aerobics classes at several community events. It will also be used as a self-running presentation at the HCC front desk.
[Student Learning Outcomes 3.1, 3.2, 3.3, 3.4, 3.5, 3.6, 3.8]

File Needed: ***WaterAerobics-03.pptx*** *(Student data files are available in the* Library *of your SIMnet account.)*
Completed Project File Name: ***[your initials] PowerPoint 3-6.pptx***

Skills Covered in This Project

- Create custom theme colors.
- Modify background fill colors.
- Change object colors on selected slides.
- Apply animation and effect options.
- Change to a widescreen slide size.

- Hide and reveal a slide.
- Use slide show navigation tools, keyboard shortcuts, and blank slides.
- Link to an online video.
- Apply a video style.
- Prepare a kiosk presentation.

1. Open the ***WaterAerobics-03*** presentation (in the **Standard (4:3)** format) from your student data files (Figure 3-97).

2. Change the slide size.
 a. Click the **Slide Size** button and select **Widescreen (16:9)**.
 b. The slide size is now 10" to 13.33".

3. Save the presentation as [your initials] PowerPoint 3-6.

4. Adjust objects to better fit the widescreen format:
 a. *Slide 1*: Increase the picture size (*Height* **4"** and *Width* **6"**).
 b. *Slide 4*: Resize the text box on the right so the text fits on four lines (Figure 3-98). Align it to the slide on the right.
 c. *Slide 4*: Right align the text box at the bottom of the slide, then extend the left end of the box to fit across the bottom of the slide.
 d. *Slide 6*: Repeat step 4c for the text box at the bottom of the slide.

Figure 3-97 Title slide in *Standard* slide size

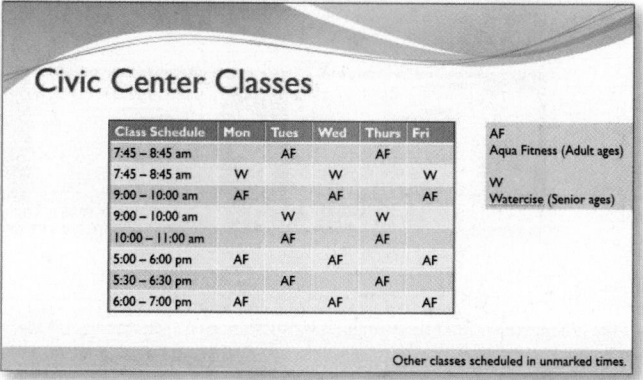

Figure 3-98 Text boxes adjusted

5. Use the *Create New Theme Colors* dialog box (Figure 3-99) to create a custom theme. Change four colors according to the *Red*, *Green*, and *Blue* numbers in Table 3-13. Name the custom theme Water and save it.

Table 3-13

	Text/Background - Dark 2	Accent 1	Accent 3	Accent 5
Red	7	53	16	255
Green	55	151	89	51
Blue	99	241	100	153

Figure 3-99 *Water* theme colors

6. Change the background colors.
 a. Click the **More** button [*Design* tab, *Variants* group] and select **Background Styles**. Click **Style 2** so a light blue is applied to the background of all slides in the presentation.
 b. Select slide 1. Use the *Format Background* pane to change the background fill. Select **Solid Fill** and choose **Dark Blue, Text 2** (fourth color/first row).

c. Change the *Font Color* for "Hamilton Civic Center" to **White, Background 1** (Figure 3-100).

d. Select slide 9. Change to the same background and text colors (steps 6 b–c).

e. Close the *Format Background* pane.

f. Select slide 3. Change the *Text Fill* color for "Fun" to **Pink, Accent 5** (ninth color/first row).

g. Select slide 4. Change the *Shading* for the table heading row to **Pink, Accent 5**.

Figure 3-100 Title slide in *Widescreen* slide size and *Water* theme colors

7. Apply the **Ripple** transition with the **From Top-Left** effect option. Apply this transition to all slides.

8. Apply animation on three slides and change options as listed in Table 3-14. Some settings will appear by default.

Table 3-14

Slide	Object	Animation Effect	Effect Options	Start	Duration
2	Bulleted list	*Fly In* (Entrance)	*From Bottom-Right, By Paragraph*	*After Previous*	*01.00*
3	Bulleted list	*Fly In* (Entrance)	*From Bottom, As One Object*	*After Previous*	*01.00*
3	*WordArt* "Fun"	*Bounce* (Entrance)	*As One Object*	*After Previous*	*02.50*

9. Hide slide 6.

10. Practice the following features using *Slide Show* view:
 a. Click **Next** and **Previous** in the control area to change slides.
 b. Click the **See all slides** button in the control area to see slide thumbnails; click a thumbnail to go to a different slide.
 c. Click the **Zoom into the slide** button in the control area to magnify the "To Wear" list on slide 8.
 d. Click the **More slide show options** button in the control area, select **Screen**, and then select **Black Screen**. Click the screen to return to the same slide.
 e. Go to the hidden slide 6.

11. Use the *Insert Video* dialog box to find and insert an online video.
 a. Display slide 5. Use the search words water aerobics exercises and select an appropriate video. For referencing purposes, write down the name of the video and online source from the lower left of the dialog box. Click **Insert**.
 b. Increase the video size if the quality remains acceptable.
 c. Apply the **Beveled Frame, Gradient** video style (*Subtle* group).
 d. Below the video, insert a text box for a source note with the name of the video and online address.
 e. Test the video in *Slide Show* view to be sure it plays correctly.

12. Use *Presenter View* to review the presentation.
 a. Select **Presenter View** on the *Slide Show* tab.
 b. Select slide 1 and begin the presentation. If you have one monitor, right-click and select **Show Presenter View**.
 c. Advance through the presentation and review the speaker notes that appear in *Presenter View*.

13. Apply timings to advance each slide after 5 seconds.

14. Use the *Set Up Show* dialog box to select the following settings for a kiosk presentation.
 a. *Show type*: **Browsed at a kiosk (full screen)**
 b. *Show options*: **Loop continuously until 'Esc'** (automatically selected)
 c. *Show slides*: **All**
 d. *Advance slides*: **Use timings, if present** (automatically selected)

15. Save and close the presentation (Figure 3-101).

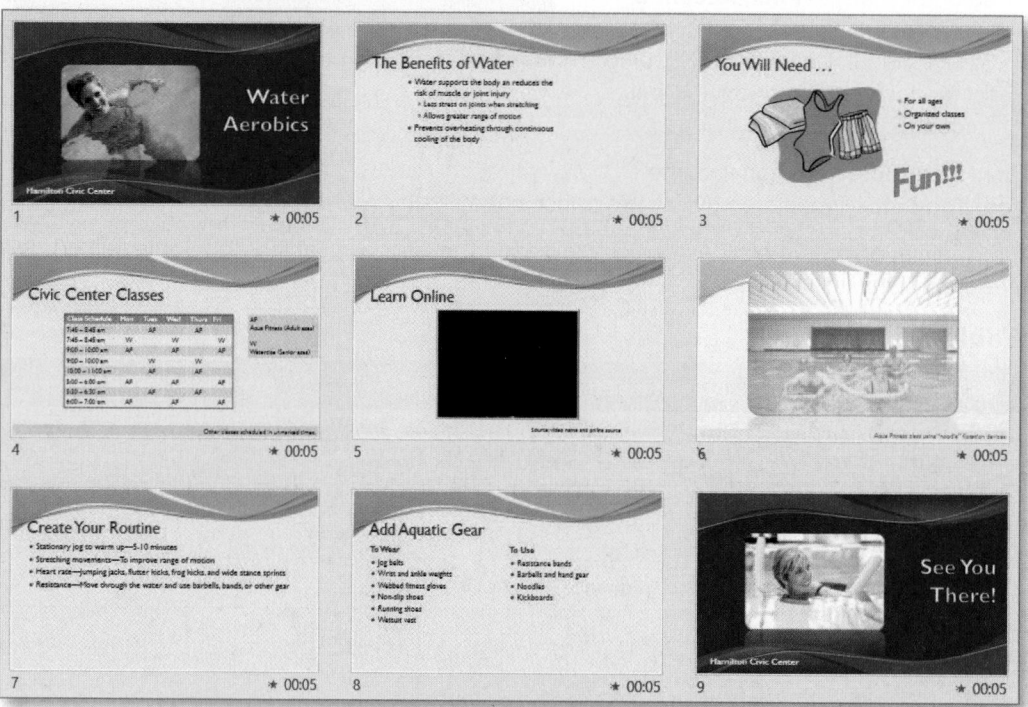

Figure 3-101 PowerPoint 3-6 completed

Improve It Project 3-7

Delivering news that employees may perceive as bad news is a difficult task. Olivia Hudson with Solution Seekers has been working to convert a formerly text-only presentation to one that is more visual. She is using pictures with brief text and transferring listed information to notes pages she will use during her presentation. She has asked you to complete a notes page, convert a list to a *SmartArt* graphic, apply custom theme colors, and add animation.
[Student Learning Outcomes 3.1, 3.2, 3.4, 3.8]

File Needed: **Announcement-03.pptx** *(Student data files are available in the* Library *of your SIMnet account.)*
Completed Project File Name: **[your initials] PowerPoint 3-7.pptx**

Skills Covered in This Project

- Create custom theme colors.
- Modify slide content with *SmartArt*.
- Create notes pages.
- Apply appropriate transitions.
- Apply animation and effect options.
- Use *Presenter View*.
- Prepare a kiosk presentation.

1. Open the **Announcement-03** presentation from your student data files.
2. Save the presentation as [your initials] PowerPoint 3-7.
3. Create custom theme colors using the name Announce. Change four colors using the numbers in Table 3-15.

Table 3-15

	Text/Background - Dark 2	Text/Background - Light 2	Accent 1	Accent 2
Red	38	255	255	204
Green	19	230	153	236
Blue	0	193	0	255

4. Format the title slide text to be more distinctive.
 a. Display slide 1 and apply **Bold** to the title and subtitle.
 b. Increase the title *Font Size* to **66 pt**. and "Big" to **96 pt**.
 c. Change the title *Font Color* to **Orange, Accent 1, Lighter 40%** (fifth column, fourth row).
 d. Increase the subtitle *Font Size* to **32 pt**. and "You" to **48 pt**.
 e. Resize the subtitle placeholder on the left so the text fits on one line (Figure 3-102).

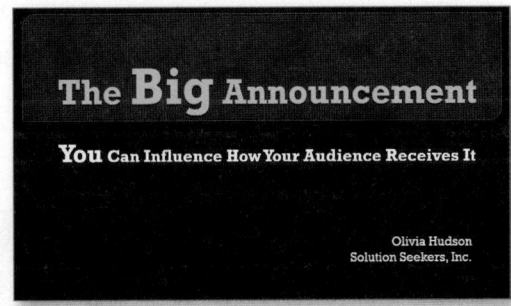

Figure 3-102 Title slide revised

5. Use the existing bulleted text to create notes.
 a. Display slide 2. If the *Notes* pane is not available below the slide in *Normal* view, click the **Notes** button on the *Status* bar.
 - Increase the size of the *Notes* pane so you can work in both panes.
 b. Copy the existing bulleted text on the slide and paste it in the *Notes* pane.
 c. Add a blank line space after the first and second lines.
 d. Select the indented text and apply bullets (Figure 3-103).
 e. Click the **Notes** button again to hide the *Notes* pane.

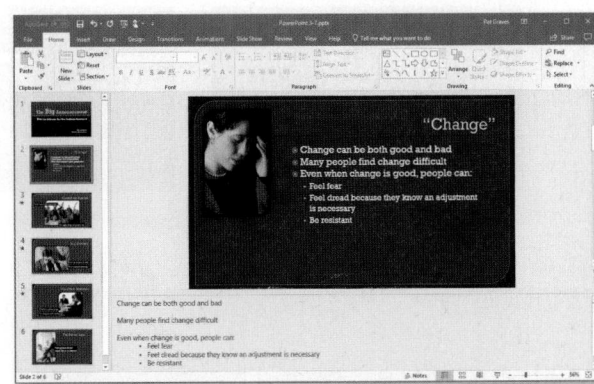

Figure 3-103 *Notes* pane expanded

6. Modify and reposition the bulleted text.
 a. Display slide 2.
 b. Select the text within the bulleted list placeholder and press **Delete**.
 c. Type the following words as three bulleted items:
 - Fear
 - Dread
 - Resistance

d. Confirm that these words appear as first-level bulleted items.
 - If your bullet shows as a small dot, the text is indented for a second-level item.
 - Click the **Decrease Indent** button [*Home* tab, *Paragraph* group] so the items change to first-level with a larger bullet.
 e. Resize the body placeholder to fit the text and move it to the lower right.

7. Insert a *SmartArt* graphic to show that "change" can be perceived as both good and bad.
 a. Insert the **Opposing Arrows** layout from the *Relationship* category.
 b. Type the text Good and Bad.
 c. Apply the **Inset** *SmartArt Style*.
 d. Resize the *SmartArt* graphic and position it as shown (Figure 3-104).

Figure 3-104 Slide 2 revised

8. Animate text boxes on slides 3–5.
 a. Display slide 3. Select the "**Do**" text box.
 b. Apply the **Wipe** animation with the **From Left** effect option.
 c. Repeat this animation for the "**Do**" text boxes on slides 4 and 5.

9. Apply the **Gallery** transition to all slides.

10. Review the presentation and speaker notes using *Presenter View*.

11. Modify the transitions by entering 00:03:00 for *After* seconds and apply the change to all slides.

12. Set up the slide show for a kiosk presentation.

13. Save and close the presentation (Figure 3-105).

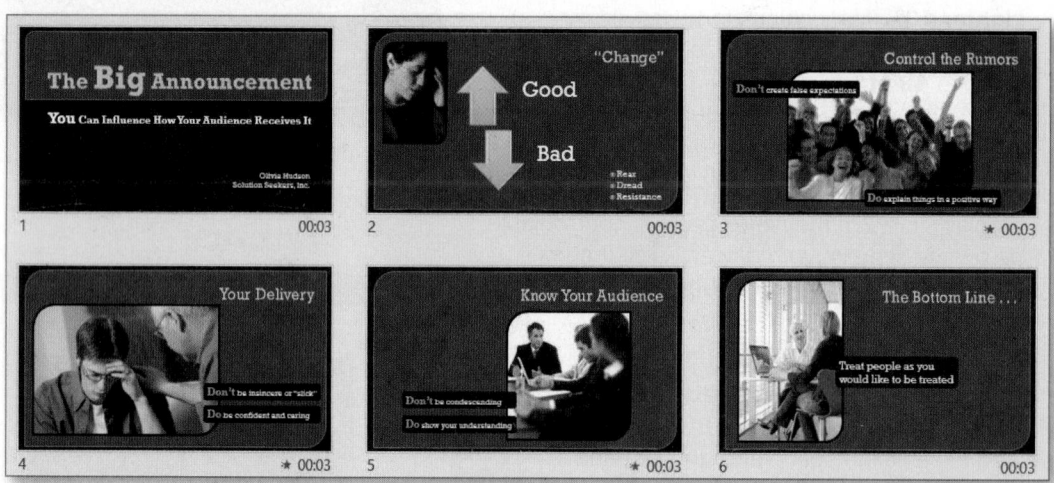

Figure 3-105 PowerPoint 3-7 completed

Challenge Project 3-8

For this project, explain the benefits of tablet computing and factors to consider when purchasing a tablet. Using sources such as www.pcmag.com, list three to four of the top-rated products and their prices. Describe common features, applications, and accessories.
[Student Learning Outcomes 3.1, 3.2, 3.3, 3.4, 3.5, 3.9]

File Needed: None
Completed Project File Name: *[your initials] PowerPoint 3-8.pptx*

Create a new presentation and save it as [your initials] PowerPoint 3-8. Modify your presentation according to the following guidelines:

- Select an appropriate theme and create custom theme colors for a high-tech appearance.
- Change to a widescreen format if necessary.
- Include pictures from www.pcmag.com or other sources and credit the source below each picture.
- Animate approximately three objects for emphasis and apply appropriate effects.
- Rehearse the presentation and save timings.
- Link to an online video and apply a video style.
- Prepare a slide listing your references and include it as the last slide in your presentation.
- Use *Package Presentation for CD* to save the presentation to a folder.

Challenge Project 3-9

Prepare a presentation to promote a student or civic organization. Use pictures and very brief text to convey the purpose of the organization. Consider using an organization chart to illustrate the officer or committee structure. Apply styles and text treatments consistently.
[Student Learning Outcomes 3.1, 3.2, 3.3, 3.4, 3.9]

File Needed: None
Completed Project File Name: *[your initials] PowerPoint 3-9.pptx*

Create a new presentation and save it as [your initials] PowerPoint 3-9. Modify your presentation according to the following guidelines:

- Select an appropriate theme, then prepare custom theme colors for your topic.
- Modify backgrounds by applying a gradient fill to all slides and a picture fill to one slide.
- Design slides with a variety of illustration techniques and minimal text.
- Add transitions and animations with appropriate effects.
- Write notes for three or more slides using the *Notes* pane or *Notes* page.
- Print notes pages.
- Include an online video if one is available and credit your source. Apply a video style.
- Prepare a slide listing your references and include it as the last slide in your presentation.
- Rehearse the presentation and use a variety of navigation techniques.
- Use *Package Presentation for CD* to save your presentation to a folder.

Challenge Project 3-10

Create a presentation about living green. Focus on ways to conserve water and other resources. Use references such as www.mygreenside.org and others. Prepare a slide listing your references and include it as the last slide in your presentation.
[Student Learning Outcomes 3.1, 3.2, 3.3, 3.4, 3.7, 3.8]

File Needed: None
Completed Project File Name: *[your initials] PowerPoint 3-10.pptx*

Create a new presentation and save it as [your initials] PowerPoint 3-10. Modify your presentation according to the following guidelines:

- Select an appropriate theme and prepare custom theme colors that fit a "green" topic.
- Modify backgrounds and use at least one picture fill.
- Design slides with a variety of illustration techniques and minimal text.
- Add transitions and animations with appropriate effects.
- Create and print notes pages.
- Include an online video about "green" living and credit your source.
- Hide one or more slides.
- Rehearse the presentation, use the pen to circle key points, and save timings.
- Modify timings as needed for a kiosk presentation.
- Prepare a kiosk presentation with looping.

Source of screenshots Microsoft Office 365 (2019): Word, Excel, Access, Powerpoint.

appendices

Microsoft Office Shortcuts

Using Function Keys on a Laptop

When using a laptop computer, function keys perform specific Windows actions on your laptop, such as increase or decrease speaker volume, open Windows *Settings*, or adjust the screen brightness. So when using a numbered function key in an Office application, such as **F12** as a shortcut to open the *Save As* dialog box, you may need to press the *function key* (**Fn** or **fn**) on your keyboard in conjunction with a numbered function key to activate the Office command (Figure Appendix A-1). The *function key* is typically located near the bottom left of your laptop keyboard next to the *Ctrl* key.

Appendix A-1
Function key

Common Microsoft Office Keyboard Shortcuts

Action	Keyboard Shortcut
Save	**Ctrl+S**
Copy	**Ctrl+C**
Cut	**Ctrl+X**
Paste	**Ctrl+V**
Select All	**Ctrl+A**
Bold	**Ctrl+B**
Italic	**Ctrl+I**
Underline	**Ctrl+U**
Close *Start* page or *Backstage* view	**Esc**
Open *Help* pane	**F1**
Activate *Tell Me* feature	**Alt+Q**
Switch windows	**Alt+Tab**

Word Keyboard Shortcuts

Action	Keyboard Shortcut
File Management	
Open a new blank Word document	**Ctrl+N**
Save	**Ctrl+S**
Open *Save As* dialog box	**F12**
Open an existing document from the *Backstage* view	**Ctrl+O**
Open an existing document from the *Open* dialog box	**Ctrl+F12**
Close a document	**Ctrl+W**
Editing	
Toggle on/off *Show/Hide*	**Ctrl+Shift+8**

Action	Keyboard Shortcut
Copy	Ctrl+C
Cut	Ctrl+X
Paste	Ctrl+V
Bold	Ctrl+B
Italic	Ctrl+I
Underline	Ctrl+U
Double underline	Ctrl+Shift+D
Small caps	Ctrl+Shift+K
All caps	Ctrl+Shift+A
Left align text	Ctrl+L
Center text	Ctrl+E
Right align text	Ctrl+R
Justify text	Ctrl+J
Single line spacing	Ctrl+1
Double line spacing	Ctrl+2
1.5 line spacing	Ctrl+5
Left Indent	Ctrl+M
Remove Left Indent	Ctrl+Shift+M
Undo	Ctrl+Z
Repeat/redo	Ctrl+Y
Insert line break	Shift+Enter
Insert page break	Ctrl+Enter
Insert column break	Ctrl+Shift+Enter
Insert non-breaking space	Ctrl+Shift+spacebar
Copy formatting	Ctrl+Shift+C
Paste formatting	Ctrl+Shift+V
Increase font size	Ctrl+Shift+. (Ctrl+>)
Decrease font size	Ctrl+Shift+, (Ctrl+<)
Insert an endnote	Alt+Ctrl+D
Insert a footnote	Alt+Ctrl+F
Update field	F9
Open Panes and Dialog Boxes	
Print area on the *Backstage* view	Ctrl+P
Open *Font* dialog box	Ctrl+D
Open *Spelling and Grammar* pane	F7
Open *Thesaurus* pane	Shift+F7

(continued)

Action	Keyboard Shortcut
Open *Navigation* pane	Ctrl+F
Open *Find and Replace* dialog box with the *Replace* tab selected	Ctrl+H
Open *Find and Replace* dialog box with the *Go To* tab selected	Ctrl+G or F5
Open *Insert Hyperlink* dialog box	Ctrl+K
Open Word Help pane	F1
Selection and Navigation	
Select all	Ctrl+A
Turn selection on (continue to press F8 to select word, sentence, paragraph, or document)	F8
Move the insertion point to the beginning of the document	Ctrl+Home
Move the insertion point to the end of the document	Ctrl+End
Move the insertion point to the beginning of a line	Ctrl+left arrow
Move the insertion point to the end of a line	Ctrl+right arrow
Switch window	Alt+Tab

Excel Keyboard Shortcuts

Action	Keyboard Shortcut
File Management	
Open a new blank workbook	Ctrl+N
Open an existing workbook from the *Backstage* view	Ctrl+O
Open an existing workbook from the *Open* dialog box	Ctrl+F12
Close	Ctrl+W
Save	Ctrl+S
Move to cell A1	Ctrl+Home
Next worksheet	Ctrl+Page Down
Previous worksheet	Ctrl+Page Up
Editing	
Cut	Ctrl+X
Copy	Ctrl+C
Paste	Ctrl+V
Undo	Ctrl+Z
Repeat/redo	Ctrl+Y
Underline	Ctrl+U
Bold	Ctrl+B
Italics	Ctrl+I
Open *Format Cells* dialog box	Ctrl+1

Action	Keyboard Shortcut
Edit mode (insertion point appears within the cell)	**F2**
Manual line break in a cell	**Ctrl+Enter**
Toggle between formula view and results view	**Ctrl+~**
Customizing Sheets	
Hide row	**Ctrl+9**
Hide column	**Ctrl+0**
Unhide row	**Ctrl+Shift+(**
Insert dialog box (cell, row, or column)	**Ctrl+plus sign (+)**
Insert worksheet	**Shift+F11**
Insert chart object	**Alt+F1**
Formula Creation	
Open *Insert Function* dialog box	**Shift+F3**
Insert a plus sign	**Shift+=**
Insert a multiplication sign	**Shift+8**
Insert an exponent sign	**Shift+6**
Insert an open parenthesis	**Shift+9**
Insert a closed parenthesis	**Shift+0**
Insert the *SUM* function	**Alt+=**
Absolute symbol toggle	**F4**
Open *Paste Name* dialog box (insert range name)	**F3**

Access Keyboard Shortcuts

Action	Keyboard Shortcut
Database File Management	
Open a new blank database	**Ctrl+N**
Open an existing database	**Ctrl+O**
Editing	
Cut	**Ctrl+X**
Copy	**Ctrl+C**
Paste	**Ctrl+V**
Working with Objects	
Open or close *Navigation Pane*	**F11**
Open selected object in the default view	**Enter**
Open selected object in *Design* view	**Ctrl+Enter**
Save a database object; if first time saving the object, opens the *Save As* dialog box	**Ctrl+S**

(continued)

Action	Keyboard Shortcut
Open the *Save As* dialog box	**F12**
Open shortcut menu for the selected object	**Shift+F10**
Working with Text and Data	
Move to next field in a table, query, or form	**Tab**
Move to preceding cell in a table, query, or form	**Shift+Tab**
Insert line break when entering data in a *Short Text* or *Long Text* field	**Ctrl+Enter**
Undo changes to current field. Undoes all changes if more than one field on current record has been changed.	**ESC**
Switch between *Edit* mode (insertion point displayed) and *Navigation* mode	**F2**
Select current column (works in *Navigation* mode only)	**Ctrl+spacebar**
Increase selection to add adjacent column to the right	**Shift+right arrow**
Increase selection to add adjacent column to the left	**Shift+left arrow**
Open *Find and Replace* dialog box	**Ctrl+F**
Open *Find and Replace* dialog box with the *Replace* tab selected	**Ctrl+H**
Find next	**Shift+F4**
Working in Design View	
Open *Expression Builder* dialog box	**Ctrl+F2**
Open *Zoom* window	**Shift+F2**
Open or close the *Properties* window for the selected control	**F4**
Show or hide *Field* list	**Alt+F8**
Switch to *Form* view from *Design* view	**F5**
Print Preview Shortcuts	
Open *Page Setup* dialog box from *Print Preview* view	**S**
Open *Print* dialog box from *Print Preview* view	**P** or **Ctrl+P**

PowerPoint Keyboard Shortcuts

Action	Keyboard Shortcut
File Management	
Open a new blank presentation	**Ctrl+N**
Open an existing presentation from the *Backstage* view	**Ctrl+O**
Open an existing presentation from the *Open* dialog box	**Ctrl+F12**
Open *Save As* dialog box	**F12**
Save	**Ctrl+S**
Editing	
Cut	**Ctrl+X**

Action	Keyboard Shortcut
Copy	**Ctrl+C**
Paste	**Ctrl+V**
Duplicate slides	**Ctrl+D**
Undo	**Ctrl+Z**
Redo	**Ctrl+Y**
Soft return, causes text to word wrap to the next line	**Shift+Enter**
Slide Movement in Normal View	
Move to first slide	**Home**
Move to last slide	**End**
Move to next slide	**Page Down** or **down arrow**
Move to previous slide	**Page Up** or **up arrow**
Move from the slide title to the body placeholder	**Ctrl+Enter**
Slide Movement in Slide Show View	
Start a presentation slide show from the beginning	**F5**
Open *Presenter View* and start a slide show	**Alt+F5**
Advance to the next slide	**N, spacebar, right arrow, down arrow, Enter,** or **Page Down**
Go to the previous slide	**P, Backspace, left arrow, up arrow,** or **Page Up**
Go to a particular slide	Slide number, **Enter**
Go to a particular slide by opening *All Slides* dialog box and selecting a slide title	**Ctrl+S**
Go to a hidden slide	Slide number, **Enter** or **H** if the next slide is hidden
Blanks the screen to black	**B** or period
Blanks the screen to white	**W** or **comma**
Zoom in	**Plus sign**
Zoom out	**Minus sign**
Stop or restart an automatic show	**S**
Ink Markup in Slide Show View	
Change pointer to pen	**Ctrl+P**
Change pointer to arrow	**Ctrl+A**
Change pointer to eraser	**Ctrl+E**
Show or hide ink markup	**Ctrl+M**
Erase markings on the screen	**E**

glossary

3D cell reference A cell address in another worksheet in the same workbook.

3D Model A three-dimensional image that can be rotated on its center axis to display the image at different angles.

3D Rotation Style effect option that includes parallel, perspective, and oblique options to create an illusion of depth.

.docx The file format of a Word document.

A

absolute cell reference A cell address with dollar signs such as B2.

Action Center A menu that displays on the right side of the Windows desktop and lists notifications, such as new email, upcoming calendar items, and software updates and notifications. The *Action Center* also contains buttons at the bottom of the menu to quickly access other Windows commands, such as *All settings, Tablet mode,* and *Airplane mode.* Click the *Action Center* button on the *Taskbar* to display the *Action Center* menu.

active cell Cell that is ready for editing, surrounded with a solid border.

adjustment handle Yellow circle used to change shape curves or points.

Advanced Filter Filter process that uses a criteria range and an optional output range.

aggregate function Function that performs calculations on a group of records such as *Avg, COUNT,* and *SUM.*

alignment Vertical and horizontal position of text, data, and objects.

All apps An area of the *Start* menu in Windows 10 that displays all app (applications) on the computer.

All Markup view The *Display for Review* view that displays all tracked changes and comments in a document.

Allow Additions property Form property that controls whether the form allows users to enter data into the database.

Allow Deletions property Form property that controls whether the form allows users to delete a record from the database.

Allow Edits property Form property that controls whether the form allows users to change data in the database.

alternate row colors Formatting option to define alternating colors for adjacent rows.

alternative text (alt text) Information about a picture or other object to make content more accessible to individuals with special needs or impairments.

AND logical operator Operator that requires that a record meet all of the individual conditions to be included in the results.

animation Movement of objects on a slide.

app Short for application; software program or Windows application or accessory.

append row Last row in a table, indicated by an asterisk; enter data values into the fields in the append row to add a new record into the table.

Application Parts Pre-built database parts that can be added into an existing database.

argument Cell reference, value, or other element required for a function.

array Range of cells in a row or a column.

Arrows Line style that provides arrowheads or other shapes for both ends of a line.

ascending order Sort order that arranges data from lowest to highest for a numeric field or from A to Z for a text field.

aspect ratio The ratio of width to height; affects slide, picture, and other object sizing.

attribute Setting or property for a cell.

Auto Outline Excel summary sheet that inserts groups based on formula locations.

AutoCalculate Status bar area that displays calculations for selected cells.

AutoComplete Feature that fills in the complete day, month, or date as you type or suggests an entry for a cell.

AutoComplete tag The notation that displays and predicts what will be typed, such as a day, month, or date. When the tag appears, press *Enter* to automatically insert the text.

AutoCorrect Feature that automatically corrects commonly misspelled words.

AutoCorrect Options smart tag Tag that appears by a word that has been automatically corrected.

AutoFilter Arrow in a header row used for sorting or filtering data.

AutoFit Formatting option that automatically adjusts column width or row height to reveal all the contents within a column or row; also referred to as *AutoFit Column Width.*

AutoFormat Feature that controls the formatting of items such as numbered and bulleted lists, fractions, ordinal numbers, hyphens and dashes, quotes, indents, and hyperlinks.

AutoNumber data type Data type used to store a unique number, automatically assigned by Access.

AutoSave Automatically saves a file stored on *OneDrive.*

Axis Horizontal or vertical boundary of plotted data in a chart.

axis title Text label for categories or values in a chart.

B

Background Style Option that changes slide background and text colors to light or dark variations.

Backstage view Area of an Office application where you perform common actions (such as *Save, Open, Print,* and *Share)* and change application options; document properties are displayed here.

balloon The object where comments display.

bar tab stop Tab that inserts a vertical line at the tab stop.

Bevel Style effect option that applies light and dark areas to create a dimensional appearance so objects and text look raised or inset.

bibliography List of the sources used in a report.

bibliography style Style that determines the formatting of sources and citations in a report.

Blank desktop database Command used to create a new database from scratch.

block format letter All parts of the letter begin at the left margin. No lines are indented or centered. Block format can be used on either business or personal business letters.

block layout Report layout option available when grouping records that displays the fields in a row and column format with the field names displayed as column heads; the grouped field displays in the left-most column but on the same row as the first record for the grouping.

bookmark Location in a document that is electronically marked and can be linked to a hyperlink or cross-reference.

border Line around text, paragraph, page, cell, table, or graphic object.

bound control Control that gets its value from a field in a table.

bound form Form that is directly connected to a table or query as the data source.

bulleted list Unordered list of items; a bullet symbol precedes each item, and a left and hanging indent controls left alignment.

business intelligence Tools, applications, and processes used to analyze data.

button Used to apply a command or open a dialog box in Office applications.

Button control Control on a form or report that performs an action when clicked; also knows as a *Command Button* control.

C

calculated control Control that gets its value from an expression.

calculated field Field that gets its value from a calculation instead of a value that is entered into the field.

caption Descriptive text that appears above or below a graphic.

caption property Field property used to create a caption that displays in the column header in datasheet view of a table and in the labels on forms and reports; captions often include spaces and multiple words and are more readable than a field name.

Cap type Line option that controls the look of the ends of lines; usually applied to single lines or arrows.

Cascade Delete Related Records Referential integrity option that allows you to delete a record from a table even if there are matching records in related tables; also deletes all matching records from related tables.

Cascade Update Related Fields Referential integrity option that allows a primary key value to be changed in a record in one table and automatically updates the foreign key values in matching records in related tables.

case Typographic term for capitalization; small letters are lowercase and capital letters are uppercase.

category axis (X-axis) Describes data shown in a chart; the horizontal axis in a column chart and the vertical axis in a bar chart.

category label Text label that describes a data series in a chart.

cell Intersection of a column and a row.

cell address Column letter and row number that identifies the location of a cell or range; also referred to as cell reference.

cell style Set of formatting elements for data in a cell.

center tab stop Tab that centers text at the tab stop.

Change Case Button used to change text from the case shown to a different case such as uppercase to lowercase.

Change Colors Gallery that displays different color combinations for *SmartArt* layouts that are based on theme colors.

character spacing Space between letters and words.

chart A visual representation of numeric worksheet data.

chart area Background rectangle area for a chart.

chart element Separate, selectable, editable object or part in a chart.

chart floor Area at the bottom of a 3D chart.

chart layout Set of chart elements and their locations.

chart object Selectable chart with clickable elements located on the worksheet.

chart sheet Chart displayed in its own tab or sheet in a workbook.

chart style Combination of colors and effects for a chart and its elements.

chart title Name or main label for a chart.

chart wall Vertical background for a 3D chart.

check box Box that allows you to choose one or more from a group of options.

Check Box control Control on a form or report used to display data for a field with a *Yes/No* data type; when used on a form, it can also accept data when a user enters a value.

circular reference Formula error in which the formula refers to the cell in which it is located.

citation Abbreviated source information in the body of the report that credits the source of information referred to in a document.

Clear Formatting Command that removes formatting from selected text and formats the text in *Normal* style.

Clipboard Location where multiple copied items from an Office file or other source such as a web page are stored.

Clipboard pane Pane that displays the contents of the *Clipboard*.

Color Saturation Option that controls the intensity of the colors in a picture; colors that are vibrant are highly saturated and colors that are muted have a low saturation level.

Color Tone Option that controls temperature values to make a picture's colors more cool or warm.

Colorful Chart option that provides varied colors for *Chart and SmartArt Styles*.

column break Formatting option that ends a column and pushes subsequent text to the next column.

Column chart Chart type that shows a comparison of values or data changes over time.

columnar layout Form or report layout that displays the fields in one column with the field names displayed to the left of the field.

Combo chart Chart type that combines two charts such as a column chart with a line chart.

comments Notations attached to text used to provide feedback or notes when reviewing a file.

Command Button control Control on a form or report used to perform an action such as *Close Report* or *Open Form*.

Command Button Wizard Tool that guides you through the steps of creating a command button control and assigning an action to the button.

Compact & Repair Database Database utility that removes unused space from a database to help improve performance; can be used to repair a database in which some objects have become corrupted.

completeness rule Data integrity rule that ensures a value is entered if required.

compound criteria Criteria used in filters or expressions that combine more than one value using the *AND* and *OR* logical operators.

Compound type Line option that provides outlines with two or more lines that vary in thickness.

Compress Pictures Command that reduces presentation file size by reducing picture resolution.

concatenated key Primary key made up of more than one field; also known as a composite key.

concatenation Combine multiple parts of an equation together into one piece; often used in an expression to combine several fields together.

conditional formatting Format settings that are applied based on rules, rankings, or other criteria.

connection Identifier and a link to external data in a workbook.

consistency rule Data integrity rule that ensures a value in one field is consistent with a value in another field.

constant A value used in a formula.

content control field Word field in which you type custom information such as the date or year.

context menu Menu of commands that appears when you right-click text or an object.

context-sensitive Describes menu options that change depending on what you have selected.

contextual tabs Ribbon tabs that become available when working on different tasks.

continuous section break Formatting option that divides a document into different sections on the same page so sections can be formatted independently of each other; can also be used at the end of columns to balance column length.

control Item on a form or report such as a text box, label, or command button; used to enter, edit, or display data, or perform tasks in the database.

control layout Structure that helps to align the different controls on a form or report.

Control Wizards Tool that directs Access to launch an available wizard when adding controls to an object in the database; for example, the *Control Wizards* tool must be turned on for the *Command Button Wizard* to activate.

Copy Duplicate text or other information.

Cortana The help feature in Windows 10 that responds to both keyboard and voice commands. *Cortana* searches not only the computer but also the Internet and displays search results in the *Cortana* menu.

criteria range Two or more rows of data used to specify advanced filter conditions.

criterion (pl. criteria) Expression entered into a query to limit and focus results or a function argument that sets a condition.

crop Trim unwanted areas of a selected picture.

cropping handles Black handles that appear on the corners and sides of pictures that you can drag to remove part of the picture.

crosshair Plus sign pointer used to draw a shape.

cross-reference Note in a document that directs readers to another location in a document.

custom dictionary Location in Office where words that you add are stored.

Cut Remove text or other information.

Cycle *SmartArt* layout type used to illustrate a continuing sequence or concepts related to a central idea.

D

Dash Type Line option that displays lines made with various combinations of dots and dashes.

Dashes Line styles that combine dots and dashes to make different patterns.

Data Entry property Form property that determines whether existing data in the database are displayed on the form.

data format rule Data integrity rule that ensures a value entered into a field matches the data type of the field.

data integrity rules A set of rules that ensures data in a database are accurate and consistent.

data label Object that displays a value for each data marker in a chart.

data marker Bar, column, slice, or other object used to graph a value in a chart.

data point A single value graphed in a chart represented by a cell.

data series A group of related values graphed by columns, bars, slices, or other objects in a chart.

data table Columnar display of values for each data series in a chart located below the chart.

data type Field property that determines the type of data that can be entered in a field, what properties can be manipulated, and how that field can be used.

data visualization Formatting that uses colored bars, color variations, or icons based on rules or rankings.

database An organized collection of integrated and related tables.

database management system (DBMS) Software that allows a user to create a database; manage the data in the database by adding, deleting, and updating records; sort and retrieve data; and create queries and reports relating to that data.

Database Properties Details and information about the database.

datasheet layout Form layout that displays the fields in *Datasheet* view.

Datasheet view View option that allows you to enter, modify, view, or delete data; available in a table, query, or form.

Date function Function that obtains the current date from your computer.

decimal tab stop Tab that aligns text at the decimal point at the tab stop.

default Setting that is automatically applied by an application unless you make specific changes.

Default Value property Field property that sets a value to automatically be entered into a field.

Delay Animation timing command used to make an animation begin at a specified time.

delimited File that separates data into columns with a special character.

delimiter Character used to separate columns.

dependent Cell that is affected by the active cell.

descending order Sort order that arranges data from highest to lowest for a numeric field or from Z to A for a text field.

Design view View option that allows you to build or modify the basic structure or functionality of a database object.

destination cell Cell location for pasted data.

dialog box Window that opens and displays additional features.

Different First Page Formatting option that displays first-page header or footer content that differs from the other headers and footers in a document.

Different Odd & Even Pages Formatting option that displays headers and/or footers that differ on odd and even pages.

dimension Number of row and columns in an array.

Display for Review The drop-down list used to select how tracked changes display.

Distribute Columns Table option that evenly distributes column width.

Distribute Rows Table option that evenly distributes row height.

document properties Information recorded in a file such as title, author name, subject, creation date, etc.

document property field Word field that displays the document property contents in the body, header, or footer of a document.

drag and drop A method to copy or move selected text or an object.

drop-down list List of options that displays when you click a button.

duplicate Create a copy of an object or a slide.

duplicate row Record in a table with the same content as another record in one or more columns.

Duration Length of time; controls the speed of transitions and animations in a slide show.

dynamic Describes results that adjust in real time to data changes.

E

Edit link A hyperlink used when sharing a file with others that allows users to edit the shared file.

Editor Pane Displays at the right side of a Word document when using the *Spelling & Grammar* feature.

Effect Formatting feature such as shadow, glow, or soft edges added to *WordArt*, shapes, or pictures.

Effect Option Command that controls the direction of slide transitions and animation movement.

embedded TrueType fonts Embedded TrueType fonts Option that saves presentation fonts for display on a different computer.

Emphasis Animation effect that calls attention to an object that remains on the slide.

endnote Reference, citation, or other text that appears at the end of a document.

Entrance Animation effect that occurs when an object appears on the slide.

Error Bar Chart element that shows margin of error or standard deviation amounts.

Excel Start page Opening screen when Excel is started.

Excel table Excel data formatted with a header row followed by data rows.

Exit Animation effect that occurs when an object leaves the slide.

expression Type of formula used to write validation rules, perform calculations, create query criteria, control macros, and group and sort data in a report.

Expression Builder dialog box Window that provides easy access to tools used to create expressions.

exporting Saving or copying data for use in another program or application.

external data Data that originated in another program or format.

extract Create a regular folder from a zipped folder.

extract range One row of labels for results of an advanced filter.

Eyedropper Feature in PowerPoint used to match colors.

F

field Collection of characters that describes one aspect of a business object or activity (a single unit of data) or one column of data.

field handle Area to select a document property of content control field.

field name Label in a header row.

field properties Description of the specific details of each field in a table; basic field properties include the *Field Name, Data Type, and Field Size.*

field width Side-to-side measurement of a column; controls how much content displays in a field.

File Explorer Window where you browse for, open, and manage files and folders (formerly called Windows Explorer).

file name extension A series of letters automatically added to a file name that identifies the type of file.

fill Color or pattern used as a background.

Fill Handle Small black square at lower-right corner of a cell or range used to complete a series or copy data.

Filter Feature that limits the data records that display in a datasheet. In Excel, a requirement or condition that identifies data to be shown or hidden.

Filter by Selection Filter option that displays only the records that match the value in specific fields you have selected.

Find Feature that searches a file to locate specific text and/or formatting.

first line indent Horizontal space between the first line of a paragraph and the left margin.

fixed width Specific number of characters assigned to a field or column.

Flash Fill Excel feature that completes column data based on the first entry.

folder A Windows feature used to store and organize files in a specific location.

font Named design of type for characters, punctuation, and symbols.

font color The color applied to selected text.

font face Specifies the shape of text.

font size Specifies the size of text.

font style Formatting applied to create bold, italics, or underlined text.

footer Displays content at the bottom of a document page, slide, or object.

footnote Reference, citation, or other text that appears at the bottom of a page.

foreign key Field in one table that is also the primary key in another table; used to create relationships between tables.

form Database object used to enter, modify, view, or delete data from a table.

Form button Tool that allows you to quickly create a form; no options are provided during the initial creation process.

Form view View option used to enter and view data.

Form Wizard Tool that guides you through the steps to create a form.

Format Painter Command that copies formatting from selected text, cells, shapes, or pictures, and applies these changes to another selection.

Format property Property that indicates the way a field displays in a table.

formula A calculation in a cell that displays a result.

formula auditing Process of reviewing formulas for accuracy.

Formula AutoComplete Feature that displays a list of function and range names after a character is typed.

Formula bar Bar below the Ribbon that displays active cell contents.

function A built-in formula.

function keys The numbered command keys (i.e., F1, F2, etc.) located near the top of the keyboard. Function keys can perform both Windows and Office application commands. Some laptops require the user to press the *function key (Fn or fn)* on the keyboard in conjunction with a numbered function key to activate an Office command.

G

gallery Group of options on a tab.

Glow Style effect option that provides a colored area around an object that fades into the background color.

Go To The feature that moves the insertion point to a specific location in a file, such as a page, bookmark, footnote, comment, or heading level.

Gradient Option that blends two or more colors or light and dark variations of the current fill color in different directions.

graphics Visual objects such as pictures, clip art, shapes, *SmartArt*, charts, and *WordArt*.

grayscale A range of shades of black in a display or printout.

Gridlines Lines that visually frame rows and columns; in Excel and PowerPoint, lines that appear behind chart elements such as columns or bars or that can be displayed on a slide as an aid to alignment.

group Area on a tab that contains related commands and options; option used to organize data in a report so that similar records appear together; a feature used to combine selected objects.

H

Handout Feature that prints 1 to 9 slides on a page.

hanging indent Additional horizontal space between second and carryover lines of a paragraph and the left margin.

header Displays content at the top of a document, slide handout, or object.

Header Row First row of a table.

hidden worksheet Worksheet whose tab is not visible.

Hierarchy SmartArt layout type used to illustrate a decision tree or top-to-bottom relationship such as an organization chart.

hierarchy of data Organization of data in a database or worksheet from the smallest to largest grouping of data.

Highlighter Highlighter Tool used to write or draw on a slide in Slide Show view.

Histogram chart Chart type that shows the distribution of data grouped by frequencies.

horizontal alignment Content positioning option that aligns material in relation to the left, center, right, or middle (justified) of the page or slide; can also refer to the position of objects in relation to each other.

hyperlink Text or an object that a reader can click to be taken to another location in the document, to a web page, or to a different file.

I

Icon Scalable Vector Graphic image that can resize or rotate with no loss of image quality.

import Transfer data from an application or browser into an application; the process of getting data from an outside source.

indent Increase the distance between the cell contents and the left boundary of the cell.

ink annotations Markings that call attention to information you mark by writing or drawing on slides.

Ink Comments Users write comments using a stylus or their finger on a touch-screen computer.

Input Mask property Property used to specify the format for data entered into a field.

Input Mask Wizard Tool that guides you through the steps to define an input mask; only available on *Short Text* or *Date* fields.

insert control Button that allows you to quickly insert a row or column into a table.

IntelliSense Tool that suggests a list of possible values when you enter an expression.

J

Join type Line option that controls the look of the connection point where two lines meet, such as the corner of a rectangle.

junction table Table created to link the two tables in a many-to-many relationship; also known as an intersection table.

justified alignment Content positioning option that aligns material with both the left and right margins.

justified layout Form or report layout option that displays the fields in a horizontal, justified layout with field names displayed above each field.

K

Kerning Space between letters in a proportional font.

keyboard shortcut Key or combination of keys that you press to apply a command.

kiosk presentation Self-running slide presentation that automatically loops.

L

label Text data in a worksheet that are not used in calculations.

Label control Control on a form or report that displays the content of the caption property of a field.

Landscape orientation Page layout option in which the page is oriented so it is wider than it is tall.

laser pointer *Slide Show* feature that displays a small dot on the screen during a presentation; also available on remote control devices.

launcher (dialog box launcher) A small square in the bottom-right corner of some groups on the *Ribbon.* When a launcher is clicked, a dialog box with more options opens.

Layout Controls the position of placeholders on a slide.

Layout view Form or report view option used to make design changes to the object and see the effects of the changes in real time.

leader Series of dots or characters that fills the blank space between text and a tab stop.

Learning Tools An immersive editing environment that adjusts how text displays on the screen. The *Read Aloud* feature is also available on the *Immersive Learning Tools* tab.

left indent Horizontal space between a paragraph and the left margin.

left tab stop Tab that aligns text at the left of the tab stop.

legend Chart element that describes colors, symbols, or textures used in a chart.

line break Formatting option that controls where lines begin and end, which can be used to keep lines together in a bulleted or numbered list or to start a new line within a cell.

line spacing Amount of space between lines of text within a paragraph.

List SmartArt layout type used to illustrate non-sequential or grouped information in a graphical list.

live preview Display option that allows you to temporarily apply and view a style or formatting feature.

Lock Aspect Ratio Command used to maintain proportion when entering object height or width sizes.

Lock Drawing Mode Feature used to draw more than one of the same shape.

Long Text data type Data type used to store alphanumeric data longer than 255 characters or text containing rich text formatting.

lookup field Field used to display a list of data values that users can select to store in the field.

loop Cycle continuously in a slide show from beginning to end and automatically repeat.

M

macro Database object used to attach code to objects and controls in a database.

many-to-many relationship Relationship between tables in a database where many rows of data in one table can be associated with many rows of data in a related table.

margin Blank space at the top, bottom, left, or right of a document; in a text box, the space between the outside of the box and the text within the box; in a table, the space between a cell border and the cell text.

marker Data point in a sparkline.

Markup area The area at the right side of a Word document that displays comments and certain tracked changes.

Master Views Group of commands that are used to make global changes to a presentation: *Slide Master, Handout Master,* and *Notes Master.*

mathematical order of operations Sequence of arithmetic operations in a formula.

Matrix SmartArt layout type used to illustrate the relationship of four parts to the whole.

maximize Increase the size of the window of an open Office file so it fills the entire computer monitor.

mean Value determined by adding all values in a range and dividing by the number of values.

Merge Cells Command that combines two or more cells in a row or column.

metadata Document properties stored with the file.

Microsoft Access The database software in the Microsoft Office suite of applications.

Microsoft account Free account that gives you access to an email account, *OneDrive* online storage area, and Office Web Apps.

Microsoft Excel The spreadsheet software in the Microsoft Office suite of applications.

Microsoft Office 2019 The suite of Microsoft productivity software that typically includes Microsoft Word, Excel, Access, PowerPoint, OneNote, and Outlook.

Microsoft Office 365 The subscription version of Microsoft Office where users pay a monthly or yearly fee to install and use the Microsoft Office applications on a computer.

Microsoft OneNote The note-taking software in the Microsoft Office suite of applications.

Microsoft Outlook The personal information management software in the Microsoft Office suite of applications that includes email, calendar, contacts, and tasks.

Microsoft PowerPoint The presentation software in the Microsoft Office suite of applications.

Microsoft Publisher The desktop publishing software in the Microsoft Office suite of applications.

Microsoft Store The online store where users can purchase and download a variety of apps (applications).

Microsoft Word The word processing software in the Microsoft Office suite of applications.

mini toolbar Toolbar with a list of formatting options that appears when you select text or right-click.

minimize Place an open Office file on the taskbar so it is not displayed on the desktop.

mixed cell reference A cell address with one dollar sign such as $B2 or B$2.

mixed punctuation Use a colon after the salutation (e.g., "Dear Ms. Vasquez:") and a comma after the complimentary close (e.g., "Best regards,"). Mixed or open punctuation can be used on either business or personal business letters.

modified block format letter Type the date line and closing lines [complimentary close, writer's name, writer's title, and return address (on personal business letters)] beginning at the horizontal midpoint. Typically, set a left tab stop at 3.25". Modified block format can be used on either business or personal business letters.

Monochromatic Color combinations containing only shades of one color; color option for Chart Styles.

multilevel list Customized list that includes a combination of numbers, letters, or bullets.

N

Name box Area in the Formula bar that displays the cell address of the active cell.

Navigation bar Area at the bottom-left corner of a table that contains buttons used to move among table records in *Datasheet* view.

Navigation menu Contains category and group settings that control the display of objects in the *Navigation Pane*.

Navigation Pane (Access) Displays all objects contained in a database.

Navigation pane (Windows File Explorer) The area on the left side of a *File Explorer* window that displays the different storage areas of the computer.

Navigation pane (Word) The pane at the left side of the Word window when the Find command is selected. The *Navigation* pane displays headings, pages, and search results.

No Markup view The *Display for Review* view that displays the final document with changes applied.

non-breaking space Formatting option that keeps words together so they are not separated by word wrap at the end of a line.

Normal template Predesigned and ready-to-use document that includes default fonts, font sizes, line and paragraph spacing, styles, and margins; new blank document.

Normal View Default view option where you enter the content of slides and move between slides as you develop them or where you create and modify a worksheet.

Notes Page View Option that displays each slide on a page with space below the slide where you can type speaker notes.

null Value in a field that indicates that nothing was ever entered in that field.

Number data type Data type used to store numbers in fields that are used in mathematical calculations.

numbered list List that arranges items in order; a number or letter precedes each item, and a left and hanging indent controls left alignment.

NumPages field Word field that lists the number of pages in a document.

O

object Major component in an Access database.

Office Clipboard Storage location for cut or copied data shared by all Office applications.

Office desktop apps The version of Microsoft Office that users download and install on a PC or Apple computer.

Office intelligent services Microsoft cloud services that provide design ideas, data analysis, editor suggestions, or search results.

Office Online The online version of Microsoft Office that is available through a web browser.

Office universal apps The version of Microsoft Office that users download and install on tablets or mobile phone devices.

OneDrive Online storage area that is a part of your Microsoft account where you can store and access documents from any computer with an Internet connection.

OneDrive folder An online storage location connected to a user's Microsoft Account that displays in the *File Explorer* window.

one-to-many relationship Relationship between tables in a database where a row of data in one table can be associated with many rows of data in a related table.

one-to-one relationship Relationship between tables in a database where a row of data in one table can be associated with only one row of data in a related table.

Online Video An image is inserted into a document or presentation that links to an online video and can be played from within an Office application.

open punctuation Punctuation after the salutation and complimentary close are omitted. Mixed or open punctuation can be used on either business or personal business letters.

operating system Software that makes a computer function and controls the working environment.

OR logical operator Operator that requires that a record meet at least one individual condition to be included in the results.

Original view The *Display for Review* view that displays the original document with none of the tracked changes applied.

outdent Negative indent that lines up information outside the left or right margins.

outline Border around selected element.

outline layout A report layout available when grouping records. Displays the grouped field and its label on a separate row at the start of each grouping. The field names are displayed as column heads above the first row of data in each grouping.

Outline view Option that expands the pane at the left of the slide area to show slide titles and bulleted text.

P

Package Presentation for CD Feature that saves a presentation and related files to a CD or a folder.

page borders A border that applies to an entire page rather than selected text or a paragraph.

page break Formatting option that controls where text on a page ends.

Page Break Preview Worksheet view that shows printed pages with dashed or dotted lines to mark where new pages start.

Page Layout Worksheet view that opens header and footer areas, indicates margin areas, and shows rulers.

page number field Word field that lists the page number.

page orientation The direction of the page. The two different orientation options are *Portrait* and *Landscape*.

paragraph alignment Formatting option that determines how a paragraph is positioned horizontally on the page.

paragraph break Formatting option that you insert when you press **Enter** at the end of a word, line, or paragraph.

paragraph spacing Amount of spacing before and after a paragraph.

paragraph symbol Icon that indicates a paragraph break.

parameter Specific phrase (entered in the *criteria* box of a query field) that displays in the *Enter Parameter Value* dialog box when a parameter query is run.

parameter query Query that asks a user to enter a specific criterion value.

Paste Place text or other objects that have been stored on the *Clipboard* in a new location.

Paste Options Gallery of choices for how data are copied.

Pattern Background color Color used with a foreground color to create a pattern.

Pattern Fill Shape Fill option that applies a mixture of two colors in various dotted or crosshatch designs.

Pattern Foreground color Color used with a background color to create a pattern.

PDF (portable document format) File format used to convert a file into a static image.

Pen Tool used to write or draw on a slide in Slide Show view; also used in Normal view to draw tables and edit border lines.

Picture SmartArt layout type used to show pictures as integral parts of many different diagrams.

Picture Effects Command used to apply effect options, such as *Shadow* or *Glow*, to pictures.

Picture Fill Shape Fill option that fills the *WordArt* or shape with a picture from a file or from the Office.com clip art collection.

PivotChart Summary chart built from a PivotTable or a range of data.

PivotTable Summary report for a range of data with interactive field and filter buttons.

pixel Abbreviated term for picture element, a single unit of information about color.

placeholder In PowerPoint, the area of a slide where you can add text, tables, charts, and pictures. In Word, text that temporarily marks a spot in a document where a citation is missing and needs to be completed.

plot area Chart element bounded by the horizontal and vertical axes.

points Font measurement of 1/72 of an inch.

Portrait orientation Page layout option in which the page is oriented so it is taller than it is wide.

Position A character-spacing option that raises or lowers text by a designated number of points.

PowerPoint Designer Provides a variety of slide layouts for listed text, pictures, and other graphics.

precedent Cell that contributes to a formula's result.

Presenter View Option that displays slides and features helpful for a speaker; can be displayed on one monitor or with a second monitor or projector that shows the presentation at full-screen size.

primary key Field that contains a unique value for each record in a table; allows one record to be distinguished from another.

print area Defined range of cells that prints.

Print Preview Print option that allows you to see how a document, spreadsheet, or database object will look when printed and lets you make changes to the printing options before printing.

Print Settings Options to control what and how printing occurs.

print title Row or column that prints on each page.

Process SmartArt layout type used to illustrate sequential steps in a process or workflow.

product Result of a multiplication formula.

program options Area in each Office application where you can make changes to the program settings.

Protected View Status of a workbook opened or copied from an Internet source.

Pyramid SmartArt layout type used to illustrate proportional or interconnected relationships.

Q

query Database object used to find data in a database. In Excel, a query is a set of definitions and filters that establishes a data connection.

Quick access (Windows File Explorer) The area at the top of the *Navigation* pane in a *File Explorer* window that displays folders or locations on a computer so users can quickly access these items. Users can pin folders or locations on a computer to the *Quick access* area of a File Explorer window.

Quick Access toolbar Area located above the *Ribbon* with buttons you use to perform commonly used commands.

Quick Analysis Tool that displays for a selected cell range with suggested command groups.

R

radio button Round button you click to choose one option from a list.

range Rectangular group of cells such as A1:B3.

Range Finder Feature that highlights and color-codes a formula cell range in Edit mode.

range name Label assigned to a single or a group of cells.

range rule Data integrity rule that ensures a value in a field falls within an established range of acceptable values.

Read Aloud The Word feature that reads text out loud and highlights each word as it is read.

Reading View Option that displays a slide show at full-screen or an alternate window size determined by the viewer.

Real-time collaboration The Word feature that allows multiple users to simultaneously edit a shared filed stored in an online location, such as *OneDrive*.

Recolor Option that changes picture colors to different monotone color variations.

record Collection of related data fields; one row of data.

record validation rule Validation rule that compares fields in the same table; entered into the *Validation Rule* property of a table.

Recycle Bin Location where deleted files and folders are stored.

Redo Repeat an action.

reference marker Number, letter, or symbol that marks a footnote or endnote in the body of a document.

referential integrity The quality of consistency in data entered into related tables; enforcing referential integrity prevents a record in one table from referencing a record that does not exist in a related table.

Reflection Style effect option that shows a mirror image below an object.

Rehearse Timings Feature that helps you to judge the pace of the presentation.

relational database Database in which data are organized into a collection of related tables.

Relationship SmartArt layout type used to illustrate concepts that are connected, such as contrasting, opposing, or converging.

Relationships window (Access) Used to create, edit, and view the table relationship in a database.

relative cell reference A cell address such as B2.

remote control Device that enables a speaker to control a slide show when he or she steps away from the computer during a presentation.

Reorder Animation Animation timing command used to adjust an animation sequence.

Repeat The command to automatically repeat the previous command used.

Replace Feature that searches a file to locate specific text and/or formatting and replace it with specified replacement text and/or formatting.

report Database object used to view and print data in a database.

Report view Report view option that shows all of the data contained in the report; displays in a continuous layout, which does not separate the data into separate pages.

Report Wizard Tool that guides you through the steps to create a report.

Required property Field property that indicates whether a value must be entered into a field or if it can be skipped and left blank.

Researcher Search for quotes, citable sources, and images about a topic that displays information from journals and web sites in the *Researcher* pane.

Reset Picture Command used to restore a picture's original characteristics and dimensions.

resize pointer Pointer used to change the size of a graphic object or a table column or row.

Resolve comment Marks a comment as resolved and replaces *Mark as Complete* on previous versions of Word.

restore down Decrease the size of the window of an open Office file so it does not fill the entire computer monitor.

Resume Assistant Connects with LinkedIn and provides assistance in Word when working on a resume.

Reviewing pane The pane at the left or bottom of the document that displays tracked changes and comments.

RGB model Typically used for computer displays; colors are formed by blending values for Red, Green, and Blue.

Ribbon Bar that appears at the top of an Office file window and displays available commands.

Ribbon Display Options A button in the upper-right corner of an Office application window that controls how the *Ribbon* displays. The options include *Auto-hide Ribbon*, *Show Tabs*, and *Show Tabs and Commands*.

right indent Horizontal space between a paragraph and the right margin.

right tab stop Tab that aligns text at the right of the tab stop.

rotation handle A circular arrow used to turn an object in different directions.

row Horizontal grouping of cells.

row height Top to bottom measurement of a row.

row selector Pointer that selects a row of a table.

row selector (Access) Box at the left of a table row. When checked, it selects that row. Also called a record selector.

ruler Vertical or horizontal guide that displays measurements within the margins of a document.

S

sans serif font One of several font typefaces with letters that do not include structural details (flair).

Save a Copy Option to save a file as a different file name when the file is saved on *OneDrive*.

Scale Character-spacing option that changes spacing by a designated percentage.

scope A worksheet set as the location for a range name.

ScreenTip Descriptive information about a button, dropdown list, launcher, or gallery selection that appears when you place your pointer on the item.

Search Feature that allows you to look for specific data values.

section break Formatting option used to break a document into different sections so sections can be formatted independently of each other.

select method Technique of selecting cell addresses to create a formula.

select query Query that locates, or selects, data in a database.

selection handle Four-pointed arrow that selects and moves objects.

serial number Value assigned to a date.

series List of labels or values that follow a pattern.

serif font One of several font typefaces with letters that feature structural details (flair).

Set Transparent Color Feature that removes one color from a picture; used to remove solid backgrounds.

Settings (Windows 10) The area of Windows 10 used to customize computer settings. The *Settings* area in Windows 10 is similar to the *Control Panel* in previous versions of Windows.

shading Fill color applied to text, a paragraph, page, cell, table, or graphic object.

Shadow Style effect option that provides dimension by inserting a shadow behind or below an object.

shape Graphic object that can be drawn, such as a line, arrow, circle, or rectangle.

shape adjustment handle Yellow circle that changes the contour of a shape.

Shape Effects Command used to apply effect options, such as Shadow or Glow, to objects.

shape fill Color that fills a shape, chart element, or graphic object.

shape outline Border around a graphic object or chart element.

shape style Set of built-in formats for shapes that include borders, fill colors, and effect components.

Share (Windows 10 *File Explorer*) The feature in a File Explorer window that allows users to share files stored online with other users.

Share pane The pane at the right side of the Word, Excel, or PowerPoint window that displays options to share a file.

SharePoint Web platform designed for collaboration via the Internet.

Short Text data type Data type used to store alphanumeric data; the maximum length is 255 characters.

Show check box Box in *Design* view of a query that indicates whether a field used in a query displays in the query results.

Show/Hide Button that displays or hides paragraph breaks, line breaks, spaces, tabs, and other formatting symbols in a document.

Shutter Bar Open/Close Button Opens and closes the *Navigation Pane* in Access.

Side to Side Page movement that scrolls horizontally through a multi-page document.

Simple Markup view The *Display for Review* view that displays the document with all tracked changes applied and a line at the left side of the document indicating where changes are made.

Simple Query Wizard Tool that guides you through the steps to create a query.

sizing handles White circles on the corners and sides of an object that are used to resize the object.

Slide Master Feature that stores information about slide backgrounds, layouts, and fonts for each theme.

Slide Show view Option that displays slides in sequence at full-screen size for audience viewing.

Slide Sorter view Option that displays slides as thumbnails.

Smart Lookup The feature that displays the definition and additional information from the Internet of a selected word or words.

Smart Lookup pane The pane on the right side of the Office application window that displays the definition and additional information from the Internet of a selected word or words when the *Smart Lookup* feature is used.

SmartArt graphics Diagram layouts used to illustrate concepts such as processes, cycles, or relationships.

SmartArt Styles Gallery that displays different effects for emphasizing shapes within *SmartArt* layouts.

Snap Assist The Windows feature that allows users to fill half or a quarter of the computer screen with an open application or window and select another open application or window to fill a different half or quadrant of the computer screen.

Soft Edges Style effect option that creates a feathered edge, which gradually blends into the background color.

soft page break Formatting option that allows text to flow to the next page when it reaches the bottom margin of a page.

Sort Feature that arranges text, table rows, or records in alphabetical or numerical order.

source Complete bibliographic reference for a book, journal article, or web page. In Excel, the source is a text, database, or other file from which data are imported.

source cell Cell data that are copied or cut.

source data Cell range with values and labels graphed in a chart.

sparklines Miniature charts embedded in a worksheet cell.

speaker notes Reminders to help the speaker present that are entered into the *Notes* pane and are visible in *Notes Pane* view.

Spelling Feature that identifies misspelled words and gives the user word choice options to correct spelling.

split button Used to apply a command or display a drop-down list of additional commands depending on where you click the button.

Split Cells Command that divides a single cell into two or more cells.

Split Form Option that allows you to view data two different ways at the same time; the top section of the form displays a columnar layout and the bottom section of the form displays a datasheet layout.

splitter bar Horizontal or vertical gray bar that divides a worksheet into panes.

spreadsheet In PowerPoint, data displayed in columns and rows to create a chart. In Excel, an individual worksheet in a workbook.

stacked layout Control layout that organizes the data vertically.

Standard Slide size option in PowerPoint that uses a more square 4:3 aspect ratio; the default size in earlier PowerPoint versions.

Standard colors Ten colors that are not affected by *Theme Color* changes.

Start Animation timing command that controls when animation begins.

Start button (Windows 10) The button located on the left of the Windows Taskbar that opens the Windows Start menu.

Status bar The area at the bottom of an Office application that displays certain file information and application commands.

stepped layout Report layout option available when grouping records; displays the fields in a row and column format with the field names displayed as column heads; the grouped field displays in the left-most column.

structured reference Name assigned to specific parts of an Excel table.

style Set of built-in formats, which include a variety of borders, shading, alignment, and other options.

style gallery Collection of preset effects for text, shapes, pictures, or other objects.

Subtotal Summary row for grouped data.

SUM Math & Trig function that adds cell values.

summary query Query that analyzes a set of records and displays summarized results.

syntax Required elements and the order of those elements for a function.

System tray The Windows area at the bottom right of the screen that displays Windows system icons.

T

tab Area on the *Ribbon* that lists groups of related commands and options. In Excel, identifier at the bottom left of a worksheet that displays the sheet name.

tab scrolling buttons Buttons to the left of tab names used to move through all worksheet tabs.

table Shows data in an organized, easy-to-read format with information arranged in columns and rows; in Access, database object that stores a collection of related records.

table of contents List of topics in a document; lists headings in the document and related page numbers.

table selector handle Handle that appears at the upper left of a table when the pointer is on a table.

Table Style Options The feature used to apply table style formatting to certain parts of a table, such as the header row, first column, or banded rows.

Table Styles Gallery of built-in table formats that includes a variety of borders, shading, alignment, and other options.

tab selector Button at the top of the vertical ruler where you select the type of tab stop you want to set on the ruler.

tab stop Marker that controls where the insertion point stops when *Tab* is pressed.

Tablet mode The Windows feature that optimizes the computer for use with a touch screen.

tabular layout Form or report layout option that displays the fields in a row and column format with the field names displayed as column heads.

target frame Window where a reader is directed when a hyperlink document or web site opens.

task pane Area at the left or right of an Office application window where you can perform tasks.

Task view The feature in Windows 10 that displays all open windows as tiles on the desktop, and users can select an item to display as the active window on the desktop.

Taskbar Horizontal area at the bottom of the Windows desktop where you can launch programs or open folders.

Tell Me The new help feature in Office applications that displays both application commands and information about commands.

template Predesigned and ready-to-use document, workbook, database, or slide presentation that includes formulas, formatting, viewing options, and sample content.

test data A set of data created to test a database application to ensure that the system performs as desired.

text box Area where you can type text.

Text Box control Control on a form or report used to display data; when used on a form, it can also accept data when a user enters a value.

Text Effects Command used to apply effect options, such as *Shadow* or *Glow*, to text.

text files Files with basic data and little or no formatting, including .txt (text) documents, .csv (comma separated values) files, and .prn (printer) files.

Text Pane Area where you enter text for *SmartArt* shapes.

text wrapping Formatting option that controls how text wraps around a graphic.

Texture Fill Shape Fill option that applies an image such as woven fabric or wood.

Theme Collection of fonts, colors, and effects that you can apply to an entire document, workbook, or presentation; provides consistent background graphics.

Theme Colors Set of background and accent colors.

ThemeFonts Pair of fonts used for a presentation's headings and body text.

Thesaurus Resource tool that lists synonyms for a selected word.

thumbnail Small picture of an image or layout.

tick marks Small lines on a chart axis to guide in reading values.

Tile picture as texture Option to format a slide background with a picture that is repeated to fill the slide.

Total row Table Style option showing color and text emphasis; in Access, a row added in the Design view of a query that specifies the aggregate function to perform, or a row added in Datasheet view of a table that aggregates values in a table column.

Touch Mode The Office applications feature that optimizes the software for use with a touch screen.

Track Changes The reviewing feature that marks changes made to a file.

Transform Style effect option used to change the shape of words.

transition Visual effect that occurs when one slide changes into another slide.

Transparency Color setting that is adjusted by percentage to allow the background to show through objects.

trendline Chart element that averages and forecasts chart data.

U

unbound control Control that is not linked to a data source.

unbound form Form that does not have a connection to a data source.

Undo Reverse an action.

Unique Records **property** Query property that directs Access to display only records that do not include duplicated values; checks all fields in the table, whether or not they have been included in the query.

Unique Values **property** Query property that directs Access to display only records that do not include duplicated values in the fields included in the query.

V

Validation Rule **property** Property used to set limits on acceptable values that can be entered into a field.

Validation Text **property** Property used to enter a custom message that displays when a validation rule is violated.

value Numerical data in a worksheet that can be used in calculations.

value axis Shows the numbers in a chart; the vertical axis in a column chart and the horizontal axis in a bar chart.

Variants Theme designs showing different color combinations.

vertical alignment Content positioning option that aligns material in relation to the top, bottom, or middle of the page or slide; can also refer to the position of objects in relation to each other.

View-only **link** A hyperlink used when sharing a file with others that allows users to only view or download a shared file.

volatile Description for function results that depend on the date and time set in the computer.

W

Weight Thickness of an outline measured in points.

white space Blank space around text and objects in a document; improves the readability of a document and prevents the document from appearing cluttered.

Widescreen The PowerPoint default slide size option that uses a 16:9 aspect ratio; a 16:10 aspect ratio is available.

wildcard character Symbol used in an expression in a query to find records that match, or in a validation rule to require

data being entered to match a specific character, number, or pattern.

Windows 10 Operating system software that controls computer functions and the working environment.

Windows desktop Working area in Windows.

Windows *Start* **menu** Menu that displays when the *Start* button in the bottom left corner of the screen is clicked. Open applications and Windows features from the *Start* menu.

word wrap Formatting option that ensures that text automatically continues to the next line when a line ends at the right margin.

WordArt Displays text as a graphic object with preset text effects that can be modified.

workbook Saved Excel file that contains worksheets.

worksheet Individual page or sheet in a workbook.

worksheet tab Identifier at the bottom left of a worksheet that displays the name of sheet.

Wrap Text Formatting tool that enables you to display the contents of a cell on multiple lines.

X

.xlsx Excel file format for workbooks.

Z

zip The Windows feature that combines files and/or folders into one compressed folder. Also, called a compressed folder.

zipped (compressed) folder Folder that has a reduced file size and can be attached to an email.

Zoom Change file display size.

index